*The Past in Hiding*

# MARK ROSEMAN

## *The Past in Hiding*

**ALLEN LANE**
**THE PENGUIN PRESS**

ALLEN LANE
THE PENGUIN PRESS
Published by the Penguin Group
Penguin Books Ltd, 27 Wrights Lane, London w8 5tz, England
Penguin Putnam Inc., 375 Hudson Street, New York, New York 10014, USA
Penguin Books Australia Ltd, Ringwood, Victoria, Australia
Penguin Books Canada Ltd, 10 Alcorn Avenue, Toronto, Ontario, Canada m4v 3b2
Penguin Books India (P) Ltd, 11, Community Centre, Panchsheel Park, New Delhi – 110 017, India
Penguin Books (NZ) Ltd, Private Bag 102902, NSMC, Auckland, New Zealand
Penguin Books (South Africa) (Pty) Ltd, 5 Watkins Street, Denver Ext 4, Johannesburg 2094, South Africa

Penguin Books Ltd, Registered Offices: Harmondsworth, Middlesex, England

First published 2000
1

Set in 10.25/14.5 pt Linotype Sabon
Typeset by Rowland Phototypesetting Ltd, Bury St Edmunds, Suffolk
Printed in England by The Bath Press, Bath

A CIP catalogue record for this book is available from the British Library

ISBN 0–713–99374–X

# Contents

# Illustrations

# Acknowledgements

My biggest debt is to Marianne Ellenbogen, the subject of this book, for embarking on our painful journey – and to her son Vivian (for whom the journey was no less painful), for staying the course to the end. I hope this book will serve to commemorate those whom Marianne lost in the Holocaust, above all her parents, Siegfried and Regina Strauss, her brother, Richard and her fiancé, Ernst Krombach.

I am grateful to the Nuffield Foundation and Keele University for financing travel to the Americas and to Israel, and the Alexander von Humboldt Stiftung for a fellowship to work in Germany. My thanks also to Jürgen Reulecke and Siegen University, my official hosts for the Fellowship; Professor Düwell and the University of Düsseldorf kindly provided additional facilities.

Alongside Marianne, a large number of individuals generously agreed to be interviewed or to provide information: Eric and Nancy Alexander, Stamford; Uri Aloni, Beit Lochamei Hagetaot; Paul Alsberg, Jerusalem; Hanna Aron, West Hartford, Connecticut; Lily Arras, Walbeck; Christian Arras, Essen; Waltraud Barkhof-Kreter, Essen; Saul and Clara Bender, Chester; Thomas Toivi Blatt, Issaquah, Washington; the late Fritz Briel, Remscheid; Wolfgang Briel, Barsinghausen; Chaja Chovers, Haifa; Jane Dalton, Romsey; Ruth Davidsohn, Haifa; Inge Deutschkron, Berlin; Edith Dietz, Karlsruhe; Ruth Elias, Israel; Gershon Ellenbogen, London; Michael Ellenbogen, Liverpool; Vivian Ellenbogen, Liverpool; Ruth Gawse, Jerusalem; Karin Gerhard, Essen; the late Tove Gerson,

Essen; David, Sandra and Rob Gray, London; Werner, Thomas and the late Hannah Hoffmann, Buenos Aires; Waltraud Horn, Bad Dürrheim; Elisabeth Jacobs, Paderborn; Hanna Jordan, Wuppertal; Ellen Jungbluth, Wuppertal; the late Meta Kamp, Niefern-Öschelbronn; Enrique Krombach, Buenos Aires; Jakov and Tsofia Langer, Kiryat Tivon; Rosemarie Lange, Bobingen; Hilde Machinek, Wuppertal; Monte and Phyllis Miller, Liverpool; Eva Morting, Sundbyberg, Sweden; Imo Moszkowicz, Ottobrunn; Elfrieda Nenadovic, Göttingen; Johannes Oppenheimer, Berlin; Lew Schloss and Trudy Schloss, Teaneck, New Jersey; Hermann Schmalstieg, Göttingen; Aenne Schmitz, Wuppertal; Armgard Schubert, Seeheim-Jugenheim; the late Eva Selig, London; Robert Selig, Denmark; Tillie Stein, Atlanta, Georgia; Ernst Steinmann, Achim; the late Liesel Sternberg, Birmingham; Reinhold Ströter, Mettmann; Uri Weinberg, Jerusalem; Hélène Yaiche-Wolf, Paris; and Kurt Zeunert, Berlin. I thank them as well as those respondents who wished to remain anonymous. I am very grateful too to a number of specialists who shared valuable knowledge and resources: Jochen Bilstein, Hanns W. Gummersbach, Jürgen Fehrs, Ulrich Föhse, Helena Fox, Monika Grüter, Gudrun Maierhof, Winfried Meyer, Gabriel Milland, Steve Paulsson, Michael Treganza and E. Thomas Wood.

I am also indebted to the archives and archivists who provided material and information: Zdenek Schindler, Academy of Sciences of the Czech Republic; Franciszek Piper, Panstwowe Muzeum, Oswiecim (Auschwitz); Edna Brocke, Judith Hess and Monika Joosten, Alte Synagoge, Essen; Beith Terezin (with thanks to Ruth Elias); Berlin Document Centre; BBC Written Archives Centre; Frau Maerten, Bundesarchiv, Berlin; Andreas Matschenz, Landesarchiv Berlin; Hermann Simon, Centrum Judaicum; Deutsche Bank, Essen; Reinhard Frost, Deutsche Bank Historisches Institut, Frankfurt; Stadtarchiv Dinslaken; Anselm Faust, Hauptstaatsarchiv Düsseldorf; Klaus Wisotzky, Stadtarchiv Essen; German Historical Institute, London; Institut für Zeitgeschichte, Munich; Vera Bendt, Frau Freidank and Leonore Maier, Jüdisches Museum, Berlin; Diane R. Spielman, Leo Baeck Institute, New York; Ulrich Borsdorf, Mathilde Jamin and Ernst Schmidt, Ruhrland Museum, Essen; David Cesarani and Jo Reilly, Wiener Library, London; Stadtarchiv Wuppertal; and Judith Kleimann, Jacob Borut and Mordechai Paldiel,

Yad Vashem, Jerusalem; Zentrum für Antisemitusmusforschung, Berlin. Benno Reicher of the Jüdische Gemeinde, Essen and Ingrid Kuschmiers of the Luisenschule–Altschülerinnenverband allowed me to benefit from their knowledge and connections.

I wrote this book while at Keele University, and had the good fortune to be in a history department that was high-powered but good-natured. Thanks to my colleagues and the office staff for making it so. Historians at Keele and elsewhere who have been particular sources of advice and encouragement on this project are: Jakob Borut, Patricia Clavin, Richard Evans, Angela Genger, Chris Harrison, Liz Harvey, Marion Kaplan, Philip Morgan, Alexander and Alice von Plato, Norbert Reichling, Colin Richmond, Nick Stargardt, Charles Townshend, Falk Wiesemann, Peter Witte and Michael Zimmermann. Colin Richmond, Nick Stargardt, Falk Wiesemann and Michael Zimmermann gave extremely generously of their time in reading and making valuable suggestions on the manuscript.

For assistance in turning the idea into a book I am very grateful to Peter Robinson of Curtis Brown, who in his good humoured way forced me to define what kind of book I was writing and then explained to others what I was about. My editor at Penguin, Simon Winder, has been a real pleasure to work with. Thanks to Volker and Marion Berghahn for making connections in the USA and for their enduring support and friendship. Thanks also to my US agent, Jill Grinberg of Anderson, Grinberg Literary Management. The manuscript benefited immeasurably from the editorial input of Joan Roseman and of Sara Bershtel of Metropolitan; I am indebted to them both for the skill, energy and time they devoted to the task.

As any writer knows, completing a project on this scale depends on the emotional support of others. In Germany, I looked to Alexander and Alice von Plato and Falk and Lisa Wiesemann. In Britain, my friend Frankie Zimmerman, my cousins Joe Hyames Mernane and Janet Davies and above all my children, Jacob, Abigail and Kate, were my significant others. Thanks too to Sarah Montagu, particularly for support with childcare during my extended residence in Germany.

Those who know me well will recognize how much the spirit of enquiry in this book draws on the intellectual environment in which I grew up. This book is respectfully dedicated to my parents, Nat and Joan Roseman.

If any one faculty of our nature may be called *more* wonderful than the rest, I do think it is memory. There seems something more speakingly incomprehensible in the powers, the failures, the inequalities, of memory, than in any other of our intelligences. The memory is sometimes so retentive, so serviceable, so obedient – at others, so bewildered and so weak – and at others again so tyrannic, so beyond controul! – We are to be sure a miracle every way – but our powers of recollecting and forgetting, do seem peculiarly past finding out.

Fanny in Jane Austen, *Mansfield Park*

# Introduction

In a very literal sense, Marianne Ellenbogen née Strauss spent her past in hiding. A German Jewess born in the 1920s, Marianne survived the Nazi killing machine by going underground. But her extraordinary journey into and out of the Holocaust had little of the passivity and isolation we associate with being hidden. Between 1941 and 1943, she and her parents were protected by contacts with the Nazi Wehrmacht's own counter-intelligence organization, the Abwehr. When Marianne's fiancé was deported to a Polish ghetto, she managed for six months to maintain a unique chain of communication to him there. And when the rest of her own family were eventually deported, she went on the run. For two years, a hitherto virtually unknown resistance group helped her to survive in the heart of Nazi Germany. She surfaced in Düsseldorf at the end of the war, joined the Communist Party and threw herself into rebuilding a better Germany.

In the months and years that followed, it was Marianne's past itself that went into hiding. In 1946 she came to Britain, married and tried to bury her memories. She led an ordinary life as housewife and mother until her death in 1996. Even her closest relatives knew next to nothing about her wartime experiences. And yet the clues to that past had not quite disappeared. For more than fifty years, an astonishing profusion of letters, diaries, official records and memories lay dormant, ready to bear witness to her survival. The tale of how they eventually came to life again is no less extraordinary than that of her survival itself.

This book is the search for a past in hiding.

## Marianne's report

In 1984, at the behest of her wartime helpers, Marianne Ellenbogen wrote one brief article about her underground life for an obscure journal, *Das Münster am Hellweg*, published in Essen, the town of her birth. Entitled 'Escape and life underground during the Nazi years of persecution, 1943–5', it began:[1]

*On a Monday morning at ten o'clock in August 1943, the two most feared Gestapo officials in Essen appeared at our house. They gave us just two hours to get ready for 'transport to the East'. At this point we were almost the last full-Jewish family left in Essen. In 1941 we had already been condemned to deportation and assigned to a transport. But at the last minute, in full view of all the other hundreds of people waiting for an unknown and frightening future, we were sent back by the Gestapo to our sealed-up house. Now, in 1943, the deportation order came like a bolt out of the blue.*

*The Gestapo officials did not let us out of their sight. The allotted two hours were filled with feverish packing of the few things that we were allowed to take with us – clothing which, in the unknown destination of a 'work camp', should be practical, warm and with luck keep us alive. Then came my moment. The two officials disappeared into the basement, probably to find some loot – all the household goods that we still possessed and did not need for day-to-day use were stored in the cellar in crates and cases. These helped to support the cellar roof and give us a bit more security from the bomb attacks since, as Jews, we were not allowed to use the public air-raid shelters. Unable to say goodbye to my parents, my brother and my relatives, I followed the impulse of the moment, ran out of the house just as I was, with some hundred-mark notes which my father had stuffed into my pocket just a few moments before. I ran for my life, expecting a pistol shot behind me any minute. To go in that way seemed to me a much better fate than the unimaginable one that might await me in Auschwitz or Łodz, in Treblinka or Izbica. But there was no shot, no one running after me, no order, no shouting!*

That evening the twenty-year-old Marianne Strauss made her way to a building in southern Essen which belonged to the 'Bund', a locally based group founded by a man named Artur Jacobs. Meanwhile, with the Gestapo still hoping they would recapture the missing girl, Marianne's family were held in an Essen prison. After a few days, they were deported to Theresienstadt.

For several weeks, Marianne Strauss hid out in Essen. But because bomb attacks and surveillance made remaining there too risky, she began to travel, staying in towns across north and central Germany with members of the Bund:

*It was decided that I should never stay for more than three weeks with any one person. We had to prevent the relatives or neighbours of my hosts from getting suspicious. In any case, I had no food coupons, so my friends carried the great burden of having to feed me from their rations. But I had some money and access to suitcases containing clothes and linen that my parents had hidden some weeks before their deportation, so I was able to barter their contents with farmers in the country in exchange for food or clothing coupons. This was an essential but very dangerous operation. I also hand-crafted countless felt flowers, which were in hot demand at various fashion shops with little to sell. In the course of time, I found a small fashion shop in Braunschweig whose owner paid for my goods largely in the so-crucial coupons. She became my main customer and I had a suspicion that she had half-guessed my situation and wanted to help.*

For almost two years Marianne Strauss travelled without papers or ration cards, never staying for longer than three weeks with any of her hosts.

*On 7 June 1944 – on my twenty-first birthday, I was . . . in Beverstedt and heard on the BBC that the occupants of the transport that had gone from Theresienstadt to Auschwitz on 18 December 1943 had been gassed there in the last few days. I knew that my parents and my brother had been on this transport to Auschwitz.*

As Germany's military situation worsened, so did the hazards of travel. Marianne was twice nearly killed by bombing raids and often only narrowly escaped detection from the Gestapo. But she survived, enduring the last weeks of the war in embattled Düsseldorf.

## A picture for the exhibition

I first saw the article some five years after it was published, in September 1989. Its arrival in the post was preceded by a call from Dr Mathilde Jamin of the Ruhrland Museum in Essen. Dr Jamin was in search of witnesses for a forthcoming exhibition on wartime life in the Ruhr. Did I know of a member of Essen's pre-war Jewish community, Marianne Ellenbogen, now living in Liverpool? It was reasonable to assume that I might at least have encountered her name: in the early 1980s I had conducted historical research in Essen, and my wife and I had been active in the town's tiny Jewish community. But most of the congregation had been post-war refugees from Eastern Europe and, with a few exceptions, Essen's pre-war Jews were present only as ghosts, their names on gravestones or memorial plaques in the Jewish cemetery. Their synagogue – the 'Old Synagogue' – once one of the finest in Germany, was now just a shell, housing another museum. So, no, I had never heard of Marianne Ellenbogen.

Dr Jamin asked whether, if Mrs Ellenbogen were amenable, I would be willing to talk to her about her experiences during the war. I readily assented. It sounded interesting. In any case, I'd enjoyed the support of the Ruhrland Museum's energetic director Professor Uli Borsdorf in the past and was happy to return the favour. And I'd just taken up a post in modern history at Keele University, so Liverpool wasn't too far away.

And then the article arrived in the post. I found it astonishing. Although I had heard of the so-called 'U-boats' in Berlin, Jews who hid in the cellars or attics of non-Jewish friends, this was the first time I had ever heard of a German Jew moving about the country in this way. I wondered what kind of young woman would have had the nerve to survive like this, to travel without papers, deal with shopkeepers and barter with farmers when any denunciation would have meant her death. And what kind of group was it that had kept her alive? I knew the research on the Ruhr in the Nazi period well but I had never heard of the

'Bund' – or at least not this particular organization, which had nothing to do with the better-known Jewish Bund in Poland. Not only was the name new to me, so was the idea of a network managing to provide a Jew with shelter in one town after another across the middle of Nazi Germany. Could this really have happened? I had grave doubts about some of the details in Marianne Ellenbogen's account, in particular the story about the BBC. Given the current state of the historical debate about what the Germans had or had not known about the Holocaust, I did not believe that the BBC could have been transmitting information with anything like that kind of precision. Even so, the interview which I had taken on partly as a favour now looked like a privilege.

But first, Mrs Ellenbogen had to agree.

Whether because of the natural circumspection of Dr Jamin's generation in relation to former Jewish residents of Germany, or because of Mrs Ellenbogen's particular sensitivity, I didn't yet know which, the museum were approaching the issue extraordinarily carefully. As a first step, Dr Jamin had asked colleagues from the Old Synagogue (the principal contact point for Essen's former Jewish residents) to ask Mrs Ellenbogen if she would be willing for the Ruhrland Museum to contact her at all in relation to the exhibition. Only then did Dr Jamin write to Mrs Ellenbogen herself. After thanking her for being 'so friendly as to hear my request' she went on:

*Your article . . . in Das Münster am Hellweg (1984) impressed me very much – and not just because you are one of only two people I have heard of who are still today in a position to report on Jews' experiences of war in the Ruhr. It seems to me that you and people in your situation were exposed just as much to the dangers and hardships of war as the German majority population, indeed even more so (for example, you could not enter the air-raid shelters). Yet these dangers and hardships must have seemed almost irrelevant compared with the terrible experience of Nazi persecution. Anyone who has understood this must be proof against the potential danger of the 'German self-pity' which an exhibition about the war might arouse – against our intentions – amongst its visitors. Partly for this reason, we would like to give the strongest emphasis to the victims of German policies and their experiences.*

After explaining how oral testimony would be used in the exhibition, and with the assurance that 'Your voice would of course remain anonymous – unless you should wish it not to be so', Dr Jamin introduced me, 'a young English historian [ . . . ] who from 1981–4 was a member of the Jewish community in Essen'. A few days later she called me to say all was well.

When I rang Marianne Ellenbogen to fix a date there was something very civilized and confident about her manner, but she did say one slightly odd thing. The Jewish festival of Tabernacles was approaching and she said that she would be unavailable on a certain date because 'the Jewish festivals are observed in this house'. I wondered about this strangely passive formulation. Did she live with children who were more Orthodox, or was there perhaps still a problem with her grasp of English?

In the autumn of 1989 I drove up to Liverpool. The address I had been given turned out to be in a leafy, prosperous-looking suburban road of solid, semi-detached 1920s houses. I arrived at the same time as a good-looking man whom I judged to be in his early fifties. Marianne appeared at the door – full of energy and charm, but looking distinctly older than he. Presumably, this was the son who observed the festivals in this house. Before I had a chance to say the wrong thing, he was revealed as Basil, Marianne's husband, six years her senior. There was some small talk and Basil hovered. He did not really want to leave us to it and wondered aloud if he could contribute something to the interview. But since he had met Marianne only after the war, and as I was then under the mistaken impression that he didn't speak German – the language in which we had to record the interview – I didn't see how he could. In any case, Marianne was clearly not keen for Basil to take part.[2] Only in retrospect did I come to see the symbolic significance of this transaction – of his desire to be involved and her desire to exclude him. At the time, I had no sense of the family burdens such memories could bring.

I had, however, been right to detect something odd in the way Marianne had alluded to the festivals on the phone. Married to an Orthodox Jewish husband, she had gone along with a level of Jewish observance that went well beyond what she was used to from her acculturated

6

German-Jewish background and what she would have chosen for herself. Later, I came to see a sadly ironic continuity here. Both in Nazi Germany and in post-war Britain, the outside world imposed her Jewish identity on her to a degree that went well beyond her own sense of its significance. From 1933 until her death, Marianne's Jewishness was both her fate and her burden.

Our conversation on that autumn day in 1989 was enormously warm and stimulating. After I had admired the antiques, beautifully made furniture and family paintings which Marianne seemed to have somehow salvaged from her parental home, we sat down to strong black coffee and swirly biscuits of a kind I usually had only ever received in Germany. Marianne had intense, jet-black eyebrows and striking dark eyes, a full smiling mouth and hair pulled back tautly behind her head in continental style. The voice was cultured and slightly husky. Like many Germans who speak English almost perfectly (my doubts on this score had been completely unfounded), her accent was delightful, particularly the 'oh' sound, as in the charming 'hello' that had greeted me on the doorstep, which took on a fragrant, sophisticated quality. I, of course, was constantly studying the housewife in her sixties to detect the qualities that had enabled the twenty-year-old girl to survive. I was struck by the strength and character of her face, her energy. She was charming with a hint of steel.

In response to Marianne's request for the questions in advance, Mathilde Jamin had sent both of us a check-list, and we obediently worked through it. Marianne talked about life in Essen during the war and the double threat of Gestapo persecution and Allied bombing. But though she would never learn to make the grammatical mistakes that I would never learn to avoid, German had become a somewhat awkward tool for her. And memory – that was a *very* awkward tool. The whole interview took on a rather dutiful character. Somehow, Marianne conveyed to me that beyond this brief encounter she would not be induced to talk about the past. She took pleasure in my company, I could see, and at one point there was just a hint that I might be her amanuensis. But really, what bonded us at the end of the afternoon was that we had survived together a painful immersion in her memory. And now it was over.

## *Conceiving this book*

In the following months and years I often thought of Marianne, and we spoke occasionally on the phone, but nothing more. That the story did not end there was almost an accident. In 1996, I was involved in the preparatory work for a TV documentary on the Allied Occupation of Germany, and I knew that Marianne had remained in Germany for a year and a half after the end of the war. Like the Ruhrland Museum before me, I thought Marianne's testimony would 'disrupt' mainstream German perceptions of what had been going on. Marianne did not want to be on camera, but was very pleased I had rung. She was a widow now (Basil had died in February), and very ill. She had thought of me a lot lately because she wanted me to look at some papers in her possession and see if they should go into a public archive. Would I come and visit her?

When she opened the front door to me in July 1996, my initial impression was that the intervening seven years had not changed her very much. There was sadly no Basil, of course; I registered that she stooped a little more and I noted the stair lift. But as far as I was concerned, it was the same face full of energy, power and charm. Later, I saw some family snaps taken in the late 1980s and realized she had lost weight since then – her recent ill health had done her the ironic favour of slimming her down. It was rather fitting, as it turned out, that the (photographic) record proved that my memory had in a small way deceived me.

The good strong coffee and the biscuits were, however, definitely the same. We went upstairs to a study piled high with books and papers. Not with ceremony, quite, but with a mixture of hesitancy and portent Marianne handed me some folded, yellowing sheets of paper on which neat lines of German text had been written in pencil. This, she said, was a letter from her fiancé, Ernst Krombach. I hadn't realized that she had had a fiancé before Basil. The letter was sent in August 1942 from Izbica which, Marianne said, was a Polish concentration camp. Considering the conditions under which it was written and the events it described, it was an enormously composed, careful and sober document. Indeed, the mixture of normality and horror, the juxtaposition of extraordinarily adverse circumstances and the writer's modest optimism, made the letter at once approachable and elusive. It was vivid, it was there in my hands, but it was also beyond imagining.

I was very conscious of Marianne's watchful eyes on me. I did not realize at the time how little is known about Izbica, a ghetto rather than a camp, which in 1942 was a point of interim resettlement for thousands of German, Austrian and Czech Jews. Neither did I realize that this was only part of a truly unique extended correspondence that Marianne and Ernst had managed to maintain between Essen and Izbica. But I said that I thought something *should* be done with the letter.

I asked Marianne how she managed to avoid the deportations that had taken away her fiancé. I had always wondered about the striking reference in her article to the family having been once nearly deported in 1941 and then reprieved. She was not sure, but she thought that the family had been protected by the Abwehr. The Abwehr – the Wehrmacht's counter-intelligence organization? Marianne was clearly somewhat nervous about the whole thing, worried that there might be something slightly shameful involved. It did seem hard to understand that the German Wehrmacht should have been trying to protect any Jews – and why her family?

I also asked how Ernst had managed to get the letter from Izbica to her (and how, as shown by the letter, she had managed to get life-saving goods to him). Marianne said that her uncle and then she herself had got to know a young SS man whose family owned a garage in Essen. Under cover of his contract work for the SS, he had taken out parcels from her to Ernst and brought back the letter. An SS man entering the ghetto, delivering parcels and returning with uncensored letters to the Jewess who commissioned him? I could only shake my head.

We went out for lunch. Despite her illness, Marianne was still driving and, after she had gingerly eased herself into the driving seat of her solid-looking Rover, drove us confidently the short distance to a nearby Chinese restaurant where we were joined by her son, Vivian, a grave, bearded man in his forties. It was Vivian who put the idea of recording his mother's life story openly on the table. After the meal, he took me aside briefly. He told me that Marianne might have only weeks to live and I should act fast. Later, I learned that he had heard this from the doctor only that morning and had spent the last couple of hours driving aimlessly around, wondering what to do with the news and his feelings.

We agreed that I would return soon with a tape recorder. In the course of 1996, Marianne and I had three long conversations, and fragments of her life gradually began to fall into place. I learned much more about the central dramas in Marianne's life – the moment of near deportation, the love affair and correspondence with Ernst, the escape from the Gestapo, the dramatic twists and turns of her two years underground, and the eighteen months spent in the ruins of post-war Germany.

These conversations were moving and enthralling, but they were anything but easy. Marianne was deeply ambivalent about talking to me. She wanted to commemorate Ernst and the help that had been given her by her friends in the Bund. But she found the act of remembering very painful. Our exchanges sometimes became rather combative. She did not want anything written about her life after 1946 when she came to England – she was worried that what she said might appear disloyal to Basil and hurt surviving relatives. She also could not bring herself to talk about what was probably the greatest tragedy in her life: the death in 1969 of her eighteen-year-old daughter Elaine, following a protracted struggle with anorexia. I insisted that we had to talk about the burden of the past on the present – about restitution, guilt and her surviving links to Germany. All right then, but we were not to probe into her family life in Britain. And so, with this uneasy agreement, we carried on. Marianne produced more documents – an extended correspondence between her and Ernst before September 1942 and a wealth of family photos. She had been a most striking-looking girl with huge, burning eyes.

As Marianne's health declined, each time she talked to me involved a major effort to psych (and drug) herself up. On a pharmacologically induced high, she would talk for hours and then by the evening would be utterly drained and take days to recover. I felt increasingly guilty that in what might be her last weeks I was adding to her burden. Did a Holocaust survivor not have a right to die in peace? Towards the end of October we had our longest, most intensive session. She kept putting off the next meeting until she felt stronger. In the meantime, I arranged that

I would go to Germany in January to try to meet some of the surviving members of the Bund and to find out what records were still available. In November, Marianne went for a spell of convalescence to a nearby hospice. The stay seemed to do her good and she returned home in December. But, unexpectedly, her condition deteriorated and she died in the early hours of 22 December 1996.

## Remembering, recording and forgetting

Marianne's death caught me unawares. I felt a deep sense of loss – and sadness that I would never be able to show her the finished product. I wondered, in fact, if there could now *be* a 'finished product'. A novelist would find in what I had already learned the plot for a marvellous survival story. But I did not want to blur fact and fiction – I wanted to write history. Quite apart from my general training and temperament, I believe that dealing with the Holocaust demands special care. One has to be very clear about what happened and what did not happen. I could not bring myself to invent details for the sake of the narrative. And that left me wondering whether I had enough material to do justice to Marianne's life. I also wondered, though I had been very hesitant to challenge her directly, whether some of the things Marianne told me could really be true.

Thus, when I took my long-planned trip to Germany just a fortnight after Marianne's death, I did so with a feeling of considerable uncertainty. My first port of call was the Hauptstaatsarchiv in Düsseldorf, which held the records from the Düsseldorf district of the Gestapo (of which Essen was part). I was lucky that this was one of only two regions in the Federal Republic where the Gestapo files had not been destroyed. When the bulging folders for Marianne's father and uncle appeared, it was clear that I had found something special. The Strauss family proved to be one of the best documented cases showing how resistance groups within high-ranking official organizations had intervened to try to protect Jews. The records even contained information about Marianne's escape.

On that and subsequent visits to Germany further remarkable sources revealed themselves. But, as in a detective story, many of the most vital clues turned out to be close to home. In early 1997, Marianne's son Vivian began what was for him the psychologically arduous process of clearing out her belongings. It was only now that he and I discovered how many important documents the Strausses had managed to deposit with friends for safe-keeping. Several times, I made journeys to Liverpool to look through the latest piles of paper that Vivian had found. Even after we had cleared the house there turned out to be another huge trunkful in the shed. The papers included some extraordinary postcards, letters and diaries from wartime Nazi Germany. I did not know whether to be more struck by their existence or by the fact that Marianne had never mentioned them while she was alive.

As in a detective story, I also felt my way, initially rather blindly, along an extending chain of witnesses. I found business contacts of her parents, distant relatives, ex-schoolmates, members of the Bund and post-war friends. It was a poignant reminder of what happened to German Jewry that my search led me across Germany, Israel, the USA and Argentina and brought me correspondents and contacts in Canada, Australia, France, Sweden, Poland and the Czech Republic. But not all my respondents were so far from home. In one instance, a conversation with the helpful archivists in Essen's Old Synagogue led to the discovery that a ninety-year-old friend of Marianne's fiancé's family was now living in Birmingham, just a couple of miles from my home.[3]

So often, the testimony of the Holocaust survivor is just one lonely voice relating a story in which almost everything and everyone described has been destroyed. But in Marianne's case, though she undoubtedly had been robbed of so much, her 'lost' world was still able to speak alongside her. It was thus possible both to be true to my craft *and* to piece together a vivid story. The gaps that remained were almost welcome, as reminders that this picture of the past had been reassembled, like a puzzle. The documentation allowed me not only to supplement but also to corroborate Marianne's testimony. All of her more implausible claims – about the Abwehr, about the underground, about the BBC – proved to be true.

At the same time, these new sources raised questions about authenticity and truth that became a central part of the story. Discrepancies began to emerge. The Gestapo's account of Marianne's flight largely mirrored her own, but there were some subtle and interesting differences which, at the time, I could not interpret. It became clear that Marianne had subtly changed some incidents, forgotten others or 'appropriated' memories that in fact belonged to other people. These changes caught my imagination, not least because they affected episodes remembered so forcefully by Marianne that they had seemed etched in stone. Even traumatic memories, it seemed, and perhaps particularly and peculiarly them, were subject to change.

Sometimes, the 'discrepancies' were not factual errors at all. Except in a few minor particulars, Marianne's memory of events on the run, for example, did not contradict the facts described in the underground diary that I found after her death. Nevertheless, the picture that emerged from the diary of what illegal life was like, and above all of what the young woman was like who had been living that life, was very different from the one she had painted for me. It became clear Marianne had lost sight of the person she had once been. The documents and witnesses thus put me on the trail not just of Marianne's past, but of the painful story of remembering and forgetting.

## Surviving Nazi Germany

As a professional historian concentrating on recent German history, one of my main preoccupations over the years has been to try to understand what went wrong in Germany between 1933 and 1945. Indeed, it was the threatening mystery of the Holocaust that provoked me into becoming a historian in the first place. But when I initially decided to write this book, it was to preserve an extraordinary survival story rather than because I expected to gain major insights into the Third Reich and the Holocaust. Marianne's life seemed too much a one-off to offer more than peripheral insights into the nightmare from which she had so unusually managed to escape. Survival was so much against the normal run of things for a Jew caught in Germany or German-occupied Europe after 1939 that in telling Marianne's story I felt guilty almost of fostering a kind of distortion. Jews did not normally thrive in the period

1938–41, have protection from the Abwehr, slip away from the Gestapo or live underground for two years. Out of the quarter of a million Jews still in Germany in 1939, fewer than 3,000 survived in hiding, and half of those were in Berlin.

At the time Marianne and I were having our first conversations, Britain and the USA were enjoying a round of German-bashing. In Britain, Germany's response to Britain's BSE crisis, the prospect of a single currency and football's European Championship were the main reasons for this latest wave. In the USA, there was a continuing, more diffuse unease at the implications of German reunification. The academic analogue to all this was the Goldhagen controversy, which gathered momentum in the summer and autumn of 1996. In his powerful study *Hitler's Willing Executioners*, published the year before, Daniel J. Goldhagen had demonstrated how widespread and wilful was German participation in the killing of Jews. Far from the 'Final Solution' being a clinical mechanical procedure carried out by a tiny few, Goldhagen argued, ordinary Germans from all walks of life showed that they shared the moral calculus which made the killing of Jews seem not only acceptable but even desirable. Powerful descriptions of death marches and forced labour buttressed the argument. Goldhagen attributed this widespread involvement to a distinctive 'exterminatory' anti-Semitism that had evolved in German culture over the centuries, creating a general German propensity to kill Jews. Goldhagen's book has been enormously influential at a popular level, and even for academics doubtful whether German anti-Semitism was so simple and direct a cause of the Holocaust the force of the book's explanation is not easily answered.

The more material and testimony accumulated, however, the more I began to feel that Marianne's story revealed, in microcosm, the complex nature of Germany's relations with its Jews. As with Viktor Klemperer, whose diaries appeared just before I began this research,[4] Marianne's story, indeed her survival, rested on the interrelationships between the Jewish and non-Jewish world. Between herself and her family on the one hand, and the non-Jewish world on the other, a whole variety of ties – ties of sentiment, of business or merely of short-term mutual advantage – were carried across the threshold of 1933 or, indeed, arose thereafter.

Even while the Strauss family was under persecution, I found nuances and differentiation I had not expected. Gestapo attempts to turn various denunciations into prosecutions collapsed because the state prosecutor or the judiciary refused to play ball. As the tax authorities squeezed the family for the special levy on Jews in 1938/9, it proved possible within the narrow limits set by the law to negotiate improvements or concessions. Even in 1941, there was still some small scope for negotiations with the city about the terms of the sale of the Strauss apartments.

As I came to know Marianne's helpers and saviours through the letters and diaries of the time, and through meetings and conversations with those still living, I learned also that the exceptional and the ordinary were closely bound up with each other. Artur and Dore Jacobs, the leaders of the Bund, were clearly exceptional personalities. But many of the individuals whom they inspired to take extraordinary risks, though upright, deeply committed and showing immense moral courage, were quite 'ordinary Germans'. Although the Bund had important distinguishing features, the values it drew on were in many ways typical of a broad grouping within the Weimar left. In short, although the drama of Marianne's survival was unique, the backdrop was so well illuminated and the cast of players so large that her story shed light on the whole theatre in which it took place.

## The burdens of the past

There were many moments – for example, when I revived some contact that had lapsed for fifty years or more, or when I discovered some discrepancy between Marianne's recollections and the documents – when I so wished that Marianne were still alive to discuss my findings. The painful truth, however, was that if Marianne had not died, many of the papers, and the names and addresses to which they helped me gain access, would have remained hidden from me. During my conversations with her she had known, as I then did not, that the house was heaving with records and mementoes. She evidently could not bring herself to confront them. Vivian told me that his mother was normally orderly, filing everything in its proper place. Yet these papers were all stuffed into envelopes and folders, nothing thrown away but nothing catalogued, in nooks and crannies all over the house. From some of the things Marianne had said to me, I do not think even she remembered exactly what was there. In other words, her story could be told only because I had been able to talk to her while she lived and gain access to her papers after she died.

For almost fifty years this knowledge, this documentation, lay dormant. No questions were asked, no discussion was allowed. In 1945, it seemed, Marianne had come out into the open – but her past had gone into hiding. A few days after Marianne's death, I had my first long talk with Vivian. I was stunned to learn that his mother had told him virtually nothing of her past. He was waiting to hear about it from a stranger, from me. At the same time, it was clear that he was fiercely protective of her memory and did not want me to intrude too deeply into her privacy. The same intimate, respectful, wary, guilty clinch that had characterized my relationship with Marianne would now continue with him. And thus I learned something of the silent, awful burdens which, in indefinable ways, the past had placed not just on Marianne but on her whole family. Those burdens of a past in hiding are also the subject of this book.

# I

# Childhood in a German-Jewish Family

Marianne told me the story of a much-prized family document. It was an elaborate family tree commissioned by her mother, Regina Strauss, and produced by a professional artist. Regina, or Ine as everyone called her, was, like her husband Siegfried, immensely proud of their ancestors' long years of respectable settlement in Germany and had carried out a great deal of research. On both sides of the family, forebears could be traced back to 1740. The assiduously collected dates and names of Strausses, Rosenbergs, Weyls, Sterns, Reisses, Behrendts and Nördlingers were incorporated into the beautiful chart of almost 200 years of births, deaths and marriages in Germany.

Marianne told me that Ine was so proud of the result that she sent it off to the Jewish Museum in Berlin for safe-keeping and display. At the time, Marianne said, she gave the document very little attention. 'All that' meant little to her as a girl. Now she wished she had been more involved. But above all she was sorry to have lost so much evidence of her family roots. She told me that on Kristallnacht[1] the Jewish Museum in Berlin went up in flames and with it the family tree. The burning of the family tree seemed to me poignantly symbolic. It represented the destruction of a German-Jewish identity. It was also full of sinister portent. Modifying Heine's famous dictum about books and people, we sense that where you begin by burning family trees you end up by burning families.

Some time after Marianne died I was researching in Berlin. I took a tour through the recently built extension to the Jewish Museum, with its striking modern design based on a fractured Star of David. Because the artefacts had not yet been installed, our guide, a final-year architecture student, talked mainly about the building's design. But he did say one or two significant things about the museum's history. I had not realized that the original Jewish Museum was created in January 1933, only six days before the Nazis came to power. I later found out that in 1936 the museum put on an exhibition titled 'Our Forebears', and it was for this exhibition that Ine submitted the family tree.[2] For me, her gesture now took on a different quality. I had made the mistake at first of seeing in it ostentatious pride. Now I saw a more conscious act of self-assertion at a time when the Nazis were trying to deny German Jews their right to call themselves German.

On 10 November 1938, the day after Kristallnacht, the museum was closed but, I now learned, had not been set alight. Indeed, a number of the museum's paintings turned up after the war and some of the former owners recovered their works. No one knows what happened to the rest. When Marianne told me the museum had gone up in flames she had, probably unconsciously, created a literary metaphor dressed up as memory. The uncertainty about what had actually happened to the family tree must have been too painfully reminiscent of her lack of final knowledge about her family's fate.

## Marianne's grandparents

Marianne must have met one of her great-grandparents, since her great-grandmother Sophie Stern died aged 100 in 1928 when Marianne was five. But Marianne's recollections go back only as far as her paternal grandparents, Leopold and Saly (Rosalie, née Stern) Strauss, as well as her mother's parents, Isaak and Anna Rosenberg. Both couples were settled in little towns on the fringe of the Ruhr valley, the Strausses in the lower-Rhinish community of Dinslaken, the Rosenbergs in Ahlen, a Westphalian market town. Both families combined positions of great respectability in their respective communities with a reasonably observant Jewish way of life.

# Marianne's Family

## Great-grandparents

| Seligman Strauss *née* Reis | Alexander Stern | Sophie néeNördlinger | Philipp Rosenberg | Therese *née* Windmüller | Kappel Weyl | Marianne, *née* Behrendt |
|---|---|---|---|---|---|---|

Seligman   Bina     Alexander   Sophie          Philipp      Therese *née*   Kappel   Marianne,
Strauss    *née* Reis    Stern       néeNördlinger   Rosenberg    Windmüller      Weyl     *née* Behrendt

## Grandparents

| Leopold Strauss | Rosalie Stern | Isaak Rosenberg | Anna Weyl |
|---|---|---|---|
| b. 30.11.1861, Hessen | b. 5.4.1867 Pflaumloch, | b. 25.5.1863 Ahlen | b. 4.1.1867 Haltern |
| d. 15.6.39 Essen | Wuerttemberg | d. 8.5.1932 Ahlen | d. 9.1.1944 Theresienstadt |
| | d. 28.5.1934 Essen | | |

## Parents

| Siegfried Strauss | Regina Rosenberg |
|---|---|
| b. 24.4.1891 Battenberg | b. 13.1.1898 Ahlen |
| d. July 1944[?] Auschwitz-Birkenau | d. July, 19444[?] Auschwitz-Birkenau |

| *Marianne's paternal uncles and aunts* | *Marianne's maternal uncles and aunts* |
|---|---|
| Alfred b. 24.4.1891 Battenberg; m. Lore *née* Dahl; d. Sept. 1944[?] Auschwitz-Birkenau, Lore died Jan. 1945 Kurzbach, nr. Breslau | Hannah b. 5.11.1894 Ahlen; m. Ernst Alexander; d. ? (deported Lodz Oct 1941); children: Alexander (Eric); Alfred(Uri); Otto (Gerald) |
| Richard b. 10.1.1893 Battenberg; d. 14.12.1916 Gumbinnen | Adolf b. 30.4.1896; m. Erna Hertz; d. Florida 1980s; son: Rolf (Ralph) |
| Bertel b. 13.6.1900 Dinslaken; m. Ferdinand Wolf; d. August 1942[?] Auschwitz-Birkenau; son: Richard (René) Wolf | Karl b. 1907; m. Diane Doutreport; d. Spain 1980s; daughter: Marie Anne |

Siegfried m. Regina 27.8.22 Ahlen
Children: Marianne b. 7.6.1923 Essen; m. Basil Ellenbogen; d. 22.12.1996 Liverpool
Richard b. 26.10.1926 Essen; d. July 1944[?] Auschwitz-Birkenau

## The Ellenbogens

Max Ellenbogen m. Gertie *née* Hamburg
children: Gershon, b. 7.1.1917 Liverpool
Basil b. 22.12.1917 Liverpool; d. 21.2.1996 Liverpool

Raymond b. 1.7.1924 Liverpool
Basil m. Marianne 29.12.1946 London
children. Vivian b. 23.11.1947, m. 2.3.1975
Elaine b. 18.1.1951; d. 29.9.1969

Leopold Strauss was the only one of eleven siblings to receive secondary education. He trained as a rabbi and teacher, and in 1896 was appointed headmaster of Dinslaken's Jewish school. He was also cantor[3] for Dinslaken's Jewish community. At the same time, he was invited by the mayor to be a teacher and later honorary director of the town's vocational school (the letter in elegant copperplate Gothic script still survived in Liverpool). He became a town councillor and served on the town's Youth Welfare Committee. When Leopold retired from teaching in 1927, the Dinslaken mayor made a formal announcement to the council and gave Leopold the town's best wishes.[4]

One of Marianne's vivid recollections was of her grandparents' wonderful garden, which, to a child at least, seemed enormous. Grandmother Saly grew apples and pears and other fruit, from which she would make vast quantities of bottled fruit and jellies. They also kept poultry, and Marianne remembered feeding the chickens and the pleasure of a fresh egg every morning for breakfast. These happy memories lay alongside the less happy experience of having to receive extracurricular Hebrew lessons and tuition in mathematics from grandfather Leopold. Coming as they did in the holidays, Marianne found the extra lessons 'very unfair', but she was compensated by the time she spent with Saly, a 'lovely person'. Saly and Marianne would go out shopping, meeting and greeting other members of the Jewish community. After Saly, a chronic asthmatic, died in 1934, Marianne used to stay in a room of her own on the second floor of the Strausses' house. 'It was very nice and very, very snug and very comfortable . . . I always loved having this room to myself, away from everything.'

Marianne had equally warm recollections of her mother's parents, the Rosenbergs, whom they visited regularly. If the family went to Dinslaken for Passover one year, they would go to the Rosenbergs in Ahlen the next. 'It was all done with great style' in Ahlen, Marianne told me. Isaak Rosenberg's father had established a successful grain and fodder business and Isaak, the fifth of seven children, had taken it on to become one of Ahlen's most prosperous citizens. He played a leading role in local civic associations such as the Bürgerschutzverein and the voluntary fire service. He was also a member of the nationalist-patriotic Kyffhäuser-Bund.[5]

Like Leopold Strauss, Isaak remained a religious man and was presi-

*Leopold and Saly Strauss at a spa*

dent of Ahlen's small Jewish community. Marianne remembered that, at Passover, Isaak would sit at the head of the table in his kittel[6] and talet.[7] Once, when very young, Marianne asked why her grandfather was wearing the kittel. He said that was what you wear when you get buried. Wearing it reminds you that life is fleeting and that everybody has to die. This was Marianne's first remembered encounter with the idea of death. When Isaak died of heart disease in 1932, the eight-year-old Marianne had her first encounter with the reality of death. The firemen's band turned out to play at his funeral.

The Rosenbergs' house, on one of Ahlen's main streets, fascinated Marianne. It was step-gabled like a Dutch house and inside there was a large winding staircase. Even as a small child Marianne had an eye for art, and remembered the top gallery being chock-a-block with old copper engravings. Halfway up the stairs was a dark room stuffed full with sacks of sultanas, currants and sugar. In the attic, there was storage for grain and a large hook outside for lifting sacks up on chains. Behind the house were offices and a yard. The family did its own slaughtering. Twice a year the butcher would come and they would make sausages and smoke the meat. Isaak used to go pheasant shooting, and Marianne remembered braces of pheasant being sent to her parents in Essen. Marianne's overall impression of Isaak was of a larger-than-life character, picking people up off the street to invite them to dinner, and with a house full of family, guests and servants.

## Marianne's parents

Though remaining observant Jews, the Strausses and Rosenbergs were part of a trend of acculturation[8] that had begun in Germany in the eighteenth century, as a result of which Germany's Jews came to resemble their Eastern European counterparts less and less.[9] Whilst Marianne's grandparents had all come from large families, for example, both couples chose to have only four children. They gave their offspring, and particularly their sons, fine-sounding Teutonic names rather than biblical ones. There was Siegfried (Marianne's father) and his twin brother Alfred, born in 1891, followed two years later by a younger brother, Richard. Only their sister Bertel, born in 1900, had a Yiddish-sounding name. The Rosenbergs for their part produced a Johannah (Hannah) (1894), Adolf (1896), Marianne's mother Regina (Ine) (1898) and Karl (1907).

Equally characteristic of the trend was that the Strausses and Rosenbergs placed greater emphasis on a good secular education than on religious instruction. Leopold sent Siegfried and Alfred to a state elemen-

*Marianne's father and uncles as children*

tary school in nearby Duisburg rather than to his own Jewish school in Dinslaken. A photo of the two boys at primary school survives, with their round, thin-lipped, intense faces and their identical sailor-suits. In 1902, the twins transferred to secondary school, a *Realgymnasium* in Duisburg-Meiderich. The Rosenbergs made similar choices. At this time, German-Jewish families probably took the education of their daughters more seriously than their non-Jewish counterparts. The typical pattern was that the girls were educated for a career which they then did not pursue after marriage. Isaak and Anna sent Ine to a convent lyceum run by Ursuline nuns, because of the good classical education on offer there. According to Marianne, her mother also absorbed much of the moral atmosphere of the place.

The Strauss boys' choice of career – the grain trade – was also characteristic of Jews in the region. For all their efforts to acculturate, German

Jews both in the Ruhr area and elsewhere retained a highly distinctive occupational profile. By the time of the First World War, the Ruhr was dominated by heavy industry, but very few of the region's Jews went into coal, steel or engineering. Instead, the majority remained in trade and, of those, by far the largest group were in clothing and food.[10]

Siegfried, Alfred and their younger brother Richard trained as apprentices to a Duisburg merchant. After completing their apprenticeships, they gained practical experience in the processing and storage of grain and fodder with the company Siegfried Heineberg, Jewish corn brokers in Düsseldorf. Some of Siegfried's references and curricula vitae survive. They tell us that he and his brother mastered, amongst other things, business correspondence, book-keeping, stock management – and telephone conversation. Evidently, telephone conversation was still considered sufficiently arcane to rank as an acquirable skill. In those days, of course, the receiver and mouthpiece were two separate parts. One of Siegfried's nephews told me that Siegfried and Alfred were such a double-act that, later, when they had their own business, one of them would do the speaking and the other the listening.[11] After a year's military service in 1910–11, Siegfried spent three years working for Heineberg as a grain, seed and animal fodder salesman. The First World War interrupted his career.[12]

For her part, Ine attended a commercial college, graduating with good results in March 1916.[13] She then trained as a teacher and was briefly employed in a commercial college in Münster, where a surviving reference suggests that she was a great success.[14] A cultured and intelligent person, in a later generation she would surely have gone to university. She had some training as a painter, and until her marriage painted for pleasure with considerable success. She was also a great linguist, one of her life-long interests being the local dialect, the Westphalian Platt.

## The call to arms

For both Siegfried and Alfred, as Marianne remembered, the First World War was a defining experience. Keen members of the Reserve before the war, both rushed to the colours and spent the whole of the war in the field. Marianne's documents include Alfred's army pay book, which shows that he joined the Reserve Infantry Regiment 220 on 1 October 1911, at the age of twenty, was called up on the second day of mobilization and rejoined the regiment for war on 30 August 1914. He served with the regiment, primarily on the eastern front, until July 1918 and then with the mine-laying Batallion 20. Siegfried, for his part, fought on the western front with Füsilier-Regiment 39 Düsseldorf. In total, about 100,000 Jews, 18 percent of the entire German-Jewish population, served in the course of the war.[15]

For the brothers, the war instilled a powerful identification with the fatherland and a strong sense of having merited official recognition and honour. Amongst Marianne's papers are hundreds of photo-cards from the front which her father and uncle collected to mark the experience. Marianne told me that her father was an officer in the German army, and this presumably was the way the family liked to think of him. In fact, the two Strauss brothers did not make it to full officer class, both remaining at non-commissioned officer level – Siegfried as corporal, his brother as sergeant. Of course, for Jews even this level of promotion was not easy to achieve and only 2,000 made it further to become officers.[16] Marianne also told me that her father had been awarded the Iron Cross. Again, this may well have become family lore, but does not seem to have been quite the truth. It is certain that both Siegfried and Alfred were among the 35,000 Jewish soldiers who were decorated for valorous service, and both received the Honour Cross of Front Fighters, but it seems that only Alfred was awarded the more prestigious Iron Cross (Second Class), on 4 April 1915.[17] Warm letters sent from his lieutenant convalescing at home to Alfred at the front testify to the esteem in which the latter was held by his superior officer.[18]

Although Siegfried and Alfred had a good war, the conflict also brought tragedy to the family. Among the family papers, I found the last correspondence between their brother Richard and their father, dating from early December 1916. On 14 December 1916, aged twenty-three years and eleven months, Richard died of malaria on a transport in East Prussia.[19] So the Strauss family felt it had made ample sacrifice for the fatherland.

We now know that the First World War and Germany's subsequent defeat were key moments in the resurgence of politically aggressive

*On the eve of war: Siegfried as soldier*

anti-Semitism.[20] In 1916, in reaction to accusations that Jews were shirking their duty at the front, the Prussian War Ministry ordered a count of all Jews in active service. The figures showed that Jews were at least as well represented as the rest of the population but, shamefully, the Ministry refused to publish them.[21] Defeat further poisoned the atmosphere, and a Reich Association of Jewish Combat Veterans (Reichsbund jüdischer Frontsoldaten; RjF) was formed with the intention of combating the defamation of Jewish participants in the war effort.[22] Yet, for the Strauss brothers and so many others like them, it was unthinkable that their services to the country should be forgotten.[23]

## Business and marriage

For a brief period after the war, Siegfried worked in Dinslaken's municipal food administration.[24] But on 26 August 1919, he and Alfred founded the grain and cattle-feed firm Gebrüder Strauss OHG, operating from Essen, then a major industrial centre of around 500,000 inhabitants in the heart of the Ruhr valley.[25] At corn exchanges in Essen, Duisburg, Cologne and elsewhere the brothers bought grain from overseas suppliers. Then they travelled around the region and sold grain mixes as cattle-feed to local farmers, retailers and other large customers.[26] It was a far from easy time to start up in business. The unsettled post-revolutionary political atmosphere and galloping inflation bankrupted many enterprises. But the brothers prospered. There is circumstantial evidence to suggest that they knew how to turn the inflation to advantage, since they invested Reichsmarks of little value in property and other fixed capital that was to make a good return in later years. In 1922 they bought land and in 1923 they made their first property deal on the Brunnenstrasse in Essen. On the other hand, they were too solid to indulge in speculation. The company's listing of its debtors and creditors shows that throughout the inflation years the company was consistently owed more by its debtors than it owed to its creditors.[27]

From the start, the brothers took a scientific approach to the right fodder mix for farm animals. With leaflets such as 'The hen is an egg machine', picturing a proud hen strutting against the background of an industrial factory, they appealed to the 1920s commitment to rationaliz-ation.[28] The other key factor in their success, according to one of the company's salesmen, was the brothers' methodical approach to selling. In 1923, the business acquired its first car, enabling the firm's salesmen to drive round and visit the thousands of farms in the area.[29]

Werner Hoffmann joined the company in April 1924, when it was already a flourishing concern. Still upright and square-shouldered despite being almost ninety when I met him in Buenos Aires in 1998, he remembered the Strauss brothers as born officer types. He and another youngster with the company, Hans Goldschmidt, used to laugh behind their backs at Siegfried's stiff military style. Alfred at least had a jovial touch in dealing with the customers; Siegfried had never been known to smile. There was no doubt that the brothers ran a tight ship. Employees were not allowed to be unoccupied for a moment. Werner remembered one example of the brothers' no-nonsense approach to the business: he was out selling in 1934 when he heard that Saly Strauss had died and rang in, offering to come back. 'There is no cause to take a holiday,' was the stern reply. He laughed at the memory. Now, with a successful business career in Argentina behind him, he said he had learned a lot about business methods from the brothers. In later years he would often catch himself applying some maxim or other that he had gained from them.[30]

By 1921, the now thirty-year-old Siegfried felt sufficiently established to consider marriage. There were various ways for Jews to meet a suitable partner at the time but a common one was to go to one of the seaside or cure resorts favoured by Jews. Norderney, a North Sea island off the Fresian coast, was a popular destination for Jews from the Ruhr, and it was here that Siegfried and Regina met, possibly introduced by a cousin. The courtship proceeded rapidly. An elegant card survives, announcing the couple's engagement in December 1921. They were married on Sunday 27 August 1922, 3 Ellul 5682 in the Hebrew calen-dar, at 1.30, in the Hotel Piper in Ahlen. Siegfried's father officiated at the wedding.

What did the pair see in each other? She was not particularly beautiful, nor he especially handsome. Both tended even then towards a certain rotundity. But by the same token, both had stature and gravitas. Their backgrounds were similar. Both were very serious people, though Nord-

*Marianne's parents at the time of their engagement*

erney would have brought out their gayer sides. In Marianne's photo collection, the snaps where her parents are smiling tend to be those taken at the seaside – at Norderney, or at the Dutch resort of Noordwijk. Marianne believed that her parents had a very good relationship. It was not an outwardly passionate marriage, and initially possibly not even a love match. 'Perhaps all the better because of it,' said a seventy-six-year-old Marianne with her own long years of marriage behind her. She felt her parents had had a great deal of respect for each other. Siegfried was not artistically inclined but admired Ine's talent, whilst she probably saw in him the honest, forceful, hard worker that he was. For Siegfried, Ine's dowry of RM60,000 was no bad thing, either, and he invested it immediately into the purchase of a marital home.

In later years, Marianne's mother would tell her that respectable people waited a little after marriage before having their first child. However, if Marianne was conceived the statistically average thirty-nine weeks before she was born, a rough calculation back from Marianne's birthday, 7 June 1923, suggests that Ine conceded less than two weeks to propriety.

About the birth itself, we know very little. The only family paper to shed some light on the occasion was a little note, dated 7 June 1923, from Marianne's father to her mother. Written on the back of one of his business cards, he thanked her 'for the new happiness which has been bestowed upon me by you'.[31] Seemingly nondescript as a historical source, in fact the card hints at three Strauss characteristics. First, Siegfried Strauss was undoubtedly very proud to have children. Second, if sentiment was articulated at all in the Strauss family then it was stiffly and formally. And, third, Siegfried was not a man to spend money on such fripperies as a greetings card, when the back of a business card would serve. Family pride, stiffness and great care with money were dominant themes in Marianne's childhood.

The house Siegfried and Ine bought in February 1922, Ladenspelderstrasse 47, was a substantial building with three stories and a cellar. The attic rooms were let out to a tenant, Fräulein Remkes, to help pay for the mortgage. A couple of months after Marianne was born, with the French occupation of the Ruhr still ongoing, the Strausses were obliged to put up a French officer for a while.[32] When Marianne's brother Richard was born in 1926, conditions became rather cramped and the maid had to sleep on a chaise longue in the living room. Eventually, the Strausses were able to help Fraülein Remkes to find a room elsewhere. In 1928, the family had a struggle to prevent the city authorities from imposing another tenant on them.[33]

The house itself was nicely furnished. There was Chippendale furniture

*Siegfried and Ine on honeymoon, 1922*

and heavy Persian carpets in many of the rooms, and a number of valuable paintings.[34] When I talked to Marianne, some of the pieces were still on display in Liverpool. A relative, Eva Selig, claimed that the house of Marianne's parents was one of the most beautiful she had visited.[35]

The neighbourhood was not particularly Jewish – indeed, there was no real Jewish quarter in Essen – which is hardly surprising since the

5,000 odd Jews in the town made up only 1 per cent of its population.[36] Poorer Jews tended to live north of the centre around the Viehofer Platz, whilst the most affluent gravitated south of the city, into Bredeney or in Rüttenscheid. The Strausses lived in between, just to the west of the centre, in Essen-Holsterhausen. Ladenspelderstrasse was a reasonably well-to-do street of new houses, in which a few other Jewish families had also found residence. Bernd Simon, who as a young German Jew had lived across the road from the Strausses, remembered them as respectable if rather distant neighbours.[37] Later, Siegfried's brother Alfred moved into a new house at number 74.

In 1997 I made a pilgrimage to Ladenspelderstrasse. I knew that the Strausses' house had been destroyed by a bomb in the war. What I hadn't bargained for was that there would be no number 47 at all. I walked up and down the street, and enlisted the assistance of a young man in one of the Ruhr's typical little street kiosks, but he couldn't help. Then an elderly resident told me that when the houses were rebuilt in a different style – squat ugly 1950s blocks – there were fewer buildings than addresses, so some numbers had been dropped. It seemed eerily appropriate for victims of the Holocaust that there should not even be a sign of the space the Strausses' house had once occupied.

## Marianne's childhood

'I wasn't a very happy child,' Marianne said, 'and didn't have a very happy temperament.' And on another occasion she said: 'My mother didn't have an easy time with me – but I didn't have an easy time with my mother.' She remembered her parents with great love and respect and tended to blame herself for her unhappy memories; indeed, she felt an enormous amount of guilt in relation to her parents, but she could not look back on the 1920s with much pleasure:[38]

'I was very dependent on my mother. We always had a nanny, later on a governess. When I was young, I missed my mother very much. My parents would go on skiing holidays and we would have a nanny. I was utterly miserable when they were away. I don't know why I was so relieved when they returned.'

*Life before Richard: Marianne at the seaside, 1925*

One of Marianne's early memories was of being 'very, very naughty indeed' when her mother was away. The nanny wanted her to put on some clothes, but Marianne 'absolutely refused'. Her grandmother was 'quite scandalized'. The memory was particularly significant because the event took place soon after her brother was born – 'I was sitting there on my brother's changing table and didn't want to put some shoes on.' Marianne told me that when she was very small she adored her father and he seemed to adore her. 'He was a wonderful dad to have around.' But as soon as her brother was born, his whole interest focused completely on the boy. In telling me this, Marianne leaped to protect her father; she was sure that the problem 'never occurred' to him, but she 'really resented' his shifting attentions which coloured her relationship with him. Again, she was self-critical, 'I wasn't an easy child by any means.' Her brother was a charming child, she wasn't so charming, and so he got a lot of attention. Richard was quieter, more serious and easier and therefore also a more cosseted child.

'We were brought up in a very autocratic way. Looking back on it, my parents were very Victorian in their attitudes. We had a very, very

*Marianne, 1925–6*

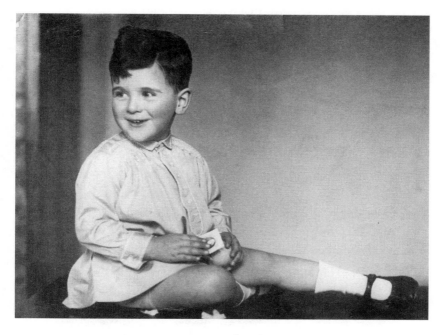

*Marianne's younger brother Richard*

austere upbringing in many ways.' When the children were young, a lot of time was spent with 'well-trained nannies' who would take them out to Essen's new Gruga park and in later years supervise their homework. When she was older, Marianne suffered from the very strong emphasis on prowess at school. She could remember having bad marks and being absolutely terrified of coming home from school. Her mother took 'all that very seriously':[39]

'My mother had a very volcanic temper, so if things didn't go the way she wanted them to go she'd let you know soon enough. And she was also a very moral sort of person, having been brought up by nuns. She'd been to a convent school and of course she had all the prejudices that went with being brought up in a convent school. Which then was transmitted on to me, who was a natural rebel. So that really was not a very easy milieu to be brought up in. The pressure formed a cloud over my childhood – I hated school I really did.'

A few letters survive which the schoolgirl Marianne wrote to her parents on family occasions. In a letter dated May 1932, the nine-year-old wrote in a painfully correct German hand:[40]

> *Dear Daddy,*
>    *Today is father's day. I thank you for all the love you have shown me. You have always worked for us. I wish you a long life, much happiness and health. I will pay good attention at school so that I can get into higher school next year and I will give you much happiness. Now I give you, dear Daddy, best wishes for today.*
>    *Your,*
>    *Marianne*

A mother's day note from the same month recorded rather stiffly: 'you are very dear to me, my Mama', and promised again 'I want always to bring you happiness. When I am bigger I will always help you.'[41] (Across the top of the note, Marianne's mother has written 'on the day my dear father died' – Isaak Rosenberg died on 8 May 1932.) Earnest promises of more work and more devotion continually recur. An undated Jewish New Year's card began with a promise to be 'always obedient and diligent'.[42] In a card for the Jewish New Year in 1935, the twelve-year-old Marianne wrote 'I promise you that I will always be good and diligent'.[43] And another note, written to offer her parents greetings for the 1936 secular new year, struck a similar chord: 'I have the firm intention that this year I will bring you only happiness. I want to make a special effort at school.'[44]

The children were given little freedom or responsibility. 'We never had pocket money because my father had the feeling that we had everything we needed, and I found that very difficult.' Looking back as a trained kindergarten teacher who had raised her own children, Marianne allowed herself to be critical of her parents on this point. As it was, she had had no sense of the value of money. Money was never short in the family – unlike so many of her contemporaries, Marianne had no special recollection of the Depression. Yet, 'here we were . . . leading a luxurious life, worry-free, on the one hand; on the other hand, every penny had to be accounted for.'[45] If friends gave her money, it had to go into a savings box. Once, she opened the box surreptitiously and took some money

*Letter, Marianne to parents, New Year 5695 (September 1934):
I have the firm intention of bringing you only happiness this
year. I will make particular efforts at school.'*

for sweets. Her mother noticed, and 'all hell broke loose – because of the dishonesty'.[46] Even in 1941, when Marianne was already eighteen and living away from home in Berlin, and when the entire world was falling apart around them, her father did not allow her to use her whole stipend[47] – she had to send some home, 'which I did religiously. One day, when I overspent, I had sleepless nights to have to explain to my father how I'd overspent. My father took that very seriously; they were very moral, everything was a moral issue.' There was a whole correspondence about the missing money. 'So that's how money was regarded, with great seriousness in a most extraordinary way.'[48] 'An awful lot was expected from us as children – probably more than most other children. It wasn't very carefree or easy going.'[49] Werner Hoffmann remembered Marianne as an intelligent child but rather withdrawn and quiet and without a large circle of friends.[50]

Marianne's social life was focused very much on the extended family. Her fondest memories, apart from those of her grandparents, were of her aunt, Lore 'Oe' Dahl, Alfred's wife. Lore Dahl, the daughter of David and Else Dahl, came from a well-established family in Wuppertal-Elberfeld. She married Alfred in 1927 when he was thirty-five and she not quite twenty. They made a much more relaxed couple than Marianne's parents. Lore had come to Alfred on the rebound. She had fallen deeply in love with a cousin of hers but, although such a match would not have been forbidden by Jewish tradition, her family were against it, above all worrying about the health of any offspring. It was a bitter irony when it transpired after her marriage that she was unable to have children. For Alfred and Lore, Richard became a surrogate son, 'as much their child as my parents'', said Marianne. 'He adored Lore and she adored him. When she came into the family, he couldn't pronounce Lore and made it Oe, as that was all he could say. So she became Oe in the family.'[51]

When Marianne and Richard went on holiday trips to Norderney with their parents, Alfred and Lore would often travel up afterwards and Richard would stay on with them. This special favouritism was not easy for the young Marianne to take, but over time, her relationship with Oe grew extremely close.[52] Marianne admired Oe's energy and enthusiasm and her talent for getting on with young people.[53]

*Marianne with grandmother Saly Strauss in Dinslaken*

After Alfred and Lore had moved into a building further down the Ladenspelderstrasse, one of the treats for the Strauss children was to go down on their own to their uncle and aunt's flat on Sunday mornings and have breakfast with them:[54]

'When we went there, sometimes they hadn't got up yet, and the greatest fun was to crawl into bed with them. They called it the Cave of Machpele, from the Bible story; my uncle made a sort of cave in the bedclothes and my brother would disappear into these bed-clothes and that was a game they played quite frequently on a Sunday morning.'

Apart from visiting family, other happy childhood memories included Marianne's dance classes. She had a teacher trained by Rudolf von Labarn and Marie Wegmann, and learned modern and group dance, coupled with a little philosophy. Marianne said she was absolutely determined to become a professional dancer, an idea that horrified her mother. Marianne also took piano lessons. Then there were regular weekend visits to the Folkwang museum, Essen's art gallery. Although the museum's behaviour to its many Jewish benefactors in the 1930s was far from laudable, Marianne maintained her affection for it up to her death and bequeathed the gallery a Chagall lithograph in her will. At weekends too, the family would often go out for coffee and cakes to one of the many pleasant cafés in southern Essen, Schwarzer Lene or the Heimliche Liebe with its spectacular views of the city forest, the Baldeney lake, the Ruhr and the Villa Hügel, the Krupp family home.

For holidays, the family would often go to Norderney for six weeks, with 'full trunks and the nanny and everybody'. Or to the Dutch resort of Noordwijk, on the North Sea near Leiden, where they stayed in an elegant hotel, the Haus der Dönen.[55] These holidays were a pleasure, though, here, too, there were memories of being at odds with her parents. Marianne told me that her father was riding on the beach in Noordwijk one day when it started to rain. 'I said, "Oh, the poor horse!", and my mother was scandalized that I worried about the horse and not my father!'

## Alexander and Alfred, Eric and Uri

My contact with one of Marianne's two surviving close relatives, her cousin Eric Alexander (formerly Alex Weinberg), began with a rather engaging letter to Vivian Ellenbogen.

> *Stamford, Lincs,*
> *19 January 1997*

*Dear Vivian,*

> *As you know, I had a phone call from a Mr Roseman. I have written down such meagre details as I can remember and I am posting a copy of these to you. I am also enclosing the copy intended for Mr Roseman. I am sending this to you rather than directly to him to give you an opportunity to consign it to the*

*wastepaper basket if you so wish. As you will see, my views about your grandfather are not very positive. However, in my view it would not be fair to the memory of your mother and to the memory of your grandmother – my favourite aunt – to concoct a distorted picture from the one I remember . . .*

*The people swallowed up by the Holocaust were human beings, not plaster-cast saints, and human beings, alas, have faults as well as virtues.*

*Best wishes and regards to your family,*

*Alex*

Eric Alexander was the oldest son of Ine's sister Hannah. Alongside the refreshing honesty, what emerged from his letter was a prickly persona with somewhat contested identity. For one thing, I did not know how to address him – was he Eric or Alex? The note to Vivian was signed Alex, the attached letter to me was signed Eric Alexander. For another, in the letter to me he managed to be extremely critical not only, as the cover-note promised, of Marianne's father but also of Germany ('every self-respecting (?) town' had a concentration camp), the hypocrisy of his parents' German-Jewish identity ('In Erkelenz[56] Hebrew was gabbled parrot fashion') and the attitudes of Eastern European Jewry ('still very much influenced by . . . the Shtetl').

In a subsequent letter, Eric Alexander invited me up to Stamford to talk about 'Germany and the whole ghostly/ghastly cavalcade'. So, on a sunny summer morning, I drove across from Birmingham to Stamford. He and his second wife Nancy lived in an attractive modern complex of flats near the city centre. In keeping with the gardens outside, which were bright with flowers, the Alexanders' flat was full of floral designs. Sofa and curtains were in chintz. There was some nice china and generally a slightly old-fashioned, genteel English feel. Nancy, a tall, graceful presence in a floral dress, had put her stamp on the apartment. Alex, kindly looking and somewhat rounder, reminded me of German-Jewish émigrés I had known from the Reform-Jewish community in which I grew up, in Leeds.

Eric Alexander had grown up as Alexander Weinberg, the oldest of three brothers, in Erkelenz, a small town to the south of Mönchen-

*Marianne with her cousins, the Weinberg boys,
in Erkelenz, 1928*

Gladbach, north-west of Cologne. His father, Ernst Weinberg, had been born and bred in the town, knew everybody, was well-connected and served on the town council. He ran the family store, A. Weyl Nachfolge, selling clothes and later toys. His war service had been even more illustrious than the Strausses'. While still a sergeant, he was with his men in a dugout when a nearby explosion destabilized some poison-gas canisters. Until he himself collapsed, Ernst repeatedly went into the dugout and dragged his men out, saving many of them from death. His commanding officer put him up for a commission and he became a lieutenant. His sabre remained on permanent display in Alex's grandmother's room. 'It was ironic,' said Alex, 'he was saving his men from gas only to be gassed himself.' 'Surely he wasn't gassed,' I said, since

Alex's parents had been killed in Łodz as far as I knew. But it is true, the fate of many of the deportees is not certain.[57] 'Łodz, Majdanek, Treblinka – who knows?' said Alex. Later I learned that many of the economically 'inactive' Jews of Łodz were gassed at Chelmno as early as January 1942.[58]

After the First World War, Ernst married Hannah Rosenberg and the boys were born: Alexander in 1921, Alfred in 1923 (just a couple of weeks before Marianne) and Otto in 1924. In 1937, as persecution worsened and it became apparent that the family store could not be maintained, the family moved to Cologne. In 1939, the boys came to Britain, Alex first and then the other two with a special transport organized by their Jewish school. Later Alex and Otto both volunteered for the British army, and it was in the army that they changed their names. Gerald (Otto) ended up fighting in Germany with the Glasgow Highlanders, Eric (Alex) was in the Middle East, interrogating German POWs. Alfred was interned as an enemy alien in Liverpool and later in Australia, whence he went to Israel. He is the only one of the brothers to have retained the name Weinberg, but in Israel the Alfred metamorphosed to Uri.

In the early part of the war it was possible for the boys and their parents to write to each other, thanks to the Red Cross, but the letters were few and far between. I had seen a letter sent out by Marianne's grandmother, Anna Rosenberg, in 1940–1, in which she said of Hannah and Ernst, 'Sadly, they very seldom hear from the boys.' I'd noted this down on my pad and Alex, when he saw it, said rather gruffly, 'Well, not at all, I should think, yeh, well, there you are.' His parents were deported to Łodz in October 1941. After the war, one of his uncles told Alex that someone had 'seen my father gathering nettles to eat, you see, but there again, whether true or not, who knows . . . It's impossible to tell. You have to excuse me for a minute . . .' And he went into the other room for a moment or two.

In the 1920s, the Weinbergs did not have a great deal of contact with the Strauss family and tended to see rather more of relatives on Ernst's side of the family, the Alsbergs. This was partly a question of distance, as Erkelenz was a good couple of hours' journey from Essen, but also because, according to Alex, Siegfried Strauss was not particularly liked in the Weinberg family. Alex's parents used to refer to a little raised area in the centre of the Strausses' sitting room as 'the heights of Siegfried'. Alex's mother later told him that in 1923–24, after the hyperinflation, the business in Erkelenz was foundering:

'My mother went to see her father in Ahlen to obtain further funds. He gave her a second dowry of – I believe – another 60,000 marks. When Siegfried got wind of this – so the story goes – he threatened to divorce Ine unless he got the same. I am not sure that Marianne even knew this story. I rather hope she did not.'

Alex confirmed Marianne's impression that the Strausses were very careful with money – though in this he felt they were very much of a piece with his grandfather Rosenberg's household. Marianne had remembered Isaak as a very generous and outgoing individual, always with guests at the table, but Alex's perception was different. He felt the Rosenbergs' wealth didn't show at all. For example, Alex's mother had told him the story of her courtship by his father, Ernst. Before Ernst's visit to inspect and be inspected by the two available Rosenberg daughters, Hannah had thought it expedient to trim the frayed linoleum floor-covering with a carving knife. Still, Alex, like Marianne, had very much enjoyed visiting the Rosenbergs. Going to Ahlen with its spacious courtyard and its horses was the highlight of the year.

Alex's own perceptions of Siegfried were particularly negative. Before the meeting he had written to me:

*When the Strauss family were together, one could not fail to see how Siegfried Strauss doted on Marianne's young brother Richard. I cannot recollect similar displays of paternal affection towards Marianne. I never discussed with Marianne her relationship with her parents, but I would not be surprised if at least for some part of her growing up period the relationship with her father was rather fraught.*

Much of this confirmed Marianne's memories, but in Alex's eyes, Siegfried appeared far more wilful and bitter and less august. And in his letter, Alex's view of Marianne's mother both reinforced and differed from hers:

*I loved my mother very much, but I always thought that aunt Ine was both better educated and more intelligent than my mother, who liked the lighter side of life. In Ahlen, they had oil paintings done very competently by Ine. My impression is in retrospect that Ine's marriage was not a happy one. I might be mistaken, but my impression is that Ine was afraid of her husband. I thought Siegfried was a petty domestic tyrant.*

About Marianne herself, Alex had little to say. As a child he had liked her very much, and in the 1930s, when Marianne had come to stay with the family, there had been a brief, very innocent relationship between them. This had come to an abrupt end when they were found holding hands. But in Alex's memory, it was the negative relationship with Siegfried which had stuck.

Since the war, Alex had had intermittent contact with Marianne. Nancy said she'd only met Marianne a couple of times, but remembered her as very charming and sophisticated. 'She was a big girl,' she said, but when she walked 'it was as if she floated. You didn't see her move.' When Nancy said Marianne had been a big girl, Alex – who clearly still had a soft spot for his cousin – gallantly said it was the cortisone.

Several times on and off the tape, Alex came back to the moment of parting with his own parents when he left for England at the age of eighteen. I wondered at what point he had learned of his parents' deaths. He said he'd always known what was coming. When he and his father parted at the station in early 1939 his father said maybe they'd see each other again, and Alex had said, coldly, 'I don't think so.' And this brusqueness, plus the fact that he'd complained his mother wasn't there – she was involved in a sweet-making course in Munich, but probably also just couldn't bear to come – still haunted Alex.

Alex had arrived in Britain with a fierce hatred of Germans. His father wrote to him that he shouldn't volunteer for the British army because the Germans would shoot him as a traitor if he were caught, but Alex was 'raring to go'. But despite feeling so anti-German, he felt at odds with his Jewishness. He felt that there were only two choices: to live in Israel, or to cease being a Jew. And since his first wife did not wish to live in Israel, he converted to the Anglican faith. He did not wish his children to go through what he had suffered.

45

Yet Alex still felt deeply tied to his former fatherland:

'I'm a German man, I suppose. I am really, what with the accent and what have you. I would have *liked* to be in Germany, yes. I might have got my chips in Russia, I suppose. Germany was my country, my father brought me up that way, you see. That's why I hated the Germans so much.'

Thus, when Alex talked to me about Siegfried, I knew that, whilst some of his dislike clearly resulted from his own observations – for example the relative neglect of Marianne – mapped on to those observations now was a complex love–hate relationship with all the values that German-Jewish fathers had stood for.

Less than a fortnight after this conversation, I was in Israel. My aim, among other things, was to talk to Uri, Alex's brother. On the phone, Uri had a much stronger accent than Alex, still clearly German but now mixed with something else – it sounded more Yiddish than German. He lived in Batei Ungari, part of Me'a Sharim, Jerusalem's ultra-Orthodox quarter and home to some of the most observant Jews in the world. Evidently, Uri's address wasn't going to be easy to find, since the house numbers did not follow any conventional order. The directions were complex: go past a print shop and round a corner to a gap in the wall; pass through into a courtyard; up some steps into another courtyard and then turn right; more steps, a left turn and the second door along the balcony was his.

The street with the print shop was full of hurrying men in black suits, some in black stockings and streimels.[59] There were signs periodically enjoining visitors to dress modestly. Then, there really was a gap in the wall, and suddenly I found myself in a different world. In the courtyard, young mothers draped in simple, heavy dresses looked up suspiciously from playing with their children. I bounded up the wooden steps and counted down the doors. Uri's was open. From the balcony, I entered straight into a room that could have been in a Polish ghetto town. A penetrating smell of a meat stew floated in from the back somewhere. The wallpaper was peeling and filthy. There was very little furniture – just a wooden table, a couple of chairs, and cupboards full of books in Hebrew. Uri, who had been sweeping out the room, put down his broom. I saw only one characteristic that constituted any kind of link with Alex's or Uri's German past: Uri's luminous blue eyes, which looked out from a face adorned with a magnificent white beard.

I'd worried whether he might have reservations about my using a tape-recorder, but Uri was very uncomplicated about such things. He began – and it takes up a good forty minutes on the tape – by telling me the story of his trip on the notorious ship the *Dunera*, which took a mixture of German prisoners of war and Jewish internees from Liverpool to Australia for internment. Uri was something I have never encountered before – a truly gifted raconteur of the old school. The story began in the middle, on the gangplank out to the ship, then swept back in widening circles of explanation before plunging to its ironic conclusion.[60]

I mentioned Alex's view that Siegfried Strauss had not been well liked in the family:

'Alex has some funny memories; well, not funny . . . He was and he was not – he was liked and he wasn't liked, you can't say. He was more exact like, you know. He was more of a soicher [a businessman] than my father. My father was a bad merchant, like me. We are too easy-going. We can't go after every penny.'

Uri's memories circled more around the amusing quirks of each individual.

'The Strauss family? Well, let's see, there were two brothers and two wives. It was known, the two brothers . . . nothing came between them . . . One said something, the other helped him a bit. The wives, it's just the same. They were not fighting. Never.'

It was Uri who told me about the Strauss brothers telephoning, one holding the receiver, the other speaking into the mouthpiece. And he had a similar account of family life in Essen:

'Yes, always my mother said, "In Essen it goes like this: Siegfried shouts 'The kids should go to bed'. The kids shout back and the women say, 'Oh, let them stay', first Oe then Ine and then Alfred says 'No, no, the kids into bed.'" That's how it was always.'

Uri's laugh was infectious. He, like Alex, had a dowry story in his pocket, but it was a different one, concerning the original dowry. Siegfried and Alfred had gone to Ahlen to collect it:

'It was the middle of the inflation. My father was there . . . The whole dowry was on the table and in Germany they had these big baskets you could lock up, like trunks. They filled up the whole basket with the dowry . . . but it didn't all fit in, so Siegfried and Alfred took a flour bag or whatever, a corn bag, and with the rest of the dowry, the corn bag was also full . . . It was a rainy day. My father never laughed so much as when the two of them, just as they got the dowry – they didn't barely say goodbye yeh – they grabbed the basket to make the train to Essen, one of them holding the bag, I don't know who held it, Alfred or Siegfried, both holding the trunk, one on each side, and running all the way to the station. When they arrived in Essen an hour later the money was only worth half. My father laughed his head off at the time.'[61]

Uri's story too captured the Strauss brothers' hard-headedness, but in a less angry way – perhaps reflecting the fact that Uri's account stemmed from his father, whilst Alex had heard his story from his mother.

Uri's take on Ine differed, also – both from Alex's and from Marianne's own memory. Whereas Alex had seen in Ine the intellectual, and Marianne remembered her mother as something of a firebrand, Uri felt that she was more relaxed. In fact, Uri's judgement on almost every aspect of family life was different from that of his brother. He did, however, share Alex and Marianne's pleasure at visiting Ahlen. But whereas both Marianne and Alex had remembered the Rosenbergs as very religious, for Uri, measured against the Me'a Sharim scale of religious observance, Isaak hadn't been so Orthodox. The really religious member of the family, he told me, had been his paternal grandfather, whom he'd never met.

Before I left, Uri asked after his brother. Though their post-war diaspora had taken them in such different directions, the two retained a great deal of affection for each other and telephoned occasionally. Uri had maintained intermittent contact with Marianne, too, though he had actually seen her only once since the war. She and Basil had come to visit him in Jerusalem, but stayed only ten minutes. Why was that? The meeting had been fraught. Uri had asked after the children, but unbeknown to him it was just a few months after Elaine's death:

'I said to Marianne, "You have a son and a daughter, how are they?" And then she told me right out. She could keep herself. I can also. But Basil broke down.'

*The Weinberg boys now (Eric Alexander and Uri Weinberg)*

On the Ellenbogens' later trips to Israel, Basil returned to visit, but Marianne did not come with him. The thought of one of her own family choosing a life so wholly alien was, I think, unbearable for her.

## The Strausses, the Jewish community and anti-Semitism

What little social contact Marianne's parents cultivated outside the family tended to be with Essen's Jewish community, which by the 1920s had grown from just a couple of hundred a century earlier to over 5,000. It had also become more affluent, largely through the success of self-employed businessmen such as the Strauss brothers, who made up a majority of the community. A growing number of Jewish professionals – particularly lawyers and doctors – added to the congregation's wealth and prestige. In 1913, a new synagogue had been consecrated, one of the grandest and most imposing works of Jewish architecture in Germany, whose striking green cupola became (and remains) a dominant feature of the Essen skyline.[62]

The community increasingly moved away from traditional Orthodox practice. The Strausses themselves were intermittent rather than regular synagogue-goers, though Marianne's mother was active in the Jewish Women's League. In this, they resembled most of the community – only the recently arrived immigrants from Eastern Europe, the so-called Ostjuden, were more observant.[63]

Apart from periodic synagogue visits, Marianne's other main contact with the community began in 1929, when she began attending the Jewish school. Located in a modern building within easy walking distance of her home, the school was quite large, with 450 boys and girls – indicating that many members of the community sent their children there, at least for the elementary years. Marianne had no particularly strong memories of the school, though her general recollection was positive. She believed she gained a very good grounding in Jewish history and Hebrew. When I later found records of her performance at the Yavne Jewish school in Cologne and the Jewish kindergarten college in Berlin, however, Hebrew turned out to be by far her worst subject.[64]

Marianne had no sense that her German-Jewish identity was in any way

*Marianne at the Jewish school, 1932 (back row, centre)*

problematic before 1933. Her memories do, however, reveal considerable social segregation. Her parents' social life was restricted to family and Jewish community. Marianne went to a Jewish school. She did not recall ever playing with non-Jewish neighbours on the street. Her cousins, too, remembered social intercourse being largely restricted to other Jews. But this does not necessarily indicate that there was a 'problem'. It could, for example, have been a sign of an active choice among German Jews to maintain their identity, to have both 'Goethe *and* Gemeinde' – both German culture and Jewish community.[65] It is often forgotten that Catholics and Protestants, too, did not mix socially at the time.

The lack of social intercourse with non-Jews does, however, limit what we can learn from Marianne's testimony. Because she had not yet reached secondary-school age and was still very much within the family orbit before the Nazis came to power, social segregation prevented her from being aware of her differentness. So, all her own memories can tell us is that anti-Semitism had not at the time reached a level which impinged on a well-protected child in an affluent family.

From the latter part of the nineteenth century, anti-Semitism had undoubtedly gained ground as a social force among broad sections of the middle class. Even in the Ruhr, one of the most tolerant regions in Germany, Jews were left bewildered and dismayed by their encounters with renewed manifestations of anti-Semitic sentiment.[66] Particularly, after the First World War, politically aggressive anti-Semitism never really went away. In Essen and elsewhere, new Jewish organizations emerged, reflecting the community's sense that it needed to assert itself.[67] On the other hand, the Weimar Republic was not a one-way street leading to Nazism.[68] It was only after 1929, in the disastrous economic and social conditions of the Depression, that extreme right-wing radicalism in the form of the Nazi Party came to dominate the political stage.

In fact, for Marianne's family, as for Marianne herself, the family history before 1933 held remarkably few clues as to what was to follow. The Strausses' and Rosenbergs' success stories before 1933 did not presage disaster. On the contrary, even the Depression was weathered by the brothers with relative ease. And as far as Marianne herself is concerned, the often subdued and occasionally contrary daughter of strict middle-class Jewish parents gave barely a hint of the independent and courageous fighter she was to become.

# 2

# Schoolgirl in the Third Reich

Marianne was always going to find the tenth year of her life a challenge. Some children stayed on at the Jewish school until school-leaving age, but Marianne's parents had long planned for her to change after the four primary years to the Luisenschule, a highly respected *Lyzeum*, or girls' grammar school, not far from their home. The Luisenschule represented not only a new academic atmosphere, but also Marianne's first venture into non-Jewish circles. So, she was inevitably going to experience 1933 as something of a shock. However, there was an additional factor: Marianne's arrival at the Luisenschule in April 1933 took place just over two months after Adolf Hitler became Reich Chancellor.

Many Jews had feared what would happen if the Nazis came to power. Their vague forebodings were more than confirmed by the rapid succession of measures that followed Hitler's appointment on 30 January 1933. First came attacks on left-wing Jews and local boycotts of Jewish businesses.[1] On Saturday 1 April there was an official national boycott, with SA (Sturmabteiling, the Nazi paramilitary wing) guards positioned outside Jewish shops to deter potential customers. Local newspapers, among them the Essen *Nationalzeitung*, published lists of Jewish doctors, businessmen and lawyers so that right-thinking citizens would know whom to avoid. Because our sense of proportion is distorted by the horrors that came later, it is hard for us to appreciate how shocked the Jewish community was in 1933 by official state involvement in such activities. The boycott was followed by laws of restriction and exclusion. Later in April, Jews were purged from the Civil Service and denied the right to practise law (though exceptions made for First World War veterans meant that many Jewish lawyers continued to practise for the time being).

Schools everywhere proved very responsive to the new regime. In neighbouring Dortmund, for example, Jewish children were excluded from school on the day of the anti-Jewish boycott, though possibly to protect them.[2] 'Wrong-thinking' and Jewish teachers were purged from all German schools a few days later. Non-Nazi youth groups were rapidly banned and youngsters encouraged, cajoled and later forced into the Hitler Youth. Marianne was thus changing schools at a most ominous time.

## Business as usual

But before we follow her into the classroom, we should look first at how her parents fared in the new conditions. For one of the defining elements of Marianne's own experience (and indeed, the reason that she continued to attend the Luisenschule) was the extraordinary insouciance with which her parents, particularly her father, met the Third Reich.

Vivian told me about the huge brown trunk in Marianne's outhouse a long time before he managed to clear a path to it. The trunk, engraved with Siegfried's initials and the number 5, was presumably the fifth in a series of cases belonging to Marianne's father. It seems that during the war it was deposited with the family banker for safe-keeping. When we finally manhandled it into Vivian's living room, we discovered a very comprehensive collection of Strauss business records which showed that the brothers had survived the 1930s in much better economic shape than I would have believed. True, in 1933 they abandoned plans for major expansion,[3] but in 1934, company turnover at RM643,432 was almost 50 per cent higher than it had been a year earlier.[4] Company profits did even better. In 1933, Alfred (for whom we have better information than for Siegfried) enjoyed pre-tax earnings of only RM11,500; his earnings in 1934 jumped to RM21,152. To give a sense of comparison, in the

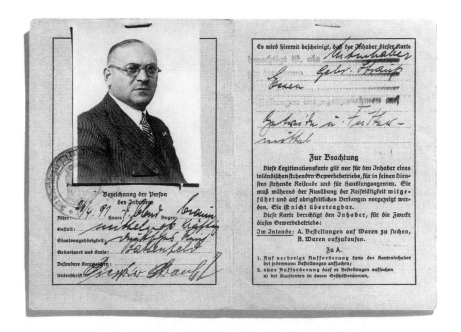

*Weathering the storm; Siegfried Strauss, 1936*

mid-1930s the pay of a top worker in the best-paid armaments sector was between RM2,500 and 3,000 a year before tax. Many workers would be earning only a tenth of what Alfred and Siegfried were taking home.[5] In August 1934, they felt able to enlist the help of the German consulate in Sofia to deal with a dispute arising out of a Bulgarian export ban.[6] Most striking of all was Werner Hoffmann's recollection that in February 1936, when he left for Argentina, the business was still operating without hindrance. As he drove round his customers for the last time in early 1936, making his farewells, he found that few could understand why he was going.[7]

The brothers' success is all the more surprising in that even after the national boycott was abandoned, 'unofficial' economic discrimination against Jewish businesses and workers increased apace. Within three years, many small business sectors would be effectively cleared of Jews. By 1936, a good fifth of the Jewish population was dependent on

*Siegfried's employee, Werner Hoffmann, and his fiancée Hanna*
*Heumann at the time of their departure to Argentina 1936*

Jewish welfare.[8] The Strauss brothers, however, possessed a number
of advantages. First, though Essen's town administration supported
anti-Jewish measures, the region was relatively tolerant. Most Jews who
lived there felt somewhat protected from the excesses they heard of
elsewhere. Indeed, up to 1938, Jewish emigration from the Rhineland
area, to which Essen belonged, was proportionately lower than for the
country was a whole.[9] Secondly, the regime was initially very hesitant
to do anything that might disrupt the food trade. But probably the most
important factor favouring the Strauss brothers was that they went to
their customers, not the other way round, and their customers were in
farms away from the public gaze.[10]

Even if they had thought of selling up, there were also serious economic disincentives to leaving the country. It was increasingly hard to get a proper price for Jewish assets. Potential customers assumed the seller would be desperate enough to accept any price. Then, the so-called Reich Flight Tax (*Reichsfluchtsteuer*) had to be paid. This tax had been introduced in 1931 to hinder the emigration of wealthy asset holders. After 1934, its main thrust changed to fleecing Jewish emigrants, and a wealthy individual like Siegfried could reckon on losing 25 per cent of his assets to the tax. But there was more. With foreign currency at a premium in the German economy, there were very tight restrictions on conversion. Again, to economic necessity was added anti-Semitic logic. The result was that a Jew in Siegfried's position leaving Germany before 1937 would be lucky to take 50 percent of his assets abroad. The only exception to these restrictions was emigration to Palestine. But Palestine, with its primitive conditions and limited business opportunities, had no appeal for a man like Siegfried Strauss, who had always been hostile towards the separatism of the Zionists.[11] After 1937, the screw was tightened further, with ever more punitive currency conversion rates being applied. For the Strauss brothers, Werner Hoffmann told me, the idea of getting out of Germany with a small remnant of their wealth 'was simply brushed aside.'[12]

But economics was only part of the explanation for the brothers' refusal to leave. Werner remembered much talk of the imminent collapse of the regime. And then there was their utter conviction that the debt to a former front-line soldier would not be forgotten. Marianne noted with a trace of irony how her father used to quote General Ludendorff's statement: 'The gratitude of the fatherland is surely yours.' Werner quoted almost word for word the same phrase about the '*Dank des Vaterlandes*'.[13] Among Marianne's surviving papers was a certificate belonging to Feldwebel Alfred Strauss, awarded on 16 April 1934, bestowing on Alfred the Remembrance Cross in 'faithful memory' of his service to the Königliches Preussiches Füsilier Regiment 39. How could anything bad happen to such loyal servants of the Reich?

In their faith, the Strausses were far from unique.[14] Often it was Jewish men rather than their wives who felt more tied to German soil, though there is no evidence that Ine thought differently from her husband.[15] Perhaps she too believed that the brothers' military background and prosperity would protect them. For a long time, there was always some hope they could cling to. After the promulgation of the Nuremberg Laws, many Jews felt they now knew the legal position and would be able to cope. During 1936, the year of the Olympics, the regime largely refrained from intensifying anti-Jewish measures. Jewish emigration remained low.[16] But even at the time, Werner Hoffmann found the brothers' confidence almost incomprehensible. For example, he remembered that when there was an amnesty for repatriating foreign accounts in 1934 or so, the brothers dutifully brought their foreign exchange holdings back into Germany. Even harder for Werner and his colleague Hans Goldschmidt to comprehend was the brothers' decision to invest in property in the mid-1930s. 'We could not understand it.'[17]

The brothers' property dealings are, indeed, the best evidence that they believed they could outlive the regime. By 1935 they had clearly decided that the prospects for their grain business were poor, at least in the short term. So, in October 1935 they bought land on the Hufeland-strasse, a street at the bottom of the Ladenspelderstrasse. Marianne remembered the excitement surrounding the building project, to which the brothers committed well over 200,000 Reichsmarks.[18] A Swiss architect, Rudolf Zbinden, was employed to build two luxury apartment blocks. Because all the business records are preserved, we can see that the brothers had no particular barriers put in their way. On one or two occasions, irate tradesmen adopted an anti-Semitic tone, but because the brothers were unflappable and never allowed themselves to be intimidated, normal courtesies were soon resumed.[19] In one of those touching examples of childhood response untouched by adult realism, Marianne assured me that the houses were the 'talk of the town' at the time.[20] In October 1936 the first tenants moved in and in 1937, with the block fully occupied, Alfred's pre-tax income was as good as in any year since the 1920s:[21]

2,999 from grain business
9,934 dividends
8,462 rents
21,395 total
20,150 after deductions.

In one sense, the brothers were far-sighted. They had chosen the one economic activity, property letting, in which Jews would be able to operate longer than any other. In another sense, of course, they had not been far-sighted at all.

Siegfried and Ine cannot have been unaware of the worsening conditions around them. In October 1933, the Nazi Veterans' Organization tried to bring a prosecution against them relating to their house-purchase ten years earlier. It came to nothing, but it must have given them pause. After the Nuremberg Laws in 1935, they were no longer allowed to employ non-Jewish maids. Non-Jewish acquaintances and neighbours began to look the other way from Marianne's family:[22]

'The neighbours never talked to us. They used to be quite friendly, ordinary people. Who'd been living there all our lives, as long as we'd been there. I can never remember ever talking to any of them after 1933. So we were completely isolated.'

On one side of the house lived a family with children of Marianne's age. Ine had been on friendly terms with the mother, a Frau Salk. 'And suddenly not a word, over the garden fence or whatever. And on the other side I don't even know – I can't remember the people or who lived there.' The only sign of life Marianne could remember from that side was wonderful music:[23]

'Somebody played the piano beautifully. I could have listened all day to whoever it was. I don't even know if it was somebody playing or if it was one of those mechanical things, it was so good. But that was the only contact with those neighbours on that side. I never saw anybody. Extraordinary, extraordinary.'

Social life was focused more and more on the family. Every Sunday relatives would visit, cousins, aunts, for tea or supper, or they would go out in the afternoon. Grandfather Leopold in Dinslaken became the object of particular attention after his wife Saly died in May 1934. But even family life began to suffer. Years earlier, Ine's cousin, Greta Rosenberg, had married a non-Jewish doctor, Dr Untieth. Marianne remembered visits to Ahlen in the 1920s when she used to play with the Untieths' daughters. Dr Untieth himself was an enormous man; in the 1920s, whenever Marianne was ill in Ahlen, he would lumber in looking more like a vet than a doctor, and she would be terrified. But now the

*The family together, 1934*

contact was broken. Grete's daughters had joined the female equivalent of the Hitler Youth, the League of German Girls (Bund deutscher Mädel or BDM). Greta would cross the road so that she would not have to say hello to her aunt, Marianne's grandmother, terrified of being implicated by the Jewish connection. Grandmother Rosenberg, of course, found this very upsetting. But such developments still did not persuade Marianne's parents that they should go. Werner Hoffmann sadly shook his head at the Strauss brothers' obstinacy. It was harder to elicit a direct view from Marianne of her parents' reluctance to leave. Once, though, Marianne described to me an argument she had after the war about whether the Holocaust could have happened in Britain, and in doing so indirectly offered a judgement of her parents:

'People just won't see it, they just will not . . . because it demands some sort of reaction or action or anything. Nobody wants to leave their home and pack up and go into the unknown. Particularly not if you're pretty well off and you've worked for it very hard and are very much self-made. And you think you've done your duty by your country. Now it's the turn of your country to do its duty by you. You're a German like everybody else. But not only that, it's sort of . . . you don't want to be inconvenienced, I don't know what you can say . . . it's something you don't want to face up to.'

The same theme recurred in my interviews with Marianne's later wartime helpers. Whenever they talked about her parents' fate, they always emphasized the fact that her father had waited too long to leave. The uniformity and emphatic way in which this view was put forward suggested that it stemmed from Marianne. Throughout her interaction with me, though, she tended to defend their behaviour and only occasionally allowed herself some veiled criticism.


## At the Luisenschule

For Marianne's parents the 1930s were unpleasant but bearable. For Marianne, the period was very different. She recalled her time at the Luisenschule as unredeemed misery. In the tape we made in 1989, she said:[24]

'Anti-semitism in Essen was always palpable . . . My childhood was very coloured by such things, particularly my experiences at school. My fellow pupils were all in the BDM and there was strong anti-Semitism in the school and in the class . . . I can remember only one or two teachers who one felt were at all distanced from the situation and were completely neutral. Never did anyone express any form of sympathy or fellow feeling.'

When we came back to the issue in 1996, she told me that 'we weren't allowed to forget that we were Jewish.' There was a lot of jeering. 'Children can be very cruel.' In fact, she was adamant that she had no positive memories of school whatsoever: 'There was nothing at all enriching about it.' In a later conversation she was even more damning: 'It was absolute hell, really.'[25] To reinforce the point, I discovered that, shortly after the war, Marianne had written a report recalling how at the age of eleven, 'I heard for the first time the word *Jew* being hissed behind my back,'[26] and how it had taken her a long while to recover the sense that there was no disgrace to being a Jew.

Marianne remained bitter about her fellow students until the end. During the 1980s, the Alte Synagoge in Essen informed her that a former fellow pupil, a Frau Barbara Sparrer,[27] had visited the exhibition in the synagogue and asked after Marianne, seeking to make contact. Would Marianne like to respond? She most certainly would not. The woman, she told me, had been 'one of her biggest tormentors'. I didn't think much more about the story until after Marianne died and I found the letter from the Alte Synagoge. I wrote to Frau Sparrer, explaining that I had found the letter and asking if she would be willing to talk to me.

Frau Sparrer lived in a very pleasant block of flats in the south of Essen. Her building was on a steep hill and with the colourful canopies over the balconies the neighbourhood might have been some Swiss holiday resort. I rang the door and she came down to meet me. Her face when I introduced myself was expressionless. We went upstairs and had coffee on the balcony, a rather cramped affair off the pleasant living room. She started off by trying to work out who I was.

'Are you, how shall I say, Israeli?' she asked.

'Do you mean Jewish or Israeli?' I responded.

She persisted: 'There are the three religions – Christianity, Jewish, Muslim – or have I got the sequence wrong?'

I clarified the difference between being a Muslim, an Israeli and a Jew, but Frau Sparrer had some difficulty understanding that I could be both English and Jewish at the same time. After I briefly mentioned the death of Marianne's daughter, Frau Sparrer looked nervously out over the balcony (we were several floors up) and said we'd better go inside. At this point I realized why she had been so expressionless downstairs. For some reason, she was paralysed with fear.

Frau Sparrer told me that she had tried to contact three Jewish fellow pupils and none had responded. The last time she saw Marianne was during the war. Nervously, she began to ask about Marianne's wartime experiences. Her questions, hesitant and broken off, were hard to follow. 'Could I then ask . . .' she began, and there was a very long pause. Then she pointed to her chest: 'Here, you know? The yellow star with the word *Jew* on it. I once saw Marianne on the street, but quite a way distant on the other side; I think it was Krupp Street, she must have been there then.'

*Hmm.*

Then she asked me a series of questions about Marianne's life after the war and about her children. She repeatedly sought to clarify my relationship with Vivian and the motive behind my project, almost as if she feared that some dossier was being put together against her. The ensuing exchanges revealed both great discomfort and much confusion:

'Now tell me; Marianne, you've just spoken about her parents . . . how is it possible, didn't they . . . Marianne must surely have in some way . . . oh, I see she lived in the – what did you say – underground?'

I confirmed that Marianne had remained in Germany illegally. 'Illegally', repeated Frau Sparrer, curiously relieved she had found the right word. 'Ah, *that's* how she saved her life.' She went on, 'There are many who left Germany early.' I agreed that there were. 'Yes? And . . .' there was another of her very long pauses, '. . . how is it possible that the parents, for example, with all the concentration camps and so on, how is it possible that her parents didn't leave in time?' Was she asking, I wanted to know, seeking to provoke her into an admission of knowledge, because it was so clear what was about to happen to them?

'Well, I know, people, I've heard that . . . but you must remember that, when I say that, I was just a child then, yes? How is it that . . . ah, now I know what I wanted to say, they said that those who had read Hitler's *Kampf* knew what was coming . . . Have you heard this said?'

'Hmm, hmm. Yes, sort of, hmm.'

We then talked about the concentration camps. Frau Sparrer had problems telling one from another and there were repeated confusions between Theresienstadt and Auschwitz, which she had visited. She had been shocked by Auschwitz, but she had an explanation: 'They did that while the German men were at the front.' And she cast doubt on the whole thing by wondering where all the bodies had gone, if there had been so many. I was able to help her out on the last point.

'They were burned,' I said.

'Ach, so.'

We moved on to Kristallnacht. Frau Sparrer remembered the devastation clearly:

'They destroyed everything. Terrible. The synagogue, it's now the museum, that was destroyed too . . . it was one of the most beautiful museums. [She meant synagogues.] Dortmund also had a beautiful synagogue . . . Yes and . . . yes what did they do? They . . . I think, they poured petrol into the synagogue and set it on fire.'

Sensing that I was dutifully being offered all this, I said that we were all agreed in condemning what had happened in retrospect, but that my interest was not in passing judgement. What I wanted to know was what her feelings, expectations and perceptions had been *at that time*. Frau Sparrer responded by asking how long Marianne was at the Luisenschule. As far as I knew, Marianne had been there until Kristallnacht. 'Yes?' said Frau Sparrer, surprised. 'But she must have . . . the parents were no longer in Essen, isn't that right?' No, the parents had still been there. Again Frau Sparrer looked surprised. When I added that Marianne had had to leave the school in 1938, she asked anxiously 'Had to? . . . What form did that take, this *having* to leave? I don't know.'

Suddenly, in a very lively voice, she launched into something else: 'Now then, you know, this probably is not appropriate here because it's not really very factual but Marianne . . . black hair, I think she had a centre parting and plait and curls . . . that's right, isn't it? Then she had a kind of old-fashioned dress and something . . . a kind of smock which, ach at that age you didn't wear any more . . . And in addition, please don't take offence, that I'm telling you this . . . she wore a little girl's petticoat, I still remember that about Marianne.'

Her good cheer remained as she remembered the day the three Jewish girls had shown their classmates a book, 'the Talmud', Frau Sparrer called it:

'That's their bible that you read from right to left, that's right isn't it? . . . They showed us that once. All three. Otherwise, you wanted to know, how we co-pupils behaved towards the Jewish girls. 1-A, 1-A. I think also –'

'What does that mean, "1-A"?'

'The best.'

Frau Sparrer told me that her father was against Hitler, that her parents protected her, that she was a sheltered girl and that her parents didn't want her to go to BDM. She said she didn't go to the younger version of the BDM, the Jungmädel, with much enthusiasm, either. Then I asked her again about the '1-A'.

'That's how I experienced it.'

'Yes. I mean, normally when one reads, er, reports about Jewish pupils at normal school in the 1930s, one could not say that the relationship was 1-A; quite the contrary.'

'No? I think it was. You mean that the Christian pupils behaved very badly towards the Jewish ones?'

'Yes.'

'That's what you want to say.'

'That pupils were discriminated against, that after a certain point they had to sit separately –'

'No. I have no memory of that. No, no . . . I normally have a good memory of where we sat. I can't remember that.'

'And that the lesson material itself made clear distinctions, for example –'

'History? Or –'

'For example,' I persisted, 'racial teaching in biology. And –'

Frau Sparrer interrupted by asking if biology was a principal subject in the curriculum at the time, something to which I did not know the answer. I then asked her how she experienced school and she said it was a good time. They had good teachers, amongst other things a priest's son, Dr Rollenberg, who taught German and history. 'Yes, well,' she said, 'so that would probably be about it. Did you have any other questions which I haven't addressed?'

I took a deep breath:

'Well, now I . . . I would like to say something that will perhaps be a little difficult for you to hear or . . . well, let me ask a question. Have you wondered, when I tell you that Marianne received your letter, why she did not reply?'

'All three did not respond. I didn't give it any thought. That was how it was, I accepted it. One didn't know what kind of fate they had faced.'

'Well, Marianne said to me, before she died –'

'That she knew me?'

'She didn't give me your name; I found out your name only when I found the letter. But she said that someone from her school had tried to get in touch –'

'That must have been me . . . and now you want to know why I did that?'

'No. It's that Marianne referred to you as one of her tormentors.'

'Me?'

'That's what she said.'

'I'm absolutely shocked . . . I don't know what she means by that. We were never together. We were in the same class and that was it.'

There was a long pause. 'Now, I want to say something to you', said Frau Sparrer, and she hit the table several times while talking. 'It was out of purely positive, human reasons. I didn't do that out of nosiness. I am really shocked about this . . . I don't know what you mean by tormentor. I was not in her parents' house, nor did I sit next to her; I can't remember that at all. How should one . . . how should one understand "tormentor"?'

The exchanges which followed contained an odd contradiction. Frau Sparrer expressed more than once amazement that the Strauss family managed to survive in the Ruhr until 1943. Yet when I tried to get at why this should be surprising, she claimed to know nothing about the deportations that would have made her see 1943 as very late for them still to be in the Ruhr. She was 'too much a child'. (In 1943 Frau Sparrer celebrated her twenty-first birthday.) Again and again, she came back to the word 'tormentor' and to the fact that her father had been against Hitler, with the implication that this provided a blanket dispensation for the rest of the family. For example, there was the time when a Jewish acquaintance of her mother wanted to make her farewells and her father insisted she be able to do so in the Sparrers' house:

'Everyone was frightened and said, "For God's sake, do anything but let a Jewess into the house." "No," said my father, "there's no question. This is where she will make her farewells."'

Who was everyone, I wanted to ask. After lots more of the same, I asked:

'Am I the first who has asked you about the past?'

'Yes, and you see that I know so little . . . I did say that on the phone, that I know very little. And I really don't know if it helped you.'

'I found it very interesting.'

Shortly afterwards I took my leave. I found myself angrily pleased at having delivered this late bit of emotional restitution. I was proud that I'd had the nerve to be so brutally open. So much of what she had told me fitted into the pattern of post-war apologia. The not having known anything. The explanation that the Jews were murdered while the German soldiers were at the front – those honest German men who would have put a stop to it. At the very time we were talking, the travelling exhibition 'Crimes of the Wehrmacht' was on in Essen. It showed just how deeply the Wehrmacht was implicated in the crimes. As in the war so now, it seemed, Frau Sparrer was ignoring the information available to her. BDM-generation girls typically took refuge behind the judgements and political positions that their parents, particularly their fathers, had held before Hitler came to power. A single moment of helping a Jew – here the graciousness with which a friend had been able to make her farewells – became the exculpatory proof of innocence. On the other hand, was I so certain that Marianne had got it right? And who was I to be the avenging angel? Had I been a German Aryan in the 1930s, would I have been braver? Guilt followed pride. I felt bad at having left Frau Sparrer in such obvious distress. Her worst fears had been realized. She was never going to look back on her school days in the same way again.

I did learn one more interesting thing from Frau Sparrer – that the Luisenschule had an Old Girls' association that held annual meetings.

In August 1997, I wrote to the organizer, Frau Ingrid Kuschmiers. A couple of months later, Dr Rosemarie Lange, living in southern Germany and a year younger than Frau Sparrer, wrote to me that Marianne Strauss had joined her class for a short period in 1938:

*I think that she came after the summer holidays after a lengthy cure by the sea. After the cure she had been kept back a year, since she started the school in 1933 whereas my class began in 1934.*

*I can remember that she lived in the Ladenspelderstrasse. Otherwise I know nothing of her family, siblings, or her father's career. That surprises me now because we sometimes cycled home together, but my journey was a lot shorter than hers. What did we talk about: school and music lessons?*

*Marianne was a pretty girl, with dark eyes, fresh skin colour, brown curly hair done up in a braid.*

Dr Lange followed with details of Marianne's last day at school after Kristallnacht and continued

*... we never heard anything more of her. I have often thought of her. Evidently, she succeeded in getting to Britain. I would be interested to hear about her subsequent life. She was the only Jewish person I ever met.*

I wrote back, intimating that Marianne had not, as Dr Lange clearly assumed in the wake of the previous correspondence, been able to escape before the war, but had survived the Nazi period inside Germany. In January 1998, Dr Lange responded:

*For your friendly letter many thanks ... You cannot know how much your letter has occupied my thoughts. I must say to you that, try as I can, I cannot recall any more memories.*

*Like most of the pupils, I was in the BDM, in a performance group, which primarily did music. Since I also had violin lessons, my leisure time after school was pretty well filled, particularly as I had to catch up on all the work I'd missed through illness.*

*Marianne thus became known to me only in September after the summer holidays. I can remember one thing clearly, that on a beautiful warm day we came out of the school gates with our bikes and Ferrucio, the Italian,[28] was there and we all said hello. I had told him that we had a Jewess in the class. I'm sure he was very pleasant to her.*

*I really do not know whether Marianne and I regularly went home together. Her way home was somewhat further than mine. In order to avoid making a big detour, she really had to go in a different direction and the tram also went her way. How strongly she was integrated into the class, I don't know. But she was actually only in our class for about eight weeks.*

*The only other thing I remember is a school excursion, in rather poor weather, with our class teacher. He was a fine man and belonged to the parish circle of Pfarrer Gräber and Gustav Heinemann.[29] (There's more that could be said on that score.) Our headmaster Dr Lindenberg was probably in the party, but he behaved correctly and was not servile, as far as I could judge that as a pupil.*
*[ . . . ]*

*I remember that she came with us on the first excursion. Whether she was attacked or isolated I don't know . . . Perhaps one didn't seek out her company. It is always hard for new people in a class to be integrated, and in her case surely particularly difficult.*
*[ . . . ]*

*What astonishes me and what I had thought was impossible is that there were Jews who survived in Germany. After everything that I've heard since then, I find it miraculous.*

I found Dr Lange's correspondence rather moving. The picture was more complicated than I had originally thought. When Marianne had referred to fellow pupils in the BDM, I had had an instant vision of ideologically committed, anti-Semitic young German girls making her life miserable. But here an implicit distinction was being drawn between those who belonged to the BDM or the party but remained correct in their behaviour, and those who were not so correct.

Other members of Dr Lange's class told me that Marianne had joined it in 1936. One, Frau Horn, was clearly one of those observant children who retain their early memories all their lives:

*Marianne Strauss belongs to the classmates whom I remember as vividly as ever after six decades. [ . . .] At the beginning of gymnastic lessons we*

*Two views of the Luisenschule:* (above) *Marianne's later school
class, probably taken in 1935 (before she joined);* (below)
*Marianne at school in 1937*

*would line up in order of size. She stood on my right and looked attentively forward at the teacher. Now and then I would look sideways and admire her beautiful dark hair, plaited into a thick braid around her head.*

*Marianne made me think. Despite the initially only slight difference, I felt she was much bigger than I and, despite being the same age, well beyond me in age and in sense. (As the youngest child I was over-protected but at the same time subject to an unusually strict upbringing. I was unworldly, lost in books and dreams.)*

*Sometimes, before the first lesson in class I would already be sitting in my place and I would see her come in. I would register with pleasure her natural but well groomed appearance. Her clothes were stylish and a little sporty, in an unostentatious, classy way. I would register too the calm look in her big dark eyes. In language lessons (French or English) I noticed that she responded more than the others and also that the teacher (of both languages) was particularly friendly towards her, both in her manner and in what she said, which of course I saw as very appropriate.*

*One lunchtime I was one of the last to leave and met a group of fellow pupils who were taking turns trying out a new bicycle. It belonged to Marianne. Although I had been standing there for only a little while, she quickly noticed me, and instead of calling me over loudly came up to me and asked quietly, 'Would you like to have a go?' Her sensitivity moved me very much, but I said shyly 'No, thanks', stood for another few minutes and then went home.*

*Once at the start of a summer trip we met accidentally in the train. My father went into a compartment where there were unoccupied seats. Opposite us sat Marianne's parents, Marianne and her brother (perhaps ten years old), who was deeply immersed in a Karl May book.*

*Marianne waited for a few minutes, then called me cheerfully, 'Come on, let's go outside to the open window!' We did that and looked out for a long time and enjoyed the trip and the wind, until Father and I had to change trains. It was only years later that I asked myself – why this often overpowering shyness towards such a delightful young human being? After all, whenever I met our neighbours, an old Jewish couple, on the street I spoke to them freely and without inhibition. And this remained so until perhaps two years after the beginning of the war. Then it was said that they, like other pensioners, fled the increasing air raids on Krupp-dominated Essen and went to the Netherlands. Not long after that, their house, like ours, was completely destroyed.*

*It was in the beginning of 1943 when, very early one morning after a long night in the air-raid shelter – the all-clear had only just been sounded – I saw Marianne again on an almost deserted street, after more than four years. We hurried from different directions and to different destinations, looked at each other without saying anything and went on, without stopping.*

*How big and how grown-up she looked now, and yet still wore her hair as she had as a child.*

Elsewhere, Frau Horn noted that when she met Marianne's father in the train he had not stood up. 'Although I assumed that he had sustained a war injury, I'm no longer sure, after such a long time, whether this really was the case.' There followed more information about Frau Horn's visiting Yad Vashem with the Society for Christian–Jewish Co-operation. In a later letter, Frau Horn added further details, remembering that there had been one occasion, but only one, when a male teacher had shouted something anti-Semitic at Marianne.

Both Frau Horn and Dr Lange were in deepest southern Germany, and not so easy to reach, but another correspondent, Waltraud Barkhoff-Kreter, was in Essen. On the phone, her gravelly voice was direct and to the point. Was she willing to meet? Certainly, come tomorrow morning at eleven.[30] And so I did. She lived in a neat block of flats on a long and rather lively street of shops and restaurants. A smiling, round-faced rather solid figure opened the door. It was clear she was still professionally active as a homoeopath – she was in the middle of a telephone consultation when I came in and there were to be several more calls in the course of our interview. I went into the sitting room and looked around. There were Chagall prints on the walls and a Menorah, the nine-armed candelabra for the Chanukah festival, on the sideboard. I remembered that Frau Barkhoff-Kreter had written that she had paid some visits to Israel. In the kitchen, making coffee, she told me about her father's pre-war contacts with the wealthy Jewish Hirschland family.

Herr Hirschland had become her godfather. After the war, Jewish friends from the USA had sent them 'care packages'.

Like her contemporaries, Frau Barkhoff-Kreter's first point of reference was Marianne's beauty:

'Yes, and then Marianne Strauss, I always admired her, a beautiful girl. I was, you know, the blonde type, with round cheeks, long arms and long legs, and Marianne Strauss was already really womanly! And to me she was beautiful. I would very much like to have been like that.'

She laughed loudly with an agreeable, slightly hoarse, smoker's laugh. Beyond that, she could remember little direct contact. What was interesting, though, is that she was a latecomer to the class, having previously been at an anthroposophical school until it was forcibly closed in 1936 and only then relocated to the Luisenschule, and her memories were closer to Marianne's. Arriving at the Luisenschule after the Waldorf school had been a shock, and she had never learned to feel at home there.

'I don't remember much of the class. When I joined as a twelve-year-old it was as if I came from another planet. And there were these girls preening themselves in their BDM uniforms.'

She pulled out a photograph of the class, taken before she or Marianne had arrived, and sure enough, a good proportion of the class was sitting there in BDM uniform.

'I wasn't old enough to realize that, for all that, they might be all right ... I was a stranger in the class, a real stranger. When school was over I would just pack my things and go.'

She also identified rather more teachers as being real Nazis than had other pupils. Though she too, made distinctions, in her vocabulary those teachers whom others had described as '*korrect*', she designated as fellow-travellers.

How was one to make sense of it all? On the specific point of dropping back a year, the evidence was in favour of Marianne having moved in 1936. With some remorse, I realized therefore that Frau Sparrer had been partially correct in remembering that Marianne had 'disappeared' from the class before 1938. She would have had no direct memories of Marianne after 1936. Nevertheless, Frau Sparrer's recollections still stuck out from the rest. The contrast between her mirthful memory of

Marianne's odd appearance and Frau Horn's paean to her sporty look seemed crass (though it was possible that Marianne's style changed between joining the school in 1933 and dropping back in 1936).

In any case, could one assume that the more positive memories were necessarily authentic? A lot of the letters contained a kind of philo-Semitism all too familiar in post-war Germany, in which the old anti-Semitic stereotypes are replaced by philo-Semitic ones.[31] Out of the hook-nosed, exploitative, rootless Jews arose brilliant minds, helpful shopkeepers and beautiful children. In such a context, the memory of Marianne's father failing to stand up had now to be interpreted as the result of a war injury. On the other hand, the stereotypical philo-Semitism was rarely accompanied by such detail about individual personalities, encounters and incidents as here. And Marianne, after all, *had* been beautiful. That was no imposition of a stereotype.

Frau Kuschmiers, the Luisenschule archivist, sent me a copy of the volume *125 Years Luisenschule 1866–1991*. The last page was devoted to 'A letter', from Jerusalem, dated August 1991, the only letter included.[32] The writer, Ruth Gawze, née Ferse, a Jewish woman one year older than Marianne, had attended the Luisenschule from 1932 to April 1938 and had managed to reach Israel early in 1939. She wrote now of her re-encounters with Essen and with the Luisenschule in the 1980s:

*I myself have positive memories of the years spent at the Luisenschule. Neither from the teachers nor my fellow pupils did I hear anti-Semitic remarks.*

Ineluctably, I found my perception of Marianne's school days changing into something more ambiguous. Perhaps, at least until Kristallnacht, the climate was not as anti-Semitic and hostile as she had said. Perhaps, in retrospect she had exaggerated.

## Jewish pupils remember school

A few months after these exchanges, I made my trip to Israel. I was there, amongst other things, to talk to two of Marianne's former Jewish fellow pupils. Ruth Gawse, born in 1922, had written the friendly letter to the Luisenschule, and Ruth Davidsohn, née Mendel, was one of the three Jewish girls in Marianne's class whom Frau Sparrer had tried to contact. I also wanted to meet Jakov, formerly Klaus, Langer, another of Marianne's contemporaries.

Ruth Davidsohn and Jakov Langer both lived in the north, Mrs Davidsohn above Haifa, in the leafy heights of Mount Carmel. I hired a car and drove up the winding, tree-lined roads, getting lost more than once, until I found her pleasant flat. In her youth, Ruth Mendel had been plain and plump. Now, a widow in her seventies, she was slim, spry and good looking. We waited on her balcony for Chaja Chovers (formerly Klara Kleimann), another of Marianne's contemporaries from Essen, to join us.[33] Ruth told me that, decades after the war, she and Chaja had met up again by chance, when Ruth was teaching traffic regulations to Israeli children. There was a pause while this sank in. We agreed with a chuckle that her teaching hadn't had much effect on Israeli driving standards.

Mrs Chovers arrived and Mrs Davidsohn served a delicious cold lunch of bread and salads, with watermelon to finish. We drank raspberry tea, something I've only had elsewhere in German youth hostels. Our conversation began with a sad acknowledgement. I showed them the photograph of Marianne as a teenager, then I showed them the photograph of Marianne a few weeks before she died. They were both shocked by how she had aged. 'Um Gottes willen! She must have suffered,' said Ruth, who kept switching between English, German and occasionally Hebrew. 'She must have suffered terribly . . . If someone had told me that that was Marianne I wouldn't have believed it.' After that, our conversation turned to school days. As it turned out, Mrs Davidsohn had been at the Luisenschule for only a year. Her memories of the place were at least as unfavourable as Marianne's. On the phone, she had already told me that all she remembered was feeling miserable and being thrown out of the religious education lessons.[34] Now, she added:

'I was *such* a bad student! . . . I had managed to get into the school. But I was bored to death there. I can remember the French lessons. To learn French, we first had to learn how to roll our r's. So we sat for hours and went "rrrr". That's how we learned French – when you think about that today . . . !'

*Chaja Chovers and Ruth Davidsohn in Israel*

Of course, there was nothing particularly National Socialist about bad French teaching, but Ruth went on:

'You noticed the anti-Semitism. And then there was the fact that I was so terribly fat, so there was *the fat Jew*, and this kind of stuff. I was happy to get out of the school. And there was something else. I was very often ill. Whether that was psychological or not, I don't know, but I was at home more often than I was at school. I think it was my parents who said, "There's no point, the child is simply miserable." But around this time, they were all thrown out.'

A little later, she reaffirmed that anti-Semitism had been evident from both staff and students. The Jewish school, which she rejoined after this one year, was much more comfortable.

I showed her the letter from Ruth Gawse, which suggested that the Luisenschule had been a positive experience. At this, Mrs Davidsohn became unsettled. She said she could remember so little, she had a 'blackout' of the period at the Luisenschule. All she could remember was being miserable, the French lessons, and the religious instruction. She could remember nothing else.

Before I left, we looked through her family photo album. There was a snap of her mother's family in 1921, a couple of years before Ruth was born. Her parents had survived, and so had an aunt, but as for the rest . . . We went down the row of comfortable faces: 'She was in Theresienstadt, deported, deported, deported, deported, deported, everyone deported . . .' And on that sad note, we parted.

Ruth Davidsohn's school memories may have been limited, but they were more than I gleaned from Mrs Gawse later in the week.[35] In an earlier letter, Mrs Gawse had written to me that she found it 'very surprising that Marianne Strauss suffered, which I did not know any-thing about and have no memory of'.[36] When I interviewed her, her recollection was so limited I felt unable to use her as a witness. Perhaps she had had a clearer memory in 1991 when she had sent the letter to the Luisenschule. If not, then it should be seen only as a gesture of conciliation – none the less meaningful for that – rather than any kind of description of the past.

On the other hand, it was clear Jewish pupils *did* have conflicting memories of school days in Essen.[37] My most reflective witness on this point was Jakov Langer. I had come across his name in Marianne's correspondence – yet another of the people from the past who had sought contact with her in the 1980s and to whom she had not responded. He lived in Kiryat Tivon, also in the northern part of Israel, and so after taking my leave from Ruth Davidsohn and Chaja Chovers I drove down to visit him.[38] The wooded, hilly country on the way to Tivon was lovely. The Langers lived in a beautiful, simple bungalow, set back from the road up some steps and surrounded by trees and a pond. It was a little paradise. I didn't yet know that Jakov Langer was a nature lover and bird-watcher and had been one of the pioneers of conservation in Israel. His wife Tsofia, a cultivated but somewhat ailing woman of Dutch origin, answered the door. A little later, Jakov himself came bounding in, shirtless, healthy and active. We sat down to a simple meal of bread and cheese. Before, while washing my hands, I'd noticed a calendar on which various dates and names had been inscribed. Here was Westerbork and a date, there was Sobibor and a date, there was Auschwitz and a date. These were the anniversaries of the dates on which family members had been deported or murdered. Jakov's father had been deported to Izbica in April 1942. His wife's family were the victims in Westerbork and Sobibor. His wife had survived in hiding in Holland. Her mother, Clara Asscher-Pinkhoff, had survived Belsen and been released to Palestine before the war ended, as part of an extraordinary deal with the Nazis. Her book *Sternkinder* had been a post-war best-seller.[39] Everywhere I turned in Israel, there were such miracles and tragedies.

Jakov Langer was born in 1924 and, like Marianne, had started secondary school soon after the Nazis came to power. For the first few years he had been in Gelsenkirchen, a period he remembered as relatively relaxed, playing with classmates and making mischief. But by 1936, when he came to Essen and transferred to the Humboldt Oberrealschule in Steelerstrasse, things were already different. His parents told him to be cautious. In 1937–8 he was the only Jewish boy out of 700 pupils. His fellow-pupils didn't talk to him much in the playground. And, one

*Jakov and Tsofia Langer in Israel*

day, he found himself sitting alone on his bench in the classroom – his neighbour must have been told to move. But, according to Jakov Langer, there was no abuse. He drew my attention to the book *A Boy in Your Situation*, written by Charles Hannam, which describes a miserable experience of persecution at the Goethe school in Essen.[40]

Langer said that he himself had 'never heard "dirty Jew" or that kind of thing. I didn't have strong contacts with fellow-pupils, that was only natural. They had been indoctrinated along those lines in the Jungvolk [the Hitler Youth's junior wing], but there was no taunting or remarks from pupils or from teachers.'

A friend of his, who had been at the Goethe school, did not share Hannam's memory, either. Langer felt that the differences were a function of individual perception or the bad luck to land in a class where there was real anti-Semitism. The fact that Langer had been sporty, though smaller than the average, may have helped. In class he was allowed to contribute normally. Only twice – during a lesson on Nazi ideology and during a biology lesson – was he asked to leave the classroom. Ironically, he was asked to guard the school gate to make sure no 'foreign elements' came into the school.

My perception of Marianne's school days had swung back again. Her recollection of misery had regained its emotional force, a force for a while diluted by the different tide of memory flowing from her non-Jewish contemporaries. It was almost shocking how differently individuals could experience the same events. Marianne's non-Jewish contemporaries had simply not understood how, for Marianne, the absence of easy interaction coupled with the odd exclusion from lessons, or outbursts from a teacher, or the occasional anti-Semitic remark in the playground, could add up to a hostile environment. For her non-Jewish contemporaries, the fact that most teachers and students behaved in a *korrekt* manner most of the time, that little overtly anti-Semitic was said or done, was evidence that the school was OK. And for some Jewish pupils, such an environment was bearable. If, like Langer, they were armed with a clear-cut interpretative framework which acknowledged the conditions shaping the behaviour of their fellow-pupils, then they were able to understand the silence around them as not particularly hostile. But for others, like Marianne, the experience overall was negative and depressing. We know that Marianne was more the rule than the exception.[41]

What made school even harder to bear for Marianne was that her parents were as keen as ever that she should perform well academically. In 1935, the Jewish newspaper *Jüdische Rundschau* felt obliged to warn parents of the situation faced by their children. It cited the example of a girl attempting to reassure her younger sister that the horse near-by would not hurt her. 'Go on,' the older girl says, 'the horse doesn't know we're Jewish.'[42] For Siegfried and Ine, however, nothing was to disrupt their daughter's education.[43]

In addition, Marianne also had ill health to contend with. Asthma and bronchitis often kept her away from school. When she was thirteen, she suffered particularly from bronchitis and was sent away for a cure.[44] This enforced absence resulted in poor marks, as she told me with regret:[45]

'Both my parents [were] very bright, particularly my mother, who'd been a high flyer and very ambitious ... To do well at school was probably the most important thing ... So I knew I was a great disappointment to my parents, and that didn't help me any.'

## Jewish youth together

There was one thing on which all the Jewish witnesses agreed: by 1935, at the latest, the only time they felt relaxed or confident or could really enjoy themselves was when they were with other Jews, above all with other Jewish youngsters. They met at Jewish youth groups, at organized events in the Jewish Youth Centre, or in each other's houses. Jakov Langer, for example, remembered bumping into Marianne occasionally at the Makkabi Hazair youth group, to which they both belonged. His most vivid memory, though, was of meeting her at a concert evening in a private house. The Langers always attended such events, being very much part of the Essen musical scene, and both Jakov (then Klaus) and Marianne were taking lessons from the same piano teacher. They chatted during the concert. 'I remember that she was pretty. That her appearance made a real impression on me – I remember that, too.'

*At Ruth Ferse's party, 1937 (Marianne and Ruth in front)*

I noticed with surprise that the Langers had a very impressive NAD stereo system, which didn't fit at all with their simple rustic life-style. Much later, in the States, when I told Hanna Aron, another contemporary, that I'd visited the Langers and Ruth Gawse she exclaimed, 'Oh, you visited the elite!' That took me aback. She was remembering them the way they had been. Herr Ferse, Ruth's father, had been a judge who had trained the later Federal President, Gustav Heinemann. Jakov's father had been a judge, too. Both his parents had been talented and enthusiastic musicians. I was going to respond that there was nothing upper-class about them now. But then I suddenly saw Jakov's stereo-system and record collection as a last echo of that German-Jewish cultural and musical life of which he and Marianne too had been a part in the 1930s.

Although in her reminiscences Marianne did not make a particular feature of the youth groups of the 1930s, we know that she took part in them and there is good reason to think that the values of the youth movement had a lasting influence on her. After 1933, Jewish youth groups continued to be allowed to operate fairly freely and took on a new significance. Whereas before 1933, only a quarter of Jewish youngsters in Germany had been organized in Jewish youth groups, now the proportion rose to over half, and by 1937 had reached around 60 per cent.[46] The youth groups were strongly influenced by the so-called free German youth, a movement that could trace its roots back to the so-called *Wandervogel* groups that emerged in the nineteenth century.[47] The *Wandervogel* had emphasized young people's right to lead themselves, removed from adult society, and had criticized modern, urban life. During the 1920s, a new German youth movement had emerged, the so-called *bündische* youth, less anarchic than the *Wandervogel* and seeking to create a separate ordered community with strong inner leadership. Surviving publications from Marianne's youth group, Makkabi Hazair – since 1934 combined with the Jewish Scouts into the JPF–MH (Jüdischer Pfadfinder–Makkabi Hazair, the largest Jewish youth organization in Germany)[48] – show that it was very much shaped by the Bündisch atmosphere. Alongside support for Zionism, it called for 'discipline, order, cleanliness, a simple life-style and clothing, calm behaviour in public, comradeship, work for the community, preparedness'.[49] Some of its dicta could just as easily have stemmed from the Hitler Youth – its emphasis on performance and effort as the principle of leadership selection, for example.[50] But whereas the Hitler Youth was increasingly regimented and controlled from above, the Jewish youth movements retained their independence. Paradoxically, the Jewish groups were probably the last in Germany to still honour the spirit of the free German youth movements of the pre-1933 period.[51] Jakov Langer remembered the group's uniform of blue shirts, with white shirts for special occasions. They would hold a roll call and march within the Youth Centre. In the 1936–8 period, Marianne's age group was very active, with regular evening and weekend meetings, talks, plays and trips.[52]

From Ruth and Chaja, I learned of another Essener of their generation, Hans Eulau, now working in the Museum of the Ghetto Fighters, Beit Lochamei Hagetaot. So, after staying over at the Langers', I drove back past Haifa to visit the museum, where Hans Eulau, now Uri Aloni, worked as a volunteer. Having learned only the day before that he was there, I turned up unannounced.[53] He received me very pleasantly, excited by the Essen connection, but also frustrated at the lack of advance notice. He had a tour group of Americans to look after, so I sat in his office and asked him questions in ten- to fifteen-minute bursts (to which he responded in faultless English) between his assignments. While we were talking, Chaja arrived. The two hadn't met before, so I felt oddly part of a kind of Essen reunion.

More strongly than any of the others, Uri Aloni emphasized the emotional and psychological reinforcement provided by the youth groups. His memory of the classroom was one of defiance; when the class had to say 'Heil Hitler', the Jewish boys shouted 'Drei Liter'. He missed not being able to go to the cinema or the public swimming baths. The youth movement was his compensation; it 'straightened our backs'. Though in his seventies, Uri Aloni had kept his 'straight back'. He had been a keen boxer in Hakoach, a Jewish sports movement, as evidenced by his flattened nose and cauliflower ears. I wouldn't have wanted to go in the ring with him in the 1930s. I wouldn't want to go in the ring with him now. He said something that I think was to be true of Marianne later, too, namely, that during the 1930s Jewish parents' and children's roles began to shift. Home had once been the place of security, but now it was a place of uncertainty. Suddenly, the parents were more unsure what to do than the children were. 'Suddenly, we knew better,' Uri said. The youth movement 'gave us just what we were lacking at home'.

Uri Aloni was at pains to point out that the youth movement had also given him a strong commitment to Zionism and a belief in the future. Clearly used to making professional presentations for visitors, he offered a smooth and well-paced account. Particularly on the subject of the youth movement, his line was so clear that I couldn't help feeling I was being given some kind of propaganda. After he left me to look after his Americans, I visited the Museum of Jewish Resistance. Its re-creation of the ghettoes was subtle and complex. But, when we came to the youth movement and its role in the resistance, the exhibition drew the same clear and direct line from the solidarity learned in Habonim or Makkabi Hazair, through anti-Nazi resistance, to the contribution of the young immigrants of the 1930s and 1940s to the foundation of the state of Israel. Here, even more than in the interviews, I had a strong sense of public ideology.

At once, my perception of the conflicting testimony changed again. I had initially been conscious of the changes and omissions in particular individuals' testimony. Then, I had realized that many discrepancies did, in fact, faithfully reflect different contemporary perceptions of events. Now, I saw how important the public context was in which individuals recalled their past. My non-Jewish German correspondents had remembered the Luisenschule within a specific German public context of post-war philo-Semitism and forgetfulness. Not only that, but when I thought about it there had been a much more specific ex-Luisenschule community which had helped to shape memory. Many of the pupils told me they had learned after the war that their teacher, Herr Schammel, had been more anti-Nazi than they had realized.[54] Their former teachers had helped disseminate the idea that the bulk of the school had resisted the tide.[55] For their part, my Israeli interlocutors were, consciously or unconsciously, speaking from the background of a battle-hardened, tenaciously self-assertive Israeli state.[56] For Marianne, however, on whom Zionism had never rubbed off very strongly, there was no such obvious public context to shape her memories.[57]

## Respite in Wyk

In Marianne's recollection, the experience from the 1930s that had given her the most emotional reinforcement had been not the youth groups but her cure in Wyk, on the North Sea island of Föhr.[58] Föhr was a health resort for respiratory diseases. The flat shores provided an ideal recreation ground for young people and there were several children's convalescent homes. The Jewish Women's League (Jüdischer Frauen-bund, JFB) had set up its own children's home there in 1927. After 1933, it began to advertise the home not only as a place of convalescence but also as a refuge for children suffering under the current political conditions.[59] During 1936, more youngsters than ever stayed at the home, nearly 300 – perhaps a sign of growing parental awareness of the strains of being in

Germany.[60] In that year, Marianne had severe problems with asthma and bronchitis, possibly exacerbated by stress. Marianne's memory was that she spent almost six months in Wyk. The usual length of a cure was seven weeks, and it is possible that Marianne had extended the time in her memory, but the comments of one of her teachers suggest that she may well have been there for longer than the customary stay.

An article written in 1937, celebrating ten years of the children's home, gives the impression of a delightful environment but a highly structured regime. Run by Clara Simons from Cologne with a team of some twenty kindergarten, school and gymnastics teachers, each day was tightly planned. For Marianne, a rather protected thirteen-year-old, such an environment was probably ideal. Even in 1936, the home was still able to offer the children such treats as trips to the small, bare but inhabited islands round about.[61] Within this child-centred regime, Marianne found being away from home and school and encountering some of the more open-minded staff especially liberating.

In particular there was Edith Caspari, whom Marianne was to meet again in Berlin during the war. Caspari, trained by the educationalist Helene Lange, was among other things a disciple of Jung and a graphologist. Marianne recalled that Caspari could gain the most astonishing insights from a small sample of someone's writing. She introduced Marianne to a new world of ideas.[62] In a letter written to Marianne in January 1943, Edith Caspari found emotional space amid the utter horror of that time (many of her closest colleagues had recently been murdered), to recall in rather literary style their first encounters:[63]

*I often still see little Marianne and her pigtails before me, just as she was when she arrived aged fifteen[64] with her father. She grew very fast and tried to enjoy life. She was frivolous in lessons and in spending money on pretty things and on the care of her own pretty body. But it is good to go through such phases too. They are not wasted. Humans are not angels. And in this period, Marianne still gave joy to other people, and not only because of her appearance (I see her still in the pretty, dark blue dress and in the colourful dressing gown).*

But while, to outsiders, Marianne was experimenting with charm and frivolity and the unusual freedom of having a little spending money, her ɔwn memory is of an independent identity that was taking shape for the first time. She arrived, as Edith Caspari observed, still a young girl, but she left on the way to maturity.

## The end of the illusion

After a lull during 1936, the pace of repression speeded up again. Between autumn 1936 and spring 1937, conditions deteriorated rapidly for many Jews. The Aryanization of Jewish firms accelerated. In February 1937, the head of the German Labour Front Robert Ley announced that a key goal of the four-year plan was to eliminate Jews from German economic life. Even so, by January 1938 only 135,000 of Germany's 525,000 Jews had emigrated. The next twelve months were to see a decisive difference, both locally and nationally.

From January 1938, Jewish citizens crossing the border into Switzerland and France had their passports confiscated, as the government attempted to restrict travel to those who were emigrating. By April 1938, only 40,000 businesses remained in Jewish hands out of 100,000 in 1933. Approximately half of all Jewish workers were now unemployed. In June 1938, Hitler ordered the Munich synagogue to be razed to the ground. Closer to home for the Strauss family, the synagogue in Dortmund was destroyed and the community cheated out of the funds they were supposed to be paid for the building.[65] From July onwards, all Jews, including infants, had to carry Jewish identity cards. In August, a new law expelled all Jewish doctors from the profession, effective from the end of September.[66] Jews were no longer allowed to own cars and the Strausses were forced to sell their smart *Wanderer*.[67] In October, Jews of Polish origin, including several hundred from Essen, were expelled from the country under appalling conditions.[68] But still Siegfried and Ine made no move to leave.

# 3

# Shattered Glass,
# Shattered Lives

On 7 November 1938, a German official at the Paris embassy was shot by Herschel Grünspan, a young Jew of Polish origin, protesting against his parents' inclusion in the October expulsions. On 9 November, at around 9 p.m., the Nazi leadership, most of whom were in Munich celebrating the fifteenth anniversary of Hitler's beer hall putsch of 1923, learned that the official, Counsellor Ernst vom Rath, had died from his injuries. Soon after the news came in, Hitler withdrew, leaving Goebbels to take the initiative and incite those present to take 'retribution'. At 10.30, the assembled Nazi, SA and SS prominence rushed off to make their telephone calls to the provinces. In this almost casual way, the stage was set for a pogrom.

In Essen, as elsewhere, local activists were deep in their cups celebrating the anniversary of the putsch. As midnight approached, SA and SS, drunk and surprised, were ordered into action and, on foot and by car, they piled off to the Essen synagogue. Thanks to the fact that one of their ranks was in charge of the carpool for the Nazi leadership in the region, the SS men managed to obtain petrol canisters and bring them into the synagogue. The fire service was so supportive that the news went round Essen in the following weeks that the firemen had 'put the fire out with petrol'. A wave of attacks on Jewish shops and homes followed, which lasted until 11 November.[1]

## Delayed reaction

On Ladenspelderstrasse, for some reason, the houses remained untouched both on 9 November and on the following days of destruction. According to one surviving Jewish witness who had lived in that part of Essen, the local district SA chief was relatively decent, and this helped spare the area.[2] Curiously, the myth of the decent local SA was relatively common in Jewish accounts of Kristallnacht. For example, the story was often told that SA units were brought in from other towns and regions to avoid local ties of friendship getting in the way of the violence. Yet subsequent research has often demonstrated such claims to be false.[3] Whatever the reason, on the night of 9 November, the Strauss family slept undisturbed.

The following morning, having no inkling of what was taking place all across Germany, Marianne went to school as usual. Rosemarie Lange wrote to me:

*Her last day at school was terrible . . . We had music lessons on the stage in the big hall. The teacher was late, and while we waited some of the girls were discussing what had happened in the town, what they'd seen and all the places that had been destroyed and smashed up. Maybe that was the first moment that Marianne heard about these things. It certainly was for me – we didn't have a radio, my parents were away at the time and the way to school led through a residential area . . . That class must have been absolute hell for Marianne. During the break, she left school unobtrusively, and we never heard from her again. I have often thought of her.*

Another correspondent, Vera Vahlhaus,[4] also described that day:

*On the morning after Kristallnacht (which neither Marianne nor I knew anything about because we lived in areas where 'nothing' had happened) I was standing on the steps by the school entrance. As Marianne Strauss came slowly towards me, another girl, Gudrun P.,[5] greeted her with the words, 'You old Jew, get lost, you've no business here,' and hit her on the head with an atlas. Without thinking, I walked over to Gudrun and shoved her head against the wall. The bell prevented me, thank God, from causing any further injury. It was the first and only time that I've ever been violent against another creature. Marianne Strauss ran from the school and I never saw her again.*

I tried to clarify the contradiction between the claim that Marianne ran away from the school before classes even started and Rosemarie Lange's account. I also asked if I could have the full name of Gudrun P. Mrs Vahlhaus wrote back:

*About the music lesson: I had had the incident with Gudrun and had to go to the headmaster. After a telephone call to my father I was sent home. I was completely out of control, and the headmaster knew I was in danger of saying or doing things that might have got my parents into trouble.*

On balance, it seems that Marianne probably did not leave school immediately and went to the music lesson as Dr Lange had said. Frau Vahlhaus would not give me Gudrun P.'s full name. She said the time for revenge was past and, although revenge was not really the point, I left it at that.

Only one of my correspondents made a point of recollecting that Marianne was *not* in school at all the day after Kristallnacht, a Mrs Gudrun Hochwald.[6] She wrote:

*In contrast to the reminiscences of Rosemarie Hahn [Lange], I do not think that Marianne appeared on the day after Kristallnacht. After the war, when the whole tragedy of the Jews became known, I often wondered about Marianne's fate, because I can't remember a conversation about it in our class. I think I sensed at the time that injustice was being done, but I was too reserved to act. Our class teacher at that time was Herr Schammel, who emerged after the war as a convinced opponent of the Nazis. He might well have talked his way into a death sentence if he had spoken openly about all the terrible things that happened that night.*

Later, I had the opportunity to interview Frau Vahlhaus. I brought along all the correspondence I had received from different Luisenschule pupils – given the uncertainties about exactly when Marianne had repeated a year, I wanted to check which of my correspondents had actually been together. I also brought a copy of the class photo that Waltraud Barkhoff-Kreter had given me in Essen. Frau Vahlhaus looked at the correspondence from Gudrun Hochwald and managed, which I had failed to do, to decipher the handwritten note of her unmarried name. She gave a start. Frau Gudrun Hochwald had been Fräulein Gudrun Plumpe, and Fräulein Gudrun Plumpe had been the girl who had attacked Marianne on the steps. Looking at the photo, she picked out a girl with glasses and identified her. I tried to find some resonance of a violent attack in the friendly letter I had received from Mrs Hochwald, in which, in addition to the section about Kristallnacht already quoted, she had written:

*Marianne sat diagonally left from me and I was always admiring her thick long plaits. I remember her as a quiet, reserved girl. Whether that was her nature or stemmed from the situation in those days, I can't say. I can't remember that she had any special status in the class. In my memory, my relationship to her was not awkward, particularly as our contact was restricted to lessons. Beyond that, there were no school activities. I don't know anything about her personal details (parents, siblings, where she lived).*

During my last lengthy stay in Germany, I asked Frau Hochwald for an interview without mentioning any details. She wasn't sure if she could remember enough to make it worth my while, she said, but I was very welcome to come. A few days later, I took the train to the sizeable industrial centre in which she lived, followed by a long taxi ride into the pleasant hills overlooking the town. As I walked towards the smart two-storey house, I felt even more peculiar than when interviewing Frau Sparrer, Marianne's 'tormentor'. I knew that if I told her of my specific interest this disclosure would distort the interview and provoke a purely apologetic response. On the other hand, I am no poker player. Frau Hochwald answered the door with a smile in which I discerned friendly politeness but also wariness. She was dressed smartly and conservatively and the house was full of expensive, very good quality heavy furniture. Her husband was there too, a friendly but firm man with a successful business career behind him, who would clearly stand no nonsense. The fact that we were to have the conversation *à trois* made me even more nervous.

The interview took the usual course. Even before I had started the tape, Frau Hochwald began by talking about Marianne's exotic beauty. And when I asked her to repeat the comment, once the tape was running, she was off on her father's positive attitude to the Jews. Apparently, Jewish employers had helped him weather the Depression. She didn't think the girls had normally worn BDM uniform in class and got into a muddle trying to explain away the photo, in which many of the girls were dressed in uniform. The photograph must have been taken on a Saturday, she claimed, although BDM girls did not attend school on Saturday. Her husband got into a similar contradiction, repeatedly asserting for most of the interview how little he was aware of politics, but when we got to his military career, he stressed his knowledge of contemporary affairs, which had got him through an important interview. And there was more sincere but apologetic detail that did not quite ring true. Frau Hochwald had, as she openly admitted, been an enthusiastic leader in the Jungmädel, the junior section of the BDM, and had risen through the ranks. But it had been an ideology-free zone, according to her. As time went on, though, I became less and less sure of my ground. Frau Vahlhaus had remembered Marianne's assailant's father as an apothecary and Nazi Party member. Frau Hochwald's father had been neither. Frau Vahlhaus had identified Gudrun Plumpe on the photo as a dark-haired girl with glasses. It was perfectly clear that the naturally blonde Gudrun Hochwald could not have been she. And when I finally put the specific accusation to Frau Hochwald, various aspects of her reaction made me pretty confident that, if she was concealing something, it was not at a conscious level.

Could I now be sure that the accusation was authentic, particularly as Marianne herself had never mentioned her last day at school? It was reasonable that Marianne's own memories should be dominated by the horrors that emerged later that day, but would she not have remembered an assault? Those who have conducted interviews in contemporary Germany know that post-war memories about Jews in the 1930s typically cluster around Kristallnacht. The historian Frank Stern has discerned in this pattern a kind of defensive forgetfulness – the long development of anti-Semitic measures and attitudes to which so many were party has been compressed in retrospect and loaded on to these few violent days.[7] Should the attack on the steps be seen as one such compressed symbolic memory, standing-in for tens of little incidents over a longer period of time that Marianne's contemporaries did not want to remember? Or had Kristallnacht really been a turning point in the schoolyard: tipping over into brutal action girls who previously had not been violently anti-Semitic, while shocking others into recognition of what was really happening? I was never going to find out.

## The assault on the Strauss family

What is clear is that soon after Marianne came home from school, the family learned that the previous night's orgy of destruction was giving way to something even more sinister. Reinhard Heydrich, the head of the Gestapo and the Sicherheitsdienst (SD), the SS security service, had given the order that as soon as the pogrom had died down a little, each district was to arrest as many Jews – in particular affluent Jews – as could feasibly be incarcerated. Initially, only healthy, male Jews were to be taken, and contact was established immediately with the concentration camps to achieve rapid transfer of the prisoners.[8] In Essen, the first Jewish men were rounded up on 10 November 1938. We know that at least 319 were taken into 'protective custody' in the police cells on the Haumannshof. As news of the round-up reached the Strauss family, Siegfried and Alfred decided to go into hiding. Marianne's great uncle Abraham Weyl (the brother of her maternal grandmother) had recently moved to Essen and was not yet well-known in the town. So Alfred and Siegfried travelled to his home at Hermann-Göringstrasse 316, Essen Bredeney, and spent two anxious days cooped up there. 'So there was hope,' Marianne said, 'that they might have been saved there. Which they might well have been had not the Gestapo put the screws on and come every few hours and said that if they didn't turn up they would take my mother and me. That brought my father and my uncle out pretty quickly, unfortunately. I don't think they would have taken us, but even so . . .'[9]

As persecution intensified, the records of the persecutors become more detailed; from this point on the Gestapo records, for example, begin to contain surprising detail on the Strausses' lives. We know from the records that the Strauss brothers eventually turned themselves in to the police on the afternoon of 12 November and were taken into protective custody as part of Heydrich's round-up. The files also include a statement Siegfried made after he gave himself up. Timed at 3 p.m. on the afternoon of the 12th, the statement runs as follows:[10]

*I have been resident in Essen since 1919. I fulfilled my military duty before the war and spent the whole war in the battlefield at the front . . .*

*By birth, I am of the Israelite religion. My ancestors have always been in Germany and I can prove this back to 1740. I possess German citizenship and feel myself a German in other respects too.*

It does not seem too much to say that we have here, preserved in the records, the last point in Siegfried's life, almost to the hour, when that proud sense of national identity could be uttered with any confidence.

Marianne's memories gain a new sharpness and depth from Kristallnacht onwards which they did not have for earlier phases of her life. Shortly after the end of the war, she recalled in a BBC broadcast 'the burning synagogues, the fear-filled days and nights in which, more clearly than ever before, we felt we were in the clutches of a power from which there was little chance of escape'.[11]

While her father was hiding, Marianne and her family began to learn what had happened to her grandparents, Leopold Strauss and Anna Rosenberg. Marianne's maternal grandmother, Anna Rosenberg, had been living alone on Adolf-Hitlerstrasse in Ahlen. Both Marianne and her cousin Uri Weinberg told me that the marauding SA came from other towns, but this was probably another myth.[12] Uri told me that Anna had a non-Jewish tenant in her house. When the SA was heard downstairs, Anna Rosenberg rushed into her tenant's rooms and hid in her bathroom. The tenant told the SA Anna had left. The men became suspicious when they found Anna's door open, but the tenant had the presence of mind to say that Frau Rosenberg was so absent-minded she regularly did such things. As Anna cowered in her tenant's bathroom, she heard her flat being destroyed.[13]

Meanwhile, Marianne and her aunt Oe telephoned Leopold Strauss in Dinslaken to see if he was all right. There was no answer. So they asked someone to drive them to Dinslaken. The house at Duisburgerstrasse 100 was empty and completely smashed to pieces. The curtains had been torn down. The mess was 'absolutely indescribable'. The bottled fruit that her grandmother had made before she died and stored in the attic, 'all beautifully, neatly labelled' was 'smashed to smithereens'. The destruction was so terrible that the conserves were dripping through the ceiling from the attic. Eventually, they found grandfather Leopold in a nearby hospital.

Of all the family members, Leopold's fate is the best documented, though some of the sources are ones to which Marianne never had access. Her own memory was dominated by her recollections of uncertainty about his welfare, and the terrible discovery of the empty house. After the war, though, Marianne's cousin obtained this description from Leopold's non-Jewish tenant, Herr Johann Mund:[14]

*The first to arrive at the house were some four to five SA men who turned up on the morning of 10 November 1938 at 9 o'clock. I opened the door and they asked me if I was Herr Strauss. I answered that they could see that I wasn't Herr Strauss. So then they went up to the first floor to look for Herr Strauss. The SA men immediately began smashing things to bits, but left after twenty to thirty minutes. Then came some twenty-five or thirty boys' who immediately took up the destruction. They pulled doors off their hinges and threw them down, smashed the jars of jam and preserves and threw clothes into the jam. Much of Herr Strauss's clothing, china and cigars were thrown out the window.*

*After they'd done this, the boys wanted to destroy the stairwell as well. I said enough was enough and they left. The things remained in the street and the house was surrounded by police. Not a single pane of glass in the house was intact when the boys left. The following morning, when the police had gone, everything on the street that was still usable was stolen. I myself swept up the glass.*

*Herr Strauss sustained severe injuries to the head. He ran to Dr Kurz, who has since died, to be bandaged and was then taken to the hospital, where he stayed for a while. After being discharged, Herr Strauss went to his son Alfred in Essen, at Hufelandstrasse 23. Shortly afterwards I and my family visited Herr Leopold Strauss. When I entered Herr Alfred Strauss's apartment I had the impression I was entering a palace.*

*On the afternoon of 10 November 1938 they had wanted to set fire to Duisburgerstrasse 100. Uniformed men pulled up in a truck loaded with straw. But since I was living in the house they decided not to set it alight.*

Johann Mund's report was inaccurate in one respect: Leopold did not manage to go straight to either doctor or hospital. At the Leo Baeck Institute in New York, I came across an account of the events in Dinslaken on 10 November by Yitzhak Sophoni Herz, teacher at the Dinslaken orphanage.[15] Herz and the children in his charge were forced into a side alley, from where they witnessed the demolition of the orphanage. A baying crowd of more than a hundred looked on, among them people who only a week before had been happy to do business with the institution. Like a medieval rite, the children were forced in procession through the streets, then herded into a schoolyard and finally into the school hall along with several Jewish women, some of them barely dressed, and some older men. Leopold Strauss was among them, as Yitzhak Herz recalled:[16]

*The retired old Jewish teacher of Dinslaken, a particularly venerable looking old gentleman (he was at one time a town councillor and head of the commercial college) sat groaning in a corner. His head was bleeding from the injuries the Nazis had inflicted upon him. With the help of a used envelope, I managed to bring some water to the suffering man. I did this in a brief moment when no one was looking, because we were in fact forbidden to leave the hall.*

Only at this point did a Nazi official in civilian clothing come to assure the detainees that they need not fear, 'they were not in Soviet Russia', and to say that the elderly Jews could be taken to the hospital. He also assured them that the cow which belonged to the orphanage was being properly looked after. A doctor arrived, who treated the elderly with 'visible compassion'. From here, Leopold must have made his way to the hospital where Marianne found him.

There was one last set of documents on the incident: among Marianne's papers I found a letter sent to Leopold Strauss twelve days after his attack. The head office of the Health Insurance Association for teachers wrote:[17]

> *Re: termination of membership*
>
> *The damnable crime against the German legate, Ernst vom Rath in Paris, has raised feelings of the greatest anger towards the Jewish population in the entire German people. Among German educators too there has been the sharpest condemnation of the fact that Jews are still members of a health insurance association belonging to an organization attached to the National Socialist German Workers' Party. Many Aryan members of the association threaten to leave if the remaining Jews are not expelled as quickly as possible.*
>
> *The Board of the Association has therefore decided to move forward the expiration date of your membership ... which will now terminate on 30 November.*
>
> *Our cancellation department in Berlin has been instructed to remove you from the list of members on that date.*

This letter was filed with three letters to Leopold Strauss from the teachers' fire insurance association. The first was a hand-written note from the Teachers' Fire Association of Rhineland and Westphalia sent in 1913, cordially welcoming Leopold in his new role as the association's district head for Dinslaken.[18] The next was an equally cordial typed note dated 1 August 1933. Evidently, Leopold had stood down and a new district administrator was elected for Dinslaken:[19]

> *We would not wish to miss the opportunity of extending to you our heartfelt thanks, both on behalf of the Association you have so strongly supported in your district and on our own behalf. All matters in your district have always been dealt with promptly and in an orderly manner. Correspondence between you and the Board has always been businesslike, calm and pleasant. Please therefore*

*accept our thanks for the efforts you have devoted to the Fire
Insurance Association. We wish you all good fortune and beg you
to retain your interest in the Association.*
   *With collegiate greetings,*
   *[Signature illegible]*

The last note was an anonymous looking circular from the by now
renamed Fire Association:[20]

*Your membership of the Fire Association of West German
Teachers and your insurance against fire damage and theft expires
– as does that of all Jewish members – on 31 December 1938.*
   *The Board.*

## Dachau and its impact

Meanwhile, Siegfried and Alfred sat in an Essen jail. Some older Jews
were released, but on 16 November, 175 'younger' Jews – including
Siegfried and Alfred – were deported to Dachau. Walter Rohr, then a
fit, young twenty-two-year-old, vividly remembered the transport. The
train became increasingly overcrowded until at some point they were
ordered to switch to a cattle car with no lights or sanitary facilities. They
arrived at Dachau at four in the morning and were sent stumbling
through the drizzle. There was no food on the first day. For Rohr, the
ensuing routine of rising at five to stand at attention for hours on end,
arduous labour, hunger and other 'horrors of life in a concentration
camp' made these 'the most gruesome days' of his life.[21]

Marianne's mother was in despair. Uri Weinberg remembered a weeping aunt Ine coming to see his parents in Cologne. The only option was
to seek clemency from the Gestapo. Ine sent her first letter on 23
November, a week after Siegfried's deportation:[22]

*My husband is forty-seven. As a non-commissioned officer he served in
the First World War from 1 August 1914 to the end of the war, and was
the recipient of several honours. Recently, he suffered from a serious
inflammation of the veins which kept him in bed for weeks. His heart*

*has suffered heavily as a result of this illness and from rheumatism. In addition, my husband is needed to administer the houses he owns. I am not informed about the business and am not in a position to pay taxes, welfare payments and other ongoing commitments.*

*The sale of land for the purpose of Aryanization has to be initiated immediately. It is our desire to emigrate to North America as soon as possible. I received the affidavit a few days ago.*

Four days later, Ine sent a second letter, the most notable feature of which was that Frau Strauss knew Siegfried Strauss's exact address down to his cell number: KL Dachau 3K, Block 21, Stube 2b. Here was the first intimation of a persistent element in Marianne's story – the startling amount of information flowing in and out of the camps. This second letter reinforced the arguments of the first; Siegfried was urgently needed to raise the money for the first instalment of the *Judenvermögen- sabgabe* or Jewish property tax,[23] a reference to the compensation pay- ments demanded of the Jewish community to cover the costs of repairing their own damaged property.[24] On 2 December, the regional Gestapo headquarters (Staatspolizeileitstelle) in Düsseldorf telegraphed Dachau that Strauss's wife had appeared with proof of his military service and had declared the family's intention to leave for the USA (the evidence she presented will have also established Alfred's intention to leave). Frau Strauss had been instructed to transfer to Dachau the money for her husband's train journey. The Dachau commandant was requested to release prisoner 29826[25] and order him to report to the Gestapo in Essen.[26]

The brothers were released together on 9 December, just over three weeks after their arrival in Dachau. In Marianne's memory, the period of internment had grown to six weeks. Elsewhere she wrote of eight weeks.[27] As so often, Marianne, Eric Alexander and Uri Weinberg all retained different memories of the event. Marianne believed that the Dachau internment was an absolutely decisive experience for her father. He came back a changed man, she said, shrunken and embittered. He never talked about what had happened to him and became very 'silent, very quiet indeed, very intractable'. I wondered whether he even talked to his wife about Dachau. Marianne did not know, and quite possibly he could share it with no one. The wife of the rabbi in nearby Dortmund remembered that 'it was an almost unbearable pain to see our friends return, their spirit so broken that they did not speak of their experiences even to their wives'.[28] For the young Marianne, the blow to her father's self-esteem was heart-rending. The most difficult thing for him, Marianne felt (perhaps only later on in life) must have been the stripping away of civilized behaviour and the confrontation with one's own naked instinct to survive. 'Because that really is the moment of truth – how you cope, how you behave, not how the others behave, though that was terrifying enough.'[29]

Typically, Uri Weinberg's memory was gentler. He did not remember that Siegfried had come back so changed, though he had certainly said little about his experiences. He remembered Siegfried volunteering that the train journey to Dachau was bearable, but that after that ' "a different wind was blowing" '. Eric Alexander, by contrast, remembered Siegfried indulging in rather unappetizing and unconvincing bravado. It wasn't so bad, Siegfried had said, the exercise had been good for them.

Other evidence, too, supports the idea that, in public at least, the fight had by no means gone out of the Strauss brothers. But in private it was another matter.

## Paying for the damage

The after-shocks of Kristallnacht continued to buffet the Strauss family. As Ine's letter to the authorities has shown, there was now the task of paying for the damage. In one of the regime's most cynical exercises, Hitler called for the Jews to pay one billion Marks to 'atone' for the destruction. The tax authorities struggled to determine the percentage of Jewish assets required to meet the figure. In the end, it was decided that 20 per cent would be required in instalments and an elaborate schedule of payments was drawn up. (Later, the rate would be raised to 25 per cent and an additional instalment required). So, the Strauss brothers were barely able to catch their breath after Dachau before they were struggling to meet the official timetable set for the new tax.

Among Marianne's papers is a letter written by Alfred Strauss on 13

December 1938, informing the south Essen tax office of the depreciation of family property since the assessment in the summer. Reading this solid businesslike document, one can hardly believe that it was written just three days after Alfred's return from Dachau. The taxes subsequently imposed show that the revisions were accepted. But the bill was still massive. In all, Siegfried, Ine and the children paid just over RM75,000, a sum in excess of Siegfried's entire earnings over the preceding three years. Alfred and Lore paid still more.[30] Together, Siegfried, Alfred and Leopold paid around 2.5 per cent of the entire Essen levy.[31]

The documents kept by the brothers on the process are revealing in a number of ways. Deadlines were tight, and the procedure full of pitfalls and humiliations. On 13 December, for example, Anna Rosenberg (whose affairs were being handled by Siegfried) ordered the Deutsche Bank in Essen and the Sparkasse Münster to make securities available for the first payment, due on 15 December. Both banks subsequently confirmed that on 14 December they had notified the relevant tax office, Beckum, that the shares were available. However, a week later Frau Rosenberg received a letter from the tax office, dated the 14th but franked 21 December, announcing that payment was late; a fine of RM117 was payable, and in addition a 'security deposit' was required equal to the full amount of the remaining payments. (Curiously this letter was dated before the due date for the first payment, and thus before it could even have been established that payment *was* overdue. Perhaps the date was an error, or the letter may have been drawn up in advance in the hope that Frau Rosenberg's payment would be late). On 4 January, Frau Rosenberg wrote, advising that she had made shares available before the due date and that her order was confirmed by the bank. Five days later the tax office responded that it did not agree and pointed out that the Deutsche Bank's letter had arrived only on 24 December, nine days after the deadline. The fine still stood, but, without any explicit acknowledgement of a modification, the penalty was reduced, based on the fact that one part of the transfer had arrived in time. On 12 January, possibly before the letter of the 9th had arrived, Frau Rosenberg wrote again, saying that there were no grounds for paying the requested security deposit, indeed that she was not in a position to pay it, since she had already made one such deposit against future payment of the Flight Tax. On the 16th she responded to the letter of the 9th, enclosing proof from the Deutsche Bank that it had indeed notified the tax office before the deadline, and appealing against the penalty. She also asked that the interest paid on the shares after their arrival in the tax office be taken into account. On the 18th, the tax office agreed that the security deposit was not necessary. On the 19th, the tax office wrote again, arguing that the note which the Deutsche Bank had sent on the 14th was insufficient; the proper form, in triplicate, had been sent only on 22 December, arriving on the 24th. However 'as a courtesy' the fine would be waived.

The subsequent instalments raised similar problems. Though the whole operation was punitive, degrading and nerve-rackingly arbitrary, there were still dim messages of hope for the Strauss family. In almost every case, letters requesting the reversal of harsh penalties, or alerting the tax office to property depreciation and so forth, were accepted. While the tone of communications from the tax office offered little comfort, letters from the Deutsche Bank continued to convey the traditional deference commanded by possession of a sizeable bank account. Where money counted, the correctness of German institutions had not yet disappeared.

But more remarkable than the remaining vestiges of correctness was the faith that the Strauss family continued to put in those institutions. The Rosenberg case again serves as an example. In October, Germany's Jews were dismayed to find that the tax had been raised to 25 per cent of their property value and thus another 5 per cent was due in a fifth instalment. Around this time, Anna Rosenberg moved to Essen and her brother, Abraham Weyl, became her trustee, though there is good reason to believe that Siegfried was keeping her accounts. On 31 October 1939, Herr Weyl wrote to the Finance Office in Düsseldorf (Oberfinanzpräsident, OFD) asking for Anna Rosenberg's fifth instalment to be waived, on the grounds that her property was over-rated, and that she herself was elderly, in ill-health and had very limited income.

The Essen tax office now responsible for Anna Rosenberg agreed to suspend collection while the matter was looked into by Düsseldorf, but warned that if Düsseldorf did not agree, Frau Rosenberg would be fined. On 10 November, Abraham Israel Weyl received a one sentence reply

*Anna Rosenberg in Essen, 1940*

from the OFD, 'I reject the application of Frau Anna Sara Rosenberg, Essen, Cäsarstr. 22, for release from the payment of 5,750.' No explanation, no nothing. But the family did not leave it there. On 14 November 1939, Abraham Weyl wrote to the Reich Finance Minister in Berlin again asking for the final payment to be waived. Simultaneously, however, the fifth instalment *was* paid as a precaution. On 9 January 1940, the OFD wrote to say that the Herr Reichsminister had rejected the application.

In this case, the family achieved nothing through their intervention. But the fact remains that even after Kristallnacht, after Dachau, they still thought they might obtain justice from the authorities. Or even more remarkably, since the law was fairly clear that Anna Rosenberg *would* have to pay, they still expected reasonableness from the civil service. And they were not yet so cowed into submission as to be frightened of asking for it. Their persistence was testimony to the enormous faith which the Strauss family had once placed in German institutions. Or perhaps the possibility that justice was no longer to be had was just too frightening to contemplate.

## *Kristallnacht as a turning point*

Kristallnacht is well known as a day on which Jewish houses of worship, public institutions and businesses were destroyed. It is also common knowledge that the pogrom marked a dramatic though somewhat unplanned radicalization of Nazi policy. But until I talked to Marianne, I had not fully realized how devastatingly the events of those days reached into the private sphere of every German-Jewish family.[32]

Yet, astonishingly, given Marianne's own memories and descriptions, when I made this observation to her, she refuted the idea. She said she didn't feel that Kristallnacht had been a turning point. The family had been aware for years of the way things were deteriorating. Then she said something odd:

'My father, we could have gone out, I used to, we had always. You asked whether there was a lot of social intercourse, there was, but with relations . . .'

Did this sentence really begin as a statement about social life in the

1930s? Or had Marianne started to tell me the family could have left the country earlier – and then changed the topic? My sense was that she could not allow Kristallnacht to be a transformative experience (though elsewhere her comments clearly indicated that it was) because she felt that her parents should have read the writing on the wall earlier. But when it came to openly articulating the criticism, she could not allow herself to do that either, and ended up telling me about social intercourse with relations.

One family member for whom Kristallnacht was indisputably a turning point was Marianne's grandfather, Leopold. Among the surviving family papers are two of Leopold's identity cards. The photo on Leopold's card from 1926 is of a vigorous, ebullient man in his prime. The Jewish Identity Pass from January 1939 depicts a man looking not thirteen but thirty years older, distinguished still, but aged and exhausted. Still lively of mind before the attack, Leopold rapidly developed Alzheimer's disease. After a miserable few months in Essen, he died on 15 June 1939 in Alfred's apartment.[33] A careful letter from Ine Strauss to a relative in New York, Fritz Stern, noted:[34]

*His state of health since the end of last year left much to be desired. He had remained healthy, calm and adaptable to change for such a long time, but the recent dislocations left their mark. And so we must allow him his eternal rest and allow ourselves to accept the loss of this good man.*

Leopold's grave can still be found in the Essen cemetery. He was the last member of the family to be given a proper burial on German soil.

## Kristallnacht and emigration

Marianne said that it was only after Kristallnacht and the imprisonment of the Strauss brothers that the family took steps to leave Germany. Initially, I did wonder if she was exaggerating their obstinacy. Was it not possible that her parents had in fact begun their efforts to leave rather earlier? But among Marianne's papers I discovered extensive correspondence with the family's American relatives, including several

Leopold Strauss, 1926 and 1939

affidavits of support filled out by Siegfried's cousin, Fritz Stern (his mother Bertha had been one of Leopold's sisters), who had been in the United States since 1907. The purpose of these affidavits was to guarantee that the Strauss family would have financial backing in America. Stern, the President of Great American Knitting Mills in Pennsylvania, with a substantial annual income of $25,000, was a credible sponsor.[35] But what was most noteworthy was the date of the very first one: 2 December 1938. This was the same day the Gestapo recorded Ine Strauss as having arrived at their headquarters with proof of Siegfried's intention to leave. Ine must have been anxiously waiting for the affidavit to arrive and gone straight to the Gestapo offices when it did so.[36] The fact that this was the earliest affidavit I found among the Strauss papers suggested strongly that it really was only the crisis provoked by Siegfried's imprisonment that had propelled the family to seek to emigrate. Incidentally, on 24 November 1938, Regina went to the local register office to get a copy of Marianne's brother Richard's birth certificate, having presumably mislaid the original. By now, every scrap of official paper had taken on a new significance. They could make the difference between acceptance and rejection of an emigration application and thus (though this was not yet fully clear) between life and death.[37]

A series of new persecutory measures gave the family further encouragement to leave. At the end of 1938, Jewish passports were declared invalid and could be reissued only with a special 'J' stamp. From 1 January 1939, Siegfried and Richard, along with all Jewish men, had to adopt the middle name Israel, whilst Ine and Marianne were assigned the middle name Sara. Siegfried had to surrender his driving licence for which, with bureaucratic thoroughness, the authorities issued him a 'confirmation of receipt'. (With the same thoroughness, Siegfried and his daughter ensured the receipt's survival until now.)[38] The car was already gone, anyway. In February 1939, the Strausses had to surrender all articles in their possession made of gold, silver, platinum, pearls or gems, with the exception of wedding rings. There is good reason to believe that they did not in fact submit all their valuables, but instead made a judicious selection, making it seem as if they had.[39]

As Siegfried's business activities were effectively limited to his responsibilities as landlord, an increasing proportion of Marianne's

*Marianne's identity pass, January 1939*

parents' time, energy and emotion could be invested in preparing for emigration; their money, however, was harder to deploy, since it was now subject to official controls. Marianne was away at college for most of this time and so did not experience much of this effort, but the considerable number of surviving family papers give a good idea of what her parents were doing. The papers include carefully cut-out sections of the Jewish newspaper, the *Jüdisches Nachrichtenblatt*, on emigration and English lessons. In May, Siegfried applied to enter New Zealand and Australia, stressing his particular skills in the grain trade. But access to these countries was extremely restricted. The Australian application was rejected in June, the refusal from New Zealand followed in July.

The Strausses also considered Britain. The Jewish Veterans' Association (RjF), informed the Jewish Ex-Servicemen's Legion in London that Siegfried was an RjF member and urged the Legion to provide 'the comrade with advice and help and all necessary information in a comradely way', adding that the assistance sought was not of a material nature. Siegfried will not have been unaware of the irony of the RjF appealing to the 'comradely' instincts of the former enemy.

In May, the family received medical certificates in English, confirming that none of them was 'mentally or physically defective in any way' and none afflicted with tuberculosis or any other 'infectious, loathsome or contagious disease', including 'favus, leprosy, framboesia or yaws, trachom, syphilis or scabies'.[40] In July 1939, the synagogue wrote letters of recommendation for the family. Marianne Strauss was:[41]

*a well-educated girl. She is intelligent, amiable and has especially good manners. She went to the Girls' High School, which she left with the finishing certificate. Since Easter 1939 she has attended the Nursery Training College in Berlin. She easily gets adapted to her surroundings and will very well fit into an English family and into English Nursery Training-College. We can recommend her from every point of view, as she seems particularly fit for the work she wants to train for.*

The German Jewish Aid Committee, based in Britain, wrote to the Strauss family on 19 July to advise that a visa application had been made on their behalf, and again on 15 August advising them to apply for a visa in Berlin.[42] On 17 August, a letter from the British Consulate-General in Cologne arrived to verify their address and finally, on 21 August, a short letter from the same source confirmed that their visas were now ready for collection.[43] The family had finally been granted permission to enter Great Britain. The sense of relief in Essen can be imagined.

Twelve days later, Britain and Germany were at war, and emigration to Britain became impossible.

# 4

# Blossoming in a
# Harsh Climate

'I really must say,' Marianne summed up for me, 'in spite of everything, the war and whatever happened . . . it was really like beginning another life. It was most enriching. It was wonderful training, a great deal of experience in every way, human, social, apart from the training itself. So, it was a very, very wonderful time for me.'[1] If I had not known better, I would have assumed Marianne was talking about her life after the war. It was scarcely credible that she was referring to the years 1939–41, when she attended the Jewish Training College for Kindergarten Teachers in Berlin.[2] Her verdict on the Yavne school in Cologne, where she studied from the end of 1938 until March 1939, was almost as positive.

Up to 1938, it had been Marianne's parents' ability to carry their prosperity and confidence through the storm that had been remarkable. While Marianne suffered at school, they had managed, like cartoon victims already over the cliff edge, to tread on air for five years of Nazi rule. Now, following Kristallnacht, the roles were reversed. At a time in which the Jewish community suffered 'social death'[3] in advance of its physical death, for Marianne 'that's when life began!'

## Changing schools

Though the formal legislation was issued only on 15 November 1938, the Luisenschule, like many other schools, seems to have dismissed its remaining Jewish pupils on the 10th. Certainly, Marianne's final school report dates from then. Naturally, along with so much else, the report is still preserved. By 1938, almost all German schools were too cowardly to grade Jewish pupils any higher than 'adequate' or 'satisfactory'. The overall judgement that 'Marianne made an effort to meet the demands of the school' and the series of 'adequate' or 'satisfactory' marks has the authentic ring of cowardly begrudging. On the other hand, the marks gain some plausibility in that Marianne did receive a 'good' for English, which Frau Horn remembered her as performing so well in, and for music, where her piano lessons had presumably stood her in good stead.[4]

For Siegfried and Ine, as soon as they could give thought to anything other than the family's survival, the question was what to do about the children's education. The Reich Education Ministry decree of 15 November 1938, forbidding Jews from attending state schools, made a return to the Luisenschule out of the question.[5] Instead, Siegfried and Ine – perhaps advised by the Weinbergs – decided to send their children to the Yavne school in Cologne. Yavne, founded in 1919, was the only Jewish secondary school in the Rhineland.

Until 1933, Yavne pupils had been recruited largely from Orthodox families. The bulk of the liberal-minded Jewish middle class sent their children to secular state schools. This changed dramatically after 1933. By 1934, pupils from non-Orthodox backgrounds accounted for 85 per cent of the new intake, and the overall number grew steadily, peaking in 1937. That youngsters from liberal backgrounds could be absorbed into a school run on Orthodox Jewish lines had much to do with the role and personality of Dr Erich Klibansky (1900–42) Yavne's headmaster from 1929. As his reputation grew, so did the proportion of youngsters coming from outside Cologne – by 1938 they made up a quarter of the school body.[6]

Marianne and her brother Richard were thus part of the growing trend of non-Orthodox outsiders seeking a safe and stimulating environment for study. They stayed with their cousins, the Weinbergs, recently installed in Cologne. Boycotts and local pressure had induced Ernst Weinberg to sell his Erkelenz shop and, like many Jews at the time, the Weinbergs had decided that the anonymity of the big city offered a better chance of protection than their close acquaintance in the small town. The three boys, Alex, Alfred and Otto, were all sent to the Yavne.

It did not surprise me by now that Marianne, Alfred and Alexander should each have different memories of the school. For Marianne, it was the first step on a personal journey of intellectual growth and liberation. She remembered above all the cultured atmosphere, the qualifications and high quality of the teachers. Partly because there were no employment prospects elsewhere, the school was staffed by a marvellous array of talent. The well-known artist Ludwig Maidner, abstract painter of the Düsseldorf school, had been at Yavne since 1935 and was Marianne's art teacher. The distinguished translator, Else Nussbaum, at the school since 1935, taught Marianne English. The staff's approach to ideas and education also appealed to her. As early as 1933, given that Jewish students' access to German universities was now severely restricted,[7] Klibansky recognized that the function of the school had changed. It was no longer to accredit youngsters for their university place, but to provide true learning.[8] In retrospect, Marianne said, 'it was the first time in my life that I enjoyed school and really got something' out of it.

Alfred, now Uri, recalled the school with similar pleasure. For him, too, it was a place of freedom. He remembered having to be very careful at his old grammar school in Erkelenz. In Erkelenz he had had to learn to judge people's character very carefully, he said. But at Yavne you felt free. He remembered that when he first joined the school, he arrived to find Klibansky teaching the class history. Klibansky asked the class a question to which Alfred, with his good grammar school education, was bound to know the answer – Frederick II. Alfred duly put his hand up, but used the description obligatory in German schools, 'Frederick the Great'. Klibansky said, 'We don't say Frederick the Great here, or if we do, we say Frederick the Great Windbag.' Alfred felt the question was designed to test which 'side' he was on: was he still (like his brother) hankering to be a German, or did he primarily see himself as a Jew?

Alfred's answer was clear, and in that one exchange he felt a stone fall from his shoulders and knew he was among friends. The school was to be an important step on his journey towards a religious Jewish life. Tears came to his eyes as he remembered Rabbi Stein, who had befriended him at Yavne; it was his first encounter with a vibrant Orthodoxy.

I had expected that Marianne, too, would recall the school as having given her a sense of a vital Jewish identity. The historian Joseph Walk noted that, partly because Klibansky managed to be Orthodox on the one hand and tolerant on the other, the school strengthened its pupils' Jewish identity, leading many to embrace religious observance and even to pass it on to their parents.[9] But Marianne said nothing of this. After she told me about the 'celebrities' on the staff, and mentioned Nussbaum and Maidner, I discovered that another distinguished teacher had been Kurth Levy, an important academic dismissed from the Oriental Seminar in Bonn, who now taught Hebrew and Latin at the school. Marianne had no memory of him or of the Hebrew lessons.[10] I wondered whether this meant she had had no positive religious experiences at the time or whether her subsequent development – be it the identity she assumed in wartime or her years of living with a more Orthodox husband after the war – had meant she forgot such experiences in later life.

For Eric Alexander, the Yavne school represented a personal defeat – the final nail in the coffin of his dream of becoming a successful German boy. He found it hard going, not least because, having attended classical grammar schools, he had not studied English and now found himself in an all-English class. He worked hard, though, and in 1939 his teacher secured him passage to Britain, so in the end Yavne served him well. But he had not made the school his own. Laughing, he told me that Alfred was 'well in with the rabbi there and I think he must have told him about me, because I remember the rabbi once passed me in the street, and if looks could kill . . .'[11]

At first, Marianne and Richard stayed in the Weinbergs' flat. After a while, though, they moved back home and commuted daily to the school from Essen. Marianne said they ended the arrangement because the flat was too small, but Eric Alexander recalled it differently. He was then about seventeen and Marianne was fifteen and they had a 'little love affair, well, you could hardly call it that really, holding hands . . . Then

Siegfried came and "ohhhh!" ' Siegfried wasn't happy about it? 'No, not at all, so she had to move out again.'[12]

Marianne might have forgotten this, but she was probably being discreet. I was later to discover that a relationship with a French prisoner of war in 1944 and a brief romance after the war were similarly passed over. What Marianne did mention was that she and Richard now had to get up at crack of dawn, and make a nearly two-hour journey every day during a very cold winter. The Kriminalpolizei would come through the trains and inspect the special authorization she said they needed to travel by rail.

## Leaving the Yavne

At Easter 1939, Klibansky managed to organize the departure of a group of children to England. The group included Marianne's class and, Marianne thought, was also open to Richard. In all, 130 children got to England in this way.[13] Alexander Weinberg had already gone with an earlier group. Now Alfred and Otto followed. Marianne and Richard did not, because Siegfried did not want them to go abroad on their own.

What on earth was Siegfried thinking of? The rabbi's wife in nearby Dortmund, for example, remembered parents literally begging the rabbi 'to send their children away as soon as possible', since the parents 'could no longer stand to see them suffer from hatred and abuse'.[14] Thanks to the various *Kindertransports* – above all to Britain – the bulk of German youngsters were getting out. By the outbreak of war, teenagers were few and far between. Of the Jews left in Germany, 75 per cent were over forty.[15] So it is hard to understand Siegfried's position. It is just possible that in March 1939, with the affidavit from Fritz Stern in his pocket, he was so confident that the US application would soon come to fruition that the risk of separating the family at this stage seemed too great. That confidence might also explain why he waited as late as May to begin applying to Britain, Australia and New Zealand. But what seems evident is that, despite Dachau, Siegfried still had not fully realized what the regime was capable of. How else to explain the fact that he thought it safer for the children to make a lengthy train journey from Essen to

Cologne every day rather than risk the danger of Alexander and Marianne holding hands?

Marianne said she didn't question her father's stance at the time. Siegfried made the decisions. However, she would have enjoyed the adventure. She felt already 'very grown up and rather restricted in my home set-up.' Her brother, who was more timid, might not have enjoyed it, she said. As to what she thought of the decision now, she made no comment.

By March 1939, Marianne had completed her fifth year of secondary school. That entitled her to the intermediate school qualification, the Mittlere Reife. The Yavne school's final report recorded her general behaviour as good but, interestingly, the marks were not so different from those of the Luisenschule. The overall grade was only adequate. Marianne did well in German and again music, but poorly in art and mathematics. In the remarks section, the report stated only that 'The school bids Marianne farewell with the best wishes for her future.'[16]

Marianne's parents were once again faced with a decision about their children's future. The local Jewish school in Essen had no higher-level education to offer. There was nowhere in Germany she could study for the Abitur, the qualifying university entrance examination, and, in any case, German centres of higher learning were closed to her. However, because of official Nazi 'support' for Jewish emigration, Jewish vocational colleges had been allowed to proliferate at a time when all other opportunities were falling away. In Berlin, in particular, there was a range of colleges offering skills useful for emigrants.[17] True, the options available specifically to girls were fairly circumscribed. There were some places at agricultural schools to prepare girls for emigration to Palestine, but the Strausses were not thinking of Palestine. There was domestic science training. There were nurses' training courses in several Jewish hospitals such as the Neonatal and Children's Hospital in Berlin. The Jewish College for Kindergarten Teachers in Berlin was unique in that it provided a state-recognized qualification.[18] Typically, the chance at an official accreditation was the crucial advantage in Marianne's parents' eyes. It was so important that Siegfried was even prepared to allow his fifteen-year-old daughter to go to Berlin, alone.

The move to Berlin was in many ways to be Marianne's liberation, but in retrospect she associated it also with the sadness of leaving Richard behind. Older children, particularly at the point where they outgrow the parental home, often lose contact with their younger siblings. In normal conditions, this can be remedied later. But one of the most painful experiences for Marianne was that there was never a later point of remedy. Even the things Marianne could tell me were not always accurate. For example, in telling me that after the Yavne school Richard was educated privately at home it is clear that she lost sight of three years of his schooling – the years, in fact, when she was largely away from home.

In December 1939, Richard celebrated his barmitzvah, a very reduced affair compared with family celebrations past. The Oberpräsident, Düsseldorf, Devisenstelle had to give his permission for Siegfried to draw RM100 from his account for 'confirmation fees,' presumably to pay the rabbi.[19] By then in Berlin, Marianne did not come back for the occasion. She said to me at one point that she could not get permission. But in a later conversation she said that she could not face the disruption and her parents had not been particularly encouraging, more interested that she should continue the course. Now, with hindsight, she was very sorry she hadn't gone. 'At the time nothing like that seemed to matter.'[20] Marianne felt guilty about losing track of her brother, and at the same time guilty towards her parents that she, and not the academically more able brother, had survived.[21]

## Kindergarten college

Now largely unknown even to experts on Jewish history, the Berlin College for Kindergarten Teachers was created in 1934 and, despite some wavering on the part of the Prussian Cultural Ministry, received state recognition. 'While Jews are still living with us,' went the official argument (and this in May 1934!), 'it would be both impractical and undesirable to deny them training for work in Jewish nurseries in proportion to the size of the population.'[22] To restrict the number of Jews obtaining a state qualification, though, the Ministry limited the intake to thirty, refused to accredit any other college within the entire Reich and insisted on extending the course to two years instead of the proposed eighteen months. At Easter 1938, the school was allowed to introduce a second class, and in summer 1938 Margarete Fraenkel,[23] previously a teacher at the school, took over as head.

Marianne's memory was that the school normally required pupils to have their Abitur and that her mother had to obtain special dispensation for Marianne to enter so young. Probably this memory reflects the sense of awe and trepidation with which Marianne went to Berlin. In fact, with her Mittlere Reife, Marianne met the minimum requirement for admission. Even so, the school normally required its pupils to be aged at least seventeen. Marianne may have been right in thinking that when she set off for Berlin in April 1939, two months short of her sixteenth birthday, she was the college's youngest entrant.[24]

When she arrived in Berlin, she found the college located at Wangenheimstrasse 36, in the affluent western Berlin district of Grünewald. It was 'a very good address, like The Bishop's Avenue', Marianne assured me, unconsciously slipping into a British register for her comparison.[25] The luxurious villa, donated by a Jewish banker, housed not only the school but also the hall of residence for girls from outside Berlin.[26] Marianne remembered the place as 'enormous, with I don't know how many really splendid 1920s bathrooms' and a large garden. The most desirable bedroom, which everybody wanted, was the 'plum room' on the top floor, a corner room with two little turrets, one of them looking down the Wangenheimstrasse, the other down the Lynarstrasse. In 1940, Marianne managed to move in there.

Here, as at Yavne, the elimination of opportunities elsewhere was a boon for the school as a glittering array of intellectuals and inspired teachers had joined the teaching staff. Aware that in different circumstances many of the students would have sought a more academic education, the college offered a far more intellectual and wide-ranging course than was usual for kindergarten teachers. An advertisement in the newsletter of the Jewish Women's League (JFB) in 1935 gives a hint of this breadth and depth:[27]

*The academic instruction covers the history of education and an introduction to educational literature, psychology and educational theory, kindergarten studies, health studies, contemporary affairs, children's literature, nature study, cultural studies, German, Hebrew, Jewish history and Jewish knowledge. Candidates will be expected to have a basic knowledge of Hebrew. The course will place considerable emphasis on arts and crafts such as music, handicrafts, drawing, modelling, needlework, gymnastics and movement.*

Marianne told me that the core teaching team at the college had all been trained at the Pestalozzi-Fröbel-Haus – the famous social-work institution founded by Helene Lange. The College director, Margarete Fraenkel, had been a pupil not only of Helene Lange but also of Jung and Adler. The Institute's board included several very prominent Jews, among them Leo Baeck. The teaching staff numbered among its ranks inspiring figures such as Hannah Karminski, a leading member of the JFB until its dissolution in 1938, who herself had trained as a kindergarten teacher and social worker. Karminski's correspondence reveals that she found teaching in the college a source of satisfaction and compensation amid her otherwise miserable and largely hopeless duties in the welfare department of the Reich Association of Jews (Reichsvereinigung der Juden, RV). There were also musicians, sociologists, specialists of all kinds. Marianne recalled 'a pupil of Gundolff – *the* translator of Shakespeare into German – who was our teacher on Shakespeare. We had a teacher just on Shakespeare . . . It was quite unheard of.'[28]

For Marianne, the college was liberation. 'Suddenly I was away from this very strict parental control. I *really* blossomed, I really sort of grew up in no time at all.'[29] Marianne was not the only student to see her studies as a liberating experience. Edith Dietz started at the College a year earlier and graduated in 1940. In her memoirs,[30] she too recalled the quality and depth of the teaching and the feeling of freedom in Berlin.[31]

The staff were well aware of Marianne's enthusiasm and responsive to her talents.[32] Her practical training outside the college, in kindergartens or with families, was equally appreciated.[33] But while Marianne was full of energy and enthusiasm, she soon found that she was 'really very innocent':[34]

'The head of the school said, "We'll throw you to the wolves, you're the youngest." So that was learning very fast, very fast indeed. Working with families and coming across their problems. People who were impoverished and demoralized. Mothers who had mental breakdowns. Children who were the result of incest. I worked in the only Jewish baby home which still existed, and the misery of the abandoned children there . . . It's just not imaginable.'

It was one of the many incongruities of this period that the conditions Marianne encountered were reminiscent of those portrayed in anti-Semitic propaganda films. Marianne had to do 'practical work in the most appalling slum conditions. I'd never known such destitution would exist among Jews . . . inadequacies, incest, anything you could think of.' Marianne remembered one particular family, 'called Fleischhammel, which was the most extraordinary name but it suited them beautifully. It was like something out of Dickens, or even worse.' She would turn up with new clothing for the children, but the next day:[35]

'. . . it was all gone, had been sold for whatever. The wallpaper was off the walls, and even during the day the cockroaches were crawling around there. I not only had to look after the children, but clean the place up, and the children didn't go to school because they had no clothes to go in. And they all slept more or less in two beds, the parents and children, and the sheets they were given away or sold or whatever. The filth was indescribable. Every day I went there I found the same thing. I took one clean lot packed one day and the next day it started all over again.'

As a sixteen-year-old who thought 'you could alter the world overnight and make decent human beings out of people' this imperviousness to assistance was hard for Marianne to bear. 'There were times when I felt quite suicidal.' At the same time, coming back each night to the very civilized existence in the Grünewald was so rewarding 'you forgot really what was going on outside. There was always something interesting going on. There were lots of interesting people still living ordinary lives in Berlin – very public well-known figures, friends of the organization. Musicians would come and give concerts and they would come and play records, we'd have get-togethers . . . folk singing, lectures . . . wonderful social things going on all the time.'[36]

Marianne's new-found independence and sociability brought her into contact with a wide circle, including a literary and cultural set. Despite the restrictions, life for her was full of undreamed-of freedom. 'When I went to Berlin I had never been out late at night, so really, I was very lucky I was of a very careful disposition. If I hadn't been, I could probably have landed in a great deal of trouble, suddenly being let off the leash as it were.'[37]

## Meeting Inge Deutschkron

In Germany, Inge Deutschkron's book *Outcast: a Jewish Girl in Wartime Berlin*[38] is the most famous autobiographical account of a so-called 'U-Boat', as the Jews protected by friends in Berlin were known. A younger generation recently learned her story anew because of the success of *From Today Your Name Is Sara*,[39] a play based on Inge Deutschkron's life. I read the book to see if there were parallels between Deutschkron's and Marianne's experiences. What I had not expected to find was that Inge Deutschkron, a year Marianne's senior, had studied at the kindergarten college at exactly the same time. I wrote to Frau Deutschkron on the off-chance that she might remember Marianne and, when a glowing tribute came back, arranged to see her next time I was in Berlin.

Inge Deutschkron lived in a large block of flats with a marvellous view over the city. She herself was clearly a toughie who didn't suffer fools gladly, but at the same time was lively and engaging. She produced a delicious late breakfast of watermelon and regaled me with the details of her Al Italia flight from Israel the previous day, including a short, miserable stopover in Milan. The final straw had been the stewardess wanting to refuse her an aisle seat, because, with her cane, she might impede the egress of the others. I'd like to have been there to see the explosion.

And then we turned to the past. It soon became clear that the college had not had the same significance for Inge Deutschkron that it had for Marianne. As a local girl, she had lived at home and missed the intensity of the boarding experience. In any case, thanks to her parents she had already been part of a lively, left-wing circle and the college's intellectual and cultural effect on her was thus far more limited. Moreover, she hadn't particularly enjoyed working in kindergarten. 'I learned that all the frustrations a kindergarten teacher has she passes on to the children. So I decided if ever I had children I would never send them to kindergarten!'[40] Nevertheless, she too remembered the villa on the Wangenheimstrasse with great pleasure. It was huge, with a lovely garden, 'just a wonderful place to live. I even remember wood panelling which shows you a rich house!'

In her book, Inge Deutschkron wrote that Frau Fraenkel 'conducted the college as though there was nothing more important in the world than to prepare young girls for their vocation.'[41] The girls lived in a separate little world, and 'acted as if nothing happened outside'. But like Marianne, she too encountered in her work with families a degree of poverty and misery she had not believed possible. 'I mean it was good,' she said, 'I saw life. From a different angle, you know.'

The main thing she remembered about Marianne was her appearance and deportment. There was something – Inge Deutschkron searched for a word – there was something *royal* about her:

'It was very intentional, of course. I mean it was not that this came natural to her. But . . . she had this wonderful hair, I don't know if that was still the case when you met her, very strong. And in a long pigtail. She wore it mostly in one, very thick. And sometimes she took that pigtail and turned it around her, what do call that?'

'Like a braid?'

'Like a braid, yes, of course that made her look even more, you know. And she was tall and slim and had a very good figure . . . I was impressed by her, I must say. And her demeanour, that's probably the word for it, it was something, so quiet, I don't know. This is also what I wrote to you, something peaceful came from her, emanated from her. She was definitely a personality, no question.'

Not only Marianne's manner and general level of education but also the quality of her clothes conveyed the impression that she came from a wealthy family. 'But I must say the girls I remember from that time, most of them were from very educated families and they were really good – it was a good place to be.'

Frau Deutschkron lived near the college's old address, though she herself never went there. So after taking the bus for a couple of stops, and then walking through still-affluent Grünewald, I found myself in front of number 36 Wangenheimstrasse. I looked up at the windows and wondered whether Marianne, in her 'plum room', had gazed out over the city from one of them.[42] The street was quiet. At lunchtime on a warm summer weekday only children and tradesmen were about. What kind of people had lived in this street then? Marianne once told me that next door to the school lived a close friend of Hermann Goering. On one occasion this friend had a party to which Goering was invited and the College members were quietly asked beforehand not to be in evidence.[43]

I walked to the other end of the street, savouring the fact that this had been Marianne's territory almost sixty years ago. A little footbridge at the end took me without warning over the Stadtring, the urban motorway that circles the city. Out of the quiet and shade of the Wangenheimstrasse I was suddenly plunged back into the noise and heat and ceaseless stream of traffic of 1990s Berlin.

## Wartime Berlin

In September 1939, the girls were in quarantine because of a case of diphtheria. On a very hot summer's day, they were sitting in the wonderful conservatory attached to the house:[44]

'I remember it was about midday,' said Marianne, 'and we were having a sewing lesson and sitting there doing some embroidery when news came over the radio that war had been declared and it was a most, really, a most devastating thing. Even though we had all thought probably that that would happen – the Germans I think wanted it – it was a devastating, quite unforgettable day.'

Initially, Marianne's life was not too affected by the outbreak of war. A curfew was introduced for Jews in Berlin from 9 p.m. to 5 a.m. in the summer months and from 8 p.m. to 6 a.m. in the winter,[45] but I don't think she took it very seriously.

Life was full of incongruities. The College members were invited to take part in air-raid precautions. Representatives of the Fliegerabwehr came and gave the students lessons in first aid and protective measures during an air raid. The girls were even issued with gas masks. 'Imagine!' said Marianne. In 1939, the regime was still protecting Jews from gas. It was also training them as air-raid wardens – Marianne's papers include a certificate confirming that Marianne Sara Strauss had taken part in a Luftschutzlehrgang (air raid course) run by the LS-Hauptschule der Ortsgruppe X/Charlottenburg (the air-raid training school of the Charlottenburg district) from 11–21 October 1940.[46] There were few actual raids, but frequent warnings that sometimes lasted all night. Marianne would have liked to stay up in her plum room, looking at the sky. But 'it was de rigueur, as soon as the bloody sirens went' that they should go down to the cellar. At first, they would sit in the cellar nearly all night, but gradually they stopped taking the warnings quite so seriously.

More incongruity: during the summer of 1940, Marianne worked at a Jewish institute for deaf and dumb children, earning her first salary.[47] The head of the institute was away at the time, leaving his three children behind. His son fell in love with Marianne, and one of the daughters had an SS officer lover. On weekends, this SS 'fellow used to come and on a Saturday night we would sit there and the lights would go out eventually, and we were all in the same room. They were quite openly going about their business and he knew who these people were and yet he was carrying on a love affair with this beautiful girl. What became of them, I don't know.'[48]

Marianne had taken the job as a means of obtaining a rather more tangible forbidden fruit – her first gramophone. She was short of money, not because of the regime's restrictions but because of her father's. With many of the family's funds frozen by the regime, each family member was granted an official personal allowance. Siegfried felt that Marianne's allowance was far too generous for a girl of her age and she was under strict instructions to send most of it home. She vividly remembered her anxiety on the one occasion when for some reason the money she sent home was a little short. The result of her father's strictures was that she didn't even have the means to buy a swimsuit in the sales, although in the heat of the summer she longed for one. 'I always was a great shopper but a very frustrated one . . . but I made up for it later on,' laughed Marianne.[49] But, still, she did want the gramophone. For the six weeks' summer job she earned RM35 and bought the cheapest, tiniest, portable wind-up gramophone she could find. Marianne was very proud to have earned it herself. Her sympathetic aunt, Oe, supplied the first records.

At some point at the end of 1940 or the beginning of 1941, the villa was requisitioned by the Gestapo. The college was allocated another building belonging to the Jewish community, this time a large house on the Mei-neckerstrasse.[50] The new accommodations were more spartan and Mari-anne found herself sharing rooms with other girls, 'quite a different thing', but still 'all right and civilized'.[51] The new location had at least one thing to recommend it; the immediate proximity of one of the world's most exciting streets, the Kurfürstendamm, full of seductive possibilities:

'On a Saturday night, we would go out on the razzle, walking along the Kurfürstendamm in twos and threes. I remember one particular occasion going with a friend window-shopping on a Saturday evening and two SS chaps were following us. We suddenly realized that we were being followed. Of course, that's how far their racial instincts went! We didn't know how to shake them off. They were obviously making overtures and making quite clear they would have liked us to join them . . . so the only way out was to get a taxi. That happened several times and in the end it became like a game of Russian roulette, a dare.'

Marianne would think 'the *Herrenrasse*, the *Herrenvolk*, and they can't even tell a Jew when they see one!' But after a while the girls felt it would be better not to tempt fate too much and grew more circumspect. In June 1941, Marianne celebrated her eighteenth birthday in Berlin.

We should not be seduced by such memories into imagining that life for Berlin's Jews was still happy. By the first winter of the war, one in four depended on Jewish welfare. The city authorities were vicious. Minor traffic offences, an infringement of the blackout or curfew, cross-ing the street at the wrong place or shopping at the wrong time could lead to very high fines of 40 marks or more, imprisonment, concentration camp or even death. Berlin was often the first to promulgate anti-Jewish legislation later adopted for the whole Reich.[52]

On the other hand, the size of the Jewish community, and the cosmo-politanism of much of the non-Jewish population, prevented Nazi measures from having the same impact in Berlin as in the provinces. Marianne said:[53]

*Marianne, 1939/40*

'In Berlin there was quite a different sort of attitude to Jews still from the rest of the country. Very much more cosmopolitan, not so narrow, somehow people behaved in a much more civilized way to us than we were expecting or knew of in the provinces; particularly after Kristallnacht, when it hit everybody what exactly might be in store.'

The sheer size of the city also meant that it was easier to be anonymous and ignore the regulations without being spotted. Thus, in the summer of 1941, it was still possible for Marianne to wander down the Kurfürstendamm without being racially attacked.

But even these special factors could not shield the community from the decisive changes of 1941.[54] Suddenly, without formal announcement, trips to the woods around Berlin were declared illegal for Jews.[55] The children remaining in the Jewish schools were forced to seek their exercise in the Jewish cemetery, the one place still open to them.[56] By the autumn of 1941, almost every store on the Kurfürstendamm carried the sign 'No entrance to Jews'. Most Berlin Jews of working age were conscripted into forced labour and suffered the humiliation and exhaustion induced by unfamiliar work, lengthy journeys to and from the factories, and a wage that after all deductions (Jews paid the highest tax rate) often barely covered the most basic needs. In July and August, Berlin Jews were denied the extra rations granted for heavy work or long hours.[57] Marianne remembered that many of the spouses of teachers at the College were conscripted into war work. 'They looked dreadful, they would hardly get any money, it was slave labour.'[58]

Shock after shock hit the community. It was suddenly announced during March 1941 that more than a thousand Jewish apartments must be vacated within five days. A further major mass eviction took place in August.[59] It rapidly became common knowledge that the Jewish official in charge of housing had pleaded for a bit more time, and had promptly been incarcerated in a concentration camp. He died there a few months later.[60] During the summer, it also became known that the RV's former chairman, Dr Otto Hirsch, had died in Mauthausen camp in June 1941.[61]

Thus, Marianne's happy memories cannot be explained by Berlin's special situation. But young people like herself were in a privileged position. The adult world ensured they were shielded as far as possible from the worst effects of persecution. Even in the terrible year 1941, the teachers at the college clearly managed to maintain their pupils' spirits. This was not just Marianne's recollection. Former pupils often retained close contact with the college. Edith Dietz, for example, qualified in 1940 and was caring full time for the often seriously disturbed children of the Berlin community. But she continued to come to classes in education and psychology.[62] Frau Fraenkel had the talent to keep her students motivated and outward-looking; she even included theology and philosophy in their curriculum. In her moving contemporary record of forced labour at Siemens in 1940–1, Elisabeth Freund writes of meeting kindergarten-college trained young women and wondering at the enthusiasm with which these women sought to continue their studies.[63]

## Berlin via Riga, Essen and New Jersey

Within this protected niche, Marianne benefited from the simple solidarity of living, studying and working together with a small group of young people. From May to August 1941 Marianne worked at the Neonatal and Children's Hospital on the Moltkestrasse in Berlin Niederschönhausen.[64] While I was researching this book, a lawyer approached the Jewish community in Essen, asking if they knew the whereabouts of a Marianne Strauss. His client, Mrs Trudy Schloss, needed to authenticate her claim to a pension for having worked in the Niederschönhausen Hospital. The name Schloss meant nothing to me at the time, but I later came across some post-war letters from Marianne's relatives, referring to her 'best friend Trude Schloss'.[65] I contacted the lawyer, sending some letters that helped to confirm the connection between the two women and asked him to pass on a letter to Mrs Schloss. She turned out to live in New Jersey, and since I was shortly to be in New York, to work in the Leo Baeck Institute, I arranged to interview her at the same time.

In August 1998, Lew and Trudy Schloss picked me up from my hotel in Manhattan in a very smart new Mazda. She was petite, with a lively, smiling and still very attractive face. He was tall, broad-shouldered and engaging, but also conveyed the air of taking no nonsense from anybody. Nothing about this couple even hinted at the horrific journeys that lay

*Lew and Trudy Schloss in New Jersey*

behind them. They had first met, in fact, in labour camps in Riga, bumped into each other again on a forced transport in and out of Stutthof – one of the most nightmarish of all the camps – and managed to meet after the war. 'Hitler was our *schadchen* [Jewish matchmaker]', said Lew in the car as we drove over the Washington Bridge on our way to New Jersey. I assumed he'd made his joke many times, but Trudy laughed and I laughed and he said he'd just thought of it.

Their house, on a typical American suburban street, was pleasant and roomy. The children's houses were much bigger, they told me. The son was personnel director for a large company and the daughter was also something high-powered. They both lived near by. By this stage I'd learned to my amazement that *both* Trudy and Lew Schloss had known Marianne, though by completely different routes, and before they knew each other. Lew, then Ludwig, Schloss had grown up near Essen in Gelsenkirchen, had moved in Essen circles and had even had a girlfriend,

Klara Stamm, who was the Strauss family maid 1940–1. And Trudy, then Trude Ullmann, had worked in Berlin as a nurse in the children's hospital and met Marianne there. I began by interviewing Lew, but although his stories were fascinating, he couldn't tell me much about Marianne's life in Essen. Had his girlfriend talked about what it was like working for the Strausses? 'No. We weren't interested in, you know, working conditions.' We all laughed. 'She was a nice looking girl.'

In the late 1930s, Lew had sometimes met Marianne socially. What did he remember of her? 'She was a little bit uppity. That I remember. She was a nice-looking girl. That's basically, you know, what you were interested in, in those days. I didn't analyse,' and he laughed again. Trudy interjected that Marianne had been fairly tall, but Lew said that compared to her, anybody was tall, and we all laughed again. Lew said Marianne had got on well with his girlfriend and hadn't treated her patronizingly. Could he remember her brother? 'No, I wasn't interested in her brother at the time.' I got the message and turned to Trudy. What were her memories of meeting Marianne in the hospital?

'Well I remember she was, like Lew said, a little bit *hochnäsig* [snooty] at times. But in Berlin it was a different story, she was with all the girls, you know, she used to talk quite a bit about home, like I guess we all did. Because let's face it, we were fifteen years old and we missed our families, all of us, you know? She was basically very, how would you say . . . ?'

'Lively,' said Lew.

'Lively,' Trudy agreed.

'Outgoing,' I volunteered.

'Vivacious,' said Lew.

'Outgoing, very outgoing,' said Trudy. 'We used to sit sometimes in the evening telling all kinds of stories. And then, once in a while, if we met a fellow or something, you know, like young girls are . . . what can I tell you?'

Trudy remembered she once had a visitor from her home town – a young man who 'never made it either'. Trudy received the message that there was someone there to see her.

'They called me, they said someone's here to visit you, a young man, so I don't have to tell you they were all very anxious to see who the young man was. But that's . . . I have *nice* memories of that.'

'Of that time, yes, Marianne did, too,' I told her.

'It was an encapsulated community,' said Lew.

The girls worked very hard, caring not just for sick children but also for youngsters whose parents were working. Sometimes if there was an air raid they had to take the kids into the shelter. But 'it wasn't really that bad. I mean we couldn't go into a lot of things, but we had each other and we used to have a lot of fun, you know, just socializing with each other'. They were limited in where they could go, and in any case felt very self-conscious in public, even before they had to wear a yellow star. Lew agreed. Jews were so conditioned, he said, that people could practically identify a Jew on sight. Jews 'were afraid, afraid to do something wrong, because you always lived with the sword over your head. Any second something could happen.'

Trudy returned to her theme. 'I couldn't say that we *suffered* in Berlin, because we had food, we didn't have to worry, we had a place to stay, it was very clean. I don't even have to tell you how particular they were, you know what I mean.'

'They were German,' said Lew.

'I remember how they used to watch us when we sterilized the instruments and everything. Ach Gott, they used to stand behind you, you know. These kinds of things you don't forget.'[66]

Marianne worked at the hospital from the beginning of May to the end of August 1941. Her report from the head of the hospital, Dr Rosenberg, was very satisfactory, attesting to her hard work, skill and conscientiousness.[67] The hospital itself survived until March 1942, and most of its staff were deported only in autumn of that year.[68] But by then Trudy was long gone. In 1940, her parents had been deported to the Gurs camp in France. Later they would be murdered in Auschwitz. In November 1941, Trudy's aunt was due to be deported to Riga and Trudy joined her rather than be left on her own in Germany. Only when they arrived did she realize the murderous conditions she had opted for.

## An exam

Memory can be a great harmonizer. Compared with Riga and Stutthof, for example, or with Marianne's years underground, it is easy to imagine that in retrospect the time in Berlin looked like paradise. That does not necessarily mean it was experienced as such at the time. But at an early stage in our conversations Marianne offered me letters from her time in Berlin, and they are the most striking evidence yet of Marianne's ability to draw sustenance from the most barren environment.

In August 1941, the Berlin community was reeling from the news that Jewish men and women aged between eighteen and forty-five were banned from emigrating. The law affecting women was particularly alarming because it clearly had no military basis. On 1 September 1941 came the proclamation that all Jews over six years of age had to wear the yellow star, and this had a much greater impact in Berlin than elsewhere. The many small evasions of regulations by Jews which Berlin's size had made possible now became much more difficult and dangerous.[69]

The Jewish Kulturbund was proscribed on 11 September 1941.[70] Then in early October came a round of eviction notices with the even more chilling instruction that those affected should not seek new apartments. The first deportation followed on 18 October 1941 to Łodz (Litzmannstadt) ghetto.[71] Hundreds were crowded into the great synagogue on the Levetzowstrasse and held there for several days before the deportation; the lack of space meant that many were left outside in the rain for hours at a time.[72] Morale among Berlin's Jews reached an all-time low.[73] Many of the children in the care of the college-trained kindergarten teachers were caught up in the deportations.[74]

Marianne returned to Essen in October, when she and her family only narrowly missed being sent to Łodz. Marianne then remained in Essen for several months, during which time she met a young man, Ernst Krombach, the son of lawyer David Krombach, the leading figure in what still remained of Essen's Jewish community. Marianne and Ernst, who had himself studied for a while in Berlin, were soon deeply in love. In February 1942, she received a letter from the RV confirming her admission to the final state exam beginning on 9 February and ending on the 20th.[75] (The letter survives among Marianne's papers, as does Ernst and Marianne's correspondence. As if circumstances had conspired to preserve every document pertaining to Marianne, Ernst at a later date returned all Marianne's letters to her, for safe-keeping.)

Marianne left for Berlin on Thursday 5 February. When I told Trudy Schloss about this trip, she was astonished and also somehow delighted. She and Lew batted the idea back and forth between them:

'Oh, she went back to Berlin and . . .'

'She did get the exam?' asked Lew.

'Oh she got her Staatsexamen? Because by that time a lot of the young nurses weren't there any more . . . But that is *interesting* that she went back to make her exam. Because I wasn't there any more at that time. You see I never knew this! . . . I have to call Ruth Arndt[76] after we finish!'

There *was* something deeply affecting about the thought of Marianne's journey. The infamous Wannsee conference, which clarified responsibility and procedures for the murder of Europe's Jewry, had taken place in Berlin a couple of weeks earlier. The deportation programme was in full swing. And yet here was Marianne returning to the Nazi capital for the sake of a qualification.

The night before her departure, Ernst put pen to paper. The unfamiliar business of communicating with Marianne by letter was rendered even more odd by the fact that at that moment Marianne was still in Essen. Ernst's pet name for Marianne was Jeanne, or Jeanny, after Joan of Arc:[77]

*Wednesday evening*

*Dearest Jeanny,*

   *Welcome to our old Heimat.[78]*

   *I hope the trip was pleasant and at least interesting. I'm not enjoying having to write to you, even though I know you're not yet physically far apart from me. I might possibly be able to get to the station tomorrow morning, but since I don't know if you'll be on your own – maybe it's better if I communicate to you this way . . .*

*Now, you must promise me something: as soon as you arrive, forget about Berlin, sit yourself down in your room, and study as hard as you can. I hope you can make up for the time you lost here. Do you feel that you've lost ground? You know by now that I'm quite capable of telling you off!*

*I was just interrupted, but now my mother is playing patience and this time, thank God, she's managed to collar my father. My parents, incidentally, are full of sympathy. They know what a sacrifice we're making!*

*So, I must stop now, my eyes are closing. There was a moderate turn-out at the gymnastics class, but it was still tiring.*

*If possible I'll write every day, sometimes more, sometimes less as time allows and events dictate.*

*Give my best wishes to our mutual friends. Here's a loving good night kiss from your*
*Ernest*[79]

*I'll write in the evenings and then get the letter to the morning train. Let me know when you've received this one.*

*Will the time pass quickly?*

Marianne wrote as soon as she reached Berlin:

*Berlin, 5 February 1942.*

*Iranischestrasse 4*[80]

*My love,*

*This is my first chance to write to you. It's already late. One person after another dropped in to break into happy screams at seeing me. (Am I being conceited to write that?!) Now I'm writing letters in my old bed; everything is as it was; at least at first sight; the same untidiness as before – Bohemian is nothing compared to this – though I'm more conscious of it now that I'm less used to it. In fact, the untidiness is like everything else – I know it all, and all so well, and yet I have to get used to it again. But let me tell you everything in order:*

*My travelling companions were awful. Did you pray to the Lord not to lead me into temptation? Three nuns especially for my entertainment. One had rattling dentures, the second drank continuously from a bottomless thermos, while the third preferred not to drink because she thought she would have to go too often.[ . . .]*

*But the journey through the white world was beautiful. Do you know what I wished . . . ? We passed by fields; sometimes there were horses pulling an old cart through the snow, once even a sleigh. The snow swallows up the colours, you see only nuances from white to black. And yet you don't get tired of looking. I think you can guess how much work I did (are you pulling a cross face?).*

*And now I'm here. Everything is as it was and yet completely different. Do you know what I mean? It's a feeling I can't explain, but maybe it's not important – tomorrow it will all look different anyway.*

*At the moment, I have the feeling that everything is too much for me. But I'm writing that only because we want to tell each other everything. It doesn't sound good, but since I'm so honest . . . !*

*Inge is tired, so I won't write any more. I hope I get a letter from you soon. I was so, so pleased to get the wallet and your photo, Ernest. Thank you. Your photo is next to me, so at least I have something of you.*

*[ . . . ]*

*Don't be angry if this letter isn't up to much; put it down to tiredness and interruptions. Sleep well, my love, and write soon to your Jeanny.*

By the time she wrote the next day, she had received her first letter from Ernst.

*Friday 6.II.1942*

*Iranischestrasse 4*

*Tel 460441*

*My dear Ernest,*

*I found your letter early this evening when I got home, tired and freezing cold. You can imagine how happy I was. Particularly as it was written under* such *difficult conditions! I'm facing similar difficulties: it's just past midnight, your Jeanny has been very good, studying until now (though not from fear of you being cross!).*

Today was a memorable, uplifting day: the big welcome assembly with Frau Dr Fraenkel in front of all the assembled students. As I sat there among them, I had to pinch my arms to see if I was dreaming. But I quickly came back to earth, thanks to the discussion of our exam subjects. For my optional subject I'm taking kindergarten theory; the compulsory subject is health studies. I haven't been able to revise either until now. Then there's educational theory and subjects which they may question me about for a 'quick check': Pestalozzi, Fröbel, school reform, and so on. You see, my love, that I didn't need your strictures at all!

Tomorrow Inge and I are going to 'sneak' into the residence of a former fellow sufferer, who took the exam last year. Have I told you about Marianne Levy? You know, I lived with her in the Wangenheimstrasse. Since then she has strapped the yoke of marriage to her fragile frame; tomorrow we shall visit her to study with her and her husband. You probably agree with all the people here who say that I won't fail the exams!

On Thursday I give a teaching demonstration. I've been assigned to a kindergarten. I'm going to do fun gymnastics with the children. I have a group of 6–8 children, as usual. Hannah Karminski, one of our teachers and the people who work at the kindergarten are the 'audience'. I hope it'll be OK. It's more a matter of luck than anything else. But I'm sure to fail in Hebrew; Frau Fraenkel tried to console me: 'The worst that can happen is that you get an unsatisfactory mark for your writing.' Poor consolation!

I wanted to visit Uta today during a free period. But I couldn't find them. They left their flat because of the cold and moved in with their parents. This morning we had our lessons in Marburgerstrasse and this afternoon in the Joachimsthalerstrasse because the Wilsnackerstrasse has been 'burned down'.

Coal is a real problem. It's freezing in the hall of residence. And travelling around in unheated trams is freezing too. The first thing we do when we get home is take a hot bath and then get into bed.

*Tomorrow, however, I'm going to be a hero and work through
the night. In the education theory exam on Monday we're afraid
they'll ask about Pestalozzi and Fröbel – lots of work to do for
that. But I see I've written about nothing but me. I hope you had
a few happy hours with Hilde. Give her best wishes from me if you
like. Above all, though, best wishes to your parents.*

*You ask if the time will pass quickly. Don't let it get you down,
my love. It's tougher for you than for me. Every day, I have some
new experience to help the time pass quickly, while for you life
follows its familiar course. But I've found that it's possible to think
of several things at the same time . . . !*

*Now I must finish. Tomorrow, another hour with you, if at all
possible.*

*A kiss from your*
*Jeanny*

At first glance, these letters are a more trustworthy source than memories related fifty years later. They are indubitably still just as they were
in 1942. Yet they raise problems of interpretation that are no less
intractable. What should we make, for example, of the fact that there is
no mention of wearing the yellow star, of official harassment or of so
many other aspects of life for Jews in Germany in 1942? How much
self-censorship is being imposed here on mail which, after all, had to
pass the surveillance of a police state? Life under the conditions of Nazi
Germany, it seems, is almost by definition unobservable. Every faint ray
of light that manages to escape from that dark era is bent out of shape
in one way or another – either filtered and refracted through long years
of memory, or else a reflection, bounced off the surface of contemporary
documents whose reliability and faithfulness we cannot know. That is
why the interplay *between* letters and reminiscences in this case is so
helpful. The letters confirm that Marianne's positive memories of her
little Berlin world were not a retrospective invention. The memories
suggest that, if she was leaving negative experiences out of the letters, it
was not because her real views were being constrained by censorship –
since they don't appear in her memories either.

On Monday 9th, Marianne reported an eventful day:

*My love,*

*The first round of terror has passed; now Lilly and I are sitting with Marianne, gorging on coffee and jam and memories of old times when everything was better! (what kind of face are you making?) ... both of them are thoughtfully being very quiet because they know that I am writing to you, my love. You should be very impressed that I'm managing to write at all, after this morning. We had three topics:*

1. *'He who seeks to lead others must be capable of great sacrifice.'[81]*
2. *The importance and scope of co-operation between the Hort [the after-school club for school-age children] the family and the school.*
3. *The depiction of child development in literature.*

*I chose the third topic to start with, and do you know which book I wanted to review? ... Fall Maurizius. But after I'd already written lots, one of the girls advised me to ask Dr Fraenkel, who said I shouldn't use the book. So then, I decided to do topic two. Of course, none of this was good and I think I've thoroughly messed up the exam. Lilly has read the essay and doesn't think so, but I've got a definite feeling.*

*Tomorrow morning there's the handicrafts or drawing exam; I'll do a drawing or a collage. In the afternoon it's written Hebrew!!!! ...*

*At five we've got lessons again and now that I've written to you I feel so much better that I'm sure they'll go very well. Only, I've got to make the big trip from Alexanderplatz to Joachimsthaler-strasse. So, I'm going to stop now. If possible I'll write again in an hour.*

*It's evening now. This is the first chance I've had to write more to you. No post from you today so now I've got to wait until tomorrow evening – an awfully long time away! I think of you all the time, Ernst, and I wish you were with me. Then we wouldn't need to write. It's strange – I thought that the things I'd like to say but can't would be easier to write, but now, with you, I'm finding I can't write them either. My letters to you always end up differently from how I wanted – maybe that will change. My love, there's so much I should say to you, but easier said than done. Anyway, you can always read between the lines!!!!*

*In the meantime, all I want is for everything that I've got to do this evening to be done so that I can sleep, sleep and sleep. I'm so tired. Two nights without sleep are making themselves felt. Incidentally, there was a promising start to the day. At around 1 a.m. Inge and I were sitting with a pile of books and sweets when we heard a sudden hullabaloo in the corridor. A guard had noticed that the hall wasn't fully blacked-out. When we heard the noise in the corridor we quickly switched off the light and fell into a 'deep sleep' in our beds. The warden's wife ran through all the rooms in a panic and couldn't find a light on anywhere. We all lay like sleeping beauties. Here and there, someone groaned sleepily as the warden's wife flung open a door (we did too, of course). That was the first blow. The second came soon after. We were supposed to be in the Wilsnackerstrasse by 9 a.m. At 8 some charitable soul found me dreaming peacefully in my bed. I swore, prayed, ran, tripped and . . . arrived on time! But I sat there the whole morning starving and desperate for a certain small room. First I hadn't had anything to eat – (later a couple of girls took pity on me) and second . . . ! And third, you're not allowed to leave the room during the exam.*

*My love, now you know everything there is to know about my bad luck. I hope that tomorrow brings me better luck and at least two letters from you!*
*Thinking of you always*
*Your*
*Jeanny*

When Ernst saw the reference to the 'round of terror' he might have thought Marianne had suffered some terrible act of persecution, perhaps a near escape from the Gestapo. But it soon becomes clear that she is referring only to her exams. Even in the Germany of the Wannsee conference, of restrictions and deportations, Marianne was able to focus all her energies and emotions on the conventional challenges of exams. There is a poignant irony in the fact that for this German Jewish girl there was only one threat worth five exclamation marks: her written Hebrew exam. Frau Fraenkel, with her knowledge of the grim events outside, tries to reassure her that the worst that can happen is a bad mark. But this, for Marianne, is only a weak consolation. By contrast, the guard checking on the light and the house warden's wife scurrying through the block in a panic, is registered merely as a comic interlude.

Marianne was not the only person to have an eventful Monday. That day, Ernst returned home to find that the elderly Frau Austerlitz, with whom the Krombachs were sharing an apartment, had died:[82]

> Sad piece of news awaited me when I got home: Frau Austerlitz had died. It's been a real challenge to write this letter because there's been so much to organize: visits to pay our condolences, the doctor, the nurse, informing the night watch, dealing with telegrams and so on. I'm continually interrupted. Only one thing really shocked me – that her death left me completely unmoved. No feelings, nothing. A sign of the times? Probably, yes. Partly also I've been expecting it for some time and so got used to the idea. It seems just the natural outcome. Whatever – it didn't frighten me.

People in their situation 'who only live for the present moment', Ernst continued, had to create a certain distance from the misery around them, though that did not mean they lost the ability or the desire to feel sympathy.[83] Marianne's reply by return of post was equally revealing:[84]

> Love,
>
> I think the death of Frau Austerlitz affected you more than you think, because as I read the opening lines of your letter I had a very odd feeling that something must be wrong. Until now I had never believed that you could sense a person's mood just from reading their letter . . .
>
> Do you remember our conversation about life and death and life?[85] You just have to find the right attitude to death and then it no longer seems so horrifying. It is both salvation and a biological necessity. That's why you weren't so disturbed, at least on the surface: it was the natural outcome. You don't need to worry about

*your feelings, love. Your attitude is the more natural one, in earlier times it was the natural attitude. Today, human beings with their 'culture' have modified these attitudes and customs. Of course we are sad when a loved one passes on; but death should be no more than a fact of nature. (I'm coming closer to your scientific approach to life.)[ . . .]In the end these issues always confront us with a problem, no matter how old we are; every opinion and every belief is simply an attempt to avoid uncertainty. Because unfortunately we try to understand everything in terms of reason and we want to know everything. How much wiser the Indians are, for example. We should learn from them. They embody so much that our modern psychology is seeking. It would be really good if, after Freud, we read something about Indian life?! I will ask around, all right? It is fantastic to be here again and I have really settled in marvellously.*

Over the next four years, Marianne's letters and diaries turned again and again to the issue of death and how to cope with it. At the college, Jungian ideas were in vogue and Marianne shows some of their influence here.[86] Another frequent theme in her writing was the lessons to be learned from pre-modern peoples whose 'natural' way of life should serve as a model. In this, she echoed a common preoccupation among youth-movement and 'life-reform' circles in Weimar.

Wednesday brought new experiences and a telling observation on the sad decline around her:[87]

*This afternoon we outsiders – there are five of us – had an educational theory lesson with Frau Dr. I really enjoy that. It's a bit of continuity that consoles me for all the other changes, makes them trivial and insignificant. Then I'm less upset by the fact that the quality of life in the hall has fallen so much. It's now an iceberg and has lost all its physical appeal. There's no intellectual life here any more, no musical evenings, no discussions about God and the world, no meetings in beautiful, cosy rooms until late at night. Whenever we 'veterans' meet, we hark back nostalgically to the time when there was still an 'elite' here. But it's only to be expected that as the external framework collapses so too does the life within.*

Nevertheless, Berlin was so rich in interesting people that, provided one was able to ignore the daily horrors, one could still have a wealth of stimulating encounters even in February 1942. There was the artist Bielefeld, whom Marianne charmed into giving her a drawing. And there was Alfred Selbiger, a former youth worker now employed by the RV, with whom she had a 'fantastic conversation' about the problems faced by young people in the current conditions. She wrote to Ernst:[88]

*He is a perfect youth movement type, and I liked him enormously. It seems the feeling was mutual because he proposed introducing me to a group with similar attitudes to his. I'm excited by the idea, of course, and I'll see what I can manage with the little time I have [ . . . ]I realized how good it would be for us to live a* bündisch *life. And if only for that reason it would be interesting to get to know the group and see if we would fit in or if all our ideas are illusions.*

On Saturday 14th Marianne wrote again. She had spent the day in Grünewald, with friends of her parents who had managed to keep their house in that elegant suburb. They had as a guest a young Chinese man who had spent five years in Germany training to be an engineer. Here was another fascinating encounter.[89]

Neither Marianne nor Ernst, however, was under any illusion that conditions would improve. Prophetically, Marianne wrote:[90]

*I often have the feeling that life is offering me as much as it can before a door is slammed shut. So much is happening and I wonder why it's different from the last 2½ years. But perhaps it just seems different because I'm living in the moment and see the fact that I'm here as a gift. If only you could always be with me! There, we don't really live – there are more choices here, even now. Perhaps it is self-centred to think like this; we have each other – unthinkable if we didn't; but nothing comes to us from the outside world. It's sad! But at least this evening we laughed as we haven't done for ages: we managed to make fun of every teacher in college.*

According to Marianne's schedule, her last oral exam took place on the morning of 20 February. Among her papers I found a telegram sent from Berlin at 15.10 on Friday 20 February to Ernst Krombach,

*Marianne's Staatsexamen certificate*

Semperstrasse 5, Essen. The text ran: 'ALL TERRORS SUCCESSFULLY OVERCOME – MARIANNE'.

One of Marianne's claims about which I was most sceptical was that the kindergarten college exams still enjoyed any official status. On 25 June 1940, the Reich Education Ministry had published a general decree stating that examinations at Jewish higher schools would no longer be regarded as state exams.[91] True, Marianne's post-war CVs and applications always referred to a 'Staatsexamen', and she assured me that she had sat the official examination. My scepticism was heightened, however, by the restitution correspondence in which Marianne was unable to authenticate the official status of her qualification.[92] But then, when her son Vivian finally worked his way through the bric-à-brac in the outhouse to the huge trunk at the back, we found her final transcript. Marianne had gained an overall mark of 'good' (though just as she had predicted, her Hebrew *had* been 'unsatisfactory', as indeed had her exam essay). But most remarkable was that the transcript came complete with the eagle and swastika stamp of the Reich and the signature of the Stadtpräsident der Reichshauptstadt Berlin. In February 1942, a month after the Wannsee conference, Jewish kindergarten teachers in Berlin *were* still graduating with the Staatsexamen, even as their potential charges were being transported to Łodz, to Minsk and to Riga.[93]

# 5

## The Family, the Gestapo,
## the Abwehr and the Banker

After the outbreak of war with Britain, the Strausses again looked to the USA for salvation. They had two advantages over many other would-be emigrants. They had an affidavit – from cousin Fritz Stern – and they could afford to pay their passage (assuming they received permission to withdraw money from their blocked accounts). Yet, when the Nazis finally stopped all Jewish emigration from Germany in August–September 1941, the Strausses were still in Essen. Marianne firmly believed that the family's American relatives had let them down. Her father pleaded with them, she said, but 'they didn't do a thing'.

The correspondence between Marianne's parents and their US relatives from 1939 to 1941 does not really bear out her view, however. The Strausses' main problem was simply timing: because their application was made so late, they were far down in the queue for US visas: number 28,972.[1] The US consulate in Stuttgart did not even call for their application papers until January 1941.[2] And submitting the papers was merely the start of a protracted second stage which would culminate in an interview at the consulate and, with luck, the visa.

Nevertheless, in January 1941 the family grew hopeful. Siegfried and Ine attended intensive lessons in English and US accountancy. A poem presented to Siegfried on his fiftieth birthday by fellow students mentions his hard work and his difficulties with English pronunciation. From May to July, the couple attended 'preparatory lessons for the profession of an Accountant'.[3] Siegfried gave the English class weekly lectures on the customs and character of the different American states.[4] A cousin, Hugo Strauss, sent them useful information on living in the USA: furniture was light and simple; people used gas stoves and refrigerators, toasters and vacuum cleaners; men's ties were narrow and brightly coloured.[5] Marianne's parents found the details so important, or so reassuring, that they typed them out again. But in July 1941, just before the family's interview in Stuttgart, all the US consulates in Germany were closed and applications would now be dealt with in Washington. There was a whole new procedure and the number of visas would probably fall sharply. The US relatives genuinely could do nothing.

It is easy to understand, though, why the Strausses felt uncertain about how much support they could expect from their American cousins. Their principal correspondents were their cousins Hugo and Grete Strauss, to whom they were very close. But Hugo and Grete themselves had reached the USA only in 1938, and as new arrivals in difficult circumstances were in no position to provide a plausible affidavit of financial support. By contrast, Fritz Stern, the relative who since 1938 had acted as Siegfried's guarantor, was, though financially very well-placed to provide support, someone whom the Strausses hardly knew.

In January 1940, the family had asked Fritz Stern to renew his affidavit. He replied fairly rapidly, on 23 February, but the uncertain post meant his letter did not arrive until mid-April. The delay was worrying enough. In May, Marianne's parents received a letter from Hugo Strauss written in January (after their own request for a new affidavit had reached the States, but before Fritz Stern had responded). Hugo wrote, trying out his English:

> Dear Folks,
>     I want to inform you that I spoke to Fritz Stern today with regard to the renewal of your affidavits. We agreed in the fact, that you should let him know as soon as this renewal is, actually necessary. If it is urgent, you may wire to him and he will send out the papers immediately. To have always best results for the common benefit, in avoiding any work, not necessary for the very moment. But don't hesitate and let me know it immediately, when

*it is the right time. Fritz is a very nice man, clearcut and short in his decisions. Let me know as soon as you make your request to him, that I may follow it up.*

Fritz may have been very nice, but wasn't there something worrying about Hugo having to reassure them? Why had Hugo written and not Fritz? Next to 'clearcut', either Siegfried or Ine has written a German translation in pencil, suggesting that they didn't know what it meant and had looked it up in a dictionary. Since their lives might depend on this man, it was important to understand every adjective.

The family's uncertainty about the help they might expect must have been heightened by Siegfried's sister's experience. Whereas Siegfried and Ine were not seeking financial assistance to enter the States, as they emphasized more than once, Siegfried's sister Bertel was in a different position. On 22 October 1940 Bertel, her husband Ferdinand Wolf and son Richard were caught up in the Bürckel-Action, in which 6,504 Jews from Baden and some 1,000 from Alsace and Lorraine were deported to various concentration camps in Vichy France.[6] Siegfried wrote to Hugo begging him to do something for them:[7]

*We are convinced that cousin Fritz and the other relations will be willing to help our dear ones with passage to the USA. You know Bertel and Ferdinand and know that they are hard-working, ambitious and undemanding and will not be a burden to you. I thank you heartily, dear Hugo and the other relatives who are working for our transfer to the USA.*

Hugo's reply, posted in January 1941 but not received by the Strausses until March, was not encouraging. He had tried all sorts of things for relatives in similar difficulties with little success. Fritz Stern was hard to contact in New York:[8]

*Luckily I reached him yesterday. He doesn't think we will be successful with the Wolfs. This is understandable given our experiences. He didn't make any promises re the fare but left the possibility open. I will . . . ask him to send an affidavit to the consulate in Marseilles. I will also try to get him to send a confirmation to the consulate about paying the fare. He is a very fine man. That is the lucky thing. Given the misfortunes that have afflicted everyone, most people won't even listen to you. I approach the thing cautiously to avoid a rejection. It is difficult to push him towards a decision. I will do my best. Fritz is my only hope . . .*

Later in the year, the Strausses were very distressed to learn via Grete Strauss that their hopes of Bertel's emigration had come to nothing. She was now interned in the Rivesault camp, separated from her husband and her son. Marianne's aunt Lore could not hide her disappointment:[9]

*We thought she would be with you in July and were so disappointed when you, dear Grete, wrote she had been unsuccessful because of the cost of the passage. Bertel and Ferdinand are so reliable that as soon as they were able to work they would certainly pay back every penny that was advanced to them.*

*If* Grete's information was correct, the Wolfs failed to escape ultimately because the American relatives had been unwilling to pay.[10] Bertel and Ferdinand were eventually murdered in Auschwitz. Their son Richard, however, escaped and survived.

Among Marianne's papers, I found a small address book. It appears to have been prepared in advance of deportation, in case she might manage to reach the USA on her own and need help. It lists at least six different sets of cousins in the USA. With so many connections, could the money not have been found? Marianne's resentment might thus have been justified in the case of the Wolfs, but is inappropriate with regard to her immediate family. Certainly, Fritz Stern did all that was asked of him for relatives he hardly knew. Not for the last time, I wondered if some of Marianne's criticism of others was in fact a deflection of the anger she felt towards her parents for having left it too late.

## Expropriation and persecution

For Marianne's parents, the period 1939–40 was characterized by the drip, drip of persecution rather than by radical change. Life was miserable but bearable. After the outbreak of war, the family was restricted to RM700 a month, which, though hardly generous, was enough to live on, particularly as Siegfried was allowed to make additional monthly transfers to pay for Marianne's schooling.[11] The introduction of rationing after the outbreak of war gave German officialdom scope to deprive Jews of food and other goods. There were no more clothing coupons for Jews,[12] and from 18 December 1939 onwards, Jews were permitted only the basic food rations and denied the supplementary card available to others. Non-rationed foods were forbidden them altogether.[13] Still, up to 1941, the Strausses had no pressing material worries, even if their standard of living had become far more modest.

In early 1941, however, the regime's threats to their well-being and survival took on a new quality. Their core assets – particularly the two blocks of flats in the Hufelandstrasse – were now in jeopardy. Not surprisingly, these smart apartment buildings were attractive to would-be 'Aryanizers', including Essen's city council. The records of the city's transactions, preserved in detail in the city archives, give an illuminating picture of the process that was set in train.[14]

The council's interest in the Hufelandstrasse seems to have arisen in autumn 1940, when a nearby hospital needed accommodation for doctors and nurses. The council first approached the brothers' architect, R. Zbinden, in November 1940, and on 5 December 1940 one councillor Schlicht sent the Oberbürgermeister a detailed description of the hospital's accommodation problems. 'For this reason, a survey of the area has been carried out to identify houses which could either be purchased or else acquired by Aryanization.'[15] At the end of December 1940, a Nazi Party official, Schwarzlose, asked the city's Land Department to find out if the brothers were willing to sell. If not, he would seek approval from the Reich Economics Minister for 'compulsory dejudification'.[16]

On 28 January 1941, Siegfried Strauss had a meeting with city officials. The minutes record the following:[17]

*Herr Strauss came to discuss the matter on the 28th of the month. He stated that there are currently 28 tenants in the two houses, only two of whom are Aryans. He requested us not to take over the properties and to acquire others in the area, in deference to the fact that he is a combat veteran and has at no time had any kind of criminal records. He believed that such a request was the more justified in that he intended to leave for America as soon as possible. In this connection, he suggested that we propose to the Currency Office an exchange whereby he would acquire the property of a German returning from the USA against the property he gave up here.*[18]

*I advised Herr Strauss that the city must pursue the purchase of the Hufelandstrasse properties as a matter of urgency and that it will if necessary seek approval for compulsory dejudification. I also rejected the idea of an application to the Currency Office. I agreed only that if Strauss identified a possible exchange, the city might support such a proposal to the Currency Office by emphasizing the public interest of the Hufelandstrasse properties.*

A day later, there was another meeting. Siegfried, with customary obduracy, reiterated his position, stressing his intent to emigrate. The official showed his ignorance of the Jewish situation by doubting that emigration was possible in wartime. Siegfried responded that several boats had recently sailed from Lisbon to the USA and again asked for an exchange with US property. The city official, on this occasion, simply said this was not feasible. Siegfried emphasized that, as First World War combatants, he and his brother enjoyed a certain level of protection against compulsory 'dejudification' and urged the city not to take over the houses at present. The officials then asked if he would be willing to part with one block and Siegfried rejected the proposal.[19] So now the city, with the backing of the regional economic chamber, began to set the wheels in motion to force the brothers to sell.

The city was not the only would-be tenant. In June 1941, the mayor received a letter from a businessman, Diplom Kaufmann Ricco Arendt:[20]

*I write to you on the advice of my father-in-law, Herr Dr Paul Redlich of the Essen Chamber of Industry and Commerce. I would be most grateful if you would allow me to visit you during business hours to discuss the following.*

*I have been trying to find an apartment in Essen since January of this year. Because I have so far failed to do so, my wife and I have been obliged to rent furnished rooms since our marriage and are at present subtenants at Billrothstrasse 32. While looking for a flat, I discovered that the most attractive houses in my area, Hufelandstrasse 23 and 25, are occupied almost exclusively by Jews. I cannot understand why here in Essen the best flats should be occupied by Jews when married couples like ourselves are obliged to live in furnished rooms. Moreover, my wife is pregnant and I therefore apply to you in the hope of possibly finding a flat by this means.*

*I await your reply as to when I may come and discuss the matter with you and remain yours,*
   *Heil Hitler*

Such everyday participation in the expropriation of Jewish property had long fuelled the Nazi Aryanization campaign.[21] Herr Arendt was no doubt disappointed to learn from the city administration that the houses were already designated for hospital use.

Aryanization was not the only weapon deployed against the Strausses. On 10 May, the local block official, an engineer called Kemmerer, together with the Gestapo, knocked on the door of Hufelandstrasse 23 late in the evening, to complain about the lack of proper blackout at a second-floor window. The window was in Alfred's flat. The consequence for an Aryan, assuming that the complaints were at all justified, would probably have been a gruff warning. Not for a Jew. Alfred Strauss was taken into custody. On 22 May, the Gestapo urged the state prosecutor to initiate proceedings. The indictment, statements and state prosecutor's response are all preserved in the Gestapo records in Düsseldorf.

According to the Gestapo, the block official, Kemmerer, claimed that:[22]

*The (NSDAP) Essen-Holsterhausen local group had entrusted him with the task of monitoring the blackout in his block. The buildings at Hufelandstrasse 23 and 25 belonged to his block. In the two houses, which were occupied only by Jews, there had often been gross infringements of the blackout regulations which had been reported to the local group.*

Within the Nazi political system, the rank and file party member often had disappointingly little power, particularly after 1934. Making a nuisance of himself about blackout regulations was one of the local block official's remaining perks. Here was a chance to flex his muscles against the wealthy owner of a big house and, what was more, a Jew. This was grist for the Gestapo's mill, which concluded that 'The suspicion that from time to time the Jews here *deliberately* fail to abide by the police blackout regulations in full is therefore probably justified.'[23]

The vague language of the memo – 'from time to time', 'fail to adhere in full', 'probably justified' – speaks for itself. And in an internal memorandum to their Düsseldorf superiors, the Essen Gestapo admitted they were seeking a prosecution 'mainly so that, if St. [Strauss] is prosecuted, he can be declared an enemy of people and the state. He owns property worth RM150,000'.[24]

In the official submission to the state prosecutor, Kriminal-Assistent Kosthorst of the Essen Gestapo did his best to establish the seriousness of the case. First, the culprit was a Jew and thus a notorious enemy of the state. It was well known that the Jews aimed to undermine the rule of law. Second, repeated breaches of the blackout law showed the infringement to be deliberate. Third, given the proximity of the hospital, patients would be endangered if a bomber saw the light.[25]

In his own submission, Alfred Strauss provided a detailed account of his military service in the First World War. He also emphasized his lack of political activity before 1933 and his understanding that it was particularly incumbent on Jews to keep the law, and that there was, therefore, no question of deliberate infringement. As for the particular accusations, Alfred noted that the window had both a blackout curtain and a blackout screen. On the evening in question, the curtain had undoubtedly been closed, but he might have forgotten the screen, so that some light could have been visible. Finally, Alfred noted that he hoped to leave for the United States in the near future and asked that no impediment be placed in the way of his emigration.

The state prosecutor dismissed the case on two grounds. In the first place, it was still only twilight when the offence had been committed. Second, there was no proof that the other breaches had been observed in Alfred Strauss's apartment. It was irrelevant that other occupants of the building might have committed the same offence.[26] The Gestapo was of course very disappointed and decided to order twenty-one days' protective custody for Alfred. The Essen police president was invited to think of further measures that might be undertaken.[27] Interestingly, while the Gestapo thought the police had agreed on twenty-one days' detention, Alfred actually spent only six days in custody, although this detail does not appear in the files. He also paid a fine of RM30.50.[28]

Just as after Kristallnacht, when the Strausses had managed to obtain some concessions from the tax authorities, the legal process conveyed mixed messages for the family. Clearly, there was still justice of a sort to be had from some servants of the state. The judicial system still enjoyed a degree of independence from Himmler's police empire. On the other hand, the grounds cited seem a woefully inadequate response to the arbitrariness of the case. For what must have been clear to the prosecutor is that the Gestapo imprisoned Alfred Strauss on the flimsiest ground – a partial failure to black-out a window, observed when it was not yet even dark.

On 26 June, the authorities' assault on the Hufelandstrasse flats entered a new phase. The Regierungspräsident in Düsseldorf informed the brothers that as of July 1941, 'on the basis of paragraph §2 of the Decree on the Utilization of Jewish Property from 3.12.1938',[29] a Dr Gilka would be appointed commissioner for their property. The state was willing to offer a purchase figure equal to the construction cost of the building. This was not the market price, but at least bore some relation to the apartments' value. The brothers bowed to the inevitable.[30]

The city file on the matter contains a small but telling indication of the atmosphere in the council offices. The housing department drafted a letter to the Hufelandstrasse tenants, to notify them that their tenancy would end at the end of October. It was addressed to 'Herrn Israel NN.' 'NN', for Nomen Nescio was a standard abbreviation, for which the real name would be substituted. Since the tenants were Jewish they would, if male, have the middle name Israel. So 'Mr Israel NN' was a playful short-hand, meaning 'to the Jew it may concern'. It is the playfulness which most disturbs.

The pace of persecution continued to accelerate. In July 1941, the US consulates were closed. August 1941 saw the ban on emigration and September the introduction of the yellow star. In early October, the Strausses left the Hufelandstrasse and moved back to their old house on

Ladenspelderstrasse.[31] In a rare moment of complaint, Ine wrote to relatives in the USA about how much they regretted having to give up their beautiful, comfortable apartment.[32] But worse was to come. Hardly had they unpacked when they were informed by a local party boss and the city official Schwarzlose that Ladenspelderstrasse too was about to be expropriated.[33] And they had hardly digested *that* when they were notified of their imminent deportation to the East.

## Snatched from the gravedigger's spade

In October 1941, Marianne was in Berlin. The first she heard of the deportation was a telegram from her parents telling her to come home immediately. The college hurriedly gave her a provisional graduation certificate[34] and Marianne arrived in Essen on 25 October.[35] The transport to which Siegfried and his family had been assigned was scheduled for 26 October 1941 and bound for Łodz, 'Litzmannstadt' in German.[36] This was the first major deportation from Essen since the expulsion of Polish Jews in 1938, and involved some 250 people.[37] It was part of a wave of transports from all over Germany, which deported 8,000 German Jews to Łodz up to the beginning of November. Ine's sister Hannah and her husband Ernst Weinberg were scheduled for a transport from Cologne as part of this wave.

Siegfried Strauss and his family may have been placed on this first list by chance, but one rather significant detail suggests otherwise. Although the Hufelandstrasse sale had been agreed upon in July, the Oberbürgermeister approved the transfer of payment only on 24 October 1941, just a few days before the deportation. Actual payment could not be made until the exchange control office in Düsseldorf had given its approval, so it seems at least reasonable to assume that Essen Council hoped to avoid paying Siegfried altogether.[38] At the same time, the city had its eye on the fine property on the Ladenspelderstrasse. Deporting the family would make expropriation easier and obviate the need to rehouse them.

The Strausses may not have known their exact destination – Marianne remembered something about a 'work camp in the East'.[39] Nor could they know the kind of conditions awaiting them. For one thing, this was the first major deportation from Essen. Marianne's parents had, of course, gained some idea of the misery which the victims of the 1940 deportations to France, in this case Siegfried's sister, had suffered. But clearly they were unaware of the true horror ahead, because when I checked in the Gestapo records I discovered, to my amazement, that Marianne was not on the deportation list.[40] I think Marianne may never have known – she certainly never said – that her parents were taking her with them voluntarily. Just as they had prevented Marianne and Richard from leaving for Britain in March 1939, so now too they placed absolute priority on keeping the family together. It is unlikely that Siegfried and Ine would have insisted had they known what they were going to.

Marianne told me they spent three tense days packing. As on other occasions, a traumatic episode had expanded in her memory – in reality she was at home for only one day.[41] The official instructions specified that each transport member could take up to RM100, one suitcase containing household goods, a complete set of clothing, bedclothes and food for eight days. Valuables, other money, jewellery (apart from wedding rings), pets and ration cards could not be taken.[42] Among Marianne's papers, tucked into the address book containing the family's foreign contacts, I found a hand-written list:

Rucksack filled with essentials
Woollen blanket and pillow with pillow case
Thermos flask
Plastic cup and plate with suitable bag (for hygiene reasons)
Cutlery and bag
Butter dish
Needle and thread in a bag
Soap, soap powder, candles, torch, toilet paper, writing
instruments, comb and washing stuff in an oilcloth bag
*Pharmaceuticals* Borax ointment, sticking plaster, burn plaster,
cotton wool, cotton bandage, absorbent cotton wool, acetate of
alumina, 'Novaletten' (Valerian in solid form), quinine for
temperatures, charcoal for constipation, diuretics, insect powder,
thermometer, scissors, tweezers
*One light suitcase* Underwear, clothing, warm slippers, shoes, two
smocks as substitute for lightweight clothing, two sleeping bags, if

possible made of easily washable coloured materials, towels and clothes

*To wear* Thick stockings, underwear, clothing, coat, raincoat with a hood in the pocket

*Address book* with addresses of relatives and friends abroad

*4 passport photos*

*Photocopies* of important papers, incl. school certificates, birth and marriage certificate

1 bag with several days' food.

On the morning of the 26th an official appeared, took the house keys and sealed up the house. Siegfried, Ine, Marianne and Richard set off on foot for the collection point in Haumannshof, site of the police headquarters and the district court. Carrying their luggage, they walked down the Ladenspelderstrasse, round the corner into the Hufeland-strasse and down to the Haumannshof. Here, a crowd of deportees awaited them.

Marianne's memory was that they queued up to board a tram taking them to the station, whence the transport would go on to Łodz:[43]

'I shall never forget the moment when we were standing there and the people were all being loaded into the tram. In front of everyone, the two Gestapo officials, notorious officials from the Gestapo headquarters in the Kortumstrasse, told my family that we were not to get on but should go back home.'

The hatred on the faces of fellow Jews as the Strausses were let go was an unforgettable experience:[44]

'We were sent back home, and that was the most dreadful experience anybody had, to hear this animal howl go up, that was really quite something which I never forgot. It took me quite a long time to get that out of my ears . . .'

So the family walked back up Ladenspelderstrasse and took the seals off their front door. Siegfried said that they had been 'snatched from the gravedigger's spade'.

Up to this point, the family's experience and behaviour was more or less the same as that of many other patriotic, well-to-do, provincial, middle-class German Jews. On 26 October 1941, however, the Strausses' story took on a new quality. What had happened – something for which Siegfried had been working but to Marianne was unexpected and inexplicable – launched the family on a different trajectory, one that in the end would enable Marianne to survive.

In retrospect, Marianne herself regarded the moment on the Haumannshof as a turning point. On one occasion, she was talking to me about the influence cast on her by left-wing friends whom she met later in the war. They were the most formative influence on her life, she said:[45]

'I felt that I had to move away from all of this Jewish ballast as I felt it then, and the hypocrisy . . . I realized how these people behaved and we were sent back you know, from this meeting point where everybody was gathered and we were in full view of everybody, quite with the intent of causing this frisson. . . . And all these things were building up and I thought I don't want anything more.'

The bitter cry of her fellow deportees took on a special significance in her memory. Marianne was torn between a feeling of injury as the object of unjust envy and wrath and a sense of unease at being unfairly privileged. This double burden of anger and guilt made the scene on the Haumannshof one of the pivotal moments of her life. She came to interpret it as a crucial stage in her alienation from the Jewish community.

## Why had the Strausses been saved?

Why was the family sent home? The Jewish community in Essen had its suspicions. When I contacted the daughter of the Essen Jewish Community's former secretary, who had settled in the States, I was shocked to hear her say with some certainty that the Strausses had bribed the Gestapo and paid a poor mother to send one of her sons in their place. She even knew the woman's name, Moszkowicz.[46] I was even more shocked as the Gestapo list of deportees to Łodz confirmed that there was indeed a young man of that name on the transport, albeit spelled slightly differently: Jakob Moschkowitz. What I found disturbing was not so much the shadow cast over Marianne's family – though, if true, the incident was distressing enough – but more the idea that places on the transports could be bought and sold. It did not fit into the conventional picture of the Third Reich at all.

By an extraordinary coincidence, I was already in touch with Imo Moszkowicz, the sole surviving member of this family. I wrote to him with some trepidation, asking about the story:[47]

*I heard that the Strauss brothers were hated for the fact that they had paid a poor woman to send one of her sons in the place of the family Strauss. Then I learned that the woman was your mother and the son your brother. I looked in* Schröter, Geschichte und Schicksal der Essener Juden, *and saw that Jakob Moschkowitz (this is how it is spelled but I assume it is your brother) really did go on this transport. On the other hand, both he and the Strauss family appear at the same time on the list [ . . .]*

*If it is not too painful for you to tackle this subject, my question to you is, do you have any memory of this? I don't understand in any case how one person – in this case your brother – can 'replace' a whole family. Were other people involved?*

The more I thought about it, the less plausible the story seemed and, when I talked to him, Imo Moszkowicz did not confirm it. Jakob wasn't his brother but his cousin, he said, and there had been some question of volunteering, but not to replace the Strauss family. His cousin, who had simply been idling his time away in Essen, had agreed to accompany two elderly ladies on the transport. Money might have changed hands, he wasn't sure. Certainly, the fact that both Jakob *and* the Strausses were on the same Gestapo list at the same time makes the substitution story particularly suspect. Imo told me that he and his friends had assumed the Strausses were protected because Marianne's father had invented the famous Krupp stainless steel, Nirrosta Stahl.[48] This was a string to Siegfried's bow I knew nothing about. In fact, as it later transpired, Imo Moszkowicz and other contemporaries had confused Siegfried with another Essen Jew, Bruno Strauss, who had indeed invented the steel.

These variant narratives suggested that it may indeed have been possible to influence the lists (and there was certainly a great deal of corruption); but above all I was being offered some insight into the way rumour worked in those fevered times. When ineffable decisions from on high could mean the difference between life and death, there was bound to be speculation about what lay behind them. Once the community had construed the Strausses' protection in a particular way, the rumour machine rapidly spread speculation as hard fact.

For Marianne, much of the background to her family's reprieve from deportation was shrouded in mystery. Siegfried Strauss remained true to his habit of not discussing his affairs with the family, or at least with the children, even though these affairs now held the key to their survival. We know that he worried about their ability to keep a secret, and the people he was dealing with had undoubtedly impressed upon him the need for discretion. The more people knew, the less plausible the enterprise. What Marianne did find out was astonishing enough. Her family, it seems, was being protected by no less an organization than the Abwehr, the counter-intelligence arm of the German Wehrmacht.

In parallel with the SD, the security organization belonging to Himmler's police empire, the Abwehr sought on behalf of the Wehrmacht to monitor foreign intelligence activity and to gain its own intelligence abroad. Most of its employees were loyal supporters of the regime. At the very top, however, the Abwehr contained a number of individuals increasingly hostile to the Nazis. Initially, the most active was General Major Hans Oster, head of the Abwehr's Central Section. In 1938, supported by his direct superior and overall chief of the Abwehr, Admiral Wilhelm Canaris, Oster developed contacts with other generals ill-disposed to Hitler, above all General Beck. Hans von Dohnanyi, the brother-in-law of the oppositional Christian, Dietrich Bonhoeffer, and himself a long-term opponent to the Nazis, joined the Abwehr in August 1939. Alongside Canaris, Oster and Dohnanyi, the other key anti-Nazi conspirator in the Abwehr was Helmuth James von Moltke, who joined its Ausland Abteilung at the outbreak of war.[49]

Nowadays, it is widely known that the Abwehr was implicated in wartime conspiracies against Hitler, and many of its leaders were executed shortly before the end of the war. Far less well known is its involvement in helping German Jews to get abroad. Almost as surprising to me was that the organization should be in contact with the Strauss brothers. The family was not particularly prominent, and their business hardly functioned on a scale that gains access to government circles. But Marianne believed that the link to the Abwehr was the family banker, Friedrich H. Hammacher.

Looking back, I realized that Marianne felt there was something unworthy about all this. There is a section in the tape of our conversation in September 1996, when Marianne was responding to my first draft. Her reaction makes it clear that she would be quite happy not to have the episode mentioned. After Marianne's death, I discovered that the Gestapo files on her father and uncle revealed an extraordinary cat-and-mouse game the Abwehr and Gestapo had played with agonizing slowness for almost two years. The material was so detailed and offered so much clarification that I cursed the fact I'd discovered it two weeks after Marianne's death. I wished I could have shown it to her to reassure her.

Later on, though, as Vivian and I worked through Marianne's papers, we found that she had copies of the Gestapo documents, sent her by researchers in the Alte Synagoge in the 1970s or 1980s. This was one of many areas where it turned out that Marianne knew or had once known more than I realized. Later still, I came across her testimony in restitution hearings in 1952 which showed she had known things that were not even in the Gestapo records. Perhaps no amount of detail could have eased her worries about being singled out for special protection.

## The Gestapo and the Abwehr

The first hint in the Gestapo files that the Strausses might escape the deportation is a telegram sent on 22 October at 8.10 p.m. from the Gestapo in Bremen to the Gestapo in Essen. Headed 'Secret' and 'Urgent. For immediate consideration', the telegram ran:[50]

*Strauss has declared himself willing to go to the USA for the Bremen office of the Abwehr division of the Oberkommando of the Wehrmacht. Since Strauss is due to be transported to Poland in an action against the Jews on 26.10.1941, the Bremen office requests that Strauss be withdrawn from the transport since he is needed for Wehrmacht purposes in the USA.*

Unsure what to do, Gestapo officials in Essen telephoned their superiors in Düsseldorf that night. Düsseldorf's Kriminalsekretär

Ommer advised them not to remove the Strausses from the deportation until he had made enquiries.[51]

The following day, Düsseldorf evidently did nothing. On the 25th, while Marianne was travelling back from her Berlin haven, Siegfried, presumably now extremely anxious about the impending deportation, went to the Gestapo headquarters in Essen. There he reported a visit by an Abwehr representative from Bremen the previous day. The visitor had been unable to come to the Gestapo in person, but had advised him to obtain confirmation that he was exempted from the transport.[52] The head of the Essen Gestapo, Kriminalrat Vaupel, cabled Düsseldorf again asking whether the Strauss family was to be 'evacuated', as the Gestapo euphemistically described deportation.[53]

The Düsseldorf officials were sceptical. But they now sought guidance from their superiors in the Reich Security Main Office (Reichssicherheitshauptamt, RSHA) in Berlin, the body that co-ordinated the activities of police and Gestapo:[54]

*It is suggested that the request from Bremen be rejected. Strauss was here and said that the man from Bremen visited him yesterday in his apartment and told him to come here today and confirm that he is released from the evacuation. The man from Bremen in question could not come himself because he had to travel further at 7.45. Strauss did not want to give the man's name. Strauss's story seems suspect. He probably just wants to evade evacuation. Strauss is very wealthy.*

*I request a clear decision. As of this moment the evacuation is still planned because Strauss's story seems too suspect.*

Whether Berlin responded during the day we do not know, but towards the evening, a senior official in Düsseldorf, Regierungsrat Ventner, felt called upon to make a decision.[55] At 7.40, Ommer cabled Essen that the Strauss family was to be given a temporary reprieve until the next available transport.[56]

The Gestapo officials in Essen did not transmit this information to the Strauss family immediately, but chose to play out the charade at the collection point. Perhaps they wanted to prolong the psychological torture. Perhaps, as Marianne suspected, they wanted to create a rift between the Strausses and the rest of the community. Perhaps they felt

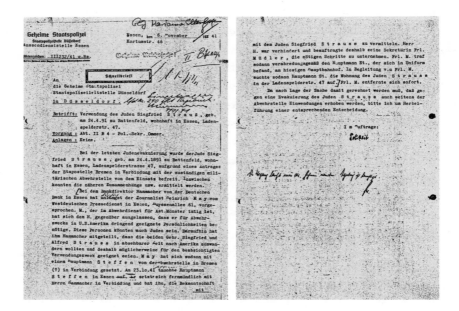

*Gestapo document of 6 November 1941 showing the fruits of its investigations into Abwehr, Hammacher and Strauss*

outwitted and sought to emphasize their power. Whatever the interpretation, they were not simply following orders. They were making up their own game.

Meanwhile, the Düsseldorf Gestapo officials tried to work out what kind of opposition they were up against and the extent of Abwehr support for Siegfried Strauss. On 28 October, they cabled their colleagues in Bremen to establish whether Siegfried Strauss's account of his dealings with the Abwehr had been correct.[57] The Bremen Gestapo cabled back on 4 November, confirming Strauss's account and asking for his family to be exempted from future transports.[58]

Unable to fathom why the Strausses should have been singled out, Essen officials now investigated the local background. They discovered that Heinrich May, a journalist for the Westdeutscher News Agency who was also working for the Abwehr office in Münster, had told Friedrich Hammacher, a Deutsche Bank director in Essen and the Strauss family's banker, that the Abwehr were looking for suitable people for intelligence work in America. These people 'could also be Jews'. Hammacher had suggested the Strauss brothers, since they were planning to emigrate to the USA in the near future. May then got in touch with a Captain Steffen, who met the Strausses in Essen on 23 or 24 October. Hammacher's secretary acted as go-between, collecting the uniformed Steffen from Essen station and taking him to Ladenspelderstrasse 47.[59]

## Historians and the Abwehr

For a long time little was known about the Abwehr's operations involving Jews. The key figures were killed before the end of the war. The few references to saving Jews in the memoirs of other Abwehr figures are often inaccurate. Recently, however, an outstanding study by Winfried Meyer has explored one particular Abwehr action, Operation Seven, in great detail.[60] Initiated by a small number of anti-Nazi conspirators at the very top of the Abwehr (including its chief, Admiral Canaris), Operation Seven saved the lives of fifteen Jews and half-Jews. Hans von Dohnanyi played the leading role.[61] The operation began in 1942, when Dohnanyi attempted to protect some Jewish colleagues from deportation. At the behest of Bonhoeffer and Canaris, further names were added to the list of protégés. The conspirators invented a cover story that the Jews would be used as agents in South America. In August and September 1942, after months of difficult negotiations and preparation, the Abwehr was able to get them into Switzerland. There the fifteen Jews survived the war, thanks as well to the Abwehr's financial assistance.

Meyer's account rightly and understandably draws attention to the heroism and principle of the men behind the rescue effort. Dohnanyi and his senior colleague Hans Oster were already under close surveillance by the SD, and it took great courage to persist with their plans. In the end, Operation Seven led to Dohnanyi's imprisonment and contributed to his execution in April 1945, though the main charge against him, as against Bonhoeffer, Oster, Canaris and Moltke, who were also all murdered in January or April 1945, was their involvement in plans to topple the regime.[62]

Elsewhere, though, the Abwehr's relationship with Germany's Jews appears to have been far less benign. Sections of the Abwehr worked closely with the SS and SD in promoting Nazi racial policy, for example, and in carrying out murders of Jews in Poland and Russia.[63] On the other occasions when the Abwehr protected Jews from deportation, the motives were far less obviously altruistic than in Operation Seven. In some cases, Jews were genuinely used to spy for the Reich, usually forced to do so by the fact that family members remained behind in Germany under threat of persecution and deportation. In other cases, the line between aiding Jews and exploiting them was very blurred, and nowhere more so than in Operation Aquilar, which was probably the source of the Strauss brothers' protection.

Operation Aquilar came into being because of a very ambiguous character, Harry W. Hamacher (no relation to the family banker, Friedrich W. Hammacher, as far as is known), the well-connected proprietor of an Aryanized travel and transport company. Well-connected in Abwehr circles, Hamacher sought official assistance to enable some Dutch Jews to emigrate. Hamacher may have been partially animated by humanitarian motives, but he was certainly making very good money out of providing assistance to desperate Dutch Jews.[64] The Abwehr representative in The Hague with whom Hamacher had contact may have had humanitarian motives, too. His primary interest, however, seems to have been in increasing the flow of intelligence from the Americas. 'Disguised' as refugees, Dutch and German Jews could plausibly travel to North and South America in a way which non-Jewish Germans could not. Canaris gave Aquilar his backing and, in April, the relevant SS official in the Netherlands gave provisional approval for the emigration of 250 people to North, Central and South America. Clearly, the story of Operation Aquilar is far from being the same sort of edifying tale as Operation Seven. Financial motives, the need for information and the desire to rescue Jews were mixed up in a not very appetizing brew. On the other hand, Aquilar was more effective. Under its auspices, 174 people managed to emigrate during 1941 and even as late as 1942, the majority to Central and South America.[65] And the inclusion of the Strauss family with all their relatives in the operation (thus leaving no hostages behind who could be used to extort information) adds credence to the idea that many of those recruited were not really expected to spy.

Although the operation was based in Holland, the Bremen office features in the telegrams in the Strauss file because it had overall responsibility for espionage in the Americas. While many would-be emigrants came from Holland, several regional Abwehr offices outside the Netherlands, including offices in the Ruhr, were notified that Jews interested in emigration were also potential recruits. Of the Abwehr representatives in the region, we know, again from Meyer, that the Heinrich May mentioned by the Gestapo had been in the Abwehr's employ since 1939. US security services had evidence that May had been gathering information about the British, French and American aircraft industries.[66]

## Bank director Hammacher

How did the Strauss brothers come to be included? One point in their favour was that the Abwehr liked to use Jews with a good war record. But there were many Jewish veterans who did not enjoy Abwehr protection. According to Gestapo records and Marianne's memory, the key link between the Abwehr and the Strauss family was the Deutsche Bank director Hammacher. Did he act out of simple loyalty to two long-standing customers with whom he had a relationship of trust and co-operation? There is no doubt that the Deutsche Bank correspondence with the brothers remained cordial and respectful to the end.

Direct information about the man is hard to come by. We know that Friedrich Wilhelm Hammacher was a manager with the Essener Credit-Anstalt from before the First World War. By the early 1930s, he had the rank of deputy director with the Deutsche Bank in Essen, becoming a departmental director sometime between then and 1937.

The clues to his role in the affair came from testimony in post-war restitution disputes between Marianne and Hammacher and from the deposition of one of Hammacher's former tenants, Hanna Aron, living in the USA. Hammacher's intervention was tied up with the purchase of the Strauss house on Ladenspelderstrasse. In a letter to the Gestapo in 1943, he stated that with permission of the Wehrmacht High Command (Oberkommando der Wehrmacht, OKW) he had capitalized his war pension to acquire Ladenspelderstrasse 47 from the 'Jew Siegfried Israel Strauss' on 30 October 1941, just four days after the aborted deportation.[67] When the Strauss family finally left Essen in 1943, Hammacher did indeed move into their house. After the war, in the context of Marianne's restitution claims against him, Hammacher emphasized his role in protecting the Strauss family, but admitted that it was linked to the house purchase:[68]

*The help which I promised before we agreed on the purchase consisted amongst other things of my providing, with the support of my friends in the Abwehr as it then was (Canaris' group), eight passports with travel visa to Sweden. The men involved are still alive, two of them in Essen.*

Hammacher claimed that the Strauss family's right to remain in Ladenspelderstrasse until their departure was enshrined in a secret codicil attached to the house sale. There is certainly no evidence that he pressured the family to leave.

Marianne's own testimony in the restitution process adds another dimension to our understanding of the conditions at the time. According to her statement to the Essen Regional Court in 1952, Schwarzlose, the party figure who informed her father in October of the imminent expropriation of Landespelderstrasse 47, was a good acquaintance of Herr Hammacher. Despite the fact that the council was about to acquire the property, she said, Herr Hammacher was subsequently allowed to purchase it.[69] Hanna Aron, who had lived with the Strausses and remained after Herr Hammacher took over the building, remembered also that he had very good connections with the Gestapo. On the Strausses' departure in 1943, he had arrived with Gestapo officials to claim some of the family's furniture.[70] This connection explained something that had been puzzling me, namely that the Gestapo reports contained nothing against Hammacher despite having identified him as the original link between the Abwehr and the Strauss family. In the restitution hearings after the war, another witness also intimated that payments had been involved.[71] Marianne herself swore under oath that there had been considerable payments under the table to keep the Gestapo sweet. Her father once told her that he had had to pay out forty-odd thousand marks to get a visa.[72]

There is a lot we will never know. Many of these statements were made in the context of restitution hearings and may not quite be what they seem: Marianne was at pains to achieve compensation, Hammacher to prove his innocence. Yet, I felt I had at least glimpsed a murky world hidden from the official records. The connections between Hammacher and the Abwehr, Hammacher and the Party, Hammacher and the city administration, Hammacher and the Gestapo were, I believe, not unusual in the Third Reich. Siegfried's protection involved a hidden local network, within which a degree of sympathy felt by a banker for an upright client merged with legal opportunities for enrichment, which in turn merged with outright corruption on the part of Gestapo and city officials. In the course of my investigation, enough such examples emerged to suggest that corruption in the Third Reich was far more widespread than has been assumed. Hanna Aron, who was not only a tenant of Hammacher's but also the daughter of the Jewish Community secretary, remembered other examples. When the last leader of the Jewish Community, Herr Ostermann, was put on a list for a future transport:[73]

'Herr Kosthorst said to Herr Ostermann, "Herr Ostermann, when you go away, I can have your briefcase." And my mother came home and she said she cried her heart out over this, that they already planned to plunder him while he was still there.'

Arthur Prinz, a leading member of the RV, wrote in his memoirs that:[74]

*... corruption had by that time become so general, even down to the lowest level, that some officials – in our own case, e.g. one of our district policemen – would tell emigrants about to break up their household just what they wished and expected to get 'for free'.*

Because there were several instances where individual Gestapo and police members were prosecuted by the Nazis for personally enriching themselves at the cost of the deportees, many historians still assume that most participants in Jewish persecution stuck to the rules. But the Strausses' case is one where private testimony undermines the official record. The full history of corruption in the Third Reich has yet to be written.

## The privilege of their own four walls

Whatever the precise reasons for their protection, the fact remains that Siegfried and his family were safe for the time being. In this, they were luckier than Ine's sister Hannah and Ernst Weinberg. True, Hannah and Ernst too were sent home from the first Cologne transport to Łodz on 21 October, but only because it was full. They were told to come back in six days and went off on 27 October.[75] When I worked through Uri (Alfred) Weinberg's collection of letters from his parents, sent by the Red Cross to his internment camp in Australia, their very last letter before deportation proved to be missing, something that upset Uri very much. But I did find a letter to him from Marianne's grandmother Anna Rosenberg, reassuring him that his parents had gone off in courage and good faith and equipped with the skills to survive. Cards came back from Łodz for a time, the last one in May 1942.[76] Subsequent enquiries through the Red Cross proved fruitless.[77]

In Essen, having failed to deport Siegfried, the Gestapo turned its attention to Siegfried's brother, Alfred.[78] Alfred now had the same nerve-racking wait as Siegfried, but at least he had a measure of confidence that the protection would extend to him.[79] In the end, the outside pressure worked again and within a few weeks Alfred and Oe quit the Hufelandstrasse and joined Siegfried and his family in Ladenspelder-strasse 47. Oe's mother Else Dahl was also officially listed as living in the house, but in fact continued to live as a tenant elsewhere, at Brahmstrasse 10.

Permission to stay in the family home was an increasingly rare privilege for Essen Jews. The city authorities had been concentrating Jews in a few designated 'Jew-houses' since 1 May 1941. In April 1942, many were forced to move to Holbeckshof, a barracks complex in the eastern suburb of Essen-Steele, favoured because it was next to the railway line. Even those not sent to the barracks were crowded into ever more dismal apartments.[80] In June 1942, Leopold Sternberg wrote from Holbeckshof to his son Walter in Chile that Walter's former employers, Siegfried and Alfred Strauss, were 'almost the only ones who still lived in their own home'.[81] Small wonder that envious rumours grew in the dwindling community about what the Strauss brothers could have done to deserve such privilege.

## Cuba

For the Strausses, the priority was to get out of Germany. In mid-October, before they knew they were to be reprieved, Siegfried had contacted his US relatives again, this time to obtain a visa to Cuba. On 17 November 1941, Siegfried wrote to Fritz Stern:[82]

*Dear Fritz,*

*The upheavals of the last few weeks have left me no time to write the letter I have been wanting to send for some time. I want to thank you and the others involved for your help and the promptness with which you acted. As you indicated in your cable of the 24th of the last month, on 14 November we received a cable from Hugo telling us that notification of our visas awaits us in the Cuban legation in Berlin. In the meantime the transfer has been partially made. The rest follows. We expect the visa's arrival any day now and hope to begin our journey as soon as possible. Alfred and Lore have their visas for Cuba and are waiting for the next opportunity to travel. My brother-in-law, Adolf Rosenberg, will have received our letters in the meantime and will know that we and our mother, who will travel with us, are well. Sadly, since the end of October we have heard very little from my brother and sister-in-law, Ernst and Hannah Weinberg. They are in the same situation as our sister Bertel. We hope very much to see you and all our relatives soon.*

*With thanks again for all your efforts and many greetings for you, dear Fritz and your family, I remain your cousin* Siegfried

*Dear Fritz, Accept my heartfelt thanks too for your help and family-mindedness and best wishes to you and yours from your cousin* Ine.

In relation to their earlier efforts to leave the country, the Strausses now faced two even more formidable obstacles. Above all, Nazi Jewish policy had now officially changed from emigration to murder. Up to 1939 or so, Nazi policy had been primarily to force Jews to leave the country. Over the next two and a half years, Nazi leaders experimented with various forms of territorial concentration of Jews. The last versions of this territorial solution were still being discussed in spring and summer 1941, when it looked as if the SS leadership was considering creating a kind of reservation on Russian soil. By then many Jews had been killed in Poland, but not yet as part of a systematic policy of extermination. During the Russian campaign from June 1941, however, the sporadically murderous operations against indigenous elites, partisans and Jews which had already characterized the occupation of Poland metamorphosed into systematic killing. A variety of SD, army, police and other units liquidated local Jewish populations with unimaginable brutality and thoroughness, wiping out half a million Russian Jews in a relatively short period (and many more over the longer term). By the end of 1941 the murder of all European Jews was firmly established as the principal goal of Nazi Jewish policy.[83]

A second hurdle which the family had to surmount was that, even assuming that with the Abwehr's help they could successfully leave the country, the Japanese attack on Pearl Harbor and Hitler's declaration of war against the USA on 11 December ended any possibility of going straight to North America. It also vastly reduced the scope for help from relatives in the States, since direct communication was now prohibited. The letter to Fritz Stern of November 1941 is, as far as we know, the last between the Strausses and their transatlantic cousins.

The only improvement in the brothers' situation was that, through the Abwehr's intervention, they regained partial control of their bank accounts. Without access to those accounts, they would never be able to find the resources necessary to obtain visas, travel documents, and foreign currency. Now, at last, in a manner not possible since October 1938, they could make their assets work for them. In 1940, the Essen tax office had put Siegfried's assets at:[84]

| | |
|---|---|
| ½ property Essen Mackensenstr. 69 | RM12,550 |
| Hufelandstr. 25 | RM82,900 |
| Ladenspelderstr. 47 | RM15,800 |
| Claim on estate of Leopold Strauss | RM5,500 |
| Current account Deutsche Bank | RM768 |
| Securities held by Deutsche Bank | RM74,742 |
| Life assurance Gerlingcompany | RM10,374 |
| | RM202,634 |
| after liabilities | RM201,501 |

Alfred, for his part, was worth some RM274,000, including RM173,000 in securities and similar.[85]

From having largely lain dormant over the past few years, Siegfried's bank account suddenly registered a series of huge transactions in November 1941, with something like RM150,000 flowing into the account and around RM100,000 flowing out again.[86] On 8 November, for example, the brothers sold Mackensenstrasse 69 to a Josef Vertschewall for RM26,000 (if the 1940 valuation is anything to go by, this seems to have been a fair price).[87]

The records of these transactions show not simply how busy the brothers were, but also how the Reich engaged in legal robbery at every turn. On 13 October, just before Siegfried's aborted deportation, Alfred had made a huge transfer of RM150,337.50 to Cuba.[88] But since foreign currency was offered at only 4 per cent of the original value, the transfer generated only 2,000 to 4,000 dollars.[89] And the punitive exchange rate was not the only problem. There were also other special taxes, levies to pay for the Jewish community's welfare bill, and so on. Alfred finally received the purchase price for Hufelandstrasse 23 in December, but out of the RM115,000 agreed, almost RM20,000 was immediately confiscated by the Reich.[90] Of the remainder, RM68,624 was placed in a blocked account for future payment of Reich Flight Tax, RM17,454.30 earmarked for the Jewish Community in Essen and RM2,000 for sundry other payments. Only RM9,544.52 was actually transferred to Alfred's account – to which, in any case, he had only partial right of access.[91] In other words, when all the deductions are made, it is clear that the Strauss brothers were able to transfer abroad only a tiny proportion of their wealth, certainly well under 1 per cent.

Still, they had no choice but to go on liquidating their assets.[92] By the beginning of 1942 virtually all the properties were gone, and the brothers' assets were largely held in the form of securities and shares in the blocked accounts.[93] Finally, in March 1942 – and only then – did the brothers accede to the official removal of their grain business from the business register.[94]

The Gestapo hovered between reluctant authorization and doing what it could to frustrate the process of emigration. On 20 November, Essen Gestapo officials informed their superiors in Düsseldorf that the Deutsche Bank had been commissioned to transfer RM4,000 to Cuba for the Strauss family and that permission had been granted by the Currency Office in Düsseldorf. All seemed in order, but the official, Horn, could not refrain from adding that, 'should the Strausses in fact *not* be permitted to leave the country, please let me know if they can now be evacuated'.[95] On the 24th, the Essen Gestapo wrote to the head of the Essen police saying that, as an exception and in the interests of the Reich, Siegfried and Regina Strauss could be issued with passports. However, a supplementary memo noted that there was as yet no passport authorization for Regina's mother. Whether it was this that prevented their departure to Cuba we do not know.[96]

Meanwhile, the Düsseldorf officials sought to establish with Berlin whether the Abwehr really intended to use the Strauss family once they were abroad. 'Berlin' in this case meant the section within Division IV (Gestapo) of the RSHA under Adolf Eichmann responsible for Jewish emigration and deportation. Pending clarification from Berlin, the Düsseldorf office provisionally assigned the Strauss brothers to a transport to Riga scheduled for 11 December.[97] The Strauss file now contains something remarkable, a direct intervention from Adolf Eichmann showing that the RSHA intended to use the family as a test case to challenge the Abwehr. In a telegram dated 2 December and addressed to the head of the Düsseldorf Gestapo, SS Obersturmbannführer Oberregierungsrat Dr Albath, Eichmann outlined the fundamental issues involved:[98]

*In response to your message of 20.11.1941, this is to inform you that the recent evacuation transports have been accompanied by a noticeable number of interventions on behalf of Jews from individual Wehrmacht offices or officers.*

*Recently, accompanied by the most diverse types of explanation, applications have been made for Jews' exemption from evacuations and for the issuance of emigration permits on the grounds that the Jews are ostensibly to be used for Abwehr purposes after their emigration.*

*In the light of experience the suspicion cannot be dismissed that, in the majority of such cases, personal interests lie behind the applications.*

*Exemption of the Jews in question from the evacuation and the issuance of an emigration permit cannot be approved prior to receipt of a letter from the OKW, specifically confirming the use of these Jews for Abwehr purposes.*

*The Abwehrstelle in Bremen should be informed that an appropriate letter from the OKW must be sent to the RSHA.*

In other words, the RSHA, which was suspicious of the whole enterprise, wanted the Abwehr to compromise itself by formally declaring its support for Jews. On 6 December, the Düsseldorf SS duly told their colleagues in Bremen that the Wehrmacht should make a formal request in relation to the Strauss brothers. In the absence of such a request, the brothers would remain on the list for a future transport. Since no formal request was received over the ensuing weeks, it would seem that telephone communication, or simply a sense that there were important institutions involved, stopped the Gestapo from pursuing its threatened course of action.[99]

Once again, then, an agonizing waiting game was underway. At every stage, the authorities took an unconscionably long time to issue the necessary permits. It was not until the end of March 1942, more than five months after the Abwehr had first offered protection, that Gestapo approval from the top in Berlin was granted (probably by now including Anna Rosenberg and Else Dahl as well).[100] Now it was the tax authorities' turn to procrastinate. On 11 May 1942, Siegfried Strauss obtained their stamp of approval allowing him to emigrate to Cuba. He sought permission from the Currency Office (ODD) in Düsseldorf to transfer funds to Cuba and to take his luggage, packed with linen, clothing and items for individual use, out of the country. The ODD did not give permission there and then and on 2 June turned to the Gestapo in Düsseldorf for confirmation.[101] Almost another three weeks passed before the Düsseldorf officials conveyed that there were no grounds for refusal.[102] That was 19 June. When Anna Rosenberg applied to Düsseldorf for permission to transfer funds to pay for *her* ticket, the ODD *again* felt obliged to seek permission from the Düsseldorf Gestapo. By the time the Gestapo gave its approval it was 8 August.[103]

In response to a request for a progress report on the case, Kriminalrat Nohles of the Essen Gestapo informed his superiors that all that was required now was the transit visas from the countries through which the Strauss family would have to pass.[104] Whether this was one hurdle too many, or there was some other complication, we do not know, but by mid-August the Strauss family knew they were not going to succeed in emigrating to Cuba.[105] Probably the formalities within Germany had taken so long that the Cuba visa had lapsed. From correspondence after the war between Marianne and one Marcus Cohn, a Basel-based lawyer who did some work for the family, we know that the family also tried to obtain exit visas to Mexico.[106] This too came to nothing.

The Gestapo's attitude began to harden, partly because of a bureaucratic mistake. On 2 July 1942, Aunt Oe's mother, Else Dahl, sought written confirmation from the police president in Essen that she was excluded from deportations. She had been told she needed such a document in order to obtain from the RV in Berlin a further document authorizing her continued presence.[107] After the usual consultation with the Gestapo the confirmation was duly given and, in September 1942, Else Dahl presented a copy to the RV. This fetched up with a different sub-section of the RSHA which had, or claimed to have, no knowledge of the approval granted the Strauss family the previous March. As a result, in October 1942 a letter arrived in Düsseldorf from this particular RSHA sub-section, asking the regional Gestapo chiefs what was going on.[108] The officials in Düsseldorf realized immediately that Berlin had got its wires crossed but sensed an opportunity once again to question the whole exemption procedure. They telegraphed Essen asking why the police president had provided Else Dahl with written confirmation, suggesting that it endangered the secrecy essential to any Abwehr operation.[109] This in turn was grist to the mill of the Essen officials, unhappy at repeatedly having to exempt the Strauss family. Essen cabled back with the background details and heartily endorsed Düsseldorf's criticisms. Indeed, they went further:[110]

*Your view that the issuance of such certificates undermines the secrecy of the grounds for emigration is most strongly to be endorsed. Moreover, the fact that the evacuation of the Jew Strauss and his family to the East has been repeatedly deferred must also have undermined the secrecy.*

So, back went a letter from Düsseldorf to the RSHA, wondering whether, in light of these facts and the changed political and military situation, the Strauss family emigration was still seen as appropriate.[111] This galvanized Adolf Eichmann's office into a new attempt on the Abwehr on 14 December 1942:[112]

*The application for exceptional approval of the emigration of the above-named Jews to the USA was passed on 23.12.1941[113] in the interests of the Reich's counter-intelligence. The emigration has not yet taken place. In view of the lengthy interval, I assume that the case is no longer of any interest. In this context, it should also be noted that as a result of the efforts of the Jews Strauss to achieve their own and their families' emigration at all cost, significant groups, particularly Jewish organizations, have learned about the exceptional treatment, so that in our view the procedure is no longer secret. Communication of your views on the matter is requested.*

Despite the provocative new tone with which Eichmann 'assumed' that there was no further need for the Strauss family, he still asked the Düsseldorf HQ to await further instructions. Over the next few months, it seems, the Abwehr bought time for the Strauss family by simply not replying.[114]

The sad fact was that at the end of 1942, four *years* after their first attempts to leave the country, the Strauss family were back to where they had started. The only sense in which they had achieved anything at all was that they had avoided the fate of their fellow Jews in Essen.

# 6

# Love Letters in the
# Holocaust

In October 1941, Marianne found herself back in Essen, away from her friends and studies in Berlin. There was the near-deportation, the reprieve, and suddenly Marianne found herself with nothing to do. And just as suddenly, she found living at home unbearable. Although she had done and experienced so much in Berlin, her parents still expected her to be the dutiful daughter.[1] She found very little to appeal to her in the Essen Jewish community. There was no cultural life any more. The waves of deportations were causing everyone to panic. And there were so few young people left. It was against this background that Marianne fell in love with Ernst.

Marianne and Ernst Krombach had had some contact in Jewish youth groups during the 1930s. A friend of Marianne's, Ute Unger, had met Ernst in Berlin in 1937 or so, while he was studying at a technical college. In 1939, long after Ernst had left Berlin, Ute became close to Marianne and informed her that Ernst 'would be perfect for her'. By May 1940 the Krombachs had moved into Hufelandstrasse, becoming tenants and neighbours of the Strausses,[2] and Marianne's aunt Oe worked alongside Ernst, organizing activities for the Jewish children still in Essen. Oe too thought Ernst and Marianne would get on well. Matchmaking friends and relatives do not always get it right, but in this case they did.[3]

Marianne did not tell me a great deal about Ernst, though she made no bones about his having been the first great love of her life. She said

*Ernst Krombach*

he was very handsome and the photos tell a similar story. The two shared a love of children. Ernst wanted to be a paediatrician and Marianne told me he would have made a very good one.[4] In Marianne's 1942 diary I later found fantasies about how she would work to support Ernst in their future life together so that he could recover the medical training denied him under the Nazis.[5] To me, she recalled his touching care for her when she had to see a doctor because of a badly swollen toe. In the summer of 1941 she had gone boating (illegally) on a Berlin lake and had afterwards dropped the boat on her toe, causing such pain that she 'nearly died'. On more than one occasion back in Essen, Josef Löwenstein, one of the remaining Jewish doctors, had to remove the nail under local anaesthetic and Ernst went with her each time and 'held my hand'.[6] Later, in one of Ernst's little notes, dated 30 March 1942, I found a tender admonishment to Marianne: 'Don't overdo it with your foot!'[7] Marianne said to me, 'I could never imagine Basil [her later husband] going with me.' But she said it laughingly, and I never had the feeling she was saying that Ernst had been *the* love of her life (though I do think it was easier for her to talk about him after Basil's death).

## The view from Buenos Aires

Marianne did not need to speak at length about Ernst, because she gave me so much to read. Letters from Ernst, copies of letters to Ernst, Marianne's diary from the time spent with Ernst – these were the only documents I had from the very beginning, all handed over at our first and second meetings. In addition, Marianne gave me letters she received at the end of the 1980s from Ernst's brother Heinz (now Enrique) Krombach from Argentina. Though he wrote several times, she could never bring herself to reply.

I wrote to Enrique, and established a warm rapport by fax and letter. His first letter, from 31 December 1996, in reply to mine of November, was in reality partly addressed to Marianne:[8]

*Thank you for your letter of 18 November. Memories are usually tied up with pain, but I have come to the conclusion that we who*

*were able to survive the terror years of the 1930s have a historical
duty to report on the events. Thus we are connected, since you as
historian have made research into the past your life's work.*

*Yes, you are of course right that Marianne's relationship with
my brother Ernst will have been the most painful episode in her
life and I tried several times to make contact. I would be very
grateful if you would tell Marianne about our correspondence
because she should and must know that she does not carry those
years alone and that our loved ones live on as long as we remember
them.*

*Your work in particular should help us preserve the memory of
our lost ones and show that the sacrifices were not in vain. One
should forgive but not forget.*

*[ . . . ]*

I could not pass this message on to Marianne. Unbeknown to Enrique,
she had died a week before he put pen to paper.

Over the following months, it became clear that memories of the
family were so painful for Enrique that he found it almost as difficult as
Marianne did to write about the past. It is true too that he did not
have much time. Although in his mid-seventies, he was still very active
professionally. In fact, I came to feel that his friendliness and generosity
towards me, though undoubtedly sincere, were almost defensive –
designed to guard himself against the pain my researches might bring.
More than six months went by before he sent me a still not very detailed
description of his brother. Enrique travelled to Germany regularly for
business reasons and I hoped to meet him there; as it turned out we only
met in June 1998, when I visited him in Buenos Aires.[9] We had arranged
that Enrique would pick me up at my hotel and I waited downstairs in
the lobby, looking through the window at the people passing by to see
if I could spot him. It seemed impossible that the man who approached
me was Enrique – the haircut and moustache made him look so Spanish.
But then I recognized the sensitive heavy-lidded eyes I had seen in a
photo of his mother. We embraced. At seventy-eight, Enrique was still
vigorous and active, though he grew increasingly melancholy as the day
went on. He propelled his new silver Escort confidently round the broad

streets of Buenos Aires, straddling lanes as is de rigueur in Argentina, and giving me an interesting condensed tour: the old synagogue, the law courts, the government quarter. Enrique conveyed the sense of someone fully at home in his adopted country.

We were now out of Buenos Aires and driving alongside a tributary of the river Plate to the town of Tigre. There were rowing clubs along the river, little cafés and pleasant bungalows. The warm weather (despite its being mid-winter in June) gave the scene a real holiday feel. We sat down at a café filled with families and groups of youngsters enjoying Saturday out. I asked Enrique if he would like to see the photos I had brought. He stiffened. 'Are there some of Ernst?' Yes. It turned out he had none. The handsome, clear-eyed boy slipped out of my wallet and tears came to Enrique's eyes. I let him keep the photos to copy them. So the tone had been set: I was there with explosive material and he was there to be hurt. I realized that, with the exception of Vivian, of all my interviewees Enrique was the most vulnerable. He was the one most likely to experience pain at the things I had to ask and the things that I could tell. Drying his eyes, Enrique plunged into the past.

Ernst's background had been strikingly similar to Marianne's. Like Marianne's parents, the Krombachs had distinguished forebears. Ernst's father, David, could trace his German ancestry back to the eighteenth century and his mother, Minna, née van der Walde, came from a wealthy, well-connected Hamburg family. Like the Strauss brothers, Krombach had volunteered at the outbreak of the First World War, and like them he had reached the rank of non-commissioned officer and earned the Iron Cross Second Class. David Krombach had come to Essen just after the war as they had, but, having a university career behind him, he followed a different career path and Abel, Herzfeld and Krombach became one of the region's better known legal practices. The Krombachs belonged to the same assimilated, patriotic wing of the Essen Jewish community as the Strausses. Unusually, even among the more acculturated Jews, David Krombach was an enthusiastic rider and was regularly to be seen exercising one of the horses belonging to an Essen-based riding club. The boys Heinz and Ernst were born in 1920 and 1921 respectively, and, like Marianne and Richard, were sent to the Jewish Volksschule. Though as with Siegfried and Ine, David and Minna pre-

*Enrique (Heinz) Krombach*

ferred a secular humanistic education at the secondary level and so sent the boys to the Goethe Gymnasium.

In Enrique's recollection, the family 'felt themselves to be completely German but lived as conscious Jews'. David Krombach was extremely active in the Jewish community, a leading member of the local and regional associations of the principal group for representing Jewish interests before 1933, the Central Association of German Citizens of the Jewish Persuasion (Central-Verein deutscher Staatsbürger jüdischen Glaubens, CV), as well as part of its national committee. He was also active in the Jewish youth associations. In 1933, he worked with his law partner and friend Ernst Herzfeld in an important Essen initiative that led to the creation of the Reich Association of German Jews (Reichsvertretung der Deutschen Juden, RV).[10]

In 1933, the Krombachs, like the Strausses, thought that the law-loving German people would surely not tolerate Nazism for long; they were certain their own credentials as citizens could not be called into question. David and Minna did not think of emigrating, though Enrique told me that as a result of some frightening and degrading incidents he himself decided as early as 1933, at the age of thirteen, that he wanted to leave. As a former front-line soldier, David Krombach was allowed to continue practising law for much of the 1930s. During this period, he became even more important in local Jewish life than before, Chairman of the Essen and Rhineland-Westphalian regional branches of the CV and, with Ernst Herzfeld, in charge of a legal-financial advice centre for the Jewish community.[11] For the Krombachs, as for the Strausses, Kristallnacht was the turning point in their attitude to emigration. Heinz left for Argentina in early 1939, but Ernst wanted to stay on with his parents until they all had US visas. In another grim parallel to the Strausses' experience, the visas never materialized.

Enrique had a great deal to tell me about his father – information augmented by a number of published tributes.[12] There was David Krombach's courage, visiting a client in an Essen jail on the day after Kristallnacht.[13] And there was David Krombach's insistence on doing everything by the book, which prevented him from reacting quickly enough to take advantage of some Chilean visas Heinz procured in Paris on the way to Argentina.[14] But as with Marianne's recollections of Richard, Enrique's memories of the younger sibling were far more patchy. In the late 1920s and early 1930s, he was the more outgoing of the two boys and spent much time outside the family in the non-Zionist Jewish Youth movement, the CV Youth.[15] Ernst was also involved, but he was far more home-based. Denied the right to take the Abitur exam, Heinz left the Goethe school before his younger brother did and, since sons of active combatants were still allowed to attend technical schools, studied away from home in a technical college in Mettweiler. Soon after Kristallnacht, he left with a youth group seeking to create a kibbutz-like community in South America.[16] So Enrique could not tell me much beyond a brief résumé of Ernst's education. In 1936 or 1937, Ernst too had been forced to leave the Goethe school before taking the Abitur and began studying as a chemist in Berlin. Kristallnacht ended his studies as well. After returning to Essen for a while, Ernst enrolled in a horticulture course at the Israelite Agricultural School in Ahlem, one of the educational institutions for Jews allowed to continue until 1942.[17] In 1941 or so Ernst returned to Essen and was drafted into forced labour in nearby Velbert.

Like Marianne, Enrique thus bore the pain of being an older sibling who had never known his younger brother properly. He felt guilt: if the brothers had been closer, Ernst might have decided to go with him to Argentina. For Enrique, the pain had become acute recently, because in accordance with Marianne's wishes and at his own request, I had forwarded to him copies of the letters Ernst had sent Marianne in 1942. Enrique was deeply impressed by the young man who emerged from the letters – this was a far more mature brother than he had known. Enrique told me how much he now missed having a brother and how well he thought they would get on. He was moved and impressed too by the degree to which Ernst had devoted himself to their parents.

The last letters Enrique received from Ernst were sent in 1941. His voice hoarse and emotional, Enrique told me that Ernst had written 'that I didn't understand him. And when I look back today I can understand why he wrote that. *Evidamente*, we had no idea what life was like for the people who could not get out.'

I asked him if still had those letters. 'Not all of them but I have one or two letters, also my father's last letter before he was transported in April 1942. He wrote, "a new task stands before us". Even as he was about to be deported, looking after others – which in the end cost my father his life – was of such significance for him that he saw a new task in it.'

Enrique went back to Germany for the first time in 1984. From then on, however, he'd returned regularly, above all to Düsseldorf, promoting co-operation between the regional governments of Buenos Aires Province and North-Rhine Westphalia (NRW). He had got on well with the then SPD parliamentary leader, Mathesen, who had been deeply moved by Enrique's life story. Enrique was even asked to inaugurate a new beer – the Krombacher Pils. These meetings were clearly extremely important to him, as was the relationship which developed with an Essen lawyer, Bernd Schmalhausen, who had devoted himself to ensuring that Essen's Jewish lawyers be properly remembered.[18]

I asked Enrique how he had found life in Argentina since the war. It would have been different in Germany, he said, much easier. Unconsciously echoing his father's sentiments, he went on that it had been an advantage not having things so easy, because it is the challenges we face that help us develop. Looking back now, he could feel content. The recognition he had received showed him that he had played his part. What recognition? Well, said Enrique, the German embassy in Buenos Aires had said that the relationship between Buenos Aires and North-Rhine Westphalia would not function smoothly without Herr Krombach. We were driving back into town in the Saturday evening twilight. I looked out of the window at the pleasant suburbs in an area once the preserve of the wealthy in Buenos Aires, touched by the irony that even now German approbation was Enrique's yardstick of success.

## The Krombachs seen from Birmingham

Even before meeting Enrique, I had heard another account of the Krombachs' family life. Through Essen's Alte Synagoge I had asked for information about the family, and the search threw up, among other things, a letter of 1945 from a lady in Birmingham to a former CV colleague, seeking information about David and Minna Krombach and the children.[19] I discovered that the author of the letter, Liesel Sternberg, was, in 1997, still in friendly contact with a member of the Alte Synagoge and, above all, that she still lived in Birmingham, within three miles of my own home. Miss Sternberg was very small and a little unsteady on her feet following two recent accidents, but she was in spirit unbowed, an alert and lively ninety-one-year-old with the strong deep voice of a singer. She had an almost comic German accent despite, as she laughingly acknowledged, almost sixty years in Britain. Born in 1905, she had grown up in Essen, attending the Luisenschule a generation before Marianne.[20] Walter, her brother, had worked for Siegfried and Alfred in the 1920s, and had then put the experience in import–export to good use in Chile, becoming director of a very substantial cork factory there. So the Strauss brothers figured in Liesel Sternberg's memory as the people who had equipped her brother for success.

Liesel had been active in the non-Zionist youth movement, which was how she had come to know David Krombach. She went to work for Krombach's partner, Herzfeld, in the late 1920s and managed Krombach's front office in the 1930s. When asked about the family her reply was full of energy and enthusiasm. David Krombach she both liked and admired exceedingly. Minna was a delightful and cultured person. Among other things, Minna and Liesel had shared a love of music. Liesel had trained as a singer and Minna was a delightful soprano:

'I liked them both very, very much. She was charming, and the house had a lovely atmosphere. It was a very affectionate household. I remember the boys when they were very small. And of course David was very eminent in Jewish life in Essen . . . the house was full of books, full of music.'

Liesel Sternberg remembered the brothers as normal, lively boys, though very different from each other. Heinz, the elder, was much more down to earth and practical; Ernst, the younger, was the more intellectual. Liesel Sternberg recalled her last encounter with the family: at a Chanukah party in the Krombachs' in December 1938. She had little sense of what the two boys were up to on that occasion, preoccupied as she was by a number of the guests, including her brother Walter, who had returned shaven-headed from Dachau just a few days before. Soon after that, she herself was in Britain, working as a maid for a family in Birmingham. She never saw the Krombachs again.[21]

## Letters between Essen and Berlin

Marianne and Ernst had so much in common by way of background, shared interests, good looks and isolation in an otherwise ageing community, that it is hardly surprising they were drawn to each other. Within two months of meeting, the two were already deeply in love. From the vantage point of 1 January 1943, after a devastating year, Marianne looked back to 'our New Year's walk last year and the church with the organ that was privy to our countless wishes. My love! I can't comprehend the awful thing that has happened!'[22]

In February 1942, Marianne's final exam at the Kindergartenseminar meant leaving behind her beloved and returning to Berlin. The correspondence between Ernst and his 'Jeanne' gives vivid insights into the nature of their burgeoning relationship. They were clearly in love. On the back of the scrap of paper carrying Marianne's exam timetable, she wrote out some lines from M. Hausmann:[23]

For each other
*You are for me and I am for you selected*
*As word for word in writing down a verse*
*Each is nothing when to the other unconnected*

Their attitudes and values had much in common. Like many influenced by the German youth movement, both Ernst and Marianne were extremely critical of conventional marriage. Their criticism did not concern the joys of free sex – indeed, the letters are chaste and never go beyond offering 'a thousand kisses' or allusions to the pleasures of the other's physical proximity.[24] Instead, they were scornful of the hypocrisy and show of the bourgeois marriage and the stereotypical roles it enforced. Ernst, for example, reported on a wedding he had recently attended in Essen:[25]

> *Incidentally, the ceremony was grotesquely typical. Quite apart from [the officiant's] stumbling reading, the inappropriateness of his clichés and phrases stood out clearer than ever. 'Remember that after the first torrent of young love . . .'(six years engaged) or: 'You, my dear groom, have taken on the duty of leading your bride carefully and surely through life . . .'(You know who wears the trousers?) Can you imagine my ironic smile? I found it terribly difficult to keep a straight face.*[26]

Marianne's attitude to marriage was if anything even more critical. Her friend Marianne Levy had 'strapped the yoke of marriage to her fragile frame'.[27] With Freudian consistency, Marianne failed to remember the married names of her formerly single friends.[28]

Both were critical of their parents. But Ernst was happy to acknowledge his parents' touching and unoppressive interest in his new love affair and to keep them informed; Marianne, by contrast, starved Siegfried and Regina of news from Berlin. Ernst, who was making the fairly typical discovery that the terrible oppressors described by his beloved were, at least in their interaction with him, 'very friendly and nice',[29] dropped in on the Strausses on Sunday 15 February:[30]

> *to congratulate your dear parents on the successes to date of their daughter, young Miss Strauss. You almost got into hot water*

*because I suddenly realized that your parents had not the faintest idea what I was talking about and had not heard from you since Tuesday!... Incidentally, their reception of me was very nice and kind (particularly worthy of note).*

In normal circumstances, their different relationships with their parents would have been of little import. But part of what burdened Marianne throughout her life was the feeling that she and Ernst had suffered different fates because he had loved his parents more than she had loved hers.

The correspondence did not always run smoothly. Not for the last time, the couple had to learn to cope with the vagaries of the mail. Marianne left for Berlin on Thursday 5 February. By the Sunday, after *three whole days*, Ernst had not received a letter:[31]

*Yesterday I was cross with you. Today too I had good reason. I have still had absolutely no mail from you! Terrible. The days seems like weeks. Actually, I didn't want to write to you today. I'm already half undressed and ready for bed. But I can't help writing. Probably the post's to blame.*

His waiting finally ended the next day. Two letters at once! To enhance Ernst's pleasure, his parents held back the second letter and gave it to him five minutes after he had read the first.[32]

In the second week, however, Ernst's principal problem was coping with Marianne's descriptions of one stimulating experience after another, many of them involving interesting men. More than once Ernst abandoned a paragraph he was writing, too churned up to continue. One young man in particular provoked his anxiety. Alfred Selbiger, with whom Marianne had had a 'fantastic conversation' about the youth movement, was someone whom Ernst himself had met and had initially been very drawn to, indeed who had provided him with something of a role model:[33]

*On the surface he makes a fantastic impression and everyone must find him sympathetic. But sadly he knows this all too well and has to struggle not to abuse those attached to him. Räqui's mother, incidentally, was also one of his 'girlfriends'...*

*Now, Jeanny, I'm counting on you! You will find the right path!*

The following day, when Marianne contrasted the lack of stimulus in Essen with all that Berlin had to offer, Ernst gave way to anxiety again. Recognizing, indeed having predicted, how different Berlin would be for her from Essen, he sought to reassure himself under cover of reassuring her:[34]

*What a difference there is between living in the backwoods with limited people and a limited horizon and living in a world where there are still real people, real experiences and real stimulus![ . . .]It is only natural that you should feel you are leading a fuller life there.[ . . .]So I will share your pleasure in your stay, but, just one thing: in all this enjoyment, don't lose your healthy common sense! (See my letter of yesterday).*

Marianne received the first of these two letters on Wednesday, and she had to take a bath to recover from the letter's contents. She resolved to send Ernst a photo of herself straight away:[35]

*This picture is proof that I think of you all the time. Doesn't that tell you everything? Doesn't it show in everything I write? But we can discuss the problem when we are together again (which thank God is very soon).*

She continued, alternating rather amusingly between contrition and irritation:[36]

*I wish I could be with you to remove all your worries. Actually, it's sad you have so little trust in me. But the fault is no doubt mine – 'seek the faults of your children in yourself' (Salzmann). Everything I've done to wrong you, my love, I'll make good.*

*Actually, a bit of jealousy never did any harm. But this seems to be too much for you. Don't worry.*

*Think of me as much as I think of you.*

On Thursday, the second of Ernst's anxious letters arrived and Marianne responded with more reassurance:[37]

*Although tomorrow threatens to be the most horrible day since ancient times, I want to write to you this evening. Today was*

*awful. My marks in Hebrew: 5! And in Jewish knowledge 4! Not
exactly uplifting! I'm quaking about the results.*

*Now to you! Another letter like yesterday's. The only good thing
is that we'll be together again soon. I'm looking forward to it so
much. It's the shining light that keeps me going. These last few
days I've realized how much we belong together. Everyone I've
met or who has impressed me or whom I've enthused about pales
into insignificance when I think of you. I'm so happy to feel this
way, my love. Because that is the only real proof of the strength of
one's feelings and ties to another person.*

*If I were with you, I could tell you everything that I want to say.
I am so fond of you.*

*Your J*

That is the last of Marianne's letters from Berlin. Ernst wrote one on
the Wednesday, noticeably more cheerful, and particularly pleased at
Marianne's response to his rather depressed musings of the weekend.
Marianne sent her telegram announcing she had passed. A card in Ernst's
handwriting, dated Monday 23 February 1942 and delivered by hand,
bears the text 'After successfully surmounting all challenges, welcome
home!'

## A secret engagement

When Marianne returned to Essen, she found the Jewish community
waiting for the next disaster and her family hoping to leave for Cuba.
The nervous, restless atmosphere at home was intolerable. So Marianne
did what came naturally – flung herself day and night into service for
the community. Inspired by her training, she set out to organize a
kindergarten for the children in the city; her first step was to buy the
equipment. In conversation with me she looked back wryly at her
enthusiasm. 'I remember going and really doing this in the very classical
manner as I had been taught.'[38] The kindergarten was established on
Hindenburgstrasse in what was then the community centre, an old
ramshackle house with one large room which might once have been a

shop. Downstairs in the basement were smaller rooms, and these Marianne converted into the kindergarten.

She had her work and she had her relationship with Ernst. First love at eighteen is often all-consuming; to be in love at a time when one is trying to 'squeeze out every last drop of experience' is something different again. The sense that theirs was a relationship for life developed fast, even though Ernst's work and Marianne's responsibilities meant that the couple could only spend the day together on Sundays. The stresses of separation in Berlin were soon forgotten; indeed, wrote Marianne in her diary, 'the separation showed us for the first time how much we belong to each other'.[39]

Marianne told me that at some point during the next six weeks they were secretly engaged. I wasn't sure how formal this understanding was, since Enrique had never heard of it. There is no explicit mention of it in the letters, but Ernst did later write of the rings they had exchanged, and in her conversations with me, Marianne certainly referred to Ernst as her former fiancé. There is a hint that they had become engaged before 26 March, since a note from Ernst hints at some secret 'theatre' in which they were both involved.[40]

A few days later, in another note, written just before going to bed after a long Sunday spent together, Ernst sighed:[41]

*Jeanne, how lovely it would be if you could be with me now or I with you! I can hardly imagine what it will be like when this is possible every day! We cannot avoid yearning for such a time – it's the logical conclusion to all our plans and feelings. But until then, we must set ourselves more modest goals. That's the only way we can get through this period until we can live just for each other.*

*10 o'clock, Jeanne. I'm quickly getting my bed ready, organizing my stuff for tomorrow, and then I'm all yours again!*

This note and others like it suggested that the relationship had not been consummated. Towards the end of 1942, Marianne confided to her diary: 'We should have spared ourselves all the barriers and all our bourgeois decency. But who could have predicted all that!'[42] However, before I came across that entry, I had already asked Marianne the delicate question. Had they . . . ? 'Alas, alas.' Marianne 'would have liked to', but Ernst was 'too much a gentleman'.[43]

The major bombing raids on Essen began on 10 March 1942.[44] The Strausses' house was not affected but the Krombachs were less lucky. We know a little about their experience because of the diary of Artur Jacobs, a non-Jew, who with his (Jewish) wife and a group of politically minded friends was making it his business to maintain links with the Jewish community and provide help where possible.[45] In spring 1942, Artur Jacobs had regular contact with the Krombachs ('Dr K'). On 13 March, Artur wrote:[46]

*At Dr K's, the house devastated – roof gone, ceilings down, windows blown in, doors torn off their hinges. 'We are experiencing Polish conditions in advance,' he said, 'One gets used to them.' No water, no heating, dirt and rubble. The last pieces of furniture also destroyed. But when one has no expectations, such disasters don't hit so hard.*

*On the morning of the disaster, they rescued the woman next door who had been trapped.*

*Their reward came quickly the following day.*

*A policeman with an officer: 'You have to quit the apartment and make room for Aryan citizens who have lost their homes.'*

*Having to move out of demolished rooms is not so bad. But that this should be their thanks, that makes one bitter.*

This was the Krombachs' relationship to their fatherland in a nutshell. David Krombach with his generous sense of duty and responsibility; the regime with its determination to drive them out.

It is striking that neither the later letters, nor Marianne's reminiscences, contain any reference to the destruction of the Krombachs' house. For ordinary non-Jewish residents, the experience of bombing raids, particularly the destruction of their homes, was the major, unforgettable experience of war. The date that one's home was hit was one of those key fixed points around which all narrative revolved. How striking an illustration of the threat facing Essen's Jews, then, that the destruction should not figure in their communications or their memories! The Krombachs and the widower Austerlitz moved from their comfortable home on Semperstrasse to cramped quarters at Lindenallee 61, joining a number of Jewish families already there.[47]

David Krombach's comment to Artur Jacobs about experiencing

'Polish conditions' in advance strongly indicates that by mid-March he was expecting to be deported. With his RV connections he will have known that the 1941 expulsions were not the end of the matter.

## Preparing for deportation

In fact, unbeknown to Marianne and Ernst, an administrative process had started which would soon tear them apart. Even as Marianne was making her way from Essen to Berlin in February 1942, a letter was travelling from Berlin to Düsseldorf demanding up-to-date statistics on the Jews in the district and the total number that could be deported. On 6 February the regional Gestapo headquarters in Düsseldorf passed the letter on to the local police and Gestapo officials, demanding an answer within twenty-four hours. On 7 February, the Essen Gestapo cabled back that 455 Jews fell into the relevant categories.[48]

A note from Ernst to Marianne dated 26 March refers for the first time to the threat of deportation, though Ernst was at pains to reassure Marianne that the danger – 'on this occasion' – seemed to have passed. Ernst and Marianne were probably unaware of the grotesque bureaucratic infighting in the background. The labour exchange, seeking to retain its conscript workers, wanted to restrict the number of deportees to 100 – a figure which would certainly have removed Ernst from the transport. But eventually the Gestapo and labour exchange compromised on 353. By 8 April at the latest, Ernst knew that he and his family, along with several hundred other Essen Jews, had been assigned to a transport due to leave for the East on 22 April.[49] All but a few of Marianne's kindergarten children were also on the list. The letter informing the victims did not, of course, tell them where they were going.

The Krombachs now had to facilitate the expropriation of their own property. A prepared form had to be filled in with details of everything they owned, including clothing, valuables and all other assets. 'No allowances would be made' if they failed to fill the forms in correctly. In addition, they had to provide RM 50 per person for conversion to zloty.[50] Many of the deportees, including the Krombachs' friend Austerlitz, had to move to the Holbeckshof barracks a few days before deportation, leaving virtually all their possessions behind them.[51]

Unseen by the human 'cargo', another set of decisions was taking place in the background. The first major wave of deportations from the Reich in October 1941 had been to Łodz, the second in November to Minsk and Riga. After the Wannsee conference, early in March 1942 Eichmann's office ordered that the bulk of deportation from the Third Reich be re-routed to ghettoes and camps in the Lublin district within the General Government, the rump area of Poland originally designated as a dumping ground for 'non-Aryan' Poles and Jews (as opposed to those areas like the Warthegau, claimed for 'Aryan' resettlement).[52] By 1942, the General Government's function for Jews had changed into an extermination centre, and the onset of transports to the region coincided with the opening of the death camp at Belzec in mid-March and the building of Sobibor and Treblinka. A series of locations – Trawniki, Piaski, Izbica Lubielska among them – were designated as temporary holding bays.[53] Initially, the Krombachs' transport was supposed to go to Trawniki, but technical difficulties meant that Ernst's destination was to be Izbica Lubielska in the Lublin administrative district.[54]

Although it became a transit point for many German, Austrian and Czech Jews in 1942, Izbica's role in the Holocaust remains almost unknown, and there is no entry for it in most Jewish encyclopedias or encyclopedias of the Holocaust. In Martin Gilbert's *Atlas of the Holocaust*, one of the few references to Izbica Lubielska appears in the context of the initial deportations to Belzec, 17 March 1942. The map shows that Izbica was roughly equidistant between Lublin and Belzec, some forty miles from the death camp.[55] As well as having drawn little attention from historians, there are very few contemporary documents about Izbica in 1942–3. According to the voluminous memorial volume for the Jewish victims of persecution (*Gedenkbuch Opfer der Verfolgung der Juden*), produced by the Federal Archive in Koblenz:[56] 'No records survive providing information about the methods adopted in the camp, about the arrivals and departures or about the fate of the prisoners who passed through.'

As we shall see, the designation 'camp' is somewhat inappropriate. And as we shall also see, some records *do* survive.

## An honourable departure

During the Krombachs' last fortnight in Essen, Ernst was freed from labour. Only now were he and Marianne able to spend almost every waking hour together. They would go for long walks through the Essen forest above Lake Baldeney. Meanwhile, Ernst's parents prepared themselves for departure. Artur Jacobs, who had long concluded that the Nazis could not be tackled by lawful means, recorded his despair at Frau Krombach's desire to stick to the rules. It would seem that Jacobs had suggested making some extralegal provision for protecting family property:

15 April
*Frau K wants to travel with 'her conscience clean' and therefore not do anything which is 'forbidden'! Should one curse, should one laugh?*

*How much immorality resides in such 'morality'! How much bourgeois pseudo-morality! Worn-out, old legalistic thinking, how weak!*

Perhaps Artur Jacobs did not understand the psychological boon to the deportee of knowing that at least one was in the clear, had done no wrong. But it is hard not to agree with Jacobs when we recall that the family failed to leave the country because of David Krombach's insistence on doing everything by the book. In an immoral society, the time for law abiding had passed.

Nevertheless, there is no disguising Jacobs' admiration for David Krombach's final words, spoken the night before the deportation:

20 April
*A final word from Dr Krombach (as, drained and overtired, he bade me farewell. Tomorrow they start on their journey[57]):*
*'We have had to shoulder many burdens. Often we thought we would go under. But we have also experienced much that gave us hope. Selfish feelings fade away – one is ashamed of them. We pull together and learn something of the power of the whole.*
*'It may be,' he added after a pause, 'that later, when we've got through this, we'll look back on this as the most important time of our lives and won't regret having gone through it, brutal as it was.'*

There are strong echoes here of David Krombach's last words to Enrique – 'A new task awaits us'.[58]

## Borrowed memory

On the night before Ernst's departure, Marianne remembered meeting Artur Jacobs in the Krombachs' apartment – a fateful encounter, as later events were to prove. At this stage, however, they did not know each other very well. Artur and David Krombach withdrew into the back room for private discussion – it may have been then that David Krombach uttered the noble sentiments noted above. Marianne helped the family to pack.

Marianne told me that she accompanied the family to the barracks in Holbeckshof and spent the night pleading with Ernst to make a run for it.[59] It seemed an astonishing act of courage to accompany them since she would have run the considerable risk of being deported too. It also crossed my mind, afterwards, to wonder what kind of escape she had in mind. She had only just met Artur Jacobs and could not yet know the possibilities he represented. But when I asked her, Marianne told me she had heard that he had offered help to the family.[60]

Among the letters from Ernst that Marianne gave me I found the following:

*20/21 April*

*Jeanne!*

*The last night in the apartment and therefore a moment of 'peace'. Ours is an unusually hard fate to shoulder, there is no doubt about that. It will certainly be hard for us, faced with all these other challenges, suddenly to find ourselves without each other – especially since we've been together every day recently, living almost like a married couple. How could we be satisfied with anything less? How rich and good it was to be together at a time of the most appalling conditions, and how great it will be when we can live together as free human beings! There are no words for the happiness that comes from our being together, a togetherness that is not bound to time or place or anything . . .*

*My dear 'love', you must know and feel that I will always be*
*with you.[. . . ]I hope that you will be able to leave Germany as*
*soon as possible. That would be a source of great comfort for me,*
*even if we are geographically further apart. We will find each other*
*again, we must. A hard test has been put before us, but in the end*
*a happy golden time awaits us! Let's look to work and people to*
*occupy and divert us, always with an eye to gathering valuable*
*experience for our future life together.*
*Jeanne, good luck! You live always and eternally in*
*Your Ernest*

I was so moved by Ernst's sentiments that it was only after Marianne's
death that I recognized a problem raised by the letter. It is clear from
the split date (20/21 April) that it was written across midnight, into the
small hours. We know that the Krombach's transport left on the 21st.[61]
The letter makes it clear that Ernst was writing in the Krombachs'
apartment and that he was alone. In other words, on the last night
before deportation, Ernst was not in the barracks and he was not with
Marianne. Jacob's entry of the 20th, incidentally, also indicates that the
Krombachs were in their apartment. Marianne's memory of accompanying the family to the barracks cannot be accurate.

Sometime after Marianne's death I was in Essen, reading a collection
of essays about Essen's Jewish life put together under the auspices of the
Alte Synagoge. In it, Hanna Aron wrote that her boyfriend was sent to
Holbeckshof with his mother. He was included on the second deportation list to Izbica on 15 June 1942. Aron wrote that the night before
deportation she went to Holbeckshof and spent the night with her friend,
pleading with him not to go. But he would not abandon his mother.[62]
This seemed strikingly close to Marianne's account. I made a point of
going through Marianne's book collection; she did not own the book in
which the account appeared. I then learned that Hanna Aron and
Marianne had known each other well at one stage, and in 1998 I visited
Hanna Aron in Connecticut. She told me that in March 1943 she, her
mother and brother had moved in with the Strausses. Not only that, but
it transpired that Hanna's friend had been Richard Fuchs, a former tutor
to Marianne's brother and someone well known to the Strauss family.

So it came to seem highly credible that Hanna had told Marianne about her last night in the barracks while living with the Strausses and that Marianne later came to believe the story was her own.[63] Marianne was very probably with Ernst earlier on the eve of his deportation, but then went home. There is a hint in letters written a few weeks later that Marianne had contemplated accompanying Ernst to Izbica and blamed her parents for preventing her from doing so. Whatever her deliberations, the trip to Holbeckshof never happened.[64]

When Vivian read my conjectures here, he was angry with me. I was challenging one of the few things which his mother had told him, and on more than one occasion. It seemed unfair to his mother when she could not answer back. And why should she invent things? This was something she remembered so vividly. It was one of the great traumatic departures in a life which had had more than its fair share. I could understand his unease and felt not entirely happy about it myself. It *was* one of those moments that Marianne had talked about as if it were yesterday. And yet, the evidence was overwhelming that she had appropriated a story that was not her own. It was only when I encountered other discrepancies in Marianne's memory that I began to discern a pattern to the changes she wrought upon the past.

## The Krombachs' journey to Izbica

On the morning of 21 April 1942 the Krombachs were deported from Essen. Marianne was waiting at the main station to give Ernst a last wave, but evidently he did not realize she was there and by the time he went to the window the train was almost out of the station. After the train had left, Marianne went back to the Krombachs' apartment with the family's loyal former housekeeper, Änne. Here she collapsed in despair.[65] She was in such a state, she said, that the alarmed housekeeper contacted her parents. In the 1980s, Enrique wrote to Marianne that Änne still remembered 'What a pretty girl you were, how much you felt for Ernst and how often you placed yourself in danger in order to do something for them.'[66]

For Marianne, the memory was of the deepest despair she had ever felt. 'That was the last time in my life,' she told me, 'that I really cried.'[67]

Our natural assumption is that the moment of separation was the last time the two lovers heard from each other. We think of deportees as cut off from the rest of the world. Possibly we *want* to think of them like this, so that we do not have to stay with the thinking, feeling, suffering participants to the end.

One of the first things Marianne gave me, however, was a padded envelope, on the front and back of which she had written 'Marianne – not to open! 29.VII.46'. The inscription suggests that while Marianne was still in Germany in 1946, she sent the envelope on ahead to Britain (possibly with other personal effects) and wanted to make sure that no one looked at the contents. Had they done so, they would have found some twenty-odd communications from Ernst dating from April to August 1942 and some lengthy, typed half-diary entries, half-letters from Marianne to him. Other Essen deportees had managed to mail an initial card from Izbica,[68] but there is no other known example of such a sustained correspondence having been preserved.

Marianne's fifty-nine single-spaced, typed A4 pages begin with an entry for 22 April 1942, the day after the Krombachs left Essen. She did not have a great deal of spare time to write. With the deportation of most of the children to Izbica, the kindergarten was closed and the community rooms were now an old-age home. The very elderly had been largely excluded from the Izbica transport, and thus found themselves left behind in Essen without family support or carers. So they were installed in the community rooms on Hindenburgstrasse, each bringing a bed, a wardrobe and a cupboard into the makeshift home. The Jewish community still had a number of nurses and Marianne joined them, initially as an unpaid auxiliary.

In her entry for 22 April 1942, Marianne wrote:

*My love, I wonder how you slept. I spent last night in your mother's bed. Änne and I had so much to do. So I had another night in your presence and that was good. I will find much to do and I am happy about that. Everyone is very kind to me and, knowing how you would be, I shall be kind to them. Oh, that I didn't manage to see you again yesterday! We three waited for the train. When you came to the window,*

-1-

den 22.4.42.

Lieber,wie Du wohl geschlafen hast?Ich habe heute nacht im Bett Deiner Mutter geschlafen.Anne und ich hatten noch so viel zu tun.So war ich noch einen Nacht in Deiner Atmosphäre und das war gut.Ich werde viel zu tun finden und darüber bin ich froh.Die Menschen sind liebevoll mit mir und ich will ihnen ein Gleiches tun im Gedanken an Dic

Dass ich Dich gestern nicht noch mal gesehen habe!wir 3 haben noch den Zug erwartet.Als Du ans Fenster kamst,war der Zug schon in weiter Ferne.Es war vielleicht besser so.Im Büro gab Herta mir Deinen Brief.Dank Dir,Lieber.Wir beide,Du und ich,wir wollen danach leben; egal,was kommen mag.Ich habe den Eindruck,dass die Sache,die geplant ist,wirklich ernst wird.Nicht zu meiner Freude.Aber es ist ha alles Schicksal und wir müssen sehen,für uns beide das beste daraus zu machen.E i n m a l     w e r d e n     w i r     w i e d e r     z u s a m m e
s e i n.

Ich werde Dir über jeden Tag einen Bericht geben.Wie ein Tagebuch. Diese Blätter werde ich dann nach einer bestimmten Zeit gesammelt schicken.So weisst Du,was hier vorgeht.Sobald ich Deine Adresse habe,bekommst Du die ersten Blätter.

Um eins mein Lieber,kann ich Dich nicht oft genug bitten: s i e h
u n d   s o r g e, d a s s   D u   g e s u n d   b l e i b s t.

23.4.42.

Mein Lieber,inzwischen sind Deine ersten beiden Nachrichten von Duisburg und Düsseldorf angekommen.Bärchen,und ich sind so glücklich mit der Post,die wir beide bekommen.Wir sind gute Freunde,und werden immer bessere werden.Über Deine zweite Karte war ich etwas beruhigter,nachdem ich nämlich vorher nur Gegenteiliges gehört hatte.Die Hauptsache ist,Lieber,dass man selbst versucht,alles leichter anzusehen und mit allem sich abzufinden und fertig zu werden.Dazu müssen wir uns erziehen,wollen wir selbst uns nicht verrückt machen. Ausserdem ist Arbeit das beste Mittel.Heute hatte ich meinen ersten Dienst-Tag im Betsaal.Jetzt kommt mir viel mehr das Unerfreuliche dort zum Bewusstsein.Aber man wird sich daran gewöhnen.Ausserdem tröste ich mich in dem Gedanken,dass jeder Tag,den man hinter sich bringt,uns beide näher zusammen führt.

Was soll ich Dir sonst schreiben?Du weisst ja alles,denn jeder Gedanke gehört Dir.

Gestern kam ein Brief an Dich von Manfred K.an,den ich gleich beantwortete.An Theodor will ich auch baldmöglichst schreiben.Schreiben hilft mir sehr über das Denken hinweg.Es ist unbedingt die Beschäftigung,die am zwingendsten die Gedanken in andere Bahnen lenkt.

Manfred schreibt,dass er jetzt in der Friedhofsgärtnerei arbeitet. Die Arbeit macht ihm Freude;vor allem das Pflanzen.Nur kann er das leider nicht immer tun,denn es müssen sehr oft Gruften geschaufelt werden.Er klagt,dass er s o sehr allein ist und Post seine einzige Abwechslung bedeutet.Ein Grund mehr für mich,ihm gleich zu antworten.

*Page 1 of Marianne's letter-diary*

*the train was already in the far distance. It was probably better so. In the office, Herta gave me your letter. Thank you, my love. We must try and live up to its sentiments no matter what may come. I have the impression that the plans here are really serious.*[69] *Not to my satisfaction. But it is all fate and we must see how we can best turn things to our advantage. One day we will be together again.*

*I shall write a report for you every day. Like a diary. After a time I shall send the pages together. So you'll know what is happening here. As soon as I have your address, you'll get the first pages.*

*There's one thing, my love, which I can't ask you enough:* be sure to look after yourself.

For his part, Ernst wrote his first postcard as the train left Essen: the address given is 'just after Mülheim' – the next station on the line – and from the postmark we see it was mailed in Duisburg, the station after that. It is from this letter that we learn that Ernst had caught a last glimpse of Marianne at Essen station:[70]

*Another quick hello from me! At the last moment, I saw you on the platform as we travelled through. I was 'visiting' with Else Bär and the Löwensteins. In Mülheim, we were joined by loads of acquaintances. The next stop seems to be Duisburg, where I will post this card.*

*Best wishes to your parents, Oe and Kurt K. To a rapid reunion!*

*Your Ernst*

Ernst's next card was sent from Düsseldorf, where the Essen deportees were kept overnight. Only now was Ernst able to ascertain where the train was actually going, though still without absolute certainty.[71]

From the historian Michael Zimmermann we know that this first leg of the transport ended in Düsseldorf Derendorf, where Jews from various parts of the region and destined for Izbica were gathered. Derendorf is now a regular, though rather desolate, train stop, currently under renovation. Whenever I flew to Germany I would land at Düsseldorf airport and take the S-Bahn into town. The train passed through Derendorf, and when we pulled into the station I would recall that this was where Ernst's group had been deposited and marched over to the abattoir near by. The station had been used by the Gestapo because of its long platform. As my S-Bahn glided off, rolling past metre after metre of desolate platform under scaffolding, one had a faint frisson of the misery of families standing in line, over-burdened with luggage and anxiety.

Ernst's train arrived there around 14.30 and the group was led by policemen (one for every twenty deportees) into the large hall of the neighbouring municipal abattoir. Now began the sifting and confiscation of much of the luggage. At the same time, court officials handed out official papers confirming that, under the Reichsbürgergesetz (Reich citizenship law) of 25 November 1941, the property of Jews leaving the country was deemed automatically to accrue to the Reich.[72]

The deportees were now restricted to taking one suitcase or rucksack with essential items, including food for fourteen days (which was supposed to comprise largely bread, flour and nuts), a woollen blanket (in which the food for the first three days was to be wrapped) and a spoon and plate. Everything else was confiscated. The German Red Cross was the beneficiary. From the thank-you letter it sent to the Gestapo, we know that the spoils in Derendorf included bandages, medicines, candles, towels, torches, washing powder, soap, razor blades, shaving cream, shampoo, toilet water, matches, eau-de-Cologne, creams, shoe polish, sewing materials, tooth brushes, tobacco and chewing tobacco, cigarettes, cigars, tea, coffee, cocoa, sweets, sausages, oranges and lemons and other fruit.[73] That was just the bounty enjoyed by the Red Cross. Confiscated clothing, by contrast, went to the National Socialist Welfare Organization. We do not have a full list of the clothing, underwear, bed linen, table cloths, umbrellas, rucksacks and pillows that were their portion, but we know that the confiscated outer clothing alone comprised 192 coats, 82 jackets, 69 ladies' jackets, 345 dresses, 181 blouses, 5 swimsuits, 330 pairs of stockings, 21 pairs of slippers, 37 hats and caps, 93 scarves, 165 ties, 171 pairs of men's trousers, 19 dressing gowns, 485 woollen items, 133 pairs and 30 single shoes, 22 pairs of over-shoes, 145 pairs of gloves and 41 scarves.

The official documents convey the impression of nameless, passive victims, having no choice but to see their belongings extracted by the Gestapo. Enrique, too, felt the Jews left in Germany could do nothing but submit to what happened to them. Yet Ernst's correspondence does not portray such passive victimhood. Undoubtedly, his cards sought to protect Marianne from some of the worst. He was also mindful of censorship. But his letter from Düsseldorf on Wednesday 22 April suggests that he had not only managed to survive and evade the demoralizing business of the plundering remarkably well, but had even been able to provide strength and good cheer to those around him:[74]

*After a second sleepless night, thousands of loving greetings. Despite minor irritations I am content. Unfortunately, not everyone was so lucky, but it was a source of satisfaction to be able to help improve the situation of others. Including the luggage business!*

An uncensored letter in August added further details and revealed that it was Ernst's position as a Jewish orderly that had helped him circumvent the worst:[75]

*Up to Düsseldorf the trip was pleasant. Taken by gendarmes and Gestapo to the abattoir; the bundles and suitcases were then checked through and much depleted. Through special care and with my armband[76] I managed to get our bundles and ourselves through the control without loss.*

Early in the morning of that same day, the Essen deportees were herded out of the Derendorf abattoir on to train Da 52. The deportees were 'lucky' in that they were transported in normal passenger cars rather than in the goods and cattle cars usually deployed outside Germany. Having boarded the train, they sat and waited for hours. Finally, they left at 11.06, stopping at Erkrath, Hagen, Soest, Paderborn, Ottbergen, Northeim, Nordhausen, Wolferode, Halle, Falkenberg, Cottbus, Sagan and Glogau, reaching Izbica two days later.[77]

Ernst's next card and a letter were written on Thursday 23 April as the train was leaving the Reich proper for German-occupied Poland:[78]

*Dearest, We travel on. Time travels too and brings us closer to the point when we can meet again! That is our consolation, that every day brings us closer. This will probably be the last time I write from the transport. It is getting harder and harder to do so. However, I learned that we will be able to write from the camp. It will be in the Lublin area, not, however, in the two places mentioned but near by.[79] As soon as we find out, you will too, of course.*

*Our separation, Jeanne? Hard! Inescapable![. . . ]What's clear is that it's harder for you than for us. For you, our absence must make itself felt from the start. For us, the challenges we face provide a distraction. I'm being open about this so that you don't worry about us. My love, we can get through many difficulties. We'll probably have it harder once we're settled and have time to reflect again.*

*I feel myself strong enough now, even if I was sometimes a bit doubtful in Essen whether I was up to this. I would be happy if you could say and think the same for yourself. To a very small extent we can draw a parallel to our separation in Berlin. But the roles are now reversed. I'm always happy to be among people I can talk to about you. I was just talking for a while with Rudi.[80][ . . .]I am not getting on particularly well with my parents at the moment. The reason: my father is too self-centred when I want to take care of others. Well, thank God I don't need them. Now, dearest Jeanne, the page is full. I've written the whole afternoon, with interruptions. Some things may be a bit confused.*

*I take you in my arms and kiss you fervently! Your Ernst*

A card sent that same day, postmarked Ostrowo, was even more upbeat:[81]

*My dear Marianne!*
*Today you are fated to hear from me again. We are in good form but would be very happy to reach our destination soon. I'll write to you all the time, of course, as soon as it's possible. The landscape has been very interesting. We are now in the General Government. One can see from the cleanliness that this was once a German area. We brought so much food with us that we haven't even got through the sandwiches. One shopping bag is still full. So do not worry. In the meantime, the train has started moving again.[ . . .]*

Even more than Marianne's letters from Berlin, these sources present us – and presented Marianne – with a problem of interpretation. Do they convey in any way the reality of conditions on the train? Clearly, Ernst was trying to reassure Marianne and, in protecting her, probably giving himself courage too. And he will also have again been mindful of the censor. Later, in a letter that went by private channels, Ernst was able to provide different details of the train journey. For example, that they had travelled twelve to a compartment[82] (which presumably meant two people per seat, not to speak of all the luggage), and that in Lublin, the wagon taking the bags of those who couldn't carry their own luggage was uncoupled and left behind.

But assuming that Ernst's early letters withheld some details, there is much we can believe. There is the strange mixture of information and ignorance. The deportees are able to communicate with Essen, send cards from the train, yet their destination is shrouded in mystery. It is clear from the letters that rumours were flying back and forth in the train – where they were going, what conditions would be like. Someone evidently claimed to know that letters would be permitted, and Ernst has chosen to believe it, but in reality no one could be certain of such things. Clearly, the deportees have no knowledge of the larger context; that their first destination is merely a holding bay before they are murdered.

Ernst's courage and generosity of spirit are evident. Obviously his parents, seeking to conserve their strength and their resources, felt he was doing too much for others, perhaps taking too many risks on other people's behalf. And then there is Ernst's ineradicable Germanness. His pleasure at the cleanliness and signs of German roots could hardly have been greater were he a young 'Aryan' travelling out to the Warthegau area of Poland reserved for German settlement, rather than a Jew condemned to the General Government ghettoes.

While she waited for news, Marianne threw herself into her new work, caring for the elderly in the Jewish community. Her task was made much lighter by the speed with which Ernst's cards arrived. The two dispatches from Duisburg and Düsseldorf reached her on 23 April. Both their upbeat content and their speedy arrival were enormously reassuring. 'Mein Lieber' Marianne tapped out on the keys of her borrowed Jewish community typewriter:

*your first two messages from Duisburg and Düsseldorf have arrived. Bärchen and I are so happy with the post we have both received. We are good friends and are becoming ever better ones. I was somewhat reassured by your second card, because what I'd been hearing was rather the opposite.*[83] *The main thing, my love, is to try to see the brighter side, to come to terms with everything and to deal with it. We must school ourselves if we are to avoid going mad. Also, work is the best answer. Today I had my first working day in the prayer hall [where the elderly were being accommodated]. I'm much more conscious now of the many grim aspects to the work there. But I'll get used to it. And also I console myself with the thought that every day we manage to get through brings us closer together.*

*What else should I write? You know everything already because all my thoughts are with you.*

Bärchen ('little bear'), incidentally, was Herta Byttiner, née Behr, then thirty-three, who worked as a typist for the Jewish Community.[84]

On 24 April 1942, Ernst's train trundled into Izbica. For an agonizing week, Marianne had no news; a card on the 30th confirmed Ernst's arrival, but gave no address. By 3 May, however, she had received two more communications from Ernst, sent on 25 and 28 April, while Ernst was taking stock of the Krombachs' new home, Izbica Lubielska, Kreis Krasnystaw, in the Lublin administrative district of the General Government.[85]

## The first exchanges with Izbica

While Marianne waited for mail she wrote about her work, her problems with the family and, of course, how much she missed Ernst:[86]

*My love, I want to spend a while longer with you before I go to bed. How will you sleep?[. . . ]I am with you in every thought. If only I could be with you fully. Does God mean well with us? We must believe in him and hope that he will help us. Only in that thought can we find solace.*

*If I could only know that you are managing to overcome everything and deal with it, I would rest easy. You must try. I will too, my love.*

*I'm so pleased that there's so much here for me to do. Every minute is taken up. At night I drop, dead tired. It's good. (Don't worry, I've remembered my promise and won't overtax myself.) Life has become harder. Two weeks ago we were happier. It is unbelievable how quickly fate can turn and strike. The main thing is not to lose sight of the light – the light of hope. We must carry our light before us. Then others will see it and live accordingly. I think I mean a lot to the old people, they're happy when they see me and that makes me happy. The place is depressing, but one must have courage and ignore the bad things with a smile. It's often awfully difficult. But if we're given time and space and everything isn't torn down as soon as it is put up, then we'll certainly be able to make many improvements. Today we finished building a medicine cupboard and one for the instruments. If we carry on working as we are we'll surely achieve something. Willy H is much better and his mother too. He's my favourite patient – you know, my son. Now that I don't have any little sons any more, I have to replace them with big ones.*

*The one thing, my love, is to take care of yourself. I can do it only in my thoughts. More tomorrow. In my letters to you I am trying every typewriter in the Community: Hindenburgstrasse, Steele, home. At the moment I'm sitting at home. In front of me on the desk I've still got your picture from Lake Baldeney in the little frame I found at your house. There are always fresh twigs next to your picture because we both want to have something from spring!*

*[. . .]*

*Now, really, a very good night, Ernest.*

Though Marianne's workload grew steadily, she relished the challenge:[87]

*The number of patients is growing[ . . .]The ward is packed to the rafters, but still not full enough for the 'management'. From time to time his lordship rushes in and gives us the benefit of his opinion. It looks as if we might be moving. But that has its advantages: you don't get out of practice, and they say that change is as good as a rest.[. . .]I may earn some pocket money; then I can send my loved ones countless parcels.*

*I can't tell you any more today. It's late and I've got to clear the decks because I'm keeping Oe and Alfred awake. I'm typing up here because I can't stand it downstairs. I get on with my parents like you do with yours. Now my wish is that you sleep well and peacefully. Every night I pray for you and I pray that we will see each other soon and that nothing but death will ever part us again.*

One of Marianne's consolations in those early days was to visit friends still living in the Holbeckshof barracks in Steele:[88]

*This morning I spent a little while in Steele. It helped me bounce back a bit. The atmosphere there is excellent. I'm just sad I can't always be there with them. I feel cut off from everyone and everything. An awful feeling. They are planning communal evenings. Someone different is in charge of organizing the evening each time. It's marvellous how quickly people can fill the gaps in their ranks, even though they're always aware of them. Don't think that people here have forgotten you.*

It was symptomatic of the divide that had grown between Marianne and her parents that, while Siegfried and Ine wanted at all costs to avoid being transferred to Holbeckshof with its lack of amenities and communal living, Marianne felt so much freer there. She revelled in the barracks' enforced communality and group spirit, and welcomed the change from the heavy material objects of the family home. Her response was a further sign of the enormous generational differences in the reaction to Nazi measures. Young people in their teens or early twenties who had not yet established a fixed way of life and had not yet acquired social status and material goods were capable of adapting to conditions simply unacceptable for older people. Within a week of Marianne writing these thoughts, for example, Artur Jacobs noted in his diary:[89]

*In the barracks [ . . .]*
*How many challenges do they have to face! Overnight, 300 people from every class, every age group, every occupation are thrown together, in a mad rush, without even the most basic things. (They can bring with them only what they are later allowed to take to the East, in effect nothing, compared with a normal existence.) No furniture, no cupboard,*

*no table, no mattresses (instead, straw sacks, sometimes filled with paper), one big stove (on which almost 100 women are supposed to do their cooking!). Under such conditions – who could expect everything to go smoothly? Particularly among people who are not used to each other and who have to learn almost everything about living together. Who could be surprised that there's constant collision, friction, discontent, reasonable and unreasonable demands?*

*They have to fix up their living area (in order to live at all), but who has any desire to make everything nice and comfortable when tomorrow it could all be over?*

*A devastating scene – the old headmaster, who is supposed to look after the children (there are still some here), sits in despair among his piled-up books, unable to come to terms with his fate.*

*'We live like dead men,' he said, 'spiritually adrift, in dirt and misery. When I think how we used to live . . .'*

*Tears welled up in his eyes.*

*What consolation can one offer? Every false word of comfort only aggravates the injury.*

The difference between Marianne's perception and that of the weeping headmaster could hardly be more stark.

There was probably some measure of illusion in Marianne's perception. She had not been forced to go to the barracks or to abandon all her possessions. Those who had, like Imo Moszkowicz, were far less romantic in their description of the place. In retrospect, Moszkowicz felt that they were being drilled for life later in Auschwitz. Undoubtedly, part of Steele's appeal for Marianne was that it was Not Home. Every experience seemed defined by the growing antagonism between her and her parents, an antagonism that sometimes led her to take some uncharacteristic stances. For example, though a great lover of children, Marianne argued to a friend in the barracks that, confronted with the choice of abandoning her husband or her children, a woman should always go with her husband. 'Parents must be able to free themselves from their children.'[90]

Finally, on 3 May, almost two weeks after the Krombachs left Essen, a letter from Ernst arrived offering a first glimpse into conditions in Izbica:

*Dearest,*

*Sadly I have not yet had any post from you. So I am waiting for something nice. What shall I write about? In terms of food and cleanliness, the conditions here are more extreme than anything we imagined; it's simply impossible to put them into words. Words could never convey the reality of life here. The Wild West is nothing to this. The attitudes and approaches to life here are so incomprehensible. Anyone not firmly grounded will find himself spiritually derailed for ever. There is neither culture nor morality, two things we once thought we could manage without. Once you experience the extremity of this place, you're cured of that particular view. It is terrible not to be able to help people. One is simply powerless in the face of it all!*

*I'm trying to give you some insight into what it's really like here. But it's impossible. I could fill twenty pages and you still wouldn't know. I'll save it until I can tell you face to face. Don't worry about me. I'm strong enough, and as long as I don't have the misfortune to go the way of all flesh, we'll see each other again. I know what to do and the thought of you keeps me going, too. I'm writing all this so openly so that you on no account pursue the plan with Bärchen. I am really happy that you do not have to be here and I pray to God every day to carry you to safety! Jeanne, I know that this is doubly hard for you. But if you trust me, you must be strong. I know that what's asked of us is almost inhuman; but we always wanted to achieve great things; so here it is, our first and probably hardest test. The word MUST stands above us and reunion is the goal that keeps us going.*

*I don't work – working is not the custom here. Where possible, I try to help, but the problems are so great and so many and my resources so limited that I can offer little in relation to what is needed. Every day I meet nice young people my own age so that I have something for myself. My love, I keep realizing that, although comparisons are possible, there is no one who is right for me as you are. The difference is so great!*

*Postal transfers are not always accepted. But we are allowed to receive money via letters and letter-parcels do get here. It's prob-*

*ably better not to send proper parcels. It is possible to put old clothes in letter-parcels. It is possible to receive food.*

*You must be terribly curious about the appearance of this place. There are 7,000 Jews, ruled by a Council of Elders, and the Council is ruled by the Gestapo. That might sound fine, but the reality is different. You might be able to sketch a rough picture of the place, but I doubt it would bear much resemblance to the reality.*

*— Now the page is used up, Jeanne!*

*[ . . . ]*

Shocked, Marianne wrote:[91]

*Your letter from 28.4 arrived today, and all I can say is we cannot, we should not, we must not lose courage and hope. We have a goal to live for and it must give us the strength to cope with every challenge. The clock keeps ticking and every move of its hands brings us a step closer to the light. God puts only the good to the test. He is always with us — let us draw solace from that. Only if we are strong can we complete the task that we have set ourselves: to help others. We should be proud, my love, that things have not been made easy for us. I feel you completely as part of me: how could I live otherwise! Don't think that it's easy for me. But let's set ourselves tasks and work and then everything will be easier. For you there must be endless things to do. Don't try and achieve everything at once. Have patience, have patience. I believe in you, always, and know that you will manage. Are all your ideals in pieces? Don't give up, even so. Later, the two of us will pick up the fragments and piece them back together. Much will be destroyed, it's war, but out of the rubble new and better things will arise. We have strong hands.*

## Reason and feeling

These and subsequent letters show how far Marianne and Ernst had advanced since Marianne's stay in Berlin. Then, the emotional tone of their correspondence had been fairly conventional, with all the repetition of sentiment, uncertainty and occasionally jealousy that separation can bring. Now, they were living on a different plane. Often the strongest evidence of their love lay in what they chose *not* to say, in their restraint, their selflessness, the determinedly optimistic tone for each other's sake. 'What struck me,' commented Ernst, when the first of Marianne's diary-letters finally reached him, 'was that independently of each other we found the same words and sentences to express our feelings of separation.'[92] Above all, the two had concluded that the language of love and feelings could only burden the other, arouse desires that could not be fulfilled, and render separation unbearable. Later, Ernst articulated this thought explicitly:[93]

*Our relationship, I feel, is the same as it ever was; no, it has become far deeper. Our yearning for each other increases in direct proportion to the length of our separation. All the more wonderful our reunion and a future life that can build on such admirable foundations. I think it's natural that we can't always suppress our feelings and now and then ignore what's rational, even if sadly the rational must predominate. Or perhaps it's that the rational is really an expression of the emotional, because each of us feels that it's better for the other this way. Always the two key factors: reason – feelings!*

From some of the letters, it is clear that theirs was not the only correspondence passing between Essen and Izbica at the time. For example, 'Bärchen', Marianne's co-worker in the Essen Community office, was corresponding with her friend Rudi Löwenstein. But like most of the Jews still in Essen, Bärchen was deported to Theresienstadt in July. Probably, no correspondence like Marianne's survived not because none existed but because by the summer of 1942 the recipients had all been deported and their property destroyed.

More unusual than the fact of getting letters through was the scale of material assistance Marianne managed to provide. After a slow start, we know that by the end of May 1942 Ernst had received a number of parcels from her. A recurrent theme in the mail from Izbica was the sheer pleasure these parcels gave their recipients – by supplementing their diet, providing capital in an environment where everything could be had for barter or money, as a sign of love and sacrifice, as a link to the outside world – in short, as the source of everything vital for Ernst's and the family's continued existence. Or rather, Ernst's letters convey that the value of these parcels went beyond what could be expressed in words. An outsider simply could not imagine their significance.[94]

Much of the communication out of Izbica from May onwards was limited to postcards with officially prescribed text by which the deportees were allowed to acknowledge receipt of parcels: 'We are healthy. We are being treated well. Deepest thanks for your post.' Marianne's papers include cards of this type sent by Ernst on 28 June, 4, 10, 17, 24 and 31 July and 8 and 14 August, but even these responses do not give an indication of the sheer volume of parcels Marianne was managing to send. From late July until the autumn Marianne developed a veritable cottage industry, begging and bartering dry goods (or being given them by sympathetic friends, family members or a friendly pastor, W. Keinath, from Wuppertal) to send to deportees in general and the Krombachs in particular. Marianne lived, she wrote, for the help she could provide Ernst and his family:[95]

*You know my life has a deeper meaning: I exist for you and the awareness that this is so has allowed me to grow and keep on growing. My greatest worry is for you and the people we both hold dear. I want to help you, help you, help you as well and as much as I can. But you must overcome your inhibitions and tell me with absolute clarity what I can do. I beg you to do this with all my heart.*

A few days later, on 11 August, Ernst noted:[96]

*Last week you really spoiled me again. A large number of parcels arrived. 131, 135, 114, 115 – those were the numbers from last week. I think the numbers themselves speak volumes for your unceasing love.*

By mid-August, then, it seems that more than a hundred small parcels had reached their addressees. By now, Marianne was dispatching them at a rate of several a day. Again and again, Ernst struggled to explain their significance.[97]

*It is incredible what you have achieved with your daily packets of love. Not just the help you give us but also the signs that you're there make me so happy. There are no words of thanks for something like this . . . It's incredible. A thousand deepest thanks for all this proof of your love, and what love it is! It's as limitless as the love we feel too! Special wishes to your parents, Oe and Alfred, and other friends. Loving greetings and countless wishes! Your Ernst*

## The ragged thread

A dramatic and inspiring lifeline was thus sustained between Ladenspel-derstrasse 47, Essen and Block III/443c, Izbica. However, soon after I began to piece together which letter had arrived when, it became clear that the lifeline was a ragged thread. This was not a correspondence in the conventional sense. On the contrary, although most of Marianne's parcels managed to reach their destination (though not in order), the post was completely erratic, sometimes taking four days, sometimes four weeks. Some letters or packages arrived completely overtaken by events, others still so fresh from the pen that the two lovers felt that they had almost touched each other.[98] For long periods they were writing to one another without knowing whether the post was arriving and without getting anything in return.

Marianne did not at first understand what caused the long intervals between Ernst's letters.[99] It gradually became clear to her, however, that there were severe constraints on what could be said and how much could be written. 'If you hear little from us, don't worry. We will, of course, write when we can,' wrote Rudi Löwenstein in June.[100]

From early May to the beginning of June, Marianne had to suffer four weeks without word from Ernst.[101] Towards the end of May she became particularly anxious because of news filtering back from other deportees:[102]

*In the last few days, vague reports have reached us about conditions there. We hear that most people have gone. Where they have gone to, nobody knows: God alone knows where you and your family are. I*

*won't say what I think, but I don't need to. Teddy [Bärchen] and I have*
*continued to write letters to the old address and send them out as before.*
*Is there any point . . .*

*Today I wrote the Council of Elders and asked for information about*
*where you are. Is there any point . . . Love, love, I pray and believe and*
*hope. Our imagination cannot keep up with reality, try hard as it might.*

Marianne's fears were not ill-founded. It is impossible to say with
certainty who was deported when, but in his study of the extermination
camps, Yitzhak Arad notes a deportation of some 400 Jews from Izbica
to Sobibor death camp on 15 May, and from Ernst's letters we will see
that there were other deportations not listed by Arad.[103] Even so, it
seems that the majority of the Essen deportees were still in Izbica in
May.

Then, miraculously, a few days before Marianne's birthday on 7 June,
a birthday card arrived from Ernst, sent on 31 May. With a whoop of
relief and renewed confidence – 'you can hardly imagine my joy', she
wrote to a friend[104] – she rounded off the first section of diary entries
and put them into the post:[105]

*Today, love, love, after five weeks the first card from you arrived. I*
*probably don't need to say how happy this made me, Ernest. I am*
*endlessly happy that you received my parcels. Now I'm full of belief and*
*courage and without more ado I am going to put these diary pages into*
*the parcel. The daily reports continue.*

For Marianne, Ernst's card was a sign that God had not abandoned
them[106] though from then to the end of July she again received very little
mail. On 6 August, a detailed letter arrived, dated 5 July, conveying an
idea of what Ernst's work was like. Another letter soon followed but,
once again, the thread slipped and became caught up in the ineffable
machinery of German censorship and the postal system. Only later did
Marianne learn that sending letters from Izbica was officially punishable
by the death penalty.[107]

At Ernst's end, although Marianne was sending post on an almost
daily basis,[108] almost ten weeks went by with no letters from Essen,
broken only at the end of June by the arrival of the parcel containing

the first part of Marianne's journal: 'That was really a piece of you, how you live and love,' he responded.[109] By then, however, Ernst had realized that personal letters were often not getting through to Izbica at all, although Marianne could not yet know this. Money orders and parcels *were* being passed, and letters hidden in parcels, such as Marianne's letter-diaries, had a chance of reaching their destinee.[110]

The misery and anxiety generated by the inconsistent post can hardly be imagined, but when letters did get through, confirming that the writer was still alive and still thinking of the other, what joy they brought. In early August, after a lengthy wait, Marianne finally received a long letter from Ernst. She had to put pen to paper straightaway:[111]

*My love, this evening Oe came back from Melitta with the letter.[112] Each such message awakens so much within me. Above all, I am so infinitely grateful for such a tangible sign that you are alive. I reach into it to find you, as you are now and in my memories. [ . . .]*

*Again and again, I read your letters, late in the evening when it's quiet all around and we too are rendered quiet by the night. Then it's our inner voice that speaks – the voice that we listen to in our dreams as well, my love. And I had the same moment with the stars as you did. God makes them speak to me at the same time as to you and in the same language. We had the same feelings here, do you remember?*

*The letters have their biggest impact on me when I read them for the first time. Then they are at their most immediate. Then I am with you and everything around me ceases to exist.*

By then, Marianne had an inkling that their communication was about to take a dramatic new turn.

# 7

# Report from Izbica

Early in 1942, or possibly even late in 1941, certainly before Ernst was deported, the Strauss family had come to know a Christian Arras, the twenty-eight-year-old son, partner and heir of the owner of a truck dealership and repair garage in Essen. Marianne's recollection was that the garage was doing contract work for the SS and that Christian himself had joined that organization opportunistically in order to enjoy the business opportunities that its contacts offered. Marianne told me that she and Ernst had met Christian and his fiancée, Lilli, at Oe and Alfred's apartment:[1]

'So he knew him and me of course, and knew where Ernst had gone. I had told him, he knew the whole story. And one day he told me that he was going there, and if I wanted to take some stuff.'

Marianne's comment sounded so innocuous, I almost missed it. Then it hit me. Christian, doing business in the General Government, had offered to take anything Marianne liked to a Jewish deportee, Ernst. Marianne wondered if Christian was supplying vehicles to Izbica – if so, it was an incredible coincidence that this little town, a tiny part of the SS killing empire, should have been serviced by someone she knew in Essen. And then there was the equally extraordinary fact that Christian was willing to perform what might prove to be a dangerous mission.

On 2 August, Marianne packed a suitcase of things for Christian to take to her lover. At last, she had something real to live for.[2] Stowed in with the clothes, foodstuffs and other items was a letter:[3]

*Actually, I don't need to write much, Ernst. What do you think of this? I've lived this moment a hundred times in my thoughts and wished, wished that I myself could bring you my love and best wishes. But we must thank God and be grateful. It is another sign that He means well with us.*

Stapled to the back of the copy of this letter, I found a copy of a 'questionnaire' which Marianne had also sent:[4]

*Here is a questionnaire so that you can answer systematically the burning questions which so concern us and which you have not or not fully answered. Above all, I beg you to be completely honest and not to think that we will find the truth a burden. Only if I really know how things are for you all can I rest easy.*

*1) What do you do during the day; work; working hours?*

*2) How are you treated?*

*3) Income?*

*4) Do you get a ration or do you have to pay for food out of your own pocket?*

*5) Can you move about freely or only with permission, and who gives the permission?*

*6) Which organization has authority there and how do you interact with it?*

*7) Exact description of the living conditions and the hygiene.*

*8) Leisure activities (books, music), friendships, attitude of the comrades to moral and ethical questions.*

*9) Can you get the food you need? In particular, what is the situation as regards fats (butter etc.)?*

*10) Do you have to pay duty on parcels and letters and what determines the level of duty?*

*11) Can you really make use of our parcels and what is most useful?*

*12) What do you need particularly for your own use?*

*13) Do all the parcels sent you reach their destination and do you feel they arrive complete???*

*14) Do you think it would be a good idea to put a contents lists in each parcel?*

*15) Do you have any idea or definite reports of the whereabouts of people sent on from there?*

*16) How many have gone? Where are Arthur and Else? So far, no news from them.*

*17) Activities and food for the children.*

*18) As far as you can tell, will you stay there or be sent on further?*

Initially, there were problems with Christian's rendezvouz with Ernst. By 17 August, however, Marianne had certain knowledge that Christian would be in Izbica two days later, and she was confident he would be able to see Ernst:[5]

*. . . the day after tomorrow he will be there. Countless wishes and thoughts accompany him. Again and again I have lived through the meeting in my mind, just as though it were happening to me. For us it is a glimpse behind the door with seven seals – and that is an understatement.*

On 26 August, a telegram arrived in Essen and the following day a postcard, both indicating that Christian would soon be back and implying that he and Ernst had indeed managed to meet.[6]

Marianne's next diary entry is dated 3 September:[7]

*My only love, Christian has now been back for a whole week. Only now can I fully comprehend what's happened. So much post! The bell rang late Saturday evening and I knew immediately who it was. And on Sunday, after I had your letters, I went to our little hill from last April. There was no one to interrupt me and YOU were with me as you were then. Love, my love.*

On 'their hill' in the Stadtwald, Marianne sat and read for hours.

In a two-page covering note, Ernst listed everything he had sent:[8]

1 Letter to your parents
1 Letter to your parents, O. and you from my father, with notes from Katzenstein
1 Letter to you from Rudi
1 Letter to you, that was lying here, that I couldn't get out, partially out of date
1 Eighteen-page report for you

1 task list for you – four pages – with two letters from my father.

The letters to Marianne's parents have not survived, nor the letters from Ernst's father which accompanied the task list. The partly out-of-date letter to Marianne may well be one of the many letters from Izbica which she saved, but it is no longer possible to identify it with certainty. The other letters have all survived and are clearly identifiable.

Rudi wrote just to thank Marianne for the things she had sent and for the unbelievable moment of contact she had arranged. Rudi's wife Grete also took the opportunity to write: 'You can hardly imagine what this means to us and how happy we were to receive your wishes through Chr.'[9] Both used the brief opportunity to ask her to maintain links with those of their relatives who had eluded deportation.

One real difference between Ernst's task list[10] and all previous communication was that he could, at last, openly name relatives and friends to contact, to provide with news, to beg for help and to engage in support; he lists name after name in Germany, Portugal, Holland, Spain and South America. If the prospect of material help from such quarters seemed somewhat illusory, since the letter also revealed to Marianne that currently no parcels or letters at all were being delivered to Izbica, there was yet hope that the conditions might change in the future. Also, it seems that the Krombachs still had a good collection of fine porcelain and other belongings in store in Essen, which could be used to reward assistance rendered. Again, taking advantage of this moment of open communication, Ernst also proposed a way of encoding information in the official postcards he was allowed to send acknowledging receipt of parcels:[11]

> If the date is at the top left, you can't send anything. Top right: possibly (i.e., cautiously try to send something). Bottom left: you can write again. If the 'the' is abbreviated to 't.'[12] you can send only small packets with a value of less than 25 zloty duty. If it is written out in full then you can send larger parcels. If the month is written as a number, then be careful, because an evacuation is imminent. If I write 1942 everything is OK, if only '42', we will certainly be evacuated. Wait till news possibly gets through. This applies from now on. (Not to my card from 22.)

Of course, such code could be of use only if the normal post started up again. Only the existence of the alternative channel opened by Christian made the suspension of communication seem less serious than it was.

But the main item in Ernst's package was the eighteen-page account of conditions in Izbica written in pencil in regular, even lines in Ernst's neat handwriting. The letter, which Marianne had handed me in June 1996, was the starting point for this book; it is one of very few extant contemporary accounts of Izbica as the Final Solution was underway, perhaps even the only one.[13] There are some post-war survivor reports which I was able to consult in Yad Vashem. There are also the recently published reminiscences of a survivor, Thomas (Toivi) Blatt, who had grown up in Izbica.[14] By email and later in a personal interview, Mr Blatt gave me further information and photographs. But Ernst's lengthy, measured, detailed contemporary report with its mixture of facts and perceptions is extraordinarily rare, not simply for Izbica, but for the experience of all German Jews deported to Poland generally.

*22/VIII.42.*

*My love, my dearest!*

*You can imagine my feelings and my joy! Everything you sent us, which for a while has removed our worries about our daily bread! The conversations and encounters, everything all at once, raised our spirits and naturally filled me with excitement. It's all so extraordinary, thoughts come thick and fast. First of all, I can't stop thinking about what this means for us. Let me say something important about this right away. Like me, you're surely wondering how we can best use this bridge for us. How can we come together? Is it something we can take upon ourselves and how could we do it? But even if we assume that it would be possible for me to return: it would be very difficult and dangerous. There would be little chance of my staying there [in Essen], given all the checks and controls and the uncertainty of how long it would be for. The most important and impossible aspect, though, is that I would be exposing my parents to grave danger, indeed putting their lives at risk. So we must put the idea out of our heads.*

*Christian told me that your journey [out of the country] is no*

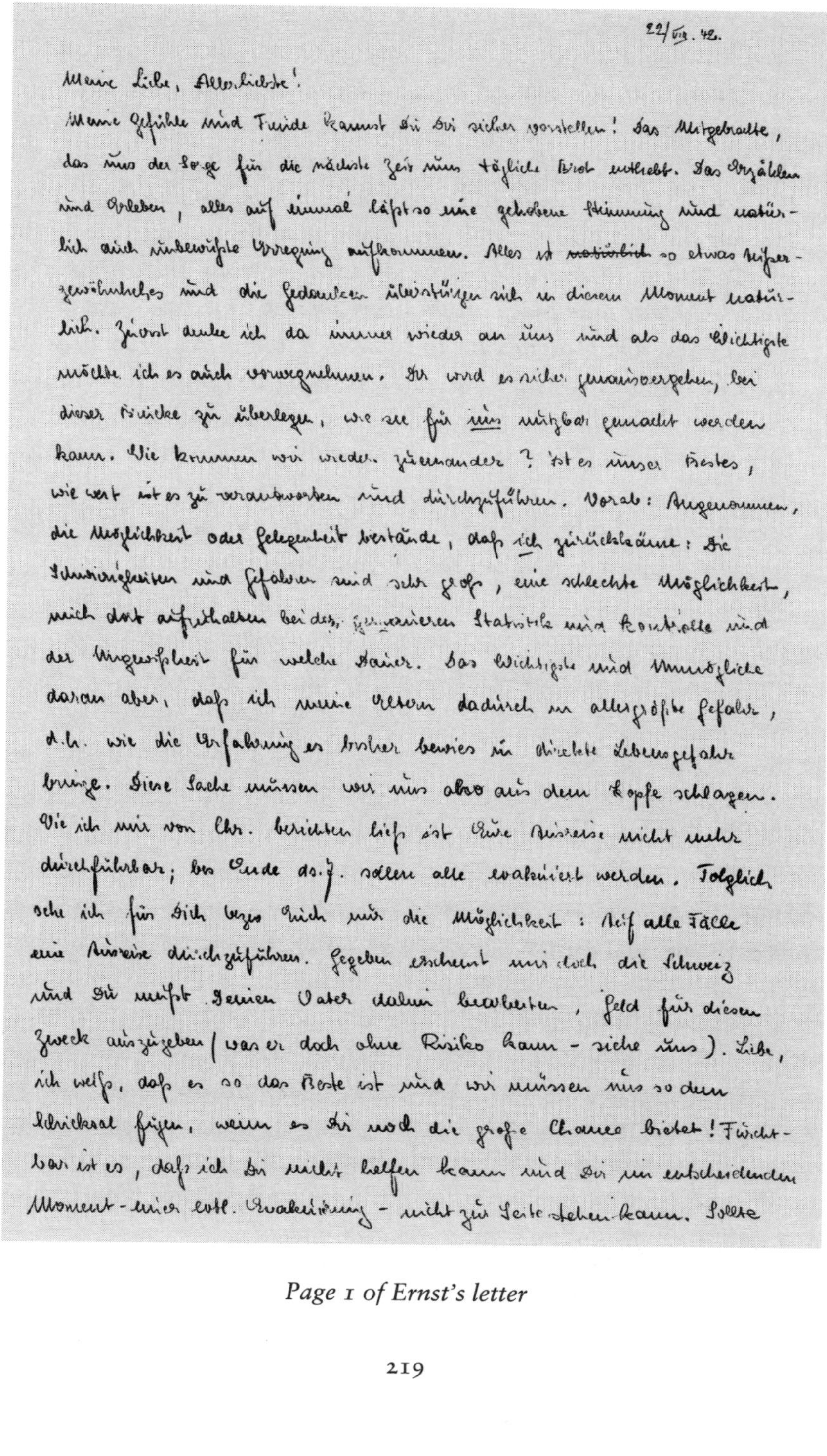

22/VII. 42.

Meine Liebe, Allerliebste!

*[Handwritten letter in German cursive]*

*Page 1 of Ernst's letter*

*longer possible and that by the end of the year everyone will have been evacuated [deported]. I see only one possibility for you and your family: at all costs get out. Switzerland seems a possibility and you must work on your father to spend money to this end (which he can do without risk, as we learned). My love, I know this is best. If fate should still offer you a chance, we must take it! It is terrible that I cannot help you and that at the crucial moment of a possible evacuation I cannot stand by your side. Should the evacuation take place around the time of Christian's second journey you will probably try to come with him.[15] As far as I can judge this seems to involve the least risk. But – as I said – from this end I can do nothing to help and I must advise you not to come here voluntarily. We must try and stay alive for each other's sake, and if you come here without being forced to do so any sensible person would think you mad. But why should I go on about it? I'll give you a report so you can see for yourself. I realize that I could just as easily write a whole novel about it – a factual novel. But I hope that I can capture the conditions on a couple of pages. It will definitely not be easy given the abnormality of life here, which lacks all formal or logical basis. Only someone who has experienced it can really understand it. Perhaps Christian will be able to make some of the incomprehensible things comprehensible. Perhaps I should begin at the beginning, directing my thoughts back four months.*

Here, Ernst gives the account of Derendorf and the crowded train compartment cited earlier and goes on:

*In the evening, we arrived in Izbica in the rain. We were received by the Jewish Police and SS and shoved into cave-like dwellings. An optimist might think of Carmen if the reality hadn't been so hard, particularly for the elderly.*

*Thus we arrived in Izbica and gradually we 'adjusted'. At this point I must describe the environment. Izbica is a village hidden in a valley. It used to be home to about 3,000 Polish Jews. Its geographical situation is superb. The 'houses' are mainly built of wood and clay and consist of one or two 'rooms'. Everything filthy and infested. A few of the houses have the luxury of beds, tables, chairs or cupboards. We ourselves live less comfortably than most but, on the other hand, we are closer to the outskirts. We look out on to greenery and freedom, in a peaceful, sunny and stink-free (no sewers) environment. 12 of us: 4 Rudis,*[16] *3 Katzensteins,*[17] *2 Meyers (relatives of Rudi's) and we 3 in a hole, 2×4 metres. At the front: 2 tables, 2 wooden benches we made ourselves, 4 chairs which we 'organized', 1 stove; at the back, on the luxury of a wooden floor (elsewhere clay) and sacks of straw the 'beds', side-by-side on the floor. As so often happens, the wives find it hard to co-operate – not least because of the limited space and the fact that three families have to share their cooking on one small wood-burning stove. This town of cave-like huts with its many hiding places would be absolute paradise for a scout group.*

*Now to the 'Jewish state'. Before the first transport arrived here, Izbica was cleansed of its Jewish residents.*[18] *I.e. the SS drove them out with weapons and clubs. The first transport arrived here in March from Czechoslovakia (from Theresienstadt where the people had been held for two months). The second transport also came from Czechoslovakia and thus the important positions were taken by the Czechs. After that the transports came thick and fast: Aachen, Nuremberg, Aachen-Düren, Breslau, Essen, Stuttgart, Frankfurt, two from Slovakia, two from Theresienstadt etc. So now there were three different categories [of Jews] here: Germans, Poles, Czechs. The German character you know: military discipline, reliable, hard-working. The Pole is the opposite: ill-disciplined, lazy, dirty, uncomradely, very good at business. One should not judge them too harshly. External conditions and pressures have made the Pole what he is. I was obliged to study the Polish character at length when I arrived. They are extremely intelligent, talented and quick on the uptake. An eight-year-old boy who has never had the opportunity to go to school writes his name with a speed and fluidity that are beyond some of our adults. Although he had certainly never seen a guitar before, he held mine correctly immediately. Even though he produced discords, he did so with rhythm. The Czechs, too, are hard to deal with. Why?*

*They see themselves solely as Czechs who were driven out of their country by the German invaders (understandably, since they were not affected until war started) and regard us as Germans. Unlike us, they had not been forced to regard themselves as Jews and led back to Judaism.*[19] *The slogan of this motley crew is: 'Sauve, qui peut' or ME, ME, and after me my relatives (nepotism without end), and forget about the rest.*

*The region contains several villages like Izbica, occupied by Polish and other evacuated Jews, Polish Aryans and a few ethnic Germans; there's no barbed wire (thank God). The district is ruled by two SS men and a sub-machine gun. The village itself is run, under SS supervision, by the so-called Judenrat, with responsibilities such as law and order, sanitation, disinfection, burial, supplies, firewood, housing, soup kitchen, etc., etc. The Judenrat is made up of leaders of the individual transports. But in the course of time so many arrived that the newcomers (the Germans, of course, including my father) were stuck in a Working Committee. The committee has no say in anything, and if anybody dares to open his mouth, he is rendered harmless by the simple expedient of being shoved on to one of the evacuation transports that leave here from time to time. The Judenrat thus consists of Czechs whose level of correctness and humanity is certainly open to criticism. Alongside it there is a Polish Judenrat, whose leader has managed to grab most of the power (i.e. over both councils). All in all, it's very difficult for us Germans who came with so many illusions about comradeship and co-operation.*

*The legal code is simple to describe: the death penalty. The hangman's assistants who haul out unfortunates and sometimes go looking for them are also Jews. Everything is forbidden; the penalty as above. Leaving the ordained district before 7 a.m. or after 7 p.m. Bartering, buying or selling or speaking to Polish Aryans. Baking bread. Buying rationed groceries such as butter, eggs, bread, potatoes, etc., etc.* Sending letters or other messages. *Leaving the city limits. Owning gold, German money or indeed any money, jewellery, silver, etc., etc. Unfortunately, such offences (if that is what they are) have cost many lives. On arrival, the last meagre possessions such as spare underclothes, suits, coats, shoes, leather goods, jewellery, wedding rings, etc. were confiscated. Some people were taken away and shot as a warning. This brings me to something that affects us both: the gold rings, our investment capital. An insufficient number was collected from our transport. So a few people were selected to collect rings. They were going to be shot.[20] The transport leader too looked as if he would lose his neck. A last attempt was made to buy up rings or slip in rolled gold. People went from house to house and took down names. At this point I sacrificed the most precious thing I have from you; our ring. You know what I am going to ask: send me another one, new! I feel the loss terribly. I miss it very much. My only consolation is the feeling that I helped and probably saved others. If it's no longer possible to send things, Christian can certainly bring it with him. If the post starts up again, put the ring in semolina (or similar), in blancmange powder (and reseal). I will always look carefully. For the moment, I hold on to your letter (which I carry around with me as a substitute) and your many larger and smaller presents (pendants,[21] pictures, etc.).*

*In the meantime, many transports have left here. Of the approximately 14,000 Jews who arrived only 2–3,000 are still here. They go off in cattle trucks, subject to the most brutal treatment, with even fewer possessions, i.e. only the clothes they are wearing. That is one rung further down the ladder. We have heard nothing more of these people (Austerlitz, Bärs, etc.) After the last transport, the men who were working outside the village returned to find neither wives, nor children, nor their possessions. (We've been somewhat lucky in any case because later transports have come in without any men. They'd already been taken out at Lublin.) If you know how, however, you can usually avoid such evacuations by going into hiding and simply reappearing after the transport has left. We learned this from the Poles ... As far as punishments or shootings are concerned the Poles are usually 'favoured' – poor consolation to us. A German is seen as more of a human being – not surprising given the ragged appearance of the Poles (who have more money than one realizes). Whenever I've had the opportunity to join the*

*police I've always refused. Mainly because of the unpleasant work:*
*Jews against Jews. But I was unable to avoid getting involved in*
*the evacuation of Polish Jews. You have to suppress every human*
*feeling and, under supervision of the SS, drive the people out with*
*a whip, just as they are – barefoot, with infants in their arms. There*
*are scenes which I cannot and will not describe but which will take*
*me long to forget. But that only as an aside, because I just thought*
*of it. Basically I have, thank God, a healthy constitution and retain*
*a balanced, clear view. I only think of these inhuman experiences*
*in my dreams.*

*Food is a principal concern for everyone here. Many go under*
*through malnutrition. There's no one here to care for them. There*
*is some 'welfare', which provides hardly any help (water soup).*
*With exemplary inhumanity, the Czechs in the Judenrat put poor*
*people on the next available transport. Various private individuals*
*give lunch to people. We and the Rudis look after needy people*
*from Essen. Those who have no money, no relatives, no acquaint-*
*ances in Germany to send them things and nothing left to sell must*
*either starve or steal. At the moment the vegetable harvest is good.*
*We three can be very content. (We're eating off your plates.)*
*Vegetable or barley soup, potatoes (pancakes or salad) sometimes*
*with meat, blancmange, cucumbers, vegetables, beans, peas. Nutri-*
*tious fare, which lacks only fats. Sometimes we buy or barter butter*
*or oil. Because we are short of fats we eat a huge amount. But*
*there's another reason too: fear of starvation and the drive for*
*self-preservation. It has become such a mania that 90 per cent of*
*conversations are about food. And when everyone talks about it*
*so much you naturally feel hungry even if you are not really in*
*need of food. For example, today I had two large slices of bread in*
*the morning with cucumber and tomato (also stolen apples and*
*carrots). For lunch, I had potatoes and cabbage. In the evening*
*potato salad, beetroot soup and semolina pudding (with milk and*
*eggs). Coffee with half a large slice of bread. It's like this every*
*day, sometimes a bit more, sometimes a bit less. I haven't wasted*
*away yet. So, a satisfactory, adequate diet.*

*That brings me to monetary values. A Reichsmark is normally*

2 zloty, on the black-market as much as 2.80. Otherwise the black-market prices are pure extortion.[ . . .]You can get everything here from whipped cream, ice-cream and chocolate to Schnapps etc. at horrendous prices but excellent quality.[ . . .]My love, I have written the whole afternoon. Tomorrow the report continues: work, hygiene etc. For today, good night! How well will I sleep?

    Yours!


                                              23/VIII.42

Dearest Jeanne!

    The report continues. I am so happy, finally to be able to write to you freely in such detail and with no pressure, just as you have doubtless long wished me to. I wish I had much more time to write. Let me not forget to touch on a subject, if only very briefly. This morning, Sunday, I dressed just as I used to with you, only more summery in trousers and shirt. I lost some time looking for a new place to live. I found a room for us three and hope also to be able to organize some furniture and even some beds (bedframes). But send things to the old address until you hear for sure, because it's not 100 per cent certain that we'll move. Even if we do move into III/440 the post will definitely be forwarded. I'm particularly happy about this move for my parents: peace and more comfort. Rudi's parents are moving into the same house. The families will each have their own room and yet be next to each other. (In the meantime unclear if it will be approved for Rudi.) Yesterday I finished by talking about the post. Only money-orders are getting through at the moment. Should parcels be resumed, please do not send silk underwear (duty too high), peppermint or fruit teas – we've got loads and can't get rid of it; everything else is desirable. Thank God neither we nor you on our behalf need have any worries about our food for a while even if the post remains blocked (and we stay here). As the owner of a sweet tooth I must say that I often enjoyed your 'sweet' parcels even more than the others. We don't spend money on sweets or biscuits, and as a non-smoker and a 'solid individual', I often yearn for something sweet. The *home-baked biscuits were wonderful. You seem to have known my weakness and gave me particular pleasure with these regular dispatches. We received no letter post, only the three cards right at the beginning. Your letters in the packages all seem to have arrived. But you must be very careful about confirming receipt of my post, because I'm taking an enormous risk in sending it. You mention having written three letters, none of which reached me. Let's hope they don't get into the wrong hands[ . . .]What a pity you didn't include a longer letter with the other things. Well, I can't complain – despite the external conditions I can call myself a happy man at the moment, the happiest man in Izbica! What you have done for us through Christian is absolutely unbelievable. But more on that later.*

*Now, you'll be certainly be interested to hear about my daily routine and my work. My father has various responsibilities on the Working Committee, has lost weight and doesn't look particularly good; he spends all day in the office and has to listen to the woes of people looking to him for help which he is ill-placed to give. At best he can reduce their misery. My mother is on the go from morning till night. She too has got thin but does an enormous amount. The cooking alone takes a great deal of time, then shopping, selling (the Poles come to the house), washing and so on. My mother has a heavy work-load. Things which are no problem on a gas stove take hours in these primitive conditions. I myself probably look the best. Some say better than I did at home. I take good care of my body because I want to survive. I eat everything which comes my way and so far, without having done anything particularly to earn them, I have had some lucky breaks. Most people suffer because they are doing unaccustomed heavy work on inadequate rations. But from the first day, I've been doing a job of my choosing (I'm still doing the same job).[22] Unlike many others I wasn't sent to a work camp or put to heavy labour with bad treatment. The earnings in these camps are meagre, usually an inadequate daily ration of a mere quarter-loaf of bread, coffee and water soup, perhaps a few zlotys a week – but usually less. I do not earn anything, or rather I earn a ration card for bread which entitles me to a 2kg loaf for 3 zlotys (4kg a month!!). Otherwise I have the advantage that I pay no rent or water rate (there are only six pumps in the whole of Izbica) and that I can use the bath (a wonderful invention, the nicest in the whole of Izbica, a shower bath) once a week for free. Sometimes I get an extra half a loaf where I work. It's a brickworks which is standing idle, a large complex of buildings and estates under the control of a German director from the SS. I work for this director as gardener in his private garden. The treatment is generous. I am cock of the roost because I have a whole harem of girls around me to whom I assign work. Thanks to my pedagogic talents I have managed to bring the Polish girls, who think any kind of work is crazy, to the point where the director is satisfied with the state of his fields. The tomatoes and cucumbers etc. we have managed to grow are real masterpieces. I get on well with the head gardener. My daily programme runs: get up 6.30 and wash; 7.00 report for work, allocation of tasks; at 8 I disappear off to the Order Police to give gymnastics lessons to the youth of Izbica. Something which provides me with stimulus and variety and contact with the police. At 10 back to the garden. 12–13 is lunch, 13–16 more work. The work is fabulous, on the hill in the open, with fresh, healthy air, surrounded by nature, almost naked, tanned – a contrast to all the misery down in the village. After work, I try to help my mother with the bartering. I am now the perfect cook, and licking the pot reminds me of times gone by. I am also a fireman and have to take part in drills twice a week.*

*Unfortunately, the day is not as rosy or calm as this suggests. We have become used to shootings. No week goes by without something happening: evacuation, round-ups of people on the street for work in the vicinity, visits from outside SS, house searches, confiscation of particular items, etc., etc. Recently on one morning alone more than twenty Polish Jews were shot for baking bread ... Our lives consist of uncertainty and insecurity. There could be another evacuation tomorrow, even though the officials concerned say that there won't be any more. It becomes more and more difficult to hide, given how few people are here now –*

*particularly as there is always a given target that has to be met. The Wild West was nothing to this!*

*'Hygiene' is a joke. Everything filthy, lice (particularly clothes lice, which spread typhus), fleas, bugs. There are few latrines. Sewage flows through unpaved streets (stench, illness). One illness is very common here: a high temperature with no other symptoms. It goes as quickly as it comes, but it leaves you weaker. Diarrhoea is equally common. Your Tamalbein has been used up already. Perhaps you could provide some more, or tar compresses. Neusamag[23] is useful too to deal with the flu symptoms brought on by sudden changes in the weather. Sometimes a cloudburst in the morning sends such floods of water through the streets that no one can venture out and the houses suddenly have 'running water'. By the afternoon, the bright sunshine makes everything dry. At the moment, the days are hot and the nights cold. Otherwise, we are adequately provided for with medicines thanks to your so thoughtfully assembled parcels.*

*There is no 'social life' here to speak of. Understandable, given the conditions, worries and the* sauve qui peut *complex. Concerts, lectures and music belong to another world; 25-zloty novels pass from hand to hand. Personal relations are limited to trade or remain purely superficial. You have to search for real friendships with a microscope. I myself don't feel the lack of these people. They have nothing to give me. There are people here from every country and of every kind. My knowledge of humanity will soon be complete! But no one even comes close to you! I'd need only to stick out my hand in this superficial place to conquer a heart or two. Conceited? No. First of all, there are more women than men. Second, my friendly manner, which stops short at a certain point, seems to exert an attraction on the girls. Perhaps it's a flaw in my character and I do it consciously, out of arrogance and confidence in our relationship. In general, I don't 'lust' after any of the girls, just after one person whom I can't find here.[ . . .]Otherwise I yearn for books, which are a rare item. The Poles have only Polish or Yiddish books. The only better-quality book I managed to lay my hands on was* Niels Lyhne *by Jacobsen. I liked it and found it* dealt with real issues in an interesting way. The style didn't suit 100 per cent. Otherwise, I've read one of the better sort of trashy novel, The Career of Doris Hart; vulgar, entertaining and many pages! I also pore over old newspapers, rescued from parcels.

That is the end of my report, or rather sketch. Christian can probably give you more detail about things I have only touched on or not mentioned at all. I have written to you as it is, authentically. But there is so much misery that it can't be put into words. A picture of Herr Simon, the father of Eugen from the Maschinenstrasse, could speak more than three volumes. Half mad with despair, undernourished, beaten black and blue, he returns at the weekend from his work outside and finds nothing: his wife, child and sister have been transported, his belongings have disappeared . . . a case of particularly bad fortune, but the daily misery here.

Jeanne, this is not for you! Many more will perish, of that I am sure. I have the will to survive, sustained by the thought of you. We can draw only one conclusion, as I did at the beginning of the letter. We need not flinch from saying that we miss and need each other almost all the time. I can't make any pretence about that. But only in my quieter moments. Otherwise, I am glad to know that you are safe. Hard as life is for us at the moment, something grand will emerge from it. This proof of our love for each other is such a foundation for our future life! If only we were at that point now! When I am with you in my thoughts and dreams, it seems like a fairy tale. What a miracle it would be to feel you in my arms again. How one learns here to see the value of life – and of bread, food, chair and bed! It would be a good lesson for some, if only it did not demand such a high price!

I have just reread your questionnaire. I think that these eighteen pages have answered it satisfactorily. It is a time of insecurity and unrest, but we will survive it with hope, confidence and . . . luck. Now you know the harsh reality of my life, but at least you have the certainty of definite knowledge. God will protect and help us as He has done so far. He will bless us and steer us in the right direction! So far I cannot complain! Stay strong and courageous

*and do not worry! Easier said than done, but trusting one another
we can do it!*

*Fondest kisses! E*

## Understanding Ernst's letter

What can have been the impact of this extraordinary letter on Marianne?
Each line, each paragraph, must have sent her spinning from horror, to
hope, to amazement at the tenacity and strength of character of the
human spirit in general and of Ernst in particular, then to fear and back
again.

What must have made the letter especially hard for her to comprehend
was its mixture of normality and horror, 'liveability' and squalor. In
part, Marianne herself was responsible for this uneven picture: amidst
general squalor, she had provided the Krombachs with riches. Thanks
to her, they were eating remarkably well. It is also clear that Ernst
himself could make no overall sense of the conditions around him; even
within the confines of this one letter, Ernst's mood and judgement seem
to fluctuate. The letter's shifting perspective shows how a contemporary
account differs from post-war testimony. In 1942, when Ernst wrote
this letter, Europe's Jews were not operating with a collective concept
of the 'Holocaust' that gave shape and 'logic' to their experiences. They
probably did not yet know what the endpoint was. Until the moment
they were selected for murder, life went on, in the nooks and crannies
between the Nazi ordinances.

To some extent, the striking juxtaposition of the bearable and the
barbaric was also a product of the Lublin region's distinctive character.
In other parts of Poland or in Lithuania, Jews were cleaned out of the
countryside and concentrated in large ghettoes. But because Lublin had
originally been designated as a Jewish reservation, the Jews were not
concentrated but dispersed into the smaller communities. This explains
the background to Ernst's experience, close to nature on the edge of a
small town with no barbed wire.

Something Marianne will not even have noticed was how German

Ernst was. A wry insight into the 'Germanness' of the deportees was provided by the native of Izbica, Thomas Blatt. When we met in Frankfurt, I showed him some of Ernst's correspondence. He pointed out the address: Block III/443c, Izbica a./Wiepiz, Kreis Krasnystaw, Distrikt Lublin, General Government. He told me that a similarly formal address figured on other German postcards he had seen, something that had bemused him for a long time because Izbica wasn't divided into blocks. But as he had recently learned from a Polish survivor, the German and Czech *Jewish* Councils had introduced blocks to improve administration.

For his part, Ernst's impressions since leaving German territory were those of a young man used to order, cleanliness, efficiency and plain-dealing, expectations which even the years of Nazi rule had not completely dispelled. In April, on the train to Izbica, Ernst's enthusiastic assertion that the order and cleanliness of the landscape showed the German influence placed him squarely within his native culture.[24] Ernst shared many of the prejudices of his countrymen, as is particularly apparent in his attitude to the Polish Jews. His reaction to the dirt and disorder is understandable, but because they fit his pre-existing prejudices, he clearly assumed that the Polish environment he encountered had always been thus, rather than being the product of war. In fact, Thomas Blatt's autobiography shows Izbica had enjoyed a thriving social and cultural life before the war, which had been wiped out by the Germans. The Izbica community had undoubtedly been poor, but conditions were transformed by the German invasion. Up to the time when many of its Polish occupants were deported in March 1942, the town was overwhelmed by the influx of Jews from all parts of the country. Ernst saw nothing of the social and religious distinctions within the Polish community, about which Blatt informs us. He never suspected that the inflated prices for goods were the result of the wealth brought there by newcomers such as himself – prices which the locals could barely afford.[25]

But alongside such prejudices, in many ways Ernst embodied all that was best about German youth. It was typical that, as a former youth leader, Ernst could not help but notice that the opportunities for hiding in Izbica made it ideal territory for a scout group. He continued to provide gymnastics instruction for the young, sought to help his parents where possible. As a humane, generous and idealistic boy, he found the commitment to ruthless self-preservation of many of those on the Jewish Council unpalatable. But the truth was, as he acknowledged, that it was often difficult to do much different. No doubt the hopeless Polish victims, shoved on to the extermination train by Ernst on the occasion when he was drafted in to help, experienced him no differently from the other orderlies involved. Still, there *was* a difference. Ernst was not about looking after number one. He was aware that there was a chance to escape – but to do so would have abandoned his parents to the next deportation train, and that he was not willing to do. In the final note that came with the report, Ernst even found time to worry whether Marianne had found a niche at home that she could call her own, where she could read and write in peace. From someone living with eight people in one room, that took more than a small degree of empathy.

Despite Ernst's protestations, Marianne must have worried whether Ernst really was painting a faithful picture of conditions. His letter was clearly designed both to deter and to reassure: Marianne should not be tempted to follow him; she should be given enough realistic detail to feel she understood; but she should not be unduly alarmed. In survivor testimonies from Izbica, I read about events in the summer of 1942 with which Ernst must have been familiar but which he does not mention here. In the testimonies deposited at Yad Vashem, the regular beatings and shootings emerge more clearly. Thomas Blatt told me that the two Gestapo officials, Engels and Klemm, beat and executed Jews on the street on a regular basis.[26] Another survivor, Hejnoch Nobel, recorded that an ethnic German called Schultz, who became Izbica's mayor, trained his Alsatian to attack people wearing white armbands (i.e., Jews) for sport. Nobel saw a woman being murdered in this way as she returned from drawing water.[27] There is much more in this vein and worse. This kind of terror is largely absent from Ernst's account, though he must have been aware of it.

I wondered whether Ernst was telling Marianne all he knew about the so-called evacuations to the East. Given that the letter is so well informed on other points, is it possible that Ernst did not know the deportation trains' destination?[28] According to Yitzhak Arad, up to August 1942 news of the activities of Belzec and Sobibor extermination camps (the destination of most of the trains removing Jews from the Lublin region) had not yet permeated much of the General Government. In August and September, Warsaw Jews arrived in Belzec and Treblinka with no idea of their imminent fate.[29] Sobibor remained so secret that in January 1943 Jews were still arriving unaware of the implications. On the other hand, Thomas Blatt says that his family heard about the Chelmno gas vans as early as December 1941, and that soon after the first major deportation from Izbica in March 1942 they learned that the unfortunates had been murdered in Belzec.[30] Blatt's account is, of course, written with hindsight, and he himself acknowledges that his family was not sure whether to believe this information. Blatt also acknowledges that the German Jews were less aware and less inclined to believe such rumours than their Polish counterparts. From August/September 1942 on, though, rumours and information about the camps and the fate of the deportees spread fairly fast through the Jews remaining in the ghettoes and labour camps of the General Government. On 20 September, an underground newspaper in Warsaw gave details of Treblinka.[31] It is thus just possible that when Ernst wrote to Marianne, he still did not know the truth – but his ignorance would not last much longer. What he did know was that those who had been taken had left only with what they had on their backs. Nothing good could come of such a departure. What could their destination be?

Ernst's last words to Marianne were written in a cover note accompanying the letters. He expressed once again his sheer amazement at what Marianne and Christian had achieved and repeated that she could not imagine the value of her supplies. Christian had told him what efforts Marianne made to assemble the parcels. Only now do we learn the full scale of the gifts she sent with Christian – a suitcase full of sweaters, jackets, food and much more. Ernst said they would sell some of the things because they needed to ensure liquid assets in case of another evacuation. Ernst asked Marianne to reward Christian generously from the Krombach property in storage in Essen.

At last, Ernst had to put down his pen:

*Although I often physically yearn for you, physical desire has taken second place to the strength and purity of our love. This despite or, rather, because of our hard separation. I had to struggle with physical desire but it is no longer a problem. Possibly it is still there, unconsciously adding to my yearning for you. I know that above all I want you as a person, and that is everything to me.*

*My love, you have no fewer worries than we do. I wish I had the strength to be with you and protect you. Daily air raids? God will and must help. Nothing else is conceivable! Every evening I pray for us. Despite the general harshness of conditions, there have always been some gestures of leniency. We all hope to return soon.*

*My dear Jeanne! Thank you for everything, everything! You are always with me, as I with you. I feel now as I did when the train was leaving. This letter must go or it will never get out and you won't get even a line from me. Anything that is missing, Christian will tell you!*

*If only I could take you in my arms and kiss you . . .*

*Eternally yours, Ernst*

## Marianne and Christian Arras

We can imagine the Krombachs' reaction when this tall German man in uniform turned up in the camp, laden with goodies. Ernst could not believe it – and neither can we. Marianne told me Christian Arras was in the SS. What kind of SS man was that?

Marianne felt very ambivalent about Christian Arras. She remembered that he and his girlfriend Lilli had come to know the Strauss family through a sale of household goods organized by Oe. Lilli and Christian were setting up house at the time and little was to be had in the shops. Lilli, a youthful and elegant young woman, whom Marianne remembered as 'a lovely girl, very nice', hit it off with Oe straight away and they became very friendly. Over the next few months Christian, too, became friendly with Alfred and Oe. Marianne remembered that Lilli and Oe shared a taste in clothes, and for her lively aunt, cut off from so much, any contact with the outside world was welcome. Moreover, there was the importance of getting cash and coupons in return for clothes and other items that the family could not use. Christian and Lilli used to bring Oe and Alfred foodstuffs 'because of course you couldn't get anything, really very nice'. But, she went on:[32]

'. . . he was an opportunist, entirely an opportunist. He became very wealthy, they were very well off, working for the SS, repairing all these things. So in a way that was how he became useful. And they were useful, but of course they were very well paid for it, and in the end they got a lot of my aunt's things, just to keep and give back after the war if they had returned. And after the war I only saw him once.'

I think, however, that Marianne herself realized that money was not a plausible explanation for Christian's action. There is no doubt that at a time when quality goods were very hard to come by, the Strauss family did provide some items on a permanent basis and others for safe-keeping which were very useful to a couple setting up home. The latter included some oil paintings, a brass chandelier, a wardrobe, a mirror and other items of exceptional quality. But there is clear post-war evidence that, unlike other recipients of Strauss family property, the Arrases regarded many of these goods as only temporarily in their possession.[33] In any case, whatever largesse the Strauss family were willing to bestow, it is unlikely that Marianne's parents would have wanted to spend heavily to benefit the Krombachs, whom they did not know particularly well. And although Ernst suggested rewarding Christian out of Krombach property, this arrangement had clearly not been worked out in advance. So it is just not credible that Christian took the parcels to Izbica for the material rewards.

Marianne had yet another interpretation of Christian's motives:[34]

'I think he just enjoyed taking risks. He was a . . . dare-devil type and would probably have been a bit of a juvenile delinquent in his time, like so many of the SS. I never trusted Christian Arras because he was too much of a wind bag. And I could never really fathom . . . why should a man like that do it? What was in it for him? I don't know . . . What was in it for him, I *assume*, was just the daredevilry of it . . .'

Christian had liked Ernst, he probably had liked Marianne, and he certainly had liked her uncle Alfred. But that, Marianne felt, wasn't enough reason to have stuck his neck out. And yet stick his neck out he certainly did.

The significance of the deed was indisputable, but it seemed that I would never be able to resolve the mystery of a man sufficiently integrated into the German killing system to be able to enter and leave an SS ghetto at will, yet sufficiently motivated to risk seeking out and helping a young Jew whom he barely knew.

## Marianne and Lilli Arras

On my first research trip to Essen in January 1997, just after Marianne's death, I was drinking tea in the office of Mathilde Jamin – the historian at the Essen Ruhrland Museum who had originally introduced me to Marianne. I asked her if I could borrow her telephone directory to see if there were still a garage or truck company run by Christian Arras, not a particularly common name in Germany. There was a stunned silence when I discovered that there was. It was too late in the day to call, but that evening I turned over and over in my mind verbal strategies to prevent an ageing SS member from putting the phone down at the mention of the past.

The following morning I rang the company and asked for Christian Arras. A suspicious voice at the other end asked who wanted him, but cheered up enormously when I said who I was. It transpired that I was talking to Christian's son, also called Christian, and that the company had been named after Christian's father, yet another Christian. (For the sake of clarity I shall refer to Christian Arras Senior, Christian Arras and Christian Arras Junior.) Clearly, Christian Arras Junior had been expecting a call from someone he was reluctant to talk to, but he certainly had no reservations about historians. His father had died some years before. His mother, Lilli, however, was still alive and would be happy to speak to me.

A day or two later, I took a train out to the little town of Geldern, near the Dutch border. I arrived early, and hung around in front of the deserted station until a new-looking dark blue BMW pulled up. Lilli Arras was tall and elegant, though of course now quite elderly, her hair neatly coiffured, her long dark coat turned up at the collar. We drove to a small village outside Geldern, to the smart bungalow that had been her and Christian's home in retirement.

On the way a strange and striking conversation unfolded. Though I

*Lilli Arras*

marvelled at what her husband had done, I was also somehow suspicious. Because of Marianne's many ambivalences – the question of
Christian's SS membership, the suggestion that he had rendered service
for family property and so on – there was something about the story that
made me uneasy. And, undoubtedly, because I was in this hyper-sensitive
state, I was particularly aware of more jarring notes during the drive to
the bungalow. As we entered her little village, we saw a most un-German
sight – houses with washing outside blowing in the wind on this chilly
snowbound day. She said the houses belonged to Aussiedler (the ethnic
Germans recently repatriated from Russia, most having few linguistic
or cultural links to their former land). There had been plans for more,
but a local resident had complained and stopped the building of further
homes. 'That was right,' she said. And then she went on to talk about
the past. The worst time, she said, was after the war – 1946, 1947, when
there had been no food. And I thought – there was a much worse time
in Germany than 1946, 1947!

But then there was one of those heart-stopping moments. Lilli began to tell me about her children, about Marianne, born in 1947. I looked at her. 'Yes,' she said, 'on purpose.' Marianne had never known that the Arras family had named their daughter after her. I saw the gesture as a sign of the friendship and respect Marianne had earned. But more, I suddenly felt that I was not just leafing through paper scraps of the past, deciphering faint imprints of past events, but was actually reconstructing a story which had never been fully told, never been fully known even by those involved. And for the first of many times I lamented that I had not been able to do the research in Germany just a few months earlier, while Marianne was still alive.

We arrived at Lilli Arras's elegantly furnished bungalow and I began taking notes. Christian had been born in 1914, Lilli four years later. Christian's father, Christian Senior, hailed from the Palatinate. Trained as a blacksmith, he had come to Essen in 1904 and set up a smithy. The company moved into transport in 1928 and took on a dealership for Magirus trucks. Christian began working for his father in the 1930s, and during the war the company had done contract work for the German army. Lilli herself hailed from a fairly modest background. Her father had been a foreman with Krupp, and there had been five children to feed. Because Lilli's father was unemployed for a significant part of her childhood, she well knew the meaning of hard times. She met Christian through one of her sisters. Apparently Christian Senior, ambitious and enterprising, rather looked down on the girl from a modest home.

Lilli Arras no longer remembered in much detail how the relationship between Christian, herself and the Strauss family had been established. For Lilli, the memory of war revolved around one thing – the bombings. On three separate occasions, the house in which she and Christian had lived was destroyed. In the worst of these, she was trapped in the cellar. The escape route to the cellar of the neighbouring house had been boarded up and she and Christian feared they would die in the flames. It was only after knocking down the barrier that they escaped. This attack, incidentally, destroyed all their furniture, including most of the things loaned to them by the Strauss family. On the next occasion, she remembers the houses toppling as bombs rained down on the street. Again and again, my questions on other subjects would lead her back to the bombings. Her wartime chronology was structured around them. At first, I was wary. Didn't she know there were worse fates? But then I understood: this, after all, had been the main threat to her own survival.

Whereas Marianne remembered the link between the families beginning with a sale of household goods, Lilli seemed to think the relationship had originated through contacts of her husband. He had come to know another member of the Jewish community, Jakob Ackermann, very well, and they had been jointly involved in black-market slaughtering in one of the large basement rooms on the Arras business premises. Yes, she acknowledged there had been property transactions. A very colourful Strauss family couch had survived the war in the Arrases' possession. Lilli told me that Alfred and Lore were at their wedding celebration, which took place on 20 February 1943 at the couple's apartment, and gave them a small telephone table as a present. On 5 March, though, all the wedding presents were destroyed in a bombing raid.[35]

I got the feeling that for Lilli the Strauss family had represented above all a touch of class. Their elegance and good manners marked them out as people of quality. Lilli remembered her first meeting with Marianne. With her plaited hair, she looked like a 'baroness from an estate', Lilli said. 'She certainly caught my eye.'[36] In one of the many letters she sent me after that first interview, Lilli remembered with particular pleasure a moment when Alfred was showing her his war decorations. She told Alfred about her own father's distinguished service in the First World War – he too had received the Iron Cross. Then, as Lilli wrote (recalling in the process of writing that Alfred's wife had been called Lore):[37] 'Herr Strauss called out "Lore come over and listen to this!" (Lore! I'd forgotten).'

It was a story full of poignant irony. The loyal German ex-soldier Alfred taking so much pleasure in the war service of another German. And the young Lilli, taking such pride in the social recognition offered her by an outcast Jew.

Lilli remembered something else from those days which confirmed the strong sense of social propriety. One day during the war, when she was living with her parents, her own house having been bombed out for the second or third time, she came across some Dutch forced labourers crowded round a large pot of 'soup', which was nothing more than white cabbage leaves in water. The young men were aged between twenty and thirty, Lilli Arras wrote,[38] 'and I said: "The educated class!" They had good clothing, expensive glasses, a sympathetic air (like you!), conversation in German.'

Here again was that sense of social order disturbed, of sympathetic, polite, established men subjected to a degrading situation. That, I think she felt, could not be *in Ordnung*.

How was it, I asked, that Christian was in a position to provide such a service for the Krombach family? Lilli had or offered only vague ideas. She said that Christian did not tell her beforehand where he was going. She remembered him going to a camp, she thought Theresienstadt, though it may well have been Izbica, with suitcases full of clothes. She thought he had bribed the guards and presented himself as an SS man. I said he didn't have to pretend, he *was* in the SS. At this point, Lilli became very agitated and the issue became a central one in our conversation (and, for a while, in our subsequent correspondence). Lilli insisted that he had been purely military, he was in the Pioniere, did his military service in Königsberg 1935–7, but was never in the SS.[39] Later, Christian Junior gave me more details. His father had done his military service in the 1930s with a Pionierbatallion and had then been called up to the army in 1939, where he had the non-commissioned rank of Schirrmeister and was responsible for the transport of a technical battalion. He was posted first to Poland, then France, then Poland again, but old man Arras had managed to have his son declared essential for the firm and got him home. It was only later in the war that Christian was called up again.

After that interview, Lilli wrote to me twice on the subject. She sent me a photo showing Christian in army uniform and his discharge certificate from prisoner-of-war camp, which clearly showed him as being army rather than, say, Waffen SS. The Berlin Document Centre (BDC), which holds the records of former SS and party members, had no file for Christian Arras. This lent credence to the idea that Marianne had got it wrong.[40] Marianne herself had said that she had never seen him in uniform.

But if he wasn't in the SS, how had he been involved in work in Izbica? Or perhaps he was working for the army near by and had managed to

*Christian Arras in Wehrmacht uniform*

bribe his way into the village? I resigned myself to the fact that we would probably never know. Lilli did, however, remember that considerable bribery had been involved for the guards to let him meet the Krombachs.[41]

The other issue was *why* Christian had taken such risks. Here, Lilli was sure that his motives were not particularly ideological; he was simply a good-hearted man. Friendships had been established and, on the basis of these friendships, Christian had wanted to perform a service. I discovered later that the Ackermann family, to whom Christian had become particularly close, had been deported on the same transport as Ernst, and it is evident from Marianne's references to 'Jakob's Friend' that Christian's visits to Izbica were also designed to assist Jakob Ackermann. When I later met Christian Junior on the premises of the family garage, he painted a similar picture of his father. He had had no interest in politics, but he had grown up in the heavily Jewish Nordviertel and Segerroth districts, and as a youngster had been friends with many Jews. Above all he was a good-hearted *Mensch*. His army record had said 'a good comrade and a poor soldier'.

When Christian returned from Izbica, Lilli remembered seeing him with a thick pile of letters – presumably the letters from Ernst – but she did not read them. Christian told her a little of what he had seen, and that had been enough. She remembered his account of a family he had visited (possibly the Krombachs) where the wife had been very ill. She remembered something about them vegetating in holes, absolutely primitive. Christian had been very shocked. And then again Lilli expressed that sense of a social order disturbed. The family had come from a 'decent house, terribly ill. Absolutely awful.'[42]

As a result of these conversations and correspondence, and in the absence of any BDC record for her husband as a party member, my attitude began to shift. But I was still far from giving Christian Arras unequivocal hero status.

## *Other voices*

After the Krombachs were deported, Marianne retained contact with
Artur Jacobs, whose diary entries about the bomb attack on the Krombachs' house we have already encountered. On 4 September, Jacobs
wrote an entry about Izbica, which made clear that Marianne had shown
him Ernst's report.[43] Over the next few days, he included several direct
quotations from Ernst's letters. On 16 September, Artur again made a
lengthy extract from Ernst's long letters whose contents had clearly both
impressed and depressed this sensitive man. But before the extract he
noted:

*Conversation with a man returned from the General Government (and
was also in I.) A simple man, straightforward, just facts. Struck me as
trustworthy – strengthened the horror of the earlier reports.*

*A tragedy is taking place that is comparable only to the tragedy of the
Armenians in the First World War. Almost more horrific.*

*One keeps on putting one's head in one's hands:*

*Is it possible? Is it humanly possible?!*

*I often feel I have been dreaming, as if it were all a horrific nightmare
and I could just wake up with a feeling of relief: Oh, if it was all only a
dream.*

*But what mind could conceive such a dream?!*

Artur's entry vividly reveals how a sensitive and sympathetic observer
of the Jewish fate gradually discovered the enormity of what was happening in the East. But it also gives us a further glimpse of Arras. For he,
surely, must be the man mentioned, since he has just returned from
Izbica and is associated with Ernst's letter. Knowing that Jacobs was a
tremendous judge of character, I considered his good opinion yet more
evidence in Arras's favour.

About ten days later, while following up information about Marianne's maternal ancestors, the Rosenbergs from Ahlen, I came across
some interviews between a local historian, Hans Gummersbach, and
Imo Moszkowicz, a Jewish-German Auschwitz survivor who stayed on
in Germany after the war.[44] At this stage I didn't know about the

rumours linking Moszkowicz's cousin and the Strausses' reprieve in 1941. What I did learn was that, though he was born in Ahlen, Moszkowicz had gone to live in Essen in 1939. As I read on, I came across a startling passage. Sometime between April 1942 (when Imo Moszkowicz's mother was deported to Izbica) and February 1943 (when Imo himself was rounded up for deportation to Auschwitz) something happened which he still remembered vividly, and yet which was so strange that it was hardly believable. For 'unfathomable reasons' a 'high-ranking military man, perhaps even an SS man' came to the family home and told them what was happening in the East:[45]

*'He reported on the extermination camps. We thought, stupidly, that he was a Gestapo spy come to draw us out[ . . .]He said he had come from the East and we should leave the country, flee! We thought this was a provocation to catch us out. We distrusted this man enormously . . . And I remember that he went away shaking his head. That's my memory. He asserted that he had met Essen families in the East, he even had with him a handwritten greeting from some Essen Jews with whom he claimed to be friendly. He had a big car-repair shop in Essen towards Altenessen. He repaired trucks for the army and went with them to the East. He accompanied the transport, he said, because he wanted to know what was going on. To outsiders he acted as though he was a 100 per cent Hitler supporter and in reality he was trying to undermine everything.'*

Unless there were several people with big repair shops in northern Essen travelling with Wehrmacht trucks to Poland, this must be Christian Arras. When I contacted Imo Moszkowicz about this, he was stunned after fifty-five years to be faced with the incident again. Thanks to his memory of the incident, at last I now had a more plausible account of how Arras came to be in the East: it was on the pretext of accompanying repaired Wehrmacht trucks. But even though the Wehrmacht contracts gave Arras an excuse for travel to Poland, he still needed enormous amount of courage (and probably not a little cash) to enter a place like Izbica.

Why did Christian Arras do it? Imo Moszkowicz himself was in no doubt, as he informed me in a subsequent letter:[46]

*I tried to find Christian Arras after liberation, hoping that he would know something of the whereabouts of my family. But at a time when neither trains nor post were working properly (and when life beckoned me!), my intention soon faded. Particularly, as it is only now, through your letter, that I have been able to dredge the name Arras from my memory. At the time it simply would not come to me.*

*Yes, he organized truck repairs for the Wehrmacht and managed personally to accompany the repaired trucks back to the East. He was concerned, I seem to remember, about a Jewish friend, whose name I no longer recall. The friend had been sent to Izbica and Arras looked for him and apparently found him.*

*Arras was a hero.*

*Did they sing his praises in Essen?*

*Ach, do you know that we who survived are guilty of committing great sins of omission since that time. Through their deeds, all those good souls kept us from absolute despair, gave us the hope that was so essential for survival. But after 1945, after the horror came to an end, they were as if paralysed, struck dumb.[ . . .]*

*I would gladly have met Arras again. Probably, though, I had the suffocating fear that I would learn more terrible things about the fate of the Essen Jews in Izbica – about the death of my mother, my siblings, my friends. And I simply did not have the strength to learn about that. My instinct for self-preservation protected me, I think, from the intolerably horrible reality, which Arras surely knew.*

*(Even now I still don't want to know the reality and I won't allow my imagination to produce a clear picture of what went on).*

When I interviewed Hanna Aron, the woman whose memory of accompanying her lover to Holbeckshof Marianne had unconsciously borrowed, I found that she too had things to tell me about Arras. This sub-community of hidden knowledge! Hanna's mother, Irene Drucker, had been the secretary to the Jewish Community. Hanna said her mother had told her about Arras, a German soldier who was giving them help and information. But she mustn't talk to anybody about it:[47]

'I think he was a good guy, he put his own life in jeopardy. Why he did it, I don't know, because there was *so* much danger in it. He must really have felt an obligation, a conscience to do this. Otherwise you wouldn't do this. They all knew that you could be taken to the camp.'

According to Hanna, the Community would organize food parcels which Christian Arras then took to Izbica.[48] She told me that his visit to the Community offices was a turning point in their awareness of conditions in the East. Once he had told them what he had seen, the Jews in Essen lost all illusion that life after deportation could be survived.

Imo and Hanna put an end to my scepticism. Clearly, no material incentive had been involved, since the poverty-stricken Moszkowicz boys had nothing to offer Christian Arras. I no longer had any doubt: Christian Arras was an unlikely hero.[49]

Yet I could sympathize with Marianne's ambivalence, echoes of which I heard in both Imo Moszkowicz's and Hanna Aron's accounts. In the atmosphere of terror, almost every gesture must have seemed suspect. I could understand that both Marianne and Moszkowicz should blur German uniforms – whether the Wehrmacht, as in this case, or railway officials, or the police – into the evil, threatening outfit of the SS. I was to find the same lack of differentiation in others interviewed. It was also easy to see why they had found Arras's actions so hard to fathom. Here, after all, was an apolitical individual, not above a bit of black marketeering, engaged in a most dangerous deed – for what? When I asked Hanna Aron if she would put into writing the positive recollections she had given me, so that I might forward them to Yad Vashem with a view to a possible recognition of Arras as 'righteous gentile', she was very reluctant:[50]

*At the time we believed he delivered the packages. Today I am not so sure any more. He also gave an account of the people who were still there. Today I must ask myself: How did he know? Was he in one of the Commandos himself? I recently read Daniel Goldhagen's book about the Commandos. Nothing would surprise me any more.*

She wrote this even though Marianne's receipt of Ernst's letters proved Arras undoubtedly *had* delivered the parcels he was given. But Arras's actions went so much against the grain of accepted knowledge about

Germans and Germany that it was hard to maintain belief in their reality. It was easier to begin doubting what one had once known as fact.

## Uncovering Ernst's fate

Sadly, Arras could not provide the lifeline that Marianne hoped. Izbica was simply a stopover on the way to the extermination camps. Ernst's survival for so many months was the result of a series of logistical hiccups in the killing machinery.[51] By April 1942, the facilities in nearby Belzec had become overwhelmed. For a time, deportations there were halted, the existing killing machinery torn down, and a new larger facility constructed. Sobibor took over briefly and there were deportations there from Izbica in May and June, but the summer offensive in the Soviet Union led to the cessation of non-military transports. In August, when Ernst wrote Marianne his letter, personnel and vehicles from the Lublin district were heavily involved in the 'Great Action' in the Warsaw Ghetto, in which 300,000 people were deported in just a few weeks, most of them to Treblinka.[52] It was not until the end of August 1942 that deportations from the Lublin district could resume in larger numbers. Even then, technical problems – for example, with the rail connection to Sobibor – limited the pace of deportations. In early October 1942, as the killing machine came closer, Izbica was again spared because the main extermination effort was to the north of the district.[53]

For Marianne, the only sign initially that things were not going well was that the post embargo continued. In early September, she wrote to the Red Cross in the General Government asking if they could forward parcels for her. A brief note from a Herr Michel, dated 14 September 1942, informed her that only parcels registered with the Presidium of the German Red Cross in Berlin could be forwarded. She should enquire in Berlin about the regulations.

Proof of Marianne's growing uncertainty about the possibility of future contact with Ernst was that, towards the end of September, she began a private diary alongside the letter diary for Ernst. Here she allowed herself bleaker reflections than she was willing to express in the letter diary. On 6 October 1942, she acknowledged for the first time that many people were saying that no one would come back from Izbica.[54] On 22 October, an extremely cautious entry in the letter-diary implies that 'our tall friend' (Christian) had been in Izbica again and that there was evidence that the Krombachs were still there. Perhaps Christian could visit Ernst soon: 'Now we hope that our tall friend will visit him because we have learned, finally, that they are still there.'[55] There is no record of news coming back.

Marianne could not have known, but in fact 22 October was the day on which the real purge of Izbica began. Overall, at least 50,000 Jews from the Lublin district were caught up in the deportation operation which ran until early November.[56] By then, most knew of their impending fate and great force had to be used. Many Jews fled from the ghettoes into the forest[57] and massive shootings followed; over 10,000 Jews were shot between October and December 1942 in the Lublin district alone.

Thomas Blatt vividly remembered 22 October 1942. The town was surrounded by SS soldiers and the Jewish leaders summoned to meet Engels, the local Gestapo chief. Many residents suspected that this was the end of Izbica. There was no longer any point in hiding because there was no longer any hope of moving freely once the operation was over. The local non-Jewish citizens would hand over anyone who tried to hide. So the Jews made their way to the station for a two o'clock deadline. Blatt did manage to hide, while the rest of his family went on. He heard screams and machine-gun fire from the station. Later, hearing talk in Yiddish, he looked out and saw groups of unguarded Jews returning to the town, some carrying pitiful belongings, others crying and covered with blood. Later he found his mother, father and brother alive and back home. The train's capacity had been too small, so Engels had made a selection. Resting his machine-gun on the shoulder of the Judenrat chairman he had mowed down a group of people and forced the others into the boxcars. They were packed so tightly that some suffocated even before the train left. Those for whom there was no room had been sent home.[58]

The Krombachs seem to have survived even this terrible operation, but there were further deportations in November.[59] On 25 November, Marianne made a coded reference to a recent visit by Christian Arras:[60]

*Today my heart is so heavy. Someone coming from there told me that there is no one left in Izbica. He kept looking round and asking, but in recent weeks everyone had gone, perhaps to nearby Lublin. Who knows! Winter draws ever closer and makes me more anxious than ever. I think always of you, of how the winter may hit you and how you will survive it. Only in such crises is one forced to acknowledge how small and insignificant one is and how powerless.*

In December came more news. Christian Arras had again had business in Izbica and again had carried post for Ernst. But the conditions he had discovered this time were very different from the last. On 30 December 1942, Marianne wrote in the private diary:

*I don't know what to write because life is pointless. You go round and round in a circle from which there is no escape.*

*News finally after four months. Our dear friend brought it again, after having had no sign of life since his last report. But this was so much more awful. There are things we know are terrible but whose horror we never fully grasp, and in that way we're protected from madness. Just sometimes there is a flash of brief, crippling insight. Then we learn the true significance of the individual person, or rather his insignificance.*

*Somewhere my trust has been punctured and I can only watch fearfully and hope the hole doesn't grow . . . I fear for you now, that you are so alone and dependent on yourself. Your mother gone, no one knows where she and all the others have ended up – no one knows their fate. God must be with you. Your father . . . died, from pleurisy, they say.*

*One says and hears and writes words whose meaning one simply does not understand! And you, you, experience the ghastly reality and you must be strong so that you don't . . . do you hear, you must! How do you look, I want to know, how do you live? It all weighs on me endlessly, the not knowing and the not being able to help! I want to be so, so close to you. And I cannot be that, even by post.*

*Despite everything, you must stay strong and preserve your spiritual foundation, because if you lose that you have given up.*

*What a poor spectacle human beings are! I can't go on!*

More than fifty years later, Marianne recalled what Arras had told her:[61]

'Of the few hundred people who went there in April 1942 there were only a handful left, about sixty people from that particular group. The rest had either been killed or sent away or just shot – tried to escape and been shot, or they just died of starvation and disease.'

Ernst was on his own, Arras reported to Marianne, his father had died, allegedly of pleurisy and his mother had disappeared. And Ernst himself? 'Ernst, he said, had been used for some medical experiment and lost his sight. Whether that was permanent or not he didn't know . . .'[62]

A copy of a very cautious letter from 8 January 1943, sent by Marianne to a Herr Austerlitz,[63] informed him of David Krombach's death, without mentioning the name. The son had been blinded as a result of an 'accident', whether irreparably so was not clear. At the same time, Marianne wrote to Emil Fuchs in Berlin to see if the RV had any means of contacting the deportees (or 'evacuees' as they were officially to be called). But Fuchs could offer no help:[64]

> Dear Miss Strauss,
>     To my very great regret I have to inform you that all, I mean all, possibility of communicating with the evacuees has been severed. For several months, every route we have tried has been barred. We suffer deeply over it. But we are helpless.
>     Accept my deepest sympathy.
>     Yours,
>     Emil Fuchs.

Typically, Marianne did not leave it there. Writing from the address of the Jewish Community office, she courageously approached the Red Cross again, asking if post could be sent to Ernst Krombach. At the end of January, she received a letter from the German Red Cross representative attached to the Generalgouverneur in Poland. In dry officialese, giving little away, it informed her that 'delivery of your letter to the above-named is not possible'.[65] One can well imagine the agonies of uncertainty that would follow the receipt of such a letter. Was it saying that letters or parcels generally could not be delivered, or that Ernst was not available to receive them? Marianne wrote again, and, on 10 February, a further letter arrived from the same office, grudgingly giving a little more information:[66]

*With reference to your letter of 1.2.1943 I hereby inform you that it is generally possible to send messages to Jews, but that in this case your message cannot be passed on.*

What did 'in this case' mean – Izbica, or specifically Ernst Krombach? Some moral constraint or some concept of public relations prevented the Red Cross from simply ignoring Marianne's letters, but they were being as unhelpful as possible. Undaunted, the tenacious Marianne wrote again:[67]

*Marianne Sara Strauss, Hindenburgstrasse 75 to German Red Cross, Kracau, 17.2.1943*

*Re: delivery of letter to Ernst Israel Krombach reference: S-O/GG J/II NR.6084/43/1*

*With reference to your letter of the 10th, I trouble you once more with the following question, to which your last letter did not provide a completely clear reply.*

*Is it generally impossible to send messages to Izbica or is Ernst Israel Krombach no longer reachable there?*

*Is there any point in seeking his current address and which office or organization would be the responsible authority?*

*Thank you in advance for your efforts.*

When no reply was forthcoming, she re-sent her request. This elicited the worst of all possible answers from the Red Cross:[68]

*With reference to your letter of 8.3.1943, I would hereby inform you that the above-named can no longer be reached at the camp and further enquiries are pointless.*

A letter that managed to be unequivocal about the pointlessness of further efforts, yet *still* avoid revealing Ernst's final fate. Realizing that nothing more was to be gained from this quarter, in April 1943 Marianne wrote to the Red Cross Head Office in Berlin to ask if there was a branch of the Swedish Red Cross in the General Government.[69] Again there was no reply and again she followed up with a further letter.[70] She was rewarded with a laconic three-liner stating that there was no Swedish organization. In all the correspondence she had received, there had been never a 'Dear' nor a 'Yours sincerely' nor even the tiniest human gesture.[71]

What exactly *was* Ernst's fate? So little is known about Izbica that it is virtually impossible to gain unequivocal information. I began to wonder, though, whether Marianne's memory of Christian Arras's report about medical experiments could be correct. Such experiments presupposed some kind of medical or research facility, which fitted less and less well with what I was learning about the place. I also noted that there was no reference to medical experiments in any of her communications or diaries at the time. For example, after giving up on the Red Cross, Marianne now turned abroad for help. I'd had no idea that German Jews were still able to communicate with friends and relatives in the neutral countries, but on 15 April 1943, and again on 16 May, Marianne wrote through the Red Cross to a former Essen community nurse, Sister Julie Koppel, living in Stockholm. Hoping that Julie Koppel's Red Cross connections would allow her to obtain further information about her beloved, Marianne provided effectively the same account of an accident as in the letter sent to Herr Austerlitz in January. Ernst, Marianne wrote, 'is said to have been blinded as a result of an accident.' Again, however, it is possible this was a neutral account to get past the censor.[72]

In his collection of tributes to Essen's Jewish lawyers, Bernd Schmalhausen's account of David Krombach contains a rather different story. According to Schmalhausen (and Enrique Krombach, who later told me exactly the same thing), Sister Julie Koppel wrote to Enrique in South America that Ernst was deliberately blinded by SS thugs after a failed escape attempt.[73] For this to be true, Julie Koppel would have needed another source of information about Izbica apart from Marianne. Yet in June 1943, Julie wrote to Marianne to say that she had no information about the Krombachs and that, though she would do her best, as things stood it was impossible to find out more.[74] From what I could tell, the letter from Koppel to Enrique no longer exists. Instead, Schmalhausen's account was based on Enrique's memory of receiving the letter.

I wrote to Thomas Blatt asking if he could remember either medical experiments or an attempted break-out by the German Jews. He was certain there had not been the former and was pretty sure there had been no escape attempts, either, at least on the part of the German Jews in Izbica.[75]

Artur Jacobs' diary offered another piece of the puzzle. On 31 December 1942, he wrote one of the bleakest entries of the war:[76]

*Marianne has just gone. I feel numb. I keep thinking: it isn't so. You're dreaming, it can't be true, and I try to erase it.*

*Dr Krombach dead, his wife gone, the boy blinded . . .*

*The other fates similar. Only a tenth of the Esseners still there, the others dead or sent further on. Frau Krombach two days after her husband's death. That is the norm. If the husband dies, the wife is sent on.*

*The boy worked in an explosives factory and lost his sight in an explosion. Where he is, what he is doing, where he lives, whether someone is helping him, in a place where it takes a supreme effort just to look after yourself, no one knows.*

*I still see his father before me, on the last day before his departure[ . . .]*

*Man dead, wife transported (who knows where? Is she even alive?) And the boy – blind!*

*The fate of the Jews is there before you in all its naked horror and hopelessness.*

Here was yet another account – blinded by an accident in an explosives factory. Or *was* this different? It was virtually what Marianne had written to Austerlitz in January 1943 and to Julie Koppel in May. Influenced by what she told me about medical experiments, I had assumed the letters offered a self-censored version of the events and not the truth. Now it seemed they might have stated the plain awful facts. If so, that meant that since the war, living on separate continents, *both* Marianne and Enrique had created private and different legends about Ernst's fate.

There was further corroboration that an accident was involved. In August 1945, Liesel Sternberg wrote to a colleague in Essen trying to trace her former employer and friend, David Krombach.[77] Liesel's letter refers to post she had just received from Enrique Krombach, who had written to her to tell her he had learned from Julie Koppel in September

1943 that Ernst had been blinded in a factory accident. In other words, at the time of writing to Liesel at the end of the war, Enrique clearly believed that his brother had been blinded in a work accident. It is unlikely that Julie Koppel wrote later with different information. It was thus clear to me that the story of the escape, as indeed the story of a medical experiment, was a later invention.

Of course, this chain of letters and diaries leads us back only as far as Arras's original report, and we will never know how accurate that was. We do not know where he obtained the information about David Krombach. 'Pleurisy' sounds like the fake causes of death supplied by Nazi concentration camps when inquiries arose. What we *can* say is that, quite independently of each other, with no communication between them to hold their memories in check, Marianne and Enrique developed different versions of Ernst's fate from a common starting point. I could not ask Marianne about this process, because she died before my discoveries. But Enrique was surprised to hear what I had learned. He agreed that he had had no new information since the war. So why should his memory have changed? As he said, it was not that his version was more bearable. On the contrary, it was more horrific than the original report. In fact, not only he but Marianne too had, in their different ways, added an extra shade of horror to the story as told them. Later, as I found out more about the fate of Marianne's own family, I was to learn that there was a discernible pattern in these revisions.

One thing was for sure: Izbica was not a place in which a blind person could survive, certainly not a blind person deprived of his family. Amid all the horror of the place, the thought of the blind Ernst dragging himself around, friendless, is unbearable. 'Oh, those beautiful eyes which looked so trustingly on the world,' wrote Julie Koppel to Marianne in June 1943. 'Oh, if only what you know were untrue. We too hope for miracles.'[78] But there were no miracles in Izbica at the end of 1942. For a brief period, Jews were allowed to work in the town again. In April 1943 the final clearance took place and the last Jews were deported to Sobibor.[79]

As far as we know, Sister Julie's letter of June 1943 was the last communication Marianne ever received about Ernst. But he did leave behind one more palpable reminder of his presence. In the very last plastic bag of documents in Marianne's house, Vivian and I found a gold ring, inscribed 'Ernest, March 1942'. It must have been the engagement ring Ernst had given Marianne before his deportation.

# 8

# Deportations, Death and
the Bund

For Marianne's parents, life in 1942 must have been one long miserable
wait under steadily worsening conditions. It is a macabre fact that, even
as the number of Jews in Germany dwindled, so the regulations making
life unliveable became ever more comprehensive. In the course of the
year, Jews were progressively denied eggs, white bread, bread rolls,
cigarettes and many other goods, and Jewish rations effectively fell to
starvation level. With their money and contacts, the Strausses managed
to get by, but they certainly did not live well. Steadily intensifying
decrees made it virtually impossible for Jews to use public transport.
Communication, too, was extremely difficult. Having had their private
telephones confiscated, Jews were now forbidden to use public phones.
In March, they were even forbidden to buy newspapers and magazines.
Segregation was rigorously enforced and Jewish houses had to be marked
with a black star. Expropriation continued – a hand-written note among
the Strauss family papers records that on 22 June 1942 they handed in
three typewriters, one remaining bicycle and their binoculars. The list
of decrees is almost endless.[1]

Within the legal framework, there were countless opportunities for
small-scale official harassment. When Else Dahl, Aunt Oe's mother,
moved to Essen at the end of 1941 a Frau Schweizer sent some of her
belongings on to her in a parcel. The parcel did not arrive. Frau Schweizer
complained to the post office, which duly informed her that the parcel
had been confiscated because the addressee was a Jew. On 8 February,

Frau Dahl wrote to the post office that she was astonished that the parcel had been confiscated because it contained her underwear. Giving chapter and verse on when and where she had bought it and confirming that if need be she still had the receipts, she asked for the underwear to be returned as she had urgent need of it.[2] A gruff four-liner came back from the post office informing Frau Dahl that the (Essen) Gestapo had confiscated the parcel. 'You will direct your application to that office.'[3]

Up until Spring 1941, as we have seen, German officialdom had occasionally displayed some vestige of its former correctness. But after the autumn there was only the unfailing politeness of the Deutsche Bank to remind the Strausses of the respect they once enjoyed. To take one example of officialdom, a senior tax inspector from the Düsseldorf Finance Office approached the Gestapo with a blunt enquiry about transferring some funds to the Strauss family. 'Before I order the Payments Office to transfer the funds, please inform me now forthwith if we can assume that these Jews will soon be evacuated.'[4] More and more, the Strausses found officials treating them as non-persons who had overstayed their welcome and who should have gone East long ago.

The family's social isolation grew. Until 1942, Richard had managed to enjoy something of a social life. From 1939 to 1941 he had attended the Jewish Volksschule in Essen. Then, denied the more academic opportunities he would normally have pursued, he had trained in metalwork, commuting daily to a Jewish workshop in Cologne.[5] But on 20 June 1942, all Jewish training schools were closed. Almost all the young Jews remaining in Cologne were deported to Minsk and murdered shortly after arrival.[6] It was at this stage, probably, that Siegfried organized private tuition for Richard. It seems that neither Richard nor Marianne had to engage in forced labour, the fate of almost all surviving Jewish youngsters at the time.

After the summer of 1942, the only relatives with whom the family were in touch were Alfred Weinberg, who received Red Cross post in his internment camp in Australia, and a distant relative in neutral Sweden. Anna Rosenberg wrote forlornly to Alfred, 'You are the only person I can write to and get a reply.' When the family sent Alfred birthday wishes in 1943, the letter was noteworthy in that the Strausses had absolutely no news about themselves to offer.

The Strausses' only social contacts were gentiles willing to run the risk of trading with them. Alongside Christian and Lilli Arras there were others, including a Catholic pair, the Jürgens. Marianne explained:[7]

'My mother got to know this Frau Jürgens. My mother fed her the most wonderful items of silver and Meissen and God knows what else in return for a piece of meat or whatever. Frau Jürgens ended up with an awful lot of things and all the furniture and the pictures which she didn't all return. But that's how these sort of relationships were . . . purely out of mutual need.'

For her part, Marianne felt more and more isolated. More than one former classmate recalled seeing her walking along on the other side of a road, wearing the yellow star, but none dared offer a sign of recognition.[8] (It did occur to me to wonder why they never remembered seeing her on the same side of the road.) In June 1942, most of Marianne's remaining young friends were taken away in a second deportation to Izbica.[9] On 20 July, all her elderly patients, together with the nurses and community workers on whom she had come to depend – Irma Ransenberg, Bärchen and the others – were loaded on to cattle trucks and deported to Theresienstadt.[10] Marianne's great uncle and aunt, Abraham and Anna Weyl, were also among the brutally dispatched human cargo. We know that after spending more than a year in Theresienstadt, most of the deportees were sent on to Auschwitz.[11]

Marianne wrote to Ernst on 21 July:[12]

*Herr O [Ostermann] is still here, otherwise it would be intolerable. Torn from everything. Did you sense from my letters how my work fulfilled and satisfied me? There is no one left within reach whom I can care for. So I will devote myself all the more to looking after you.*

For a while, Marianne's principal activity was collecting goods for her parcels. She told me:[13]

'I had developed a whole . . . I wouldn't call it an industry, there wasn't enough of that to go around, but a sort of occupation, trying to find people who would give me foodstuffs to send away. Non-Jewish people, friends of friends and that sort of thing. It was amazing, there were one or two people who really were very kind. There was an old lady who had a very nice grocery shop, well it was at that time a grotty little shop in a side street somewhere. She became very rich during the war with all the black-market dealing. She also was dealing in all directions, but she knew what she was doing and she used to give me stuff, dry goods, like peasum,[14] that sort of thing . . . Some dry goods were not very highly rated on the coupon side – we did quite well with that.[ . . .]

'People said try so and so, that priest or whatever – because the church was still the most likely way of getting some sort of echo. One always hoped that there was something someone might be able to do, hoping against hope.'

But by the autumn, when it became clear that no post was getting through, even this activity lost its purpose.

Marianne still did some clerical work for the Community.[15] She played a vital role answering enquiries from Jews who had emigrated about family members they had left behind.[16] Like Ernst, Marianne could not escape becoming a minor cog in the Nazi machinery. With the bulk of the community now deported to Łodz, Minsk, Izbica or Theresienstadt, there were a series of smaller-scale deportations to mop up the Jews left behind, and Marianne was given the responsibility of informing those assigned to the next transport. She remembered in particular one middle-aged lady:[17] 'who lived on her own, to whom I had to bring this news. She just nodded, she didn't say anything, and the next day they found her dead. She had hanged herself.'

## Imo Moszkowicz and the Hindenburgstrasse

After summer 1942, the only Jews left behind were a few privileged individuals and those conscripted into essential war work. True, some life returned to the rooms at Hindenburgstrasse 22 when the remaining Jews from Holbeckshof moved in there, but, unlike the children or the elderly, they did not require special help. There was little Marianne could do for them:[18]

*The sad remnant is moving tomorrow from Steele to 22. The bachelors, fifteen of them, will be in the main room, the couples are in the other*

*room and in 88. So there'll be some life in the place, which was com-*
*pletely dead last week. Those coming here are not particularly happy*
*about it and you can't blame them. They lived so much more freely*
*there.*

In the summer of 1997 I gained an unexpected insight into Marianne's
effect on this group. The sixteen-year-old Imo Moszkowicz was among
the new residents of the Hindenburgstrasse. Imo has already surfaced
several times in this book, wherever his memories shed light on Marianne's story. However, my discovery of quite how intricately his life had
been interwoven with Marianne's was much more dramatic than might
appear from his intermittent appearances in this narrative.

It began with my visit to the historian Hans Gummersbach. From Dr
Gummersbach I learned that Imo Moszkowicz had grown up in Ahlen
and had some memories of the Rosenbergs – Marianne's maternal
grandparents, aunts and uncles. In 1939, Imo came to Essen. Then I
discovered that Imo's mother and most of his siblings were deported to
Izbica on the same transport as Ernst. Imo and Marianne had in
fact both been at Essen station seeing off the train. More dramatic still
was Imo Moszkowicz's encounter with Christian Arras, an encounter
he still remembered, but could hardly believe, fifty years later. Because
I was so taken with these connnections, Dr Gummersbach lent me the
video of a television programme he had made about Imo Moszkowicz's
life.

I didn't have a video player in Germany, and so had to wait a week
before seeing the tape. In the meantime, without realizing I was about
to uncover yet another link between Imo and Marianne, I went to
Wuppertal to interview Hanna Jordan, a celebrated stage designer. I
wanted to talk to her because I knew that she had been a friend of people
who had assisted Marianne. She herself, as it turned out, had vivid
memories of meeting Marianne during Marianne's underground years.
A few days later, I flew back home and finally watched the video. The
film followed Moszkowicz from his Ahlen childhood, through the years
in Essen to his deportation to Auschwitz in February 1943. Surviving
both Auschwitz and the subsequent death marches, Moszkowicz elected
to stay in Germany after the war. The second half of the film pursued

the handsome and charismatic Moszkowicz in his blossoming post-war career as theatre director and master of the new medium of television, for which he made over a hundred productions. And there in the film was yet another connection to Marianne: Moszkowicz's close collaborator on countless projects was Hanna Jordan, whom I had just interviewed in an entirely different context.

The film made clear just how reluctantly – and only after decades of silence – Moszkowicz had begun to delve into the past. But I could not refrain from writing to him. Almost immediately, back came a fax:[19]

> Dear Doctor Roseman,
> I just received your letter. In a flash it shoved me back into that past which I – so unsuccessfully! – seek to flee. Is Marianne Strauss still alive?

So he *had* known her. Imo promised to send a detailed answer before he took up a visiting professorship at the Academy for the Performing Arts in Graz. He concluded:

> The Hanna Jordan connection, your mention of Ernst Krombach, Christian Arras, Izbica, simply take my breath away. A photo of Arras would help my vague memories.

A day or two later, I received a six-page fax. He began with Marianne herself:[20]

> I am trying very hard to transpose myself back to those years when I was in Marianne Strauss's presence. But I'm dredging up shadows rather than concrete facts.
>     Marianne was adored by all who knew her. She mastered the challenges of the time with such ease and unaffectedness. If I am not mistaken, she wore her hair round her head in a braid, adding an extra touch to her good looks.

The letter then repeated the widely held misperception that Siegfried had invented a particular steel for Krupp and had therefore been protected. For Imo Moszkowicz, there was another unexpected link – that Marianne was the niece of Carlos (Karl) Rosenberg of Ahlen, someone with whom he had become a close friend in the post-war period.

*Imo Moszkowicz*

He talked at length about the Essen deportation and about Arras. He
went on:

*Almost unbelievable, it seems to me, is the fateful link to my
Hanna Jordan. I am simply speechless and have no further comment! I simply note that in Hanna's presence I often had to think
of Marianne Strauss – Hanna had almost exactly the same kind of
aura. Perhaps she also made me unconsciously aware of my failure
to look for Marianne Strauss after the war.*

*'Does the name Marianne Strauss mean anything to you?' you
ask me, and in doing so have hit a central element in my reflections
on my own memories. You must understand that in our world at*

*that time, Marianne was an extraordinary phenomenon – and not just in terms of her appearance.*

*[. . .]*

*Marianne comes (came?) from a very good background, from an assimilated, almost goyish family, very rich and well educated. I, on the other hand[ . . . ]come from a very poor, more or less religious. East European cobbler's family. From my earliest childhood I have suffered from the difference between Eastern and Western Jews. I understood that the Yiddish of my parents was not pleasant to Western ears because it sounded like debased German. Also kaftans and Peikeles [Peyot – the long side-curls worn by very Orthodox Jews], which hardly anyone wore in the Western world, were seen as repellent – a pretext for the racist propaganda of* Der Stürmer *and the carnival associations.*

Imo argued that the Nazis' failure to discriminate between Eastern and Western Jews did not end the divisions and recriminations within the community:

*Even as a child I already felt burdened by the way the others distanced themselves from us, and this depressed me deeply. Even during the most dangerous times, when the gas chambers were working to full capacity, there was no real mixing of Eastern and Western Jews. One must remember that at that time, in 1938, as the Polish Jews were driven out of Germany across the Polish border, not even the German Jews living in safety abroad protested. Because many Western Jews were not unhappy to be relieved of this Eastern Jewish burden – by Hitler! – while they as German or stateless Jews could, for a while at least, enjoy the fruits of this contemptible distinction.*

*But Marianne approached us in a way that broke down all these awful barriers. Although she could have got out abroad years before, she didn't. She took up with us outcasts and used her privileged status only when the situation was life-threatening.*

*Or was it just love for Ernst Krombach which bound her to that time and place?*

*In my memory, Marianne has become a symbol of my dream of*

*unconditional Jewish unity. The way she turned this dream into reality in the most awful hell helped to stabilize my shaky belief in the necessity of Judaism.*

*For that I admire her, honour her, and have held her in my feelings and my memory through all the years.*

He concluded:

*'Anything which you can remember from that time in Essen, would interest me,' you write. I have ventured back into those years for Marianne's sake; but I find it very painful. I had made a firm decision never to do it again. The Essen of those times, it's true, is always in my consciousness. But writing or speaking about it demands such an effort. It forces me to sink back into the past (which is always with us), and that I find unspeakably difficult.*

*Only in honour of Marianne Strauss have I overcome my inhibitions and accepted the heavy duty of the historical witness. Perhaps also because as a young man, hungry for life, I felt such a strong attraction to her, one that it would be fair to call love.*

*And this indescribable feeling has been brought back into life by your letter.*

*For that, I thank you very, very much.*

*As long as there is memory, however painful it may be, then all those who once were still exist:* Non omnis moriar, *says Horace in his Odes.*

Imo Moszkowicz's letters and his painful wonder at the hidden links brought out of the shadows fifty-seven years later made me feel, for a moment, like part of the story, a small link in the chain. Of course, there are always coincidences waiting to happen, connections and associations lurking round the corner, some to be discovered, others to remain forever hidden. But this was something more. The unwillingness or inability to face the past, the silence after 1945, had created a barrier to the resumption or resolution of relationships and friendships. Though I deeply regretted not being able to bring all these connections to Marianne, I wondered if she, had she been alive, could have coped with all this past brought back to life.

In any case, did Imo Moszkowicz's idealized Marianne, his almost literary construction of her as a bridge between East and West, bear any relationship to her own reality? For her, the interactions in the Hindenburgstrasse were far less significant. She did note in her diary some of the meetings with the boys in the Hindenburgstrasse. On 17 November, in deepest despair at the lack of news from Ernst, she recorded a meeting with the youngsters for an oneg Shabbat (an oneg, literally 'delight', is a Sabbath study-meeting). Marianne evidently went with much reluctance, protesting that out of respect to those who had been transported to the camps they should not enjoy their unearned freedom. With a little self-irony, she recognized something 'puritanical, blue-stocking' about her opinions, and in the end was able to enjoy the get-together. The group read 'Angst' by Stefan Zweig and sang old songs. But it is clear her thoughts were elsewhere.

## 'Does God mean well with us?'

One can see why the sixteen-year-old Imo felt the way he did about Marianne. It was not just her beauty. Her serenity and confidence, her openness and strength were inspiring. She proved there were still Jews who did not look bowed or crushed, despite everything the Third Reich had thrown at them. At the same time, she was alive to the worries of others and totally committed to providing help. She represented the best kind of Jewish elite. It's not surprising Imo should have fantasized that, had she wished to, Marianne could easily have left the country.

On the other hand, there seemed to be a kind of irony here. For Imo, Marianne stabilized his belief in Judaism. But for Marianne, Jewishness often seemed so irrelevant. It was surely no accident that at the kindergarten college, Hebrew and Jewish studies should have been her worst subjects. It was Marianne who had told me about the division between her and the community triggered by the cry of envy on the Haumannshof. And yet here she was figuring in Imo Moszkowicz's memory as a symbol of Jewish unity.

But when I looked again at Marianne's diary and correspondence from 1942, I realized that religion meant more to Marianne then than at any time before or since. It was noticeable how often God was mentioned in Marianne's letters to Ernst. In April she asked, 'Does God mean well with us? We must believe in him and hope that he will help us. Only in that thought can we find solace.'[21] When Ernst's card arrived in time for her birthday, she saw it as a sign from heaven. 'The Lord will help us, my love, I build my hopes on that.'[22] This is very different from the letters she wrote in Berlin or her diary entries in later years. In the whole of her 1944 diary, for example, God is mentioned only once.

In 1942, Marianne referred to the Jewish festivals as they occurred. Sometimes she noted simply that they were not being celebrated. But she also drew hope from the texts traditionally read on the day. On 21 May, she referred to the festival of Shavuot (Pentecost) and the associated period of reflection and contemplation.[23] The next major festival in the calendar is Rosh Hashanah, the Jewish New Year, and to celebrate the day, Marianne selected a present to send to Ernst as soon as the opportunity allowed. On the most solemn day of all, Yom Kippur, the Day of Atonement, Marianne wrote how consoling the prayers were, how much hope they gave. And she copied out in her letter diary for Ernst the Haftorah[24] portion from the prophet Isaiah read on the morning of Yom Kippur.[25] In his long report, as we know, Ernst distinguished between German Jews and their Czech counterparts. 'Unlike us,' he wrote, the Czech Jews 'had not been forced to regard themselves as Jews and led back to Judaism.' The implication was that the Nazis, by forcing Jewish identity to the fore, had effected among German Jews a positive, subjective return to Judaism as well. Ernst clearly felt Marianne would understand and identify with this proposition.

It is easy to make the mistake of assuming that other people have one unchanging identity. By contrast, having himself grown up in Weimar Germany, the historian Arno Klönne wrote of the identity of Jewish youth in Weimar and Nazi Germany:[26]

*From my own experience I know that there's something one might call shifting consciousness. In a single year it was possible to go through three phases of self-identification all within the same youth organization: secular Jewish nationalism with a socialist tinge, German-focused anti-fascism, and a religious Jewish phase.*

In later life, Marianne lost sight of the nourishment she had once drawn from her Jewish identity. But for a while in 1942 her Judaism was a real source of comfort and strength.

## The depths of despair

Through October and November 1942, as Ernst's silence continued and the rumours and news grew worse, Marianne became ever more miserable. She often felt she was living in a dream. The blurring of reality and nightmare became complete following an operation on her toe. The old injury from Berlin had been giving her trouble – potentially a huge handicap when all forms of transport were forbidden to Jews. But where was she to go for treatment? There were no Jewish doctors left. There was, however, a Catholic hospital in Essen Steele and Aunt Oe, bolder than Regina, finally suggested they make an appointment there without giving too many details. The surgeon asked no questions and a date was set for Marianne's third operation at the end of September 1942.[27] Apparently, a fragment of bone had broken off and was floating loose in the toe. Marianne was given chloroform and the surgeon removed the fragment, the size of a pea. She told me that the traumatic experience of waking up from the operation, linked to her terror of having said something to reveal her identity, gave her a fear of anaesthetics she never lost.

In her diaries, I discovered her contemporary account of the experience, which continued to haunt her for weeks. She had had a vision, 'like a dream', she wrote on 7 October, that made her aware of 'how brutal life is, how badly mankind deals with it and yet that God is merciful enough to allow mankind to live'.[28] She was standing before a kind of divine court, a young boy clad in only a shirt was wandering around and playing a tune; she could sense the presence of others but not see them. And then suddenly:[29]

*It is as if in this one minute my life were to be judged, as if in this single minute of CONSCIOUSNESS it were to be subjected to God's unsparing judgement; but I am no longer just me but to be held to account for*

*the whole of humanity. The judgement: 'You are not fit to count as*
*enlightened beings . . . but I will be merciful and tolerate you as before.'*
*The deathly fear from that moment has still not gone.*

This epiphany, part nightmare, part prophecy, occupied her thoughts
for weeks. On 18 October, she wrote in her private diary the bleakest
entry yet:

Sunday, 18th October
*My love, and now I don't know how I can write out of myself everything*
*that lies so deeply within me. All the terrible fear that crawls around me.*
*How should I fight it when the weapons and strength I need to confront*
*it dwindle and dwindle? At night when I lie awake or sit upright in bed*
*it creeps over me, closer and closer, all the horror. And then I experience*
*everything that makes your life intolerable and threatens to destroy all*
*of you physically and spiritually. And I curse my powerlessness and*
*retreat into prayer, which gives me only a little consolation and you not*
*even that. How long will God stand by and watch it all! I wish this*
*awful life would come to an end. And still we accept whatever comes*
*and grab it indiscriminately, knowing full well that all we're being*
*offered are temporary expedients.*

Now the shocks followed fast upon each other. At the end of the year,
Christian Arras brought back the terrible news that Ernst had been
blinded and was on his own. Then, just when Marianne must have
thought she could not take any more, a letter arrived from Edith Caspari,
her former teacher in the kindergarten college, written on 31 December.[30]
Edith described the horrors which had hit the Berlin community.
Mothers had been deported, leaving their children behind. In one case,
a fourteen-year-old child had been left on its own because it had diphtheria at the time of deportations. But what will have depressed Marianne beyond words was the news about her many friends and teachers.
The inspirational Hannah Karminski, her former teacher and examiner,
had been held as a hostage and subsequently deported with five hundred
other RV employees. Karminski died on the transport, although Edith
Caspari would not have known this at the time.[31] Other hostages had
been shot, including Alfred Selbiger, Marianne's handsome conversation

partner of February of whom Ernst had been so jealous. The book of Job was now 'our book', wrote Edith Caspari, concluding the letter with a heartfelt 'Farewell! Let us hope for a better New Year! Remain my Marianne!'

This was the end. The news was so devastating, so appalling, the sense of helplessness so overwhelming that there was nothing to be done, nothing to be said. After typing out a final entry, Marianne abandoned the letter-diary:[32]

New Year 1943

*New Year. And one so different from what we had imagined and hoped. What one year can do to a person, one day, one hour even . . . don't think, don't think! Our New Year's walk last year, the church with the organ privy to our countless wishes. My love! I can't comprehend the awful thing that has happened! To be with you, to help you, to protect you! My love, my love, what have I done! That I didn't stand by you or bring you out of danger! We should have spared ourselves all the barriers and all our bourgeois decency. But who could have predicted all that! What the year brought us – and what will this one bring? I pray, pray, pray that God will give you back to me, very, very soon. Your dear, good eyes . . . I can't think about it or imagine it. And the way I found out! – but that is irrelevant.*

*How wonderfully the year began for us, and how it has ended! Shooting stars and other signs – are they good or bad omens? I don't know anything any more, don't want to know anything, don't want to think any more. Only you. To help you, to liberate you.*
God must help us!

## The Bund

In these months of despair a force entered Marianne's life that was to be her spiritual salvation even before it saved her physically. But to understand it, we need to cast our eyes back briefly to the early 1920s. The term 'Bund' (meaning 'league' or 'federation') is common to numerous organizations. Perhaps best known is the socialist Jewish Bund, with its many supporters in Poland and Russia. In post 1949 West Germany, the shorthand 'Bund' came to be used to denote the Federal Government as opposed to the individual states. Neither of these has anything to do with the Bund in Marianne's story, which is not well known and was never a large organization. Even at its peak, the *Bund. Gemeinschaft für sozialistisches Leben*, the League. Community for Socialist Life, never had more than a few hundred members.

The Bund emerged in Essen in the early 1920s out of a group attending the Volkshochschule lectures of Artur Jacobs. The Volkshochschulen, literally Higher Education Institutions for the People, were created after the First World War, seeking to advance the cultural and educational level of the working class. Jacobs, the son of a craftsman, and from a very pious Protestant background, had been active in the German youth movement before the First World War. Despite his modest origins, he had managed to attend university and trained as a school teacher. But he proved too radical for the conservative parents of Essen and, taking early retirement, Jacobs became an enthusiastic and inspirational lecturer in the Volkshochschulen. In 1924, the close and persisting contacts with his students were formalized with the creation of the Bund.[33]

The Bund was one of a small number of left-wing circles in Weimar Germany that sought to bring together Marxist thinking about society with Kant's view of the objective ethical laws governing the individual.[34] Jacobs combined a belief in the historical mission of the proletariat with an intense concern for the moral choices that face individuals in their daily lives. 'He who puts into practice the most modest idea,' Jacobs declared in 1929, 'is closer to the truth than he who merely researches or declaims the most sublime.'[35] The Bund's members were as likely to discuss marital relationships or a group member's work problems as the development of the world economy.[36]

The 'socialist life' of the Bund's title was thus meant to convey a dual programme of campaigning for a better society and experimenting with new ways of living, or 'life reform', in Weimar parlance. The Bund's core members developed a regular pattern of Sunday meetings in which the group would spend the whole day together, discussing, eating, walking, playing music and dancing. During the 1920s, Bund members bought, built or rented so-called 'Bund houses'. The 'Blockhaus' in Essen was completed in 1927; there was also a second Essen house, in the Dönhof and one in Wuppertal. Some of the Bund members lived in them as collectives (though without the free love practised by their 1960s successors).[37]

The group sought also to find a new relationship to physical movement and the body. Artur Jacobs' Jewish wife Dore, née Marcus, had been trained in eurhythmics and began to develop her own philosophy of dance and movement, aimed particularly at non-professional dancers. In 1925, Dore Jacobs' school for rhythm and movement was formally constituted. Many later members came to the Bund via instruction at Dore's school or after seeing some of her pupils perform. It was not uncommon during the Weimar period for dance and movement to be seen as part of the political struggle, and no left-wing festival was complete without its dance group and theatre presentations. There was also a broad shift at that time away from narrow intellectuality and towards a reaffirmation of man's natural energy and physicality. But it was rare that a consciously political organization and a dance group should be as closely tied as here. The Bund's aim was to create a socialist way of life which would incorporate the whole person – body, mind and soul.[38] In contrast to their 1960s counterparts' use of drugs, the Bund members were hostile to all forms of artificial intoxication, including alcohol.

The Bund was influenced by the notion of the *Orden* or order, a popular concept in Weimar Germany. An *Orden* consisted of a group bound together by a common oath under the natural authority of a charismatic leader. The Bund drew on this cultural attraction to charismatic leadership and Artur and Dore were held in awe by the other members. The Bund was thus a kind of hybrid. It was a circle of friends rather than a formal organization. At the same time, it was a very tight-knit group of people who spent much time together, in some cases living together, who discussed everything and who swore a solemn oath or 'commitment' to one another.[39] *Verpflichtung*, or commitment, was the key concept. Initially just the core members, the so-called Inner Circle, ceremonially committed themselves, swearing an oath to the Bund. At later annual festivals, newcomers joined the ranks of the *Verpflichteten*. The group's excursions – every summer, for example,

*Artur and Dore Jacobs in 1964*

they would go to the same retreat in the Sauerland – provided an opportunity for members from further afield to bond with the core members and absorb the group's atmosphere.

One feature of the Bund that most impressed newcomers was its ability to transcend the class barriers that were otherwise so insurmountable in Weimar Germany. A number of the Bund's leading figures were teachers who had risen from modest backgrounds. Others, particularly some of the women, came from educated, bourgeois households, while many others were workers. The middle class Tove Gerson, for example, remembered being awe-struck in her first dance class by the way Dore related to a worker in the group:[40]

'The idea that without any awkwardness you could say to a worker,

"Fritz, come on show us [how you'd drive in that prop]", I'd never seen that. I was a bourgeois and the fact that we were working together there, in a flash I suddenly saw the Bund's attitude to the social question.'

The group was also more conscious than most of gender issues and was committed to equality in marriage. One of the most incisive and progressive pamphlets published by the Bund was the tract *Mann und Frau als Kampfgenossen* (*Man and Woman as Comrades in the Struggle*), which appeared in 1932.[41] This awareness of gender gave it a strong appeal for women (though, ironically, so did Artur's patriarchal role as father of the movement). Moreover, Dore's work with dance and movement offered women the chance themselves to become dance and gymnastics teachers, a career increasingly recognized as a profession in the 1920s and 1930s. Equally important for the shaping of the Bund's identity was the fact that gender issues were the most direct and challenging area of daily life in which to apply and test its principles.[42]

Racism was another core area of concern to the Bund. Remarkably, as early as 1920, Artur Jacobs wrote an article about racism in education which rejected selection based on racial or ethnic principles.[43] The presence in the group of Jewish and half-Jewish members, including Dore, sharpened the group's sensibility to such issues.[44]

## The Bund in the Third Reich

After 1933, the challenges to the members' commitment became tougher. Many similar left-wing circles collapsed under the pressures, whether because they had underestimated the regime and took part in foolhardy protest actions, or because Nazi infiltration resulted in the group's destruction, or because opportunism and fear led to quiescence and silence. By and large, the Bund did not engage in open resistance. But its commitment to maintaining group meetings and communication and its low-key efforts to undermine and expose racism and fascism in the outside world demanded courage enough. In the early years, Bund members also protected individuals on the run from political persecution, and helped them get out of the country.[45]

For someone so idealistic and humane, Jacobs always had an extraordinary degree of political insight. For example, he worried that the very honesty and civil courage of many Bund members might lead to dangerous acts of opposition or a failure to make proper risk assessments. Lisa Jacob, one of Dore Jacobs' first pupils and a founder member of the Bund, recalled:[46]

*Artur Jacobs taught us (and not a few tears flowed in this 'extra tuition') to fight the enemy with his own weapons. Faith in human decency or in the propriety of the judiciary was completely inappropriate. We learned to keep secrets, lie, camouflage and mislead.*

Lisa was Jewish by background, and these lessons were later to save her life. In intensive workshops, the group systematically analysed the various elements of National Socialist ideology. Jacobs developed 'seventeen points', a kind of intellectual catechism listing all the weaknesses of the National Socialist creed. Another of the Bund's founder members and influential figures was Ernst Jungbluth. His widow Ellen recalled in an interview that the great strength of both Artur Jacobs and Ernst was their thoroughness. They never treated a particular incident, a mistake or a problem as a one-off accident but always went back to its roots. Group members would take part in role plays, acting out how they would respond to a specific eventuality, an interrogation, for example, and getting the group to criticize. They repeated the appropriate answers over and over again until they could say them in their sleep.[47]

Even in the Nazi years, the Bund groups managed to maintain their regular meetings and these were crucial in helping individuals find the right balance between personal safety and activism.[48] Above all, the Bund broke through each individual's sense of isolation. In an early post-1945 publication, the Bund tried to make foreign friends aware of just what it had meant to live in a situation where you could trust no one. Where anyone, any neighbour was a potential enemy. Where there was no free press, just a constant stream of lies and deceptions.[49] In Germany, unlike other countries that had national resistance movements against German occupation, there was no consensus of oppositional feelings or ideals that found a broad echo, no national ethos that could unite resistance.[50]

In contrast to many other left-wing opponents of Nazism, the Bund recognized from the start that the Nazi movement's anti-Semitism was at the heart of the problem. Particularly after Kristallnacht, the Bund showed its true colours. As Tove Gerson recalled, Artur's slogan was: 'Step forward and break through the isolation of the Jews.' It was liberating to know what one should do. Tove Gerson remembered, for example, having to run the gauntlet of a baying mob to visit a wealthy Jewish family in their destroyed apartment on the day after Kristallnacht. But her solidarity was not enough to prevent the couple from later committing suicide. Artur Jacobs' private diary contains ample testimony of his refusal to look the other way.[51]

When the deportations started, the Bund gave the deportees what assistance it could, helping them carry their luggage, offering psychological support and sending parcels to the ghettoes. In 1983, the German Radio Station WDR broadcast a moving selection of letters between Trude Brandt, who had been deported from Posen to Poland in 1939, and Lisa Jacob who, with the assistance of other Bund members, regularly sent her parcels of food and clothing.[52] In 1941, Artur Jacobs recorded his last conversation with a woman on the transport to Minsk. She thanked him for his help:[53]

*'What for? For the tiny assistance that was more of a help to us than to you? We must thank you for being able to discharge a tiny portion of our guilt. It's more a token of goodwill than anything more material, but one suffocates if one does nothing . . .'*

*She (after weeks of holding herself together and forcing herself to appear calm) burst into tears. 'You don't know what comfort you give me.'*

Most of the group's Jewish members managed to leave the country before the war. Others, like Dore Jacobs, lived in a 'privileged mixed marriage' (a mixed marriage where the male partner was not Jewish and the children had not been raised as Jews) and were for the moment safe from deportation. April 1942 brought the group's biggest challenge yet, when Lisa Jacob was put on the deportation list to Izbica. But the Bund had long prepared for this eventuality. Lisa went underground, to be fed and supported by the other Bund members for three years.

## Marianne and the Bund

Marianne's first contact with the Bund had come much earlier, in 1933. In that year, Marianne and other Jewish pupils had been prohibited from receiving further dance lessons at the Folkwangschule. Marianne's parents sent her to train with Lisa Jacob and Dore Jacobs. One of Marianne's most endearing traits, so far as I was concerned, was her confident, dismissive judgement, particularly on things cultural, about which she was so knowledgeable. Whenever former Bund members talked to me about Dore Jacobs' marvellous approach to movement and dance I would replay in my mind Marianne's verdict: 'Utterly boring!' She said it was not nearly as constructive, lively or imaginative as the classes she had taken at the Folkwangschule. But at least the instruction gave Marianne her first contact with Bund members, in the communal house in the Dönhoff.

After a while, Marianne had discontinued the dance lessons and lost contact with the Bund. In the Krombachs' flat the night before Ernst's deportation, she was reintroduced to Artur Jacobs. He invited Marianne to call on him if she needed advice or support. Soon after, when Marianne was working in the nursing home with one of the community nurses, Artur came in with food coupons and again offered help. From time to time, Bund members would bring coupons or food for the home. Artur asked Marianne to keep him informed of developments because he was compiling a dossier on Nazi policies.[54] In the spiritual and emotional vacuum left by Ernst's deportation, Marianne did seek out Artur and his wife, at first hesitantly, then quite frequently. 'They always made me very welcome, and for me it was an enormous moral help, you know, to be able to talk about this dreadful business and unburden myself.'

Some passages from Artur Jacobs' remarkable diary have been quoted earlier. I was first alerted to the diary's existence when I discovered that Dore Jacobs, now a widow, had in the 1960s or 1970s sent Marianne an extract from it as a keepsake of Artur. As I gradually made contact with the surviving members of Jacobs' group, I asked them about the diary. None of them knew where it was, but one thought there might be something in the Essen city archive. Sure enough, the loose-leaf volumes, some in their original state, some copied out later, were in a large cardboard box in the vaults. They were to turn out to be one of the most dramatic sources for this book. The diary jumps between thoughts about Goethe, lyrical reflections on nature, moving accounts of Artur's attempts to support Essen Jews and extracts from an equally moving correspondence with Artur's son Gottfried, trapped in Holland and suffering terribly from the German occupation. There are also powerful insights into the Nazi system, a record of his growing awareness of the unique monstrosity of the Final Solution and acute descriptions of people he had met, including the Krombachs – and Marianne.

We first learn what Jacobs thought of Marianne in a diary entry written in August 1942. The entry is itself an extract from a letter Jacobs had just written to his son Gottfried. In the 1930s, Gottfried had been sent by his parents to the safety of the Netherlands, but now found himself living under German occupation and drafted into forced labour. His sad letters to his parents must have been almost unbearable to them. In June 1942, Gottfried had written that he fainted at work from under-nourishment and was not sure he could continue to bear the demands placed on him. In July, he had sent an even more distressing letter, describing the deportation of his lover, Gina, from Holland. Artur sought various ways to persuade Gottfried to shake off his depression and throw himself into helping others. Finally, he tried a positive role model:[55]

*Yesterday evening a young girl was with me, whose best friend had to go to the East. She has always had a rich and varied life with many friends, books, music etc. Now everything has been taken from her. And how does she live? I asked her. She told me: from early to late I sit in the office, then at home, to help my mother, then I make up parcels [inserted in pencil below 'for deported Jews'] and then I think how else I can help. By then, it's usually after midnight. This is not the life I was used to, but it satisfies me. The only unsatisfying thing about it is that it is much too little.*

*Hers is certainly not a happy life in the usual sense of the term. But isn't it nevertheless worth living? And don't you think that it can yield moments of deep satisfaction that a worry-free, 'happy' life can never offer? And what a different complexion life has when it triumphs over such difficult conditions!*

Although Marianne was not named, the details and her explicit mention in other entries make her almost certainly the person described. As in Imo Moszkowicz's memory, here, too, Marianne Strauss emerges as a role model. To earn the respect of a man as rigorous with himself and others as Artur Jacobs was some achievement.

In early September, Artur's diary is full of comments about Izbica and excerpts from Ernst's letters. On the 18th it refers to the meeting with Christian Arras and a further quotation from Ernst. Then on the 22nd:[56]

> *Singing with Marianne Str.*
>
> *Folk songs and serious ones from Brahms.*
>
> *That's what she wished. But one does it with ambivalent feelings.*
>
> *How could someone so caught up in the thick of things,* * for whom life consists of nothing but waiting for something terrible to happen or hearing about something terrible that's already happened, how could she open herself up to this beautiful serious world. It seems so far away, so unreal, like a cruel joke?!*
>
> *A front-line soldier, hearing these old songs for the first time, suddenly began to cry – so terrible, so unnerving, so unsettling was the contradiction . . .*
>
> *Yes, crying seems almost more natural than such carefree immersion in the stream of feeling that flows from the songs.*

> * *She was awaiting her deportation [Pencil addition at bottom of page].*

Although Marianne's self-discipline was implicit in the restraint of her own letters, it was clearly evident to perceptive outside observers as well. As Uri Weinberg told me in Jerusalem, 'She could keep herself. I can also.' The soldier weeps, but Artur and Marianne, with iron self-control, kept their feelings and thoughts to themselves.[57] Just as in Berlin, but now in even more difficult circumstances, Marianne managed to concentrate on the present and set aside her burdensome knowledge of terror and loss. This capacity for self-control and ruthless focusing was a crucial weapon in her armoury for survival and was later transmuted into a strategy for dealing with the past.

In November, Marianne visited Artur Jacobs, seeking courage to face an impending Gestapo interrogation. Jacobs noted:[58]

*Earlier with Marianne – in personal difficulties. She has to attend tomorrow. Perhaps something minor – perhaps not. One has to be ready for anything.*

*She was very calm.*

Meeting Marianne on 31 December, just after the desperate news about Ernst had reached Essen, Artur Jacobs could only shake his head at Marianne's rigid composure:[59]

*Strange the way the girl is, with her apparent calm.*

*Terrible things must be going on inside – how could it be otherwise?*

*But on the outside she keeps up the conventions, like a suit of armour that prevents the failing body from collapsing.*

*How much more natural one would find any kind of wild cry. But perhaps this is the best part of conventional behaviour. Otherwise, such a young person would fall apart.*

*And yet one senses that she is frozen, rather than finding release in sorrow and experiencing new life and depth.*

*On the one hand total pessimism, which brusquely rejects every consoling word, every tiny trace of hope, even the smallest shadow of a possible way forward. On the other, a web of illusions in which the soul staggers around like a drunkard, with no sense of reality.*

Marianne herself was aware of how strange her calm demeanour must have seemed to others. She noted in her diary:[60]

*Sometimes they must all think that the most important things barely affect me (that's the feeling I have), but I push everything deep down and let no one near.*

If Jacobs was impressed with Marianne, she, for her part, was increasingly influenced by the Bund. To me she said, 'It really was the most formative influence on my life.'[61] In her diary and letters of the time she was naturally extremely cautious about mentioning her contacts with the group. True, we find a former nurse of the Jewish Community, Sister Tamara (not Jewish herself), with whom Marianne was in correspondence, expressing her pleasure in spring 1943 at learning that Marianne had found a regular sanctuary at the Blockhaus in Essen-Stadtwald.[62] But for the most part, contemporary evidence of the Bund's influence on Marianne is less direct. From November 1942, for example, Marianne's diary displays a new interest in the wider political and military picture. Of course, the changing military situation began to offer a glimmer of hope with the result that, in any case, world news was now more palatable and worthy of note. Nevertheless, it is noticeable that, from then on, Marianne's diary is interspersed with descriptions of national and international affairs. Elements of the Bund's ethical teaching also appear from this time. Here she is, writing in her diary in response to a new threat from the Gestapo:

*Yesterday they gave me a moment of fear. I received some orders, well, I can tell you the details later, I hope it's all sorted out. But the thing about it is: one simply has to submit to whatever happens. The question of lawful or unlawful is an illusion. One has to build one's own ethical code to live by. It is so important that one can justify one's actions to oneself and say: it was right. Whatever the consequences. The world is unpredictable and unjust and therefore one must be at peace with oneself.*

This approach to ethics and the law was exactly that of Artur Jacobs and the Bund – bow to force majeure when one had to, but live by one's own ethical code as far as one was able.

As Marianne sought to regain her footing after the shocking news from Izbica, she adopted Jacobs' strategy of trying to identify the root of the problem so as to make it more manageable. 'Explain, investigate, prove, understand, everything, everything. Not this permanent state of being thrown out of balance,' she wrote in January.[63] And during spring 1943, a little of her old vigour gradually returned.

## Family tensions

For Marianne, drawing closer to the Bund meant pulling away from her parents. Rather than forging family unity, the stress and strains of everyday life served further to inflame the tensions. In November 1942, conflict worsened after Marianne received a summons to visit Gestapo HQ.[64] The Gestapo had, it seems, confiscated two letters addressed to her which contained some money. The interrogation, Marianne noted in her diary, was not very serious. But, as she also noted:[65]

*It was the perfect opportunity to open my box of letters and diary entries and to go through everything and read it most carefully. Afterwards they could claim such pious reasons for having done so; for example, that there should be no incriminating material in case of a search, or worrying about me . . .*

At first, I thought it was the Gestapo who had searched through Marianne's things. But then I realized that it was the family who had done so. Marianne was left feeling violated and bitter; it felt, she said, like a rape. As a result, she cut herself off from them, and removed all her things from the house. In her diary, she wrote:[66]

*Unspoken and spoken accusations against the bad, cold daughter who shows her loved ones only ingratitude, egotism and lack of trust. I am used to them, and they affect me no more now than before.*

Fifty years later we can feel more sympathy with desperate parents, anxious about their daughter's activities at a time of such danger, seeking to understand what was going through her mind. As Dore Jacobs reported, the Bund itself had a similar philosophy:[67]

*Leave no one to their own devices. Don't rely blindly on even the most dependable; for example, in relation to their room, their letters and papers. Periodic checks essential (we called it 'house cleaning').*

In their concern that nothing should jeopardize their plans to leave the country, Marianne's parents must have seen her as rather selfish. Every risk she took could affect the fate of her brother, her parents, her aunt and uncle, her grandmother and Lore's mother. But we can also sympathize with Marianne. Her every impulse moved her to help others. Moreover, she was only nineteen and faced with the common teenage challenge of emotional disengagement from rather overbearing parents. It was her tragedy that her fight for independence had to take place under such horrendous conditions. A few days later, the violation was still very much on her mind:[68]

*I think with horror of the events of last Thursday and want to thrust them away from me as far as possible, but the memories are more resistant than I would like and make everything even more difficult than it would otherwise be. Also, they ensure that there is nothing left to tie me to my parents. I feel more burdened than I can say. I wish there were some way to make a physical separation so that I would not be continually reminded how unnatural our relationship is.*

I wonder if Marianne ever looked back at this passage. In the light of later events, it must have been unbearable.

## The Strausses observed

As 1942 became 1943, the family's protective bubble grew thinner and thinner. The remaining 'privileged' members of the community were picked off one by one for deportation. When Marianne's former boss in the Jewish Community, Fritz Ostermann, was deported to Theresienstadt in June 1943 with his wife Else and the last remaining Community officials, the Strauss family were left behind as probably the last full-Jewish family in the city, perhaps in the region.[69]

Another major source of anxiety was the increasingly intensive bombing. The industrial Ruhr area, with Essen at its heart, was a prime target for the Royal Air Force. On the night of 5 March 1943, Essen suffered something quite outside its previous range of experience. In little over an hour, 50,000 civilians were rendered homeless, 1,600 injured and 479 killed. A further 20,000 had to leave their homes temporarily. Hardly had the town begun to recover when it suffered another massive raid a week later, on 12 March. In that one night, Essen was hit by

500,000 explosive bombs and 200,000 incendiary devices, over five times the number of incendiaries dropped during the whole of 1942. For the next few weeks there was something of a lull as other cities in the region received the same treatment, but in May and July there was more heavy bombing – in July there were another 509 deaths in Essen.[70]

Denied access to the public air-raid shelters, the Strauss family took refuge in their own cellar, surrounded by packing cases full of their belongings. In our conversations, Marianne remembered the air raids as a time of terror. But she also remembered watching from the windows and fantasizing that an aeroplane might touch down and lift them away from it all.[71]

'My uncle Alfred being such a war buff, he had a map on the wall and would put little stickers in, hoping that the British would soon be licking the Germans. Every night he would sit with this map, like a general. That was his pastime, hoping for the best. Well, it kept him busy, he didn't have much else to do, unfortunately.'

Barely once in the whole of the war do the bomb attacks figure in Marianne's letters or diary. Even Artur Jacobs, so selfless and universal in his perspective, became obsessed by them for a while in 1943. It is a sign of how enormous were the other threats and pressures on Marianne that even the most damaging raids did not feature as significant events in her wartime experience.

With the growing housing shortage in Essen, the Strauss family had to share their home with even more people. Marianne told me that in March 1943 she rescued the secretary to the Jewish Community, Irene Drucker, who had become homeless, and brought her home with her son and daughter. When a mixed-marriage couple, the Rosenbergs, were assigned to a second room a month or so later, the Strausses effectively lost the use of their own ground floor.

When I was given Hanna Aron's phone number in Connecticut, and told that she had known Marianne, I did not immediately realize that Hanna was Irene Drucker's daughter, and thus someone who could give me a brief glimpse inside the Strauss household during the family's last months in Essen. In August 1998, I took a Greyhound bus down from New York to Hartford, Connecticut. That evening, Mrs Aron and I had dinner in my hotel in Farmington, and I began to learn about her life.

*Hanna Aron in Connecticut*

Though very lively, round-faced and cheerful at seventy-three, she had recently had a stroke, so I was a little worried when she drove off into the night whether she would get home. Happily, the following morning she returned to take me to her house, where we were due to tape an interview.[72]

Hanna gave the same kind of feisty account of herself as had Marianne's schoolfriends whom I interviewed in Israel. Born in 1925, she was two years younger than Marianne. In 1940–1 she had gone to the Yavne school in Cologne, and she too had found it a marvellous experience. The school was 'beautiful . . . so many lights went on, it was just gorgeous. Not the building but the people.' For a brief period after April 1942, Hanna, her parents Bernhard and Irene and her younger brother Wolfgang had been assigned to the Holbeckshof barracks. But because Hanna's mother was a convert to Judaism and thus 'racially' an Aryan, the family was allowed to return home.

In June 1942, Hanna's friend Richard Fuchs was on the deportation list to Izbica, and it was then that Hanna spent the much-discussed night with him in Holbeckshof, pleading with him to go underground. Hanna told me that on the morning of the deportation, the deportees were made to stand on the platform in the pouring rain for hours. When the train finally arrived from Cologne, where it had taken other deportees on board, the Essen Jews were soaking wet. As they boarded the train, somebody shouted that there were corpses on board. Some of the infirm pushed on to the train in Cologne must have died in the time it had taken to get to Essen.

A couple of weeks after losing Richard Fuchs, Hanna lost her father. Bernhard Drucker had been conscripted into clerical work in a warehouse in Essen-Katernberg. He died when a heavy load fell from a crane under mysterious circumstances. Another Jewish conscript was to die in similar fashion not long after. Hanna's sixteen-year-old brother Wolfgang was working on the same site and had to endure the experience of one hospital after another refusing to take his father. By the time a Catholic hospital finally deigned to admit him, it was too late.

And then came the massive air raids of March 1943. Living near the Krupp factory, the Druckers were very exposed to the risk of destruction. Hanna had a vivid memory of the night her house went up:

'We were in there and every time a bomb came down you'd hear this szhszhszhszhszh boom! This went on for twenty minutes, and it was just awful [. . .] My brother threw down a mattress from the third floor and he threw down some clothes, which we put into a big basket and that was all we saved. We couldn't save anything else. The house was burning, we had to get out. This was during the night [. . .] Krupp's had a shoe-repair shop and we sat there, all by ourselves, just crying. The next morning I don't know whether my mother went to work. I think she tried to go. And my brother and I, we were sitting alone [. . .] and Marianne came and said, you can come to us we will give you a room'.

Like an angel, Marianne had appeared, scooping the family off the pavement and inviting them back to live in Ladenspelderstrasse.

'So my mother somewhere found a *Schubkarre*, what's this in English?'
'A cart.'
'Yes, to take the little leftovers that we had because this was far away: Holsterhausen. So we pushed them on a cart, my brother and I, to

Holsterhausen . . . and so we got there and the Straussen gave us there
a front room. I remember the front room was empty, I don't think it
was empty before, they must have done this quickly. I give them so much
credit for this, you know. We had nothing, of course.'

Her mother managed to organize a couple of beds after a few weeks
and Hanna's brother slept on the floor on a mattress. By this time the
other tenants, the Rosenbergs, had moved in:

'Now there were three women who had to share the kitchen, Frau
Strauss, Frau Rosenberg and my mother. You can imagine . . . But Frau
Strauss, the *kleine* Frau Strauss, she must have been very tolerant. I can
tell you one thing, when we were in the barracks, it was always terrible
to cook in the main kitchen, but here in the Strauss house it was OK.
Everybody got along because everybody made an extra effort to get
along, you knew you couldn't get on each other's nerves.'

Hanna said Ine had been wonderful and very generous. Generous in
what sense? 'Well in sharing, the sense of, you know, women in the
kitchen, it's not easy to do. She also shared food.' Did they have food,
then? 'They had food. If you had money, you had food.' In retrospect,
Hanna felt Ine was a rather subservient wife:

'Looking back at it some years afterwards, she was the typical traditional housewife who did what the husband says. I think she got up
when he said get up and she lay down when he said lie down. Was this
Marianne's impression?'

'Not absolutely.'

'Because I always thought of her as a very obedient wife, you know. I
did not see this in my parents, but of course my parents' situation was
different. Siegfried was a big heavy strapping guy, she was a little itsy
bitsy of a woman. In public at least she always seemed to be doing what
he wanted. She was definitely the traditional housewife, no question
about it. Marianne always had fights with her father. Loud fights.'

How did Hanna know? Had the noise come down from upstairs, I
wondered. Hanna said it had. She had a notion that Marianne's mother
used to leave the room when there was a fight. What did they fight
about? Hanna said it was more ideological than anything else:

'Marianne at that time was very much into Communism. Socialism,
to put it in a more acceptable word today, you know. Communism at

that time was not a bad thing. It is today. But at that time it was not a bad thing. And Marianne really fought for the idea of equality among the people.'

This fitted very well with the impression Marianne's writings gave of her developing identity. In 1943, she must have been testing out the Bund's ideas against her parents. Not surprisingly, the solid businessman Siegfried Strauss didn't like the sound of it at all. Hanna had some sympathy for Siegfried:

'It must have been terrible, you know, for the men too, can you imagine? To be at home day after day. First of all, with your wife; I mean, I married you for better or worse but not for lunch and here you have the men sitting there all day long. And with no outlet, nowhere to go really, nothing to do. It must have been terrible.'

But for company, Hanna preferred Alfred and Lore. They were not quite so stiff as Siegfried and Ine.

After we finished the interview, I took some photos of Hanna outside her house. She lived in the sort of classic leafy American suburb that I knew from a thousand films. It was an area where one would be absolutely lost without a car. When Hanna had her stroke, she told me that the brief spectre of carlessness had been a terrifying prospect. In this area, I felt, to take away your car ownership was almost to take away your citizenship. Not for the first or last time, I heard an odd echo. For a moment, I caught a glimpse of the ageing process as a malevolent regime, gradually, incrementally laying down new restrictive laws and ordinances – shutting down this right, that pleasure, blocking off opportunities and marking out the victims.

That evening, a friend of Hanna's collected me from the hotel and drove me to the temple. At the synagogue, I met up with Hanna, her son Michael and Michael's wife and children. Hearing Hanna's enthusiastic participation in the service was a particular pleasure. It established a different kind of connection to her former self, giving a different resonance to the answers she had given to my questions about Jewish identity. For Hanna, those 'lights that went on' in the Yavne had never gone out.

I had agreed to give a brief talk after the service about Marianne's story and about Hanna's relationship to her. Afterwards, I didn't feel particularly happy with my talk. I wasn't sure that you could turn a

Holocaust experience into Sabbath evening fare. It seemed somehow American to believe that you ever could. But Hanna looked radiant. Earlier, she had told me about the crying fits she had had in past years about 'how they destroyed us'. If the public narration of the past gave her some satisfaction, I felt she was well entitled to it.

There was one other remarkable moment in the question and answer session. Someone stood up and said he had been a good friend of Heinz Krombach. They had taken gymnastics classes together in the Krombachs' front room. It seemed I could arrive on any foreign shore in the world and find that a small piece of Marianne's past had washed up there.

# 9

# The Escape

For almost four and a half years the Strauss family had sat and waited. Their attempts to leave the country had met with reversal after reversal. But sometime in spring 1943, they gained new reason to hope. Marianne's recollection was that the Abwehr had obtained visas for them to go to Sweden. The records show, though, that the Gestapo believed the family was poised to go to Switzerland.[1] Since I knew that Switzerland had become the prime destination for the Abwehr's protective efforts, I thought that Marianne had probably misremembered. Subsequently, however, I found ample evidence that the family had indeed set its sights on Sweden. The Abwehr may have deliberately kept the Gestapo in the dark. The Gestapo's information was that the Strauss family was due to depart on 30 August 1943. Possibly the Gestapo was as misinformed about the timing as about the destination.

The Deutsche Bank records in Frankfurt show that in May 1943 Siegfried emptied his account with the Deutsche Bank – showing that he really was expecting to leave the country very soon.[2] He sold his last assets – RM65,000 in securities held in his blocked account – with the proceeds going to a notary, Ivor Morting, in Sweden, the son-in-law of Ine's distant relative Grete Sander. The Deutsche Bank confirmed the instruction on 10 May, noting that the securities had been accepted by the Deutsche Golddiskontbank at the usual exchange rate of 4 per cent. With a loss of value of 96 per cent, the transfer produced only 4,368 Swedish kronor.[3] Another transfer of RM32,626.95 netted some 2,192 kronor.[4] On 2 June, Alfred wrote to the Deutsche Bank, asking for his remaining bank holdings to be converted too. Because he had to pay RM21,908 flight tax, his assets of over RM75,000 were reduced to a yield of just 3,700 kronor.[5]

There is further evidence that the family was poised to leave. On 23 June, Sister Tamara wrote to Marianne, rather incautiously naming her destination: 'I personally fear very much that I shall not find you there in late autumn. For *you* I wish *deeply* that you soon land in Sweden,'[6] and going on to enthuse about the qualities of the country and the possibilities for Marianne to use her child-caring talents and energies there. She also hoped that Marianne would convey a message to her former colleague, Julie Koppel.

On 2 July, bank director Wilhelm Hammacher wrote to the Gestapo asking permission to buy the Strausses' furniture. The letter explained that the family would soon be emigrating, and that Hammacher himself had been bombed out. Attached was a note signed by Siegfried Strauss, listing the furniture he wished to sell.[7] On 19 July the Gestapo agreed.[8] The family also deposited goods in various places for collection after the war. The Jürgens received for safe-keeping several trunks, containing clothes, linen, silver, pictures, chairs, other furniture and some Persian rugs. Business papers were left with Herr Hammacher.[9]

The Bund gave Marianne its good wishes and a more practical offer. Artur Jacobs told her that, if it came to the crunch, she should turn to the Bund for help. Something which Marianne never told me, and which I can no longer fully corroborate, was reported to me by Bund member Tove Gerson. Tove, by 1943 safe in the USA with her half-Jewish husband, herself heard it only after the war from another Bundist, Else Bramesfeld, a life-long friend of Marianne's who died long before I had a chance to meet her. So the story, at two removes, may be apocryphal, but it has the ring of Artur Jacobs' honest clarity. Apparently, Artur said to Marianne, 'You can't save your parents, but you can save yourself.'[10]

Everything seemed set for emigration, yet Marianne did take one precautionary step, though we know neither why nor how she did it. On 12 August 1943 she obtained – or perhaps renewed – an international postal ID card, made out to Marianne Strauss, leaving out the obligatory

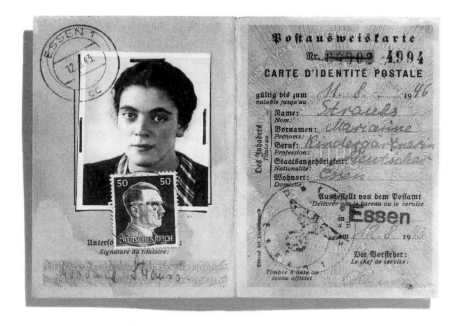

*Marianne's wartime pass*

'Sara' and thus all visible sign that she was Jewish. The card identified her as a *Kindergärtnerin*, resident in Essen.

## The SS, the Abwehr and the Strauss brothers

Until July 1943, the Gestapo's efforts to pierce the Strauss brothers' protective shield continued to fail. On 27 May, the Düsseldorf Gestapo sent a telegram to Berlin, stating that there seemed little prospect of the Strauss family leaving Germany and asking if they could be included in the next deportation to Theresienstadt.[11] From other Gestapo files we know that a transport was due to leave on 16 June 1943.[12] But when Eichmann replied on 9 June, stating that he had again approached the Oberkommando of the Wehrmacht, he once more asked the Düsseldorf office to hold fire.[13] Nevertheless, the local officials may have been encouraged by Eichmann's involvement to think the matter would be soon resolved. They fielded an enquiry from the Düsseldorf Finance Office as to whether the Strausses would soon be evacuated[14] with a telephone call to say they would hold off replying formally for about three weeks. They clearly hoped that three weeks was sufficient time for Eichmann to confirm the Strausses' deportation.[15] But by the end of July, they were still unable to respond.

As Eichmann's interventions in the Strausses' case have shown, the RSHA had been questioning the Abwehr's use of Jewish agents ever since 1941. In February 1942, Heinrich Himmler complained directly to Hitler about it. In summer 1942, however, the Abwehr's chief, Admiral Wilhelm Canaris, had been able to regain some of the initiative. An espionage disaster and the death of several German agents had led Hitler to make a wild comment proposing the use of 'criminals or Jews' for such work. But by early 1943, the SD began Operation 'Deposit Account', reviewing the Abwehr's use of Jews as agents. In June 1943, Dietrich Bonhoeffer, at that stage held in an army prison in Berlin-Tegel, was interrogated on the matter. It seems that sometime in July Hitler also explicitly rejected using Jews for espionage work.[16]

Then, Himmler made a rather surprising deal with the increasingly powerless Canaris. Himmler had his own reasons for not wanting to dissolve the Abwehr completely – not least the fact that he was putting out peace feelers, and needed the Abwehr to act as go-between with the Allies. The Abwehr was allowed to survive, but the quid pro quo was that it should stop using 'unreliable elements' as agents. A reorganization followed. Hans von Dohnanyi was imprisoned and placed under investigation. Hans Oster was suspended and placed under house arrest. The registry of the Abwehr's Bremen section indicates that it received key instructions concerning the use of Jewish agents in mid-July. On 24 July, Bremen responded by letter, appending a ten-page list of the Jewish informants run by the Bremen office which has not been preserved but which, presumably, identified the Strauss brothers by name.[17]

Death sentences come in different forms. On 6 August 1943, unbeknown to the Strauss family, theirs arrived in Düsseldorf in the form of a short telegram, signed by Eichmann's deputy SS-Sturmbannführer Günther. It announced that the Wehrmacht High Command was 'no

*Gestapo telegram – Wehrmacht has no further interest in the Strauss family*

longer interested' in Siegfried and Alfred Strauss. There were no objections, 'insofar as existing guidelines allow', to including the Strauss family as well as their dependants in the evacuations.[18] A couple of days later, these instructions were passed on to Essen, but with a macabre twist. The draft text of the letter to Essen said that there was now no reason to *include* the Strauss family in the evacuation measures. Perhaps the Gestapo officials were confused by their own euphemisms, mixing up 'emigration' (survival) with 'evacuation' (murder). In any case, a stroke of the pencil hastily changed the reprieve to a death sentence:[19]

*There are no longer any grounds for ~~including~~ excluding the Strauss brothers and their families ~~in~~ from the evacuation measures.*

The Essen Gestapo was instructed to prevent the Strauss family's emigration and to await further directions with regard to a transport to Theresienstadt. An additional memo on 8 August, some two months after the initial enquiry, advised the Düsseldorf Finance Office to abandon the transfer of funds.[20]

Whether Siegfried and Alfred received warnings of the change in their status, we do not know. Marianne's memory was that, up to the end, they were still expecting to leave in a few days' time. They may have suspected something was wrong on 30 August, if that really was their departure date, since they did not receive their passports. On that same day, Kriminalsekretär Kosthorst of the Essen Gestapo telephoned his superiors in Düsseldorf to warn them that the Strauss family might well try to make a run for it; it was decided to imprison them on the 31st.[21] The family was once again within reach of the 'gravedigger's spade'.

Could they, should they, have got away earlier? Were they still finessing, waiting for the last transfers of money to be effected, however pitiful the amount to be paid into the Swedish accounts? In May, Siegfried had authorized the sale of his final assets. But Alfred's transfer of assets, though initiated in June, was not finalized until 24 August.[22] Had the brothers really been waiting for the funds to clear? According to a letter from Wilhelm Hammacher after the war, 'The chance to leave the country had existed since the beginning of 1943. Why the unfortunate victims should have hesitated so long is something I wonder about to this day.'[23] But Hammacher's testimony is not really to be trusted. In the context of Marianne's restitution claims on Strauss family property in his possession, he had a strong interest in emphasizing the quality of his aid. The failure, he was trying to argue, lay not in the degree of support provided but in the family's own unwillingness to leave. I was not sure if I should simply discount his letter. What held me back from doing so, though, was that Hammacher's assertion was so reminiscent of the Strauss family's reluctance to leave in the earlier period. It is just possible that their assets were still delaying their departure in 1943.

Amongst Marianne's papers I found a copy of a letter sent in 1961 from Ernst Dahl, Lore's brother in Canada, to Marianne's cousin René Wolf in France. These two, together with Marianne, were Alfred and Lore's surviving legal heirs. From Ernst Dahl's letter, I learned that in the summer of 1943 Alfred had not simply transferred money to Sweden – he had sent on some of his suits. I understood Alfred's logic: if the brothers were going to live in Sweden and seek employment there, they would need respectable clothing. After reading about so many family disappointments, I found this evidence of careful bourgeois planning right up to the end almost unbearable.

The clothes arrived in Stockholm and awaited their owner for the rest of the war.[24]

## A few minutes before 12

Among Marianne's papers are several drafts of the article she published in *Das Münster am Hellweg*. With very minor differences they all say that on 31 August at 10 a.m. two of the most feared members of the local Gestapo, Kriminaloberassistent Kosthorst[25] and Kriminaloberassistent Hahn, appeared at Ladenspelderstrasse 47. They gave the family two hours to prepare for a forthcoming transport. The arrival of the Gestapo, Marianne wrote, was like a bolt from the blue. Up to that moment, the family had still been expecting to get away in the next few days. Now, in just two hours, they had to adjust to their new fate and scramble everything together for deportation.

Shortly before midday, Marianne's father passed her a few hundred marks, which she stuffed into the pocket of her tracksuit.[26] Meanwhile, the Gestapo went down into the cellar to inspect the substantial family belongings stored there in packing cases. Seizing her chance, and without being able to say goodbye to the family, Marianne slipped down the stairs to the front door and left:

'I ran for my life, expecting a pistol shot behind me any minute. But it had always seemed to me better to end my life like that than to await an unimaginable fate in Auschwitz or Łodz, Treblinka or Izbica. But there was no shot, nobody running after me, no order, no shout!'

In our conversations, Marianne added a few details to the picture. She told me that when the Gestapo arrived, a friendly churchman, Pastor Keinath, was visiting the family.[27] He hid on the balcony and tried to get away while the Gestapo were down in the cellar. Unfortunately, the stairs squeaked. Marianne said that when the Gestapo appeared, Keinath looked like a ghost. After answering questions he was allowed to go. Marianne's memory was that he got away with a heavy fine, which the church paid, perhaps because Keinath's wife was related to Bishop Galen. We know that Keinath survived because Marianne remained in friendly contact with him until his death, and afterwards continued to correspond with his family.[28] What struck me as odd about this story at the time was that if Keinath had tried and failed to escape while the Gestapo were in the cellar, it seemed almost unimaginable that, having apprehended him, *both* officials would later have returned to the cellar, or that Marianne herself would have attempted and succeeded with exactly the same ruse.

The family were not told the destination of the transport. They were given to understand, though, that it was Theresienstadt.[29] Marianne's mother put on her one pair of sensible footwear, a sturdy pair of walking shoes. But one of the Gestapo men said it wasn't worth her putting the boots on, they'd have them off her at the police station before she was sent away. Marianne erupted. Weren't they taking enough of the family's property without taking the clothes off their backs as well? She remembered the Gestapo official standing on the stairs and drawing a pistol. Marianne said, go on shoot me, it's better than going off on a transport. In our last interview, she said that it was this episode that made her realize she would be a liability for her family.[30]

In our conversations, Marianne added that when the Gestapo arrived, her father had slipped her a wad of 200-mark notes which he had in the house, 'which was naturally illegal'[31]. She couldn't remember the exact amount, but felt that it ran to several thousands. 'I swore that he would get it back in its entirety when he came back.'[32] She told her father she wanted to run and asked if she could take Richard. Her father agreed, but Richard wouldn't go. In Marianne's written account, when the Gestapo went into the cellar (again), she saw her moment, caught sight of her mother in the kitchen and gave a brief wave. Her mother nodded, the front door opened noiselessly, and she was gone.

Once she had made it down the street, Marianne criss-crossed through different parts of Essen so that, if she were being followed, her pursuers would not know where she was headed. She kept to side-streets, put on a scarf and even varied her usual gait. She telephoned from a call box to a contact number her father had given her. She remembered having heard that it belonged to the head of the Canaris group, who lived with his butler in some style. 'I don't know who answered the phone, a man answered, and I asked if I could speak to so and so.' Marianne used a code she'd been given. She was not sure if the person at the other end knew what she was talking about. If he did, he did not let on. Marianne told him her family was in jail in Essen. Then she hung up quickly and ran on.

I asked her if she could remember what went through her mind as she left the house. She said she only had one thought:[33]

'To get away. I was expecting any minute now, absolutely – I was quite clear about that – that there would be some shooting and I would have had it. But that's what I wanted . . . To go to one of the camps was to me one of the most horrifying, nightmarish things and I just could not, I just could not do that.'

For the rest of that day she stayed with a former assistant of David Krombach. Later, I learned that she may also have dropped in on Martin Schubert, a Krupp manager with links to the Bund.[34] As night fell, Marianne made her way to Essen-Stadtwald. Jacobs had suggested that in the event of having to make a run for it, Marianne should go to the Blockhaus to stay with Sonja Schreiber, which she now did.

Thinking about Marianne's escape, it struck me that this was not a period of technological surveillance. Nowadays – though ironically this is truer of a country like Britain, where the lack of a public commitment to civil liberties has allowed video and close-circuit cameras far greater intrusion than in Germany – it would not be possible to run away from the house and not be spotted. The Gestapo staffs were surprisingly limited and, indeed, the same two or three officials have surfaced regularly in this story. They relied for their effectiveness on denunciations from the public.[35] The fact that no police reinforcements were used also shows that the Gestapo was accustomed to depending on the passivity of its victims. Two officials were considered quite enough to keep an eye on the eight members of the Strauss entourage.

## The Gestapo reports Marianne's disappearance

Only at 11 o'clock on the morning after the escape did the Essen Gestapo summon the courage to cable their superiors in Düsseldorf:[36]

> *Telegram. Gestapo Essen Office to Stapoleitstelle Düsseldorf, 1.9.1943 11.07*
>
> *Re: Evacuation of the Jews Strauss.*
>
> *Refers: Telephone instructions from 30.8.1943.*
>
> *The Jewess Marianne Sara Strauss, born 7.6.1923, resident here Ladenspelderstrasse, due to be taken into custody for the purpose of evacuation to Theresienstadt, has escaped. A letter to her parents found here, runs: 'I am not going with you, I am taking my life, God protect you, Marianne.'*
> *Signed, Nohles*

Because I found these documents only after Marianne's death, I couldn't ask her about the suicide note. The Gestapo officials may have invented it – no copy of the note appears in her file. A dead Jew was less of an admission of failure than one on the run. I discovered that after the war the Gestapo official Kosthorst himself disappeared, faking his own suicide with a note, so perhaps Marianne's too stemmed from his imagination.[37]

On the same day, the Düsseldorf Gestapo (now based in nearby Ratingen because of bomb damage to their headquarters) cabled Theresienstadt:[38]

*Urgent, present immediately.*

*Re: change of address of Jews to Theresienstadt*

*Refers: Telegram 31.8.1943*

*For technical reasons the Transport of the Jews in the above-mentioned telegram cannot take place on 6.9.1943 but only on 9.9.1943. Consequently, the transport will arrive in Theresienstadt on 8.9.1943 with the normal timetabled D-Train at 2.57.*
*Confirmation is requested.*

Not noticing that Düsseldorf had designated an arrival time a day before departure, Theresienstadt cabled back acceptance. Only a day later was the error spotted in Düsseldorf and a correction made.

The mere three-day delay shows that the Gestapo assumed Marianne would not last long on her own. They did not believe anybody would shelter her for any length of time. As Marianne learned later from the Druckers, after sealing up the Strauss family apartments Gestapo officials kept returning to Ladenspelderstrasse 47 at different times of the day and night in the expectation of finding her there.[39]

On 3 September, Kosthorst evidently felt compelled to make a lengthier report about the escape:[40]

*On 31 August 1943, accompanied by Kriminaloberassistent Hahn, I made my way to the apartment of the Jews Strauss. I informed them of the impending expulsion to Theresienstadt. I gave the Jews a fixed-time period by which to pack the things to take with them. During the packing, I supervised the family of Siegfried Israel Strauss living on the first floor (five people). Kriminalober-assistent Hahn supervised the family of Alfred Israel Strauss (three people) on the second floor. For the purpose of taking food for the journey I allowed the Jewess Marianne Sara Strauss to go to the kitchen in the ground floor. She then left the house in an unsupervised moment. After about five minutes, her absence was noticed. The aforementioned farewell note was discovered in the hall.*
*Signed, Kosthorst.*

This was slightly different from Marianne's account. Marianne had remembered the corrupt officials rooting around for loot among the family possessions in the cellar. Kosthorst seemed to be concealing the dereliction behind a picture of the humane Oberkriminalassistent allowing the daughter of the house to get food. His trust had been abused by the deceitful Jewess. Encountering this document in the reading room of the Düsseldorf State Archives, it struck me that I was probably the first person to read it who knew it contained a lie.

Not long after seeing the Gestapo records, I spoke with Lilli Arras. She had met Marianne once or twice after the war and Marianne had told her about her escape. Completely unprompted, Lilli told me how the Gestapo had been with the family and Marianne had asked to go and get bread and had then disappeared. Suddenly, it seemed the Gestapo story was true. And that on this point Marianne's account was inaccurate.

## Later echoes of the escape

Lilli Arras was not the only person to whom Marianne had said something about what happened that day. When I talked to her friends from Liverpool and surviving relatives, I found that they generally knew about her escape even if they knew little else about her past. By and large, their recollections closely resembled Marianne's written account: the Gestapo in the cellar, her quick escape down the stairs and out of the front door. Some understood that she might have gone through a back door or climbed out of a window. Her second cousin, Robert Selig, emailed me from Denmark:[41]

*Marianne never mentioned her past and any information I have about it comes from other sources, mainly my parents. As far as I know, she lived in Essen with her parents, her grandmother and her younger brother Richard. The Gestapo (or possibly other police) came to arrest them, but Marianne climbed out of a window at the rear of the house and escaped. She wanted to take her brother with her, but her mother would not allow it as he was thought to be too young. She spent the*

Essen, den 3. September 1943.

Betrifft: Flucht der Jüdin Marianne Sara S t r a u s s ,
geboren am 7. 6. 1923 in Essen, wohnhaft hier, Laden=
spelderstr. 47.

--------

Am 31. 8. 1943 begab ich mich mit dem Krim.-Ober-Assistenten
H a h n in die Wohnung der Juden S t r a u s s , um sie von
der bevorstehenden Abschiebung nach Theresienstadt in Kenntnis
zu setzen. Ich gab den Juden eine befristete Auflage zum Packen
der mitzunehmenden Sachen. Während des Einpackens beaufsichtigte
ich die Angehörigen der in der 1. Etage wohnenden Familie Sieg=
fried Israel Strauss (5 Personen), während Krim.-Ober-Assistent
H a h n die in der 2. Etage wohnenden Angehörigen der Familie
Alfred Israel Strauss (3 Personen) beaufsichtigte. Zwecks Mit=
nahme der Reiseverpflegung hatte ich der Jüdin Marianne Sara
Strauss gestattet, die im Erdgeschoss gelegene Küche aufzusuchen.
Sie hat dann in einem unbewachten Augenblick das Haus verlassen.
Nach etwa 5 Minuten wurde ihr Fehlen festgestellt. Im Hausflur
wurde der bereits erwähnte Abschiedsbrief vorgefunden.

Krim.-Sekretär.

Geheime Staatspoli
Staatspolizeitelli.tle Düsseldorf
Außenbienstelle Essn        - 6. SEP. 1943   Essen, den 3. September 1943.
II B 4/4472/43.
B

Urschriftlich

der Staatspolizeileitstelle Düsseldorf

in

R a t i n g e n

gemäss fernmündlicher Anordnung vorgelegt.

Im Auftrage:

*Gestapo report on Marianne's escape*

*next years living underground until she walked into a British camp near the front line.*

I assumed the details that differed from Marianne's original had simply been misreported by the listeners. Indeed, the story of her walking into a British camp near the front line was so at odds with what actually happened that Marianne could never have asserted it. But among her restitution papers I found a declaration made by Marianne herself in 1961 to the effect that she had jumped out of a window. This made me wonder if Selig's comment that Regina had been unwilling for Richard to go had also emanated from Marianne.[42]

## Flight from memory

The escape was one of the two most vivid and traumatic episodes of Marianne's life. The memory never really left her. Above all, it stood under the twin stars of liberation and betrayal. It was both the moment of decision, when her survival was balanced on a knife-edge, and the moment when she abandoned her family, probably for ever. It was a moment etched into Marianne's consciousness.

And yet her account of the escape began to change relatively early on. In 1984, when her article was published in *Das Münster am Hellweg*, it was no surprise that a woman in her sixties should have lost track of a few details of an event that had happened over forty years before. But, in fact, in the context of restitution proceedings we find Marianne making a written declaration as early as 1957, and under oath referring to the Gestapo as being in the cellar.[43] A few years later, she made another declaration containing a slightly different version; this time she left the house by the window.[44] Within a few years of the end of the war, the details were slipping and changing.

Three key aspects of leaving the house were ambiguous. There was the issue of how premeditated the escape was. In Marianne's published account, her escape appeared as a last-minute decision, with her father slipping her cash just before. In her verbal account to me she said she had received the money early on, and her decision to leave was made after she had the altercation with the Gestapo on the stairs. Then there was the question why Richard did not go with her. In the published account, the issue is not raised. In conversation, Marianne said that Richard did not want to come. The Seligs heard that Ine would not allow it. Finally, there was the question of how she got out of the house. The episode of Marianne asking whether she could get some bread seemed too powerful and memorable to have 'gone into hiding' from her memory.

At this stage, I had no real theory about why Marianne should have lost this particular memory. But I was already beginning to feel that the traumas of separation were at once the most painful and the most elusive events in Marianne's enormous collection of sad memories. I could see strong echoes of the way Marianne's account of Ernst's departure had evolved. Here was another painful moment of separation. Perhaps, too, here was another 'borrowed' journey in the sense that Pastor Keinath's attempted escape while the Gestapo was in the cellar had metamorphosed into her own path to flight, just as Hanna Aron's night in Holbeckshof had become her own last journey with Ernst. But why should Marianne have been borrowing other people's journeys? That I did not yet understand.

## And that was it

I had read and heard Marianne's own accounts. I had consulted those close to her to whom she had spoken at various times from the 1940s to the 1980s. And I had worked through the Gestapo records with all their astounding (though sometimes mendacious and often misleading) detail. I felt I had found more evidence about an escape from an ordinary house in wartime Nazi Germany than even the most obsessive historian could require.

Then I spoke to Hanna Aron:[45]

'As a matter of fact, the day they were picked up I had played hooky.[46] And I had gone to a movie theatre in Essen West, which was of course forbidden. I had taken off my star, gone to see the movie, come back home and when I came in the door – there are the stairs, there, just like these stairs. When you came into the house you could see right into the kitchen and up the flight of stairs – when I came in I immediately saw Mr Hahn from the Gestapo standing there. I knew him quite well and he knew me. And I went to the right, past the kitchen, into our room because I'd seen him and, boy, was I in dire straits because I had taken the star off! Well, I put it on and he came into the room right away, and he saw that I had just put it on there with a pin. And he said to me, "You know, I could send you to camp right away." I don't know, I think I apologized, I must have, very low key, being so afraid. Somebody must have called my mother at work. It certainly wasn't me, because "You stay in the room!" So of course I did, being so afraid. I think it was Rosenberg who called my mother and she came home. And when she walked into our room, Herr Hahn came in again and told her what had happened. That he had caught me without the star and so forth.

'But before my mother came home, before, Marianne opened the door of the room. She looked in and I was sitting there, you know, very afraid, just sitting there, frightened. Marianne opens the door, looks in, and makes a movement with her head, doesn't say anything. Leaves the door a little bit ajar. And I think, what the heck is she doing now?! I am in so much trouble already! I didn't think any more about her. Then my mother was home and when Hahn came into the room she said to him, "Herr Hahn can we leave?" And he said, "Yes, you can leave." And she took me and we went to these friends that we had in Essen West. Later we came home, it was dark already and we had of course the curfew[ . . .]

'We came back and Herr Rosenberg, Fritz, was all upset. "My God, Frau Drucker, you don't know what happened!" "What happened, what is so terrible?" "Marianne ran away! And if they catch her, they'll kill her!" And my mother smiled and said, "Thank God, at least she got away." So then he told us that by the time they were ready to leave, everybody had their things together, Marianne was not there, she was not to be found, and then they realized the front door was open. She had left through the front door, carrying nothing with her, leaving the front door ajar not to make any noise. And she must have gone out of the house very silently, you know. And Rosenberg was so upset about it and my mother said to him, "Fritz, you know, I can't get very excited about it, it's good for her that she left."

[. . . ]

'The next day the Gestapo came, they took everything that wasn't nailed down. They took the artwork, they took the huge steamer trunks that weren't in the basement. I saw it myself. And they worked hard at it because those trunks were heavy.'

Hanna wasn't sure where the Gestapo were at the point when Marianne left. She felt that Marianne had probably left just after poking her head round Hanna's door. Later, it occurred to me that this raised the problem that Hanna and her mother seemed to have gone out between the moment Marianne left the house and the moment when others found the door ajar. I wrote to her about this, and she said that she and her mother found the door open and left it so. But whether this was a genuine memory or something she felt she had to come up with to fit my question, I wasn't sure.

Her memory pushed the evidence forward a little on two points. One, Marianne had certainly used the door and not the window. Second, no one in the house mentioned that Marianne had left a note. 'No, nothing, nothing, absolutely nothing,' Hanna said. 'She just looked into my room and afterwards I realized she had been saying goodbye.' So it did look as if this element of the Gestapo communication might have been a lie.

Hanna said that when her mother came home she saw Ine in the kitchen. And what did Ine say?

'Well, I don't know but I think they embraced, cried a little bit.'

'Did your mother say this, or this is just a sense that you have?' I asked.

'No, this is what my mother said. First of all, you couldn't do very much in front of the Gestapo, and you didn't want to let yourself go. Because once you start crying, you can't stop. So I think Ine pretty much kept a stiff upper lip and my mother probably also, you know. They just hugged each other, and that was it.'

# 10

# Memories Underground:
# August 1943 – Spring 1944

For a long time, my perception of the dangers and stress of Marianne's escape was focused on what lay behind her, on the risks and pain of leaving. I thought of the trauma of abandoning her parents and Richard. I imagined her spine arched in anticipation of the pistol shot from behind. I thought of the chance that someone on Ladenspelderstrasse might see her running and do what the Gestapo relied upon Germany's citizens to do: inform on her. These were the threats, the uncertainties that I imagined going through her head.

But when after some months I listened again to the tape Marianne and I had made in September 1996, I heard something which had not initially caught my attention. Marianne said of the Bund's offer to help her:[1]

'Maybe somebody else would have felt squeamish about it and thought, well, people say these things and they don't mean them. But I took that risk, you see. And I thought, if they don't want me they can say so. But by that time I knew Artur well enough to think I could believe that they did mean it. And there you are, they saw me through.'

She sighed audibly on the tape and I realized the obvious. At the moment of escape, Marianne was not at all sure if the Bund would be willing or able to help her. She was fleeing into the unknown. What she faced was as uncertain and threatening as what lay behind her was traumatic and dangerous.

The day before Marianne's escape, Bund members had held one of their summer meetings. Artur Jacobs was full of concerns. A few days earlier, a card had arrived from his son's Amsterdam landlady to say that Gottfried had been missing for weeks. Artur had sent letters to the German consul and to the police in Amsterdam. Now at the end of August came the news of Gottfried's arrest.[2] But typically, his anxieties about Gottfried did not prevent Artur from taking the keenest interest in his neighbours, and in Marianne's fate in particular. The Bund would remain true to its word.

A day or two after her escape Artur noted in his diary:[3]

*Marianne is in the Blockhaus. She eluded disaster at the last minute.*

*What an upright, mature, intelligent, active, courageous young person! And one discerns hardly a glimmer of what she's going through!*

*What people like her have learned to deal with! And with unbroken courage.*

*That young people of this calibre can still evolve, even in such an environment should make us think. It is proof, surely, that good seeds will germinate in the most unpropitious soil.*

*Marianne: again and again, she simply amazes me. The thought of all she carries on her shoulders! She stands there unbowed, with her heavy burden and an uncertain and difficult life before her . . .*

*What sources does she have to draw on? First, there is the boundless energy of the young; second, a certain caution in expressing her views which she has learned to practise since childhood; and, not least, the strength built up during a long period of suffering and growth.*

## The Blockhaus

On the evening of 31 August 1943, Marianne arrived at the Blockhaus. When I went there in the summer of 1997 to take photographs, I realized that it was only a quarter of a mile away from where I had once lived in Essen. The hill which Marianne must have climbed was one I had walked up and down many times. But the Blockhaus had never caught my attention – and I would not have understood its significance even if it

*The Blockhaus*

had. Now, of course, the little wooden building, clearly unchanged since Marianne's time, was bursting with significance. And yet, for passers-by, it was a nondescript structure, perhaps slightly out of place, on an ordinary suburban street with little Sunday traffic. The Dore Jacobs school, which – with the exception of the Nazi years – had used the Blockhaus as its premises since 1927, was closed for the summer holidays. So I was left to contemplate alone the irony that of all the buildings in which Marianne had lived, the only one to have survived was made entirely of wood.

In May 1999, I was back at the Blockhaus, this time to interview Karin Gerhard, the Dore Jacobs school director. Inside, I discovered that the building was almost exactly as it had been during the war. Seeing my excitement, Frau Gerhard gave me a tour. For once, I was able to move through rooms in which Marianne had lived during that time – the little kitchen, the bedroom where she stayed, the hall where the Catholic church had held services. For a moment, the past was so present it was hard to breathe.

Almost immediately after her arrival, Marianne cut and bleached her hair because she had heard from Frau Drucker that the Gestapo had put up a wanted poster for her.[4] Many who met her during the war years retained an abiding vision of Marianne's vital, animated face and her reddish hair. For the moment, though, Marianne had little human contact with anyone apart from her host, Sonja Schreiber. Marianne felt immediately that the forty-nine-year-old Sonja had taken on responsibility for her; indeed, Sonja became her substitute mother.[5]

Sonja Emmi Schreiber was one of many socially conscious middle-class women drawn to the Bund. Born in 1894, the daughter of an Essen town councillor, she attended Marianne's school, the Luisenschule, some thirty years before Marianne. She studied in Bonn and at the left-leaning Frauenakademie in Düsseldorf, and was a member of the free German youth movement. After the First World War she taught at an experimental, non-denominational school in Essen-Rellinghausen. Like many others, she was drawn to Artur Jacobs' circle by his lectures on Kant at the Volkshochschule; she became one of the Bund's founders and a member of its inner circle.[6]

From 1927 until the last years of her life, Sonja lived in the Blockhaus. Dore's school was closed down after 1933 and the practice rooms in the building were handed over to the Catholic church in Essen-Stadtwald. The church held services there and organized a kindergarten in the building. But Sonja lived on in the rooms upstairs, which became a place of refuge for those helped by the Bund. In 1940, Sonja had been denounced to the Gestapo for publicly declaring her outrage at the treatment of the Jews, and had only narrowly escaped with a warning.[7] But the experience did not make her hesitate to help Marianne.

During the day, Marianne was confined to those rooms:[8]

*I could leave the house for short walks only after dark. I was known in Essen, and denunciation represented the biggest threat to my safety and to that of everyone involved in my escape. During the day I had to stay in my little room because the kindergarten brought many outsiders into the house. Cooking soon became my responsibility and I cooked for the*

*Sonja Schreiber*

*first time in my life, mainly vegetables and salads, and above all cabbage, and also whatever Sonja got on her rations and as gifts from our friends. She shared everything with me, the danger above all.*

Only after seeing the house myself and discovering how small it was did I realize that a short, narrow staircase and a closed door were all that separated Marianne from those who might betray her.

## Last contacts with her parents

While Marianne was in the Blockhaus, her parents, brother, aunt, uncle, grandmother Anna Rosenberg and great aunt Else Dahl were held in the cells at police headquarters. A Bund member, Grete Ströter, who was at this stage living with the Jacobs in the Bund house in the Dönhof, visited the family in prison and gave them a gift from Marianne. In this way, Siegfried and Ine received silent reassurance that their daughter was free and safe with friends. Marianne told me that the contact was rendered a little easier because of another unexpected twist in the story. One of the warders turned out to be a wartime comrade of Alfred Strauss and, possibly with a bit of bribery, was willing to close an eye now and then.[9]

Even so, a visit to imprisoned Jews in 1943 was an act of enormous courage. Unfortunately, by the time I came to interview Bund members, Grete Ströter had died. I did speak to her husband, Reinhold, but he had been away in Hamburg at the time and had heard about her prison visit only after the event. Grete, like many of the Bund members, had been so discreet about her heroism that others such as Ellen Jungbluth and her step-daughter Ursula heard about her action only from me. 'Typical Grete!' said Ursula Jungbluth.

Marianne told me that the family was held for three weeks while the Gestapo returned to Ladenspelderstrasse day and night in the hope of finding her.[10] In fact (just as in relation to her father's imprisonment in Dachau and the time she had spent in Essen before the aborted deportation) a traumatic time had again expanded in her memory: her parents were held for just over a week. Marianne was dreadfully afraid that she had exposed her family to all kinds of torture. 'I put my parents at risk, I put my whole family at most dreadful risk; the Gestapo could have done anything they wanted with them.

'I don't even know how big the[ir] cell was. Quite frankly I didn't ask too many questions. I really didn't want to know. Because there was nothing I could do about it. And I had nightmares, as you can well imagine.'[11]

Aware that her parents were detained at least in part to put pressure on her, Marianne asked herself over and over whether she should give herself up:

'And then my, I don't know what it was, whether I was just yellow or whether it was my better sense, or a combination of both got the better of me and I thought: there's nothing I can do. If I join them that only does the Gestapo a favour, not my parents or me, because the Gestapo can then send them off to wherever they send them to. Whereas this way, my family is still here, while the Gestapo's hoping that they come across me somewhere so they won't have to report to Düsseldorf to the headquarters that out of eight people one went missing. That really pleased me.'

Among Marianne's restitution papers is a statement from Julia Böcker, who was ostensibly already incarcerated at police headquarters and witnessed the Strauss family's imprisonment. She wrote that she was surprised at the jewellery and other goods the Strauss family still had in its possession:[12]

*One day after they were brought in, the family was stripped completely by the Gestapo and taken into another cell. They were given only a blanket to cover themselves with. Then Gestapo officials Kosthaus [sic] and Hahn made a thorough search of the cell in which they had been previously held. They even cut through the straw mattresses to search for jewellery. Then they packed all the items they had found into the family's suitcases and took the cases with them. They left behind only underwear and clothes which the Strausses were allowed to put on again after the search.*

However, there is considerable doubt over the veracity of Frau Böcker's testimony. Another statement that she made at the same time suggesting Lore Strauss was murdered in Auschwitz was certainly not true.[13] She also claimed she could 'still assert today with absolute certainty' that Lore had a diamond ring – something which Marianne knew not to have been the case. In a subsequent statement, she dealt with the problem of how she could have known what the Gestapo took by claiming there had been a small hole in the wall through which she observed them.[14] Just as conveniently for Marianne's restitution claims, Frau Böcker claimed to have overheard the Gestapo men saying that they wanted the Strauss suits because they were 'very good suits'. The suspicion is, therefore, that Frau Böcker was a rather too obliging witness, perhaps in return for a small consideration.

Herr Hammacher also claimed to have had contact with the family in captivity. According to him, with the help of his chauffeur he was able 'continually to smuggle groceries and other goods into the prison'.[15] Marianne was sceptical. It was tendered, after all, as part of an attempt by Hammacher to strengthen his case at a post-war restitution tribunal. On the other hand, if anybody had the connections to smuggle goods into the prison, it was bank director Hammacher.

Occasionally, Marianne ventured out in the evening to try to stir the family's influential contacts into action. She wrote:[16]

*As long as my parents were in jail, I had some hope that I would be able by telephone to activate the influential figures who had protected us for so long. But in the end . . . this proved unsuccessful.*

The last time she tried to call, she 'was given a very strong indication that it would be very dangerous to contact them again. So I didn't', she said, 'and that was that'.[17]

The protection offered by Marianne's parents' world – the quiet relationships between established Jews and high-placed resistance circles – had thus indubitably failed. Now Marianne had to put her faith in the ethical socialism of the 'proletarian' Bund. Yet in a way, she none the less owed her good fortune to her father, at least in part. It was precisely because he had been a well-connected bourgeois member of the Jewish community that Marianne had been able to benefit from the Bund's protection. For a start, Artur Jacobs' concern for the plight of Essen's Jews had led him inevitably to such community leaders as David Krombach. Consequently, Jacobs was far more likely to meet those who moved in the Krombachs' circle. And as we know, only someone with clout and money, such as Siegfried Strauss, could have evaded deportation until 1943. The other Jews, the mass fodder of the deportations, were too numerous, too unknown, caught up too early in the process to have had the chance of falling into the Bund's protective net. By late 1943, with so few Jews left and clear signs that Germany was losing the war, it was psychologically possible for a group to take on the danger of sheltering individuals. This is not in any way to belittle the enormous risks taken by the Bund; but Siegfried's power and that of the circles he moved in had bought Marianne time. So now, the beautiful middle-class Jewish girl passed into the hands of the pro-proletarian Bund.

## The family dispatched

On 6 September, the Gestapo contacted the German railway authorities in Mönchen Gladbach:[18]

*To facilitate a prisoner transport we request that on 9 September 1943 (Thursday), two 3rd-class compartments in the time-tabled train DmW 311, if possible at the front of the train, be kept free and marked 'reserved'. Brief written confirmation is requested.*

The train was due to reach Dresden at around ten at night. The Strausses would travel on from Dresden just after midnight and arrive in Theresienstadt shortly before three in the morning. Pre-war Theresien-stadt, or Terezin, to give it its Czech name, was a small garrison town some forty miles north of Prague. In 1930, it had had just over 7,000 inhabitants. The garrison consisted of a number of barracks, many of them still as primitive as when they were built 150 years earlier, and a number of equally primitive private homes. Into these buildings, tens of thousands of Jews were concentrated in the first deportations in 1942. By 1943, there were over 40,000 people pressed into a ghetto 700m by 500m. Theresienstadt was designated a 'show camp' for prominent and aged Jews and some First World War veterans, but it was a model camp only in comparison with the benchmarks set by Auschwitz or Treblinka.

On 9 September, the family's hour had come. Maria Jürgens, who had enjoyed such profitable exchanges of food for family Meissen and silver, was at Essen station, whether by chance or design we do not know, and saw the family escorted on to the train. When Marianne met Maria a few days later, her description made it clear that the family, though deprived of most of their possessions, were travelling with at least some of their cases.[19] (Yet more evidence that Frau Julia Böcker had exaggerated.) A Gestapo memo from 21 September records that

'The transport took place smoothly and without incident. The Jews were escorted by Polizeisekretär Waldbillig and Polizeisekretär Pütz.'[20] RM770.42 was confiscated from the Strauss family, of which RM450 was handed over to Theresienstadt. On file is the receipt provided by Theresienstadt for the RM450.[21] The balance was paid to the Finance Office in Düsseldorf. Everything correct and in order.

One interesting legal point. I was puzzled that the Strausses' property was confiscated under the Reich Interior Ministry circular of 4 July 1942 concerning 'control of property of Jews of German nationality who have assisted measures hostile to people and nation'. The Krombachs' property had been taken away under the Reich Citizenship Law of 25 November 1941, whereby the holdings of Jews leaving the country were deemed automatically to have accrued to the Reich. Why was that law not invoked here? The answer is logical: Theresienstadt was a part of Czechoslovakia which had been made a German protectorate, and thus was not formally foreign territory. The 1941 law did not, therefore, apply, so a different decree was required.[22]

An internal Gestapo memo gave instructions for information about the family to be transferred to file cards and the remaining paperwork to be archived. The Strauss files were closed.[23]

## The hissing bomb

In the Blockhaus, Marianne was now isolated from all former friends and family. Her life in September 1943 – a life of confinement indoors, apart from a few breaths of air in the evening – briefly resembled what we imagine a life in hiding might be like, influenced by the account of Anne Frank; a life of inactivity, of frustration, perhaps also, as in the case of Anne Frank, of intense inner life. And of waiting for denunciation, discovery or liberation, whichever came first. Such extended waiting vigils undoubtedly did take place in Nazi Germany. In Berlin in particular, there were people hidden in friends' apartments, sharing a two- or three-room flat until the end of the war.[24] However, in Marianne's case, her period of immobility was quite short. Indeed, of the very small number of Jews who survived in hiding, even fewer were able to stay in one spot.[25] Ironically, what often endangered the fugitives and, certainly, what dislodged Marianne was the increasing intensity of Allied air raids. Whether Marianne could have coped with two years' enforced idleness is another question.

One evening, an incendiary bomb fell on the Blockhaus gymnasium. Before it went off, Marianne told me:

'I summoned the courage to grab the hissing bomb, cross the long hall to the window and throw it into the garden, where it exploded immediately. Possibly, I saved the Blockhaus, whose memory is so precious to me, from burning down.'

This incident brought the precariousness of Marianne's position home to everyone. Made of wood, the Blockhaus was particularly vulnerable in an air raid. And since Marianne was still so close to home, she ran a great risk of being identified any time she went outside. Behind the scenes, the Bund's inner circle debated what to do. Artur and the others felt that it was simply too dangerous for her to stay in the Blockhaus. Her time of relative security thus came to an end within a few weeks.

None the less, even after Marianne was forced to start moving, Sonja remained a pivotal figure and the Blockhaus Marianne's physical and psychological base and refuge.[26] Indeed, the weeks she spent with Sonja in September 1943 marked the beginning of a life-long friendship. After Sonja died on 27 June 1987, Marianne wrote the warmest of tributes to her Bund friends, acknowledging Sonja's love and concern for others and reminding them of what she herself owed her former protector. 'I would so have liked to embrace her once more.'[27]

## Marianne on the run

From October 1943 until February 1945, Marianne's life was characterized by a series of short stays with Bund members, occasionally with family friends or distant relatives, punctuated by journeys across Germany by train and tram. During the two years she made more than thirty, very probably more than fifty such journeys.

A novelist would accompany Marianne on her journey from place to place, family to family. The narrative would start in Braunschweig and

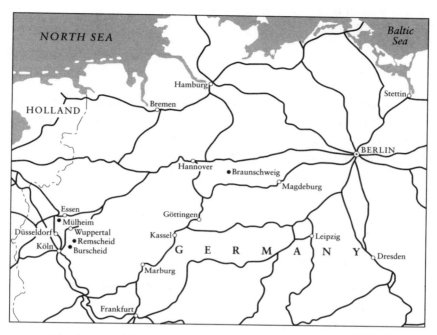

*North-central Germany in the 1930s (including principal rail*
*connections and towns where Marianne stayed)*

then move on to Göttingen, taking Marianne from the Morgensterns to
the Gehrkes, the two families the Bund leadership initially entrusted
with Marianne's care. Then, in the shorter days of winter 1943–4, when
it was easier to avoid being recognized, the story would follow her back
closer to home, as she moves between Remscheid, Wuppertal, Mülheim,
Essen and Burscheid. Here we would join her on the trams which she
used to travel between her hosts, rather than the more intensively policed
Reichsbahn.

But although we know Marianne's general destinations, we cannot
recapture Marianne's time underground in anything like a continuous
narrative, particularly in the period before April 1944. Marianne
recalled some episodes very clearly, but many were no longer accessible
to her memory. Some of her hosts had vivid memories to offer me, others
had died or were too ill to meet. What we can do is attempt to construct

a composite picture of her life underground in those first few months, and of what it meant for Marianne.

## Trams and trains

First of all, it meant travelling in a police state without a pass. Lisa Jacobs, the Jewish Bund member in hiding since the Izbica transport of April 1942, had managed to obtain a forged identity pass, which carried her own photo but the biographical details of a non-Jewish Bund friend. After the war, Lisa wrote a small paean to this document:[28]

*The pass was my most priceless possession. Life and death depended on its existence. I carried it in my shoulder bag, which I never let out of my sight. At night it always lay next to me. To grab it during an air-raid warning or when a visitor arrived became a reflex.*

That 'priceless possession' was precisely what Marianne did not have. Her only usable ID was the international postal ID card she had somehow obtained before she went underground. On the left is a beautiful photo of Marianne with her hair up in a plait, big eyes looking coolly, but somehow also vulnerably, at the photographer. Superimposed on the lower part of the photo is a green 50-pfennig stamp with a solemn-faced Hitler gazing into the distance. Officially, the pass could only accredit the holder at post offices; it offered little protection elsewhere. Effectively, Marianne was travelling without papers.

Official controls to check papers were common on trains and trams at the time. When uniformed men boarded the train, Marianne sometimes stayed in the toilet and got off at the next station to avoid a check. Once or twice she moved slowly through the overcrowded train ahead of the guards and, luckily, reached a station before they reached her. In her deposition to the restitution authorities in the 1950s, Marianne mentioned two occasions when she was caught by the police on a train. Both times she managed to get away, once because of police inattention and the second time because she managed to escape in the press of the crowd as she left the station.[29] On trams, too, several times she edged slowly to the back as the control came in from the front.[30]

Listening to Marianne talk about her travels, it was almost impossible to imagine what it had been like. But what she said reminded me that earlier in the year I had been travelling from Dortmund to Essen – a stretch of track Marianne must have covered many times – with a British TV journalist and a German colleague. At the time, we had just been talking to an Auschwitz survivor and I had still been feeling overwrought from his unbearable testimony. At Dortmund station we ran for the S-Bahn, catching it with no time to buy a ticket. There are no conductors on the S-Bahn, but occasionally teams of men in plain clothes make surprise swoops through the train. Coupled with the gruelling interview behind us, I found the tension of travelling without a ticket almost unbearable. We weren't caught, but now hearing Marianne's account made me think of my reaction to this experience. What was the worst that could have happened to us? A 40 mark fine. For Marianne, the checks were about life and death.

Along with her own stories, I gradually collected a series of anecdotes which Marianne had told others – Bund members she had spent time with during the war, German friends she had spoken to immediately after the war, friends in Britain to whom she had let slip the odd snippet. In an affidavit to the German restitution authorities in support of Marianne's claim for compensation for loss of freedom, one of her former Bund friends, Hanni Ganzer, described a time when Marianne was stopped by the police on the train to Bremen and was only able to get away by chance.[31] The late Fritz Briel, a Bund member from Remscheid, vividly recalled Marianne's account of one narrow escape. She had hidden in the toilet on a train while a check was being carried out. Suddenly, there was a knock on the door, and when she opened it three young SS men were standing there. Evidently Marianne bawled them out: 'How dare you frighten a young girl like that?' The alarmed SS men never did check her papers.[32] (Incidentally, they were unlikely to have been SS. The blurring of uniforms in memory had probably taken place here, too.)

In 1997, while attending Marianne's stone-setting[33] in Liverpool, I discovered that Sol and Clara Bender, close friends of the Ellenbogens who lived in nearby Chester, also had something to tell me. Shortly before the end of her life (and during the period of our interviews),

Marianne had dropped in after one of her trips to Chester's antique shops, sat down and, for the first time in their many years of friendship, talked freely about the war years. The Benders wished they had noted down what she said, but some of what she related had stuck, especially her description of playing hide and seek at a station with guards and ticket inspectors.[34] A cinematic image came to mind of Marianne moving warily with the crowd, eyeing the guards and officials around her.

Then, when I went to the States, I heard another anecdote from Lew and Trudy Schloss. Before I even got to switch the tape recorder on they wanted to tell me the story which had stuck in their minds for the last fifty-odd years. It was when Marianne called on them in Essen unannounced in 1945 – the one time they'd seen her since the war. This is the version of the story I managed to get on tape:[35]

TRUDY: *I was startled when all of a sudden she rang the doorbell, do you remember?*

LEW: *Well, there were so few Jews there – you, and me and a few others.*

And here was Marianne, looking so like a German, they said, she could have been Scholtz Klink (the most senior woman in the Nazi movement, head of the National Socialist Women's League). They both laughed.

LEW: *When she came, she told us at the time that one of the reasons she survived was that she masqueraded as a Nazi; not as a Nazi, as an agent.*

TRUDY: *I don't know if this is true, I don't know.*

LEW: *She told us that she would go into compartments in trains where the hierarchy of the Nazis and the Gestapo officers would travel. That impressed us at the time and this is what I, we, both had foremost in our minds: that she told us that she survived because she was in the lion's den, and whenever somebody asked her what she was doing she said, 'I can't tell you that because I am under direct orders of the Führer.' Now I don't know if that's true . . .*

TRUDY: *But that's the story we remember . . .*

LEW: *But this is what I remember distinctly . . .*

[ . . . ]

TRUDY: *This is the story we didn't forget.*

LEW: *This was so unique at the time but, you know, since I survived under all kinds of circumstances, it made perfectly good sense to me that somebody could have done this. And certainly, when she walked in, I mean all she needed was to put on the uniform and she would have fitted perfectly.*

TRUDY: *She really looked like a German. When she walked in that time in our house I couldn't believe it.*

The memory of that incident was so strong that we came back to it a third time after lunch:

TRUDY: *In fact, we were sitting there and were absolutely . . .*

LEW: *Stunned . . .*

TRUDY: *Stunned when she told us that story. And how she used to sit in first class in the train, and they used to ask her . . .*

LEW: *It was always first class.*

TRUDY: *. . . and they used to ask her, you know what she was doing . . .*

LEW: *Direct order from Hitler,* direkter Befehl von Hitler. *Something like that.* Sie kann nicht darüber reden.

TRUDY: *And she told us, she used to dress very well, in order to look, you know.*

LEW: *How she managed to do that . . . ?*

TRUDY: *I don't know how she managed all that, I have no idea.*

Marianne's cousin Eric Alexander had another story. Some while after I had visited him and his wife in Stamford, I called him up to check on another matter, the call was almost over, and then he suddenly remembered Marianne telling him something. Shortly before the end of the war, a Gestapo officer in Düsseldorf had asked for her papers but then let her go, even though she didn't have satisfactory identification. Marianne had sensed that the official knew something was not in order, but the end of the war was so obviously imminent that he let her go.[36]

Thus, I gradually pieced together a mosaic of Marianne's daily life. Each of her interlocutors had held on to a fragment of her experiences, sufficiently arresting (or rather not) to lodge firmly in the listener's memory, sometimes for more than fifty years. But each fragment was different. Some of the differences were small enough to guess that they might be the same story, changed in the remembering, but often my impression was that Marianne had dropped into the laps of her friends one precious little pearl and no more. When I told Lew and Trudy what I knew of Marianne's survival, for example, they were struck that in the summer of 1945 she had said nothing to them about the Bund. She gave them her train story and that was their ration.

## Marianne's hosts

On most occasions, Marianne's arrival at her destination meant putting herself in the hands of strangers – strangers whose background, experience and way of life often had little in common with her own. Not all Marianne's hosts were members of the Bund. Friends and family connections of the Strausses could also sometimes be used. There was a distant relative in Beverstedt, near Bremen. There was Grete Menningen, a sister of Marianne's former nursing colleague, Irma Ransenberg, who lived in Barmen in a mixed marriage and was comparatively safe until the regime's policy on mixed marriages hardened in summer 1944.[37] Emilie Busch, a resident of Wuppertal Elberfeld, was Oe's former housekeeper, and on several occasions Marianne was able to spend a few days in her little top-floor flat. But the Bund members were her principal protectors during the period. For Marianne it was a miracle

*that in this fearful time there was always a safety net waiting to catch me; people who were complete strangers were willing to expose themselves to such dangers for my sake and for the sake of human rights.*

What kind of people were her Bund helpers? Although each of her hosts – the Gehrkes in Göttingen, the Morgensterns in Braunschweig, the Briels in Remscheid, the Zenkers in Mülheim and the Schmitzes in Burscheid – were, of course, individuals in their own right, they also had much in common with one another. They were nearly all working class in origin, though the Morgensterns presented a colourful exception here, since Carlos, the husband, came from a very simple background, but his wife, Karin, was upper class. Theirs was an 'extraordinary marriage', Marianne said, 'so ill matched, yet it was very good and it worked.'[38] Almost all had had only limited formal education, having left school after the basic four years of secondary education to earn a living. For the most part they were fifteen to twenty years older than Marianne and married with small children. Generally of modest means, they typically lived in small apartments. Often they did not have a spare room and could offer Marianne only a couch.

Like Marianne, many had been influenced by the free German youth movement, but usually by groups on the left-wing of the youth spectrum such as the Naturfreunde (literally, Friends of Nature) or pacifist groups. Most had gravitated to left-wing parties in the 1920s. Some were members of the Social Democratic Party (SPD), whereas the Morgensterns, the Briels and the Zenkers were committed Communists. Some had encountered the Bund first through gymnastics lessons or seeing a troupe of Dore Jacobs' pupils perform. Others had attended Bund lectures at the Volkshochschulen in Essen or Wuppertal and had been won over.

It was all a million miles away from Marianne's own milieu, yet in many of her hosts she found inspiring, self-educated conversation partners and role models. Often, the men were away, either like Gustav Gehrke or Carlos Morgenstern because they were called up, or because the bombing had induced the wives to move out of town whilst the men stayed near their factories. Thus, it was the women of the Bund – above all Sonja Schreiber, Maria Briel, and later Meta Steinmann[39] – who meant most to Marianne.

Maria Briel, for example, was born in 1905 to a large family and soon learned the meaning of hardship and independence. Her father, a craftsman, died of tuberculosis in the early years of the First World War. Maria trained as a secretary and worked as office girl in a factory while she attended lectures at the Volkshochschule. Here she made her first contacts with the pacifist and anti-militarist movement, and ultimately with the Bund. It was, she recalled, a personal liberation. She went on long hikes with her new-found spiritual companions. 'That was the beginning of a wonderful time, I really felt, for the first time, that I had found my feet, that I was someone, that I had become "me"!'[40]

*Maria Briel*

Her husband Fritz Briel, born in 1907, also came from a working-class family. After the First World War, he apprenticed as a joiner and discovered the Bund in the 1920s. Both he and Maria attended monthly meetings at the Remscheid Volkshochschule and also maintained regular contact with the Essen group.[41] In 1933, they distributed anti-Nazi leaflets, but soon realized the risk of this kind of activity. Indeed, both were briefly imprisoned by the Nazis. Despite the danger and the hostility of many of their relatives, the Briels maintained their Bund links throughout the 1930s. Another Bund member, Grete Dreibholz, whose sister was married to the left-wing Jewish playwright Friedrich Wolf, made them aware of the Jewish community's problems.

Of all the relationships Marianne formed in the first months on the

*Fritz Briel in recent times*

run, she was probably closest to the Briels. In her short article on her experiences during the war, she made special mention of their fearlessness and generosity. And Maria Briel, like Sonja Schreiber, also became a kind of substitute parent for Marianne.

Because Maria died in the early 1990s and her husband Fritz was already very poorly when I was in Germany, I never came to meet her and had only a telephone conversation with him. I did have a pleasant meeting with their son Wolfgang, born in 1940, but he remembered little of the war years. Luckily, an extended video interview with Maria made in 1990 survives.[42] I was struck immediately by her sense of quiet strength. Her face was too severe to be charming, her spectacles were thick and chunky, but there was something very sympathetic about the

*Ellen Jungbluth*

whole. Extremely self-contained, modest and unheroic, volunteering nothing more than what was asked, Maria Briel was a real presence.

The only one of Marianne's hosts during her first year in hiding I managed to meet personally was Aenne Schmitz, with whom Marianne stayed in the spring of 1944. My first contact was with a rather shaky, nervous voice at the other end of the telephone. I wanted to arrange an interview, but Frau Schmitz was not sure she was up to it. Blind and living alone, she was understandably very reluctant to let a stranger into her apartment. Through the intercession of another Bund member, Ellen Jungbluth, it was arranged that we would both go to Frau Schmitz's home.

By the time the taxi had deposited me outside Frau Schmitz's flat it was already dark and very cold. I rang the bell, was ushered in, and immediately found myself in a scene of some confusion. Frau Jungbluth, physically rather frail-looking herself, whispered me into the spare room.

*Aenne Schmitz*

Frau Schmitz had had a turn for the worse and the doctor was with her. It was not clear whether we would be able to talk. With the cold gloom of a Wuppertal winter evening outside, I could not have had a starker reminder of how little time I had left to complete the project. How melancholy it was to see these once indomitable women reduced to such fragile and vulnerable selves. The doctor came out, consulted with Frau Jungbluth, and concluded Frau Schmitz might be well enough to have a brief chat. Round-faced and rather flustered, she greeted Frau Jungbluth warmly as she heard her voice. She was totally blind.

Aenne Schmitz had been born in 1906 into a working-class family.[43] Her mother was very religious, her father had been a Social Democrat and it was to him that young Aenne was most strongly drawn. Whilst her mother and siblings went to church, she would go for nature walks with her father, 'which upset my mother very much'. In the early 1920s, Aenne joined the Young Socialists and at nineteen became a member of the SPD, 'And I still am today,' she said. She was apprenticed as a

327

book-binder and also trained to become a member of the Workers' Samaritans' League.

In 1928, she joined the Bund. Her first experience of the group had been at a left-wing festival, an 'L-L-L' (Lenin, Liebknecht, Luxemburg) celebration in Barmen. Dore Jacobs' dance group performed a piece about the impact of machines on human beings and Frau Schmitz could still remember vividly the great effect the simulated mechanical motions on stage had had on her. Invited by Ernst Jungbluth, she joined a Volkshochschule group in Wuppertal and later came to lectures given by Artur Jacobs in Essen. At the mention of his name, Frau Schmitz became animated. 'Artur already saw the dangers, already saw the dangers,' she said in a quavery voice. Aenne's future husband, August, also joined the Bund.

In the early Nazi years their flat was used as a stop-off point for left-wingers who were being spirited out of the country. Frau Schmitz never knew their names, but she had a spare room with a couch and was thus able to help them hide for a day or two. They also had the advantage that their neighbours were either Social Democrats, old Kaiser loyalists or, at least, not ardent Nazis. At one stage, though, August was arrested and imprisoned for six months. Frau Schmitz could still remember the house-search, the jackbooted figures rifling through their books. Like the Briels, the Schmitzes did not allow the experience to frighten them into silence.

Meeting Aenne Schmitz was a memorable and moving occasion, but in one sense it was rather a failure. Because I knew that the Bund members who were blind communicated with each other by sending tapes, I had assumed that Frau Schmitz had a cassette recorder in good working order, and foolishly omitted to bring my own. In fact, her bulky tape machine had only a short lead, which would not stretch to where we were sitting, and had no external microphone. So although I recorded a tape, on replaying it at home all I could hear was distant murmuring. As Frau Schmitz's voice grew more tired, even the murmurs gradually disappeared behind the hiss of the tape.

## Cover stories

Sheltering Marianne, even for a couple of weeks, was not an act to be taken lightly. Above all, it meant finding a way to explain to neighbours, relatives – one's own children – who this stranger was. In the case of the Morgensterns in Braunschweig this was not so complicated. They lived in a rather isolated house on the edge of the town, and while Carlos was away Marianne and Karin lived a secluded life, eating the produce of the garden and, Marianne said, giving each other support and solace. With her kindergarten training, Marianne also enjoyed looking after the two daughters. At the Gehrkes, there was a problem in the form of Hedwig's mother-in-law, a 'terrible old tartar', to whom the truth could not be told. Hedwig found it difficult to explain away Marianne's presence, and during a later stay in 1944 the tensions were to reach breaking point.

When Artur Jacobs approached the Briels on Marianne's behalf, they did not hesitate. 'We were frightened, but we thought, it'll be fine.'[44] But it was no easy matter. They lived fairly centrally in a small apartment in Remscheid and in neighbouring apartment blocks there were a number of convinced Nazis as well as some right-wingers who had fought for the Phalangists in the Spanish Civil War. Not all the Briels' relatives were reliable either, and a cover story had to be invented for their benefit as well. Even their son, Wolfgang, then only three years old, had already picked up that the world was full of enemies and hidden dangers. Maria Briel remembered:[45]

'When he went out he asked "Mother, are the Ms [the name of some family acquaintance] on *our* side?" Although we never said anything, children soak up what is going on. He knew not everything was kosher.'

The principal problem was how to explain why such a physically fit young girl was not working. Artur Jacobs came up with the idea of borrowing a child from some other Bund members and presenting Marianne as a young mother. 'When we had the child here,' said Maria Briel, 'the neighbours said, "She's the spitting image of her mother"!' Some of Fritz Briel's acquaintances who bumped into Fritz on a walk with the attractive young Marianne decided that there was something

*Marianne underground with Wolfgang Briel*

illicit but enviable going on: Fritz remembered them ribbing him afterwards about his new 'Freundin'.

Proof that the cover stories worked for the Briels, at least, came when Marianne visited them some time after the war. Maria Briel remembered:

'When Marianne was here, my sister-in-law said, "Oh, I haven't seen you for a long time." "Yes," Marianne said, "Back then I was here illegally.". . . My sister-in-law didn't even know what "illegal" meant! Though we'd been swimming in illegals!'

With the Schmitz family, things were a little easier. Because they were bombed out in 1943, Aenne, her sister and two-year-old son Jürgen moved to live with their aunt in Berringhausen, a small village north of Burscheid. Burscheid itself is a modest town in the Bergisch region south of the Ruhr, not far from Cologne. The local squire helped the sisters obtain an apartment in an old farmer's house, just across the way from their aunt. The old lady who lived there then died, and it was here that Ernst Jungbluth made several visits. Ernst and Aenne went for a walk through the woods and Ernst said, 'I would like to introduce a friend to you'. 'Of course!' was the reply. But even in such a relatively secluded situation there were still authorities to deal with. The local mayor wanted to know who Marianne was. Aenne explained that she was an Essen resident who'd lost her papers in the bombing, and was coming to stay permanently. Since she eventually planned on returning to Essen, she didn't want to register properly in Burscheid. 'I was very confident. We lived freely there,' was how Aenne Schmitz recalled a conversation which could have cost her life.[46]

Sometimes, Marianne had to arrive without warning. Her grandmother had a distant cousin who had married a non-Jew and lived on the land in Beverstedt, near Bremen. All Marianne knew of them was their address, and she knew this only because some family packing cases had been sent there for safe-keeping. One day, Marianne simply turned up at the house. The husband was a ship's purser on the Bremen line, 'a real rough diamond', but they agreed to look after her and she stayed with them on several occasions.[47]

## Between freedom and danger

I had assumed that when Marianne stayed with her hosts she would resume her Blockhaus routine, hiding in bedrooms and spare rooms and taking brief, nervous constitutionals in the early evening. But when Maria Briel's interviewer on the video asked her if it was true that she had hidden a Jewish girl in her apartment, she said, 'You couldn't say hidden, she lived openly with us, she could do that because she had changed her appearance and had no acquaintances here.'[48]

So, Marianne was not tucked away in an attic. At the Briels she slept on a fold-up bed in the living room. By day, Maria Briel said, 'We didn't stay in our apartment. No, we went out . . . we didn't act as though we were hiding someone. She lived completely openly.'

This was my first real inkling of the freedom that Marianne had wrung from her situation. Talking to me on the phone, Fritz Briel remembered Marianne as 'very courageous and cheeky' and, of course, very good looking.[49] Maria, too, was struck by Marianne's apparent lack of anxiety or concern. Of course, there were fearful moments – for instance when they had to go to the air-raid shelter.[50]

'The only time she showed fear was when we had to go into the air-raid shelter. She had no papers, and I know that the landlady, our landlady, once said, as we went down into the cellar, we had our bed clothes, you know, she said, "Ach, Marianne, she always crawls right under the bedclothes."'

If they had been asked there for their papers, it would have been disastrous. Maria remembered other moments too:[51]

'I know that we had to be careful to make sure we stayed on good terms with the landlady . . . She was angry once, Marianne had motioned to me, I was cleaning the steps and she motioned to me that I should come and listen to the English broadcaster, and then the landlady came and said, "Two women in the house and still they leave a bucket on the steps." She was really angry!'

As the story of the encounter with the landlady indicates, the Briels and Marianne listened to the BBC together, despite the consequences of being caught, particularly once the BBC began to broadcast more information about Nazi treatment of Jews.

One story Maria told (which Marianne, with her typical reticence, had never mentioned) was about Marianne's romance with a French prisoner of war. Near the apartment was an air-raid shelter that had been flooded. Conscript labourers assigned to clear the shelter included a young French soldier. Although it was strictly forbidden for Germans to make contact with the foreign conscripts, a friendship, actually signs of something more than friendship, began to develop between Marianne and the young man. This was the one event during Marianne's stay that had even the courageous Briels chewing their fingernails.[52]

Each of Marianne's hosts conjured a similar image. Aenne Schmitz remembered her gaiety and had a strong visual memory of her cheerfully washing the red dye into her hair of an evening. Indeed, so many of my interlocutors had a vivid memory of Marianne's hair colour that I began to feel there was some point that I was missing. To be sure, the result clearly looked attractive – Aenne recalled that the village boys had been *very* interested in the newcomer. Marianne's looks had been almost too good. A bit plainer, a bit more discreet, would have been better. But, still, there was something about the way Marianne's red hair shone like a beacon through different people's memories that I did not understand. But then, in the wonderfully written reminiscences of a Polish-Jewish survivor, Janina Fischler-Martinho, I came across a passage in which she describes running into her family's former manicurist, Lola, who – thanks to her liaison with an Aryan – has metamorphosed into something far more confident:[53]

*She had had her hair hennaed. Today, a woman turns from a deep brunette into a golden blonde from one day to the next and nobody turns a hair ... But in those days, to change the colour of one's hair marked one as a female bold as brass, a pioneer, a revolutionary – almost. A mass of fiery, coppery, glinting waves and ripples. We were speechless with wonder and astonishment at the audacity and splendour of that transformation.*

In Marianne's case, the point was not so much that people were struck by the sudden transformation. After all, many of them had never known

Marianne in her previous dark-haired incarnation. It was rather the boldness – under normal circumstances, the vulgarity – of changing one's hair colour that was the thing. There was, I realized, a kind of excited complicity among my respondents, in having been party to this brash subterfuge.

The same themes of beauty, transformation and freedom emerged powerfully from the testimony of Hanna Jordan. In her post-war career, Hanna Jordan had become a celebrated stage designer. On the day I visited her, I found her just back from her travels, ensconced in a sizeable apartment full of art, interesting clutter, fluffy toys and two noisy parrots. Hanna's mother had been Jewish, but she herself had become a Quaker after the war. Still, there was something Jewish in her style which I immediately felt at home with. She had a garrulousness, a sort of cosmopolitanism with attitude, which came as a welcome break from the steady, calm seriousness of many of my interviewees. I went to see her, expecting to learn something about her own fate during the war (I knew that she had had some contact with the Bund then). What I hadn't expected was that she herself had met Marianne.

Hanna Jordan was two years older than Marianne, having been born in Wuppertal in 1921, the daughter of two lively minded, left-wing parents.[54] None of her family were ever members of the Bund, but her parents moved in the same kind of circles, were regular participants in the Volkshochschule courses in Wuppertal and came to know a number of Bund members well. From an early stage they were deeply impressed by the Bund's seriousness and strictness. In the 1930s, Hanna was sent away to Holland to attend a school run by Quakers for the children of people subject to persecution in Nazi Germany. It was an experience that helped forge Hanna's own political and religious identity, and provided the basis for personal contacts, some of which continue until this day. She then rejoined the family, living in the progressively more circumscribed conditions attached to being a *Mischling 1. Grades* (first degree half-Jew).

In 1942, Hanna had direct experience of the Bund's willingness to help. In that year some Jewish relatives, a youngish couple with their son, were placed on the deportation list. The Bund offered to protect them. Hanna went to see the pair to give them the message, but they were too frightened to respond and, finally, the three were transported to the East and never heard of again. At the end of 1942, Hanna's mother was caught in one of the Berlin operations and interned, prior to deportation. Under the rules then in force, as a partner in a so-called 'privileged' mixed marriage, Frau Jordan should not have been imprisoned. Hanna's father travelled to Berlin and furnished the necessary papers to get her out shortly before she was due to be dispatched to the East.

The conversation took a new turn, and I was suddenly surprised and excited to learn that Hanna had met Marianne. Really? When was that? Had they met while Marianne was living underground? I thought it must have been then, because until that time Marianne had not had contact with Bund circles outside the Jacobs and Sonja Schreiber in Essen. But Hanna thought not:

'Well, I don't think that it can have been when she was hidden, because she would not have been able to go out, she couldn't have visited anybody. We experienced that ourselves, my parents and I, when we were hiding towards the end of the war. You stayed where you stayed, hidden, you couldn't move . . .'

Well, I went on, what impressions of Marianne had she retained?

'The main thing, which naturally made a particular impression on me as a woman, but also impressed all of us, was that she was so beautiful. I have never seen such a beautiful person, unbelievable. When you saw her, you thought, that's how I'd like to look. She had frizzy red hair tied at the back and a beautiful face, dark brown eyes . . . an absolute treat for an artist. She spoke very well, spoke beautifully, she moved, she had something that you don't usually find, but you held your breath and you looked and thought, My God! And I don't know, whether I've dreamed it or whether she really did, at some point, have black hair instead of red or . . .'

'Yes, she did.'

'Could that have been while she was hidden?'

'While she was hidden she had red hair.'

'She was red, then! I know her red and black, but I can't remember when red and when black.'

'So you *did* meet her in her the underground period!'

'Well, I mainly remember her red.' And then she went on: 'I can't remember any more, but that is not just a sporadic memory but a very personal impression of someone who was with us more than once and who stayed strongly in our memory – someone whom we spoke of later. I remember a very intelligent person, a very clever person, a very sensible person, she had a real personality, and impressed us very much. At that time, you know, that really stuck. I would very much have liked to meet her again.'

This unusually generous tribute struck me not just because it was the strongest testimony yet of the enormous impression Marianne made on those around her. It was clear from Hanna's memory and other details that the main contact between the two *must* have been during Marianne's time underground. Despite living in conditions of permanent threat and uncertainty, Marianne had managed to convey such a sense of liveliness and freedom that Hanna Jordan could not initially believe that her memory dated from Marianne's illegal period. Hanna, as she herself said, had good reason to know what it was like being in hiding, because she too had to go underground in the closing months of the war.

I realized that, for someone like Marianne, 'hiding' was a misnomer. She was living in many ways a very unhidden life, 'passing' as a red-haired Aryan. Her identity was in hiding, but she herself was out in the open.

## Food and money

Though she may have given a carefree impression, Marianne was very conscious of what she was asking of her hosts. Not only did she compromise their safety but, since as a non-person she did not qualify for ration cards, the Bund members had to feed her from their own limited resources. Some, like Karin Morgenstern and Hedwig Gehrke, grew food in their gardens. Others were less well placed. Bund members who were not actually putting Marianne up helped by providing some of their own ration cards. But the brunt still fell on her hosts.[55]

Marianne tried to alleviate the burden by eating, whenever possible, at a restaurant or inn that did not ask for food coupons. In Braunschweig there was a smart restaurant where you could get a decent *Stammgericht* without ration cards. But, of course, this meant mixing with strangers in public. On one occasion, the restaurant was very crowded and she had to join a table with a high-ranking Wehrmacht officer. Marianne, being Marianne, played 'Russian roulette' and engaged in a mixture of flirtation and debate. In doing this she was following the Bund policy of imparting political education through one-to-one conversations. She had an idea that the handsome officer guessed there was something odd about her position, but everything remained charming and there were no consequences.[56]

Of course, even if coupons were not an issue, eating a meal in a restaurant required money. I assumed that Marianne bankrolled her time underground from the wad of notes her father had given her. When I asked about this, she insisted that she never touched that money.[57] Mindful of the seriousness with which her father took money and property, and determined to prove herself the dutiful daughter, perhaps also to keep her parents alive in symbolic form, she jealously guarded the billfold and put it in a savings account after the war:[58]

'I didn't really need much money. My friends wouldn't have wanted me to *pay* for what they did for me – it would have been an insult more than anything. So I did whatever I could to make up for it, above all going into the countryside and bartering for food.'

Marianne started going to Essen periodically to visit Maria and Wilhelm Jürgens, the acquaintances of her parents who were storing some of the family's trunks. Here she collected household goods, linen and suchlike which she could use for barter. She would then embark on the 'necessary but dangerous enterprise' of taking the goods to the farmers in the country and bartering them for whatever you could get:[59]

'Persian rug – a hundred grams of bacon. Three eggs for a tailored suit – that sort of rate. The story told after the war that the pigsties were plastered with Persian rugs is quite true. Really, the farmers survived the war with absolutely everything you could think of. You were entirely at the mercy of the farmers and what they would give you.'

The problem with obtaining the family goods for barter was that she had to break open the seals of the trunks at the Jürgens':[60]

'Once I had done that, they started to rob them systematically. Well,

I can't blame them . . . They probably said to themselves that my parents would never come back, and I'd probably be found anyway, so there wasn't much risk.'

On one occasion, arriving at the Jürgens' while Wilhelm was still in bed, Marianne saw her brother's alarm clock, a Barmitzvah present, on the bedside table. But she could say nothing.[61] In fact, the Jürgens provided her with a unique insight into the double standards of at least part of Christian Germany during this period. The Jürgens lived quite near the Blockhaus. The Blockhaus hall was used as a temporary place of worship and, as devout Catholics, Herr and Frau Jürgens would go there for Sunday services. While staying in the Blockhaus, Marianne would, from her hidden vantage point, see the Jürgens come in to prayer:[62]

'They would come to the service . . . and it was really quite ironic that they were praying there in this hall and I could see them coming in and praying. Little did they know that I was just round the corner from them. They went to church and they prayed, then they went home and robbed a little more.'

In addition to bartering the family property, Marianne had learned all kinds of skills as part of her kindergarten training, including making artificial flowers out of felt and leather. (Vivian and I found that a few of the patterns had survived among her things.) She was able to collect the scraps she needed from cases she had deposited with friends. The shops had nothing to sell, and were delighted to buy Marianne's confections. In this way she managed to earn both money and ration cards. In particular, she found a small fashion shop in Braunschweig, whose owner became her main customer because she was prepared to pay for most of the goods in coupons. Marianne had a distinct sense that this woman understood her predicament and wanted to help.[63] Marianne may have had other customers, too. Aenne Schmitz remembered providing Marianne with food but being unable to help her out with cash. She did not enquire about Marianne's own source of money or where she went on her regular journeys during the week. She says she once saw a train ticket to Frankfurt and remembers Marianne making the leather flowers.

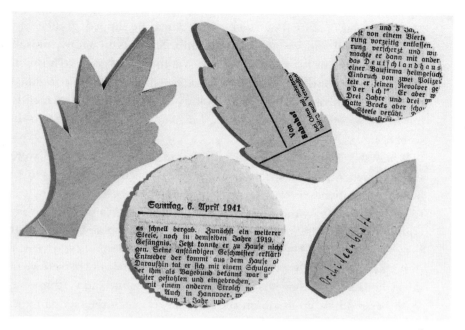

*Marianne's patterns*

## Ill health

One of Marianne's biggest fears was that she might fall ill. 'God forbid anything happened and you needed a doctor.' Her first stroke of ill luck came in Göttingen, while tending Hedwig Gehrke's bees. She was stung on the eyelid, potentially a very dangerous place. Luckily, the swelling went down by itself. During air raids, Marianne was almost more afraid of being injured than of dying. As Maria Briel remembered:[64]

'Marianne was frightened, you know, she was frightened, she must have been thinking, for God's sake, just let me not end up in a hospital! And that was a time when there was an air-raid warning every day, when the bombs fell every day.'

In winter 1943 in Wuppertal, a minor disaster struck. Wuppertal is a very hilly town, with many steps carved into the hills to connect the levels. It was a very cold winter and the roads and pavements were frozen. Marianne was coming down some steps when she slipped, grabbed on to the iron rail and wrenched her thumb. She was in agony, unsure whether she had dislocated or broken it. Yet the risk of going to hospital was too great. Marianne was in despair. The injured thumb continued to swell and throb and began to look as if it would be permanently out of joint. After a couple of days, Marianne decided she had to do something.

When she arrived at a nearby Protestant hospital, the staff were surprised when she said she was not covered by insurance and was there as a private patient. Surprise turned to horror when she asked the doctors to set the thumb without anaesthetic. 'Without an anaesthetic they couldn't *possibly* dream of doing that.' Marianne explained that, after her experience with her toe, she was terrified of anaesthetics; what she didn't say, of course, was that she was fearful of betraying herself when anaesthetized. Did they suspect anything? Marianne didn't think so. With her red hair up in a bun, she looked every inch the German girl. Eventually, the staff agreed. There were three doctors and two nurses and 'it was like a medieval procedure', she said. 'I don't think I made a peep, and they were absolutely staggered at this . . . they set my thumb, but it never healed properly.'

In the longer term, stress and poor nutrition did no favours to her health. Because of the rationing, most of her diet consisted of bread and potatoes, with a distinct shortage of fats and proteins.[65] But in this particular deprivation, Marianne was no different from many other Germans at the time.

## Games and poison

Trying to imagine the daily struggle to survive in such circumstances, to cope with the kind of fear she must have felt, I asked Marianne where she had found the nerve. 'I'm a fighter, otherwise I wouldn't be here now,' she said. The whole thing had been like a game of chess. 'I wanted to outwit them, it was like a game. I made a very conscious effort never to show fear . . . I couldn't do it now, but then I felt I had nothing to live for.'[66]

In our interview in 1989, she had said, 'For me, the most important thing was to outwit the Nazis whatever happened. I pitched my understanding and my will against their stupidity and their bureaucratic rules.'

Marianne told me that she carried cyanide with her: 'My hope was that I would never be found alive by the Gestapo. I always had enough medication with me, on my person, so that I could take my life at any time. That was the most important thing for me — that I would either get out of this inferno healthy or not at all.'

Marianne mentioned the cyanide several times. It had clearly given her a sense of control, a way to decide the means of her own death, a way to avoid the degradation of incarceration in a concentration camp. The Polish resistance fighter, Jan Karski, in *Story of a Secret State* described his feelings when a nun placed a cyanide capsule under his pillow:[67]

*After her departure, I felt a surge of courage and determination. I was now armed against the worst contingencies. The poison gave me a sense of luxury, a feeling that I had a magic talisman against the eventualities which I had dreaded most — torture and the possibility that I might crack and betray the organization.*

Marianne said something similar: 'That helped me very much, this possibility. I was not a victim and had it in my power in some way to control my fate — although I was of course completely dependent on others.'

But I thought I detected in Marianne's repeated mention of the poison another resonance, too. When I spoke to her in October 1996, she was tired of life. Every time we met she was drugged up to give her extra energy. She'd said to me about the 'game' she played against the Nazis that she 'couldn't do it now'. Perhaps in 1996 she wished she still had the courage and means to determine her final fate.

## *The diary*

In early December 1997, almost a year after Marianne's death, I was staying with Vivian on what must have been my third visit to go through Marianne's papers. On previous occasions, we had scaled mountains of restitution files and waded through great swaths of post-war reports and correspondence from the Bund. This time, I'd stayed over on Friday night to go through the bulk of the remaining documents. It had also given me the chance to join in Vivian's fiftieth birthday celebrations. Secretive as his mother, Vivian asked me in advance not to discuss our finds with the family and friends at the celebration.

Preparing for my visit, Vivian had sorted through several boxes of papers and unearthed a lot of personal material. There was Marianne's commonplace book from school and her little striped address book with family contacts overseas. I started ploughing through yet more restitution files, but Vivian said he wanted me to look at something. It was another little square, hard-backed notebook, with the same abstract red and blue design as the commonplace book and the same green bound spine. I hadn't finished the file I was working on, but Vivian persisted.

Opening it, I found unruled pages covered with Marianne's handwriting. I had still not fully mastered her Gothic script and the book did not immediately yield its contents. Opening a page at random I made out a heading, 'Mülh., 31.9.44'. 'Mülh.?' Mülheim? Then I went back to the beginning. The first entry was 20 April 1944. I turned to the end, 10 September 1944. No, there was an additional entry folded in from February 1945. Then I realized that there was a typed insert at the beginning as well. The first entry was dated 18 April 1944, Remscheid. And there were typed letters folded in between the pages, some typed during the war, some after. 'Vivian!' I shouted, 'Do you realize what this is?!'

Driving back home that night it was hard to contain my excitement. The idea that we could gain an insight into Marianne's state of mind *while she was on the run* was staggering. Almost as amazing, indeed almost eerie, was the fact that Marianne had never told me about the diary. She could not have failed to appreciate its significance for my book. Perhaps she had withheld it, but if so, why? Because it was too personal? I did not think it could be more personal than her correspondence with Ernst which she had given me. Perhaps she simply could not face looking for it, unearthing it amid all the other papers. Perhaps she had forgotten that she still had it. Either interpretation was possible, not least because the diary pages were so pristine and well-preserved as to make clear that they had been very little read since the war. Either way, the diary surfacing like this opened a window not only on her years on the run, but also on her reluctance to confront the past.

# II

# Underground Chronicles:
# April 1944 – April 1945

The typewritten entry folded into the beginning of the diary was headed 18 April 1944, Remscheid:

*Beautiful being on one's own in the open air. Sun, hills, meadows and woods. With all my senses I relish lying on the earth, relaxed, my mind wandering, and yet feeling more connected to myself than I have for a long time! How good, how healing friendship with nature is – no words, no need to say anything; just yielding oneself up to it and listening. There's so much to learn here for our relationships with other people.*

*Thoughts wander with the brook and buzz with the bees. How good it is to be alone, to find oneself again. The distance from others, from everyday life, the communion with the wind as it slips through the grass and trees, with the hare as it trustingly looks for food just a couple of steps away from me, pointing with its long ears. Listening to the noises of this little world, one is so grateful that it consists of nothing more than a little patch of earth: a sun-drenched meadow, with a stream chattering through it, surrounded by tall pine trees. In this defined space the heart is full of reverence, the gaze is not distracted by the diversions of daily life; the trees bar one's gaze from straying further.*

*What a powerful experience it is: looking, listening, being with oneself. How much we need this in our everyday life!*

*. . . I keep thinking of a conversation. It was about how to find one's*

self. Does one manage it through turning outwards – devoting oneself to the community – or turning inwards – self-exploration in the peace of solitude? This is not an easy question. A whole lifetime would not suffice to answer it. The important thing is to confront whatever task stands before us, master it and allow ourselves to be sustained by so doing. Facing up to our responsibilities necessarily brings us into the community, makes us links in the chain and no longer just separate individuals. But we will always remain separate beings. How could we find repose, if we were never alone! We need the chance to rest, to draw on our inner reserves. And it is good that this is so, because the strength that we draw on in such moments will benefit the community later. Fields cannot be sown every year. Sometimes they need to lie fallow to gather strength for new seed and future harvests.

My thoughts travel on through time and space. How incomprehensible and awful it is; the enclosed, dreamy peace here, this little world within a larger one in which, every moment, countless fates are sealed. All the people out there, so intensely in our thoughts and yet so far away and so alone; beyond all knowledge, beyond all feeling, how difficult the present is for them, that same present which brings one such happiness and fulfilment. And it makes one think that it is impossible to come through unscathed. How can one get away without sacrifice or pain when, every second, pain and sacrifice is demanded of so many others? What does life hold in readiness? How fortunate that we can only grope our way to the future, blindfolded, step by step.

For that reason we must learn to live so that we can greet tomorrow without regrets, without having to repair what we have done. Every day must be a lifetime; complete, worthwhile; filled with duty, love, and at least one good honest deed and one good thought, one loving word. Each day, something must happen so that one can say in the evening: today I helped to make the wheel turn a little further.

And that reminds me of a thought I had yesterday when I was working in the garden. I thought suddenly how many centuries and how many people were necessary to transform the primordial earth into the soil we plant today. And the thought that what we do now may be of use to those that follow us showed me that life is worth living.

Recognize life's law and act accordingly.

The hand-written diary proper begins on 20 April 1944, two years to the day since Marianne had last seen Ernst:

*How my thoughts are with you today! More than for a long time. Two years lie like a chasm between then and now; two years of events, of experiences, of difficulties, pain, horror, and so little that was good. Today you are so much in my feelings, my blood, my heart. It has all come back to me again, so vividly – your being, your love, your understanding. Oh, my love, if only you were always so close to me! Then my flight, my restless searching, would not be necessary. How even and steady everything would be! Often I think with fear and guilt how, how it is possible that I could lose you so. You know, what we experienced, what we shared, all the good things you left in me – I am always aware of them. You could say they are your legacy. They will be there as long as I live and as long as I can pass them on to others; but you, you as a living person, you I can't reach any more.*

*[. . . ]*

*Oh, how I yearn to have my friend next to me. If only I could rest my head on his shoulder and close my eyes and feel how good that is.*

*But then it's the other way round; then I wish with all my heart to draw him in to me completely, to embrace him, to give, to give and to feel.*

*Oh, my love, how heavy I feel! But perhaps somewhere you sense this too, and know what I'm feeling.*

*. . . My thoughts travel back, back down the road we took together – the most beautiful time of my life. The first period of being alone was still filled by you; we were so together and yet so far apart. Then came the knowledge of your fate and I had only one thought – to help you and be close to you. And then there was nothing, no word, and slowly you slipped away from me. I didn't want you to go and held on to you desperately. But there are forces stronger than will. And then came a new life; challenges, danger, demands on every part of me. I had to relinquish even the things I wanted to hold on to. I had to have my hands free to master new challenges . . .*

*And so two years have passed. If you were to find me now? What would that be like? How different we are now. What we share is the past, but the present is something we're experiencing on our own. We have nothing in common there but the past that lives on within us. And the future, could we sustain it together? I don't know! I know only that I would like to preserve you inside me, just as I have over these last two years. And a whole lifetime won't change that, no matter what happens.*

Marianne wrote both of these entries in Remscheid, while she was staying with the Briels. The next lengthy account dates from Whitsun. Marianne was taking part in a Bund study trip in the Bergisch area, near Remscheid. The entry begins confusingly enough:

Whitsun, [28/29] May 1944

*Marvellous days outside in the Bergisch Land. Whitsun conversation about WA. One hopes that all the Easter wounds have been healed. But have they? The effort is too great! Only we three are aware of it.*

It took me a while to figure out that WA was Marianne's abbreviation for *Weltanschauung* or 'view of the world'. But for the moment the 'Easter wounds' remained a mystery. The Whitsun entries continue on 2 June, headed 'at the dam; extract from a letter':

*The rain is streaming down, but still how beautiful it is: camping by the lake. How one lives when close to nature, to weather and time, to the animals and the sounds of solitude. I can't tell you how beautiful it is! At first, I was worrying about the weather and thinking I could enjoy it and feel happy only if everything were bathed in sunlight. But now I realize that's not true. Everything, including oneself, is more alive when the clouds and the rain and the wind are all about. I feel like the grass and the leaves, exposed, utterly open to the elements. It's beautiful! Beautiful, beautiful, beautiful.*

*To be totally oneself, without distortion, without a mask, without qualification. To open oneself fully, to forget oneself and only then to find oneself.*

*To be all senses; feeling, seeing, hearing. And to want nothing; to just take what comes; to taste and enjoy it.*

*Waking up in the dawn after an astoundingly warm and good night in the tent; bathing in the reservoir in the morning, surrounded by the mist as it moves across the water. And then hiking through the pouring rain;*

*woods, fields, meadows. At one point a rain-drenched cart, otherwise no
sounds, no evidence of people near by. The path led across a hill through
wisps of cloud, then through a wood rich with the fragrance of wet pines.
At one point, a horse out to pasture whinnied happily at the unexpected
interruption of its isolation. It sniffed me up and down, chewed at my
sprig of broom and walked with me to the end of the pasture. Elsewhere,
I surprised a couple of cows. Behind a gorse-covered hill two farms squat-
ted together, like children huddled in the rain. A thousand good thoughts
wandered with me through mist and rain, above all the strong desire to
have a friend by my side, someone to share the experience with me.*

*Sometimes on the way you explore a stretch through the woods and
then have to retrace your steps to the main path. You must erase this
detour from your memory so that later you don't lose your way home.
And it occurred to me that life's often like that; you can take a wrong
path and so easily lose sight of your goal. It's so good to be able to blank
out the mistake until you can find the right path. Then you can look at
your mistake, evaluate it, and above all, learn to accept it.*

Afternoon

*[. . .]*

*I spent a lot of time with farmers today. I wanted to experience people,
smell life and hear what they had to say. Oh, what a muddle you get to
hear! You need so much time and patience and education! It's easy to
get frightened. Learn, understand, and believe with conviction – is that
the secret to conquering this fear?*

The following day

*[. . .]*

*You know, I'd like to say something about the Whitsun days. Those few
days were beautiful. I keep thinking of the discussions about WA, a
topic I'm sure you've often pondered and talked about. An endless
topic. Much became clear, much more was just touched on and lightly
dislodged, to keep rolling forward like a heavy stone. You don't know
where it will end up, you just feel it rolling inside you. In those conver-*

*sations, questions came up that I've been thinking about for a long time. I've made heavy weather of them in the past, but now much was clarified and many uncertainties removed.*

*WA. What are we to understand by the term? Where can we find a WA? What should it look like?*

As I gradually reclaimed these first few entries from Marianne's beautiful but near-impenetrable Gothic script, I felt like an archaeologist stumbling on ancient gold, untarnished and unaltered. The pages were almost pristine. Her writing was so composed that hardly anything was crossed out in the whole diary. There is barely an ink smudge. Possibly, she drafted every entry before inscribing it; often, the entries are extracts from letters she was writing.

In deciphering the diary's contents I felt I was bringing something to the surface that had been doubly hidden, actually three times hidden. The diary had emerged so unexpectedly and unannounced from the clutter in Marianne's house in Liverpool. Its steady, even lines, written behind enemy lines, as it were, had survived a life in hiding in Nazi Germany. Most of all, these first entries were enough to reveal an account strikingly at odds with the world in which it had been composed – or at least with the image we have of that world. I saw already, for example, that my preconceptions about hiding had prevented me almost completely from understanding the freedom Marianne had wrested from the situation. But I also saw that Marianne herself had since lost sight of the life she had once lived and, above all, who she had once been.

Nothing in our interviews had prepared me for the fact that Marianne had been able to do something so light-hearted and independent as camping. Obviously, I could see at once the attraction of doing so. Like many influenced by the youth movement, Marianne was a nature lover. In her situation, with human society so dangerous and unpredictable, solitude in nature offered a vital respite from threat, subterfuge and disguise. But, still, I found such unencumbered freedom of movement almost incredible. We have to pinch ourselves to recall that one unlucky check of her papers would see Marianne unceremoniously switched between two worlds that do not seem to exist in the same universe – the world of camping and the world of the camps.

If Marianne's actions were remarkably carefree, her reflections were anything but. The comments of those who knew her at the time had not prepared me for the diary's maturity, perceptiveness and sophistication. Particularly when writing about Ernst, Marianne evinced a self-awareness that was truly admirable. She recalled her love for him, but at the same time acknowledged the distancing that had necessarily taken place. A year earlier, she had noted in her Essen diary that others might feel she was heartless because of the way she pushed painful issues deep down out of reach. Now, with the metaphor of 'freeing her hands', she was again conscious that the psychological mechanism of displacing painful issues was crucial to her survival. Perhaps most impressive was that she could feel her love and debt to Ernst as strongly as ever, but at the same time wonder if their separate experiences (assuming Ernst had survived) would in fact have made them incompatible.

The diary reveals for the first time that Marianne suffered enormous guilt at surviving, even while she herself was still on the run. There was that striking passage as she wondered 'with fear and guilt' how she could have allowed Ernst to go. Guilt slips easily into fear and back again. When she asks how she could be enjoying such peace and beauty while others are suffering unknown and unspeakable horrors, she wonders fearfully if sacrifice or pain must one day inevitably be her lot, too.

Often, Marianne's preoccupations and judgements do not seem to correspond to her predicament as we understand it. Someone picking up the diary without knowing its background would have no sense that Marianne was on the run. Keeping a diary was in itself, of course, an extremely risky act, as Marianne was well aware. So, she camouflaged some details, never named her hosts and conversation partners, and avoided specifying her address or giving details of her personal identity. To a certain extent, therefore, we have to read between the lines and imagine the thoughts and feelings left out because of her fear of discovery.

But take, for example, the paragraph in which her enjoyment of solitude leads to thoughts about whether one really can find oneself in isolation. The issue of how to reconcile individual freedom with the needs of the community was for the Bund, as for Kant, a central preoccupation. When Marianne exhorted herself to recognize life's 'law' and 'act accordingly', she, in line with her Bund mentors, expressed the Kantian belief in an objective moral imperative which governs action in any situation; men become truly free when they recognize and act on what is objectively right. In various guises, Marianne's diary throughout 1944 was full of reflection on this issue. Cast out of the community by racial laws, on the run, her family imprisoned and facing God knows what fate, her lover blinded, probably dead, Marianne was preoccupied with general reflections about the place of the individual in society; as though such generic philosophical choices were her problem! Yet, as later entries show, her pursuit of these questions was real and earnest. Marianne was redefining, or perhaps burying, her direct experience within the broader framework of the Bund's Kantian questions about self and society.

On 28 April, Marianne noted a recent report that the women in a technical school were doing much better than the men, most of whom were disabled veterans. 'What consequences,' noted Marianne with feeling, 'the depleted physical capacity of a people can have for its spiritual development!' Obviously, she could not have been hoping that Germany would win the war. But she expresses no sense of being an outsider, that it is not her society. One is reminded, too, of what she wrote on 18 April about working in the garden and imagining the thousands of generations who had worked the same soil before her. She unselfconsciously found solace in the idea that her garden work had reconnected her to hundreds of years of settlement and working the soil beneath her. In doing so, she ironically adopted a vision of continuity used by many anti-Semitic conservatives against the 'rootless' Jew. And she ironically adopted this vision of continuity at the very time when the anti-Semites had *turned* her into a rootless Jew.


## On the move again

During the Whitsun meeting, the Bund leaders must have decided Marianne should leave the Ruhr again. Marianne's first port of call was not a Bund member at all, but her distant relatives in Beverstedt, the cousin who had 'married out' and her 'rough diamond' of a husband. In a diary entry influenced by the news of D-Day, which came that same day, Marianne described her train journey north:

On 6 June

*In B.*

*Journey through a fateful night. Ignorant of what was happening – and yet so closely linked to the events of the world. On the surface one is still uninvolved, but how long before one is sucked into the whirlpool? Will one survive the struggle?*

The train journey took her to Bremen, where she spent the day before travelling on to Beverstedt.[1] Wartime Bremen was a subdued place, but Marianne was still entranced and invigorated by the echoes of its mercantile, cosmopolitan Hanseatic past. She chanced on a restaurant in the Böttcherstrasse, and her description provides some of the earliest evidence of a love of historic objects that was to be Marianne's life-long passion:

*I had lunch in the beautiful old restaurant. Wonderful old Worpsweder furniture, hand-crafted lamps, stained glass windows and on the walls old, blue-painted tiles, tin and porcelain plates, wood-cuts and paintings – some of which were so old they were painted on wood and metal.*

Here amongst the beautiful old furniture she first heard the news:

*Here I first heard of the invasion; I had travelled through the night in blissful ignorance. It's strange and frightening to think that one can experience moments, hours, of such security whilst others are waging such decisive struggles. And yet how much one is involved, inextricably involved! It is so much better to live in danger!*

Later in the afternoon, it was on to Beverstedt. The following day Marianne celebrated her twenty-first birthday. In her 1980s article, Marianne wrote that the day brought her some horrific news:[2]

*On 7 June 1944 – on my twenty-first birthday, I was back in Beverstedt and heard on the English broadcast that the 18 December 1943 transport from Theresienstadt to Birkenau-Auschwitz had been gassed there in the last few days. I knew that my parents and my brother had been on this transport. And so I had an unforgettable birthday present.*

But there is no diary entry for 7 June and on the 8th, still full of the Whitsun discussions with the Bund, Marianne wrote calmly and at length about *Weltanschauungen*. Could she really have heard such horrific news about the family?

## WA

Marianne's lengthy notes on 8 June about 'WA' again reconnected to the Bund conversations at Whitsun. One of Marianne's Bund friends wrote to me of the great fascination the Bund's meetings exerted:[3]

*One returned home as if laden with gifts, in the awareness that one had come a little closer to real independent thought.*

Marianne's intellectual activity throughout the summer of 1944 was dominated by the questions the Bund meeting had raised for her. She was, literally, running with an idea.

On 8 June, for example, Marianne embarked on a detailed description of the meaning of a *Weltanschauung*, outlining the seven components that any self-respecting WA should contain. A month later, ensconced in Göttingen, she would still be grappling with the same issues. Waking up very early one morning and unable to go back to sleep, she wrote a letter to some friends, which she then noted in her diary:

I. *'Basic principles'; that is the basic question, and one must begin by asking 'what actually is a basic principle?' A basic principle is a formula that provides an objective guideline for a particular area of life (do you agree?)*
*And I think we have said something decisive here: an objective guideline.*

*Was* there something 'decisive' in writing 'an objective guideline'? We may well feel astonished that to someone in Marianne's situation this dry, ponderous exercise meant anything at all. But it is clear that for her these concerns were more than an intellectual game. She sought a core belief or set of principles strong enough to provide assurance in a world full of threats and horrors. One sentence in her ensuing reflections (which go on for pages) is underlined: 'We evolve basic principles to give us confidence and a guiding rule.'

In the 8 June entry, she comments on the absence of objective principles in her time:

*We live in a time without* Weltanschauung. *Lessons and slogans are taken from all corners, thrown together, all jumbled up, and no one looks to see whether they really fit together. This is no basis on which to build a coherent view. The last two centuries, with all their technological developments, have challenged mankind with radically new challenges – challenges which have yet to be mastered. Technology has changed the whole structure of the world and dislocated basic concepts and values.*

*That's why we can't talk of a WA in our time. Above all, a WA has to evolve organically.*

In this passage the Nazi era practically disappears from view, absorbed into the generic problems of our 'technological' age. Curiously, many German conservatives in the immediate post-1945 period articulated this very argument as an explanation for what had gone wrong in Germany, not least as a way of suppressing awareness of the Nazis' unique crimes.[4] Marianne's adoption of it is more surprising, particularly as it seems too ready-made, too fully formed, to be just her own view, and presumably stems from the Bund. Neither she nor they had the conservatives' reasons for wanting to deny the Nazis' distinctiveness. But perhaps the Bund as a whole, like Marianne, sought to master the oppressive threats they faced by redefining them in general historical and societal terms. Valid insight thus merged with a form of psychological 'threat-management'.

## Dreams, films and broadcasts

If Marianne sought by day to conquer her fears through philosophical reflection, her dreams were not so easily controlled. In Beverstedt, the morning after writing the entry above, Marianne woke early and reached for her pen:

9.6.44

6°

*I've woken up from a dream which I feel I must write down: it includes two portraits of H., which represent him clearly, amazingly clearly.*

*I'm sitting with a few friends when H. enters the room with a young woman, his wife, to tell us about two episodes in his life and 'work'.*

*In the first he's still a young man, a boy in fact, taking part in a fire drill. He and several comrades are dressed in firemen's uniforms, black, with a steel helmet. In the dream, a new person appears to tell us what we are watching: In his youth, H. belonged to a fire fighters' unit. His own responsibilities were modest; but there was someone else who could climb up the ladder particularly high. Everyone was amazed by this person and everyone admired him. When he reached the ladder's dizzy heights he could even fire a shot, that is, he could stand without holding on. H. couldn't bear this. He had to achieve what the other person could do. One day he managed it. He stood on the top rung with a revolver and fired a shot. But he hit a street lamp which hung above him and put out the light. As we looked round in the dimness, we saw rubble strewn everywhere; walls, remains of houses, torn up streets, all jumbled together. Somewhere there was a blacked-out tram. H. climbs down from the ladder and dares the others to match his feat. Some other young man volunteers, makes it to the top, and as he comes down again, H. shakes his hand with a calm expression and reaches for a box which he opens. The young man thinks that he will receive a medal [with an asterisk here, and at the bottom of the page, Marianne had added the comment 'i.e. I think that'], but H. simply puts something in the box and closes it. I don't remember any more of this bit of the dream.*

355

2. *We are still sitting together, H. and his young wife among us. He thinks about what else he can do to impress us. Then above us, at a window, we see a man's head, a beautiful, intelligent looking face. H. calls up immediately, 'V.Mst. I would like to talk to you.'*

*The man's face darkens, he seems unsettled. Then he comes down accompanied by two other men and greets H . . . One of his companions gives M. something and I see that it's a revolver.[5] Then the four go into a room [with an asterisk here, Marianne inserts the comment 'H. on his own'] and after this we only hear their voices.*

*H. attacks v.M. over the invasion and holds him responsible, but v.M. proves intelligently and clearly that no other outcome was possible and that it was the logical consequence of all that has already happened. He is completely calm, considered and clear. I imagine I see him smiling, while H.'s voice is loud and agitated. As v.M. finishes his remarks, H. says only, 'I don't understand that, I am not with you.'*

*Then they come out of the room. H. with his chest puffed out and head held high, looking as if he's just won a battle. Behind him is M. with an indulgent smile which to me signals wisdom. Now I notice that he has no uniform and is wearing knickerbockers. His companions stand behind him and he gives them back the revolver. H. sees it and threatens him but M. stays calm, pauses for a second and says: 'This is only because I want to go with you.' H. says nothing. I understand that if H. had tried to shoot him . . .*

Marianne breaks off here at this point, leaving the ending very unclear. The 'H.' is clearly Hitler. 'V.Mst.' or 'v.M.' or 'M.', may be von Manstein, one of Hitler's leading generals. The dream powerfully captures Hitler's character, particularly as a younger man. His shot at the light was a masterful metaphor of Hitler's assault on the German and European order. The armed stand-off between Hitler and Germany's military leaders (though probably indicating that Marianne shared the widely held, though erroneous, view that the army was not deeply implicated in Nazi crimes) anticipated by little more than a month their failed military attempt on Hitler's life. The dream is a masterpiece of precise observation of the Nazi regime, quite different from the normal run of Marianne's daytime reflections, in which she rarely mentioned politics.

Although she never admitted it to me, throughout her life Marianne was to experience in dreams the horror of what she overcame by day.[6]

What Marianne *did* find unbearable by day (and not for the first time) was living with narrow-minded, provincial relatives – in this case the Beverstedt cousins. With typical contempt for the couple's petty-bourgeois outlook, she fumed about their limitations. From her diary entries it is clear that she tried to introduce them to the Bund's ideas while they, unsettled, tried to pick holes in her idealism.[7] After a few days of this, Marianne's restless spirit could stand it no longer and she set off on an expedition that was as risky as it was typical. It was a three-hour journey to the cinema. The film, *The Secret of Tibet*, was, she wrote afterwards to a friend, 'really marvellous, and if I had decided not to take the risks involved in such a journey I would have missed something'.[8]

For Marianne, who felt so limited in where she could go and what she could do, the glimpse of this other universe was overpowering. Afterwards, even wandering round the provincial port of Wesermünde assuaged a little of her thirst for the wider world. The town was grey and ugly, to be sure:[9]

*But the sea and the winds of the world. In wartime there's not much going on, but one still senses a little of the wide world coming in with the tide as it laps the shore. I walked a long way along the dyke and took deep breaths of the sea breeze wafting in over the Weser. The current is strong in the river estuary. You could imagine you were already at sea. There's sand on the shore, the air smells of salt and seaweed, gulls are flying over the water and big ships move on the water. Over in the distance, the river winds its way past Oldenburg, past Blexen. There's a small church, a windmill, so far away, like toys. I enjoyed the walk very much and closed my eyes to absorb it all.*

Just before she left Beverstedt, Marianne wrote one little diary entry of a completely different kind. A line and a half at the bottom of a page runs: '20 June. Horrific! What will happen now? I'm thinking of my second dream on 9 June . . .' The immediacy and pithiness of that cryptic 'horrific!' breaks through the diary's normal tone. What had happened?

There is good reason to think that this was a reference to some

*Marianne's underground diary – at the bottom of the page is the oblique reference to the murder of her parents* extraordinary and horrific news. It seems it was now that Marianne heard the BBC broadcast containing information about a Theresienstadt – Auschwitz transport which she knew included her parents. The broadcast – the full story of which will be unravelled later – was transmitted on 16 June and contained the prediction that the occupants of the transport would be gassed on 20 June.[10] It was on 20 June that Marianne wrote the horrified entry above. She was in some way reminded of her vivid dream – probably because of its disturbingly accurate representation of Hitler's wild radicalism. Had the dream in some way been a portent? What dark forces she must have felt were governing a world in which a broadcasting service from London could be predicting the precise date of the murder of her family.

## Göttingen with Hedwig and Meta

Almost immediately, though, Marianne's normal tone reasserted itself. Here she is, a day or two later, by now ensconced with Hedwig Gehrke in Göttingen:

Gö. 25 VI

*Days with He. Marvellous sunshine; garden, bees and child. How attractive the city is! But the people!*

In her conversations with me, too, Marianne recalled the pleasures of working in Hedwig Gehrke's garden, tending her bees and helping to look after her child. Göttingen also had other distractions. Marianne went to the cinema, seeing among other things *Nora*, based on the Ibsen play. But the social problems of living with Hedwig's mother-in-law continued, though whether the diary's cryptic 'But the people!' referred to old Frau Gehrke, or to the middle-class Göttingen population, so much less attractive to Marianne than the more anti-Nazi Ruhr working class, is not clear.

The final straw at the Gehrkes, Marianne told me, were the bugs. While on leave from the front, Gustav Gehrke, a skilled joiner, had converted the attic. The conversion was 'beautiful, absolutely beautiful',

Marianne said, although it did get very warm in the hot summer of 1944. But then Marianne started breaking out in awful blisters. Since there was no question of consulting a doctor, it took a while for the cause to emerge. One night, Marianne felt something moving in her bed. Turning the light on, she discovered the woodwork crawling with bugs, which she thought Gustav had probably brought back from the front. Hedwig was so appalled that she practically threw Marianne out. (Marianne never quite clarified this, perhaps not wishing to say that Hedwig assumed Marianne had imported the bugs!)

Thanks to help from other Göttingen Bund members, I tracked down Gustav and Hedwig Gehrke. I knew that the couple, now in their eighties, had broken with the Bund. Another Bund member wrote to me that while on leave from the front, Gustav had said to him that they had fooled themselves with their abstinence from alcohol and tobacco. 'Probably the events of war smashed his youthful ideals,' he wrote.[11] When I rang, Gustav answered and was clearly not sure his wife would want to talk to me at all. Hedwig did come to the phone, but was so poorly and depressed that she was able to tell me little more than that she remembered Marianne staying with her. Evidently the Bund had disappointed her after the war, and Marianne too, she said, had never been in touch again. 'Life is hard,' Hedwig Gehrke told me. She sounded more drained and sad and ill than anyone I have ever spoken to. I wished her well and left it at that.[12]

On or soon after 20 July – the day of the attempted assassination of Hitler – Marianne moved in with Meta Steinmann.[13] Years after the war, Meta, by then remarried as Kamp, published an account of her experiences during the Third Reich for her children and grandchildren. Marianne lent me her copy of the book, and it was thanks to this that I managed to find Frau Kamp. I thought the Göttingen city administration might have had a hand in funding the book's publication, and the friendly staff at the town's cultural affairs department were indeed able to provide me with Frau Kamp's address. It turned out that both Meta Kamp and her younger sister, Elfrieda Nenadovic, had been influential in local politics after the war. Frau Nenadovic was still active in cultural affairs and local history at the time I established contact.

Meta was born on 24 July 1907, one of five children, into a working-

*Meta Kamp and granddaughter*

class family.[14] Her grandfather had been a carpet weaver and a highly respected, well-educated Social Democrat; her parents (her father was a tailor, her mother a housewife) were both Social Democrats and also active in the local workers' chorus. Meta, a bookworm from an early age, became a convinced Social Democrat herself in the 1920s. She and the man who was later to become her husband, Ernst Steinmann, were both enthusiastic members of the youth movement, above all the Naturfreunde.[15] Abstinence from alcohol and tobacco and a commitment to further education are indicative of the group's high-mindedness. Meta remembered reading Dostoevski, August Bebel, Kant ('not all of which we understood') and many other writers.

Meta's contact with the Bund developed during the 1930s through Carlos Morgenstern. Meta felt that, of all her comrades in Göttingen, she had perhaps been the one who most closely identified with the Bund and early on intuited what they were about. Sonja Schreiber was her 'spiritual adviser', and Meta was deeply impressed by Artur Jacobs' personality. She had the feeling of 'coming home', she said, 'as if I had been waiting for such an experience'.[16] Sadly for Meta, she found that her husband did not share her enthusiasm. Their first great source of confrontation was the issue of sexual equality. Meta read the Bund pamphlet: *Man and Woman as Comrades in the Struggle* – and this, for husband Ernst, raised in a traditional farming family, was too much to take. Thus Meta made her spiritual journey very much alone, an independence reinforced by the fact that for much of the 1930s Ernst was working as a mechanic on building sites across Germany.

In 1936, Meta's father was arrested and imprisoned by the Nazis for a few months, his name having been divulged by a former Social Democratic comrade during interrogation. Meta, as her sister told me, learned to be particularly careful, not least because of the hostile neighbourhood. One of the residents in the neighbouring block, a certain Herr Flohr, was or had been a commandant of Moringen concentration camp. The local Block leader lived on the second floor of Meta's own building and was always on the look-out for activities to denounce.[17] Nevertheless, during the war Meta and the other local Bund members tried to put the group's philosophy into practice, providing food to foreign forced labourers – and taking in Marianne.

In order not to endanger her family, and mindful of her husband's lack of commitment, Meta told no one that Marianne was Jewish. Instead, she invented a story that Marianne had been bombed out in Essen and lost her family, becoming psychologically unstable. Her doctor had advised her to move to a new location to recover. The neighbours were fed this tale and it rapidly made the local rounds.

Meta's published account and her conversations with me contained many warm memories of Marianne. Like many other Bund members, she recalled Marianne's beauty and, of course, that hair . . . Its colour, she wrote in her memoir, was a 'warm brown with a reddish sheen'. And Marianne, she wrote, was 'basically a happy, life-affirming young person'.[18] Talking to me, Meta recalled with amazement Marianne's confidence and cheerfulness. But along with the amazement, she seemed to be asking an unspoken question. Frau Kamp could not really understand how Marianne could have been quite so cheerful. Indeed, at the time, she felt some consternation that Marianne was too convivial and gay for someone who had ostensibly lost her family in the bombing:[19]

'When she was so cheerful and confident, sometimes I had to wink at the neighbour with a sad face and point to my head. Which was supposed to imply, "The poor girl is completely confused!"'

At other times, though, Marianne sat quiet and despondent, and although they did not discuss things much, Frau Kamp caught a glimpse of the turmoil beneath.

Meta's book describes a dramatic episode. One day, Marianne was out walking with Meta's son, Ernst junior. The pair were stopped by police and ordered to show their papers. If they had been exposed, it would have meant certain death for Marianne and dire consequences for Meta's family. But Marianne was so jokey and friendly that in the end the patrol decided not to bother and allowed the two to continue unhindered.

Through Meta I obtained young Ernst's phone number, and when I finally caught up with him, now sixty-seven and living near Hamburg, what I really wanted to know was how *he* had coped with that moment. I was astonished to learn that he had no recollection of the incident, though he didn't doubt it had occurred. How could a moment when his life had hung in the balance disappear from his memory? But, as his mother reminded me, none of the family knew Marianne was Jewish. So Ernst had had no idea of the danger he was in, nor of the courage being shown by his companion. The incident was almost a non-event – they were asked for papers, but then didn't have to show them. Thoroughly forgettable.

Another occasion, however, had impressed itself on Ernst's memory. In 1944, he was one of many teenage anti-aircraft auxiliaries. One day he was in the flak emplacement when Marianne suddenly appeared to ask if he had his mother's watch. Evidently, Meta had been upset about losing it, and to relieve her anxiety Marianne had come over to ask if Ernst had got it. As Ernst remarked to me, even ordinary civilians were wary of venturing into designated military areas, so for Marianne – 'that took quite a lot, you know?' 'She had a lot of guts', was his comment on the girl, though just how much he found out only after the war, when

*Marianne in underground years*

his mother revealed Marianne's true identity.[20] Incidentally, Ernst felt guilty for years at having lost his mother's watch. Twenty years later he finally got round to buying her a new one.

After hearing the BBC broadcast, Marianne must have been consumed with worry about her parents. Meta's much younger sister Elfrieda told me a moving story about this. In July 1944 Elfrieda was on labour service in Upper Silesia. While she was visiting Göttingen, Meta told her that she had a young guest staying who wished to ask Elfrieda something about Upper Silesia. And so the two went for a walk. Elfrieda found Marianne very nice and lively, but wondered what she wanted. It soon came out. 'Have you heard of a camp there for political unreliables?' Marianne asked. In this cautious way, Marianne sought to find the truth of the BBC report about Auschwitz. Elfrieda, of course, did not know why Marianne was asking, nor had she heard of Auschwitz, so could offer little enlightenment. But they agreed a code by which she would communicate anything she found out. Once back in Upper Silesia, she asked around. A farmer confirmed that special trains came through continually to the camp, but more than that he could not say. In any case, Elfrieda told me, her base was relatively far from Auschwitz. Like her brother, it was only after the war that she understood the significance of the encounter: with her seemingly casual question, Marianne had been trying to confirm whether Theresienstadt deportees really were being murdered.[21] Not until 1945 did Elfrieda realize how 'spirited' and fearless Marianne had been. Her confident manner had been Marianne's protection, Elfrieda said. That and the fact that she 'didn't look Jewish'.[22]

## The trials of friendship

Marianne's diary entry from 13 July contained yet another revelation, in the form of excerpts from a letter sent to her by Sonja Schreiber. Sonja gave vent to gentle but firm criticism of Marianne's behaviour in relation to the Briels; in forming a close friendship with Fritz Briel, Marianne, it seems, had been careless of Maria. She also commented on Marianne's relationship with someone called Hermann:

'. . . And something else, while I'm dispensing maternal advice: I was somewhat perturbed by the fact that you're venturing to advise Hermann on his personal relationships. Really, the only person who can and should give such advice is someone with maturity and experience, someone who has gained first-hand insights into such difficult problems. I hope you have not entangled yourself in difficulties. I also think you should be a little more circumspect towards a man who has a close relationship with another woman. You have known both sides for far too short a time.' – How right she is! And that's why it's doubly painful!

A letter from a Hermann Schmalstieg is also folded in at this page. Though the tone of the letter is friendly, the writer was clearly concerned at unsolicited advice Marianne had given his girlfriend, Berti. He did not question Marianne's insight, but rather the inappropriateness of her seeking to advise someone whom she hardly knew, on the basis of so little knowledge and experience.[23] Had she thought through the conversation, he wanted to know, since such things required careful thought. Had she discussed it with Hedwig? (Evidently, Hedwig Gehrke was a mutual friend.) He included part of a subsequent letter from Berti to himself, which showed how unhappy she was about the affair.

Of course, I found all this, the diary and letters, only after Marianne's death. Whenever she and I had spoken about Bund members, she had alluded to tensions only with Mrs Gehrke senior, Hedwig's mother-in-law. For the rest, the Briels, the Schmitzes and so on took on an almost saintly quality. Some were closer and more powerful presences, Maria Briel, for example, or Sonja Schreiber; others, such as the Morgensterns, more distant, if only because Marianne had had little contact with them after the war. But there was never a hint of problems between them. Now I looked back into the diary and realized that I had failed to spot the significance of various other passages. When Marianne had talked at Whitsun about 'Easter wounds', of which 'only we three are aware'[24] this was not, as I had thought at first, some kind of quasi-religious reference, but a hint of conflict between herself and the Briels.

If the letter from Sonja was correct, the cause of friction, it seemed, was often, ironically, Marianne's desire to help her hosts. She had been thrust suddenly into intimate familial situations and confronted with other people's marriages in a way that was new to her. (Ernst, too, had written from Izbica about the novelty of living side by side with other families. Nazi policies and the dislocations of war had the effect of roughly pushing aside the screens that normally shielded family life from view.) In addition, as we know, part of the Bund's philosophy was that its moral and political values should be applied just as much to marriage and private life as to the public arena. Its members were engaged in the experiment of creating a moral community, and there was a tradition of open discussion about relationships.[25] For Marianne, who felt her inactivity and her dependence so keenly, here was a forum in which she felt she could actively help. But the impact of the beautiful, headstrong girl had evidently been explosive.

The next couple of weeks were spent in various attempts to make things better. On Sunday 16 July, Marianne noted 'a lovely, clarifying, open exchange with Hermann; Hedwig was there. That was how I wanted it', but 'nevertheless everything in me is dark and heavy'. A letter to Sonja followed, excerpted in the diary. She wrote to the Briels, too.[26] And she wrote to Berti, with more harmless advice on how to decorate her room. Her suggestion was to pick some landscapes by Van Gogh:

Göttingen, 5 August

*(Letter to Berti)*

*The 'Landscape with Vegetable Garden' is one of his peaceful pictures, although he often applies the paint tube directly to the canvas out of impatience and a desire to capture the object completely. How far he penetrates beneath the surface and how much renunciation of self! The painter completely submerging himself in the subject!*

*This is something one senses in his pictures, and that is why I love them so (not all of them!). Also because they are so life-like (through the thick layers of colour), so luminous, so vivid and so immediate.*

For someone like Marianne, so knowledgeable, so conscious of material artefacts and so aware of the environment around her, what torture it must have been to live for two years with virtually no possessions and with no base of her own.

As part of her peace mission, Marianne made a weekend excursion into the Harz mountains to spend time with Hermann Schmalstieg and Berti. In her published account from the 1980s, Marianne made only a brief reference to Hermann Schmalstieg and he did not surface at all in our conversations. Initially, therefore, I made no particular effort to find him. When Meta Kamp mentioned that Hermann was still alive and gave me his address I was, of course, glad to make the connection. But only after discovering the diary did I realize that Marianne had met him more than once in 1943–4 and that they corresponded regularly. As a result, I contacted Herr Schmalstieg on several occasions by telephone or letter, each time with a fresh batch of questions, and finally interviewed him in 1999, at what may prove to be the Bund's last summer meeting.

Like so many in the Bund, Schmalstieg had been born into a modest working-class family.[27] In his teens during the 1920s, he had also been an enthusiastic member of the Naturfreunde. Also like many Bund members, he first came in contact with the group through gymnastics. Responding to a notice advertising classes in Göttingen, run by Georg Reuter, a Bund member, Hermann soon came to realize that there was more than simply physical exercises on offer: here was a movement seeking answers to fundamental questions about life.[28] Though he never lived in the Bund's heartland, the Ruhr area, Hermann retained regular contact through the meetings and Bund holidays, which continued to be held during the Nazi years. These meetings made such an impression on him that after the war he took an entirely new career path, giving up his job as a laboratory technician and becoming a youth worker in order to help shape a different generation of Germans.

During the war, Hermann Schmalstieg worked at the Technische Hochschule in Braunschweig. Because of the air raids, his research section, which tested audio and radio equipment for the military, moved to the Auerhahn mountain, near Goslar in the Harz mountains. Hermann was quartered in a lonely forester's cottage, in an isolated romantic area, ideal for hiding the young Marianne, and it was doubtless there that she went in July 1944. Hermann Schmalstieg had a vivid memory of her visit, and of one incident in particular. In the morning, he left Marianne in the cottage while he went off to work. No one was supposed to know she was there, since a highly sensitive technical project for the military was in the vicinity. Returning home from his day's work, Hermann's blood ran cold. Marianne had opened the windows wide and was sitting with her legs dangling outside, singing happily.[29]

For her part, Marianne's record of the experience was quite different. Lonely, with the recent news of her family behind her, she evidently began to have feelings for Hermann that troubled her:

Monday, 31.7

*Weekend in the Harz*

*Conversation with Hermann in connection with a remark I once made: 'The only things of value in life are things one has called forth from oneself; knowledge that comes from the self.'*

*[ . . . ]*

*Early morning on a superb, beautiful day, and a growing attraction to a somehow familiar and yet so alien person. Around me the open peacefulness; pine-dark hills and valleys.*

*To feel so divided! Torn back and forth between heart and reason; so close to despair; the abyss so near. At such moments you feel a loneliness without end or, more accurately, you become clearly aware of how lonely you are. Help is to be found only within. From the clear, objective forces which lie within. For human beings, the greatest challenge is to keep these forces alert at all times, at every moment, to never lose the clear judgement of one's critical faculties ('critical', in a good sense). But how close the danger is! If you are not endlessly vigilant. You have to keep renewing that judgement; it's never simply to hand.*

*But it is so difficult; so difficult, so difficult, so difficult! The heart is so powerful; far too strong a counterweight. Often the weight of reason is not sufficient to balance it. How true the saying: 'Two souls dwell, ach, in my breast.'*

*The struggle of I against me is so difficult and so lonely.*

*If one could only learn to say an unequivocal 'Yes' to loneliness!*

*Perhaps one asks too much, too much from people and from things?*

*And each step, each new piece of knowledge, each new rung on the ladder, involves so much pain.*

*To be able to love, to love, to love, to love; uninhibited, unfettered by one's own conscience, unchallenged by the world outside! But the fact that it's never possible, that I'm never allowed to love, that it always brings so much pain – surely this must mean something?*

*If only one weren't always desperately waiting for something, always wanting. If only one could let go of the branch, give oneself up, completely and without reservation; give oneself up to something, perhaps that's the secret. Perhaps that's also the way to the other person. If only one could!*

*[ . . . ]*

*Yesterday during our walk, the conversation about* Weltanschauung. *The Jewish question: How is such an attitude possible, given such intellectual capacity and judgement! If only he knew! Oh, my stupid heart.*

A couple of hours later.

*Goslar, on the market place.*

*Ernest, I think I might have lost you now. Or, did you let me go? Forever?*

*Will you draw me to you again? Who knows?*

*[ . . . ]*

*This old town is beautiful in its harmonious style. For writing poetry, dreaming and losing oneself.*

It is not absolutely certain that the conversation Marianne refers to is the same conversation, the one with Hermann, with which the entry opens, but it seems likely. Clearly, whoever was with her on the walk had stirred feelings of love – and of guilt in relation to Ernst. Taking this entry in conjunction with the letters, I wondered if there had been more than friendship between Hermann Schmalsteig and Marianne. Meta Kamp thought not, but, enclosing transcripts of some of the diary and letters I had found, I wrote to Hermann Schmalstieg and, after apologizing for presenting him with what might be emotionally painful, I asked him whether he could fill in the background.

Hermann Schmalstieg was touched by my letter, but was adamant that there had been no affair. He had been going out with Berti at the time, a vulnerable girl, now long dead, who suffered feelings of inferiority and needed constant reassurance. He remembered Marianne and Berti meeting. Looking back, Hermann was amazed that under the conditions of war and Nazi terror a private life had been possible at all.

*To come back to Marianne, she really was a delightful person. I had no idea how close she felt to me until I read the thoughts in her diary. I mean the thoughts and feelings which she wrote in her diary after a conversation with me. Yes, the diary opened up a world of which I was completely unaware at the time. I myself was too preoccupied with Berti, with the events of the war and the work in the institute. Reading Marianne's thoughts and feelings as an older person today, one could gain the impression that her behaviour towards me was more than just friendly. But on my part this really wasn't the case. I've already explained why not. Nevertheless I am moved by Marianne's thoughts. That is because what appears in the diary entries is also my world, one which I've carried around fixed within me, for almost a lifetime.*

When we finally met at the Bund conference at the Rüspe in the Sauerland, I found Hermann Schmalstieg a little unsteady on his feet but still with youthful charm and, above all, an enthusiastic innocence, despite being in his nineties. He was accompanied by his attractive wife, she only in her sixties and looking younger still. Hermann told me again how deeply moved he had been to learn of Marianne's feelings for him.

In my letters, I posed some delicate questions, curious whether he realized the full implications of some of Marianne's remarks:

*One entry of 31.7.1944, which* perhaps *referred to a conversation with you, raised the question for me whether you actually knew at the time that Marianne was Jewish. Or was this information withheld for your safety?*

Of course he had known that she was Jewish, he wrote. And as far as I can tell, the Bund members who protected Marianne *did* generally know this. But Marianne wrote that her 'stupid heart' had left her with strong feelings for someone with intolerable views on the Jewish question, prompting the only entry in the whole diary making even an oblique reference to her Jewish identity. Her remark 'If only he knew!'

either meant 'he' did not know she was Jewish or that 'he', with his views about Jews, did not realize she loved him. But if Hermann Schmalstieg now registered the implication of Marianne's remarks, he did not let on to me.

## Where to now?

A diary entry from late August begins with yet another brief encounter:

26. VIII.44

*'It's coming to an end, everything's coming apart,' the dentist said. Shame – I'd like to have got to know him better. And I had the feeling he wanted to know more about me. Perhaps at some later time. Who knows!? Sometime, when we can put our cards on the table.*

But the tone soon changes, introducing an unexpected twist:

*Later, in the train*

*[. . .]Farewell to Gö. Where to now?*
*Never have I felt the burdens of my life so acutely as I do now. Homelessness, loneliness. I'm suspended in space! How will the heart-to-heart with Karin go?*
*[. . .]*
*Journey into the unknown. After Goslar into the Harz . . . and then? Ach, if only I could rest with someone's loving heart.*
*But could I? One's own nature is so torn, so ambivalent. One wants to surrender oneself but also to fight; to be carried along but also to set the direction.*

Marianne had never even hinted to me that the chain of helpers had been close to breaking. Only the diary revealed that in late summer 1944, after four weeks with Meta Steinmann, Marianne really did not know where she should go next. For a while in Göttingen, she had been anxiously awaiting a letter from Karin Morgenstern. Now, it seemed that Karin was camping in the Harz mountains and some kind of clarification was needed between them before a decision could be made about Marianne's future.

That evening Marianne slept under the open sky:

Evening [in the Harz]

*Marvellous to drift along! Just water, sky and God – and the unknown depths below. Evening above the water. Solitude and peace. You feel all your problems flow away. Forests and sky, sun and moon, the untapped harmony of the universe. But life?*

Sunday!

*[. . .]*

*Yesterday evening brought a short conversation with Karin, to be continued this morning, and a walk with the other two friends though the moonlit summer evening. We talked about Karin and the difficulty of being with her, above all because of the way she takes every favour for granted. The conversation ended on a positive note.*

*I'm so preoccupied, thinking about life in this difficult, bloody time. Future; tests and dangers, how are they to be mastered?*

*To be* whole! *And to master the horror through* reason!

In a letter to Meta Steinmann it emerged that the conversation with Karin Morgenstern had been far from satisfactory.[30] Tensions persisted between Marianne, Karin, and the other two Bund members in the mountains. From shorthand in the diary and some information provided by Hermann Schmalstieg, it seems the others were Hermann and Lene Krahlisch, a couple from Mülheim. The problems were apparently compounded by the fact that not only was Marianne's arrival unexpected but Lene's mother also turned up unannounced. Nevertheless, from the Harz mountains, Marianne now travelled back to Braunschweig with Karin.

Hints at tensions in her relations with Bund friends continue for some weeks. Tucked into the front of the diary I found a letter in someone else's hand addressed to 'Liebe Anya' and clearly directed to Marianne.

23.9.1944

Dear Anya,

I wonder how things are with you? Did you arrive at L's[31] safe and sound? I hope the journey went well. In my thoughts I was with you so much – I'm sure that helped. How are you settling in?

I wanted to send you a parcel but they wouldn't take it. Now I have to pack a smaller one. And send you a little bread and some groceries in it.

Something is weighing on my mind that I wanted to tell you before you started living there. I've had the strong sense that you, in yourself, if you know what I mean, have somehow been thrown off kilter. Recently.

That's the feeling I get from your latest letters. It may partly be the result of ~~the weeks being so insecure~~ of your external situation being so insecure – as you waited for K's[32] letter and didn't know where to go. But M, if we are secure inside, have confidence and know where others stand in relation to us, then we can stay on an even keel.

One has to learn to stop seeing oneself[33] as the centre of everything and learn to share more of others' lives.

If you want to take part.

If you want to live with a family.

It's not always easy – but it is something that can be learned.

And so I wanted to say something to you about living together, as a community.

Our whole life consists of experimenting and testing.

But not, as you tend to do when living with others, laying down the law unilaterally. Something which expresses itself in so many small things.

To be sure, M is young and the world is open to her. And she wants to conquer all by 'force'. But that's not the right way.

One must be able to adapt to other people – that has to be learned. One must listen to others and learn how to fit oneself into their lives.

And not always react with a critical attitude to everything that doesn't suit you.

*I have some misgivings about you going to L. You will be thinking, is that —-'s [the letter-writer's] business . . .*

*Yes, I feel that I must say something to you about it.*

*You see, I'm able to say when something doesn't suit me or, more to the point, when I believe something isn't right. But not everyone can do that. You remember that I too had to learn to tell you when I didn't think something was right. Not everyone learns so quickly. Usually, people think, 'the couple of weeks are soon past and then we'll be on our own again'.*

*No, it should be a proper life together.*

*And since you exert a very powerful influence on people, even when you're wrong and aren't seeing things properly, you must always ask yourself, 'Is that right?' and, 'Am I allowed to do that?'*

*What I find troubling is that in conversation you see that something you've done is wrong and say yes, yes but afterwards you act just as you want, just as you had before.*

*That's not the point of living and experimenting together. The point is to act on the principles one has already accepted and then experiment further.*

*I've often found it so draining. Perhaps you do it without realizing. But it's very depressing for the people you're living with.*

*And when I think of L, she's not a very strong person[ . . .]*

*I think I've expressed myself clearly.*

*Will you write to me what you think?*

*For today, loving greetings.*

The signature is unclear, and in any case is probably a code. Comparison with other letters does not help identify the handwriting. The letter is not fluent enough to be from Sonja. Most likely, it came from Hedwig Gehrke.

Poor Marianne! What utter loneliness she must have felt in such moments. When those on whom her life depended were exasperated with her, who was there left to turn to? With the exception, perhaps, of the time she actually spent with Meta, this whole period since Beverstedt now seemed so much more conflict-laden and unsettled than I had realized.

It was, above all, the letter to 'Anya' that prompted me to ask Hermann Schmalstieg whether he thought the Bund friends really understood Marianne's situation. When Marianne and Karin Morgenstern had their quarrel in the Harz, Karin had even accused Marianne of not understanding the difficulties of *her* position. Of course, Marianne was not the only one in danger. The heroism of the Bund members is without question. In that sense, they were all in the same boat. But unlike her friends, Marianne had no choice but to continue being heroic. If they stopped defying the regime, they would be safe from persecution. If she stopped defying the regime, she would be murdered. I wondered if Marianne's hosts had made sufficient allowance for her special predicament. Yet, when I considered the situation from their angle, it was clear that they actually found it hard to cope with and contain Marianne. They experienced her not as vulnerable, but as powerful. As Hedwig wrote, they had to learn to say 'no' to her. The indomitable character that was essential for Marianne's physical and psychological survival did not make life easy for her hosts.

## The front creeps closer

During an air raid over Braunschweig at the end of August, Marianne and Karin took refuge in a shelter and Marianne penned a letter to Sonja in the anxious hours of the night. She had been on the run for a whole year:

Bra.[34] 29/30.VIII

*Night in the shelter*

*One has the feeling that the war is coming closer with every day. How much it devours and how frighteningly small are the personal sacrifices we've made until now!*

*Eberhardt [Jungbluth – recently killed in battle] – I still can't believe it! Sometimes you wonder if it always strikes the best of them! (But that's an unworthy thought; it just strikes doubly hard.)*

*All that's left are the happy thoughts and memories that allow those we have lost to live on. The more they were loved, the more they stay with us. Isn't that so? And I feel we have a duty to do our utmost to live properly, in memory of the dead (because their lives and being are somehow interwoven with ours; on one level they've died and taken part of us with them, but they've also left much behind; though we often don't recognize its value because of the pain).*

*. . . and to do our utmost to live, mindful of our own death because we are part of an unending cycle.*

*That's never been so clear to me as it is now. I've often thought such things but never felt so fulfilled by them.*

*A remarkable year lies behind me, one in which I've won – and lost – an enormous amount. (But where does the idea of winning begin and the idea of losing leave off?) Is there not a loss entailed in winning and a win in each loss?*

*[. . .]*

*The shelter has now emptied. Next to me, two people are talking about the war. Which is never more present than in moments of danger. 'What do you think, will we still win the war?' The other shakes her head: 'What, now? Impossible!' Do many people think like that?*

*Strange, people at night; quite different from by day!*

Signs of the approaching front were ever more apparent; the air-raid warnings unceasing. Marianne's diary entries became more intermittent and her thoughts preoccupied by the mounting chaos around her. Paradoxically, life was now as much under threat from the Allies as from the Nazis. When I interviewed her for the Ruhrland Museum in 1989, Marianne said that the last few months of the war were the most taxing and stressful:

'All these factors built up: the never-ending travelling, the fact that I could never come to rest, the ever-growing danger of being caught or recognized, on top of the problems I shared with the rest of the population – finding food, staying healthy, avoiding the bombs. In the last months of the war and of my illegal existence they all had an effect on me which I was aware of only much later.'

Marianne's first port of call after Braunschweig was Mülheim in the Ruhr, just a few miles from her home in Essen. Here she stayed with

Lene Krahlisch (probably the 'L' of Meta's letter), one of her Bund hosts whom she completely forgot after the war and never mentioned in her article:[35]

Mülheim, 31.9.44

*(Letter to Meta)*

*I've been with Lene for a week now, a very eventful, unsettling week that has given me little chance to rest. The journey here was better than I'd feared. We left early in the morning and arrived late at night. The trains were packed. Every time you meet other people, you are moved and shaken by what they tell you. Dramatic experiences and fates seared by the relentlessness of war. People torn apart, separated from their families, often without a clue to where to find them. Refugees fleeing battles on the borders, or fleeing bombs. The stories they tell are often so horrific that you're left trembling with fear about your own fate.*

*Travelling has become dangerous. Massive attacks can happen any time. Some people have already been through such horrors. Yes, the war has come very close. The front is not far, and day and night you can hear the thunder of the guns.*

Here was further evidence that Marianne made no mental distinction between herself and 'the Germans'. The refugees evoke her sympathy and also elicit anxious identification with their plight. Their dreadful experiences make her fear for her own safety.

As defeat seemed increasingly certain, the regime became even more radical. Half-Jews and Jews in mixed marriages were now targeted for deportation and murder. Typically, Marianne tried to help those around her. Her friend, Grete Menningen, had been relatively protected until the early summer of 1944 because she was married to a non-Jew. She lived in Barmen and had been able to put Marianne up once or twice. But now Grete, too, was assigned to a transport. Marianne told me that, through the help of another Bund friend, Else Bramesfeld, someone was eventually found who lived in an isolated house near Remscheid and was willing to hide Frau Menningen.[36]

Marianne herself struggled to make a virtue of the constant tension and threat. In Duisburg, she was caught up in one of her worst air raids yet:

15.X.44

*Attacks day and night. Yesterday and last night Duisburg. The bombs just kept falling. One dies a thousand deaths. And people manage to put up with it!*

*How salutary the way one's sense of values changes in moments of acute danger. All your own worries seem so tiny. You no longer cling so rigidly to external things. You feel your way, testing, exposed to everything. We should learn from this for our ordinary lives. Really learn: to be detached from everything, to be able to let go. Only then can one live properly and die properly.*

Monday, 16.X.44

*Still filled with the horror of the previous few hours I went to the cinema yesterday afternoon, because I simply could not relax. My thoughts kept wheeling round and round what had happened.*

By the end of October, Marianne was in Remscheid, probably staying with the Briels again:

30.X.44 Rem.

*(Letter to Lene)*

*Yes, these are difficult, bad times. Fear of what is to come creeps up on you. Essen must have been awful. I was so happy when Maria brought news on Thursday that everyone there is well and in good shape. During the raid on Monday evening, I was sitting in a train between D.–S.[37] It was absolutely dreadful. The planes rumbled overhead, flying very low. Any minute a bomb could have fallen on us. You can imagine the panic. I learned what an effect on others it has if one stays completely calm. I surprised myself with the strength I could convey by staying calm and speaking calmly. Women, trembling, clutched on to my hands, but then they too calmed down. I only hope I'll have the same strength when things really depend on it. But that demands so much!*

31.X

*Another day has passed! At midday it seems there was another attack on Essen. I worry so much about our friends! Every day brings new tests. I listen to every rumour and am always on the move.*

*Half-sedentary, half-nomad.*

The image of Marianne sitting in the train providing solace to the women around her is extraordinary, and conveys vividly her divided sense of identity. On the one hand, she feels part of the wider community, and it is natural that she should provide others with assistance. On the other hand, she does not yet consider this the real test. What was probably the high-point of terror in the whole war for those around her is for Marianne just a rehearsal for the challenges she fears are yet to come.

At the beginning of November a letter must have arrived from Meta, bringing not only news that the Göttingen friends were still alive, but also, evidently, some welcome praise for Marianne herself, acknowledging her strength and spirit at such a difficult time. Such words, so important to Marianne after so many difficult encounters, prompted her to put pen to paper straight away.

Friday, 3.XI.44

*(From a letter to Meta)*

*I can't tell you what pleasure your delightful letter gave me! I was a little worried not to have heard from you for so long. The times are so uncertain and one's life so dependent on the bigger picture – at least that's how things are here.[ . . .]*

*Now to your letter: are you sure that you're seeing me properly? I don't feel my thoughts and deeds merit anything like so much praise! I keep learning how much I'm still at the beginning. In that, you're right. Yes, it is time that I do something productive with my life, though not to give (as you think) but to learn – to learn the inner peace and balance required for true freedom and the discovery of the true, clear path to oneself and others. Objective actions are surely the secret. So much confusion in personal things, and in humanity as a whole, would be*

*resolved instantly if everyone heard the call of necessity and simply acted*
*on it! One can and must confront mankind with the basic command: 'Do*
*what you see is necessary; do what it is most important for you to do!'*

## The diary and identity

With that, and another small entry from 11 November 1944, the diary
proper comes to an end. Over the months from April to November 1944
a voice had emerged which I had not heard in any of the interviews. Had
I read the diary first, I might have been able to make out faint echoes in
some of the things Marianne said to me. But, as it was, my image of the
girl on the run had been quite different from the self-portrait she painted.
My overriding awareness of that monstrous thing, the Holocaust, and
the knowledge that Marianne's flight had been triggered because she
was a Jew, had led me to assume that while on the run she would see
herself primarily as a Jew in hiding and as a victim caught among her
tormentors. My conversations with Marianne had not challenged this
image. True, she never paraded her victimhood. She was very conscious
of the difference between her experiences and those of people in the
camps. But nothing she had said to me revealed, as the diary now
suggested, that at the time Marianne had not in any way seen herself or
her problems in light of Jewish persecution.

Of course, the diary itself raises problems of interpretation. Fear of
discovery may have led to suppression of some issues and thoughts.
Marianne may have deliberately omitted, for example, anything that
identified her as Jewish. But there are too many sustained observations
and judgements (and also too many indiscretions) to see the diary as a
document written in terror, in fear of calling a spade a spade. Moreover,
as we shall see, Marianne's post-war writing, when the Gestapo had
ceased to be a threat, continued in the same vein.

The more important issue surrounding the diary's 'authenticity',
though, is what was the relationship between the entries, on the one
hand, and Marianne's identity and experience, on the other. The diary
is not a stream of consciousness or unmediated outpouring of emotion
but a remarkably composed document. It was clearly influenced by a

genre of reflective journal-keeping that sought to probe the essence of things, rather than record the day-to-day.[38] Thus Marianne often uses the third-person construction 'one' rather than the more immediate 'I'.[39] The diary was also clearly a way of regaining balance, finding her feet, a deliberate counterweight to the fears of the day. She was able to apply (and be quite conscious of applying) a kind of psychological censorship. The letters to Ernst from 1942 showed her capacity to exclude from her writing the daily threats and humiliations, and to focus on what was enriching or constructive. This did not mean that, off the page, Marianne was not aware of those threats or that they did not influence her sense of her identity.

Should we see Marianne's sustained reflections on *Weltanschauung*, then, as just 'flights' of fancy, an effort to hide from being in hiding? Did her dreams gave a better account of what she was going through than her measured daytime reflections? There *was* undoubtedly a degree of escapism here, a refusal to connect the dots in her increasingly well-informed picture of Nazi terror. But the diary also reports authentic experience that did not reinforce a sense of identity as a Jewish victim of Nazi persecution. For one thing, as the war went on, Marianne was increasingly surrounded by German suffering of one sort or another, and she was guiltily, fearfully conscious that she had so far come through the war 'unscathed', while the number of refugees, evacuees, war-wounded, and war-dead grew around her. In her descriptions of encounters with refugees on the train, what comes through is that Marianne saw herself as one of very many people displaced by war. Of course, for us, the moral significance of being an accidental victim of the machinery of war and of being sought out for a programme of genocide is quite different. But Marianne's awareness of others' suffering was probably an important factor in her survival.[40]

Something else that emerges from the diary is how disorientating it must have been constantly to pretend to be someone else. For Marianne, 'passing' involved maintaining at least *three* identities. She herself and those fully in the know were aware that she was a Jew on the run (although, as noted, this barely seemed to define her identity for herself or them). To Elfrieda Wahle, Ernst Steinmann and others, Marianne as Bund member was a politically endangered Aryan, keeping her head down, but not belonging to that most dangerous category – the Jew. And for the wider world, she was quite simply an ordinary German. That last identity kept changing its specific character: sometimes she was a young woman with a child, sometimes a distant relative and sometimes a bombed-out victim. Small wonder that, occasionally, Marianne ached to end the role-playing and simply be herself. The problem was, as she herself acknowledged, that she was no longer sure what that was. In September, for example, she wrote:[41]

*I love the 'I' too much; all the different 'I's within me. And the true person one should be and wants to be somehow gets lost. One is always playing a role to oneself and to others. One is never really 'I'.*

This comment also reveals perhaps the most subtle and important part of Marianne's experience. With our awareness of the Holocaust, we assume that persecution was the fundamental fact in Marianne's life. Of course, in many ways, it was: it had robbed her of family and friends and sent her into hiding. But for Marianne, a young woman just entering maturity, encountering new ideas and new people, it was not always easy to tell which of her fears and problems were in fact the product of war. Was the loss of the 'I' the result of trying to decide who she was or rather of having to be in hiding? She was not sure. In early August, she wrote, for example:[42]

*All one's personal difficulties and problems – don't they stem from the chaos of our time? Events fly by so fast that one follows them in an exaggerated state of wakefulness and tension. Aren't one's own problems inextricably interwoven with all this?*

To us, the connection seems so obvious – how could friendships and relationships be other than fraught in such circumstances? But Marianne's insight is phrased as a question; she could not be certain of what is now obvious. And on reflection, we can see that *not* everything she said or experienced, *not* every feature of her life and interactions, could be ascribed to persecution. It was Marianne's tragedy to experience the process of growing up, of finding herself, in those horrific conditions. Marianne had an advantage enjoyed by few other Jews passing as Aryans; a very positive 'Aryan' role model. Looking back on some of the personal difficulties she experienced with her hosts, I realized that the Bund members' refusal to make allowances for Marianne's special predicament had a powerfully uplifting aspect. For Marianne, the letters from Hedwig and Sonja, critical though they were, signalled that they treated her as one of the group. No distinctions were being made. In other words, the Bund provided her not only with safe houses but, even more important, it offered her an identity. More and more, as the diary makes clear, Marianne saw herself as one of them, a fighter for a better Germany. From our interviews, I learned her debt to the Bund; from the diary, I learned that for a while during the war she became, at least subjectively, *part* of the Bund.

## The last weeks on the move

As 1944 came to a close, travelling became even more risky as a result of air attacks on the railways and the increasing surveillance by Gestapo and criminal police on trains, stations and public places. According to a Bund member from Düsseldorf, towards the end of 1944 Marianne almost fell into the hands of the criminal police and only escaped by good luck.[43] The number of safe houses dwindled rapidly. In January 1945, Sonja Schreiber was sent into a rural area with her school. Artur and Dore Jacobs went to ground in southern Germany. It was now too risky to travel as far as Braunschweig, Göttingen or Bremen.[44]

On 31 December 1944, Marianne was at Wuppertal-Vohwinkel station, waiting for a train to Solingen-Wald to stay with a woman associated with the Bund called Reni Sadamgrotzky, when suddenly the station came under direct attack in a bombing raid. The following day, by which time she was ensconced at Reni's in Solingen-Wald, waves of bombers suddenly flew over while they were eating lunch; bombs exploded around the house as they fled to the cellar. The house received a direct hit while they were in the cellar and the whole estate was destroyed in minutes. Happily, Reni and Marianne emerged unharmed.[45]

Marianne's restitution testimony reveals that in January 1945 she paid a brief visit to Hammacher, her father's bank manager. She wanted to make it clear that at least one of the family had survived. Whether

her purpose was to establish later claims to the house (which, she knew by then, had been destroyed), or to prevent the bank from doing anything with the records of the family's accounts, I am not sure. In her testimony, she said that she had wanted to ascertain the current state of the family property and finances. She did not tell Hammacher where she had come from or where she was going, and the whole visit lasted no more than ten minutes. There is no evidence that the bank director informed anyone else about it.[46] Marianne also used her visit to Essen to drop in on the Jürgens. This time, she said, there was 'a spanking new table cloth with my mother's monogram' on the dining table, and she had to bite her lip to keep silent.[47]

By February 1945, the Allies had reached the left bank of the Rhine. In view of the war situation, where was best for Marianne to go? Her friends advised her to try Düsseldorf, which they believed would soon fall to the Americans. A Remscheid Bund member, Greta Dreibholz, had an old friend in Düsseldorf, Hanni Ganzer, a teacher at a girls' grammar school. Marianne wrote in *Das Münster am Hellweg*:

*On a cold February night I stood at the station in Ratingen because the unceasing shelling meant that the trains couldn't get any closer to Düsseldorf. I waited with many other refugees till dawn, at which point a couple of trucks ventured into the city centre. A driver took me along. I was carrying all the property I had gathered or swapped in the suitcase which had accompanied me on all my travels over the last two and a half years.*

At six in the morning, Marianne knocked on the door of a woman she had never met. Marianne knew that she was confronting the stranger with new and serious risks. It turned out she was lucky to have arrived just then, as Hanni Ganzer was generally in the house for only an hour or so in the early mornings and spent the rest of the day in the air-raid shelter. Hanni read Greta's letter and said without hesitation 'Of course you can stay.'[48]

*Else Bramesfeld and Hanni Ganzer, after the war*

## Holed up in Düsseldorf

The Bund had calculated that Marianne would soon be liberated. True enough, the Americans reached the western part of the city, on the left bank of the Rhine, on 3 March, only a few weeks after Marianne's arrival. The left bank was now governed by a mayor appointed by the Americans. But Marianne was in the main part of Düsseldorf, east of the Rhine, and the Wehrmacht destroyed the remaining bridges across the river. The city's Nazi leaders[49] and the Wehrmacht decided to make a last stand; Marianne thus found herself trapped in a bastion of resistance with no escape in view. By April, large parts of the Ruhr were under Allied control, but Düsseldorf was still holding out.

The Bund had made a disastrous mistake. Though 20 February saw the last massive bombing raid on Düsseldorf, the city was now under ceaseless artillery bombardment from the left bank and daily attacks from low-flying American fighters. The city centre dissolved into a crazy world of rubble and craters. During March, gas, electricity and water supplies were cut off.[50]

For more than six weeks, Marianne and Hanni slept on chairs in the air-raid shelter, sometimes spending up to twenty-three hours a day underground. If possible, during the day, Marianne would leave her protector to herself. Whenever there was a lull she would come out of the shelter, sometimes to order a meal from one of the few inns still functioning. In the shelter, Marianne was protected from American shells, but not from the other threat in those last desperate weeks: the incessant patrols searching for deserters and 'enemies' of the state. The offices of the local chief of the NSDAP and other party functionaries were next door to the shelter where Marianne and Hanni spent their time.[51] In addition to Party and Gestapo, army units were also combing the city (though largely looking for male deserters).

At this stage, run-ins with the authorities could go either way. Some officials, mindful that it would not be a bad thing to have post-war witnesses to their humanity, were already tending to play it safe. If Eric Alexander's reminiscence is correct, Marianne *was* stopped on one occasion but not detained. By contrast, the final days of the Reich also saw many party members and others engage in a last outpouring of violence and rage. In Düsseldorf, the killings went on to the very end. On 15 April 1945, just two days before the city fell, an army unit found Moritz Sommer, a Jew, in hiding. The seventy-two-year-old Sommer was hanged in public on the Oberbilker Markt.[52]

We gain a brief glimpse into Marianne's feelings in the inferno from the draft of a letter she wrote to Maria, which is folded into the diary. The draft may have been written just before she moved to Düsseldorf:

Sunday evening, 18.2.45

*(To Maria)*
*I've just got home. Despite two air-raid warnings, the journey was easy and quick, and I want to sit down to write to you.*

*I must say how lovely the few hours with you were. For me, they set some thoughts rolling and I want to send you my best wishes in acknowledgement. I felt the enormous weight, which presses down on me all the time, day and night, lift from my shoulders for a few hours.*

*We live with a thousand fears, with danger always just around the corner, with constant premonitions of death by one means or another.*

*And this evening, while I was sitting in the train and thinking over our conversations, I started wondering why we have such a fear of death. Surely, death is the culmination of life, biologically and spiritually. Fulfilment and release. Shouldn't we in fact fear life rather than death? In life, so many goals and expectations we set ourselves remain unfulfilled.*

*Perhaps what is so frightening is that death has its own laws. It doesn't ask whether we still have jobs to do, or more accurately, whether we still believe we have a job to do. When the time comes, death cuts the thread, sometimes without notice, sometimes after a warning, sometimes with our full knowledge.*

Death's law.

*Who knows what law governs our existence? Where we find fulfilment and completion? When we have to cease being here? We often imagine we should be spared because we still have so much to do in the years ahead and we sense enormous energy within ourselves, demanding to be used. But isn't this arrogant and inappropriate? Self-deception! Our true work often lies not in the great challenges but in the smaller ones that we so easily overlook. If only we could always remember this! If only knowledge, and living according to that knowledge, weren't two separate things!*

*I would like to thank you for all your love and to say (it's easier in writing) how happy I am that you are there!*

Never had Marianne written so under the shadow of death.

In a letter written shortly after the war, she looked back on this period.[53] In post-war safety, Marianne's tone was heroic:

*Life in the face of death is very different – much more intense, truer, more naked. I wrote like someone possessed in order to keep a record of the crazy, dreamlike, unbelievable life of those days. I hope I'll soon be able to show you my diary entries, Meta.[54] So many thoughts about you are inter-woven with them. . . The greater the danger, the stronger the will to live and the more productive one's thinking and actions.*

But then this thought slipped out: 'In this last period I often gave up hope of surviving. And who knows what would have happened had the war lasted longer!'[55]

*The impressions I gathered during those eight weeks of almost intimate life with the motley crew in the air-raid shelter . . . it's incredible, when I think back. There was little that was positive in the experience.*

Marianne wrote of the egotism and lack of common sense she observed around her, and the tension:[56]

*Almost every night there was a raid in search of deserters. I always had to reckon with the possibility of being caught at the last minute, after surviving so many other dangers. It was an incredible feeling.*

Finally, though, on 17 April 1945, the Bund's job was done. A US 97th Infantry battalion entered Düsseldorf and the city capitulated quietly, without further resistance. Marianne was saved.

## The Bund and Marianne

As we know, Marianne was not the only Jew to survive under the Bund's protection. Lisa Jacob had been in hiding since April 1942. Other Jews had been hidden by the Bund for at least part of the war. A woman called Eva Seligmann hid in the Blockhaus for a while. Hannah Jordan was briefly protected by Bund contacts. Dore Jacobs was under threat after September 1944 when, with some inconsistency, the regime began deporting Jews of mixed marriages. In all, perhaps some eight Jews (and half-Jews) were saved by the group. But, given the length of time and the fact that she was not previously known to any of her hosts, protecting Marianne must rank as their finest achievement.

How did they manage it? The Bund had a number of remarkable advantages. Few other left-wing organizations had been so conscious of the dangers of Nazi racism so early, possibly because Jews had played a prominent role in the group.[57] In any case, Artur was an extraordinary leader – an idealist, but at the same time a master tactician. With scrupulous attention to detail, he laid down rules and procedures for every eventuality.[58] And he practised what he preached. The transcript of his interrogations by the Gestapo – again on file in Düsseldorf – in which he kept returning and adding extra detail in a tone designed to match their assumptions, is a masterpiece.[59] Indeed, several members of the Bund were interrogated by the Gestapo[60] yet no charges were ever brought and monitoring of Jacobs' mail never revealed anything of an incriminating nature.[61]

Studies of people who helped Jews in the Holocaust have often drawn attention to the importance of informal networks.[62] The Bund in this sense was a rather odd hybrid, as much a collection of friends as an organized body. There was no official structure, but there was the rigour of its emphasis on the ethics of the everyday act and a strong internal hierarchy. Unlike other groups, which seemed large but in fact had an active core of only a few members, Bund members were all active, all committed.[63]

The Bund was an odd hybrid, also, in the way it combined dance and politics. Though Dore's school was soon closed, gymnastics lessons provided a basis for activity which could be maintained even into the early years of the war. This gave members a chance to communicate and to conceal their other activities. When Gestapo officers carried out searches and found papers about dance and physical movement, they didn't know what to make of them.[64]

Additionally, the movement's ownership of the so-called Bundeshäuser, where like-minded people could be tenants, ensured a relatively safe framework for meetings and communication in the early years. The Blockhaus, the house in the Dönhoff, where Grete Ströter lived, and the Jacobs' house in Wuppertal remained key addresses for much of the war. The group meetings there and in the wild were crucial in helping members establish the right balance between personal safety and commitment.[65] Above all, the group broke through the sense of isolation that characterized daily life in Nazi Germany.[66] By the time Marianne was on the run, regular group meetings had largely ceased. But even then, as we have seen, the Bund's gatherings once or twice a year could be a crucial source of moral support. Finally, the Bund was lucky. Every member I spoke to had a near-miss story to offer, and Marianne had plenty of her own.

In one of the Bund's post-war bulletins, an article asserted that the Bund members were neither particularly adventurous nor possessed of particular physical courage. And they were well aware of the consequences of what would happen if they were caught.[67] A booklet in memory of August Schmitz, produced by the Bund, offered a comment that could serve for many of its members:[68]

*It is astounding how someone possessing no extraordinary gifts could grow, work and influence those around him.*
*'Man grows in his actions and with his tasks.'*
*He exemplifies this truth.*

In her 1980s article and conversations with me, Marianne suppressed, perhaps even had forgotten, her personal wrangles with various of her hosts. As a result, what she felt about the Bund probably became slightly distorted in her memory. The way she presented her friends then was as miraculous, almost saintly people. Whereas at the time, I think, Marianne knew that the real miracle lay in the fact that they were, in many ways, quite ordinary human beings who, well-led, well-organized, well-hidden and powerfully motivated, found the extraordinary courage and commitment to risk their lives to save hers.

## Marianne and the Bund

To dwell on the Bund's qualities is not to question Marianne's own contribution to her survival. Jews in Nazi Germany often said how easy it was to spot one another. Nervous looks, a self-effacing gait, the consciousness of being a pariah all revealed the mark of Cain – or perhaps we should say of Abraham. Marianne under pressure was all coolness and confidence. Hers was an astonishing performance.

What was the relationship between the performance and the person? The diary suggests that Marianne was 'passing' not only on the outside, but also within her most intimate self. She refused to internalize the category 'Jew' which the Nazis imposed on her. In the company of the Bund and inspired by their philosophy, she sloughed off her former identity and slipped into being one of them. To the extent that her

Jewishness was the key reason for her persecution and that she was not really free to redefine her identity, we might say she was in hiding from what she was. But if so, the self-deception undoubtedly helped her to pass as an Aryan.

In addition to her own qualities, Marianne had three other things in her favour. She had capital – her access to the family trunks for bartering was crucial. She had skills and could make things to sell. Above all, she was a woman. As Marianne's youth-group friend Jakov (Klaus) Langer in Israel pointed out:[69]

*A man would have been lost. I don't mean that he would not have had the manual skill [to produce felt flowers etc.], but he could not have ventured on to the street.*

It was hard enough to explain why a young healthy girl should not have been in employment or in some kind of uniform. But a young man neither in uniform nor working long hours in a factory would have been impossible.

Jakov Langer raised a question I had not considered. Why had the Bund not found Marianne somewhere she could stay for the duration? After all, Lisa Jacob spent the last six months of the war, perhaps longer, at a guest-house in Bodensee run by Bund sympathizers. Marianne's friend, the half-Jewish Grete Menningen, was placed with someone for the last nine months of the war. Of course, they were both older than Marianne, and a neighbour seeing them would perhaps not find it so odd that they were not at work. Even so, was there no remote house where she could have stayed? Perhaps the Bund did not believe her suitable for a lengthy stay in hiding. Artur Jacobs was so conscious of human qualities and human frailties. Had he recognized that Marianne was not reliable enough, perhaps also too disruptive a presence, to stay in hiding? Hermann Schmalstieg's experience of finding her sitting on the window ledge, singing, legs dangling through the open window, might have served as a warning. The very energy that had helped Marianne survive on the edge prevented her from living quietly and unobtrusively. She was outstanding at passing, but she would have been hopeless at staying in hiding.

# 12

# Living Amid the Ruins

As Marianne and I worked through her last months in Düsseldorf, I was looking forward to the day the Allies arrived. I wanted to share in the exhilaration of the moment of liberation. But I didn't get the pay-off I was expecting. Marianne said she had learned for so long to be cautious that when the end of the war came she felt no release. Indeed, for ten days or so, she said, she did not believe she was safe:[1]

'I couldn't believe it. I simply couldn't believe it. I couldn't believe or trust this magic. It took about ten days before my friend could persuade me to register myself officially.'

Of course, I knew that as the battlefront shifted from one locality to another, it was often not clear for a day or two whether the Allies really were in control.[2] And even after the Nazis were finally and definitively gone from the scene, old habits of caution died hard. Ellen Jungbluth recalled with some amusement the very first Bund summer meeting after the war. They were holding a political discussion in the forest on one of their walks and someone said automatically, 'Just check and make sure that no one is coming.' To which the response was: 'Wait, we can shout out as loud as we want to, now!' 'Oh, yes, you're right!'[3]

But still I found Marianne's testimony odd. Even if the first day after the Americans arrived was a day of caution, wouldn't the second have been the day of joy? After Marianne died, I came across a letter she wrote to Bund friends in Göttingen just a few weeks after the end of the war:[4]

*And while a thousand small and big things were happening . . .
salvation came ever closer – but from the East and not, as we had
expected, from the West. I continue to marvel at this strategic and
tactical coup.*

*And one day, there they were. For eight weeks we had expected
them daily. Rumours and pronouncements followed thick and fast,
often contradicting each other. Then, one summer afternoon when
we had given them up for the day, the Americans arrived.*

*The 'historical moment' passed without fanfares. Everyone felt
an enormous sense of release. But that was more of an unconscious
feeling. It's often hard to see the full significance of such an event
as it happens. How should we evaluate it and where does it fit in?
It wasn't obvious at the time that this was a turning point. Instead,
one simply flowed into a new set of circumstances. Something had
ended, but the thing that was beginning wasn't clear at all. Once
you understand this, however, you needn't be disheartened –
indeed you* cannot *be disheartened – even though the reality is so
different from what many had hoped for.*

*We too have to keep relearning this truth, rather than think that
we have to drive things forward, do more, achieve more.*

Apart from showing what an insightful observer Marianne had
become, this letter does, to some extent, convey more of what we might
have expected. Here she does express a sense of salvation. But the letter
contains a new surprise – the salvation is presented in collective terms.
Under daily bombardment from across the Rhine, in a city where the
most basic services had ceased functioning, the whole population had
of course been in great danger. But still the end of the war meant
something different for Marianne than for her neighbours, yet she makes
no distinction. At the very end of this passage, Marianne does allude to
some differentiation; but it is between the mass of Germans and us, as
Bund members, not herself as a Jew.

I thought of Marianne's perception when I spoke to the two of her
friends who had also experienced the end of the war in the Ruhr. One
was Hanna Aron, who as a half-Jew had initially been protected from
deportation, and later was in hiding in Essen. As the war ended, she was

in Essen. She recalled with delight the moment the Allies arrived in the city. She donned her yellow star and went out to greet them:[5]

'The troops came up Zweigert Strasse and Hufelandstrasse, that's how they came in. I was at the Hufelandstrasse with my star, needless to say, and I said "hello" to these boys, and I was so happy. And they said, "Oh, no, you can't be here, they were all killed! You can't be a Jew, that's impossible!" I saluted them, but the neighbours didn't take that so well, you know?'

'How do you mean?'

'Well, they didn't like us to give them a good hello, you know. They didn't realize that we *had* to give them a good hello.'

For Hanna Aron, her feelings at liberation only deepened the division between herself and the resentful neighbours.

Ludwig, later Lew, Schloss had had the most appalling wartime experiences. Beginning in Riga, he was moved from one labour or concentration camp to another. For a few weeks he was in Stutthof, by common account one of the most bestial sites, even by the Nazis' unique standards. Lew and his father were then sent to Buchenwald and, in 1944, as two of a group of mainly foreign conscripts, to a factory in Bochum. They were within spitting distance of their hometown of Gelsenkirchen. It transpired that Lew's father had known the brother of their Bochum foreman well. And through this personal link they were able to make contact with the outside world. Someone they knew sent them civilian clothing, which the foreman brought in. Lew and his father hid the clothes, along with false papers, in the factory cranes. One day, they changed into the clothes and walked out of the plant in broad daylight. They awaited the end of the war in Essen. Like Hanna, Lew had no doubt about the meaning of the event. On 10 April the Americans moved in, on the 11th he was working for them, on the 12th he had an American uniform. Hanna Aron told me virtually the same story. The Americans set up headquarters in the Nazi Gauleiter's old house in Bredeney, and the very next day Hanna told her mother she was going there to get a job. She 'marched right in' and said she wanted to work as a secretary. Not a woman to be denied, she got the job.

If we contrast these memories with Marianne's letter, we would say that Hanna Aron and Lew Schloss experienced the end of the war as

Jews, while Marianne experienced it as a German. Marianne's letter sustains the tone of the wartime diary, even though the Gestapo and denunciation were no longer any threat. So Marianne's self-presentation during the war was evidently not simply enjoined by self-censorship. She really had understood herself as a member of the Bund, as a young German thinking about how to create the better society of the future.

On the other hand, Marianne's letter was addressed to other Bund members. Mindful of the dangers and privations they too had faced, she may well have been averse to pleading any special privilege as a victim of persecution. In this context, Marianne was all Bund, and probably deliberately underplaying the facets of her identity that did not connect with the Bund members. As the letter goes on there is a distinct sense of clubbiness and a slightly literary bravado.

Putting the letter to one side for a moment, when we contrast what Marianne said to me with the testimonies of Hanna and Lew, what strikes us is how much clearer a story Hanna and Lew have to tell. As comfortably-off, well-integrated Americans in Connecticut and New Jersey, Hanna Aron and Lew Schloss recall the end of the war as a moment of American–Jewish amity. They can, as it were, draw a direct line from the people they were then to their identities today. Whereas Marianne, no less comfortably off but perhaps more uneasy about her past, seemed not to want to acknowledge the end of the war. I wondered if, once again, her memory was shaped by her sense of guilt and loss. Perhaps, in retrospect, she could not allow herself to have experienced the end of the war as a liberation, when it underlined the reality of her family's murder.

What is certain is that the ambivalence in Marianne's testimony is symptomatic of her memories and descriptions of the post-war years in Germany. More than any other phase of Marianne's life, these years refuse to take on a stable shape. One minute they appear as a burst of creative energy and optimism, a time when Marianne was able to commit her energies to building a new Germany. Then, the kaleidoscope of memory twists just a degree or two, and the bright world of cultural life and activism gives way to far more sombre hues of loss and disorientation.

## *The activist*

'From the moment of liberation,' Marianne wrote just after she arrived in Britain, 'I could be active again, and the year and a half in Düsseldorf forms some of my brightest and dearest memories.'[6] Almost fifty years later her judgement was just the same. To me, Marianne described the post-war years – apart from the uncertain days at the beginning – as a time of great joy and enthusiasm. The energy which had been stifled for so long could at last be unleashed.

Liberation brought three important benefits almost immediately. First, *Lebensraum*, living space, was no longer the privilege of the Aryans. For more than three years, Marianne had not had a room to herself and, since August 1943, not even a shared room. Now, Marianne gained a large bed-sitting room in Hanni's apartment at Lindenstrasse 223; Hanni moved her big weaving loom into the front room.[7] 'Now that I finally have my own four walls,' she wrote to friends, 'I'm a completely new person. A room is almost the mirror of one's personality, a piece of oneself.'[8]

Despite its visible scars of war, Marianne loved her new home. To begin with, she furnished it with some old furniture dragged out of a cellar, carefully covering the odd blemish with a table cloth or a vase. But soon after the end of the war, Marianne visited the Jürgens to pick up the furniture and trunks her parents had deposited. Here, she had a most unpleasant surprise. The Jürgens claimed that her parents had given them the possessions! Marianne had to enlist the help of the authorities to reclaim what was hers. 'There was a terrible kerfuffle about that; it was dreadful, really dreadful,' she said.[9] In fact, it was the start of a miserable fifteen-year struggle over family property that was one of the low points of Marianne's post-war life. But by January 1946, Marianne was able to write to Hugo and Grete Strauss in the States:[10]

*I have a very pretty room which I have furnished with furniture that was in safe-keeping with acquaintances. This furniture and a few old family pictures (from my mother's side) are about the only things I have left. It is good, to have saved something of the old atmosphere and the old good family tradition.*

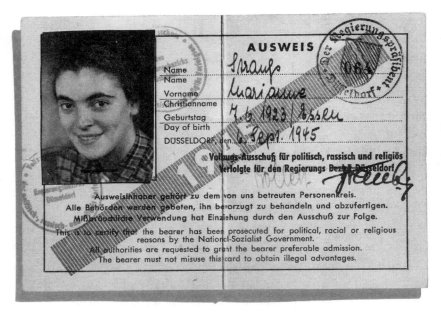

*Marianne's post-war pass*

A second major post-war bonus was food, not that there was so much of it. For the next three years, German cities were to suffer periodical bouts of real hunger, and nowhere worse than in the Ruhr. Marianne wrote in May 1945 that, 'the food situation is very very bad'. She received no potatoes, only two pounds of bread and less than a quarter-pound of fat per week, and even this meagre allowance required long hours of queuing. 'How good that I no longer have to live illegally! I would simply starve, because even with the best will in the world, you cannot feed two on these rations.'[11]

But Marianne was no longer dependent on others to eat. In that sense, the end of the war brought a decisive improvement. She had her first encounter with society at large when she went to get ration cards. She felt very strange walking into an office and registering as a legitimate person. 'How did you get through the war?' they asked her. The officials were very embarrassed; they'd never encountered anything like her.[12]

Marianne's position in relation to official allocations – foodstuffs,

398

housing, clothes – was transformed overnight. Suddenly, racial discrimination was replaced by privileged treatment for victims of the Nazi regime. In September, Marianne received an official pass from the Regierungspräsident in Düsseldorf, authenticating her as a victim of persecution. She was entitled to the rations normally reserved for someone employed in heavy labour. Marianne could still remember the enormous pleasure of the first loaf she obtained with her own ration card. She was beholden to no one over how much or when she ate. The result, predictably, was that she made a pig of herself on this 'wonderful bread' and became 'quite sick'.[13]

The third great benefit of the post-war period was that Marianne could work and pay her own way. Her wartime experiences had given her an absolute dread of being dependent on others. She wrote to the Strausses in the States about the possibility of emigrating there:[14]

*What is important for me, however, is that I have the opportunity to work and enjoy full material independence. I say this so bluntly because over the last few years I have gathered enough experience of living with other people and of what can happen to good friendships when one is materially dependent on the other.*

Like her wartime admirer Imo Moskowicz, Marianne had hoped to find a job in the theatre. But whilst Imo was to make his decisive step to stardom in Düsseldorf, Marianne failed in her attempts to find a job in theatre management there. Instead, her route to employment took a rapid and unexpected turn. Within a couple of weeks of the end of the war, Marianne went to the Düsseldorf labour exchange to enquire about possible job openings. The entire labour administration had been deeply implicated in the Nazis' forced-labour programme and was anxious to forestall major purges of its personnel. So the director of the Düsseldorf branch was overjoyed to discover this young woman, who would, as a Jew, enhance the exchange's reputation. Here, again, the tide had turned, and Marianne was now a sought-after item. With no qualifications, she found herself employed as a careers adviser, generally a highly trained profession.[15] Incidentally, I had thought nothing of Marianne's going to the labour exchange for work until Hanna Aron and Lew Schloss told me they had immediately gone to the Allies in search of employment.

Yet again, Marianne's behaviour conveyed a different sense of identity from theirs.

Marianne's memory of her work was very ambivalent. Almost from the beginning she had doubts about the value of what she was doing.[16] Initially, her job was to assist young female school graduates to find employment, but she was soon moved into a special new section. As she wrote to her cousins:[17]

> *My office has to help all those who suffered in the Nazi era get back to work and their careers. That sounds very good, but it's very difficult. On the one hand, the labour force is substantially reduced because of the incredible decline in the German economy (consequence of the war, removal of German competition).[18] On the other hand, the people I'm looking after are physically and psychologically in need of recuperation. They have to find their way back to normal life slowly. Time, patience and sympathy are needed to find the right way forward. The stories I hear at my desk every day are beyond description.*
>
> *The work is not as satisfying as one would wish because we don't have the resources to provide the kind of help that is needed.*

To me, she said the job was 'very bureaucratic and not my cup of tea at all. I'm not cut out to be a civil servant. I'm anti-authoritarian.'[19] Her rapid rise in the profession was 'resented, naturally' by all the 'long-established pen-pushers who'd been there long before'. Moreover, Marianne found it very peculiar working alongside people whose wartime role she knew very well. The director 'saw me as his life saver', she said:[20] 'He had been very much involved with slave labour for Mannesmann and Krupp and all those other great people who were employing all the slave labour they could lay their hands on.'

And here she was working with these 'polite and friendly colleagues' day in, day out. But none of this could gainsay the importance of financial independence.[21]

In addition to work, there was politics. Just three weeks after the end of the war, a fired-up Marianne told Meta Kamp that 'our work has begun' and spoke of her 'impatient, burning desire to act'.[22] From almost the first day of peace, Marianne was travelling around the Ruhr, meeting

Bund activists. In one May weekend alone – at a time when public transport was still largely out of service – Marianne was in Essen, Mülheim and Wuppertal, talking with different local Bund leaders about the possibilities for reshaping society:[23]

> *In Mülheim the friends are working very, very actively in the factories and, it seems, with success. They can influence decisions and bring about important changes and improvements. All within narrow limits of course, but it's still a beginning.*

One reason Marianne took the labour exchange job was the hope that it would enable her to gain access to youngsters and influence them. Beyond working for the Bund, she also joined the Communist Party.[24] She had seen the courageous way in which the Communists had thrown themselves into resistance against the Nazis. Many of the most active and idealistic Bund members – like the Zenkers and the Morgensterns and, probably most important for her, Ernst Jungbluth – were Communist Party (KPD) members. Within a short period, Marianne was being trained as a youth leader for the Communist-backed youth movement, the Freie Deutsche Jugend (FDJ). With her credentials as a victim of persecution, her Bund contacts and her enthusiasm she soon gained access to the men (and they were very largely men) who played a decisive role in the local political scene.

Hanna Aron heard through the grapevine that Marianne was very left wing. Being rather anti-Communist herself, she went to visit Marianne in Düsseldorf with some trepidation. What she found confirmed her worst fears:[25]

'Her whole apartment was decorated with the red flags. I mean, I walked in there and thought I was in Russia, honestly. Hammers and sickles all over and the red flags. This was just before the break-up of the Allies and so forth, so I wasn't an enemy of the Russians, but I just thought it was going a little bit too far.'

One of Marianne's boyfriends at the time, Johannes Oppenheimer, remembered falling under Marianne's political influence, though he was her senior by several years.[26] Marianne, he recalled, had links with a Düsseldorf Communist group which was just being reestablished, and she dragged him along to meetings.[27] Oppenheimer found some of them interesting, including one with the dramatist Müller-Schlösser, but he soon felt that the KPD was not for him, as a party 'egotistical and fairly unconcerned about the common good', and he stopped attending.[28] Although both Aron and Oppenheimer were struck by Marianne's Communist affiliations, Marianne's writings show that it was the Bund, far more than the KPD, which influenced her outlook and ideas.

Alongside politics, there was education and there was culture. Marianne was enormously conscious of the gaps in her knowledge and read voraciously. She also thought of pursuing a medical career (or so she asserted later in one of her restitution claims), and to that end studied Latin.[29] She remained extremely interested in the theatre – and Düsseldorf was a good place for theatre lovers at the time. As early as July 1945, the Düsseldorf Schauspielhaus was operating again. Its first director was Wolfgang Langhoff, an inspiring though cantankerous Communist who had spent many years in the Burgermoor and Lichtenburg concentration camps. And outside the theatre, too, post-war Düsseldorf offered a very animated cultural life. (The British, who had taken over control of the town from the Americans at the beginning of June 1945, encouraged considerable freedom.)

In January 1946, Marianne ended a letter to relatives saying she would happily write more:[30]

> But time is pressing, there is always so much to do. There's not enough space in my diary for all my appointments. The days pass in a whirl and I come home in the evening and drop into bed exhausted.

New professional opportunities were opening up. In February 1946, Marianne wrote to her cousin Alex Weinberg that she had received a series of good offers from both the military government and the provincial German administration, 'astounding, given the shortage of career opportunities here; and so I have the freedom and the burden of choice'.[31]

## *Marianne as missionary*

Marianne began to write as a freelance theatre critic for the *Düsseldorfer Nachrichten* and as a cultural correspondent for the KPD paper *Freiheit*, and in April 1946 gave up her job with the labour administration to concentrate on writing.[32] She also began to write pieces for the BBC's German language transmission to the British Zone of Occupation, in particular for the *Letter Box* programme. In February, Marianne sent in her first piece, 'Youth problems in Germany'.[33] The basic proposition was that German youngsters had been so misled and disillusioned that they had lost sight of core values. Particularly in the last years of the war, the errors and misjudgements of the adult generation had exposed them to terrible hardship. Now, young people simply wanted to follow their own road. But this, said Marianne in strikingly Bundist tones, was to misunderstand freedom:

*The individual who holds to a firm line and does not allow himself to be driven by his desires, drives and instincts is the one who is really free. 'In the ties that bind us, lies our freedom!' – a great truth! But our youth does not yet understand it. Young people are fighting for their own interests. For too long they were forced into a community which was not really a community at all. So now they think only of their own needs at the expense of the good of all.*

Youth had to be persuaded, she concluded, that personal happiness does not derive from satisfying one's impulses, but only from 'serious, responsible work'.

Marianne clearly felt a sense of mission towards Germany. She framed her piece as a letter from a German woman, explaining the situation in her country to an English friend. In many ways sympathetic to the situation of young Germans, she implicitly criticized one of the most hypocritical features of post-war German life – the common complaint by adults about young people's loss of values with no reference to their own responsibility for the crimes of the recent past. Interestingly, however, when the BBC broadcast the letter in April, it presented Marianne not as a typical German but as a young Jewish woman and a

*Marianne after the war*

spokeswoman for the 'Freie deutsche Jugend'.[34] The British, not Marianne, chose to identify her this way.

Praise from the programme's producers prompted a very happy Marianne to submit her two perhaps most impressive pieces.[35] One was entitled 'Taking responsibility for a meaningful life. From a letter to a young student'. In it, she responded to the complaint of a 'young student' (Marianne at this stage herself was not quite twenty-three!) about the difficulties of studying in post-war conditions, and also to reports on the radio about a recent student conference at Göttingen. Marianne argued that young people today were waiting for a leader or for a philosophy to tell them what to do, instead of beginning with themselves. Her young correspondent had forgotten, she argued, the meaning of taking responsibility for oneself:

*True, they speak of democracy – just as they used to speak of National Socialism. But they still surround these concepts with lots of words without really giving them living meaning. What is stopping young people from being creative themselves and building something new? This is something I often ask myself.*

Of course, the Bund was not the only group to see the emptiness in post-war political rhetoric and attitudes. Others too, particularly on the left, criticized the empty phrase-making and the dutiful and rather nominal acceptance of democracy.[36] A more distinctive Bund line, though, emerged in the second half of Marianne's piece, as she sought to explain why young people were not more active, reflective or creative. Why were so many all appearance and no substance?

*What is it that prompts young people to strike such a pose? I have no other explanation than that they simply lack a sense of awe: for the life force that is everywhere present. That is why they cannot be creative. When people cease to listen, they become deaf to the eternal process of renewal and awakening. They live on the surface, they see but they understand nothing. And so they can only reproduce and not actively shape the self.*

This insight, she went on, seemed to her to explain the behaviour not only of the young people she was addressing, but of humanity as a whole.

Far more than any Communist line, Marianne's counsel expressed the Bund's efforts to fuse post-religious spirituality with practical, democratic commitment. Her article ended with an appeal to the young '*werde wesentlich*' – lead a responsible life never losing sight of the essential.

Another piece, 'Fate has turned', was broadcast by the BBC on 27 August. It began by describing the queues for food in the cities and the despair and criticism to which food shortages gave rise:[37]

*Hunger is terrible and many are only now getting to know its brutal ways. On the streets, German children ask Occupation soldiers, 'You, got bread?' We are reminded of the last years of the war, when grey columns of tired, ragged prisoners from all nations dragged themselves along the same streets where Germans now go hungry. The prisoners' eyes were fixed on the ground in search of every cigarette butt Germans had casually thrown away. Perhaps a couple of puffs would still their fearsome hunger. And we are reminded as well of the wretched foreign conscript worker, nervously approaching the well-dressed Germans on the street, whispering, 'You, got bread?' How readily one turned away, because it was forbidden to give anything to these 'sub-humans' and because a full stomach allowed the 'sleeping beauty' of one's own conscience to slumber on.*

*And today? Today the same Germans on the street, no longer the secure master race, find themselves mired in the distress and the misery of those to whom they once threw cigarette butts.*

*Does that make them think? Do they wonder whether some balancing force of justice is at work? One only has to stand in the long queues in front of the shops to hear that they do not!*

*We Germans have a difficult, difficult time before us. We had better hope that we won't be subjected to equal retribution; we had better hope that the world's conscience will not remain as passive as did the conscience of many Germans when things were the other way round. We had better hope that someone will help us. But we had better hope too that we will not forget the way things were.*

*Once we grasp the situation and judge it properly, we'll find it easier to understand and to bear and other nations will find it easier to help us out of our distress.*

Rarely in Germany in 1946 were the sufferings of the German population so openly and clearly placed in the context of the sufferings
Germany had inflicted yesterday. It is noteworthy that Marianne again
presents herself not as victim, but as one who shares Germany's collective
fate. Clearly, this was partly a literary device. Marianne had calculated
that the message would be much more powerful if delivered not as
accusation from outside – the victim Jew accusing the former oppressors
– but from inside: 'we Germans'. But the very fact that, in the interest of
creating a new Germany, she *wanted* to speak as a German, that her
primary instinct was not to speak out as Jew or as victim is what
impresses itself on our consciousness.

Was this a marvellous testimony to her generosity of spirit and her
ability to distinguish between active perpetrators and bystanders? Was
it an act of self-denial? Or was it, in fact, both, the expression of a young
woman increasingly unsure of who she was and which way her life was
taking her?

## *The displaced person*

Naturally, from the moment the war ended, Marianne had a burning
interest in tracing her immediate family:

'One of my first steps after the war was to open a German bank
account in the hope that maybe they would come back and I could
proudly present my father with the money he'd given me, which seemed
like a lot of money in those days. I don't know, now it probably wouldn't
be much at all.'

It is hard to know how hopeful she really felt. Probably, the survival
of the money had became a symbol of the survival of the family. In
fulfilling her father's admonitions to practise probity and economy,
Marianne had consciously or unconsciously kept something of him alive
within herself.

Almost immediately after the war Marianne wrote to the Strauss
family lawyer in Basel, Marcus Cohn, to tell him she was still alive.
Through Cohn, other surviving relatives learned of Marianne's whereabouts. It was probably in this way that in September 1945, Grete

Sander was able to establish contact from Sweden, offering help and hoping that Marianne had heard some news. It was now that Marianne learned that her parents had managed to get letters out of Theresienstadt to Grete in Sweden; she also obtained her first information about the fate of uncle Alfred and Aunt Lore.[38] In March and April 1946, more information arrived from Erna Ogutsch, the wife of the cantor in Essen, who had been in Theresienstadt and could tell Marianne more about the experiences of her parents and brother and her uncle and aunt. She also had news about some of Marianne's former teachers from Berlin. One had been murdered at Auschwitz, another had survived the camps and gone to Sweden. 'It was good,' Frau Ogutsch reassured her young correspondent, 'that you did not come to Theresienstadt. Your own experiences were hard enough.' Cousins on her father's side, the Ansbachers, wrote from Frankfurt in April 1946. They too had been with Marianne's parents in Theresienstadt.

By the summer of 1946, having heard from Grete Sander, Erna Ogutsch and the Ansbachers, Marianne knew most of what she would ever learn of the fate of her parents, her brother, her aunt and her uncle. (Of Ernst and family she discovered no more than she had in 1943.) In most cases, this was still far from definite knowledge. 'It is agonizing to think about,' she wrote to Hugo Strauss, 'a thousand speculations about a thousand possible different horrible ends. If one knew for sure, everything would be easier.'[39]

At what point, I asked her, did she give up hope?[40]

'I didn't learn ever for definite. There was never, there was always . . . I don't know, for many years, I still thought somebody would turn up. But then I thought rationally that if they were going to turn up they would have turned up in Essen. I knew enough people even if I wasn't living there, and they knew where I was, there wouldn't have been any difficulty with that. And pretty soon it became very clear that it really was an exception for somebody to come back. But I always thought that being a big family somebody might have survived, my brother or Ernst, somebody who was younger, who maybe had more physical or moral resilience or ruthlessness, which they didn't have. Ruthlessness was probably the most important ingredient of survival they didn't have.'

The first of the family with whom she had an actual meeting was her cousin Otto Weinberg, now a proud Lt Corporal Gerald Alexander of the 1st Battalion Glasgow Highlanders. The only one of the three brothers to be stationed in Germany, Gerald managed to locate Marianne in August 1945.[41]

Marianne's attitude to such revived contacts, though, was often mixed. She felt her family had let her down where friends had prevailed. Writing to Alfred in 1947 about her pleasure at seeing Gerald, she said:[42]

> From the start, we spent many happy hours together and I can tell you that I really enjoyed having some family by me (although in general I don't believe in blood ties but in ties of choice. In difficult times they always proved themselves where the family failed to help.)

Nevertheless, she did seek to reestablish contact with relatives who had managed to get out of Germany. She regained contact with her maternal uncle Karl, now a decorated war hero, living in Brussels, and with her cousins on her mother's side, the Weinberg boys. Marcus Cohn informed surviving relatives in the USA that she was alive – her father's cousin Hugo Strauss, her maternal uncle Adolf Rosenberg, and Lore's brother Ernst Dahl – and they got in touch with her over the next months. More distant cousins in Britain – the Oppenheimers and the Seligs – also surfaced. Marianne learned (though when, we are not quite sure) that her cousin Richard, now René, Wolf – the son of her father's sister Bertel and her husband Ferdinand Wolf, both interned in France and later murdered in Auschwitz – had also survived. He had made an epic journey across France and Spain as a fifteen-year-old, fought with the French Foreign Legion and entered Germany as part of the French force of occupation. Marianne also made unsuccessful enquiries to trace the child left behind by Lore's sister Ilse when she and her husband were deported from France.

But often, when the family did make contact, one of their first steps was to cement a kind of pact of silence about the past. Karl Rosenberg, for example, helped enforce that silence. Karl had been considered the 'black sheep' of his family, but whatever his misspent youth, he had had an adventurous and heroic war. Trained in Britain, he was parachuted into France to fight alongside the French resistance. Now living with his wife Diane in Brussels, he wrote in the warmest fashion to Marianne. After receiving a letter in reply, he wrote back in November 1945:[43]

*We are fine, that's the main thing. What happened, happened. I feel as you do, that it was a hard school and I too am happy that I've come through it – one is stronger for life as a result. But I want to forget it and only think of the here and now. Life is so short, why make it harder than it already is?*

A couple of months later Marianne wrote to her cousin Alex:[44]

*You'll have heard much about me and about our fate in recent years. It's unnecessary to talk about it. We have no time to think about the past because the present demands all our strength. There is an enormous amount of reconstruction work to do and we're tackling it with courage and hope.*

And evidently she must have written something similar to Erna Ogutsch, because the latter responded:[45]

*It is good that you have satisfying work that demands all your thoughts and attention so that you don't have to think about the sadness of recent years. I force myself to look to the future.*

When I asked Marianne whether her work colleagues tried to talk with her about the past she replied:[46]

'Not then, no, they never talked about it, never. They just knew I was Jewish and that I had come back, one of those that had come back . . . but it was never discussed. They were all terrified, naturally. There was no reference ever, no question, nobody wanted to know anything because it was all too uncomfortable. And the people who came back from the concentration camps, all they were interested in was getting a job, earning a living, restoring a normal life. And that's all I was interested in, to restore a normal life. I didn't seek out, wanting to ask questions, I didn't want to go into all my past history. I wanted to forget it as quickly as possible and get on with a normal life and make something . . . make up for lost time.'

It is one of the ironies of Marianne's life that although she continually exhorted the Germans to remember, she herself sought to forget. Her 'forgetting' was not 'thoughtless', to use her term, but it was relentless. She avoided almost every connection with her former life. Despite living so close to Essen, for example, she rarely went back there.

She was not sure she had anything in common with her family any more. As she wrote to Hugo and Grete Strauss:[47]

> *It's good finally to be able to build a bridge across the time and physical distance which divides us. Above all, it's good to feel meaningful contact reviving again. Between us lies not just the ocean but also the monstrous experiences of the last few years.*

Apologizing to her cousin Alex Weinberg in February 1946 for not having written before, she said she had been extremely busy, but also that it was 'not very easy after the long years of such different experiences to find a point of contact'.[48] On several occasions when more distant relatives and family friends located her, she did not follow it up at all.

Reading the correspondence between Marianne and her relatives in Britain, Australia and the USA, we begin to see that she was doubly displaced. On the one hand, she knew she was no longer the person her relatives had known. On the other, in the privacy of the correspondence, she revealed an increasing unhappiness at her situation in Germany. Karl began by reporting Gerald's comments on meeting her:

> *Otto told me that you were doing very well, and that you wanted to stay in Germany. In my view, everyone should shape their life as they wish. When I heard that you wanted to stay there I thought, you know best what's right for you. But I see from your letter that you would gladly leave Germany. I hope it is understood that nowhere would you be looked after better than with us.*

The offer from Karl and his wife Diane could not have been warmer or more affectionate, but there is no evidence that Marianne responded to it.

In January 1946, Marianne wrote to Hugo and Grete Strauss, thanking them for the parcel they had sent:[49]

> *I cannot tell you, my dears, how much pleasure your loving parcel gave me! It contained real treasures – things I haven't seen for such*

*a long time – and I had a real day of celebration. I'm surprised I*
*didn't get indigestion! The stockings and scarf are wonderful. It's*
*impossible to get them here. All textiles, shoes etc. are unobtain-*
*able. Germany is in every respect so poor!*

What echoes must she have heard in her own thanks now that *she*
was the recipient of parcels full of unobtainable treasures! These echoes
led her to give a succinct and poignant account of her wartime experience. At the end she concluded:

*Few have survived these horrors and returned. Only now do we*
*really learn what went on – but it needs to be broadcast to the*
*world with far more emphasis and far louder than it has been.*
*Much too little is being done here to compensate for all the suf-*
*fering.*

*The few survivors have one thing in common; they have lost*
*their loved ones. That common fate binds us, but often it's the only*
*thing we share. The ties are not strong. Everyone thinks and*
*worries about himself and wants to catch up on all that he's missed*
*in the last few years. Judaism, religion, does that still exist out*
*there? There's no trace of it here.*

Marianne said she was thinking of leaving Germany, perhaps only for
a period, but she had trepidations. 'Having finally regained my freedom,'
she explained, 'I value it extremely highly and am very reluctant to enter
into a new dependence.'

To Alex, she wrote in February:[50]

*More and more I feel the desire to leave Germany, at least for a*
*while. There are no prospects here for young people and there's a*
*lot I'd like to learn to be able to give real help.*

She had lots of good job offers but, 'Naturally I see all that now as
temporary. I yearn for any possibility of leaving Germany as quickly as
possible.'

It is hard to square all this with her cheerful missive to Alfred Weinberg
in 1947, looking back on the time in Germany as one of the 'brightest
and most beautiful memories' of her life.

## Half-way house

The ambivalence of Marianne's position is equally apparent in her friendships. After the Nazi years, one of the luxuries of the post-war period was her freedom to socialize as she chose. It would not be long before such an engaging, lively and attractive young woman made new friends. One day, soon after she began working at the labour exchange, a young man appeared seeking advice. By chance, she had seen him arrive:[51]

'I remember he was pushing a bicycle and left it standing outside in the compound which was very brave, because anything on wheels would move very quickly . . . On my way home in the afternoon I saw him on the Koenigsallee pushing this bike. He came over – he'd seen me, I don't know if he'd been waylaying me, I'm not sure; anyway he came up grinning and was pushing his bicycle and chatting and talking and that's how we got to know each other.'

The man was Johannes Oppenheimer. He was living with a lively group of four *Mischlinge* who had survived the war as labourers in the Organization Todt (OT), the enormous organization entrusted with road and fortification building named after the transport minister Fritz Todt. They were all highly gifted and intent on educating themselves for successful professional careers. 'They had a pretty grotty flat the four of them,' Marianne remembered fondly. 'And trying to make their futures in their very different ways.' Two of them, Johannes Oppenheimer and Wilhelm Jacob, became life-long friends.

Marianne had told me various things about their lives before the war, but when I spoke to Johannes Oppenheimer, retired Vice President of the Federal German Court of Administration, what struck me was how inaccurate most of her information had been. Johannes Oppenheimer was born in Berlin in the closing months of the First World War of a Jewish father and a Protestant mother. His father held a senior position as Oberregierungsrat in the Prussian finance administration until forced into early retirement in 1935. After a failed suicide attempt, he later died in Auschwitz. Johannes Oppenheimer began training as a chemist but was called up in 1939. In 1940, his office duties in the army enabled him to see a communication to the effect that all *Mischlinge 1 Grades* were to be dismissed from the service. In his eighties still every bit the German jurist, Herr Oppenheimer said to me, 'That surprised me, because it differed from the legal position.' But it had been a 'special directive of the Führer'. Oppenheimer dutifully communicated his situation to his superiors, was transferred to the reserve and in November 1940 dismissed. Prevented from continuing his studies, he was drafted into the OT and sent first to Paris, and then elsewhere in France, building fortifications, often in very poor conditions. Shortly after D-Day, he was recalled to Paris and trained to supervise foreign conscripts who were to be taken to Germany for work. Even a half-Jew could thus find his place in the hierarchy of racial subordination. However, the unit was transferred to Wuppertal before Herr Oppenheimer had to perform this duty. Finally, in the middle of February 1945, he ended up in Düsseldorf in an OT camp, where he stayed till April.

Recognizing his administrative abilities, the camp leader asked Oppenheimer to be his deputy and the latter accepted. He 'didn't want to promote the war but wanted to help maintain order'. I didn't keep a precise count, but in our conversation Herr Oppenheimer must have said the word *Ordnung* about thirty times. His success in improving conditions for the many foreign conscripts in the camp was borne out, he said, by the fact that after the war had ended he and the other half-Jewish OT conscripts were able to continue living side by side with the now liberated 'DP's, (displaced persons). Finally, in May 1945, his friend Kurt Zeunert, another OT conscript, prevailed upon the authorities to assign them an apartment that had formerly belonged to some Nazis. Here, sharing two rooms, a kitchen and a toilet, five, then later four of the half-Jewish survivors of the Organization Todt formed the bachelor household Marianne so much enjoyed visiting.

Johannes Oppenheimer remembered meeting Marianne in the labour exchange, although he had forgotten about arriving by bike. He remembered that the bicycle itself had been sold to him by a 'crooked OT comrade'. And that he had no lock[52] – hence the 'reckless' act of leaving the bike unsecured at the labour exchange gates. Marianne, he wrote to me:[53]

*was indeed a remarkable person, about nineteen years old [actually*
*twenty-two] when we met. That was in May or June 1945 soon*
*after the end of hostilities in Düsseldorf. If my memory serves,*
*Eduard Marwitz, a so-called quarter-Jew, took me with him to the*
*Düsseldorf labour exchange as so-called 'victims of Nazi per-*
*secution' to get advice from 'Sister Marianne Strauss'[ . . .]*

*She was very friendly towards us and showed an ease in dealing*
*with people which suggested a maturity far beyond her years.*

'We became friends and were often together outside work,' he added.
'I fell in love with her for a while and she did not reject my advances.'
But 'we did not have a really close relationship'.[54] By the end of the
year, whatever love affair had existed between them had fizzled out.
Marianne, always very reticent about her relationships, admitted there
had been more than friendship between them, 'but that didn't really
work at all, we were too different in temperament'.[55]

Johannes Oppenheimer recalled what he knew about Marianne at the
time:[56]

*That she was Jewish was clear from the start. She must have been*
*in a concentration camp and looked after children or the sick as a*
*nurse. How she came to survive the end of the war in Düsseldorf*
*I have no idea; I heard nothing about Düsseldorf relatives.*

In other words, despite the fact that they had met within a month or
two of the end of the war, he learned next to nothing about her wartime
experiences or her life before the war, and what he thought he knew
was wrong. Acknowledging the great gaps in their knowledge of each
other, Herr Oppenheimer wrote:

*From the present vantage-point I find it hard to understand why we*
*did not talk more about our earlier lives and about our fate in the Nazi*
*period. But apparently all that wasn't important once we had got it*
*behind us and felt liberated; we lived and thought only in the present,*
*and looked somewhat hesitantly but full of hope into the future.*

In a subsequent interview, I asked again why they had talked so little
about the past:

'I don't know why, we had no reason to be silent. We thought of the future. That we had lost relatives was not so dramatic, because ordinary Germans had also lost relatives. We did not see any particular literary material in that. We did not have the feeling we had special reason to complain. I don't even know what happened to Marianne's parents.'

Now I understood why, when referring to his application to the labour exchange, Herr Oppenheimer had placed the phrases 'victim of persecution' and later again 'victim of racial persecution' in quotation marks. To him they were only legal categories and not real ones.

The other member of Oppenheimer's entourage whom Marianne got to know well, and who remained an enduring friend, was Wilhelm Jacob. Once again, Marianne's information about his past life was largely inaccurate, as I learned when I talked to Wilhelm Jacob's widow, Dr Elisabeth Jacob, née Kühne, the daughter of a former Prussian general.[57] Wilhelm Jacob was born in Kösslin, near Danzig, in 1916. His father, Emil, had married a non-Jewish hairdresser from a high-class establishment in the town. Wilhelm wanted to study medicine and spent eight semesters in Zurich. In 1938, while he was studying there, his father was murdered at a police station. The family could no longer support Wilhelm financially and the Swiss predictably chucked him out. He returned to Kösslin and got a job driving a truck collecting rags, working for a man Frau Jacob called a 'decent Nazi', who became a master butcher after the war and maintained friendly contact with the Jacobs. 'You see,' said Frau Jacob to me, 'the mass of the people were not such rabid Nazis!' Like Oppenheimer, Wilhelm Jacob was called up to the OT where, his widow told me drily, he 'protected his life and his glasses'. Engaged in building bridges and laying railway tracks in France, perhaps the saddest thing for Wilhelm, who had dreams of becoming a musician, was that the work ruined his hands. 'But', continued Frau Jacob – a general's daughter to the core – 'from the point of view of survival it was not the worst place to be.' He had ended up in the same OT camp as Oppenheimer, and after the war shared the house with him. He completed his medical studies in Düsseldorf and met Elisabeth Kühne in the process. 'Wilhelm,' Marianne remembered, 'was very Prussian, which was quite amusing, being half Jewish and marrying a general's daughter, it was quite incongruous.'

Whatever Wilhelm may have known about Marianne's history, his widow Elisabeth, with whom Marianne developed a close friendship which lasted from the 1940s until Marianne's death, had no knowledge of it at all. As with the others, Frau Jacobs had constructed her own picture based on signs and assumptions, telling me, for example, that Marianne's relatives had owned a string of department stores – no uncommon thing among wealthier German Jews, but not true of any of the Strauss family.

It is hard not to see this network, the only friendships outside the Bund that survived the immediate post-war years, as symptomatic of Marianne's situation in post-war Germany. It seems entirely appropriate that the people she attached herself to as friends should have been half-Jews. This was a group who did not regard themselves as Jewish, in many ways German to the core, yet they shared a sense of having been defined as outsiders. The group was marked by a common loss of relatives and friends and at the same time by an absolute unwillingness to dwell on their losses or talk about the past.

## Marianne, the Bund and post-war society

To add to Marianne's feeling of displacement, she was becoming increasingly frustrated with what she was able to achieve in Germany. Material conditions were dispiriting enough. Only 7 per cent of Düsseldorf's buildings had been undamaged – and Düsseldorf was in a much better state than Essen.[58] In Marianne's age group there were 172 women for every 100 men (not that Marianne was ever going to have to worry about the competition). In the winter of 1945–6, the rationing system virtually collapsed – and worse was to come a year later.[59] Small wonder that so many non-Jewish Germans were also keen to leave the country.

In addition, the Bund as a whole was becoming disenchanted with its role in post-war Germany. Understandably, and with considerable justification, the members felt that history had proved them right. As the Bund proudly announced to its overseas well-wishers and contacts:[60]

*What has proved itself above all is the idea. The Bund, its approach to education, its structure, its principles, its view of human beings and its attitude to history all gave each individual the strength to carry on and resist the thousand-fold temptations and influences of the National Socialist un-spirit and the general weakening of character.*

Surely, its members reasoned, this wartime achievement proved how vital the Bund was for the challenges that lay ahead.[61] And yet from early on we find the Bund members having to acknowledge that they were not enjoying the resonance they had expected. 'Our flock has dwindled,' commented Artur Jacobs as early as 1947, 'one often feels very lonely. We are having to stand against the current just as we did during the twelve years of Nazism.'[62]

Partly, the Bund felt, the problem was that the Germans were not willing to confront their past:[63]

*Everything is judged only from the perspective of today as though there had been no past, no provocation of war, no Lydices, no extermination camps, no arbitrary decrees, no millions murdered.*

The Bund also made the painful discovery that they themselves were now seen as implicated in the past. Most young people wanted nothing to do with any kind of organized movement or party, and rituals such as oath-swearing were anathema to a deeply disillusioned generation of youngsters. The Bund itself later acknowledged:[64]

*As a result of National Socialism the younger generation were very intolerant of hierarchical structures. For all their undoubted interest in the Bund, they could not commit themselves to new ties.*

Artur Jacobs and the other Bund members, insightful as they were, probably could not comprehend, though, how thoroughly out of place the group seemed in the post-war years. I managed to locate and interview a number of young people (of Marianne's age or a little younger) who had come into contact with the Bund in the late 1940s. They had been enormously impressed by what Artur Jacobs and his friends had achieved. Some of them told me that their subsequent choice of career and political orientation were strongly influenced by contact with the

Bund. But they could not cope with the Bund's hierarchical character, its 'inner circle', its veneration for Artur Jacobs and the way youngsters were supposed to sit at his feet. They found the Bund leadership over-sensitive to criticism.[65] And, although unwilling to be directly quoted, some children of the founding Bund generation expressed similar senti-ments. None of them could be persuaded to become full-fledged Bund members.[66]

As a charismatic movement, the Bund's other problem was that some of the fight had gone out of its leaders. Both Artur and Dore had been emotionally and physically drained by their wartime experience. Artur was now nearing seventy, mentally still at the height of his powers, physically no longer really in a position to lead a vibrant movement. Dore, though younger, would never again be completely healthy and had to conserve her strength. They were also, as Maria Briel related in an interview, deeply troubled by the impact the war had had on their son Gottfried (he later committed suicide).[67] A bitter argument between Carlos Morgenstern and Artur Jacobs further weakened the group. The former wanted the Bund to be more politically active and eventually broke away from the group.[68] Artur, by contrast, felt increasingly that the Bund's role should lie predominantly on the spiritual–intellectual plane. He devoted more and more of his time to thinking and writing, culminating in the book *Die Zukunft des Glaubens* (*The Future of Belief*).[69] It is an enormously impressive text, but far too wooden and out of kilter with the times to have much resonance when it finally appeared posthumously in 1971.

So it is not surprising that Marianne had growing doubts about whether she was doing any good. She shared with other Bund members the belief that the great mass of Germans had learned nothing from the past. She bemoaned the political shallowness of the young. She felt that many of the left-wing leaders who might have given guidance were far too fixated on material reconstruction, to the detriment of spiritual renewal.[70] And, like the Bund, steeped in a tradition of searching for organic unity of purpose, she probably also found some of the signs of an emergent pluralist society, with its party politics and interest groups, rather disheartening. A letter to cousin Alex in February 1946 contains her most comprehensive critique yet of German society:[71]

*You can imagine how happy I was, after the endless years of being condemned to do nothing, finally to have a clear set of tasks, to know that I was needed and to take part as an equal. I plunged in with real enthusiasm and tried with holy zeal to do my best towards rebuilding. But increasingly one recognizes how illusory were the hopes we placed in Germany's ability to develop and change. Sometimes I feel that the Germans have learned nothing. Party-political interests are more important to them than united reconstruction. Will they ever learn to pull together? Will they ever learn real political convictions rather than just allow themselves to be driven by material interests and gather round the bowl that promises the best meal? Will they ever learn to be tolerant? Unity can emerge only from a foundation of tolerance – the prerequisite for creating new values.*

*On the one side there are the politically active, with their short-sightedness and dissension. Ranged against them is the unending number of politically indifferent, who represent an even bigger danger than the first group. In part, they are simply ignorant of political matters. But many have resolved on the basis of National Socialism never to tie themselves to a political line so that 'afterwards they're not the ones who did it'. They forget that National Socialism would have failed in 1933 if fewer people had stood on the sidelines.*

*There is so much talk today about 'democracy' and 'freedom'. The German people are far from being mature enough for democracy and freedom. They must be steered slowly along the right road. It's good that there's a military government in Germany to prevent anarchy (even though it also hinders healthy economic reorganization and regeneration, which is less smart).*

But as Marianne's political engagement began to falter, her life was gaining new purpose.

## *Basil*

On 25 November 1945, Marianne received an intriguing letter:

*Captain B. K. Ellenbogen RAMC 13 (BR) FDS BAOR*
*25 Nov. 1945*
*Dear Miss Strauss,*
*I do not know who you are, but I called here to let you know that*
*your cousin Ernst Dahl (now in Canada) has received news of you*
*through your relative in England. I was given this information by*
*a Canadian officer who knows your cousin. Your cousin's address*
*in Canada is:*
    *Ernie (Ernst) Dahl*
    *c/o Dominion Bridge Coy.*
    *Ottawa Canada*
*I called here this morning too at 11.15, but there was no one in. I*
*should like to meet you, but unfortunately I do not live here but in*
*München Gladbach. However, I should try my best to call on you*
*again sometime, perhaps during next week.*
    *With best wishes*
    *B. K. Ellenbogen*
    *Captain BAOR*

Ernst Dahl, Aunt Lore's younger brother, had gone to Canada before
the war. Having received Marianne's address (probably from Marcus
Cohn), Ernst asked a Canadian officer stationed in Germany to
make contact with her. In the end, the officer had no time to follow up.
Instead, a young Jewish doctor with the British Forces, Captain Basil
Ellenbogen, offered to go. Captain Ellenbogen had made it his mission
to seek out Jews in Germany and offer help where possible. On his
own initiative, he had sought permission to visit Belsen, an experience
recorded in some shocking photographs which survive to this day.
Correspondence in his files attests to the moving and conscientious work
he put in to establishing contact between camp survivors and their
relatives overseas.

Basil Ellenbogen was born in Liverpool in December 1917, the second of three boys. His father, Max, was a credit draper selling clothing and furniture on credit. Basil's grandfather, Gershon, had come from Lithuania and Max, whose first language was not English, still did all his adding up in Yiddish. A pious man, learned in Jewish law, Max had married Gertie Hamburg from Cardiff, the daughter of the cantor at the Cardiff synagogue, and the two had settled in Liverpool. The three boys Gershon, Basil and Raymond were all very bright. Gershon won a scholarship to read classics at Cambridge. Basil and Raymond both went to Liverpool University, where Basil read medicine and Raymond dentistry.

Basil was very different from the people Marianne was mixing with in Germany. Not particularly politically engaged, he was a committed Orthodox Jew. He had been prominent in Jewish student life at university, and for a while chaired the national Jewish student federation. A handsome, witty man, he was popular with women, but apart from a deep attraction to a cousin, he had not experienced a serious relationship before he was called up.

Marianne told me that when Basil came to her apartment she was out at a Communist Party meeting. Knowing their later marriage had been difficult and that a major bone of contention had been the issue of Jewish observance – he was much more Orthodox in practice than she – I found it hard not to see already in this very first non-meeting a symbol of the problems ahead. Basil sought out Marianne because she was Jewish and he wanted to help Jewish people. Marianne was not at home because she was a Communist or, more precisely, because of the political mission she felt the Bund had given her. In a way, the war had brought them together almost on false pretences. He was pursuing an identity which she had sloughed off. But on reflection, this is probably too rigid an interpretation. Marianne's identity, her affiliations and her sense of the future were still much in flux. And love has a way of building bridges between the most unlikely shores.

On Marianne's return, Hanni Ganzer told her that a marvellous-looking man had been to see her. For his part, Basil had apparently been impressed by the various things that Marianne had managed to reclaim – the quality furniture and family portraits. This was not the picture of misery and destitution he was used to finding. On the Saturday, he came back. As she watched a khaki hat ascend the stairs, Marianne thought at first it belonged to one of the other officers she knew. Then suddenly this 'glorious chap' appeared. She was twenty-two, he twenty-eight. It was love at first sight. 'It took over. I knew it would. I wasn't very happy about it, but there was nothing I could do.'[72]

Over the following months, Marianne and Basil came to see more and more of each other. They would take romantic walks along the Rhine, looking out at the devastated bridges. They went to the opera and saw, amongst other things, *Cosí fan tutte*. Marianne introduced Basil to some of the prominent figures in the post-war Jewish community. By April 1946, when Basil learned that he was to be demobilized, they were deeply in love. Before Basil left, Marianne put together a little book of memories and photos for him to take along. In the accompanying letter, dated 19 April, Marianne wrote (in English):

> *Do not forget*
> *Düsseldorf*
> *And . . .*
> *Marianne*

At the time Basil was demobilized, Marianne was perhaps not yet committed to spending her life with him. Her uncle Adolf Rosenberg had cabled from New York that he had sent two affidavits of support to the American Consulate in Stuttgart and that he was able and happy to pay her passage when required. In April 1946, Marianne was still interested in following this up. A day after writing her farewell letter to Basil she informed the US consulate that Adolf had sent the affidavits and that her family had been about to emigrate to the USA in 1941 when the consulate was closed. Was a new registration necessary, or was the old quota number still appropriate?[73] But when the necessary forms came back in June, Marianne did not fill them out. Her desired destination had by then become clear: she wanted to join Basil in England.

## The struggle to get to Britain

The fact that Marianne spent the next six months in Germany was due solely to difficulties the authorities put in the way of her coming to Britain. As she was about to discover, the UK was opposed to special immigration arrangements for German (or other European) Jews. There was a strong anti-Semitic unwillingness to respond to Jewish moaning. There was a principled (but, in view of recent events, scarcely defensible) refusal to make racial distinctions between different groups of Germans. Above all, there was a reluctance to create a precedent of 'special treatment' for European Jews that might in any way bolster their demands to be allowed into Palestine.

In early 1946, Marianne's relatives, the Oppenheimers, made a first attempt to obtain permission for her to come to Britain and failed. Then in March Marianne's cousin Gerald Alexander approached the British Interest Branch of the military government in Lübbecke.[74] The response from the Passport Control Officer was a sure indication of how little the British authorities were listening to the particular sufferings of German Jews. 'A scheme will shortly be put into operation by which distressed persons in Germany may come to England, provided that relatives there can give them a home. The conditions of this scheme will shortly be published.' Reading thus far, Gerald must have felt fairly confident, 'but', the letter went on, 'unless Miss Marianne Strauss has parents in England, I am afraid she will not fall within the limitations of this scheme.'[75]

On 22 March, Basil took up the case, noting that:[76]

> since the parents of Miss Strauss are dead, she will not be eligible for entry into England. This appears to be a particularly harsh decision, since being an orphan would incline one to consider her more a 'distressed' person than one whose parents are, fortunately, still alive.

Basil's letter may have crossed with a further note from the Passport Control Office, offering no more hope than the previous one and helpfully pointing out that 'There are, unfortunately millions of distressed persons in Europe in the same situation as your cousin.'[77] Certainly, Marianne could be assured she was not the only victim of British indifference to the plight of European Jews. When a British rabbi applied early on to go to Berlin to minister to Jewish survivors there, a visa was denied because British citizens were not supposed to provide help to Germans.[78]

A growing collection of letters, applications, health reports and other documentation built up in Marianne's files over the following months. When the couple became engaged in June 1946, the emphasis in the applications shifted from seeking to be united with relatives to wishing to marry Basil. But after being informed by the Public Safety Officer in Düsseldorf that a visa could be expected in six to eight weeks,[79] Marianne heard in July that she did not fall under the category of distressed persons and that 'no travel is at present allowed under these circumstances'.[80]

Marianne grew more and more impatient. Schemes were afoot to marry Basil in Belgium and travel from there to Britain. In October, Basil wrote to his Member of Parliament. Noting that several German brides had already reached the country, he went on:[81]

> *It appears to me scandalous that after five months no visa should have been granted, and indicative of the chaotic state of military government in Germany. May I add that as a doctor, I worked amongst the concentration camp victims at Sandbostel (and unofficially at Belsen) and saw the fate that my fiancée had averted but which had befallen her family. She has herself endured much hardship during the war and all the years of Nazi rule – is it not time that British democracy be extended to include her?*[82]

Finally, in November 1946, the authorities relented, allowing Marianne to enter as a German national, on the basis that she was going to marry Basil. Among Marianne's papers we find a reference from the *Freiheit* attesting to her journalistic ability and a charming farewell letter from the paper's editorial board hoping 'from our hearts that England may give you all that we are at present still denied in Germany'.[83] Hanni Ganzer too had many moving wishes to send to her young friend.[84]

On or soon after 20 November, Marianne finally arrived in England. Basil's solicitor, a family friend who had been involved in the legal battle for more than six months, felt compelled to write a personal note to his client:[85]

> *The world is in such a terrible state as far as relations between communities and peoples are concerned that one is particularly happy as one goes through it in these days to find that personal relations can be so satisfactory in a tortured universe . . .*
>
> *It was good to see Miss Strauss in the flesh – really here – and it seemed to me at once that you will both be very happy and are in for an interesting time. At any rate, my wishes will follow you. There are so many frustrations nowadays in jobs one does and activities we all want to do, that when one sees one object attained it is all the more satisfying.*
>
> *So – sincerest wishes for all your future happiness, and that Miss Strauss will enjoy being amongst us in England, as I am sure she will after all her experiences.*

# 13

# The Fate of Marianne's Family

Marianne and Basil made rapid plans for their wedding. Given that Marianne's visa would expire within two months unless she married a British national, speed was of the essence. The ceremony took place at London's Hampstead Garden Suburb synagogue on Sunday 29 December and the newlyweds honeymooned in Torquay. Liverpool was where they intended to live. They moved in briefly with Basil's parents, but soon found a flat in the attic of a Victorian house. The flat had previously been occupied by some of Basil's friends. Following her mother's example rather than her advice, Marianne conceived within a few months of the marriage, and Vivian was born on 23 November 1947.

Several months before Vivian's birth, in the summer of 1947, Basil's brother Gershon brought Marianne some remarkable letters from Sweden. With the information they contained, Marianne was as well informed about her family's fate as she would ever be.

## Marianne's testimony

Marianne herself shared only some of this knowledge with me. By the 1990s, she had forgotten various details, subtly changed others, and some she probably deliberately withheld. From the papers in her possession and other sources, I had to reconstruct a picture not only of what

*The young marrieds – Marianne and Basil*

had happened to her family, but also what exactly she had once known.

Marianne knew her parents had been deported from Theresienstadt to Auschwitz in December 1943. As we've seen, in her published account she claimed to have heard this on the run. Her even more startling claim was that, while staying with her relatives in Beverstedt on her birthday, 7 June 1944, she had been listening to the BBC and heard that the occupants of her parents' particular transport had been gassed. This is what she told me in our conversation for the museum in 1989:[1]

'Throughout the war and particularly during my illegal phase we listened to the English broadcasts. That was, of course, extraordinarily dangerous because the opening bars of the Beethoven Symphony [the BBC's call sign] were very distinctive. One had to be careful to turn the volume right down and lie with one's ear next to the speaker. But for my parents and family, and later for me and my friends living illegally, it was a lifeline to hear the real war situation.[. . . ] And so on one such lunchtime transmission, we were listening to the broadcast and heard that the transport from 18 December 1943 to Birkenau-Auschwitz had been gassed there in the last few days. I knew that my parents and brother had been on that transport to Auschwitz. So, I had an unforgettable birthday.'

Of all Marianne's revelations about communication, I found this the hardest to believe. Surely she could not have obtained such precise details about which transport her parents were on? And surely, the BBC did not broadcast information about gassings with this kind of precision?

While I was in Düsseldorf just after Marianne died, Dr Angela Genger from the Düsseldorf Museum of Persecution showed me a list they had of deportees to Theresienstadt. From this, I gained the name of a Czech expert on Theresienstadt, Miroslav Karny, who led me to an ongoing project to enter information about all the inmates into an electronic database.[2] I contacted the group by email, and received the following communication from Zdenek Schindler:

*A list of our (not yet fully authenticated) data follows. The list needs an explanation:*

*1. First datum is a code of a transport. VII/4 means Düsseldorf, 9.9.1943*[3]

2. *The transport number of a person follows*
3. *[Next in line] is the code of transport from Terezin and the personal number.*
4. *I have added also the destination and the date of deportation from Terezin (please, check it)*

| | | | | |
|---|---|---|---|---|
| VII/4 3 | Ep 128 (Auschwitz 9.10.1944) | Dahl \ Else | born 25.01.1883 | Died ? |
| VII/4 8 | Dz 1870 (Auschwitz 15.5.1944) | Jaffe \ Gertrude | born 27.06.1903 | Died ? |
| VII/4 9 | Er 881 (Auschwitz 16.10.1944) | Liebrecht \ Reha | born 12.01.1942 | Died ? |
| VII/4 67 | | Rosenberg \ Anna | born 04.01.1867 | Died 09.01.1944 Terezin |
| VII/4 1 | El 497 (Auschwitz 29.9.1944) | Strauss \ Alfred | born 24.04.1891 | Died ? |
| VII/4 2 | Ep 127 (Auschwitz 9.10.1944) | Strauss \ Lore Rosa | born 16.08.1907 | Died ? |
| VII/4 5 | Ds 2215 (Auschwitz 18.12.1943) | Strauss \ Regina | born 13.01.1896 | Died ? |
| VII/4 6 | Ds 2216 (Auschwitz 18.12.1943) | Strauss \ Richard | born 26.10.1926 | Died ? |
| VII/4 4 | Ds 2214 (Auschwitz 18.12.1943) | Strauss \ Siegfried | born 24.04.1891 | Died ? |

*total 9 persons*

Siegfried, Regina and Richard *had* been deported together on 18 December 1943, leaving Regina's mother, Alfred, Lore and Lore's mother behind. The seventy-seven-year-old Anna Rosenberg had then died in Theresienstadt on 9 January 1944. At the time, I thought this news about Anna was something Marianne had not known. Later I was to discover that this was just one of many facts about the family's life in the ghetto which Marianne *had* in fact known. (Gertrude Jaffe and Reha Liebrecht, incidentally, were the other people transported with the Strauss family from Essen in September 1943.)

So Marianne's information about her parents' transport had been correct. When we spoke about this, she could no longer remember exactly how she had found out. But it is known that, as a 'show camp', Theresienstadt was still allowed postal contact with the outside world. Other inmates remembered, for example, that Theresienstadt inmates could write once every eight weeks, and outside correspondents could write in to the camp once every four weeks.[4] In fact, the regulations varied and there were always many restrictions and limitations, but there is no doubt that post could go in and out.[5] It thus seems likely that either the Strauss family or someone else had sent a letter to an address in Germany that allowed Marianne to learn of their departure.

Subsequent research in Britain and Germany confirmed that, on this rare occasion, the BBC really did broadcast precise information about the fate of a particular transport, a fact of which even much of the specialist literature on the Third Reich seems unaware. The circumstances surrounding the broadcast were quite unusual. The underground resistance movement within Auschwitz had obtained advance knowledge that the people on the December transport from Theresienstadt would be held 'in quarantine' for a period of several months and later murdered. Wanting to convince outsiders of the credibility of their revelations about Auschwitz, the resistance sought to present as much detailed information as possible. The fact that it was able to forecast the impending murder of the occupants of a specific transport was important. In April 1944, Rudolf Vrba and Alfred Wetzler, two Slovakian Jews in the camp underground, hid between the inner and outer perimeter fences and after several days succeeded in escaping. They took with them a wealth of facts and figures from the camp, including the details of the December transport. By the end of April they had written a meticulous report, which delivered in sober language by far the most comprehensive description of Auschwitz-Birkenau yet available to the outside world.[6] One copy reached Dr Jaromir Kopecky, the diplomatic representative in Switzerland of the Czech government, sometime in May. Kopecky showed a copy to the Swiss-based General Secretary of the World Jewish Congress, Gerhard M. Riegner, who had already played a vital role in informing the Allies about the Holocaust.

Because of the urgency and clarity of Vrba and Wetzler's prediction that thousands of Czech citizens would be murdered on 20 June, Kopecky and Riegner decided to inform the Czech government in exile in London. Kopecky made a request to British and US broadcasters: 'Please, broadcast promptly the most urgent warning possible to the German murderers who are managing the slaughter in Upper Silesia.'[7]

This message was sent on 14 June with the help of Elizabeth Wiskemann, the British legate in Bern. On 15 June it was deciphered in London. We know that the first BBC broadcast of the news was made in its Czech and Slovak service on 16 June. On the 17th, a more comprehensive version with a more emphatic warning was transmitted.[8] And on or about this date, a German transmission was made, which is what Marianne must have heard. We don't have the direct transcripts of the German service, but we do find the following item in the BBC's German Service records:[9]

*Here is an important announcement. News has reached London that the German authorities in Czechoslovakia have ordered the massacre of 3,000 Czechoslovakian Jews[10] in gas chambers at Birkenau on or about June 20th. These Jews were transported to Birkenau from the concentration camp at Theresienstadt on the Elbe last December.*

*Four thousand Czech Jews who were taken from Theresienstadt to Birkenau in September 1943 were massacred in the gas chambers on March 7th. The German authorities in Czechoslovakia and their subordinates should know that full information is received in London about the massacres in Birkenau. All those responsible for such massacres from the top downwards will be called to account.*

Marianne's diary entry on the 20th – 'Horrific! What will happen now?' – so different in tone from the measured entries preceding it, must have referred to this news.

Why should Marianne in her memory have displaced the date of receiving the news from the 16th or 17th back to 7 June, thereby inventing the notion of her 'unforgettable birthday present'? As in her account of Ernst's death, she had added a slight 'literary' slant to the truth. The shocking nature of the birthday 'present' brought out even more poignantly the horrible contrast of those times: that she could be living in comparative security while her parents had suffered the most hideous fate. A day that should have been shared by her family brought news that the family would never be together again.

We are all familiar with the experience that sometimes the facts don't seem powerful enough in the retelling. We feel the need to add something extra to the story to give it greater punch, though the perceived need might well spring as much from our insecurity as from the insufficient interest of what we have to tell. In Marianne's case, it seems hardly credible that she should have felt the need to embellish her account, but perhaps with the passage of time she had come to feel some lack in the emotional power of the facts and begun, wittingly or not, to add extra details.

On the other hand, Marianne's version omitted perhaps the most gruesome feature of the events – that when she heard the broadcast, the gassings *had not yet taken place*. She had obliterated the traumatic four-day waiting between the broadcast on the 16th or 17th and her diary entry on the 20th; in much the same way, her most painful separations and partings – from Ernst and her parents – had been slightly reworked in her memory.

Incidentally, Marianne was far from the only person in Germany to monitor this broadcast. It was received by the SS in Auschwitz and may have been responsible for delaying the killings for a few weeks. They took place on 11–12 July 1944.[11] Again, although not widely known, this BBC broadcast seems to have been important for other Jews still in Germany (by now almost exclusively Jews of mixed parentage, those in mixed marriages or the very few in hiding). On 20 August, Viktor Klemperer noted in his diary:[12]

*I heard: Some time ago many Jews (three hundred? three thousand?) are said to have been brought out of Theresienstadt and afterwards the English radio reported the gassing of this transport. The truth?*

Klemperer did not know. The broadcast did not end Marianne's uncertainty, either. Like Klemperer, but far more urgently, she was confronted with the choice of whether or not to believe what she had heard. As the memories of Frau Nenadovic indicated, Marianne probed gently where she could to find out more.

## Marianne's documents

I learned about the BBC broadcast from Marianne directly. What I did not learn from her, and discovered only after her death, was that once the war was over she found out quite a lot about how her parents had lived before they were murdered.

As we know, her parents were initially deported to Theresienstadt in September 1943. By that point an extension to the railway line had been built, bringing new inmates directly into the ghetto. For most, the first shock was the *Schleuse* (sluice), the one-, two- or three-day processing period in dark, unhealthy conditions, during which they were robbed of most of what they still had. It is possible that, because they came in a tiny privileged transport, the Strauss family was spared the lengthy processing. But they were not spared the plunder.

We know about the plunder because of letters Vivian and I came across which had been sent to Marianne in March and April 1946 by Frau Erna Ogutsch, the widow of the former Essen cantor. Erna Ogutsch, by then working as a librarian in a DP camp in Bavaria, gave Marianne detailed information about the family's life in Theresienstadt and the circumstances of their departure.[13] The Ansbachers, cousins of Siegfried and Alfred from Frankfurt,[14] also wrote at around the same time; they had maintained regular contact with the Strausses in Theresienstadt.

According to Frau Ogutsch, when the Strausses arrived, the guards found money in Ine's possession. Despite their imprisonment in Essen, the Strausses had still managed to hold on to some of their money. Ine was sentenced to four months' imprisonment. According to Erna, however, Ine in prison had 'more, much more food than we had. She was allowed to work as a cleaning woman and *was completely content*.[15] Ine Strauss, working as a cleaning woman and 'completely content'? Erna Ogutsch was undoubtedly sensitive to the psychological needs of her reader. But, perhaps, in a world turned upside down, it was a credible assertion.

With few exceptions, men and women were not allowed to stay together in Theresienstadt, and so Siegfried, Alfred and Richard were immediately separated from Lore, Else Dahl and Anna Rosenberg. According to Frau Ogutsch, Alfred, Siegfried and Richard lived in the Hanover barracks and Lore and the two grandmothers in the Hamburg barracks. The possibility of meeting was limited to certain times of day, between work and curfew. Conditions were, however, easing a little in this respect, thanks to the Danish government's request to inspect the camp. Another resident of the Hamburg barracks remembered, for example, that as of autumn 1943 one no longer needed a pass to leave the building.[16]

Conditions had been at their worst in 1942, when Theresienstadt had been completely unprepared for the influx. The Strauss family were lucky to the extent that, since September 1942, a number of steps had been taken to improve matters. Nevertheless, housing remained overcrowded and extremely primitive, often double or treble bunks in large dormitories. Compared with even the vastly reduced circumstances of their last years in Essen, the conditions must have been a terrible shock. The Strausses did not experience the worst of the water shortage, which had been resolved by 1943, but they must have been forced to accept the most degrading washing conditions in which tens, sometimes hundreds of people shared the same lavatory and wash basin.[17] In the Hamburg barracks, for example, where Lore, Else and Anna lived, the lavatories were at the distant end of an arcade and far too few.[18] Obviously, misery for an elderly person with any kind of infection.

There were also far too few doctors – one for every 1,600 people, many of whom were the vulnerable young or the vulnerable elderly. Typhus, scarlet fever, jaundice, measles and, particularly, enteritis swept through the ghetto. For the Strauss brothers, the anarchy of corruption, despite the many regulations, and the constant individual battles for survival must have been almost as intolerable. The family was also exposed to the infamous census on 10–11 November, when the ghetto's population was made to stand outside in the rain for some fifteen hours, an ordeal which several of the elderly did not survive.[19]

Apart from Erna Ogutsch's reference to Regina's diet in prison, we do not know how the Strausses fared with nourishment. For newcomers, the food was often awful. Even the official rations fell below absolute minimum levels of necessary protein. To make matters worse, the wide-

spread corruption ensured that a substantial portion of the food allocation never became available for general consumption. Anyone who tried
to protest was removed on the next transport.[20] But what I learned from
Erna's letters was that the Strausses did have the one thing vital to
keeping body and soul together – regular parcels from outside. Provided
they contained no written messages, parcels could be sent to Theresienstadt frequently and were distributed daily.[21] But the Strausses were
possibly the last Jews to be deported from the Ruhr: who was still
outside, supplying them with such precious commodities?

## Parcels for the Strauss family

Erna Ogutsch wrote that in 1944 Lore, 'often had news and parcels
from you and once, for her birthday, a small book, perhaps E.T.A.
Hoffmann or someone like that.' Because the polite German word for
'you', *Ihnen*, can also mean 'them', it took me a moment to realize that
Frau Ogutsch meant that the parcels came from Marianne. To confirm
the point, the Ansbachers, too, wrote of Marianne's beneficence, 'All
your parcels arrived and gave your loved ones much pleasure.'[22] So,
suddenly, from these very last letters in her house, I learned that while
Marianne was on the run, she had still been assembling food parcels
and sending them to Theresienstadt. Yet she had never mentioned this
in any of her testimony, even though one would have thought that proof
of Marianne's continued freedom would have given her parents the
greatest consolation, and would comfort her memory of them, too.

When Vivian learned that his mother had been providing for her
parents even while in hiding, he was overcome. It was not just her
heroism, her truly remarkable resourcefulness. It was that he should
discover this only now. His reaction made me aware of the strange
symmetry between his experience and his mother's. Both, it seemed,
were condemned to find out about their parents' lives via a posthumous
paper trail. The same letters which in 1946, two years after the Strausses'
murder, had told Marianne about her parents' experience in Theresienstadt, now in 1997, a year after his mother's death, told Vivian about
who his mother had been.

The Ansbachers' letter contained another surprise. 'Is the name Christian familiar to you? He was a friend of yours and did a great deal of good.'[23] Christian Arras again! When I had spoken to Lilli Arras, she had vaguely remembered sending parcels to the family in Theresienstadt. On one such occasion, she was so brutally shouted at by the clerk in the post office that she simply walked out, too nervous to complete the transaction. She also thought that Christian Arras had visited Theresienstadt once. I was unable to confirm his visit and had rather discounted it. But now the Ansbachers' cryptic comment made it much more likely. Either the Strauss family had simply talked about his help or, more probably, they were still somehow the beneficiaries of his good offices in Theresienstadt. The exact details will never be known.

These striking revelations almost paled into insignificance beside another batch of documents Vivian and I had already turned up; the postcards Basil's brother, Gershon, had brought back from his trip to Sweden in 1947. In Stockholm, Gershon had met Grete Sander who had, it seemed, received some 800 Swedish kronor from the Strauss family. She gave Gershon several cards which on his return he forwarded with a cheery letter: 'We had a most interesting time, particularly in Stockholm, but it came so expensive that I am personally more relieved than disappointed at the ban on foreign travel!'[24]

At this stage, I had not yet discovered who Grete Sander was, and for a while pursued a false trail.[25] But then I learned from Eric Alexander that Grete had lived in München Gladbach, near Krefeld, and was a relative on his side of the family. The family connection to Marianne was so distant that without looking at Eric Alexander's letter I can never quite get it right: Grete Sander was Marianne's mother's sister's husband's sister's husband's sister.[26] Grete would never have featured in this story but for one vital fact: she had emigrated to Sweden, a neutral country with which direct postal contact was possible from Germany.[27]

The first card, complete with Hitler's stern visage on the 15-pfennig stamp, was something I had never expected to see – a postcard from Marianne's father in Theresienstadt. Siegfried's card is dated 1 October, but postmarked 12 January 1944, so apparently lay around for three months before being dispatched. With the rigorous censorship operating in the camp, Siegfried had little choice but to be upbeat. Only the *absence*

*Postcards from Theresienstadt to Sweden*

of news tells us that the postcard was not sent from a family holiday in Norderney or Nordwijk:[28]

> Dear Grete,
>
> We arrived here fine and are healthy and hope the same of you and your children. My address is Hauptstrasse 1.
>
> We often see Hans Orgeler's parents and Luise Saul. We would be very glad to hear from you soon. All send their best wishes.

The card did contain one crucial piece of information for the recipient: the address. Later cards indicated that Grete was now able to act both as benefactor and as an important intermediary to Strauss relatives in the States. Parcels were not only being sent from Sweden but also from the USA, commissioned by Hugo Strauss. According to Alfred's cards in 1944, parcels were being sent via Lisbon, received by him (it is not clear whether Siegfried was in Theresienstadt long enough to benefit) and confirmed by mail to Sweden. A post-war letter from Grete Sander to Marianne suggested that Grete Sander had also sent numerous parcels from Sweden direct.[29] Another post-war letter, from the family's Swiss lawyer Marcus Cohn to Hugo Strauss, listed items sent to Theresienstadt between May and December 1944. That made me wonder whether 'Lisbon' was in fact Alfred's neutral code for the USA, and whether Hugo's gifts were in fact coming via Switzerland.[30] In 1947, Cohn evidently also still had in his possession some postcards from Theresienstadt, which Alfred had sent to Switzerland on 10 July and 21 August 1944.[31] The most likely scenario, if 'likely' is a word that can be used in such an astonishing context, is that Alfred wrote to the family in neutral Sweden. They passed on the details to relatives in the USA who, in turn, commissioned the family lawyer in neutral Switzerland to send parcels, receipt of which was confirmed via Sweden.

## Deportation to Auschwitz-Birkenau

Most of the postcards I found had been sent by Alfred in 1944, after his brother had gone. Siegfried's upbeat postcard to Frau Sander, written on 1 October 1943, will have been doubly misleading to its recipient since, by the date of the postmark, 12 January 1944, Siegfried had already been deported to Auschwitz. In her letter to Marianne after the war, Frau Ogutsch confirmed that Marianne's parents were indeed deported in December 1943, and ended by suggesting that Marianne should get in touch if she wanted to know more. Marianne rarely responded to such invitations, but in this case was evidently spurred on to respond almost by return.[32] She wanted to know why her parents been singled out for transport in December 1943. In April Erna wrote again:[33]

> You ask why your parents were transported to Birkenau as early as December. There were continual transports. Already in autumn 1942 so many from our transport[34] were sent on, mainly older people. Then there were several large transports in January 1943, including my sister and again many from Essen of every age. There was a constant coming and going. Always the spectre of a transport hanging over us. It is possible that the punishment of your mother led to the earlier transport. In May 1944 there were again many.

And here Erna listed the Essen families who had been transported to Auschwitz – including Rudi's father, Dr Josef Löwenstein, Liesel Sternberg's father Leopold, Marianne's friend Irma Ransenberg, and many others.

In fact, for much of 1943 there were no transports out of Theresienstadt. During the summer, Eichmann even declared that the ghetto would be spared further deportations. But on 6 September 1943, just four days before Siegfried and his family arrived, 5,000 ghetto occupants were deported and the whole place was plunged into uncertainty again, an uncertainty which would last until the end of the war. December 1943 – when Siegfried, Ine and Richard were carted off – was a new peak. In that month over one-eighth of the inhabitants were caught up in deportations.[35]

We do not know in what condition Siegfried, Ine and Richard travelled to Auschwitz. Frau Ogutsch wrote that when Lore was deported the following year, she went off reasonably well equipped (adding, sadly, 'But what good did it do?'). So it is possible that Marianne's parents, too, had possessions as they boarded the train. But since suitcases had to be handed over before departure, that may have been the last they saw of them.

Nor do we know if they had any idea what awaited them. Ever since hearing Christian Arras's information about Izbica they must have dreaded being sent on to Poland. Yet it seems most Theresienstadt inmates did not really know about Auschwitz until December 1944. Between September 1943 and October 1944 there had been occasional 'postcard actions' from Birkenau to Theresienstadt, orchestrated by the Nazis. On at least one occasion, in June 1944, recipients of such cards in Theresienstadt were allowed to reply, though the replies never reached the original writers, most of whom had been killed in the interval.[36] Because of this, the Theresienstadt Jews were far less well informed than the remnants of the Polish Jewish community. Whatever the case, the specific fate of Marianne's parents' transport beggared belief even in a world in which the unbelievable happened every day.

Ruth Elias, a Czech woman who had been in the same barracks as Lore, was on the Strausses' transport.[37] In her published autobiography she provides a vivid account of the departure. Unlike the ordinary train carriages in which the Strauss family had travelled from Essen, they were now sent in cattle cars. SS guards called out the names of the travellers and then chased them on to the trucks, yelling, 'Faster, faster, you Jewish swine!' The cattle cars were filled with fifty, sixty people, sometimes more. There was no straw on the floor, and in any case there was no room to lie down. The deportees were held in semi-darkness. There were two pails on the floor, one filled with water; the other supposed to be a toilet. Since it was virtually impossible to empty the pail out of the small windows, the stink became unbearable.

Elias could not remember whether she spent one night or two on the train – in fact it was two. In the late afternoon of the third day the train stopped, the doors were wrenched open and the inmates confronted with yelling kapos and barking dogs. They had to jump down from the cars and line up in groups of five. Ruth Elias asked one of the men standing near by the name of the place:[38]

*Without looking at me, he said, 'Auschwitz.'*

*That meant nothing to me. It was the name of one of many towns in*

*Poland. I didn't know how deeply Auschwitz would be engraved into my very being, so indelibly that it could never be erased.*

More evidence that the Theresienstadt deportees really did not know what awaited them.

In this abnormal world, the 'normal' next step should have been the selection. Siegfried and Ine would probably have been sent one way, to immediate death; Richard, the other, to work. But this was no ordinary transport. For the December transports were the second tranche of two very large waves of deportations from Theresienstadt to the Auschwitz-Birkenau 'family camp', one of the most bizarre elements of the Nazi murder programme.[39] *'Familienlager BIIb'* was established in September 1943 with the arrival of 5,006 Jews from Theresienstadt.[40] In his memoirs Rudolf Vrba recalled:[41]

*Nobody who survived Camp A in Birkenau will ever forget September 7, 1943, for it was unlike any day we had ever known. That morning we felt wonder, elation, nostalgia and overwhelming amazement as we gazed on a sight which most had forgotten existed and the rest doubted if they would ever see again.*

*Into Camp B beside us, separated from us by only a few strands of wire, poured men, women and children, dressed in ordinary civilian clothes, their heads unshaven, their faces bewildered, but plump and unravaged. The grown-ups carried their luggage, the children their dolls and their teddy-bears; and the men of Camp A, the Zebra men who were only numbers, simply stood and stared, wondering who had tilted the world, spilling a segment of it on top of them.*

*[. . .]*

*The SS men treated them with consideration, joking with them, playing with the children.[. . .]I noted that each of them, even the youngest children, who were about two years of age, had been tattooed with a special number that bore no relation to Auschwitz; and each had a card on which was written: 'six months' quarantine with special treatment'.*

Soon after the arrival of the September transportees, the camp underground learned that the official transport list was headed, 'SB – Transport of Czech Jews with six months' quarantine'.[42] The underground knew that SB was an abbreviation for *Sonderbehandlung*, 'special treatment', itself usually a euphemism for murder. But it was not clear what was intended. In contrast with other transports to Auschwitz, no selection was carried out. All those who arrived were taken to the camp. They retained their personal property, their hair and their clothes. How exceptional these conditions were can be gleaned by comparing them with the fate of 1,260 Jewish children and 53 carers who arrived from Theresienstadt on 7 October. All were gassed on the day of their arrival.[43] On 16 and 20 December, the second wave from Theresienstadt entered Birkenau, amongst them Siegfried, Regina and Richard. They too had the symbol SB6, i.e. special treatment after six months,[44] against their names in the camp files (though, unlike the camp underground, they themselves will not have known this). They, too, arrived in the 'family camp', this strangely privileged area in the heart of the most horrific place of the twentieth century. No one knew why they had this special status.[45]

In Auschwitz terms, the inmates were thus immensely privileged and the sight of them called forth 'nostalgia'. But here is the same experience described from the point of view of the arrivals themselves, not yet having learned the Birkenau scale of horror by which to calibrate their good fortune:[46]

*Our pitiful human column in rows of five, flanked by SS men with their rifles at the ready, began to move. Not a word was said. Totally intimidated, we moved forward like automatons. Koni and I had only one thought: Stay together; don't lose sight of each other. The column came to a halt in front of a large building, and we were ordered to undress. Undress? Here we were, women and men and children all together. We couldn't do that! But when the SS men used their whips, we obeyed. It was shortly before Christmas, and the temperature hovered between 10 and 14 °F (−10 to −15 °C). Then the men were separated from the women, and we were led into a large room where showerheads were attached to the ceiling. Ice cold water poured down on us. There was no way to avoid the downpour since we were crowded together like sardines. We cursed. There was no soap; there were no towels. When we came out, we were sopping wet. They threw some clothes at us. There was no sign of my fur-trimmed winter coat that had cost me so much bartered bread. Instead, I was handed a flimsy dark-blue silk dress and a lightweight coat; no underwear, no stockings, just wooden clogs.*[47] *Before we were led into the shower room, we had to bundle our own clothes and shoes together and turn them in. We never got them back.*

Thinking of Marianne's parents in the cold reminded me of one of Eric Alexander's letters to me:[48]

*As I am writing this, another conversation comes to mind, so grotesque and tragic that you could be forgiven for thinking that I made it up. I do distinctly remember Ine saying to my mother that if they were ever taken away, she would make sure that she would take her Persian lamb fur coat with her, because if there was anything she disliked, it was being cold.*

*Such lovely uplifting conversations. They talked about this kind of thing without believing what they were saying.*

In three-tiered wooden bunks, with no mattresses and nothing but a thin blanket, the new arrivals tried to make themselves warm. Their first food since leaving Theresienstadt was not to come till the following day, when they were also tattooed. The 1,137 men from the train were given the numbers 169969 to 171105 and the 1,336 women and girls numbers 72435 to 73700.[49] I hoped I would be able to identify the precise numbers the Strausses were given and find some record of them in the Auschwitz archives. But it is not clear how precise a list was kept. Certainly the Strausses' names are not included among the 50,000 or so which survive on the Auschwitz lists. Since new lists are being discovered in Russia, it is just possible that their names may be found in the future.[50]

The daily routine was also unlike that in any other part of Birkenau. According to some accounts, the new inmates were allowed to write to family every fortnight and receive parcels. The men did not have to report to work and a school was opened for the children under the leadership of the inspirational Fredy Hirsch. The children also had a small garden area and, initially, somewhat better food than the rest of the camp.[51] With the exception of the Camp Elder, the Jewish inmates themselves ran the camp administration. Best of all, because the men's and women's barracks were in the same enclosure, families could meet during the evening visiting hour in the Lagerstrasse.

The inmates, unaware of their relative privilege, felt they were enduring the most horrific experience of their lives. The diet consisted of little more than watery soups, and hunger and disease took an enormous toll. Within the first six months, more than 1,000 of the 5,000 who arrived in September had died of 'natural causes'.[52] There was roll call early in the morning, which involved standing outside in skimpy clothes in freezing weather, sometimes for hours, until all had been accounted for. Senseless, backbreaking work, moving rocks, was their daily lot. One of the most shocking experiences for the second wave of inmates was meeting their former Theresienstadt comrades who had been deported in September. As Ruth Elias recalled:[53]

*These people had changed completely their behaviour. We had known each other, we had been friends, after all, and one of them had become* Blockälteste, *a person in charge of a block with 400 people or more. Someone approached him as a friend, but he told him: 'We don't play games here,' and started making a speech: 'You've come to a place from which you will not return.' The people we had known became unrecognizable. Those I had known as civilized persons behaved like savages, and it was difficult to explain the change that had come over them.*

And over the next few weeks, rumours about gas chambers and ovens became part of the arrivals' consciousness. The rumours became more urgent and the whole meaning of the camp experience for the December arrivals changed dramatically in March when, almost exactly six months after the arrival of the first transport, instructions came from the RHSA that the September deportees were to be killed. In the camp, the Nazis attempted to maintain the illusion that those affected were being transferred to labour camps in the interior. All were instructed to send postcards to acquaintances; those capable of work were transferred to quarantine camp BIIa, the men in one set of blocks, women in another; and all were allowed to take their things with them. None the less, the suspicions of the underground hardened. On 4 March, the head of the

445

Auschwitz underground confided his thoughts to Rudolf Vrba, telling him that the group had all been told to write postcards and post-date them by one month. The Sonderkommando had been ordered to stoke the furnaces for 4,000 on the night of 7 March and the SS men had been talking about a special job.[54] The underground leaders hoped that the size of the operation, the certainty of it, and the fact that there were some thirty members of the underground in the group might provide the basis for an uprising. They decided that Fredy Hirsch, the inspirational youth leader who had done so much for the youngsters on the transports, was the man who might enjoy enough confidence throughout the camp to lead the uprising. After Vrba talked to Hirsch, the latter went off, ostensibly to consider, and poisoned himself.

All the September deportees were killed in one night, 7/8 March or, in the Jewish calendar of that year, on Purim, the festival commemorating the defeat of the wicked Haman who had plotted to kill all the Jews. Just as there had been no selection on arrival, there was no selection now (with the exception of a few twins, on whom Mengele practised his experiments, and some medical personnel).[55] From then on, according to the witnesses cited by the historian Otto Dov Kulka, it was clear to those left behind that the life span of transports brought to the special camp was pre-determined at precisely six months. Camp life continued, with concerts and theatrical performances, youth and educational work,[56] but now many inmates were fully aware that they were doomed to extinction. However, A. Schön recollected that even weeks after the March murders, members of the December group remained unaware of the deaths of their compatriots. Their self-delusion was reinforced by the arrival of the victims' post-dated postcards (25–27 March);[57] which also served to convince those still in Theresienstadt that Birkenau was a reasonable camp.[58]

With that, we are almost done, but for one more, tiny glimpse into the lives of the Strauss family. Among the cards received by Grete Sander in Sweden was one in a wild pencil scrawl from Regina Strauss, Labour Camp Birkenau, near Neuberun (Oberschlesien). Dated 15 April, it said:[59]

*Dear Grete, I am healthy, things are fine, I hope to hear often from you. With best wishes, your Regina*

As we know, cards were sometimes sent to deceive. The designation 'Work Camp Birkenau' was misleading, since this was no work camp. The address 'near Neuberun' was chosen deliberately by the authorities so that no one receiving a card from the family camp would link it with Auschwitz.[60] The dates were also often deceptions and the writers murdered before the cards reached their addressees. In this case, though apparently written in April, the card was postmarked 23 June and may have been sent out deliberately at a time when the Nazis knew that the Vrba/Wetzler report was receiving considerable international attention.[61] My initial feeling of having discovered a miraculous conduit of communication was therefore soon replaced by the insight that virtually nothing interpretable was being communicated. That Ine was healthy is only just possible. That she was still alive in April, the putative date of the card, is quite probable. That she was 'doing fine' is impossible. That a wild scrawl was not her normal way of writing is certain. From Frau Ogutsch and others, Marianne learned after the war that Richard, too, had managed to send one card back to Theresienstadt. And we also know that Grete Sander was able to convey to Lore that she had heard from Ine[62] and also send parcels to Auschwitz.[63]

But Ine will not have received them. In June (though then delayed to July), it was the December transport's turn to be eliminated. The imminent prospect of the murders was what Marianne had heard announced on the radio. What the underground had not predicted, however, and Marianne never knew, was that this time there was a selection. It is possible that this was the result of the publicity about the killings. But in any case, the Nazis were growing more aware of the need to conserve labour.[64] So, unlike the March killings, where all had been sent to the gas chambers without exception, in June those deemed fit to work were taken to labour camps in Germany.[65] According to the historian H. G. Adler, himself a Theresienstadt survivor, of the 2,503 people transported to Auschwitz from Theresienstadt on 18 December 1943, some 443 survived, and of the two December transports overall 705, 13 percent, survived.[66] I do not know what Marianne would have made of this, if she had lived long enough for me to tell her that this was the case. Possibly some of the Strausses, perhaps Richard, made it through at this stage. If they did, there is no trace of them in the records.

These two six-month quarantine periods surely form one of the most bizarre and macabre twists in the Auschwitz chronicle. What can have been the purpose of this murder by clockwork? One thing is clear: the killings were planned from the very beginning. It now seems certain that the family camp was one of the actions the RSHA undertook to conceal the murder programme. There was some fear that Red Cross representatives visiting Theresienstadt might also wish to see Auschwitz. The family camp, the mail facilities, the receipt of parcels sent under the auspices of the International Red Cross and so on were all part of an elaborate smoke screen. In May 1944, for example, Himmler agreed to conduct a tour of inspection of 'one Jewish labour camp [in Birkenau]' with representatives of the German and International Red Cross.[67] Not until the Red Cross decided that a visit to Theresienstadt on 23 June 1944 had 'satisfied all expectations' and that a further visit to Auschwitz was unnecessary did the regime decide to wind up the special family camp and dispose of its last inmates.[68]

Among all the Holocaust's grotesqueries, this must rank as one of the strangest. There is something about the 'special treatment' within the 'special treatment' that seems to capture the Holocaust's essence. What makes the Holocaust so singular and so impenetrable is the macabre interplay between procedure, irrational hatred and murderous brutality. In this case, a special procedure was imposed on the general pattern; the virtues of murder were carefully weighed up against the importance of public relations; a precise timetable of premeditatedly delayed murder was substituted for the usual clockwork. The story of the Theresienstadt transports stands as a symbol for the impenetrability of the whole.

From another perspective, the family camp was for the Strausses the final phase of their privileged status, though they will not have experienced it as such. As well-connected, affluent Jews, the men boasting a distinguished war record, they had long escaped the treatment received by other Jews. Through their connections they had escaped early deportation. When they were deported, they went to Theresienstadt, the ghetto for *Prominente*, prominent Jews. And now, along with other inmates of that ghetto, they still had a limited, special worth, essentially as propaganda. But at each stage, the value of their prominence had diminished. Initially, it had ensured them relative freedom and prosperity. Then, in 1941–3, in increasingly straitened circumstances, they had continued to enjoy the privilege of the use of part of their home and part of their savings. Then, in Theresienstadt, privilege had spared them the extermination camps. Now it meant just a few extra months of life in excruciating conditions.

What sense can they have made of it all? Would Siegfried have seen in the 'Germanness' of the enterprise around him the ultimate repudiation of his cherished beliefs? Or would he simply have shaken his head at the circumstances which had allowed a band of criminals to subvert the strengths of his German homeland? Throughout her life, Marianne tortured herself wondering how they had reacted to the concentration camps. Yet at no time did she mention what must have been the single, dazzling ray of light for her parents: that they went to the gas chambers knowing their daughter had escaped and was probably still alive.[69] One of them had managed to outwit the Nazis. From our perspective, Marianne's survival must have been their sole consolation. Yet Marianne seemed to take no comfort from this at all.

## Alfred and Lore in Theresienstadt

Meanwhile, the rest of the family was still in Theresienstadt. Anna Rosenberg died of 'old age', as Erna Ogutsch put it, three weeks after her daughter's deportation.[70] Both Alfred and Oe found useful jobs to do. Alfred supervised the queues at the post counter, where parcels were collected. This explains the frequency with which he managed to send post out to Grete Sander. With assistance from Herr Ogutsch, Oe was able to gain a position in a children's home. She moved in and took charge of about fifteen boys. According to Erna Ogutsch, who worked as a nurse across the way and spent much time with Oe in the summer of 1944, Oe found genuine fulfilment in her work. How much contact Alfred and Oe had with each other, we do not know.

In March 1944, Alfred Strauss wrote a card acknowledging receipt of a parcel.[71] A month later, he sent a lengthier postcard, which yet again sat for three months before it was sent off:[72]

*Alfred and Lore in happier times*

*Dear Frau Sander,*

*I acknowledge with thanks the packet sent from Lisbon to our brother. He and his family are not here. We three are healthy and hope the same is true of you and your family. Aunt Anna died 8.1.1944 after a short illness. My wife and her mother were with her to the last. Have you heard from Siegfried and his wife? We would be very happy to hear from you very soon. Many thanks, dear Frau Sander, and best wishes also from my wife and my mother-in-law.*

*Your Alfred Strauss*

In May or June 1944, Alfred received a postcard that Siegfried had sent from Birkenau in January. These delays! This was a time when it was possible for letters sent from German troops on the Eastern front to reach their destination within a few days. We also know that, in May, Alfred and Lore received a card from Richard, which seemed to suggest that he was on his own but gave no address.[73] On 3 June, Alfred wrote to Frau Sander:[74]

*I hope that my card of April has reached you. For the parcels sent from Lisbon I thank you most warmly. They are very valuable to us. My brother wrote in January that he and his family are well and that they receive post punctually. We three are also well and hope that this is true of you and your family.*

*For now, accept my best wishes also from my wife and my mother-in-law!*

*Your Alfred Strauss*

In July, he wrote again:[75]

*Dear Frau Sander! I hope my cards of 7/6 and 24/6 have reached you. Have you heard anything from my brother? What else do you hear from our relatives? Please tell my cousin Hugo that we are delighted with his Lisbon parcels, which are very valuable to us. Please send best wishes to all our loved ones, accept our thanks and good wishes for you and your family from my wife, my mother-in-law and myself.*

451

Alfred's postcard of August 1944 was anxious that letters sent to his brother should have his birth date on the parcel. In all probability, though, Siegfried was already dead:[76]

> *Dear Frau Sander, I hope that you and the family are well and I can report the same of us. You will have received my last card of 24/7. For the parcels of sardines from Lisbon which we were particularly delighted to receive, many thanks. If you write to my brother in Birkenau do not forget his date of birth (24.IV.91).[ . . .]*

A short card, dated 18 September 1944, confirmed that they still had no news of Siegfried and family.[77] It was Alfred's last communication.

I tried to contact Grete Sander and her family to find out what it had meant to them. I learned that Grete's nephew, Paul Alsberg, had been Chief Archivist for the Israeli government, had done some work on the family tree, and might have information. He told me that Grete herself, 'an extraordinarily active and intelligent woman,' had died, but her daughter, Erna Morting, was still living in Sweden.[78] I wrote to Mrs Morting in Sundbyberg to ask her what she remembered. But other than a fascinating snippet of information about the Strausses' Swiss bank accounts and a rather sad hint that there had been recriminations from Marianne about money after the war, she could add little. Her closing comment was that she, her husband and her mother had been in such financial difficulties during the war that there was little they could do other than send some parcels to deported relatives. Clearly, it was impossible to have survived the Holocaust and not feel guilty.

I also telephoned Gershon Ellenbogen, but, as the gay tone of his original letter implied, he had passed on the postcards without realizing what they were and was rather taken aback to discover fifty years later that he had been so casual with the last signs of life from Theresienstadt and Auschwitz. Typically, Marianne had never explained what he had given her.

## The deportation of Alfred and Lore

It is not clear why the closing stage of the war should have seen another major wave of deportations from Theresienstadt. The Nazis probably felt some fear of the former Jewish military officers in the camp. Most of the officers were now deported.[79] Whatever the reason, the new wave of deportations began on 28 September. Because those dispatched in the first of the transports were selected for work fitness, it was widely believed within Theresienstadt that they really were going to some new camp or labour centre.[80] During the journey, the men were enjoined to send their wives postcards confirming that they had reached their ostensible destination and that food and accommodation were good and the work not too harsh. In reality, the transports, as before, were going to Auschwitz-Birkenau. Over the next few weeks, a whole series of transports followed, the last on 23 and 28 October. The scale of the operation is clear from the figures: on 28 September there were still 29,481 people in Theresienstadt, a month later only 11,077.[81]

On 29 September, eleven days after writing his last postcard, Alfred was deported. By the time the authorities deigned to frank and send his missive, not only Alfred but Lore and her mother too had gone to Auschwitz. Frau Ogutsch wrote to Marianne that when Lore was included on one of the very last transports out of Theresienstadt (on 9 October[82]), Lore's mother Else volunteered to go with her.

## The end of two journeys

When the final Theresienstadt transports arrived in Birkenau, they were subject to a selection. We do not know if Alfred survived it, but Else Dahl cannot have done. In Marianne's letter to Hugo and Grete Strauss dated January 1946, she assumed that Alfred, Oe and Else had all died in Birkenau. But later that year, Marianne told me, Erna Ogutsch wrote to her from a hospital in Sweden, where she had ended up after liberation, completely emaciated and almost dead. According to Marianne, Frau

Ogutsch had been in Birkenau and knew that Oe had been selected to work and dispatched to some distant concentration camp:[83]

'She witnessed how my aunt was shot by the SS on the retreat. As the Russians were marching forward, they [the SS] emptied the concentration camps of the ones who were still there and drove them away, and whoever sat down by the wayside was shot. And apparently she just couldn't make it and she just sat down and they shot her. And I think a few miles later the people who were still alive – within a matter of probably hours – were rescued, they were liberated. So she really could, just for a matter of a few hours, have survived the war. That is the only story I have of all these near relations where I know what happened up to the end.'

Oe 'was not a well woman ever', Marianne pointed out, 'but she was pretty tough and resilient, so I think that if it hadn't been for that, she might well have been here even now. She was born I think in 1906 or 1909[84] and so there would certainly have been the possibility that she would still be around.' Marianne told me that Frau Ogutsch said Oe's last words to her had been, 'tell Alfred what happened to me'.[85] Marianne said she would find Erna Ogutsch's letter for me, but never did. I rather think she could not bear to look for it.

Though Vivian and I had gone through most of the papers in her house, we failed to find the Ogutsch letter. But we did find a number of contradictory references to Oe's death. In the 1950s, another survivor, Frau Julia Böcker, made a rather different statement:[86]

*Declaration under oath*

*I saw Frau Lore Strauss from Essen, earlier resident Hufelandstrasse 23, arrive in the concentration camp in Auschwitz. All occupants of this transport were gassed immediately after their arrival.*

*I can say with certainty that Frau Lore Strauss, whom I knew from Essen, was among the people who were gassed on 22 November 1944.*

This report simply cannot be true. We know that Oe left Theresienstadt on 9 October and that the gassings stopped in Auschwitz on 2 November 1944. We have already seen that the same witness made an inaccurate statement regarding family possessions.[87] It is of course possible that Oe had been killed after disembarking from the October transport. According to H. G. Adler, there were only twenty-two survivors of the 1,600 people on the transport that left for Auschwitz on 9 October 1944.[88] But even this figure is a little suspect. We know that other healthy younger people were selected for work from this transport.

In 1978, Marianne filled out 'pages of testimony' for Yad Vashem. These recorded the deaths of her parents and brother at Auschwitz, date probably June 1944, and of her grandmother at Theresienstadt, date unknown. Evidently, she had forgotten by this point that Anna died in January 1944. For Alfred, she had put a question mark next to the date of death, followed by 1944, but for Oe's place of death she had entered Treblinka or Maidanek 1945. Treblinka, however, had been shut down as a killing centre after the 1943 uprising and Maidanek was not a destination for Jews sent from Auschwitz in the last months of its existence. So neither of these could be correct. It suggested that during the 1970s Marianne had lost track of the letter describing the death of her aunt.[89]

In the 1980s, Marianne received another set of Yad Vashem memorial pages, this time in German and sent by the Alte Synagoge in Essen. Marianne dutifully filled out this set as well. For her parents and brother, this time she did not guess at a date but wrote simply that they had been transferred from Theresienstadt to Auschwitz and had been recorded as dead in May 1945. She recalled the precise date of her grandmother's death, and for Oe she wrote that she had been shot by the SS at Treblinka in the final days of the war.[90] As noted already, this is not possible since Treblinka no longer existed.

In the very last plastic bag of papers, the one in which we also found Ernst's ring, Vivian and I finally found Frau Ogutsch's letter, which indeed contained many details of the Strausses' experience in Theresienstadt. What Erna Ogutsch's letter did not contain was the one item Marianne had described to me, namely the account of Oe's death. Indeed, it could hardly have done so – Frau Ogutsch had never left Theresienstadt, and when she wrote to Marianne it was not from Sweden but from a DP camp in Bavaria.

But the plastic bag contained another letter, dated May 1 1946 from Ludwig Ansbacher and his wife Selma.

Ludwig explained the coincidence which had brought them news of Marianne:[91]

*Your best friend Trude Schloss, who was with you in Berlin, went from here to Bremerhaven and from there to America. Her uncle, a good friend of mine, was with her. We talked; he said here is my only surviving relative. I asked the girl where she was from, she said I come from Essen. Can you imagine what I was feeling? I asked her then, and as luck would have it she was able to tell me about you. I went home straight away and told Aunt Selma; naturally she was very excited.*

Selma Ansbacher added that their daughter Sigrid had been deported from Theresienstadt a few days after Oe and her mother. On 22 December 1944, Selma and Ludwig, still in Theresienstadt, had received a letter from Sigrid sent on 19 October. Through an agreed secret code, they were able to figure out that Sigrid was in Auschwitz. Sigrid had written that she had met Oe there. Selma continued:

*When we were liberated by the Russians and the war came to an end, we knew that something awful had taken place in Auschwitz. We arrived in Frankfurt on 22 June and found none of our dear children here. But let me tell you straight away that Sigrid is alive and has been in Sweden since July last year. But our dear Heinz never came back. I know that you are on your own. How often we talked about you in Theresienstadt. Your parcels all arrived and gave your loved ones much pleasure. We were together every day.*

The next section of the letter made clear that it was the Ansbachers' daughter who had been working with Lore:

*Now I have to tell you something very, very sad. We have been in contact with our Sigrid since last October. We discovered through Julius, my husband's brother in America, that Sigrid was alive and Sigrid discovered through America that we had been saved. Sigrid wrote and told us her awful story, all the places she was taken. She was with aunt Lore until 24 January 1945 in Kursbad b/ Trachenburg über Breslau.*

Frankfurt den 1. Mai 1946

Liebe Marianne!

Wir erfuhren von einem Fräulein Trude
Schlass durch einen Zufall Deine Adresse.
Wir freuen uns daß Du G"tt sei Dank am
Leben bist. Erinnerst Du Dich unser? Mein
lb. Mann ist der Vetter Deines lb. Vaters
u. Onkel Alfred und waren wir in
Theresienstadt mit Deinen lb. Eltern u.
Richard u. Tante Lore u. Onkel Alfred
zusammen. Wir kamen schon 1 Jahr
vorher mit unserer Sigrid dorthin.
Leider kamen alle Deine Lieben schon
sehr bald nach Auschwitz und zwar am
18. Dez. 1943. Deine lb. Großmutter ist
bald darauf in Theres. gestorben. Im Mai
1944 kam einmal eine Karte an Onkel
Alfred von lb. Richard. Wir entnahmen
daraus, daß er allein ist. aber wir wußten damals nicht genau, wo er ist, denn
es war keine Adresse angegeben Anfangs
Oktober 1944 kam Onkel Alfred weg u.
Tante Lore mit ihrer Mutter kam 14 Tage

*Extract from the Ansbachers' letter*

The letter went on to explain that Sigrid had gone from Auschwitz to the Gross-Rosen concentration camp. Even before this letter emerged, I had begun to think that Gross-Rosen might have been Lore's destination. Much less well-known than some of the other camps, it has begun to receive more attention from Western historians only in the last few years. In the latter stages of the war its network of satellite work camps made it one of the largest labour constellations in Germany. The use of female labour (almost exclusively Jewish women) in the Gross-Rosen satellites began in 1944. Thirty-nine female labour camps were created in the course of that year and another three in 1945, absorbing some 26,000 women prisoners.[92] I already knew of one inmate, Felice Schragenheim, who had been on the same transport as Oe and was sent to a Gross-Rosen sub-camp, as had been two survivors of Birkenau family camp, Ruth Klüger and her mother.[93]

My problem was that Kursbad does not appear as a location in any accounts of the camp. But a number of indications began to suggest that the Ansbachers had got the name slightly wrong. Under the rubric of 'Operation Bartold', four new sub-camps of Gross-Rosen were created in late autumn 1944 to build fortifications against the advancing Red Army. These four camps were Birmbäumel, Hochweiler, Kurzbach and Schlesiersee. In addition to the similarity of the name, other facts suggested that it was Kurzbach and not Kursbad that marked the end of Lore's journey. Kurzbach, which was indeed north of Breslau, was opened in November 1944, around the time that Lore would have been transferred from Auschwitz, and it closed 20–21 January, just when Sigrid remembered her having been killed.[94] Other sources confirm that the inmates of Birnbäumel, Christianstadt, Hochweiler and Kurzbach were marched to Bergen Belsen, where Sigrid ended up.[95]

The 1,000 women in Kurzbach came mainly from Hungary and Poland. German Jews such as Lore Strauss and Sigrid Ansbacher were in the minority.[96] The women were quartered in the stables of a large estate, surrounded by barbed wire and watched over by Wehrmacht soldiers. Because they worked in the open, visible to the general population, they wore civilian clothes rather than striped convict uniforms. Like Sigrid Ansbacher, most of the women were in their early twenties or even younger. But even for them the extremely taxing work must have been barely manageable in their undernourished state. For Oe, it must have been torture, as testimony preserved in Yad Vashem confirms.[97] The women knew, though, that prisoners deemed no longer capable of working were either shipped back to Auschwitz or sent to the Gross-Rosen main camp, where they were murdered by injection. The only redeeming feature compared with other camps was that, by and large, the female overseers in the women's camps seem not to have murdered inmates for sport or for minor misdemeanours.[98]

Towards the end of January, the Red Army moved closer and all four Operation Barthold camps were shut down. Selma wrote:

*Then the Russians came and the inmates had to flee with the SS. Aunt Lore had typhus and lay in the sick bay and here comes the terrible thing, Marianne; Aunt Lore was shot. Sigrid wrote that it was terrible. Aunt Lore said she should tell everything to Uncle Alfred. Our Sigrid suffered terrible things, she was in the KZ Gross-Rosen, Mauthausen and finally in Bergen-Belsen. There she got typhus and arrived in Sweden in July with a weight of five stones, a girl of seventeen.*

The effect of reading this letter was heightened by the fact that it was virtually the last document left to find. It seemed the end of two journeys. That the letter was so well hidden away conveyed anew how dreadfully painful the memory had been. For several weeks I was involved in a fruitless search for Kursbad, unaware that the letter itself contained a misremembering. But I knew immediately that Oe's fate was not quite what Marianne had told me. As in her memory of Ernst's fate, so here she had gently embellished the original with a literary touch. Unlike her treatment of Ernst's death, though, she had not rendered Oe's more brutal. Rather, by moving Oe's death from the camp's sick bay, still some months away from the end of the war, to a forced march just a few hours before liberation, she had intensified the picture of senseless waste.

# Living with a Past in Hiding

From an early stage in my conversations with Marianne I knew that I wanted to ask her about her post-war life in Britain. Having read many survivor autobiographies or biographies which took their subjects' lives no further than the liberation or the end of the war, I had often felt I was being offered a false sense of closure. It was obvious that survivors' problems long outlived the war.[1] Indeed, the condition of *being* a survivor was one that existed only after 1945.[2] For me, Marianne's post-war life raised many questions. I wanted to understand how a woman with the courage to take on the Nazis had felt confining her strength and talent to her home and family. I wanted to understand the irony behind her comment that 'the Jewish festivals are celebrated in this house'. Had she been a martyr to her Jewishness all her life? And I wanted to understand the tragedy, the unspeakable (the word comes up unbidden) tragedy, that having lost her parents and her brother Marianne should lose her daughter. In short, I wanted to understand how Marianne's past reached into her post-war life.

The problem was that these issues, or most of them, were precisely the reason why Marianne did *not* want to talk about her life in Liverpool. She had brought me in to commemorate the heroism of her friends and helpers, to remember her lost family and to create a memorial for Ernst. She saw no logic in advancing beyond 1945 and, indeed, believed it would cause pain to others if she did so. I tried to persuade her that to understand her persecution one had to make sense of the way the past had hounded her to the present. Reluctantly, Marianne accepted that we might look at some specific aspects of what the Germans call *Vergangenheitsbewältigung*, dealing with the past. Restitution, for example, was an area on which she provided information. But we were not to pry into her private life in Britain. Nearly all my arguments with her, and subsequently with Vivian, were about determining the precise boundary between *Vergangenheitsbewältigung* and privacy.

## Evidence of a settled life

Marianne's first months in England were far from easy. Encountering Basil's parents, with whom she and Basil lived in 1947, was a culture shock. She found their form of Orthodox piety very different from her own liberal background and their attitudes very old-fashioned. 'To my in-laws a dowry was very important. Quite incredible! They had attitudes which go back to ghetto years, ghetto life. A dowry was something that was quite essential.'[3] If I had known more about her own family background at that stage, I would have pointed out that Siegfried had not objected to his 60,000 marks, either.

Basil and Marianne soon moved into an attic flat, but it was the 'most primitive flat you can imagine', Marianne said. There were 'tiny little English fireplaces for the servants' quarters. There was no fridge, no proper heating and these two small open fireplaces. There was a very primitive bathroom with a gas heater which exploded now and then with great aplomb and terrified the wits out of me. The water tank in one of the rooms (for the whole house) made a great deal of noise.' Every morning, the heavily pregnant Marianne had to go down to the cellar and carry two buckets of coal up several flights of stairs. Never having learned to light a coal fire, her first efforts were a disaster. Someone told her to fan it, but nothing happened. In the end, she used more fire lighter than coal. It was an icy cold winter and droplets froze on her nose.[4]

Over 1946–7, Marianne taught German literature at what would now be A-level standard in a Liverpool girls' school. Despite her fractured English and their fractured German, all passed. She stopped working, however, after Vivian was born in November 1947. It was a lonely period. Basil was studying hard to become a consultant physician and had little free time. Marianne did not get on with her parents-in-law. Being on the top floor, it was hard to get the baby any fresh air. She remembered one day leaving the pram in the garden while she sat upstairs. Looking down, she saw that Vivian had managed to crawl out of the pram and was hanging by his harness. How she managed to get down the stairs so fast, she did not know!

All this was delivered as a fond recollection of early adversity, not imbued with any existential misery. What came through, in fact, was how quickly Marianne adapted to her new life. Married to someone settled in England, she avoided many of the problems of survivors finding their feet in a new country. The English language came easily to her – she learned 'with great aplomb', she might have said. Just nine months after leaving Germany she dreamed in English for the first time. When she woke up, she knew she had arrived.

I had been prepared to see her domestic role as the trap from which she had *not* managed to escape. But I soon realized that Marianne did not see her life this way at all. On the contrary, creating her own family was a mission she took up gladly. In 1949, she and Basil bought a pleasant four-bedroomed semi in the Allerton district of Liverpool, where she was to spend the rest of her life. In January 1951 their second child, Elaine, was born. Marianne's cousin René, writing to her in 1950, was clearly surprised by the speed with which she had settled down:[5]

> I am personally astonished that you are buying a new house. From my perspective, I have put my savings in liquid form, i.e. money. My idea is never again to allow oneself to be settled anywhere. But in England perhaps one thinks differently about this problem.

One might observe that attitudes towards house-buying were different in England and France and Marianne's gesture was therefore less significant than it appeared to René. But Marianne really did settle into her new life in Britain with remarkable speed and enthusiasm. She and Basil soon acquired a circle of close friends in Liverpool that lasted forty years or more. By marrying a 'local', Marianne had gained access to a settled circle, many of them from Liverpool's sizeable Jewish medical scene. The Millers and the Benders, whom I interviewed, were soon enormously impressed with Marianne's learning and culture, her knowledge of English literature (which put most English speakers to shame) and her expertise on antiques.[6] The Millers told me that Marianne knew England much better than they did. No matter how obscure the village, Marianne would know where there was a nice coffee shop and the address of a good antique dealer.[7]

For his part, Vivian recalled a rich and stable family life. Like any good 1950s middle-class family, they always ate a proper dinner together. Friends of the children remembered the family dinners as good-humoured, civilized affairs where one had to be on one's best behaviour. Not only Vivian but also other family and friends confirmed Marianne's prowess and creativity as a cook.

Many authors have commented on the fact that in the USA it is easy to be an immigrant and still feel American, but in England (or indeed in Britain) to have a foreign accent or manner was, until recently at least, to be clearly not English.[8] Marianne certainly retained a foreign air. Vivian remembered feeling quite protective of her (particularly in relation to schoolmates) because of this. Yet Marianne did not appear displaced or stateless. There is no evidence that she felt cut adrift as she had in post-war Germany. Rather, she conveyed an air of gracious cosmopolitanism.[9]

A remarkable coincidence brought me some extra insights into Marianne's family life in the 1950s and 60s. In autumn 1998, I asked my final-year students at Keele University to look at some of the contradictory testimony from Marianne's fellow school pupils. Before the seminar, one of the students, Rob Gray, knocked on my office door and said that the name Marianne Ellenbogen had rung a bell. He had checked with his parents and it was as he had thought: for almost the entire 1950s and 1960s his father and aunts had grown up literally next door to the Ellenbogens. I travelled to London to interview Rob's father, David Gray, and to Romsey to talk to his aunt, Jane Dalton, about their memories of the Ellenbogen family.[10] Jane, for a while a close friend of Elaine, remembered Marianne in the early 1960s as a glamorous and slightly racy mum. There were exciting trips for Jane and Elaine in

*Modelling photo from the 1950s*

*The proud parent – Marianne and family in Stratford*

Marianne's convertible, for example, or they were left to enjoy themselves at a funfair and once, famously, Marianne used contacts to get them tickets to a Beatles concert.[11]

Like many German-Jewish émigrés, Marianne missed aspects of German life and retained a soft spot for German landscape. She quoted Heine's dictum to me:

> *Think I of Germany in the night*
> *I sleep no more until daylight*

Marianne felt a painful mixture of nostalgia and aversion for locations that had been frequented by her family. In 1970 she and Basil visited Ahlen for the first time since the war. They went to the Dutch resort of Nordwijk, too, and stayed at the family's regular old hotel, the Haus der Dönen. The hotel was being converted to flats and not much frequented but was still beautiful, 'still very grand' and absolutely 'bang on the sea'. Marianne rarely went back to Essen. Returning there in response to an invitation to Essen's former Jewish citizens, she could not face the official reception.[12] Unlike other émigrés, however, she did have a way of maintaining links with Germany that were both strong and not too painful, namely through her relationships with the Bund. Warm correspondence with various Bund members continued up to her death. Some of her Bund friends visited her in Liverpool, others she met on occasional trips to Germany. Vivian remembered meeting Hanni Ganzer and others in the Black Forest.

## Between secrecy and restitution

Towards the end of what proved to be our last lengthy conversation, I asked Marianne about her battle for compensation from the German government. Like most people, I had only a vague sense of what was involved. I assumed that 'it' was a single something which you managed to 'get' or not, though obviously the exact amount would depend on what you had lost and what you had suffered. But Marianne said that restitution became 'more and more involved and difficult, the more they unravelled the whole thing. The law was still very raw, very much at the beginning. It was all very difficult, very involved; nothing was very clear. Oh God, it went on for years.'

The process took a heavy toll:[13]

'I remember sitting up night after night, writing reams and reams of letters. I've still got all that correspondence lying around, about restitution. Absolutely dusty old things lying around . . . It went on for years and years and years and years and years. I went to Germany every eight months or so to keep an eye on things and speed things up . . . There were many court cases.'

It was only after Marianne's death, when Vivian began to unearth those 'absolutely dusty old things' lying around, that I realized that I had had absolutely no conception of what was involved. Scattered around the house were enough files, folders, boxes, stuffed envelopes and loose piles of papers to form a private archive. And as I waded through the letters, affidavits and court proceedings, something of the

*Marianne and family visit the Bund in 1963.*

simply enormous demands of the process began to emerge. There were demands on her purse (because, as in any legal process, there was outlay before compensation), demands on her time, demands on her energy and health and, above all, emotional demands. The first letters date from September 1945, when Marianne applied in Düsseldorf for an advance to help re-equip her room.[14] The last legal letters date from the 1970s. For almost thirty years restitution was on her mind, with a particularly intense phase which extended from 1950 to the mid-1960s.

The problems were legion. The law itself began to take shape only in the late 1940s. Adequate legislation on many issues emerged only in the mid-1950s. Initially, Marianne used British lawyers who, in turn, dealt through German colleagues, and the dual chain in an uncertain law field proved disastrous. It was not until 1956, after a most acrimonious correspondence and a trip to Germany, that she finally ditched her 'worse than useless' lawyers (a judgement which the documentation

467

suggests not to have been unfair) and engaged Carl Hermann, a distinguished advocate in Cologne who was handling restitution cases for the
big Jewish concerns of Ullstein and Wertheim.[15]

By the mid-1950s, the Strausses' major property sales had been dealt
with, but for the rest work had only just begun. An idea of the scale
involved can be gained from a far from exhaustive list her lawyer
presented her in 1958 of still unresolved claims:[16]

*Claims in the name of Siegfried Strauss*
Loss of liberty; Household goods; Gold and silver; Insurance
policies;
Special payments (Reich Flight Tax; Judenvermögensabgabe;
Other payments, including payments to the Jewish community,
social payments, payments arising from racially based tax rates);
Transfer damages (damages arising from the emigration to
Sweden; damages arising from transfers to Cuba); Professional
losses, including damages arising from enforced closure of the
business.
*Claims in the name of Regina Strauss*
Loss of liberty; Gold and silver goods; Judenvermögensabgabe;
Securities.
*Claims in Marianne's own right*
Loss of liberty; Damages in her education and training; Damages to
health; Gold and silver; Judenvermögensabgabe; Damages to her
career.
*Claims in the name of Richard Strauss*
Gold and silver; Damages to his education and training;[17]
Judenvermögensabgabe.

Sundry other issues were also listed at the end. Not included in the
list are the property matters already dealt with as well as all the claims
being handled by René Wolf's lawyers in which he and Marianne were
co-beneficiaries – particularly with regard to the estates of Alfred and
Lore Strauss and Leopold Strauss. On these, too, Marianne was regularly
consulted and had to provide declarations, estimates and lists.

But what constituted the biggest challenge was the mix of moral,
emotional and psychological problems interlaced with the purely legal
complexities. Marianne was torn between needing to delve into the

documents and wishing to forget what had happened, and torn too between her desire to preserve the family wealth and her distaste at haggling over the remains.[18] Particularly painful for her were cases where her memory or her experiences were challenged. For example, Marianne wished to claim compensation for her loss of liberty, both as a wearer of the yellow star from 1941 to 1943 and for her years underground. Marianne noted 'with amazement' in January 1957 that, despite the well-known Nazi directive of September 1941, the Restitution authorities in Essen wanted *proof* she had worn the yellow star between 19 September 1941 and 31 August 1943.[19] However, the job of finding witnesses to prove something that Nazi law had required was small beer compared with what followed. Hermann wrote apologetically to Marianne in June that, based on recent court decisions, the official at the Düsseldorf Restitution Office believed that Marianne's underground years did not constitute loss of liberty or living under inhuman conditions. The official would, however, accept her claim if she could prove that she had worn the yellow star while on the run.[20] Not surprisingly, Marianne could scarcely believe what she was reading. To have worn the yellow star while passing as an Aryan would have been madness. She responded by return with a moving and powerful account of the stresses of life underground.[21]

Nevertheless, on 5 December the state rejected Marianne's claim for compensation, arguing that the presence of her circle of friends and her ability to earn ration points by selling felt flowers meant that her life was not, as the law required, of or below the level of a prisoner.[22] In other words, Marianne's extraordinary courage in breaking through the constraints of wartime life was now being used to prove that the conditions had been bearable.[23] It was only by dint of further representations, which Marianne found enormously taxing and stressful, and a court hearing in May 1958, that a compromise was reached. And this was just one claim under one of the many headings of restitution.[24]

In some cases, the emotions of yesterday were aroused particularly acutely, and nowhere more so than with the family banker, Hammacher, and with the Jürgens. In the case of Hammacher, Marianne had already suffered the shock in the early post-war months of finding him ensconced in a flat with many of the family possessions. Now there was the question whether they had been purchased at a fair price or under duress. Hammacher, however, did have something to offer Marianne's lawyers – considerable help in tracing Deutsche Bank documentation about the transfer of family funds to Sweden. So Marianne was faced with the problem of whether to accept a compromise figure from Hammacher for the family goods he had received, in recognition of his efforts in tracking down the funds.[25] After some months, Marianne agreed to the compromise, though the tone of her English solicitor's letter to their German lawyer indicates the depth of her bitterness.[26]

The single most painful and upsetting case for Marianne had to do with the Jürgens. In the immediate post-war period, Marianne had gone to reclaim the furniture and trunks left in trust with them, but the Jürgens claimed that these were a gift from her parents. 'I had to get the authorities to come to the house and say you have to give it back. It was all really dreadful.'[27]

What was?

'Well, the way they behaved, it was so undignified, so absolutely awful, I felt, I really felt as if I was in the wrong, stealing what was really legally theirs, terrible, really terrible. Amazing how people can behave.'

In conversation, she returned to the Jürgens several times. She particularly resented that she should have been depicted as the importunate claimant, 'because it throws such a bad light on what's your right. So, that was all pretty awful. Really awful. And what hurt me most was that they didn't give me all the family portraits back.'

As I discovered from the documents, her claim against the Jürgens went on for years. From October 1950 we find a deposition by Frau Jürgens to the Office for Restitution, Essen, the only document I found among all the restitution papers that has Marianne's annotations all over it. Clearly, what was extraordinarily painful was that Maria Jürgens made public Marianne's poor relationship with her parents (something Marianne could scarcely deny) and used it to claim that Marianne had no knowledge of the arrangements between Regina Strauss and the Jürgens:[28]

*The applicant, Frau Marianne Ellenbogen née Strauss, was not informed about the personal relationships I had with her parents, particularly as she was on very poor terms with them. At that time, I did the Strauss parents great favours without compensation. During the war, as the food supply, particularly for Jews, was very difficult, I kept them well supplied with food.*

Here were all the burdensome strands of the past coming together. The mixture of truth and lies must have cut her to the quick. She had covered Maria Jürgens' statement with underlining and exclamation marks, often doubled, which grew ever larger through the document, until the final paragraph, which is adorned by two huge exclamation marks as large as the paragraph itself.

Restitution also imposed a strain on relations between the various branches of the family. She fell out with Adolf Rosenberg over the Ahlen inheritance (as indeed did Karl, who ended up taking legal action against his brother); with Hugo Strauss over money deposited in a US account; there were irritable exchanges with Lore's brother Ernst Dahl and an angry letter to Erna Morting about money Anna Rosenberg had deposited in Switzerland. Marianne's underlying feeling that the extended family had not done enough for her parents and brother no doubt influenced her attitude. Probably, too, she was deflecting the anger she felt towards her parents on to relatives who were a more acceptable target. Certainly, the documents suggest that on occasion she was less than indulgent towards her relatives. On the other hand, her many years of close co-operation with René Wolf proved an essential ingredient of her success. René's indefatigable efforts on both their behalfs in relation to Alfred and Lore often helped her with regard to her own claims. Given the similar situations of Alfred and Siegfried, often all her own lawyer had to do was simply duplicate René's successful applications.

Overall, Marianne pursued restitution with determination, perseverance and great success. Apart from René's assistance, she was also aided by the huge range of documentation the family had managed to deposit with the bank, the Jürgens and others. By 1967, when the last significant payments were handed over, Marianne had received many hundreds of thousands of Deutschmarks:

'I've not inherited this to squander it or use or do whatever with it but to hand it on, to make something with it. And that's really why I started buying antiques, selling antiques as well, not an awful lot but also selling. And investing the money so that I could feel that I had done right by my parents – that I had not done, what so often happens, that one generation builds up something and the next generation tears it down. That's what they usually say. . . . And I really do think that I haven't done too badly in that respect.'

She had been her father's daughter.

## Silence and suffering

Looking at Marianne's ability to adapt to her new surroundings, the energy with which she threw herself into motherhood, her ease with the English language and culture, her circle of friends, the success with which she tackled the complexities of restitution, would anybody knowing her in the 1950s and 1960s have said that she was struggling to cope with the past? I think probably not. Vivian was hesitant about delving into the minutiae of his childhood, but it did not seem that Marianne had flinched every time she saw a policeman, or told her children always to have their passports with them, or kept a suitcase ready-packed in the bedroom – characteristics which many other second-generation survivors noted of their parents.

As in the war years, she gave no impression of being vulnerable or a victim. She was formidable. I certainly found her so. Even in our last interview, weeks before her death, Marianne never gave me cause to feel that I was powerful or that she was fragile. She was very self-controlled and, as I and others experienced, quite ready to control others.

Was this self-control, though, merely the iron lid on boiling turmoil beneath? Marianne certainly did show signs of stress. Up to the 1980s, she was an extremely heavy smoker. Despite her asthma, she would smoke upwards of forty cigarettes a day. Most of her acquaintances also commented on her rows with Basil. But neither smoking heavily nor shouting at one's spouse are the preserves of a Holocaust survivor. More significant as an indicator of Marianne's pain (and of the control she had to exert) was her silence. Just as in the immediate post-war period so now, Marianne hid her past behind an almost complete blackout. Even those closest to her found their questions deflected and discouraged. I was never able to ask Basil what he had or had not learned. But from the urgent instructions on the packets full of letters that Marianne had sent on ahead of her in 1946 – 'Marianne, private, not to open' – through to her unwillingness to include Basil in our conversation in 1989, I deduced that she was little more forthcoming with him than with others. To close family friends, the Millers, the Benders and other relatives she imparted, at best, snippets of information. And of course, the wartime letters and diaries lay untouched and unread for forty years. Indeed, Marianne's habit of secrecy, of divulging past information a nugget a time, became such a habit that it extended to every area of her life. Her grandchildren would find her as loath to disclose her chopped-liver recipe as to provide information about Nazi Germany for a school project. (She *did* provide a recipe for chopped liver. But they discovered that it lacked her secret ingredients.)

Yet the past would not disappear. Marianne's accounts and memories have already made clear her complicated feelings towards her family. They were compounded by her sense that she had let the Bund down after the war. Bruno Bettelheim reminds us that rescued Jews often felt they had to prove they were worthy of having been saved.[29] Marianne said:

'After the war, after it was finished I always felt that I let the Bund down, because I took on an entirely humdrum, bourgeois existence bringing up a family and not really doing anything else – not being, you know, a politically active person, which I had intended to be after the war. You know, when I was in Düsseldorf first after the war I joined the party and did whatever I thought was expected of me. I didn't enjoy it, but I felt I had that obligation. *I* had taken on that commitment[ . . .]But I couldn't say I was committed – that I was convinced that that was the way for me. When I got married, and I really had no choice in taking that step, I felt I also have a life to live at last and I have to live the sort of life that means something to me, bringing up my children. I always felt guilty about it because it didn't leave me any sort of leeway, any time for doing something else, which I knew would have been important to them [the Bund]. They never *said* anything. But I felt I let them down.'

For Vivian and Elaine, the past made itself felt above all as unearthly, heavy silence. They learned early not to ask questions for fear of upsetting their mother. They dimly sensed but could not see the forces pressing down on Marianne's shoulders. Vivian said that as a youngster he was aware of his mother's guilt-feelings towards her parents, and above all her brother. But when I asked him why he thought this, he volunteered only that that was what *he* would feel were he in her situation. The one thing he did strongly remember was his mother sitting up during the night, typing away at her restitution correspondence, and himself having a keen sense that she was engaged in something burdensome and painful.

Jane Dalton, Elaine's friend and neighbour, gave me an extraordinary, brief glimpse into Marianne's inner world. During the summer months when the windows were open, she said, you would hear Marianne crying out loudly in German in her sleep. This was to repeat itself several times over the years. On the other side of their road lived the German consul in Liverpool and his wife (with whom Marianne was on very friendly terms). Sometimes, the consul's wife would have nightmares too, and fearful German would echo from both sides of this suburban Liverpool street.

Yet almost as arresting as this image was the fact that Vivian had no memory of his mother's nightmares at all. Indeed, he challenged the assertion and I had to go back to Jane to confirm it. If Jane was right, this seemed to me a telling example of the way the children learned to hide from signs of their mother's pain.

## Mastering the past

Thinking about Marianne's life after the war made me look again at the wartime experiences that had now become memories. Clearly, her situation could not be compared with that of a survivor of the camps. She had not suffered the arbitrary brutality, the powerlessness or the shame and degradation which were the camp inmate's daily fare.[30] She had not had to endure seeing the extremes to which people were driven

in order to survive. Nor did she have to reconstruct her essential humanity after the war.[31] No one was more conscious of this difference than
Marianne herself:[32]

'That was something I always feared when thinking of ending up in a
concentration camp – how I would behave, whether I'd behave like a
civilized human being, how long it would take before I wouldn't care
any more how civilized I was, and survival become the main thought, as
it did for so many. That you just did anything in order to survive . . .'

The difference between camp survivors' memories and Marianne's
was reflected in the quality of her testimony. Her flow of speech was not
impaired by memory, as was that of some survivors.[33] What she had to
tell did not defy her capacity of expression.[34] She spoke, and wrote,
when she had to, smoothly and articulately. She did not weep in the
telling or pause mid-sentence, nor did she have to adopt the mechanical
voice of the automaton.

Yet her own past had been traumatic enough. Bruno Bettelheim could
have been describing her when he wrote that to be considered a survivor
it was not necessary to have been in the camps:[35]

*Having to live for years under the immediate and continuous threat of
being killed for no other reason than that one is a member of a group
destined to be exterminated, and knowing that one's closest friends and
relatives are indeed being killed – this is sufficient to leave one for the
rest of one's life struggling with the unsolvable riddle of 'Why was I
spared?'*

A central feature of Marianne's psychological predicament was that
her traumatic memories revolved remarkably little around what had
happened to herself. Her wartime friends had been astonished by the
insouciance with which she brushed off the threats to her life and liberty.
I myself sometimes found it hard to remember how much danger she
had faced. In her testimony, Marianne devoted precious little emotional
energy to describing the close shaves with police and Gestapo. The most
detailed account of a near arrest came not from Marianne but from
Meta Kamp. Instead, Marianne's most vivid and painful stories had to
do with leaving or losing her family and fiancé. Almost equally powerful
were the moments when Marianne learned of their fates. Even in her

diary, it is only the news of her parents on the BBC that broke through the normal tone. And also in her diary, guilt already vied with fear as her predominant emotion.

Marianne's long years of silence over these incidents suggest that she fought to prevent the past from taking control of the present. But the way her memory altered events also suggests that the present reached back to try to take control of the past. All memory is subject to change. In inconsequential matters of information Marianne's memory was prone to the usual inaccuracies. But when she related incidents as if they had happened yesterday, incidents which seemed to be permanently etched into her consciousness, the differences between what she said and what I later learned to be true took on a different significance. Lawrence Langer has argued that it is inappropriate to talk about inaccuracy in Holocaust testimony and has talked of the survivor's 'insomniac memory' – the memory that never goes away.[36] But Marianne's memory suggests that even those traumatic memories which were always with her were subject to change. Moreover, the alterations followed certain common patterns, adding to my sense that what was happening in her mind was no accident.

One thing I'd noticed was that in a number of cases a kind of polarization had taken place in her testimony. On the one hand, there were small exaggerations or magnifications of experience. Particularly where there had been some traumatic event, the circumstances surrounding that event had often taken on slightly larger dimensions in Marianne's memory. Periods of time were doubled or trebled: the duration of her father's internment in Dachau after Kristallnacht in 1938 became in her memory six weeks; in reality it was three. Similarly, after her flight in 1943, her family was imprisoned in Essen just over a week; Marianne remembered the period as three weeks. Something true not only of her own testimony but that of other Jewish witnesses was that uniform wearers of very different provenance metamorphosed in memory into 'SS men'. Wehrmacht soldiers, railway officials, ordinary police on the trains and other figures became fused with the archetypal threat figure: the SS man. This was evident in both Marianne's and Imo Moszkowicz's memories of Christian Arras. On the other hand, in contrast to these forms of magnification, there were occasions where time had served to diminish or underplay past events. This was most marked in relation to the Bund, where Marianne's desire not to tarnish their memory had led her to forget or suppress the arguments and tensions that I discovered in the diary.

More interesting than this tendency of memory to expand or diminish the good and the bad, however, were the various points in her personal narrative where the chain of events, as described by her, did not match with the events as described by other sources. The most striking and consistent pattern was the reworking or obscuring of episodes of separation and loss. Marianne's memory was that she had accompanied Ernst to the barracks; in reality she had left him in his apartment. In her memory of her own escape, she believed she had slipped out of the house while the Gestapo men assessed the loot in the basement. In reality, she had asked them if she could get bread for the journey and had left the house while ostensibly in the kitchen. In her memory, she had heard on the BBC that her parents had already been murdered. She had forgotten the waiting period between the announcement and the date on which the gassings were due to take place. All these partings or farewells – *the* central traumas of Marianne's life – had subtly changed.

Marianne, it seemed, 'defused' traumatic and guilt-ridden partings by amending them. In Ernst's case, she adopted Hanna Aron's story and, in so doing, sought to delay the moment at which she had let Ernst go. In the story of her own escape, she again adopted a story – this time taking Pastor Keinath's attempted route out of the house for her own. For a while I wondered why escaping down the stairs and locating the Gestapo in the cellar had seemed preferable as a memory to asking for bread and slipping out of the kitchen. Did Marianne wish to deny the fact that her escape depended on a gesture of humanity from the Gestapo? It is possible, but unlikely, since she was very alive to the nuances of goodness and evil in those around her. I came to the conclusion that Marianne had invented an escape route that her brother could have taken with her. Both could have sneaked down the stairs whilst the Gestapo were in the cellar. Fetching bread from the kitchen was a ruse which allowed the escape of only one.

What was the point of these changes? Even if they had been true, would they have made her any less 'guilty'? From our perspective, she was not guilty anyway. From Marianne's perspective, even if she *had* slipped out of the house by a route which Richard could have taken, even if she *had* spent the night with Ernst, she would probably not have felt any less guilty after the war. She might well have felt the need to make other changes to cope with the past. The important thing was to impose some mastery on the moments that caused such pain.

In other words, it seemed to me that the inaccuracies in Marianne's memory were evidence of her pain and loss and a sign that she had sought to control the past within her, just as she sought to limit communication about it to the outside world. The stories had gently been changed into metaphors. As 'parables' of her and her families' fate they were very slightly more bearable.

As the past moved further and further away, the painful reliving of these separations began to be joined by a new emotion that she commented on several times, namely, a sense of disconnection from the past. The murders of her family and loved ones were not just senseless – they also began to become more remote. Probably this new 'parting', a separation enforced by time and distance, occasioned new feelings of guilt. Indeed, there are hints in the wartime diary entries that in relation to Ernst Marianne felt this guilt at 'letting go' of memory as early as 1944. So she began to embellish the stories of her loved ones' fates. Ernst's horrible accident became a medical experiment – just as Enrique, a couple of thousand miles away in Buenos Aires, invented the image of the SS stabbing. Marianne 'rescheduled' the announcement of her parents' death to her birthday, whereas there were in fact some ten days between birthday and broadcast. She moved Lore's shooting forward from January 1945 to a few hours before liberation. We might well feel that the changes themselves were trivial – the original facts were awful and poignant enough. Here again, the 'gesture' of reworking the past, in this case to try and keep it alive, was the important thing.

I did not know whether such changes were deliberate or unconscious. But after Marianne died, I listened again to my conversation in September 1996 and was struck by a passage I had forgotten. Marianne was talking about returning with Basil to Noordwijk:[37]

'So, that was going back to traces of my childhood. I didn't like doing that ever. And, er, I never, I'm not a person who likes looking back anyway. I don't like to look back on what went on before, all these experiences, which are bound up with one's existence, because I always find I get very unsettled. I always think that one's memory's always different from the reality of it. And, not only is that *mostly* the case, it's not always, but you certainly are frightened of it that it's always the case, that you always are disappointed.'

Vivian, too, told me he recalled his mother making similar comments. It seemed to me, therefore, that Marianne saw herself as more the victim than the master of her memory.

## Losing touch with the past

Once, when Marianne and I were looking at old photographs of the Strauss family in the Gruga Park or at Norderney, I asked her what she felt. She felt nothing, she said. It was like looking at somebody else's life. 'My life seems to be fragmented in so many different parts, it's as if it's not me.'[38] It made me realize anew how many abrupt changes in her environment and identity Marianne had endured between 1933 and 1946. As a child, she had been an acculturated Jew, not particularly aware of her Jewishness. The Nazis forced her Jewish identity to the fore, initially at school as a stigma, but more positively in the late 1930s and early 1940s as a source of identity (though still very much within a German intellectual and cultural framework). During 1941–2, she referred often to God, cited portions of the Bible, and observed the Jewish calendar. With the Bund, she had acted out three identities – the ordinary 'Aryan' for outside consumption, the fellow-comrade with her hosts, and the Jewish girl the regime sought to murder her for being. But while 'passing', she increasingly saw herself as the Bund fighter. After the war, she was torn between the activist and the exile. Finally, she came to Britain as Jewish wife and mother. Given so many transitions, it was not surprising that Marianne should feel disembodied.

It is perhaps also not surprising that Marianne should have lost sight of some of her earlier incarnations. Yet it did not seem accidental that the two 'selves' which had slipped from view were the religious self and the wartime Bund fighter. As far as the latter was concerned, I felt that what blocked Marianne's vision of the person she had been in the diary was the same thing that had made the diary so unexpected for *me*: namely, the public perception of the Holocaust that emerged after the war. As a 'claimant' to special treatment – post-war rations, access to Britain, restitution – Marianne had been encouraged to present herself as Jewish victim. When she broadcast, the BBC chose to label her as a young Jewess talking to the Germans. The family members with whom Marianne re-established contact after the war of course viewed her in this light. And in the Anglo-Jewish circles in which she moved in Liverpool, particularly once public discussion of the Holocaust became more open, this was how she must have been seen. In this post-war context, it was perhaps inevitable that her wartime self-image as Bund comrade should disappear from view.

Marianne's experience here may be a sign that people who survived by 'passing' as an Aryan were prone to wartime shifts in their self-image. We are familiar with the idea that Jewish children taken in by non-Jewish parents or institutions sometimes underwent a permanent change of identity and emerged from the war as Christians. Adults rarely underwent such permanent conversions. But it may be that, like Marianne, for a while they too did not just *pretend* to be someone else, but really took on a new identity, an identity which they then discarded some time after the war. (We can rarely observe such changes because we usually only have oral testimony at our disposal – and interviews are ill-placed to reveal to us what the memory has hidden. Marianne's diary provided a very unusual window into her wartime state of mind.) On the other hand, few Jews passing as Aryans had such positive role models to emulate as Marianne found in the Bund. Few had such a strong motive to take on a new identity within as well as without. Moreover, afterwards it was not only the pressures of victimhood that compelled Marianne to abandon her wartime role. Had Marianne been a man actively embraced during the war by a non-Jewish political grouping, it is hard to imagine an equivalent post-war reabsorption into an observant Jewish household. Such feats of domestic adaptation are seldom expected of men. So the discontinuities Marianne underwent seemed to me possibly unique, but certainly the experience of a woman.

Having abandoned the political activist, Marianne was also unable to reconnect to the earlier self who had talked and thought seriously about God. It was clear from things she said that the Bund's influence blocked her way back. In addition, the Ellenbogens' Jewishness was so alien to her own and Basil's expectations (though Basil was in no sense an intolerant man), so at odds with hers, that Jewish religious life became conflict-laden and difficult. And when Elaine died, Marianne gave up on religion completely.

## Elaine's death

In June 1968, Marianne started a letter to her Bund friends. It was summer but she did not feel at all summery:[39]

> *Even the sunshine cannot make the world look any more bearable today. Elaine has been in hospital for almost five months and there has been no improvement in her condition or her weight. As long as she is so negative in her attitude to life, all we can do is hope and pray.*

Marianne talked about what a strange disease anorexia was and went on:

> *My thoughts and well-being are so completely entwined with hers. Often I ask myself how we have managed to survive this long year, from one day to the next existing and hoping. And who knows for how much longer and what is still to come!*
> *And the world around us looks so sad, after . . .*

And here the letter ended, unsent, joining the growing pile of papers in Marianne's house. On 29 September 1969, the eighteen-year-old Elaine died.

'For my own part', Vivian said of his mother, 'I felt it was an extreme injustice, I still do, for somebody who'd been through what she'd been through and lost what she'd lost, to have to suffer losing a child as well, although nobody should have to lose a child.'[40]

I was never able to probe the question of a connection between Elaine's death and Marianne's experiences.[41] The matter was too painful for

Marianne to discuss. Vivian's feelings were also still extremely raw. After Marianne's death, Vivian's distress was compounded by the discovery of letters Elaine had written but not sent to his parents during her stay in hospital. He had never read them, and his parents had denied any such letters existed. Twice Vivian told me a story in the first person, but when I quizzed him about it, he looked at me confused and said 'No, not me, her.' Vivian had theories about Elaine's death, but refused to discuss them with me. I raised the matter with some of the Ellenbogens' family friends and with Jane Dalton, Elaine's girlhood neighbour and friend. I even managed to gain contact with Elaine's psychiatrist. A family friend, he had been asked by Basil to destroy his case notes and could not bring himself to talk about it.

I do know that Elaine's death almost destroyed Marianne. She lost all remnants of her religious faith. The marriage survived, despite hints from Basil to Vivian that it went through a very rocky patch in the wake of the tragedy. But Marianne's life was never the same again.

How far Vivian was aware of it I do not know, but the loss of his sister represented an eerie reprise of his mother's loss of her brother Richard. Both mother and son had lost an eighteen-year-old younger sibling. Both felt that the child who had died had been brighter and more promising than them. Both felt enormous guilt towards their sibling – Marianne felt she had abandoned Richard; Vivian felt that his studies had prevented him giving Elaine enough attention when she was ill. For both Vivian and Marianne, the deaths also intensified a sense of guilt towards their parents. Vivian had long felt that he fell short of Basil and Marianne's academic expectations. After Elaine's death, it was incumbent upon him to do twice as well. Incumbent on him also to survive – in 1971 Vivian was involved in a near-fatal car crash and felt intense guilt at the burden of worry he was placing on his parents. And because he so often felt guilty, he, like his mother, was unable openly to acknowledge how important his survival had been for his parents' happiness. Just as the knowledge that Marianne was free must have been the one comfort for Siegfried and Ine as they faced their deaths, so I knew that in her later years Marianne's principal source of happiness was Vivian's family and children. And, of course, Vivian felt angry with his parents, as Marianne had with hers – she because they had held

*Coffee and cakes with the Bund. Clockwise from left: Tove Gerson, Else Bramesfeld, Doris Braune and Marianne*

Richard back in the country for too long, he because they had withheld much that Elaine had communicated to them. That anger could never be properly dealt with for either of them.

## Seeking recognition for the Bund

Another source of sadness in the latter part of Marianne's life was her failure to have the Bund included among the ranks of 'righteous gentiles'. In 1984, Lisa Jacob sought to have her Bund saviours recognized in Yad Vashem, the museum and memorial to the victims of the Holocaust in Jerusalem. Marianne supported the application and added those from the ranks of her own helpers who were not on Lisa's list. But when the Commission for the Designation of the Righteous considered the Bund at its session on 28 January 1986, the outcome was inconclusive and the matter fizzled away. In 1994, Basil and Marianne were in Jerusalem. Lisa Jacobs having died, Marianne felt it was up to her to pursue the case. In March, she and Basil met Mordechai Paldiel, the director of that part of Yad Vashem which deals with recognition, to make another attempt. Again, she failed to achieve her goal.

Marianne was very bitter and disappointed to have again failed her friends, as she saw it, and I too felt frustrated on her behalf. When visiting Israel in 1998, I arranged to meet Paldiel to ask him about the case. Even before I met him, however, I already had a fair idea of what had gone wrong. The very peculiarities of the Bund that had helped it elude the Gestapo now perplexed those who were in a position to award it honours. I had already discovered that the major history of resistance and persecution in Essen did not mention the Bund – except to belittle reference to its achievements made in an earlier study.[42] It really was remarkable that in a thick, well-researched book focusing purely on Essen, the Bund should warrant nothing more than one condescending footnote. As a circle of friends that did not resemble a formal political grouping and as a dance movement in which seemingly unpolitical women played a major role, the Bund failed to fit the image of what resistance was supposed to look like.

What I now discovered was that Yad Vashem had made various enquiries in Germany to try to substantiate Lisa's claims – Dr Paldiel handed over the file of letters to prove the point – and all their enquiries had drawn a blank. No one knew of the Bund, the group no longer had links to senior people in the SPD who might have been able to speak for them, and the claims sounded so implausible. In addition, Dr Paldiel had not been clear who was gentile and who was Jewish in the Bund – an essential piece of information in a programme designed to reward gentiles. And, no doubt, as Dr Paldiel regretfully acknowledged, there had been probably been a degree of scepticism on their part, and they had let the matter drop.

Then something unexpected happened. Since I had indicated my willingness to help put the case together, Dr Paldiel handed me their file. 'Look through that,' he said, 'take copies of what you need, and do what you can.' Suddenly, the responsibility for pursuing the case rested on *me*. My first duty, I told him, was to this book, but afterwards I would indeed make the case to Yad Vashem. Perhaps I shall be able to fulfil Marianne's wish, albeit posthumously.

## Marianne's story

While she was alive, Marianne herself never volunteered – and I never managed to elicit – any kind of judgement or view of her life overall. The forays we made into the post-war years were confined to particular details. She told no over-arching story. I suspected that, if Elaine had survived and prospered, Marianne might just have managed a happy ending. Her post-war family would have given some meaning to her wartime survival. But Elaine's death precluded this. Although Vivian and his children were very precious to Marianne, indeed in the final years her principal source of pleasure, she could not call her post-war life a success.

Marianne was an intensely private person. Even if she had been able to put a more positive gloss on her biography, she might well still have chosen to say little about her post-war life. Divulging *any* personal information came hard to her. During my final research trip in Germany, long after Marianne had died, I rang Liverpool and spoke to Vivian's wife. I was wondering what Marianne would have made of all the connections I had uncovered. 'She would have hated it,' was the friendly but regretful reply. Probably she would.

Shortly before completing the book, I learned from Vivian just how hard he had worked to keep his mother reasonably composed while talking to me. Looking back to the day of our first meeting, I was suddenly confronted by the blindingly obvious fact that it had been *Vivian* who had persuaded us to record her story. When Marianne and I had set off to have lunch with him, we had been considering what to do with Ernst's letters. By the time lunch was over, we were talking about a book. Recognising Vivian's role reassured me that the impulse for the book had come not just from me – but it did not stop me worrying whether I was doing what Marianne herself had wanted.

Yet ever since the war, Marianne knew there was a story she wanted to tell. In January 1946, sensing the communication gap between herself and her overseas relatives, Marianne wrote to Hugo and Grete Strauss:[43]

*Last photo of Marianne, Liverpool, October 1996*

*What I went through, experienced and learned in those two years – one day I will write a whole book about it; a single fate that gives an insight into the general political, spiritual and cultural constellation of Germany in the Nazi period.*

She never wrote her book, but it is surely significant that she threw none of her papers away. I learned from her friends that before I made contact Marianne had already been looking for someone to translate the documents. After we began working together, there had been the incident when Marianne dropped in on the Benders and launched into an account of her years underground. Clara Bender said to me, 'you could almost feel her heaving a sigh and saying I must get this down on paper.'[44] In January 1997, when visiting Mathilde Jamin at the Ruhrland Museum, I read a letter Marianne had written in December, just a week away from death. Marianne wrote of her desire 'to do justice to everything and not to leave too much unfinished business behind'. She went on:

*Mark Roseman and I have been working through my memories. Currently this is still in a very rough form and sketchy. We'll see what form it takes. It is a binding duty and burdens me greatly.*

What was it that Marianne wanted told? Above all, she was concerned to show the value of friendship and the heroism and selflessness of the Bund. When Marianne wrote to Mathilde Jamin about her 'binding duty' (doubtless the last time in her life she used the Bund's word *Verpflichtung*) it was to commemorate what her helpers had done. At the same time, she was not ashamed of admitting that she herself had been a fighter and that she herself had contributed to her survival. One of the titles she suggested for the book was the Dylan Thomas quotation, 'Do not go gentle into this good night'.[45] She never sang her own praises, but there was no denying that her courage and stubborn refusal to be subdued had been an essential precondition of staying alive.

Her other concern was more universal. The Holocaust, she said, could have happened anywhere. She had bitter arguments with her father-in-law about whether it could have taken place in Britain:

'I said to him, "Oh, well, you're lucky, it could have happened here." The reaction was absolutely explosive. "Of *course* it could not happen here. This is a democratic country." The usual sort of piffle. I mean . . . it's indescribable that people think . . . it can happen anywhere. It's happening anywhere, it's happening everywhere.'

On one occasion, I asked her if Christian Arras had made any comment to her about what he had seen in Izbica. She didn't remember any specific observations. And then she said:[46]

'The Germans, or anybody in that situation if it comes to that, you look at television every night and you see the atrocities that are going on now everywhere, in every part of the world. Well, after a while, you become immune. It's the most dreadful thing and I could never understand – and I still don't – how people come to think that six million makes an enormous difference from sixty or six thousand. It's what you do, not how many you do it to – *that* is at the root of the thing. The enormity for me lies in the fact that it happened at all – and that it is still happening. And that's what matters. That – is – what – matters. Yes. And nothing else. Not the six million. And those people in Izbica, they're

26 GARTH DRIVE
LIVERPOOL, L18 6HW

30. Nov. 1996/
14. Sec. 1996/

Liebe Frau Dr. Jamin,

von Herzen Dank für Ihren lieben, freundschaftlichen Brief, der seit einigen Monaten (mit vielen anderen) auf meinem Arbeitstisch auf Antwort wartet. Zu viel hat sich während meiner Krankheit angesammelt — und Allem gerecht zu werden in begrenzter Zeit und nicht zu viel "unfinished business" zu hinterlassen, gibt mir schlaflose Nächte.

*Last letter to Mathilde Jamin*

488

Augenblicklich bin ich wieder
in ˅Marie Curie Centre (auf
etwa 14 Tage) um mich etwas
auszuruhen; so finde ich
endlich Zeit Ihnen zu danken -
nicht nur für's Brief - auch
für den so reichhaltigen Katalog.
Vieles darin erweckt alte Er=
innerungen.
Mit Mac ˅Rosenun arbeite wir
meine Erinnerungen, augenblicklich noch sehr roh und
"sketchy". Wir werden sehen

not six million they're, what, a few, a handful of people, they're the epitome of what happened then to six million and more and is still happening. And that's it.'

I think she would have liked to use this statement to end the book.

For Marianne, man's inhumanity to man was the important issue, far more significant than the difference between killing sixty people or six million. I was not sure I could agree. I could see that to lose one's mother, one's father, one's brother and one's first love, was to sustain a loss, and to learn something about others' capacity for evil, that made the overall numbers almost irrelevant. To that extent, the murders of the Krombachs in Izbica and the Strausses in Auschwitz encapsulated the killings of all. But to kill six million required such a commitment, such a 'utopian' project of murder, such an infrastructure and such broad involvement and co-operation. It was not just the sheer numbers involved, but even more the aspiration to genocide that was so distinctive. Man's basic potential for inhumanity seemed a necessary part of the explanation, but very far short of a sufficient one.

The idea that every modern society is equally poised to commit genocide also did not ring true to me, even if all contain some of the elements that made the Holocaust possible.[47] At the time of our discussions, I wondered if Marianne had ever really come to terms with the Holocaust's scale or the extent of German society's involvement. In retrospect, I think she may have been provoked into such a blanket assertion of the Holocaust's universality. She could not stand the complacency she found in Britain. It reminded her too strongly of the naïve trust in one's homeland that had proved so misplaced in Germany. Above all, the simplistic anti-German attitudes she encountered in Britain were too much at odds with her own experience.

Marianne knew that there was an 'other' Germany, a Germany of culture and ideas, of idealism and public service, whose values had influenced both Jews and non-Jews. Marianne saw the Bund's intellectual world as in many ways typically Weimar. She knew that the tradition of integrity and public service which guided David Krombach was as German as it was Jewish. She did not deny that other facets of German society and culture had the potential to call forth great evil, particularly in the wake of the political, economic and cultural crisis of the early

1930s. She could not doubt the depth and breadth of German anti-Semitism. But from her I gained the insight that, in their different ways and different generational styles, Artur and Dore Jacobs, David Krombach, the young Ernst and (though she would never have claimed this) the young Marianne herself were the very best of Germans.

Marianne experienced enormous variation in human responses to herself and her family. Despite the threats and dangers, some had found the freedom to offer selfless assistance; others had provided help, but only in return for material rewards; many others had cold-shouldered the family and some had had a hand in their murder. Marianne knew that a remarkable range of relationships had been struck up or maintained with her family at a time when Jews were publicly vilified. The bank director, the priest, the Wehrmacht soldier, the Catholic family and of course the Bund, to name but some. Not all of these relationships were 'bought' by the Strausses' wealth and not all were so unique. It was understandable that, for Marianne, the crucial distinction should not be between the 'Germans' and others, but between one individual and another.

The Bund members themselves would have rejected the idea that it was a question of individuals. What proved itself, they wrote after the war, was 'the idea', the principles they shared. Certainly, the fact that they were a group, working together, was crucial, both in giving each individual confidence and strength and in making joint action possible. For all their German roots, they do seem to offer a more universal message of hope. An informal network of upright and courageous individuals, inspired by a common idea, may be able (given some luck) to uphold standards of decency, provide support for the persecuted and elude capture, even in a dictatorship.

Some time after Marianne's death, Vivian and I made our final foray to her house in search of documents. The house was cold and dilapidated. After Elaine's death, Marianne had not been able to tolerate work being done in the home. When I met her, despite her love of cooking she was still making do with a primitive 1950s kitchen. With so many of Marianne's possessions already removed, it was apparent that in fact the whole house needed renovating. There were serious settlement cracks in the back bedrooms. It was as if the whole structure were gradually sinking under the weight of her unmasterable past. Standing in the empty house, I was reminded of Marianne saying that she felt she had lived a series of lives, and that she was increasingly disconnected from all of them. She had suggested a second title for this book, a quotation from Rückert's poem, set by Mahler: 'Ich bin der Welt abhanden gekommen', 'I am lost to the world'.[48]

And yet it was impossible to think of Marianne as lost, or as a victim, for long. The house, forlorn as it appeared, held out another message. Marianne had insisted on her privacy. The subsidence had not been dealt with because she did not want workmen in; she had calculated, rightly, that the walls would hold up for as long as she needed them. Looking at the now defunct stair-lift reminded me that she had managed to look after herself pretty well to the last. Only two days before her death she had still been out and about. She had been resolute in relation to me, insisting on setting the boundaries. I could not help a wry smile when I thought how successfully Marianne had thwarted my efforts to bridge her pre- and post-war lives. She had kept the latter largely off limits.[49] The past *had* been unmasterable for her, yet she had managed it in the best way she could and had remained a fighter – resolute, dignified and in control. Marianne had succeeded, in the end, in telling her story. It seemed entirely fitting, almost a tribute to her, that some parts of her past should for ever remain in hiding.

# *Abbreviations*

| | |
|---|---|
| ADStE | Gestapo Aussendienststelle (Gestapo Branch Office) Essen |
| AfWGE | Amt für Wiedergutmachung (Office of Restitution), Essen |
| AS | Alfred Strauss |
| ASE | Alte Synagoge, Essen |
| BAB | Bundesarchiv, Berlin |
| BDC | Berlin Document Centre |
| CH | Carl Hermann |
| CV | Central-Verein deutscher Staatsbürger jüdischen Glaubens (Central Association of German Citizens of the Jewish Persuasion) |
| DB | Deutsche Bank |
| DBE | Essen branch of the Deutsche Bank |
| DBF | Deutsche Bank Historisches Zentrum, Frankfurt |
| DRK | Deutsches Rotes Kreuz (German Red Cross) |
| EK | Ernst Krombach |
| EP | Ellenbogen Papers |
| HStAD | Hauptstaatsarchiv, Düsseldorf |
| JFB | Jüdischer Frauenbund (Jewish Women's League) |
| JPF–MH | Jüdischer Pfadfinder–Makkabi Hazair (combined Jewish Scouts and Maccabi Hazair Youth Group) |
| JSK | Jüdisches Seminar für Kindergärtnerinnen und |

|  | Hortnerinnen, Berlin (College for Kindergarten Teachers, Berlin) |
| --- | --- |
| KPD | German Communist Party |
| KriPo | Kriminalpolizei (Criminal Police) |
| LBINY | Leo Baeck Institute, New York |
| LG | Landgericht (State Court) |
| LGD | Landgericht Düsseldorf |
| LGE | Landgericht Essen |
| ME | Marianne Ellenbogen |
| MS | Marianne Strauss |
| NRW | North-Rhine Westphalia |
| NSDAP | Nationalsozialistische Deutsche Arbeiterpartei (National Socialist German Workers' Party – Nazi Party) |
| ODD | Oberfinanzpräsident, Düsseldorf, Devisenstelle (Currency Section of the Finance Office, Düsseldorf) |
| OFD | Oberfinanzpräsident, Düsseldorf (Finance Office, Düsseldorf) |
| OKW | Oberkommando der Wehrmacht (Armed Forces High Command) |
| OT | Organisation Todt |
| RjF | Reichsbund jüdischer Frontsoldaten (Reich Association of Jewish Combat Veterans) |
| RSHA | Reichsicherheitshauptamt (Reich Security Main Office) |
| RV | Reichsvertretung der deutschen Juden, later Reichsvereinigung der Juden in Deutschland (Reich Association of German Jews, later Reich Association of Jews in Germany) |
| RW | René Wolf |
| SD | Sicherheitsdienst (Security Service of the SS) |
| SStr | Siegfried Strauss |
| StAE | Stadtarchiv, Essen |
| StAE NJ AJD | Stadtarchiv, Essen Nachlaß Jacobs, Artur Jacobs diary |
| StaPo | Staatspolizeileitstelle (Gestapo Main Office) |
| StaPoD | Staatspolizeileitstelle Düsseldorf |

| | |
|---|---|
| StAW | Stadtarchiv, Wuppertal |
| VE | Vivian Ellenbogen |
| WGK | Wiedergutmachungskammer (Court for restitution matters) |
| YVJ | Yad Vashem, Jerusalem |

# Dramatis Personae

*Eric Alexander* (formerly *Alex Weinberg*), oldest of the three Weinberg brothers, Marianne's cousins on her mother's side.

*Gerald Alexander* (formerly *Otto Weinberg*), youngest of the Weinberg brothers, Marianne's cousins on her mother's side.

*Nancy Alexander*, Stamford, second wife of *Eric*.

*Uri Aloni*, (formerly *Hans Eulau*) contemporary of Marianne's from Essen in the 1920s and 1930s.

*Paul Alsberg*, distant relative of Marianne's. His aunt, *Grete Sander*, played an important role as addressee for family letters from Theresienstadt and Auschwitz-Birkenau.

*Hanna Aron* (née *Drucker*), near contemporary of Marianne's from Essen. Hanna's mother, *Irene Drucker*, worked with Marianne at the Jewish Community Office 1942–3. Hanna, Irene and Hanna's brother *Wolfgang* lived with Marianne for six months March–September 1943.

*Christian Arras*, soldier who acted as courier for Marianne to Izbica; also the name of his father. His son, also *Christian*, continues the family truck business.

*Lilli Arras*, wife of *Christian Arras*, Marianne's courier to Izbica.

*Waltraud Barkhoff-Kreter* (née *Kreter*), contemporary of Marianne's at the Luisenschule.

*Saul* and *Clara Bender*, friends of the Ellenbogens in Liverpool.

*Thomas Toivi Blatt*, Sobibor survivor who grew up in Izbica.

*Else Bramesfeld*, Bund member.

*Fritz* and *Maria Briel*, Bund members living in Remscheid. Their son, *Wolfgang*, was a small child when Marianne stayed with the family.

*Chaja Chovers* (formerly *Klara Kleimann*), contemporary of Marianne's from the Essen Jewish community.

*Jane Dalton* (née *Gray*), lived next door to the Ellenbogens in the 1950s.

*Ruth Davidsohn* (née *Mendel*), Jewish fellow-pupil of Marianne's at the Luisenschule.

*Inge Deutschkron*, journalist and author of *Ich trug den gelben Stern*; a contemporary of Marianne's at the College for Kindergarten Teachers in Berlin.

*Edith Dietz*, near contemporary of Marianne's at the College for Kindergarten Teachers in Berlin.

*Greta Dreibholz*, Bund member in Remscheid.

*Ruth Elias*, author of *Triumph of Hope*; at Theresienstadt at the same time as the Strauss family and took the same transport to the Family Camp in Auschwitz.

*Basil Ellenbogen*, Marianne's husband.

*Elaine Ellenbogen*, Marianne's daughter.

*Gershon Ellenbogen*, older brother of *Basil*.

*Raymond Ellenbogen*, younger brother of *Basil*.

*Vivian Ellenbogen*, Marianne's son.

*Hanni Ganzer*, friend of the Bund, living in Düsseldorf; Marianne's last protector before the end of the war.

*Ruth Gawse* (née *Ferse*), near contemporary of Marianne's in the Essen Jewish community; at the Luisenschule until 1938.

*Karin Gerhard*, Essen; successor to Lisa Jacobs as Director of the Dore Jacobs school.

*Tove Gerson*, Essen; Bund member who was in the USA during the war years.

*David, Sandra* and *Rob Gray*, London; Rob was my student who alerted me to the fact that his father David had grown up living next door to the Ellenbogens in Liverpool. Rob's mother Sandra had also met the Ellenbogens on many occasions.

*Werner* and *Hanna* (née *Heumann*) *Hoffmann*; Werner was an employee of the Strauss brothers from 1924 until he left Germany for Argentina in 1936 with his fiancée Hanna. They have a son, *Tomas*.

*Waltraud Horn*, non-Jewish contemporary of Marianne's at the Luisenschule.

*Lisa Jacob*, Jewish member of the Bund, also in hiding.

*Artur* and *Dore* (née *Marcus*) *Jacobs*, founding members and leaders of the Bund.

*Elisabeth Jacobs*, wife of *Wilhelm Jacobs*, one of the group whom Marianne met in Düsseldorf after the war.

*Mathilde Jamin*, historian at the Ruhrland Museum who made the original contact to Marianne.

*Hanna Jordan*, near contemporary of Marianne's. Her quaker parents had close links to Bund circles. Hannah met Marianne during the war and she (herself half-Jewish) was protected by the Bund for a brief period. After the war worked in theatre with *Imo Moszkowicz*.

*Ellen Jungbluth* (formerly *Ellen Hube*, née *Brandt*) Wuppertal Bund member since the 1930s, had only limited contact with Marianne, but after the war married *Ernst Jungbluth*, one of the Bund's central figures. In the last decade or more Ellen has been the central figure ensuring the Bund's survival.

*Meta Kamp*, (formerly *Meta Steinmann*, née *Wahle*) Bund member and Marianne's main host in Göttingen. Her sister *Elfrieda Nenadovic* and son *Ernst Steinmann* also had contact with Marianne.

*Hermann* and *Lene Krahlisch*, Bund members from Mülheim; Lene protected Marianne in October 1944.

*David Krombach*, father of Marianne's fiancé, *Ernst*. Died in Izbica 1942.

*Enrique* (formerly *Heinz*) *Krombach*, Buenos Aires; brother of *Ernst* who left Germany before the war.

*Ernst Krombach*, Marianne's fiancé.

*Minna* (*Minne*) *Krombach*, *Ernst's* mother; disappeared from Izbica November 1942.

*Rosemarie Lange* (née *Hahn*), Bobingen; non-Jewish contemporary of Marianne's from the Luisenschule.

*Jakov* (formerly *Klaus*) and *Tsofia Langer*, Kiryat Tivon; Jakov was in Marianne's youth group and managed to leave Germany just after the outbreak of war.

*Rudi* and *Grete Löwenstein*, friends of Ernst in Izbica; they had come to Essen in 1938. Rudi's father, *Josef*, had operated on Marianne's toe in 1941.

*Hilde Machinek*, Wuppertal, Bund member.

*Grete Menningen* (née *Ransenberg*), sister of *Irma Ransenberg*. Because she was in a mixed marriage she was protected from deportation until 1944 and sheltered Marianne a couple of times. In 1944 Marianne helped her find safety.

*Monte* and *Phyllis Miller*, Liverpool; friends of the Ellenbogens.

*Eva Morting*, Sundbyberg, Sweden; daughter of Marianne's very distant relative *Grete Sander*. Eva was married to *Ivor Morting*, notary.

*Imo Moszkowicz*, Ottobrunn; celebrated TV and theatre director after the war; met Marianne in 1942 before being deported to Auschwitz in 1943.

*Elfrieda Nenadovic* (née *Wahle*), Göttingen; younger sister of *Meta Kamp*; met Marianne in July 1944.

*Johannes Oppenheimer*, Berlin; one of Marianne's half-Jewish friends in Düsseldorf after the war, who later became a distinguished judge.

*Irma Ransenberg*, nurse with Jewish community; worked with Marianne in the home for the elderly until Irma's deportation July 1942.

*Adolf Rosenberg*, Marianne's maternal uncle who emigrated to the USA in 1941.

*Anna Rosenberg*, Marianne's maternal grandmother.

*Isaak Rosenberg*, Marianne's maternal grandfather.

*Karl* (later *Carlos*) *Rosenberg*, Marianne's maternal uncle who fought with the resistance in France.

*Hannah Rosenberg*, see *Hannah Weinberg*.

*Reni Sadamgrotzky*, friend of the Bund, living in Solingen.

*Grete Sander* (née *Alsberg*), Marianne's distant relative who was the Strauss family correspondent in Sweden.

*Lew* (formerly *Ludwig*) and *Trudy* (née *Ullmann*) *Schloss*, Teaneck, New Jersey; both had met Marianne independently before they knew each other. Lew came from Gelsenkirchen and his former girlfriend worked for the Strausses. Trudy met Marianne in the Children's Hospital in Berlin in 1941.

*Hermann Schmalstieg*, Göttingen; Bund member based near Goslar during the war, for whom Marianne may have had a secret passion.

*Aenne Schmitz*, Wuppertal; Bund member (along with husband *August*) with whom Marianne stayed for a while in the small village of Berringhausen.

*Eva Selig*, London; distant cousin of Marianne's on her mother's side.

*Robert Selig*, Denmark; son of *Eva*; provided me with a family tree of the Rosenbergs and some anecdotal evidence about Marianne.

*Tillie Stein*, Atlanta, Georgia; second cousin of Marianne's on her father's side who provided me with information about the Strausses.

*Ernst Steinmann*, Achim; son of *Meta Kamp*; encountered Marianne in 1944.

*Fritz Stern*, Siegfried's cousin (Fritz's mother, Bertha Strauss, was a sister of Leopold Strauss). Resident in the USA since 1907 and a US citizen since 1915. Successful businessman; the Strausses' guarantor in their efforts to emigrate to the USA.

*Liesel Sternberg*, Birmingham; former employee and friend of *David Krombach*.

*Alfred Strauss*, Marianne's paternal uncle.

*Leopold Strauss*, Marianne's paternal grandfather.

*Lore (Oe) Strauss* (née *Dahl*), wife of Alfred and Marianne's aunt by marriage.

*Regina (Ine) Strauss* (née *Rosenberg*), Marianne's mother.

*Richard Strauss*, Marianne's paternal uncle who died in the First World War.

*Richard Strauss*, Marianne's younger brother.

*Rosalie (Saly) Strauss* (née *Stern*), Marianne's paternal grandmother.

*Siegfried Strauss*, Marianne's father.

*Grete Ströter*, Essen; Bund member; visited the Strausses in prison in September 1943.

*Reinhold Ströter*, Mettmann; Bund member; formerly married to *Grete*.

*Alex Weinberg*, see *Eric Alexander*.

*Alfred Weinberg*, see *Uri Weinberg*.

*Ernst Weinberg*, husband of *Hannah*, Marianne's uncle by marriage, father of *Alex*, *Alfred* and *Otto*, deported to Łodz 1941.

*Hannah Weinberg* (née *Johannah Rosenberg*), Marianne's maternal aunt, mother of *Alex*, *Alfred* and *Otto*, deported to Łodz 1941.

*Otto Weinberg*, see *Gerald Alexander*.

*Uri Weinberg* (formerly *Alfred Weinberg*), second of the three Weinberg brothers, Marianne's cousins on her mother's side.

*Abraham* and *Anna Weyl*, Marianne's great-uncle and great-aunt (Abraham was Anna Rosenberg's brother); moved to Essen 1938, deported to Theresienstadt 1942.

*Bertel Wolf* (née *Strauss*), Marianne's paternal aunt, married to *Ferdinand Wolf*.

*René* (formerly *Richard*) *Wolf*, Marianne's cousin (son of her father's sister *Bertel*); survived the expulsions to French concentration camps and service in the French Foreign Legion and played a major role assisting in Marianne's restitution claims.

*Hélène Yaiche-Wolf*, Paris; daughter of *René Wolf*.

*Kurt Zeunert*, Berlin; member of the group of part-Jewish survivors whom Marianne befriended in Düsseldorf.

# Notes

## Introduction

1. Marianne Ellenbogen, 'Flucht und illegales Leben während der Nazi-Verfolgungsjahre 1943–1945', *Das Münster am Hellweg*, vol. 37 (1984), pp. 135–142. Reprinted in Alte Synagoge (ed.), *Stationen jüdischen Lebens. Von der Emanzipation bis zur Gegenwart* (Verlag J. W. Dietz Nachf., Bonn, 1990), pp. 248–252.
2. Only years later did I learn that Basil was in fact a fluent German speaker – a fact which merely underscored Marianne's wish to keep her memories shielded from him.
3. Sadly, Mrs Liesel Sternberg died before publication of the book.
4. Viktor Klemperer, *Ich will Zeugnis ablegen bis zum letzten*, vol. 1: *Tagebücher 1933–1941*; vol. 2: *Tagebücher 1942–1945* (Aufbau-Verlag, Berlin, 1995).

## 1   *Childhood in a German-Jewish Family*

1. Several authors choose not to use this label to describe the events of 9 November 1938 because it belittles the real violence and terror on that day. Indeed, the term *has* contributed to obscuring the reality of what went on, but since the discovery that this is so is the theme of a later chapter, it is appropriate to retain the customary label, at least for now.
2. With many thanks to Dr Vera Bendt for her assistance. See Hermann Simon, *Das Berliner Jüdische Museum in der Oranienburgerstraße. Ges-

*chichte einer zerstörten Kulturstätte* (Stadtgeschichtliche Publikationen II ed. Berlin Museum, Berlin, 1983).

3. In the Orthodox Jewish service, it is the cantor or chazan, and not the rabbi, who leads the congregation in prayer.

4. The following sources for Leopold's career were consulted: Tillie Stein to author, 16.1.1998 and 8.9.1999; LBINY, *Jüdische Bibliothek* (Hamburg), no. 324, 31.12.1931; *Jüdisches Nachrichtenblatt*, 30.6.1939; Kurt Tohermes and Jürgen Grafen, *Leben und Untergang der Synagogengemeinde Dinslaken* (Verein für Heimatpflege 'Land Dinslaken' e.V., Dinslaken, 1988), p. 60; Bürgermeister, Dinslaken, to Leopold Strauss, 1.8.1903; *Dinslakener Generalanzeiger*, 1.4.1927.

5. Information about Isaak Rosenberg was provided by Marianne, her cousins Eric Alexander and Uri Weinberg and Hans W. Gummersbach, 'Sozialhistorische und soziologische Forschungen zur jüdischen Minderheit in der westfälischen Stadt Ahlen vor und während der Zeit des Nationalsozialismus unter besonderer Berücksichtigung lebensgeschichtlicher Selbstzeugnisse' (PhD, University of Paderborn, 1996). Gummersbach's principal source was Marianne's uncle, Karl Rosenberg.

6. The white garment worn on some religious occasions and in which one is buried.

7. The prayer shawl worn by the officiant and by married men for morning prayers.

8. The clumsy term acculturation is preferred to assimilation because the latter implies a loss of identity, which was not the case here. See Marion Kaplan, 'Tradition and transition: the acculturation, assimilation and integration of Jews in Imperial Germany, a gender analysis', in *Leo Baeck Year Book*, vol. 28 (1982), pp. 3–36.

9. Amongst the wealth of studies on the evolution of Jewish identities in Germany, see Reinhard Rürup, *Emanzipation und Antisemitismus. Studien zur 'Judenfrage' der bürgerlichen Gesellschaft* (Vandenhoeck & Ruprecht, Göttingen, 1992); Trude Maurer, *Die Entwicklung der jüdischen Minderheit in Deutschland. Neuere Forschungen und offene Fragen* (Niemeyer, Tübingen, 1992); Helmut Berding, 'Antisemitismus in der modernen Gesellschaft: Kontinuität und Diskontinuität', in Jörg K. Hoensch, Stanislav Biman and L'ubomir Liptak (eds.), *Judenemanzipation – Antisemitismus – Verfolgung in Deutschland, Österreich-Ungarn, den böhmischen Ländern und in der Slowakei* (Klartext, Essen, 1999), pp. 85–100; Falk Wiesemann, 'Jewish burials in Germany – between the Enlightenment and the authorities', *Leo Baeck Institute Year Book*, vol. 37 (1992), pp. 17–31, at p. 31. For the region, see Michael Zimmermann, 'Die Assimi-

lation und ihre Relativierung. Zur Geschichte der Essener jüdischen Geme-
inde vor 1933', in Dirk Blasius and Dan Diner (eds.), *Zerbrochene
Geschichte. Leben und Selbstverständnis der Juden in Deutschland* (Fischer
Taschenbuch Verlag, Frankfurt am Main, 1991), pp. 172–186.

10. Avraham Barkai, 'Die sozio-ökonomische Situation der Juden in Rheinland und Westfalen zur Zeit der Industrialisierung (1850–1914)', in Kurt
Düwell and Wolfgang Köllmann (eds.), *Rheinland-Westfalen im Industriezeitalter*, vol. 2: *Von der Reichsgründung bis zur Weimarer Republik*
(Peter Hammer, Wuppertal, 1984), pp. 86–106.

11. Interview, Uri Weinberg, Jerusalem, 30.7.1998.

12. Werner Hoffmann to author, 29.4.1997; Industrie und Handelskammer
für die Stadtkreise Essen, Mülheim & Oberhausen, 26.4.1939, 'Bescheini-
gung', signed Dr Herbig; copy, CH to Oberstadtdirektor Essen, 9.5.1959,
Entschädigungsantrag der Frau Marianne Ellenbogen geb. Strauss . . .
nach Siegfried Strauss 50, 8/St 24 a (statement of Paul Petry); Siegfried
Heineberg, Düsseldorf, 'Zeugnis', 7.1.1919.

13. Befähigungs-Diplom, 9.3.1916.

14. Quabecks Handelsschule, 1.4.1918, reference for Regina Rosenberg,
signed F. Pratje.

15. John Dippel, *Bound Upon a Wheel of Fire. Why Leading Jews Stayed in
Nazi Germany* (Basic Books, New York, 1996), p. 17.

16. Ibid.

17. When Ine interceded with the Gestapo on Siegfried's behalf in 1938 and
listed the reasons for which he deserved release from his post-Kristallnacht
imprisonment, she named various decorations but not the Iron Cross,
which she undoubtedly would have, had he received it.

18. On Alfred, see his pay book and several letters from Lieutenant Kiss to
Sergeant Strauss, July and August 1918.

19. HStAD RW58 74234, file Alfred Strauss; Staatliche Kriminalpolizei,
Kriminalpolizeistelle Essen, Strafanzeige 12.5.1941, Aussage von Alfred
Strauss.

20. And indeed of a populist, right-wing politics in general. See Peter Fritzsche,
*Germans into Nazis* (Harvard University Press, Cambridge, Mass.,
1998).

21. Dippel, *Bound Upon a Wheel of Fire*, p. 20.

22. Saul Friedländer, 'Political transformations during the war and their effect
on the Jewish question', in Herbert A. Strauss (ed.), *Hostages of Modernisation: studies on Modern Anti-Semitism 1870–1933/39. Germany–Great
Britain–France* (Walter de Gruyter, New York and London, 1993),
pp. 150–164.

23. This is not to claim that Nazism was inevitable in 1918. For recent work on the Jews and anti-Semitism in Weimar, see below, notes 66–68.

24. Copy, CH to Oberstadtdirektor Essen, 9.5.1959, Entschädigungsantrag der Frau Marianne Ellenbogen geb Strauss . . . nach Siegfried Strauss 50, 8/St 24 a (statement of Paul Petry).

25. The date of founding the business is taken from René to ME, 12.3.1955; a copy of the registration in the family possession, however, places the official registration date at 30.9.1919.

26. Werner Hoffmann to author, 29.4.1997.

27. File, Salta GmbH I Liqu. documents in folder 'Zuwachssteuererklärung Mackensenstr. [Brunnenstrasse] 69; Debitoren und Creditoren. Waren und Inventarbestand'.

28. Undated (clearly 1939) CV, 'Lebenslauf Siegfried Strauss Essen, Laden-spelderstr. 47'.

29. 'Debitoren und Creditoren. Waren und Inventarbestand'.

30. Interview, Werner Hoffmann, Buenos Aires, 19.6.1998; Werner Hoffman to author 29.4.1997.

31. SStr to Ine, 7.6.1923.

32. The French occupied the Ruhr at the beginning of 1923 to enforce reparations transfers.

33. SStr to Mieteinigungsamt der Stadt Essen, 23.6.1928.

34. Typewritten 'Aufstellung über Mobilar und Hausrat u.s.w. *Siegfried Strauss*'.

35. Unsigned copy, *Eidesstattliche Versicherung*, produced by Frau Selig, May 1955.

36. Trude Maurer, 'Reife Bürger der Republik und bewußte Juden: die jüdische Minderheit in Deutschland 1918–1933', in Hoensch, Biman et al. (eds.), *Judenemanzipation*, pp. 101–116, at p. 112.

37. ASE, INo.75, Bernd Simon, 29.08.94, a236.

38. Interview, ME, 10.9.1996.

39. Interview, ME, 31.10.1996.

40. MS to her father, 3.5.1932.

41. MS to her mother, 7.5.1932.

42. Undated New Year's card with Magen David on front, MS to parents.

43. MS to parents, 1 Tischri 5695.

44. MS to her parents, 5695.

45. Interview, ME, 31.10.1996.

46. Ibid.

47. Marianne's father's money was by then frozen in blocked accounts. He was allowed to draw a certain amount each month, including monthly

transfers to Berlin to pay for Marianne's tuition there. This is the 'stipend' referred to.

48. Interview, ME, 31.10.1996.
49. Interview, ME, 10.9.1996.
50. Werner Hoffmann to author, 5.3.1997.
51. Interview, ME, 31.10.1996.
52. Ibid.
53. Ibid.
54. Ibid.
55. House of the Dunes.
56. The small town south of Mönchen-Gladbach where the Weinberg boys grew up.
57. NS-Documentationszentrum der Stadt Köln (eds.), *Die jüdischen Opfer des Nationalsozialismus aus Köln. Gedenkbuch* (Böhlau Verlag, Cologne, 1995), pp. 490–49, 536–537.
58. Phillippe Burrin, *Hitler and the Jews: the Genesis of the Holocaust* (Edward Arnold, London, 1994), p. 126.
59. The hats worn by some very traditional Jews.
60. Benzion Patkin, *The Dunera Internees* (Cassell Australia, Stanmore, N.S.W., 1979) confirms all the details Uri gave me.
61. I should point out that in 1922 the daily falls in currency value were still pretty modest; nevertheless, it's a nice end to a good story.
62. Michael Zimmermann, 'Zur Geschichte der Essener Juden im 19. und im ersten Drittel des 20. Jahrhunderts. Ein Überblick', in Alte Synagoge (ed.), *Jüdisches Leben in Essen 1800–1933* (Klartext, Essen, 1993), pp. 8–72.
63. Ibid., pp. 32–33.
64. Photo and description in Hermann Schröter, *Geschichte und Schicksal der Essener Juden. Gedenkbuch für die jüdischen Mitbürger der Stadt Essen* (printed by the city of Essen, Essen, 1980), pp. 109–110. At some point, it moved to the Herkulesstrasse and then to Frohnhausen. In 1978 *Das Münster am Hellweg* published an account of the school.
65. On this, see Kaplan, 'Tradition and transition'.
66. Berding, 'Antisemitismus', pp. 85–91; Reinhard Rürup, 'Jüdische Geschichte in Deutschland. Von der Emanzipation bis zur nationalsozialistischen Gewaltherrschaft', in Blasius and Diner, *Zerbrochene Geschichte*, pp. 79–101, at pp. 94ff.; Zimmermann, 'Zur Geschichte der Essener Juden'.
67. Angela Genger, 'Hakoah – Die Kraft. Ein jüdischer Turn- und Sportverein in Essen', in Alte Synagoge (ed.), *Zwischen Alternative und Protest. Zu Sport- und Jugendbewegungen in Essen 1900–1933* (Exhibition cata-

logue, Essen, 1983), pp. 8–25, at p. 13; Zimmermann, 'Zur Geschichte der Essener Juden', p. 36.

68. Recent work on Jews in the Weimar Republic includes Michael Brenner, *The Renaissance of Jewish Culture in Weimar Germany* (Yale University Press, New Haven, 1996); Friedländer, 'Political transformations'; Anthony Kauders, *German Politics and the Jews: Düsseldorf and Nuremberg, 1910–1933* (Clarendon Press, Oxford, 1996); Donald L. Niewyk, *The Jews in Weimar Germany* (Manchester University Press, Manchester, 1980).

## 2   Schoolgirl in the Third Reich

1. Marion Kaplan, *Between Dignity and Despair: Jewish Life in Nazi Germany* (Oxford University Press, Oxford and New York, 1998), p. 18.

2. Testimony of Marta Appel, née Insel, in Monika Richarz, *Jewish Life in Germany: Memoirs from Three Centuries* (Indiana University Press, Bloomington and Indianapolis, 1991), p. 351.

3. Alfred Strauss, income tax return for 1932; Copy, ME to René, 19.11.1961; J Clemens, estimates; folder, 'Mischanlage'.

4. Copy, CH to Drs Kessler and May, 8.6.1962.

5. International comparisons are notoriously difficult, since they involve not only converting currencies fixed in the 1930s at rather artificial exchange rates but also taking into account different standards of living. In 1937, when Alfred earned around RM20,000 before tax, this was equivalent to dollar income of around $8,000. Their cousin, Fritz Stern, a successful businessman in the USA, was at that stage earning three times this amount. So by US middle-class standards, the Strausses' was not a great income. The sterling value of Alfred's earnings in 1937 would have been about £1,600. This was a fair middle-class income in the UK at the time. By way of comparison, a skilled engineering worker in Britain would be earning less than £200 a year. See Statistisches Reichsamt (ed.), *Statistisches Jahrbuch für das Deutsche Reich 1932* (Berlin, 1932); and *1939/1940* (Berlin, 1940), sections on German prices, earnings, currency rates, foreign prices, foreign earnings.

6. Copy, Gebr. Strauss to Deutsche Gesandtschaft, Sofia, 27.6.1934; Deutsche Gesandtschaft to Gebr. Strauss, 2.8.1934; draft, Declaration re Winterhilfswerk. October 1934–March 1935; 'Mitgliederverzeichnis, Großmarkt für Getreide und Futtermittel e.V., Essen 1.4.1936.

7. Werner Hoffmann to author, 5.3.1997.

8. Dirk von Laak, ' "Wenn einer ein Herz im Leibe hat, der läßt sich von einem deutschen Arzt behandeln". Die "Entjudung" der Essener Wirtschaft von 1933 bis 1941', in Alte Synagoge (ed.), *Entrechtung und Selbsthilfe. Zur Geschichte der Juden in Essen unter dem Nationalsozialismus* (Essen, Klartext, 1994), pp. 12–30, at p. 22; Kaplan, *Between Dignity and Despair*, pp. 24–31.

9. Kurt Düwell, *Die Rheingebiete in der Judenpolitik des Nationalsozialismus vor 1942* (Ludwig Röhrscheid Verlag, Bonn, 1968), p. 191.

10. I am indebted to Jacob Borut for this insight.

11. On the economic measures, see Raul Hilberg, *Die Vernichtung der europäischen Juden* (Fischer, Frankfurt am Main 1993) vol 1, pp. 140–141, 149; Avraham Barkai, *From Boycott to Annihilation: the Economic Struggle of German Jews, 1933–1943* (University Press of New England, Hanover, 1989), pp. 99–100, 144; Kaplan, *Between Dignity and Despair*, p. 71.

12. Werner Hoffmann to author, 5.3.1997.

13. Ibid.

14. Marta Appel, in Richarz, *Jewish Life in Germany*, p. 356.

15. Marion Kaplan, 'Jewish women in Nazi Germany: daily life, daily struggles, 1933–39', in Peter Freimark, Alice Jankowski and Ina S. Lorenz (eds.), *Juden in Deutschland: Emanzipation, Integration, Verfolgung und Vernichtung* (H. Christians Verlag, Hamburg, 1991), pp. 406–434, at p. 420.

16. Barkai, *Boycott*, p. 100.

17. Interview, Werner Hoffmann, 19.6.1998

18. Including land costs. The figures of Hufelandstrasse 25 are taken from typewritten sheet 'Gestehungskosten Hufelandstr. 25'.

19. See, for example, Theodor Kruse, to Strauss brothers, 17.10.1936; Alfred and Siegfried Strauss to Th. Kruse, 17.10.1936; letters from Kruse to brothers, Dec. 1936 and Feb. 1937.

20. The family papers did at least include a clipping from the *Essener Allgemeine Zeitung* of 20.8.1936 with the headline, 'Neubauten in der Hufelandstraße'.

21. File, Einkommenssteuer, Einkommensteuerbescheid für Alfred Strauss 1937.

22. Interview, ME, 31.10.1996.

23. Ibid.

24. Interview, ME, 1989.

25. Interview, ME, 31.10.1996.

26. Undated, untitled typewritten manuscript, evidently for broadcast on the BBC, produced some time in 1946.

27. Not her real name. References that follow are from an interview on 28.7.1997.

28. A guest of the family whom she had previously mentioned.

29. Dr Lange here refers to people associated with the oppositional 'Confessing Church'. Heinemann later became Federal President in post-war Germany.

30. Interview, Waltraud Barkhoff-Kreter, Essen, 23.6.1999.

31. On the characteristic philo-Semitic patterns in post-war discourse, see Frank Stern, *Am Anfang war Auschwitz. Antisemitismus und Philosemitismus im deutschen Nachkrieg* (Bleicher Verlag, Gerlingen, 1991), pp. 227ff.

32. Letter from Ruth Gawse, August 1991, printed in *125 Jahre Luisenschule 1866–1991*.

33. Interview, Ruth Davidsohn, née Mendel, and Chaja Chovers (Klara Kleimann), Haifa, 27.7.1998.

34. Telephone conversation with Ruth Davidsohn, Israel, 18.10.1997.

35. Interview, Ruth Gawse, née Ferse, Jerusalem, 30.7.1998.

36. Ruth Gawse to author, July 1997.

37. Interviews with Uri Aloni (Hans Eulau), in the Museum of Kibbutz Lochamei Hagetaot, 28.7.98, and Lew Schloss and Trudy Schloss, nee Ullmann, Teaneck, New Jersey, 11.8.98.

38. Interview, Jakov (Klaus) Langer, 27.7.98, Kiryat Tivon.

39. Clara Asscher-Pinkhof, *Star Children* (Wayne State University Press, Detroit, 1986).

40. Charles Hannam, *A Boy in Your Situation* (Adlib Paperbacks/André Deutsch, London, 1988).

41. Arbeitsbericht des Zentralauschusses der deutschen Juden für Hilfe und Aufbau, Reichsvertretung der Juden in Deutschland, July to December 1934, p. 24, cited in Werner T. Angress, 'Jüdische Jugend zwischen nationalsozialistischer Verfolgung und jüdischer Wiedergeburt', in Arnold Paucker (ed.), *Die Juden im nationalsozialistischen Deutschland* (J. C. B. Mohr/Paul Siebeck, Tübingen, 1986), pp. 211–232, at p. 213.

42. Cited in Ruth Röcher, *Die jüdische Schule im nationalsozialistischen Deutschland 1933–1942* (Dipa, Frankfurt am Main 1992), p. 69.

43. Unsigned copy, *Eidesstattliche Versicherung*, May 1955, produced by Frau Selig.

44. A medical questionnaire carried out in April 1940 by the Reichsvereini-

gung der Juden in Deutschland in 1940 – presumably to support applications for emigration – has been preserved and records Marianne's medical history.

45. Interview, ME, 31.10.1996.
46. Arnold Paucker, 'Zum Selbstverständnis jüdischer Jugend in der Weimarer Republik und unter der nationalsozialistischen Diktatur', in Hans Otto Horch and Charlotte Wardi (eds.), *Jüdische Selbstwahrnehmung. La Prise de conscience de l'identité juive* (Max Niemeyer Verlag, Tübingen, 1977), pp 111–128, at p. 115.
47. Jutta Hetkamp, *Die jüdische Jugendbewegung in Deutschland von 1913–1933* (Lit, Münster and Hamburg, 1994), p. 32; Zimmermann, 'Zur Geschichte der Essener Juden', pp. 54–55.
48. Kaplan, *Between Dignity and Despair*, p. 111.
49. LBINY, Bundesleitung des JPF–MH (ed.), *Unser Weg zum Volk. Ein Beitrag zur Ideologie des Makkabi Hazair*, (Berlin, 1936), p. 25.
50. LBINY, Bundesleitung des JPF–MH (ed.), *Unser Weg im Zionismus. Eine Sammelschrift des jüdischen Pfadfinderbundes Makkabi Hazair* (Berlin, no date).
51. Jakov Langer to author, 16.3.1997.
52. Jakov Langer to author, 25.2.1997.
53. Interview, Uri Aloni (Hans Eulau), in the Museum of Kibbutz Lochamei Hagetaot, 28.7.98.
54. For instance, Dr Lange, Frau Horn, and Frau Hochwald.
55. For example Dr Martha Jenke in her farewell speech to the school in 1956, in *Mitteilungen der Altschülerinnenbund der Luisenschule Essen*, vol. 30 (1998), pp. 50–51 and vol. 31 (1999) pp. 51–52.
56. See also Moshe Zimmermann, 'Vom Jischuw zum Staat – die Bedeutung des Holocaust für das kollektive Bewußtsein und die Politik in Israel', in Bernd Faulenbach and Helmut Schütte (eds.), *Deutschland, Israel und der Holocaust. Zur Gegenwartsbedeutung der Vergangenheit* (Klartext, Essen, 1998), pp. 45–54.
57. As I was to realize later, the British context served rather to enhance her feeling of disembodiment. See pp. 479ff.
58. Interview, ME, July 1996.
59. *Blätter des Jüdischen Frauenbundes (BJFB)*, vol. 9 (1933), no. 5, p. 11.
60. *BJFB*, vol. 13 (1937), no. 7, p. 1.
61. Ibid.
62. Interview, ME, 31.10.1996.
63. Edith Caspari to MS, 8.1.1943.
64. This is probably an error. If Marianne had been fifteen, she would have

been in Wyk in 1938. There is no certain proof that Marianne was in fact in Wyk in 1936, the date Marianne remembered; but there is a fitness questionnaire Marianne completed in 1940 which said that her bronchitis had become particularly bad at age thirteen, which suggests that she had remembered correctly. See note 44 above.

65. Max Eschelbacher, *Der zehnte November 1938* (Klartext, Essen, 1998), p. 32.
66. On the worsening conditions, see Saul Friedländer, *Nazi Germany and the Jews: the Years of Persecution, 1933–1939* (Pheonix Giant, 1997); Barkai, *Boycott*, pp. 121–130; Dippel, *Bound Upon a Wheel of Fire*, pp. 209–222, 234.
67. René Wolf to May, 14.2.1958.
68. Schröter, *Geschichte und Schicksal*, p. 52.

## 3   Shattered Glass, Shattered Lives

1. Events in Essen are chronicled in Michael Zimmermann, 'Die "Reichskristallnacht" 1938 in Essen', in Alte Synagoge, *Entrechtung*, pp. 66–97.
2. Information from Mrs Liesel Sternberg, Birmingham.
3. Gummersbach, 'Ahlen', pp. 176ff.
4. Not her real name.
5. Not her real name.
6. Not her real name.
7. Stern, *Am Anfang war Auschwitz*, p. 204.
8. Zimmermann, ' "Reichskristallnacht" ', p. 78.
9. Interview, ME, 31.10.1996.
10. HStAD RW58,45264, 'Einlieferungsanzeige', 12.11.1938.
11. Undated, untitled typewritten manuscript, evidently for a BBC broadcast, produced some time in 1946.
12. See note 3 above.
13. Information from Uri Weinberg.
14. René to ME, 18.5.1961, copy attached: 'Eidesstattliche Erklärung, 11.5.1961', from Johann Mund.
15. Yitzhak Sophoni Herz, *Meine Erinnerung an Bad Homburg und seine 600jährige jüdische Gemeinde (1935–1942)* (privately published, Rechovoth, Israel, 1981), pp. 284–294, cited in Anselm Faust, *Die 'Kristallnacht' im Rheinland. Dokumente zum Judenpogrom im November 1938* (Schwann, Düsseldorf, 1987), pp. 81ff.
16. Ibid.

17. Krankenunterstützungskasse des NS Lehrerbundes KUK Hauptverwaltung, Bayreuth, to Leopold Strauss, 22.11.1938.

18. Brandkasse der Lehrer Rheinlands u. Wesfalens, Bochum, to Leopold Strauss, 19.12.1913.

19. Brandkasse westdeutscher Lehrer a.G., Bochum, to Leopold Strauss, 1.8.1933.

20. Brandkasse westdeutscher Lehrer a. G, Bochum, to Leopold Strauss, 'date as postmarked', [1938].

21. English original in Archive Ernst Schmidt, Ruhrland Museum, file 19–490. See also Walter Rohr, 'Die Geschichte meines Lebens', in Ernst Schmidt, 'Walter Rohr – 1938 aus Essen vertrieben, 1945 als US-Soldat zurückgekehrt', Alte Synagoge, *Entrechtung*, pp. 98–117, at pp. 106ff.

22. HStAD RW58, 45264, letter from Ehefrau Siegfried Strauss to Gestapo Essen, 23.11.1938.

23. HStAD RW58, 45264, letter from Ehefrau Siegfried Strauss to Gestapo Essen, 27.11.1938.

24. Schröter, *Geschichte und Schicksal*, p. 53.

25. Ibid., p. 368.

26. HStAD RW58, 45264, draft of letter from the Stapo IIB4 5629/38 dated 2.12.1938 to the KL Dachau.

27. She said six weeks to me. See also file Restitution 'A', CH to ME, 4.12.1956, annex: CH, Cologne, to Stadtverwaltung Essen, Amt für Wiedergutmachung, 12.10.1936.

28. Marta Appel, in Richarz, *Jewish Life in Germany*, p. 355.

29. Interview, ME, 10.9.1996.

30. Typed sheet: 'Abschrift, Judenvermögensabgabe Familie Siegfried Strauss'; figure includes bank charges and stock exchange taxes.

31. The total tax paid by Essen's 2,000 Jews was RM6,903,000: Schröter, *Geschichte und Schicksal*, p. 5.

32. For Essen more generally, see Schröter, *Geschichte und Schicksal*, p. 53; Zimmermann, 'Reichskristallnacht', p. 78.

33. Sterbeurkunde, Standesamt Essen-Rüttenscheid, 15.6.1939.

34. Draft, Ine Strauss to Fritz Stern, 19.6.1939.

35. United States Lines Affidavit of Support, signed 2.12.1938.

36. A slight mystery is offered by Ine's comment in her letter to the Gestapo on 23 November, in which she stated that she already had the affidavit in her possession. Probably she had received a cabled confirmation by then from Fritz Stern that he had provided an affidavit, but the actual document took a little longer to arrive.

37. Geburtsurkunde, Essen, 24.11.1938.

38. 'Empfangsbescheinigung', Essen 2.1.1939.
39. On what they submitted, see CH to ME, 21.2.1958, annex: Übersicht über die Entschädigungs- und Rückerstattungssachen der Frau Marianne Ellenbogen; copy, WGK beim LGE, Beschluß RüSp 58/54, 23.1.1956.
40. Herbert Schein, MD, 'Medical certificate', Essen, 9.5.1939.
41. Copy, 'Recommendation', Vorstand der Synagogen-Gemeinde Essen, 27.7.1939.
42. German Jewish Aid Committee, Immigration Section, Ref BA 4382 to SStr, 19.7.1939 and 15.8.1939.
43. British Consulate-General, Cologne to Siegfried and Alfred Strauss, 21.8.1939.

## 4 Blossoming in a Harsh Climate

1. Interview, ME, 10.9.1996.
2. Sozialpädagogisches Seminar zur Ausbildung von jüdischen Kindergärtnerinnen und Hortnerinnen in Berlin.
3. For use of the term, see Kaplan, *Between Dignity and Despair*.
4. Luisenschule zu Essen, Schuljahr 1938/9 Abganszeugnis für MS, 10.11.1938.
5. Schröter, *Geschichte und Schicksal*, p. 110.
6. Information from Dieter Corbach, *Die Jawne zu Köln. Zur Geschichte des ersten jüdischen Gymnasiums im Rheinland und zum Gedächtnis an Erich Klibansky 1900–1942* (Scriba Verlag, Cologne, 1990); Joseph Walk, 'Das jüdische Schulwesen in Köln bis 1942', in Jutta Bohnke-Kollwitz, Willehad Paul Eckert, Frank Golszewski and Hermann Greive (eds.), *Köln und das rheinische Judentum. Festschrift Germania Judaica 1959–1984*, (Cologne, 1984), pp. 415–426.
7. By the Law Against Overcrowding of Schools and Universities of 25 April 1933.
8. Walk, 'Jüdisches Schulwesen', p. 420.
9. Ibid.
10. See the reminiscences of Anni Adler in Barbara Becker-Jakli (ed.), *Ich habe Köln doch so geliebt. Lebensgeschichten jüdischer Kölnerinnen und Kölner* (Volksblatt Verlag, Cologne, 1993), pp. 182, 205.
11. Interview, Eric Alexander, Stamford, 16.7.1998
12. Eric Alexander to author, 17.1.1997; interview, Eric Alexander, Stamford, 16.7.1998.

13. Walk, 'Jüdisches Schulwesen', speaks of seventy (p. 422), but Corbach, *Jawne*, p. 29, refers to the higher figure.
14. Marta Appel in Richarz, *Jewish Life in Germany*, p. 359.
15. Hilberg, *Vernichtung*, vol. 1, p. 153.
16. Authenticated copy of the Abgangszeugnis from the Jawne Schule, 30.3.1939.
17. Joseph Walk, *Jüdische Schule und Erziehung im Dritten Reich* (Verlag Anton Hain, Frankfurt am Main, 1991), p. 225.
18. Röcher, *jüdische Schule*, p. 219.
19. Deutsche Bank Historisches Zentrum, Frankfurt (DBF) F67/56, Der Oberfinanzpräsident Düsseldorf, Devisenstelle, to Siegfried Israel Strauss, 23.11.1939.
20. Interview, ME, 31.10.1996.
21. Ibid.
22. Bundesarchiv, Berlin (BAB), R4901, 10575/42, document 6, memo, 25.5.1934; document 7, circular, Prussian Ministry for Science, Art and Education to Herren Oberpräsidenten, 27.7.1934.
23. Marianne and other contemporaries referred to Frau Fraenkel as 'Dr', but it seems that this title was purely honorary. Information from her son via Gudrun Maierhof.
24. 'Die Kindergärtnerin und Hortnerin', in LBINY, *BJFB*, vol. II (1935), no. 3, p 6.
25. The Bishop's Avenue is a road of very expensive houses in Hampstead, north London. Marianne's comparison here reminded me that her knowledge of British social geography was now at least as good as her sense of place in Germany.
26. LBINY, *BJFB*, vol. 13 (1937), no. 2, p. 13.
27. 'Die Kindergärtnerin und Hortnerin', in LBINY, *BJFB*, vol. II (1935), no. 3, p. 6.
28. On Hannah Karminski (1897–1942), see Richarz, *Jewish Life in Germany*, p. 342, note 8; correspondence is LBINY AR330 (ex. A.154) LOC. K1/6/E Hannah Karminski, circular letter, 2.7.1939; interview, ME, 31.10.1996.
29. Interview, ME, 31.10.1996.
30. Her testimony was recorded in Switzerland in 1946, see Zentrum für Anti-Semitismusforschung A.15, Edith Dietz, 'Freiheit am Ende des Weges' (recorded 1946 in Zurich). An abbreviated version was later published – Edith Dietz, *Den Nazis entronnen. Die Flucht eines jüdischen Mädchens in die Schweiz. Autobiographischer Bericht 1933–1942* (Dipa Verlag, Frankfurt, 1990).

31. Dietz, 'Freiheit', p. 18.

32. Copy, RV, Abteilung Zentralwohlfahrtsstelle, 23.7.39; Jüdisches Seminar für Kindergärtnerinnen und Hortnerinnen, Berlin (JSK), 'Zeugnis', 20.10.1941, signed Margarethe Fraenkel.

33. 'Zeugnis' from Rosie Zenik [?] Berlin Charlottenburg Uhlandstrasse 179, 28.7.1939. See also reference from Henriette Klein, Berlin, 10.12.1939.

34. Interview, ME, 31.10.1996.

35. Ibid.

36. Ibid.

37. Interview, ME, 10.9.1996.

38. Inge Deutschkron, *Outcast: a Jewish Girl in Wartime Berlin* (Fromm International, New York, 1989). German edition, *Ich trug den gelben Stern* (Deutsche Taschenbuch-Verlag, Munich, 1995).

39. *Ab Heute Heißt Du Sara.*

40. Interview, Inge Deutschkron, Berlin, 28.5.1999. In addition to the interview, some information stems from Inge Deutschkron, *Mein Leben nach dem Überleben* (DTV, Munich, revised edn, 1995).

41. Deutschkron, *Ich trug den gelben Stern*, p. 64.

42. I have slightly stretched the truth here. In fact, number 36 did not match Marianne's description, whereas number 45 did. I stood in front of 45 and thought that changes in the street numbers meant that 'this' was the house. But with the help of Frau Leonore Maier of the Jewish Museum and Herr Andreas Matschenz of the Landesarchiv Berlin I was able to find out that there had been no number change and 36 was still where it always had been. It is possible that the house has been rebuilt, of course.

43. Interview, ME, 31.10.1996. The comment about Goering was off the tape.

44. Ibid.

45. Erica Fischer, *Aimée & Jaguar: a Love Story, Berlin 1943* (paperback edition, Bloomsbury, London, 1996), p. 70.

46. Interview, ME, 31.10.1996.

47. Jüdische Wohlfahrts- und Jugendpflegestelle, Taubstummenheim und Gehörlosenschule, Berlin-Weissensee, Parkstrasse 22, report, 20.9.1940 and additional note Jüdische Gemeinde zu Berlin eV, Jüdische Wohlfahrts- und Jugendpflegestelle to Jüdisches Seminar für Kindergärtnerinnen und Hortnerinnen, Berlin, Wangenheimstrasse 36, 24.9.1940.

48. Interview, ME, 31.10.1996.

49. Ibid.

50. This may indeed have been its original home, since the College's founding address was in Meineckerstrasse.

51. Interview, ME, 31.10.1996.

52. Carola Sachse (ed.), *Als Zwangsarbeiterin 1941 in Berlin: die Aufzeich-nungen der Volkswirtin Elisabeth Freund* (Akademie Verlag, Berlin, 1996), p. 112; Wolf Gruner, *Judenverfolgung in Berlin 1933–1945. Eine Chronologie der Behördenmaßnahmen in der Reichshauptstadt* (Edition Hentrich, Berlin, 1996), pp. 9–11.

53. Interview, ME, 31.10.1996.

54. Dietz, 'Freiheit', p. 21.

55. Sachse, *Als Zwangsarbeiterin 1941 in Berlin*, p. 96.

56. Ibid, p. 116.

57. Gruner, *Judenverfolgung*, p. 78.

58. Interview, ME, 31.10.1996.

59. Gruner, *Judenverfolgung*, p. 79.

60. Sachse, *Als Zwangsarbeiterin 1941 in Berlin*, p. 82.

61. Ibid., p. 92.

62. Dietz, 'Freiheit', p. 82.

63. Sachse, *Als Zwangsarbeiterin 1941 in Berlin*, pp. 51–52, 58, 79–80. In the course of 1941, however, the women became too tired and their courses came to an end (p. 89).

64. Jüdische Kultusvereinigung zu Berlin e.V., Säuglings und Kinderheim, to JSK, Marburgerstr. 5, 6.10.1941.

65. Ludwig and Selma Ansbacher, Frankfurt, to MS, 1.5.1946. Marianne knew Trudy (then 'Trude') in Berlin by her maiden name Ullmann, but she married very soon after the war, so Marianne had the opportunity to see her in Germany as Mrs Schloss.

66. On the demanding nature of the course, see also Ruth Arndt, cited in Ingrid Littmann-Hotopp, *Bei Dir findet das verlassene Kind Erbarmen. Zur Geschichte des ersten jüdischen Säuglings- und Kleinkinderheims in Deutschland (1907 bis 1942)* (Edition Hentrich, Berlin, 1996), pp. 90–91.

67. Jüdische Kultusvereinigung zu Berlin e.V., Säuglings und Kinderheim, to Jüdisches Seminar für Kindergärtnerinnen und Hortnerinnen, Berlin, Marburgerstr. 5, 6.10.1941.

68. Littmann-Hotopp, *Bei Dir findet das verlassene Kind Erbarmen*, p. 114.

69. Dietz, 'Freiheit', p. 21.

70. Richarz, *Jewish Life in Germany*, p. 447, note 1.

71. Sachse, *Als Zwangsarbeiterin 1941 in Berlin*, p. 149.

72. Richarz, *Jewish Life in Germany*, p. 448, note 4.

73. Camilla Neumann, née Salinger, in Richarz, *Jewish Life in Germany*, p. 435.

74. Dietz, 'Freiheit', p. 24.
75. RV Abteilung Fürsorge, 19.1.1942.
76. Trudy was still in close contact with her former fellow-nurse, Ruth Arndt, who now lives in California.
77. EK to MS, 'Mittwoch Abend' [4.2.1942].
78. As noted above, Ernst had studied in Berlin in the 1930s and Marianne had come to know some of his former friends.
79. Sometimes he signed himself Ernst and sometimes Ernest.
80. According to the *Wegweiser durch das jüdische Berlin* (Berlin, 1937), p. 13 Iranischestrasse 3 is listed as the Kindergarten and Hort of the Jewish Community. This was presumably the last home of the Seminar. Iranischestrasse 4 must have been the place of the halls of residence. I am grateful to Dr Jörg H. Fehrs for this information.
81. An asterisk links this quotation to Ilmenau.
82. EK to MS, 'Monday' [9.2.1942].
83. Ibid.
84. MS to EK, 11.2.1942.
85. In German, as in English, the normal phrase would be 'life and death'.
86. MS to EK, 17.2.1942.
87. MS to EK, 11.2.1942.
88. MS to EK, 13.2.1942.
89. MS to EK, 14.2.1942.
90. Ibid.
91. Walk, *Jüdische Schule*, p. 323
92. See, for example copy, Hermann to Regierungspräsidenten, Dezernat für Wiedergutmachung, 28.2.1958.
93. This was to be the last exam. On 1.4.1942, the College was disbanded. BAB R4901, 10575/41, Stadtpräsident der Reichshauptstadt Berlin to Reichsminister für Wissenschaft, Erziehung und Volksbildung, 23.4.1942.


5   *The Family, the Gestapo, the Abwehr and the Banker*

1. Dippel, *Bound Upon a Wheel of Fire*, pp. xix, 222.
2. Copy, SStr to Fritz Stern, 16.1.1941.
3. Certificate, dated 30.7.1941.
4. Copy, SStr to Grete and family, 5.3.1941.
5. Hugo Strauss to Siegried and Ine, 31.1.1939.
6. Copy, RW to Ernst Dahl, 22.7.1960.
7. Copy, SStr to Hugo, Essen, 9.12.1940.

8. Hugo Strauss to SStr and family, 7.1.1941.

9. Copy, AS (Lore) to Uncle Markus and family, 6.9.1941; see also copy in Siegfried's hand, Fritz Stern to Strauss family, 9.5.1941.

10. Copy AS to Marcus Strauss and family, 6.9.1941.

11. DBF F67/56, various memos from the Zollfahndungszweigsstelle, Essen, later from the Oberfinanzpräsident, Düsseldorf, Devisenstelle (ODD).

12. Sachs, *Als Zwangsarbeiterin 1941 in Berlin*, p. 123.

13. Joseph Walk, *Das Sonderrecht für die Juden im NS-Staat* (C. F. Müller, Heidelberg, 1981), pp. 312, 314, 328.

14. I am indebted to Michael Zimmermann, as for so much, for alerting me to the documents in the Essen Stadtarchiv. Those documents cited without a class-mark are in the Ellenbogens' possession.

15. StAE Rep. 102/1/33, Stadtrat Schlicht to Herrn Oberbürgermeister Dillgardt, 5.12.1940.

16. StAE 45 – 2515, Schwarzlose to Grundstücksamt, 23.12.1940.

17. StAE 45 – 2515, memo: E d29/1/1941.

18. This was the only way to circumvent the punitive currency conversion rates.

19. StAE 45 – 2515, Vermerk 25–2–1047/40 E d4/2/1941. And again in February, EP, Schwarzlose to Siegfried Israel Strauss, 8.2.1941.

20. StAE 45 – 2515, letter from Dipl. Kaufm. Ricco Arendt to Oberbürgermeister, 3.6.1941.

21. Wolfgang Dressen, *Betrifft: 'Aktion 3'. Deutsche verwerten jüdische Nachbarn* (Aufbau Verlag, Berlin, 1998).

22. HStAD RW58 74234, Alfred Strauss, Kripo Essen, Strafanzeige, 12.5.1941.

23. Ibid.

24. HStAD RW58 74234, ADStE to StaPoD, 26.5.1941.

25. HStAD RW58 74234, Alfred Strauss, Kripo Essen, Strafanzeige, 12.5.1941.

26. HStAD RW58 74234, copy of judgment to ADStE, signed Oberstaatsanwalt i.A. Dr Cohausz, 22.5.1941.

27. HStAD RW58 74234, ADStE to StaPoD, 26.5 1941.

28. Note from Polizei Präsident, Essen, 5.6.1941.

29. Reichsgesetzblatt I S. 1709.

30. StAE 45 – 2515, SStr to Hernn Oberbürgermeister, 4.7.1941; memo, 25–2–1047/40; StAE document 17817 Beurkundungsregister A Nr 49/41; Beurkundungsregister A Nr 50/41 verhandelt Essen.

31. Copy, SStr to Gilka, 17.9.1941.

32. Copy, SStr (Ine) to Grete and family, 4.9.1941.

33. Copy [draft] ME to LG Essen, Wiedergutmachungskammer (WGK), 2.10.1952. There is more than one copy of this document; only in one is the head of the Wohnungsamt identified by name.
34. Copy, JSK, 'Zeugnis' Fräulein Marianne Sara Strauss.
35. The date is clear from copy of a letter to EK, dated 25.10.1942.
36. Schröter, *Geschichte und Schicksal*, p. 346.
37. HStAD RW36, 19, StaPoD to Aussendienstellen, 11.10.1941; Schröter, *Geschichte und Schicksal*, p. 56.
38. StAE, Rep 102/I/33, copy Der Oberbürgermeister als Preisbehörde St.A. 34–5 Gr.1643, Genehmigung, 24.10.1941, signed Dr Zwick, Direktor.
39. Interview, ME, 1989.
40. HStAD RW58, 45264, memo headed 'Dauerdeint: Essen 25.10.1941', clearly lists those due for transportation as Siegfried Strauss, Regina and Richard. The deportation list in Schröter, *Geschichte und Schicksal*, p. 368 also does not list Marianne.
41. Interview, ME, 1989.
42. HStAD RW36, 19, StaPoD to Aussendienstellen, 11.10.1941.
43. Interview, ME, 1989.
44. Interview, ME, 10.9.1996.
45. Ibid.
46. Telephone conversation with Hanna Aron, 20.10.97.
47. Author to Imo Moszkowicz, 24.10.1997.
48. Interview, Imo Moszkowicz, Munich, 14.6.1999.
49. Winfried Meyer, *Unternehmen Sieben. Eine Rettungsaktion für vom Holocaust Bedrohte aus dem Amt Ausland/Abwehr im Oberkommando der Wehrmacht* (Verlag Anton Hain, Frankfurt am Main, 1993), pp. 100–102; Heinz Höhne, 'Canaris und die Abwehr zwischen Anpassung und Opposition', in Jürgen Schmädeke and Peter Steinbach (eds.), *Der Widerstand gegen den Nationalsozialismus* (Munich and Zurich, 1985), pp 405–416, at p. 407; Eberhard Bethge, *Dietrich Bonhoeffer. Theologe. Christ. Zeitgenosse* (Chr. Kaiser Verlag, Munich, 2nd edn, 1967), pp. 702–708.
50. HStAD RW58, 45264, telegram Bremen to ADStE, 22.10.41.
51. HStAD RW58, 45264, telegram ADStE to StaPoD, 25.10.1941.
52. HStAD RW58, 45264, StaPoD to RSHA, 25.10.1941.
53. Ibid.
54. Ibid.
55. See HStAD RW58, 74234, memo II B 4/71.02/Strauss Düsseldorf, [25]. 10.1941, added in typescript to StaPoD telegram to RSHA, which is a copy of the telegram in the Siegfried Strauss file.

56. HStAD RW58, 45264, memo headed 'Dauerdeint: Essen 25.10.1941'.

57. HStAD RW58, 74234, draft of StaPoD IIB4 to StaPo Bremen, 28.10.1941.

58. HStAD RW58, 74234, telegram, Bremen to StaPoD, 4.11.41.

59. HStAD RW58, 74234, ADStE to StaPoD, 6.11.1941.

60. Meyer, *Unternhmen Sieben.*

61. For this and the following sections, the sources used, other than Meyer, *Unternehmen Sieben* and Bethge, *Dietrich Bonhoeffer*, are Elisabeth Chowaniec, *Der 'Fall Dohnanyi' 1943–1945* (R. Oldenbourg Verlag, Munich, 1991), pp 10–17; Christoph Strohm, *Theologische Ethik im Kampf gegen den Nationalsozialismus. Der Weg Dietrich Bonhoeffers mit den Juristen Hans von Dohnanyi und Gerhard Leibholz in den Widerstand* (Christian Kaiser, Munich, 1989), pp. 231–289.

62. Meyer, *Unternhmen Sieben*, p. 336; Bethge, *Bonhoeffer*, pp. 898ff.

63. Meyer, *Unternhmen Sieben*, pp. 100–102; the proportion of active opponents is based on Höhne, 'Canaris und die Abwehr', p. 407.

64. Meyer, *Unternhmen Sieben*, pp. 206ff.

65. Ibid., pp. 213, 223.

66. Ibid., pp. 209–212, 235.

67. HStAD RW58, 74234, letter from Wilhelm Hammacher DBE to ADStE, 2.7.1943.

68. Copy, W. Hammacher to CH, 27.6.1957.

69. See note 33 above.

70. Interview, Hanna Aron, West Hartford, Connecticut, 7.8.1998.

71. Copy, Öffentliche Sitzung des II.WGK beim LG Dortmund, Dortmund, 4.11.1960.

72. 'Eidesstattliche Erklärung', signed ME, Liverpool, 14.11.1961.

73. Interview, Hanna Aron, West Hartford, Connecticut, 7.8.1998.

74. LBINY, SAFE ME805, Arthur Prinz, *Plunging Into Chaos.*

75. NS-Documentationszentrum der Stadt Köln (eds.), *Die jüdischen Opfer des Nationalsozialismus aus Köln. Gedenkbuch* (Böhlau Verlag, Cologne, 1995), pp. 490–491, 536–537.

76. YVJ file 0.48/1630.2 Archiv 13390, very tattered mail, no envelope, from Rosenberg/Strauss to Alfred Weinberg, Essen, 5.11.1941.

77. YVJ file 0.48/1630.2 Archiv 13390, George Morel Delegate in Australia and New Zealand of the IRC to Alfred Weinberg, Internment Camp, 20.8.1942.

78. Schröter, *Geschichte und Schicksal*, p. 379.

79. HStAD RW58, 45264, AStDE to StaPoD, 7.11.1941, and enclosure, Bremen Nr 7137, 6.11.41, 1800 hrs.

80. ASE, AR.8043, Leopold to Walter Sternberg, 20.3.1942.

81. ASE, AR.8043, Leopold to Walter Sternberg, 8.6.1942.

82. Copy, SStr to Fritz Stern, 17.11.1941.

83. The somewhat later Wannsee conference in January 1942, once viewed as the moment at which murder policy was decided on, is now seen more as establishing responsibility and procedure.

84. HStAD RW 58, 45264, return from Finanzamt Essen Süd to ADStE, 5.6.1941.

85. Copy, Finanzamt Essen-Süd to Schroetter, 7.2.195[2?].

86. Rheinisch-Westfälische Bank, Filiale Essen, Tagesauszüge, SStr 60 723.

87. Copy, 'Teil-Beschluss in der Wiedergutmachungssache der Erben nach SStr und AS . . .', Gericht der Wiedergutmachung des LGE, Essen, 1.9.1953.

88. The fact that Alfred was able to make the transfer on that date raises questions. Had the contact with the Abwehr begun earlier in October? In which case, it is not obvious why the Abwehr representative visited on the 24th. Possibly, the brothers were able to use their assets *before* Abwehr intervention, but this seems unlikely. Possibly the date in the restitution papers is wrong.

89. RW to ME, 12.3.1955, attached schedule in respect of AS; copy, RW to May, 19.5.1961, annex, copy, Hammacher to Schroetter, 14.8.1951.

90. Copy, RW to Oberstadtdirektor Essen, Gutachterausschuß für Grundstückswerte, 3.3.1954; copy DBE to RW, 12.6.1963.

91. WGK des LGE, Beschluß Rü Sp 18–54 Rü 1171–50 in der Rückerstattungssache der Erben nach dem Kaufmann AS, Essen, 15.5.1956.

92. DBE to LGD, 7. Entschädigungskammer, 5.3.1965; Meyer to Schroetter, 21.5.1952, enclosures: copy of letter from lawyer Beyhoff to SStr, 29.1.1942; excerpt from Abtretungserklärung from SStr, 19.11.1941.

93. Copy, Finanzamt Essen Süd to Schroetter, 7.2.1955.

94. RW to ME, 12.3.1955, attached listing of claims in respect of AS.

95. HStAD RW 58, 74234, ADStE Abt II B 4 IA, telegram to StaPoD, 20.11.1941.

96. HStAD RW 58, 74234, copy with Geheim stamp ADStE II B 4 to Polizeipräs Abt II, 24.11.1941. We also do not know what the situation was in relation to Lore's mother, Else Dahl.

97. HStAD RW 58, 74234, StaPoD draft telegram to RSHA IV B 4, 20.11.1941 (Eichmann) (sent 21.11.1941).

98. HStAD RW 58, 74234, RSHA IV B 4 b 3182/41g (1445), telegram to StaPoD, SS Obersturmbannführer Oberreigerungsrat Dr Albath persönlich, 2.12.1941, signed Eichmann.

99. HStAD RW58, 74234, draft, StaPoD to StaPo Bremen, 6.12.1941; draft StaPoD to ADStE, 8.12.1941; additional memo 10.1.1942, noting that no response has yet been received from Bremen.

100. HStAD RW58, 45264, StaPoD to ADStE, 24.3.1942, betrifft den Juden Siegfried Israel Strauss.

101. HStAD RW58, 74234, ODD Gen. Abt III/Ausw./Tal to StaPoD, 2.6.1942.

102. HStAD RW58, 74234, StaPoD II B 4 to ODD, 19.6.1942.

103. HStAD RW58, 74234, ODD Gen. Abt III/Ausw./Tal to StaPoD, 20.7.1942.

104. HStAD RW58, 74234, RSHA IV B 4 a 3182/41g (1445) to StaPoD, 16.7.1942; ADStE to StaPoD telegram 10.8.1942; draft, StaPoD to RSHA, 12.8.1942.

105. EK, Izbica report.

106. Hugo Strauss to ME, 27.3.1948, annex: invoice from Marcus Cohn, Austrasse, Basel dated 19.5.1947.

107. HStAD RW58, 74234, ADStE II B 3 – 285/42g to StaPoD, 6.11.1942.

108. HStAD RW58, 74234, RSHA IV B 4 a 3028/42, letter to StaPoD 5.10.1942, signed Moes.

109. HStAD RW58, 74234, draft telegram StaPoD to ADStE, 14.10.1942.

110. HStAD RW58, 74234, ADStE II B 3 – 285/42g to StaPoD, 6.11.1942.

111. HStAD RW58, 74234, draft StaPoD II B 3/Tgb Nr 421/42g/Strauss to RSHA IV B 4 a, 18.11.1942.

112. A copy of his letter to Abwehr is in HStAD RW58, 74234, RSHA telegram to StaPoD, 19.12.1943.

113. This date does not correspond to any particular document in the Gestapo files. It may correspond to a decision within the RSHA that the Strausses should be at least temporarily reprieved. The formal approval of the Strausses' exemption, as noted above, was sent to Düsseldorf only in March 1942.

114. HStAD RW58, 74234, RSHA Roem 4 B 4 – 3182/42g (1445) to StaPoD 19.12.1943, signed Eichmann; Meyer, *Unternehmen Sieben*, p. 421.

## 6   Love Letters in the Holocaust

1. Interview, ME, 31.10.1996.
2. Oberbürgermeister der Stadt Essen to Alfred Israel Strauss, 23.4.1940.
3. Interview, ME, July 1996.
4. Interview, ME, 31.10.1996.

5. MS, private diary, 10/11.10.1942.
6. Interview, ME, 31.10.1996.
7. Postcard, EK to MS, 30.3.1942.
8. Enrique Krombach to author, 31.12.1996.
9. This section draws also on interviews Enrique recorded with Angela Genger and Benno Reicher, ASE, reference IN 002, 10.6.1983 and IN 260, 26.10.1987.
10. On Herzfeld and the RV's creation, see Otto Dov Kulka (ed.), *Deutsches Judentum unter dem Nationalsozialismus*, vol 1: *Dokumente zur Geschichte der Reichsvertretung der deutschen Juden 1933–1939* (Mohr Siebeck, Tübingen, 1997), pp. 56–63; LBINY file ME 287 Herzfeld.
11. Schröter, *Geschichte und Schicksal*, pp. 48, 193, 623.
12. Enrique's account of his father's life in 'Dr David Krombach, ein Leben aus dem Glauben', in Schröter, *Geschichte und Schicksal*, pp.193–194; Bernd Schmalhausen, *Schicksale jüdischer Juristen aus Essen 1933–1945*, (Klartext, Essen, 1994), pp. 81f.; E. G. Lowenthal, *Bewährung im Untergang. Ein Gedenkbuch* (Deutsche Verlags-Anstalt, Stuttgart, 1965), p. 110.
13. Lowenthal, *Bewährung*, p. 110.
14. ASE interview, IN 260, 26.10.1987; ASE interview, IN 002, 10.6.1983.
15. The CV Youth was later renamed and absorbed into the 'Ring – League of German Youth' (Ring – Bund jüdischer Jugend). On the German-Jewish wing of the youth movement, see Kulka, *Deutsches Judentum*, p. 466.
16. Enrique Krombach to ME, 20.6.1988.
17. See *50 Jahre Jubiläum der Schüler der Israelitischen Gartenbauschule Ahlem* (no date, no place), in the Wiener library, London.
18. See Schmalhausen, *Schicksale*.
19. ASE AR 4434, Liesel Sternberg to Dr Alexander, 20.8.1945.
20. Interview, Liesel Sternberg, Birmingham, 11.9.1997.
21. Sadly, Mrs Sternberg has since died. Britain was distinctive in admitting many Jewish refugees as domestic servants; see Tony Kushner, *The Holocaust and the Liberal Imagination: a Social and Cultural History* (Blackwell, Oxford and Cambridge, Mass., 1994), pp. 90–118.
22. Letter-diary, final entry, New Year's Day 1943.
23. Undated pencilled note in Marianne's handwriting on the back of the timetable.
24. EK to MS, 'Sonntag Abend' [8.2.1942].
25. Ibid.
26. The couple were Harry and Grete Höllander, neé Levy. Both were soon

deported and murdered; see Schröter, *Geschichte und Schicksal*, pp. 590, 387.

27. MS to EK, 6.2.1942.
28. MS to EK, 8.2.1942.
29. EK to MS, 'Sonntag Abend' [8.2.1942].
30. EK to MS, 'Montag Abend noch 7 Tage!' [16.2.1942].
31. EK to MS, 'Sonntag Abend' [8.2.1942].
32. EK to MS, 'Dienstag' [10.2.1942].
33. EK to MS, 'Montag' [16.2.1942].
34. EK to MS, 'Dienstag, noch 6 Tage' [17.2.1942].
35. MS to EK, 18.2.1942.
36. Ibid.
37. MS to EK, 19.2.1942.
38. Interview, ME, 31.10.1996.
39. MS, private diary, 5.2.1943.
40. Hand-posted letter from EK to MS, 26.3.1942.
41. EK to MS [pencilled date is 30.3.1942. This is a Monday, and from the card which followed, I think the date has been added by MS, and is the day she received it. I think the letter was written late the day before].
42. Letter-diary, final entry, New Year's Day 1943.
43. Interview, ME, July 1996.
44. Essen Alte Synagoge (ed.), *Essen unter Bomben: Märztage 1943* (Klartext Verlag, Essen, 1984), pp. 46–47.
45. Artur and Dore Jacobs' role is explored more fully below. See pp. 269 ff.
46. StAE, Nachlaβ Jacobs, Artur Jacobs diary (henceforth StAE NJ AJD), 13.3.1942. A number of later references place it beyond doubt that 'Dr K' is David Krombach.
47. Schröter, *Geschichte und Schicksal*, pp. 380–402.
48. Michael Zimmermann, 'Die Deportation der Juden aus Essen und dem Regierungsbezirk Düsseldorf', in Ulrich Borsdorf and Mathilde Jamin (eds.), *Überleben im Krieg. Kriegserfahrungen in einer Industrieregion 1939–1945*, (Rowohlt, Hamburg, 1989), pp. 126–143.
49. Schröter, *Geschichte und Schicksal*, p. 380.
50. All this from Zimmermann, 'Deportation der Juden', pp. 127–131.
51. StAE NJ AJD, 14.4.1942.
52. Franciszek Zabecki, *Wspomnienia dawne i nowe* (Warsaw, 1977), p. 45.
53. In full: Lublin, Belzyce, Izbica Lubielska, Kamionka, Luszawa, Ostrow, Piaski, Rejowiece and Zamosc. The standard work remains Hans-Günther Adler, *Der Verwaltete Mensch. Studien zur Deportation der Juden aus Deutschland* (JCB Mohr/Paul Siebeck, Tübingen, 1974).

Adler's extraordinary painstaking research has never been given the acknowledgement it deserves.

54. Postcard from Ernst Israel Krombach, III/418, Transport Essen Izbica a.d. Wilpez, krs Krasnyetaw b. Lublin, Gen. Gouvern., Post Ältestenrat., 25.4.1942.

55. Martin Gilbert, *The Macmillan Atlas of the Holocaust* (Macmillan, New York, 1982), p. 91.

56. *Gedenkbuch Opfer der Verfolgung der Juden* (Bundesarchiv, Koblenz, 1986), pp. 1759ff.

57. The main part of the journey began only on 22 April. But the Essen Jews were taken on 21 April to spend a night in Düsseldorf before deportation.

58. Schmalhausen, *Schicksale*, p. 82.

59. Interview, ME, July 1996.

60. It is possible that she had known Jacobs for longer, since she said in a letter to Yad Vashem in 1984 that she met Jacobs in 1941.

61. See note 57 above.

62. 'Erinnerungen an das Lager am Holbeckshof', in *Stationen jüdischen Lebens*, pp. 232–235.

63. Interview, Hanna Aron, West Hartford, Connecticut, 7.8.1998. See also Mark Roseman 'Surviving memory: truth and inaccuracy in Holocaust testimony', *British Journal of Holocaust Education* (1999); 'Erinnerung und Überleben: Wahrheit und Widerspruch in dem Zeugnis einer Holocaust-Überlebenden', *BIOS*, vol. 11 (1998), no. 2, pp. 263–279.

64. MS, letter-diary, 26.4.42.

65. Interview, ME, July 1996.

66. Enrique Krombach to ME, Buenos Aires 28.5.1989.

67. Interview, ME, 10.9.1996.

68. MS, letter-diary, 30.4.1942.

69. This is clearly an oblique reference to Cuba.

70. Postcard, 21.4.1942, 'nach Mülheim', postmarked Duisburg.

71. Postcard, 'Wednesday early' [22.4.1942].

72. Zimmermann, 'Deportation der Juden', p. 132.

73. Ibid., p. 135.

74. Postcard, 'Wednesday early' [22.4.1942], postmarked Düsseldorf.

75. EK to MS, 22.8.1942. This is the first of two letters sent on that day. This one, an eighteen-page account which must be one of the most remarkable contemporary documents of the Holocaust, will be referred to henceforth as 'Izbica report', the other as 'Arbeitsbericht'. See the following chapter.

76. I.e., as one of the Jewish orderlies.

77. Zimmermann thought the transportees were then taken on to the extermination camps Belzec, Kulmhof, Sobibor, Maidanek or Treblinka within a few days. However, it is clear from EK's letters that this was not the case.

78. Letter, Thursday, 23.4.1942

79. We do not know to what he refers.

80. Dr Rudolf Löwenstein, b. 6.3.1900 in Essen Steele. He had practised as a doctor in Soest until 1938; after his licence was withdrawn, he had moved to Essen. Rudi was deported with his wife Grete (Margarete, née Katzenstein), b. 18.9.1901, and his son Klaus, b. 16.3.1930. His daughter Klara, b. 9.6.1932, seems to have survived, though she too was deported – see the deportation list in Schröter, *Geschichte und Schicksal*, p. 392; see also Ingrid Niemann and Ludger Hülskemper Niemann, *Vom Geleitbrief zum gelben Stern. 450 Jahre jüdisches Leben in Steele* (Klartext, Essen, 1994), p. 172, note 94.

81. Postcard, Ostrowo, 23.4.1942.

82. EK talks of a *coupé*, which suggests they were in passenger carriages, although Michael Zimmermann states that they were in goods trucks.

83. The first reports from Düsseldorf, as Jacobs noted, were very negative.

84. See Schröter, *Geschichte und Schicksal*, pp. 40, 472, 500. I discovered that Herta's sister had emigrated to Birmingham and was living just a mile and a half away from my home, in a nursing home. Sadly, though, in the opinion of the nursing staff, her physical and mental state precluded an interview. She has since died.

85. Postcard from Ernst Israel Krombach, III/418, Transport Essen Izbica a.d. Wilpez, krs Krasnyetaw b. Lublin, Gen. Gouvern., Post Ältestenrat., 25.4.1942.

86. MS, letter-diary, 24.4.1942.

87. MS, letter-diary, 30.4.1942.

88. MS, letter-diary, 26.4.1942.

89. StAE NJ AJD, 5.5.1942.

90. MS, letter-diary, 26.4.42.

91. MS, letter-diary, 3.5.1942.

92. Pencil-written letter EK to MS, 5.7.1942.

93. Pencil-written letter EK to MS, 9.8.1942.

94. Postcard, 31.5.1942.

95. MS, letter-diary, 6.8.1942.

96. Letter, 11.8.1942.

97. Ibid.

98. Letter in pencil from 11.8.1942.

99. In copy of letter to 'Hetty', 29/30.6.1942. Ernest is here referred to as Arthur – a name in which he also signed some of his cards. I was not able to ascertain Hetty's identity.
100. Unsigned note from 3.5.1942, probably from Rudi Löwenstein.
101. Entry: 'Pfingstmontag, den 25.5'.
102. MS, entry 'Mittwochabend' [27.5.1942].
103. Yitzhak Arad, *Belzec, Sobibor, Treblinka – the Operation Reinhard Death Camps* (Indiana University Press, Bloomington, 1987), pp. 383, 390. On what EK knew, see the next chapter.
104. Copy, MS, letter to Hetty, 29/30.6.1942.
105. MS, letter-diary, 4.6.1942.
106. MS, letter-diary, 7.6.1942.
107. EK, 'Izbica report', p. 6.
108. MS, letter-diary, 29/30.6.1942.
109. Letter from EK, 5.7.1942.
110. EK, 'Izbica report'.
111. Copy, MS, letter to Hetty, 6.8.1942.
112. From other references, it seems likely that this refers to Melitta Levy, a young woman of about Marianne's age, who with her rather older husband Kurt had been one of the couples Marianne enjoyed visiting in the Holbeckshof and who now, after the July deportations, had been moved into the Jewish Community building at Hindenburgstrasse 22. See Schröter, *Geschichte und Schicksal*, pp. 428, 447. Both were eventually deported to Auschwitz on the last major Essen transport of 1 March 1943. It is not clear why Ernst was sending letters via Melitta (or why Marianne was sending messages via Hetty). Possibly they wished to avoid attracting attention by sending too many letters to the same addressee.

## 7   Report from Izbica

1. Interview, ME, 31.10.1996.
2. MS, letter-diary, 2.8.1942.
3. The surviving copy of the letter has no heading or date. Typed on it is simply 'Mit Christian'.
4. No heading, attached to the above.
5. MS, letter-diary, 17.8.1942.
6. MS, letter-diary, 27.8.1942.
7. MS, letter-diary, 3.9.1942.
8. Letter in pencil from EK [from Izbica], 23.8.1942, henceforth 'cover note'.

9. Hand-written note from Rudi and Grete Löwenstein, 21.8.1942.

10. Letter in pencil, dated 22/23.8.1942, henceforth 'Task list'.

11. Ibid.

12. In German, the convention is to write the date in the form 'Izbica, the 9th August 1942'.

13. E. Thomas Wood and Stanislaw M. Jankowski, *Karski: How One Man Tried to Stop the Holocaust* (John Wiley & Sons, 1994) suggest that in 1942 Polish underground fighter Jan Karski visited Izbica and not Belzec, as Karski claimed.

14. Thomas Toivi Blatt, *From the Ashes of Sobibor. A Story of Survival* (Northwestern University Press, Evanston. Ill., 1997). Mr Blatt kindly also sent me a copy of *Sobibor, the Forgotten Revolt: a Survivor's Report* (HEP, Issaquah Wash., 1996).

15. I.e. should the Strauss family be deported, Marianne might well choose to accompany Christian to Izbica.

16. See previous chapter, note 80 and text.

17. With whom the Krombachs had been living before deportation.

18. This is something of an exaggeration. Perhaps two-thirds of the town's Jews had been deported.

19. Ernst's comment in German is 'Sie sind nicht so wie wir auf das Judentum gestossen worden und zu ihm zurückgeführt worden.'

20. This section is not clear in the German. It seems that the members of the transport had to come up with a certain amount of gold to avoid its leaders being shot.

21. In the German, the list of presents include 'Nuss-Maske', the meaning of which eluded me.

22. This is hard to square with his earlier letter in which he said he did not work, it was not customary. Perhaps he had now forgotten his first weeks of idleness.

23. Evidently a brand of medicine.

24. Postcard, Ostrowo, 23.4.1942

25. Blatt, *Ashes*, pp. 16ff.

26. Thomas Blatt to author, 19.2.1997.

27. YVJ, Hejnoch Nobel, b. 1.2.1896 in Izbica, testimony 19.5.1946.

28. As an example of the quality of Ernst's information, with the aid of the historian Peter Witte, I was able to establish that his listings of the transports to Izbica was highly, possibly completely accurate.

29. Arad, *Belzec, Sobibor, Treblinka*, p. 243.

30. Blatt, *Ashes*, p. 33.

31. Arad, *Belzec, Sobibor, Treblinka*, p. 244.

32. Interview, ME, 10.9.1996; supplementary information interview, ME, 31.10.1996.

33. Christian and Lilli Arras to MS, 7.9.1946.

34. Interview, ME, 31.10.1996.

35. The first massive raid on Essen took place on 5 March 1943, when 442 planes bombarded the city for about an hour. Some 50,000 residents lost their homes and another 20,000 had to move out temporarily. *Essen unter Bomben*, p. 26.

36. Interview, Lilli Arras, 10.1.1997.

37. Lilli Arras to author, 30.1.1997.

38. Ibid.

39. Interview, Lilli Arras, 10.1.1997; Lilli Arras to author, 1.3.1997.

40. Herr Bartnick, Bundesarchiv, section III Z 4 to author, 26.2.1997.

41. Lilli Arras to author, 1.3.1997.

42. Interview, Lilli Arras, 10.1.1997.

43. StAE NJ AJD, 4.9.1942.

44. Conversation between Gummersbach and Moszkowicz recorded June 1988, reproduced in Gummersbach, 'Ahlen', p. 250.

45. Ibid.

46. Imo Moszkowicz to author, 2.9.1997.

47. Interview, Hanna Aron, West Hartford, Connecticut, 7.8.1998.

48. Email, Hanna Aron to author, 27.9.1999.

49. After completing the manuscript, I discovered Christian's De-Nazification Panel report from the post-war period. This too confirmed that he had been a member of neither the SS nor the Nazi Party. See HStAD NW 1005–6. 11 119.

50. Email, Hanna Aron to author, 27.9.1999.

51. ASE Izbica 4431, Archiv der Zentralen Stelle der Landesjustizverwaltungen in Ludwigsburg, Akten, Vermerke des Unterabteilungsleiters Türk, Chef der Unterabteilung Bevölkerungswesen und Fürsorge in der Inneren Verwaltung beim Distriktchef von Lublin, 20.3.1942; Dieter Pohl, *Von der 'Judenpolitik' zum Judenmord: der Distrikt Lublin des Generalgouvernements 1939–1944* (Lang, Frankfurt am Main, 1993), p. 119.

52. This was the deportation of most of the ghetto's inmates, not the assault against the Warsaw Underground, which took place in May 1943. See Israel Gutman, *Resistance: the Warsaw Ghetto Uprising* (Mariner, Boston and New York, 1994).

53. Christopher Browning, 'Foreword', in Blatt, *Ashes*, pp. xiii–xix, at pp. xvi–xvii; Pohl, *Judenpolitik*, pp. 128–139.

54. MS, private diary, 'Sonntag' [4.10.1942]; entry 'den 12.[10.42]'.

55. MS, letter-diary, 22.10.1942.
56. Pohl, *Judenpolitik*, p. 138.
57. Ibid., p. 137.
58. Blatt, *Ashes*, p. 42
59. Pohl, *Judenpolitik*, p. 165.
60. MS, private diary, 25.11.1942. By this time most of the deportees to Izbica had been murdered.
61. Interview, ME, 31.10.1996.
62. Interviews, ME, 10.9.1996, 31.10.1996.
63. Presumably Carl Austerlitz, in Glogau, brother of a close friend of the Krombachs.
64. Emil C. Fuchs to MS, 8.1.1943.
65. Deutsches Rotes Kreuz (DRK), Der Beauftragte beim Generalgouverneur, Krakau, to Marianne Sara Strauss, 26.1.1943.
66. DRK, Der Beauftragte beim Generalgouverneur, Krakau, to Marianne Sara Strauss, 10.2.1943.
67. Copy, Marianne Sara Strauss, Hindenburgstr. 75, to DRK Krakau, 17.2.1943.
68. DRK, Der Beauftragte beim Generalgouverneur, Krakau, to Marianne Sara Strauss, 13.3.1943.
69. Copy, Marianne Sara Strauss, Hindenburgstr. 75, to DRK Präsidium, Berlin, 1.4.1943.
70. Copy, Marianne Sara Strauss, Hindenburgstr. 75, to DRK Krakau, 13.4.1943.
71. DRK, Presidium Berlin VII/4 Br.-Pu. to Marianne Sara Strauss, 15.4.1943.
72. Copy, MS to Julie Koppel, 16.5.1943.
73. Schmalhausen, *Schicksale*, pp. 81–82.
74. Julie Koppel to MS, 25.6.1943.
75. Thomas Blatt to author, 11.3.1997.
76. StAE NJ AJD, 31.12.1942.
77. ASE AR 4434, Liesel Sternberg to Dr Alexander, 20.8.1945.
78. Julie Koppel to MS, 25.6.1943.
79. Blatt, *Ashes*; YVJ Nobel, Hejnoch, testimony, 19.5.1946.


## 8   Deportations, Death and the Bund

1. Walk, *Sonderrecht*, pp.364–387; Fischer, *Aimée & Jaguar*, p. 89; inter-view, Hanna Aron, West Hartford, Connecticut, 7.8.1998; hand-written note, 'An jüdische Kultusvereinigung, Synagogengemeinde Essen e.V.,

Essen', 19.11.1941, signed Siegfr. Isr. Strauss, with added note of when the objects were handed in.

2. Copy, Else Sara Dahl to Postamt Wuppertal-Barmen, 8.2.1942.
3. Postamt 1, Essen, to Frau Else Sara Dahl, 16.2.1942.
4. HStAD RW58, 74234, OFD to StaPoD, 7.6.1943.
5. EK to MS, 'Sonntag Abend', 8.2.1942.
6. Corbach, *Jawne*, p. 29.
7. Interview, ME. 10.9.1996.
8. Interview, Frau Sparrer, 28.7.1997; Waltraud Horn to author, 26.2.1998.
9. Transport to Izbica, 15.6.1942. See Schröter, *Geschichte und Schicksal*, pp. 403f.
10. Schröter, *Geschichte und Schicksal*, p. 686.
11. On the deportation, see Michael Zimmermann, 'Eine Deportation nach Theresienstadt. Zur Rolle des Banalen bei der Durchsetzung des Monströsen', in Miroslav Karny, Raimund Kemper et al. (eds.) *Theresienstädter Studien und Dokumente* (Edition Theresienstädter Initiative Academia, 1994), pp. 54–73, at. p. 56; *Stationen jüdischen Lebens*, p. 246; copy of MS to Julie Koppel 16.5.1943; StAE NJ AJD, 25.7.1942.
12. MS, letter-diary, 21.7.1942.
13. Interview, ME, 31.10.1996.
14. Dried peas.
15. MS, letter-diary, 31.7.1942.
16. War Organization of the British Red Cross and Order of St John, postal message scheme, enquirer Klaus Langer to Erich Israel Langer, 17.9.1942. Copy in possession of the author.
17. Interview, ME, 1989; interview, ME, July 1996.
18. MS, letter-diary, 31.7.1942.
19. Imo Moszkowicz to author, 29.8.1997.
20. Imo Moszkowicz to author, 2.9.1997.
21. MS, letter-diary, 24.4.1942.
22. MS, letter-diary, 7.6.1942.
23. Whether in her community Shavuot was presented in this light we do not know. More usually, Shavuot – which among other things commemorates the giving of the ten commandments – is associated with study rather than contemplation.
24. In the Jewish morning service on the Sabbath and festivals, and also in the afternoon service on the Day of Atonement, a section of the Five Books of Moses, the Torah, is read from the scrolls. For each Torah portion there is an appropriate Haftorah, a selection from the remaining post-Mosaic books of the bible, which is also read.

25. Isaiah, chapter 57, verse 14 to chapter 58, verse 14. In her transcription, Marianne wrongly cites the second part of the passage as chapter 58, verses 1–4.

26. Paucker, 'Zum Selbstverständnis jüdischer Jugend,' p. 114.

27. MS, letter-diary, 28.9.1942.

28. MS, letter-diary, 7.10.1942.

29. MS, private diary, 3.10.1942.

30. Edith Caspari to MS, 31.12.1942. The letter was folded in Marianne's private diary.

31. Richarz, *Jewish Life in Germany*, p. 342, note 8. Caspari talks of eighteen escapees, Richarz of twenty.

32. There is an additional blank sheet with the letter-diary which looks as if it has faint lines of typing on it. Whether this is a faded carbon of further entries or whether it had simply rubbed off from existing entries is impossible to say.

33. Else Bramesfeld, Doris Braune et al. (eds), *Gelebte Utopie: Aus dem Leben einer Gemeinschaft, Nach einer Dokumentation von Dore Jacobs* (Klartext, Essen, 1990). Henceforth *Gelebte Utopie*.

34. The best known being the Internationaler Sozialistischer Kampfbund (ISK), also known as the Nelsen-Bund. There were, in fact, a number of similarities between the ISK and the Bund, see Werner Link, *Die Geschichte des Internationalen Jugend-Bundes und des Internationalen Sozialistischen Kampf-Bundes. Ein Beitrag zur Geschichte der Arbeiterbewegung in der Weimarer Republik und im 3. Reich* (Meisenheim am Glan, 1964).

35. Artur Jacobs, *Der Bund* (Bund Verlag, Essen 1929), p. 41.

36. *Gelebte Utopie*, p. 63.

37. *Gelebte Utopie*; Zum Gedenken an Artur Jacobs, 'Worte zur Gedenkstunde für Artur Jacobs im Bundeshaus am 17. März 1968', in unpublished Bund Manuscript pp. 7–8 (Sonja Schreiber); interviews with Meta Kamp, Ursula Jungbluth.

38. *Gelebte Utopie*; unpublished, printed and bound volume, produced by the Bund in 1989 'Für Lisa Jacob'. The volume contains the article 'Leben und Lernen mit Lisa Jacob', by Ellen Jungbluth.

39. A point also made by Monika Grüter's excellent dissertation 'Der "Bund für ein sozialistisches Leben": Seine Entwicklung in den 20er Jahren und seine Widerständigkeit unter dem Nationalsozialismus' (Examensarbeit, University of Essen, 1988), pp. 59ff.

40. Interview Tove Gerson, Essen, 8.1.1997.

41. Der Bund, *Mann und Frau als Kampfgenossen* (Bund series 'Die Bresche', Essen, 1932).

42. Der Bund. Gemeinschaft für sozialistisches Leben (ed.), *Aus der illegalen Arbeit des Bunds. Zweiter Auslandsbrief* (printed pamphlet, 1948), p. 3.

43. A point made by Grüter: 'Bund', p. 46.

44. *Zweiter Auslandsbrief*, p. 5.

45. Interview, Aenne Schmitz, Wuppertal, January 1997.

46. 'Zum Gedenken an Artur Jacobs', p. 13 (Lisa Jacob).

47. 'Worte zur Gedenkstunde für Artur Jacobs', p. 13; conversation with Ellen Jungbluth, 13.7.1999.

48. Interview, Tove Gerson, Essen, 8.1.1997.

49. *Zweiter Auslandsbrief*, pp. 8f.

50. Der Bund. Gemeinschaft für sozialistisches Leben (ed.), *Leben in der Illegalität. Dritter Auslandsbrief* (printed pamphlet 1948), p. 3.

51. Interview, Tove Gerson, 8.1.1997; video by Jochen Bilstein with Frau Briel, Herr Jost, 9.11.1990.

52. *Sie wußten was sie taten*, WDR broadcast.

53. StAE NJ AJD, 8.11.1941.

54. Interview, ME, 10.9.1996.

55. StAE NJ AJD, 10.8.1942.

56. StAE NJ AJD, 22.9.1942.

57. Ibid.

58. StAE NJ AJD, 20.11.1942.

59. StAE NJ AJD, 31.12.1942.

60. MS, private diary, 26.1.1943.

61. Interview, ME, 10.9.1996.

62. Schwester Tamara to MS, 23.6.1943.

63. MS, private diary, 26.1.1943.

64. MS, private diary, 17.11.1942.

65. MS, private diary, 23.11.1942.

66. Ibid.

67. Dore Jacobs, 'Ein Auslandsbrief', in *Gelebte Utopie*, pp. 109–121, at p. 112.

68. Folded, typed sheet in MS private diary.

69. 'Liste der am 25 Juni 1943 von Düsseldorf nach Theresienstadt evakuierten Juden', Gestapo document kindly provided by Michael Zimmermann.

70. *Essen unter Bomben*, pp. 26–47.

71. Interview, ME, 31.10.1996.

72. Some information here was gleaned in a telephone conversation with Hanna Aron, 20.10.97; the remainder in the interview in West Hartford, Connecticut 7.8.1998.

## 9   The Escape

1. See the note attached to HStAD RW 58, 74234, draft StaPoD IIB 4/Tgb Nr 248/43/Strauss, telegram to StaPo Prag, Polizeigefängnis Theresienstadt, letter sent 31.8.1943.
2. Copy, RW to May, 19.5.1961, annex; copy, Hammacher to Schroetter, 14.8.1951.
3. DBF F67/56, copy, DBE to SStr, 10.5.1943; SStr to DB, 10.5.1943; copy, DBE to SStr, 18.5.1943. In Marianne's papers, see DBE to LGD, 7 Entschädigungskammer, 5.3.1965 and attached letter describing the contents of DB's communication to the lawyer Schroeter of 6.7.1955.
4. Copy, CH to AfWGE, 19.7.1963.
5. Copy, Schroetter to Koplowitz, 18.4.1955, containing copy of Alfred Strauss to DBE, 2.6.1943; copy, RW to May, 19.5.1961, annex, copy, Hammacher to Schroetter, 14.8.1951.
6. Schwester Tamara to MS, 23.6.1943.
7. HStAD RW 58, 74234, letter from Wilhelm Hammacher in Firma DBE to ADStE, 2.7.1943.
8. HStAD RW 58, 74234, draft letter, StaPoD to ADStE, 19.7.1943.
9. Interview, ME, 31.10.1996.
10. Interview Tove Gerson, Essen 8.1.1997.
11. HStAD RW 58, 74234, draft telegram, StaPoD to RSHA IV B 4, 27.5.1943.
12. See HStAD microfilm A28, StaPoD II B 4 to RSHA IV B 4, 9.6.1943.
13. HStAD RW 58, 74234, telegram, Berlin Chef d. SIPO und d. SD Roem 4 B 4 Kl., signed Eichmann to StaPoD, 9.6.43.
14. HStAD RW 58, 74234, OFD to StaPoD, 7.6.1943.
15. Ibid., memo *verso*, 10.6.1943.
16. Meyer, *Unternehmen Sieben*, pp. 241, 411–412.
17. Ibid., pp. 412, 417.
18. HStAD RW 58, 74234, telegram, RHSA IV B 4a to StaPoD, 6.8.1943 (it may have been sent 5.8.1943).
19. HStAD RW 58, 74234, draft telegram, StaPoD to ADStE, 9.8.1943.
20. HStAD RW 58, 74234, draft of letter to Herr OFD, 9.8.1943.
21. Memo attached to HStAD RW 58, 74234, draft StaPoD to StaPo Prag, 31.8.1943.
22. Copy, Schroetter to Koplowitz, 18.4.1955, containing copy of AS to DBE, 2.6.1943; copy, RW to May, 19.5.1961, annex, copy, Hammacher to Schroetter, 14.8.1951.

23. Copy, Hammacher to CH, 27.6.1957.
24. Copy, Ernst Dahl to RW, 3.3.1961.
25. Marianne slightly misremembered his name.
26. Marianne's description of the garment was a 'ski suit', but it was clearly closer to a modern tracksuit than a padded ski suit.
27. Interview, ME, July 1996.
28. Sadly, I was not able to add any details about Pastor Wilhelm Keinath. He and his wife Margarethe died before I began my researches and left no children. Marianne remained in contact with his niece, Frau Hedda Keinath. I contacted Frau Keinath, but she owed to Marianne what she knew about her uncle's past connections with the Strauss family and could add nothing.
29. Interview, ME, 1989.
30. Interview, ME, 31.10.1996.
31. Interview, ME, 1989.
32. Interview, ME, 31.10.1996.
33. Ibid.
34. Information from Angela Genger, Düsseldorf.
35. Robert Gellately, *The Gestapo and German Society*, (Oxford University Press, Oxford, 1990).
36. HStAD RW58, 74234, ADStE to StaPoD, 1.9.1943.
37. Typed manuscript provided by Michael Zimmermann, 'Gespräch mit Herrn Borghoff über die Ermittlungsverfahren 1964 bis 1986 zu den Deportationen der Juden aus dem Gebiet der Gestapoleitstelle Düsseldorf'.
38. HStAD RW58, 74234, draft telegram, StaPoD IIB, Ratingen to Police Prison in Theresienstadt FAO SS-Hauptsturmführer Dr. Seidl., 1.9.1943 (sent 2.9.1943).
39. Copy, AfWGE, in der Wiedergutmachungssache Marianne Ellenbogen nach Siegfried Strauss, witness statement from Erna Rosenberg, 9.11.1959.
40. HStaD RW58 74234 Betriff: Flucht der Jüdin Marianne Sara Strauss geboren am 7.6.1923 in Essen Wohnhaft hier Ladenspelderstr. 47, Essen 3.9.1943.
41. Email, Robert S. Selig to author, 24.8.1998.
42. ME, Eidesstattliche Erklärung (Declaration under Oath), 14.11.1961.
43. ME, Eidesstattliche Erklärung (Declaration under Oath), 22.5.1957.
44. Declaration under Oath, 14.11.1961.
45. Interview, Hanna Aron, West Hartford, Connecticut 7.8.1998.
46. Hanna was working as a seamstress at the time.

## 10 *Memories Underground: August 1943 – Spring 1944*

1. Interview, ME, 10.9.1996.
2. StAE NJ AJD, entries for 25, 26 and 29/30.8.1943.
3. Extract reproduced in a letter from Dore Jacobs to ME 24.9.73. The September extracts are missing from the copy of the diary in the Essen City Archive. They are, however, present in another copy of the diary in the Blockhaus.
4. Interview, ME, July 1996.
5. ME, 'Flucht', p. 140.
6. Biographical information from an unpublished Bund Manuscript, 'Zum Gedenken an Sonja Schreiber' (Doris Braune and others) (no date [1987]).
7. HStAD RW 58, 1808.
8. See copy, ME to CH, 3.2.1958, annex: Eidesstattliche Versicherung.
9. Interview, ME, 31.10.1996; undated carbon copy (1983), 'Flucht und illegales Leben während der Nazi-Verfolgungsjahre 1943–45 der Marianne ELLENBOGEN STRAUSS.'
10. Interview, ME, 1989.
11. Interview, ME, 31.10.1996.
12. Copy, Julia Böcker, 'Eidesstattliche Erklärung', Essen, 26.2.1955.
13. Ibid. See below, chapter 13, note 87.
14. Copy, witness statement of Julia Böcker, 28.3.1955.
15. Copy, ME to LGE, in Sachen Ellenbogen/Hammacher, 2.10.1952.
16. ME, 'Flucht', p. 140.
17. Interview, ME, 31.10.1996.
18. HStAD RW 58, 74234, draft letter StaPoD II B 4/Tgb Nr 248/43g/Strauss to Bahnhof M-Gladbach 6.9.1943.
19. According to Frau Jürgens in 1960; see copy, Öffentliche Sitzung des II. WGK beim LG Dortmund, 4.11.1960.
20. HStAD RW 58, 74234, StaPoD II B 4/Tgb Nr 248/43g/Strauss, draft memo, Düsseldorf, 21.9.1943.
21. HStAD RW 58, 74234, Quittung, Theresienstadt 10.9.1943.
22. Zimmermann, 'Eine Deportation nach Theresienstadt'; HStAD RW 58, 74234, draft, StaPoD to RSHA IV B 4, Düsseldorf, 21.9.1943 (posted 24.9.1943).
23. HStAD RW 58, 74234, StaPoD, memo, 21.9.1943.
24. Kaplan, *Between Dignity and Despair*, pp. 207ff.
25. Konrad Kwiet and Helmut Eschwege, *Selbstbehauptung und Widerstand*.

*Deutsche Juden im Kampf um Existenz und Menschenwürde 1933–1945* (Hans Christians Verlag, Hamburg, 1984), p. 154.

26. Emphasized particularly in a typewritten early draft of ME's article in *Das Münster am Hellweg*; presumably for reasons of space, the paragraph was omitted from the final draft.

27. Reprinted in 'Zum Gedenken an Sonja Schreiber'.

28. Jacob, ' "Der Bund" ', p. 112.

29. ME, 'Eidesstattliche Erklärung', 22.5.1957; copy CH to Oberstadtdirektor, Essen, 4.6.1957.

30. Interview, ME, July 1996.

31. 'Eidesstattliche Erklärung', 25.9.1957, signed Johanna Ganzer.

32. Telephone conversation with Fritz Briel, Remscheid, 10.1.1997.

33. In Jewish ritual, the stone-setting, which takes place up to a year after the burial, is accompanied by a short ceremony and a eulogy and concludes the formal period of mourning.

34. Interview, Sol and Clara Bender, Chester, 17.10.1997.

35. Interview, Lew and Trudy Schloss, Teaneck, New Jersey, 11.8.98.

36. Telephone conversation with Eric Alexander, 21.8.98.

37. Born Margarete Ransenberg, 27.9.1881, Schröter, *Geschichte und Schicksal*, p. 686.

38. Interview, ME, 31.10.1996.

39. See chapter 11, pp. 359ff.

40. ASE, A6418, copy of Ruth Kotik, 'Ein Vorläufer alternativer Lebensformen: Der Bund – Gemeinschaft für sozialistisches Leben.' 16.11.1984, 20.15–21.00 WDR3.

41. 'Hilfe für Juden war für die Briels selbstverständlich', *Bergische Morgenpost*, 21.4.1994.

42. Video, Frau Briel, Herr Jost, 9.11.1990, made by a historian of Remscheid, Jochen Bilstein, Wermelskirchen, in whose possession the video resides.

43. Interview, Aenne Schmitz, January 1997.

44. Video, Frau Briel, Herr Jost, 9.11.1990.

45. Ibid.

46. Interview, Aenne Schmitz, January 1997.

47. Interview, ME, July 1996.

48. Video, Frau Briel, Herr Jost, 9.11.1990.

49. Telephone conversation, Fritz Briel, January 1997.

50. Video, Frau Briel, Herr Jost, 9.11.1990.

51. Ibid.

52. Interview with Maria Briel, in Jochen Bilstein and Frieder Backhaus, *Geschichte der Remscheider Juden* (Remscheid, 1992), p. 135.

53. Janina Fischler-Martinho, *Have You Seen My Little Sister?* (Valentine, Mitchell, London and Portland, Oreg., 1998), p. 236.
54. This and following information from my conversation with Hannah Jordan, Wuppertal, 29.7.1997.
55. Interview, ME, July 1996.
56. Ibid.
57. Ibid.
58. Interview, ME, 31.10.1996.
59. Ibid.
60. Ibid.
61. Interview, ME, July 1996.
62. Interview, ME, 31.10.1996.
63. ME, 'Flucht', p. 138.
64. Video, Frau Briel, Herr Jost, 9.11.1990.
65. See copy, ME to CH, 3.2.1958, annex: Eidesstattliche Versicherung.
66. Interview, ME, July 1996.
67. Jan Karski, *Story of a Secret State* (Houghton Mifflin, Boston, 1944), p. 185.

## 11   Underground Chronicles: April 1944 – April 1945

1. Typed letter folded into the diary headed 'Beverstedt, den 12. Juni 44'.
2. ME, 'Flucht', p. 139.
3. Hermann Schmalstieg to author, 4.5.1997.
4. Mark Roseman, 'The organic society and the Massenmenschen. Integrating young labour in the Ruhr mines 1945–1958', in Robert Moeller (ed.), *West Germany Under Construction: Politics, Society, and Culture in the Adenauer era* (Ann Arbor, University of Michigan Press, 1997), pp. 287–320.
5. The alternation between 'v.Mst', 'M' and v.M' are in the original.
6. See chapter 'Living with a Past in Hiding', p. 474.
7. Typed letter, headed 'Beverstedt, den 12. Juni 44.'
8. Ibid. *Geheimnis Tibet* deals with Schäfer's expedition to Tibet in 1940, and not with the escape to Tibet of Heinrich Harrer in 1944, as portrayed in the film *Seven Years in Tibet*.
9. Incidentally, Marianne said that she was writing the above while sitting in a little wood on an old tree trunk. But the letter which contains all this is typed (and contains several mistakes and crossings out, suggesting that she typed as she thought and was not writing it up later), so I wondered if

she was travelling around with a portable typewriter. On the other hand, the typeface here is not the same as that in her first letter in April, nor the later ones from Düsseldorf, so she may well have borrowed a portable from her hosts and taken it into the woods with her.

10. See chapter 13.
11. Hermann Schmalstieg to author, 10.10.1998.
12. Telephone conversation, Hedwig Gehrke, 21.1.1997.
13. The date from telephone conversation with Elfrieda Nenadovic, neé Wahle, 24.1.97.
14. The following information is taken from Meta Kamp, *Auf der anderen Seite stehen* (privately published, Göttingen, 1987) and from telephone conversation with Meta Kamp, 24.1.1997.
15. Kamp, *Auf der anderen Seite stehen*, p. 11.
16. Telephone conversation with Meta Kamp, 24.1.1997.
17. Telephone conversation with Elfrieda Nenadovic, 9.12.1997.
18. Kamp, *Auf der anderen Steite stehen*, p. 45.
19. Telephone conversation with Meta Kamp, 24.1.1997.
20. Telephone conversation with Ernst Steinmann, 24.1.1997.
21. Telephone conversation with Elfrieda Nenadovic, 24.01.1997.
22. Ibid.
23. Letter from Hermann Schmalstieg, 12.7.1944.
24. See p. 347.
25. Hermann Schmalstieg to author, 2.4.1998.
26. MS, diary entry, 31.7.1944.
27. The following information derives from a telephone conversation with Hermann Schmalstieg, 24.1.1997, subsequent letters from him to me, 4.5.1997, 2.4.1998 and 10.10.1998, and an interview 25.8.1999.
28. Hermann Schmalstieg to author, 4.5.1997.
29. Telephone conversation with Hermann Schmalstieg, 24.1.1997.
30. MS, diary entry, Friday, 3.11.1944 (from a letter to Meta).
31. Lene Krahlisch in Mülheim.
32. Presumably Karin Morgenstern.
33. 'Oneself' is underlined in pencil (the rest of the letter is in ink) suggesting that, while she was reading, Marianne wanted to emphasise this section for herself.
34. Braunschweig.
35. Another one of her wartime helpers who later slipped from view was Albert Schürmann, whom Marianne thanked in a submission made on behalf of Ernst Jungbluth after the war, but who did not surface in her later article. See Stadtarchiv Wuppertal (StAW) Wiedergutmachungsakte,

Jungbluth, Ernst, 115, 24, statement from Marianne Strauss, Düsseldorf 24.8.1945. It is unknown what Schürmann's role was.

36. See ME, 'Flucht', p. 139; diary, Mülheim, 31.9.1944 [Brief an Meta].

37. Possibly Düsseldorf and Solingen.

38. I am grateful to Michael Zimmermann for this insight.

39. This is not always apparent in my translation. The repetition of 'one' (in German 'man') was so clumsy in English, that I have rendered it sometimes as 'you', sometimes as 'we', occasionally as 'I', depending on the context.

40. Interview, ME, 31.10.1996.

41. MS, diary entry, Braunschweig, 2.9.1944

42. MS, diary entry, 9.8.1944.

43. Copy, Johanna Ganzer, 'Eidesstattliche Erklärung', Düsseldorf, 25.9.1955.

44. ME, 'Flucht', p. 140.

45. Ibid., p. 139.

46. Copy, draft, ME to Landgericht Essen, 2.10.1952.

47. Copy, ME to RW, 14.10.1960.

48. ME, 'Flucht', p. 141.

49. Gauleiter Florian, Kreisleiter Walter and police president Korreng.

50. Peter Hüttenberger, *Düsseldorf. Geschichte von den Anfängen bis ins 20. Jahrhundert*, vol. 3, *Die Industrie- und Verwaltungsstadt* (Schwann, Düsseldorf, 1989), pp. 635–646.

51. Copy, Johanna Ganzer, 'Eidesstattliche Erklärung', Düsseldorf, 25.9.1955.

52. Hüttenberger, *Düsseldorf*, pp. 631, 648.

53. In diary, copy MS to Meta, Hedwig, Elli and Hermann [Meta Kamp, Hedwig Gehrke, Elli Schlieper and Hermann Schmalstieg] 30.5.1945.

54. Unfortunately, this later diary does not seem to have survived.

55. Copy, MS to Meta, Hedwig, Elli and Hermann, 30.5.1945.

56. Ibid.

57. A comprehensive study shows that those who helped Jews were more likely to have had Jewish friends before the war than the bystanders. Samuel P. Oliner, *The Altruistic Personality. Rescuers of Jews in Nazi Europe* (The Free Press, New York, 1998), p. 115.

58. Unpublished Bund manuscript, 'Zum Gedenken an Artur Jacobs'. Here, 'Worte zur Gedenkstunde für Artur Jacobs im Bundeshaus am 17. März 1968', p. 13 (Lisa Jacob).

59. HStAD RW 58, 1593 (Jungbluth); RW 58, 19223 (Jacobs); RW 58, 71703 (Jacobs).

60. Jacob, '"Der Bund"', p. 109; HStAD RW 58, 19223, various papers.

61. HStAD RW 58, 71703 Jacobs, Dr Artur, copy of statement dated 6.8.1944, and attached note Gestapo AStE IV 3 a 6812/44 to StaPoD.
62. Oliner, *Altruistic Personality*, p. 130.
63. *Dritter Auslandsbrief*, pp. 9–10.
64. Comment by Herr Jost in video, Frau Briel, Herr Jost, 9.11.1990.
65. Interview, Frau Gerson, Essen, 8.1.1997.
66. *Zweiter Auslandsbrief*, pp. 8f.
67. *Dritter Auslandsbrief*, p. 5.
68. 'Unsere toten Freunde – Lebenszeugnisse des Bundes' (anonymous unpublished printed booklet from the Bund, no date).
69. Interview, Jakov Langer, 27.7.1998.

## 12   *Living Amid the Ruins*

1. Interviews, ME 1989; July 1996.
2. See, for example, Klemperer, *Tagebücher 1942–1945*, pp. 750–760.
3. Interview, Frau Jungbluth, 29.7.1997.
4. Copy MS to Meta, Hedwig, Elli and Hermann, 30.5.1945, folded into diary.
5. Interview, Hanna Aron, West Hartford, Connecticut, 7.8.1998.
6. YVJ, file 0.48/1630.2, archiv 13390, MS to Alfred Weinberg, 26.6.1947.
7. Interview, ME, 31.10.1996.
8. Copy, MS to Meta, Hedwig, Elli and Hermann, 30.5.1945.
9. Interview, ME, 31.10.1996.
10. Copy, MS to 'Meine sehr Lieben [Hugo and Grete Strauss], 24.1.1946, folded into diary.
11. Copy, MS to Meta, Hedwig, Elli and Hermann, 30.5.1945.
12. Lisa Jacob had a similar story to tell; see ' "Der Bund", Gemeinschaft für sozialistisches Leben und meine Rettung vor der Deportation', in *Das Münster am Hellweg*, vol. 37 (1984), pp. 105–134.
13. Interview, ME, July 1996.
14. Copy, MS to 'Meine sehr Lieben' [Hugo and Grete Strauss], 24.1.1946.
15. Interview, ME, July 1996.
16. Copy, MS to Meta, Hedwig, Elli and Hermann, 30.5.1945 [postscript from 8 June].
17. Copy, MS to 'Meine sehr Lieben' [Hugo and Grete Strauss], 24.1.1946
18. It is interesting that Marianne subscribed to the widely held myth that German industries were being shut down because of Allied fear of competition.

19. Interview, ME, 31.10.1996.
20. Ibid.
21. Arbeitsamt Düsseldorf, 'Zeugnis', Düsseldorf, 30.4.1946.
22. Copy, MS to Meta, Hedwig, Elli and Hermann, 30.5.1945.
23. Ibid.
24. Interview, ME, July 1996.
25. Interview, Hanna Aron, West Hartford, Connecticut, 7.8.1998.
26. Telephone conversation with Johannes Oppenheimer, 27.3.1997.
27. Johannes Oppenheimer to author, 3.3.1997.
28. Telephone conversation with Johannes Oppenheimer, 27.3.1997.
29. Copy, ME to Koplowitz, 4.2.1956.
30. Copy, MS to 'Meine sehr Lieben' [Hugo and Grete Strauss], 24.1.1946.
31. Copy, MS to Alex [Eric Alexander, formerly Alex Weinberg], 4.2.1946, folded into diary.
32. According to copy, ME to CH, 9.1.1956 [sic = 1957], she left the job in January, but a surviving reference from the Arbeitsamt Düsseldorf suggests that she was there until 30 April 1946. Though I contacted various people who had worked for the *Freiheit* at that time, only the wife of the paper's former editor, Gerd Leo, vaguely remembered her. A few of Marianne's manuscripts are preserved, though it is not always possible to identify the newspaper in which they were published.
33. Copy, MS to Braun, BBC, 2.2.1946.
34. BBC, German Service, Funkbriefkasten Programme no. 48, 12.4.1946, transcript.
35. Copy, MS to Christina Ogilvy, 12.7.1946.
36. Roseman, 'The organic society'.
37. The text here is taken from Marianne's own copy. The transmission date confirmed by undated postcard from G. H. Gretton, BBC, evidently enclosed with some other letter or parcel.
38. Grete Sander to MS, 22.8.1945.
39. Copy, MS to 'Meine sehr Lieben' [Hugo and Grete Strauss], 24.1.1946.
40. Interview, ME, 31.10.1996.
41. YVJ file 0.48/1630.2, archiv 13390, letter from ME to Alfred, 26.6.1947.
42. Ibid.
43. Karl Rosenberg to MS, 18.11.1945.
44. MS to Alex [Eric Alexander, formerly Alex Weinberg], 4.2.1946, folded into diary.
45. Erna Ogutsch to MS, 20.4.1946. We don't have Marianne's letter, but Erna Ogutsch thanks her for her letter of 31.3.1946.

46. Interview, ME, 31.10.1996.

47. Copy, MS to 'Meine sehr Lieben' [Hugo and Grete Strauss], 24.1.1946.

48. Copy, MS to Alex [Eric Alexander, formerly Alex Weinberg], 4.2.1946.

49. Copy, MS to 'Meine sehr Lieben' [Hugo and Grete Strauss], 24.1.1946.

50. Copy, MS to Alex [Eric Alexander, formerly Alex Weinberg], 4.2.1946.

51. Interview, ME, 31.10.1996.

52. Telephone conversation with Johannes Oppenheimer, 27.3.1997.

53. Johannes Oppenheimer to author, 3.3.1997.

54. Ibid.

55. Interview, ME, 31.10.1996.

56. Johannes Oppenheimer to author, 3.3.1997.

57. Including Jacob's place of origin, the fate of his father and so forth. The following is based on a lengthy telephone conversation with Frau Elisabeth Jacob, 24.1.1997.

58. Hüttenberger, *Düsseldorf*, p. 660.

59. Ibid pp. 667–668

60. *Zweiter Auslandsbrief*, p. 2.

61. Ibid.

62. 'Erster Auslandsbrief', p. 7.

63. Ibid.

64. *Gelebte Utopie*, p. 15.

65. Interviews with Helmut and Helga Lenders, Düsseldorf; Kurt and Jenni Schmit, Wuppertal; Alisa Weyl, Meckenheim.

66. Much more will be explored here in my and Norbert Reichling's forthcoming publication on the Bund.

67. Video, Frau Briel, Herr Jost, 9.11.1990.

68. Information from Reinhold Ströter, Mettmann.

69. Artur Jacobs, *Die Zukunft des Glaubens. Die Entscheidungsfrage unserer Zeit* (Europäische Verlagsanstalt, Frankfurt am Main, 1971).

70. Copy, MS to Meta, Hedwig, Elli and Hermann, 30.5.1945.

71. Copy, MS to Alex [Eric Alexander, formerly Alex Weinberg], 4.2.1946.

72. Interview, ME, July 1996.

73. Copy, MS to Herrn Generalkonsul des Amerikanischen Konsulats, Düsseldorf, 20.4.1946.

74. Copy, Gerald Alexander to Officer i/c British Interests Branch CCG (BE), Lübbecke.

75. Passport Control Office c/o Political Division CCG Lübbecke BAOR, to L/Cpl G. Alexander, 14.3.1946.

76. Copy, Cap. B. K. Ellenbogen to Passport Office, 22.3.1946.

77. Passport Control Officer, Lübbecke to L/Cpl G. Alexander, 25.3.1946.

78. Ursula Büttner, *Not nach der Befreiung. Die Situation der deutschen Juden in der britischen Besatzungszone 1945–1948* (Hamburg, 1986), p. 17.

79. Copy, Basil Ellenbogen to Scholefield-Adams, 20.10.1946.

80. HQ Military Government, North Rhine Region, Deputy Inspector General Senior Public Safety Officer (J. T. Baldock), 5.7.1946 to 320 Detachment Mil. Govt, attention of Public Safety.

81. Copy, Basil Ellenbogen to Scholefield- Adams, 20.10.1946.

82. Many German Jews at the time were deeply upset that it was no easier for them to come to Britain than for non-Jewish Germans. See Gerda Rother to MS, 2.11.1946.

83. *Freiheit* Hauptschriftleitung, Düsseldorf Pressehaus, to MS, 1.11.1946; *Freiheit* Hauptschriftleitung, Düsseldorf, to MS, 4.11.1946, signed G. Eisenhütte, Gerhard Leo, Nora Leibnitz and another.

84. Hanni Ganzer to MS, undated.

85. Herbert Perrett to Ellenbogen, 21.11.1946.


### 13 The Fate of Marianne's Family

1. Interview, ME 1989.

2. 'Project of Automated Data Processing of Terezin Prisoners', conducted by the Institute of Information Theory and Automation at the Academy of Sciences of the Czech Republic, in co-operation with the Terezin Initiative Foundation and the Terezin Memorial.

3. This is a correction. In the original communication, Dr Schindler put a date in December. Two transports had the same code.

4. Fischer, *Aimée & Jaguar*, p. 196.

5. Hans-Günther Adler, *Theresienstadt 1941–1945. Das Antlitz einer Zwangsgemeinschaft. Geschichte. Soziologie Psychologie* (J. C. B. Mohr/ Paul Siebeck, Tübingen, 1955), p. 124.

6. The Vrba report: 'The extermination camps of Auschwitz (Oswiecim) and Birkenau in Upper Silesia' [1944, author Rudolf Vrba] microfiched in the Leo Baeck Institute, New York.

7. On the Czech connection and Kopecky's role, see Miroslav Karny, 'The Vrba and Wetzler report', in Yisrael Gutman and Michael Berenbaum (eds.), *Anatomy of the Auschwitz Death Camp* (Indiana University Press, Bloomington and Indianapolis, 1994), pp. 553–568, at p. 557.

8. These details from Karny, 'Vrba and Wetzler report', pp. 557–558.

9. BBC Written Archive Centre, German Service, Sonderbericht scripts Jan.

1943 – Apr. 1945. I am very grateful to Gabriel Milland for this reference.

10. In describing all the occupants as Czech, the report echoed the Auschwitz camp's own description of the transport, but it was misleading, since the Jews were not just of Czech origin. See Adler, *Theresienstadt*, p. 53.

11. Danuta Czech, *Kalendarium der Ereignisse im Konzentrationslager Auschwitz Birkenau 1939–1945* (Rowohlt, Hamburg, 1989), pp. 800– 801.

12. Klemperer, *Zeugnis. Tagebücher 1942–1945*, p. 565.

13. Erna Ogutsch to MS, 22.3.1946.

14. Ludwig's mother was a sister of Siegfried's mother, Rosalie, née Stern.

15. Erna Ogutsch to MS, 22.3.1946.

16. Ruth Elias, *Triumph of Hope. From Theresienstadt and Auschwitz to Israel* (John Wiley & Sons, New York, 1998), p. 97.

17. Adler, *Theresienstadt*, pp. 129 and 316ff.

18. Elias, *Triumph of Hope*, p. 95.

19. Adler, *Theresienstadt*, p. 157; Elias, *Triumph of Hope*, p. 197.

20. Adler, *Theresienstadt*, pp. 339ff.

21. Fischer, *Aimée & Jaguar*, p. 196.

22. Ludwig and Selma Ansbacher to MS, 1.5.1946.

23. Ibid.

24. Gershon Ellenbogen to Marianne and Basil Ellenbogen, 12.9.1947.

25. Schröter, *Geschichte und Schicksal*, p. 710 refers to a Grete Sander from Essen who went to Sweden and for a while I believed her to be the woman in question.

26. Marianne's mother Ine's sister, Hannah, was married to Ernst Weinberg. Ernst Weinberg's sister, Helene Weinberg, married Alfred Alsberg. Alfred Alsberg's sister became Grete Sander by marriage.

27. Eric Alexander to author, 9.7.1997.

28. Postcard, SStr to Grete Sander.

29. Grete Sander to MS, 22.8.1945.

30. Hugo Strauss to ME, 27.30.1948, annex: invoice from Marcus Cohn, Austrasse, Basel, dated 19.5.1947.

31. Marcus Cohn to ME, 19.5.1947.

32. We do not have the letter, but Erna Ogutsch thanks her for her letter of 31.3.1946. See Erna Ogutsch to MS, 20.4.1946.

33. Erna Ogutsch to MS, 20.4.1946.

34. The transport from Essen to Theresienstadt in July 1942.

35. Adler, *Theresienstadt*, p. 158.

36. Ibid., p. 46.

37. Elias, *Triumph of Hope*, p. 105. Elias does not give the exact date of the

transport. But from her own dating, and from the circumstances of the transport, we know that she went on one of the big December transports. She and her partner missed the first of these and went a few days later. According to Danuta Czech's *Kalendarium*, there were only two big transports in that month, one arriving in Auschwitz on 16 December and one arriving on the 20<sup>th</sup>. The latter, we know, was the one which took the Strausses to the camp. Elias also notes that they arrived 'shortly before Christmas', and her tattooed number is one of those assigned to this transport, all facts confirming she was on the same train.

38. Elias, *Triumph of Hope*, P. 106.
39. The following information stems largely from the Vrba report, 'The extermination camps of Auschwitz (Oswiecim) and Birkenau in Upper Silesia'; Adler, *Theresienstadt*, pp. 53–56, 692; Rudolf Vrba and Alan Bestic, *I Cannot Forgive* (Sidwick & Jackson/Anthony Gibbs and Phillips, London, 1963); Otto Dov Kulka, 'Ghetto in an annihilation camp: Jewish social history in the Holocaust period and its ultimate limits', in *The Nazi Concentration Camps. Proceedings of the Fourth Yad Vashem International Historical Conference Jerusalem, January 1980* (Yad Vashem, Jerusalem, 1984), pp. 315–330; Czech, *Kalendarium*; Martin Gilbert, 'What was known and when', in Gutman and Berenbaum, *Anatomy*, pp. 539–552; Miroslav Karny, 'The Vrba and Wetzler report', in ibid., pp. 553–568; Nils Keren, 'The family camp', in ibid., pp. 428–441.
40. Czech, *Kalendarium*, p. 600
41. Vrba and Bestic, *I Cannot Forgive*, pp. 180ff.
42. Adler, *Theresienstadt*, p. 53.
43. Czech, *Kalendarium*, p. 670.
44. Michael Zimmermann has pointed out to me that sometimes 'special treatment' meant that people were *not* murdered. I.e. the special treatment in this case may have meant the six months *before* murder.
45. Kulka, 'Ghetto', p. 318.
46. Elias, *Triumph of Hope*, p. 107.
47. According to information provided by Ruth Elias in a letter, those on the September transport were allowed to keep their own clothes. Those on the December transport were not.
48. Eric Alexander to author, 18.7.1998.
49. Czech, *Kalendarium*, p. 684.
50. Staatliches Museum Auschwitz-Birkenau (ed.), *Sterbebücher von Auschwitz. Fragmente*, vols. 1 and 2 (Verlag K. G. G. Sauer, Munich, London, Paris etc., 1995); Dr Franciszek Piper, Panstwowe Muzeum, Oswiecim to author, 26.5.1997.

51. Czech, *Kalendarium*, pp. 600ff.

52. Kulka, 'Ghetto', p. 318.

53. Cited in Keren, 'Family camp', p. 430.

54. Vrba and Bestic, *I Cannot Forgive*, p. 185.

55. Czech, *Kalendarium*, pp. 700ff; Kulka, 'Ghetto', p. 318.

56. Kulka, 'Ghetto', p. 324.

57. A. Schön, 'Co byl Birkenau' (Ms. 1945), cited in Adler, *Theresienstadt*, p. 730.

58. Adler, *Theresienstadt*, p. 128.

59. Postcard, Regina Strauss, Arbeitslager Birkenau, bei Neuberun (Oberschlesien) 15.4.1944, franked Berlin 23.6.1944, to Grete Sander, Stockholm.

60. Gilbert, 'What was known and when', pp. 548.

61. Karny, 'The Vrba and Wetzler Report', pp. 558ff.

62. Erna Ogutsch to MS, 20.4.1946.

63. Grete Sander to MS, 22.8.1945.

64. Though this did not prevent them from subjecting the Hungarian Jews to the most intensive murder programme yet. In two months in the summer of 1944 300–400,000 Hungarian Jews were murdered, one-third of the total number of people murdered during Auschwitz's existence. See Deborah Dwork and Robert Jan van Pelt, *Auschwitz: 1270 to the Present* (W. W. Norton, New York and London, 1996), p. 343.

65. Kulka, 'Ghetto', p. 318.

66. Adler, *Theresienstadt*, pp. 53–56, 692.

67. Kulka, 'Ghetto', p. 329.

68. Ibid, p. 319.

69. It is not known exactly when they received the last sign of life from Marianne. The letter from the Ansbachers might suggest that Marianne's parcels to Theresienstadt began before her parents were deported. If so, they left for Auschwitz knowing she was still well. Thereafter, they are very unlikely to have heard any news of her.

70. Erna Ogutsch to MS, 22.3.1946.

71. Postcard, AS Hauptstr. 195/1, Theresienstadt Protektorat, to Grete Sander, 22.3.1944, franked 4.4.1944.

72. Postcard, AS geb. 24.IV.1891 Hauptstr. 195/1, Theresienstadt Protektorat, to Grete Sander, 3.4.1944, franked 20.7.1944.

73. Ludwig and Selma Ansbacher to MS, 1.5.1946.

74. Postcard, AS geb 24.IV.1891 Hauptstr. 195/1, Theresienstadt Protektorat, to Grete Sander, 3.6.1944, franked 8.7.1944.

75. Postcard, AS Hauptstr. 195/1, Theresienstadt Protektorat, to Grete Sander, 24.7.1944, franked 31.8.1944.

76. Postcard, AS Hauptstr. 195/1, Theresienstadt Protektorat, to Grete Sander, 25.8.1944, franked 12.9.1944.
77. Postcard, AS geb 24.4.1891, Theresienstadt Hauptstr. 195/1, to Grete Sander, 18.9.1944, franked 12.10.1944.
78. Professor Paul Alsberg to author, 29.7.1997.
79. Cited in Adler, *Theresienstadt*, p. 185.
80. Ibid., p. 187.
81. Ibid., p. 191.
82. Felice Schragenheim, whose fate has become famous through the book *Aimée & Jaguar*, was deported on the same transport as Oe and her mother, namely transport EP, 9 October 1944. Listed in Fischer, *Aimée & Jaguar*, p. 197, as passenger number EP 342 on 9.10.1944.
83. Interview, ME, 31.10.1996.
84. Actually, 16.08.1907.
85. Written notes, off the tape, interview, ME, 31.10.1996.
86. Copy, declaration, Julia Böcker, Essen Stadtwald, Drosselstrasse 51, 26.2.1955.
87. Frau Böcker was not to blame here, I suspect. Marianne and her cousin René wanted to establish for the courts that Oe had predeceased Alfred so as to avoid problems with the inheritance and Frau Böcker was an obliging witness. Marianne knew, though, that Alfred had probably died first.
88. Adler, *Theresienstadt*, p. 694.
89. Several sheets bearing the heading 'Yad Vashem Daf-ed. A page of testimony'.
90. Several sheets bearing the heading 'Yad Vashem Daf-ed. Gedenkblatt' and dated July 1983.
91. Ludwig and Selma Ansbacher to MS, 1.5.1946.
92. Isabel Sprenger, *Groß-Rosen. Ein Konzentrationslager in Schlesien* (Böhlau Verlag, Cologne, Weimar and Vienna, 1996), pp. 261–262.
93. Ruth Klüger, *Weiter leben. Eine Jugend* (Wallstein, Göttingen, 1992).
94. Gudrun Schwarz, *Die nationalsozialistischen Lager* (revised edn, Fischer, Frankfurt am Main, 1996), p. 198; Internationaler Suchdienst, Arolsen, *Vorläufiges Verzeichnis der Haftstätten unter dem Reichsführer-SS 1933–1945* (1969), p. 110.
95. Israel Gutman (ed.), *Encyclopaedia of the Holocaust* (Macmillan, London, 1990), p. 625.
96. Details on Kurzbach in Sprenger, *Groß-Rosen*, pp. 263ff.
97. Cited in Sprenger, *Groß-Rosen*, p. 282.
98. Ibid. p. 284.

## Living With a Past in Hiding

1. The value of incorporating the post-1945 period has been marvellously demonstrated recently by an autobiographical account, sadly not yet available in English: Ruth Klüger, *Weiterleben*.

2. The literature about Holocaust survivors is vast. Texts cited in this chapter are Martin S. Bergmann, Milton E Jucovy and Judith S. Kestenberg (eds.), *Kinder der Opfer. Kinder der Täter* (Fischer, Frankfurt am Main, 1995); Bruno Bettelheim, *Surviving the Holocaust* (Flamingo, London, 1986); Cathy Caruth (ed.), *Trauma: Explorations in Memory* (Johns Hopkins University Press, Baltimore, 1995); Israel Charny (ed.), *Holding on to Humanity: the Message of Holocaust Survivors: the Shamai Davidson Papers* (New York University Press, New York, 1992); Shoshana Feldman and Dori Laub, *Testimony: Crises of Witnessing in Literature, Psychoanalysis and History* (Routledge, London, 1992); Roger S. Gottlieb, *Thinking the Unthinkable: Meanings of the Holocaust* (Paulist Press, New York, 1990); Henry Greenspan, *On Listening to Holocaust Survivors: Recounting and Life History* (Praeger, Westport, Conn., 1998); Geoffrey Hartmann (ed.), *Holocaust and Remembrance – the Shapes of Memory* (Blackwell, Oxford, 1995); Lawrence L. Langer, *Holocaust Testimonies: the Ruins of Memory* (Yale University Press, New Haven, 1991); Dalia Ofer and Lenore J. Weitzman (eds.), *Women in the Holocaust* (Yale University Press, New Haven and London, 1998); Gabriele Rosenthal (ed.), *The Holocaust in Three Generations: Families of Victims and Perpetrators of the Nazi Regime* (Cassell, London and Washington, DC, 1998).

3. Interview, ME, 31.10.1996.

4. Ibid.

5. RW to ME, 13.1.1950.

6. Interview, Sol and Clara Bender, Chester, 17.10.1997; interview, Monte and Phyllis Miller, Liverpool 17.10.1997.

7. Interview, Monte and Phyllis Miller, Liverpool 17.10.1997.

8. See Marion Berghahn's sensitive exploration, *German-Jewish Refugees in England: the Ambiguities of Assimilation* (Macmillan, London and New York, 1984), esp. pp. 173ff; Rebekka Göpfert, *Der jüdische Kindertransport von Deutschland nach England 1938/9* (Campus, Frankfurt am Main and New York, 1999), pp. 186ff; on the pressures on wartime German-Jewish refugees to be English, Kushner, *Holocaust and the Liberal Imagination*, pp. 57ff.

9. Berghahn too talks about the way the diffuseness of British identities allowed German-Jewish refugees to feel both at home and 'cosmopolitan'. Berghahn, *German-Jewish Refugees*, p. 176.

10. Interviews David and Sandra Gray, London, 30.1.1999; Jane Dalton, née Gray, 6.2.1999.

11. Interviews, VE, 5.12.1997; David and Sandra Gray, 30.1.1999; Jane Dalton, 6.2.1999.

12. Marianne told the Millers that she went back to Germany and went into the fish shop where her parents used to shop. The owner nearly collapsed at seeing her. Interview, Monte and Phyllis Miller, Liverpool 17.10.1997. But I do not know if this was in the immediate post-war years or later.

13. Interview, ME, 31.10.1996.

14. MS to Düsseldorf Vollzugsausschuß der rassisch, politisch und religiös Verfolgten in Düsseldorf, 12.9.1945.

15. Interview, ME, 31.10.1996.

16. CH to ME, 21.2.1958, annex: 'Übersicht über die Entschädigungs- und Rückerstattungssachen der Frau Marianne Ellenbogen'.

17. This was inapplicable, as it turned out, since this particular claim could not be inherited.

18. This was a common dilemma. See Berghahn, *German-Jewish Refugees*, p. 208.

19. Copy, ME to CH, 9.1.1956 [sic = 1957].

20. CH to ME, 4.6.1957.

21. Copy, ME to CH, 8.6.1957.

22. Copy, Regierungspräsident 14 I, vol ZK 620 480, Teilbescheid in der Entschädigungssache der Frau Marianne Ellenbogen, 5.12.1957.

23. Copy, CH to LGD Entschädigungskammer, 13.12.1957.

24. Copy, '*Persönlich!*', ME to Hermann, 28.12.1957; ME to CH, 3.2.1958, annex: Eidesstattliche Versicherung.

25. G. Meyer to ME, 21.1.1952.

26. Copy of letter, ME to G. Meyer, 18.9.1952; copy of letter G. Meyer to Schroetter, 18.9.1952.

27. Interview, ME, 31.10.1996.

28. AfWGE, Eing. 12.10.1950, In der Wiedergutmachungssache Strauss ./. Jürgens, Geschäftsnummer Rü 1190/50, signed Maria Jürgens.

29. Bettelheim, *Surviving*, p. 37.

30. This is not to argue that the camps brought out only selfishness – as Bettelheim movingly shows.

31. See Charny, *Shamai Davidson Papers*, p. 35.

32. Interview, ME, 10.9.1996.

33. Friedhelm Böll, 'Halblar o callar sobre la persecucion nazi en Alemania', *Historia Antropologia y Fuentes Orales*, vol. 20 (1998), no. 2, pp. 45–52.

34. See Dori Laub, 'Truth and testimony: the process and the struggle', in Caruth, *Trauma*, pp. 61–75, at p. 68.

35. See 'Trauma and reintegration', in Bettelheim, *Surviving*, pp. 31–48.

36. Langer, *Holocaust Testimonies*, p. xv.

37. Interview, ME, 10.9.1996.

38. Written notes off the tape, interview, ME 31.10.1996.

39. Unfinished letter, ME to Sonja [Schreiber], Hanni [Ganzer] and Else [Bramesfeld], 11.6.1968

40. Interview, VE, 5.12.1997.

41. Eating disorders are far from unknown among second-generation survivors, but there is no easy connection between the two syndromes. The literature on anorexia reveals how diverse its causes can be. On second-generation survivors, see Bergmann et al., *Kinder*; Shamai Davidson, 'The clinical effects of massive psychic trauma in families of Holocaust survivors', in *Journal of Marital and Family Therapy*, vol. 6 (1980), no. 1, pp. 11–21; Rosenthal, *Holocaust in Three Generations*. On anorexia, see R. L. Palmer, *Anorexia Nervosa: a Guide for Sufferers and their Families* (Penguin, Harmondsworth, 1989), p. 6; Hilde Bruch, *The Golden Cage: the Enigma of Anorexia Nervosa* (Open Books, London, 1978). I am also grateful to Helena Fox, a psychiatrist specializing in eating disorders, for information.

42. Hans-Josef Steinberg, *Widerstand und Verfolgung in Essen* (Hanover, 1969) referring to Günther Weisenborn, (ed.), *Der lautlose Aufstand. Bericht über die Widerstandsbewegung des deutschen Volkes 1933–1945*, (Rowohlt, Hamburg, 1953), pp. 102–103.

43. Copy, letter to US relatives (not named but clearly Hugo Strauss), 24.1.1946.

44. Interview, Sol and Clara Bender, Chester, 17.10.1997.

45. Written notes off the tape, interview, ME, 31.10.1996.

46. Interview, ME, 31.10.1996.

47. See Zygmunt Bauman, *Modernity and the Holocaust* (Polity Press, Cambridge, 1991); Mark Roseman, 'National Socialism and Modernisation', in Richard Bessel (ed.), *Fascist Italy and Nazi Germany: Comparisons and Contrasts* (Cambridge University Press, Cambridge, 1996), pp. 197–229.

48. Written notes, off the tape, interview, ME, 31.10.1996.

49. Marianne's relationship with Basil, for example, remained largely a mys-

tery to me, as did Basil himself. I could, of course, have asked his surviving relatives more questions but, given Marianne's strictures, it seemed wrong to do so. I am grateful, though, for the information provided by Gershon, Raymond and Michael Ellenbogen.

# Bibliography

The bibliography is restricted to works cited in the text. Interview partners and archives consulted are listed in the acknowledgements. Unpublished sources listed in the endnotes with no archival attribution are Marianne's own papers.

*50 Jahre Jubiläum der Schüler der Israelitischen Gartenbauschule Ahlem* (no date, no place) (held in Wiener library, London)

Adler, Hans-Günther, *Theresienstadt 1941–1945. Das Antlitz einer Zwangsgemeinschaft. Geschichte. Soziologie. Psychologie* (J. C. B. Mohr/Paul Siebeck, Tübingen, 1955)

— *Der Verwaltete Mensch. Studien zur Deportation der Juden aus Deutschland* (J. C. B. Mohr/Paul Siebeck, Tübingen, 1974)

Alte Synagoge, Essen (ed.), *Essen unter Bomben: Märztage 1943* (Klartext, Essen, 1984)

— *Stationen jüdischen Lebens. Von der Emanzipation bis zur Gegenwart* (Verlag J. W. Dietz Nachf, Bonn, 1990)

— *Jüdisches Leben in Essen 1800–1933* (Klartext, Essen, 1993)

— *Entrechtung und Selbsthilfe. Zur Geschichte der Juden in Essen unter dem Nationalsozialismus* (Klartext, Essen, 1994)

Andreas, Nachama and Julius H. Schoeps (eds.), *Aufbau nach dem Untergang. Deutsch-Jüdische Geschichte nach 1945* (Argon Verlag, Berlin, 1992)

Angress, Werner T., 'Jüdische Jugend zwischen nationalsozialistischer Verfolgung und jüdischer Wiedergeburt', in Arnold Paucker (ed.), *Die Juden im nationalsozialistischen Deutschland* (J. C. B. Mohr/Paul Siebeck, Tübingen, 1986), pp. 211–232

Arad, Yitzhak, *Belzec, Sobibor, Treblinka – the Operation Reinhard Death Camps* (Indiana University Press, Bloomington, 1987)

Barkai, Avraham, 'Die sozio-ökonomische Situation der Juden in Rheinland und Westfalen zur Zeit der Industrialisierung (1850–1914)', in Kurt Düwell and Wolfgang Köllmann (eds.), *Rheinland-Westfalen im Industriezeitalter*, vol. 2, *Von der Reichsgründung bis zur Weimarer Republik* (Peter Hammer, Wuppertal, 1984), pp. 86–106

— *From Boycott to Annihilation. The Economic Struggle of German Jews, 1933–1943* (University Press of New England, Hanover, 1989), pp. 99–100

Bar-On, Daniel, *Legacy of Silence: Encounters with Children of the Third Reich* (Harvard University Press, Cambridge, Mass, 1989)

Bauman, Zygmunt, *Modernity and the Holocaust* (Polity Press, Cambridge, 1991)

Becker-Jakli, Barbara (ed.), *Ich habe Köln doch so geliebt. Lebensgeschichten jüdischer Kölnerinnen und Kölner* (Volksblatt Verlag, Cologne, 1993)

Benz, Wolfgang, 'Zielsetzung und Maßnahmen der deutschen Judenverfolgung', in Jörg K. Hoensch, Stanislav Biman and L'ubomir Lipták (eds.), *Judenemanzipation, Antisemitismus, Verfolgung* (Klartext, Essen, 1999), pp. 131–141

Berding, Helmut, 'Antisemitismus in der modernen Gesellschaft: Kontinuität und Diskontinuität', in Hoensch et al., *Judenemanzipation*, pp. 85–100

Berghahn, Marion, *German-Jewish Refugees in England: the Ambiguities of Assimilation* (Macmillan, London and New York, 1984)

Bergmann, Martin S., Milton E. Jucovy and Judith S. Kestenberg (eds.), *Kinder der Opfer. Kinder der Täter* (Fischer, Frankfurt am Main, 1995)

Bethge, Eberhard, *Dietrich Bonhoeffer. Theologe. Christ. Zeitgenosse* (Chr. Kaiser Verlag, Munich, 1967)

Bettelheim, Bruno, *Surviving the Holocaust* (Flamingo, London, 1986)

Bilstein, Jochen and Frieder Backhaus, *Geschichte der Remscheider Juden* (Wermelskirchen, 1992)

Blasius, Dirk and Dan Diner (eds.), *Zerbrochene Geschichte. Leben und Selbstverständnis der Juden in Deutschland* (Fischer Taschenbuch Verlag, Frankfurt am Main, 1991)

Blatt, Thomas Toivi, *From the Ashes of Sobibor: a story of survival* (Northwestern University Press, Evanston, Ill., 1997)

Böll, Friedhelm, 'Halblar o callar sobre la persecucion nazi en Alemania', *Historia Antropologia y Fuentes Orales*, vol. 20 (1998), no. 2, pp. 45–52

Borsdorf, Ulrich and Mathilde Jamin (eds), *Überleben im Krieg. Kriegserfahrungen in einer Industrieregion 1939–1945* (Rowohlt, Hamburg, 1989)

Bramesfeld, Else, Doris Braune et al. (eds), *Gelebte Utopie: Aus dem Leben einer Gemeinschaft, Nach einer Dokumentation von Dore Jacobs* (Klartext, Essen, 1990)

Brenner, Michael, *The Renaissance of Jewish Culture in Weimar Germany* (Yale University Press, New Haven, 1996)

— *Nach dem Holocaust. Juden in Deutschland 1945–1950*, (Beck, Munich, 1995)

Burgauer, Erica, *Zwischen Erinnerung und Verdrängung – Juden in Deutschland nach 1945* (Rohwohlts Enzyklopädie, Rheinbek, 1993)

Brewer, W. F., 'What is biographical memory?', in D. C. Rubin (ed.), *Autobiographical Memory* (Cambridge University Press, Cambridge, 1988), pp. 25–49

Bruch, Hilde, *The Golden Cage: the Enigma of Anorexia Nervosa* (Open Books, London, 1978)

Bundesleitung des Jüdischen Pfadfinderbundes Makkabi Hazair (ed.), *Unser Weg zum Volk. Ein Beitrag zur Ideologie des Makkabi Hazair* (Berlin, 1936)

— *Unser Weg im Zionismus. Eine Sammelschrift des jüdischen Pfadfinderbundes Makkabi Hazair* (Berlin, no date)

Burrin, Phillippe, *Hitler and the Jews: the Genesis of the Holocaust* (Edward Arnold, London, 1994)

Büttner, Ursula (ed.), *Not nach der Befreiung. Die Situation der deutschen Juden in der britischen Besatzungszone 1945–1948* (Hamburg, 1986)

— *Die Deutschen und die Judenverfolgung im Dritten Reich* (Hamburg, 1992)

Caruth, Cathy (ed.), *Trauma: Explorations in Memory* (Johns Hopkins University Press, Baltimore, 1995)

— *Unclaimed Experience: Trauma, Narrative and History* (Johns Hopkins University Press, Baltimore and London, 1996)

Charny, Israel (ed.), *Holding on to Humanity: the Message of Holocaust Survivors: the Shamai Davidson Papers* (New York University Press, New York, 1992)

Chowaniec, Elisabeth, Der *'Fall Dohnanyi' 1943–1945* (R. Oldenbourg Verlag, Munich, 1991)

Conway, M. A. et al. (eds.), *Theoretical Perspectives on Autobiographical Memory* (Kluwer Academic Press, Dordrecht, 1992)

Corbach, Dieter, *Die Jawne zu Köln. Zur Geschichte des ersten jüdischen Gymnasiums im Rheinland und zum Gedächtnis an Erich Klibansky 1900–1942* (Scriba Verlag, Cologne, 1990)

Czech, Danuta, *Kalendarium der Ereignisse im Konzentrationslager Auschwitz Birkenau 1939–1945* (Rowohlt, Hamburg, 1989)

Davidson, Shamai, 'The clinical effects of massive psychic trauma in families of Holocaust survivors', *Journal of Marital and Family Therapy*, vol. 6 (1980), no. 1, pp. 11–21

Davidson, Shamai (ed.), *Holding on to Humanity – the Message of Holocaust Survivors* (New York University Press, New York, 1992)

Der Bund. Gemeinschaft für sozialistisches Leben (eds.), *Aus der illegalen Arbeit des Bunds. Zweiter Auslandsbrief* (printed pamphlet, 1948)

— *Leben in der Illegalität. Dritter Auslandsbrief* (printed pamphlet, 1948)

Deutschkron, Inge, *Ich trug den gelben Stern* (Deutsche Taschenbuch-Verlag, Munich, 1995), translated as *Outcast: a Jewish Girl in Wartime Berlin* (Fromm International, New York, 1989)

Dietz, Edith, *Den Nazis entronnen. Die Flucht eines jüdischen Mädchens in die Schweiz. Autobiographischer Bericht 1933–1942* (Dipa Verlag, Frankfurt am Main, 1990)

Dippel, John, *Bound Upon a Wheel of Fire: Why Leading Jews Stayed in Nazi Germany* (Basic Books, New York, 1996)

Dressen, Wolfgang, *Betrifft: 'Aktion 3'. Deutsche verwerten jüdische Nachbarn* (Aufbau Verlag, Berlin, 1998)

Düwell, Kurt, *Die Rheingebiete in der Judenpolitik des Nationalsozialismus vor 1942* (Ludwig Röhrscheid Verlag, Bonn, 1968)

Dwork, Deborah and Robert Jan van Pelt, *Auschwitz: 1270 to the Present* (W. W. Norton, New York and London, 1996)

Elias, Ruth, *Triumph of Hope. From Theresienstadt and Auschwitz to Israel* (John Wiley & Sons, New York, 1998)

Ellenbogen, Marianne, 'Flucht und illegales Leben während der Nazi-Verfolgungsjahre 1943–1954', *Das Münster am Hellweg*, vol. 37 (1984), pp. 135–142

Eschelbacher, Max, *Der zehnte November 1938* (Klartext, Essen, 1998)

Faust, Anselm, *Die 'Kristallnacht' im Rheinland. Dokumente zum Judenpogrom im November 1938* (Schwann, Düsseldorf, 1987)

Feldman, Shoshana and Dori Laub, *Testimony: Crises of Witnessing in Literature, Psychoanalysis and History* (Routledge, London, 1992)

Gottlieb, Roger S., *Thinking the Unthinkable: Meanings of the Holocaust* (Paulist Press, New York, 1990)

Fischer, Erica, *Aimée & Jaguar: a Love Story, Berlin 1943* (paperback edn, Bloomsbury, London, 1996)

Fischler-Martinho, Janina, *Have You Seen My Little Sister?* (Valentine, Mitchell, London and Portland, Oreg., 1998)

Friedländer, Saul, 'Political transformations during the war and their effect on the Jewish question', in Herbert A. Strauss (ed.), *Hostages of Modernisation. Studies on Modern Anti-Semitism 1870–1933/39, Germany–Great*

*Britain–France* (Walter de Gruyter, New York and London, 1993), pp. 150–164

— *Nazi Germany and the Jews: the Years of Persecution 1933–1939* (Pheonix Giant, London, 1997)

Fritzsche, Peter, *Germans into Nazis* (Harvard University Press, Cambridge, Mass., 1998)

*Gedenkbuch Opfer der Verfolgung der Juden* (Bundesarchiv Koblenz, 1986).

Gellately, Robert, *The Gestapo and German Society* (Oxford University Press, Oxford 1990)

Genger, Angela, 'Hakoah – Die Kraft. Ein jüdischer Turn- und Sportverein in Essen', in Alte Synagoge (ed.), *Zwischen Alternative und Protest. Zu Sport- und Jugendbewegungen in Essen 1900–1933* (Exhibition catalogue, Essen, 1983), pp. 8–25

Gershon, Karen, *Postscript: a Collective Account of the Lives of Jews in West Germany Since the Second World War* (Victor Gollancz, London, 1969)

Gilbert, Martin, *The Macmillan Atlas of the Holocaust* (Macmillan, New York, 1982)

— 'What was known and when', in Gutman and Berenbaum, *Anatomy*, pp. 539–552

Gill, Anton, *The Journey Back from Hell. Conversations with Concentration Camp Survivors* (HarperCollins, London, 1989)

Göpfert, Rebekka, *Der jüdische Kindertransport von Deutschland nach England 1938/39. Geschichte und Erinnerung* (Campus Verlag, Frankfurt and New York, 1999)

Goldhagen, Daniel J., *Hitler's Willing Executioners. Ordinary Germans and the Holocaust* (Abacus, London, 1997)

Greenspan, Henry, *On Listening to Holocaust Survivors: Recounting and Life History* (Praeger, Westport, Conn., 1998)

Gruner, Wolf, *Judenverfolgung in Berlin 1933–1945. Eine Chronologie der Behördenmaßnahmen in der Reichshauptstadt* (Edition Hentrich, Berlin, 1996)

Grüter, Monika, 'Der "Bund für ein sozialistisches Leben": Seine Entwicklung in den 20er Jahren und seine Widerständigkeit unter dem Nationalsozialismus' (Examensarbeit, University of Essen, 1988)

Gummersbach, Hans W., 'Sozialhistorische und soziologische Forschungen zur jüdischen Minderheit in der westfälischen Stadt Ahlen vor und während der Zeit des Nationalsozialismus unter besonderer Berücksichtigung lebensgeschichtlicher Selbstzeugnisse' (PhD, University of Paderborn, 1996)

Gurewitsch, Bonnie, *Mothers, Sisters, Resisters: Oral Histories of Women*

*Who Survived the Holocaust* (University of Alabama Press, Tuscaloosa and London, 1998)

Gutman, Israel (ed.), *Encyclopaedia of the Holocaust* (Macmillan, London 1990)

— *Resistance. The Warsaw Ghetto Uprising* (Mariner Books, Boston and New York, 1994)

Gutman, Israel and Michael Berenbaum (eds.), *Anatomy of the Auschwitz Death Camp* (Indiana University Press, Bloomington and Indianapolis, 1994)

Hannam, Charles, *A Boy in Your Situation* (Adlib Paperbacks/André Deutsch, London, 1988)

Hartmann, Geoffrey (ed.), *Holocaust and Remembrance – the Shapes of Memory* (Blackwell, Oxford, 1995)

Henschel, Hildegard, 'Gemeindearbeit und Evakuierung von Berlin', in *Zeitschrift für die Geschichte der Juden* (Tel Aviv), vol.9 (1972), nos. 1/2, pp. 33–53

Hetkamp, Jutta, *Die jüdische Jugendbewegung in Deutschland von 1913–1933* (Münster and Hamburg, Lit, 1994)

Hilberg, Raul, *Die Vernichtung der europäischen Juden* (Fischer, Frankfurt am Main, 1993)

Höhne, Heinz, 'Canaris und die Abwehr zwischen Anpassung und Opposition', in Jürgen Schmädeke and Peter Steinbach (eds.), *Der Widerstand gegen den Nationalsozialismus* (Munich and Zurich, 1985), pp. 405–416

Hoensch, Jörg K., Stanislav Biman and L'ubomír Lipták (eds.), *Judenemanzipation, Antisemitismus, Verfolgung* (Klartext, Essen, 1999)

Hüttenberger, Peter, *Düsseldorf. Geschichte von den Anfängen bis ins 20. Jahrhundert*, vol 3, *Die Industrie- und Verwaltungsstadt* (Schwann, Düsseldorf, 1989)

Internationaler Suchdienst, Arolsen, *Vorläufiges Verzeichnis der Haftstätten unter dem Reichsführer-SS 1933–1945* (1969)

Jacob, Lisa, ' "Der Bund", Gemeinschaft für sozialistisches Leben und meine Rettung vor der Deportation', *Das Münster am Hellweg*, vol. 37 (1984), pp. 105–134

Jacobs, Artur, *Die Zukunft des Glaubens. Die Entscheidungsfrage unserer Zeit* (Europäische Verlagsanstalt, Frankfurt am Main, 1971)

Jacobson, Kenneth, *Embattled Selves: an Investigation into the Nature of Identity, Through Oral Histories of Holocaust Survivors* (Atlantic Monthly Press, New York, 1994)

Kamp, Meta, *Auf der anderen Seite stehen*, (privately published, Göttingen, 1987)

Kaplan, Marion, *The Jewish Feminist Movement in Germany* (Greenwood Press, New York, 1979)

— 'Tradition and transition: the acculturation, assimilation and integration of Jews in Imperial Germany: a Gender Analysis', *Leo Baeck Institute Year Book*, vol. 27 (1982), pp. 3–36

— 'Jewish women in Nazi Germany: daily life, daily struggles, 1933–39', in Peter Freimark, Alice Jankowski and Ina S. Lorenz (eds.), *Juden in Deutschland: Emanzipation, Integration, Verfolgung und Vernichtung* (H. Christians Verlag, Hamburg, 1991), pp. 406–434

— *Between Dignity and Despair: Jewish Life in Nazi Germany* (Oxford University Press, New York and Oxford, 1998)

Karny, Miroslav, 'The Vrba and Wetzler Report', in Gutman and Berenbaum, *Anatomy*, pp. 553–568

Karski, Jan, *Story of a Secret State* (Boston, Houghton Mifflin, 1944)

Kauders, Anthony, *German Politics and the Jews: Düsseldorf and Nuremberg, 1910–1933* (Clarendon Press, Oxford, 1996)

Keren, Nils, 'The family camp', in Gutman and Berenbaum, *Anatomy*, pp. 428–441

Klemperer, Viktor, *Ich will Zeugnis ablegen bis zum letzten*, vol. 1, *Tagebücher 1933 – 1941*; vol. 2, *Tagebücher 1942–1945* (Aufbau-Verlag, Berlin, 1995)

Klüger, Ruth, *Weiter leben. Eine Jugend* (Wallstein, Göttingen, 1992)

Kogon, Eugen, *Der SS-Staat. Das System der deutschen Konzentrationslager* (21$^{st}$ edn, Wilhelm Heyne Verlag, Munich, 1989)

Konieczny, Alfred (ed.), *Die Völker Europas im KL Groß-Rosen* (Staatliches Museum Groß-Rosen, Walbrzych, 1995)

Kulka, Otto Dov, 'Ghetto in an annihilation camp. Jewish social history in the Holocaust period and its ultimate limits', in *The Nazi Concentration Camps: Proceedings of the Fourth Yad Vashem International Historical Conference Jerusalem, January 1980* (Yad Vashem; Jerusalem 1984), pp. 315–330

— *Deutsches Judentum unter dem Nationalsozialismus, vol. 1, Dokumente zur Geschichte der Reichsvertretung der deutschen Juden 1933–1939* (Mohr Siebeck, Tübingen, 1997)

Kushner, Tony, *The Holocaust and the Liberal Imagination: a Social and Cultural History* (Blackwell, Oxford and Cambridge, Mass., 1994)

Kwiet, Konrad and Helmut Eschwege, *Selbstbehauptung und Widerstand: Deutsche Juden im Kampf um Existenz und Menschenwürde 1933–1945* (Hans Christians Verlag, Hamburg, 1984)

Laak, Dirk von, ' "Wenn einer ein Herz im Leibe hat, der läßt sich von einem deutschen Arzt behandeln". Die "Entjudung" der Essener Wirtschaft von 1933 bis 1941', in Alte Synagoge, *Entrechtung*, pp. 12–30

Langer, Lawrence L., *Holocaust Testimonies: the Ruins of Memory* (Yale University Press, New Haven 1991)

Laub, Dori, 'Truth and testimony: the process and the struggle,' in Caruth, *Trauma* pp. 61–75

Link, Werner, *Die Geschichte des Internationalen Jugend-Bundes und des Internationalen Sozialistischen Kampf-Bundes. Ein Beitrag zur Geschichte der Arbeiterbewegung in der Weimarer Republik und im 3. Reich* (Meisenheim am Glan, 1964)

Littmann-Hotopp, Ingrid, *Bei Dir findet das verlassene Kind Erbarmen. Zur Geschichte des ersten jüdischen Säuglings– und Kleinkinderheims in Deutschland (1907 bis 1942)* (Edition Hentrich, Berlin, 1996)

Lowenthal, E. G., *Bewährung im Untergang Ein Gedenkbuch* (Deutsche Verlags-Anstalt, Stuttgart, 1965)

Lütkemeier, Hildegard, 'Einrichtungen der Jugendwohlfahrt für Kinder im Vorschulalter in jüdischer Trägerschaft in Deutschland 1919–1933' (Hausarbeit, Erziehungswisenschaft, Universität Dortmund, 1991)

Maurer, Trude, *Die Entwicklung der jüdischen Minderheit in Deutschland. Neuere Forschungen und offene Fragen* (Niemeyer, Tübingen, 1992)

— 'Reife Bürger der Republik und bewußte Juden: die jüdische Minderheit in Deutschland 1918–1933', in Hoensch et al., *Judenemanzipation*, pp. 101–116

Meyer, Winfried, *Unternehmen Sieben. Eine Rettungsaktion für vom Holocaust Bedrohte aus dem Amt Ausland/Abwehr im Oberkommando der Wehrmacht* (Verlag Anton Hain, Frankfurt am Main, 1993)

Niemann, Ingrid and Ludger Hülskemper Niemann, *Vom Geleitbrief zum gelben Stern. 450 Jahre jüdisches Leben in Steele* (Klartext, Essen, 1994)

Niewyk, Donald L., *The Jews in Weimar Germany* (Manchester University Press, Manchester, 1980)

NS-Documentationszentrum der Stadt Köln (eds.), *Die jüdischen Opfer des Nationalsozialismus aus Köln. Gedenkbuch* (Böhlau Verlag, Cologne, 1995)

Ofer, Dalia, and Lenore J. Weitzman (eds.), *Women in the Holocaust* (Yale University Press, New Haven and London, 1998)

Oliner, Samuel P., *The Altruistic Personality: Rescuers of Jews in Nazi Europe* (The Free Press, New York, 1998)

Palmer, Robert L., *Anorexia Nervosa: a Guide for Sufferers and their Families* (Penguin, Harmondsworth, 1989)

Patkin, Benzion, *The Dunera Internees* (Cassell, Stanmore, N. S. W, 1979)

Paucker, Arnold, 'Zum Selbstverständnis jüdischer Jugend in der Weimarer Republik und unter der nationalsozialistischen Diktatur', in Hans Otto Horch and Charlotte Wardi (eds.), *Jüdische Selbstwahrnehmung. La Prise de conscience de l'identité juive* (Max Niemeyer Verlag, Tübingen, 1977), pp. 111–128

Pohl, Dieter, *Von der 'Judenpolitik' zum Judenmord: der Distrikt Lublin des Generalgouvernements 1939–1944* (Lang, Frankfurt am Main, 1993)

Richarz, Monika, *Jewish Life in Germany: Memoirs from Three Centuries* (Indiana University Press; Bloomington and Indianapolis, 1991)

Röcher, Ruth, *Die jüdische Schule im nationalsozialistischen Deutschland 1933–1942* (Dipa, Frankfurt am Main, 1992)

Rohr, Walter, 'Die Geschichte meines Lebens', in Ernst Schmidt, 'Walter Rohr – 1938 aus Essen vertrieben, 1945 als US-Soldat zurückgekehrt', in Alte Synagoge, *Entrechtung*, pp. 98–117

Rohrlich, Ruby (ed.), *Resisting the Holocaust* (Berg, Oxford, 1998)

Roseman, Mark, 'National socialism and modernisation', in Richard Bessel (ed.), *Fascist Italy and Nazi Germany: Comparisons and Contrasts* (Cambridge University Press, Cambridge, 1996), pp. 197–229

— 'The organic society and the Massenmenschen: integrating young labour in the Ruhr mines 1945–1958', in Robert Moeller (ed.), *West Germany under Construction: Politics, Society, and Culture in the Adenauer Era* (University of Michigan Press, Ann Arbor, 1997), pp. 287–320

— 'Erinnerung und Überleben: Wahrheit und Widerspruch in dem Zeugnis einer Holocaust-Überlebenden', *BIOS*, vol. 11 (1998), no. 2, pp. 263–279

Rosenthal, Gabriele (ed.), *The Holocaust in Three Generations: Families of Victims and Perpetrators of the Nazi Regime* (Cassell, London and Washington, DC, 1998)

Rürup, Reinhard, 'Jüdische Geschichte in Deutschland. Von der Emanzipation bis zur nationalsozialistischen Gewaltherrschaft', in Blasius and Diner, *Zerbrochene Geschichte*, pp. 79–101

— *Emanzipation und Antisemitismus. Studien zur 'Judenfrage' der bürgerlichen Gesellschaft* (Vandenhoeck & Ruprecht, Göttingen, 1992)

Sachse, Carola (ed.), *Als Zwangsarbeiterin 1941 in Berlin: die Aufzeichnungen der Volkswirtin Elisabeth Freund* (Akademie Verlag, Berlin, 1996)

Schmalhausen, Bernd, *Schicksale jüdischer Juristen aus Essen 1933–1945* (Klartext, Essen, 1994)

Schröter, Hermann, *Geschichte und Schicksal der Essener Juden. Gedenkbuch für die jüdischen Mitbürger der Stadt Essen* (City of Essen, Essen, 1980)

Schwarz, Gudrun, *Die nationalsozialistischen Lager* (revised edn, Fischer, Frankfurt am Main; 1996)

Simon, Hermann, *Das Berliner Jüdische Museum in der Oranienburgerstraße. Geschichte einer zerstörten Kulturstätte* (Stadtgeschichtliche Publikationen II ed., Berlin Museum, Berlin 1983)

Sophoni Herz, Yitzhak, *Meine Erinnerung an Bad Homburg und seine 600jährige jüdische Gemeinde (1335–1942)* (privately printed, Rechovoth (Israel), 1981)

Sprenger, Isabel, *Groß-Rosen. Ein Konzentrationslager in Schlesien* (Böhlau Verlag, Cologne, Weimar and Vienna, 1996)

Staatliches Museum Auschwitz-Birkenau (ed.), *Sterbebücher von Auschwitz. Fragmente*, vols. 1 and 2 (Verlag K. G. Sauer, Munich, London, Paris etc., 1995)

Steinberg, Hans-Josef, *Widerstand und Verfolgung in Essen* (Hanover, 1969)

Stern, Frank, *Am Anfang war Auschwitz. Antisemitismus und Philosemitismus im deutschen Nachkrieg* (Bleicher Verlag, Gerlingen, 1991)

Strohm, Christoph, *Theologische Ethik im Kampf gegen den Nationalsozialismus. Der Weg Dietrich Bonhoeffers mit den Juristen Hans von Dohnanyi und Gerhard Leibholz in den Widerstand* (Christian Kaiser, Munich, 1989)

Tec, Nechama, *When Light Pierced the Darkness: Christian Rescue of Jews in Nazi-Occupied Poland* (Oxford University Press, New York and Oxford, 1986)

Tohermes, Kurt and Jürgen Grafen, *Leben und Untergang der Synagogengemeinde Dinslaken* (Verein für Heimatpflege 'Land Dinslaken' e.V., Dinslaken, 1988)

Vrba, Rudolf and Alan Bestic, *I Cannot Forgive* (Sidwick & Jackson/Anthony Gibbs and Phillips, London, 1963)

Walk, Joseph, *Das Sonderrecht für die Juden im NS-Staat* (C. F. Müller, Heidelberg, 1981)

— 'Das jüdische Schulwesen in Köln bis 1942', in Jutta Bohnke-Kollwitz, Willehad Paul Eckert, Frank Golsczewski and Hermann Greive (eds.), *Köln und das rheinische Judentum. Festschrift Germania Judaica 1959–1984* (Cologne, 1984), pp. 415–426

— *Jüdische Schule und Erziehung im Dritten Reich* (Verlag Anton Hain, Frankfurt am Main, 1991)

Weisenborn, Günther (ed.), *Der lautlose Aufstand. Bericht über die Widerstandsbewegung des deutschen Volkes 1933–1945* (Rowohlt, Hamburg, 1953)

Wiesemann, Falk, 'Jewish burials in Germany – between the Enlightenment and the authorities', *Leo Baeck Institute Year Book*, vol. 37 (1992), pp. 17–31

Wood, E. Thomas, and Stanislaw M. Jankowski, *Karski: How One Man Tried to Stop the Holocaust* (John Wiley & Sons, New York, 1994)

Zabecki, Franciszek, *Wspomnienia dawne i nowe* (Warsaw, 1977)

Zimmermann, Michael, 'Die Deportation der Juden aus Essen und dem Regierungsbezirk Düsseldorf', in Borsdorf and Jamin, *Überleben im Krieg*, pp. 126–143

— 'Die Assimilation und ihre Relativierung. Zur Geschichte der Essener jüdischen Gemeinde vor 1933', in Blasius and Diner, *Zerbrochene Geschichte*, pp. 172–186

— 'Zur Geschichte der Essener Juden im 19. und im ersten Drittel des 20. Jahrhunderts. Ein Überblick', in Alte Synagoge, *Jüdisches Leben in Essen 1800–1933*, pp. 8–72

— 'Eine Deportation nach Theresienstadt. Zur Rolle des Banalen bei der Durchsetzung des Monströsen', in Miroslav Karney, Raimund Kemper et al. (eds.), *Theresienstädter Studien und Dokumente* (Edition Theresienstädter Initiative Academia, 1994), pp. 54–73

— 'Die "Reichskristallnacht" 1938 in Essen', in Alte Synagoge, *Entrechtung*, pp. 66–97

Zimmermann, Moshe, 'Vom Jischuw zum Staat – die Bedeutung des Holocaust für das kollektive Bewußtsein und die Politik in Israel', in Bernd Faulenbach and Helmut Schütte (eds.), *Deutschland, Israel und der Holocaust. Zur Gegenwartsbedeutung der Vergangenheit* (Klartext, Essen 1998), pp. 45–54

# Index

# The Medical Basis of Psychiatry

**GEORGE WINOKUR, M.D.**

The Paul W. Penningroth Professor and Head,
Department of Psychiatry
The University of Iowa, Iowa City, Iowa

**PAULA CLAYTON, M.D.**

Professor and Head, Department of Psychiatry,
University of Minnesota Medical School,
Minneapolis, Minnesota

1986

W. B. SAUNDERS COMPANY

Philadelphia, London, Toronto, Mexico City, Rio de Janeiro, Sydney, Tokyo, Hong Kong

W. B. Saunders Company:    West Washington Square
                           Philadelphia, PA 19105

**Library of Congress Cataloging-in-Publication Data**

The Medical basis of psychiatry.

  1. Psychiatry.  2. Biological psychiatry.
I. Winokur, George.   II. Clayton, Paula J., 1934–
[DNLM: 1. Mental Disorders.  2. Psychopathology.
WM 100 M4883]
RC454.M335  1986        616.89        86-1739
ISBN 0-7216-1306-3

*Editor:*  William Lamsback

*Production Manager:*  Frank Polizzano

*Manuscript Editor:*  Barbara Hodgson

*Illustration Coordinator:*  Kenneth Green

*Page Layout Artist:*  Joan Sinclair

*Indexer:*  Barbara Hodgson

The Medical Basis of Psychiatry                    ISBN   0-7216-1306-3

Last digit is the print number    9    8    7    6    5    4    3    2    1

# CONTRIBUTORS

GENE G. ABEL, M.D.

Department of Psychiatry, Emory University School of Medicine, Atlanta, Georgia

*Sexual Disorders*

RICHARD ABRAMS, M.D.

Professor of Psychiatry, University of Health Sciences/The Chicago Medical School; Consultant, North Chicago Veteran's Administration Medical Center, Chicago, Illinois

*Phenomenology of Coarse Brain Disease*

HAGOP SOUREN AKISKAL, M.D.

Professor of Psychiatry and Associate Professor of Pharmacology, University of Tennessee, Memphis; Director, Mood Clinic, Northeast Mental Health Center, Associate Director, Baptist Memorial Hospital Sleep Disorders Center, Memphis, Tennessee

*Mood Disturbances; Diagnosis in Psychiatry and Mental Status Examination*

NANCY C. ANDREASEN, M.D., Ph.D.

Professor of Psychiatry, University of Iowa College of Medicine, University of Iowa Hospitals and Clinics, Iowa City, Iowa

*Thought Disorder*

REMI CADORET, M.D.

Professor of Psychiatry, University of Iowa College of Medicine, University of Iowa Hospitals and Clinics, Iowa City, Iowa

*Antisocial Personality*

C. ROBERT CLONINGER, M.D.

Professor of Psychiatry and Genetics, Washington University Medical School; Attending Psychiatrist, Barnes and Jewish Hospitals, St. Louis, Missouri

*Somatoform and Dissociative Disorders*

WILLIAM CORYELL, M.D.

Professor of Psychiatry, University of Iowa College of Medicine, University of Iowa Hospitals and Clinics, Iowa City, Iowa

*Schizoaffective and Schizophreniform Disorders*

iii

THOMAS J. CRAIG, M.D., M.P.H.

Professor of Psychiatry and Behavioral Science, College of Medicine, State University of New York at Stony Brook; Staff Psychiatrist, State University Hospital at Stony Brook, Stony Brook, New York

*Epidemiology of Psychiatric Illness*

RAYMOND R. CROWE, M.D.

Professor of Psychiatry, University of Iowa College of Medicine, University of Iowa Hospitals and Clinics, Iowa City, Iowa

*Paranoid Disorders*

ELKE D. ECKERT, M.D.

Associate Professor of Psychiatry, University of Minnesota School of Medicine; Attending Psychiatrist, University of Minnesota Hospitals, Minneapolis, Minnesota

*Anorexia Nervosa and Bulimia*

SUSAN E. FOLSTEIN, M.D.

Associate Professor of Psychiatry, Johns Hopkins School of Medicine; Active Staff, Johns Hopkins Hospital, Baltimore, Maryland

*Emotional Disorders in Children*

BARRY D. GARFINKEL, M.D.

Associate Professor and Director, Child and Adolescent Psychiatry, University of Minnesota Medical School, Minneapolis, Minnesota

*Major Affective Disorders in Children and Adolescents*

ELLIOT S. GERSHON, M.D.

Chief, Clinical Neurogenetics Branch, National Institute of Mental Health, Bethesda, Maryland

*Genetics of Psychiatric Disorders*

LYNN R. GOLDIN, Ph.D.

Senior Staff Fellow, Clinical Neurogenetics Branch, National Institute of Mental Health, Bethesda, Maryland

*Genetics of Psychiatric Disorders*

DONALD W. GOODWIN, M.D.

Professor and Chairman, Department of Psychiatry, University of Kansas Medical School, Kansas City, Kansas

*Alcoholism*

FRITZ A. HENN, M.D., Ph.D.

Professor and Chairman, Department of Psychiatry and Behavioral Sciences, College of Medicine, State University of New York at Stony Brook; Psychiatrist in Chief, State University Hospital at Stony Brook, Stony Brook, New York

*The Neurobiologic Basis of Psychiatric Illnesses*

BARRY LISKOW, M.D.

Associate Professor of Psychiatry, University of Kansas Medical School; Chief Alcohol Dependence Treatment Unit, Kansas City Veterans Administration Medical Center, Kansas City, Missouri

*Alcoholism*

DOYNE W. LOYD, M.D.

Assistant Professor of Psychiatry, University of South Carolina School of Medicine; Chief of Consultation Liaison Psychiatry, Dorn Veterans Hospital, Columbia, South Carolina

*Schizophrenia*

THOMAS B. MACKENZIE, M.D.

Associate Professor of Psychiatry and Medicine, University of Minnesota Medical School; Attending Psychiatrist, University of Minnesota Hospitals, Minneapolis, Minnesota

*Obsessive-Compulsive Neurosis*

RONALD L. MARTIN, M.D.

Professor of Psychiatry, Vice Chairman for Education and Training, Director of Residency Training, University of Kansas School of Medicine; Attending Psychiatrist, University of Kansas Medical Center, Kansas City, Kansas

*Use of the Laboratory in Psychiatry*

JAMES E. MITCHELL, M.D.

Associate Professor of Psychiatry, University of Minnesota School of Medicine; Attending Psychiatrist, University of Minnesota Hospitals, Minneapolis, Minnesota

*Anorexia Nervosa and Bulimia*

GEORGE E. MURPHY, M.D.

Professor of Psychiatry, Washington University School of Medicine; Attending Psychiatrist, Barnes Hospital, St. Louis, Missouri

*Suicide and Attempted Suicide*

HENRY A. NASRALLAH, M.D.

Professor and Chairman, The Ohio State University College of Medicine; Attending Psychiatrist, The Ohio State University Hospitals, Columbus, Ohio

*Special and Unusual Psychiatric Syndromes*

RUSSELL NOYES, JR., M.D.

Professor of Psychiatry, University of Iowa College of Medicine; University of Iowa Hospitals and Clinics, Iowa City, Iowa

*Anxiety and Phobic Disorders*

JOHN I. NURNBERGER, JR., M.D., Ph.D.

Department of Psychiatry, Indiana University, Indianapolis, Indiana

*Genetics of Psychiatric Disorders*

BRUCE PFOHL, M.D.

Associate Professor and Director of Medical Student Training in Psychiatry, University of Iowa College of Medicine; University of Iowa Hospitals and Clinics, Iowa City, Iowa

*Personality Disorders*


MICHAEL K. POPKIN, M.D.

Professor of Psychiatry and Medicine, University of Minnesota Medical School; Director, Psychiatry Consultation Service, University of Minnesota Hospitals, Minneapolis, Minnesota

*The Organic Brain Syndromes Presenting with Little or No Cognitive Impairment; Organic Brain Syndromes Presenting with Global Cognitive Impairment: Delirium and Dementia*


SHELDON H. PRESKORN, M.D.

Professor and Vice Chairman of Psychiatry, University of Kansas School of Medicine— Wichita; Chief, Psychiatry Service, Wichita Veterans Administration Medical Center, Wichita, Kansas

*Use of the Laboratory in Psychiatry*


JOANNE L. ROULEAU, M.D.

Department of Psychiatry, Emory University, School of Medicine, Atlanta, Georgia

*Sexual Disorders*


FREDERICK S. SIERLES, M.D.

Associate Professor and Director, Medical Student Education in Psychiatry and Behavioral Science, University of Health Sciences/The Chicago Medical School; Staff Psychiatrist, Veterans Administration Medical Center, Chicago, Illinois

*Phenomenology of Coarse Brain Disease*


MARK A. STEWART, M.D.

Ida P. Haller Professor of Child Psychiatry, University of Iowa College of Medicine, Iowa City, Iowa

*Conduct Disorders and Hyperactivity*


MICHAEL ALAN TAYLOR, M.D.

Professor and Chairman, Department of Psychiatry and Behavioral Sciences, University of Health Sciences/The Chicago Medical School, Chicago, Illinois

*Motor Behavior; Phenomenology of Coarse Brain Disease*


LUKE Y. TSAI, M.D.

Professor of Child Psychiatry, University of Kansas School of Medicine; Director, Division of Child Psychiatry, University of Kansas Medical Center, Kansas City, Kansas

*Infantile Autism and Schizophrenia in Childhood*

MING T. TSUANG, M.D., Ph.D.

Professor of Psychiatry, Harvard Medical School and Director, Harvard Program in Psychiatric Epidemiology; Director of Psychiatric Epidemiology and Genetics, Harvard Medical School Department of Psychiatry, Massachusetts Mental Health Center; Chief of Psychiatry, Brockton/West Roxbury Veterans Administration Medical Center, Brockton, Massachusetts

*Schizophrenia*

CHARLES VAN VALKENBURG, M.D.

Consultant, Minneapolis Veterans Administration Medical Center, Minneapolis, Minnesota

*Anxiety Symptoms*

RAFIQ WAZIRI, M.D.

Associate Professor of Psychiatry, University of Iowa College of Medicine, Iowa City, Iowa

*The Amnestic Syndrome*

JOSEPH WESTERMEYER, M.D., Ph.D.

Professor of Psychiatry, Adjunct Professor of Anthropology and Psychology, University of Minnesota; Director of Alcohol–Drug Treatment Program, University of Minnesota Hospitals, Minneapolis, Minnesota

*Drug Abuse*

# PREFACE

One dictionary defines psychiatry as the branch of medicine that deals with mental, emotional, and behavioral disorders, but another defines it as the branch of medicine that relates to brain, gland, and nerve diseases. The one thing that the definitions have in common is that they both note that psychiatry is relevant to *diseases* or *disorders*. Psychiatry is a branch of medicine and a psychiatrist is a specialist in that field. The practice of psychiatry is related to the diagnosis and treatment of people with disorders that fit a definition of a medical illness and are associated with emotional or behavioral changes of sufficient severity as to cause a disruption of the person's life and behavior.

For practical purposes our definition of what constitutes a psychiatric illness is simply a medical illness with major emotional and behavioral aspects. The definition of an illness is always arguable, of course, but beyond that it is generally true that the study of medicine in the literature divides its presentation of illness and disease into a definition, epidemiology, signs and symptoms, etiology, and treatment. Because an overlap of symptoms occurs, there is usually a section on differential diagnosis. The presentation of material in this text will therefore assume that psychiatric problems are analogous to other medical problems and will follow the familiar paradigm.

What then is the role of psychosocial factors in medicine and in psychiatry? They are of considerable importance if the evidence indicates that illnesses in themselves create social disturbances or social incapacities, or that social problems are relevant to the etiology or the cause of the illness. In other words, they can be quite significant depending on the circumstances.

Likewise, consider the role for psychotherapy in medicine and in psychiatry. If psychotherapy is nonspecific and applicable to a wide range of medical and psychiatric problems, it probably does not need to be discussed in a text concerned with the medical bases of diseases. However, when it proves to be an effective treatment for any of the reasonably well-defined illnesses it is included in the discussion.

One additional issue needs to be considered. How does one best present the illnesses that are seen in psychiatry? We have found it most useful for the mode of presentation to parallel the way in which a person learns clinical medicine. Similar to the idea that ontogeny recapitulates phylogeny, a medical student or resident learns clinical medicine by seeing patients as well as reading books. One starts to learn by seeing patients and then categorization occurs. This is the way in which clinical material becomes alive for the student who then returns to the text to read about an illness. Rather than present introductory chapters on etiology and classification and then launch into the pictures of the clinical states, we believe that the best way to present the material is to describe the clinical entities first. After that, chapters dealing with specific kinds of circumstances, such as symptom clusters or various biological or psychosocial etiologies, become far more meaningful. These realities have contributed to the organization of this book.

In the final analysis we are interested in specific psychiatric illnesses or entities. The frontispiece of this book, which comes from Hobbes' *Leviathan*, describes this very well. We are not interested in *Leviathan* per se. We are not interested in the "psyche." We are interested in specific psychiatric illnesses; that is, what is inside the *Leviathan*. As with medicine, psychiatry deals not on the basis of "soma" or symptoms but on the basis of specific diagnoses.

G.W.
P.C.

# CONTENTS

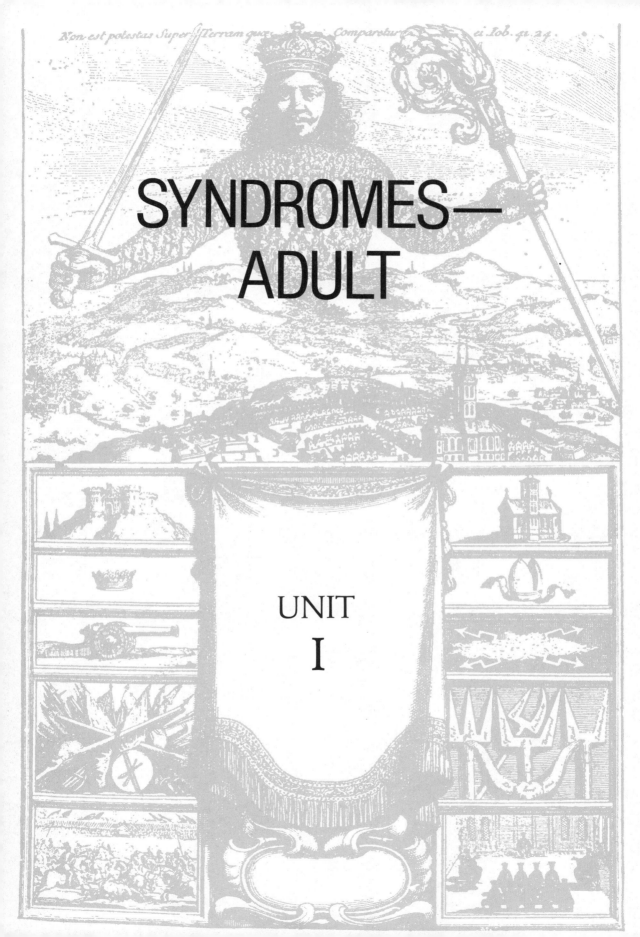

SYNDROMES—
ADULT

UNIT
I

# ORGANIC BRAIN SYNDROMES PRESENTING WITH GLOBAL COGNITIVE IMPAIRMENT: DELIRIUM AND DEMENTIA

*by* Michael K. Popkin, M.D.

## INTRODUCTION

Hoping to achieve a new clarity in an area long beset by uncertainty and controversy, the developers of the *Diagnostic and Statistical Manual of Mental Disorders*, third edition (DSM-III), coined the broad rubric organic mental disorders (OMDs). This term spans a *heterogeneous* group of disorders linked by two common elements: brain dysfunction and associated behavioral or psychological abnormality. More so than the disorders described in any other section of DSM-III, these conditions are critically positioned at the interface of psychiatry and medicine. Only in this section of DSM-III must the clinician address etiology together with the de-

scriptive features of thought and behavior. Here alone the clinician is expected to demonstrate "by means of the history, the physical exam or laboratory tests, the presence of a specific organic factor judged to be etiologically related to the abnormal mental state" (DSM-III, p. 101).

Are OMDs medical conditions or psychiatric conditions, or both? Clinical problems of this kind have historically been regarded as psychiatric until a specific pathophysiology has been established. After such clarification the individual disorders have been perceived as within the province of medicine or neurology. Recently, however, psychiatry is changing course, displaying heightened interest in the clinical correlates and management of brain dysfunction, well explained or not. This development, spurred in part by the rapid growth of technology concerned with imaging, visualizing, and understanding the brain, anticipates that much more psychopathology will likely be encompassed within the OMDs section of DSM-IV. It gives no hint of earlier proclivities to relinquish this realm to other medical disciplines.

Today's "functional" psychiatric disorders are the conditions for which cerebral pathology has not yet been shown to be a necessary causal factor (Lipowski, 1984). Yet altered levels of neurotransmitters, changes in receptor affinities, neuroanatomic and computed tomography (CT) scan aberrations, and genetic factors have been identified as associated features of many of the "functional" disorders. Such developments necessitate the rethinking of earlier constructs of organicity. As knowledge of brain function continues to accelerate, the age-old functional vs. organic dichotomy should become increasingly forced, if not meaningless. "Organic" and "functional" are not mutually exclusive conditions; rather, they are best viewed as inextricably intertwined. Such a perspective is partially embodied in the 1980 DSM-III and its revisionist approach to OMDs.

DSM-III "liberalized" the concept of organicity, no longer requiring cognitive or intellectual impairment as a sine qua non (Lipowski, 1984). As a result, the OMDs framework was broadened to include a range of clinical presentations (affective, delusional, and altered personality) that may be caused by (1) brain dysfunction (primary or secondary), (2) ingestion of an exogenous toxic substance, or (3) withdrawal from certain abused substances. In short, DSM-III proposes that an OMD can simulate almost any psychiatric disorder. Work by investigators such as Hall, Gardner, Stickney, LeCann, and Popkin (1980) and Koranyi (1979) has underscored that psychiatric symptomatology is *nonspecific*. These authors have shown the high frequency with which physical illnesses take a psychiatric guise or contribute to psychiatric symptomatology. Their work exemplifies that clinicians have responsibility to consider carefully "organic" explanations for much, if not all, psychopathology. To overlook such factors may condemn the patient to inappropriate treatment and the risk that physical illness and its central nervous system (CNS) impact may become irreversible. Accordingly, OMDs are the concern of all psychiatric practitioners, not only those who research or study specific cerebral disturbances.

The term *organic mental disorder* is used in DSM-III both generally and specifically. First, it signals a theoretical umbrella, incorporating a diverse cluster of brain syndromes. Second, it refers "to a specific organic brain syndrome in which the etiology is known or presumed" (DSM-III, p. 101). DSM-*II* relied exclusively on the terminology "organic brain syndromes" (OBSs) or simply "brain syndrome." In DSM-III, *organic brain syndromes are constellations or psychopathological clinical pictures without reference to etiology*. At least one critic (Taylor, in press) has assailed such distinctions on conceptual and practical grounds. Arguing the "OMD is a vestige of the notion that there are behavioral syndromes divorced from brain function," Taylor proposes eliminating the OMD–OBS distinction. (He also wisely proposes operationally defining many of the diagnostic criteria and expanding the list of subcategories.) Whether the changes introduced by DSM-III in the OMDs section will facilitate study of the clinical correlates of brain dysfunction remains to be seen. One major stumbling block may be DSM-III's silence regarding what satisfies the etiological requirement. No guidelines are presently offered; this is especially troublesome in cases of novel associations not previously identified or reported.

Despite the apparent nosologic complexity, the universe of choices regarding a given OBS is surprisingly limited. The clinician contemplating such a diagnosis must choose from among but seven specific clinical syndromes. These can be divided into three major groups: (1) *global disturbances of cognition* (delirium and dementia), (2) *selective cognitive deficits* (amnestic syndrome and hallucinosis), and (3) the *"functional equivalents"* (organic affective syndrome, organic delusional syndrome, and organic personality syndrome). In addition to these seven specific syndromes, there are two general syndromes (intoxication and withdrawal) associated with substance use and a residual category, atypical or mixed organic brain syndrome. In this and the two chapters that follow, these three major groups of organic brain disturbances are examined in detail.

## BRAIN SYNDROMES WITH GLOBAL COGNITIVE IMPAIRMENT: DELIRIUM AND DEMENTIA

### Historical Perspective

Delirium and dementia are the two common neuropsychiatric syndromes manifested by global cognitive impairment; they have been appreciated since antiquity. The two terms first appear within the writings of Celsus, a Roman aristocrat of the first century A.D. Heralding an ironic pattern that persisted for centuries, Celsus used the term delirium "inconsistently" (Lipowski, 1980). He identified it as a marker of the imminence of death and as an unfavorable sign in small bowel disease (Lipowski, 1980). Araetaeus, in the second century, distinguished "dotage," or senile dementia, as a chronic OMD (Lipowski, 1980). Although descriptions of the two conditions appeared with some consistency in the writings of physicians through the centuries, constructs now in use did not emerge until recently. A series of twentieth-century theorists and investigators, including Bonhoeffer (1910), Wolff and Curran (1935), and Engel and Romano (1944), have shaped and refined earlier constructs leading to the present-day clinical entities as set forth in DSM-III. Structured cognitive examinations, such as M. Folstein, S. Folstein, and P. McHugh's Mini-Mental State (1975), offer a rapid screening instrument to heighten recognition of cognitive impairment. Nonetheless, such disturbances are still best appreciated by the clinical examination, by the careful assessment of the mental status, and the benchmark cognitive decline. The diagnoses are more than academic exercises of DSM-III and International Classification of Diseases, Ninth Revision (ICD–9); they carry prognostic significance. The cognitively impaired, specifically those with delirium, have sharply increased fatality rates compared with cognitively intact persons (Guze and Cantwell, 1964; Rabins and Folstein, 1982).

Interest in cognitive impairment has grown since the 1970s. Investigations of de-

mentia continue to predominate; delirium remains something of a "stepchild," studied infrequently, as Lipowski (1967) noted.

### Editors Comment

*A new screening battery for the detection of abnormal mental decline in older persons has recently shown a correct classification of 89 per cent of cases with a high degree of probability (Eslinger P, Damasio A, Benton A, VanAllen M: JAMA 253:670–674, 1985). The battery takes a short time to administer (10 to 15 minutes) and is a combination of three tests: visual retention, controlled oral word association, and temporal orientation.*

## DELIRIUM

### Definition

Delirium is *"a psychiatric syndrome characterized by a transient disorganization of a wide range of cognitive functions due to widespread derangement of cerebral metabolism"* (Lipowski, 1980, p. 34). Perception, information processing, goal-directed thought, and memory function are disrupted. The stable, constant grasp of internal and external reality gives way to a sequence of fragmented experiences that cannot be successfully integrated by the patient. Abrupt in its onset and relatively brief in duration, delirium is marked by disturbances of attention, the sleep–wake cycle, and psychomotor activity (DSM-III). Difficulties in sustaining attention, awareness, and maintaining an adequate level of arousal are the hallmark of the disorder (not simply disorientation, as is sometimes mistakenly assumed). The disorder shows wide variability from patient to patient and from moment to moment in the same individual. It is presumed to be fully reversible but entails diffuse dysfunction of the cerebral hemispheres, the reticular activating system, and the autonomic nervous system (Wells and Duncan, 1980).

The term delirium is derived from the Latin *de lira*, meaning "out of the furrow" or off the track. In their classic work (1959), Engel and Romano called delirium "a syndrome of cerebral insufficiency." They likened it to other medical insufficiencies: renal, cardiac, hepatic, and pulmonary. Lipowski's definitive monograph (1980) is comparably titled *Delirium: Acute Brain Failure in Man.*

## Etiology and Pathogenesis

Delirium can be evoked by any process, disorder, or agent that disrupts the integrity of the CNS and diffusely impairs its functioning at a cellular level. Thus the list of potential etiologic factors is extensive, if not nearly limitless (see Lipowski for a full accounting, 1980). It is frequently difficult for the clinician to confirm a suspected etiology. Not only are most deliria short-lived, but they are also often the product of multiple factors converging to precipitate a final behavioral outcome. Causal disorders or factors may be either intrinsic to the CNS (tumor, trauma, bleeding, seizure disorder, or infection) or extracranial in origin. The latter group includes medical illnesses involving organs other than the CNS, medications, and toxic substances.

In my experience as a psychiatric consultant in a tertiary care hospital, the most common causes of delirium are fluid and electrolyte disturbances, drug toxicity, infections, and vascular events. The first two predominate. In the case of fluid and electrolyte disturbances, the clinical picture of delirium may antedate by as much as 24 to 48 hours the emergence of aberrant electrolyte values. Behavioral resolution may then be accompanied by clearly abnormal electrolyte values, reflecting disparities between peripheral and central events (i.e., lags involving the blood–brain barrier). With particular reference to metabolic disorders, it is important to appreciate that the *rate of change* may be more crucial than the extent of laboratory abnormality involved. For example, cognitive dysfunction secondary to uremic changes may be expected with blood urea nitrogen (BUN) values greater than 60 mg/ml. Yet many patients with end-stage renal disease have BUN levels that are greater than or equal to 100 mg/ml without evidence of OMD. Conversely, with rapid elevation of the BUN, as in acute renal failure, delirium is common. Similarly, many patients with chronic obstructive lung disease (COPD) routinely have $Pco_2$ values that are greater than or equal to 55 mm Hg. Were this range of value to result rapidly, delirium

would be invariable. This capacity in metabolic and insufficiency disorders to obviate OMD through gradual adjustment should not obscure the general principle that the more pronounced or severe the pathogenic factor, the greater the likelihood that delirium will occur.

Although many theories have been propounded over the years, surprisingly little is understood of the pathogenesis of delirium. The known electroencephalographic (EEG) changes in delirium (to be reviewed later) have prompted some to argue that substrate deficiencies, particularly of glucose and oxygen, are crucial to pathogenesis. Other "speculations" have cited disrupted synaptic transmission, false transmitters, compromised blood–brain barrier, altered cerebral blood flow, and biochemical changes, particularly in those pathways subserving sleep–wake cycles. Lipowski (1980) notes that delirium is not a failure of cerebral energy metabolism; rather, he suggests that it is a final common pathway for a variety of pathophysiologic processes and mechanisms. What these share appears to be a disruption, particularly in the usual relationship of cortical and subcortical structures. Given that delirium is principally a disorder of attention and arousal, it is difficult to minimize the role of the reticular activating system (RAS) in its pathogenesis. The RAS is responsible for alertness, wakefulness, and responsivity to external stimuli. Although delirium impacts the brain as a whole, any proposed account of its pathophysiology must literally begin with the state of the RAS, which in turn influences the extent of cortical excitability.

## Epidemiology

With the exception of dementia, the epidemiology of OMDs has received little systematic investigation. The majority of available data has emerged from studies of the population of medical-surgical patients referred for psychiatric consultation. In most settings, 20 per cent to 25 per cent of such referrals are assigned a psychiatric diagnosis of OMD by the consultants. Not surprisingly, delirium and dementia account for upward of three quarters of such OMD cases. The prevalence of delirium and other OBSs in the larger (unreferred) medical-surgical inpatient population has been estimated at *10 per cent to 15 per cent* (Engel, 1967). Often a transient episode in a protracted illness course, delirium can be overlooked. It undoubtedly occurs with greater frequency in the elderly; estimates of the prevalence of delirium in the hospitalized elderly have ranged from one third to one half (Lipowski, 1983). Impaired hearing and vision, brain damage, increased vulnerability to hypoxia, and decreased drug metabolism all play a role.

Other groups at increased risk for developing delirium are those with preexisting CNS dysfunction or injury and those with substance abuse problems. There is no substantial evidence to support the idea that certain personality features heighten the vulnerability to delirium. It is agreed however, that certain factors, including sensory deprivation, immobilization, extreme psychologic stress, and immaturity of the brain, can predispose to delirium.

## Pathology

The neuropathologic changes associated with delirium are nonspecific and largely reversible in patients who survive. There may be evidence of cerebral edema with widening of perivascular and perineuronal spaces. On microscopic examination there may be noted "swelling of the neurons of the cerebral cortex and hippocampus, some dissolution of the Nissl granules and generalized pallor" (Wells and Duncan, 1980). Such changes fail to point to a specific etiology.

## Clinical Picture

*Disturbances of attention and awareness* are central to the clinical presentation of delirium. The delirious patient has difficulty shifting, focusing, and sustaining attention to environmental stimuli. Thus the usual capacity to regulate one's attention at will is impaired. All critical components of attention are altered; these include alertness and the readiness to respond to stimuli, directiveness, and selectiveness (Lipowski, 1980). These core changes, directly linked to a reduced awareness of surroundings and self, have long been described as a "cloud-

ing of consciousness." This term is included in the A criteria for delirium in DSM-III, although it has been chastized as "obsolete, vague and redundant" (Lipowski, 1983). Lipowski alternatively suggests that the attentional deficits are best regarded as manifestations of a *disorder of wakefulness or arousal* (1983). A somewhat more speculative explanation of the attentional difficulties in delirium would emphasize that the barriers or psychological mechanisms normally used to screen and prioritize incoming stimuli are lowered or rendered inoperative (much as disinhibition may become apparent in areas of impulse control). As a consequence, the delirious individual is flooded with incoming stimuli that he or she can no longer structure by selectively attending to some of the input. The result is chaos, with the delirious patient focusing on seemingly inconsequential or inappropriate stimuli or ineffectually endeavoring to scan the suddenly overwhelming environment.

No matter what the explanation for the attentional disturbances, the clinical encounter is likely to be thwarted by a patient who is unable to maintain meaningful engagement with the examiner. The patient's level of awareness may vary from modest deficits in recognizing details to stupor and, eventually, coma. Change in arousal and level of vigilance may range from lethargy to agitation. The delirious patient seems given to "drifting off" or apparently grasping and responding to only fragments of the dialogue. The persistent examiner usually finds it necessary to attempt repeatedly to refocus the patient's attentional process. This sequence is instructive in itself. Interviews with the delirious are often characterized by their brevity; this should not preclude adequate appreciation of the syndrome.

Accompanying the difficulties in attention and awareness is an invariable *disturbance of the sleep–wake cycle.* The delirious patient commonly naps or sleeps during daytime hours and is awake "all night long." Nocturnal insomnia, bewilderment, and restlessness are often striking parts of a prodromal pattern. The reversed sleep–wake cycle is one of four B criteria for delirium in DSM-III. Of note, it is only necessary to have two of the four (incoherent speech, altered motor activity, and perceptual disturbances, in addition to the sleep–wakefulness change). Thus this feature is not a requisite per DSM-III. Nonetheless, it sharply colors the clinical picture.

Cognitive dysfunction is always heightened by fatigue and minimized by ample sleep. Patients with global cognitive impairment (delirium or dementia) are at their best after a good sleep. They are likely to be at their worst when they have been awake for many hours and the latter part of their day arrives. In this phenomenon, called *sundowning*, reduced sensory input and fatigue combine to unmask organicity in nighttime hours. The disturbance in the sleep–wake cycle also contributes to the lucid intervals that can be observed in delirium. Clinical features, especially early on, tend to fluctuate over the course of a day; this may relate to the intrinsic pathophysiology of the disturbance, but the sleep cycle factor undoubtedly explains much of the variation.

*Perceptual abnormalities* are common in delirium. These encompass misperceptions, illusions, and hallucinations; none have been extensively studied despite their apparent ubiquity in delirium. As the delirious patient sustains the attentional and awareness problems mentioned earlier, he or she struggles to achieve or regain a satisfactory grasp of the situation and is always at least mildly disoriented in time. In this sequence the patient is also prone to misperceive and, specifically, to mistake the unfamiliar for the familiar. Confronted with an overwhelming experience, patients are often likely to misidentify strangers as family members and the hospital room as home. This intriguing process seems to be quite adaptive—converting the threatening to the known. Less comforting are the propensities to perceive objects as too big, too small, moving or flowing together. Patients are also inclined to misread or mistake common objects: spots for insects, folds in the bedcovers for snakes, or a bedpost for a rifle. Finally, in terms of hallucinations, Lipowski (1980) proposes that visual hallucinations occur in 40 per cent to 75 per cent of deliria. Auditory and tactile hallucinations are somewhat less common. Most important, hallucinations are neither diagnostic nor pathognomonic for delirium. In addition, they do not distinguish between delirium and dementia (Rabins and Folstein, 1982).

*Disturbances of thinking* are routinely posited as part of delirium. Yet the DSM-III criteria for delirium do not address this issue as such. Thought is disorganized and fragmented; reasoning is defective. Generally, thought processes are slowed; they may be impoverished as well. The capacity to assess and problem-solve is dramatically reduced. Frequently, the patient experiences "oneiroid" or dreamlike imagery, which is disturbing and reinforces the disruption in the sleep–wake cycle. Ideas of persecution are possibly the most common form of delusions in delirium, although patients are perhaps equally inclined to believe that their hallucinations are real. As a rule, delusions are transient and not highly developed in delirium.

All delirious patients experience *memory impairment*. They manifest difficulties in receiving, retaining, and recalling; these are usually readily demonstrable deficits. Engel and Romano (1959) proposed that serial subtraction of numbers was the most valuable bedside test for the diagnosis. Remote memory is often relatively intact (to the examiner's surprise). Patients are subsequently able to recall only bits and pieces of their delirium.

*Motor activity* may be increased or decreased in delirium. This is associated with two clinical variants—hyperactive and hypoactive—which seem to occur in equal percentages (Lipowski, 1980). In addition, speech and nonverbal behavior are often altered.

The clinical picture in delirum also normally entails affective lability, fine to coarse irregular tremor at 8 to 10 seconds, asterixis, multifocal myoclonus, and various signs of autonomic dysfunction (e.g., nausea, vomiting, flushing, blood pressure changes). Other neurologic signs are comparatively uncommon.

## Clinical Course

Delirium has a sudden onset, involving no more than hours or a day or two at most. Prodromal symptoms may occur but are usually appreciated only in retrospect. These may include restlessness, impaired concentration, hyperacusis, insomnia, vivid dreams, and nightmares (DSM-III, p. 106). Fluctuation in symptoms is a characteristic feature of the course. The severity of the symptoms varies, most often being greatest at night with lucid intervals likely to be observed in the morning. These unpredictable fluctuations facilitate clinical diagnosis; they are not features of other OBSs.

Any variety of behavior can be encountered in delirium. In a given patient, the particular clinical presentation is probably determined by an interplay of four factors: (1) the premorbid personality, (2) the nature and locus of the insult rendered to the CNS, (3) the environment in which the delirious individual is placed, and (4) the reactive response to the recognition of the impairment. Although the insult rendered is possibly most important, there is little question that the mode of responding to cognitive disorganization often carries the day in terms of the resulting clinical picture. Many consultation requests are occasioned by consultees' dilemmas with agitated, paranoid, or depressed patients who in fact are suffering from an unrecognized delirium. Perceiving that their cognitive integrity has been violated or lost, patients respond in personalized, if not idiosyncratic, fashion. Some become despondent, others phobic, anxious, paranoid, or hysterical. Those who are conversant with altered consciousness may be less alarmed than those who have never experienced loss of control. In any case, the clinician is obligated to explore the question of reactive response. Hackett and Weisman (1960) have shown that dialogue anticipating the likelihood of delirium can clinically modify the resulting course. Delirium is marked by wide clinical variability, even in the same patient.

Most deliria are short-lived, on the order of a week. A longer process suggests that the syndrome has shifted to another, more enduring OBS or that death is imminent. Recovery is usually complete unless the underlying disorder cannot be redressed. The issue of psychological outcome of delirium has recently been raised. Mackenzie and Popkin (1980) suggested that the patient's lack of clear and correct information about his or her delirium may impede assimilation of the event. Blank and Perry (1984) found that postdelirium psychological outcome was associated with psychological processes manifest during the delirium.

## Laboratory Findings

The brain dysfunction underlying the clinical picture of delirium can be demonstrated by EEG. The typical abnormality is relative slowing of the EEG background activity (with or without superimposed fast activity—found in hyperactive delirium). The EEG can be useful diagnostically if serial tracings are done and the changes in background activity are consonant with changes in attention, awareness, and cognition (Lipowski, 1980). A diffusely slow tracing can help to make the diagnosis, but a normal or fast record does not rule it out (Pro and Wells, 1977).

Organic causative factors are identified in perhaps 80 per cent of cases (Lipowski, 1982). Specific laboratory studies must be directed to the evidence for associated physical illness or drug intoxication. In the absence of specific indications of etiology, initial measures should include electrolyte determinations, drug screen, hepatic and renal function studies, blood gas analyses, urinalysis, and an electrocardiogram.

## Differential Diagnosis

Although some psychotic disorders may involve hallucinations, delusions, and the like, it is seldom difficult to recognize that one is dealing with an OBS. Accordingly, the differential for delirium primarily involves dementia. This distinction should center on the features of disordered attention and arousal, which are not expected to be at issue in dementia. Yet distinguishing the conditions can be problematic despite examining factors such as rate of onset, fluctuating course, and sleep–wake cycle alterations. Rabins and Folstein (1982) argue that "altered cognition and consciousness alone can validly distinguish them [delirium and dementia]." In some instances, delirium may be superimposed on dementia. Watchful waiting and a provisional diagnosis are occasionally indicated when the diagnoses cannot be immediately clarified. DSM-III also includes factitious disorder with psychological symptoms in the differential diagnosis of delirium. Likewise, "pseudodelirium" has to be considered (Lipowski, 1983).

## Treatment

The first step after diagnosis of delirium should be the determination and correction of the underlying causes. Special attention must be directed to fluid and electrolyte status, hypoxia, anoxia, and diabetic problems. This search for an etiology is not always a rewarding process. While the workup proceeds, or after it has been effected, clinical management of the delirious patient requires attention to several points. The delirious patient should have a constant attendant both to monitor behavior and to provide reorientation and assurance. The room environment should ensure that the patient is neither excessively stimulated nor deprived of external stimuli. My preference is to avoid adding medications, especially when the etiology of the delirium is unclear. Additional agents may only compound the OBS. However, the patient's agitation and penchant for pulling intravenous lines and assaulting the staff may force the issue. In such instances, low-dose neuroleptics—usually haloperidol—are effective. (If physical restraints are used, chemical restraints must be invoked as well.) In daily amounts between 2 and 15 mg orally (or half as much intramuscularly), most delirious patients become tractable. The elderly require the more modest doses. Generally, one third to one half of what would be used to contain a psychotic disorder works satisfactorily in agitated delirium, although occasionally larger amounts are needed. If possible, the neuroleptic should be administered at night so as to facilitate sleep and help restore the disrupted sleep–wake cycle. Orientation cues, night lights, the presence of family members, and a primary nurse are all helpful in management.

## DEMENTIA

### Definition

The term dementia is derived from the Latin dement, meaning "to be out of one's mind." Like delirium, this OBS is characterized by global dysfunction. Its essential feature is broad-based intellectual decline; DSM-III (1980) stipulates that the loss of intellectual abilities in dementia must be of sufficient severity to interfere with social or occupational function. Thus the DSM-III definition permits or tolerates a modest degree of cognitive fall away with advancing age—so long as it does not compromise the individual's overall functioning. The specific DSM-III diagnostic criteria for dementia include a critical loss of intellectual ability, memory impairment, and at least one of the following: impaired abstract thinking, impaired judgment, disturbance of higher cortical function, or personality change. These deficits must occur in "a state of clear awareness" (Lipowski, 1984); this removes the question of delirium or intoxication from diagnostic consideration.

Dementia has traditionally signaled an irreversible and usually progressive process presumed to be associated with neuron loss. "Cell death" thus precluded the prospect of reversibility. DSM-III, however, chose to restrict the concept of dementia to descriptive parameters. As one of the OBSs dementia is but a clinical constellation of symptoms devoid of the prior prognostic connotations. It may be transient, static, or progressive. Which of these courses is encountered will prove a function of the underlying pathology.

Of all the OMDs in DSM-III, only dementia can be diagnosed in the absence of evidence for a specified etiology. The organic factor can be presumed "if conditions other than OMD have been reasonably excluded and if the behavioral change represents cognitive impairment in a variety of areas."

DSM-III divides the dementias into three principal groups: (1) primary degenerative dementia (PDD), (2) multi-infarct dementia (MID), and (3) dementias arising from other etiologies. In this schema the clinician may only diagnose PDD or MID by exclusion—after all other etiologies or pathophysiologic processes have been ruled out. (Recent technological advances, such as positron emission tomography and nuclear magnetic resonance, are helping to distinguish PDD and MID on grounds other than clinical history and physical examination.)

Primary degenerative dementia encompasses Alzheimer's disease, or dementia of the Alzheimer type (DAT), and Pick's disease. The former is the most common dementing illness; the latter can only be distinguished from DAT by direct examination of brain tissue. Although DSM-III still technically offers presenile and senile categories, such a distinction is unnecessary. Alzheimer's disease and "senile dementia" are now regarded as one disease. Multi-infarct dementia signals disturbances attendant to cerebrovascular disease. For both PDD and MID,

DSM-III identifies "phenomenological subtypes" when the clinical picture is complicated by depression, delusions, or superimposed delirium. The remaining dementing illnesses span a wide range from processes primarily affecting brain tissue with or without observable features such as abnormal movements (e.g., normal pressure hydrocephalus, Huntington's chorea, Creutzfeldt-Jakob disease, progressive supranuclear palsy, and Wilson's disease) to the dementias associated with diseases that do not usually attack the brain directly. The latter are called *secondary dementias* and encompass the behavioral sequelae of, for example, infection, endocrine disorder, and drug toxicity. In some constructs, depression and pseudodementia fall within this category as well.

## Etiology and Pathogenesis

### Primary Degenerative Dementia

Although considerable advances have recently been made in understanding the neurobiological features of DAT, "the pathogenesis and aetiology of Alzheimer's Disease remain *unknown territory*" (Deakin, 1983, my emphasis). Genetic factors have been shown to be instrumental in at least a portion of Alzheimer's cases. Heston, Mastri, Anderson, and White (1981) found in a study of 125 autopsy-proven cases of DAT that 40 per cent were familial. Pick's disease is regarded as hereditary, most likely an autosomal dominant (Spar, 1982). Genetics, however, do not account for the majority of DAT. Efforts to identify causal factors have focused on neurotransmitters, viruses (especially slow viruses), aluminum toxicity, and immune system dysfunction.

Since the 1970s many studies have demonstrated that the amount of acetylcholine found in the brains of patients with DAT is substantially reduced (Kokmen, 1984). These changes, as reflected by marker enzymes (choline acetyltransferase and acetylcholinesterase), entail loss or destruction of cholinergic neurons in specific areas (especially the basal forebrain and the nucleus basalis of Meynert). It has also been shown that temporary memory deficits can be produced in healthy, young volunteers by interfering with CNS cholinergic activity. Physostigmine, a cholinomimetic, reverses such deficits. Together with the biochemical findings, these data have led to a cholinergic hypothesis concerning DAT (Coyle, Price, and DeLong, 1983). Identification of cholinergic abnormalities gave promise of a ready treatment, but to date, trials of acetylcholine precursors have been unrewarding in DAT patients. More recently, other subcortical nuclei and their transmitter systems have been implicated in DAT (Besson, 1983). These include the locus ceruleus (noradrenergic), the raphe nucleus (serotonergic), and the substantia nigra (dopaminergic). The etiological significance of these changes and associated biochemical abnormalities remains to be clarified.

The transmissibility of DAT has been at issue for some time. In one study, inoculation of scrapie (a slow virus) into the CNS of certain mice induced neuritic plaques akin to those of DAT (Bruce and Fraser, 1975). This study, however, stands alone in the literature. Yet Creutzfeldt-Jakob disease is a transmissible encephalopathy of humans with a long incubation period. Subacute sclerosing panencephalitis and post-encephalitic Parkinson's disease can culminate in dementia. These examples serve to keep the issue of a viral etiology for DAT alive (if tenuously).

Aluminum toxicity has been suggested as a cause of DAT. An extremely small excess of aluminum has been consistently found in the brains of patients succumbing to DAT. Aluminum may induce in animals brain lesions similar to those in DAT, but these "tangles" are morphologically distinct (Wisniewski, Terry, and Hirano, 1970). As with other theories, the aluminum hypothesis is unresolved.

Defects in the immune system have also been proposed to underlie DAT. This prospect is linked to well-known declines of immunologic competence with aging, the immunologic origin of amyloid in senile plaques, and increased levels of brain reactive antibodies in DAT (Watson and Seiden, 1984).

### Multi-infarct Dementia

As a result of the elegant neuropathologic work of Tomlinson, Blessed, and Roth (1970), it has been generally appreciated that cerebral atherosclerosis does not account for the typical, insidiously progressive dementia of old age. When vascular disease is responsible for dementia, it is through the occurrence of multiple small or large cerebral infarcts. Hence the term multi-infarct dementia has been introduced to more clearly convey the pathogenic process that is involved. MID has been estimated to account for 10 per cent to 20 per cent of all cases of dementia. Complicating the situation is the fact that at autopsy, DAT and MID are found to coexist in perhaps 20 per cent of cases (Tomlinson et al., 1970).

Most cerebral infarcts are caused by thromboembolism from extracranial arteries and the heart (Hachinski, Lassen, and Marshall, 1974). Direct or in situ occlusion of cerebral vessels is a much less frequent event. In either case, the compromised blood supply results in the death of cells and subsequent encephalomalacia. Hypertension commonly underlies MID; Corsellis (1969) observed that it was unusual for autopsy to reveal an arteriosclerotic etiology for dementia unless there was hypertension exceeding 210/110 mm Hg.

Early identification of MID is crucial because vigorous intervention should serve to minimize or retard progression of the condition. A single infarct seldom, if ever, yields a dementia; rather, it is the cumulative impact of multiple, often small lesions (état lacunaire) that evokes the dementiform process. A minimal volume of brain destruction of 60 ml, with particular involvement of the corpus callosum and the temporal and occipital lobes, has been adequately defined (Torack, 1978). Arteriosclerosis is often more prominently developed in one part of the body than in another. Thus the status of peripheral and retinal vasculature do not invariably coincide with the condition of the cerebral vessels.

### Remaining Dementias

More than 50 diseases have been identified that can cause dementia (Haase, 1977). The list of causes continues to grow and has been reviewed in detail by Haase (1977). Causes of dementing illnesses span a gamut that includes genetic, viral, traumatic, and toxic factors. As with delirium, etiology may often be multifactorial. Among the list of causes, special attention should be briefly directed to certain disorders. They underscore the fact that widely disparate patho-

genetic mechanisms may each result in the final common pathway of dementia (as a clinical syndrome).

Huntington's chorea is a *hereditary* disorder characterized by dementia and choreiform movements. It is inherited as an autosomal dominant with high penetrance. Approximately half the offspring of an affected person will develop the disease. Creutzfeldt-Jakob disease is an *infectious* disease caused by slow virus; it has been transmitted by corneal transplantation and by performing craniotomy or autopsy. Its clinical course is generally fulminant once it becomes manifest. Normal pressure hydrocephalus is often a sequelae of *injury* to the brain, with resultant impaired absorption of cerebrospinal fluid. It presents with a clinical triad including dementia, ataxia, and incontinence. Finally, the *toxicity* of drugs and alcohol can be critical to the pathogenesis of dementia. DSM-III's dementia associated with alcoholism exemplifies this point.

### Epidemiology

Community surveys have found that 4 per cent to 5 per cent of the population over age 65 are severely demented (i.e., the extent of intellectual decline precludes independent living). An additional 10 per cent suffer mild to moderate dementia. Prevalence rates for severe forms increase to approximately 20 per cent by age 80 (Brody, 1982). Recent data also suggest that after age 85, the incidence of dementia plateaus or declines (Jarvik, Ruth, and Matsuyama, 1980). In all major postmortem series, DAT has been reported as accounting for between 50 per cent and 60 per cent of cases of severe dementia (Terry and Katzman, 1983). Multi-infarct dementias account for approximately another 20 per cent of these severe cases.

### Primary Degenerative Dementia

At present, genetic factors are the only known risk for PDD. In a small number of families, DAT presents as though it were a straightforward autosomal dominant disorder (Cook, Ward, and Austin, 1979). Jarvik et al. (1980) reported incomplete concordance among identical twins. In general, the risk to siblings of an affected person has been gauged at about 7 per cent up to age 75 (Heston and White, 1980). Estimates of risk for children of DAT probands are not yet available because of the lack of long-term followup studies. Heston and White (1983) emphasize that the risks of developing DAT are age-specific. Since DAT "will eventually affect 20–30 per cent of those living long enough" (Heston and White, 1983), the main impact of having an affected first-degree relative is an increased risk of developing the disease earlier in life (vs. someone without a DAT-affected relative). Of considerable interest is that DAT occurs predictably in patients with Down's syndrome (trisomy 21) who survive to age 40. Heston and Mastri (1977) found that relatives of probands with histologically confirmed DAT had an increased incidence of dementing illness, Down's syndrome, and hematologic malignancies. Given the known 20-fold increased risk of leukemia in Down's, the Heston–Mastri study suggested that the common denominator in the group of diseases (DAT, Down's, and hematologic malignancies) may have been an inherited microtubular abnormality.

A recent case control study (Heyman et al., 1984) exploring epidemiologic aspects of DAT found a significantly higher frequency of prior thyroid disease among female patients vs. controls and an increased history of severe head injury among patients vs. controls. It did not corroborate differences in the frequency of hematologic malignancies in the families of patients and controls.

More uncommon than DAT, Pick's disease also has a different distribution of age at onset. Risks in terms of inheritability are much less defined than for DAT.

### Multi-infarct Dementia

Multi-infarct dementia occurs more frequently in men than in women. Genetic factors may contribute; the most significant predisposing factor is arterial hypertension. Although it can affect individuals in their 40s, MID usually begins in the seventh or eighth decade of life.

### Remaining Dementias

Table 1–1 presents data from six major studies conducted between 1972 and 1982. Subjects assigned provisional diagnoses of dementia were further examined by psychiatrists and neurologists. Specific etiologies were sought to account for the clinical presentations. Methodologies were not uniform in the studies; no postmortem examinations were conducted. Overall, 39 per cent of the confirmed dementias were assigned a specific etiology according to criteria of inclusion. Fourteen per cent of the confirmed dementias were attributed to MID; the remaining 47 per cent were presumed to be cases of DAT. Table 1–2 (Popkin and Mackenzie, 1984) details those 15 per cent of dementias identified as having a "potentially reversible" etiology. Seven specific medical disorders accounted for 90 per cent of the reversible conditions. These were normal pressure hydrocephalus (31 per cent); tumors and cysts of the CNS (21 per cent); drug toxicity (12 per cent); subdural hematoma (9 per cent); thyroid dysfunction (8 per cent); alcoholism (5 per cent); general paresis (4 per cent). Of nonreversible etiologies other than MID and DAT, Huntington's chorea accounted for 3 per cent; trauma, 2 per cent; Creutzfeldt-Jakob disease, Parkinson's disease, and encephalitis, 1 per cent each. These distributions emerged in secondary and tertiary referral centers; those encountered in a primary care setting may differ markedly.

---

TABLE 1–1.   Evaluations for Provisional Diagnosis of Dementia

| | No. in Original Sample | Confirmed Dementia | Specific Etiology Established (Diagnosis by Inclusion) | Diagnosis by Exclusion | |
|---|---|---|---|---|---|
| | | | | MID | DAT |
| Marsden, Harrison (1972) | 106 | 86 (81%) | 40/86  (47%) | 8/86  (9%) | 38/86  (44%) |
| Freeman (1976) | 60 | 59 (98%) | 21/59  (36%) | 5/59  (8%) | 33/59  (56%) |
| Victoratos et al. (1977) | 52 | 49 (94%) | 25/49  (51%) | 5/49  (10%) | 19/49  (39%) |
| Smith, Kiloh (1981) | 200 | 164 (82%) | 62/164  (38%) | 22/164  (13%) | 80/164  (49%) |
| Rabins (1981) | 41 | 41 (100%) | 21/41  (51%) | 8/41  (20%) | 12/41  (29%) |
| Delaney (1982) | 100 | 100 (100%) | 27/100  (27%) | 22/100  (22%) | 51/100  (51%) |
| Totals | 559 | 499 (89%) | 196/499 (39%) | 70/499 (14%) | 233/499 (47%) |

**TABLE 1–2.** Etiologies Assigned to Potentially Reversible Dementias (n = 77 or 15%) and Their Actual Clinical Outcomes

| Studies: | Marsden, Harrison (n = 86) | Freeman (n = 59) | Victoratos* et al. (n = 49) | Smith, Kiloh (n = 164) | Rabins* (n = 41) | Delaney (n = 100) | Total (%) | Cumulative (%) | Outcomes No Change (%) | (If Reported) Partially Improved (%) |
|---|---|---|---|---|---|---|---|---|---|---|
| Normal pressure hydrocephalus | 5 | 7 | 1 | 8 | 1 | 2 | 24 (31) | 31 | 12 (55) | 6 (27) |
| Tumors/cyst of CNS | 8 | 0 | 0 | 3 | 0 | 5 | 16 (21) | 52 | 8 (50) | 5 (31) |
| Drug toxicity | 2 | 5 | 0 | 0 | 0 | 2 | 9 (12) | 64 | 0 (0) | 0 (0) |
| Subdural hematoma | 0 | 2 | 1 | 0 | 1 | 3 | 7 (9) | 73 | 0 (0) | 5 (100) |
| Hypothyroidism | 0 | 1 | 0 | 2 | 1 | 0 | 4 (5) | 78 | 0 (0) | 1 (33) |
| Alcoholism | 0 | 0 | 1 | 0 | 0 | 3 | 4 (5) | 83 | 0 (0) | 0 (0) |
| General paresis | 0 | 1 | 1 | 0 | 0 | 1 | 3 (4) | 87 | 1 (50) | 1 (50) |
| Hyperthyroidism | 0 | 0 | 0 | 0 | 1 | 1 | 2 (3) | 90 | 0 (0) | 0 (0) |
| Hepatic encephalopathy | 0 | 1 | 0 | 0 | 0 | 1 | 2 (3) | 93 | 0 (0) | 0 (0) |
| Fungus | 0 | 0 | 0 | 0 | 0 | 2 | 2 (3) | 96 | 0 (0) | 2 (100) |
| Lead | 0 | 0 | 0 | 0 | 0 | 1 | 1 (0.2) | 96 | 0 (0) | 0 (0) |
| Other | 0 | 0 | 1 | 0 | 0 | 2 | 3 (4) | 100 | 0 (0) | 2 (100) |
| Total | 15 | 17 | 5 | 13 | 4 | 23 | 77 — | — | 21 (27) | 22 (29) |

* Outcomes not reported by authors.

## Pathology

Beginning with work by Roth, Tomlinson, and Blessed (1967), much evidence has been gathered that establishes a direct relationship between the severity of the clinical picture of dementia and the severity of neuropathologic change. The extent of intellectual loss has been quantitatively associated with the density of senile plaques and neurofibrillary tangles, the volume of brain softening, and the mass of tissue loss (Wells and Duncan, 1980).

### Primary Degenerative Dementia

In 1907, Alois Alzheimer described neurofibrillary tangles and senile plaques in brain tissue from a 51-year-old woman who died after a 4-year course of profound intellectual decline and behavioral change. These classic features of the disease are most prominent in the hippocampus. The tangles are masses of neurofibers arranged as paired helical filaments (Terry and Katzman, 1983); the plaques are derived from degenerative neurites and granulovascular degeneration. The biochemical nature of the amyloid in these plaques is not yet clarified. Plaques and tangles are not unique to DAT. They are found in small numbers in normal aging. In most cases of DAT, there is generalized cortical atrophy, most marked in the frontal and temporal lobes. The ventricles may be enlarged.

The microscopic findings in Pick's disease are dramatically different from those in DAT. Affected cells have *Pick's bodies*, collections of the components of the normal cell in disarray. In most cases, plaques and tangles are conspicuous by their absence (Lishman, 1978). The gross appearance of the brain is characteristic, with marked reduction of frontal and temporal lobes. Involvement of the parietal and occipital lobes is unusual.

### Multi-infarct Dementia

The brain may demonstrate generalized or localized atrophy. On microscopic examination, effects of ischemia and infarction are apparent. Cystic softenings, reactive gliosis, and necrotic degeneration are common. The cerebral vasculature itself may show a range of changes.

### Remaining Dementias

The cellular pathology of dementia is a function of the underlying disease; given 50 or more etiologies, this topic is too extensive for the current chapter. The interested reader is referred to Tomlinson's review of the pathology of dementia (1977).

## Clinical Picture

Memory dysfunction is the most prominent feature of a dementia. Often insidious in its presentation, it may begin with difficulties in short-term recall and in the acquisition and retrieval of new information. There is no problem with maintenance of attention, arousal, and awareness. As the dementing illness progresses, memory impairment becomes more pronounced and interferes with remoter memories. Early coping mechanisms may involve excessive use of lists, schedules, and notes to contend with forgetfulness in daily life. Loss of interest and initiative are also relatively early signs, resulting in less than usual standards of performance. Distractibility is increased, and the patient is prone to fatigue readily. Thinking is comparably impaired in dementia, with a poverty of associations and inability to generate new constructs. Perseveration is frequent; intellectual capacity/flexibility is compromised. Paranoid ideation is common, as is delusional thinking. Speech shows similar deficits, with great reliance on clichés or "old tapes." Paraphasic errors and difficulty in word finding are common. Constructional ability is almost always disturbed.

As the dementing illness proceeds, impaired judgment and impulse control are often manifest, together with sweeping personality shifts. Because of changes in the frontal lobes, the individual becomes disinhibited; inappropriate sexual and social actions may first prompt medical attention. There is increasing inattention to the rudiments of self-care; incontinence may develop. When taxed beyond his or her cognitive capacity, the demented patient is prone to show marked, intense affective response. Emotional lability can dominate the later clinical picture. Memory dysfunction becomes profound; the individual loses the capacity to effect meaningful interchanges.

Eventually behavior becomes "futile and aimless" (Lishman, 1978).

## Clinical Course

The initial presenting features and the ensuing course of a dementia are functions of the specific etiology of the disorder. Primary degenerative dementia is, for the most part, insidious in its onset and steadily progresses to death over an interval of several years. Fifty per cent of patients with DAT present between ages 65 and 69. Earlier onset is associated with severer illness and, subsequently, shorter courses. For DAT manifesting between ages 55 and 74, the average survival time is about 8.5 years (Heston and White, 1983). Pick's disease presents somewhat earlier, with a peak incidence at age 55. Average survival is slightly longer than 7 years. (In all PDD, dating onset with precision is clearly difficult.) During the early phase the neurologic examination may remain normal. As cognitive and behavioral changes become more manifest, signs of neurologic dysfunction also emerge. Aphasia, apraxia, and agnosia usually appear. "Primitive reflexes" are characteristic of most diffuse brain disease and depend on the speed of the course and the extent of brain injury. In PDD, disturbances of posture, gait, muscle tone, and extensor plantar responses are common as the dementia proceeds. In the final phase of PDD, as the patient becomes bedridden, gross neurologic disability is often seen, together with grand mal seizures (reported in up to 75 per cent of cases).

In MID, the onset is typically abrupt, earlier than in DAT, and the course shows stepwise decrements over time with an uneven progression. The cognitive deficits, especially early in the course, may be selective rather than diffuse. Focal neurologic signs are common, and associated features include dysarthria, dysphagia, and pseudobulbar palsy. Time to death varies widely (Lishman, 1978); generally, the course is slower than in DAT. The personality may be preserved until late in the course owing to the patchy nature of the insults. Seizures have been found in approximately 20 per cent of cases. Birkett (1972) found that neurologic abnormalities predicted MID more accurately than any mental feature.

The courses of the remaining dementias are variable. Table 1–2 details the observed outcomes of a series of potentially reversible dementias. Only 44 per cent of these cases proved reversible in fact as well as in theory. Duration of the dementing process and the time of its detection are crucial to outcome in the reversible cases. The longer a process remains uncorrected, the less likely full restitution becomes.

Finally, as with delirium, the course of any dementing illness is strongly colored by the patient's premorbid personality, the precise neuroanatomical location and extent of brain lesions, and the crucial element of reactive response to cognitive and neurologic impairment.

## Laboratory Findings

Based on data from studies presented in Tables 1–1 and 1–2, it has recently been suggested that a battery consisting of a CT scan, drug screen, thyroid functions, and serology will suffice to identify 90 per cent of the potentially reversible etiologies of dementing processes (Popkin and Mackenzie, 1984). Additional studies should proceed only from a combination of clinical acumen and the patient's individual history. Exhaustive laboratory testing is reserved for those few cases with decidedly atypical courses.

Two sets of investigators (Fox, Topel, and Huckman, 1975; Freeman and Rudd, 1982) have found that demented patients with lesser degrees of atrophy on CT scans had a greater likelihood of having a treatable disorder. A normal CT scan does not rule out dementia; neither do abnormalities on a scan establish a diagnosis of dementia. Scanning has shown differences between DAT and MID. Ventricular dilatation is greater in DAT; changes in temporal zones are more frequent in MID. Of note, positron emission tomography and nuclear magnetic resonance imaging both appear capable of distinguishing DAT from MID (Besson, 1983). Oxygen utilization is reduced in both conditions, but this is more generalized in DAT.

One of the clearest physiologic correlates of DAT is symmetrical, usually diffuse slowing of the EEG (Terry and Katzman, 1983). If the diagnosis of dementia is uncertain, the

EEG may prove useful if focal or diffuse dysfunction is found. However, dementia can be advanced and the EEG remain unremarkable (Wilson, Musella, and Short, 1977).

## Differential Diagnosis

In the studies detailed in Table 1–1 presumed diagnoses of dementia were confirmed in 89 per cent of cases. Restricting the data to those four studies with truly provisional diagnoses, dementia was confirmed in 86 per cent of cases. The majority of patients receiving a primary psychiatric diagnosis other than dementia were diagnosed as depressed. Remaining diagnoses included a cadre of OMDs (particularly delirium) and schizophrenia. These categories reflect the differential diagnosis for an apparent loss of intellectual abilities. The distinctions between dementia and delirium have been discussed earlier. Emil Kraepelin first called schizophrenia by the term *dementia praecox*. Cross, Crow, and Owen (1981) have demonstrated cognitive decline in type II schizophrenics; careful history should help to identify such patients. However, distinguishing dementia from depression can be difficult. Data from followup studies underscore the point. Ron, Toone, Garralda, and Lishman (1979) found that as many as 30 per cent of original diagnoses of dementia cannot be supported on reexamination several years later. They concluded that unappreciated affective disorders chiefly explained the outcomes they observed.

The term *pseudodementia* has been used to describe cognitive dysfunction appearing in depressed patients (especially the elderly). This mimicry of dementia by an affective disturbance usually begins more discretely and progresses more rapidly than dementia. There may be a preceding history of affective illness, and performance on cognitive testing is often variable and marked by poor motivation. Mood disturbance is more pervasive in depression and accompanied by complaints of memory dysfunction. (The latter are uncommon in dementia.) In contrast to earlier work (McAllister, 1981), Rabins, Merchant, and Nestadt (1984) reported in a 2-year followup study that patients with "the dementia syndrome of depression" can be readily identified (vs. irreversibly demented patients) by a standard clinical history and examination. In those instances in which the question of depression vs. dementia cannot be resolved, a trial of antidepressants is warranted. It also must be recalled that affective illness arises in as many as 25 per cent of patients with progressive dementias. These secondary depressions are often benefited by antidepressant medication.

Although psychometric tests may identify mild cases of DAT (Storandt, Botwinick, Danziger, Berg, and Hughes, 1984), dementia is a clinical diagnosis. Evidence to establish the diagnosis is derived from clinical interview, a reliable corroborative history, physical examination, and laboratory workup. Within the hospital setting, memory dysfunction often goes unrecognized (Jacobs, Bernhard, Delgado, and Strain, 1977). Most memory-impaired patients defend vigorously against revelation of their deficits. Those with longer courses may become facile at evading the examiner's efforts. Careful review of the medical record usually provides indication of cognitive difficulties. This prospect can be confirmed by an examination that presumes cognitive dysfunction is at issue and offers the patient a forum for sharing his or her concerns about this. Because the diagnosis of dementia is often revealed by changes in function over time and because the patient often cannot provide such history, a corroborative history is crucial.

## Treatment

Once the diagnosis of dementia has been confirmed, the clinician's focus must be first directed to the question of etiology. The foremost considerations are the identification and resolution of potentially reversible processes. Data from Tables 1–1 and 1–2 indicate that as few as 7 per cent of dementias are actually reversed (e.g., restitution achieved). Yet the obligation to be circumspect remains; to miss a potentially reversible etiology borders on negligence. Ironically, the preoccupation with correcting treatable or reversible dementias may have contributed to a pattern/practice of "writing off" those patients with irreversible dementing disorders (Wells, 1984).

The need for general supportive care of the demented has been long recognized. Provisions must be made for security, stimulation, patience, and nutrition. Symptomatic treatment should reduce reliance on lost functions and maximize use of residual functions. The history of drug therapy for dementia is replete with reports of initial success, eventually followed by observations of failure (Torack, 1978).

Although Hydergine (dihydrogenated ergot alkaloid) has been used extensively in dementia, resultant improvements are "generally modest and clinically unimportant" (Kokmen, 1984). As noted previously, drugs enhancing cholinergic activity in the CNS have not proven helpful in reversing the signs and symptoms of dementia. However, double-blind crossover studies have demonstrated that physostigmine can facilitate memory in some DAT patients but not others (Terry and Katzman, 1983). Work is currently under way using gangliosides in DAT; such agents may produce increased sprouting and regeneration of injured nerve cells.

Psychotropic medications in the demented should be reserved for (1) the control of agitated, assaultive behavior; (2) paranoid ideation and other psychotic features; (3) the improvement of mood state; and (4) facilitating impaired sleep, thereby minimizing organicity. Generally, low-dose neuroleptics should be used for all save number 3 and given at night in order to aid sleep. In the face of known CNS dysfunction, my preference is for thiothixene (Navane) or thioridazine (Mellaril), beginning with modest amounts and slowly increasing as needed. In terms of treating depressive disorders superimposed on dementia, nortriptyline works satisfactorily, in my experience, in doses between 50 and 75 mg daily. There is a significant risk of heightening the underlying cognitive dysfunction with this agent. Supportive psychotherapy can be of benefit to some demented patients (Wells and Duncan, 1980).

Increasing attention is being directed in the literature to the needs of the family of the demented patient. The family requires vigorous education regarding the dementing process; they likewise need assistance and support in implementing treatment plans. Caring for the demented patient is a full-time task. The increasing responsibilities as the disease evolves are likely to prove stressful. Caretakers require their own support systems and regular respite. Day care may assist patients and families alike (Fisk, 1983). While the search for pharmacologic treatments that can facilitate memory function continues, it is important to recall that demented patients can be helped in a variety of ways. Poor prognosis should not be equated with resignation or abdication of responsibility for vigorous care and management.

## REFERENCES

Besson J: Dementia: Biological solution still a long way off. Br Med J 287:926–927, 1983.

Birkett DP: The psychiatric differentiation of senility and arteriosclerosis. Br J Psychiatry 120:321–325, 1972.

Blank K, Perry S: Relationship of psychological processes during delirium to outcome. Am J Psychiatry 141:843–847, 1984.

Bonhoeffer K: Exogenous psychoses (1910). Reprinted in Hirsch SR, Shepherd M (eds):Themes and Variations in European Psychiatry. Bristol, John Wright, 1974, pp. 47–52.

Brody JA: An epidemiologist views senile dementia: Facts and fragments. Am J Epidemiol 115:155–162, 1982.

Bruce ME, Fraser H: Amyloid plaques in the brains of mice infected with scrapie: Morphological variation and staining properties. Neuropath Appl Neurobiol 1:189–202, 1975.

Cook RH, Ward BE, Austin JH: Studies in aging of the brain. IV. Familial Alzheimer's disease: Relation to transmissible dementia aneuploidy and microtubular defects. Neurology (NY) 29:1402–1412, 1979.

Corsellis JAN: The pathology of dementia. Br J Hosp Med 2:695–702, 1969.

Coyle JT, Price DL, DeLong MR: Alzheimer's disease: A disorder of cortical cholinergic innervation. Science 219:1184–1190, 1983.

Cross AJ, Crow TJ, Owen F: $^3$H-Flupenthixol binding in postmortem brains of schizophrenics: Evidence for a selective increase in dopamine $D_2$ receptors. Psychopharmacology (Berlin) 74:122–124, 1981.

Deakin JFW: Alzheimer's disease: Recent advances and future prospects. Br Med J 287:1323–1324, 1983.

Delaney P: Dementia: The search for treatable causes. South Med J 75:707–709, 1982.

Diagnostic and Statistical Manual of Mental Disorders, ed 3. Washington, DC, American Psychiatric Association, 1980.

Engel G, Romano J: Studies of delirium. II. Reversibility of the encephalogram with experimental procedure. Arch Neurol Psychiatry 51:378–392, 1944.

Engel G, Romano J: Delirium: A syndrome of cerebral insufficiency. J Chronic Dis 9:260–277, 1959.

Engel GL: Delirium. In Freedman AM, Kaplan HI (eds): Comprehensive Textbook of Psychiatry, ed 1. Baltimore, Williams & Wilkins, 1967, pp. 711–716.

Fisk AA: Management of Alzheimer's disease. Postgrad Med 73:237–241, 1983.

Folstein M, Folstein S, McHugh P: "Mini-mental state":

A practical method for grading the cognitive state of patients for the clinician. J Psychiatric Res 12:189–198, 1975.

Fox JH, Topel JL, Huckman MS: Use of computerized tomography in senile dementia. J Neurol Neurosurg Psychiatry 38:948–953, 1975.

Freeman FR: Evaluation of patients with progressive intellectual deterioration. Arch Neurol 33:658–659, 1976.

Freeman FR, Rudd SM: Clinical features that predict potentially reversible progressive intellectual deterioration. J Am Geriat Soc 7:449–451, 1982.

Guze SB, Cantwell DP: The prognosis in organic brain syndromes. Am J Psychiatry 120:878–881, 1964.

Haase GR: Diseases presenting as dementia. In Wells CE (ed): Dementia, ed 2. Philadelphia, FA Davis, 1977.

Hachinski VC, Lassen NA, Marshall J: Multi-infarct dementia: A cause of mental deterioration in the elderly. Lancet 2:207–209, 1974.

Hackett TP, Weisman AD: Psychiatric management of operative syndromes. I. The therapeutic consultation and the effect of noninterpretive interventions. Psychosom Med 23:267–282, 1960.

Hall RCW, Gardner ER, Stickney SK, LeCann AF, Popkin MK: Physical illness manifesting as psychiatric disease. II. Analysis of a state hospital inpatient population. Arch Gen Psychiatry 37:989–995, 1980.

Heston LL, Mastri AR: The genetics of Alzheimer's disease. Arch Gen Psychiatry 34:976–981, 1977.

Heston LL, Mastri AR, Anderson E, White J: Dementia of the Alzheimer type: Clinical genetics, natural history and associated conditions. Arch Gen Psychiatry 38:1085–1090, 1981.

Heston LL, White J: A family study of Alzheimer's disease and senile dementia: An interim report. In Cole JO, Barrett JE (eds): Psychopathology in the Aged. New York, Raven, 1980.

Heston LL, White JA: Dementia: A Practical Guide to Alzheimer's Disease and Related Illnesses. New York, WH Freeman, 1983.

Heyman A, Wilkinson WE, Stafford JA, Helms MJ, Sigman AH, Weinberg T: Alzheimer's disease: A study of epidemiological aspects. Ann Neurol 15:335–341, 1984.

Jacobs JW, Bernhard MR, Delgado A, Strain JJ: Screening for organic mental syndromes in the medically ill. Ann Int Med 86:40–46, 1977.

Jarvik LF, Ruth V, Matsuyama SS: Organic brain syndrome and aging: A six-year followup of surviving twins. Arch Gen Psychiatry 37:280–286, 1980.

Kokmen E: Dementia—Alzheimer type. Mayo Clin Proc 59:35–42, 1984.

Koranyi EK: Morbidity and rate of undiagnosed physical illness in a psychiatric clinic population. Arch Gen Psychiatry 36:414–419, 1979.

Lipowski ZJ: Delirium: Clouding of consciousness and confusion. J Nerv Ment Dis 145:227–255, 1967.

Lipowski ZJ: Delirium: Acute Brain Failure in Man. Springfield, IL, Charles C. Thomas, 1980.

Lipowski ZJ: Differentiating delirium from dementia in the elderly. Clin Gerontologist 1:3–10, 1982.

Lipowski ZJ: Transient cognitive disorders (delirium, acute confusional states) in the elderly. Am J Psychiatry 140:1426–1436, 1983.

Lipowski ZJ: Organic mental disorders: An American perspective. Br J Psychiatry 144:542–546, 1984.

Lishman WA: Organic Psychiatry. Oxford, Blackwell, 1978.

Mackenzie TB, Popkin MK: Stress response syndrome occurring after delirium. Am J Psychiatry 137:1433–1435, 1980.

Marsden CD, Harrison MJG: Outcome of investigations of patients with presenile dementia. Br Med J 2:249–252, 1972.

McAllister TW: Cognitive functioning in the affective disorders. Compr Psychiatry 22:572–586, 1981.

Popkin MK, Mackenzie TB: The provisional diagnosis of dementia: Three phases of evaluation. In Hall, RCW, Beresford TP (eds): The Handbook of Psychiatric Diagnostic Procedures. Jamaica, NY, Spectrum, 1984.

Pro JD, Wells CE: The use of the electroencephalogram in the diagnosis of delirium. Dis Nerv Syst 38:804, 1977.

Rabins PV: The prevalence of reversible dementia in a psychiatric hospital. Hosp Comm Psychiatry 32:490–492, 1981.

Rabins PV, Folstein MF: Delirium and dementia: Diagnostic criteria and fatality rates. Br J Psychiatry 140:149–153, 1982.

Rabins PV, Merchant A, Nestadt G: Criteria for diagnosing reversible dementia caused by depression. Br J Psychiatry 144:488–492, 1984.

Ron MA, Toone BK, Garralda ME, Lishman WA: Diagnostic accuracy in presenile dementia. Br J Psychiatry 134:161–168, 1979.

Roth M, Tomlinson BE, Blessed G: The relationship between quantitative measures of dementia and of degenerative changes in the cerebral grey matter of elderly subjects. Proc R Soc Med 60:254–259, 1967.

Smith JS, Kiloh LG: The investigation of dementia: Results in 200 consecutive admissions. Lancet 1:824–827, 1981.

Spar JE: Dementia in the aged. Psychiatric Clin N Am 5:67–86, 1982.

Storandt M, Botwinick J, Danziger WL, Berg L, Hughes CP: Psychometric differentiation of mild senile dementia of the Alzheimer type. Arch Neurol 41:497–499, 1984.

Taylor MA: DSM-III organic mental disorders. In Tischler, G (ed): Diagnosis and Classification in Psychiatry. Cambridge, Cambridge University Press, in press.

Terry RD, Katzman R: Senile dementia of the Alzheimer type. Ann Neurol 14:497–506, 1983.

Tomlinson BE: The pathology of dementia. In Wells CE (ed): Dementia, ed 2. Philadelphia, FA Davis, 1977.

Tomlinson BE, Blessed G, Roth M: Observations on the brains of demented old people. J Neurol Sci 11:205–242, 1970.

Torack RM: Pathologic Physiology of Dementia. Berlin, Springer-Verlag, 1978.

Victoratos GC, Lemmon JAR, Herzeberg L: Neurological investigation of dementia. Br J Psychiatry 130:131–133, 1977.

Watson WJ, Seiden HS: Alzheimer's disease: A current review. Can Fam Physician 30:595–599, 1984.

Wells CE: Diagnosis of dementia: A reassessment. Psychosomatics 25:183–188, 1984.

Wells CE, Duncan GW: Neurology for Psychiatrists. Philadelphia, FA Davis, 1980.

Wilson WP, Musella L, Short MJ: The EEG in dementia. In Wells CE (ed): Dementia, ed 2. Philadelphia, FA Davis, 1977.

Wisniewski H, Terry RD, Hirano P: Neurofibrillary pathology. J Neuropathol Exp Neurol 29:163–176, 1970.

Wolff HG, Curran D: Nature of delirium and allied states: The dysergastic reaction. Arch Neurol Psychiatry 51:378–392, 1935.

# chapter 2

# THE AMNESTIC SYNDROME

*by* Rafiq Waziri, M.D.

## DEFINITION

The amnestic syndrome is characterized by (a) moderate to severe degree of inability to remember recently observed or experienced events after the onset of the illness (anterograde amnesia); (b) mild to moderate inability to remember minor or important and significant events or both, that occurred before the onset of the illness (retrograde amnesia); (c) lack of insight and confabulation, which refers to the fabrication of stories to fill in gaps in recent memory; and (d) absence of significant other cerebral dysfunctions, such as aphasias, apraxias, or clouding of consciousness. The amnestic syndrome may be called Korsakoff's psychosis, the amnesic–confabulatory psychosis, and the Wernicke-Korsakoff syndrome.

## ETIOLOGY AND PATHOGENESIS

The most common causes of the amnestic syndrome are (a) alcoholism in association with thiamine deficiency; (b) brain trauma (by concussion, crush, or penetration); (c) cerebral anoxemia, especially associated with carbon monoxide poisoning; (d) vascular occlusions leading to brain infarct; (e) viral encephalitis affecting specific brain areas; (f) tumors involving diencephalic structures; (g) seizures—especially those of the temporal lobe origin; (h) degenerative diseases, such as Alzheimer's, when affecting predominantly the temporal lobes.

## ANATOMICAL PATHOLOGY

With such diverse etiological correlates it would be unlikely that a single, discrete locus for a brain lesion leading to the syndrome will be uncovered. In the first half of this century, brain autopsies done on alcoholics who had suffered a Wernicke's encephalopathy with the resultant amnesic symptoms implicated pathology of the mammillary bodies (Brierly, 1977) either solely or in conjunction with other lesions in the diencephalic structures (fornix and the gray matter in the walls of the third ventricle). Since the 1950s the limbic structures, especially the hippocampus, and the amygdaloid nucleii, have been the subject of intense research as sites for the pathology of memory processes. The studies of Scoville and Milner (1957) on the memory defects produced in subject H.M., by bilateral removal of amygdaloid nucleii and the hippocampal formation, led to the hypothesis that the hippocampal formation was essential in the mediation of learning and short-term memory. Studies on similarly operated subjects, who developed moderate to severe defects in memory processes (Milner, 1970), appeared to confirm the original observations. Occlusion of posterior cerebral artery, which results in hippocampal damage and Korsakoff-type of memory defect (Van Buren and Borke, 1972), provided further support for this idea. The studies of Victor, Adams, and Collins (1971) raised serious questions about the role of the hippocampus as an important site for memory processing. The authors reported elaborately on 245 alcoholics who had suffered from the Wernicke-Korsakoff syndrome. Eighty-one of these patients died either about a week after the onset of their encephalopathy (44 cases) or an average of 3.2 years after the onset of the illness (37 cases). In 62 of these cases, brain autopsies revealed gross neuropathologic changes in various parts of the brain, the majority (74 per cent) having abnormalities in the mammillary bodies. Fifty-three had microscopic brain examinations, and of these, 43 had sections through the dorsomedial thalamic nucleii and the mammillary bodies. Of these 43 subjects, 5 had no memory problems in their postencephalopathy period. The brains of these 5 subjects all showed lesions in the mammillary bodies but not in the dorsomedial thalamus. Few had extensive hippocampal lesions. Victor et al. (1971) proposed the idea that lesions of the dorsomedial nucleii were essential in the pathogenesis of Korsakoff's syndrome. Support for an important role for the dorsomedial thalamus as an important station for memory processing has come from surgical lesions placed specifically in this locus, resulting in severe memory disturbances of the Korsakoff type (Spiegel, Wycis, Orchinik, and Freed, 1955). Victor et al. (1971) found no consistent lesions in the limbic structures, other than in the mammillary bodies, that correlated with Korsakoff's syndrome.

If the diencephalic dorsomedial nucleus of the thalamus is the site for memory processing, then what is the explanation for the severe recent memory and learning deficits that ensue after surgical removal of the hippocampal formation in humans? Horel (1978), in a careful review of the pathologic neuroanatomy associated with memory disturbances, considers neither the limbic system nor the dorsomedial nucleus of the thalamus as structures that mediate short-term memory and learning. He postulates that the anterior portion of the inferior temporal gyri sending fibers by way of the temporal stem to the dorsomedial nucleii are involved in short-term memory and learning. In monkeys, where selective lesions of the hippocampal formation is easily accomplished without the destruction of the temporal stem, no memory deficits (for certain tasks) are noted when this site is removed. The only defects noted postsurgery are disturbances of spatial orientation. Similarly, lesions of the mammillary bodies or the fornices have led to no defects in learning or memory in animals. Fibers from the inferior temporal cortex traverse through the temporal stem to end up partially in the dorsomedial nucleus (pars magnocellularis); hippocampectomy in humans destroys the temporal stem, severing the input from the temporal cortex to the diencephalic structures. In animals, lesions of the thalamus that involve the magnocellular part of the dorsomedial nucleus result in learning deficits. In monkeys with cooling probes placed in the temporal lobes, the hippocampal formation, and the amygdaloid nucleii, learning and memory show severe decrements only when the anterior part of the inferotemporal gyrus or the fibers emanating from this area are cooled to 6° C. These functions return to normal levels of performance when the temperature is raised back to normal (Horel and Pytko, 1982). Zola-Morgan and Squire (1984) studied monkeys with lesions either in the temporal stem or conjointly in the hippocampus–amygdaloid complex. They showed that in learning tasks modeled on human memory for reward–nonreward discrimination, only lesions of the conjoint hippocampus–amygdaloid complex produce memory deficits; lesions in the temporal stem were associated with defects of visual pattern discrimination. It appears that lesions at different sites in the brain lead to different types of memory disturbance. As yet, evidence that pathology of the inferior temporal gyrus by itself can cause memory disturbances in humans is scanty. The observations of Penfield and Jasper (1954) that electrical stimulations of the cortex of the temporal lobe evokes memories, and those of Bickford, Mulder, Dodger, Svien, and Rome (1958) that stimulation of white matter of the middle temporal gyrus produces amnesia, are of interest and provide support for the importance of the temporal lobe and its cortex in memory mechanisms. Further evidence

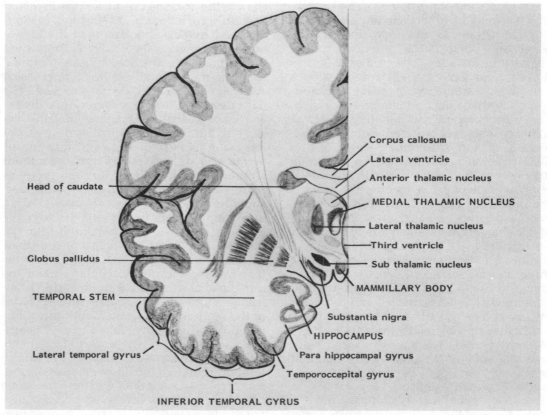

**FIGURE 2–1.** Coronal section passing through the mammillary bodies. Capital letters are used for structures putatively important in mediating memory processes.

for the role of these structures as important sites for the mediation of memory in humans could come from using the techniques of transitory cooling of these areas during neurosurgical procedures. Thus the controversy as to what is the essential locus of memory pathology in the brain remains unresolved. Figure 2–1 is a coronal section of the brain in which pathologic anatomy of several structures (their names in capital letters) have been implicated with the amnesic syndrome.

Other neuropathologic conditions associated with memory disturbances of the Korsakoff type in the presence or absence of various degrees of cognitive dysfunction also have been mostly associated with lesions of the limbic or diencephalic structures. Tumors most commonly produce amnesic symptoms when they are located in the walls or floor of the third ventricle. Craniopharyngiomas and cysts in the third ventricle that exert pressure on dorsomedial nu-

cleii and the hypothalamus produce anterograde amnesia, as well as retrograde amnesia and confabulation in the presence of relatively intact cognitive functions.

Head trauma, resulting in either negative or positive acceleration of the brain and consequent posttraumatic amnesia, probably affects the axial structures of the brain more than it affects the outer structures. The pathology may be due to localized hemorrhage, edema, or actual shearing of connecting fibers important in the mediation of memory. In the majority of cases, posttraumatic amnesias are not permanent, and various degrees of restitution of functions occur in the months or years after the trauma. Generally, with the passage of time the extent of retrograde amnesia shrinks more quickly than that of the anterograde amnesia (Russell, 1971; Whitty and Zangwill, 1977).

Occlusion of posterior cerebral arteries, which supply the hippocampi, part of globus pallidus, and the area through which temporal lobe fibers traverse to midline structures, can produce an amnesia similar to that of Korsakoff's syndrome. Viral encephalitis resulting in variable degrees of Korsakoff's syndrome is sometimes associated with neuropathology in the limbic and diencephalic structures (Glaser and Pincus, 1969).

In the initial stages of Alzheimer's disease, when the temporal lobes are more affected, amnesia and learning problems are the salient features. This occurs before the pathology becomes extensive and other cognitive dysfunctions become predominant. In these cases the cortices of temporal lobes, in addition to the hippocampal formation, are the main sites of degeneration. Temporal lobe seizures and electroconvulsive treatment (ECT) produce transient amnesias of both the retrograde and the anterograde type. In the first instance, in addition to a pathophysiology of temporal lobes, resulting in localized seizure activity, there may be structural pathology. In the case of ECT, only a pathophysiologic state exists, which affects not only the temporal lobes locally, but also the whole nervous system in a global fashion.

## CLINICAL PICTURE

Chronic alcohol intoxication associated with thiamine deficiency manifesting as an acute confusional state is accompanied by (a) ocular dysfunction and nystagmus, paralysis of lateral and conjugate gaze with strabismus and diplopia; (b) various degrees of cerebellar dysfunction with wide-based stance and short-stepped gait; and (c) polyneuropathy with disturbance of sensory and motor function. The confusional state is characterized by disturbances of awareness, attention, and motivation; disorientation to time, place, and person; and inability to recall recent or remote occurrences. Before the advent of thiamine therapy, a majority of these patients died within 10 days of the onset of symptoms. Brain autopsies in these cases showed lesions in the cerebellum, the dorsal motor nucleii, the paraventricular structures of the thalamus, and the hypothalamus. Lesions of the mammillary bodies were quite severe (Victor et al., 1971). Questions have arisen as to what brings about this pathology in the brain. Severe thiamine deficiency, as seen in Wernicke's encephalopathy, does lead to diencephalic lesions in monkeys without being associated with alcohol intoxication. However, chronic alcoholics, not having suffered overt Wernicke's encephalopathy, end up having memory disturbances that are intermediate between those of normals and those of the Korsakoff's patients (Butters and Cermak, 1980). Thus it would appear that the concomitant deficiency of thiamine and the toxic levels of alcohol may be synergistic in the pathogenesis of the amnesic syndrome.

Those who survive the acute period of the Wernicke's encephalopathy end up with memory problems of various degrees and duration. The description of amnesia with polyneuritis in alcoholics (and some non-alcoholics) by Korsakoff (1889) still is unsurpassed. The memory difficulties are manifested by a decreased or lack of ability to learn and recall new information for more than a few minutes in the post-illness period. Also, there is difficulty in recalling experiences and events that have occurred before the onset of the illness.

In anterograde amnesia, immediate or instantaneous (as tested by recall within several seconds) memory may be relatively intact, indicating that registration of perceptions is fairly normal. Recent memory, dating back from a few minutes or hours to weeks, is moderately or severely deficient. This is sometimes referred to as "rapid forgetting." A patient may not remember that an hour earlier he had undergone a painful lumbar puncture or that he had eaten breakfast or shaken hands with a doctor, whom he greets again as if he has seen him for the first time. He may be repeatedly shown the way to his house or room and yet cannot find his way back where he came from or loses his way in the streets or the hospital corridors. This disorientation to place and person extends to time and date. The patient may be reading the newspaper with apparent interest and attention and a few minutes later not remember what he had read and start reading the same item again with interest. The patient may remember his name and recognize his close relatives if he lives with them but may not know what their occupation is, how many children they have, or when he last saw them. His memory may show less deficiency if he is given cues about what he has learned recently, i.e., he shows "responsiveness to recognition probes." Such patients may or may not have insight into their memory defects. Some, being aware of their problems, complain about inability to remember and are upset about it. Others are partially aware and mostly deny any disability, while still others are totally unaware and express puzzlement when confronted with evidence for their memory deficits. Insight into illness generally diminishes as the post-illness period of amnesia is prolonged. However, despite the severity of amnesia, patients are still able to learn with frequent practice, even under limited conditions, certain specified tasks (Piercy, 1977; Hirst, 1982). They are better at learning skills than learning facts. Memories of events or experiences antecedent to the illness are generally better preserved than those of recent events or experiences.

The nearer retrograde amnesia is temporally to the illness, the severer it is. Habitual functions, such as speech, reading, writing, getting dressed, or riding a bicycle, that were learned in childhood and adolescence remain intact. Memory for remote events may be fairly good but may show various degrees of disorganization in the temporal and spatial context. A patient may remember that the four presidents before Nixon were Johnson, Kennedy, Eisenhower, and Truman, but he might not remember the temporal order in which they occupied the office. He may remember that there were two wars after World War II but might say that the war in Korea came after the war in Vietnam, or he may think that General McArthur was in the war in Vietnam. He may remember that his children were married but may not remember their spouses' names or their wedding dates. He may know the names of the states bordering his own state but may make mistakes in their geographical relationships to one another. Significant and dramatic events in his life many years before the onset of the illness may be remembered but with embellishment from other events in the life of the patient. When the patient recounts these events, there is a fictional and, at times, fantastic tinge to the story.

Patients with severe or moderate antero-grade amnesia and with partial or complete loss of insight, when asked questions about their recent activities or experiences, will not state that they cannot remember, but will embark on long, circumlocutory stories that are not factual. The stories may contain elements of actual events experienced by the patient in the past. This confabulatory tendency is manifested generally without any element of doubt; when confronted with the facts, the patient may either express puzzlement, show anger, or accuse the interviewer of trying to confuse or persecute him. It is this lack of insight that gives such patients the designation of having a "psychosis." Confabulations can also be prompted in patients by asking them leading questions. The examiner may ask the patient who has been in the hospital for weeks, "Didn't I see you in the park yesterday?" The patient could respond, "Sure, wasn't it a beautiful day? Oh, the kids flying kites and playing with their Frisbees! My friend Johnny and I were playing with our dog, Snapper, and he was such a card . . . " and so on. While telling this story, the patient may express facial emotions appropriate to the content of what he is recounting. It is quite likely that this fictitious presentation is made up from fragments of a repository of old memories or events that may have been experienced by the patient.

The following case is an example of the amnesic syndrome: The patient is a 37-year-old married white male house painter who had abused alcohol since his teenage years. In the past 4 to 5 years he had shown signs of alcohol addiction and had suffered twice from withdrawal (delirium tremens). About 3 months before his hospitalization, while drinking heavily for weeks, he had undergone a period of confusion, hallucinations, inability to walk without holding on to objects and had complained of seeing double and having visions. He had been admitted to a local hospital for about 3 weeks, treated with vitamins, enriched diet, benzodiazepines, and thioridazine. When he went home, his wife noted that he did not know his way around the house, did not remember names, and could not recognize some of his friends and relatives. An hour after having been served breakfast, he would ask if he were going to have breakfast soon. He had no memory of the events that led to his hospitalization or of his hospital stay. He had no memory about his job. Two or 3 weeks after discharge from the local hospital, he was able to find his way around the house and was able to remember the names of his children but could not remember their ages or birthdays. Sometimes he would misidentify one of his children with another. At times his memory would be slightly better than at other times. Two weeks before admission he and his children had gone to the park, which was a few blocks from his house. While the children were playing, he walked away and then could not find his way to them or to his house. Two hours later he was found many blocks away from the park and had no memory of where he had been. He was readmitted to the hospital. In the hospital he was noted to appear older than his stated age. He was casually dressed, pleasant, and sociable. He was not oriented to time, place, or person. He had no insight as to why he was in the hospital. He knew the town from which he had come but could not remember the address of his house. His memory for recent events was practically nil. His memory of events before the onset of his illness was severely diminished for up to 3 to 4 years antecedent to the illness. He could not remember what he had done as a house painter, where he had lived, and what kinds of cars he had driven. His memory for remote events was patchy, e.g., he knew the year of his marriage but did not remember what church he was married in. When asked how was it that he could not remember the name of the church, he answered, "Oh, I am not interested in churches. Why don't you go and find out from the records?"

In the hospital he continued to be disoriented and was not able to find his bed or the bathroom unassisted. He could not retain the names of nursing staff, medical students, or doctors for more than a few minutes. When the doctor who had introduced himself to the patient and had shaken hands with him an hour earlier saw him and asked him if he had known the doctor before, he would say, "Sure, you are Dr. Johnson, who mended my broken knee after the car accident." (His wife reported that indeed about 12 years ago he had had a car accident and a Dr. Johnson had taken care of him.) Every time the doctor saw the patient, the patient would behave as if he had seen the doctor for the first time in his life. A few days after admission, this conversation took place between the doctor and the patient:

Doctor (D): Hi, Mr. McD. Do you remember me?
Patient (P): Sure, you are Dr. Barry. (Not the correct name.)
D: Where did we meet?
P: You are David's brother, aren't you? And David is a good friend of mine.
D: How are you feeling today?
P: Oh, fine . . .
D: Do you have any memory problems?
P: No.
D: Can you tell me what you did since you woke up this morning?
P: (Hesitates for several seconds) Sure. I woke up, took a good shower, and then had breakfast.
D: What did you have for breakfast?
P: Oh, I had two eggs sunny side up, two pancakes with bacon, a glass of orange juice, and a cup of coffee. (Actually, he had a boiled egg, cereal with milk, orange juice, and coffee.)
D: What did you do after breakfast?
P: Oh, I was here and there.
D: Did you go out of here?
P: Yep.
D: Did you drive a car?
P: Yep.
D: Can you tell me where you went?
P: (He hesitates, as if searching his memory.) Sure. My friend Bill and I got into the car and were driving around, when we came to a crossing. The light was still yellow when we tried to cross, but sure as heck, here comes a Cadillac driven by a dame with a flowered hat on top of her head, bearing down on us as if she owned the damn street. Before you know it, her car has taken off half the front of our car. A few minutes later there are policemen and they take us to the hospital, where they take care of my broken knee and my friend's broken nose and shoulder. Then we end up in front of the judge, who gives me a lecture on how to drive my car. The judge is actually the same one who sent one of my friends to jail for twenty years. Now, jails weren't for sissies and perverts. A lot of good, hardworking people ended up there because they wanted to be unionized . . . (The wife later corroborated part of the story of the car accident at the crossing and the court appearance about 12 years ago.)
D: Then how did you get here?
P: Why, on my own steam.

*D:* What would you say if I told you that in the past few days you have never left the hospital?

*P:* (Looking puzzled) Then I won't believe you.

After 3 weeks of hospitalization the patient's condition remained essentially unchanged, although he was able to recognize some of the staff better than others and was able to find his way in the ward. He lived as if in a perpetual present time, where everything around him was novel and worthy of interest. If in the past hour he had suffered frustrations and had burst out in tears, he had no memory of them and behaved as if nothing was wrong and nothing was bothering him.

This case is illustrative of a severe amnestic syndrome. The amnesia in patients who have suffered from the Wernicke-Korsakoff illness is graded from severe to mild. The severer the amnesia, the greater the probability that other cognitive functions will also be disturbed to some degree.

The amnestic syndromes resulting from other pathogenetic causes will also manifest themselves with various degrees of intensity and associations with other cognitive dysfunctions.

After the acute state of Wernicke's alcoholic encephalopathy has subsided with vigorous vitamin therapy, progressive improvement in midbrain, cerebral, and cerebellar dysfunctions occurs in a period ranging from a few hours to several weeks in most cases. Neurologic signs, such as ophthalmoplegia, disequilibrium, and nystagmus, disappear within a few weeks. The delirious–confusional state lasts somewhat longer and may take a few months to clear. When the confusional state has cleared up, the signs of amnesic syndrome become evident in more than 80 per cent of patients who have survived the acute state. Of these subjects, about 50 per cent improve completely or significantly within the next year, while the other 50 per cent have minor or no improvement in their amnesic syndrome (Victor et al., 1971). The extent of residual memory deficits depends on the extent of structural changes in the brain brought about by thiamine deficiency in association with other nutritional deficiencies that result when alcohol is chronically abused.

The clinical picture of amnesia secondary to trauma differs in accordance with the degree and site of damage. A concussive episode that results in a short- or long-term period of unconsciousness may also result in anterograde and retrograde amnesia of various intensities. Confabulation may not be as frequent, and the rate of recovery from the amnesia may be faster than what is observed in Korsakoff's psychosis (Russell, 1971). Carbon monoxide poisoning and other hypoxic states produce amnesias that are rarely pure, since other than diencephalic structures may be involved and other cognitive dysfunctions are also manifest. These observations are true also of amnesias secondary to encephalitis. Tumors in the region of the third ventricle tend to produce a purer form of the amnesic syndrome. In these cases the onset of the illness is gradual and the removal of tumor leads to a quicker amelioration of the memory problems than observed with the Wernicke's-Korsakoff syndrome.

Amnesias caused by temporal lobe seizures and ECTs manifest themselves during the ictal and postictal periods, lasting for a few minutes to a few hours or several days. In these cases, too, other cognitive functions may be impaired to a certain extent, although for a shorter time than the memory functions. Occasionally patients who have received ECT have relatively extensive retrograde amnesias and tend to have less problem with anterograde amnesia.

## LABORATORY FINDINGS

There are no specific laboratory tests that would help in the diagnosis of amnesia. Studies of structural changes by pneumoencephalography, x-rays of the brain, and computed tomography may help in localizing lesions caused by tumors, vascular occlusion, or trauma to the brain that may relate to the amnesic syndrome. None of these techniques are refined enough, however, to uncover lesions that are pathognomonic of the amnesic syndrome. Even postmortem neuropathologic studies have not been definitive enough to provide a reliable guide for diagnosis. Clinical examination and neuropsychological testing are the mainstays of diagnosis.

## DIFFERENTIAL DIAGNOSIS

Amnesias of the psychogenic type (Ganser's syndrome, fugue states, conversion reactions, malingering, multiple personality) are generally differentiated from organic amnesias by their relationship to traumatic and stressful situations, by their being either of the purely retrograde or purely anterograde type, and by their rather abrupt onset after a traumatic psychological experience occasionally associated with mild head trauma. In Ganser's syndrome, memory defects are manifested by the subject, who in response to questions will give approximate answers; for example, a man age 26 who is in prison, whose wife's name is Mary, and who has three children (two sons and one daughter) will say that he is 25 years old, that his wife's name is Miriam, and that he has four children (one son, three daughters). In fugue states, the individual has no memory of his past; he maintains that he does not remember his name, family, address, job, or age. When confronted with evidence about these aspects of his past life, he appears puzzled and confused. He is able to assume and remember a new name; his recent memory is generally intact. He learns new information and retains it normally. The fugue state is frequently due to an untenable situation facing the patient, and it seems to provide him with an escape mechanism by which he "wanders away" from unpleasant circumstances. Fugue states of shorter duration are known to occur as a postictal complication of temporal lobe epilepsy. Fugue states are most often observed in soldiers facing battles or in those who have been defeated or who have suffered shell shock. Dysfunctions of memory as a conversion reaction are akin to the disturbances of motor or sensory functions in hysterical subjects. In malingering, where memory losses are simulated, these losses are patchy and at times exaggerated. Such subjects would claim that they cannot read or write because they have forgotten how to. Malingering in such cases is generally associated with circumstances in which the subject gains financially or avoids punishment. Subjects with multiple personalities, while assuming a new personality, may say that they do not remember what the "other" person has said or done. Whereas in fugue state the subject loses his past identity, in the case of multiple personality the subject gains new identity and memories. The subject may have some inkling into the identity of the other person or persons; however, he seems to be somewhat forgetful of what the others have done. The memory for the others may become clearer with hypnosis or suggestion.

## TREATMENT

The brain lesions that produce the amnesic syndrome are various; hence treatment would include, initially, the removal, if possible, of the lesioning process, be it vitamin deficiency and alcoholism or a growing tumor exerting pressure on the paraventricular structures. The long-term treatment of patients with amnesic syndrome is mostly ameliorative rather than curative. Once brain structures have been damaged and their functions impaired, it is unlikely that complete restitution of function will occur, especially in the older individual. Nevertheless, with passage of time, slow progress in many cases has been observed. If no improvement of memory function has occurred within the first year or two with memory-enhancing psychological maneuvers, it is unlikely that significant further progress in memory functions will ensue. Repetition of tasks in a fairly uniform and relaxed environment, avoidance of frustrating experiences, and provision of appropriate rewards and incentives as psychological aids may help the patient. Drugs to enhance memory, such as cholinergics, magnesium pemoline, and, more recently, neuropeptides, have not been tested rigorously enough to be used routinely in patients with the amnesic syndrome. The memory-enhancing status of these drugs at this time is still equivocal at best.

### REFERENCES

Bickford RG, Mulder DW, Dodge HW, Svien HJ, Rome HP: Changes in memory function produced by electrical stimulations of the temporal lobe in man. Res Publ Assoc Res Nerv Ment Dis 36:227–243, 1958.

Brierly JB: Neuropathology of amnestic states. In Whitty CWM, Zangwill OL (eds): Amnesia. London, Butterworth, 1977, pp 199–223.

Butters N, Cermak LS: Alcoholic Korsakoff's Syndrome: An Information-Processing Approach to Amnesia. New York, Academic, 1980.

Glaser GH, Pincus JH: Limbic encephalitis. J Nerv Ment Dis 149:59–66, 1969.

*Hirst W: The amnesic syndrome: Descriptions and explanations. Psychol Bull 91:435–460, 1982.

*Horel JA: The neuroanatomy of amnesia. A critique of the hippocampal memory hypothesis. Brain 101:403–445, 1978.

Horel JA, Pytko DE: Behavioral effects of local cooling in temporal lobe of monkey. J Neurophysiol 47:11–22, 1982.

*Korsakoff SS: Psychic disorders in conjunction with peripheral neuritis (1889). Trans Victor M, Yakovlev PI. Neurology 5:394–406, 1955.

*Milner B: Memory and the medial temporal regions of the brain. In Pribram KH, Broadbent DE (eds): Biology of Memory. New York, Academic, 1970, pp 29–50.

Penfield W, Jasper HH: Epilepsy and the Functional Anatomy of the Human Brain. Boston, Little, Brown, 1954.

Piercy MF: Experimental studies of the organic amnesic syndrome. In Whitty CWM, Zangwill OL (eds): Amnesia. London, Butterworth, 1977, pp 1–51.

Russell WR: The Traumatic Amnesias. Oxford, Oxford University Press, 1971.

Scoville WB, Milner B: Loss of recent memory after bilateral hippocampal lesions. J Neurol Neurosurg Psychiatry 20:11–21, 1957.

Spiegel EA, Wycis HT, Orchinik LW, Freed H: The thalamus and temporal orientation. Science 121:770–772, 1955.

Van Buren JM, Borke RC: The medial temporal substratum of memory. Anatomical study in three individuals. Brain 95:599–632, 1972.

*Victor M, Adams RD, Collins GH: The Wernicke-Korsakoff Syndrome. Philadelphia, FA Davis, 1971.

Whitty CWM, Zangwill OL: Traumatic amnesia. In Whitty CWM, Zangwill OL (eds): Amnesia. London, Butterworth, 1977, pp 118–135.

Zola-Morgan S, Squire LR: Preserved learning in monkeys with medical temporal lesions: Sparing of motor and cognitive skills. J Neurosci 4:1072–1085, 1984.

*References with asterisks are important in terms of understanding the description, history, neuropathology, and neuropsychology of the amnestic syndrome.

# chapter 3

# THE ORGANIC BRAIN SYNDROMES PRESENTING WITH LITTLE OR NO COGNITIVE IMPAIRMENT

*by* Michael K. Popkin, M.D.

Cognitive impairment is not required as an essential feature of an organic brain syndrome (OBS) in the *Diagnostic and Statistical Manual of Mental Disorders*, third edition (DSM-III). This striking departure from prior nosological constructs has, from the outset, drawn criticism, especially that of blurring the usual boundaries between organic and functional psychopathology (Roth, 1981). Diagnostic criteria mandating global or selective cognitive deficits are absent from three of the seven specific OBSs in DSM-III. These are (1) *organic affective syndrome*, (2) *organic delusional syndrome*, and (3) *organic personality disorder*. For each, DSM-III specifies that cognitive impairment, if present, will be no more than mild. Features other than cognitive dysfunction may thus be the sole symptoms of each of the three disorders. If cognitive impairment is more

than mild, a diagnosis of delirium or dementia becomes the principal choice. These three disorders were initially (if transiently) designated "symptomatic functional syndromes" by Lipowski (1978), who noted that "there is little doubt that these syndromes may at times follow cerebral disorder and may remit following its resolution." The use of the term symptomatic recalled Wernicke's turn-of-the-century definition of symptomatic psychoses as those dependent on a physical illness.

## DEFINITIONS AND GENERAL OBSERVATIONS

Changes in mood, thinking, and personality have long been associated with cerebral disorders. It is briefly inviting to think of the three OBSs with little or no cognitive impairment as "functional equivalents," signaling the extent to which they may resemble and overlap with standard functional disorders. However, the diagnostic criteria for the three disorders are not merely transpositions of the usual DSM-III criteria for affective disorder, schizophrenia, or personality disorder combined with the organic mental disorder (OMD) requirement to demonstrate "an organic factor etiologically related to the abnormal mental state" (p. 101). Careful examination shows major differences; these extend well beyond the presence of criteria excluding delirium, dementia, and other OBSs.

A diagnosis of organic delusional syndrome requires that delusions attributed to an organic factor *predominate* in a clinical presentation without evidence of delirium, dementia, or hallucinosis. Nothing further is specified regarding the delusions. The B and C criteria of schizophrenia (DSM-III, p. 189), which address the deterioration of function and the duration of the illness process, are not mentioned. A diagnosis of organic affective syndrome (depressed) rests on the identification of *dysphoria* (attributed to an organic factor) as the *predominant* clinical feature and requires the presence of only two of eight B criteria (DSM-III, p. 214) governing major depressive disorder. There is to be no evidence of delirium, dementia, hallucinosis, or delusions. In contrast, a DSM-III diagnosis of major depressive episode requires that dysphoria be *prominent* and that *four* of the B criteria be satisfied. Parallel observations apply to the criteria for manic presentations of organic affective syndrome as well. Even a cursory glance at the elements of organic personality syndrome suffices to indicate that it shares surprisingly little with any of the 12 personality disorders coded on Axis II of DSM-III. It principally requires evidence of one of the following changes in behavior and personality (attendant to a specific organic factor or process): (1) emotional lability, (2) impaired impulse control, (3) apathy, or (4) suspiciousness.

The rationales that underlie the specific elements of these diagnostic criteria are, regrettably, not presented or clarified in DSM-III. Equally problematic is DSM-III's failure to address what might satisfy the required etiological relationship in these three and other OBSs. As a consequence, considerable latitude has been extended to the clinician's subjective judgment.

The category *organic affective syndrome* is an outgrowth of the concept of "secondary depression," which appeared in the late 1960s. The original "Feighner et al." criteria (1972) included among secondary depressive disorders those arising in the context of life-threatening or incapacitating medical illness. The major focus, however, was directed to those depressive syndromes beginning after the onset of other nonaffective psychiatric illness. The depression that follows the resolution of an acute schizophrenic episode is a ready example of such a secondary disorder.

Andreasen and Winokur (1979) argued for excluding preexisting medical illnesses from the category of secondary affective disorder in order to achieve a more homogeneous clinical entity; Klerman (1981) favored expanding the concept to include "not only the affective states secondary in time to other well-defined psychiatric syndromes but also secondary to, or associated with, *concomitant* systemic medical disease or drug reactions." Organic affective syndrome is an indirect product of this dialogue. It provides a discrete DSM-III category for medical affective disturbances and has been designed with the assumption that physiologic or biologic variables engender these affective disturbances. It seems to look past the perplexing question of reactive or psychological response to medical illness. Organic affective syndrome is a broad overinclusive category at present.

As has been noted by Kathol and Petty (1981) and Klerman (1981), diagnosing affective disorder in the face of medical-surgical illness is a difficult task; many of the usual guideposts, particularly vegetative functions, are confounded by the physical illness process itself. One cannot rely with certainty on such parameters as impaired sleep, impaired appetite, weight loss, and reduced energy to diagnose mood disorder in the patient with malignancy, a collagen vascular disease, or respiratory insufficiency. This led Stewart, Drake, and Winokur (1965) to conduct their study of depression among the medically ill "based entirely on psychological symptoms." Such diagnostic dilemmas have impeded vigorous investigation of "medical depression."

Few data aside from prevalence estimates are presently available to characterize these conditions; little is known of their natural course, outcome, and treatment response.

The category *organic delusional syndrome* addresses schizophrenia-like presentations associated with organic disorders. These disturbances may involve the central nervous system (CNS) directly or indirectly. Kraepelin and Bleuler both viewed schizophrenia as the clinical outcome of an *organic* cerebral pathologic process. Studies using computed tomography (CT) scanning (Luchins, 1982), brain electrical activity mapping (BEAM) (Morihisa, Duffy, and Wyatt, 1983), evoked potential (Morstyn, Duffy, and McCarley, 1983), and positron emission tomography (PET) (Buchsbaum et al., 1982), together with the earlier work of Johnstone et al. (1976, 1978) and Cross, Crow, and Owen (1981), lend increasing credence to the early postulates. Without the technology for sophisticated brain imaging, the early German theorists could only look to presumed relationships between known organic disorders (including alcoholism) and paranoid or schizophrenia-like states. These "models" apparently served quite well. Over the ensuing years the literature has documented any number of medical disorders, brain trauma, and drugs capable of evoking schizophrenic symptomatology. Substance-induced disorders have recently come to the fore and may be the most common cause of the syndrome (Lipowski, 1984).

The category *organic personality syndrome* traces its origins to the 19th-century recognition of behavioral change in end-stage neurosyphilis. Subsequently, the outbreak of encephalitis in 1918 and the extensive number of World War I brain injuries focused attention on the question of specific lesions of the CNS and concomitant changes in personality and behavior (Lipowski, 1980b). The DSM-III category of organic personality syndrome has been specifically constructed to encompass the frontal lobe syndromes (Blumer and Benson, 1975). These consist of two types: (1) a "pseudodepressed" convexity syndrome with "negative symptoms," in which patients are impoverished in thought and action alike; and (2) "pseudopsychopathic"—with dysfunction in the orbitomedial areas of the frontal lobes—in which patients are disinhibited, impulsive, puerile, and often intensely labile. Focal brain lesions involving other areas of the cortex merit no special status as yet in DSM-III, although other "regional cortical syndromes" are well described (Taylor, in press).

Despite its recognition of the diversity with which organic disorders may psychiatrically present, DSM-III offers no organic equivalent for anxiety disorders. The omission is surprising, since a range of problems, including endocrinopathies, substance abuse, and tumors, are known to give rise to recurrent or persistent anxiety or panic attacks. Mackenzie and Popkin (1983) have defined and formulated diagnostic criteria for an organic anxiety syndrome. In a similar fashion, DSM-III does not address organic counterparts for a number of other clinical problems; at present, these must be classified as *atypical* OBSs (*without evidence of reduced cognitive performance*) (author's emphasis).

## ETIOLOGY

An explicit goal of liberalizing the OMDs section of DSM-III was to encourage reporting of associations of disturbances in mood, thinking, and personality with cerebral disorders. This in turn was expected to stimulate further investigation of causative and pathogenetic relationships (Lipowski, 1980a). These intentions remain to be fulfilled, but it is appreciated that a wide range of diseases, substances, and trauma can evoke each of the OBSs presenting with little or no cognitive impairment. In the tertiary care setting, however, a modest number of physiologic factors account for the majority of cases.

Endocrinopathies, drugs, direct lesions of the CNS, and infections are the causes for most *organic affective disorders*. This list of etiologies applies to both depressive and manic forms of organic affective disorder (although the second is far less prevalent). Thyroid dysfunction and cortisol aberrations are both well known for evoking mood change; affective disturbances have been described in a full complement of endocrine conditions (Popkin and Mackenzie, 1980). Substance-induced mood disorders are encountered frequently in the hospital setting. Surprisingly, DSM-III makes no attempt to distinguish these from the general grouping of organic affective disorders. To the contrary, it identifies reserpine, methyldopa, and some hallucinogens as prominent etiological factors for organic affective syndrome (p. 117). It would appear instructive to categorize such conditions as substance-induced OMD, affective type, and reserve the organic affective category for endogenously mediated phenomena. This seemingly technical distinction may carry treatment implications; for example, steroid-induced mood disorders respond promptly to neuroleptics but may be exacerbated by tricyclics (Hall, Popkin, and Kirkpatrick, 1978). Only a small number of drugs (especially antihypertensives, oral contraceptives, barbiturates, and ethanol) precipitate depressive symptoms with any frequency (Whitlock and Evans, 1978). Other "offenders" in the tertiary care hospital include steroids and several chemotherapeutic agents.

Work by Robinson et al. (1984) clarifies the association of stroke and affective disorder of the depressive type. Krauthammer and Klerman (1978) did not identify vascular events (e.g., hemorrhages, cerebrovascular accidents) as a significant etiological factor in "secondary mania." Lishman (1978) noted the elevation of mood after at least one type of vascular event, the rupture of anterior communicating artery aneurysms. Associations of mood disorder with multiple sclerosis, viral illness, and pancreatic carcinoma are well described. The first is a point of controversy—is the affective condition reactive or a direct function of demyelination? The last is a puzzle—are neuropeptides the underlying mechanism?

Etiologic factors in *organic delusional syndrome* include drugs, metabolic disorders, a range of CNS conditions (e.g., encephalitis, head trauma, epilepsy, and tumor), and a number of other conditions, including systemic lupus erythematosus, vitamin $B_{12}$ deficiency, porphyria, and Huntington's chorea. Substance-induced delusions are probably the most common etiology; stimulants dominate the clinical picture, although L-dopa and steroids are common offenders on medical-surgical services. In psychiatric consultation work, organic delusional syndrome is most likely to be encountered in patients with epileptic disorders. The emergence of schizophreniform features in patients who have had epilepsy

for 15 or more years is well recognized (Davison and Bagley, 1969); considerable controversy still surrounds the pathogenesis of such clinical phenomenology.

In contrast to the first two conditions, *organic personality syndrome* is predominantly the result of head trauma or structural damage to the brain. The latter may involve vascular insults (particularly subarachnoid bleeds), tumors, poisoning, and psychosurgery. At present postconcussive phenomenology must be grouped in DSM-III as either organic personality syndrome or atypical OBS. The diagnosis of organic personality syndrome is commonly extended to numbers of hospitalized epilepsy patients as well.

## EPIDEMIOLOGY

Epidemiologic studies using DSM-III criteria and systematically examining all three of the OBSs under discussion are not yet available, to my knowledge. In the consultation psychiatry setting, the three disorders account for approximately 15 per cent to 20 per cent of all OMD cases. Technical problems of diagnosis aside, it can be expected that organic affective syndrome is the most common of the three and organic delusional syndrome, the least common. A number of investigators have estimated the prevalence of depression in the medically ill to range between 20 per cent and 30 per cent. Moffic and Paykel (1975) used the Beck Depression Inventory and found 24 per cent of a group of medical inpatients scored at or above a cutoff point of 14 within 1 week of admission to a teaching hospital. (A cutoff point of 14 has been reported by Beck [1967] to differentiate reliably between depressives and non-depressives.) Few of these patients were, however, identified by their physicians as depressed. Schwab et al. (1967) concluded that "at least 20%" of a series of medical inpatients were depressed. To date no published studies of medical depression use DSM-III criteria; nor did most preceding studies take pains to separate reactive processes from "purely" physiologic depressions, i.e., those with an identified (organic) etiology. The association of depression and medical illness need not imply an etiologic relationship. In reviewing the available studies of "medical depression," certain intriguing observations about risk factors appear with consistency. First, there is no evidence of the usual female preponderance in affective illness; rather, the incidence of depression in the medically ill appears independent of gender. Neither is there usually a prior history of mood disorder in the patient or in his or her family. In a similar vein, data regarding secondary mania suggest a negative family history and late onset. The overall severity of these constellations appears less pronounced than that found in "functional" major depressive or manic episodes. Suicide is generally regarded as uncommon in the medically ill; however, there is evidence that patients with specific illnesses, particularly respiratory disorders, constitute high-risk groups for suicide (Mackenzie and Popkin, in press).

In the absence of formal epidemiologic inquiries, the work of Hall et al. (1980) and Koranyi (1979) does offer some perspective. Hall et al. reported data from the exhaustive medical evaluation of 100 psychiatrically disturbed subjects of lower socioeconomic strata admitted to a research ward in lieu of commitment to a state mental hospital. Forty-six per cent were judged to have medical illnesses that directly accounted for or greatly exacerbated their behavioral symptoms. Of this group, one third had a schizophreniform presentation, another third presented with affective features, and less than one tenth had personality disorders. (In retrospect these would now be assigned per DSM-III to the respective three OBS categories under discussion.) Of the medical conditions manifesting as psychiatric disease (or evoking psychiatric constellations), endocrinopathies were predominant. Disturbances of the CNS, hematologic disorders, and cardiovascular disturbances accounted for most of the remaining cases. Koranyi (1979) studied some 2000 subjects referred to his psychiatric clinic; 43 per cent had major medical illness. In 18 per cent of those with medical illness, the presenting psychopathology was judged to be caused by the physical disease. In 51 per cent, the medical condition contributed substantially to the behavioral picture; in the remaining 31 per cent the two disorders were judged independent though concurrent. Koranyi found that the frequencies of medical conditions in psychiatric patients by organ system were as follows: (1) cardiovascular, (2)

CNS, (3) endocrine/metabolic, and (4) gastrointestinal. Although Hall's work dealt with a specific socioeconomic population, Koranyi's data are more broad-based. Together they signal that the psychiatrist and the primary care physician alike must conscientiously consider organic etiologies for a sizable fraction of psychiatric presentations in either the inpatient or outpatient setting.

## PATHOLOGY

Investigators have pursued the neuroanatomical basis of psychiatric illness throughout the course of modern psychiatry, but precise anatomical correlates for psychiatric disorders have proven elusive (Ross and Rush, 1981). Studies of the psychopathology arising with "organic" disorders show that the *site* of CNS lesions and the *nature of the pathologic process* are crucial to resultant behavioral presentations. Flor-Henry and Koles (1980) proposed that both mood and thought disorder relate to alterations of the frontotemporal regions of the brain. Numerous studies of temporal lobe epileptics have led to the suggestion that right-sided lesions are more frequently associated with affective changes and those on the left, with schizophreniform presentations (Flor-Henry, 1976; Bear and Fedio, 1977). Studies of patients with unilateral brain damage have consistently indicated that left hemisphere lesions are associated with dysphoria, hopelessness, and self-depreciation; in contrast, right hemisphere damage is correlated with indifference, euphoria, social disinhibition, and placidity (Sackeim et al., 1982). While some argue for hemispheric asymmetry in the expression of positive and negative emotions (Sackeim et al., 1982), others (Ross and Rush, 1981) emphasize that both hemispheres participate in affective disorders, each modulating certain features. Studying brain-damaged patients, the latter authors observed that in the right hemisphere a loss of ability to express emotion correlated with more anterior lesions and a loss of emotional recognition with more posterior lesions. In contrast, Kiloh (1980) focuses exclusively on the limbic system and its interconnections, viewing laterality issues with reservation and implying that no one nucleus has a monopoly on a specific behavior.

In this confusing picture, the work of Robinson et al. (1984) is noteworthy. Studying mood disorders in stroke patients without preceding psychiatric disorder, they found that behavioral changes were a function of the location of the hemispheric lesion. Severity of depression was greatest in patients with left anterior lesions (vs. all others). In addition, "the severity of depression correlated with the proximity of the lesion on CT scan to the frontal pole" in this group. In the group with right hemisphere lesions, the reverse trend was found. The more posterior the lesion, the more pronounced the depression. Right anterior lesions were accompanied by apathy or undue cheerfulness. Thus intrahemispheric lesion location seems to be critical to mood disorder in stroke patients.

In analogous work, Levine and Grek (1984) studied patients manifesting delusions after right cerebral infarction. No particular site or size of lesion was associated with particular delusions; however, there was a relationship between delusions and all measures of brain atrophy. The authors concluded that the emergence of delusions depended on premorbid brain atrophy; thus they argue that the state of the left hemisphere determines the response to right cerebral infarction.

The literature includes a number of neuropathologic accounts of the psychiatric manifestations of cerebral tumors (Haberland, 1965; Malamud, 1967). Factors including site of the cerebral pathology, rate of tumor growth, and amount of tissue compromised are critical to the behavioral sequelae, which span a full gamut of psychopathology. (The interested reader is referred to Lishman's review [1978] of the psychopathology accompanying cerebral tumors.) Davison and Bagley (1969) compiled a comprehensive account of schizophrenia-like psychoses associated with CNS disorders. This work reflects how varied may be the pathology evoking what would now be called organic delusional syndrome.

Discussing personality changes with frontal and temporal lobe lesions, Blumer and Benson (1975) note that in addition to *localization*, the *nature of the lesion* is important. "Frontal personality disorders result from destructive lesions, whereas temporal personality changes are the product of *irritative* (epileptic) disorders." In addition to studies of war-injured and neurosurgical patients, the consequences of frontal lobe injury on personality can be appreciated by reviewing the psychosurgery or lobotomy literature. The "pseudo-depressed" type of frontal lobe personality alteration appears to result from pathology affecting the prefrontal convexity and its connections to the basal ganglia and thalamus. These latter sites have also been implicated in subcortical dementia (e.g., Parkinson's disease, Huntington's chorea). The "pseudopsychopathic" presentation involves lesions of the orbital frontal lobe (Blumer and Benson, 1975). The personality changes appearing late in the course of temporal lobe epilepsy are associated with varied types of pathology (tumors, vascular insults, infections, scars from trauma). Blumer and Benson (1975), however, caution that in most cases of frontal lobe disorder, pathology "fails to respect anatomical boundaries."

## CLINICAL PICTURE AND COURSE

For two of the disorders at hand, the clinical picture is straightforward. The patient presenting with an organic delusional syndrome has overt delusions, an identified organic etiologic factor, and no evidence of delirium or dementia. Associated features of a schizophreniform process may be encountered. Hallucinations may be present, although Davison and Bagley (1969) noted that auditory and tactile hallucinations are less common in "organic" vs. true schizophrenics. Catatonic symptoms were found to be more common in the organic group. Of interest, Davison and Bagley also comment on the low incidence of primary delusions in the organic group. Persecutory delusions are suggested (DSM-III, p. 114) to be the most common type of delusions.

The patient assigned a diagnosis of organic personality syndrome is "not himself." Although not seriously cognitively impaired and not manifesting major mood or thought disorder, the individual will be recognized by family and friends as changed, different, particularly in terms of lifelong emotional responsivity and general demeanor. Emotional lability and incontinence (such as seen in pseudobulbar palsy patients), poor capacity for impulse control, and altered (usually reduced) initiative are prominent. Inattention and indifference are often striking contrasts to what has gone before. The spectrum ranges from those appearing lethargic and apathetic to those who have ostensibly lost all social graces (if once present). Although the clinician is unlikely to miss such features, the premorbid picture as described by family and friends is crucial to a full appreciation of the psychopathology.

Abnormal mood judged to be the consequence of an organic factor is the essential feature of an organic affective syndrome. The disturbances of mood may closely resemble those in a depressive or manic episode, and clinical phenomenology may be the same as in a manic or depressive episode. Lipowski (1980a) argues that the presence of an organic factor should *antedate* the mood disturbance. In practice the diagnosis is often less than straightforward; as noted earlier, assessing the presence and extent of affective symptomatology in the physically ill is problematic. DSM-III skirts this problem by its emphasis on the organic etiologic factor. More explicit criteria concerning the actual affective features of the diagnoses are needed. Endicott (1984) has proposed substituting alternative associated symptoms in order to diagnose major depressive episode in the patient with malignancy. (She suggests fearfulness or depressed appearance to replace the parameter of weight change/appetite; social withdrawal instead of sleep dysfunction; brooding or self-pity instead of the loss of energy criterion; and "cannot be cheered up" in place of the impaired concentration parameter.) Presumptively, these changes could apply to a diagnosis of organic affective syndrome as well. They leave unaddressed the critical issues of reactive response to a physiologically induced mood disorder or how the clinician meaningfully distinguishes organic affective syndrome in the cancer patient from major depressive episode or adjustment disorder with depressed mood.

The clinical course of the three OBSs without cognitive dysfunction depends predominantly on the etiology of the specific disorder. Drug-induced disturbances are perhaps the most likely to remit promptly; metabolic- and endocrine-related disturbances may do likewise when corrected.

The conditions linked to destruction, permanent compromise of CNS tissue, are most likely to have ongoing behavioral sequelae. In general, organic affective syndromes should be short-lived; in contrast, the non–drug-induced organic delusional and organic personality disorders are more chronic states. DSM-III fails to comment on the course of organic delusional syndrome. Systematic data from cohort studies on the clinical course of the organic affective and delusional syndromes are needed.

## LABORATORY FINDINGS

Evidence of CNS or systemic disease is required for any of the three diagnoses. No specific approach has been formulated to date. However, history and physical with neurologic examination, CT scan, sleep-deprived electroencephalography, electrocardiography, urinalysis, blood counts, and a battery of blood chemistry studies sufficed in Hall et al.'s study (1980) to identify 90 per cent of cases in which unrecognized medical illness presented as psychiatric disease. Foster et al. (1976) demonstrated that patients with medical-associated depression had significantly less rapid eye movement (REM) activity during REM sleep compared with patients with primary depression. Such quantification of REM density has not yet been used as a marker for organic affective disorder. Clinical acumen must guide routine investigations in the search for an organic etiology. When the patient is age 35 or older and without a personal or familial history of psychiatric illness, the search for an organic factor should be more extensive.

## DIFFERENTIAL DIAGNOSIS

The diagnosis of organic personality syndrome can be primarily confused with dementia and organic affective syndrome. Personality changes may be among the initial features of a dementing illness, but in time the intellectual decline serves to distinguish the two. Likewise, the patient with an organic affective disorder may display personality alteration; the predominance of mood disturbance is the diagnostic "cutting edge." Organic delusional syndrome must be distinguished from such processes as schizophrenia and paranoid disorder. This may prove problematic at times. Delusions may arise in organic affective syndrome as well, but they are mood congruent and not the predominant feature. The dilemmas of differentiating organic affective syndrome from other affective disorders have been previously discussed. Lipowski (1980b) suggests not diagnosing organic personality syndrome unless behavioral changes have persisted for 1 month. No duration criteria presently apply in DSM-III to any of the three disorders under discussion.

## TREATMENT

### Correcting the Medical Problem

The treatment of OBSs presenting with little or no cognitive impairment has been largely neglected in the literature. Once an etiologic factor for an OBS has been identified, efforts to resolve or minimize the pathophysiologic process must follow. In some instances, correcting the medical disorder alone may suffice. For example, behavioral changes caused by a parathyroid adenoma can be expected to abate with surgical removal of the tumor and restoration of eucalcemia. In other instances, medical treatment may not redress the psychiatric disturbance. Time may be a critical variable in this process. Vitamin $B_{12}$ deficiency takes more than a year to develop, but if it is permitted to go uncorrected at some point, irreversible neuronal loss will result. In perhaps the only such study extant, Tonks (1964) found that three factors predicted whether restoration of euthyroid status would result in cessation of affective changes associated with hypothyroidism. He observed that full clearing of the psychiatric picture was likely if (1) the patient was over age 60, (2) the presentation involved cognitive impairment, and (3) the process was less than 2 years in duration.

### Management of the Psychopathology per se

Treatment of the OBS psychiatric disturbances per se has not been well researched. Little specific therapy is available for organic personality disturbances; one can treat the underlying disease, structure the environment, support and educate family members, and reserve neuroleptics for agitation or psychotic outbursts. There is evidence that agents, including lithium (Dale, 1980; Williams and Goldstein, 1979) and propranolol (Yudofsky, Williams, and Gorman, 1981; Elliot, 1976), may be useful in the management of patients with CNS damage and problems in impulse control. Patients with organic delusional syndrome benefit from neuroleptic medication to attenuate delusional ideation and preclude flagrant decompensation. My clinical experience has found thiothixene (Navane) the best choice in patients with known CNS lesions or dysfunction. (In contrast, haloperidol [Haldol] has seldom been helpful in such patients.) No clear explanation for these observations is available; however, it is interesting to note that Navane has not to date been associated with increased seizure activity. I find that two thirds of standard amounts (e.g., dose for schizophrenia) will contain delusional thinking and schizophreniform behavior in OBS patients, especially epileptics.

Perhaps most distressing is the absence of guidelines regarding the treatment of organic affective disturbances. Davies et al. (1971) found that 13 per cent of psychiatric patients treated with antidepressants became confused. When tricyclics are used in the medically ill, one third of drug trials must be discontinued owing to side effects, principally delirium (Popkin, Callies, and Mackenzie, 1985). Falk, Mahnke, and Poskanzer (1979) reported that lithium prophylactically averted steroid-induced affective disorders in a group of multiple sclerosis patients. Veith et al. (1982) and Glassman et al. (1983) have demonstrated that tricyclics will not significantly alter left ventricular function in patients with known cardiac disease; Lipsey et al. (1984) reported that nortriptyline proved useful in some mood disorders associated with stroke. (The study has numerous limitations and requires replication with a larger sample.) Thus to date the efficacy of antidepressants in treating organic affective syndrome remains unclear. Prospective studies with more specific diagnostic criteria are needed; the clinician is often confronted with dilemmas that demand choices be made despite diagnostic impasses.

## REFERENCES

Andreasen NC, Winokur G: Secondary depression—familial, clinical and research perspectives. Am J Psychiatry 136:62–66, 1979.

Bear D, Fedio P: Quantitative analysis of interictal behavior in temporal lobe epilepsy. Arch Neurol 34:454–467, 1977.

Beck, AT: Depression: clinical, experimental and therapeutic aspects. New York, Hoeber Medical Division, Harper & Row, 1967.

Blumer D, Benson DF: Personality changes with frontal and temporal lobe lesions. In Benson DF, Blumer D (eds): Psychiatric Aspects of Neurologic Disease. New York, Grune & Stratton, 1975, pp 51–170.

Buchsbaum MS, Ingvar DH, Kessler R, et al: Cerebral glucography with positron tomography: Use in normal subjects and in patients with schizophrenia. Arch Gen Psychiatry 39:251–259, 1982.

Cross AJ, Crow TJ, Owen F: H$^3$-Flupenthixol binding in postmortem brains of schizophrenics: Evidence for a selective increase in dopamine $D_2$ receptors. Psychopharmacologia 74:122–124, 1981.

Dale PG: Lithium therapy in aggressive mentally subnormal patients. Br J Psychiatry 137:469–474, 1980.

Davies RK, Tucker GJ, Harrow M, et al: Confusional episodes and antidepressant medication. Am J Psychiatry 128:95–99, 1971.

Davison K, Bagley C: Schizophrenia-like psychoses associated with organic disorders of the CNS: A review of the literature. Br J Psychiatry, Special publication #4, Current Problems of Neuropsychiatry, Herrington RN (ed), 1969, pp 113–184.

Elliot FA: The neurology of explosive rage. Practitioner 217:51–60, 1976.

Endicott J: Measurement of depression in patients with cancer. Cancer 53:2243–2248, 1984.

Falk WE, Mahnke MW, Poskanzer DC: Lithium prophylaxis of corticotropic induced psychosis. JAMA 241:1011–1012, 1979.

Feighner JP, Robins E, Guze SB, et al: Diagnostic criteria for use in psychiatric research. Arch Gen Psychiatry 26:57–63, 1972.

Flor-Henry P: Lateralized temporal-limbic dysfunction and psychopathology. Ann NY Acad Sci 280:777–795, 1976.

Flor-Henry P, Koles ZJ: EEG studies in depression, mania and normals: Evidence for partial shifts of laterality in the affective psychoses. Adv Biol Psychiatry 4:21–43, 1980.

Foster FG, Kupfer DJ, Coble P, et al: Rapid eye movement sleep density: An objective indicator in severe medical-depressive syndromes. Arch Gen Psychiatry 33:1119–1123, 1976.

Glassman AH, Johnson LL, Giardina EGV, et al: The use of imipramine in depressed patients with congestive heart failure. JAMA 250:1997–2001, 1983.

Haberland C: Psychiatric manifestations in brain tumors. Akt Frasen Psychiat Neurol 2:65–86, 1965.

Hall RCW, Gardner ER, Stickney SK, et al: Physical illness manifesting as psychiatric disease. Arch Gen Psychiatry 37:989–995, 1980.

Hall RCW, Popkin MK, Kirkpatrick B: Tricyclic exacerbation of steroid psychoses. J Nerv Ment Dis 166:738–743, 1978.

Johnstone EC, Crow TJ, Frith CD, et al: Cerebral ventricular size and cognitive impairment in chronic schizophrenia. Lancet 2:924–926, 1976.

Johnstone EC, Crow TJ, Frith CD, et al: The dementia of dementia praecox. Acta Psychiatr Scand 57:305–324, 1978.

Kathol RG, Petty F: Relationship of depression to medical illness. J Affective Disord 3:111–121, 1981.

Kiloh LG: Psychiatric disorders and the limbic system. In Girgis M, Kiloh LG (eds): Limbic Epilepsy and the Dyscontrol Syndrome. New York, Elsevier, 1980.

Klerman GL: Depression in the medically ill. Psychiatr Clin North Am 4:301–317, 1981.

Koranyi EK: Morbidity and rate of undiagnosed physical illness in a psychiatric clinic population. Arch Gen Psychiatry 36:414–419, 1979.

Krauthammer C, Klerman GL: Secondary mania. Arch Gen Psychiatry 35:1333–1339, 1978.

Levine DN, Grek A: The anatomic basis of delusions after right cerebral infarction. Neurology (NY) 34:577–582, 1984.

Lipowski ZJ: Organic brain syndromes: A reformulation. Compr Psychiatry 19:309–322, 1978.

Lipowski ZJ: A new look at organic brain syndromes. Am J Psychiatry 137:674–678, 1980(a).

Lipowski ZJ: Organic mental disorders: Introduction and review of syndromes. Section 20.1 in Kaplan HI, Freedman AM, Saddock BJ (eds): Comprehensive Textbook of Psychiatry, ed 3. Baltimore, Williams & Wilkins, 1980(b).

Lipowski ZJ: Organic mental disorders—an American perspective. Br J Psychiatry 144:542–546, 1984.

Lipsey JR, Robinson RG, Pearlson GD, et al: Nortriptyline treatment of poststroke depression: A double-blind study. Lancet 1:297–299, 1984.

Lishman WA: Organic Psychiatry. Oxford, Blackwell, 1978.

Luchins DJ: Computed tomography in schizophrenia. Arch Gen Psychiatry 39:859–860, 1982.

Mackenzie TB, Popkin MK: Organic anxiety syndrome. Am J Psychiatry 140:342–344, 1983.

Mackenzie TB, Popkin MK: Suicide in the medical patient. In Schubert D (ed): Depression in the Medical Patient. In press.

Malamud N: Psychiatric disorder with intracranial tumors of limbic system. Arch Neurol 17:113–123, 1967.

Moffic HS, Paykel ES: Depression in medical inpatients. Br J Psychiatry 126:346–353, 1975.

Morihisa JM, Duffy FH, Wyatt RJ: Brain electrical activity mapping (BEAM) in schizophrenic patients. Arch Gen Psychiatry 40:719–728, 1983.

Morstyn R, Duffy FH, McCarley RW: Altered P300 topography in schizophrenia. Arch Gen Psychiatry 40:729–734, 1983.

Popkin M, Callies A, Mackenzie T: The outcome of antidepressant use in the medically ill. Arch Gen Psychiatry 42:1160–1163, 1985.

Popkin MK, Mackenzie TB: Psychiatric presentations of endocrine dysfunctions. In Hall RCW (ed): Psychiatric Presentations of Medical Illness. Jamaica, NY, Spectrum, 1980, pp 139–156.

Robinson RG, Kubos KL, Starr LB, et al: Mood disorders in stroke patients: Importance of location of lesion. Brain 107:81–93, 1984.

Ross ED, Rush AJ: Diagnosis and neuroanatomical correlates of depression in brain-damaged patients. Arch Gen Psychiatry 38:1344–1353, 1981.

Roth M: Discussion. In Miller NE, Cohen GD (eds): Clinical Aspects of Alzheimer's Disease and Senile Dementia. New York, Raven, 1981.

Sackeim HA, Greenberg MS, Weiman AL, et al: Hemispheric asymmetry in the expression of positive and negative emotions: Neurologic evidence. Arch Neurol 32:210–218, 1982.

Schwab JJ, Bialow M, Brown JM, et al: Diagnosing depression in medical inpatients. Ann Intern Med 67:695–707, 1967.

Stewart MA, Drake F, Winokur G: Depression among medically ill patients. Dis Nerv Syst 26:479–485, 1965.

Taylor MA: DSM-III organic mental disorders. In Tischler G (ed): Diagnosis and Classification in Psychiatry: Cambridge, Cambridge University Press, in press.

Tonks CM: Mental illness in hypothyroid patients. Br J Psychiatry 110:706–710, 1964.

Veith RC, Raskind MA, Caldwell JH, et al: Cardiovascular effects of tricyclic antidepressants in depressed patients with chronic heart disease. N Engl J Med 306:954–959, 1982.

Whitlock FA, Evans LEJ: Drugs and depression. Drugs 15:53–71, 1978.

Williams KH, Goldstein G: Cognitive and affective responses to lithium in patients with organic brain syndrome. Am J Psychiatry 136:800–803, 1979.

Yudofsky S, Williams D, Gorman J: Propranolol in the treatment of rage and violent behavior in patients with chronic brain syndromes. Am J Psychiatry 138:218–220, 1981.

# chapter 4

# BIPOLAR ILLNESS

by Paula J. Clayton, M.D.

The affective disorders are disorders of mood. In the past, numerous terms, usually dichotomous, have been used to distinguish these disorders. One major separation made on the basis of genetic and clinical differences that seemed viable was the separation of the mood disorders into unipolar affective disorder and bipolar affective disorder. Unipolar affective disorder refers to patients who have depression only. Bipolar affective disorder refers to patients who have episodes of both mania and depression, or episodes of mania only.

Mania is derived from a Greek word meaning "to be mad." Hippocrates is credited with introducing psychiatric diagnoses into medical nomenclature. Two of the six diagnoses that Hippocrates proposed were mania and melancholia. In his classification, mania referred to acute mental disorders without fever and melancholia, to a wide variety of chronic mental illnesses. In the first century, Aretaeus noted that depression and excitement often alternated in the same person, and therefore might represent different aspects of the same illness. Although it is difficult to tell from the classification systems how pervasive this idea of cycling became in the centuries thereafter, the term mania remained prominent in all. For hundreds of years the diagnosis of mania seemed to have been used primarily for an illness with an acute onset and with a mood of merriment or rage or fury (Menninger, Mayman, Pruyser, 1977).

In 1686, Bonet used the term maniaco-melancholicus to characterize a group of patients. In the 1850s, Falret adopted the term circular insanity and Baillarger, double-form insanity for similar patients (Sedler, 1983). In 1874, Kahlbaum referred to patients with cyclothymia. Kraepelin (1921) drew on and synthesized the various approaches to nosology bequeathed to him from the preceding centuries. Beginning in 1883, he published nine editions of his textbook on psychiatry, and it was he who separated dementia praecox from manic-depressive illness using clinical descriptions and the natural history of the illnesses.

If we could assume that names are given to illnesses in an attempt to organize clinical observations, then it must be said, from the long history of the term mania, that the recognition of mania and the occurrence of mania were apparent to clinicians throughout history.

In 1957, Leonard was the first to suggest that bipolar and unipolar forms of affective illness may be different, separate illnesses. Perris (1966) and Angst (1966) confirmed Leonard's evidence on this point. The first American researchers to place emphasis on this distinction were Winokur, Clayton, and Reich (1969).* Although bipolar illness was, initially, separated from unipolar illness on the basis of differences in age of onset, course, family history, and response to treatment, this separation may not, in the end, prove valid. Data are beginning to accumulate that suggest that the two illnesses may be different forms of the same disorder, with bipolar illness being a severer, earlier onset form than recurrent unipolar.

## Editor's Comment

*In fact, the separation of unipolar from bipolar illness may go back to Dr. Carl Lange in Denmark in 1895 (Periodiske Depressioner, Copenhagen, 1895). Dr. H. I. Schou presented Lange's views in 1927 (Acta Psychiatr et Neurol 2:345, 1927). Dr. Schou was a coauthor of a paper (Pederson A, Poort R, Schou H: Acta Psychiatr et Neurol 23:285–319, 1947) that presented data on periodical depression. Schou and his coauthors said, on page 287, that "periodical depression has no manic phases and differs from manic-depressive psychoses with regard to heredity as well as distribution of somatic types and prognosis." They added that manic-depressive patients were more likely chronic and disabled in contradistinction to periodic depressives, who were more likely to be discharged and recovered. Certainly Leonard's contribution is undeniable, but clearly, there had been some rumblings in the field before that time.*

## DEFINITION

Manic-depressive disease, or manic-depressive illness, is the old term for the *Diagnostic and Statistical Manual of Mental Disorders*, third edition (DSM-III), disorder bipolar affective disorder, which includes patients with mania and depression or mania only. Each episode is classified as mixed, manic, or depressed. A manic episode requires a mood change that is predominantly elevated, expansive, or irritable as well as at least 1 week of at least three of the following symptoms: (1) increased activity or physical restlessness; (2) more talkative than usual or pressured speech; (3) flight of ideas or racing thoughts; (4) inflated self-esteem, including grandiosity; (5) decreased need for sleep; (6) distractibility; and (7) excessive involvement in activities that have a high potential for unrecognized painful consequences (e.g., buying sprees, sexual indiscretions, foolish business investments, reckless driving). The episode can be characterized with or without psychotic features, and the psychotic features can be characterized as either mood congruent, which involves delusions or hallucinations that are consistent with inflated worth, power, and knowledge, or mood incongruent, which involves delusions and hallucinations that are not consistent with this elevated mood, such as persecutory delusions, thought insertion or delusions of

being controlled, and catatonic symptoms, such as stupor, mutism, negativism, and posturing. The depressive episode also has a mood change, distinct features, and a 2-week duration. These characteristics are outlined in Chapter 5. For either diagnosis there is no requirement of disability or hospitalization.

The DSM-III classification does not include hypomania as part of the bipolar spectrum or the diagnosis of bipolar II, which usually refers to patients with clear episodes of depression and episodes of hypomania. Because recent evidence indicates that patients with a diagnosis of bipolar II are a heterogeneous group or closer to unipolar patients, it seems reasonable to continue to separate it.

## Editor's Comment

*The definition of a bipolar II illness requires that the individual have a significant depressive episode of major proportions and a history of hypomania but not meet the criteria for mania. A recent study (Coryell W, Endicott J, Andreasen N, Keller M: Br J Psychiatry 145:49–54, 1984) suggests that bipolar II illness is seen in families of bipolar probands and at other times in families of unipolar depressive probands. However, there also is a set of bipolar II patients who breed true within families, which may indicate that bipolar II illness, in fact, may be simply a personality disorder superimposed on a major depression.*

## ETIOLOGY

At the present time it is evident that genetic factors play a significant role in the etiology of bipolar affective disorder. There are no other data as strong as those in the genetic area, although they are currently of limited predictive value. With new genetic techniques it seems likely in the future that the entire human genome will be mapped. With this map and DNA probes for linkage markers, transmission and linkage to specific chromosomal markers will be possible (Gershon, Nurnberger, Nadi, Berrittini, and Goldin, 1983). The reports on the Older Amish Pedigree (Kidd, Gerhard, Kidd, Housman, and Egeland, 1984) illustrates such possibilities.

In addition to the genetic factors, biochemical, neuroendocrine, neurophysiologic, and sleep abnormalities have been reported, but whether these are specific to bipolar affective disorder or overlap with recurrent unipolar disorder findings is questionable. Besides the confusion of always including some not-yet-identified bipolar patients in unipolar studies (at least 10 per cent) one must always consider if the abnormalities described in any particular report occurred during a unipolar or bipolar depression, during a mania, or during a well state and under what conditions (e.g., on lithium maintenance). Because there are few unequivocal findings, a limited discussion of these issues, as well as of animal models or other disease models that mimic mania, follows.

## Genetics

There is no doubt that bipolar affective disorder is familial; that is, it runs in families, with close relatives being more likely to be affected than are unrelated subjects. Three types of studies contribute to the extent of the genetic knowledge of this illness: (1) family studies of patients with affective disorder, (2) adoption studies, and (3) twin studies.

### Family Studies

Family studies were originally anecdotal. Falret's 1854 article on circular insanity (Sedler, 1983) noted that by interviewing the parents of patients, he obtained compelling evidence as to the hereditary disposition in the illness. He concluded that circular insanity was very heritable. He could not decide, however, whether it was more heritable than any other type of mental illness, although he was inclined to think so.

Based on studies by Angst and Perris and his own work, Winokur (1978) summarized the literature and reported that in bipolar patients, 52 per cent could be expected to have a parent with an affective disorder, 54 per cent could be expected to have two generations of members affected, and 63 per cent could be expected to have an affective illness in the parents or an extended family member. He reported the incidence of mania in the first-degree relatives as between 4 per cent and 10 per cent. Thus, even in bipolar patients, the majority of affected

relatives have unipolar depression, although almost all this excess is in women (Winokur and Crowe, 1983).

The most thorough study, by Gershon et al. (1982), looked at schizoaffectives, bipolar Is, bipolar IIs, unipolars, and normal controls. The authors concluded that the most common disorder in the relatives of all probands was unipolar affective disorder, and that since there was bipolar illness in the relatives of all ill probands, there was probably genetic overlap between types. In the bipolar probands, the morbid risk in parents and offspring for schizoaffective disorder was 1.2 per cent; for bipolar affective disorder, 9.2 per cent; and for unipolar disorder, 12.3 per cent. Similar figures in siblings of bipolars for schizoaffective disorder was 0.8 per cent; bipolar affective disorder, 6.9 per cent; and unipolar disorder, 18.1 per cent. The normals had little illness except unipolar affective disorder (5.7 per cent in siblings and parents and children). The authors also looked at how the number of affected parents related to illness in the adult children. To do this they combined the schizoaffectives, the bipolar Is and IIs, and the unipolars. If one parent was ill, the risk of having an ill child was 27 per cent compared with 74 per cent if both parents were ill. When they excluded one family with the highest number of ill offspring, the risk if two parents were affected was reduced from 74 per cent to 57 per cent. Among the siblings of probands, the risk was 24 per cent if no parents were ill and 32 per cent if one parent was ill (not significantly different). Merikangas and Spiker (1982) reported similar results in adult offspring in a report of assortative mating, as did Waters, Marchenko, Abrams, Smiley, and Kalin (1983). Gershon et al. (1982) found no significant differences in illness in the relatives when the probands and controls were separated by sex and no increase in alcoholism, drug abuse, or sociopathy in the relatives of patients with these affective disorders as compared with controls. Winokur, Clayton, and Reich (1969) noted the occurrence of compulsive gambling in the fathers and brothers of some bipolar patients, but without control rates they could not comment further.

Studies of *children* (age varies from 6 to 17) of bipolar parents have yielded conflicting results. Even the best studies that included children of bipolars and controls assessed blindly and with strict criteria do not lend themselves to clear interpretation, although in the most negative study (Gershon et al., 1985), out of 76 children, there were three with mania or hypomania (by National Institute of Mental Health criteria), and they were all from bipolar families. The probability of assortative mating in bipolar parents and purposely choosing two well parents for controls make any negative findings impressive, as that combination should maximize differences.

As with the studies of children, studies of assortative mating have produced variable results. Here, too, blind structured assessment of spouses of bipolars and controls is essential. Also, because bipolar studies probably will have equal numbers of male and female spouses, and affective disorder rates are always higher in women, sex of spouses must be controlled for. Merikangas (1982) summarized the literature and concluded that there probably was assortative mating in affective disorder (not separated by polarity) but that the magnitude of the problem was unknown. Later, Merikangas, Bromet, and Spiker (1983) indicated that when assortative mating occurred, it predicted a poorer outcome at followup. Waters et al. (1983) confirmed an increased prevalence of affective disorders in spouses of bipolars, although their interpretation of results was unduly guarded.

To date no firm statement can be made about the association between bipolar affective disorder and either X linkage or HLA antigens. Some studies have not confirmed a linkage, so the ones that do must be explained by genetic heterogeneity. Recently, Nadi, Nurnberger, and Gershon (1984) reported that in cultured skin fibroblasts, bipolar patients and those relatives with a history of unipolar or bipolar illness had increased muscarinic receptors compared with unaffected relatives and controls. This finding is consistent with a theory of cholinergic mechanisms (see later) being involved in bipolar illness, but it needs replication.

### Adoption Studies

There is only one study of adoptees with bipolar illness. Mendlewicz and Rainer (1977) reported that 31 per cent of biologic parents and 12 per cent of adopted parents of hospitalized bipolar adoptees had an affective disorder. This percentage in biologic parents was comparable to the risk they reported in parents of nonadopted bipolar patients. There are studies of unipolar adoptees and of completed suicide in adoptees that are not specific to bipolar illness.

### Twin Studies

Nurnberger and Gershon (1982) summarized the twin studies on affective disorders, although not by polarity. The best study that dealt with bipolar illness was that of Bertelsen, Harvald, and Hauge (1977), who reported that starting with a bipolar twin, the concordance for 55 pairs of monozygotic twins was 0.67 and for 52 pairs of dyzygotic twins was 0.20. This concordance was higher in bipolar than in unipolar index twins. As an extension of that study, Fischer (1980) dealt in greater detail with bipolar illness in 28 pairs of monozygotic and 35 pairs of dyzygotic twins. When the monozygotic twins were looked at for concordance for affective psychosis only, the concordance was 75 per cent for monozygotic compared with 20 per cent for dyzygotic. However, when other psychosis, severe affective personality disorder, or completed suicide was added as "illness," the concordance for monozygotic twins rose to 96 per cent and for dyzygotic twins, to 49 per cent. There was thus only one pair of monozygotic twins who were discordant. Fischer also discussed the issue of discordance in monozygotic twins with one being bipolar and the other being schizophrenic. There were only two pairs from two studies that reported such twins, and she reported in detail these case histories.

To summarize, bipolar affective disorder is a genetic illness. The extent of assortative mating and the extent of illness in children are unclear, but adolescent and adult children have high rates of illness that varies directly with assortative mating.

### Biochemical and Neuroendocrine Parameters

The depressant effect of reserpine when given for hypertension and the euphoric effects of a monoamine oxidase inhibitor when given for tuberculosis led to the development of the "biogenic amine hypotheses" for the etiology of depression.

The classic amine hypothesis stated that in depression, there was a functional deficit of either norepinephrine or serotonin at critical synapses in the central nervous system and implied that, conversely, an excess of such amines was associated with mania. More recently, it has become evident that the third biogenic amine, dopamine, is also important in the affective disorders and that other neurotransmitters or neuromodulators, such as the cholinergic system, the GABAergic system, and the endorphin system, may be implicated in affective disorders. A recent review (Petty and Sherman, 1984) indicates the state of confusion concerning GABA (gamma-aminobutyric acid). Janowsky et al. (1983) suggested that an affective state may represent a balance between central cholinergic and adrenergic neurotransmitters and that depression may be a disorder of cholinergic predominance and mania, the opposite. There is no consistent body of evidence to date, however, to confirm that the two poles of illness (mania and depression) are biologic opposites of each other. Clinically, there are many mixed states that have not been dealt with from a putative biologic standpoint.

In the same way, early observations of the affective state of patients with excesses or deficiencies of corticosteroids (Cushing's syndrome and Addison's disease) led to the measurement of corticosteroids in the plasma and urine of patients with depression. Some depressed patients had elevated levels of corticosteroids that returned to normal with recovery. Capitalizing on the endocrine challenge test for the diagnosis of Cushing's disease, Carroll et al. (1981) began systematically to evaluate the dexamethasone suppression test in depressed patients. They reported that about 40 per cent of depressed melancholic inpatients and outpatients given 1 mg of dexamethasone at 11:00 P.M. failed to suppress cortisol at either 4:00 or 11:00 P.M. the next day. In most of the studies the bipolar and the unipolar depressed patients were similar and manics were suppressors. Controversy over this test, owing to many difficulties, emerged. Most recently, for instance, Stokes et al. (1984), using data from the collaborative study of the psychobiology of affective disorders, showed that patients in the manic state had the highest percentage of nonsuppression. Use of this test by clinicians as a biologic marker for primary depression has been questioned, but everyone agrees that a significant minority of bipolar and unipolar depressed patients have elevated corticosteroid levels, some (not necessarily the same) are nonsuppressors after dexamethasone and that in these, with recovery, the test returns to normal. The manic state needs further clarification. Because the neuroendocrine system is related to the amine and immune systems, attempts to integrate findings are now emerging. Noting a relationship between serotonin activity and production of anterior pituitary hormones, Meltzer, Arora, Tricou, and Fang (1983) reported that serotonin activity in platelets in unipolar, bipolar, and schizoaffective depressed inpatients was significantly decreased but varied independently of those patients who were dexamethasone nonsuppressors. They are expanding their data to look also at the relationship between neuroendocrine function and lymphocytic function. Schleifer et al. (1984) also recently reported decreased functional capacity of lymphocytes (that is, they did not respond as well to appropriate mitogen stimulation) as well as generalized reduction in peripheral lymphocytes in depressed (polarity not given), drug-free inpatients compared with controls. These findings have not been replicated.

As mentioned, there is not a clear picture of whether the other pole of illness, mania, is the opposite biochemically from depression either at neuroendocrine baselines or with provocative tests. Amsterdam et al. (1983) looked at a full neuroendocrine test battery in bipolar patients and healthy subjects. They measured baseline levels of luteinizing hormone (LH), follicle-stimulating hormone (FSH), thyroid-stimulating hormone (TSH), prolactin (PRL), growth hormone (GH), cortisol, thyroxine ($T_4$), and triiodothyronine ($T_3$) in 22 bipolar outpatients (14 of whom were currently depressed and 8 of whom were hypomanic) and appropriate controls. They used four provocative tests (thyrotropin-releasing hormone, gonadotropin-releasing hormone, insulin tolerance, and dexamethasone suppression). All assays were measured by radioimmunoassay. For the most part, they found no difference between the depressed and the hypomanic patients at baseline and minimal differences at baseline between the subjects and the patients. Only when they looked at the distribution of abnormal responses did a highly significant difference emerge. Twelve patients (54.5 per cent) but no normal subjects demonstrated abnormalities in two or more tests. The most useful tests in these patients were the dexamethasone suppression test and the measurement of TSH and PRL after protirelin. This last finding of a blunted response of TSH to protirelin has been observed in frankly manic patients and is the same as that which is reported in depressed patients (Extein, Pottash, Gold, and Cowdry, 1982).

In conclusion, these studies indicate abnormalities and variability in biochemical and neuroendocrine function, but they do not shed any light on a specific neurobiology of bipolar illness, either mania or depression.* A recent article from the collaborative study by Swann et al. (1983) on monoamine metabolites in cerebrospinal fluid of manic inpatients reached the same conclusion. The only difference in both sexes between the manics and the controls was an elevated level of 3-methoxy-4-hydroxyphenylglycol (MHPG) in the manic patients, which again has been reported in depressed inpatients.

## Editor's Comment

*A recent study by Lewis and McChesney (Arch Gen Psychiatry 42:485–488, 1985) presents data that there are significantly fewer titrated imipramine binding sites on platelet membranes in patients with bipolar illness when compared with controls. Replication of this finding would be a meaningful advance in knowledge.*

## Sleep and Other Electrophysiology Parameters

The sleep parameters of depressed patients are well known. Both unipolar and bipolar depressed patients have shortened rapid eye movement (REM) latency, higher REM density, and problems with sleep continuity (Kupfer, 1983). Sitaram (1983) reported that in remitted "depressed" patients, arecoline (an acetylcholine agonist) induced REM sleep significantly more rapidly than in normal controls. Some of the remitted affective disorder patients and normal controls also had an amphetamine chal-

lenge test. There was a negative correlation between arecolinergic REM induction and amphetamine-induced behavioral excitation. That is, those former patients who had REM induction sooner were also less likely to develop an elation or excitation with intravenous (IV) amphetamines, again suggesting a reciprocal relationship between the cholinergic and catecholamine systems even in the well state.

Original reports of evoked potential response differences between bipolar and unipolar patients were not replicated. A recent report (Iacono et al., 1983) of bipolar and unipolar patients in remission but on medication showed decreased electrodermal activity compared with controls that was not due to the effects of medication (lithium and imipramine), but no differences between the remitted bipolars and unipolars. Because these electrodermal activities are mediated through the cholinergic system, this is another implication of this system in the affective disorders.

## Animal Models

Robbins and Sahakian (1980) reviewed the animal models for mania, including a thoughtful discussion of how to relate clinical symptoms to animal behavior, criteria for the ideal animal model of a syndrome, and a discussion of models produced by drugs, lesions, and behavioral manipulations. Their own research emphasized the amphetamine-induced model and is particularly interesting in light of the clinical studies of amphetamine-induced symptoms and syndromes in humans (see next section).

## Secondary Mania

Krauthammer and Klerman (1978) thoroughly reviewed the literature on secondary mania. They required specific criteria to include cases as mania. The major causes were drugs, metabolic disturbances, infection, neoplasm, and epilepsy.

Besides the mania that is precipitated by antidepressants, mania has also been reported during treatment with corticosteroids, cocaine, and L-dopa and during the spontaneous use of amphetamines and KHAT, a leaf used as part of the culture of people of North and South Yemen. Tatetsu (1963, 1972) reported on 131 Japanese patients who, because it was legal and available, used methamphetamine after World War II. The most common diagnoses in both the acute and the stationary stage in these addicted patients (30 to 90 mg/IV/day) were either manic-depressive illness or manic-depressive illness with schizophrenia-like features. The paranoid delusions that develop are compatible with a diagnosis of manic-depressive illness. A recent report (Gough and Cookson, 1984) indicated that after the use of KHAT, a patient became manic with elation, hyperactivity, pressured speech, diminished appetite, poor sleep, and delusions. The patient was called schizophreniform. The drug screen was positive for amphetamines but negative for other drugs.

Another report (Arnold et al., 1980) described a patient given baclofen, which is structurally related to GABA and presumably acts as a GABA agonist or as an inhibitor of substance P, for cervical myelopathy who developed a manic-like syndrome 1 day after he discontinued the drug. The symptoms were elevated mood; talking loudly, rapidly, and volubly; gesturing expansively, ordering members of the family and hospital personnel around; distractibility; sexual preoccupation; and grandiose delusions. After baclofen was readministered, along with haloperidol, the manic episode resolved.

Mania developing after specific left and right intercerebral pathology (Jampala and Abrams, 1983) has also been reported and critically reviewed.

As with the neurobiology and electrophysiologic findings, these animal and human models provide evidence for this illness being a biologic brain disorder but emphasize the complexity, diffuseness, and variability of the syndrome rather than clarify the cause.

## EPIDEMIOLOGY

All calculations of bipolar affective disorder are underestimates, since to calculate the prevalence of lifetime risk requires that the patient have an identifiable mania and a majority of patients, particularly women, begin with depressive episodes (Angst, 1978). Perris (1969) and Angst (1974); Angst,

Felder, Frey, and Stassen, (1978), respectively, reported that 16 per cent and 13 per cent to 16 per cent of their patients who had had three previous episodes of depression still became bipolar. A study of manic episodes in older people (Shulman and Post, 1980) indicated that a mean of 10 years elapsed between the first depressive episode and the first manic episode. Akiskal et al. (1983), in a younger sample, reported that 20 per cent of 206 depressed outpatients switched to bipolar I or II an average of 6.4 years after the initial identification. If the illness began at a younger age, the switch was earlier. Krauthammer and Klerman (1979) estimated a similar switch rate.

Factors besides young age found to be associated with a change of polarity from unipolar to bipolar (Akiskal et al., 1983) were hypersomnic and retarded phenomenology, psychotic depression, and postpartum episodes. A family history of bipolarity or a pharmacologic hypomania produced by antidepressants were also predictive of a bipolar outcome. The mean age at which the switch occurred was 32. The average number of previous episodes was two to four.

Boyd and Weissman (1981), in reviewing studies of bipolar affective disorder, estimated that the lifetime risk for bipolar I disorder was between 0.2 per cent and 0.9 per cent. These estimates probably were not age corrected. In the same way, the epidemiologic catchment area (ECA) study (Robins et al., 1984) estimated the lifetime risk to be 0.6 per cent. Thus the frequency of illness is similar to schizophrenia. The incidence of bipolar disorder per 100,000 per year varies enormously between studies. Using modern diagnostic techniques, Myers et al. (1984) reported a 6-month prevalence for manic episode to be between 0.4 per cent and 0.8 per cent. In all these studies the distribution of males to females was about equal.

There are no data to suggest that unipolar mania differs from the bipolar disorder. Unipolar mania was said to be rare and to constitute only 2 per cent to 5 per cent of all the patients in this category. Nurnberger, Roose, Dunner, and Fieve (1979), however, reported that 16 per cent of a group of bipolar patients had never been hospitalized or treated for depression, and Abrams, Taylor, Hayman, and Krishna (1979) reported that 18 per cent of patients hospitalized for affective disorder (not necessarily bipolar) were unipolar manics. Pfohl, Vasquez, and Nasrallah (1982) reported the highest percentage (33 per cent) based on a chart review. Interestingly, Kraepelin (1921) originally reported that 17 per cent of his 900 manic-depressive patients were exclusively manic. Some feel that the longer or the more closely the patient is followed, the more likely it will be that depression is recognized. In my own experience, unipolar mania is uncommon.

## Risk Factors

Bipolar illness is the disease of much earlier onset and much more limited risk. The onset is usually from the teens to the 50s, with the average age of onset being 30. At least 20 per cent of bipolars become ill by the age of 20 (Clayton, 1981). Numerous studies have indicated that in the teenage years, bipolar illness can be mistakenly called schizophrenia, antisocial personality, or borderline personality disorder. Actually, there should be more adolescents diagnosed as bipolar (either manic or depressive) than as schizophrenic. The literature on late-onset bipolar illness is confusing because some of the patients discussed had episodes of depression before age 50 but did not become manic until after age 50. If read carefully, even here the age of onset of the first affective episode is usually before 50. In keeping with this young age of onset, Akiskal et al. (1983) found that depression in a person under age 25 was highly correlated with a bipolar outcome in followup. A psychotic depression or any severe depression in a teenager should always be considered potentially the onset of a bipolar illness. The same is true of a schizoaffective illness (Joyce, 1984). This is important because of the implications for treatment in the acute episode and the willingness to consider maintenance therapy if such episodes recur.

The sex ratio shows only a slight preponderance of women over men. There are no racial differences in the incidence or prevalence of this illness. A fair amount of recent literature indicates that both Hispanics and blacks (Jones, Gray, and Parson, 1981, 1983; Keisling, 1981) have high rates of bipolar affective disorder when inpatients are studied

and that it is frequently misdiagnosed as schizophrenia. In the ECA study (Robins et al., 1984) there were no differences in the lifetime prevalence of mania by race, and in fact, in the St. Louis data, there seemed to be an excess of mania in the blacks. In the same data set, mania was equally prevalent in urban or rural residents but was significantly more prevalent in non-college graduates than in college graduates. These race and education findings may be related. Interestingly enough, there is little comment on the marital status of bipolars. In the collaborative study there were significantly more single bipolars than single unipolars, a fact also mentioned in the reports on race and bipolar illness. Young age of onset probably correlates with singleness.

The data on immigration status of bipolars are controversial.

Periodicity of this illness is true for some patients, with fall and winter depression being most frequently described. The suicide rate is highest in April. Onset of illness should be recorded for each episode in order to highlight patterns of illness.

Although Akiskal et al. (1977) identified 46 outpatients (2.3 per cent of the outpatient population) as cyclothymic and reported that 22 per cent became bipolar in the followup period, others (MacVane, Lange, Brown, and Zayat, 1978; Lumry, Gottesman, and Tuason, 1982) have found that bipolars who are well or stabilized on lithium have personalities similar to those of controls. Bech et al. (1980) suggested that lithium mutes the cyclothymia and causes bipolars to test more like unipolars. Others (Jamison, Gerner, Hammen, and Padesky, 1980; Targum, Dibble, Davenport, and Gershon, 1981) indicated that even in remission, manics evaluate themselves in a positive way. Still others (Akiskal et al., 1983; Matussek and Feil, 1983) emphasized the achievement orientation personality of the bipolars. Thus no personality trait or feature can be identified as a risk factor, and as yet no childhood features are predictive of bipolarity. Perhaps cyclothymia is an early manifestation of the illness, rather than a personality trait. Akiskal, Hirschfeld, and Yerevanian (1983) and Pritz and Mitterauer (1984) concur. It seems more likely that personality traits associated with early-onset recurrent depression will identify bipolars.

## CLINICAL PICTURE

As previously emphasized, the typical bipolar patient starts with an episode of pure depression. Angst (1978) reported that the ratio of depression to mania in the first episode was 3:1 for women and 3:2 for men. Depression is well described in the chapter on unipolar affective disorder. Most, but not all, investigators report inconsistent and minimal differences in symptoms in bipolar and unipolar depressives.

Mania or mixed manic and depressive state is the hallmark of this illness (Winokur et al., 1969). The mania can begin suddenly with the development of a full-blown syndrome over hours (causing some to posit a substance in the bloodstream), or it may be a more gradual state, developing over days. It seldom takes weeks to develop. A history of a change in the patient's behavior is usual, although unless the onset is sudden, close relatives miss the first indications. Mania may begin with a short period of depression. Some suggest that early in the course of illness, episodes are likely to be precipitated by life events, but as the illness continues, there are fewer precipitants. Mania can be preceded by any life event, including bereavement, although most studies looking at causal links with stress have failed to show a significant relationship.

The picture can vary from an excited, talkative, loud, overreactive, somewhat amusing individual to a completely disorganized, intrusive psychotic. The mood is always elated, angry, or irritable. Many patients appear overly confident, bragging, self-aggrandizing, and happy but become irritable when their ideas are not enthusiastically endorsed. Frequently they become most angry at those who are closest to them, particularly their spouses. They interrupt conversations but dislike being interrupted themselves. They are distractible. Racing thoughts, pressured speech, circumstantiality, irrelevancies, flight of ideas characterize thoughts and language. Decreased need for sleep or insomnia, increase in sexual thoughts, and an increase in alcohol intake are all common in the manic patient. During the full-blown syndrome there may be episodes of depression lasting from minutes to hours. Grandiose ideas and delusions are common and are probably the basis for the symptoms of excessive telephone calls, extravagances, and excessive writing. One or two themes usually predominate. The themes may be religious, political, financial, sexual, or persecutory. All varieties of psychotic symptoms have been reported in the manic patient. The best documentation of this is probably the Carlson and Goodwin (1973) study on the evolution of a manic episode. At the height of the manic episode, patients exhibited unusual psychomotor activities, incoherent thought processes, and delusions and hallucinations that were bizarre and idiosyncratic. They found that besides hyperactivity, extreme verbosity, pressure of speech, grandiosity, manipulativeness, irritability, euphoria, labile mood, hypersexuality, and flight of ideas, 75 per cent had delusions that were either of control or sexual, persecutory, or religious; 75 per cent had assaultive or threatening behavior; 70 per cent had distractibility, loose associations, and a fear of dying; 60 per cent were intrusive; 55 per cent had somatic complaints; 55 per cent had some delusions, 50 per cent had religiosity; 45 per cent used the telephone excessively; 45 per cent had regressive behavior (urinating or defecating inappropriately and exposing themselves); 40 per cent demonstrated symbolization or gesturing; 40 per cent had auditory and visual hallucinations; and 35 per cent were confused. Confusion is a well-documented symptom of acute mania. In a chart review, 58 per cent of 31 manics (Clayton, Pitts, and Winokur, 1965) were reported either to be disoriented or to have memory lapses. Kraepelin (1921) used the term delirious mania.

Research on manic symptomatology has been intensive since the 1970s. Andreasen (1974, 1979a, 1979b) looked at thought disorder in manics and found that besides being overinclusive, both behaviorally and conceptually, manics were tangential and had derailment, incoherence, and illogicality that was equally as prominent as in schizophrenics. The manics were more likely to have pressured speech, distractibility, and circumstantiality. The schizophrenics more frequently had poverty of speech and poverty of content of speech. Harrow, Grossman, Silverstein, and Meltzer (1982) confirmed and extended this, indicating that at followup, in partial remission, almost half continued to have thought pathology. Brockington, Hillier, Francis, Helzer, and

Wainwright (1983) reported similar followup findings. Catatonic features during a manic episode have been well documented by Abrams and Taylor (1976). Pope and Lipinski's (1978) comprehensive article emphasized that between 20 per cent and 50 per cent of well-validated bipolar cases have psychotic symptoms, including hallucinations, delusions, catatonia symptoms, and schneiderian first-rank symptoms, as illustrated in the following case.

A 22-year-old, single man was referred for consultation. He gave a clear history of episodes of psychosis beginning in May and June at age 17, after graduation from high school. He was going with a group to Israel, and in anticipation of this trip he got excited and developed insomnia. On the airplane he developed the idea that his peers were sending messages by some strange visual communication. He thought that their facial expressions told other stories and began to think that he could read their thoughts and minds. He also developed the idea that something was visibly wrong with him and that security guards in Israel noted this. In the midst of this he lost track of time and became convinced that they couldn't go to the Wailing Wall because it was Friday, when indeed it was Wednesday, so he refused to leave his room. After that he included the group leader in his scheme, thinking "they" were trying to fool him and retain him in Israel. He remembered that his thinking was loud and fast and that he was angry. He was hospitalized in Israel and returned to a hospital in the United States. His second episode occurred in April, 2 years later. In the second and third episodes his psychotic symptoms were grounded in the grandiose delusion to save the world. He began to write a book. He also wrote clever but disjointed letters to the governor that pertained to fighting crime (this was probably originally based on some incident like an attempted rape in his dorm). He developed the idea that one way to help crime and stabilize the financial market was to construct more jails, so he began to buy stock in construction companies. He believed that he would become famous for this plausible plan. Finally, because of his letter writing, the police decided that he might be dangerous and he was committed. Again, he remembered being excited, needing no sleep, talking fast, and not eating. His third episode occurred again in April of the next year and had a similar theme. Each time he was diagnosed as manic and was put on lithium and a major tranquilizer, but he objected to taking lithium continuously. When I saw him he was on no medicine. He was depressed with slowed thinking, difficulty concentrating, and difficulty making decisions. He had intermittently returned to a difficult college and had completed courses but had not completed his degree. He felt discouraged about that and thought that it was useless to go to school or work. He was thin and distraught looking. In retrospect, he stated that he probably was depressed in high school in the *spring* of his senior year, when his grades fell and he didn't do as well on the swimming team and developed a great deal of interpersonal difficulty with his father. His mother had recurrent bipolar affective disorder, but he has always blamed his father for his illness.

In the past 2 years he has been on lithium and an antidepressant. He graduated from college and subsequently is taking additional courses in electronics. His mental state is stabler than it was in the preceding 5 years, but he is far from well adjusted. He complains that he never smiles. He remains single, lives at home, and is dependent on his family. He would very much like to be married with children and have a reasonable job. He has had numerous long trials of psychotherapy. At one point, because of side effects (alopecia, tremor), he wanted to stop lithium. We discussed the symptoms that we should anticipate if he gets manic. He voluntarily listed the following symptoms: racing thoughts, distractibility, grandiosity, driving faster and in more of a hurry, talking faster, excessive buying and long-distance telephone calls, increased humorousness with free associations and punning, playing records louder, listening to music and bothering more people in the household and becoming evangelistic. He did not think that his sexual interest had changed (it is always high) or that he had weight loss or increased energy.

## COURSE

Bipolar illness is definitely a recurring illness. Bratfos and Haug (1968) found in a 6-year followup that 7 per cent of 42 patients recovered without relapse, 48 per cent had one or more episodes, and 45 per cent had chronic courses. Grof, Angst, and Haines (1974) reported that virtually every patient had a recurrence. There are no comparable data from an outpatient clinic, although the lithium/placebo studies show high relapses when such patients are put on placebo, and therefore complement these data.

The clearest data on the characterization of the illness come from the collaborative study of Grof et al. (1974). Patients were treated for their affective episodes and received no prophylactic treatment between episodes. The investigators were particularly interested in documenting numbers of episodes, lengths of episodes, and other details pertaining to episodes. The average manic episode lasted for about 3 months and the average depressive episode, for about 4 months. The duration of episodes did not change remarkably with increasing numbers of episodes. Initially, with each episode, the interval between the episodes tended to decrease. However, once the patient had gone through a number of episodes, perhaps more than five, the duration of the cycle—defined as the time from the beginning of one episode to the beginning of the next—became stable. Thus the duration of the time between attacks had a tendency to decrease and the course deteriorated, but it ultimately bottomed out at a cycle every 6 to 9 months. The authors concluded that the most useful way to predict a patient's future course was by his past course, e.g., if a patient had three episodes in the past 2 years, his short-term future course would be similar.

The relationship between age of onset and course is a controversial issue. Carlson, Davenport, and Jamison (1977) found no difference in course or prognosis between adolescent bipolars and late-onset (after 45) bipolars (very different from most early/late-onset diseases). An interesting and tentative finding from the work of Grof et al. (1974) was that there may be an extinction of the pattern of episodes after a certain number. The authors found that although the total number of episodes in a lifetime varied from 2 to more than 30, and 42 per cent of them had more than 10 episodes, still the median number was 9 whether the patient had been studied for 5 or 40 years (Angst, Felder, and Frey, 1979). This means that while the short-term prognosis of bipolar affective disorder may be poor, the long-term course may be better. Winokur (1975) suggested the same thing from a different data base. Here, however, the studies on lithium maintenance would speak against this, for they show that even patients up to age 65 who have recurrent bipolar illness relapse if lithium is discontinued.

The occurrence of chronicity in bipolar disease is not a moot point. Grof, Angst, and collaborators did not characterize the social disabilities of their patients. Without stating so specifically, they give the impression that between episodes the patients were relatively free of symptoms other than minor mood swings. Winokur et al. (1969) painted a picture more similar to that of Bratfos and Haug (1968). In a 2-year followup of 28 patients, 14 per cent were well in every way, 46 per cent had additional episodes and were well in between, 29 per cent never achieved more than a partial remission of symptoms, and 11 per cent were chronically ill. There were only four patients who were in the first episode of the illness, and in these four, one had a partial remission, two had complete remissions with subsequent episodes, and one remained entirely well. Welner, Welner, and Leonard (1977) reviewed a large number of studies of bipolar illness and indicated that chronicity, if defined as presence of symptoms, social decline, or both, occurred in at least one third of the bipolar patients. Chronic mania, however, is uncommon. The only more favorable outcome comes from Petterson's study (1977) of a group of patients treated in Sweden. She observed the clinical, social, and genetic aspects of 123 patients for approximately 5 years. At the end of the study a large number of patients showed more satisfactory work capacity and better social adaptation. This was a group treated by a single investigator. It may be that in treating chronically ill patients who require maintenance therapy, psychological skills are an essential ingredient to a more favorable outcome.

## Complications

The most serious consequence of this illness is suicide. Not dividing patients by polarity, a summary of the relationship between suicide and primary affective disorder showed that the suicide risk among patients with affective disorder was more than 30 times greater than that of the general population (Guze and Robins, 1970). Between 10 per cent and 15 per cent of all deaths of patients with affective disorder were accounted for by suicide (Tsuang, 1978). In bipolar disease, as in unipolar disease, there is a trend for the suicide to occur early in the illness and less frequently as the disease continues (Tsuang, 1978). Several recent studies have found lower suicide rates in unipolars and bipolars (Petterson, 1977; Khuri and Akiskal, 1983; Martin, Cloninger, Guze, and Clayton, 1985). Morrison (1982) found lower rates in unipolars but not in bipolars. The followups in these studies were sufficiently long to consider that this could be a positive result of lithium and of other acute and maintenance therapies.

Suicide attempts have been reported to be

higher in bipolars, especially men (Woodruff, Clayton, and Guze, 1972; Johnson and Hunt, 1979). And everyone reports an increased mortality among bipolar patients over and above that which is due to suicide. The cause of this is unclear, although one report (Lilliker, 1980) showed increased prevalence of diabetes in hospitalized bipolars compared with *all* other hospitalized patients such as schizophrenics, alcoholics, and retarded. Both Bratfos and Haug (1968) and Angst (personal communication) reported that these patients develop dementia at a higher frequency than would be expected compared with appropriate age-matched controls, but without autopsy findings it is unclear if this is Alzheimer's disease.

Some have indicated that bipolar patients' marriages ended in divorce more frequently than those of unipolars or appropriate controls (Brodie and Leff, 1971). Even in those not ending in divorce, 53 per cent of well spouses compared with 5 per cent of the bipolar patients indicated that they would not have married the spouse, and 47 per cent of the well spouses compared with 5 per cent of the patients would not have had children had they known about the bipolar illness before making these decisions (Targum et al., 1981). The illness impacts on marriage, job, childrearing, and all aspects of life. In addition, there may be an increased association between heavy drinking and acute mania and between pathologic gambling and a bipolar diagnosis (McCormick, Russo, Ramirez, and Taber, 1984). Once more, Petterson (1977) reported better social and medical outcomes. In her data the distribution of marital state and frequency of marriage were largely in agreement with the general population. In several cases there were divorces that occurred in connection with the patient's illness, but there were also reconciliations that were attributed to lithium treatment. Bipolar patients had fewer children and more childless marriages than the general Swedish population, but she believed that because the numbers were small, social and regional factors could account for this. The finding of decreased fertility was also reported by Baron, Risch, and Mendlewicz (1982). With regard to criminality, her patients had fewer convictions than expected in comparison with the general population, a finding replicated in other studies. An interesting set of studies (London and Taylor, 1982), however, indicates that symptoms of mania are more common in forensic settings than was generally thought. In studying patients admitted to St. Elizabeth's Hospital in Washington, D.C., the authors found that 11 of the 13 attempted crimes against the president of the U.S., so-called "White House cases," were diagnosed as affective disorder and the majority of them were bipolar.

In summary, although numerous problems can be anticipated with the development of a bipolar affective disorder, there is some hope that maintenance therapy can significantly alter the course of the illness.

## DIFFERENTIAL DIAGNOSIS

As indicated, there are many disorders that have similar ages of onset, type of onset, percentage single, symptoms, course, and outcome, including high chronicity and suicide. Only family history can reliably distinguish the bipolar. Pritz and Mitterauer (1984) emphasize well the spectrum of mood phenomenon in the bipolar spectrum. Symptoms are not absorbed from the patient; they are elicited. Therefore, all symptoms, including mood, should be asked of the patient.

### Schizophrenia

Schizophrenia and mania are alike in many ways. The symptoms of a current episode can be similar in mania and schizophrenia. There is not one symptom that is pathognomonic for either, although the mood of merriment, elation, ecstasy, or even irritability is much more likely to occur in the manic than in the schizophrenic, but there are some hypochondriacal or grandiose schizophrenics who maintain a haughty, elated effect. Studies of diagnostic criteria for mania (Young, Abrams, Taylor, and Meltzer, 1983) indicated that the triad of symptoms—manic mood, rapid or pressured speech, and hyperactivity—are robust, so that perhaps any patient with all three symptoms should be considered manic regardless of number or content of other symptoms.

Mania, for the most part, should have a relatively sudden onset, with the only extended prodromal being a depressive syndrome, and should be characterized as a change from the person's premorbid self. Schizophrenia should be more insidious, but it, too, can begin with depression *or* anxiety.

The course of the illnesses could be similar. At least one third of bipolar patients have either social disabilities or symptoms that may be more than just low-grade depressive symptoms. Still, all studies show significantly better followup outcome in manics than in schizophrenics. Both have high suicide rates, with 10 per cent to 15 per cent dying by suicide.

The most reliable difference in these two illnesses is the family history. Although both are hereditary/familial, at least 50 per cent of manic patients should have some family history of an affective disorder (mania or depression). Studies of schizophrenics show a significant but less striking increase in schizophrenia in their families but no increase in affective disorder over the population prevalence of about 6 per cent to 8 per cent.

## Paranoid Schizophrenia

After the teenage years many manics are misdiagnosed as paranoid schizophrenics. This seems to be particularly true with blacks and Hispanics. Again, the other indications of a manic syndrome, such as previous episodes, mode of onset, and family history, should help to differentiate patients.

## Catatonic Schizophrenia

Since, when looking at catatonic symptoms, patients are more frequently bipolar or manic than any other diagnosis, all patients in whom the diagnosis of catatonic schizophrenia is entertained should be carefully evaluated for depressive and manic symptoms, previous episodes, and family history. Some manics become mute when their thoughts go so fast that they cannot speak. A "flat affect" is not uncommon or unusual in a bipolar treated with or maintained on phenothiazines. The amytal interview may still be useful in uncovering depressive delusions, disjointed manic thoughts, or disorientation (organicity).

## Schizoaffective

Using the research diagnostic criteria (RDC) definition of schizoaffective, which splits patients into schizoaffective mania and schizoaffective depression, all studies show that the schizoaffective manics (Clayton, in press) are similar to manics, especially mood incongruent mania as defined in DSM-III. They all agree that the schizoaffective manic probably has an earlier age of onset and a more malignant course, but the biologic markers and the family history data indicate that they are in the bipolar spectrum. Joyce (1984) also concluded that patients with teenage onset have *more* schizophrenic symptoms. Because schizoaffective mania is so much like mania, it probably is wise not to use it for manic patients and to reserve it for schizoaffective depressives only.

On the other hand, schizoaffective depressives, who are usually a smaller group, seem to be a conglomerate of many different patients, such as schizophrenics, depressives, the spectrum of anxiety disorders with secondary depression, and alcoholics or drug abusers with secondary depression (Clayton, 1983). When schizoaffective manics are removed from schizoaffective depressives, there are almost no schizoaffective depressed who become bipolar at followup. It is a much more unstable diagnostic entity, but it should be retained to reflect uncertainty. Previous episodes of "pure" mania or depression and family history again help to discriminate.

## Organic Mental Disorders

Because at least one third of manics have either disorientation or some memory blanks during an episode, it might be easy to think of mania as a toxic state. Although certain drugs, as shown, can precipitate manic episodes, usually even these syndromes are treated with neuroleptics or lithium, or both. In a first episode it may be impossible to distinguish or to make a definitive diagnosis. Previous history and family history should be useful in confirming a diagnosis. It is most difficult in a catatonic stupor. It is important not to be sidetracked by the confusion of mania and delay treatment for a long time (1 week) while completing extensive organic workups.

### Personality Disorders (Antisocial, Borderline) and Alcohol and Drug Abuse

There are many presentations of bipolar disorder. Twenty per cent begin in the teenage years. Akiskal (1983) indicated that the clinical presentation of adolescents with bipolar disorders, in decreasing frequency, are "psychosis," alcohol and drug problems, "moodiness," suicidal ideation or attempt, academic failure, philosophic brooding, obsessional brooding, somatic complaints, school phobia, "hyperactivity," stupor, and flagrant antisocial behavior. Although the last was extremely uncommon, it can occur. As before, a change in behavior would be the key to distinguishing the manic from the typical sociopath. It is easy if the sociopathic behavior is manic—that is, stealing with some grandiose plan in mind—but less easy if it is typical of all adolescent antisocial acts. The same can be said of alcohol or drug problems, school phobia, and borderline personality diagnoses. Here again the premorbid adjustment should be stable, and this should be a change in behavior that could not have been expected or anticipated. Depressive symptoms, or, less commonly, manic symptoms, should be present if inquired about. These things, coupled with a family history of affective disorder, should help in making the proper diagnosis.

### Suicide Attempter

Because a suicide attempt may be trivial or serious in a bipolar depressive or manic (rarely), all suicide attempters should be considered potential unipolar or bipolar patients. Onset, symptoms, previous history, premorbid adjustment, and family history should help in making a diagnosis. Again, all suicidal or psychotic teenage depressives should be considered potential bipolars with all that that implies.

### TREATMENT

No psychosocial management can be accomplished with a patient in the manic state. The patient is talkative, irritable, irritating, sexually aroused, confident, expansive, and completely lacking in insight or good judgment. Because of his uplifted mood, he feels no need of treatment and refuses with vehemence offers of assistance. Hospitalization is necessary and frequently entails commitment. The patient must be protected against the serious social and medical consequences of this state. In my opinion, because of the manic's intrusiveness and his potential for creating conflict, it is almost always possible to think of him as being dangerous to himself. In the collaborative study of depression in St. Louis, the first death in the followup period was in a manic who was killed in a fight in a bar. If manics have other illnesses, like hypertension, that are controlled by medication, those illnesses get out of control as the manic neglects his medications, creating another reason for hospitalization.

When the manic is hospitalized his excessive energy is easy to handle if he is given space to roam and not confined to a locked room. This does not mean that he can be on an unlocked unit, since he is capable of excessive spending even while in the hospital. The manic patient is also intrusive and speaks in an uncensored way so that he can provoke arguments anywhere, including the hospital. In addition, enormous bills and bad feelings can develop in the manic patient if telephone usage is not restricted. Hospitalization is also welcomed by the relatives, who are worn down and exasperated by the manic's behavior and relieved to know that he is being protected in the hospital.

In treating the manic patient, the physician should always remember that certain interpersonal traits are part of the manic illness. Janowsky et al. (1970, 1974) outlined a series of interpersonal behaviors that they had originally thought were part of the manic's premorbid personality but later discovered to be symptoms of the manic episode. In addition to the classic manic symptoms of hyperactivity, push of speech, flight of ideas, irritability, distractibility, poor judgment, and increased social contact, they found that manic behavior included such things as the testing of limits, flattery, shifting responsibility for their actions to others, exploiting other's soft spots, dividing the staff, and provoking anger. These traits led to marked interpersonal, marital, and ward conflict. Therefore, in treating the patient one must take into consideration these symptoms and behaviors and respond to them as if they were part of the illness. This is best done by setting limits in an unambivalent, firm, and rather arbitrary way.

In acute mania the efficacy of lithium is well accepted. With this in mind, the following choices are available, although the order may be debatable and may depend on the severity of the presenting symptoms: (1) lithium, (2) a neuroleptic plus lithium, (3) a neuroleptic, (4) electroconvulsive therapy (ECT). Most studies comparing lithium with chlorpromazine or lithium, chlorpromazine, and haloperidol indicate that lithium is superior to either in terms of earlier discharge. These studies, however, also indicate that chlorpromazine, haloperidol, and other such neuroleptics control the hyperactivity/excitement of the acutely manic patient more quickly than does lithium because lithium takes longer to act. Some maintain that, clinically, the end result is superior with lithium alone, whereas others maintain that haloperidol alone is sufficient for the acute illness. Because there have been a few isolated reports that the combination of haloperidol and lithium can produce adverse side effects, lithium or a neuroleptic should be the first choice (Garfinkel, Stancer, and Persad, 1980; Dunner, 1983). It should be remembered, however, that some investigators believe that bipolars are at increased risk for tardive dyskinesia (Rosenbaum, Niven, Hanson, and Swanson, 1977; Kane, Struve, Weinhold, and Woerner, 1980; Rush, Diamond, and Alpert, 1982), so if a neuroleptic is chosen, close monitoring is indicated.

Before beginning treatment with lithium, the patient should have a complete medical workup, including a physical examination, tests for thyroid and renal function (blood urea nitrogen and creatinine), a white blood cell count, and electrocardiography. Other medications should be recorded, particularly the use of diuretics. Lithium is not contraindicated, however, in patients with hypertension alone. Lithium should not be started in a pregnant woman. The issue of becoming pregnant while on lithium maintenance is discussed later. Patients should be monitored daily for symptoms of toxicity, such as tremor, nausea, vomiting, diarrhea, and confusion. Lithium levels should be monitored frequently. Symptoms of toxicity necessitate immediate change in the lithium dose. In general, however, if the dose is raised gradually, toxicity can be avoided.

The usual starting dose of lithium in acute manic attack is 300 mg three times a day, which is gradually raised until a blood level of 1.0 to 1.2 mEq/L is achieved. Improvement typically occurs in 8 to 10 days. Keeping in mind the natural history, without lithium, manic attacks usually lasted about 3 months. With the old "treatments," hospitalization was typically 6 to 7 weeks, and if we assume that the patient had symptoms for at least a week before admission, the patient was near the end of his attack when he was discharged from the hospital. With lithium, improvement occurs more rapidly, and patients are discharged from the hospital long before the illness has run its course. The most common mistake in treating the acute manic attack is to discharge the patient too early, only to have him readmitted shortly after discharge. The manic should have a marked decrease in his symptoms and an awareness about his illness and be thoroughly committed to continuing lithium before discharge (Young, Nysewander, and Schreiber, 1982). In addition, his family should be educated and understanding about the illness.

McCabe (1976) compared manics treated with ECT with untreated matched controls who were gathered before the introduction of ECT. In a second paper (McCabe and Norris, 1977) a third group of patients treated with chlorpromazine was added. McCabe found that both ECT and chlorpromazine were far superior to no treatment in acute mania when measured by duration of hospitalization, condition at discharge, and social recovery, but there were no significant differences between the two treatments. He did not, however, have a comparison group of patients treated with lithium. The main purpose of these papers is to remind physicians that electrotherapy is still an efficacious alternative in the treatment of mania and may be the treatment of choice in certain cases (e.g., in a patient for whom lithium is contraindicated because of known renal or cardiac disease and in whom neuroleptics are considered potentially dangerous because of some sensitivity, like a neuroleptic malignant syndrome). It also should be considered in those patients who have had such frequent episodes that lithium is not efficacious. Many authors have shown that the rapid cycler is a poor responder to most pharmacotherapy, and there have been no studies treating such patients with electrotherapy.

Finally, L-tryptophan (Brewerton and Reus, 1983) or 5-hydroxytryptophan may be a useful adjunct for the treatment of acute mania.

## Treatment of the Depressive Episode

This is well covered in Chapter 5 and will not be replicated.

## Maintenance Therapy

Everyone agrees that lithium is an effective prophylactic agent. Not only does it significantly decrease the number of manic episodes, but it also decreases the number of depressive episodes. Many believe that this later finding is true because if lithium decreases the number of manic episodes—since it is frequently a biphasic or triphasic illness—it automatically decreases the potential for depressive episodes. Also, the quality of the episodes that do occur is changed (shorter, less severe) and hospitalization is avoided. Because mood swings still occur, however, patients on maintenance lithium need to be followed regularly so that the physician can add a phenothiazine or an antidepressant if necessary. Most people agree that lithium plasma levels should be maintained between 0.4 and 0.8 mEq/L, with the preference to be 0.6 mEq/L (Coppen, Abou-Saleh, Milln, Bailey, and Wood, 1983). New data indicate that lithium can be given in a single bedtime dose. Controversy reigns over whether this is better for the kidney; however, most agree that compliance is increased with a single daily dose. This can be either lithium carbonate or a sustained release lithium. Again, there is lack of agreement about which of these two preparations is superior. The association between relapse and plasma lithium levels is still unclear partially because the half-life of lithium is short and plasma levels fall quickly with missed doses and rise rapidly with extra doses, giving spurious impressions of compliance. Red blood cell lithium may be a better indicator than plasma lithium of brain lithium. However, red blood cell/plasma lithium studies still are inconclusive and should only be used as a research tool.

As mentioned earlier, all investigators have found that "rapid cyclers" (three episodes per year) have the poorest lithium response. They relapse quickly. Studies indicate that the more quickly the relapse occurs after beginning maintenance therapy, the more likely a second relapse will occur. The converse is also true; that is, the longer the patient is maintained without relapse, the better is his long-term prognosis. Early relapse is not correlated with anything else, such as sex, age, age of onset, family history (Fleiss, Prien, Dunner, and Fieve, 1978; Clayton, 1978).

The question of when to start maintenance therapy and how long to continue it is unanswered. Everyone would agree that a patient with two severe manic or depressive episodes within a certain period should be started on maintenance therapy. Some would automatically start every patient on maintenance therapy after his second manic or schizoaffective manic episode. Age, age of onset, severity of episodes, length of episodes, and many other factors must be considered in making a decision. In like manner, it is unclear whether patients should stop maintenance therapy. Some people say no; even up to age 65 relapses occur if the drug is discontinued. Others believe that short drug holidays in the safest months of the year are possible. A recent (Sashidharan and McGuire, 1983) study looked at the recurrence of affective illness after withdrawal of long-term lithium treatment. The authors were particularly interested in rebound. They found that 16 of 22 subjects had recurrences of affective illness after lithium withdrawal, with a mean relapse rate of 13.3 months and a range of from 1 to 67 months. Interestingly enough, they reported that half of their subjects continued to have manic or depressive episodes while on maintenance therapy, and when they compared that with the number of episodes that occurred after drug discontinuation, there were no significant differences. As might be expected, those who had been without episodes for the longest period before discontinuation were the least likely to experience relapse.

Recently, a 45-year-old successful businessman came for consultation about a decision to stop lithium. He had had several manic episodes in his 20s and finally became well stabilized on lithium. He had discontinued it at age 37 and done well for 3 years. He then developed a severe prolonged depression during which time he shot himself in the chest in his psychiatrist's office. After his recovery from depression with ECT he was stabilized on lithium and had done well. Again he wanted to stop lithium because of weight gain and tremor. Although this might be possible at the appropriate time of the year and if followup treatment was rigorous, in his case, it was not encouraged.

The consequences of relapse have to be weighed against the discomfort of continuing treatment, since it is seldom that lithium therapy is without some side effects. On maintenance lithium, thyroid and renal functions need to be monitored yearly. Jamison and Goodwin (1983) have outlined the therapeutic issue surrounding maintenance therapy with lithium, including patient and physician compliance. This is an important point because when the literature on studies of maintenance therapy is reviewed, there are far more relapses in treatment studies from collaborative studies of multiple impartial investigators than in studies reported by individual therapists treating a cohort of patients. It is definitely a disorder in which therapy and management make a difference.

## Side Effects

The side effects of lithium are numerous and disturbing to the patient but seldom deleterious to his health. Many patients complain of tremor while on lithium. This can be treated with 10 mg of propranolol, although it need not be given on a regular basis but can be taken by the patient before those situations that might prove embarrassing. Weight gain is a problem. Almost 50 per cent of patients gain some weight, and weight gains of up to 30 kg have been reported. Weight gain, for the most part, is due to increased caloric intake and not water weight and needs to be treated with a low-carbohydrate diet. Patients should be warned not to treat an increased thirst with calorie-laden drinks. Some patients develop polyuria and polydipsia, and some patients cannot concentrate their urine. If this occurs, an adjustment in the dose of lithium should be made. Careful studies of long-range effects do not indicate permanent kidney damage. Memory problems, tiredness, and a dulling of senses have been reported to be present while the patient is on lithium, although these could also be symptoms of a low-grade depression. There is no antidote for this, although again lowering the lithium dose should be considered. Some patients report diarrhea. A few patients develop hypothyroidism while on lithium. If this occurs, thyroxin needs to be added to the drug regimen. A few develop leukocytosis. Finally, some patients develop alopecia.

Because of small samples, there are no statistically significant differences between delivery outcome in women on lithium and on other psychotropic drugs. Still, since there are reported prenatal deaths and congenital malformations in babies of women on lithium, lithium should be discontinued, if possible, in early pregnancy (Kallen and Tandberg, 1983).

## Other Treatment Therapies

Carbamazepine may be useful in the treatment of the acute mania in those patients who are unable to tolerate either lithium or neuroleptics and in the treatment-resistant rapid cyclers (Post, 1982; Post, Uhde, Ballenger, and Squillace, 1983; Nolen, 1983; Kishimoto, Ogura, Hazama, and Inoue, 1983). Carbamazepine also has been used as a maintenance therapy for bipolar illness. Although the numbers are small in all studies, it seems to be a worthwhile second choice for select patients. It has been used alone, with lithium, with neuroleptics, or with tricyclic antidepressants and has been reported efficacious in all situations, in reducing both the number of episodes and the quality of episodes if they did occur (shorter duration, less severe). The average daily dose varies across studies from 100 to 1200 mg, and the average blood level to be achieved varies between 6 and 12 $\mu$g/ml.

Another anticonvulsant, valproic acid amide, has also been said to be efficacious as a maintenance therapy for bipolar patients (Puzynski and Klosiewicz, 1984). When used at a dose of about 1500 mg a day, there was a significant reduction in the number of episodes, particularly manic, and in the severity of episodes. With valproic acid, the treatment was given alone, with other drugs only being added as necessary for the mood swings. Each of these drugs has specific side effects, and laboratory monitoring should be done before initiation of treatment and regularly during the treatment. Others (Ahlfors et al., 1981) have cautiously recommended the use of long-acting phenothiazines for maintenance in the patients whose illness is primarily manic.

There is no doubt that bipolar illness is a devastating and difficult illness to treat, but the gratitude of patients who achieve remission justifies the concern, the patience, the tolerance, the persistence, the imagination, and the good judgment such treatment takes. And remembering the natural history, a certain number of patients will achieve long remissions.

## REFERENCES

Abrams R, Taylor MA: Catatonia. A prospective clinical study. Arch Gen Psychiatry 33:579–581, 1976.

Abrams R, Taylor MA: Importance of schizophrenic symptoms in the diagnosis of mania. Am J Psychiatry 138:658–661, 1981.

Abrams R, Taylor MA, Hayman MA, Krishna NR: Unipolar mania revisited. J Affective Disord 1:59–68, 1979.

Ahlfors UG, Baastrup PC, Dencker SJ, Elgen K, Lingjaerde O, Pedersen V, Schou M, Aaskoven O: Flupenthixol decanoate in recurrent manic-depressive illness. A comparison with lithium. Acta Psychiatr Scand 64:226–237, 1981.

Akiskal HS: The bipolar spectrum: New concepts in classification and diagnosis. In Grinspoon L (ed): Psychiatry Update, vol 2. Washington, DC, American Psychiatric Press, 1983.

Akiskal HS, Djenderedjian AH, Rosenthal RH, et al: Cyclothymic disorder: Validating criteria for inclusion in the bipolar affective group. Am J Psychiatry 134:1227–1233, 1977.

Akiskal HS, Hirschfeld RMA, Yerevanian BI: The relationship of personality to affective disorders. A critical review. Arch Gen Psychiatry 40:801–810, 1983.

Akiskal HS, Walker P, Puzantian VR, King D, Rosenthal TL, Dranon M: Bipolar outcome in the course of depressive illness. Phenomenologic, familial, and pharmacologic predictors. J Affective Disord 5:115–128, 1983.

Amsterdam JD, Winokur A, Lucki I, Caroff S, Snyder P, Rickels K: A neuroendocrine test battery in bipolar patients and healthy subjects. Arch Gen Psychiatry 40:515–521, 1983.

Andreasen NC: Thought, language, and communication disorders. I. Clinical assessment, definition of terms, and evaluation of their reliability. Arch Gen Psychiatry 36:1315–1321, 1979a.

Andreasen NC: Thought, language, and communication disorders. II. Diagnostic significance. Arch Gen Psychiatry 36:1325–1330, 1979b.

Andreasen NJC, Powers PS: Overinclusive thinking in mania and schizophrenia. Br J Psychiatry 125:452–456, 1974.

Angst J: Zur Atiologie und Nosologie endogener depressiver Psychosen. Mongraphien aus desm Gesamtgebiete der Neurologie und Psychiatrie. Berlin, Springer-Verlag, 1966.

Angst J: Discussion. In Angst J (ed): Classification and Prediction of Outcome of Depression. New York, Symposia Medica Hoechst 8, F. K. Schattauer Verlag, 1974.

Angst J: The course of affective disorders. II. Typology of bipolar manic-depressive illness. Arch Psychiat Nervenkr 226:65–73, 1978.

Angst J: Course of unipolar depressive, bipolar manic-depressive, and schizoaffective disorders. Results of a progressive longitudinal study. Fortschr Neurol Psychiatr 48:3–30, 1980.

Angst J: The course of affective disorders. Paper prepared for the Consensus Development Conference on Mood Disorders: Pharmacologic Prevention of Recurrences. National Institutes of Health, Bethesda, MD, April 1984.

Angst J, Arnold ES, Rudd SM, Kirshner H: Manic psychosis following rapid withdrawal from baclofen. Am J Psychiatry 137:1466–1467, 1980.

Angst J, Felder W, Frey R: The course of unipolar and bipolar affective disorders. In Schou M, Stromgren E (eds): Origin, Prevention and Treatment of Affective Disorders. New York, Academic, 1979.

Angst J, Felder W, Frey R, Stassen HH: The course of affective disorders. I. Change of diagnosis of monopolar, unipolar, and bipolar illness. Arch Psychiatr Nervenkr 226:57–64, 1978.

Arnold E, Rudd S, Kirshner, H. Manic psychosis following rapid withdrawal from baclofen. Am J Psychiatry 137:1466–1467, 1980.

Avery D, Winokur G: Mortality in depressed patients treated with electroconvulsive therapy and antidepressants. Arch Gen Psychiatry 33:1029–1037, 1976.

Ballenger JC, Post RM: Carbamazepine in manic-depressive illness: A new treatment. Am J Psychiatry 137:782–790, 1980.

Baron M, Risch N, Mendlewicz J: Differential fertility in bipolar affective illness. J Affective Disord 4:103–112, 1982.

Bech P, Shapiro RW, Sihm F, Nielsen B-M, Sorensen B, Rafaelsen OJ: Personality in unipolar and bipolar manic-melancholic patients. Acta Psychiatr Scand 62:245–257, 1980.

Bertelsen A, Harvald B, Hauge M: A Danish twin study of manic-depressive disorders. Br J Psychiatry 130:330–351, 1977.

Boyd JH, Weissman MM: Epidemiology of affective disorders. A reexamination and future directions. Arch Gen Psychiatry 38:1039–1046, 1981.

Bratfos O, Haug J: The course of manic-depressive psychosis. Acta Psychiatr Scand 44:89–112, 1968.

Brewerton TD, Reus VI: Lithium carbonate and L-tryptophan in the treatment of bipolar and schizoaffective disorders. Am J Psychiatry 140:757–760, 1983.

Brockington IF, Hillier VF, Francis AF, Helzer JE, Wainwright S: Definitions of mania: Concordance and prediction of outcome. Am J Psychiatry 140:435–439, 1983.

Brodie HKH, Leff MJ: Bipolar depression—A comparative study of patient characteristics. Am J Psychiatry 127:1086–1090, 1971.

Carlson GA, Davenport YB, Jamison K: A comparison of outcome in adolescent and late-onset bipolar manic-depressive illness. Am J Psychiatry 134:919–922, 1977.

Carlson GA, Goodwin FK: The stages of mania. A longitudinal analysis of the manic episode. Arch Gen Psychiatry 28:221–228, 1973.

Carroll BJ, Feinberg M, Greden JF, Tarika J, Albala AA, Haskett RF, James NMcI, Kronfol Z, Lohr N, Steiner M, de Vigne JP, Young E: A specific laboratory test for the diagnosis of melancholia. Standardization, validation, and clinical utility. Arch Gen Psychiatry 38:15–22, 1981.

Clayton PJ: Bipolar affective disorder—Techniques and results of treatment. Am J Psychother 32:81–92, 1978.

Clayton PJ: The epidemiology of bipolar affective disorder. Compr Psychiatry 22:31–43, 1981.

Clayton PJ: A further look at secondary depression. In Clayton PJ, Barrett JE (eds): Treatment of Depression: Old Controversies and New Approaches. New York, Raven, 1983.

Clayton PJ: DSM-III: The Affective Disorders. *Diagnosis and Classification in Psychiatry.* Cambridge, Cambridge University Press, in press.

Clayton PJ, Pitts FN Jr, Winokur G: Affective disorder. IV. Mania. Compr Psychiatry 6:313–322, 1965.

Coppen A, Abou-Saleh M, Milln P, Bailey J, Wood K: Decreasing lithium dosages reduces morbidity and side-effects during prophylaxis. J Affective Disord 5:353–362, 1983.

Dunner DL: Drug treatment of the acute manic episode. In Grinspoon L (ed): Psychiatry Update, vol 2. Washington, DC, American Psychiatric Press, 1983.

Extein I, Pottash ALC, Gold MS, Cowdry RW: Using the protirelin test to distinguish mania from schizophrenia. Arch Gen Psychiatry 39:77–81, 1982.

Fischer M: Twin studies and dual mating studies in defining mania. In Belmaker RH, van Praag HM (eds): Mania, an Evolving Concept. New York, Spectrum, 1980.

Fleiss JL, Prien RF, Dunner DL, Fieve RR: Actuarial studies of the course of manic-depressive illness. Compr Psychiatry 19:355–362, 1978.

Garfinkel PE, Stancer HC, Persad E: A comparison of haloperidol, lithium carbonate and their combination in the treatment of mania. J Affective Disord 2:279–288, 1980.

Gershon ES, Hamovit J, Guroff JJ, Dibble E, Leckman JF, Sceery W, Targum SD, Nurnberger JI Jr, Goldin LR, Bunney WE Jr: A family study of schizoaffective, bipolar I, bipolar II, unipolar, and normal control probands. Arch Gen Psychiatry 39:1157–1167, 1982.

Gershon ES, Nurnberger JI Jr, Nadi SD, Berrittini WH, Goldin LR: Current status of genetic research in affective disorders. In Angst J (ed): The Origins of Depression: Current Concepts and Approaches. Berlin, Springer-Verlag, 1983.

Gershon ES, McKnew D, Cytryn L, Hamovit J, Schreiber J, Hibbs E, Pellegrini D: Diagnoses in school-age children of bipolar affective disorder patients and normal controls. J Affective Disord 8:283–291, 1985.

Gough SP, Cookson IB: KHAT-induced schizophreniform psychosis in UK. Lancet 1:455, 1984.

Grof P, Angst J, Haines T: The clinical course of depression: Practical issues. In Angst J (ed): Classification and Prediction of Outcome of Depression. New York, Symposia Medica Hoeschst 8, F. K. Schattauer Verlag, 1974.

Guze SB, Robins E: Suicide and primary affective disorders. Br J Psychiatry 117:437–438, 1970.

Harrow M, Grossman LS, Silverstein ML, Meltzer HY: Thought pathology in manic and schizophrenic patients. Its occurrence at hospital admission and seven weeks later. Arch Gen Psychiatry 39:665–671, 1982.

Iacono WG, Lykken DT, Peloquin LJ, Lumry AE, Valentine RH, Tuason VB: Electrodermal activity in euthymic unipolar and bipolar affective disorders. A possible marker for depression. Arch Gen Psychiatry 40:557–565, 1983.

Jamison KR, Gerner RH, Hammen C, Padesky C: Clouds and silver linings: Positive experiences associated with primary affective disorders. Am J Psychiatry 137:198–202, 1980.

Jamison KR, Goodwin FK: Psychotherapeutic issues in bipolar illness. In Grinspoon L (ed): Psychiatry Update, vol 2. Washington, DC, American Psychiatric Press, 1983.

Jampala VC, Abrams R: Mania secondary to left and right hemisphere damage. Am J Psychiatry 140:1197–1199, 1983.

Janowsky DS, El-Yousef MK, Davis JM: Interpersonal maneuvers of manic patients. Am J Psychiatry 131:250, 1974.

Janowsky DS, Leff M, Epstein RS: Playing the manic game: Interpersonal maneuvers of the acutely manic patient. Arch Gen Psychiatry 22:252, 1970.

Janowsky DS, Risch SC, Judd LL, Parker DC, Kalin NH, Huey LY: Behavioral and neuroendocrine effects of physostigmine in affect disorder patients. In Clayton PJ, Barrett JE (eds): Treatment of Depression: Old Controversies and New Approaches. New York, Raven, 1983.

Johnson GF, Hunt G: Suicidal behavior in bipolar manic-depressive patients and their families. Compr Psychiatry 20:159–164, 1979.

Jones BE, Gray BA, Parson EB: Manic-depressive illness among poor urban blacks. Am J Psychiatry 138:654–657, 1981.

Jones BE, Gray BA, Parson EB: Manic-depressive illness among poor urban hispanics. Am J Psychiatry 140:1208–1210, 1983.

Joyce PR: Age of onset in bipolar affective disorder and misdiagnosis as schizophrenia. Psychol Med 14:145–149, 1984.

Kahlbaum K: Die Katatonie oder das Spannugsirresein. Berlin, 1874.

Kallen B, Tandberg A: Lithium and pregnancy. A cohort study on manic-depressive women. Acta Psychiatr Scand 68:134–139, 1983.

Kane J, Struve FA, Weinhold P, Woerner M: Strategy for the study of patients at high risk for tardive dyskinesia. Am J Psychiatry 137:1265–1267, 1980.

Keisling R: Underdiagnosis of manic-depressive illness in a hospital unit. Am J Psychiatry 138:672–673, 1981.

Khuri R, Akiskal HS: Suicide prevention: The necessity of treating contributory psychiatric disorders. Psychiatr Clin North Am 6:193–207, 1983.

Kidd KK, Gerhard DS, Kidd JR, Housman D, Egeland JA: Recombinant DNA methods in genetic studies of affective disorders. Clinical Neuropharmacology, vol 7, abstr suppl 1, New York, Raven, 1984, pp 198–199.

Kishimoto A, Ogura C, Hazama H, Inoue K: Long-term prophylactic effects of carbamazepine in affective disorder. Br J Psychiatry 143:327–331, 1983.

Kraepelin E: Manic-Depressive Insanity and Paranoia. Edinburgh, E & S Livingstone, 1921.

Krauthammer C, Klerman GL: Secondary mania. Manic syndromes associated with antecedent physical illness or drugs. Arch Gen Psychiatry 35:1333–1339, 1978.

Krauthammer C, Klerman GL: The epidemiology of mania. In Shopsin B (ed): Manic Illness. New York, Raven, 1979.

Kupfer DJ: Application of the sleep EEG in affective disorders. In Davis JM, Maas JW (eds): The Affective Disorders. Washington, DC, American Psychiatric Press, 1983.

Lilliker SL: Prevalence of diabetes in a manic-depressive population. Compr Psychiatry 21:270–275, 1980.

London WP, Taylor BM: Bipolar disorders in a forensic setting. Compr Psychiatry 23:33–37, 1982.

Lumry AE, Gottesman II, Tuason VB: MMPI state dependency during the course of bipolar psychosis. Psychiatry Res 7:59–67, 1982.

MacVane JR, Lange JD, Brown WA, Zayat M: Psychological functioning of bipolar manic-depressives in remission. Arch Gen Psychiatry 35:1351–1354, 1978.

Martin R, Cloninger C, Guze S, Clayton P: Mortality in a follow-up of 500 psychiatric outpatients. II. Cause-specific mortality. Arch Gen Psychiatry, 42:58–66, 1985.

Matussek P, Feil WB: Personality attributes of depressive patients. Results of group comparisons. Arch Gen Psychiatry 40:783–790, 1983.

McCabe MS: ECT in the treatment of mania: A controlled study. Am J Psychiatry 133:688, 1976.

McCabe MS, Norris B: ECT versus chlorpromazine in mania. Biol Psychiatry 12:245, 1977.

McCormick RA, Russo AM, Ramirez LF, Taber JI: Affective disorders among pathological gamblers seeking treatment. Am J Psychiatry 141:215–218, 1984.

Meltzer HY, Arora RC, Tricou BJ, Fang VS: Serotonin uptake in blood platelets and the dexamethasone suppression test in depressed patients. Psychiatry Res 8:41–47, 1983.

Mendlewicz J, Rainer JD: Adoption study supporting genetic transmission in manic-depressive illness. Nature 268:327–329, 1977.

Menninger K, Mayman M, Pruyser P: The Vital Balance. The Life Process in Mental Health and Illness. New York, Penguin Books, 1977.

Merikangas KR: Assortative mating for psychiatric disorders and psychological traits. Arch Gen Psychiatry 39:1173–1180, 1982.

Merikangas KR, Bromet EJ, Spiker DG: Assortative mating, social adjustment, and course of illness in primary affective disorder. Arch Gen Psychiatry 40:795–800, 1983.

Merikangas KR, Spiker DG: Assortative mating among in-patients with primary affective disorder. Psychol Med 12:753–764, 1982.

Morrison JR: Suicide in a psychiatric practice population. J Clin Psychiatry 43:348–352, 1982.

Myers JK, Weissman MM, Tischler GL, Holzer CE, Leaf PJ, Orvaschel H, Anthony JC, Boyd JH, Burke JD Jr, Kramer M, Stoltzman R: Six-month prevalence of psychiatric disorders in three communities: 1980–1982. Arch Gen Psychiatry 41:959–967, 1984.

Nadi SD, Nurnberger JI Jr, Gershon ES: Muscarinic cholinergic receptors on skin fibroblasts in familial affective disorder. N Engl J Med 311:225–230, 1984.

Nolen WA: Carbamazepine, a possible adjunct or alternative to lithium in bipolar disorder. Acta Psychiatr Scand 67:218–225, 1983.

Nurnberger J, Roose SP, Dunner DL, Fieve RR: Unipolar mania: A distinct clinical entity? Am J Psychiatry 136:1420–1423, 1979.

Nurnberger JI, Gershon ES: Genetics. In Paykel ES (ed): Handbook of Affective Disorders. Edinburgh, Churchill Livingstone, 1982.

Perris C: A study of bipolar (manic-depressive) and unipolar recurrent depressive psychoses. Acta Psychiatr Scand 42:1–188, 1966 (suppl 194).

Perris C: The separation of bipolar (manic-depressive) from unipolar recurrent depressive psychoses. Behav Neuropsychiatry 1:17–24, 1969.

Petterson U: Manic-depressive illness. A clinical, social and genetic study. Acta Psychiatr Scand [Suppl] 269, 1977.

Petty F, Sherman AD: Plasma GABA levels in psychiatric illness. J Affective Disord 6:131–138, 1984.

Pfohl B, Vasquez N, Nasrallah H: Unipolar vs. bipolar mania: A review of 247 patients. Br J Psychiatry 141:453–458, 1982.

Pope HG Jr, Lipinski JF Jr: Diagnosis in schizophrenia and manic depressive illness. A reassessment of the specificity of "schizophrenic" symptoms in the light of current research. Arch Gen Psychiatry 35:811–828, 1978.

Post RM: Editorial. Use of the anticonvulsant carbamazepine in primary and secondary affective illness: Clinical and theoretical implications. Psychol Med 12:701–704, 1982.

Post RM, Uhde TW, Ballenger JC, Squillace KM: Prophylactic efficacy of carbamazepine in manic-depressive illness. Am J Psychiatry 140:1602–1604, 1983.

Prien RF: Long-term prophylactic pharmacologic treatment of bipolar illness. In Grinspoon L (ed): Psychiatry Update, vol 2. Washington, DC, American Psychiatric Press, 1983.

Pritz WF, Mitterauer BJ: Bipolar mood disorders: An affected sibling study. I. Genetic background and course of illness. Psychopathology 17:67–79, 1984.

Puzynski S, Klosiewicz L: Valproic acid amide in the treatment of affective and schizoaffective disorders. J Affective Disord 6:115–121, 1984.

Robbins TW, Sahakian BJ: Animal models of mania. In Belmaker RH, van Praag HM (eds): Mania, an Evolving Concept. New York, Spectrum, 1980.

Robins LN, Helzer JE, Weissman M, Orvaschel H, Gruenberg E, Burke JD, Regier D: Lifetime prevalence of specific psychiatric disorders in three sites. Arch Gen Psychiatry 41:949–958, 1984.

Rosenbaum KM, Niven RG, Hanson HP, Swanson DW: Tardive dyskinesia: Relationship with primary affective disorder. Dis Nerv Syst 38:423–426, 1977.

Rush M, Diamond F, Alpert M: Depression as a risk factor in tardive dyskinesia. Biol Psychiatry 17:387–392, 1982.

Sashidharan SP, McGuire RJ: Recurrence of affective illness after withdrawal of long-term lithium treatment. Acta Psychiatr Scand 68:126–133, 1983.

Schleifer SJ, Keller SE, Meyerson AT, Raskin MJ, Davis KL, Stein M: Lymphocyte function in major depressive disorder. Arch Gen Psychiatry 41:484–486, 1984.

Sedler MJ: Falret's discovery: The origin of the concept of bipolar affective illness. Am J Psychiatry 140:1127–1133, 1983.

Shulman K, Post F: Bipolar affective disorder in old age. Br J Psychiatry 136:26–32, 1980.

Sitaram N: Faster cholinergic REM sleep induction as a possible trait marker of affective illness. In Davis JM,

Maas JW (eds): The Affective Disorders. Washington, DC, American Psychiatric Press, 1983.

Stokes PE, Stoll PM, Koslow SH, Maas JW, Davis JM, Swann AC, Robins E: Pretreatment DST and hypothalamic-pituitary-adrenocortical function in depressed patients and comparison groups. A multicenter study. Arch Gen Psychiatry 41:257–267, 1984.

Swann AC, Secunda S, Davis JM, Robins E, Hanin I, Koslow SH, Maas JW: CSF monoamine metabolites in mania. Am J Psychiatry 140:396–400, 1983.

Targum SD, Dibble ED, Davenport YB, Gershon ES: The family attitudes questionnaire. Patients' and spouses' views of bipolar illness. Arch Gen Psychiatry 38:562–568, 1981.

Tatetsu S: Methamphetamine psychosis. Folia Psychiatr Neurol Jpn 17:377–380, 1963 (suppl 7).

Tatetsu S: Methamphetamine psychosis. In Ellinwood EH, Cohen S (eds): Current Concepts on Amphetamine Abuse. DHEW Publ No (HSM) 72-9085. Washington, DC, 1972, pp 159–161.

Tsuang MT: Suicide in schizophrenics, manics, depressives, and surgical controls. Arch Gen Psychiatry 35:153–155, 1978.

Tsuang MT, Woolson RF: Mortality in patients with schizophrenia, mania, depression and surgical conditions. Br J Psychiatry 130:162–166, 1977.

Waters B, Marchenko I, Abrams N, Smiley D, Kalin D: Assortative mating for major affective disorder. J Affective Disord 5:9–17, 1983.

Welner A, Welner Z, Leonard MA: Bipolar manic-depressive disorder: A reassessment of course and outcome. Compr Psychiatry 18:327–332, 1977.

Winokur G: The Iowa 500: Heterogeneity and course in manic-depressive illness (bipolar). Compr Psychiatry 16:125–131, 1975.

Winokur G: Mania and depression: Family studies and genetics in relation to treatment. In Lipton MA, DiMascio A, Killam KF (eds): Psychopharmacology: A Generation of Progress. New York, Raven, 1978.

Winokur G, Clayton PJ, Reich T: Manic depressive illness. St. Louis, C. V. Mosby, 1969.

Winokur G, Crowe RR: Bipolar illness. The sex-polarity effect in affectively ill family members. Arch Gen Psychiatry 40:57–58, 1983.

Woodruff RA Jr, Clayton PJ, Guze SB: Suicide attempts and psychiatric diagnosis. Dis Nerv Syst 33:617–621, 1972.

Young MA, Abrams R, Taylor MA, Meltzer HY: Establishing diagnostic criteria for mania. J Nerv Ment Dis 171:676–682, 1983.

Young RC, Nysewander RW, Schreiber MT: Mania ratings at discharge from hospital: A follow-up (brief communication). J Nerv Ment Dis 170:638–639, 1982.

# chapter 5

# UNIPOLAR DEPRESSION

*by* George Winokur, M.D.

## DEFINITION

Unipolar depression is an affective disorder characterized by low mood and associated symptoms, such as loss of interest and energy, anorexia and weight change, sleep disturbance, feelings of unworthiness and self-condemnation, trouble thinking and concentrating, and suicidal ideation. It occurs in patients who have never suffered a mania. Synonyms for unipolar depression in the *Diagnostic and Statistical Manual of Mental Disorders*, third edition (DSM-III), are major depression and dysthymic disorder. Synonyms in the International Classification of Diseases (ICD)-9 system are major depressive disorder, reactive depressive psychosis, and neurotic depression.

## EPIDEMIOLOGY

A medical student who flunks a major anatomy examination or a woman who is passed over for a good position in favor of a less qualified man very well may be unhappy and "depressed." No doubt these kinds of circumstances occur in the lives of most people; and if one considered this unhappiness as a depression, the risk for this would be 100 per cent. Such events and responses ordinarily are short-lived, and the person is not incapacitated for daily life. In the case of true unipolar depression, the

person should be considered different from his usual self and have some degree of incapacity impairing his function in job or social life. A person could conceivably have a depression and continue to function in an ordinary fashion, but this is unusual. Social incapacity in a depression often brings an individual to seek help.

Unipolar depression is a common illness in the population. Compared with other kinds of psychiatric disorders, it occurs 8 times as frequently as bipolar illness and possibly 12 times as frequently as incapacitating schizophrenia. Table 5–1 gives a breakdown of the expectancy for a depression in the lifetime of people selected from the population.

Robins et al. (1984) have published data on the lifetime prevalence of psychiatric illnesses in three epidemiologic catchment areas. The lifetime prevalence is the proportion of persons in the population who have experienced a disorder up to the date of assessment. The lifetime prevalence for a

**TABLE 5–1. Lifetime Illness in Control Populations**

| Study | Risk for Depression (%) | | |
|---|---|---|---|
| | MALES | FEMALES | TOTAL |
| Iowa | 3.8 | 11.9 | 8.1 |
| New Haven | 12.3 | 25.8 | 18.0 |
| Iceland | 9.4 | 14.4 | 12.0 |

major depressive episode varies between 3.7 per cent and 6.7 per cent over the three catchment areas. The lifetime prevalence for dysthymia (minor depressive disorder) varies between 2.1 per cent and 3.8 per cent. In contrast, the lifetime prevalence for a manic episode is between 0.6 per cent and 1.1 per cent. Some of these diagnoses may overlap because the authors did not deal with "diseases," but with syndromes.

In Table 5–1, note the difference in the proportions of the population at risk for a depression, dependent on the individual study. The reasons for this are obvious. The study in Iowa dealt with a population of relatives of psychiatrically well surgical patients (Tsuang, Winokur, Crowe, 1984). Thus the relatives presumably were not related to anybody who had had a psychiatric illness. The New Haven and the Iceland population studies were done out in the community, and no effort was made to evaluate the people who come from psychiatrically well families (Weissman and Meyers, 1978; Helgason, 1979). Many studies show that psychiatric illnesses run in families; therefore, one would expect that the purified population in the Iowa study would contain less illness than the other two populations. In any event, there is a threefold difference between the highest and the lowest proportion at risk for males and a twofold difference among females. There are other differences in the epidemiologic studies. In the Iowa population, the person had to be ill for at least 4 weeks in order to qualify for a diagnosis, whereas a much shorter time constraint was used in the New Haven study. Also, different methods were used in obtaining the populations.

However, some things are clear. Within each study, females are more likely to be affected with unipolar depression than are males. All studies take into account both hospitalized and nonhospitalized patients in the population. In the Iceland study, about 48 per cent of males and 37 per cent of females with major affective disorders (bipolar plus unipolar) were never admitted to any hospital. Presumably, many of these people would have been seen by family practitioners, although some may have escaped medical notice.

There has been a plethora of studies looking at the prevalence, at any point in time, for unipolar depression (Boyd and Weiss-man, 1981). This prevalence varies between 1.0 per cent and 10.8 per cent.

Annual incidence studies in unipolar depression are numerous; these vary between 247 and 7800 cases per 100,000 per year. In a series of incidence studies, between 130 and 201 men and between 320 and 500 women per 100,000 per year began receiving treatment for depression for the first time.

## CLINICAL PICTURE

Although a depressive syndrome may be chronic, the person presenting himself to the hospital or clinic usually complains of an acute change. In a sense, the patient considers himself changed in some way from his usual state. A good question to ask a patient, then, would be whether he is different from his usual self.

A person may be diagnosed as depressed if he describes his state of mind as being dysphoric and uses such terms as feeling depressed, sad, blue, despondent, hopeless, irritable, down in the dumps, fearful, worried, discouraged, and worthless. Having described himself as being that way, other symptoms are necessary. Common symptoms in depression include poor appetite or weight loss, difficulty in sleeping, energy loss or fatigability, agitation or retardation, loss of interest in usual activities, as well as loss of interest in sexual matters, feelings of worthlessness or guilt, and complaints of not being able to think or concentrate. Recurrent thoughts of death or suicidal ideas also are presented by depressive patients (Feighner et al., 1972). Such symptoms are, in part, seen in patients who have experienced personal tragedies. For example, bereavement may produce a syndrome that resembles depression (Clayton, Herjanic, Murphy, Woodruff, 1974). This is, in a sense, a normal reactive depression. Such symptoms as suicidal thoughts, retardation, and feelings of worthlessness usually are not seen in a depression associated with grief. A person ordinarily gets over such a depression in a short period of time, but sometimes it is prolonged. Other circumstances may also produce for a short period a mental state that fulfills a depressive syndrome. Thus a parent whose child suffered an injury might show depression, but this would not be considered a depressive illness. Also, such an episode would be short-lived. A time constraint is needed on the diagnosis of depression, and various have been used. A conservative time constraint would be the presence of depressive symptoms for 1 month continuously.

Many studies have systematically evaluated the clinical status of depressed patients. Table 5–2 presents the common symptoms in 100 unipolar depressive patients. Although there were twice as many females in this group of 100 as males, there were no meaningful differences between the sexes regarding the frequency of symptoms (Baker, Dorzab, Winokur, Cadoret, 1971).

Some of the symptoms deserve special comment. When a patient complains of impaired concentration, it is quite possible that his boss or spouse or close friends will not have noted any difficulty in his thinking. However, he believes that he is neither tracking nor concentrating as well as he did before he became depressed. The differences are subtle, and studies have shown that the difficulties in thinking are demonstrable on psychological tests (Stromgren, 1977). For purposes of diagnosis, the important thing is that the patient himself recognizes a difference.

Decision making is often impaired in depressive patients. This creates some difficulty in dealing with such patients. As an example, a patient who had shot himself through the mouth and lived to tell the tale appeared with his wife in the office of a psychiatrist after medical treatment for the effects of the gunshot wound. This was a few months after the suicide attempt, and he was still as depressed as he had been before. When he was told that he would have to come into the hospital for treatment of his depressive illness, he was unable to make up his mind to do this. Instead, he vacillated back and forth over the idea of what would be best for him. This kind of uncertainty and difficulty making a decision are fairly typical of patients who have unipolar depressions, although usually the circumstances are not as dramatic as in the case described.

The sleep difficulties in unipolar depression are characteristic of the disorder. Although some patients complain of having trouble getting to sleep, the hallmark symptom is terminal insomnia. The individual says that he can fall asleep all right but wakes after a few hours and cannot get back to sleep; or he complains of getting up several hours earlier in the morning than is his usual habit and is not able to get back to sleep. This is terminal insomnia. Often during these periods of wakefulness, the patient will ruminate over past guilt and difficulties in his life.

Table 5–3 shows symptoms that occur often during a depressive episode but not in the majority of patients. Most are seen equally in males and in females, but females are more than twice as likely to complain of inability to cry, and males are twice as likely to complain of multiple somatic symptoms during the depressive illness only. Some of the symptoms deserve special note. Diurnal variation describes mood change over the course of the day. A person who has this symptom awakens in the morning and feels quite depressed or agitated or inert. As the day wears on, he or she improves, sometimes almost to normality. There are probably no pathognomonic symptoms of depressive illness, but this one would come as close to being specific as any.

Anxiety attacks occur frequently during a depressive episode. In unipolar depression these are associated only with the episode itself. Unlike in other illnesses (agoraphobia, panic disorder), the anxiety attack is not present on a long-term or chronic basis.

**TABLE 5–2.** Symptoms of Index Episode Occurring in More Than 50% of Patients

| Symptoms | No. and Percentage of Patients (N = 100) |
|---|---|
| Reduced energy level | 97 |
| Impaired concentration | 84 |
| Anorexia | 80 |
| Initial insomnia | 77 |
| Loss of interest | 77 |
| Difficulty starting activities | 76 |
| Worry more than usual | 69 |
| Subjective agitation | 67 |
| Slowed thinking | 67 |
| Difficulty with decision making | 67 |
| Terminal insomnia | 65 |
| Suicide ideation or plans | 63 |
| Weight loss | 61 |
| Tearfulness | 61 |
| Movements slowed (subjective perception) | 60 |
| Increased irritability | 60 |
| Feels will never get well | 56 |

**TABLE 5–3.**  Symptoms of Index Episode Occurring in 10% to 50% of Patients

| Symptoms | No. and Percentage of Patients (N = 100) |
|---|---|
| Diurnal variation | 46 |
| Difficulty finishing activities once started | 46 |
| Prominent self-pity | 45 |
| Inability to cry | 44 |
| Constipation | 43 |
| Impaired expression of emotions | 42 |
| Ruminations of worthlessness | 38 |
| Decreased libido | 36 |
| Anxiety attacks | 36 |
| Difficulty doing activities once started | 35 |
| Ruminations of guilt | 32 |
| Complains more than usual | 28 |
| Any type of delusion | 27 |
| Phobias during depression only | 27 |
| Multiple somatic symptoms during depression only | 25 |
| Communication of suicidal ideas, plans, or attempts | 22 |
| Place major blame for illness on others | 19 |
| At least one depressive delusion | 16 |
| Death wishes without suicidal ideation | 16 |
| Suicide attempts | 15 |
| Other delusions | 14 |
| Obsessions during depression only | 14 |
| Depersonalization and derealization | 13 |
| Ruminations of sinfulness | 12 |

Often a depressive patient is delusional. Delusions seen in depressives are of two types. The first comprises depressive delusions, which include delusions of guilt, sinfulness, worthlessness, and failure. A man who cheated on his income tax in 1927 entered the hospital in 1957. He was guilty about having cheated and believed that he was being persecuted by the government because of this. He thought that this was appropriate because he had been such a dishonest person. This type of depressive delusion is called a mood congruent delusion because it is consistent with a state of mind of the depressed individual. Other types of delusions seen in depression are mood incongruent delusions, which have nothing to do with feelings of guilt or worthlessness. It is important to recognize that even in the presence of mood incongruent delusions and hallucinations, a diagnosis of unipolar depression may be made as long as the individual shows the appropriate symptom picture, a relatively acute onset, and no suggestion of another illness (e.g., schizophrenia, alcoholism, organic brain syndrome).

Table 5–4 shows mental status signs exhibited by patients being admitted to the hospital at the time of their first episode. What is notable is that almost half the patients show no clear signs of the illness. Formal thought disorder in the mental status consists of blocking or circumstantiality. No patient in this group shows tangentiality or loosening of associations. Again, males and females are not different from each other in showing these signs, although there is a slight increase in retardation of movements and speech in men.

Some differences in the clinical picture are related to other variables. Patients who are admitted after having had previous episodes are different from those who are admitted with a first episode. First-episode patients are more likely to complain of subjective agitation and tearfulness and less likely to complain of constipation, inability to cry, inability to express emotions, trouble making decisions, and slowed thinking. Perhaps some of the most striking clinical differences are seen in young (under 40) patients when they are compared with older depressive patients. Agitation is more common in the older group, and retardation is more common in the younger group (Winokur, Morrison, Clancy, Crowe, 1973).

Finally, some statement should be made about the concept of the "endogenous" depression. Such a depression is considered to be physiologic, or somatic, or coming from within the body. It is ordinarily differentiated from neurotic-reactive depressions, which are presumed to be the result of difficult life stresses. Symptoms that are especially seen in endogenous depressions include diurnal variation, delusions, psychomotor retardation, early-morning awak-

**TABLE 5–4.**  Mental Status Findings at Index Episode

| Findings | No. and Percentage of Patients (N = 100) |
|---|---|
| Mental status without evidence of agitation, retardation, or formal thought disorder | 45 |
| Agitation | 30 |
| Psychomotor retardation | 19 |
| Formal thought disorder | 8 |
| Both agitation and retardation | 6 |

ening, marked guilt, hopelessness, and hallucinations. Symptoms that are seen in the neurotic-reactive type of unipolar depression include initial insomnia, emotional lability, blaming others, many somatic complaints, and a stormy life-style with difficulties in marriage, school, and job (Mendels, 1968; Kay, Garside, Beamish, Roy, 1971). In endogenous depression, the concept has to do with a specific definable illness; in neurotic-reactive depression, the concept is related to a set of symptoms that are either a response to life events or a life-style that remains unchanged over years. Many studies have shown difficulties in separating these types of depression. There is an overlap of symptoms between the endogenous and the neurotic-reactive (Kendell, 1968). Nevertheless, it is conceivable that these concepts do identify a certain group of patients at one or the other end of a continuum. The separation into two diagnoses, endogenous versus neurotic-reactive, may have some usefulness in predicting course as well as in prescribing treatment.

The clinical picture is composed of depressive affect and a number of related symptoms. Some patients, however, simply have the affect and relatively few or even none of the related symptoms. This clinical presentation suggests a depressive personality. Patients with a depressive personality look on the dark side of life and view circumstances with extreme pessimism. Often such people are mistrustful and seem to have little capacity for pleasure. They are excessively critical and full of derogatory comments about themselves and their friends. Minor defeats lead them to conclude that their entire life has been a failure. An innocent or insignificant comment causes them to feel slighted. They have been described as being unaggressive, kindly people who are vulnerable or, alternatively, as ill-humored people who are surly, bitter, suspicious, and irritable. Because they have received what they consider to be the short end of the stick, they are often malicious and jealous of other people's success (Schneider, 1959; Akiskal, in press). They chronically feel this way. On occasion they will go from showing a depressive personality to being incapacitated with the full assortment of symptoms. The relationship of the depressive personality to the clear and unequivocal

depressive syndrome with incapacitation is difficult to determine. Some believe that these depressive personalities are a minor form of a depressive illness; others believe that they exist independently of major depressive syndromes. A relationship of the depressive personality either with significant incapacitating depressive syndromes or with a presence of major depressive illness in the family would lead one to believe that the depressive personality is, in fact, a kind of *forme fruste* of unipolar depressive illness.

### Some Illustrative Cases

### CASE HISTORY 1

**Present Illness:** Mrs. A., aged 40 and white, was admitted in 1939. Her illness had begun 9 months earlier, when she expressed "queer ideas." She wrote letters to her minister and others stating that if anything happened to her, somebody should take care of her child. She worried about finances, started to sleep poorly, and lost her job taking care of children. She had ideas of reference and believed that people were talking about her. She became more irritable and complained of pain in the abdomen, which led her to the hospital.

At admission, her mental status was striking. She appeared weak and tired. Her facial expression was sad and downcast. On occasion she would moan and whimper to herself. She refused to eat or drink, saying that she was unable to swallow. At times she would become excited and squirm around in bed. Her stream of talk was such that she often would not answer questions; and if she did, she would answer them in a weak voice. She would respond if spoken to sharply. Her mood was such that she appeared very depressed. She cried and at other times would become agitated. She expressed no delusions or hallucinations on questioning. Her sensorium was such that she fluctuated in and out of orientation.

**Past History:** In 1917, 22 years before, she had had a nervous breakdown similar to the present illness. At that time she was mute, restless, wept, picked at her clothing, and had to be cared for. This condition cleared up in 6 months, but she was left more irritable than before. In 1922 she married for economic reasons, and in 1924 her first child was stillborn after a difficult labor. In 1925 and 1929 she had normal pregnancies, and in 1931 she had a gastroenterostomy performed for a perforated gastric ulcer.

Mrs. A. was a nervous person, irritable, given to talking a lot about inconsequential things. She had few friends. She took disappointments hard. She worked hard and conscientiously. Her heterosexual interest was minimal, and she only married her husband for economic advantages, which, unhappily, did not ensue.

As regards family history of psychiatric disease, her father was quite possibly a chronic alcoholic.

**Course of Illness:** Mrs. A. had a similar illness at age 18 from which she recovered. In 1939 (index admission) she was admitted to a psychiatric hospital because of weakness, emaciation, weight loss, and confused behavior. She was tube fed and gained 10 lbs. She then felt considerably stronger. However, she became more depressed and had poor contact with other people. With sedative medication, she improved to the point where she could eat by herself and she talked more. She was not well, however, and was transferred to a state hospital.

## CASE HISTORY 2

Mrs. A.F. was admitted in June 1939 to a psychiatric hospital. Her illness apparently started around February 1939, when she learned that a foster brother had absconded with money from a company for which he was working. She cried a great deal about this and stated that it was her own fault. She believed this because her foster brother had had behavior problems and she had not given him adequate support. She gave voice to a number of self-deprecatory ideas and self-accusations.

At admission to the hospital her attitude and general behavior indicated profound depression, mostly associated with her guilt about her interaction with her foster brother. She was somewhat agitated and expressed suicidal ideas on occasion. She was uncomfortable with her attitude toward religion, and she inquired whether she was a bad person because of her failure to believe implicitly in the Bible and in God. She also wondered whether she had started her children off wrong and blamed herself for preventing her husband from attending theology school. Because of the persistence of these self-condemnatory symptoms, she was admitted to the hospital.

Her mental status was replete with many ideas of self-accusation and many self-deprecatory delusions. She protested vehemently that all of her troubles were of her own making and because she was constantly self-centered. She conceived of herself as a "congenital defective" who should expect no more than she was getting. Her outlook was dismal, and she stated that she would end her days in an "asylum with the most violent type of mental disease which I justly deserve because I am such a despicable character."

**Past History:** Mrs. A.F. was always considered a reactive kind of a person and might have had a previous depression 4 years earlier, when her husband lost his job. At this point she worried over the circumstances, was depressed, blamed herself for coming to the city in which she lived, seemed absentminded and preoccupied. After several months she stopped worrying and returned to normal.

She was talented. She graduated from college and was described as an energetic person who enjoyed social activities. It is noted that when she was a very young child, she was fearful of dogs and other animals, but this phobia did not persist.

**Course of Illness:** Mrs. A.F. remained in the hospital for about 2 months and continued profoundly depressed throughout her hospitalization. She was started on Metrazol convulsive therapy (the predecessor of electroconvulsive therapy) and showed dramatic improvement after the second treatment. Although she slipped back somewhat, she was discharged less depressed than on admission. After being out of the hospital for one day, she was readmitted. There was an exacerbation of depressive affect and self-deprecatory ideas. She believed that she would spend the rest of her days in a mad house. She was given another series of Metrazol therapy treatments (this time seven; the first time, five). There was a marked improvement in her mood after the first treatment, and this affective improvement was maintained. Interestingly, there was an attempt to determine whether there was any organic impairment from the Metrazol treatments, and it was noted that she did better on an IQ test (I.Q. 134) than she did at the time of her first hospital admission (I.Q. 124). She was discharged as well after 3 weeks in the hospital and was followed up in 1940, 1941, 1942, 1943, and 1944. She continued well and functional during all of those followups.

## CASE HISTORY 3

**Present Illness:** Mr. M.H., 47 years old, was admitted August 1938. His illness had been noted for about 1 year. In February 1937 he had fallen from a bridge, and this was rumored to be a suicide attempt. He began to scratch all parts of his body and stated that he had lost his soul and had sinned. On several occasions he said that he wanted to die; once he was found with a gun, and another time he took a rope into a building but left it there. A month before admission he was found clinging to the inner edge of a cistern; he had intended to commit suicide but then thought better of it. He was restless and wandered. He refused food even when he stated that he was hungry.

His mental status showed retardation, speaking slowly, and perseverating in thinking. His general mood was one of depression, and ideas of guilt and unworthiness were expressed. On occasion he said that people made noises and did things to make him angry, but that this was done to punish him. There was no evidence of hallucinations.

**Past History:** Mr. M.H. was born in Norway and moved to the United States as a young child. His wife died of tuberculosis 19 years before his illness. He was described as a congenial, well-liked person, interested in school activities, and an officer in church organizations.

**Family History:** A brother had had a nervous breakdown. He was not hospitalized and he improved. The family was considered intelligent, stable, and successful in business. A nephew was admitted to the same hospital as a patient with a diagnosis of depression.

**Course of Illness:** At admission Mr. M.H. was in a semistuporous state. He was tearful and agitated and said that his children would be better off without him, that he wanted to go away and live in a little shack. He said that he used to be goodhearted, but that he was currently bad. He talked of losing his soul and of committing crimes. He was transferred to a long-term state mental hospital after a couple of weeks of hospitalization. Seven years after his admission to the hospital, an attempt was made to follow him up. His daughter responded to the inquiry by saying, "I am answering your letter . . . regarding the health of my father, which has been real good these past years and does not show any signs of mental or physical complaints."

## CLINICAL COURSE

The first episode of unipolar depression is usually, but not invariably, reported as occurring after puberty. Table 5–5 shows the cumulative proportion of patients for age of first episode. In this table, males and females are combined, as the ages of onset were not significantly different for the two sexes (Dorzab, Baker, Winokur, Cadoret, 1971).

A fifth of the patients first become ill in their teens, and by the time they are age 65, almost all of them who are going to fall ill have had an episode. Some people, however, do have their first episodes even after age 70. The median age of onset for unipolar depression is 37 years. If a depressive person has a family history of unipolar depression or a family history of alcoholism, the age of onset is usually earlier, probably around age 33. If there is no family history of either alcoholism or depression, the age of onset is later. These "sporadic" cases normally start in the late 30s or early 40s, or even at an older age.

Unipolar depressive illness shows multiple episodes. Single-episode cases are seen; but if one follows patients for more than 15 years, single-episode illnesses are rarely observed (Angst et al., 1973). If one follows patients for a period of 20 years, the average number of episodes in unipolar depression is five or six.

Treated episodes are relatively short, around 3 months' duration, but untreated episodes often last longer, in bygone days about 6 to 13 months or longer. The length of each episode of depression generally remains constant throughout the individual's lifetime, but cycle length—defined as the time from the beginning of one episode of depression to the beginning of the next—shortens from episode to episode.

Age seems to play a role in the clinical course. As women grow older, their episodes are likely to become longer. Thus women with age show a considerable amount of chronicity. As men grow older they seem to show an increasing number of episodes but not necessarily chronicity (Winokur and Morrison, 1973). There may be a limitation to the mean number of episodes in the unipolar depressive group. As noted earlier, unipolar depressives in followup have five to six episodes. This is true whether they are followed for 20 years or for 25, 30, or 35 years. This self-limitation in the mean number of episodes may indicate that after a certain number of episodes, the illness has run its course and the future will be good for the absence of occurrences.

Some unipolar depressives go on to show a mania (bipolar illness) some time in the future. This occurs in about 5 per cent of unipolar depressive patients followed for a period of 3 to 5 years. Following the patients for up to 40 years would indicate that about 10 per cent of unipolar patients convert to bipolarity in the course of time (Winokur, Tsuang, Crowe, 1982).

In a group of untreated seriously ill depressives admitted to the hospital and followed for a period of 3 to 5 years, about 30 per cent will remain chronically ill. This will be more common in females, about 36 per cent, as compared with males, 26 per cent. By about 5 years, 70 per cent to 75 per cent

**TABLE 5–5.** Age of Onset in Unipolar Depression: Cumulative Proportion of Ill People

| Age | Proportion (%) |
| --- | --- |
| 10–19 | 19 |
| 20–29 | 39 |
| 30–39 | 54 |
| 40–49 | 73 |
| 50–59 | 87 |
| 60–69 | 96 |
| 70–79 | 100 |

Mean age of onset 37.3 years.

of depressives will have had a recovery. If one follows a group for 15 years, 85 per cent will have recovered. One of the most interesting things about chronicity in depressed patients is that a group of patients may be chronically ill for a period of 10 years, but if one follows them for another 10 years, most will have recovered. "Late-onset" patients (i.e., after 50), who have their first episode at that point, often remain ill for prolonged periods but ultimately recover spontaneously. Thus chronicity is a limited affair that may last for up to 10 years but does not continue indefinitely. It is important to emphasize that these observations refer only to the natural history of untreated unipolar depression; with treatment, chronicity is less of a problem (Winokur, 1974).

Some findings suggest that a family history of alcoholism in a unipolar depressive predicts an absence of chronicity. In other words, if alcoholism exists in a first-degree family member, a depressed patient is not likely to have an unremitting illness; rather, it will be an illness that is more variable.

In bipolar affective disorder, a short-term followup indicated that a high proportion of patients remained chronically ill but had superimposed exacerbations or episodes on this baseline state (Winokur, Clayton, Reich, 1969). This course was termed "partial remission with episodes." Such a finding has also been reported in unipolar illness. In a 2-year followup of unipolar depressives, a "subsyndromal" picture is reported as an underlying problem. This means that the full set of depressive symptoms are absent but may recur at any point; in fact, the patient may exhibit the full clinical picture of depression off and on during the followup but never be completely asymptomatic. This course is termed a "double depression" (Keller, Lavori, Endicott, Coryell, Klerman, 1983).

If one follows a group of unipolar depressives for a prolonged period, 35 years, and compares them with a group of controls, it is clear that the controls will have fared better (see Table 5–6). Most of the controls will be considered to have no disability at the time of a 35-year followup, whereas slightly more than half the depressed patients will be considered severely or moderately disabled. In this case the disability would take into account employment status, physical health, and the presence of psychiatric symptoms. Nonetheless, as may be noted from Table 5–6, 46 per cent had no psychiatric disability of any sort (Winokur and Tsuang, 1975).

In any discussion of the course of the illness, one must keep in mind some severe consequences. In unipolar depression these would be suicide and mortality from natural causes. A number of studies have shown a remarkably consistent finding. In groups of patients chosen for the diagnosis of affective disorder (usually unipolar depression plus bipolar illness), about 14 per cent to 16 per cent of the deceased patients will have died by suicide. In one study a large group of unipolar depressives who were admitted to the hospital between 1935 and 1940 were chosen as subjects and followed for 35 to 40 years. These were compared with a group of controls who were followed for approximately the same length of time. Table 5–7 shows the suicide rates for the two groups. What is clear is that suicide risk for patients who have a unipolar depressive illness is far greater than the risk that one would expect from the general population (Winokur and Tsuang, 1975).

The risk for suicide in patients with unipolar depression is highest shortly after discharge from hospital or treatment. The question of mortality is a more difficult one to answer. There have been a variety of studies of mortality in the affective disorders. One investigation showed that the survival rate in patients with unipolar depression is shortened. One of the causes of the increased mortality in such patients is unnatural deaths. These include suicides

TABLE 5–6. Psychiatric Disability After a 35-Year Follow-up

| | No. Followed Up | Disability (%) | | |
|---|---|---|---|---|
| | | SEVERE | MODERATE | NONE |
| Unipolar depressives | 145 | 26 | 28 | 46 |
| Controls | 83 | 0 | 11 | 89 |

**TABLE 5–7.  Incidence of Suicide Among Proband and Control Groups in a 30- to 40-Year Followup Study**

| Item | Depressives | Controls |
|---|---|---|
| No. followed up | 182 | 109 |
| No. of suicides | 14 | 0 |
| Percentage of suicides | 7.7 | 0.0 |
| No. deceased at followup | 132 | 37 |
| Percentage of suicides among total deceased | 10.6 | 0.0 |

and accidents. It is possible, however, that other causes of death are implicated. For the first decade after admission to a hospital (in the years when relatively little treatment was available), the increased number of deaths in depressives, when compared with the general population and a control group, was about twofold (Tsuang, Woolson, Fleming, 1980).

Finally, it is important to assess whether or not patients with a diagnosis of unipolar depression change the character of their illness over time. When one deals with diagnoses that are made primarily on the basis of a clinical evaluation, some error is likely to be present. As noted earlier, in about 10 per cent of the cases there is a change in diagnosis to bipolar illness. Changes to other diagnoses are considerably less common. About 5 per cent of unipolar depressives in a 30- to 40-year followup will earn a diagnosis of schizophrenia. If one simply evaluates medical records, 84 per cent of unipolar depressives, on readmission, will earn the same diagnosis (Tsuang, Woolson, Winokur, Crowe, 1981). This kind of stability of psychiatric diagnosis in the case of the unipolar depressive group is reassuring. The lack of change to another diagnosis is evidence of a true illness.

## ETIOLOGY

Both biologic and psychosocial factors have been implicated in the cause of unipolar depression. This seems quite rational because clinicians have separated unipolar depression into those types that might be considered endogenous (having origin within the organism) and those that might be considered neurotic-reactive. A reasonable definition of neurotic-reactive depression would be a depression seen in a person

who either has life events that provoke the syndrome or a history of multiple neurotic or personality difficulties (a stormy lifestyle) that culminate in a depressive episode (Klerman, Endicott, Spitzer, Hirschfeld, 1979). In this definition, such people have had symptoms of personality difficulties but do not meet criteria for a true diagnosis of a personality disorder. Thus they are people with problems in living.

A model for a reactive depression is seen in widows and widowers who develop a depressive syndrome after the death of their spouses. A third of the bereaved survivors meet criteria for depression. Women and men are equally likely to show a depression after bereavement, which is different from the sex ratio in a clinic or hospital. Such depressions may last for a considerable period, sometimes a year or longer. Some differences in clinical symptomatology exist between hospitalized depressives and patients who suffer depression after bereavement; suicidal thoughts, retardation, and feelings of hopelessness and worthlessness are far less common in bereavement depressions. Likewise, these patients are less likely than ordinary depressives to show loss of interest in personal relationships. Nevertheless, the bereaved depressive meets reasonable criteria for depression, indicating that depression can occur because of precipitating factors (Clayton, Halikas, Maurice, 1972).

The role of precipitating factors or life events in the depressed patient who is either hospitalized or seen in the clinic is more difficult to assess. Regardless of whether the patient is defined as endogenous or neurotic-reactive, some data suggest that life events are likely to occur around the onset of the illness (Paykel, 1982). Studies have shown that life events are more likely to occur in psychiatric patients who have a depressive syndrome, when compared with people selected from the general population. More specifically, these kinds of life events are separations from important people in the individual's background. This appears to be consonant with the bereavement studies described previously. One of the problems in assessing the importance of life events is the difficulty in determining the onset of a depressive episode. Some of the things that might be particularly unpleasant to an individual could in fact be brought on as a consequence of the symptoms that are seen in the illness itself (e.g., losing a job or experiencing a marital problem). In other words, the depression may produce life events as well as be caused by them, and until a good method exists for evaluating the onset of depression, it may not be possible to determine the strength of the contribution of life events.

Other etiologic possibilities that are related to psychosocial events include the idea that early parental loss may lead to affective disorder later in life. Here the findings are mixed, with many studies showing that early parental loss is in fact related and other studies showing that early parental loss has no bearing on the subsequent development of a depression. Interestingly, most of the studies have not controlled for the possibility that early parental loss, either through death or disturbed family relationships, might be due to the presence of the illness itself in the parent. Therefore, a relationship of early parental loss and adult depression may indicate a familial (genetic) factor just as much as an environmental factor.

Genetic factors have been well studied in unipolar depression. After bipolar and unipolar illnesses were separated in the mid-1960s, it was possible to do genetic and family studies with an independent assessment of each of the illnesses. Before that time most of the studies had been performed on mixed groups of unipolar depressives and bipolar patients. To suggest a genetic factor in an illness, one would need to demonstrate more illness in the families of unipolar depressives than in the families of a control population. It would be well to perform such a study blindly, with the investigator not knowing the diagnosis of the index case (the patient whose family is evaluated). Further, such a study should use valid and systematic criteria for the diagnosis of a family member.

Table 5–8 shows the results of a study in which bipolars, unipolar depressives, and controls were selected (Winokur et al., 1982). These cases were then followed up for 35 to 40 years and a systematic family study was accomplished. This investigation was performed by researchers who were blind to the diagnosis of the index case. It is noteworthy that a far higher proportion of relatives of unipolar depressives were also ill with unipolar depression than is found in the relatives of the controls. The

**TABLE 5–8.  Unipolar Depression in First-Degree Relatives**

| Index Cases | No. of Relatives | No. (%) Blindly Interviewed with Unipolar Depression |
|---|---|---|
| Unipolar (N = 203) | 416 | 34  (8.2) |
| Control (N = 160) | 541 | 25  (4.6) |

| Index Cases | No. of Deceased Relatives | No. (%) with Unipolar Depression Confirmed by Charts |
|---|---|---|
| Unipolar (N = 203) | 606 | 13  (2.1) |
| Control (N = 160) | 322 | 1  (0.3) |

controls were surgical patients who were admitted at approximately the same time as the unipolar depressives. The ratio of ill family members in the unipolar depressives to the ill family members in the controls, when personally examined, is about 2:1. Deceased relatives were also evaluated. Psychiatric records were obtained on deceased relatives of unipolar depressives. There were 13 charts of relatives who were admitted with the same illness, a far higher number than was found in the deceased relatives of the control group. There the ratio is 7:1. The conclusion is that there is a much higher family history of unipolar depression in the family members of unipolar depressives than one would expect from studying the normal population. Another important type of genetic study is concerned with a comparison of concordance for depression in monozygotic versus dizygotic twins. Because monozygotic twins entertain all of the same genes and dizygotic twins only 50 per cent, one would expect a higher concordance rate in the monozygotic group. A study by Bertelson, Harvald, and Haug (1977) in Scandinavia shows this to be true. In the monozygotic pairs of unipolar depressives, 43 per cent were concordant. In the dizygotic pairs, only 19 per cent were concordant. Other twin studies show similar findings.

Such studies as those described do not prove a genetic factor beyond a shadow of doubt. The way to prove a genetic factor would be by conducting adoption or linkage and association studies. In adoption studies, children of parents with affective disorder who were adopted away at an early age would be more likely to have the illness than would children who were adopted but born of normal biologic parents. Such a study has been reported by Cadoret (1978), in which a higher proportion of adopted children of parents with unipolar illness themselves had unipolar illness than did adopted children of parents who had no psychiatric illness. Nevertheless, more studies of unipolar depression using the adoption technique are needed. Linkage and association studies have been reported for bipolar illness. A linkage study would indicate that two genes, that of a genetic marker and that of a psychiatric illness, are next to each other on the same chromosome. Therefore, within a family (but not in the population) the marker and the illness would be found together more often than one would expect by chance alone. Association indicates that some seemingly unrelated genetic trait is more likely seen in persons who have a particular illness than in persons from the general population. To accomplish an association, a group of depressives would be compared with an appropriate control population. Studies of linkage and association would be useful, and some have been attempted, but no unequivocal findings in unipolar depression have emerged as yet.

Another point should be made about the family or genetic studies. Depression can be classified on the basis of family background. Implicit in such a classification is that a specific type of family history of psychiatric illness has etiologic significance. Unipolar depressive illness can be divided into three groups. The first group is called depression spectrum disease, which is a depression in an individual who has a first-degree relative who has alcoholism or sociopathy. Such an individual may or may not have a relative with depression. A second group is that of familial pure depressive disease. This is a depression in an individual who has a family history of depression but not of alcoholism or sociopathy. The third group is sporadic depressive disease, which is a depression in an individual who has no family history of alcoholism, antisocial personality, or depression. None of these depressives should have a family history of mania.

When one divides patients into these kinds of familial subtypes, there are some differences in the clinical picture. One of the most striking differences is that in many studies, a clinical diagnosis of neurotic-reactive depression is related to a family history of alcoholism (depression spectrum disease). Alternatively, a family history of depression only (familial pure depressive disease) is related to a clinical diagnosis of endogenous depression. Thus, clinically and familially, some differences do exist in these groups. A patient with a depression spectrum disease is likely to have a stormy life history, with multiple marital and social problems. This is less likely in a patient with familial pure depressive disease. Sporadic depressive disease patients are differentiable from the other two groups on a later age of onset (Winokur, 1982).

The evidence for a genetic factor in unipolar depression is strong. In regard to etiology, this does not tell us anything about the proximal cause of the illness. All it tells us is something of the distal etiology and indicates that there are significant biologic factors that must, by definition, come into play in causing the illness. There are three sets of data that may shed some light on the proximal etiology of the illness.

One set concerns the biogenic amine hypotheses. These hypotheses were formulated because of the observation that a drug such as reserpine, which depletes the brain of amines, was associated with the development of a depressive syndrome. Biogenic amine hypotheses are best viewed as two hypotheses rather than as one. The first assumes that a decrease in catecholamines at important synapses in the central nervous system is associated with a depression. The other hypothesis is similar but considers the indole amines to be important factors. Such drugs as the monoamine oxidase inhibitors would decrease the breakdown of the monoamines, and therefore be efficacious in the treatment of depression. The tricyclic antidepressants would prevent reuptake of the monoamines, and therefore, likewise, be associated with a remission from a depressive state. Various of the tricyclic antidepressants have differential effects in preventing reuptake of specific monoamines, and therefore may be differentially efficacious in the treatment of certain depressions. Because some patients may respond to one antidepressant and not to another, this has given rise to the idea that certain kinds of depressive illnesses are associated with functional deficits of certain kinds of monoamines. The results of a large recent study reveal that some unipolar depressed patients show raised levels of 5-hydroxyindoleacetic acid, the metabolite of serotonin, in spinal fluid and that some show high levels of 3-methoxy-4-hydroxyphenyl-glycol (MHPG), a metabolite of the catecholamines (Koslow et al., 1983). The same study showed raised levels of vanillylmandelic acid, normetanephrine, metanephrine, norepinephrine, and epinephrine in urine in depressives. Such findings have not been invariable, and they have not been consistently related to specific kinds of affective disorder (e.g., bipolar versus unipolar). Nevertheless, the biogenic amine hypotheses are viable at the present time. They may well be involved in the etiology of all the affective disorders, and even specifically in unipolar depression.

Recent findings have related receptor differences in the central nervous system to depressive illness. An example is that there may be reduced numbers of platelet imipramine binding sites in depression when compared with controls. Platelet binding sites may reflect those in the brain. Another reported finding is a decrease in serotonin uptake in platelets in depressed patients, even after recovery (Meltzer, Arora, Tricou, Fang, 1983).

A second set of biologic findings relevant to depression is related to the endocrine system. Serious or endogenous depressions have been associated with an abnormal response to dexamethasone. Whereas a normal person has a marked reduction in circulating cortisol in response to a 1-mg challenge with dexamethasone, some depressed patients escape the effect of the dexamethasone and show high serum cortisol levels. This response is seen in about 50 per cent of endogenous depressives. In some studies, patients with a family history of depression but not of alcoholism (familial pure depressive disease) are particularly noted to show abnormal nonsuppression. The finding of the abnormal dexamethasone test is paralleled by the finding that some depressive patients have high hourly plasma cortisol concentrations compared with controls (Sachar, 1975; Carroll, Curtis, Mendels, 1976; Schlesser, Winokur, Sherman, 1979). These findings suggest an abnormality in the hypothalamic-pituitary-adrenal axis, but the specific location of the "lesion" is unknown.

At one time an abnormal dexamethasone suppression test was considered specific for depression. However, reports have come out indicating that specificity is not quite as great as was previously thought, and that some patients with obsessional neurosis, schizophrenia, anorexia nervosa, and Alzheimer's disease are abnormal suppressors. Nevertheless, the test is a good lead, since the response is commonly different in depressives as compared with controls.

Another abnormal endocrine response in depression is deficient thyroid-stimulating hormone (TSH) response to an infusion of thyrotropin-releasing hormone (TRH). This is not seen in all cases, and there is no reason to believe that the person with the abnormal cortisol response will have the abnormal TSH response to TRH. In other words, the two endocrine abnormalities may not be highly correlated. There is a possibility that the low TSH response to TRH continues after recovery, but this is not certain (Kirkegaard et al., 1975).

One problem with biologic studies is that there is no way to examine directly the organ that is considered responsible for the depression—the brain. One studies blood, urine, and spinal fluid, whereas it would be important to determine the pathophysiology of the brain during depression. At present there is no satisfactory answer to the problem.

Another set of data is promising. Studies have shown that there is an abnormally short onset of rapid eye movement (REM) sleep in seriously ill depressives. REM sleep is associated with dreaming in a healthy individual. In patients with major depressions or endogenous depressions, the onset of REM sleep is far shorter than in the normal population. This shortened REM latency is not seen in patients who have secondary depressions to serious medical illnesses or other psychiatric illnesses. Also, it seems that patients who have a family history of alcoholism as well as a depression (depression spectrum disease) are less likely to have a shortened REM latency (Kupfer, 1976; Akiskal, 1983).

None of the findings have provided final answers to the etiology of unipolar depression, but they have stimulated a great deal of research and have considerable heuristic value.

## DIFFERENTIAL DIAGNOSIS

The syndrome of depression is common and is seen in a number of conditions. Usually when one refers to unipolar depression, one means an illness that is primary. In other words, such a depression occurs in the absence of another illness that might be associated with it. Figure 1 shows a system that may be used for differential diagnosis.

Secondary depression occurs in the presence of another medical or psychiatric illness (Winokur, 1972). A number of psychiatric illnesses, including such diverse conditions as schizophrenia, antisocial personality, alcoholism, anxiety states, and organic brain syndromes, will at some point in their development be associated with a full-fledged depressive syndrome. If the individual who suffers this depressive syndrome has had a preexisting psychiatric illness, then such a depression can be called secondary. In this circumstance the appropriate way to look on the depression is simply as a concomitant of the primary illness. Thus the clinician must be cognizant of the fact that appropriate treatment is that of the primary illness; a person with alcoholism or somatization disorder who develops a secondary depression may be best served by emphasizing the treatment of the primary disorder.

The meaning of a secondary depression is unknown. Such a depression is conceivably a reaction to being chronically ill with another psychiatric illness. In a sense, then, such a depression resembles a neurotic-reactive depression.

Just as there are secondary depressions associated with psychiatric illness, so also do secondary depressions exist in the context of serious medical illnesses (Stewart, Drake, Winokur, 1965). When discussing secondary depressions in medical illness, it is not meant that the medical illness itself is clearly related to the depression in any physiologic way, but simply that the secondary depression occurs in the course of medical illness. Like a secondary depression to a psychiatric illness, this kind of secondary depression may be a reaction to a serious medical problem. When compared with primary depressives, patients with secondary depression to medical illness are less likely to be suicidal and less likely to have a family history of depression.

Thus the differential diagnosis in secondary depression is a matter of some significance. What is necessary is a systematic evaluation of the patient to determine whether another diagnosis might be made, either medical or psychiatric. *The simple finding of a depressive syndrome is not meaningful in terms of diagnosis. Evaluating a depressive syndrome must be done in the context of a full medical and psychiatric workup.*

Another major factor in differential diagnosis concerns the induced depression. Some circumstances are commonly associated with depression either as a cause or as a concomitant; seemingly, there is a biologic relationship between the depressive syndrome and the medical circumstance. An example of this is withdrawal from alcohol in a chronic alcoholic. A high percentage of such patients develop a depressive syndrome. The depressive syndrome lasts for

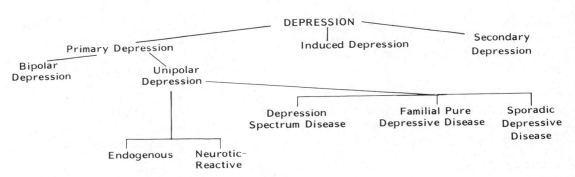

**FIGURE 5–1.**

only a discrete period of time (several days), after which it will dissipate itself. Other depressions are seen in alcoholics, secondary depressions that occur in the course of drinking. These are associated with interpersonal difficulties. An alcoholic in the midst of a drinking bout may be extruded from the home and develop depressive symptoms and suicide trends. This kind of depression is different from the withdrawal syndrome of depression. Likewise, certain medical illnesses and kinds of treatments seem to be associated with a depressive syndrome. As an example, patients treated with steroids may develop a depression. Hypertensives who are taking reserpine have been reported to develop depressive syndromes. These are induced depressions. They are not secondary. The implication in these kinds of depressive syndromes is that they result from some kind of physiologic interaction between the host and the medical or treatment circumstances. Again, the differential diagnosis is made by obtaining a full medical and psychiatric history.

In some cases it is difficult to determine whether a depression is secondary or induced. Such would be the case of a depression developing in the course of Alzheimer's disease, vascular disease affecting the brain, or Huntington's disease.

Finally, there are the primary depressions. Bipolar depression occurs in an individual who has a history of mania. This, then, is to be separated from unipolar depression. Significant treatment implications may be involved in this separation. The unipolar depressions may be divided into either endogenous or neurotic-reactive, depending on the presence of such endogenous symptoms as early-morning awakening, marked weight loss, diurnal variation, lack of energy, lack of interest in things, inability to feel pleasure. The neurotic-reactive depression is associated with a lifelong history of stormy life-style. Again, it is important to make a differential diagnosis of these types, since there may be treatment implications.

One could make a familial subtype diagnosis. Depression spectrum disease is seen in an individual who has a family history of antisocial personality or alcoholism. Depression may or may not be seen in such families. Familial pure depressive disease is seen in an individual who has a family history of depression and nothing else, and sporadic depressive disease is seen in an individual who has a negative family history for alcoholism, antisocial personality, and depression. Again, such a subclassification may have treatment and etiologic meaning and may be useful for predicting the course.

In a differential diagnosis one thing must be kept in mind: the course of the illness. As described earlier, a clear depression is seen in patients who are being withdrawn from alcohol. This depression is short-lived, lasting for 1 to 2 weeks. Most sets of criteria for the diagnosis of unipolar depression use a time constraint. In other words, an individual must be ill for a period of time before he or she earns the diagnosis. A reasonable time constraint would be 1 month. In a differential diagnosis this would remove patients who had withdrawal syndromes and some of the patients with induced depressions as well as many who are experiencing life events that make them acutely unhappy but that do not necessarily provoke a unipolar depression.

## LABORATORY FINDINGS

Some laboratory tests performed in unipolar depression have shown abnormal findings that are associated with a depressed state. Perhaps the best known is the 1-mg dexamethasone suppression test, discussed earlier, under Etiology. This test is accomplished in the following way. One milligram of dexamethasone is administered to a patient at 10:30 P.M. The next morning at 8:00 the patient's blood is drawn for a determination of serum cortisol. This determination is repeated at 4:00 P.M. A level of cortisol in the blood above 5 $\mu$g/dl at either 8:00 A.M. or 4:00 P.M. is considered an abnormal test. When dexamethasone is administered to nondepressives, their cortisol levels at those times the next day are usually quite low, well below 5 $\mu$g/dl and generally in the range of 1 to 2 $\mu$g/dl. Table 5–9 shows some of the results in various types of patients (Schlesser et al., 1979). Investigators have found some groups of patients with endogenous depression to have as high as 50 per cent abnormal nonsuppressors. Patients who have familial pure depressive disease have been noted to be abnormal in some studies in 70 per cent to 85 per cent of

**TABLE 5–9.**  Proportion of Abnormal Nonsuppressors in Various Psychiatric Illnesses

|  | Proportion Nonsuppressors (%) |
|---|---|
| Unipolar depression, primary | 45 |
| Bipolar depression | 85 |
| Secondary unipolar depression | 0 |
| Mania | 0 |
| Schizophrenia | 0 |

cases. Neurotic-reactive depressives and secondary depressives are generally considered to be normal suppressors, as are patients with depression spectrum disease. Certainly not all studies are in agreement with these subtype findings, but most agree that patients with major depressions are more likely to be nonsuppressors than are normal controls or other psychiatric patients. Specificity of the test is not perfect, and the test may not be reliable in patients with recent weight loss, endocrine disturbances, pregnancy, and hepatic and renal disease or in those who are on such drugs as phenytoin (Dilantin). Nevertheless, most studies do support the finding that unipolar depressives whose illness is severe enough to get them admitted to the hospital have a high likelihood of abnormal nonsuppression. The use of the dexamethasone suppression test for practical purposes is controversial. Some believe that it could be used for diagnostic purposes in those cases where the clinical picture is unclear. However, the lack of specificity makes this questionable. The test might also be used as an aid in determining whether the patient has improved. Normalization of the dexamethasone test might indicate that the person is no longer suffering from the illness. Recent findings, however, have indicated that patients who have multiple episodes and admissions vary over time (Coryell and Schlesser, 1983). When depressed during one admission, they will be nonsuppressors; at other admissions, and with equal severity, they will be normal suppressors. This makes the use of the test as a monitor for improvement a dubious prospect. The test generally is considered important because it is an abnormal finding associated with psychiatric illness, and this abnormal finding may in fact provide a clue to the proximal etiology of the disease.

Other endocrine tests have been reported to be abnormal besides the blunted TSH response to TRH. Growth hormone abnormalities have been noted. In one study a decreased drop in blood glucose to insulin injection after recovery has been reported in familial pure depressives and bipolar depressives when compared with depression spectrum patients (Lewis, Kathol, Sherman, Winokur, Schlesser, 1983). None of these findings are validated well enough for use in diagnosis or in monitoring progress in treatment, but they do indicate areas in which laboratory findings might be useful in the future.

One finding that may be clinically useful comes from the sleep laboratory (Kupfer, 1976). REM sleep shows a less-than-normal latency period in depressives. Other sleep disturbances have also been reported. Patients with secondary depression have been noted to have normal REM latency, as have patients with depression spectrum disease. Like the endocrine tests, the sleep laboratory tests show considerable promise in testing out pathophysiology of the illness that we call unipolar depression and in helping to make clinical evaluations.

Most depressed hospitalized patients have a medical workup of some sort. The finding of abnormal electrolyte tests or of abnormal plasma and serum levels is usually an indication that something else besides depression may be wrong with the patient. This does not mean that a patient cannot have two illnesses—a medical illness and a depression—but certainly no ordinary laboratory finding that is obtained on admission has been strongly associated with depression. Thus abnormal findings in plasma, serum, urine, or spinal fluid should be pursued, since they may indicate another illness that may be responsible for the depression or that may exist independent of the depression.

## TREATMENT

For practical purposes, treatment may be divided into four major headings: general management, psychological therapy, pharmacologic therapy, and other somatic therapies.

### General Management

General management is an important area. The person with unipolar depression is at some risk for suicide. Further, in the midst of his depression, he is likely to be irritable or hard to manage. Such a person has the potential of turning family relationships or social situations into disasters.

If a person is judged to be a suicidal risk, he or she must be protected. This can be done by having him enter a hospital. Often a patient with a depression is indecisive and will not make such a decision on his own. The physician should take the responsibility for such a decision by strongly advising the responsible people in the patient's life that they must have him in the hospital, even if he is opposed. This sounds easy, but often the family is reluctant to take the responsibility for committing the patient to the hospital against his will. Thus there is a stand-off: the doctor reluctant to take care of the patient if he is not fully protected by being in a hospital and the family recognizing that the patient is at risk but unwilling to make the appropriate moves. On rare occasions the physician will go to the courts and recommend commitment. Most of the time, however, the physician is constrained to do the best he can with a patient who is not being optimally cared for. These kinds of ambiguities and uncertainties make the management of depressives difficult at times. There is no final answer; one must attempt to use good judgment.

Patients who are depressed have considerable difficulty with concentration and thinking. Consequently, it seems unreasonable to force them into situations where they have to be responsible for much intellectual work. Often depressed patients will vegetate unless they are pushed into some kind of activity, but the activity ought to be more physical than cerebral. Thus a physician is unlikely to suggest that the patient go to a book club while depressed and report on something he has read. Rather, the physician might suggest that the patient involve himself in such physical activity as might be reasonable. Insisting on intellectual activity may well make the patient more depressed.

In the midst of a depression the patient may want to make major decisions. Because of irritability, divorce may seem to be an appropriate response to a marital conflict. Quitting a job that the depressed patient believes he can no longer perform is hardly uncommon. Patients should be discouraged from making major changes in their lives during the period of depression. Once they are well, they will again become free agents and can make any decisions they want. But while they are depressed, it seems unreasonable to support their burning bridges or making foolish decisions that might come back to haunt them. One of the largest problems in managing the depressed patient is that he often finds reasons for his depression. Because depression is akin to being unhappy, it seems reasonable to him that something terrible may have caused the state. The patient who believes that his condition is due to disturbed life events may not be correct, and the physician should attempt to prevent him from acting on false premises.

It is well to deal with the depressed patient as if he were a collaborator, rather than as if he were a totally dependent individual. Thus it is often useful to discuss the illness with the patient and point out to him that although he is ill at the present time, all available evidence indicates that he will get well, that he will be as well as he ever was, and that he will not end up as a patient on the chronic ward of a state hospital. The patient often believes that he is going to lose his mind permanently. It is important to reassure him that this is not an end point of unipolar depression. In a sense, dealing with a depressive is similar to dealing with an intelligent diabetic. The more he knows about his illness, the better off everybody is likely to be. It is interesting to note that a retarded depressed patient may lose a good bit of his retardation during a discussion with a physician. Giving the patient reassurance that he will get better may make for an acute improvement. The patient will feel better for a short period of time. This kind of reassurance, however, is no permanent treatment for the depression. The next day the patient will be back to where he was before the discussion.

One thing should be mentioned about the family. Often the wife or the parents or the children are prone to take blame themselves for the depressed relative. There are no data to support the idea that anybody's behavior causes a depression. The family should be reassured that the depression is best looked on as an illness, that they are not to blame, and that their sympathetic understanding will be useful. It will not cure the depression, but it may help with the management.

Intense exploration into personal problems during a depression may be contraindicated. Constant questioning of the person's behavior may make him feel more guilty and depressed.

During a depression the patient may need to visit the physician more frequently than usual. When he feels frightened or guiltier or more ashamed and in need of reassurance, the patient may ask to be seen more often. The physician should honor this request.

## Psychological Therapy

Psychotherapy as a treatment for unipolar depression, after a time in the "yellow leaf," has once more become a viable concept. A variety of specific psychotherapies have been used recently to treat depressives (Rush, 1982). At this point in time, cognitive therapy has been extensively investigated. Cognitive therapy is based on the concept that a depressive regards himself in a negative fashion. The individual thinks of himself as being worthless and believes that life can never be worthwhile again. In cognitive therapy the person offering the treatment attempts to use both verbal and behavioral techniques to help a patient recognize that these negative viewpoints (cognitions) are related to feeling states and behavior. The cognitive therapy is an effort to help the patient examine the circumstances and recognize that his ideas about himself are not consistent with reality. Self-condemnatory distortions may be expressed; when the patient realizes that they are inappropriate, the therapist suggests the substitution of a more reality-oriented concept. A high percentage of patients in cognitive therapy show marked improvement. That certain patients receive a great deal of benefit from cognitive therapy seems to be supported by the available evidence. Clarification of what specific kinds of patients with unipolar depressions might receive benefit is necessary at this point. Would they be patients who have had multiple somatic treatments with failure? Would they be patients who have mild depressions? Would they be patients who were reactive-neurotic, rather than endogenous? Answers to these questions are needed in order to determine the place of cognitive therapy in the treatment of unipolar depression.

Another kind of psychotherapy that has been reported to be useful is interpersonal psychotherapy. This kind of psychotherapy seems related to the idea that depression resembles unhappiness. Interpersonal psychotherapy is offered as a way to improve the patient's social functioning by increasing the ability to deal with stresses and by helping the patient to manage personal and social consequences of the depression. In interpersonal psychotherapy, special techniques have been developed for managing depressed patients who have experienced grief and loss, interpersonal deficits, and marital problems. Some studies of interpersonal psychotherapy in depressives suggest that it may be as effective as pharmacologic treatments. Antidepressant medication used in combination with interpersonal psychotherapy may be particularly effective. The patients in whom this technique has been used have generally been mildly depressed outpatients. Again, whether this technique would be useful in severely retarded or agitated inpatients is open to question.

## Pharmacologic Therapy

For seriously ill depressives, specific antidepressant drug therapy is probably the most common treatment. These antidepressant drugs are related to the biogenic amine hypotheses, which have been previously discussed. Two classes are used. The first of these are the tricyclic antidepressants, which prevent reuptake of biogenic amines and thus increase the concentration of these amines at the synaptic junction. The other type of drug is the monoamine oxidase inhibitor, which prevents breakdown of the biogenic amines at the synaptic junction.

The tricyclic antidepressants are most frequently used. These drugs include amitriptyline, nortriptyline, which is a metabolic product of amitriptyline, imipramine, desipramine, which is a metabolic product of imipramine, and doxepine. These drugs differentially prevent reuptake of the different neurotransmitters. Desipramine prevents reuptake of norepinephrine very well, whereas amitriptyline prevents the reuptake of serotonin more effectively. Two of the drugs, amitriptyline and doxepin, are particularly sedative. Because of this, they are valuable in patients who might need a certain amount of sedation or who have sleep difficulties. A large proportion of the dose given at night might well be effective in producing a better sleep pattern. Imipramine or desipramine are less likely to be sedative. Thus a retarded patient might be considered a good candidate for these two drugs. Some of the tricyclics are associated with weight gain. The use of desipramine might be indicated if that becomes a problem, since less weight gain has been reported with this drug. Improvement is expected to occur in about 3 weeks, but the data indicate that it may occur within 1 week and continue thereafter.

The tricyclic drugs are given by starting the individual at about 50 to 75 mg in divided doses. In a few days the dose is raised to 150 mg a day. This is a reasonable dose for effectiveness. Some people metabolize tricyclics in aberrant ways; if this is suspected, blood levels may be obtainable for the drugs. After the individual has been built up to a dose of about 150 mg a day, it is possible to give a larger proportion at night, to help the patient fall asleep. If the person does not improve at this level after a period of time, the dose may be increased to 200 or 300 mg a day.

Side effects of these drugs have been noted. Lowered blood pressure and heart arrhythmias may be seen with some of the drugs, and this could be an adverse effect for a person with cardiac problems. Hypotension is an important effect, and often patients on the tricyclics will fall and suffer fractures. This can be a problem for elderly patients with fragile skeletal systems. On rare occasions confusional states and disorientation occur. Withdrawal of the medicine is usually accompanied by an improvement of these symptoms. Common side effects are dry mouth, inability to urinate, and constipation. Some drugs cause more potent side effects than others.

The monoamine oxidase inhibitors are not usually first-choice treatment for depression because of their possibly serious side effects. The drugs most commonly used are tranylcypromine sulfate, isocarboxazid, and phenelzine. Usually treatment is started by giving one 15-mg tablet of phenelzine on the first day, and the dose is increased over the

next several days to 60 mg a day. In the case of tranylcypromine sulfate, over a period of a few days the dose is raised to about 30 mg in 10-mg doses. Side effects include lowered blood pressure and sometimes marked fatigue. A serious side effect is related to the presence of tyramine, which is found in some foods and beverages (e.g., aged cheese, red wine, pickled herring, and chocolate). Monoamine oxidase in the gastrointestinal tract inactivates tyramine. If monoamine oxidase inhibitors are given and the tyramine is not inactivated, severe headaches and hypertension and death can result.

Monoamine oxidase inhibitors may be particularly useful for depressed patients who are somewhat atypical. These might be patients who show marked anxiety or do not show the classic symptoms described in depression. In other words, there is some reason to believe that the neurotic-reactive type of patient might be particularly responsive to monoamine oxidase inhibitors.

## Electroshock Therapy

For years, electroshock, or electroconvulsive therapy (ECT), was used as an effective treatment in depression. As originally given, electrodes were placed on each temple and a current was passed between them. A grand mal seizure occurred, with the ordinary train of changes seen in any convulsion. Further, vertebral fractures occurred in the early days of ECT, as well as considerable confusion. Today ECT is far less traumatic to watch or to experience. It is usually administered three times a week. Before the treatment the patient is given nothing by mouth after supper until the treatment the next morning. About 30 minutes before the treatment, the patient is given atropine, which dries up secretions. At the time of treatment a rubber mouthpiece is inserted to ensure a good airway. Oxygen is given from a face mask. Electrodes are placed on the patient's temples and the physician injects a short-acting anesthesia, methohexital, until the patient is asleep. Through the same needle, a muscle relaxant is injected. After about 45 to 60 seconds, a current is administered and the patient has a modified convulsion. Often it is virtually impossible to tell that a convulsion has occurred because of the effectiveness of the muscle relaxant. After the convulsion the face mask is placed over the patient's face and oxygen is given to the person. Within 50 to 80 seconds after the convulsion, breathing occurs. The patient then rests for a short while and eats breakfast. ECT is a safe treatment. The major side effect has to do with memory loss, which occurs for events around the period of time of the treatments. This occurs if the electrodes are placed bitemporally. Within several weeks, however, the patient has recalled most of the things that he has forgotten. Certainly after a few weeks have passed, the patient's ability to retain new memories is as good as it ever was. If the electrodes are placed unilaterally, less acute confusion results, but some clinicians believe that the efficacy is reduced as compared with the bilateral method. The average number of treatments administered is between 6 and 12. The patient is usually given treatments while hospitalized, but outpatient ECT has been used with success.

The effect of ECT is of considerable importance. When compared with antidepressant drug therapy, ECT tends to be equal in producing improvement (Homan, Lachenbruch, Winokur, Clayton, 1982; see Table 5–10). Of particular interest is that *marked* improvement is more likely to result with ECT than with antidepressant medication. Likewise, if one follows patients who have been treated with ECT and compares them with patients who have been followed after receiving adequate antidepressant therapy, a difference can be seen in the number of suicide attempts after treatment. Fewer patients with ECT (1 per cent) than with antidepressant therapy (7 per cent) are likely to attempt suicide during hospitalization and followup (Avery and Winokur, 1978), indicating that ECT may be more effective than antidepressant therapy. This possibility is relevant to the idea that perhaps there are certain kinds of patients in whom ECT should be the treatment of choice. These would be middle-aged men who have shown marked suicidal trends. Such men who were diagnosed as having unipolar depression are at particularly high risk for suicide; perhaps these patients should be given the most effective treatment for a marked recovery (i.e., ECT).

## Prevention

A continuation of tricyclic medication has been associated with prevention of relapse in unipolar depression (Glen, Johnson, Shepherd, 1984). Usually the individual who has improved may be kept on 75 to 150 mg of tricyclic medication in an attempt to provide prophylaxis against subsequent attacks. The plasma level for amitriptyline should vary between 60 and 230 mg/ml. Another drug, lithium carbonate, may also be of use. It has been effective in preventing depressive episodes in patients with unipolar depression who have had multiple episodes in the past (Coppen et al., 1971). The individual may be kept on a dose that produces a serum level of about 0.6 to 1.0 mEq/L for a long period.

In summary, a milder outpatient depression is a consideration for psychotherapy and a severer depression that necessitates hospitalization is a reasonable candidate for ECT. Antidepressant drug therapy may be considered in both groups.

## REFERENCES

Akiskal H: Diagnosis and classification of affective disorders: New insights from clinical and laboratory approaches. Psychiatr Develop 2:123–160, 1983.

Akiskal H: Boundaries of affective disorders: Implications for defining temperamental variance, atypical subtypes, and schizoaffective disorder, in Tischler G (ed): *DSM-III: An Interim Appraisal.* Washington, DC, American Psychiatric Press, in press.

Angst J, Baastrup P, Grof P, Hippius H, Poldinger W, Weis P: The course of monopolar depression in bipolar psychoses. Psychiatr Neurol Neurochir 76:489–500, 1973.

Avery D, Winokur G: Suicide, attempted suicide and relapse rates in depression. Arch Gen Psychiatry 35:749–753, 1978.

Baker M, Dorzab J, Winokur G, Cadoret R: Depressive disease: Classification and clinical characteristics. Compr Psychiatry 12:354–365, 1971.

**TABLE 5–10.    Treatment Results in Hospitalized Unipolar Depressives**

|  | ECT (%) (N = 76) | Antidepressant Medication (%) (N = 101) |
|---|---|---|
| No improvement | 8 | 6 |
| Moderate improvement | 49 | 82 |
| Marked improvement | 43 | 12 |

Bertelson A, Harvald B, Haug A: Danish twin study of manic depressive disorders. Br J Psychiatry 130:330–351, 1977.

Boyd J, Weissman M: Epidemiology of affective disorders: A re-examination and future directions. Arch Gen Psychiatry 38:1039–1046, 1981.

Cadoret R: Evidence for genetic inheritance of primary affective disorder in adoptees. Am J Psychiatry 135:463–466, 1978.

Carroll B, Curtis G, Mendels J: Neuroendocrine regulation in depression. II. Discrimination of depressed from non-depressed patients. Arch Gen Psychiatry 33:1051–1058, 1976.

Clayton P, Halikas J, Maurice W: The depression of widowhood. Br J Psychiatry 120:71–77, 1972.

Clayton P, Herjanic M, Murphy G, Woodruff R: Mourning and depression: Their similarities and differences. Can Psychiatr Assoc J 19:309–312, 1974.

Coppen A, Noguera R, Bailey J, Burns B, Swani M, Hare E, Gardner R, Maggs R: Prophylactic lithium in affective disorders. Lancet 2:275–279, 1971.

Coryell W, Schlesser M: Dexamethasone suppression test response in major depression: Stability across hospitalizations. Psychiatry Res 8:179–189, 1983.

Dorzab J, Baker M, Winokur G, Cadoret R: Depressive disease: Clinical course. Dis Nerv Sys 32:269–273, 1971.

Feighner J, Robins E, Guze S, Woodruff R, Winokur G, Munoz R: Diagnostic criteria for use in psychiatric research. Arch Gen Psychiatry 26:57–63, 1972.

Glen A, Johnson A, Shepherd M: Continuation therapy with lithium and amitriptyline in unipolar depressive illness: A randomized, double blind, controlled trial. Psychol Med 14:37–50, 1984.

Helgason T: Epidemiological investigations concerning affective disorders, in Schou M, Stromgren E (eds): Origin, Prevention, and Treatment of Affective Disorders. New York, Academic Press, 1979.

Homan S, Lachenbruch P, Winokur G, Clayton P: An efficacy study of electroconvulsive therapy and antidepressants in the treatment of primary depression. Psychol Med 12:615–624, 1982.

Kay D, Garside R, Beamish P, Roy J: Endogenous and neurotic syndromes of depression: A factor analytic study of 104 cases. Clinical Features. Br J Psychiatry 115:377–388, 1971.

Keller M, Lavori P, Endicott J, Coryell W, Klerman J: Double depression: Two year follow-up. Am J Psychiatry 140:689–694, 1983.

Kendell R: The Classification of Depressive Illness. London, Oxford University Press, 1968.

Kirkegaard C, Norlein N, Lauridsen U, et al: Protirelin stimulation test and thyroid function during treatment of depression. Arch Gen Psychiatry 32:1115–1118, 1975.

Klerman G, Endicott J, Spitzer R, Hirschfeld R: Neurotic depressions: A systematic analysis of multiple criteria and meanings. Am J Psychiatry 136:57–61, 1979.

Koslow S, Maas J, Bowden C, Davis J, Hanin I, Javaid J: CSF and urinary biogenic amines and metabolites in depression and mania. Arch Gen Psychiatry 40:999–1010, 1983.

Kupfer D: REM latency—a psychobiological marker for primary depressive disease. Biol Psychiatry 2:159–174, 1976.

Lewis D, Kathol R, Sherman B, Winokur G, Schlesser M: Differentiation of depressive subtypes by insulin insensitivity in the recovered stage. Arch Gen Psychiatry 40:167–170, 1983.

Meltzer H, Arora R, Tricou B, Fang V: Serotonin uptake in blood platelets and the dexamethasone suppression test in depressed patients. Psychiatry Res 8:41–47, 1983.

Mendels J: Depression: The distinction between syndrome and symptom. Br J Psychiatry 114:1549–1554, 1968.

Paykel ES: Life events and early environment, in Paykel ES (ed): Handbook of Affective Disorders. Edinburgh, Churchill Livingstone, 1982, pp 146–161.

Robins L, Helzer J, Weissman M, Orvaschel H, Gruenberg E, Burke J, Regier D: Lifetime prevalence of specific psychiatric disorders in three sites. Arch Gen Psychiatry 41:949–958, 1984.

Rush J: Short-term Psychotherapies for Depression. New York, Guilford Press, 1982.

Sachar E: Neuroendocrine abnormalities in depressive illness, in Sachar E (ed): Topics in Psychoendocrinology. New York, Grune & Stratton, 1975, pp 135–156.

Schlesser M, Winokur G, Sherman B: Genetic subtypes of unipolar primary depressive illness distinguished by hypothalamic-pituitary-adrenal activity. Lancet 1:739–741, 1979.

Schneider K: Clinical Psychopathology. New York, Grune & Stratton, 1959.

Stewart M, Drake F, Winokur G: Depression among medically ill patients. Dis Nerv Syst 26:1–7, 1965.

Stromgren L: The influence of depression on memory. Acta Psychiatr Scand 56:109–128, 1977.

Tsuang M, Winokur G, Crowe R: Psychiatric disorders among relatives of surgical controls. J Clin Psychiatr 45:420–422, 1984.

Tsuang M, Woolson R, Fleming J: Premature deaths in schizophrenia and affective disorders: An analysis of survival curves and variables affecting the shortened survival. Arch Gen Psychiatry 37:979–983, 1980.

Tsuang M, Woolson R, Winokur G, Crowe R: Stability of psychiatric diagnosis, schizophrenia and affective disorders followed up over a 30 to 40 year period. Arch Gen Psychiatry 38:535–539, 1981.

Weissman M, Meyers J: Affective disorders in a U.S. urban community: The use of research diagnostic criteria in an epidemiological survey. Arch Gen Psychiatry 35:1304–1311, 1978.

Winokur G: Family history studies. VIII. Secondary depression is alive and well and . . . Dis Nerv Syst 33:94–99, 1972.

Winokur G: Genetic and clinical factors associated with course and depression: Contributions to genetic aspects. Pharmacopsychiatr Neuropsychopharmacol 7:122–126, 1974.

Winokur G: The development and validity of familial subtypes in primary unipolar depression. Pharmacopsychiatria 15:142–146, 1982.

Winokur G, Clayton P, Reich T: Manic Depressive Illness. St. Louis, CV Mosby, 1969.

Winokur G, Morrison J: The Iowa 500: Follow-up of 225 depressives. Br J Psychiatry 123:543–548, 1973.

Winokur G, Morrison J, Clancy J, Crowe R: The Iowa 500: Familial and clinical findings favor two kinds of depressive illness. Compr Psychiatry 14:99–107, 1973.

Winokur G, Tsuang M: The Iowa 500: Suicide in mania, depression, and schizophrenia. Am J Psychiatry 132:650–651, 1975.

Winokur G, Tsuang M, Crowe R: The Iowa 500: Affective disorder in relatives of manic and depressed patients. Am J Psychiatry 139:209–212, 1982.

# chapter 6

# SCHIZOPHRENIA

*by* Ming T. Tsuang, M.D., Ph.D., and
    Doyne W. Loyd, M.D.

## DEFINITION

In 1896, before Bleuler coined the term *schizophrenia* (1908), Kraepelin (1919) described an illness characterized by hallucinations, delusions, and thought disorder. He termed this disorder *dementia praecox* (after Morel), since it appeared to have an early onset (praecox) of an irrecoverable mental deterioration (dementia), although later he found that a small percentage of these patients recovered fully.

In regard to symptomatology, Kraepelin felt that "one must on principle beware of attributing characteristic significance to a *single morbid phenomenon*" (Kraepelin, 1919, p. 261). He also said, "Unfortunately, there is in the domain of psychic disorders no single morbid symptom which is thoroughly characteristic of a definite malady." Diagnosis must include the "*total clinical picture*, including development, course and issue" (p. 261).

Bleuler (1911/1950) thought that schizophrenia encompassed, but was not necessarily limited to, Kraepelin's "dementia praecox." He named four fundamental symptoms (Bleuler's four As): autism, ambivalence, abnormal thought associations, and abnormal affect. Evidence of any of these was sufficient for the diagnosis of schizophrenia. Bleuler considered delusions and hallucinations to be accessory symptoms that were not essential to the diagnosis. He used the term schizophenia, which literally means split mind, because his four As reflected incongruent relationships

(splitting) between thought, emotion, and behavior. Outside the medical community, schizophrenia is commonly thought to mean "split personality," or multiple personality, but these expressions have no direct relationship with the diagnostic term schizophrenia.

To Bleuler, affective symptoms were not incompatible with schizophrenia, but schizophrenic symptoms were incompatible with affective disorder. He believed that schizophrenics never recovered fully. Always some residual evidence of the fundamental symptoms of schizophrenia could be found.

Bleuler's four fundamental symptoms of schizophrenia became the basis of the American definition of schizophrenia and remained so for many years until the *Diagnostic and Statistical Manual of Mental Disorders*, third edition (DSM-III), supplanted DSM-II. There were many interpretations of the meaning of these four symptoms, and many clinical pictures seemed to fit within these varying definitions of schizophrenia. Bleuler himself stated: "Dementia praecox comprises the majority of psychoses heretofore designated as functional" (Bleuler, 1911/1950, p. 271). And so in American psychiatry, before DSM-III, schizophrenia was more often diagnosed than other psychoses.

Morton Kramer (1961), at the National Institute of Mental Health, noticed that the hospital incidence of schizophrenia in the United States significantly exceeded that of Great Britain (28.0 vs. 17.9 per 100,000 population). In turn, in the hospitals of Great Britain, affective disorder was diagnosed much more often than in U.S. hospitals (36 vs. 7 per 100,000; rates for the U.S. group include manic-depressive psychosis and psychotic depression). Kramer questioned whether these differences were real or just artifacts of diagnostic definition or practice. He also noted that "studies are needed which will lead to the development of diagnostic standards for psychiatric disorders" (Kramer, 1961, p. 157).

The U.S.–U.K. project was begun to determine the source of these differences (Cooper et al., 1972). To gather information from the patients, psychiatrists used a structured interview, a combination of the Present State Examination (PSE) and the Mental Status Schedule. The International Classification of Diseases (ICD)-8 glossary was used as a reference standard to make each diagnosis. Two hundred fifty hospital patients in Brooklyn, New York, and 250 hospital patients in London were examined. The rates of schizophrenia and manic-depressive illness were similar in the two cities when project diagnoses were used: 81 (32 per cent) of the New York group and 65 (26 per cent) of the London group received a project diagnosis of schizophrenia. However, the rates using hospital diagnoses were quite different: 163 (65 per cent) of the New York group, but only 85 (34 per cent) of the London group, received hospital diagnoses of schizophrenia. Sixty-two (38 per cent) of the New York patients with a hospital diagnosis of schizophrenia received a project diagnosis of affective disorder, including 20 patients with mania.

The International Pilot Study of Schizophrenia, a larger international collaborative project, also considered the problem of classification (World Health Organization, 1973). In nine countries (five developed and four developing) 1202 patients were examined with the PSE. The diagnosis of schizophrenia was made in three ways—clinical judgment, computer assessment of PSE data (CATEGO), and cluster analysis. Three hundred six patients were diagnosed as being schizophrenic by all three methods. Restricted affect, poor insight, audible thoughts, widespread delusions, incoherent speech, unreliable information, bizarre delusions, and nihilistic delusions were characteristic of these 306 schizophrenics. Depressed facies, elation, and waking early (all affective symptoms) were not. Carpenter, Strauss, and Bartko (1973), who were U.S. participants in this study, incorporated these findings from the International Pilot Study into a system for diagnosing schizophrenia, which they termed the Flexible System.

At about the same time, researchers at Washington University, St. Louis, were concerned with the need for operational definitions of psychiatric disorders. Based on the research literature, they developed criteria for 15 disorders, including schizophrenia (Feighner et al., 1972). Subsequently, Spitzer's group in New York, in collaboration with the St. Louis group, refined and elaborated on these diagnostic systems in the Research Diagnostic Criteria (RDC) (Spitzer, Endicott, Robins, 1978). They defined 25 diagnoses, several with multiple subclassifications.

Several factors shaped the development of Feighner criteria and RDC, and somewhat later DSM-III (American Psychiatric Association, 1980). First, it was already clear that Americans diagnosed schizophrenia much more frequently than did Europeans. Second, additional research from a variety of sources showing that some patients called schizophrenic did not recover, but that others recovered fully, had begun to accumulate (Robins and Guze, 1970). The recovered group seemed to be characterized by abrupt onset of illness, prominent affective symptoms, family histories of affective disorder, precipitating events, and concern with dying or guilt. As a result of these findings, patients who met criteria for affective disorder were excluded from the diagnosis of schizophrenia, and an insidious onset, operationalized as 6 months of symptoms, was required for the diagnosis of schizophrenia (Feighner and DSM-III only). Table 6–1 contains DSM-III criteria for schizophrenia.

Schizophrenia has traditionally been divided into a number of categories. Tsuang and Winokur (1974) have developed criteria (see Table 6–2) for paranoid and hebephrenic schizophrenia. By their criteria, all of the patients must first have fulfilled Feighner criteria for schizophrenia. Then, by application of subtyping criteria, they are divided into paranoid, hebephrenic, and undifferentiated subtypes. These criteria separate patients by outcome better than other criteria for these subgroups (Kendler, Gruenberg, Tsuang, 1984). In general, the

**TABLE 6–1.    DSM-III Criteria for Schizophrenia**

A.  At least one of the following during a phase of the illness:
1.  Bizarre delusions (content is patently absurd and has no possible basis in fact), such as delusions of being controlled, thought broadcasting, thought insertion, or thought withdrawal
2.  Somatic, grandiose, religious, nihilistic, or other delusions without persecutory or jealous content
3.  Delusions with persecutory or jealous content if accompanied by hallucinations of any type
4.  Auditory hallucinations in which either a voice keeps up a running commentary on the individual's behavior or thoughts or two or more voices converse with one another
5.  Auditory hallucinations on several occasions with content of more than one or two words, having no apparent relation to depression or elation
6.  Incoherence, marked loosening of associations, markedly illogical thinking, or marked poverty of content of speech if associated with at least one of the following:
    a.  Blunted, flat, or inappropriate affect
    b.  Delusions or hallucinations
    c.  Catatonic or other grossly disorganized behavior.
B.  Deterioration from a previous level of functioning in such areas as work, social relations, and self-care.
C.  Duration: Continuous signs of the illness for at least 6 months at some time during the person's life, with some signs of the illness at present. The 6-month period must include an active phase during which there were symptoms from A, with or without a prodromal or residual phase, as defined below.
    *Prodromal phase:* A clear deterioration in functioning before the active phase of the illness not caused by a disturbance in mood or a substance use disorder and involving at least two of the symptoms noted below.
    *Residual phase:* Persistence, after the active phase of the illness, of at least two of the symptoms noted below, not caused by a disturbance in mood or a substance use disorder.
    *Prodromal or Residual Symptoms*
1.  Social isolation or withdrawal
2.  Marked impairment in role functioning as wage earner, student, or homemaker
3.  Markedly peculiar behavior (e.g., collecting garbage, talking to self in public, hoarding food)
4.  Marked impairment in personal hygiene and grooming
5.  Blunted, flat, or inappropriate affect
6.  Digressive, vague, overelaborate, circumstantial, or metaphorical speech
7.  Odd or bizarre ideation, or magical thinking, e.g., superstitiousness, clairvoyance, telepathy, "sixth sense," "others can feel my feelings," overvalued ideas, ideas of reference
8.  Unusual perceptual experiences, e.g., recurrent illusions sensing the presence of a force or person not actually present
D.  The full depressive or manic syndrome (criteria A and B of major depressive or manic episode), if present, developed after any psychotic symptoms or was brief in duration relative to the duration of the psychotic symptoms in A.
E.  Onset of prodromal or active phase of the illness before age 45.
F.  Not a result of any organic mental disorder or mental retardation.

Adapted from Diagnostic and Statistical Manual of Mental Disorders, ed. 3. Washington, DC, American Psychiatric Association, 1980.

paranoid group has a better outcome than the hebephrenic and undifferentiated groups and as good an outcome as that of the manic comparison group (Kendler et al., 1984). For example, 21 of 33 (64 per cent) of the paranoid group at 35- to 40-year followup were not occupationally disabled because of psychiatric illness compared with 11 of 40 (28 per cent) of the hebephrenic group and 41 of 102 (40 per cent) of the undifferentiated group. By comparison, 65 of 86 bipolars (76 per cent) were not occupationally disabled. The DSM-III criteria for paranoid, disorganized (hebephrenic), and undifferentiated schizophrenia are similar to the Tsuang-Winokur criteria. DSM-III, however, requires the absence of systematized delusions for hebephrenic schizophrenia. Tsuang-Winokur criteria have almost the opposite exclusion criterion: even

though patients may be preoccupied with paranoid symptoms, they exclude the diagnosis of paranoid schizophrenia when hebephrenic symptoms are prominent. These differences may explain the superior predictive validity of Tsuang-Winokur criteria, but replication is needed.

Both Feighner and DSM-III criteria for schizophrenia are relatively crude and in need of further refinement. Both are much more reliable, however, than broad criteria and are generally better than broad criteria at predicting the outcome of schizophrenia (Helzer, Brockington, Kendell, 1981; Stephens et al., 1982). By carefully excluding affective disorder and other good prognosis psychoses, such as schizophreniform disorder and brief reactive psychosis, they also improve the prediction of appropriate treatment. In the absence of a classification sys-

**TABLE 6–2. Tsuang-Winokur Criteria for Hebephrenic and Paranoid Schizophrenia**

I. Hebephrenic (A through D must be present)
  A. Age of onset and sociofamilial data (one of the following)
    1. Age of onset before age 25
    2. Unmarried or unemployed
    3. Family history of schizophrenia
  B. Disorganized thought
  C. Affect changes (either 1 or 2)
    1. Inappropriate affect
    2. Flat affect
  D. Behavioral symptoms (either 1 or 2)
    1. Bizarre behavior
    2. Motor symptoms (either a or b)
      a. Hebephrenic traits
      b. Catatonic traits (if present, subtype may be modified to hebephrenia with catatonic traits)
II. Paranoid (A through C must be present)
  A. Age of onset and sociofamilial data (one of the following)
    1. Age of onset after 25 years
    2. Married or employed
    3. Absence of family history of schizophrenia
  B. Exclusion criteria
    1. Disorganized thoughts must be absent or of mild degree, such that speech is intelligible.
    2. Affective and behavioral symptoms, as described in hebephrenia, must be absent or of mild degree.
  C. Preoccupation with extensive, well-organized delusions or hallucinations

Adapted from Tsuang MT, Winokur G.: Criteria for subtyping schizophrenia: Clinical differentiation of hebephrenic and paranoid schizophrenia. Arch Gen Psychiatry 31:43–47, 1974.

tem based on etiology, it is important that a diagnosis perform two basic functions: the prediction of outcome and the prediction of treatment. Both are essential aspects of practical day-to-day clinical medicine.

## ETIOLOGY

A variety of noxious psychological influences that disturbed ego functioning have been thought to cause schizophrenia. Society, social class, "schizophrenogenic" mothers, double-blinds, and other abnormal patterns of communication or behavior in the family have been implicated. At times it has even been suggested that schizophrenia is actually a healing process or a beneficial spiritual experience rather than an illness. After critically reviewing these

theories, Wing (1978a) and Leff (1978) concluded that advocates of these various explanations for schizophrenia had produced little evidence in their support.

Regarding the cause of schizophrenia, Kraepelin's (1919) comment many years ago still seems to hold: "The causes of dementia praecox are at the present time still wrapped in impenetrable darkness" (p. 224). Many factors are probably relevant to the process of schizophrenia, but their causal relationships are unclear. In the following sections, evidence for the most important of these are reviewed.

## Family Studies

A variety of studies over the years have demonstrated a fourfold increase in the rate of functional psychosis in the families of patients with psychosis compared with the families of patients without psychosis. Most research suggests that the increased rate is illness-specific; that is, the increased risk in the families of patients is significant for the illness from which the patient suffers (for example, Guze et al., 1983; Scharfetter and Nusperli, 1980; Tsuang, Winokur, Crowe, 1980). Table 6–3 summarizes the risk for schizophrenia from the older literature (Tsuang and Vandermey, 1980). The figures clearly show that the more closely a person is related to a schizophrenic, the greater is that person's risk of having schizophrenia. This suggests that schizophrenia is a familial disorder. Familial disorders may result from environmental factors or genetic factors, or both.

## Twin Studies

If schizophrenia were due entirely to genetic factors, in monozygotic twin pairs who have identical genes, the intrapair concordance for schizophrenia would be 100 per cent; in same-sex dizygotic twin pairs who share 50 per cent of their genes, the intrapair concordance would be 50 per cent. In the absence of such a clearly defined relationship, substantially higher concordance rates for monozygotic than dizygotic twins suggests a genetic contribution to the causation of schizophrenia, assuming that environmental influences peculiar to monozygotic

**TABLE 6–3.   Risk to Relatives of Schizophrenics**

| Relation | Risk (%) |
|---|---|
| *First-degree relatives* | |
| Parents | 4.4 |
| Brothers and sisters | 8.5 |
|   Neither parent schizophrenic | 8.2 |
|   One parent schizophrenic | 13.8 |
| Fraternal Twin | |
|   Opposite sex | 5.6 |
|   Same sex | 12.0 |
| Identical twin | 57.7 |
| Children | 12.3 |
|   Both parents schizophrenic | 36.6 |
| *Second-degree relatives* | |
| Uncles and aunts | 2.0 |
| Nephews and nieces | 2.2 |
| Grandchildren | 2.8 |
| Half siblings | 3.2 |
| *General population* | 0.8 |

Adapted from Tsuang MT, Vandermey R: Genes and the Mind: Inheritance of Mental Illness. Oxford, Oxford University Press, 1980.

twins could not explain the difference. Kendler (1983) has reviewed the evidence for environmental influences peculiar to monozygotic twins that might make their likelihood of developing schizophrenia greater than that of dizygotic twins and has concluded that there is little evidence of such a difference.

Kendler (1983) has summarized nine twin studies from eight countries involving 401 monozygotic twin pairs and 478 dizygotic twin pairs. Overall, 211, or 53 per cent, of the monozygotic twin pairs were concordant for schizophrenia, whereas only 74, or 15 per cent, of the dizygotic twin pairs were concordant. This significant difference between concordance rates for the two types of twin pairs strongly implicates genetic factors in the causation of schizophrenia.

## Adoption Studies

Environmental factors can confound family and twin studies. They can be eliminated in part by studying children of schizophrenics who were not raised by their schizophrenic parent. Heston (1966) compared the rates of schizophrenia in 47 adopted-away children of schizophrenic mothers with 50 adopted-away children of non-schizophrenic mothers. Five of the children of schizophrenic mothers were found to have schizophrenia at followup compared with none of the control group.

A series of studies known as the Danish-American Adoption Study of Schizophrenia demonstrated that 173 biologic relatives of adoptees with schizophrenia had significantly higher rates of schizophrenia (6.4 per cent) than 174 biologic relatives of control adoptees without schizophrenia (1.7 per cent) and 74 nonbiologic adoptive relatives of schizophrenics (1.4 per cent) (Kety et al., 1978).

In utero influences may confound adoption studies. Because paternal half siblings have different mothers, their comparison eliminates such an influence. Kety et al. (1978) found that 8 of 63 paternal half siblings of schizophrenic adoptees (12.7 per cent) had definite schizophrenia on interview compared with only 1 of 64 paternal half siblings of control adoptees (1.6 per cent).

Monozygotic twins raised apart provide a unique opportunity to separate genetic factors from environmental factors. Gottesman and Shields (1972) have summarized eight such investigations. Eleven of 17 monozygotic twin pairs reared apart (65 per cent) were concordant for schizophrenia.

In sum, family studies, twin studies, and adoption studies suggest a significant genetic component in the causation of schizophrenia. Genetic factors alone, however, cannot explain schizophrenia; otherwise, monozygotic twin pairs would be 100 per cent concordant for schizophrenia. Other factors must play an important role.

## Abnormalities of Brain Structure and Function

In 1927 Jacobi and Winkler (Weinberger and Wyatt, 1982) reported enlarged ventricles in 18 of 19 schizophrenics studied with pneumoencephalography. Subsequently, more than 30 studies reported similar results (Weinberger and Wyatt, 1982). These results were, by and large, ignored until recent work using computerized axial tomography (CAT) scans confirmed that, as a group, schizophrenics had larger ventricles than did controls.

Johnstone et al. (1976) reported that 17 institutionalized schizophrenics had, on the average, larger ventricles than eight matched controls. Patients with the larger ventricles had more cognitive impairment, fewer positive symptoms of schizophrenia, and more negative symptoms (see Clinical Picture for definition). Subsequent work by several researchers suggests that, depending on the population studied, between 20 per cent and 50 per cent of schizophrenics may have enlarged ventricles (Luchins, 1982).

Enlarged ventricles do appear to be related to negative symptoms of schizophrenia, cognitive impairment, poor performance on neuropsychological testing, and poor response to treatment (Andreasen et al., 1982; Golden et al., 1980; Johnstone et al., 1976; Weinberger et al., 1980). But ventricular enlargement may not be confined to schizophrenia. It has also been reported in mania, schizoaffective disorder, and adolescent obsessive-compulsive disorder (Behar et al., 1984; Nasrallah, McCalley-Whitters, Jacoby, 1982; Rieder et al., 1983).

Several lines of evidence suggest that schizophrenics may have abnormalities of brain function. Total brain blood flow might be reduced in schizophrenia (Mathew et al., 1982; Ariel et al., 1983). Regional blood flow measurements suggest a particular reduction in frontal blood flow (Ariel et al., 1983; Buchsbaum and Ingvar, 1982). Glucose metabolism, as measured by positron emission tomography, is a more direct indicator of regional metabolism than of regional blood flow. Such studies have also shown a relative reduction in metabolic activity in the frontal areas of schizophrenics compared with controls (Buchsbaum et al., 1982; Farkas et al., 1984).

A number of investigators have postulated left hemisphere dysfunction in schizophrenia. Gur (1979) concluded from her own work and a review of the literature that schizophrenics had dysfunctional left hemisphere, overactivation of the dysfunctional hemisphere, and failure to shift processing to the right hemisphere. Left hemisphere dysfunction may include an attentional deficit (Niwa et al., 1983).

Regional cerebral blood flow studies can be used to measure task-related changes in regional brain activity. In schizophrenics, Gur et al. (1983) found no flow asymmetries for a verbal task in which controls showed an increase in left hemisphere flow, and greater left hemisphere increases than right hemisphere increases for a spatial task in which controls showed a larger right hemisphere increase. Left temporal lobe epilepsy has been associated with an increased risk of a psychosis with schizophrenic symptomatology, and right temporal epilepsy, with an increased risk of affective symptoms (Flor-Henry, 1983).

These studies of regional brain dysfunction and structural brain defects in schizophrenia should not be considered definitive. They are not without faults. For example, see Sheppard et al.'s (1984) criticism of the hypofrontality hypothesis.

Eye tracking dysfunctions have been reported in 8 per cent of a normal population, 40 per cent of bipolars, and 50 per cent to 85 per cent of schizophrenic patients. More recently, Holzman et al. (1984) blindly studied parents of these patients and reported that 55 per cent of parental pairs of schizophrenics, compared with 17 per cent of parental pairs of bipolars, had similar smooth-pursuit eye movement dysfunction. They speculated that this may represent a trait phenomenon and a familial marker of vulnerability in a class of schizophrenics.

Many neurotransmitter systems have been implicated in schizophrenia, including serotonin, norepinephrine, dopamine, and gamma aminobutyric acid (GABA) (Snyder, 1982). Endorphins, enkephalins, prostaglandins, pineal deficiency, wheat sensitivity, and hypersensitivity to various allergins have played roles in other theories (Horrobin, 1979).

Most of these relationships remain highly speculative, but the dopamine theory has aroused consistent interest over the years. The primary evidence for the role of dopamine has been that positive symptoms (hallucinations and delusions) of schizophrenia are reduced by antipsychotics, and this reduction is roughly proportional to the ability to block dopamine receptors. In addition, amphetamines, which are dopamine agonists, may produce a paranoid psychosis indistinguishable from paranoid schizophrenia (Ellison and Eison, 1983). On the other hand, no defect in dopaminergic systems of schizophrenics has been identified, and drugs effective in schizophrenia are also effective in mania, psychotic depression, and schizophreniform psychoses. Thus some investigators, at least, doubt that "the lesion" of schizophrenia lies in dopamine pathways (Henn, 1982; Snyder, 1982).

## Family and Social Environment

Whether schizophrenia is a genetic illness or an environmental illness is not the important question. The true issue is what constellation of environmental factors may interact with what genetically determined factors to produce the disorder. Environmental factors could be of any sort. In this section family and social environment is considered.

No psychosocial factors have been identified that clearly play a role in causing schizophrenia. Many factors have been postulated, including low socioeconomic status and stressful life events, and none clearly proven. However, some old and some relatively new research on the role of family factors in the exacerbation of the illness suggests that certain family interactions worsen the illness and result in increased rates of relapse (Leff, 1976). Stressful life events may predispose to an acute resurgence of symptoms (Leff et al., 1983), and low levels of social stimulation may increase social withdrawal and deterioration of self-care (Wing, 1978b).

To investigate the relationship between emotional environment in the family and relapse of schizophrenia, researchers divided families into high-expressed emotion (High EE) and low-expressed emotion (Low EE) groups. Expressed emotion was defined in terms of number of critical comments, amount of hostility, and degree of emotional overinvolvement with the patient.

In a series of studies in which a total of 128 schizophrenic patients and their families were investigated, 13 per cent (9 of 71) from Low EE families relapsed after 9 months. In the High EE families, 51 per cent (29 of 57) relapsed over a 9-month period. In the latter group, relapse rates were lower for those patients who had spent less than 35 hours/week in face-to-face contact with the family (28 per cent) than for those who spent more than 35 hours/week in such contact (69 per cent) (Leff, 1976). Two recent studies designed to reduce expressed emotion in families have demonstrated reduced relapse rates in the treated families (Falloon et al., 1982; Leff et al., 1982). It is hoped that further studies will clarify whether this is specific to schizophrenia or is also true of bipolar patients and their families.

Chronic institutionalization with little so-

cial stimulation may also increase schizophrenic deterioration. This deterioration may be reversed to some degree with increased social stimulation, but too much social stimulation may cause a relapse (Wing, 1978b).

In sum, high amounts of expressed emotion in the families of schizophrenics and greater exposure to expressed emotion increase relapse rates in schizophrenics. Family treatment designed to reduce expressed emotion appears to reduce these relapse rates. Schizophrenics have increased social deterioration with low levels of social stimulation, but high levels of stimulation increase the chance of relapse.

## EPIDEMIOLOGY

A pooled estimate of disease expectancy (lifetime risk) culled primarily from the European literature is about 0.8 per cent (Cooper, 1978). Using narrow criteria for schizophrenia that excluded acute schizophrenia, reactive psychoses, and affective disorders, Helgason (1964) found the expectancy of schizophrenia to be about 0.7 per cent in 5395 Icelanders. Using broad American criteria, the expectancy of schizophrenia in the United States has been found to be as high as 3 per cent (Cooper, 1978). This higher number is consistent with the finding that more inclusive criteria, such as the New Haven Schizophrenic Index, diagnose schizophrenia several times more often in a given patient sample than do narrow criteria, such as DSM-III (Stephens et al., 1982).

Schizophrenia has been found in all cultures. In industrialized societies, schizophrenics tend to belong to lower socioeconomic groups (Cooper, 1978). Dunham's work (1965) suggests that the excess of schizophrenics in the lowest socioeconomic group results either from downward drift or from the schizophrenic's failure to move into a higher class. Goldberg and Morrison (1963) found that the social class distribution of the fathers of schizophrenics did not differ from that of the general population. Male schizophrenics tended to have lower job achievement than did fathers, brothers, and other male relatives. Whereas fathers tended to rise in job status, schizophrenic sons tended to fall into jobs of lower and lower status or become disabled.

## What Causes Schizophrenia

Simple genetic or environmental theories have not been adequate to explain schizophrenia. A number of factors that reflect our present understanding of schizophrenia have been reviewed. However, other relevant factors, such as seasonality of birth (Watson et al., 1984), perinatal injury, and twins discordant for schizophrenia (Shields and Gottesman, 1977), have not been discussed. With the resurgence of interest in the careful examination of the many physiologic, psychological, and social factors relevant to the pathogenesis of schizophrenia, a great expansion of our knowledge of the pathology of schizophrenia is expected, but a simple theory that can explain but one type of data or that cannot generate testable hypotheses should raise doubt.

## CLINICAL PICTURE

Each person with schizophrenia is unique. However, there are certain similarities between individuals with schizophrenia; otherwise, we could not use a classification system. The vignettes that follow illustrate many of the clinical features of schizophrenia that are described subsequently.

### Some Illustrative Cases

### CASE HISTORY 1

M.C. is a 25-year-old male high school graduate who lives with his parents and receives social security disability income. His grades in high school were average but not as good as those of his siblings. He never dated and had few friends. After high school he worked at one job for about 2 years, but he has not been able to hold a job since then for more than a few months, although several of his father's friends have hired him as a favor.

His first psychiatric admission at age 20 followed a period of withdrawal during which he refused to eat with his family and became hostile for no clear reason. His family brought him to the hospital after he became agitated. The records do not describe any clear hallucinations or delusions but do note that he had flat affect, talked little during his hospitalization, and laughed to himself at times. He was treated with an antipsychotic and became quite agreeable, although he still was somewhat withdrawn. He returned home and attempted to return to his work but was fired because he made too many mistakes.

His second hospitalization, at age 22, followed a similar episode, except that this time he complained of being God or the devil and of being influenced by spirits. His account was fragmented and vague. Again he responded to an antipsychotic.

One year later, while his antipsychotic dose was being reduced, he became withdrawn, refused again to eat with the family, refused to bathe, and over a period of several weeks took nearly every pill he could find in his parents' home. He could give no rational explanation for his behavior. In between acute episodes he had blunted affect, talked little during psychiatric evaluations, and often smiled peculiarly when answering questions with his usual one- or two-word answers, as if something funny had just happened and he were trying to suppress a giggle. His family reported that he seldom left the house and had no social life.

### CASE HISTORY 2

R.F. is a 58-year-old male who lives with his parents and has never married. He lives on disability income, although he claims that he does not need it and tore his last check into shreds in a fit of anger that terrified his aging parents. He has a 30-year history of believing that government agents have replaced most of his internal organs with artificial ones. He also believes that two teams of scientists continually experiment on him. At an examiner's first contact with this patient, he refused to answer most questions, replying, "You know, you know," in a hostile tone of voice and with a sarcastic smile. He insisted that the examiner belonged to the "gold team" because his last name began with two *l*s and because he had asked some questions twice. When informed that the examiner's last name began with only one *l*, the patient still insisted that the examiner belonged to the gold team. The patient would allow the examiner to talk with him only for 10 to 15 minutes at a time and then would become even more hostile and insist that the doctor leave the room. During these brief interviews the patient admitted that at times, external forces would control his mind and body, causing him to think thoughts and perform actions against his will. He indignantly insisted that these were violations of his rights by the experimenting scientists.

The family reported that no other family members had ever had a similar illness. After 4 days in the hospital he signed himself out against medical advice, despite the encouragement of his relatives to stay for treatment.

The first patient meets Tsuang-Winokur (Tsuang and Winokur, 1974) criteria for hebephrenic schizophrenia. Onset of symptoms occurred before age 25; he is unmarried and unemployed. His thinking has been disorganized during acute exacerbations; otherwise, he shows poverty of speech. His affect is flat, except when he smiles inappropriately. He has behaved bizarrely, as by taking all the pills in the house without a rational explanation and by having purposeless, withdrawn behavior.

The second patient meets criteria for the paranoid subtype. No first-degree relative has had schizophrenia. He has no disorganized thoughts or hebephrenic symptoms, and he is preoccupied with a well-organized delusional system. Table 6–4 summarizes essential differences between hebephrenic and paranoid schizophrenia.

## Symptomatology

First-rank symptoms are particularly common in schizophrenia, although they may occur in other psychoses as well. They are often referred to in the general literature on schizophrenia, and several are specifically referred to in section A of DSM-III criteria for schizophrenia. Thus some knowledge of these symptoms is important to the understanding of the clinical picture of schizophrenia, even though researchers do not agree on definitions of these symptoms.

### First-Rank Symptoms

Mellor's (1970) descriptions of first-rank symptoms are as follows:

- *Audible thoughts:* Voices speak the patient's thoughts out loud.
- *Voices arguing:* Two or more voices argue or discuss, usually with the patient as the subject, who is often referred to in the third person.
- *Voices commenting:* A voice describes or comments on the patient's activities as he performs them.
- *Somatic passivity:* Some outside agency imposes sensations on the patient, often by some extraordinary means, such as x-rays.
- *Thought withdrawal:* Some outside agency withdraws the patient's thoughts. Usually the patient feels for a time that his mind is empty.
- *Thought insertion:* Some outside agency inserts thoughts into the patient's mind.
- *Thought broadcasting:* The patient feels that his thoughts escape into the environment and are overheard by other people. The patient may ascribe this to telepathy but usually distinguishes this from the belief that others can read his mind.
- *Made feelings:* Some outside agency imposes on the patient feelings that are not his own.
- *Made impulses (drives):* The patient experiences the drive or impulse to act as coming from some outside agency.
- *Made volitional acts:* The patient's actions are,

**TABLE 6–4.    Characteristics of Hebephrenic and Paranoid Schizophrenia**

| Clinical Features | Hebephrenic | Paranoid |
|---|---|---|
| Age of onset before age 25 yr | Likely | Less likely |
| Marriage | Less likely | More likely |
| Employment | Less likely | More likely |
| Family history of schizophrenia | More likely | Less likely |
| Disorganized thought: tangential, illogical, incoherent, or irrelevant speech; loose associations; blocking; or other formal thought disorders | + + | + or − |
| Affect changes: inappropriate affect; giggling; self-absorbed smiling; mood inconsistent with expressed ideas; flat affect; frozen, expressionless, impenetrable face | + + | + or − |
| Behavior symptoms | | |
|   Bizarre behavior; unusual, unpredictable, irresponsible, purposeless, or withdrawn behavior not in keeping with sociocultural norms | + + | + or − |
|   Motor symptoms, hebephrenic traits: habitual mannerisms of an ordinary character, usually involving a single part of the body, e.g., grimaces, tics, moving lips soundlessly, fidgeting with fingers, hand wringing, thigh rubbing, etc. | + + | + or − |
|   Catatonic traits: physical activity of an extraordinary and abnormal character, usually involving the whole body, e.g., posturing, stereotyping, waxy flexibility, negativism, stupor, hyperkinesis, etc. | + | − |
| First-rank symptoms of Schneider, other hallucinations, or delusions | + or − | + + |

Traits present to a marked degree or of a persistent nature, + +; present to a mild degree or of a transient nature, +; absent, −.

Adapted from Tsuang MT, Winokur G: Criteria for subtyping schizophrenia: Clinical differentiation of hebephrenic and paranoid schizophrenia. Arch Gen Psychiatry 31:43–47, 1974.

he believes, completely controlled by an out-side force. He may feel as if he were a robot or a zombie.

- *Delusional perception:* The patient attributes a private meaning to a normal perception. The meaning is delusional and is not simply re-lated to a previous personal experience.

Schneiderian first-rank symptoms consist of particular kinds of hallucinations and de-lusions. A *hallucination* is a false perception in the absence of real sensory stimuli. Pa-tients may also have *illusions,* which are mis-perceptions of real external stimuli. A *de-lusion* is a fixed false belief that the believer maintains even in the face of considerable evidence or likelihood to the contrary.

First-rank symptoms are not usually con-sidered to be present unless the patient gives an unequivocal delusional interpre-tation of his experience; that is, the patient has a firm belief in the reality of the unreal experience and the experience is not a nor-mal one in the patient's culture and occurs in clear consciousness. Whispering voices that cannot be understood or occasional sin-gle words or phrases are also not considered as Schneiderian first-rank symptoms and are not characteristic of schizophrenia.

## Negative Symptoms

Negative symptoms are also common in schizophrenia, particularly in non-paranoid forms. Until recently, reliable definitions of negative symptoms have been unavailable. Andreasen (1982) has classified negative symptoms into five groups and described their rating. They are:

1. Affective flattening or blunting
   a. Unchanging facial expression
   b. Decreased spontaneous move-ments
   c. Paucity of expressive gestures
   d. Poor eye contact
   e. Affective nonresponsivity
   f. Inappropriate affect
   g. Lack of vocal inflections
2. Alogia
   a. Poverty of speech
   b. Poverty of content of speech
   c. Blocking
   d. Increased latency of response
3. Avolition–apathy
   a. Poor grooming and hygiene
   b. Impersistence at work or school
   c. Physical anergy

4. Anhedonia–asociality
   a. Decrease in or lack of recreational interests or pleasure from recrea-tional activities
   b. Lack of sexual interest or activity
   c. Decreased ability to feel intimacy or closeness
   d. Decrease in or lack of relationships with friends and peers
5. Attentional impairment
   a. Work inattentiveness
   b. Inattentiveness during mental sta-tus examination
   c. Subjective complaints of inatten-tiveness

Many of the symptoms are self-explana-tory. Some require explanation. *Affect* refers to emotion expressed by the subject and ob-served by the examiner (DSM-III glossary). *Blunted affect* is a marked reduction in the amount of affect. *Flat affect* refers to the ab-sence of affect. *Inappropriate affect* is affect that is strikingly inconsistent to circum-stance or content of thought.

*Poverty of speech* means that speech is ex-tremely reduced in amount; for example, the patient says very little in response to questions that, with an ordinary person, would elicit considerable talk. *Poverty of con-tent of speech* refers to speech that is devoid of content. Despite normal verbal produc-tion, nothing seems to be said. *Blocking* is when speech is interrupted before a thought has been completed, and the patient cannot recall what he or she was saying or had in-tended to say before the interruption of thought (DSM-III definition). In *latency of re-sponse* there is an abnormally long delay be-tween a question and the patient's response to the question. *Physical anergy* refers to physical inactivity, such as sitting and doing nothing for long periods.

## Other Symptoms

There are a variety of other schizophrenic symptoms in addition to first-rank symp-toms and the negative symptoms described by Andreasen. *Loose associations* is the term applied to thought production in which there is no recognizable relationship be-tween ideas. Thoughts appear unconnected or, at best, obliquely related to one another. Tangentiality, derailment, word salad, and talking past the point are related terms that apply to abnormal relationships between ideas.

*Delusions* (defined previously) can be of many sorts. *Paranoid delusions* may include beliefs that one is being persecuted, harassed, spied on, poisoned, or in some other way plotted against. The patient may name his family, friends, or some specific organization, or he may not know who the perpetrators are.

In *ideas of reference* the patient believes that events that are of no obvious relevance to him refer personally to him. For example, he may believe that people are talking about him when they pass him on the street or that radio or TV programs or newspaper articles are about him.

*Catatonic* symptoms, including negativism, mutism, waxy flexibility, posturing, catatonic excitement, and catatonic stupor, may be present. *Negativism*, loosely defined, refers to the refusal of the patient to comply with requests. More narrowly defined, it refers to the active resistance on the part of the patient to most or all demands made on him. *Mutism* is self-explanatory; the patient does not talk; it may be accompanied by catatonic *stupor*, in which the patient is unresponsive and immobile although conscious. Catatonic *excitement* occurs when the patient becomes hyperactive. During the excited phase he may be destructive or violent. This differs from the hyperactivity of mania in that other manic symptoms, such as euphoria, are not present and the patient does not meet criteria for mania (see DSM-III for the definition of mania). *Waxy flexibility* may be elicited by first instructing the patient that he does not have to cooperate and then, while distracting with conversation or questions, placing a limb of the patient in some position. If waxy flexibility is present, the patient will hold the position for at least several minutes. *Posturing* refers to the holding of unusual positions for long periods.

Schizophrenics may also display *mannerisms*, which are goal-directed movements that are stilted, bizarre, or out of context. *Stereotypies* are repetitive non–goal-directed movements that are more complex than a tic.

None of the symptoms are pathognomonic of schizophrenia; they all may occur in other disorders. Kraepelin's (1919) original work and *Fish's Schizophrenia* (Hamilton, 1984) are good sources for more detailed descriptions of the symptomatology of schizophrenia.

## COURSE AND OUTCOME

Both Kraepelin (1919) and Bleuler (1911/1950) thought that recovery from schizophrenia was rare. Identifying criteria that might predict the course of illness has been difficult. Narrow criteria, such as those in DSM-III, have been more successful at separating good-prognosis patients from poor-prognosis patients than have broader criteria (Helzer et al., 1981; Stephens et al., 1982).

Thirty-five to forty years after admission, Tsuang, Woolson, and Fleming (1979) followed up 186 schizophrenics, 86 manics, and 212 depressives diagnosed by Feighner criteria, which are similar to DSM-III criteria (Feighner et al., 1972). Thirty-three of the schizophrenics met Tsuang-Winokur criteria for paranoid subtype, and 40, for hebephrenic subtype (Kendler et al., 1984). Table 6–5 summarizes their outcomes. Schizophrenics had significantly poorer outcomes in all three areas examined than did manics and depressives.

Manfred Bleuler (1978) personally followed 208 schizophrenic patients for more than 20 years. All living patients were included in the followup who had been in a relatively stable psychiatric condition, or "end state," for at least 5 years. Fifty-six patients were excluded because they either were dead or had not reached a stable end state. Twenty per cent of the remaining 152 patients recovered fully. They were able to reassume former social and family roles, were regarded by their families as rational, and had no psychotic symptoms on examination. Thirty-three per cent of the patients had mild "end states." They could converse sensibly about topics other than their hallucinations and delusions. Overt behavior was normal, and they were usually able to work. However, they continued to have definite schizophrenic symptoms. Forty-seven per cent had moderate to severe end states, characterized by marked psychiatric symptoms and marked impairment in most or all role functioning.

In Bleuler's series of patients, 62 per cent had acute onsets of less than 6 months' duration. Acute onset and undulating course

**TABLE 6–5.  Comparative Outcome of Schizophrenics, Manics, and Depressives**

| | Schizophrenia (%) | | | Mania (%) | Depression (%) |
|---|---|---|---|---|---|
| | PARANOID | HEBEPHRENIC | TOTAL | | |
| Work-disabled from psychiatric illness | 36 | 72 | 58 | 24 | 17 |
| Severe psychiatric symptoms | 36 | 62 | 54 | 29 | 22 |
| Residence in county home or mental hospital | 39 | 77 | 40 | 17 | 13 |

Schizophrenia, $N = 186$; paranoid subtype, $n = 33$; hebephrenic subtype, $n = 40$; mania, $N = 86$; depression, $N = 212$.

were both associated with a more favorable outcome than were insidious onset and chronic course. Bleuler described several combinations of course and outcome similar to those later described by Ciompi.

Ciompi (1980) began with an initial sample of 1642 schizophrenics and followed up the 289 surviving patients. Followup was as much as 50 years after hospitalization. End states were defined with Bleuler's criteria (Bleuler, 1978). At followup 27 per cent of the patients had recovered fully, 22 per cent had mild symptoms, 24 per cent moderately severe symptoms, 18 per cent severe symptoms, and 9 per cent uncertain outcome.

Of the 289 cases, mode of onset, course type, and end state (followup status) were known for 228 (79 per cent). Onset was divided into two types, acute and chronic (insidious); course type, into undulating (episodic) and simple (continuous); and end state, into recovery or mild end state and moderate or severe end state. Table 6–6 summarizes the resulting eight course combinations.

Acute onset was associated with a better outcome than insidious onset, and episodic course was associated with a better outcome than continuous course. Of those patients

who would probably receive the DSM-III classification of schizophrenia early in the course of their illness (patients with insidious onset or acute onset with continuous course), 40 per cent were recovered or had a mild end state at followup. Of the acute onset group with episodic course, 68 per cent were recovered or had a mild end state.

The onset of schizophrenia is usually insidious (66 per cent in Ciompi's series of patients if schizophreniform psychoses are excluded). Schizophrenics, particularly males, may have conduct disturbances as children, lower IQ, lower school grades, and completion of fewer grades (Offord, 1974; Robins, 1966). Fifty per cent to seventy per cent of schizophrenics may have had certain schizoid personality traits, such as aloofness, few close friends, and less involvement in social activities than their peers (Slater and Roth, 1969). In children at high risk for schizophrenia, Fish (1977) has described a syndrome involving dysregulation of physical growth; motor, visual-motor, and cognitive development; proprioception; and vestibular responses. Several such children developed overt schizophrenia by early childhood. Other investigators have reported

**TABLE 6–6.  Course of Schizophrenia**

| Mode of Onset | Course Type | End State | No. (%) of Patients ($N = 228$) |
|---|---|---|---|
| Acute | Episodic | Recovery/mild | 58 (25.4) |
| Acute | Episodic | Moderate/severe | 27 (11.9) |
| Acute | Continuous | Moderate/severe | 19 (8.3) |
| Acute | Continuous | Recovery/mild | 12 (5.3) |
| Insidious | Continuous | Moderate/severe | 55 (24.1) |
| Insidious | Continuous | Recovery/mild | 23 (10.1) |
| Insidious | Episodic | Recovery/mild | 22 (9.6) |
| Insidious | Episodic | Moderate/severe | 12 (5.3) |

From Ciompi L: Catamnestic long-term study on the course of life and aging in schizophrenics. Schizophr Bull 6:606–618, 1980.

similar findings (Erlenmeyer-Kimling et al., 1982).

Usually, by the time the patient with schizophrenia consults a psychiatrist, deterioration from the previous level of functioning has been under way for months or years. In a group of 52 non-paranoid schizophrenics defined by Tsuang-Winokur criteria (Tsuang and Winokur, 1974) positive or negative symptoms, or both, had been present for an average of 1 year before admission (Pfohl and Winokur, 1982a).

Positive symptoms tend to be less persistent than negative symptoms (Pfohl and Winokur, 1982a, 1982b) and may serve to precipitate admission to a psychiatric hospital. Certain negative symptoms, such as avolition, may also begin early in the course of the illness. But in contrast to positive symptoms, negative symptoms may become more and more prominent as the illness progresses. In the Iowa 500 followup study, only 12 of 120 patients (10 per cent) originally diagnosed as being non-paranoid schizophrenics received the diagnosis of paranoid schizophrenia at followup 35 to 40 years later. However, 22 of 54 paranoid schizophrenics (41 per cent) received the diagnosis of non-paranoid schizophrenia at followup (Tsuang et al., 1981).

Depression is common in the course of schizophrenia. Over a 6- to 12-year span, Guze et al. (1983) reported that 25 of 44 schizophrenics (57 per cent) had one or more depressive episodes. Relatives of these schizophrenics were not at increased risk of affective disorder compared with relatives of schizophrenics without depressive episodes. It is important to note that these schizophrenics had an otherwise typical course of schizophrenic symptoms. Their illness did not appear to begin with affective symptoms and was not episodic.

One aspect of the course of an illness is the stability of the symptoms over time as reflected in diagnostic stability. Personal interview of 93 of 117 living patients who had been diagnosed schizophrenic 35 to 40 years earlier and who met Feighner criteria on chart review confirmed the diagnosis in 86 (93 per cent). Only 4 of the 93 (4 per cent) were found to have affective disorder at followup (Tsuang et al., 1981). Guze et al. (1983) have reported similar results in a prospective followup of 19 narrowly defined schizophrenics. None were rediagnosed affective disorder.

Mortality in schizophrenics is elevated compared with the general population (Ciompi, 1980; Tsuang and Woolson, 1977). A good portion of the increased mortality is due to suicide. Tsuang (1978) found that 10 per cent of the deceased schizophrenics died by suicide; this represents 4 per cent of the total sample of 195 who could be traced to either death or present residence. Schizophrenics have an increased risk of death owing to physical illness as well. However, a reported decreased risk for cancer death appears to be an artifact of inappropriate statistical analysis (Tsuang, Woolson, Fleming, 1980).

To summarize:

- Acute onset and episodic course are associated with better outcome than are insidious onset and chronic course.
- Acute onset is more likely to be associated with an episodic course than is insidious onset. As a result, many patients with an acute onset of schizophrenic symptoms will not qualify for a DSM-III diagnosis of schizophrenia.
- Impaired role functioning is much more likely to occur in schizophrenia than in affective disorders.
- Tsuang-Winokur criteria for paranoid and hebephrenic schizophrenia separate schizophrenia into three groups: paranoid, hebephrenic, and undifferentiated. The paranoid group has an outcome similar to that of the affective disorder group and significantly better than that of the other two schizophrenic subgroups.
- Schizophrenics have increased rates of mortality, primarily by suicide.
- Hebephrenic symptoms tend to be more enduring than paranoid symptoms.

## DIFFERENTIAL DIAGNOSIS

### General Principles

The making of a differential diagnosis presumes an understanding of certain basic principles of diagnosis. In general, medical diagnoses cannot be based on a single dimension, such as cross-sectional symptomatology, course, family history, response to treatment, or laboratory findings. Usually, the more dimensions along which an illness has been defined, the more reliably it can be differentiated from other disorders.

Specific basic considerations in the differential diagnosis of schizophrenia are as follows:

- Establish clear sensorium, the absence of

which precludes any immediate diagnosis of schizophrenia.

- Use reliable, narrow definitions of symptoms, such as those described under Clinical Picture.
- Carefully determine the course of each symptom, including mode of onset, first occurrence, and course.
- If possible, gather information on psychiatric illness in other family members.
- Determine response to any treatment that may have been given in the past.
- Specifically review symptoms of bipolar affective disorder and major depressive disorder, since the exclusion of these two disorders is required for the diagnosis of schizophrenia.
- Specifically exclude drug-induced psychosis or any other organic psychosis.
- Be patient and observe until relevant diagnostic information can be gathered.
- Carefully rate the presence or absence of features required by DSM-III for the diagnosis.
- Remember that most symptoms of schizophrenia can occur in other disorders. We are looking for characteristic *patterns* of course and symptoms. Pathognomonic features do not exist.

Usually, after these steps are carefully executed, application of DSM-III criteria to the information gathered will clarify the diagnosis and help to avoid ludicrous labeling of individuals as schizophrenic, such as that reported by Rosenhan (1973).

## Disorders to Be Considered in the Differential Diagnosis

The differential diagnosis of schizophrenia should include.

- organic mental disorder
- bipolar affective disorder
- major depressive disorder
- schizophreniform disorder
- atypical psychosis
- schizoaffective disorder
- brief reactive psychosis
- schizotypal personality disorder
- paranoid disorder
- paranoid personality
- borderline personality disorder

This list includes most of the disorders that are likely to share symptomatology with schizophrenia.

Less commonly, the following may be confused with schizophrenia: somatization disorder, agoraphobia, obsessive-compulsive disorder, antisocial personality disorder, atypical anxiety disorder, and atypical depressive disorder.

Almost every major psychiatric disorder is included in the list. This is partially because schizophrenia was once broadly defined and partially because many disorders share symptoms with schizophrenia, or have symptoms that may be confused with those of schizophrenia.

Symptoms found in schizophrenia are hallucinations, delusions, thought disorder, and a miscellaneous group that includes other negative and catatonic symptoms. Any of these symptoms may be found in other disorders.

In a study of 116 consecutively admitted patients with hallucinations, Goodwin, Alderson, and Rosenthal (1971) found that only 32 (28 per cent) had schizophrenia. Abrams and Taylor (1981) examined 111 manics who met Feighner criteria, RDC criteria, and DSM-III criteria for mania. Only 42 (38 per cent) had none of the following symptoms: formal thought disorder, catatonic symptoms, auditory hallucinations, persecutory delusions, and first-rank symptoms. Andreasen (1979) found similar patterns of "thought-language-communication disorder" in 45 schizophrenics and 32 manics, including poverty of content of speech, tangentiality, derailment, incoherence, illogicality, loss of goal, and perseveration.

Research reviewed in the Definition, Clinical Picture, and clinical Course and Outcome sections of this chapter suggests that course and outcome of symptoms is the primary factor that differentiates schizophrenia from other psychoses. When based on symptoms alone, particularly isolated symptoms, the diagnosis of schizophrenia has often been erroneous (Pope and Lipinski, 1978). This was Kraepelin's basic position many years ago (Kraepelin, 1919). The importance of establishing not only symptoms, but also their pattern and course has been recognized by DSM-III, which in many cases requires a specific course of symptoms for the diagnosis of a given disorder, particularly for schizophrenia.

## Specific Sources of Confusion in the Differential Diagnosis

There are many case reports of organic mental disorders being confused with schizophrenia or schizophreniform disorder. Most of the confusion appears to result from two fundamental essentials in the diagnosis of schizophrenia being ignored.

1. For the diagnosis of schizophrenia, symptoms *must* occur in clear consciousness. Otherwise, an organic mental disorder cannot be excluded, and the diagnosis of a functional disorder, such as schizophrenia, must be deferred. In addition, drug-induced psychoses, which may not result in a marked impairment in sensorium, must be excluded.

2. The symptoms of schizophrenia and their duration are relatively specific, as noted earlier. Most reported cases of organic mental disorders confused with schizophrenia do not show a typically schizophrenic course of symptoms. For example, in an acute brain syndrome, symptoms begin much more abruptly and may include visual hallucinations or bizarre behavior resulting from clouded consciousness rather than first-rank symptoms or systematized delusions that are more typical of schizophrenia. In a chronic brain syndrome, symptoms that might be confused with negative symptoms result from intellectual deterioration. The schizophrenic typically can describe the course of hallucinations and delusions over the duration of the illness. The patient with a brain syndrome recalls only vaguely what has occurred. (The problems of differentiating organic illness from schizophrenia have been discussed in more detail by Hall, 1980, and Lishman, 1978.)

Several organic mental disorders may resemble schizophrenia more closely than other organic mental disorders, particularly temporal lobe epilepsy, amphetamine psychosis, and alcoholic hallucinosis. In temporal lobe epilepsy (complex partial seizures), delusions and hallucinations (including auditory hallucinations) may follow a course resembling that of schizophrenia, except that the changes occur after the onset of complex partial seizures (in one series an average of 14 years after the seizures began) (Slater and Beard, 1963). Amphetamine abuse may produce a paranoid psychosis with visual, auditory, and tactile hallucinations. Unlike the insidious onset typical of DSM-III schizophrenia, the psychosis may begin relatively abruptly (e.g., during a several-day course of high intake of amphetamines) and resolve within a few days after cessation of drug use (Ellison and Eison, 1983; Grinspoon and Bakalar, 1980).

Transient hallucinations and delusions may occur frequently in alcoholics. In Victor and Hope's (1958) work, 15 of 76 patients had onset of hallucinations while still drinking. In the patients for whom the time of the last drink could be determined, 32 (60 per cent) had onset of hallucinations within 12 to 48 hours of the last drink. In the 75 patients for whom the duration of hallucinations could be determined, 64 (85 per cent) had a duration of hallucinations of 6 days or less. Only 8 of the 75 (11 per cent) had a duration of symptoms longer than 6 weeks. Schuckit and Winokur (1971) found no increase in the incidence of schizophrenia in the relatives of alcoholics with hallucinosis. Also, the patients were no more likely than other alcoholics to have a history of schizophrenia. Thus alcoholic hallucinosis differs from schizophrenia in that it occurs after prolonged alcohol abuse and is usually of abrupt onset and short duration.

In recent years a number of hallucinogens have become commonly abused, and drug abuse is common in psychiatric patients. Overall, 30 per cent of 335 consecutive admissions to one hospital had histories of drug abuse and 15 per cent were currently abusing drugs (Fischer et al., 1975). It can be difficult to distinguish between individuals with preexisting psychiatric illness who may abuse drugs and drug abusers who may have prolonged psychoses (Tsuang, Simpson, Kronfol, 1982). Morbidity risks for schizophrenia in the families of 45 drug abusers with prolonged psychoses (at least 6 months of symptoms without return to previous levels of functioning) were similar to those in the families of 46 schizophrenics (6.5 per cent and 6. 8 per cent, respectively). In addition, families of drug abusers with prolonged psychosis had increased risk for affective disorder, suggesting that this group of patients with psychosis was genetically heterogeneous. The psychoses of the patients, however, resembled schizophrenia in terms of course and symptomatology. Because chronic psychoses in drug abusers may begin at an earlier age than those in non-drug abusers, some authorities have suggested that drug abuse precipitates the illness in the genetically predisposed (reviewed in Tsuang et al., 1982, and Bowers and Swigar, 1983). In sum, a psychosis in a drug abuser that does not remit on prolonged cessation of drug abuse and that otherwise meets DSM-III criteria for schizophrenia probably is schizophrenia.

Affective disorder, particularly mania, was often diagnosed as schizophrenia in the New York sample of the U.S.–U.K. study (Cooper et al., 1972). Abrupt onset and the predominance of affective symptoms usually distinguish bipolar affective disorder from schizophrenia (Pope and Lipinski, 1978). Manics may have many symptoms, such as paranoid delusions and thought disorder, that once were considered indicative of schizophrenia. Flight of ideas may be confused with loose associations, but these rarely occur without other symptoms of mania, such as euphoria, decreased sleep, and hyperactivity. Schizophrenics occasionally may sleep badly and have episodes of hyperactivity, but these symptoms are usually secondary to delusions and hallucinations or part of catatonic symptomatology and are unaccompanied by the typical euphoria, grandiosity, and social hyperactivity of the manic.

Major depressive disorder may involve paranoid delusions, usually mood-congruent. Sometimes mood-incongruent delusions occur, but more typical symptoms of depression normally precede them. Patients with depression may report hearing voices or having other hallucinations. These reports are typically fragmented; the experiences are not of many months' duration, and they occur within the context of a predominantly affective constellation of symptoms. Occasionally, at first examination, the clinician may have difficulty establishing the course of symptoms. In such a case, more information needs to be gathered before the final diagnosis is decided. The nosologic place for affective disorder with mood-incongruent features needs further clarification (Coryell, Tsuang, McDaniel, 1982).

In schizophrenia, episodes of depression usually occur along with other schizophrenic symptoms and within the context of an otherwise typical schizophrenic illness (Guze et al., 1983). If such episodes do not occur, the diagnosis of schizophrenia should be reevaluated. The social withdrawal, lack of interest, and psychomotor retardation of depression may resemble schizophrenic social deterioration and thought disorder. A careful history will reveal whether these symptoms occur in the context of a typical depressive illness, with other symptoms such as poor appetite, terminal insomnia, and self-reproach, and whether the onset of a depressed mood preceded the marked withdrawal, lack of interest, and psychomotor retardation.

Schizophreniform disorder, by DSM-III criteria, has the same symptoms as schizophrenia, but they are of shorter duration. It thus appears to function as a residual category for those patients with typically schizophrenic symptoms who have an abrupt, rather than an insidious, onset. However, schizophreniform disorder has historically been used for individuals who do have some of the symptoms of schizophrenia but who differ from schizophrenics in ways other than mode of onset and duration (Tsuang and Loyd, 1985). For example, emotional turmoil and intellectual confusion or perplexity may be prominent; psychosocial stressors may play a larger role than in schizophrenia; premorbid adjustment is usually good. Nonetheless, the most important distinctions between the two disorders may remain mode of onset and duration of episode.

Atypical psychosis is a residual category, as defined by DSM-III. When DSM-III is carefully applied, many patients called schizophrenic in years past will fall into this category. The main identifying characteristic of this group is that they do not fit into any more rigorously defined category. Using this category rather than forcing a choice between the more carefully defined categories is important because it reminds the physician that more information needs to be gathered before deciding on course of treatment and counseling the patient and family as to future outcome.

Schizoaffective disorder differs from schizophrenia in that both affective and schizophrenic features are equally prominent (Tsuang, Dempsey, Rauscher, 1976; Tsuang and Loyd, 1985). The affective symptoms do not occur in an otherwise typical schizophrenic course of illness, or vice versa. Rather, both categories of symptoms occur together. Schizoaffective patients may also have a relatively abrupt onset and fail to meet the duration criterion for schizophrenia.

Brief reactive psychosis (Tsuang and Loyd, 1985) should not be confused with schizophrenia, except in the case where the history cannot be obtained. Otherwise, the history of an abrupt onset psychosis with rapid resolution of symptoms should distinguish the two. One difficulty may arise— confusion of a preexisting personality disorder with the prodromata of schizophrenia. If the psychotic symptoms are of brief duration, we doubt the diagnosis, despite the fact that DSM-III allows for only a brief duration of psychosis if prodromal symptoms have been present for some time. Schizophrenics are usually psychotic for many months before coming to the psychiatrist (see the Clinical Picture and the Course and Outcome sections of this chapter).

Paranoid disorder is relatively rare (Winokur, 1977). It may be confused with paranoid schizophrenia and perhaps rightly so, since the boundaries between the two are unclear (Kendler and Tsuang, 1981). In paranoid disorder only a single, well-encapsulated delusional system occurs. The delusions of paranoid disorder are plausible in the sense that they could occur. There are no hallucinations, bizarre or fantastic delusions, or negative symptoms, as in typical schizophrenia, and delusions are not fragmented (unsystematized).

Schizotypal personality disorder may be genetically related to schizophrenia. However, the symptoms never quite reach the stage of full-blown delusions or hallucinations. The patient may appear suspicious and superstitious. He may complain of vague ideas of reference and have few social contacts. But no symptoms such as those described under category A of schizophrenia are unequivocally present.

Paranoid personality should not be confused with schizophrenia, since no delusions, hallucinations, changes in affect, thought disorder, or other schizophrenic symptoms, as described in DMS-III and elsewhere in this chapter, are present. Initially, one might suspect that delusions lie behind the suspiciousness, guardedness, and hostility, but none can be found.

Borderline, histrionic, and other personality disorders have been confused with schizophrenia when broad criteria were applied. Strict application of DSM-III criteria, using reliable and narrow definitions of features as described in other sections of this chapter, obviates such errors. Although some of the symptoms of these disorders resemble the prodromata of schizophrenia,

these patients do not develop narrowly defined symptoms in category A of the DSM-III criteria for schizophrenia; however, they may be more susceptible to brief reactive psychoses.

In one group of patients, the mentally retarded, the diagnosis of schizophrenia may be difficult even if all the recommendations in this chapter are carefully followed. Schizophrenic features are, by and large, symptoms that only the patient can report. Patients with severe communication defects may not be able to communicate the symptoms to the observer. Less frequently, it may be difficult to differentiate misperceptions of events, or fantasy, from delusions or hallucinations (Wright, 1982).

The diagnosis of schizophrenia must be based on the presence of specific symptoms and a specific course of symptoms. DSM-III specifies these symptoms and their course. Other disorders differ from schizophrenia if symptoms are narrowly defined and their course is taken into account. When the history and psychiatric examination of a psychotic patient do not reveal a pattern of symptoms and symptom duration that clearly corresponds to a well-defined DSM-III disorder, it is prudent to use the category of atypical psychosis.

## TREATMENT

In the treatment of schizophrenia the following modalities should be considered: hospitalization, administration of antipsychotics, social and family therapy, individual psychotherapy, and rehabilitation.

Hospitalization is used for four basic reasons: (1) diagnostic evaluation, as described in the Differential Diagnosis section of this chapter; (2) regulation of medication; (3) reduction of danger to the patient or others; and (4) other acute management problems. Rarely is the hospital used for chronic care as in the past. Lengthy hospitalization has not been found to be more effective than brief hospitalization (Caton, 1982), although some authors have reported minor differences (Hargreaves et al., 1977).

Antipsychotics reduce relapse rates in schizophrenia. Davis's (1975) review of the older literature indicates that relapse rates are two to four times higher in the placebo-treated groups than in the drug-treated groups. For example, Hogarty et al. (1974a) found that 80 per cent of placebo-treated patients had relapsed by the end of 2 years compared with 48 per cent of the drug-treated group. Hogarty and Ulrich (1977) found that the placebo-treated group was 2½ to 3 times more likely to relapse over a 3-year period than the treated group. Chronic schizophrenics may relapse if antipsychotics are discontinued, even after several years' remission (Cheung, 1981). After 2 to 3 years of treatment without relapse, 65 per cent of 43 patients withdrawn from medication had an exacerbation of symptoms during the next year (Hogarty et al., 1976).

The principles of antipsychotic use are (Klein et al., 1980; Perry, Alexander, Liskow, 1981):

- **Define target symptoms.**
- **Choose an antipsychotic with the profile of side effects least likely to exacerbate other medical problems. If an antipsychotic has proven beneficial in the past, it may be restarted, or the dose increased. If an antipsychotic in adequate dose has not proved beneficial in the past or has particularly troublesome side effects, choose an antipsychotic from another class.**
- **Increase medication as tolerated and observe target symptoms for several weeks. Evaluation of the effect of an antipsychotic may take up to several weeks of observation on a therapeutic dose of that antipsychotic.**
- **If there has been no change in target symptoms after this time, consider further increases in medication if side effects are tolerable, or change to a different class of antipsychotics. In either case, reevaluate target symptoms and appropriateness of diagnosis.**
- **Avoid polypharmacy.**

During the course of treatment with antipsychotics, acute extrapyramidal symptoms—dystonia, akathisia, and pseudoparkinsonism—may occur in 40 per cent to 60 per cent of patients (Perry et al., 1981). Dystonic reactions are involuntary tonic muscle contractions of a striated muscle group and typically involve muscles of the head and face. Akathisia is a subjective feeling of restlessness and may be expressed by pacing, rocking from foot to foot, or other motor activity and, at times, by insomnia. Pseudoparkinsonism is the production of an extrapyramidal syndrome that is virtually indistinguishable from Parkinson's disease, including tremor, rigidity, akinesia, and parkinsonian gait. These symptoms may be treated with anticholinergics (Perry et al., 1981). Prophylactic use of anticholinergics for acute extrapyramidal syndromes is usually unnecessary.

Prolonged administration of antipsychotics may produce a late-onset dyskinetic syndrome known as tardive dyskinesia. This syndrome consists of involuntary dyskinetic movements, frequently involving the mouth, lips, and tongue. The prevalence has been estimated at about 20 per cent of patients chronically treated with antipsychotics (Kane and Smith, 1982). Withdrawal of antipsychotics may reverse the dyskinesia in about 37 per cent of cases (Jeste and Wyatt, 1982).

Once target symptoms have been reduced to a low level, the dose should be slowly reduced while target symptoms are carefully observed. The maintenance dose of medication that will keep target symptoms reduced to a satisfactory level is highly individual and can be determined only by trial and error (Baldessarini and Davis, 1980). If the patient is noncompliant and medication is clearly indicated, consider use of a long-acting (1 to 3 weeks) depot antipsychotic administered intramuscularly. In any case, determination of the lowest necessary maintenance dose is important, since risk for tardive dyskinesia and other chronic side effects (e.g., cornea and lens changes) may be related to total lifetime dose of antipsychotics (Baldessarini and Davis, 1980; Kane and Smith, 1982).

Lithium has been suggested for the treatment of schizophrenia. However, the effectiveness of lithium in the treatment of DSM-III schizophrenia, which excludes schizoaffective disorder, has not been clearly established (Jefferson, Greist, Achermann, 1983). Electroconvulsive therapy has also not proved to be effective in chronic schizophrenia (Kendell, 1981). Depression, sometimes termed postpsychotic depression, is common in schizophrenia (Guze et al., 1983); it usually responds to antipsychotics alone (Knights and Hirsch, 1981). A role for antidepressants in the treatment of depression in schizophrenia has not been clearly established (British Medical Journal, 1980).

After a review of the literature on psychotherapy for schizophrenia and other disorders, the American Psychiatric Association Commission on Psychotherapies (1982) concluded:

Psychotherapy as the sole therapeutic modality seems to be useful in such conditions as some psychoneuroses, personality disorders, and maladjustments. Psychotherapy alone has been shown to be less effective for the major affective disorders and much less so for schizophrenia. The prototypic relationship between psychotherapy and pharmacotherapy seems reciprocal, favoring psychotherapy for personality disorders and favoring pharmacotherapy for psychotic disorders. For many conditions the interrelationship seems to be additive. (p. 227)

As a rule, schizophrenics have many social problems. Assistance in dealing with social agencies and such matters as finances and family stress is as important for the schizophrenic as it is for any handicapped individual. For example, marked social isolation appears to produce more schizophrenic deterioration. On the other hand, too much social stimulation may produce an increase in florid symptoms (Wing, 1978b). If counselors and relatives do not understand the need for the schizophrenic to control social stimulation and the protective nature of some social withdrawal, they may place too much pressure on him to engage in social activities. Two recent studies suggest that in cases where the schizophrenic lives with his family, family therapy designed to reduce the level of expressed emotion may reduce relapse rates (Falloon et al., 1982; Leff et al., 1982).

Regular followup visits for monitoring symptoms, medication compliance, medication side effects, and social problems are advisable and can reduce hospitalization rates (American Psychiatric Association Commission on Psychotherapies, 1982; Hogarty et al., 1974b). Too vigorous an intervention, however, particularly in the symptomatic patient, may be worse than no intervention (Goldberg et al., 1977).

Unfortunately, rehabilitative programs specifically tailored to the needs of schizophrenics, and of proven efficacy, are rare or nonexistent (Meyerson and Herman, 1983). Clinically, in practice, a rehabilitative program for a patient with schizophrenia is tailored to the particular handicaps of that patient. This may involve day care of a low intensity (Linn et al., 1979), sheltered employment, and sheltered housing (Bennett, 1978). It may be important to involve the patient's family in the process of rehabilitation, at least insofar as to enhance the family members' understanding of the specific limitations of their relative and the nature of the schizophrenic process (Bennett, 1978).

Basic behavioral management, consisting of clearly specified and appropriate rules, clearly specified positive and negative consequences of specified behaviors, and, to the extent possible, education of the patient as to the nature of his illness, is important for any treatment in any residential or hospital setting. During an acute phase of the illness, these rules should be simple and limited in number. In the chronic phase of the illness, during which the patient usually resides outside the hospital, an appropriate management strategy may need to involve family and, occasionally, employers (Wing, 1978c).

In conclusion, the optimum treatment for schizophrenia may include:

- **Careful diagnostic evaluation.**
- **Hospitalization for acute management if necessary, such as with the suicidal, homicidal, or assaultive patient, the patient who requires intensive observation to evaluate and determine target symptoms, or the patient who requires skilled nursing care and intensive medical management.**
- **Antipsychotics in an appropriate dose and dose form.**
- **Supportive psychotherapy; monitoring of symptoms, medication side effects, and compliance with medication; and assistance with social problems such as finances, housing, employment, and family conflicts.**
- **Recognition of the sensitivity of the schizophrenic to overly intrusive therapies and other social stresses.**
- **Education of the family about schizophrenia and, if relevant, family therapy to reduce expressed emotion.**

## REFERENCES

Abrams R, Taylor MA: Importance of schizophrenic symptoms in the diagnosis of mania. Am J Psychiatry 138:658–661, 1981.

American Psychiatric Association: Diagnostic and Statistical Manual of Mental Disorders (DSM-III), ed. 3. Washington, DC, American Psychiatric Association, 1980.

Andreasen NC: Thought, language, and communication disorders. II. Diagnostic significance. Arch Gen Psychiatry 36:1325–1330, 1979.

Andreasen NC: Negative symptoms in schizophrenia:

Definition and reliability. Arch Gen Psychiatry 39:784–788, 1982.

Andreasen NC, Olsen SA, Dennert JW, et al: Ventricular enlargement in schizophrenia: Relationship to positive and negative symptoms. Am J Psychiatry 139:297–302, 1982.

American Psychiatric Association, Commission on Psychotherapies: Psychotherapy Research: Methodological and Efficacy Issues. Washington, DC, American Psychiatric Association, 1982.

Ariel RN, Golden CJ, Berg RA, et al: Regional cerebral blood flow in schizophrenics: Tests using the Xenon Xe 133 inhalation method. Arch Gen Psychiatry 40:258–263, 1983.

Baldessarini RJ, Davis JM: What is the best maintenance dose of neuroleptics in schizophrenia? Psychiatry Res 3:115–122, 1980.

Behar D, Rapoport JL, Berg CJ, et al: Computerized tomography and neuropsychological test measures in adolescents with obsessive-compulsive disorder. Am J Psychiatry 141:363–369, 1984.

Bennett D: Social forms of psychiatric treatment, in Wing JK (ed): Schizophrenia Towards a New Synthesis. New York, Grune and Stratton, 1978.

Bleuler E: Dementia Praecox or the Group of Schizophrenias. New York, International Universities Press, 1950 (originally published as a volume of Aschaffenburg's Handbuch in 1911, trans. Zinkin J).

Bleuler M: The Schizophrenic Disorders: Long-term Patient and Family Studies. New Haven, CT, Yale University Press, 1978 (originally published in 1972, trans. Clemens S).

Bowers MB, Swigar ME: Vulnerability to psychosis associated with hallucinogen use. Psychiatry Res 9:91–97, 1983.

British Medical Journal: Use of antidepressants in schizophrenia. Br Med J i:1037–1038, 1980.

Buchsbaum MS, Ingvar DH: New visions of the schizophrenic brain: Regional differences in electrophysiology, blood flow, and cerebral glucose use, in Henn FA, Nasrallah HA (eds): Schizophrenia as a Brain Disease. New York, Oxford University Press, 1982.

Buchsbaum MS, Ingvar DH, Kessler R, et al: Cerebral glucography with positron tomography: Use in normal subjects and in patients with schizophrenia. Arch Gen Psychiatry 39:251–259, 1982.

Carpenter WT, Strauss JS, Bartko JJ: Flexible system for the diagnosis of schizophrenia: Report from the WHO international pilot study of schizophrenia. Science 182:1275–1278, 1973.

Caton CLM: Effect of length of inpatient treatment for chronic schizophrenia. Am J Psychiatry 139:856–861, 1982.

Cheung HK: Schizophrenics fully remitted on neuroleptics for 3–5 years—to stop or continue drugs? Br J Psychiatry 138:490–494, 1981.

Ciompi L: Catamnestic long-term study on the course of life and aging in schizophrenics. Schizophr Bull 6:606–618, 1980.

Cooper B: Epidemiology, in Wing JK (ed): Schizophrenia Towards a New Synthesis. New York, Grune & Stratton, 1978.

Cooper JE, Kendell RE, Gurland BJ, et al: Psychiatric Diagnosis in New York and London: A Comparative Study of Mental Hospital Admissions. London, Oxford University Press, 1972. (Institute of Psychiatry, Maudsley Monographs, no. 20).

Coryell W, Tsuang MT, McDaniel J: Psychotic features in major depression: Is mood congruence important? J Affective Disorder 4:227–236, 1982.

Davis JM: Overview: Maintenance therapy in psychiatry. I. Schizophrenia. Am J Psychiatry 132:1237–1245, 1975.

Dunham HW: Community and Schizophrenia: An Epidemiological Analysis. Detroit, Wayne State University Press, 1965.

Ellison GD, Eison MS: Continuous amphetamine intoxication: An animal model of the acute psychotic episode. Psychol Med 13:751–761, 1983.

Erlenmeyer-Kimling L, Cornblatt B, Friedman D, et al: Neurological, electrophysiological, and attentional deviations in children at risk for schizophrenia, in Henn FA, Nasrallah HA (eds): Schziophrenia as a Brain Disease. New York, Oxford University Press, 1982.

Falloon IRH, Boyd JL, McGill CW, et al: Family management in the prevention of exacerbations of schizophrenia: A controlled study. N Engl J Med 306:1437–1440, 1982.

Farkas T, Wolf AP, Jaeger J, et al: Regional brain glucose metabolism in chronic schizophrenia: A positron emission transaxial tomographic study. Arch Gen Psychiatry 41:293–300, 1984.

Feighner JP, Robins E, Guze SB, et al: Diagnostic criteria for use in psychiatric research. Arch Gen Psychiatry 26:57–63, 1972.

Fischer DE, Halikas JA, Baker JW, et al: Frequency and patterns of drug abuse in psychiatric patients. Dis Nerv Sys 36:550–553, 1975.

Fish B: Neurobiologic antecedents of schizophrenia in children: Evidence for an inherited, congenital neurointegrative defect. Arch Gen Psychiatry 34:1297–1313, 1977.

Flor-Henry P: Determinants of psychosis in epilepsy: Laterality and forced normalization. Biol Psychiatry 18:1045–1057, 1983.

Goldberg EM, Morrison SL: Schizophrenia and social class. Br J Psychiatry 109:785–802, 1963.

Goldberg SC, Schooler NR, Hogarty GE, et al: Prediction of relapse in schizophrenic outpatients treated by drug and sociotherapy. Arch Gen Psychiatry 34:171–184, 1977.

Golden CJ, Moses JA, Zelazowski R, et al: Cerebral ventricular size and neuropsychological impairment in young chronic schizophrenics: Measurement by the standardized Luria-Nebraska neuropsychological battery. Arch Gen Psychiatry 37:619–623, 1980.

Goodwin DW, Alderson P, Rosenthal R: Clinical significance of hallucinations in psychiatric disorders: A study of 116 hallucinatory patients. Arch Gen Psychiatry 24:76–80, 1971.

Gottesman II, Shields J: Schizophrenia and Genetics: A Twin Study Vantage Point. New York, Academic Press, 1972.

Grinspoon L, Bakalar JD: Drug dependence: Nonnarcotic agents, in Kaplan HI, Freedmab AM, Sadock BJ (eds): Comprehensive Textbook of Psychiatry, ed. 3. Baltimore, Williams & Wilkins, 1980.

Gur RE: Cognitive concomitants of hemispheric dysfunction in schizophrenia. Arch Gen Psychiatry 36:269–274, 1979.

Gur RE, Skolnick BE, Gur RC, et al: Brain function in schizophrenic disorders. I. Regional blood flow in medicated schizophrenics. Arch Gen Psychiatry 40:1250–1254, 1983.

Guze SB, Cloninger R, Martin RL, et al: A follow-up and family study of schizophrenia. Arch Gen Psychiatry 40:1273–1276, 1983.

Hall CW: Psychiatric Presentations of Medical Illness: Somatopsychic Disorders. New York, SP Medical and Scientific Books, 1980.

Hamilton M: Fish's Schizophrenia, ed. 3. Bristol, John Wright & Sons, 1984.

Hargreaves WA, Glick ID, Drues J, et al: Short vs. long hospitalization: A prospective controlled study. VI. Two-year follow-up results for schizophrenics. Arch Gen Psychiatry 34:305–311, 1977.

Helgason T: Epidemiology of mental disorders in Iceland. A psychiatric and demographic investigation of 5395 Icelanders. Acta Psychiatr Scand 40:173, 1964 (Suppl).

Helzer JE, Brockington IF, Kendell RE: Predictive validity of DSM-III and Feighner definitions of schizophrenia: A comparison with Research Diagnostic Criteria and CATEGO. Arch Gen Psychiatry 38:791–797, 1981.

Henn FA: Dopamine: A role in psychosis or schizophrenia, in Henn FA, Nasrallah HA (eds): Schizophrenia as a Brain Disease. New York, Oxford University Press, 1982.

Heston LL: Psychiatric disorders in foster home-reared children of schizophrenic mothers. Br J Psychiatry 112:819–825, 1966.

Hogarty GE, Goldberg SC, Schooler NR, et al: Drug and sociotherapy in the aftercare of schizophrenic patients. II. Two year relapse rates. Arch Gen Psychiatry 31:603–608, 1974a.

Hogarty GE, Goldberg SC, Schooler NR, the Collaborative Study Group: Drug and sociotherapy in the aftercare of schizophrenic patients. III. Adjustment of nonrelapsed patients. Arch Gen Psychiatry 31:609–618, 1974b.

Hogarty GE, Ulrich RF: Temporal effects of drug and placebo in delaying relapse in schizophrenic outpatients. Arch Gen Psychiatry 34:297–301, 1977.

Hogarty GE, Ulrich RF, Mussare F, et al: Drug discontinuation among long term, successfully maintained schizophrenic outpatients. Dis Nerv Syst 37:494–500, 1976.

Holzman PS, Solomon CM, Levin S, et al: Pursuit eye movement dysfunctions in schizophrenia: Family evidence for specificity. Arch Gen Psychiatry 41:136–139, 1984.

Horrobin DF: Schizophrenia: Reconciliation of the dopamine, prostaglandin, and opoid concepts and the role of the pineal. Lancet 1:529–531, 1979.

Jefferson JW, Greist JH, Achermann DL: Lithium Encyclopedia for Clinical Practice. Washington, DC, American Psychiatric Press, 1983.

Jeste DV, Wyatt RJ: Therapeutic strategies against tardive dyskinesia. Arch Gen Psychiatry 39:803–816, 1982.

Johnstone EC, Crow TJ, Frith CD, et al: Cerebral ventricular size and cognitive impairment in chronic schizophrenia. Lancet 2:924–926, 1976.

Kane JM, Smith JM: Tardive dyskinesia: Prevalence and risk factors, 1959 to 1979. Arch Gen Psychiatry 39:473–481, 1982.

Kendell RE: The present status of electroconvulsive therapy. Br J Psychiatry 139:265–283, 1981.

Kendler KS: Overview: A current perspective on twin studies of schizophrenia. Am J Psychiatry 140:1413–1425, 1983.

Kendler KS, Gruenberg AM, Tsuang MT: Outcome of schizophrenic subtypes defined by four diagnostic systems. Arch Gen Psychiatry 41:149–154, 1984.

Kendler KS, Tsuang MT: Nosology of paranoid, schizophrenic, and other paranoid psychoses. Schizophr Bull 7:594–610, 1981.

Kety SS, Rosenthal D, Wender PH, et al: The biologic and adoptive families of adopted individuals who became schizophrenic: Prevalence of mental illness and other characteristics, in Wynne LC, Cromwell RL, Matthysse S (eds): The Nature of Schizophrenia: New Approaches to Research and Treatment. New York, John Wiley & Sons, 1978.

Klein DF, Gittelman R, Quitkin F, et al: Diagnosis and Drug Treatment of Psychiatric Disorders: Adults and Children. Baltimore, Williams & Wilkins, 1980.

Knights A, Hirsch SR: "Revealed" depression and drug treatment of schizophrenia. Arch Gen Psychiatry 38:806–811, 1981.

Kraepelin E: Dementia Praecox and Paraphrenia. Huntington, NY, Robert Krieger, 1971 (facsimile of 1919 edition, trans. Barclay RM).

Kramer M: Some problems for international research suggested by observations on differences in first admission rates to the mental hospitals of England and Wales and of the United States. Proceedings of the Third World Congress of Psychiatry 3:153–160, 1961.

Leff J: Schizophrenia and sensitivity to the family environment. Schizophr Bull 2:566–574, 1976.

Leff J: Social and psychological causes of the acute attack, in Wing JK (ed): Schizophrenia: Towards a New Synthesis. New York, Grune & Stratton, 1978.

Leff J, Kuipers L, Berkowitz R, et al: A controlled trial of social intervention in the families of schizophrenic patients. Br J Psychiatry 141:121–134, 1982.

Leff J, Kuipers L, Berkowitz R, et al: Life events, relatives' expressed emotion and maintenance neuroleptics in schizophrenic relapse. Psychol Med 13:799–806, 1983.

Linn MW, Caffey EM, Klett J, et al: Day treatment and psychotropic drugs in the aftercare of schizophrenic patients. Arch Gen Psychiatry 36:1055–1066, 1979.

Lishman WA: Organic Psychiatry: The Psychological Consequences of Cerebral Disorder. Oxford, Blackwell Scientific, 1978.

Luchins DJ: Computed tomography in schizophrenia: Disparities in the prevalence of abnormalities. Arch Gen Psychiatry 39:859–860, 1982.

Mathew RJ, Duncan GC, Weinman ML, et al: Regional cerebral blood flow in schizophrenia. Arch Gen Psychiatry 39:1121–1124, 1982.

Mellor CS: First rank symptoms of schizophrenia. Br J Psychiatry 117:15–23, 1970.

Meyerson AT, Herman GS: What's new in aftercare? A review of recent literature. Hosp Community Psychiatry 34:333–342, 1983.

Nasrallah HA, McCalley-Whitters M, Jacoby CG: Cerebral ventricular enlargement in young manic males: A controlled CT study. J Affective Disorder 4:15–19, 1982.

Niwa SI, Hiramatsu KI, Kameyama T, et al: Left hemisphere's inability to sustain attention over extended time periods in schizophrenics. Br J Psychiatry 142:477–481, 1983.

Offord DR: School performance of adult schizophrenics, their siblings and age mates. Br J Psychiatry 125:12–19, 1974.

Perry PJ, Alexander B, Liskow BI: Psychotropic Drug

Handbook, ed. 3. Cincinnati, Harvey Whitney Books, 1981.

Pfohl B, Winokur G: The evolution of symptoms in institutionalized hebephrenic/catatonic schizophrenics. Br J Psychiatry 141:567–572, 1982a.

Pfohl B, Winokur G: Schizophrenia: Course and outcome, in Henn FA, Nasrallah HA (eds): Schizophrenia as a Brain Disease. New York, Oxford University Press, 1982b.

Pope HG, Lipinski JF: Diagnosis in schizophrenia and manic-depressive illness: A reassessment of the specificity of "schizophrenic" symptoms in the light of current research. Arch Gen Psychiatry 35:811–828, 1978.

Rieder RO, Mann LS, Weinberger DR, et al: Computed tomographic scans in patients with schizophrenia, schizoaffective, and bipolar affective disorder. Arch Gen Psychiatry 40:735–739, 1983.

Robins E, Guze SB: Establishment of diagnostic validity in psychiatric illness: Its application to schizophrenia. Am J Psychiatry 126:983–987, 1970.

Robins L: Deviant Children Grown Up. Baltimore, Williams & Wilkins, 1966.

Rosenhan DL: On being sane in insane places. Science 179:250–258, 1973.

Scharfetter C, Nusperli M: The group of schizophrenia, schizoaffective psychoses, and affective disorders. Schizophr Bull 6:586–591, 1980.

Schuckit MA, Winokur G: Alcoholic hallucinosis and schizophrenia: A negative study. Br J Psychiatry 119:549–550, 1971.

Sheppard GP, Jutai J, Manchanda R, et al: Frontal-lobe hypofunction in schizophrenia. Lancet 1:970–971, 1984 (letter).

Shields J, Gottesman II: Obstetric complications and twin studies of schizophrenia: Clarification and affirmation. Schizophr Bull 3:351–354, 1977.

Slater E, Beard AW: The schizophrenia-like psychoses of epilepsy. I. Psychiatric aspects. Br J Psychiatry 109:95–150, 1963.

Slater E, Roth M: Clinical Psychiatry. Baltimore, Williams & Wilkins, 1969.

Snyder SH: Neurotransmitters and CNS disease: Schizophrenia. Lancet 2:970–973, 1982.

Spitzer RL, Endicott J, Robins E: Research diagnostic criteria: Rationale and reliability. Arch Gen Psychiatry 35:773–782, 1978.

Stephens JH, Astrup C, Carpenter WT, et al: A comparison of nine systems to diagnose schizophrenia. Psychiatry Res 6:127–143, 1982.

Tsuang MT: Suicide in schizophrenics, manics, depressives, and surgical controls: A comparison with general population suicide mortality. Arch Gen Psychiatry 35:153–155, 1978.

Tsuang MT, Dempsey M, Rauscher F: A study of "atypical schizophrenia": Comparison with schizophrenia and affective disorder by sex, age of admission, precipitant, outcome, and family history. Arch Gen Psychiatry 33:1157–1160, 1976.

Tsuang MT, Loyd DW: Other psychotic disorders, in Cavenar JB et al (eds): Psychiatry. Philadelphia, J.B. Lippincott, vol. 1, 70:1–17, 1985.

Tsuang MT, Perkins K, Simpson JC: Physical diseases in schizophrenia and affective disorder. J Clin Psychiatry 44:42–46, 1983.

Tsuang MT, Simpson JC, Kronfol Z: Subtypes of drug abuse with psychosis: Demographic characteristics, clinical features, and family history. Arch Gen Psychiatry 39:141–147, 1982.

Tsuang MT, Vandermey R: Genes and the Mind: Inheritance of Mental Illness. London, Oxford University Press, 1980.

Tsuang MT, Winokur G: Criteria for subtyping schizophrenia: Clinical differentiation of hebephrenic and paranoid schizophrenia. Arch Gen Psychiatry 31:43–47, 1974.

Tsuang MT, Winokur G, Crowe RR: Morbidity risks of schizophrenia and affective disorders among first degree relatives of patients with schizophrenia, mania, depression, and surgical conditions. Br J Psychiatry 137:497–504, 1980.

Tsuang MT, Woolson RF: Mortality in patients with schizophrenia, mania, depression, and surgical conditions. Br J Psychiatry 130:162–166, 1977.

Tsuang MT, Woolson RF, Fleming JA: Long-term outcome of major psychoses. I. Schizophrenia and affective disorders compared with psychiatrically symptom-free surgical conditions. Arch Gen Psychiatry 36:1295–1301, 1979.

Tsuang MT, Woolson RF, Fleming JA: Premature deaths in schizophrenia and affective disorders: An analysis of survival curves and variables affecting the shortened survival. Arch Gen Psychiatry 37:979–983, 1980.

Tsuang MT, Woolson RF, Winokur G, et al: Stability of psychiatric diagnosis: Schizophrenia and affective disorders followed up over a 30- to 40-year period. Arch Gen Psychiatry 38:535–539, 1981.

Victor M, Hope JM: The phenomenon of auditory hallucinations in chronic alcoholism: A critical evaluation of the status of alcoholic hallucinosis. J Nerv Ment Dis 126:451–481, 1958.

Watson GC, Kucala T, Tilleskjor C, et al: Schizophrenic birth seasonality in relation to the incidence of infectious diseases and temperature extremes. Arch Gen Psychiatry 41:85–90, 1984.

Weinberger DR, Llewellyn BB, Kleinman JE, et al: Cerebral ventricular enlargement in chronic schizophrenia: An association with poor response to treatment. Arch Gen Psychiatry 37:11–13, 1980.

Weinberger DR, Wyatt RJ: Brain morphology in schizophrenia: In vivo studies, in Henn FA, Nasrallah HA (eds): Schizophrenia as a Brain Disease. New York, Oxford University Press, 1982.

Wing JK: Reasoning About Madness. London, Oxford University Press, 1978a.

Wing JK: Social influences on the course of schizophrenia, in Wynne LC, Cromwell RL, Mattysse S (eds): The Nature of Schizophrenia: New Approaches to Research and Treatment. New York, John Wiley & Sons, 1978b.

Wing JK: The management of schizophrenia, in Wing JK (ed): Schizophrenia Towards a New Synthesis. New York, Grune & Stratton, 1978c.

Winokur G: Delusional disorder (paranoia). Compr Psychiatry 18:511–521, 1977.

World Health Organization: The International Pilot Study of Schizophrenia, vol 1. Geneva, World Health Organization, 1973.

Wright EC: The presentation of mental illness in mentally retarded adults. Br J Psychiatry 141:496–502, 1982.

# SCHIZOAFFECTIVE AND SCHIZOPHRENIFORM DISORDERS

*by* William Coryell, M.D.

## DEFINITION

The term schizoaffective disorder implies a mixture of schizophrenic and affective (depressive or manic) symptoms.

Ambiguous terminology has impeded the accumulation of knowledge in psychiatry, particularly for efforts to clarify the boundary between schizophrenia and affective disorders. The number of terms proposed to label such patients reflects the failure of any one definition to meet with wide acceptance. Moreover, differing definitions have attached to certain of these terms, definitions that, until recently, were purely descriptive; they provided no clear rules for inclusion and exclusion, and therefore did not lend themselves to use by other researchers. The recent introduction of the Research Diagnostic Criteria (RDC) (Spitzer, Endicott, Robins, 1978) and the *Diagnostic and Statistical Manual of Mental Disorders*, third edition (DSM-III) (American Psychiatric Association, 1980), have remedied the situation somewhat, and for the first time, researchers have attempted to replicate one another using the same definitions.

Yet the term schizoaffective remains a source of confusion. According to the RDC, a diagnosis of schizoaffective disorder requires a full affective syndrome (i.e., dysphoria plus five symptoms from a possible eight) and at least one feature of five traditionally associated with schizophrenia. Several of these features, such as thought broadcasting, thought insertion, and delusions of passivity, are Schneiderian first-rank symptoms (Taylor, 1972). Other features of RDC schizoaffective disorder concern the temporal relationship of symptoms. Thus a patient is considered schizoaffective if any delusion or hallucination (other than those typical of mania or depression) occurs when the affective syndrome is either absent or relatively mild.

DSM-III, on the other hand, provides no criteria for schizoaffective disorder and applies the term only to those patients who cannot be otherwise classified. Instead, most patients with RDC schizoaffective disorder have DSM-III affective disorder with mood-incongruent psychotic features.

Any discussion of schizoaffective disorder, then, requires that the term be qualified by the system—RDC, DSM-III, International Classification of Diseases (ICD), or others. Although there is considerable variety (see Tables 7–1 and 7–2), most definitions used since the 1970s have several features in common. They require either the coincidence of schizophrenic and affective symptoms or the occurrence of an affective syndrome at one point and a schizophrenic syndrome at another. In the interest of readability, the term schizoaffective is used generically in this chapter, in a fashion generally consistent with the preceding definition. DSM-III major depression (or mania) with mood-incongruent psychotic features is included under this heading; almost no data exist to describe DSM-III schizoaffective disorder.

## ETIOLOGY

Many demonstrable organic insults can produce syndromes suggesting schizoaffective disorder. Identification of a cause, however, precludes the diagnosis, and in DSM-III, the diagnosis becomes one of organic affective disorder or organic delusional disorder. The etiology of schizoaffective is, by definition, unknown.

The question then becomes, does schizoaffective disorder share its unknown etiology with schizophrenia, with affective disorder, or with neither? Or does schizoaffective disorder simply label a genotypically mixed group made up partly of affective disorder patients and partly of schizophrenics? Because both schizophrenia and affective disorder are heritable, family studies offer one approach to this question. The relevant hypotheses can be tested in the following ways: (1) If schizoaffective disorder is simply a variant of affective disorder (Clayton, Rodin, and Winokur, 1968; Pope, Lipinski, Cohen, Axelrod, 1980), then schizoaffective probands should have no more familial loading for schizophrenia than do affective disorder probands. (2) If schizoaffective probands have simply a variant of schizophrenia, as implied in the formerly used DSM-II (American Psychiatric Association, 1968), their families should contain no more affective disorder than the families of schizophrenic probands. (3) If schizoaffective patients have a condition separate from both schizophrenia and affective disorder, the other two situations should obtain and their families will be loaded for schizoaffective disorder, provided this condition is,

likewise, familial. Because schizophrenialike symptoms may have different implications when they coexist with depressive syndromes than when they coexist with manic ones (Clayton, 1982), this review summarizes studies in three groups: those that isolated schizoaffective manics, those that isolated schizoaffective depressives, and those that did neither.

Those studies that did not separate schizoaffective manic patients from schizoaffective depressed patients consistently failed to support the first hypothesis (Table 7–1); in eight out of eight studies, relatives of schizoaffective probands were more likely to have schizophrenia than were the relatives of affective disorder probands. The same was true in two of the three studies that considered schizoaffective depression apart. On the other hand, three studies considered schizoaffective mania separately and none found schizophrenia among relatives of schizoaffective probands.

Although fewer studies included schizophrenia cohorts for comparison, they are consistent in finding higher rates of affective disorder in the families of schizoaffective probands than in the families of schizophrenics.

### Editor's Comment

*Another possibility is that the phenomenon of secondary psychotic depression causes the diagnostic dilemma of schizoaffective depression and the confusing patterns of illness in families. That is, besides schizophrenia with secondary depression, patients with such illnesses as obsessive-compulsive disorder, panic disorders, and alcoholism develop psychotic depression and are diagnosed cross-sectionally as schizoaffective depressed. Only unbiased followup of patients by a nontreatment assessor could clarify the issue. Predictably, family studies would find many psychiatric disorders in the relatives (Clayton, 1983).*

Thus the second of the hypotheses—that schizoaffective disorder is altogether a variant of schizophrenia—can be rejected.

Attempts to address the third hypothesis, that there is a "third psychosis," present special problems. Most relatives are, by necessity, diagnosed in retrospect, particularly if their lifetime diagnosis involves an episodic condition. Although past depressive episodes can be reliably assessed (Andreasen et al., 1981), the existence and na-

**TABLE 7–1.**   Rates of Illness Among Relatives of Probands with Schizoaffective, Mood-Incongruent, or Atypical Psychoses: Comparisons to Probands with Affective Disorder or Schizophrenia

| | Proband Diagnosis | | |
|---|---|---|---|
| | AFFECTIVE DISORDER | SCHIZOAFFECTIVE OR EQUIVALENT | SCHIZOPHRENIA |
| *Schizoaffective probands not divided by polarity* | | | |
| Reference (definition of schizoaffective disorder used in study) | | | |
| Angst J, 1973 (author's def.) | | | |
| No. of probands | 254 | 73 | — |
| MR%* − schizophrenia | 1.4 | 5.9 | |
| MR% − affective disorder | 13.3 | 7.1 | |
| MR% − schizoaffective | 0.7 | 3.8 | |
| Tsuang et al., 1976 (author's def.) | | | |
| No. of probands | 325 | 85 | 200 |
| % FH** + for schizophrenia | 0.5 | 1.3 | 1.3 |
| % FH + for affective disorder | 8.3 | 7.6 | 3.1 |
| Suslak et al., 1976 (author's def.) | | | |
| No. of probands | 37 | 10 | — |
| MR% − schizophrenia | 0.9 | 4.0 | |
| MR% − affective disorder | 12.5 | 6.5 | |
| Tsuang et al., 1977 (author's def.) | | | |
| No. of probands | 289 | 52 | 183 |
| MR% − schizophrenia | 0.5 | 0.9 | 1.3 |
| MR% − affective disorder | 8.3 | 11.8 | 3.2 |
| Mendlewicz et al., 1980 (author's def.) | | | |
| No. of probands | 110 | 55 | 55 |
| MR% − schizophrenia | 2.5 | 10.8 | 16.9 |
| MR% − affective disorder | 34.0 | 34.6 | 8.6 |
| Scharfetter, 1981 (author's def.) | | | |
| No. of probands | 89 | 40 | 102 |
| MR% − schizophrenia | 3.3 | 13.5 | ~7.4 |
| MR% − affective disorder | 11.4 | 4.4 | ~1.0 |
| MR% − schizoaffective | 3.4 | 2.5 | — |
| Baron et al., 1982 (RDC) | | | |
| No. of probands | 85 | 50 | 50 |
| MR% − schizophrenia | 0.3 | 2.2 | 7.9 |
| MR% − affective disorder | 25.2 | 18.9 | 5.1 |
| MR% − schizoaffective | 3.1 | 2.2 | 2.3 |
| Gershon et al., 1982 (RDC) | | | |
| No. of probands | ? | ? | — |
| MR% − schizophrenia | 0.2 | 3.6 | — |
| MR% − affective disorder | 22.6 | 31.0 | — |
| MR% − schizoaffective | 0.9 | 6.1 | — |
| *Schizoaffective mania vs. mania (vs. schizophrenia)* | | | |
| Abrams and Taylor, 1976 (RDC) | | | |
| No. of probands | 78 | 10 | — |
| % FH + for schizophrenia | 0 | 0 | — |
| % FH + for affective disorder | 14.4 | 13.9 | |
| Pope et al., 1980 (RDC) | | | |
| No. of probands | 34 | 52 | 41 |
| % FH + for schizophrenia | 0 | 0 | 9.8 |
| % FH + for affective disorder | 32.4 | 40.4 | 9.8 |
| Rosenthal et al., 1980 (RDC) | | | |
| No. of probands | 28 | 25 | — |
| MR% − schizophrenia | 0 | 0 | — |
| MR% − affective disorder | 24.8 | 24.6 | — |
| *Schizoaffective depression vs. depression (vs. schizophrenia)* | | | |
| Coryell et al., 1982 (DSM-III) | | | |
| No. of probands | 221 | 95 | 235 |
| MR% − schizophrenia | 0.5 | 1.6 | 2.8 |
| MR% − affective disorder | 13.0 | 8.2 | 5.8 |

**TABLE 7–1.** (*continued*)

| | Proband Diagnosis | | |
|---|---|---|---|
| | AFFECTIVE DISORDER | SCHIZOAFFECTIVE OR EQUIVALENT | SCHIZOPHRENIA |
| Abrams and Taylor, 1983 (DSM-III) | | | |
| No. of probands | 14 | 17 | 31 |
| MR% − schizophrenia | 0 | 0 | 1.6 |
| MR% − affective disorder | 12.9 | 19.3 | 6.8 |
| Endicott et al., in press (RDC) | | | |
| No. of probands | 275 | 23 | — |
| MR% − schizophrenia | 0 | 3.0 | — |
| MR% − affective disorder | 35.9 | 25.2 | — |
| MR% − schizoaffective | 0.3 | 1.0 | — |

$$* \text{ Morbid risk \%} = \frac{\text{no. of relatives with a disorder}}{\text{no. of relatives at risk for that disorder}}$$

$$** \text{ \% Family history positive} = \frac{\text{no. of probands with a family history of a disorder}}{\text{total no. of probands}}$$

ture of psychotic symptoms apparently cannot (Orvaschel, Thompson, Belanger, Prusoff, Kidd, 1982; Rosenthal et al., 1979). Unless a researcher evaluates the relative during a psychotic episode, or unless records taken during that episode are available, the distinction between mood-congruent and mood-incongruent psychotic features, and thus the precise diagnosis, will be elusive. Indeed, the five studies that made this diagnosis in relatives yielded mixed results (Table 7-1).

Other approaches to familial psychopathology may be more germane to the third hypothesis. Cohen, Allen, Pollin, and Hrubec (1972) described a large series of monozygotic twin pairs and found a higher concordance rate for schizoaffective disorder than for manic-depressive disorder or schizophrenia. Moreover, among pairs concordant for any psychosis, there was 100 per cent concordance for the specific diagnosis. This would argue powerfully for a third psychosis, except that the medical records of each twin were assessed to gather information about co-twins; this allowed substantial rater bias. Although there are no blindly rated twin studies with which to gauge this effect, Tsuang (1975) did describe a series of blindly diagnosed sibling pairs, the results of which lead to very different conclusions. Of the 35 pairs concordant for any psychosis, only 4 (11.4 per cent) were concordant for schizoaffective disorder. Of 17 siblings with schizoaffective disorder, 5 (29.4%) had a co-sibling with schizophrenia,

8 (47.1 per cent) had a co-sibling with affective disorder, and only 4 (23.5 per cent) had a co-sibling with schizoaffective disorder. Moreover, those schizoaffective siblings with affective disorder co-siblings were significantly older at onset than were the schizoaffective siblings with schizophrenic co-siblings. These findings are quite consistent with a fourth hypothesis, that some schizoaffective patients are genotypically schizophrenic while others are genotypes for affective disorder.

## EPIDEMIOLOGY

Most community surveys have not described rates of schizoaffective disorder. Given the many definitions in use and the low concordance across these definitions (Brockington and Leff, 1979), such rates would have been widely disparate. Only two community surveys have appeared using the same diagnostic system; Weissman and Myers (1978) found a 0.4 per cent lifetime prevalence for RDC schizoaffective disorder, whereas Vernon and Roberts (1982) found 0.8 per cent. These figures were based on only three and four cases, respectively, however, and none of these were ill when interviewed.

Brockington and Leff (1979) found ten patients who met at least three of eight definitions for schizoaffective disorder from approximately 222 consecutive admissions; six (2.7 per cent) met RDC criteria for schizoaf-

**TABLE 7–2.** Course of Illness Among Patients with Schizoaffective, Mood-Incongruent, or Atypical Psychoses: Comparisons to Probands with Affective Disorder or Schizophrenia

| | Affective Disorder | Schizoaffective or equivalent | Schizophrenia |
|---|---|---|---|
| *Schizoaffective disorder not divided by polarity* | | | |
| Angst et al., 1970 (author's def.) | | | |
| No. of patients | 172 | 72 | — |
| % reduction in no. of episodes with lithium | 66.3 | 40.0 | — |
| Tsuang et al., 1976 (author's def.) | | | |
| No. of patients | 325 | 85 | 200 |
| % recovered | 58 | 44 | 8 |
| Angst, 1980 (author's def.) | | | |
| No. of patients | 254 | 150 | — |
| % with "full remission" | 39 | 27 | — |
| Himmelhoch et al., 1981 (author's def.) | | | |
| No. of patients | 409 | 34 | — |
| "Improved within 2 months" | 39.7 | 5.9 | — |
| Rzewusha and Angst, 1982 (author's def.) | | | |
| No. of patients | 50 | 50 | 50 |
| % of intervals with affective residual symptoms | 26.0 | 13.4 | 2.8 |
| % of intervals with paranoid residual symptoms | 0 | 1.5 | 28.1 |
| | | | |
| *Schizoaffective mania vs. mania (vs. schizophrenia)* | | | |
| Brockington, Wainwright, and Kendell, 1980 (author's def.) | | | |
| No. of patients | 66 | 30 | 53 |
| % recovered | 94 | 77 | 34.0 |
| Abrams and Taylor, 1976 (RDC) | | | |
| No. of patients | 78 | 10 | — |
| Mean treatment response (4 = full remission) | 3.2 | 3.5 | — |
| Pope et al., 1980 (RDC) | | | |
| No. of patients | 18 | 35 | 27 |
| % with "marked improvement" after treatment | 79 | 73 | 7.3 |
| % with "excellent" globally assessed outcome | 44 | 26 | 0 |
| Rosenthal et al., 1980 (RDC) | | | |
| No. of patients | 28 | 25 | — |
| Probability of remaining well at 16 wk | 70 | 86 | — |
| van Praag and Nijo, 1984 (RDC) | | | |
| No. of patients | 21 | 10 | 19 |
| % with "good" treatment responses after 6 wk | 62 | 40 | 5 |
| Grossman et al., 1984 (RDC) | | | |
| No. of patients | 33 | 15 | 47 |
| % with "good" overall functioning | 33 | 13 | 9 |
| | | | |
| *Schizoaffective depression vs. depression (vs. schizophrenia)* | | | |
| Brockington, Kendell, and Wainwright, 1980 (author's def.) | | | |
| No. of patients | 66 | 75 | 53 |
| % recovered | 94.0 | 69.3 | 34.0 |
| Coryell et al., 1982 (DSM-III) | | | |
| No. of patients | 149 | 43 | 171 |
| % recovered during followup | 57.1 | 32.6 | 7.0 |
| Abrams et al., 1983 (DSM-III) | | | |
| No. of patients | 14 | 17 | 31 |
| % improvement at discharge | 80.7 | 92.7 | 34.5 |
| van Praag and Nijo, 1984 (RDC) | | | |
| No. of patients | 29 | 12 | 19 |
| % with "good" treatment response after 6 wk | 69.0 | 50.0 | 5.3 |
| Coryell et al., in press (RDC) | | | |
| No. of patients | 330 | 24 | — |
| % recovered during followup | 54.8 | 29.2 | — |
| Grossman et al., 1984 (RDC) | | | |
| No. of patients | 48 | 24 | 47 |
| % with "good" overall functioning | 38 | 8 | 9 |

fective disorder (one manic and five depressed). These figures are similar to those derived from consecutive admissions seen by me over a several-year period; of 388 patients, 11 (2.8 per cent) met RDC criteria for schizoaffective disorder (1983). In a more recent series of 56 consecutively admitted, nonmanic psychotics, 31 per cent had RDC schizoaffective disorder, depressed type (unpublished data). In the same series, only ten met RDC criteria for schizophrenia. Thus, while conditions meeting one or more definitions for schizoaffective disorder may be rare in the community, they constitute a meaningful proportion of conditions of psychotics admitted to psychiatric hospitals.

Some have used prevalence data to address an additional epidemiologic hypothesis—that schizoaffective disorder represents the chance coexistence of schizophrenia and affective disorder. According to Brockington and Leff (1979), this chance coexistence should occur only once in a year in Great Britain, yet they found ten in 1 year in only three hospitals.

## CLINICAL PICTURE

A description of the clinical picture seen in schizoaffective disorder is circular by necessity. Most definitions of schizoaffective disorder depend entirely on the clinical picture, and since these definitions vary so markedly (Brockington and Leff, 1979), the associated clinical picture will also vary markedly, depending on the label. By definition, then, patients with RDC schizoaffective disorder or DSM-III affective disorder with mood-incongruent psychotic features can exhibit in cross section any symptom characteristic of schizophrenia and any symptom characteristic of affective disorder. Such a patient may report low mood, anorexia, insomnia, fatigue, and thoughts of suicide, as well as thought broadcasting, delusions of passivity, and hallucinations in all spheres. He may exhibit euphoria, hyperactivity, recklessness, and grandiosity, as well as blunted affect, bizarre behavior, catatonia, and loose associations. Various researchers, with uneven results, have tried to correlate the relative preponderance of schizophrenic-type symptoms to family history and outcome.

Croughan, Welner, and Robins (1974) found that schizoaffective patients with two or more types of psychotic symptoms had a poorer outcome than those having only one type. According to Brockington, Kendell, and Wainwright (1980), passivity phenomena and hallucinations, in particular, predicted a more malignant course for "schizomanic" patients. On the other hand, neither Pope et al. (1980) nor Abrams and Taylor (1981) found any relationship between the number or type of first-rank symptoms in manics and outcome or family history.

Because these patients suffer from psychosis, an associated loss of insight, and, often, severe psychomotor disturbance, many are poor historians. This feature deserves special emphasis. At the time of admission, affective symptoms may be altogether overshadowed by the patient's delusional preoccupation, hallucinations, or bizarre behavior. Indeed, at this point such patients often deny affective symptoms that they later recall and that other informants describe when questioned carefully. The distinction between affective, schizoaffective, and schizophrenic psychosis, therefore, must not depend on the patient interview alone. In all cases the clinician must seek knowledgeable informants to learn whether affective symptoms preceded the psychotic ones. Serial interviews of the patient are also more useful than is generally appreciated (Dysken, Kooser, Havaszti, Davis, 1979).

## CLINICAL COURSE

The prognosis for schizoaffective disorder appears to be somewhat worse than that for affective disorder (Table 7–2), although this may be less true of manics than of depressives. In two of six studies, schizoaffective manics fared slightly better than typical manics, while only one of the six studies of schizoaffective depression found outcome in that group superior to that in depressives. Five studies failed to separate schizoaffective depression from schizoaffective mania, and none of these found a superior outcome in the schizoaffective group.

Because lithium is generally thought to be effective in mania and much less so in schizophrenia, acute and prophylactic response

**TABLE 7–3.  Outcome with Lithium Therapy in Patients with Schizoaffective (or Equivalent) Mania: Comparisons to Patients with Manic Disorder**

|  | Manic Disorder | Schizoaffective Mania |
|---|---|---|
| Schou et al., 1954 (author's def.) |  |  |
| No. of patients | 30 | 8 |
| % with "+ effect" acutely or prophylactically | 40.0 | 25.0 |
| Baastrup and Schou, 1967 (author's def.) |  |  |
| No. of patients | 51 | 15 |
| % reduction of no. of episodes with lithium | 95.2 | 71.3 |
| Zall et al., 1968 (author's def.) |  |  |
| No. of patients | 33 | 10 |
| % with "complete recovery" | 78.8 | 10.0 |
| Aranoff and Epstein, 1970 (author's def.) |  |  |
| No. of patients | 7 | 6 |
| % with "unequivocal" acute response | 71.4 | 33.3 |
| Johnson, 1970 (author's def.) |  |  |
| No. of patients | 19 | 11 |
| % in "remission" | 79.0 | 9.1 |
| Prien et al., 1974 (author's def.) |  |  |
| No. of patients | 86 | 5 |
| % without episodes during 1 yr of prophylaxis | 60.5 | 40.0 |
| Pope et al., 1980 (RDC) |  |  |
| No. of patients | 13 | 20 |
| % with "marked" improvement | 92.3 | 80.0 |
| Rosenthal et al., 1980 (RDC) |  |  |
| No. of patients | 27 | 15 |
| Probability of remaining well after 16 wk | 0.70 | 0.86 |

to this drug affords another view of schizoaffective mania. With one exception, lithium studies describing five or more schizoaffective patients report poorer responses in that group than in more typically manic groups (Table 7–3).

Patients with schizoaffective depression might also be compared with more typical depression in terms of tricyclic antidepressant response. Such a comparison would probably be uninformative, however, since the presence of psychosis per se appears associated with a poor response to these agents (Glassman, Kantor, Shostak, 1975). On the other hand, electroconvulsive therapy (ECT) is quite effective in psychotic depression (Coryell and Zimmerman, 1984). Unfortunately, few studies compare ECT response in schizoaffectives to that in typical depressives.

As noted earlier, the diagnosis of schizoaffective disorder may be more important in nonmanic cases. Although other subdivisions of schizoaffective disorder may also be important, they have received little study. Specifically, schizoaffective patients so defined because of the persistence of schizophrenia-like symptoms between affective episodes may constitute a different group from those defined solely by the presence of first-rank symptoms in the midst of an affective syndrome. Indeed, the studies finding the largest outcome differences between affective disorder and schizoaffective disorder were those that defined the latter disorder by the persistence of schizophrenia-like symptoms between affective episodes (Angst, Weis, Grof, Baastrup, Schou, 1970; Himmelhoch, Fuchs, May, Symons, Neil, 1981; Johnson, 1970; Zall and Therman, 1968). In contrast, one of the few studies finding a superior outcome for schizoaffective disorder explicitly excluded subjects with psychotic symptoms persisting between episodes (Rosenthal, Rosenthal, Stallone, Dunner, Fieve, 1980). Moreover, 12 of the 75 schizodepressives followed by Brockington, Kendell, and Wainwright (1980) had had a history at intake of "schizophrenic symptoms in the absence of affective symptoms"; they were twice as likely as the remaining schizodepressives to have a followup diagnosis of schizophrenia (66.7 per cent vs. 34.9 per cent).

Such comparisons serve only to summarize the literature; their simplicity can be misleading, since there are many shades of "improved" and "recovered." In light of the most tenable hypothesis on etiology, some schizoaffective patients should have a course typical of psychotic affective disorder; the psychosis may be profound, but the eventual recovery is complete. Others may display a waxing and waning of symptoms, which might be perceived initially as recovery and relapse but which eventually evolve into the chronicity and avolition characteristic of narrowly defined schizophrenia.

Patients, as well as families and physicians, need to know which course to expect. Unfortunately, most work to date has been limited to determining the prognostic position of schizoaffectives as a group compared with reference groups with affective disorder or schizophrenia. As noted earlier, there have been only scattered attempts to subdivide schizoaffective patients in terms of outcome.

With the scarcity of data bearing directly on this problem, it is reasonable to deduce some guidelines. Demographic features more characteristic of schizophrenia than of affective disorder are probably also more characteristic of schizoaffective patients with relatively poor prognoses. Among these features are an early (before age 30) and insidious onset, a family history negative for clear affective disorder or positive for clear schizophrenia, a chronic unremitting course, and prodromal traits such as social isolation, peculiar behavior, and longstanding role impairment. The converse of these features should indicate a relatively good prognosis.

## LABORATORY FINDINGS

As yet there are no generally accepted roles for laboratory tests in the clinical distinction between schizophrenia and depression, and the laboratory, therefore, has little to offer in subdividing schizoaffective disorders. Some tests may eventually prove useful in this way, however; among these are the thyroid-releasing hormone stimulation test (Kirkegaard, Bjorum, Cohn, Lauvidsen, 1978) and the dexamethasone suppression test (DST) (Carroll et al., 1981). So far, the latter test shows the most promise as a diagnostic aid. As used in psychiatry, it is a modification of a test long used to screen for Cushing's disease; 1 mg of dexamethasone is given at 11 P.M., and blood

samples for cortisol assay are drawn the next day at 8 A.M., 4 P.M., and 11 P.M. Post-dexamethasone cortisol values over 4 or 5 μg/dl generally indicate an abnormal resistance of the hypothalamic-pituitary-adrenal axis to suppression by exogenous steroid (nonsuppression). By 1984, researchers had published 13 English-language studies in which DST results in patients with depression were compared with those of at least five schizophrenics (Coryell, 1984). Together, these studies described 233 schizophrenics and 658 depressives. The mean and medium rates of false positive tests in schizophrenics were 13.3 per cent and 11.1 per cent, respectively. Five of these studies showed 100 per cent specificity—none of the schizophrenics in those studies were nonsuppressors. In contrast, the mean and median rates of nonsuppression among comparison patients with depression were 52.4 per cent and 48.0 per cent, respectively, and in no case did the depressives have nonsuppression rates less than 44 per cent. These data are encouraging and indicate a potential role for the DST in the differential diagnosis of ambiguous psychoses such as schizoaffective disorder. Three studies, however, had rather high false positive rates (Coppen et al., 1983; Meltzer, Fang, Tricou, Robertson, Piyaka, 1982; Banki and Arato, 1983)—22 per cent, 40 per cent, and 50 per cent, respectively. If these represented prevailing rates, the DST would be of little use clinically. Because reasons for these aberrant rates are presently obscure, the diagnostic use of DST results in psychotic states must remain tentative.

## DIFFERENTIAL DIAGNOSIS

As with other conditions seen by psychiatrists, the differential diagnosis when affective and psychotic symptoms coexist should begin with the distinction between conditions that arise from demonstrable lesions (organic illness) and those that do not (functional illness). Depressive, manic, and schizophrenic syndromes can be produced by a variety of identifiable insults, and the differential for each of these conditions is provided in more detail in the corresponding chapters. With those other possibilities in mind, there are several general features that should increase the suspicion that psychiatric symptoms are arising from an organic condition. Moderate to severe "depressions" with only two or three of the possible eight criteria symptoms (American Psychiatric Association, 1980) should raise such suspicions, as should the appearance of affective or psychotic symptoms in an elderly individual with no prior psychiatric history. Confusion that is out of proportion to the depressive symptoms and that features approximate answers rather than refusal or reluctance to answer also increases the possibility of medical illness as etiology. Likewise, "catatonia" in an individual with no recent or remote history of affective disorder or schizophrenia should be considered undiagnosed until a full syndrome can be identified.

Several conditions are of particular note in the differential of schizoaffective syndromes. High doses of exogenous steroids may produce conditions in which symptoms of affective disorder, schizophrenia, and delirium alternate rapidly. Liability to this condition is dose related, and symptoms typically resolve within 3 weeks, rarely lasting longer than 6 (Lewis and Smith, 1983). The crucial feature here is the history of high doses of steroids preceding the onset of the symptoms. Because this history is almost always apparent, diagnosis is usually not a problem. Patients with persistent symptoms, particularly those with a prior history of similar symptoms not preceded by steroid ingestion, may, however, have a purely functional condition (Lewis and Smith, 1983).

Amphetamines and other sympathomimetics may produce hyperactivity, euphoria, racing thoughts, and pressured speech typical of mania shortly after ingestion. A "crash" may occur after several days of continuous amphetamine ingestion and often features dysphoria, hyperphasia, hypersomnia, and extreme irritability—a picture that may resemble depression. These conditions rarely, of themselves, lead individuals to seek psychiatric help. Between these two phases of amphetamine intoxication, however, a psychosis may emerge that is indistinguishable from paranoid schizophrenia in cross section. Delusions typically resolve within several days to 1 or 2 weeks, and simple observation for this period usually clarifies the diagnosis. There is little evidence that individuals who develop

this condition have any particular predilection to schizophrenia. Several studies, in fact, have induced this condition in volunteers with no history of schizophrenia or schizoid features (Griffith, Cavanaugh, Held, Oates, 1970; Angrist, Shopsin, Gershon, 1972).

Phencyclidine (PCP) intoxication may be more difficult to recognize. The diagnosis is frequently missed, even by those who are familiar with its presentation (Yago et al., 1981). This may be due in part to the protean nature of the symptoms; paranoid delusions in a clear sensorium may alternate with marked depressive symptoms, or these syndromes may coexist with or without evidence of delirium. In one Los Angeles emergency room, 78.5 per cent of involuntary psychiatric admissions had detectable PCP in the admission blood sample. In only 21 per cent of these cases was there an initial diagnosis of PCP psychosis; a diagnosis of schizophrenia was given to more than a third of these cases and primary affective disorder to another third (Yago et al., 1981). Drug screening available to most clinicians is probably inadequate for the detection of clinically significant PCP levels (Analine, Allen, Pitts, Yago, Pitts, 1980), since the drug is highly lipophilic and is secreted in only minute quantities over an extended period. However, this condition often involves certain physical symptoms that may help to distinguish it from functional psychosis— slurred speech, ataxia and nystagmus, ptosis, hypertension, analgesia, and hyperreflexia. The level of suspicion should also depend in large part on the patient's demographic features and the pattern of drug use in his subculture.

Temporal lobe epilepsy may also produce affective psychosis, schizophrenia-like psychosis, or a mixture of the two (Flor-Henry, 1969), and the syndromes can closely resemble their functional counterparts (Slater and Beard, 1963). History is crucial, therefore, in the differential diagnosis. In both of the two largest series describing temporal lobe epilepsy and psychosis, a mean delay of 14 years existed between the onset of clinically manifest epilepsy and psychosis (Flor-Henry, 1969; Slater and Beard, 1963). In only 3 of the 69 cases described by Slater and Beard (1963) did the psychosis and epilepsy begin in the same year; in all other cases the psychosis followed the epilepsy, usually by many years. Thus the likelihood that epilepsy lies at the base of a new case of psychosis is greatly reduced when there is no history of clinically manifest seizures.

## TREATMENT

Clinicians should consider the hypotheses described previously when selecting treatment. The most efficient approach, the one most consistent with followup and family history data, assumes that schizoaffective patients have either schizophrenia or affective disorder. The clinician must weigh the probability of one of these illnesses over the other using all available data—demographics, both present and past psychopathology, premorbid or prodromal features, and family history.

Greater weight should be given to the affective disorder alternative, particularly in treatment-naive patients, since treatment of affective disorder is generally more specific than treatment of schizophrenia. For instance, ECT is much more effective for psychotic depression than for schizophrenia, and the prophylactic value of lithium in affective disorder is clearly established, while there is relatively little support for its use in schizophrenia. In contrast, neuroleptics ameliorate psychotic symptoms regardless of the underlying disorder. Because of the risk of tardive dyskinesia with chronic neuroleptic treatment, other, potentially more specific approaches—lithium, tricyclic antidepressants, monoamine oxidase inhibitors, and ECT—should be given preference unless indications for chronic neuroleptic treatment are clear.

Nevertheless, acute treatment usually requires antipsychotics unless ECT is given. In the absence of clear indications for long-term use of neuroleptics, these drugs should be gradually discontinued when delusions remit. The clinicians should then determine whether lithium or a tricyclic antidepressant will provide adequate protection against relapse. This will require careful surveillance, particularly in the first 6 months, when the risk of relapse is the highest (Keller, Shapiro, Lavori, Wolfe, 1982). Because relapse is likely to involve a loss of insight, the family's help will be important in this effort. After one or more episodes they will learn the early warning signs and help the patient to seek early intervention.

More judgments are necessary when relapse does occur. Was the relapse preceded by poor compliance? If so, does the patient find the side effects peculiar to that drug intolerable, or does he or she simply require more time to develop the acceptance and habits necessary for adequate compliance? Because the options for effective prophylaxis are limited, it is important not to abandon a given drug prematurely. Also, it must be remembered that prophylactic efficacy may require time to develop. In fact, maintenance therapy may take several years to show clear effects for depression or hypomania (Dunner, Stallone, Fieve, 1982).

If, with these cautions in mind, tricyclic antidepressants and lithium appear ineffective, carbamazepine might be considered before chronic neuroleptics. Several controlled trials have found this agent effective in patients with affective disorders resistant to more conventional treatment (Ballenger and Post, 1980; Okuma et al., 1979, 1981).

## SCHIZOPHRENIFORM DISORDER

Langfeldt coined the word schizophreniform in 1939 (Langfeldt, 1939) to describe schizophrenia-like psychoses with relatively good prognoses. He intended this to be a heterogeneous group that would include "exogenically precipitated psychosis," as well as cases, "belonging to the manic depressive group of psychosis" (Langfeldt, 1982). Indeed, the words schizophreniform and schizoaffective have been used interchangeably through much of the subsequent literature. The definition found in DSM-III is original, however; it separates schizophreniform disorder from schizophrenia solely on the basis of a duration of less than 6 months, including the prodromal phase. DSM-III thus sets schizophreniform disorder apart both from affective disorder with mood-incongruent psychotic features and from schizoaffective disorder. This departure from convention must be borne in mind in any review of recent literature on atypical schizophrenia. The preceding section under schizoaffective disorder describes schizophreniform disorder equally well, according to common usage before DSM-III. This section is therefore restricted to studies using the DSM-III definition.

Table 7–4 summarizes all such studies as of 1984 (Coryell and Tsuang, 1982; Fogelson,

**TABLE 7–4.    DSM-III Schizophreniform Disorder: Studies of Validity***

| Study | No. with SF | Comparison Groups | Design | Results |
|---|---|---|---|---|
| Helzer et al., 1981 | 7 (of 134 admissions with psychosis: 5.2%) | 19 with schizophrenia | Systematic followup averaging 6.5 yr | SF patients had significantly better "combined social status score" and "outcome regression score," less percentage of time in hospital; more manic symptoms |
| Coryell and Tsuang, 1982 | 93 (of 810 admissions studied: 11.5%) | 86 bipolar AD, 203 unipolar AD, 214 schizophrenia | Chart followup averaging 3.1 yr; family history study | 16% of SF patients recovered vs 8% of S patients and 58% of AD patients; SF resembled S patients more than AD patients in terms of MR for S and AD |
| Fogelson et al., 1982 | 6 (of 50 consecutive admissions: 12%) | None | Individual case reports | Outcome, response to treatment, family and DST results (5/6 abnormal) lead to conclusion that SF is atypical AD |
| Weinberger et al., 1982 | 35 (of 128 c̄ CT scans: 27.3%) | 17 schizophrenia, 23 affective disorder, 27 other disorders, 26 neurologic controls | Computerized tomography study (CTs routinely obtained) | SF group had distribution of ventricular to brain ratio indistinguishable from those for S group, significantly less than controls, less (but not significantly) than other psychiatric illnesses |
| Targum, 1983 | 21 (of 145 admissions: 14.5%) | 76 unipolar AD, 10 bipolar AD, 24 other disorders, 14 schizophrenia | Neuroendocrine evaluation (DST and TRH-ST) c̄ 6 mo followup of only SF patients | % with: |

|  | +DST+ | Blunted TRH-ST+ |
|---|---|---|
| AD | 44 | 32 |
| SF | 24 | 29 |
| S | 7 | 7 |

Neuroendocrine test results predicted outcome among SF patients

* AD, affective disorder; SF, schizophreniform disorder; S, schizophrenia; DST, dexamethazone suppression test; TRH-ST, thyroid-releasing hormone stimulation test.

† With certain exceptions, a positive DST and a blunted TRH-ST may be specific to major depression.

Cohen, Pope, 1982; Helzer, Brockington, Kendell, 1981; Targum, 1983, Weinberger, DeLisi, Perman, Targum, Wyatt, 1982). Two things are immediately apparent. First, few studies have been done; second, the results of those that have been done lead to no consensus. According to three, schizophreniform disorder defines an intermediate or heterogeneous group (Coryell and Tsuang, 1982; Helzer et al., 1981; Targum, 1983). One found no difference between schizophrenia and schizophreniform disorder (Weinberger et al., 1982), while still another concluded that schizophreniform disorder simply represented "atypical affective disorder" (Fogelson et al., 1982).

Consensus may not be forthcoming for several reasons. First, the distinction between schizophrenia and schizophreniform disorder often hinges on the presence of a prodromal syndrome, and many of the components of this syndrome (i.e., social isolation, blunted affect, and digressive speech) shade gradually into the normal spectrum of behavior. Many acutely psychotic patients are unable to give valid accounts of such features in retrospect. Affective syndromes are also difficult to assess in patients who are delusional or hallucinating. Even when such patients report typical depressive symptoms, these are often attributed to understandable effects of acute psychosis. A careful history taken from knowledgeable informants will remedy these problems to some extent. Unfortunately, few studies describe the availability of such informants or the thoroughness with which they were interviewed. Reasons for discordance across these studies are, therefore, hard to trace.

In light of this, the clinician must maintain doubtfulness about the true nature of schizophreniform disorder in a given case. As with schizoaffective disorder, he should use all the clinical data available to weigh the likelihood of schizophrenia over an affective disorder, giving at least initial weight to the presumption that the overall course and treatment response will ultimately suggest affective disorder.

## REFERENCES

Abrams R, Taylor MA: Importance of schizophrenic symptoms in the diagnosis of mania. Am J Psychiatry 138:658–661, 1981.

American Psychiatric Association: Diagnostic and Statistical Manual of Mental Disorders, ed. 2. Washington, DC, American Psychiatric Association, 1968.

American Psychiatric Association, Committee on Nomenclature and Statistics: Diagnostic and Statistical Manual of Mental Disorders, ed. 3. Washington, DC, American Psychiatric Association, 1980.

Analine O, Allen RE, Pitts FN, Yago LS, Pitts AF: The urban epidemic of phencyclidine use: Laboratory evidence from a public psychiatric hospital in-patient service. Biol Psychiatry 15:813–816, 1980.

Andreasen NC, Grove WM, Shapiro RW, Keller MB, Hirschfeld RMA, McDonald-Scott P: Reliability of life-time diagnosis. Arch Gen Psychiatry 38:400–405, 1981.

Angrist B, Shopsin B, Gershon S: Metabolites of monoamines in urine and cerebrospinal fluid, after large dose amphetamine administration. Psychopharmacologia 26:1–9, 1972.

Angst J, Weis P, Grof P, Baastrup PC, Schou M: Lithium prophylaxis in recurrent affective disorder. Br J Psychiatry 116:604–614, 1970.

Ballenger JC, Post RM: Carbamazepine in manic-depressive illness: A new treatment. Am J Psychiatry 137:782–790, 1980.

Banki CM, Arato M: Amine metabolites in neuroendocrine responses related to depression and suicide. J Affective Disord 5:223–232, 1983.

Brockington IF, Kendell RE, Wainwright S: Depressed patients with schizophrenic or paranoid symptoms. Psychol Med 10:665–675, 1980.

Brockington IF, Leff JP: Schizo-affective psychosis: Definitions and incidence. Psychol Med 9:91–99, 1979.

Brockington IF, Wainwright S, Kendell RE: Manic patients with schizophrenic or paranoid symptoms. Psychol Med 10:73–83, 1980.

Carroll BJ, Feinberg M, Greden JF, Tarika J, Albala AA, Haskett RF, James NM, Kronfol Z, Lohr N, Steiner M, de Vigne JP, Young E: A specific laboratory test for the diagnosis of melancholia. Arch Gen Psychiatry 38:15–22, 1981.

Clayton PJ: Schizo-affective disorders. J Nerv Ment Dis 170:646–650, 1982.

Clayton P: A further look at secondary depression, in Clayton P, Barrett JE (eds): Treatment of Depression: Old Controversies and New Approaches. New York, Raven Press, 1983.

Clayton PJ, Rodin L, Winokur G: Family history studies. III. Schizo-affective disorder, clinical and genetic factors including a one to two year follow-up. Comp Psychiatry 9:31, 1968.

Cohen SM, Allen M, Pollin W, Hrubec Z: Relationship of schizo-affective psychosis to manic depressive psychosis and schizophrenia. Arch Gen Psychiatry 26:539–546, 1972.

Coppen A, Abou-saleh M, Milln P, Metcalfe M, Harwood J, Bailey J: Dexamethasone suppression test in depression and other psychiatric illness. Br J Psychiatry 142:498–504, 1983.

Coryell W: The use of laboratory tests in psychiatric diagnosis: The DST as an example. Psychiatr Develop 3:139–159, 1984.

Coryell WH, Tsuang MT: DSM-III schizophreniform disorder: Comparisons with schizophrenia and affective disorder. Arch Gen Psychiatry 39:66–69, 1982.

Coryell W, Zimmerman M: Outcome following ECT in primary unipolar depression: A test of newly proposed response predictors. Am J Psychiatry 141:862–867, 1984.

Croughan JL, Welner A, Robins E: The group of schizoaffective and related psychoses. II. Record studies. Arch Gen Psychiatry 31:632–637, 1974.

Dunner DL, Stallone F, Fieve RR: Prophylaxis with lithium carbonate: An update. Arch Gen Psychiatry 39:1344–1345, 1982.

Dysken MW, Kooser JA, Havaszti JJ, Davis JM: Clinical usefulness of sodium amobarbital interviewing. Arch Gen Psychiatry 36:789–794, 1979.

Flor-Henry P: Psychosis and temporal lobe epilepsy. Epilepsia 10:363–395, 1969.

Fogelson DL, Cohen BM, Pope HG: A study of DSM-III schizophreniform disorder. Am J Psychiatry 139:1281–1285, 1982.

Glassman AH, Kantor SJ, Shostak M: Depression, delusions and drug response. Am J Psychiatry 132:716–718, 1975.

Griffith JD, Cavanaugh T, Held J, Oates JA: Experimental psychosis induced by the administration of *d*-amphetamine, in Costa E, Gavattini S (eds): Amphetamine and Related Compounds. New York, Raven Press, 1970.

Helzer JE, Brockington IF, Kendell RE: The predictive validity of DSM-III and Feighner definitions of schizophrenia: A comparison with RDC and CATEGO. Arch Gen Psychiatry 38:791–797, 1981.

Himmelhoch JM, Fuchs CZ, May SJ, Symons BJ, Neil KS: When a schizoaffective diagnosis has meaning. J Nerv Ment Dis 169:277–282, 1981.

Johnson G: Differential response to lithium carbonate in manic-depressive and schizoaffective disorders. Dis Nerv Sys 9:613–615, 1970.

Keller MB, Shapiro RW, Lavori TW, Wolfe N: Relapse and major depressive disorder. Arch Gen Psychiatry 39:911–915, 1982.

Kirkegaard C, Bjorum N, Cohn D, Lauvidsen UG: Thyrotrophin-releasing hormone (TRH) stimulation test in manic depressive illness. Arch Gen Psychiatry 35:1017–1021, 1978.

Langfeldt G: The schizophreniform states. London, Oxford University Press, 1939.

Langfeldt G: Definition of "schizophreniform psychoses." Am J Psychiatry 139:703, 1982 (letter).

Lewis DA, Smith RE: Steroid-induced psychiatric syndromes. J Affective Disord 5:319–332, 1983.

Meltzer HY, Fang BS, Tricou BJ, Robertson A, Piyaka SK: Effect of dexamethasone on plasma prolactin and cortisol levels in psychiatric patients. Am J Psychiatry 139:763–768, 1982.

Okuma T, Inanaga K, Otsuki S, Sarai K, Takahashi R, Hazama H, Mori A, Watanabe S: Comparison of the antimanic efficacy of carbamazepine and chlorpromazine: A double blind control study. Psychopharmacology 66:211–217, 1979.

Okuma T, Inanaga K, Otsuki S, Sarai K, Takahashi R, Hazama H, Mori A, Watanabe S: A preliminary double blind study on the efficacy of carbamazepine in prophylaxis of manic depressive illness. Psychopharmacology 73:95–96, 1981.

Orvaschel H, Thompson WD, Belanger A, Prusoff BA, Kidd KK: Comparison of the family history method of direct interview. J Affective Disord 4:49–59, 1982.

Pope HG, Lipinski JF, Cohen BM, Axelrod DT: "Schizoaffective disorder": An invalid diagnosis? A comparison of schizo-affective disorder, schizophrenia and affective disorder. Am J Psychiatry 137:921–927, 1980.

Rosenthal NE, Rosenthal LN, Stallone F, Dunner DL, Fieve RR: The validation of RDC schizoaffective disorder. Arch Gen Psychiatry 37:804–810, 1980.

Rosenthal NE, Rosenthal LN, Stallone F, Fleiss J, Dunner DL, Fieve RR: Psychosis as a predictor response to lithium maintenance treatment in bipolar affective disorder. J Affective Disord 1:237–245, 1979.

Slater E, Beard AW: The schizophrenia-like psychoses of epilepsy: Psychiatric aspects. Br J Psychiatry 109:95–150, 1963.

Spitzer RL, Endicott J, Robins E: Research diagnostic criteria: Rationale and reliability. Arch Gen Psychiatry 35:773–786, 1978.

Targum SD: Neuroendocrine dysfunction in schizophreniform disorder: Correlation with 6 month clinical outcome. Am J Psychiatry 140:309–313, 1983.

Taylor MA: Schneiderian first-rank symptoms and clinical prognostic features in schizophrenia. Arch Gen Psychiatry 26:64–67, 1972.

Tsuang MT: Genetics of affective disorder, in Mendels J (ed): The Psychobiology of Depression. New York, Spectrum Publications, 1975, pp 85–100.

Vernon SW, Roberts RE: Use of the SADS-RDC in a tri-ethnic community survey. Arch Gen Psychiatry 39:47–52, 1982.

Weinberger DR, DeLisi LE, Perman GP, Targum S, Wyatt RJ: Computed tomography and schizophreniform disorder and other acute psychiatric disorders. Arch Gen Psychiatry 39:778–783, 1982.

Weissman MM, Myers J: The affective disorders in a U.S. urban community. Arch Gen Psychiatry 35:1304–1311, 1978.

Yago KB, Pitts FM, Burgoyne RW, Aniline O, Yago S, Pitts AS: The urban epidemic of phencyclidine (PCP) use: Clinical and laboratory evidence from the Public Hospital Emergency Service. J Clin Psychiatry 42:193–196, 1981.

Zall H, Therman PG: Lithium carbonate: A clinical study. Am J Psychiatry 125:549–555, 1968.

# chapter 8

# OBSESSIVE-COMPULSIVE NEUROSIS

*by* Thomas B. Mackenzie, M.D.

## DEFINITION

Obsessive-compulsive neurosis is a chronic mental disorder dominated by obsessions and compulsions that does not result from an affective disorder and is not a precursor of schizophrenia.

An obsession is a recurrent, intrusive mental experience recognized by the subject as originating in his mind and as being unreasonable or improbable. It may take the form of a thought, a fear, a doubt, an image, an impulse, or a feeling. The experience is distressing, and attempts to change the content or form of the mental experience, if taken, are not successful.

A compulsion, also called an obsessional ritual, is a behavior such as counting, checking, or avoiding that is recurrent, stereotypic, purposeful in appearance and recognized by the patient as originating from within himself. Great importance may be assigned to conducting the ritual in a fixed manner, and any interruption or deviation may force repetition of the entire sequence. Completion of the behavior is variably accompanied by a reduction in anxiety.

Synonyms for the obsessive-compulsive neurosis are obsessive-compulsive disorder, obsessional states, and anancastic states, disorders, or conditions. The *Diagnostic and Statistical Manual of Mental Disorders*, third edition (DSM-III), classifies obsessive-compulsive neurosis among the anxiety disorders. Contrary to the practice of some authorities (Kringlen, 1970), this chapter treats obsessive-compulsive neurosis and phobic disorders as separate conditions.

## ETIOLOGY

There is no satisfactory etiologic explanation for the occurrence of obsessive-compulsive neurosis. Family and twin studies point to familial transmission (Insel, Hoover, Murphy, 1983b; McGuffin and Mawson, 1980). However, as Insel et al. (1983b) have noted, the rarity of the disorder has precluded adoption or reared-apart twin studies to determine the relative contributions of genetic vs. environmental factors.

A biologic etiology is suggested by several lines of evidence. Flor-Henry, Yendall, Koles, and Howarth (1979) reported that obsessive-compulsive neurotics demonstrated neuropsychological and electroencephalographic (EEG) disturbances indicative of left frontal lobe dysfunction. Further support for a cerebral abnormality derives from the observed association between obsessional behavior and neurologic illness (Grimshaw,

1964) and from the more frequent history of abnormal birth events in obsessional patients than in psychiatric controls (Capstick and Seldrup, 1977). However, efforts to detect systematic neuropsychological or neuroanatomical abnormalities in patients with the disorder have failed (Insel, Donnelly, Lalakea, Alterman, Murphy, 1983a; Rapoport et al., 1981). Thus, while a specific biologic deficit may account for a fraction of obsessive-compulsive neurosis, at the present time this explanation has limited application.

Psychological theories of obsessive-compulsive neurosis postulate the existence of pathologic anxiety as a result of either conflicts involving expression-inhibition of drive states or linkage with stimuli that unconditionally generate anxiety. Both views explain the performance of rituals in terms of their capacity to reduce anxiety. Beech and Liddell (1974) have contested this reasoning, pointing out that as many as 40 per cent of rituals do not reduce anxiety, that obsessionals can suspend rituals under certain circumstances, and that therapeutic prevention of rituals does not inevitably cause uncontrolled anxiety.

Beech and Perigault (1974) have proposed that obsessive-compulsive neurosis is initiated by an abnormality in arousal whereby emotional states have enhanced intensity and duration. They hypothesize that obsessions are generated as a means of explaining or communicating a disturbance in arousal. This theory, the authors contend, is consistent with the accounts offered by some patients of increasing emotional instability before the appearance of obsessive-compulsive behavior. It also questions the symbolic importance often assigned to obsessive-compulsive phenomena by psychological theorists. Efforts by Beech, Ciesielski, and Gordon (1983), using visual evoked potentials to demonstrate central nervous system dysfunction indicative of a disturbance in arousal, have offered only partial support for this hypothesis.

## EPIDEMIOLOGY

Obsessive-compulsive neurosis is an uncommon disorder. Woodruff and Pitts

(1964) estimate the prevalence in the general population to be 0.05 per cent. Based on his analysis of the literature, Black (1974) cited an incidence of 0.3 per cent to 2.9 per cent of psychiatric outpatients and 0.1 per cent to 4.0 per cent of inpatients. A tabulation of 11 studies by the same author showed the ratio of men to women to be 49:51.

Study of the occurrence of mental illness in the relatives of obsessional neurotics has been confounded by a lack of control populations and the absence of agreed operational definitions. Thus Brown (1942) reported a 7 per cent prevalence of obsessional neurosis in the first-degree relatives of patients with that diagnosis. The incidence of obsessional neurosis was less than 0.5 per cent in relatives of anxiety and hysterical neurotics (Brown, 1942). Rosenberg (1967), however, found only two persons who had been treated for obsessional neurosis among 547 first-degree relatives of his obsessive neurotics. Likewise, Insel et al. (1983b) failed to find any cases of obsessive-compulsive neurosis among the parents of 27 patients with the disorder.

Rosenberg (1967) reported that 9.3 per cent of first-degree relatives had received psychiatric treatment. Coryell (1981) noted that at least 40 per cent of obsessive-compulsive neurotics had a history of psychiatric illness in first-degree relatives.

## PATHOLOGY

The defining feature of obsessive-compulsive neurosis is the presence of obsessions. Obsessions generally involve themes of dirt contamination (excreta, germs, semen, blood, illness), aggression (physical or verbal assault, accidents, calamities, wars), inanimate-impersonal (locks, leaking substances, mathematical figures and their totals), sex (sexual advances, incestuous impulses, competence), or religion (the existence of God, violation of religious canons, blasphemous thoughts), in decreasing order of frequency (Akhtar, Wig, Varma, Dwarka, Verma, 1975). They are often accompanied by a dysphoric mood (Goodwin et al., 1969). At least half of the patients have more than one obsession (Akhtar et al., 1975) and the content of these changes over time (Goodwin, Guze, Robins, 1969). Women are more likely to show fears of contamination than are men (Dowson, 1977), and persons of low intelligence tend to have less structured and less abstract ideation (Ingram, 1961).

Three quarters of obsessive-compulsive neurotics experience compulsions (Akhtar et al., 1975). These involve cleaning (51 per cent), avoiding (51 per cent), repeating (40 per cent), checking (38 per cent), completeness (11 per cent), and meticulousness (9 per cent) (Stern and Cobb, 1978). The latter authors found that 40 per cent of patients had little resistance to carrying out the ritual, but that 80 per cent felt that the ritual was silly or absurd. Stern and Cobb (1978) reported that reassurance from others had no effect on the ritual in 50 per cent of patients and that 88 per cent of rituals occurred in more than one place. Only 8 of 45 patients had a single type of ritual.

Compulsions may be classified according to whether they involve controlling an obsession or yielding to it. A worse prognosis has been linked to those with yielding compulsions (Akhtar et al., 1975). They may also be classified into rituals that resemble everyday activities or involve bizarre/magical components. According to Capstick and Seldrup (1977), patients with the latter more frequently give a history of abnormal birth, raising the possibility of an association between bizarre content and cerebral damage.

Obsessive-compulsive neurotics appear to have a higher than average intelligence. Whether this reflects their intrinsic endowment, or the overrepresentation of upper- and middle-class patients among obsessional neurotics is not clear (Black, 1974).

Premorbid obsessional traits, such as indecisiveness, orderliness, rigidity, punctuality, scrupulosity, and conscientiousness, are by no means ubiquitous among obsessive-compulsive neurotics, being absent in 16 per cent to 36 per cent of cases (Black, 1974). Moreover, the same traits can be retrospectively identified in 53 per cent of non-obsessional psychiatric patients (Kringlen, 1965).

Obsessional patients are consistently reported to have an unusually high celibacy rate, ranging from 40 per cent to 50 per cent (Black, 1974). Men show a higher rate of celibacy than do women (Ingram, 1961). Further, Kringlen (1965) observed that among those who married, the relationship was bad or extremely bad in 25 of 90 cases.

## CLINICAL PICTURE

The average age of onset for obsessive-compulsive neurosis in men and women is in the early 20s (Black, 1974). Three quarters of patients have symptoms by age 30 (Black, 1974). The disorder commonly has a childhood onset, and Kringlen (1965) noted that half of his adult patients had become ill before age 20 and one fifth of them, before puberty. Although the symptoms and clinical picture of the childhood disorder are virtually identical to those of adult patients (Rapoport et al., 1981), it has been suggested that in children, the onset is more likely to be sudden (Elkins, Rapoport, Lipsky, 1980).

Ingram (1961) noted a significant precipitating factor in 70 per cent of his obsessional patients, as opposed to 50 per cent of his anxiety neurotics. He found that the most common precipitants in women were pregnancy and childbirth. In each case similar symptoms were noted: fears of harming the child with consequent washing and avoidance rituals. Black (1974) cited sexual experiences, marital difficulties, and bereavement as additional precipitants in both sexes.

According to Pollitt (1975), the most common initial symptoms are fears and rituals. The same author described the intrusion of the first symptom as sudden and dramatic (Pollitt, 1975). Kringlen (1970) described an acute onset in 65 per cent of women and 40 per cent of men. Symptoms are frequently disguised by the patient to avoid ridicule. The disguise can be maintained for long periods if the behavior involves an activity such as checking or avoidance. Cleaning, however, is usually readily evident, especially in family settings, where the bathroom may be occupied for hours at a time (Stern and Cobb, 1978).

The interval between onset of symptoms and psychiatric treatment is typically lengthy; the average duration between onset and consultation being 7.5 years (Pollitt, 1975). If hospitalization is necessary, it tends to take place in the mid-30s (Kringlen, 1965) and is often related to the emergence of depression (Marks, Stern, Mawson, Cobb, McDonald, 1980).

## CLINICAL COURSE

Black (1974) reviewed outcome studies completed before the development of effective behavioral and pharmacologic therapies. Among outpatients, 114 of 190 (60 per cent) followed up for 1 to 14 years were asymptomatic, much improved, or improved. Forty per cent showed slight or no improvement or were worse. Patients who had been hospitalized showed a slightly worse symptomatic outcome; 142 of 309 (46 per cent), when followed for 1 to 20 years, were asymptomatic, much improved, or improved.

Pollitt (1957) reported that among his cohort of inpatients and outpatients, 50 per cent had showed a phasic course, with episodes lasting for approximately 1 year. He noted that most of this group had three or fewer attacks. In contrast, Ingram (1961) reported that at followup, only 13 per cent of his inpatients had a phasic course marked by periods of recovery.

Grimshaw (1965) has pointed out that there may be a dissociation of symptomatic outcome and social and occupational adjustment. Thirteen per cent of his socially recovered outpatients remained unchanged or were worse as far as symptoms. He concluded that many patients maintained social adaptation in face of severe symptoms (Grimshaw, 1965).

According to Ingram (1961), factors associated with a negative prognosis include childhood symptoms, compulsions, and a lengthy interval between onset and treatment. An episodic course, mild or atypical symptoms, and precipitating factors are favorable prognostic signs (Black, 1974; Goodwin et al., 1969). Evidence on the contribution of personality to outcome is mixed. On the one hand, Kringlen (1965) concludes that obsessive premorbid personality is associated with a poor prognosis. On the other hand, Pollitt (1957) assigns a positive prognostic significance to the presence of moderate obsessional traits. The content and form of obsessional phenomena appear to be irrelevant to prognosis (Akhtar et al., 1975).

The most common complication of obsessive-compulsive neurosis is depression (Goodwin et al., 1969). Nearly one third of obsessive-compulsive inpatients develop depression in the course of their illness (Ro-senberg, 1968). Marks et al. (1980) reported that 38 of 40 chronic obsessive-compulsive ritualizers accepted for a clinical study were depressed. According to Insel (1982), mood change correlates weakly with obsessive-compulsive symptoms. This agrees with Marks et al. (1980), who noted that even after substantial and sustained improvement in rituals and social adjustment, their patients had a strong tendency to have depressive episodes. Despite the high incidence of depression in obsessive-compulsives, the risk of suicide is lower than that observed in other neurotics (Rosenberg, 1968; Coryell, 1981).

The development of schizophrenia at followup in obsessive-compulsive neurotics has been described in anywhere from 0.0 per cent to 12.3 per cent of patients (Black, 1974). The reported incidence of schizophrenia in obsessive-compulsives has steadily fallen since the 1960s (Black, 1974), suggesting that the earlier reported association of obsessive-compulsive neurosis and schizophrenia was substantially a reflection of diagnostic practices.

According to Kringlen (1970), misuse of alcohol and drugs frequently occurs, but typical patterns of substance abuse rarely emerge.

## LABORATORY

No laboratory determination is diagnostic of obsessive-compulsive neurosis. However, a number of investigators have made important observations. Compared with normal controls, obsessive-compulsive neurotics had less total sleep, more awakenings, a decreased percentage of delta sleep, and a 50 per cent reduction in rapid eye movement latency (Insel et al., 1982a). On the latter measure, they resembled depressed subjects (Insel et al., 1982a). The same investigators noted that 6 of 16 patients with chronic, severe obsessive-compulsive neurosis showed nonsuppression on the dexamethasone suppression test (Insel et al., 1982a). Four of the six nonsuppressors showed significant depression. In a related study, a number of the same patients showed a diminished growth hormone response to intravenous clonidine similar to that observed in depressed patients (Siever et al., 1983). Thoren et al. (1980a) noted normal cerebrospinal fluid concentrations of 5-hydroxyindoleacetic acid, homovanillic acid, and 3-methoxy-4-hydroxyphenylglycol in patients participating in a clomipramine treatment study.

Neuropsychological testing of obsessive-compulsive neurotics has yielded inconsistent results. Flor-Henry et al. (1979) reported neuropsychological deficits indicative of left frontal dysfunction in 11 adults. Children with severe obsessive-compulsive disorder exhibited disturbances in spatial orientation and maze-solving abilities (Behar et al., 1984). In contrast, Insel et al. (1983a) found no significant abnormalities in adult patients using standard neuropsychological instruments.

Contemporary EEG studies using strict diagnostic criteria have produced variable results. Mild nonspecific abnormalities were observed in 10 per cent of patients by Insel et al. (1983a) and Rapoport et al. (1981). On the other hand, Jenike and Brotman (1984) discovered abnormalities consistent with partial complex seizures in 4 of 12 patients. Because patients with organic mental disorders had been excluded in all three studies, it is not clear what accounts for this difference. Computerized tomography of the head has been generally unrevealing (Insel et al., 1983a; Rapoport et al., 1981). An exception to this may be children with severe obsessive-compulsive disorder who, according to Behar et al. (1984), show a higher than expected frequency of ventricular enlargement compared with controls.

An association of blood group A and obsessive-compulsive neurosis has been observed (Rinieris, Stefanis, Rabavilas, Vaidakis, 1978). Other investigators (McKeon and McColl, 1982) have not been able to confirm this finding, and its reliability and meaning remain unestablished.

## DIFFERENTIAL DIAGNOSIS

Obsessions must be distinguished from two related phenomena: phobias and delusions. A phobia is a persistent, unreasonable fear of an object, activity, or situation that generates avoidance behavior. Anxiety is usually in proportion to the probability of encountering the phobic stimulus and can be virtually eliminated by avoidance. The act of avoiding need not conform to fixed rules. The imagined consequences of encountering the stimulus are overwhelming anxiety and personal danger. In contrast, the distress associated with obsessions is not directly related to the probability of encounter or occurrence. Unlike phobias, virtually any situation can serve to enhance the intrusion of obsessions. Compulsive behaviors, such as checking, avoiding, and washing, are rarely executed once but must be repeated in exactly the same way many times. The imagined consequences of an encounter often exceed feeling frightened or being hurt, extending to catastrophic, even absurd, consequences, such as killing someone, getting tetanus, or transmitting leukemia.

Obsessive-compulsive experiences are distinct from delusions in that their irrationality and self-origin are recognized by the patient. The presence of delusions, hallucinations, or disturbance in progression of thought is indicative of a psychotic process.

Distinguishing obsessive-compulsive neurosis from depression is complicated by the fact that at least one third of obsessives become depressed (Rosenberg, 1968) and as many as 25 per cent of depressives develop state-dependent obsessional symptoms (Gittleson, 1966). Further, obsessive-compulsive neurotics show sleep and endocrine abnormalities resembling those seen in depression (Insel et al., 1982a; Insel et al., 1982b; Siever et al., 1983). According to Black (1974), obsessional illness is heralded by anxiety, fears, and rituals and the onset is often sudden. In contrast, depression usually has an insidious onset (Black, 1974). If obsessions appear during a depression, they often show a diurnal variation in intensity and frequently involve themes such as suicide and homicide (Gittleson, 1966). Depressive symptoms in obsessionals appear in relationship to the dysfunction created by the core symptoms. Signs of melancholia are rarely present unless a major depression has set in as a complication. The observation that eight times as many primary depressives have a family history positive for depression as do obsessive-compulsive neurotics (Coryell, 1981) may be of assistance in ambiguous cases.

## TREATMENT

Treatment studies of obsessive-compulsive neurosis are plagued by two factors: the rarity of the syndrome and the fact that when encountered, the disorder is typically in its chronic stages. Approaches to treatment fall into four categories: (1) psychotherapeutic, (2) behavioral, (3) pharmacologic, and (4) psychosurgical.

It is generally conceded that the response of obsessive-compulsive neurosis to intensive, dynamically oriented psychotherapy has been disappointing (Salzman and Thaler, 1981). Nonetheless, certain guidelines have been advanced with respect to interacting with obsessive-compulsive patients. The patient should be apprised that he has a well-known illness that may improve spontaneously, that he is not losing his mind, and that impulses to act destructively will almost certainly not be carried out (Goodwin et al., 1969).

Since the 1960s behavioral therapy has emerged as the treatment of choice for obsessive-compulsive neurosis with rituals. In vivo exposure with response prevention has been effective in 60 per cent to 75 per cent of patients followed up at 2 years (Cobb, 1983). The treatment involves immersing the patient in a situation that provokes obsessional experiences and then preventing ritualization. Substantial improvement can be observed after 20 daily sessions lasting for 1 hour (Marks, Hodgson, Rachman, 1975). This technique showed greater success in patients with overt ritualistic behavior, in vivo exposure being most effective in reducing anxiety, and response prevention, in reducing rituals (Steketee, Foa, Grayson, 1982). Relaxation techniques are ineffective in the treatment of obsessive-compulsive neurosis (Marks et al., 1975). One quarter of patients may reject exposure-response prevention therapy and 20 per cent may need retreatment at followup (Steketee et al., 1982). Disturbances in mood are poorly responsive to behavioral therapy (Marks, 1981), and treatment failure or early relapse has been correlated with severe depression and conviction that fears were realistic (Foa, 1979).

To date the most effective psychotropic agent in the treatment of obsessive-compulsive neurosis is the tricyclic compound clomipramine hydrochloride. In at least four double-blind, placebo trials, clomipramine has been shown to produce significant symptomatic improvement (Marks, 1983). Treatment effects were observed in patients with and without rituals (Insel et al., 1983c). A therapeutic window for the parent compound and its primary metabolite, desmethyl clomipramine, has been reported (Stern, Marks, Mawson, Luscombe, 1980). The drug appears to exert a maximum effect at 10 to 18 weeks (Marks et al., 1980), and discontinuation of the drug may be rapidly followed by relapse (Thoren, Asberg, Cronholm, Jornestedt, Traskman, 1980b).

A controversy has arisen over whether clomipramine exerts an anti-obsessional or antidepressant effect. Marks et al. (1980) found that among patients concurrently treated with in vivo exposure, clomipramine produced a significant effect only in those subjects who initially had a depressed mood. Other investigators have not found an association between depression and outcome when clomipramine was the only treatment (Thoren et al., 1980b; Insel et al., 1983c).

There are abundant open trials and case studies that report the efficacy of virtually every major psychotropic agent (Insel and Murphy, 1981). Monoamine oxidase inhibitors have been recommended for patients with associated phobic anxiety or panic attacks (Jenike, Surman, Cassem, Zusky, Anderson, 1983). Loxitane was found to be effective in a case where paranoid ideation was prominent (Bulkeley and Hollender, 1982). Lithium was successfully used in a case where depressive symptoms were prominent (Stern and Jenike, 1983). Carbamazepine was associated with modest improvement in one of four patients with electroencephalograms suggestive of temporal lobe epilepsy (Jenike and Brotman, 1984).

Early studies of electroconvulsive therapy yielded unimpressive results. However, the recent successful use of this modality in a single patient (Mellman and Gorman, 1984) has called attention to the need for controlled studies of electroconvulsive therapy in obsessive-compulsive neurosis.

For patients with obsessive-compulsive neurosis refractory to other therapies, a bimedial leukotomy aimed at interrupting thalamofrontal fibers thought to play a role in maintaining anxiety may be considered. Tan, Marks, and Marset (1971) noted that 24 leukotomy patients showed a significant postsurgical reduction in symptoms when compared with 13 matched controls. The improvement was most marked in the first

3 months but continued over 5 years. A compilation of six studies revealed that 89 of 110 leukotomy patients were at least improved, and one half of those improved were in complete remission (Tippin and Henn, 1982).

## REFERENCES

Akhtar S, Wig NN, Varma NN, Dwarka P, Verma SK: A phenomenological analysis of symptoms in obsessive-compulsive neurosis. Br J Psychiatry 127:342–348, 1975.

Beech HR, Ciesielski KT, Gordon PK: Further observations of evoked potentials in obsessional patients. Br J Psychiatry 142:605–609, 1983.

Beech HR, Liddell A: Decision-making, mood states and ritualistic behavior among obsessional patients, in Beech HR (ed): Obsessional States. London, Methuen, 1974, pp 143–160.

Beech HR, Perigault J: Toward a theory of obsessional disorder in obsessional states, in Beech HR (ed): Obsessional States. London, Methuen, 1974, pp 113–141.

Behar D, Rapoport JL, Berg CJ, Denckla MB, Mann L, Cox C, Fedio P, Zahn T, Wolfman MG: Computerized tomography and neuropsychological test measures in adolescents with obsessive-compulsive disorder. Am J Psychiatry 141:363–368, 1984.

Black A: The natural history of obsessional neurosis in obsessional states, in Beech HR (ed): Obsessional States. London, Methuen, 1974, pp 19–54.

Brown F: Heredity in the psychoneuroses. Proc R Soc Med 35:785–790, 1942.

Bulkeley NR, Hollender MH: Successful treatment of obsessive-compulsive disorder with loxitane. Am J Psychiatry 139:1345–1346, 1982.

Capstick N, Seldrup J: Obsessional states: A study in the relationship between abnormalities occurring at the time of birth and the subsequent development of obsessional symptoms. Acta Psychiatr Scand 56:427–431, 1977.

Cobb J: Behavior therapy in phobic and obsessional disorders. Psychiatr Devel 4:351–365, 1983.

Coryell W: Obsessive-compulsive disorder and primary unipolar depression. J Nerv Ment Dis 169:220–224, 1981.

Dowson JH: The phenomenology of severe obsessive-compulsive neurosis. Br J Psychiatry 131:75–78, 1977.

Elkins R, Rapoport J, Lipsky A: Obsessive-compulsive disorder of childhood and adolescence. J Am Acad Child Psychiatry 19:511–524, 1980.

Flor-Henry P, Yendall LT, Koles ZJ, Howarth BG: Neuropsychological and powerspectral EEG investigations of the obsessive-compulsive syndrome. Biol Psychiatry 14:119–130, 1979.

Foa EB: Failure in treating obsessive-compulsives. Behav Res Ther 17:169–176, 1979.

Gittleson NL: The phenomenology of obsessions in depressive psychosis. Br J Psychiatry 112:261–264, 1966.

Goodwin DW, Guze SB, Robins E: Follow-up studies in obsessional neurosis. Arch Gen Psychiatry 20:182–187, 1969.

Grimshaw L: Obsessional disorder and neurological illness. J Neurol Neurosurg Psychiatry 27:229–231, 1964.

Grimshaw L: The outcome of obsessional disorder: a follow-up study of 100 cases. Br J Psychiatry 111:1051–1056, 1965.

Ingram IM: Obsessional illness in mental hospital patients. Br J Psychiatry 107:382–402, 1961.

Insel TR: Obsessive-compulsive disorder—Five clinical questions and a suggested approach. Compr Psychiatry 23:241–251, 1982.

Insel TR, Donnelly EF, Lalakea ML, Alterman IS, Murphy DL: Neurological and neuropsychological studies of patients with obsessive-compulsive disorder. Biol Psychiatry 18:741–751, 1983a.

Insel TR, Gillin C, Moore A, Mondelson WB, Loewenstein RJ, Murphy DL: The sleep of patients with obsessive-compulsive disorder. Arch Gen Psychiatry 39:1372–1377, 1982a.

Insel TR, Hoover C, Murphy DL: Parents of patients with obsessive-compulsive disorder. Psychol Med 13:807–811, 1983b.

Insel TR, Kalin NH, Guttmacher LB, Cohen RM, Murphy DL: The dexamethasone suppression test in patients with primary obsessive-compulsive disorder. Psychiatry Res 6:153–160, 1982b.

Insel TR, Murphy DL: The psychopharmacological treatment of obsessive-compulsive disorder: A review. J Clin Psychopharmacol 1:304–311, 1981.

Insel TR, Murphy DL, Cohen RM, Alterman I, Kilts C, Linnoila M: Obsessive-compulsive disorder: A double blind trial of clomipramine and clorsyline. Arch Gen Psychiatry 40:605–612, 1983c.

Jenike MA, Brotman AW: The EEG in obsessive-compulsive disorder. J Clin Psychiatry 45:122–124, 1984.

Jenike MA, Surman OS, Cassem NH, Zusky P, Anderson WH: Monoamine oxidase inhibitors in obsessive-compulsive disorder. J Clin Psychiatry 44:131–132, 1983.

Kringlen E: Obsessional neurosis: A long term follow-up. Br J Psychiatry 111:709–722, 1965.

Kringlen E: Natural history of obsessional neurosis. Semin Psychiatry 2:403–419, 1970.

Marks IM: Review of behavioral psychotherapy. I. Obsessive-compulsive disorders. Am J Psychiatry 138:584–592, 1981.

Marks IM: Are there anti-compulsive or anti-phobic drugs? Review of the evidence. Br J Psychiatry 143:338–347, 1983.

Marks IM, Hodgson R, Rachman S: Treatment of chronic obsessive-compulsive neurosis by in vivo exposure: A two year follow-up and issues in treatment. Br J Psychiatry 127:349–364, 1975.

Marks IM, Stern RS, Mawson D, Cobb J, McDonald R: Clomipramine and exposure for obsessive-compulsive rituals. I. Br J Psychiatry 136:1–25, 1980.

McGuffin P, Mawson D: Obsessive-compulsive neurosis: Two identical twin pairs. Br J Psychiatry 137:285–287, 1980.

McKeon JP, McColl D: ABO blood groups in obsessional illness—state and trait. Acta Psychiatr Scand 65:74–78, 1982.

Mellman LA, Gorman JM: Successful treatment of obsessive-compulsive disorder with ECT. Am J Psychiatry 141:596–597, 1984.

Pollitt J: Natural history of obsessional states. Br Med J 1:194–198, 1957.

Pollitt J: Obsessional states. Br J Psychiatry 9:133–140, 1975 (spec).

Rapoport J, Elkins R, Lancer DH, Sceery W, Buchsbaum MS, Gillin JC, Murphy DL, Zahn TP, Lake R, Ludlow

C, Mendelson W: Childhood obsessive-compulsive disorder. Am J Psychiatry 138:1545–1554, 1981.

Rinieris PM, Stefanis CN, Rabavilas AD, Vaidakis NM: Obsessive-compulsive neurosis, anancastic symptomotology and ABO blood types. Acta Psychiatr Scand 57:377–381, 1978.

Rosenberg CM: Familial aspects of obsessional neurosis. Br J Psychiatry 113:405–413, 1967.

Rosenberg CM: Complications of obsessional neurosis. Br J Psychiatry 114:477–478, 1968.

Salzman L, Thaler FH: Obsessive-compulsive disorders: A review of the literature. Am J Psychiatry 138:286–296, 1981.

Siever LJ, Insel TR, Jimerson DC, Lake CR, Uhde TW, Aloi J, Murphy DL: Growth hormone response to clonidine in obsessive-compulsive patients. Br J Psychiatry 142:184–187, 1983.

Steketee G, Foa EB, Grayson JB: Recent advances in the behavioral treatment of obsessive-compulsives. Arch Gen Psychiatry 39:1365–1371, 1982.

Stern RS, Cobb JP: Phenomenology of obsessive-compulsive neurosis. Br J Psychiatry 132:233–239, 1978.

Stern RS, Marks IM, Mawson D, Luscombe DK: Clomipramine and exposure for compulsive rituals. II. Plasma levels, side effects and outcomes. Br J Psychiatry 136:161–166, 1980.

Stern TA, Jenike MA: Treatment of obsessive-compulsive disorder with lithium carbonate. Psychosomatics 24:671–673, 1983.

Tan E, Marks IM, Marset P: Bimedial leucotomy in obsessive-compulsive neurosis: A controlled serial enquiry. Br J Psychiatry 118:155–164, 1971.

Thoren P, Asberg M, Bertilsson L, Mellstrom B, Sjogvist F, Traskman L: Clomipramine treatment of obsessive-compulsive disorder. II. Biochemical aspects. Arch Gen Psychiatry 37:1289–1294, 1980a.

Thoren P, Asberg M, Cronholm B, Jornestedt L, Traskman L: Clomipramine treatment of obsessive-compulsive disorder. I. A controlled clinical trial. Arch Gen Psychiatry 37:1281–1285, 1980b.

Tippen J, Henn FA: Modified leukotomy in the treatment of intractable obsessional neurosis. Am J Psychiatry 139:1601–1603, 1982.

Woodruff R, Pitts FN: Monozygotic twins with obsessional illness. Am J Psychiatry 120:1075–1080, 1964.

# chapter 9

# SOMATOFORM AND DISSOCIATIVE DISORDERS

*by* C. Robert Cloninger, M.D.

The most prominent features of some psychiatric disorders are physical complaints that cannot be explained by known pathophysiologic mechanisms. Such unexplained physical complaints are common in all medical practices, so physicians must learn to recognize psychiatric disorders that mimic physical disorders. Such psychiatric disorders cannot be reliably recognized simply by excluding physical disorders or by treatment trials. Physical disorders may fail to respond to routine treatments or may go unrecognized because of atypical presentation or limitations of available assessment procedures. In addition, patients often present with combinations of physical and psychiatric symptoms that challenge the diagnostic and therapeutic skills of the most astute and patient physician.

One of the major innovations of the third edition of the American Psychiatric Association's *Diagnostic and Statistical Manual of Mental Disorders* (DSM-III) was its classification of psychiatric disorders associated with prominent physical complaints. DSM-III distinguishes five groups of disorders ac-

**TABLE 9–1  DSM-11 Criteria Used in the Differential Diagnosis of Symptom(s) Suggesting Physical Illness**

| Classification | Physical Mechanism Explains the Symptoms | Symptoms Are Linked to Psychological Factors | Symptoms Initiation Is Under Voluntary Control | Obvious Recognizable Environmental Goal |
|---|---|---|---|---|
| Somatoform and dissociative disorders | No | Yes | No | Variable |
| Factitious disorders | Variable | Yes | Yes | No |
| Malingering | Variable | Variable | Yes | Yes |
| Psychological factors affecting physical condition | Yes | Yes | No | Variable |
| Undiagnosed physical illness | Variable | Variable | No | No |

Based on Hyler and Spitzer, 1978

cording to the role of known pathophysiologic mechanisms, psychological conflict, and voluntary control over symptoms (Table 9–1). The somatoform disorders refer to illnesses in which there is no known physical disorder or pathophysiologic mechanism to explain symptoms and in which psychological conflicts are currently assumed to lead to involuntary formation of physical signs and symptoms. These somatoform disorders include several explicitly described syndromes or discrete clinical disorders: Briquet's syndrome (also called somatization disorder or chronic hysterical neurosis), conversion disorder (or acute hysterical neurosis, conversion type), psychogenic pain disorder, hypochondriasis (or hypochondriacal neurosis), and other atypical somatoform disorders. In this chapter, each of these categories of somatoform disorder is considered. Conversion disorders and dissociative disorders are often referred to collectively as acute hysterical neurosis because of similarities in their clinical course and in theories about their etiology. Accordingly, dissociative disorders are described here along with conversion disorders.

## BRIQUET'S SYNDROME (SOMATIZATION DISORDER OR CHRONIC HYSTERIA)

### Definition

Briquet's syndrome has been described by Guze and his associates (Perley and Guze, 1962; Guze, 1967; Woodruff, 1967) as a chronic syndrome of recurrent symptoms in many organ systems that begins before age 30 and is associated with psychological distress but no physical disorder. It is associated with excessive surgery and medical attention for a wide variety of medically unexplained complaints. Characteristic symptoms include frequent pains, gastrointestinal symptoms, sensorimotor conversion symptoms and dissociative reactions, sexual and menstrual problems, and a belief that the patient has been sickly most of his or her life. Anxiety and depressive symptoms are frequently associated with the recurrent physical complaints. Personal and social problems are also commonly observed in such patients. In 1962, Perley and Guze described 59 symptoms in 10 groups as char-

acteristic of Briquet's syndrome and required at least 20 medically unexplained symptoms in 9 groups for diagnosis (Table 9–2). These patients were initially labeled as having hysteria or hysterical neurosis, but later the name Briquet's syndrome was suggested in order to distinguish this chronic polysymptomatic disorder from acute conversion and dissociative reactions. The name recognizes the early work of the French physician Briquet, who described a similar syndrome in 1859 (Purtell, Robins, Cohen, 1951; Guze, 1967; Mai and Merskey, 1980).

In order to facilitate clinical applications, an attempt was made in DSM-III (American Psychiatric Association, 1980) to simplify the original criteria of Perley and Guze. DSM-III also suggested the alternative name of somatization disorder. Depressive symptoms and panic attacks were omitted from the criteria to avoid overlap with depressive and anxiety disorders. The remaining 37 symptoms that best discriminated persons with Briquet's syndrome from others were retained. Requirements about the number of groups were dropped because this was found to add little information: the total number of somatization symptoms is highly correlated with the number of somatization groups. Finally, to reduce possible sex bias owing to the impossibility of menstrual and pregnancy symptoms in men, men were diagnosed who had 12 unexplained symptoms compared with the criterion number of 14 in women.

The DSM-III criteria for somatization disorder require a history of medically unexplained physical symptoms of several years' duration, beginning before age 30. These include at least 14 complaints in women and 12 in men of the following 37 symptoms: sickly, difficulty swallowing, loss of voice, deafness, double vision, blurred vision, blindness, fainting, unconsciousness, amnesia, seizures, trouble walking, paralysis or weakness, urinary retention, abdominal pain, nausea, vomiting, abdominal bloating, food intolerance, diarrhea, dysmenorrhea, menstrual irregularity, menorrhagia, hyperemesis gravidarum, sexual indifference, frigidity, painful intercourse, back pain, joint pain, extremity pain, genital pain, dysuria, other pain except headaches, shortness of breath, palpitations, chest pain, and dizziness.

**TABLE 9–2    Symptom Items for Guze's Criteria for Briquet's Syndrome**

| | |
|---|---|
| **Group 1** | **Group 6** |
| Headaches | Abdominal pain |
| Sickly most of life | Vomiting |
| **Group 2** | **Group 7** |
| Blindness | Dysmenorrhea |
| Paralysis | Menstrual irregularity |
| Anesthesia | Amenorrhea |
| Aphonia | Excessive bleeding |
| Fits or convulsions | **Group 8** |
| Unconsciousness | Sexual indifference |
| Amnesia | Frigidity |
| Deafness | Dyspareunia |
| Hallucinations | Other sexual difficulties |
| Urinary retention | Vomiting nine months pregnancy or |
| Ataxia | hospitalized for hyperemesis gravidarum |
| Other conversion symptoms | **Group 9** |
| **Group 3** | Back pain |
| Fatigue | Joint pain |
| Lump in throat | Extremity pain |
| Fainting spells | Burning pains of the sexual organs, mouth or |
| Visual blurring | rectum |
| Weakness | Other bodily pains |
| Dysuria | **Group 10** |
| **Group 4** | Nervousness |
| Breathing difficulty | Fears |
| Palpitation | Depressed feelings |
| Anxiety attacks | Need to quit working or inability to carry on |
| Chest pain | regular duties because of feeling sick |
| Dizziness | Crying easily |
| **Group 5** | Feeling life was hopeless |
| Anorexia | Thinking a good deal about dying |
| Weight loss | Wanting to die |
| Marked fluctuations in weight | Thinking of suicide |
| Nausea | Suicide attempts |
| Abdominal bloating | |
| Food intolerances | |
| Diarrhea | |
| Constipation | |

The criteria for Briquet's syndrome consider 21 other symptoms besides those included in somatization disorder: headaches, anesthesia, hallucinations, fatigue, panic attacks, anorexia, weight loss, marked fluctuations in weight, constipation, amenorrhea, other sexual difficulties, nervousness, fears, depressed feelings, inability to carry on regular duties because of feeling sick, crying easily, hopelessness, thinking a good deal about dying, wanting to die, thinking of suicide, and suicide attempts. These 21 symptoms occur in 8 of the 10 groups delineated by Perley and Guze.

It is possible to satisfy the criteria for Briquet's syndrome and not somatization disorder as defined in DSM-III because the criteria for Briquet's syndrome include more than 20 symptoms that do not contribute to a diagnosis of somatization disorder. It is also possible to satisfy the criteria for so-

matization disorder and not Briquet's syndrome because the 14 symptoms required for somatization disorder are insufficient to satisfy the requirement of at least 20 for Briquet's syndrome. In clinical practice, discordance between the diagnosis of Briquet's syndrome and somatization disorder can be substantial. Among 123 women who received either diagnosis in a recent followup and family study of somatization disorder, only 63 per cent received both diagnoses, 21 per cent had somatization disorder only, and 16 per cent had Briquet's syndrome only (Cloninger, Martin, Guze, Clayton, in press). Men and women with somatization disorder only had a variety of heterogeneous disorders, particularly anxiety and personality disorders. There was familial aggregation for Briquet's syndrome but not for somatization disorder alone. Thus the agreement of the simplified DSM-III criteria, and other briefer screening criteria (Reveley et al., 1977), with the full criteria is too low for definitive diagnosis. The diagnosis of Briquet's syndrome may influence clinical decisions about treatment and risk for suicide, so clinicians are encouraged to use the full Briquet's syndrome criteria rather than any briefer criteria. Actually, the criteria for Briquet's syndrome are not substantially more time-consuming to administer than the DSM-III criteria because nearly all the additional items should be routinely elicited in psychiatric assessments.

## Etiology

Briquet's syndrome is familial: it is observed in 10 per cent to 20 per cent of the female first-degree relatives of probands with Briquet's syndrome, a fivefold to tenfold increase over the lifetime risk of the disorder in women in the general population (Woerner and Guze, 1968; Cloninger, Reich, Guze, 1975; Coryell, 1980; Cloninger et al., in press). The male relatives of women with Briquet's syndrome also show an increased risk of antisocial personality and alcoholism (Woerner and Guze, 1968; Cloninger et al., 1975). A recently completed blind family interview study in St. Louis has confirmed the familial nature of Briquet's syndrome in women and the association with antisocial personality in male and female relatives. In contrast, men with many somatic complaints were found to be clinically heterogeneous and did not aggregate in families with either male or female somatizers (Cloninger et al., in press). This suggests that somatization in women often has a common etiology with antisocial personality, but not somatization in men.

This familial aggregation could be caused by genetic factors, environmental influences, or both. Recently, an adoption study of somatoform disorders in Sweden has shown that the contributions of both genetic and environmental influences are substantial (Bohman, Cloninger, von Knorring, Sigvardsson, 1984). Two discrete types of somatoform disorders were distinguished in Swedish women using comprehensive lifetime medical records (Cloninger, Sigvardsson, von Knorring, Bohman, 1984). One of these disorders, high-frequency somatization, was characterized by frequent headaches, backaches, and gastrointestinal and gynecologic complaints associated with psychiatric disability (Figure 9–1). Extensive overlap with Briquet's syndrome was suggested by available psychiatric evaluations. Women who were adopted away at an early age had a fivefold increase in high-frequency somatization disorder if their bio-

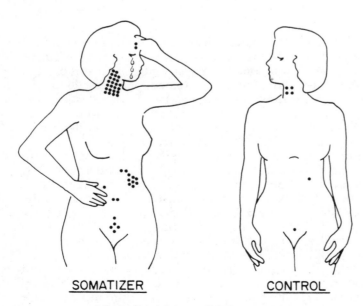

**FIGURE 9–1.** Distribution and number of sick leave occasions in Swedish high-frequency somatizers and control non-somatizers.

SOMATIZER                    CONTROL

• I Somatic sick leave / IO person years
6 I Psychiatric sick leave / IO person years

CLASSIFICATION OF PREDISPOSITION
TO TYPE I (High Frequency) SOMATIZATION        OBSERVED FEMALE ADOPTEES

| Congenital | Postnatal | Row Total (N) | Row % of Type I Somatizers |
|------------|-----------|---------------|----------------------------|
| Low | Low | 379 | 2.1% |
| Low | High | 359 | 4.7% |
| High | Low | 68 | 7.4% |
| High | High | 53 | 13.2% |

**FIGURE 9–2.** Cross-fostering analysis of type 1 (high frequency) somatization in Swedish adopted women (Bohman et al., 1984). "Congenital" refers to variables about biologic parents, whereas "postnatal" refers to variables about rearing experiences and adoptive placement. Classification of predisposition depended on whether the set of background variables were more like the average characteristics of adoptees with type 1 somatization (classified as high) or with type 2 or no somatization (classified as low).

logic parents were antisocial or alcoholic. Low social status of the adoptive parents also increased the risk of somatoform disorders in the adopted children. This indicates that both biologic and psychosocial influences contribute to the development of this disorder. The interaction of these genetic and environmental contributions was studied in a cross-fostering analysis (Figure 9–2), which considers the possible combinations of genetic background (high or low risk) and of postnatal background (high or low risk). The analysis showed that both genetic and environmental background contribute to the risk of somatization regardless of the other.

Studies of the biologic and adoptive parents of hyperactive children have also provided evidence for genetic factors that are shared by Briquet's syndrome and attention-deficit disorder with hyperactivity in children. Briquet's syndrome and antisocial personality are increased in the biologic parents of hyperactive children in intact families, but not in the adoptive parents of other hyperactive children (Cantwell, 1972; Morrison and Stewart, 1973).

Objective experimental tests indicate that individuals with Briquet's syndrome have low pain thresholds (Bianchi, 1973) and an information-processing pattern characterized by distractibility, difficulty distinguishing target and nontarget stimuli, and impaired verbal communication (Ludwig, 1972; Bendefeldt, Miller, Ludwig, 1976; Almgren, Nordgren, Skantze, 1978; Flor-

Henry, Fromm-Auch, Tapper, Schopflocher, 1981). This attentional deficit is associated with their failure to habituate to repetitive stimuli (Mears and Horvath, 1972). Flor-Henry et al. (1981) compared the neuropsychological function of patients with Briquet's syndrome with normal controls, psychotic depressives, and schizophrenics who were matched to the Briquet's patients for age, sex, handedness, and full-scale intelligence. Compared with the normal controls, the Briquet's patients had a bilateral and symmetrical pattern of frontal lobe impairment. This anterior cerebral impairment was substantially greater than posterior cerebral impairment, but the Briquet's patients exhibited some bilateral, but principally nondominant (right-sided), posterior temporal deficits in most cases also. The patients with Briquet's syndrome had greater dominant hemisphere impairment than did the psychotic depressives, as expected from their relationship to antisocial personality, and they had less nondominant hemisphere disorganization than did the schizophrenics. This characteristic pattern of neuropsychological impairment allowed patients with Briquet's syndrome to be distinguished from each of the other contrast groups.

Shapiro (1965) and Horowitz (1977) have suggested that this "hysterical" information-processing pattern explains many of their clinical features. Their "global deployment of attention" leads to vague, nonspecific labels for experience; their "impressionistic grouping of constructs" leads to unclear and incomplete statement of ideas and feelings, circumstantial or partial patterns of association, and distortion of new information to fit earlier preconceptions. Their tendency to respond quickly and impulsively to external stimuli without sustained critical examination leads to suggestibility, shallowness, lability, and diminished reflective self-awareness. Schalling (1978) and her associates (1973) have shown that monotony avoidance and impulsivity are positively associated with somatization or somatic anxiety but not with obsessional traits or anticipatory anxiety. Thus somatization, impulsivity, and the hysterical information-processing pattern tend to occur in the same individual, as is observed in patients with Briquet's syndrome and their biologic relatives.

The hysterical information-processing deficit may underlie the frequent somatic complaints, mental status findings of vagueness and circumstantiality, as well as many social and personal problems that are prominent in patients with Briquet's syndrome and their biologic relatives (Horowitz, 1977; Cloninger, 1978; Flor-Henry et al., 1981). This pattern of information processing is associated with the use of what psychoanalysts describe as the defense mechanisms of repression and denial. Shapiro (1965) describes repression as "the loss not of affect, but of ideational contents from consciousness, the failure of once-perceived contents to achieve the status of conscious memories." Schafer (1948) suggested that excessive reliance on repression and denial hampers the development of broad intellectual and cultural interests, impairs the ability for independent and creative thinking, and leads to emotional lability, immature interpersonal attachments, and a crisis-oriented life-style. In contrast, Shapiro suggested that the appearance of repression and the associated clinical problems are a consequence of the information-processing pattern. It is likely that the same neurobiologic phenomena are simply being described at different levels of observation so that arguments about whether the egg or the chicken came first are moot.

The perception of somatic sensations can be increased by selective attention and improves with practice or conditioning. Adam (1967) showed that individuals could be taught to perceive gastrointestinal move-ments that they were unaware of previously. Autonomic activity can be conditioned to signals that can occur below the level of awareness. For example, heart rate can be conditioned to vary with signals that subjects are not aware of consciously (Lacey, Smith, Green, 1955). Transient physiologic disturbances associated with autonomic hyperactivity, muscle tension, or hyperventilation are associated with somatic symptoms and occur frequently in the general population (Mayou, 1976; Kellner and Sheffield, 1973). Examples of such somatic symptoms include tension headaches, irritable bowel syndrome, and sensory changes, such as paresthesias (Weintraub, 1983). Presumably, the frequency of such physiologic disturbances or symptoms can be modified by selective attention and conditioning. Patients with Briquet's syndrome show rapid and marked responses to suggested shifts of their attention (Scallet, Cloninger, Othmer, 1976) and frequently experience symptoms associated with such physiologic disturbances.

Social modeling and operant conditioning of sick role behavior can influence the frequency and intensity of somatization and are discussed later in relation to conversion symptoms and chronic pain states.

## Epidemiology

### Age

The full Briquet's syndrome develops gradually. It is rarely diagnosable before age 14 (Robins and O'Neal, 1953). In the majority of cases, characteristic symptoms begin during adolescence and full criteria are satisfied by age 25 (Purtell et al., 1951; Guze and Perley, 1963). The hysterical information-processing pattern and histrionic personality traits are usually recognizable during adolescence in those cases (about 70 per cent) in whom they are ever prominent (Cloninger and Guze, 1970). Kimble, Williams, and Agras (1975) found histrionic personality and Briquet's syndrome highly correlated in adult women but noted that teenage girls with histrionic personality rarely fulfilled the criteria for Briquet's syndrome. Guze, Woodruff, and Clayton (1973) found that among psychiatric clinic patients, the number of symptoms characteristic of Briquet's syndrome was unimodally distributed in women and peaked during the 20s, followed by a gradual decline. In men, on the other hand, there was a gradual increase in the number of symptoms with age, reaching a peak in the 50s and then declining. There was a significant sex difference under age 40 but not thereafter. Similar findings have been observed in different age cohorts of psychiatric outpatients in Sweden also (Lindberg and Lindegard, 1963), but in the absence of prospective studies, it remains uncertain whether such patterns reflect differences between various birth cohorts or actual clinical changes with age within birth cohorts. In any case, in patients who develop Briquet's syndrome, the characteristic symptoms are recurrent and lead to chronic disability.

### Lifetime Risk in Women

Several studies now suggest that the lifetime risk for Briquet's syndrome or somatization disorder is about 2 per cent in women when age of onset and method of assessment are taken into account. Cloninger et al. (1975) found that 3 of 153 white women who had just experienced normal child deliveries had Briquet's syndrome. By counting the 59 unaffected women younger than age 25 as being, on average, only half through their lifetime risk period, the lifetime risk was estimated as 2.4 per cent plus or minus 1.4 per cent.

The prevalence of Briquet's syndrome or somatization disorder is underestimated in studies relying on interviews by non-physicians. The diagnostic criteria require a judgment of whether or not the symptoms are medically explained. This judgment requires medical training to develop the skill to assess critically the description of the symptoms, diagnostic evaluations, and putative physical diagnoses. Psychiatrists and other physicians can do this reliably even in patients with multiple chronic medical illnesses (Woodruff, 1967; Reveley et al., 1977). Patients with Briquet's syndrome, however, often attribute symptoms to a variety of physical disorders, and non-physicians are unable to critically evaluate such assertions adequately. As a result, when non-physicians accept medical explanations offered by patients without properly judging their plausibility, Briquet's syndrome is underdiagnosed. In addition, people may be less motivated to describe somatic complaints to non-physicians. The sensitivity (proportion of true cases recognized) of non-physicians compared with psychiatrists is 55 per cent for Briquet's syndrome and 41 per cent for DSM-III somatization disorder (Robins, Helzer, Croughan, Ratcliff, 1981). Specificity (proportion of non-cases properly diagnosed) remains high (97 per cent to 99 per cent) for non-physicians for both Briquet's syndrome and somatization disorder.

This underestimation of prevalence by non-physicians may account for the low prevalence estimates of Briquet's in large-scale population surveys that use non-physician interviewers. Weissman, Myers, and Harding (1978) obtained followup interviews on 511 adults in 1975–76 (all over age 25) out of an original sample of 1095 adults identified in 1967. The followup sample differed significantly from the original population in that there were fewer non-white and low socioeconomic subjects. They found only two women with definite Briquet's syndrome. However, this is an underestimate owing to the biased attrition and the fact that interviews were done by non-physicians. Correcting for sensitivity and specificity of non-physician interviewers, the lifetime risk for Briquet's syndrome is about 1.6 per cent in women. Similarly, in a more recent epidemiologic study using non-physician interviewers, the lifetime risk of somatization disorder was reported as only 0.2 per cent to 0.3 per cent of women, but this does not correct for underdiagnosis by non-physicians.

Comprehensive medical records are the most sensitive method for recognizing Briquet's syndrome or somatization disorder because they are unaffected by inconsistent self-reports (Martin, Cloninger, Guze, 1979). Using complete lifetime medical records in Sweden, high-frequency somatization disorder was observed in about 3 per cent of 859 women in the general population. This is only slightly higher than estimates of Briquet's syndrome based on comprehensive assessments by psychiatrists using personal interviews supplemented by selected medical records.

### Sex Differences

Briquet's syndrome is diagnosed predominantly in women, but infrequent cases in men do occur. In a recent study in St. Louis, 4 per cent of 74 psychiatric outpatients with

Briquet's syndrome were men. Some clinicians have suggested that this sex difference is artifactual. Warner (1978) found that male and female professionals tend to label men as antisocial and women as hysterical even when they have identical clinical features. Others have noted that the criteria for Briquet's syndrome were biased against diagnosis of men because some of its characteristic symptoms are inapplicable to men (e.g., pregnancy and menstrual complaints). Also, men generally report fewer symptoms than do women, and it has been suggested that there should be compensation for this response bias in the number of reported symptoms required for diagnosis in men (Temoshok and Attkisson, 1977).

DSM-III reduced the number of symptoms required to diagnose somatization disorder from 14 in women to 12 in men. This compensates for the inapplicable gynecologic symptoms but not for the general response bias in number of somatic complaints. Somatization disorder is much rarer in men than in women unless the number of somatic complaints required for diagnosis in men is reduced to half the number required in women (14 to 7). The symptoms characteristic of somatization disorder were counted in a recent study of psychiatric outpatients and their relatives (Cloninger et al., in press). The cumulative frequency distributions of these counts are shown in Table 9–3 for probands at followup and for the relatives of definite non-somatizers. Using the DSM-III criterion of 14 unexplained symptoms in women, the prevalence of so-

matization disorder was 22 per cent in outpatient women compared with 2.9 per cent in the female relatives of non-somatizers. Using the DSM-III criterion of 12 unexplained symptoms in men, the prevalence of somatization disorder in the relatives of non-somatizers was only 0.3 per cent, making the disorder more than ten times as prevalent in women as in men. If the required minimum symptom count for men was reduced to 7 or 8, the prevalences in men and women were about the same. However, these men with 7 to 11 somatic complaints had a wide variety of anxiety and personality disorders and did not aggregate in families with female somatizers. This suggests that the sex difference in somatization in the United States has practical clinical significance.

It is interesting that a study of 75 subjects with Briquet's syndrome in Greece included 21 men and 54 women (Rinieris, Stefanis, Lykouras, Varsou, 1978). Further cross-cultural studies are needed to evaluate the importance of cultural influences on sex role stereotypes about the expression of somatization.

### Socioeconomic Associations

Briquet's syndrome is more common in individuals who have low socioeconomic, occupational, and educational status (Robins, 1966; Cloninger and Guze, 1970; Guze, Woodruff, Clayton, 1971a). Low occupational status of either biologic or adoptive parents increased the risk of high-frequency

**TABLE 9–3**  Frequency of Somatization Disorder Symptoms

| Symptoms Count | Probands of Followup | | Relatives of Non-Somatizers | |
| | Men (N = 129) Cum. Col. (%) | Women (N = 277) Cum. Col. (%) | Men (N = 375) Cum. Col. (%) | Women (N = 479) Cum. Col. (%) |
|---|---|---|---|---|
| 20+ | — | 2.5 | — | 0.2 |
| 16–19 | 3.1 | 12.3 | — | 1.5 |
| 14–15 | 3.1 | 22.0* | — | 2.9* |
| 12–13 | 6.2 | 25.6 | 0.3 | 4.0 |
| 8–11 | 17.8* | 48.4 | 2.7* | 11.7 |
| 4–7 | 40.3 | 76.5 | 12.5 | 35.5 |
| 2–3 | 47.3 | 85.9 | 13.6 | 38.2 |
| 0–1 | 100.0 | 100.0 | 100.0 | 100.0 |

Relatives were excluded if the proband had 14 (women) or 8 (men) symptoms, whether the symptoms were judged medically explained or not, in order to best approximate a general population sample by excluding probands with medical and somatoform disorders.
* Percentages of subjects in each sex with somatization disorder if the criterion was taken as 14 and 8 medically unexplained symptoms in women and men, respectively.

somatization disorder in adopted Swedish women (Bohman et al., 1984).

## Pathology

By definition, patients with Briquet's syndrome have no known pathologic abnormalities to explain their symptoms. The disorder often leads to surgery. Pathologic reports of surgically removed tissues are typically characterized as normal or describe coincidental abnormalities.

## Clinical Picture

The most discriminating clinical feature is a medical history complicated by recurrent unexplained problems and the subjective complaint of sickliness. However, the chief complaint at a particular time need not be a physical complaint. Often the chief complaint involves social problems, a suicide attempt, or a non-psychotic agitated depression. Frequently, patients with Briquet's syndrome are unable to specify a single chief complaint and instead describe many problems that are, at best, vaguely related (Purtell et al., 1951). In order to avoid misdiagnosis and inappropriate treatment, it is necessary to review the history of hospitalizations and outpatient medical care as well as conduct a careful review of systems in all patients, regardless of their most prominent presenting symptoms, because of the variability and vagueness of chief complaints in Briquet's syndrome.

No one symptom or sign is pathognomonic of Briquet's syndrome; the cardinal feature is the chronic polysymptomatic pattern of physical complaints. Nevertheless, some symptoms are highly characteristic and discriminate Briquet's disorder from other psychiatric disorders. These include the complaint of sickliness for most of a patient's life, or a history of voluntary sterilization before age 30, or repeated surgery for unexplained pain. Individual symptoms or behaviors such as these suggest the possibility of Briquet's disorder but are an inaccurate basis for diagnosis because they are not frequent enough in Briquet's disorder and too common in other conditions. It is necessary to consider combinations of two or more symptoms in evaluating the possibility of Briquet's disorder.

Three symptom clusters have been identified that distinguish patients with Briquet's syndrome from patients with other psychiatric or medical disorders (Reveley et al., 1977). One syndrome, occurring in 30 per cent of outpatients with Briquet's disorder, is the combination of onset of a complex illness before age 26, back pain, abdominal pain, and suicidal thoughts. This syndrome is similar to the symptom pattern that is characteristic of high-frequency somatizers in Sweden, as noted earlier. The second syndrome, occurring in another 28 per cent of outpatients with Briquet's disorder, was the combination of recurrent vomiting and the conversion symptom ataxia. The third syndrome, occurring in most other patients with Briquet's syndrome, is the onset of a complex illness before age 26, back pain, painful menstrual periods, and either sexual indifference or conversion reactions. The presence of one of these symptom clusters should lead to especially careful consideration of the possibility of Briquet's syndrome, including detailed review of past medical records.

Recurrent somatic complaints lead to repeated hospitalizations for observation, laboratory tests, x-rays, and surgery. A wide variety of specialists may be consulted because of the range of unexplained complaints. Abdominal, pelvic, and back pain often lead to frequent gynecologic surgery: dilatation and curettage, uterine suspension, and hysterectomy. Gastrointestinal complaints lead to frequent x-rays and laparotomies. Complaints of headaches, fits, and other sensorimotor problems lead to neurologic evaluations. Psychiatrists are often consulted because of agitated depressions, suicide attempts, and interpersonal problems.

On mental status examination, histrionic personality traits and the hysterical information-processing deficit described earlier are prominent in most cases. Such patients are circumstantial, imprecise, and inconsistent historians. They recall their current situation and past history as a series of separate elements mixed together or mingled without sorting, discrimination, or apprehension of functional relationship and temporal order. As a result, it is useful to obtain collateral information from other observers and from records.

Social maladjustment is prominent in

most cases also. This may include juvenile delinquency, frequent divorce or marital separations, child neglect and inconsistent parenting, and low job productivity. Interpersonal relations are often shallow and chaotic.

## Clinical Course

The course of illness in Briquet's syndrome or somatization disorder is chronic, with fluctuation in the frequency and diversity of symptoms but without complete remission (Guze and Perley, 1963; Guze, Cloninger, Martin, Clayton, in press). The most floridly symptomatic phase is usually early adulthood, but aging does not lead to remission. Prospective longitudinal studies have confirmed that 80 per cent to 90 per cent of patients have a similar clinical picture and the same diagnosis over many years (Perley and Guze, 1962; Guze et al., in press). This stability of clinical picture and consistency of diagnosis is observed for both Briquet's syndrome and DSM-III somatization disorder (Cloninger et al., in press). Some clinicians have questioned whether this is a consequence of the requirement of many years of past sickliness. However, the course of somatoform disorders in the relatives of chronic somatizers is also chronic; there is no excess of individuals with acute or episodic disorders (Woerner and Guze, 1968). Also, chronic somatizers show qualitatively different neurophysiologic responses than do acute somatizers (Mears and Horvath, 1972). Although individual symptoms may wax and wane, these clinical, familial, and neurophysiologic observations indicate that the underlying disorder is a stable trait with a chronic course.

## Laboratory Findings

Patients with Briquet's syndrome are not immune to other medical illnesses, so laboratory tests are useful to document concurrent illnesses objectively. However, no specific laboratory tests are available for diagnosis of Briquet's syndrome itself. Some nonspecific laboratory tests include low pain thresholds (Bianchi, 1973) and failure to habituate to repetitive stimuli (Mears and Horvath, 1972), but these are not sufficiently discriminating for use in routine clinical practice.

## Differential Diagnosis from Physical Disorders

The individual symptoms encountered in Briquet's syndrome and somatization disorder are nonspecific. In other words, they occur in many different medical disorders so that the differential diagnosis of the individual symptoms encompasses all of clinical medicine. Three features help to distinguish Briquet's syndrome from physical disorders: (1) involvement of multiple organ systems, (2) early onset and chronic course without development of physical signs of structural abnormalities, and (3) absence of characteristic laboratory abnormalities of other physical disorders. Medical disorders that begin with nonspecific functional and sensory abnormalities with transient or equivocal physical signs may present diagnostic problems. Multiple sclerosis and systemic lupus erythematosus are classic examples of conditions that are often misdiagnosed early in their course. However, they seldom satisfy the multisystem requirements for diagnosis of Briquet's syndrome; only about 14 per cent of female medical inpatients have the range of symptoms characteristic of Briquet's syndrome even when symptoms are counted that may be medically explained (Reveley et al., 1977). Even patients with multiple coincident disorders can be distinguished by attention to the onset, course, and associated physical and laboratory findings of individual complaints (Woodruff, 1967). Two conditions that are associated with metabolic disturbances affecting multiple organ systems—porphyria and hypercalcemia—present clinical pictures that are most likely to be confused with the full Briquet's syndrome.

Acute intermittent porphyria (AIP) and other hepatic porphyrias may resemble Briquet's syndrome with a history of recurrent pains and neurologic disturbances. AIP is due to a hereditary partial deficiency of porphobilinogen (PBG) deaminase, which leads to the accumulation of PBG and its precursor, delta-aminolevulinic acid, in blood and their excretion in urine. Like Briquet's syndrome, AIP is familial. Carrier status, demonstrated by assay of erythrocyte PBG de-

**TABLE 9–4**    Utility of Psychiatric Criteria for Distinguishing Conversion and Dissociative Reactions from Physical Disorders

| Putative Diagnostic Criteria | Predicts No Physical Disorder |
|---|---|
| Briquet's syndrome | Yes |
| Prior history of conversions | Yes |
| Prior history of recurrent somatic complaints | Yes |
| Current anxiety or dysphoria | No |
| Emotional stress before onset | |
|    any | No |
|    previous history of conversions with conflict resolution | Yes |
|    with symbolism | No |
| Secondary gain | No |
| Partial improvement with suggestion or sedation | No |
| MMPI profile type | No |
| Histrionic personality | |
|    with prior history of conversions | Yes |
|    no prior history of conversion | No |
| La belle indifference | No |

MMPI, Minnesota Multiphasic Personality Inventory.

aminase, is inherited as an autosomal dominant disorder. Carriers may complain of mood swings and pains even when their urine PBG levels are within the normal range (Bissell, 1982; Stein and Tschudy, 1970). Factors that increase the demand for heme synthesis lead to overproduction of heme precursors and clinical symptoms. Drugs such as alcohol and barbiturates that induce the microsomal cytochromes in liver often precipitate acute attacks. Other drugs that precipitate attacks include chlordiazepoxide, imipramine, and estrogens. Recurrent painful premenstrual exacerbations occur in some women and resolve with onset of menstruation. As in Briquet's syndrome, clinical symptoms are uncommon before puberty and carrier status is more often expressed in women than in men. PBG can be converted to a dark compound called porphobilin in the bladder; this is accelerated by exposure of voided urine to light, so some patients may notice that their urine darkens after voiding. PBG and its precursor appear to have neurotoxic effects. Neuropathic changes are variable, with patchy demyelination of peripheral nerves and focal degeneration of autonomic nerves. Acute attacks usually include complaints of abdominal, back, or extremity pain. Tachycardia, anorexia, nausea, and vomiting are also frequent. Constipation is often a chronic problem in carriers and may be exacerbated during acute attacks. In such cases, x-rays often reveal a paralytic ileus. Neuropsychiatric symptoms include seizures, paralysis, con-

fusion, and psychotic behavior. Routine laboratory tests are usually normal except for slight elevation of serum transaminase activity, even during acute attacks. Urine PBG levels are elevated during attacks, and this may be documented by rapid qualitative methods (Schwartz-Watson or Hoesch tests). In 20 per cent to 30 per cent of carriers, however, urine PBG levels are within normal limits when they are not in acute distress. In these cases, only assay of erythrocyte PBG will identify carriers (Bissell, 1982). Other types of hepatic porphyrias are associated with elevated levels of serum porphyrins that lead to skin abnormalities not seen in Briquet's syndrome or in acute intermittent porphyria.

Various causes of hypercalcemia may present with symptoms that cross-sectionally suggest Briquet's syndrome. These include a large number of nonspecific symptoms in many organ systems: (1) central nervous system—lethargy, depression, emotional lability, confusion, and drowsiness; (2) neuromuscular system—easy fatigability, weakness (especially of the proximal muscles), joint pains, pruritus; (3) gastrointestinal system—anorexia, nausea, vomiting, constipation, dyspepsia; (4) cardiovascular system—hypertension, arrhythmias; (5) renal system—polyuria, stone diathesis. Early onset and course of illness in Briquet's disorder distinguishes it from most causes of hypercalcemia, such as hyperparathyroidism, vitamin D or A toxicity, diuretic therapy, and cancer. Also, serum calcium is routinely tested by most physicians, so hypercalcemia is seldom mistaken for Briquet's syndrome.

Chronic systemic infections, such as brucellosis and trypanosomiasis, may present a picture suggestive of chronic somatization disorders. Although they are uncommon in general, they should be considered in patients who live in endemic areas or who have a history of relevant exposures, such as brucellosis in slaughterhouse workers. After returning from his voyage on the *Beagle* in 1836, at age 27, Charles Darwin was described as sickly and hypochondriacal by his friends, family, and physicians of the time, who could find no physical explanation for his chronic complaints of fatigue, recurrent abdominal pain, vomiting, abdominal bloating, palpitations, dizziness, chest pain, and insomnia. Darwin withdrew socially and remained a semiinvalid attentively ministered by his wife at home until his death of heart disease at age 73. Some psychiatrists have suggested that Darwin had hysterical or hypochondriacal neurosis, and his social withdrawal and acceptance of his wife's careful attention to his needs have been offered as evidence of his neurosis. It is known, however, that in 1835 in South America he had extensive bites from the insect *Triatoma infestans*, the most frequent carrier of the trypanosome of Chagas' disease (De Beer, 1980). This American trypanosome was not discovered until 1909, and the disease was not described by Chagas until 1916. The acute phase of this infestation is seldom recognized, and in the chronic phase there may be effects in multiple organ systems, with the cardiovascular and gastrointestinal systems most prominent clinically, as in Darwin's case (Macedo, 1982). With more sophisticated diagnostic methods and chemotherapy, such chronic infections have become uncommon in industrial societies.

Neurologic and other medical disorders that must be differentiated from conversion and dissociative reactions are discussed later because they seldom present with symptoms in multiple organ systems.

## Differential Diagnosis from Psychiatric Disorders

The psychiatric disorders that must be considered in the differential diagnosis of Briquet's syndrome include the anxiety disorders, the affective disorders, and the schizophrenic disorders. The most difficult distinction is between anxiety disorders and Briquet's syndrome. Patients with Briquet's syndrome present with recurrent panic attacks in most cases. Similarly, features of generalized anxiety disorder (motor tension, autonomic hyperactivity, apprehensive expectation, and vigilance and scanning phenomena) are common in Briquet's syndrome. Age of onset and course are of little help in differentiating anxiety disorders from Briquet's disorder. Patients with anxiety disorders also often have disease fears and hypochondriacal disease convictions. Conversion and dissociative symptoms, sexual and menstrual problems, social maladjustment, and histrionic personality traits are the major distinguishing features. Men are more likely to have anxiety disorders than somatoform disorders also. The distinction may be difficult in individual cases, but it is clinically important because the family history and clinical management of Briquet's syndrome are different from that of anxiety disorders (Guze, Woodruff, Clayton, 1971b).

Patients with unipolar and bipolar affective disorder may present with multiple somatic complaints associated with depressive syndromes. In fact, the chief complaint in depressive disorders is often a physical complaint like headache, gastrointestinal distress, or other pain. These complaints are transient, however, and resolve with the treatment of the depression, whereas in Briquet's syndrome the physical complaints persist regardless of the mood state.

Patients with schizophrenia sometimes present initially with somatic complaints. Only later are they found to have systematized delusions and hallucinations in addition to their somatic complaints. Some of their somatic complaints may be due to somatic hallucinations and delusions, but this is often difficult to resolve. There is no familial aggregation of schizophrenia and Briquet's syndrome so the somatic complaints appear to be symptomatic of schizophrenia.

Patients with antisocial and histrionic personality disorders often have associated Briquet's syndrome or somatization disorder. These disorders aggregate both within individuals and within families (Cloninger et al., 1970, 1975) and may have a common pathogenesis in many cases. Such personality disorders do not preclude an additional diagnosis of Briquet's syndrome or somatization disorder.

Occasional patients with Briquet's syndrome or somatization disorder may be found to produce some of their symptoms factitiously or to malinger. Even when this is documented for some occasions, the patient may insist that the symptom occurs spontaneously on other occasions. Such claims are difficult or impossible to resolve, and the distinction often has little or no practical consequence in clinical management.

## Treatment and Clinical Management

The optimal treatment of Briquet's syndrome or somatization disorder is unknown. Claims of superiority of particular methods of management have often varied with the vogue of the times. A review of treatment studies (Scallet et al., 1976) shows that psychotherapeutic approaches, including psychoanalysis, dynamically oriented psychotherapy, behavior therapy, and group therapy, have no superiority over eclectic psychotherapy that mainly involves education about their illness, reassurance, and redirection of their attention from somatic complaints to work on improving social skills. Somatic therapies such as use of anxiolytics, electrosleep therapy, and electroconvulsive therapy have limited and transient benefits (Scallet et al., 1976). Patients with Briquet's syndrome or somatization disorder have a high rate of utilization of health care services so it is essential that all physicians understand the principles involved in their clinical management.

The first phase of clinical management must be the establishment of the diagnosis and of a therapeutic alliance. Patients with Briquet's syndrome or somatization disorder often change doctors after a short time or may go to several doctors at the same time. They quickly reject the conclusion that there is nothing wrong with them physically and seek another evaluation and more tests from another physician. They also quickly reject the suggestion that their symptoms are due to psychological distress or psychiatric disorder if this is equated with the absence of a physical basis to their complaints. Therefore, it is useful to inform a patient

who is suspected of having somatization that you recognize that they are ill and uncomfortable, but before beginning treatment, it will be necessary to see them at least a few times to know them more fully, to review their medical history carefully, and to obtain records of prior diagnostic evaluations and treatments. This communicates your empathy and willingness to evaluate their complaints seriously and is essential to establishing their confidence in your subsequent diagnosis and treatment plan. It also provides the time needed to properly evaluate alternative diagnoses; if neglected initially, the patient is likely to reject any reassurance that they are not physically ill because you do not really know enough about them. Thorough evaluations can be carried out in most cases without additional invasive tests. The time taken to carefully review and document the patient's history initially will pay long-term benefits in accuracy of diagnosis and effectiveness of compliance with followup and treatment. Considering the frequency and cost of the use of health care services by these patients, the time required is easily justified.

The second step is to explain to the patient that they have Briquet's syndrome or somatization disorder and what this means. It is essential to communicate to the patient that they have a real disorder that leads to their experiencing characteristic symptoms that distinguish their disorder from other disorders that lead to progressive physical deterioration and from other psychiatric disorders that do not have such prominent physical complaints. Many patients are reassured that their disorder has been recognized by physicians as a valid entity, that it has a name, that it is heritable, and that it does not lead to progressive physical deterioration. However, they will not be much reassured by this information alone because they are uncomfortable, disabled, and seeking relief of their discomfort and help to reduce their disability. It is important to communicate a realistic treatment plan and goals both for the sake of the patient and yourself.

The goal of treatment in Briquet's syndrome is to educate the patient to manage his or her own life more effectively, not for the physician to cure and relieve all symptoms passively. If a passive cure is promised or expected, both the patient and the physician will be frustrated and disappointed.

Realistic goals include reduced frequency and severity of physical complaints, improved social adjustment, and reduced cost and frequency of medical treatment.

These goals can usually be achieved by adherence to a few treatment principles. First, it is essential to limit the number of doctors the patient is seeing. Often a primary-care physician alone can effectively manage a patient with Briquet's syndrome. Alternatively, patients with prominent psychosocial problems do best when seen by both a psychiatrist and a primary-care physician on different occasions but with close consultation. An important behavioral management principle is to schedule regular visits that are neither increased nor decreased in frequency in response to somatic complaints.

Second, it is essential that invasive or costly diagnostic evaluations and treatments only be undertaken in response to objective evidence, and not in response to subjective complaints alone. Of course, patients with Briquet's syndrome or somatization disorder are not immune to physical disorders. A physician who is responsible for all the health-care needs of a patient over many years has much more knowledge of his usual status in order to recognize the emergence of another disorder. Sometimes a patient may be frustrated with the physician for not doing more tests or not prescribing a desired medication and threaten to change physicians. This should be met with an empathetic but firm response that such a change would be unfortunate because the physician knows her history well and this knowledge permits the physician to be most effective in carrying out his commitment to providing the best possible care of the patient in the long run. A thorough annual physical examination and routine tests provide reassurance.

Third, it is essential to recognize that patients with Briquet's syndrome or somatization disorder usually have much discomfort from anxiety or depressive symptoms that are often associated with many personal and social problems. They often have limited social skills and methods for dealing with stressful or difficult interpersonal problems. Often their physical complaints are precipitated or exacerbated coincident with increasing stress. They often have information-processing deficits that make it difficult for them to recognize the relationship between their physical complaints and social problems. When the information-processing deficit is not too great, it may be possible for them to improve their skill at recognizing what is upsetting them when they experience an exacerbation of somatic symptoms. Even if this is not accomplished, it is possible to modify the patient's behavior by simple behavioral management techniques. The physician should show little interest and attention in physical complaints and great interest in personal and social problems (Morrison, 1978). Alternative ways of dealing with social and personal problems can be concretely discussed by reviewing the advantages and disadvantages of each of several possible courses of action and inaction. The goal is to improve the patient's problem-solving skills by concrete, nondirective discussion to practical problems of immediate interest. It may be helpful for the patient to keep a diary of her activities, symptoms, and associated circumstances in order to identify recurrent factors that precipitate symptoms or reinforce sick role behavior. Operant conditioning of sick role behavior is discussed in detail in relation to chronic pain later. Actual direction and advice must be avoided; direct advice fosters dependence rather than increased self-esteem and facilitates manipulation of the therapist by the patient. In addition to teaching problem-solving techniques, the patient can be taught that regular brief periods of rest and relaxation may reduce tension and that this will indirectly reduce sensitivity to pain, muscle spasms, and other factors associated with somatic discomfort. A wide variety of relaxation techniques are available at little or no cost (Scallet et al., 1976). The combination of instruction in relaxation techniques and training in problem-solving and social skills may help the patient to deal with psychosocial stress with less disability from physical discomfort.

Fourth, the prescription of medication should be kept to a minimum and carefully monitored. Wheatley (1962, 1964, 1965) has shown that low doses of anxiolytic drugs provide some symptomatic improvement in these patients in a series of double-blind clinical trials with general practitioners. Chlordiazepoxide, phenobarbital, amobarbital, and the phenothiazine pericyazine were compared in various trials. Chlordiazepoxide was recommended because of safety, patient preference, and equivalent effectiveness in symptom relief (Wheatley, 1965). The best results were obtained by optimistic doctors using low doses of medication regardless of which anxiolytic drug was used. The preferred regimen was chlordiazepoxide, 5 mg three times daily. The response to placebo tablets was uniformly poor, and it was concluded that the use of placebo tablets is of little value in the treatment of somatizers. Other drugs besides anxiolytics may be preferable in some cases. Some patients with Briquet's syndrome as adults have a history of attention-deficit disorder with hyperactivity as children; these adult hyperkinetics often are dramatically improved on stimulants, such as methylphenidate, amphetamine, and the non-euphoriant pemoline (Wender, Reimherr, Wood, 1981). Other patients without childhood inattention, hyperactivity, and impulsivity do not tolerate such stimulants. More patients show improvement on antidepressants, but the effective doses are often lower than usually required in primary major depressive disorders: Mann and Greenspan (1976) reported rapid improvement on 25 to 50 mg of imipramine. However, patients with Briquet's syndrome or somatization disorder are often erratic about taking medication; develop drug dependence on sedatives, analgesics, and euphoriant drugs; and may attempt suicide by overdosing. Accordingly, it is important to teach relaxation techniques in order to minimize the need for medication. Medication should be selectively prescribed in the lowest effective dosage schedule and discontinuation trials undertaken regularly.

Fifth, it is useful to maintain contact with family members. Patients with Briquet's disorder are such poor observers and historians that information from others involved in their lives on a daily basis is often needed for the physician to know what is really happening. Family members can assist the physician maintain compliance with therapy and alert the physician to emerging social problems, doctor shopping, medication abuse, or forms of noncompliance with therapy.

Finally, it is essential that the physician place firm limits on excessive or manipulative demands by the patient (Murphy and Guze, 1960; Murphy, 1982). These limits should be guided by the preceding principles with an attitude of optimism and confidence that such patients can eventually reduce their disability and discomfort, learn to cope more effectively with their problems, and avoid unnecessary medical and social complications.

## CONVERSION AND DISSOCIATIVE REACTIONS (ACUTE HYSTERIA)

### Definition

A conversion reaction is a sudden, temporary loss or alteration in sensorimotor function or some other physical functions in response to psychological conflict. The classic examples of conversion reactions are sensorimotor abnormalities that suggest neurologic disorders. These include sensory losses, such as blindness, deafness, anosmia, anesthesia, and analgesia, or sensory alterations, such as diplopia and dysesthesias. Other classic examples often involve motor abnormalities alone, such as paralysis, ataxia, dysphagia, and aphonia, or in combination with disturbances of consciousness or sensation, such as pseudoseizures and unconsciousness. Thus the classic conversion reactions involve the special senses or voluntary nervous system, but DSM-III also includes some disturbances of the autonomic nervous system or endocrine system when these disturbances appear to be direct symbolic expressions of psychological conflict. For example, disgust or rejection of particular situations or activities may be symbolized by recurrent psychogenic vomiting; or the wish for pregnancy may be symbolized by pseudocyesis (false pregnancy). Many clinicians prefer to reserve the term conversion reaction for the classic sensorimotor disturbances because autonomic and endocrine disturbances more often have a chronic course (Cloninger, in press). Conversion disorder is not diagnosed in DSM-III when symptoms are limited to pain (see psychogenic pain disorders later) or sexual dysfunction.

Conversion symptoms are not diagnosed simply by the exclusion of neurologic or other physical disorders. An essential element of the diagnosis is that there is a close temporal relationship between the onset of the symptom and an environmental precipitant that appears to involve a psychological conflict or need of the patient. Judgments about such precipitation are often uncertain unless the chain of events is repeated, so the diagnosis of a conversion reaction is unreliable unless the symptom is recurrent. DSM-III (1980) also permitted diagnosis of conversion disorder when there was no identifiable environmental precipitant, but the symptom enabled the individual to obtain "secondary gain." Secondary gain refers to the patient obtaining additional support or avoiding undesired activities because of the symptom. This has little diagnostic value, however, because many patients with medical illnesses obtain such secondary gain from their illness. Accordingly, the 1980 DSM-III criteria are being revised to exclude diagnosis based on secondary gain and to distinguish between isolated and recurrent conversions.

A dissociative reaction is a sudden, temporary, psychogenic loss of memory, alteration in consciousness, or alteration in identity. When there is an alteration in consciousness, important personal events cannot be recalled and the patient may be disoriented, perplexed, and wander aimlessly. When there is an alteration in identity, the person may forget his usual identity, travel to a new location, and assume a new identity temporarily; this is called a fugue. An uncommon example of a dissociative disorder is the phenomenon of multiple personality: the existence of two or more fully integrated personalities within an individual, each of which is dominant at different times and with unique memories, complex social activities, and behavior patterns. Transition between personalities or the onset of amnesic or fugue states is usually precipitated by psychosocial stress, such as marital quarrels, personal rejection, or events associated with a high risk of injury or death. Thus both conversion and dissociative states are typically precipitated by severe psychosocial stress, but it is often difficult to elicit the relevant history before treatment without collateral informants. Both conversion and dissociative states suggest the possibility of neurologic disorders and are characterized by abrupt onset and resolution. Accordingly, they are sometimes grouped together as acute hysteria or hysterical neurosis.

## Etiology

Dissociative and conversion reactions appear to depend, in at least some cases, on descending or corticofugal inhibitory brain mechanisms. This was initially suggested in 1963 by Hernandez-Peon, Chavez-Ibarra, and Aguilar-Figueroa based in part on a study of a patient with hysterical hemianesthesia, using averaged electroencephalographic (EEG) responses evoked by painful stimuli. No somatosensory responses were evoked by stimulation of the anesthetized side, but stimulation of the healthy side evoked normal responses. The inhibition was relative, operating only up to a certain level of stimulus intensity. Active inhibition was indicated by responses returning to normal with anesthesia. Similar findings have been obtained with visually evoked responses in 14 patients with hysterical blindness (Behrman and Levy, 1970). A longitudinal study of a patient with depersonalization revealed little or no fluctuation in skin conductance during the dissociative state (Lader, 1969), but she reverted to a state of marked agitation with frequent spontaneous fluctuations in skin conductance when the depersonalization state remitted.

These observations all support the hypothesis that conversion and dissociative reactions may be precipitated by excessive cortical arousal, which in turn triggers reactive inhibition of signals at synapses in sensorimotor pathways by way of negative feedback relationships between the cerebral cortex and the brainstem reticular formation (Berlyne, 1967; Hernandez-Peon, 1961). This accounts for the consistent temporal relationship between stressful events and the onset of acute hysteria (Raskin, Talbott, Meyerson, 1966), the reduction in anxiety and autonomic activity during conversion and dissociative states (Lader, 1969), and the effectiveness of sodium amobarbital infusions—and other methods of sedation that are discussed later—in relieving the symptoms (Frumkin, Ward, Grim, 1981).

Before these modern physiologic studies were possible, detailed clinical studies of patients with conversion and dissociative reactions were a major impetus to the development of many psychodynamic concepts by Janet (1907) and Freud (1964). Both men thought that the development of hysterical symptoms was the result of disturbing mental associations becoming unavailable to consciousness by voluntary recall. Janet proposed that hysterical symptoms could arise when forces that normally serve to integrate mental function fail and some functions escape from active central control. This theoretical process was referred to by Janet as dissociation. In contrast, Freud suggested that there was an active process by which disturbing mental associations were removed from conscious awareness. This active process of removal from availability to voluntary recall was called repression and was conceived as a mechanism to protect the patient from emotional pain arising from either disturbing external circumstances or anxiety-provoking internal urges and feelings. The theoretical formulation of Freud is remarkably analogous to contemporary theories based on more refined neurophysiologic data.

Current psychodynamic theory suggests that conversion symptoms are a direct symbolic expression of the underlying psychological conflict, rather than an undifferentiated reaction to stress. Primary gain is defined in terms of the effectiveness of a conversion symptom in reducing anxiety by symbolic expression of the repressed wish. In practice, however, the evaluation of symbolism is usually difficult or impossible in brief consultations (Raskin et al., 1966). Social learning, mimicry, and suggestion also appear to influence at least the form of conversion phenomena: patients with conversions often have been exposed to a model for their symptom (Raskin et al., 1966). The model may have been the illness of another person, a previous illness, or even concurrent physical disease. For example, individuals with epilepsy may also develop pseudoseizures that simulate their usual fits or a seizure by one person in a school or factory may herald "mass hysteria" in which conversion symptoms spread like contagion (Temoshok and Attkisson, 1977).

Individuals differ in their susceptibility to conversion and dissociative reactions. Individuals with histrionic, antisocial, or dependent personality disorders or with Briquet's syndrome are more likely to develop acute hysterical symptoms than others (Guze et al., 1971a; American Psychiatric Association, 1980). Increased susceptibility to conversion and dissociative reactions is found in individuals with low sedation thresholds, frontal lobe trauma or impairment, or dominant cerebral hemisphere dysfunction (Shagass and Jones, 1958; Slater, 1948; Flor-Henry et al., 1981). However, conversions may occur in individuals with no associated psychopathology or neuropsychological deficits.

Most studies have not distinguished between individuals with single and recurrent conversions, and these groups may be qualitatively distinct but overlapping populations. Acute hysterics habituate normally to repetitive sound stimuli whereas chronic hysterics do not (Mears and Horvath, 1972).

Most patients with conversion reactions have bilateral symptoms, but left-sided symptoms predominate when the symptoms are unilateral (Stern, 1977; Galin, Diamond, Braff, 1977). The left-sided predominance is more pronounced in women than in men (Flor-Henry et al., 1981). Flor-Henry et al. (1981) suggest that this asymmetrical distribution of unilateral conversion reactions and of psychogenic pain (Merskey and Watson, 1979) is a direct consequence of brain neural organization. Wyke (1967) studied the effects of brain lesions on the rapidity of upper limb movement and found that left hemisphere lesions produced both ipsilateral and contralateral abnormalities, whereas right brain lesions had only contralateral effects. Similarly, in studies of discriminative touch sensibility, Semmes (1968) found ipsilateral deficits with left hemispheric lesions but contralateral deficits with right hemispheric lesions. Thus brain dysfunction is likely to be associated with either bilateral or left-sided sensorimotor symptoms.

## Epidemiology

Estimates of the incidence and prevalence of conversion and dissociative reactions depend greatly on whether they are based on treated cases or on self-report of past symptoms regardless of treatment. A past history of one or more classic conversion or dissociative reactions was found in 27 per cent of 100 normal postpartum women (Farley, Woodruff, Guze, 1968) and in 30 per cent of 50 medically ill women (Woodruff, 1967). Most of these symptoms remitted quickly without treatment but were clearly recalled because of the dramatic and severe nature of the symptom. When the same interview was given to psychiatric outpatients, about 25 per cent had a past history of conversions (Guze et al., 1971a), which is similar to the risk in the general population. This suggests that the association of conversion and dissociative reactions with psychopathology may be greatly influenced by treatment-seeking behavior.

In contrast, treated cases of conversion or dissociative reaction are uncommon. The incidence of treatment for conversion reactions over a 10-year period was 22 per 100,000 in New York and 11 per 100,000 in Iceland (Stefansson, Messina, Meyerowitz, 1976). The hospital incidence in New York during the same period was 4.5 per cent for conversions. Dissociative reactions appear to be even more uncommon than conversions: only 1.3 per cent of all admissions to an Air Force medical center were for dissociative reactions (Kirshner, 1973). Even in treated samples, however, a high proportion of patients in some settings have some conversion symptoms observed when assessment is systematic: about 25 per cent of all men in a Veterans Administration neuropsychiatric hospital in Appalachia had one or more conversions at some time during their hospitalization (Weinstein, Eck, Lyerly, 1969).

Although it is often said that conversion and dissociative reactions are becoming less common, available data suggest no actual change (Stephens and Kamp, 1962). Some psychiatrists may now see fewer patients with acute hysteria than in the past because they are now often referred to neurologists or internists (Chodoff, 1974). Among patients referred for psychiatric consultation in medical centers, about 14 per cent are referred because of conversion symptoms (Ziegler, Imboden, Meyer, 1960; McKegney, 1967).

Patients with acute hysteria are most often adolescents or young adults (Ziegler et al., 1960; Guze et al., 1971a), but patients of all ages may present with conversions (Temoshok and Attkisson, 1977). Women outnumber men by a factor of 2:1 (Stefansson et al., 1976) to 5:1 (Ziegler et al., 1960). Acute hysteria is more common in lower socioeconomic groups (Hollingshead and Redlich, 1958; Stefansson et al., 1976). Fewer patients with 1 or more years of college report a history of conversion or dissociative reactions

than those with less education (Guze et al., 1971a). The incidence of treatment for acute hysteria may be higher in rural areas than in urban areas (Temoshok and Attkisson, 1977). Interpreting these differences is difficult because they are based on series of treated cases, and the vast majority of all conversion and dissociative reactions appear to remit spontaneously without treatment.

## Pathology

By definition, there are no pathologic findings that account for the symptoms.

## Clinical Picture

Conversion and dissociative reactions are not syndromes or discrete disorders with their own characteristic clinical picture. They are individual symptoms occurring in response to stress in a wide variety of psychiatric or medical disorders. Nevertheless, the diagnosis may be useful to distinguish individual psychogenic symptoms from individual symptoms of physical disorders. The fundamental clinical issue is to identify the associated clinical features that permit an accurate distinction from symptoms of physical disorders.

Investigators who have followed patients for several years after a diagnosis of conversion or dissociative reaction have identified those features that permit a reliable distinction from physical disorders. Several studies have found that a previous history of conversion or other unexplained physical complaints is the most reliable predictor that the patient will not later be proven to have a physical disorder (Gatfield and Guze, 1962; Slater, 1965; Perley and Guze, 1962; Raskin et al., 1966; Purtell et al., 1951; Guze et al., 1971a; Bishop and Torch, 1979). The diagnosis of conversion or dissociative reactions is unreliable in the absence of a definite history of Briquet's syndrome or a past history of transient unexplained symptoms that recur in association with well-defined precipitants.

Patients with Briquet's syndrome or a past history of conversion or dissociative reactions are not immune to physical disorders. Thus the presence of prior hysterical symptoms is not a sufficient basis for diagnosis. The evaluation of emotional stress is a difficult but necessary part of the clinical assessment. Events that are obviously stressful often precede the onset or exacerbation of physical disorders as well as various psychiatric disorders and do not distinguish true conversions from initially undiagnosed physical disorders (Raskin et al., 1966; Watson and Buranen, 1979). However, Raskin et al. (1966) reported success in distinguishing conversion symptoms from physical disorders by judgments about whether the symptoms appeared to solve a psychological conflict brought about by a precipitating stress. Their judgment was highly dependent on the patient's report of prior conversion symptoms or transient somatic complaints: that is, an event that would be trivial for an average individual was judged to be significant because it was reportedly associated with somatic symptoms in the past. Thus clinical judgments about psychogenic stress seem to be reliable only when the sequence of events has been repeated.

The *complete* resolution of symptoms by suggestion, hypnosis, or intravenous infusion of sedatives like amobarbital is useful in distinguishing conversion and dissociative reactions from physical disorders. For example, psychogenic amnesia often clears, whereas organic amnesia is often worsened with amobarbital infusions (Ward, Rowlett, Burke, 1978; Frumkin et al., 1981). Physical disorders may be exacerbated by associated anxiety, and *partial* improvement with reassurance or sedation often occurs in such cases. Such concurrent anxiety or partial improvement with reduction of anxiety may lead to misdiagnosis of physical disorders (Gatfield and Guze, 1962; Watson and Buranen, 1979). For example, Gatfield and Guze (1962) found that 21 per cent of 24 patients diagnosed as conversion reactions on a neurology service had definite neurologic diseases 3 to 10 years later to explain the original symptoms. All these diagnostic errors were due to temporary partial improvement with medical evaluation or sedation that had falsely suggested psychiatric illness.

Signs and symptoms that appear inconsistent with known anatomical distributions or that vary from one examination to another are frequent in patients with conversion reactions (Weintraub, 1983). Such judgments are notoriously unreliable because of limitations in knowledge of pathophysiology, marked variation in the presentation of physical disorders, and limited methods for objective assessment. Patients with undiagnosed physical disorders are often in distress and may exaggerate or misrepresent their symptoms. Consequently, patients with both physical disorders and somatoform disorders may be difficult to evaluate.

The diagnosis of conversion disorder is often suspected if patients are dramatic or suggestible. Such findings are associated with conversions but, like inconsistent signs and symptoms, are not a reliable basis for diagnosis in the absence of past history of recurrent psychogenic symptoms.

## Clinical Course

The course of conversion and dissociative reactions depends on the organ system that is affected. Classic pseudoneurologic symptoms, including sensorimotor conversions and psychogenic amnesia or fugue states, are characterized by their abrupt onset and resolution. The duration of the individual attack is usually short and self-limited. Occasionally, pseudoneurologic symptoms may become chronic or recurrent, especially when the precipitating stress is chronic or recurrent, when there is associated chronic psychopathology, or when persistence of the symptom is reinforced by secondary gain. Patients with pseudoseizures are more likely to have recurrences than are patients with paralysis or aphonia (Hafeiz, 1980; Weintraub, 1983). The overall course of illness is dominated by the course of any underlying physical or psychiatric disease. For example, multiple personality disorder is often associated with chronic psychopathology, but the individual transitions usually are brief.

Endocrine disturbances are often chronic and misdiagnosed physical disorders. For example, most patients with symptoms suggestive of pseudocyesis can be shown to have an objective endocrine disturbance, most often a prolactinoma, with radioimmunoassays of serum prolactin (Cohen, 1982).

In contrast, patients with psychogenic vomiting, like psychogenic pain patients, usually have a chronic course. Psychogenic vomiting is seldom debilitating, despite its chronicity (Rosenthal, Webb, Wruble, 1980; Wruble, Rosenthal, Webb, 1982), whereas psychogenic pain is often disabling (Blumer and Heilbronn, 1982).

## Laboratory Findings

Acute hysteria is not associated with abnormal laboratory findings. The results of neurophysiologic tests and other laboratory findings largely depend on any associated psychopathology or physical disease.

## Differential Diagnosis

General aspects of the clinical picture that aid in differential diagnosis were noted earlier, but differential diagnosis in individual cases depends on the particular symptoms. Marked weakness in the presence of normal deep tendon reflexes may suggest the possibility of a conversion reaction, but myasthenia gravis, periodic paralysis, myoglobinuric myopathy, polymyositis, and other acquired myopathies must be considered. In myasthenia gravis, weakness may come and go, but typical attacks last for weeks rather than for hours or days. Myopathies are usually associated with prominent myalgia, and muscle enzymes assays and electromyography permit differentiation. Also, discolored urine is observed with myoglobinuria. Attacks of weakness in periodic paralysis are usually precipitated by exercise or by eating a large meal but may also be precipitated by frightening experiences or injections of epinephrine. Potassium metabolism is altered in periodic paralysis, and many cases are inherited as a mendelian dominant. Weakness of arms and legs is seen early in acute idiopathic polyneuritis of the Guillain-Barré type.

Sudden unilateral blindness owing to optic neuritis may be confused with a conversion reaction, since the funduscopic examination is normal in both conditions. Diminished direct light reflex usually permits a differentiation, and many patients with optic neuritis later develop other signs of multiple sclerosis.

Apparent dissociative phenomena, including amnesia, fugue, and multiple personality, may either result from complex partial seizures owing to a temporal lobe focus or be secondarily generalized from another brain region (Mayeux, Alexander, Benson, Brandt, Rosen, 1979; Schenk and Bear, 1981). Prolonged or repetitive complex partial seizures with continuous interictal confusion have been documented in episodes lasting for as long as 3 days. Depression and anxiety may herald the onset of fugue caused by such complex partial seizures, and apparently, psychogenic behavior responds to anticonvulsant therapy (Mayeux et al., 1979).

A detailed, practical guide to the differential diagnosis of a wide variety of specific conversion, dissociative, and pain symptoms has been presented by Weintraub (1983).

## Treatment

The diagnosis and treatment of conversion and dissociative reactions must be approached with caution and respect for the patient for two major reasons. The differentiation of physical and psychogenic symptoms is unreliable early in the course of illness, so the physician must observe carefully and avoid premature conclusions based on inadequate data. If the symptom is truly psychogenic, the patient is in distress and the symptom has an adaptive role. Relief of the symptom and treatment of associated psychosocial problems may have a major impact on later adjustment. If a patient is told that there is nothing "real" wrong with him, he will often deteriorate rather than improve. If the symptom is relieved but the associated psychosocial problems that precipitated the symptom are not recognized and managed, the symptoms may recur. Improper management can have serious consequences, leading to chronic disability. In contrast, proper management can be rewarding because of the rapid and complete resolution of the symptoms.

As soon as possible after conversion and dissociative reactions are suspected, it is important to obtain collateral information about the circumstances associated with the onset of symptoms. The patient's own account is often incomplete or inaccurate before treatment, and this information can expedite treatment.

Once a presumptive diagnosis of conversion or dissociative reaction is made, the first phase of treatment is the reassurance and relaxation of the patient. Many patients are reassured by a calm and thorough history and physical examination. Some patients who remain overtly agitated may benefit from mild sedation. It is nearly always countertherapeutic to tell the patient initially that the symptom is psychogenic. It is more helpful to suggest to the patient that from your examination, you are confident that the symptom will disappear quickly and completely. It is also useful to suggest that the symptom may already be beginning to disappear. As long as the patient does not become more agitated, recent events and feelings may be discussed without drawing any specific causal connection with the symptom. If the patient becomes more agitated, he should be reassured and encouraged to relax quietly for a short while before continuing with further discussion.

If this conservative approach of reassurance and relaxation does not result in remission of the symptom, then an amobarbital (Amytal) interview has both diagnostic and therapeutic value. A 10% solution of Amytal Sodium is slowly injected intravenously; 500 mg of Amytal Sodium diluted in sterile water to 5 ml is injected at a maximum rate of 1 ml/min. Before the infusion begins the patient should be informed that you expect the conversion or dissociative symptom to disappear with this treatment. During the infusion the physician should suggest that the symptom is beginning to disappear. The patient can be asked to try to recall the circumstances preceding the onset of the symptom, and it can be suggested that the medication being infused will help this recall. When the patient's words begin to slur, administration should be stopped and the patient observed. Often the removal of the symptom is accompanied by recall of the precipitating stress, which is expressed with much crying and sighing. The patient can be reassured that he will be able to discuss what was upsetting him without so much distress later and that the symptom will not recur.

Suggestion, hypnosis, Amytal Sodium, and other relaxation treatments are all effective in the first, acute phase of treatment (Weintraub, 1983; Hafeiz, 1980; Frumkin et al., 1981). Although some have suggested that amobarbital is more effective than other approaches (Frumkin et al., 1981), Hafeiz (1980) found that other relaxation techniques as well as 10 mg of methylamphetamine injected intravenously were more effective than a 5% solution of amobarbital. Regardless of the particular technique used, the emphasis in this phase is on rapid relief of the symptom to prevent reinforcement of its persistence by secondary gain, to identify and recall precipitating psychosocial stressors, and to establish a therapeutic alliance. The treatment of acute hysteria is a psychiatric emergency requiring both empathy and a push for rapid resolution because the risk of recurrence and chronic disability are strongly associated with the prior duration of symptoms before treatment (Hafeiz, 1980).

The second phase of treatment is to support the patient and help him to recognize and cope with the psychosocial stress that initially precipitated the symptom. If the precipitating stress is unlikely to recur and the patient has no major underlying psychopathology, then this phase of treatment is likely to be brief, with little risk of recurrence. On the other hand, persistent stress or associated psychopathology may require long-term psychiatric treatment. The duration and type of treatment at this phase must be individualized according to these associated factors.

## PSYCHOGENIC PAIN (CHRONIC IDIOPATHIC PAIN)

### Definition

Pain is one of the most frequent and difficult symptoms that a physician must evaluate. It is a subjective experience, and a patient's pain threshold varies with his attention, mood, fatigue, and suggestion. In other words, there is always an interaction between physical stimuli and psychological state in the perception of pain, so the distinction between physical (pathogenic) and psychogenic pain is moot. Even when clinicians attempt to rate the etiology of chronic pain on an organic-nonorganic continuum based on comprehensive diagnostic data, the agreement among different raters is, at best, moderate; in a study of 100 consecutive patients referred to a pain clinic, Fordyce, Brana, and Holcomb (1978) found the interjudge correlation for such ratings was only 0.57 even though the raters had access to the same data. In a followup study of patients diagnosed as having psychogenic pain, Slater (1965) found that acute pain proved to result, in most cases, from physical disorders. When the pain remains unexplained despite repeated observation over 6 months, psychological factors that lead to persistence or exacerbation of the pain often develop. Nevertheless, obscure organic pathology may remain unrecognized. For example, Hendler, Uematesu, and Long (1982) used thermography to evaluate 224 consecutive patients with no radiologic, neurologic, orthopedic, or laboratory abnormalities to explain their chronic pain. Abnormal results of thermography in 19 per cent led to revised diagnoses of reflex sympathetic dystrophy, nerve root irritation, and thoracic outlet syndrome. Other series have found up to 54 per cent abnormal thermograms (Weintraub, 1983). Thus attempts to evaluate the causes of pain according to the Cartesian mind/body dichotomy are doubtful in principle and unreliable in practice.

DSM-III criteria for psychogenic pain are identical to those for conversion disorder except that the symptoms are limited to pain. The required judgments about psychogenicity have proved to be impossible in most patients, and it is now recommended that the pathogenic/psychogenic distinction not be attempted (Williams and Spitzer, 1982). Patients with chronic (6 months') preoccupation with pain are recognized as having idiopathic pain disorder if the pain is unexplained after extensive evaluation or if the functional impairment or complaints are grossly in excess of what would be expected from the physical findings. Such patients are clinically heterogeneous in terms of their pre-pain psychopathology, but most have a characteristic pattern of psychiatric symptoms and pain-related behaviors that appears to be learned or conditioned by the consequences of their recurrent complaints about pain.

## Etiology

Pain-related behavior may be learned by either operant or classical conditioning. Operant conditioning occurs when certain behaviors are reinforced (increased in frequency or strength) through contingent rewards or when particular behaviors are decreased in frequency or strength by punishment or inhibition. For example, the frequency and intensity of pain-related complaints may be reinforced by increased attention from friends and relatives, relief from carrying out undesirable activities such as hard physical labor or undesired sexual obligations, the pleasurable effects of analgesics given as needed for pain, the possibility of monetary gain from litigation or disability compensation. At the same time, health-related behaviors may be inhibited by instruction by physicians, lawyers, and well-meaning associates not to work and to assume an invalid role or by the need to remain sick in order to collect compensation. Classical conditioning can also occur with chronic pain patients so that ordinary neutral objects begin to evoke pain-related behavior. A pain patient's bedroom or work area may evoke an increase in pain if earlier experience with these settings has been associated with pain. Such learned behavior cannot be eliminated by relief or correction of the original source of pain, so separation from such conditioned stimuli and behavioral modification in pain centers may be necessary.

Demoralization and learned helplessness, as described by Seligman (1975), may account for the prominence of depressive symptoms in many patients with chronic pain. Such patients appear anergic, anhedonic, dependent, and helpless after prolonged periods in which they are unable to achieve rewards for initiating health-related behavior (Morse, 1983).

There is some evidence that prior social models and cultural attitudes may predispose some individuals to developing chronic pain-related behavior. Apley (1975) studied 1100 British schoolchildren and found that half of those with chronic unexplained abdominal pain had a close relative with chronic pain compared with such a family history in only one eighth of children with a clear physical explanation for their abdominal pain. It is believed that the Irish and Anglo-Saxons have greater pain tolerance than southern Mediterranean ethnic groups, suggesting substantial ethnic differences. Some empirical studies confirm these cultural and ethnic stereotypes about pain tolerance (Woodrow, Friedman, Siegelaub, Cohen, 1972), but others do not. Flannery, Sos, and McGovern (1981) found no significant difference in episiotomy pain among five ethnic groups (blacks, Italians, Jewish, Irish, and Anglo-Saxon Protestants). Zborowski (1969) found that ethnic differences are more prominent in first-generation immigrants than in later generations.

Neurons in the cerebral cortex and medulla can inhibit the firing of trigeminal and spinal pain transmission neurons. The activity of this descending pain inhibition system is mediated, at least in part, by endorphins, which are endogenous opiatelike compounds. Serotonin has an inhibiting effect on pain perception and is probably the neurotransmitter of the descending inhibitory pathways that arise in the raphe nucleus of the medulla (Posner, 1982). Accordingly, it is interesting that endorphins and serotonin metabolites are decreased in the cerebrospinal fluid of chronic pain patients (von Knorring, Almay, Johansson, Terenius, 1979). The extent of the reduction in endorphins correlates with the tendency to augment the intensity of incoming sensory stimuli as measured by the slope of the amplitude of averaged evoked EEG potentials in response to increasing stimulus intensities. Thus what appears to be an overdramatized description of pain in relation to physical abnormalities is associated with an objective neurophysiologic tendency to augment sensory input. It is unclear whether the amplification or abnormally decreased inhibition of pain in such patients is a cause or an effect of the observed clinical state. Regardless of the original direction of effects, there are objective neurophysiologic and biochemical differences between patients with chronic pain and patients with other psychiatric and medical conditions.

## Epidemiology

Few epidemiologic data are available about chronic pain patients, but the number of pain control facilities indicates that such patients are not uncommon. In 1979 the Pain Clinic Directory, published by the American Society of Anesthesiologists, listed 285 pain control facilities in the United States. Most of the patients in such facilities have mala-daptive pain-related behavior conditioned by the consequences of their chronic complaints (Brena and Chapman, 1983).

## Pathology

Many postural and gait abnormalities can be caused by chronic misuse of braces, collars, and ambulatory devices by pain patients. Low activity and poor postural habits may lead to contractures and myofibrositis. Prolonged inactivity can also lead to osteoporosis, overweight, and circulatory and respiratory disorders. Abuse of aspirin and phenacetin can lead to gastric, renal, or hepatic damage. Thus pain-related behavior may in turn cause added nociceptive stimulation, creating a vicious cycle of progressive deterioration.

## Clinical Picture

Patients with chronic pain-related behaviors manifest a life-style that has been characterized as the "disease of the Ds" (Brena and Chapman, 1983): (1) dramatic display in describing the painful experience: vague, diffuse complaints that are often inconsistent with documented organic pathology or known pathophysiologic mechanisms; (2) disuse and degeneration of various body functions as consequences of the pain-related behavior; (3) drug misuse and doctor shopping; (4) dependency: passivity and learned helplessness, which lead to demoralization and depression; (5) disability: pain-contingent financial compensation or desire for compensation through litigation and disability claims.

Blumer and Heilbronn (1982) evaluated a consecutive series of 129 patients with chronic unexplained pain and compared them with 36 patients with chronic rheumatoid arthritis who were receiving gold therapy. They noted that the chronic idiopathic pain patients had many more of the Ds than did the patients with chronic rheumatoid arthritis (Table 9–5). They also noted that such patients seemed unable to appreciate and verbalize their feelings. This inability to read one's own emotions has been called alexithymia (Nemiah, 1978). Although nearly all the patients showed depression and dependency after the onset

**TABLE 9–5   Clinical Features of Chronic Pain Patients**

**Somatic complaints**
  Continuous pain of obscure origin
  Hypochondriacal preoccupation
  Desire for surgery and passive medical cures
**Solid citizen**
  Denial of conflicts
  Idealization of self and of family relations
  Ergomania (prepain): "workaholism," relentless activity
**Depression**
  Anergia (postpain): lack of initiative, inactivity, fatigue
  Anhedonia: inability to enjoy social life, leisure, and sex
  Insomnia
  Depressive mood and despair
**History**
  Family (and personal) history of depression and alcoholism
  Past abuse by spouse
  Crippled relative
  Relative with chronic pain

Based on Blumer D, Heilbronn M: Chronic pain as a variant of depressive disease: The pain-prone disorder. J Nerv Ment Dis 170:381–406, 1982.

of pain, only 12 per cent had a history of depression before the onset of pain. The most prominent depressive symptoms are anergia, insomnia, and anhedonia, which are typically attributed to the pain; diurnal variation, loss of weight, and psychomotor retardation are unusual. Patients with chronic idiopathic pain had a history of more chronic overtime at work before onset of pain compared with those with rheumatoid arthritis (50 per cent vs. 28 per cent) and more often took no annual vacation (48 per cent vs. 22 per cent). A careful history from the patient and family members often reveals that the symptoms are almost identical with pain learned from a previous experience or observation. Patients often seek passive cures by physicians without accepting their own responsibility for modifying pain-related behavior, setting up what Berne (1964) called the pain game, in which the doctor inevitably fails and feels guilty if he accepts the patient's premise that the doctor is responsible for the pain and its consequences.

Women tend to complain of pain in the face, abdomen, or genital region, whereas men usually complain of pain in the back or chest (Weintraub, 1983). Prepain psychopathology, if any, is highly variable: major affective disorders, alcoholism, Briquet's syndrome, and various anxiety states and personality disorders are the most common associated diagnoses.

## Course

The course of illness depends on associated psychopathology, prior duration of pain, and extent of external reinforcement. Patients with lifelong adjustment problems, as in Briquet's syndrome, or pending or continuing monetary compensation are unlikely to improve regardless of treatment (Brena and Chapman, 1983). If there are many operantly conditioned pain-related behaviors, remission is unlikely without treatment in which the patient is removed from her usual environment and these contingencies are modified before the patient's return.

## Laboratory Findings

Infrared thermography is useful in identifying changes in vascular flow associated with some cases of chronic pain. According to available studies, there is reduced vascular flow and lower temperature in the anatomical region of pain that is undetected by other tests (Hendler et al., 1982). There is a low correlation between thermographic findings and clinical symptoms (Weintraub, 1983). Also, changes in vascular flow may be psychologically induced or learned, as in autogenic training or biofeedback, so that the question of original psychogenicity remains moot.

## Differential Diagnosis

Several medical syndromes are characterized by chronic pain that cannot be diagnosed by routine evaluations, including electromyography, myelography, and tomography of affected regions. These include sympathetic reflex dystrophies and myofascial pain syndromes, such as tension headaches (Posner, 1982). Thermography is abnormal in these disorders.

## Treatment

All physicians need to be knowledgeable about the first phase of pain management—the prevention of learned illness behavior associated with pain. Often chronic pain-related behaviors are, in part, iatrogenic and preventable. Prevention involves attention to behavioral management principles in prescription of medication, providing disability statements to employers and others, and educating the patient and his family about illness behavior.

Brena (1983) has summarized the following guidelines for use of drugs in chronic pain patients: (1) The use of any sedative or antianxiety drug has no lasting benefit and is a potential iatrogenic problem because of frequent misuse and complications. The patient and his family should be informed that such drugs can cause depression and foster dependency. (2) The use of opiates should be limited to nonambulatory patients in cases of clear pathogenic pain. When the decision to use opiates is made, the drug must be given in doses high enough to provide effective analgesia. (3) In cases of chronic pain associated with a nonprogressive, noninvasive pathologic process of long duration, the drug of first choice is a tricyclic antidepressant, such as amitriptyline or doxepin, not sedatives or antianxiety medication. Depression, whether endogenous or reactive, should be treated with tricyclic antidepressants. If a rheumatic-type inflammatory process is documented, a nonsteroidal anti-inflammatory drug may be added. This permits encouragement of activity rather than inactivity. (4) No drug for chronic pain should be prescribed on an as-needed basis. Time-contingent prescriptions are less likely to lead to drug misuse through conditioning. Demands from the patient should be resisted, and drugs should never be prescribed, even temporarily, without proper assessment and followup. (5) Patients should be informed about possible drug reactions and complications in order to increase the likelihood that they will comply with prescribed limits. (6) Alternative treatment approaches, such as relaxation therapies, should be provided. Many patients requesting drugs for sleep and muscle spasms will have no further need for drugs after they have learned relaxation skills.

It is important for the physician to encourage appropriate activity rather than inactivity in order to avoid fostering sick role developments. The physician should explain the importance of normal activities of daily living in preserving physical and mental adjustment and should return the patient to activity that is appropriate for his physical status. This requires accurate assessment of physical limitations because premature or excessive activity can cause later avoidance of activity. Any statement of disability from the physician, whether to the patient, the family, employers, lawyers, or others, should be objectively documented, not based on subjective complaints alone, and should always be time-limited rather than indefinite. Most often operantly conditioned pain behavior is promoted by the patient's medical ignorance or misunderstanding, which the physician can correct. The patient and his family should be informed when pain is not a symptom of a progressive disease and when physical activity can be increased without risk of harm. The meager rewards of chronic pain behavior are ultimately self-defeating and should be contrasted with those of effective well behavior. Disability benefits are generally adequate only for subsistence; depression and dependency accompany relief from responsibility; sympathy from others is usually brief and gives way to avoidance; and pain behaviors are not effective ways to communicate needs and feelings accurately to others.

In patients with chronic pain who have already developed conditioned pain-related behavior, it is important for the doctor and the patient to realize that the benefits of somatic treatment of any underlying physical disease will be independent of the benefits of psychiatric treatment of the learned sick role behaviors. Elimination of the original cause of the pain will not extinguish the conditioned sick role behavior and subjective complaints may actually intensify.

The goals of psychiatric treatment of chronic pain are to replace pain-related behavior with normal activity and to counteract the Ds by detoxifying patients misusing medication, decreasing subjective pain intensity, increasing activities of daily living, teaching competent coping skills to deal with impairment and suffering, and providing vocational evaluation and rehabilitation. It is often useful to have the patient keep a diary of her daily activity, pain, and associated circumstances in order to identify any patterns suggesting conditioned behavior. This can be supplemented by interviewing family members. A wide variety of treatment strategies may be useful, including relaxation and biofeedback, cognitive therapy, behavior modification, and structured milieu-group therapy programs (Brena and Chapman, 1983). When conditioned pain behaviors are extensive, individual outpatient treatment is often unsuccessful, and it may be necessary to remove the patient from his usual setting, evaluate and treat him in a pain clinic or comprehensive pain control facility, educate the family, and restructure the environment before returning the patient home. Pain centers are medical facilities for diagnosis and treatment that are staffed by a team of physicians, psychologists, physical and occupational therapists, and consulting medical specialists. About 70 per cent of patients who go through such pain control programs are improved (Brena and Chapman, 1983). Many of the refractory patients have continuing disability compensation or associated chronic psychopathology, such as personality disorders, drug dependence, or Briquet's syndrome.

## HYPOCHONDRIASIS AND OTHER SOMATOFORM DISORDERS

Hypochondriasis has been conceptualized in four ways that are supported by data (Barsky and Klerman, 1983). First, hypochondriasis is conceptualized as a psychiatric syndrome composed of "functional" somatic complaints, fear of disease, body preoccupation, and the persistent pursuit of medical care despite reassurance. Second, according to psychodynamic theory, the patient is disturbed by problems of anger and hostility, orality and dependency, low self-esteem, guilt, and masochism. Third, the cognitive set the patient uses to assess body sensations tends to amplify and augment normal body sensations so that the patient has a low threshold and tolerance of physical sensations, often misinterpreting normal sensations as an indication of disease. Fourth, hypochondriasis is socially learned sick role behavior and indirect interpersonal communication that is reinforced by success in eliciting caretaking and other secondary

gains from the sick role. These features are all characteristic of the somatoform disorders in general, and serious doubt exists about whether there is a discrete disease entity corresponding to hypochondriacal neurosis.

The DSM-III criteria for hypochondriasis or hypochondriacal neurosis require preoccupation with an unrealistic fear or belief of having a serious disease and impaired social or occupational function despite medical evaluation and reassurance. The concept that such patients have an augmenting perceptual style and often misinterpret normal sensations is mentioned in the DSM-III description, but it is not part of the criteria.

Until the late nineteenth century, hypochondriasis was associated specifically with complaints involving the hypochondriac region of the abdomen—that is, below the costal cartilages—rather than with regionally nonspecific morbid disease preoccupation (Cloninger et al., 1984). The DSM-III criteria are essentially the same as proposed by Gillespie in 1928, who believed that hypochondriasis was an independent, discrete disease entity. Kenyon (1976) concluded from an extensive literature review and a controlled study of 512 psychiatric patients with hypochondriacal symptoms that hypochondriasis was always a secondary part of another syndrome, usually a depressive illness. In addition, Bianchi (1973) carried out a principal-components analysis of 235 psychiatric patients and identified one component that corresponded to a distinct group of female patients who had a syndrome of multiple somatic complaints, unnecessary surgery, and psychogenic pain associated with a low pain threshold. Bianchi concluded that these women had Briquet's syndrome and that other aspects of hypochondriasis were ancillary symptoms of other primary psychiatric disorders. For example, those scoring high on his disease conviction component usually had endogenous depressions and those with disease phobias usually had an anxiety neurosis.

It is important to note that most studies of hypochondriasis have been done in psychiatric patients rather than in the general population except for the recent Stockholm Adoption Study of somatoform disorders (Sigvardsson et al., 1984; Cloninger et al., 1984; Bohman et al., 1984). It may well be that few patients with hypochondriasis ever see psychiatrists because they believe that the symptoms of psychiatric patients are imaginary, not real, whereas they know that their own suffering is real. More studies with general or primary-care populations are needed before any conclusions about other somatoform disorders can be drawn.

## REFERENCES

Adam G: Interception and Behavior. Budapest, Akademiai Kiado, 1967.

Almgren PE, Nordgren L, Skantze H: A retrospective study of operationally defined hysterics. Br J Psychiatry 132:670–673, 1978.

American Psychiatric Association Task Force on Nomenclature and Statistics: Diagnostic and Statistical Manual of Mental Disorders, ed 3. Washington, DC, American Psychiatric Association, 1980.

Apley J: The Child with Abdominal Pains. Oxford, Blackwell, 1975.

Barsky A, Klerman G: Overview: Hypochondriasis, bodily complaints, and somatic styles. Am. J. Psychiatry 140:273–283, 1983.

Behrman J, Levy R: Neurophysiological studies on patients with hysterical disturbances of vision. J Psychosom Res 14:187–194, 1970.

Bendefeldt F, Miller LL, Ludwig AM: Cognitive hysteria. Arch Gen Psychiatry 33:1250–1254, 1976.

Berlyne DE: Arousal and reinforcement, in Divine D (ed): Nebraska Symposium on Motivation. Lincoln, University of Nebraska Press, 1967, pp 1–110.

Berne E: Games People Play. New York, Grove Press, 1964.

Bianchi GN: Patterns of hypochondriasis. A principal components analysis. Br J Psychiatry 122:541–548, 1973.

Bishop ER Jr, Torch EM: Dividing "Hysteria": A preliminary investigation of conversion disorder and psychalgia. J Nerv Ment Dis 167:348–357, 1979.

Bissell DM: Porphyria, in Wyngaarden JB, Smith LH Jr (eds): Cecil's Textbook of Medicine, ed 16. Philadelphia, WB Saunders Co, 1982, pp 1121–1126.

Blumer D, Heilbronn M: Chronic pain as a variant of depression disease: The pain-prone disorder. J Nerv Ment Dis 170:381–406, 1982.

Bohman M, Cloninger CR, von Knorring A-L, Sigvardsson S: An adoption study of somatoform disorders. III. Cross-fostering analysis and genetic relationship to alcoholism and criminality. Arch Gen Psychiatry 41:872–878, 1984.

Brena SF: Drugs and pain: Use and misuse, in Brena SF, Chapman SL (eds): Management of Patients with Chronic Pain. New York, Spectrum, 1983, pp 121–130.

Brena SF, Chapman SL (eds): Management of Patients with Chronic Pain. New York, Spectrum, 1983.

Briquet P: Traite clinique et therapeutique a l'hysterie. Paris, J-B Balliere & Fils, 1859.

Cantwell D: Psychiatric illness in the families of hyperactive children. Arch Gen Psychiatry 27:414–417, 1972.

Chodoff P: The diagnosis of hysteria: An overview. Am J Psychiatry 131:1073–1078, 1974.

Cloninger CR: The link between hysteria and sociopathy: An intergrative model of pathogenesis based on clinical, genetic, and neurophysiological observations, in Akiskal HS, Webb WL (eds): Psychiatric Diagnosis: Explorations of Biological Predictors. New York, Spectrum, 1978, pp 189–218.

Cloninger CR: Diagnosis of somatoform disorders: A critique of DSM-III, in Tischler GL (ed): Diagnosis and Classification in Psychiatry. New York, Cambridge University Press, in press.

Cloninger CR, Guze SB: Psychiatric illness and female criminality: The role of sociopathy and hysteria in the antisocial woman. Am J Psychiatry 127:303–311, 1970.

Cloninger CR, Martin RL, Guze SB, Clayton PJ: Somatization disorder in men and women: A prospective follow-up and family study. Am J Psychiatry, in press.

Cloninger CR, Reich T, Guze SB: The multifactorial model of disease transmission. III. Familial relationship between sociopathy and hysteria (Briquet's syndrome). Br J Psychiatry 127:11–22, 1975.

Cloninger CR, Sigvardsson S, von Knorring A-L, Bohman M: An adoption study of somatoform disorders. II. Identification of two discrete somatoform disorders. Arch Gen Psychiatry 41:863–871, 1984.

Cohen LM: A current perspective of pseudocyesis. Am J Psychiatry 139:1140–1144, 1982.

Coryell W: A blind family history study of Briquet's syndrome. Further validation of the diagnosis. Arch Gen Psychiatry 37:1266–1269, 1980.

De Beer G: Charles Darwin, in Encyclopedia Britannica Macropedia, vol 5. pp 492–496. Chicago, Encyclopedia Brittanica Inc. 1980.

Farley J, Woodruff RA Jr, Guze SB: The prevalence of hysteria and conversion symptoms. Br J Psychiatry 114:1121–1125, 1968.

Flannery RB, Sos J, McGovern P: Ethnicity as a factor in the expression of pain. Psychosomatics 22:39–50, 1981.

Flor-Henry P, Fromm-Auch D, Tapper M, Schopflocher D: A neuropsychological study of the stable syndrome of hysteria. Biol Psychiatry 16:601–626, 1981.

Fordyce WE, Brana SF, Holcomb RJ: Relationship of patient semantic pain descriptions to physician diagnostic judgments, activity level measures, and MMPI. Pain 5:293–303, 1978.

Freud S: Standard Edition of the Complete Psychological Works of Sigmund Freud. London, Hogarth Press, 1964.

Frumkin LB, Ward NG, Grim PS: A possible cerebral mechanism for the clearing of psychogenic symptoms with amobarbital. Biol Psychiatry 16:687–692, 1981.

Galin D, Diamond R, Braff D: Lateralization of conversion symptoms: More frequent on the left. Am J Psychiatry 134:578–580, 1977.

Gatfield PD, Guze SB: Prognosis and differential diagnosis of conversion reactions (A follow-up study). Dis Nerv Sys 23:1–8, 1962.

Gillespie R: Hypochondria: Its definition, nosology, and psychopathology. Guys Hosp Rep 78:408–460, 1928.

Guze SB: The diagnosis of hysteria: What are we trying to do? Am J Psychiatry 124:491–498, 1967.

Guze SB, Cloninger CR, Martin RL, Clayton PJ: A follow-up and family study of Briquet's syndrome. Br J Psychiatry, in press.

Guze SB, Perley MJ: Observations on the natural history of hysteria. Am J Psychiatry 119:960–965, 1963.

Guze SB, Woodruff RA Jr, Clayton PJ: A study of conversion symptoms in psychiatric outpatients. Am J Psychiatry 128:643–646, 1971a.

Guze SB, Woodruff RA Jr, Clayton PJ: Hysteria and antisocial behavior: Further evidence of an association. Am J Psychiatry 127:957–960, 1971b.

Guze SB, Woodruff RA Jr, Clayton PJ: Sex, age, and the diagnosis of hysteria (Briquet's syndrome). Am J Psychiatry 129:745–748, 1973.

Hafeiz HB: Hysterical conversion: A prognostic study. Br J Psychiatry 136:548–551, 1980.

Hendler N, Uematesu S, Long D: Thermographic validation of physical complaints in "psychogenic pain" patients. Psychosomatics 23:283–287, 1982.

Hernandez-Peon R: Reticular mechanisms in sensory control, in Rosenblith WA (ed): Sensory Communication. New York, Wiley, 1961.

Hernandez-Peon R, Chavez-Ibarra G, Aguilar-Figueroa E: Somatic evoked potentials in one case of hysterical anesthesia. EEG Clin Neurophysiol 15:889–892, 1963.

Hollingshead AB, Redlich FC: Social class and mental illness. New York, Wiley, 1958.

Horowitz MJ (ed): Hysterical Personality. New York, Jason Aronson, 1977.

Hyler S, Spitzer R: Hysteria split asunder. Am J Psychiatry 135:1500–1504, 1978.

Janet P: The Major Symptoms of Hysteria. New York, Macmillan, 1907.

Kellner R, Sheffield BF: The one week prevalence of symptoms in neurotic patients and normals. Am J Psychiatry 130:102–105, 1973.

Kenyon F: Hypochondriacal states. Br J Psychiatry, 129:1–14, 1976.

Kimble R, Williams JG, Agras S: A comparison of two methods of diagnosing hysteria. Am J Psychiatry 132:1197–1199, 1975.

Kirshner LA: Dissociative reactions: An historical review and clinical study. Acta Psychiatr Scand 49:698–711, 1973.

Lacey JI, Smith RL, Green A: Use of conditioned autonomic responses in study of anxiety. Psychosom Med 17:208–217, 1955.

Lader MH: Psychophysiology of anxiety, in Lader M (ed): Studies of Anxiety. Br J Psychiatry Special Pub No 3, 1969.

Lindberg BJ, Lindegard B: Studies of the hysteroid personality attitude. Acta Psychiatr Scand 39:170–180, 1963.

Ludwig AM: Hysteria: A Neurobiological theory. Arch Gen Psychiatry 27:771–786, 1972.

Macedo V: Chagas' disease (American trypanosomiasis), in Wyngaarden JB, Smith LH Jr (eds): Cecil's Textbook of Medicine, ed 16. Philadelphia, WB Saunders Co, 1982, pp 1728–1731.

Mai FM, Merskey H: Briquet's treatise on hysteria. A synopsis and commentary. Arch Gen Psychiatry 37:1401–1405, 1980.

Mann HB, Greenspan SI: The identification and treatment of adult brain dysfunction. Am J Psychiatry 113:1013, 1976.

Martin RL, Cloninger CR, Guze SB: The evaluation of diagnostic concordance in follow-up studies. II. A blind follow-up of female criminals. J Psychiatr Res 15:107–125, 1979.

Mayeux R, Alexander MP, Benson DF, Brandt J, Rosen J: Poriomania. Neurology 29:1616–1619, 1979.

Mayou R: The nature of bodily symptoms. Br J Psychiatry 129:55–60, 1976.

McKegney FP: The incidence and characteristics of patients with conversion reactions. I. A general hospital consultation service sample. Am J Psychiatry 124:542–545, 1967.

Mears R, Horvath TB: "Acute" and "chronic" hysteria. Br J Psychiatry 121:653–657, 1972.

Merskey H, Watson GD: The lateralization of pain. Pain 7:271–280, 1979.

Morrison JR: Management of Briquet's syndrome (hysteria). West J Med 128:482–487, 1978.

Morrison JR, Stewart MA: The psychiatric status of the legal families of adopted hyperactive children. Arch Gen Psychiatry 28:888–891, 1973.

Morse RH: Pain and emotions, in Brena SF, Chapman SL (eds): Management of Patients with Chronic Pain. New York, Spectrum, 1983, pp 47–54.

Murphy GE: The clinical management of hysteria. JAMA 247:2559–2564, 1982.

Murphy GE, Guze SB: Setting limits. Am J Psychother 14:30–47, 1960.

Nemiah JC: Alexithymia and psychosomatic illness. J Clin Exp Psychiatry 25–37, 1978.

Perley MJ, Guze SB: Hysteria—the stability and usefulness of clinical criteria. N Engl J Med 266:421–426, 1962.

Posner JB: Pain, in Wyngaarden JB, Smith LH Jr (eds): Cecil's Textbook of Medicine, ed. 16. Philadelphia, WB Saunders Co, 1982, pp 1940–1948.

Purtell JJ, Robins E, Cohen ME: Observations on clinical aspects of hysteria. JAMA 146:901–909, 1951.

Raskin M, Talbott JA, Meyerson AT: Diagnosis of conversion reactions: Predictive value of psychiatric criteria. JAMA 197:102–106, 1966.

Reveley MA, Woodruff RA Jr, Robins LN, Taibleson M, Reich T, Helzer J: Evaluation of a screening interview for Briquet Syndrome (Hysteria) by the study of medically ill women. Arch Gen Psychiatry 34:145–149, 1977.

Rinieris PM, Stefanis CN, Lykouras EP, Varsou EK: Hysteria and ABO blood types. Am J Psychiatry 135:1106–1107, 1978.

Robins E, O'Neal P: Clinical features of hysteria in children. Nerv Child 10:246–271, 1953.

Robins LN: Deviant Children Grown Up. Baltimore, Williams & Wilkins, 1966.

Robins LN, Helzer JE, Croughan J, Ratcliff KS: National Institute of Mental Health Diagnostic Interview Schedule: Its history, characteristics, and validity. Arch Gen Psychiatry 38:381–389, 1981.

Rosenthal RH, Webb WI, Wruble LD: Diagnosis and management of persistent psychogenic vomiting. Psychosomatics 21:722–730, 1980.

Scallet A, Cloninger CR, Othmer E: The management of chronic hysteria: A review and double-blind trial of electrosleep and other relaxation methods. Dis Nerv Sys 37:347–353, 1976.

Schafer R: Clinical Application of Psychological Tests. New York, International Universities Press, 1948.

Schalling D: Psychopathy-related personality variables and the psychophysiology of socialization, in Hare RD, Schallings D (eds): Psychopathic Behavior: Approaches to Research. New York, John Wiley, 1978, pp 85–106.

Schalling D, Cronholm B, Åsberg M, Espmark S: Ratings of psychic and somatic anxiety indicants—interrater reliability and relations to personality variables. Acta Psychiatr Scand 49:353–368, 1973.

Schenk L, Bear D: Multiple personality and related dissociative phenomena in patients with temporal lobe epilepsy. Am J Psychiatry 138:1311–1316, 1981.

Seligman MEP: Helplessness. San Francisco, WH Freeman, 1975.

Semmes J: Hemispheric specialization: A possible clue to mechanism. Neuropsychologia 6:11–16, 1968.

Shagass C, Jones AL: A neurophysiological test for psychiatric diagnosis: Results in 750 patients. Am J Psychiatry 114:1002–1009, 1958.

Shapiro D: Neurotic Styles. New York, Basic Books, 1965.

Sigvardsson S, von Knorring A-L, Bohman M, Cloninger C: An adoption study of somatoform disorders: I. The relationship of somatization to psychiatric disability: Arch Gen Psychiatry 41:853–859, 1984.

Slater ETO: Psychopathic personality as a genetical concept. Br J Psychiatry 94:277–282, 1948.

Slater ETO: Diagnosis of hysteria. Br Med J 1:1395–1399, 1965.

Stefansson JG, Messina JA, Meyerowitz S: Hysterical neurosis, conversion type: Clinical and epidemiological considerations. Acta Psychiatr Scand 53:110–138, 1976.

Stein JA, Tschudy DP: Acute intermittent porphyria. A clinical and biochemical study of 46 patients. Medicine 49:1, 1970.

Stephens JH, Kamp M: On some aspects of hysteria: A clinical study. J Nerv Ment Dis 134:305, 1962.

Stern DB: Handedness and the lateral distribution of conversion reactions. J Nerv Ment Dis 164:122–128, 1977.

Temoshok L, Attkisson CC: Epidemiology of hysterical phenomena: Evidence for a psychosocial theory, in Horowitz MJ (ed): Hysterical Personality. New York, Jason Aronson, 1977, pp 145–222.

von Knorring L, Almay BGL, Johansson F, Terenius L: Endorphins in CSF of chronic pain patients, in relation to augmenting-reducing response in visual averaged evoked response. Neuropsychobiology 5:322–326, 1979.

Ward N, Rowlett D, Burke P: Sodium amylobarbitone in the differential diagnosis of confusion. Am J Psychiatry 135:75–78, 1978.

Warner R: The diagnosis of antisocial and hysterical personality: An example of sex bias. J Nerv Ment Dis 166:839–845, 1978.

Watson CG, Buranen C: The frequency and identification of false positive conversion reactions. J Nerv Ment Dis 167:243–247, 1979.

Weinstein EA, Eck RA, Lyerly OG: Conversion hysteria in Appalachia. Psychiatry 32:334–341, 1969.

Weintraub MI: Hysterical Conversion Reactions: A Clinical Guide to Diagnosis and Treatment. New York, Spectrum, 1983.

Weissman MM, Myers JK, Harding PS: Psychiatric disorders in a U.S. urban community: 1975–76. Am J Psychiatry 135:459–462, 1978.

Wender PH, Reimherr FW, Wood DR: Attention deficit disorder ("Minimal Brain Dysfunction") in adults: A replication study of diagnosis and drug treatment. Arch Gen Psychiatry 38:449, 1981.

Wheatley D: Evaluation of psychotherapeutic drugs in general practice. Psychopharmacol Bull 2:25–32, 1962.

Wheatley D: General practitioner clinical trials: Phenobarbitone compared with an inactive placebo in anxiety states. Practitioner 192:147–151, 1964.

Wheatley D: General practitioner clinical trials: Chlordiazepoxide in anxiety states. II. Long-term study. Practitioner 195:692–695, 1965.

Williams JBW, Spitzer RL: Idiopathic pain disorder: A critique to pain-prone disorder and a proposal for a revision of the DSM-III category psychogenic pain disorder. J Nerv Ment Dis 170:410–419, 1982.

Woerner PI, Guze SB: A family and marital study of hysteria. Br J Psychiatry 114:161–168, 1968.

Woodrow KM, Friedman GD, Siegelaub AB, Cohen MF: Pain tolerance according to age, sex and race. Psychosom Med 34:548–556, 1972.

Woodruff RA Jr: Hysteria: An evaluation of objective diagnostic criteria by the study of women with chronic medical illnesses. Br J Psychiatry 114:1115–1120, 1967.

Wruble LD, Rosenthal RH, Webb WL: Psychogenic vomiting: A review. Am J Gastroenterol 77:318–321, 1982.

Wyke M: Effect of brain lesions on the rapidity of arm movement. Neurology 17:113–120, 1967.

Zborowski M: People in Pain. San Francisco, Jossey-Bass, 1969.

Ziegler FF, Imboden JB, Meyer E: Contemporary conversion reactions: A clinical study. Am J Psychiatry 116:901–910, 1960.

# chapter 10

# ANXIETY AND PHOBIC DISORDERS

*by* Russell Noyes, Jr., M.D.

## ANXIETY DISORDERS

### Definition

Anxiety is an emotion that anticipates danger but lacks a clearly identified object. It is accompanied by increased alertness and physiologic arousal that prepares the organism for action. In this sense, it has adaptive potential. Pathologic anxiety represents an inappropriate response to a nonthreatening environment and causes impairment in functioning. When used in the psychopathologic sense, the term may refer to a symptom, a syndrome, or a disorder. The anxiety syndrome is made up of psychological, somatic, and behavioral symptoms or dimensions.

### History

The recent history of anxiety disorders is dominated by competing beliefs about the nature of these disturbances. In 1871, Da Costa published a classic description of an affliction he observed among soldiers of the Union Army. He believed that it represented an abnormal reaction to exertion and gave the label "irritable heart" to what later became known as Da Costa's syndrome. In 1895, Freud separated anxiety neurosis from neurasthenia, a category that Beard had popularized. He believed that anxiety was the primary disturbance and early on claimed that sexual repression was an important etiologic factor. In the absence of a clearly defined cause or organ system abnormality, there continues to be uncertainty about whether anxiety disorders are medical or psychiatric. During World War II they were more frequently diagnosed and treated by psychiatrists. Yet many internists continue to speculate on the nature of functional heart disturbances with little regard for the role of anxiety.

### Classification

Two anxiety disorders are described in the *Diagnostic and Statistical Manual of Mental Disorders*, third edition, DSM-III (American Psychiatric Association, 1980).

Panic disorder is named for its essential feature—recurrent anxiety, or panic attacks. These attacks are characterized by the sudden onset of intense, unprovoked anxiety, together with symptoms of autonomic nervous system hyperactivity.

A. **At least three panic attacks within a 3-week period not caused by marked physical exertion or life-threatening circumstances.**

B. Panic attacks consisting of discrete periods of apprehension or fear accompanied by at least four of the following symptoms:
  1. dyspnea
  2. palpitations
  3. chest pain or discomfort
  4. choking or smothering sensations
  5. dizziness, vertigo, or unsteady feelings
  6. feelings of unreality
  7. paresthesias (tingling in hands or feet)
  8. hot and cold flashes
  9. sweating
  10. faintness
  11. trembling or shaking
  12. fear of dying or going crazy

Generalized anxiety disorder is characterized by generalized, persistent anxiety of a chronic nature. Symptoms of the disorder are grouped under the headings of apprehensive expectation, vigilance and scanning, motor tension, and autonomic hyperactivity.

A. Generalized, persistent anxiety is manifested by symptoms from three of the following four categories:
  1. Motor tension: shakiness, jumpiness, trembling, tension, muscle aches, fatigability, inability to relax, fidgeting, restlessness, easy startle, etc.
  2. Autonomic hyperactivity: sweating, heart pounding or racing, dry mouth, dizziness, light-headedness, paresthesias (tingling in hands or feet), hot or cold spells, frequent urination, diarrhea, nausea, lump in the throat, flushing, pallor, etc.
  3. Apprehensive expectation: anxiety, worry, fear, rumination, anticipation of misfortune to self or others, etc.
  4. Vigilance and scanning: hyperattentiveness resulting in distractibility, difficulty in concentrating, insomnia, irritability, impatience, etc.

Although patients with panic disorder commonly experience anxiety symptoms between attacks, the diagnosis of generalized anxiety disorder is reserved for patients who do not have attacks. The diagnosis of both disorders depends on the exclusion of physical or mental disorders that might be responsible for anxiety symptoms.

These two disorders were formerly regarded as one illness. They were separated when anxiety syndromes were observed that appeared differentially responsive to drugs. Preliminary data suggest that generalized anxiety disorder has fewer autonomic symptoms and an earlier, more gradual onset (Anderson, Noyes, Crowe, 1984). Family and twin studies also support the separation.

The existing classification assumes that anxiety and depression are separate illnesses. However, many patients report a mixture of anxious and depressive symptoms. This, together with the fact that the disorders respond equally to certain drugs, suggests that they might be one illness. Although the issue is not settled, recent investigations indicate that they are distinct. Multivariate analyses have separated anxious and depressed patients on the basis of clinical features (Roth and Mountjoy, 1982). Also, followup studies show a more favorable outcome for depressive disorders (Coryell, Noyes, Clancy, 1983); family studies show an increase in anxiety, but not depressive disorders, among the relatives of anxious patients (Crowe et al., 1983).

## Etiology

### Genetic Factors

Although the cause of anxiety disorders is unknown, genetic factors appear to be important. A greater prevalence of anxiety disorders exists among the relatives of patients with anxiety neuroses. Roughly 25 per cent of the first-degree relatives suffer from the same disorder compared with 2 per cent of control relatives (Crowe et al., 1983). Female relatives are at greater risk than males, and male relatives have a higher risk of alcoholism. Twin studies provide further evidence for the importance of hereditary factors. Monozygotic twins have a higher concordance rate than dizygotic twins. The monozygotic concordance rate is roughly 50 per cent compared with 15 per cent for dizygotic pairs (Torgersen, 1983).

### Biologic Factors

The search for an inherited vulnerability has taken root in certain biologic abnormalities found in anxious patients. These disturbances resemble the well-known physiologic response to stress. Epinephrine is released from the adrenal medulla under stressful conditions, and increased adrenergic activity can be demonstrated in anxious patients (Uhde, Boulenger, Vittone, 1984). Epinephrine acts on beta-adrenergic receptors so it is not surprising that beta-blocking drugs reduce anxiety symptoms while beta-stimulating agents increase them. Whether the production of epinephrine is specific to anxiety or important in the etiology of these disorders is unknown.

When physiologic changes associated with anxiety are measured, they confirm clinical observation of anxious patients (Lader, 1976). Heart rate and forearm blood flow are increased and finger pulse volume is decreased. Sweat gland activity and muscle activity are increased and salivary gland activity is reduced. Electroencephalography shows increased beta and diminished alpha activity. Such changes reflect an increase in sympathetic nervous system tone. Study of patients with anxiety disorders indicates that they adapt slowly and respond excessively to stimulation.

Poor exercise tolerance has been observed in patients with anxiety disorders. In performing equal work, they consume more oxygen and produce more lactic acid than do normal subjects. This observation led to induction of panic attacks by infusing sodium lactate. Infusions of this kind provoke panic attacks in more than 70 per cent of patients with panic disorder compared with 5 per cent of normal subjects. The laboratory induction of attacks provides a research tool with which to study the mechanisms of anxiety. Although changes in lactate and calcium metabolism were originally thought to be responsible for these attacks, noradrenergic (NA) activation of the central nervous system appears to be a more likely explanation (Leibowitz et al., 1985).

Some investigations have shown that 30 to 50 per cent of patients with panic disorder or agoraphobia have mitral valve prolapse (Klein and Gorman, 1984). This minor valvular defect has been identified by echocardiography in about 5 per cent of the general population. An association between mitral prolapse and panic disorder is suggested by the observation that both run in families, are more prevalent in women, and occur in similar proportions of the population. When present, symptoms of mitral valve prolapse are similar to those of panic disorder. It has been suggested that an autonomic vulnerability to panic disorder may be activated by

mitral prolapse, accounting for the link between them. However, it is unclear whether the observed relationship between these disorders is a real one. In recent family and commmunity surveys, no association was found. Conceivably, a selection bias has operated to increase the numbers of patients with both conditions being referred to centers where studies are being done.

### Personality Factors

A personality vulnerability to anxiety states is believed to exist, although the personality of these patients has received little study. In clinical practice the premorbid personality is often characterized by trait anxiety (Spielberger, 1966). Persons with trait anxiety are highly reactive to their surroundings and develop anxiety symptoms in response to stressful circumstances. They tend to be apprehensive, worrisome, easily upset, and uneasy in unfamiliar surroundings.

Patients with anxiety disorders are more neurotic and introverted than normal or depressed patients (Kerr et al., 1972). However, personality tests that measure such characteristics are influenced by the symptomatic state of the patient and may not accurately reflect their premorbid or asymptomatic functioning. Traits of dependency and immaturity are also more common in anxiety states than in depression.

### Social Factors

The literature dealing with neurotic illness (a group of disorders including anxiety) and its relationship to environmental stress is extensive but inconclusive. Although these disturbances have been found to be more prevalent among women and unmarried persons, no association between this ill-defined category and social class has been found. Associations between life events and the risk of neurotic illness have been reported, but they are small and have little clinical importance (Andrews and Tennant, 1978). Studies of social network variables have emphasized perceived satisfaction with social relationships as a factor in neurotic illness. This area of research has methodological problems and few studies have examined individual disorders.

## Epidemiology

### General Population

Anxiety disorders approach depressive disorders in frequency of occurrence. The 6-month prevalence of panic disorder, according to the Epidemiologic Catchment Area project, is 0.4 per cent to 1.0 per cent (Myers et al., 1984). A corresponding estimate from New Haven for generalized anxiety disorder is 2.5 per cent. These figures are consistent with earlier estimates ranging from 2 per cent to 5 per cent for anxiety neurosis (Marks and Lader, 1973). However, because it is difficult to distinguish between a disorder and anxiety that represents a normal response to environmental stress, higher figures are obtained when minimal criteria for a case are used.

Community surveys indicate that only a proportion of persons with anxiety symptoms seek treatment for them and that, according to the type of treatment sought, a spectrum of severity exists. Roughly one third report mild symptoms for which they seek no treatment. Another third, with symptoms of intermediate severity, receive treatment from family physicians, while those with the severest symptoms come to the attention of psychiatrists.

### Practice Populations

Patients with anxiety disorders account for as many as a quarter of patients who see their doctors for psychiatric problems (Kedward and Cooper, 1966). Anxiety states make up about 10 per cent of a cardiologist's practice and a similar proportion of psychiatric outpatients. Rarely are such patients treated as inpatients.

### Sex and Age Distribution

Women are more commonly affected with anxiety disorders in a ratio of 2:1. However, in psychiatric populations, men and women are more equally represented, suggesting that men suffer from a severer form of the disorder. Anxiety disorders begin in early adult life, with the age of onset ranging from 15 to 35 years. The average is about 25 years (Marks and Lader, 1973).

Anxiety disorders are not uncommon among children. Of British children on the Isle of Wight, 1.7 per cent were diagnosed as having anxiety neuroses (Rutter, Tizard, Whitmore, 1970). Surveys of psychiatric morbidity among the aged show that the prevalence of anxiety states remains high after age 60 (Roth and Mountjoy, 1980). Although the majority represent illnesses that began in early adult life and persisted into old age, a proportion have their onset after age 60.

## Neurochemistry and Neurophysiology

### Animal Models

One approach to understanding central nervous system mechanisms in anxiety involves animal models. A conflict test is commonly used in which animals are conditioned to inhibit food-seeking behavior in response to a signal for punishment. Benzodiazepines bring back the suppressed behavior despite the occurrence of punishment. Learned helplessness has been conceptualized as a model of anxiety as well as of depression. It consists of a loss of response to escapable shock after exposure to inescapable shock. The induction of learned helplessness is prevented by antidepressants and, once induced, may be reversed by them.

Studies of the locus ceruleus in monkeys have yielded evidence for involvement of the NA system in anxiety (Redmond, 1979). The locus ceruleus is the major NA nucleus located in the pons, with projections to the cerebral cortex, cerebellum, limbic system, and spinal cord. Electrical and pharmacologic activation of the locus produces behaviors like those observed in monkeys that are exposed to threats in the wild. In contrast, electrical lesions and pharmacologic inhibition of this nucleus abolishes those behaviors. Also, drugs that increase or decrease locus ceruleus activity are drugs that have anxiogenic and anxiolytic properties in humans.

### Chemical Induction

Another strategy for studying mechanisms involves chemical induction of anxiety. Although a variety of adrenergic agents are capable of producing anxiety symptoms, yohimbine provokes a response most like pathologic anxiety syndromes. This alpha-adrenergic blocking agent produces anxiety symptoms in nonanxious as well as anxious patients (Guttmacher, Murphy, Insel, 1983). It is one of the drugs that provokes fear in monkeys when applied to the locus ceruleus.

### Neurotransmitters

Clues to the neurobiology of anxiety have come from study of the action of pharmacologic agents that reduce anxiety. The discovery of benzodiazepine receptors on the nerve cells of human brain has major importance in this regard. The existence of receptors suggests that an endogenous compound resembling the benzodiazepines may act as a specific mediator of anxiety. A number of compounds have been considered possible endogenous ligands but, as yet, none have been confirmed.

Benzodiazepine receptors are functionally linked to the neurotransmitter gamma aminobutyric acid (GABA). Because GABA mediates transmission in nearly a third of synapses in the brain, its influence is extensive (Hoehn-Saric, 1982). Benzodiazepines appear to enhance GABA-mediated inhibition at presynaptic and postsynaptic sites throughout the central nervous system. This potentiation may be related to the antianxiety effect of benzodiazepines.

Evidence for the involvement of the NA transmitter system has already been presented. The locus ceruleus contains nearly half of the NA neurons in the brain. The effects of norepinephrine are mediated by two kinds of receptors that, according to their pharmacologic properties, are labeled either alpha or beta receptors. Drugs that increase locus ceruleus activity and release norepinephrine, such as yohimbine and piperoxane, induce anxiety in animals and humans, whereas drugs that inhibit the locus ceruleus, such as clonidine and benzodiazepines, reduce anxiety.

There is also evidence for involvement of the serotonergic system in the mediation of anxiety. Present evidence suggests that at least three transmitter systems are involved in the production of anxiety. The precise function and relative importance of these systems remains unknown.

### Clinical Picture

Anxiety or panic attacks are characterized by the sudden onset of extreme anxiety and autonomic arousal like that caused by life-threatened danger. Most attacks occur spontaneously and may even awaken a person from sleep, although they may be provoked by strong emotion, excitement, or even physical exertion. They last from minutes to hours and may vary in frequency from several times daily to once or twice yearly. The person having a panic attack reports that he feels suddenly frightened for no reason. He may feel as though electricity is passing through his body. His heart may pound as though leaping from his chest, and he may feel blood rushing to his face. His legs may feel wobbly, and a sense of imbalance may cause him to grab something for support.

Anxiety of panic proportions is accompanied by a feeling of impending doom or the thought that something terrible is about to happen. Patients feel that they may lose control of themselves (e.g., faint, urinate, or cry out) or have a serious accident or illness (e.g., a heart attack or stroke). At the height of their anxiety, many feel that they are about to die.

During attacks, patients are visibly distressed and show obvious physiologic signs of anxiety. They are often pale, with fearful expression and pleading manner. Many have a rapid pulse and labored breathing and are diaphoretic and tremulous. Their behavior is motivated by an overpowering impulse to escape from circumstances that are perceived as being dangerous. This takes many to emergency rooms in search of life-saving interventions.

Between attacks, most patients experience some degree of generalized anxiety. They find themselves worried, anxious, and fearful. Many ruminate about unfortunate events that might happen, such as injury or death. Others experience tightness and aching in their muscles as well as trembling. They are restless, cannot relax, and wear out easily. During the day many patients are keyed up and irritable; at night they sleep poorly. Some find that their attention is dominated by symptoms.

Associated features include agoraphobic, depressive, and depersonalization symptoms. Agoraphobic and depressive symptoms are described elsewhere. Depersonalization often accompanies panic attacks but may occur fleetingly on its own. It consists of a feeling of strangeness or unreality concerning the individual or his environment. Patients often describe feeling as though they are detached from themselves or their surroundings. They may feel empty, as though cut off from their emotions.

## Course and Complications

### Onset

Commonly, a spontaneous panic attack is the abrupt, initial manifestation of panic disorder, although many patients report a period of increasing generalized anxiety. Regardless of its timing, the first attack often leaves a lasting and painful impression. Precipitating events or circumstances are often associated with the onset of symptoms (Noyes et al., 1980). These include emotionally disturbing events, such as the death of a family member, divorce, and financial loss. Physical illness, surgical procedures, and events associated with hormonal change, such as pregnancy, childbirth, and menopause, may also be associated with initial symptoms.

### Course

Typically, anxiety disorders follow a chronic, fluctuating course, although remissions and exacerbations are experienced by some patients. Most report that their symptoms are reactive to life circumstances and that they are severest during periods of environmental stress. A favorable outcome is found in half of psychiatric patients and two thirds of general medical patients (Greer, 1969). Thus, despite a degree of subjective distress associated with continuing symptoms, most patients report little social impairment. It is uncommon for patients to be unable to work. More often they report some loss of efficiency as a result of poor concentration or easy fatigability. Some find that worried preoccupation with health diverts attention from pleasurable pursuits.

Few predictors of outcome have been identified for anxiety disorders, although premorbid personality, precipitating events, and the environmental setting are important for neurotic illness in general (Sims, 1975). Duration of illness is, of course, predictive. Half of the patients who have had symptoms for less than 1 year will become free of them thereafter (Noyes et al., 1980). This is unlikely in patients who have experienced symptoms continuously for 3 or more years. Treatment, although effective in

the short run, has not been shown to influence the long-term outcome of anxiety disorders.

### Complications

The most common complications of anxiety disorders are depression and alcohol dependence. Secondary depression—that is, depression that begins after the primary disorder is well established—develops in about half the patients with anxiety disorders (Clancy et al., 1978). Such depression is usually mild and reactive to environmental circumstances. In some it is precipitated by distressing events; in others it is associated with worsening symptoms. Depression may explain the increased risk of suicide in anxiety disorders (Coryell, Noyes, Clancy, 1982).

Alcohol dependence may complicate anxiety disorders, although it is not known how frequently this occurs (Woodruff, Guze, Clayton, 1972). Patients who use alcohol in an effort to control their symptoms may become dependent on it. Likewise, a small proportion of patients who use benzodiazepines find themselves increasing the dose to achieve the same effect; others have difficulty discontinuing their use. Dependence on these drugs occasionally results from the overzealous prescribing of physicians.

Whether physical illness is a complication of anxiety disorders remains a critical but unanswered question. The finding of excess mortality in panic disorder patients followed for 35 years suggests this possibility (Coryell et al., 1982). A portion of the excess is due to cardiovascular disease in men. Anxiety is frequently identified in patients with physical illnesses such as hypertension and coronary artery disease, but the nature of the association remains uncertain. Followup studies have yielded contradictory results with respect to the prevalence of these and other conditions in anxious patients (Wheeler et al., 1950; Noyes et al., 1978).

## Differential Diagnosis

### Physical Illness

The differential diagnosis of anxiety disorders includes a variety of physical as well as psychiatric illnesses. A number of cardiac, neurologic, and endocrine disorders are commonly associated with organic anxiety syndromes (Dietch, 1981). Because an organic etiology may be overlooked in patients with anxiety symptoms, these disorders are sometimes missed. The initial workup should, therefore, include a physical examination and appropriate laboratory testing.

The most common cardiac conditions associated with recurrent attacks are angina pectoris and cardiac arrhythmias. Angina is characterized by episodes of chest pain, dyspnea, and palpitations that are precipitated by exercise or emotional stress. The diagnosis may depend on coronary arteriography when symptoms are atypical. Cardiac arrhythmias may cause palpitation, chest discomfort, dyspnea, and faintness. The diagnosis of an arrhythmia is made by identifying the abnormal rhythm during an attack. A portable monitor may facilitate this.

Hyperthyroidism is the most common endocrine disturbance associated with an anxiety syndrome. Symptoms include palpitations, insomnia, sweating, heat intolerance, increased appetite, and diarrhea. Signs include tachycardia, tremor, weight loss, and warm, moist skin. A diffuse goiter and exophthalmus are often present. The diagnosis is established by tests of thyroid function. Pheochromocytoma is an uncommon, cathecholamine-secreting tumor of the adrenal medulla. Flushing and headache are prominent and sustained hypertension is present in most patients who have this type of tumor. A urine metanephrine assay is usually diagnostic.

Hypoglycemia is seldom associated with anxiety symptoms. It is accompanied by sweating, weakness, hunger, tremor, and headache and may be confirmed by measurement of blood glucose levels during an acute episode. Reactive hypoglycemia is identified by an oral glucose tolerance test. The disorder may be diagnosed if the glucose level falls below 45 mg/dl. Hypoparathyroidism is associated with anxiety symptoms in a minority of cases. Symptoms include muscle cramps and parethesias of the hands, feet, and mouth. Carpopedal spasm is a diagnostic sign. Useful diagnostic tests include serum calcium and phosphorous levels.

Caffeine may be associated with anxiety symptoms when the daily intake exceeds 250 mg. Brewed coffee contains 90 to 120 mg, tea and instant coffee 70 mg, and cola drinks 20 mg. The diagnosis is confirmed when symptoms disappear after discontinuing the drug. Other substances that may produce anxiety symptoms include nicotine, cocaine, and alcohol. Medications that may cause anxiety include ephedrine, aminophylline, amphetamines, methylphenidate, phenmetrazine, levodopa, antihistamines, indomethacin, and thyroid preparations. Withdrawal from benzodiazepines, barbiturates, and other sedative hypnotics, opiates, tricyclic antidepressants, and neuroleptics may be associated with anxiety symptoms.

### Psychiatric Illness

Anxiety symptoms may accompany almost any psychiatric disorder. Most commonly they are associated with affective disorders, phobic disorders, obsessive-compulsive disorder, and posttraumatic stress disorder. Anxiety symptoms are often prominent in patients with depression, making the differential diagnosis difficult. Anxiety disorders have an earlier onset, and when anxiety symptoms appear for the first time after age 40, they are commonly part of a depressive syndrome. Because anxiety disorders are chronic, a history of discrete episodes suggests depression. A family history of depression suggests an affective disorder diagnosis.

Anxiety symptoms are also shared by phobic disorders (Woodruff et al., 1972). Simple phobics are distinguished by having little anxiety outside of the feared situation. Both social phobias and agoraphobia have panic attacks, making them difficult to distinguish from panic disorder. Patients with panic disorder may be uneasy in crowds or when traveling or alone yet not avoid these situations. The diagnosis of agoraphobia requires phobic avoidance. In obsessive-compulsive disorders, anxiety is associated with obsessions and compulsions.

Anxiety symptoms are prominent in posttraumatic stress disorders. Emotionally traumatic events are associated with the onset of these disorders and form their mental content. The diagnosis depends on establishing a connection between a traumatic event and the ensuing disturbance.

# Treatment

## Medical Management

Effective treatment of panic and generalized anxiety disorders rests on establishing and communicating the diagnosis. Unfortunately, many patients are convinced that they are physically ill, despite evidence to the contrary. Consequently, they resist the idea that their problem may be psychiatric. Other patients reject an anxiety disorder diagnosis because it implies weakness or responsibility for symptoms. Too often, to avoid unpleasant confrontation, patients are told only that they have no physical disease. Although reassuring, this gives them little information about their illness or its treatment.

Of course, examination and reassurance are important initial steps when patients present with acute symptoms. These measures not only rule out more serious illness, but also have an important anxiety-relieving function. In the face of persisting symptoms, education becomes important. Discussion of the diagnosis and prognosis forms a basis for understanding and accepting the condition.

## Drug Therapy

Except in the mildest cases, drug treatment should be considered for patients with anxiety disorders. It may provide temporary control of acute symptoms and long-term reduction of chronic ones. The goal is control rather than permanent relief of symptoms. This is because the relapse rate after effective drug therapy is nearly 90 per cent (Rickkels, Case, Diamond, 1980). The most useful drugs belong to four classes: the benzodiazepines, tricyclic antidepressants, monoamine oxidase inhibitors, and beta-adrenergic blocking agents (Noyes, 1983).

The benzodiazepines are among the most widely prescribed drugs in the United States. These drugs are especially effective with generalized anxiety but reduce panic attacks as well (Noyes et al., 1984). Diazepam, the standard among a great number of similar drugs, is an ideal agent for the relief of acute symptoms. It acts promptly with little sedation. A dose of 10 to 40 mg daily may be prescribed initially, and once control over symptoms has been established, it may be reduced and discontinued over several weeks to a few months. Because of effects on coordination and mental alertness, patients should be cautioned about driving or performing tasks requiring concentration. They should also be warned that diazepam enhances the effects of alcohol.

In addition to their effectiveness, the benzodiazepines are well tolerated. Successful suicide resulting from an overdose is uncommon. However, two problems associated with their use dictate caution in prescribing them. First, although many patients report continuing benefit, studies have yet to establish that tolerance does not develop. Second, dependence may develop. Withdrawal phenomena, including abstinence syndromes, deliria, and seizures, have been documented in a proportion of patients (Schopf, 1983). The risks of dependence may be minimized by (a) not prescribing benzodiazepines for patients who abuse alcohol or drugs or who have personality disorders; (b) prescribing drugs that are slowly absorbed and long-acting; (c) alerting patients to the potential risks and setting limits on the amount of drug prescribed; and (d) considering other drugs and alternative forms of treatment.

The tricyclic compound imipramine is not only a standard antidepressant, but an antianxiety agent as well. First reported more than 20 years ago by Klein and Fink, the drug's anxiety-relieving properties received little attention until recently (Zitrin et al., 1983). Imipramine blocks panic attacks and may relieve generalized anxiety as well. The dose is the same as that for depression: 150 to 300 mg daily at bedtime. Anxiety symptoms are relieved gradually, and improvement may not be maximal for 6 to 10 weeks. Because some patients are sensitive to its side effects, the drug is often started at a dose of 25 mg and increased by 25 mg every 3 days. Common side effects include dry mouth, constipation, postural hypotension, tremor, and blurred vision.

Once a patient has responded to imipramine, the dose may be gradually reduced to a maintenance level where improvement is sustained. After 6 months it should be gradually discontinued to assess continuing need. Other tricyclic compounds may also be effective, and the more sedative drugs, such as doxepin, have antianxiety effects in low dose. Imipramine is a relatively safe drug for long-term administration; the risk of cardiac arrhythmias is minimal in patients without heart disease. Still, a number of patients gain weight on the drug, and an overdose, taken in a suicide attempt, may be life-threatening. This is a serious consideration in patients with an increased risk of suicide (Coryell et al., 1982).

Possibly the most effective drug for patients with panic disorder is the monoamine oxidase inhibitor phenelzine (Sheehan, Ballenger, Jacobson, 1980). It may also carry the greatest risk. Originally, the drug was shown to be effective in atypical depressions with prominent anxiety symptoms. Like imipramine, it is capable of blocking panic attacks but may also reduce generalized anxiety symptoms. The recommended dose is 45 to 90 mg daily. Patients are instructed to eliminate foods containing tyramine (e.g., red wine and certain cheeses) from their diet. Tyramine, if ingested in sufficient quantity, interacts with the drug to cause a hypertensive crisis. Such crises may have serious consequences, but they seldom occur if the diet is followed. Patients who are not responsible in such matters should not receive the drug. Side effects of phenelzine include dizziness, tremor, diarrhea, and tiredness.

Beta-adrenergic blocking drugs, such as propranolol, also have anxiety-reducing properties. These were first observed in patients with functional tachycardia. Beta-blockers are not as effective as the benzodiazepines, but patients with prominent autonomic symptoms may respond (Noyes, 1982). Palpitations and tremor are particularly suitable target symptoms. The dose of propranolol is 40 to 320 mg daily in divided doses. A fall in resting heart rate accompanies the beta-adrenergic blockade and provides a means of monitoring the drug's activity. Side effects include dizziness, nausea, and fatigue. Propranolol is well tolerated and free of potential for psychological dependence. It is a safe drug provided it is not given to patients with asthma or heart disease.

### Self-regulatory Therapies

Self-regulatory techniques that have been used to reduce generalized anxiety include relaxation, biofeedback, and meditation (Goldberg, 1982). Jacobson, in 1938, introduced a method of progressive muscle re-laxation that is effective and widely used. His method depends on the systematic tensing and relaxing of muscle groups. In addition to the changes in muscles, relaxation reduces sympathetic nervous system activity. Electromyographic biofeedback facilitates muscle relaxation by providing patients with information about the electrical potentials of certain muscle groups. In the treatment of generalized anxiety, it is usually the frontalis muscles that are monitored. Although this technique has proved effective, the mechanism of anxiety reduction is uncertain, and controlled studies have yet to demonstrate unique superiority.

Transcendental meditation is the most widely practiced method of altering subjective states. Although mastery requires lengthy practice, its basic principles can be learned in one or two sessions. Transcendental meditation produces a physiologic state of restful alertness different from sleep or wakefulness that is associated with reduced oxygen consumption. According to Benson (1975), this physiologic state is similar to that associated with muscle relaxation. He called it the "relaxation response" and described a technique for achieving it. Although self-regulatory techniques are useful adjuncts, they are probably not adequate for most chronically anxious patients by themselves.

### Cognitive Therapy

Cognitive therapy is based on the cognitive model of anxiety, according to which anxiety-provoking thoughts and images are the primary disturbance (Beck and Emery, 1985). These cognitions center on the theme of personal danger. The anxious patient systematically misconstrues innocuous situations, exaggerates the probability of harm, and persists in thoughts and images of physical or psychological injury. Cognitive therapy of anxiety disorders is designed to modify these abnormal thoughts and images. Typically, the therapist elicits unrealistic cognitions, analyzes the faulty logic, and explores alternative ways of thinking. Few studies have examined the value of this therapy in anxiety disorders, although it has been found useful in depression.

### Psychotherapy

Patients with anxiety disorders may benefit from supportive psychotherapy. As has been mentioned, reassurance about the meaning of symptoms and education about the nature of the illness often bring considerable relief. Such measures, in the hands of a sympathetic physician, often restore morale and self-confidence. Beyond this, exploration of the circumstances surrounding the onset of symptoms often reveals factors of importance in their development or continuation that had escaped the patient's notice. Also, when marital conflict or job dissatisfaction exists, counseling may be called for. Chronic anxiety symptoms often cause patients to become less effective in coping with interpersonal difficulties. Because such patients are dependent and unassertive, they often drift into emotionally unhealthy relationships. With emotional support, patients may recognize maladaptive patterns and find ways to change them. Where personality difficulties are associated with an anxiety disorder, intensive therapy designed to produce personality change may be recommended.

## PHOBIC DISORDERS

### Definition

Fear is a disquieting feeling that danger is close at hand. Unlike anxiety, the object of this painful emotion is clearly recognized. It is composed of three elements: an unpleasant subjective state, physiologic arousal, and avoidant behavior. Fear represents an adaptive response to danger that is important for survival among animals and capable of improving performance among humans. When fear causes impairment, it is said to have reached phobic proportions. A phobia is fear that is disproportionate to the actual danger, cannot be explained away, is beyond voluntary control, and leads to avoidance of the feared situation.

### History

Although morbid fears have been described from antiquity, psychiatric interest in them appears to have been recent (Marks, 1969). One reason may be the relative mildness of these disturbances, but another may be the difficulty in separating them from other illnesses, particularly affective disor-

ders. The first account of a phobic syndrome is credited to Westphal. In 1871 he published a monograph describing three men who feared public places. He named the disorder agoraphobia, a Greek word meaning "fear of the market place." Although still in use, the term is a misnomer; the agoraphobic fears separation from a source of security, not open spaces.

As detailed clinical descriptions of psychiatric syndromes appeared near the end of the nineteenth century, attempts were made to classify phobic disorders. Certain authorities considered phobias and obsessions manifestations of a single disorder, while others regarded them as symptoms of affective illness. In 1895, Freud separated phobias from obsessions and suggested a classification based on the extent of actual danger involved. The current classification was introduced by Marks (1970), who distinguished between phobias of external objects (e.g., storms) and internal circumstances (e.g., heart disease).

### Classification

Three phobic disorders are described in DSM-III (American Psychiatric Association, 1980). Agoraphobia is a disturbance involving multiple fears of being alone or in public places. In such places the agoraphobic is afraid that help might not be available in case of sudden incapacitation. Common fears include crowded stores, restaurants, and theaters; travel by car, bus, or train; passing over bridges, through tunnels, or being on elevators.

A.  The individual has marked fear of, and thus avoids, being alone or in public places from which escape might be difficult or where help might not be available in case of sudden incapacitation, e.g., crowds, tunnels, bridges, public transportation.

B.  There is increasing constriction of normal activities until the fears or avoidance behavior dominates the individual's life.

C.  Not due to other psychiatric disorder.

Social phobia is characterized by multiple fears of situations involving exposure to public scrutiny (DSM-III, American Psychiatric Association, 1980). In the phobic setting the social phobic is afraid that he might behave in an uncontrolled manner, causing humiliation or embarrassment. Feared situations include speaking or acting in public, eating or drinking in public restaurants, writing in the presence of others, and using public restrooms.

A. **A persistent, irrational fear of, and compelling desire to avoid, a situation in which the individual is exposed to scrutiny by others and fears that he or she may act in a way that will be humiliating or embarrassing.**
B. **Significant distress because of the disturbance and recognition by the individual that his or her fear is excessive or unreasonable.**
C. **Not due to other mental disorder.**

Simple phobia is characterized by a persistent irrational fear of a specific object or situation (DSM-III). Unlike the more diffuse or generalized phobic disturbances already described, simple phobias are usually single. The objects of such phobias commonly hold some potential for physical harm (e.g., snakes, rats, storms, heights, deep water), but the phobic person's reaction to them is excessive.

A. **A persistent, irrational fear of, and compelling desire to avoid, an object or a situation other than being alone, or in public places away from home, or of humiliation or embarrassment in certain social situations. Phobic objects are often animals, and phobic situations frequently involve heights and closed spaces.**
B. **Significant distress from the disturbance and recognition by the individual that his or her fear is excessive or unreasonable.**
C. **Not due to other mental disorder.**

Illness phobias (e.g., cancer, heart disease) fall into a separate category that is difficult to distinguish from hypochondriasis. Little information about such phobias is available.

## Etiology

### Genetic Factors

Agoraphobia is familial. Roughly 20 per cent of first-degree relatives are at risk for agoraphobia or panic disorder, which, according to one study, is a milder variant of the disorder (Noyes et al., in press). The risk for agoraphobia or panic disorder is highest among female relatives, being nearly 35 per cent among female siblings. A 3:1 sex ratio among affected relatives is similar to the sex ratio of agoraphobics in the general population. Among male relatives there is an increased risk of alcohol disorders.

Evidence for the influence of genetic factors comes from twin studies showing a higher rate of concordance in monozygotic twins than in dizygotic twins. A concordance rate of 50 per cent for anxiety and phobic disorders was found among monozygotic twins compared with 15 per cent in dizygotic pairs (Torgersen, 1983). In this study, agoraphobics constituted the largest group of probands, but social phobics were included as well. In a smaller series, which excluded animal phobias, a concordance rate of 88 per cent for phobic symptoms was found in monozygotic twins compared with 38 per cent for dizygotic pairs.

### Biologic Factors

Biologic mechanisms involved in panic disorder and agoraphobia are discussed under the etiology of anxiety disorders.

### Personality Factors

The personality of phobic patients has received little study. Nevertheless, certain traits are commonly observed among agoraphobic patients, the most common being dependence on others and avoidance of difficult situations (Mathews, Gelder, Johnston, 1981). Such traits might, if they existed before the development of agoraphobia, be part of a personality predisposition to the disorder. However, many patients claim that they were independent and self-reliant before becoming ill, suggesting that their dependency is a result of their condition. Childhood separation anxiety may be a predisposing factor or simply an early manifestation of the disorder (Gittleman and Klein, 1984).

Early dependence predisposing to later phobic avoidance could represent a learned response to parental behavior. Retrospective studies suggest that agoraphobics are more often exposed to maternal overprotection (Mathews et al., 1981). Of course, such studies are difficult to interpret because the overprotective parent-child interaction could just as easily stem from the child's anxiety as the parent's. Unstable family backgrounds are reported by some agoraphobics.

Social phobics have been described as socially ill at ease and withdrawn. Many possess traits like those of the avoidant personality described in DSM-III. Tendencies toward interpersonal sensitivity and avoidance of intimate relationships may predate the social phobia. One study rated the parents of social phobics as relatively uncaring but overprotective, suggesting a link between the disorder and parental attitudes.

### Learning Factors

Certain phobias arise in association with traumatic events (Goldstein and Chambless, 1978). For example, an individual may develop a fear of deep water after nearly drowning. This is an example of classical conditioning in which a conditioned stimulus (water) is paired with an aversive stimulus (drowning) so that the former acquires aversive properties and elicits a fear response. Classical conditioning is rarely involved in the development of agoraphobia, but a substantial proportion of simple phobias can be linked to conditioning events. Even so, these events are probably not necessary or sufficient, since most persons exposed to traumatic events do not become phobic.

Vicarious learning may also play a role in the development of phobic disturbances. If a person observes fear in another, he may become fearful in the situation himself. Studies have shown that children often have the same fears as their mothers. A few phobic patients recall experiences that suggest such learning may have played a part in the acquisition of their fear.

## Epidemiology

### General Population

The six-month prevalence of phobic disorders, as estimated by the Epidemiological Catchment Area project, is 5 per cent to 6 per cent in New Haven and St. Louis, making them the most prevalent disorders among women (Myers et al., 1984). An earlier estimate of nearly 8 per cent was made in Burlington, Vermont (Agras, Sylvester, Oliveau, 1969). Such figures can be expected to vary because there is no sharp distinction between fears and phobias and because the impairment associated with most phobias in the general population is minimal. In the Vermont survey, for example, only 3 per cent of phobics were severely disabled and only 1 per cent were receiving treatment at the time of interview.

Simple phobias are the most prevalent, followed by agoraphobia and social phobia.

The 6-month prevalence estimate for simple phobia is 5 per cent; for agoraphobia it is 3 per cent (Myers et al., 1984). The most common simple phobias in the general population are storms, animals, and heights. Phobias of illness, injury, and death are likewise common.

### Practice Populations

Few phobias are ever treated. Most persons simply adapt to the limitations imposed on them by having to avoid certain objects or situations. Consequently, despite their prevalence, phobic disorders make up only about 2 per cent to 3 per cent of psychiatric outpatients. Although simple phobias are the most prevalent, the majority of persons seeking treatment have the severer and disabling agoraphobia.

Although irrational fears are common in children, phobias are uncommon. The proportion reporting specific fears decreases with age, and more girls have fears than do boys. In one study of 10-year-old chilldren, 0.7 per cent were found to have clinically significant and disabling phobias (Rutter, Tizard, Whitmore, 1970). These most commonly involved animals, darkness, heights, disease, dirt, and school. According to the Vermont survey, new phobias seldom develop after age 50, and after 60 the prevalence rapidly declines, suggesting that many long-standing phobias remit with advancing years (Agras, Sylvester, Oliveau, 1969).

### Sex and Age Distribution

Agoraphobia is predominantly a female disorder. The ratio of women to men is roughly 3:1. Simple phobias are also more prevalent among women, but social phobias affect men and women equally (Amies, Gelder, Shaw, 1983). The age of onset also differs according to type of phobia. Simple phobias have their onset in childhood, the majority beginning before age 7. Agoraphobia, on the other hand, usually begins in late adolescence or early adult life, with most beginning between ages 15 and 35. Social phobias begin in adolescence. Most have their onset between ages 10 and 25.

## Clinical Picture

### Agoraphobia

The life of the agoraphobic is dominated by multiple fears having as a common theme separation from a source of security. This separation may involve space or time. When the person's dwelling is a source of security, his fear increases the farther he goes from it. On account of this, some agoraphobics avoid traveling beyond their communities, others remain within their neighborhoods, and still others are confined to their homes. When the source of security is the agoraphobic's spouse or trusted companion, his fear increases when he is alone.

Confined places involve separation in terms of time. Patients are disturbed by finding themselves in situations they might not be able to get out of quickly, for example, elevators, tunnels, bridges, and public transportation, such as buses, trains, and planes. Crowded places, such as stores, restaurants, theaters, and churches, are especially disturbing, not only because rapid exit might be difficult, but also because uncontrolled behavior (e.g., screaming, running out) in such settings might result in embarrassment. Patients commonly avoid such places as stores and theaters or go when there are few shoppers or they can sit near the exit.

In a crowded store the agoraphobic often begins to feel sweaty and flushed. His legs become wobbly and he feels light-headed. He may notice that his heart is pounding and that his breath is short. As his anxiety rises, he experiences an overpowering urge to leave the store. Unless they avoid situations that evoke discomfort or leave promptly when symptoms arise, many experience panic attacks in such places. Attacks are accompanied by the thought that some catastrophic event or sudden incapacitation is about to take place. Thus the patient may fear loss of control (e.g., fainting, urinating, or crying out) or death from illness or accident (e.g., heart attack, stroke, or choking).

The agoraphobic is distressed not only by certain phobic situations but also by the anticipation of having to confront them. Thus a housewife may begin to feel anxious as soon as she thinks of going shopping. Some anticipatory anxiety and scanning of surroundings for phobic objects is present much of the time. The agoraphobic is often preoccupied with arranging his activities so as to minimize his discomfort and maximize his sense of self-control. Some are comforted by having a family member go into crowded stores or restaurants with them. However, most avoid such places, with the result that activities are increasingly restricted.

In addition to their phobic symptoms, patients with agoraphobia experience generalized anxiety and panic attacks as described elsewhere. Consequently, in addition to psychological distress, they experience somatic symptoms indicative of autonomic hyperactivity and motor tension. Associated features include depressive symptoms, depersonalization, and obsessions. Studies disagree on whether impairment in sexual functioning is more common among agoraphobics (Mathews et al., 1981). Sexual problems sometimes begin after the onset of phobic symptoms, suggesting that they are secondary to the phobic disturbance.

### Social Phobia

The social phobic suffers from one or more fears that have as their common theme exposure to public scrutiny. In feared settings, socially phobic persons fear embarrassment or humiliation resulting from some uncontrolled action. The most commonly feared situations are speaking or performing in public and eating in public. Others include writing in public and using public toilets. The phobic response may extend to social gatherings, persons of the opposite sex, or persons in authority. As a result of his fear, the social phobic has a strong desire to avoid such situations or persons. Unlike the agoraphobic, who feels confined by a crowd but is indifferent to the reaction of individuals within it, the social phobic fears a disapproving response of persons that he feels may be critically attending to his actions.

In the feared situation, the social phobic reacts much like the agoraphobic, with overwhelming anxiety of panic proportions. Often he is afraid that autonomic disturbances will expose his anxiety to others. For this reason he is commonly troubled by blushing, sweating, and trembling, which he believes cause disapproval. Also, the social phobic fears that some anxiety-related impairment in his performance (e.g., stammering, lapse of memory) may lead to criticism. A vicious cycle may be created in which irrational fear impairs performance, generating still further anxiety and avoidance of phobic situations. Like the agoraphobic, the social phobic experiences anticipatory anxiety when forced to enter phobic situations and avoids them if possible.

### Simple Phobia

The simple phobic usually fears a single object or situation. Contact with that object may cause the phobic person to fear physical injury. Intense fear may be accompanied by sweating, trembling, and other signs of autonomic excitation. The degree of distress varies with the prevalence of the feared object and the extent to which avoiding it interferes with important activities. Apart from contact with the feared object or situation, the simple phobic is usually free of symptoms.

## Course and Complications

### Onset and Course

Agoraphobia most often begins suddenly with an unprovoked panic attack. Less commonly, a period of gradually increasing anxiety symptoms precedes the initial attack. With repeated attacks many patients become fearful of settings in which they occur and begin to avoid them. The progression from panic attacks to phobic avoidance suggests that attacks are the primary disturbance and that phobic symptoms develop as a learned response. A substantial proportion of agoraphobics report precipitating events or circumstances. These may involve separation, as in leaving home, bereavement, and divorce, or major life changes, such as marriage, pregnancy, and childbirth. Given the variety of precipitants, it is unlikely that they are specific to the disorder.

Agoraphobia follows a fluctuating course, with some patients experiencing remissions and exacerbations. Most experience persisting symptoms, however, and few patients will experience significant remissions after a year of continuous symptoms. Followup studies show that little change occurs in untreated agoraphobics, but that fluctuations in symptoms occur over time (Agras, Chapin, Oliveau, 1972). The illness is highly reactive to life circumstances so that symptoms are worse at times of environmental stress. Symptoms are often aggravated by physical illness and fatigue or by the use of caffeine and alcohol.

The disability associated with agoraphobia ranges from mild to severe. A substantial proportion of agoraphobics in the general population experience little impairment. They go to stores and travel despite a degree of discomfort, which they minimize by restricting travel and shopping when crowds are small. On the severe end of the spectrum, a proportion of agoraphobics are housebound. Under these circumstances they are unable to work and become dependent on their families. When family relationships are harmonious, adaptation to this impairment may be made without difficulty, but when disharmony has existed, serious conflict may develop (Mathews et al., 1981). Sexual dysfunction may contribute to marital problems.

Many agoraphobics attempt to hide their affliction to avoid the disapproval that they believe might result if others were to learn of it. Others claim that family members and physicians have not understood their illness. They themselves sometimes wonder if they simply lack willpower. Agoraphobics report that symptoms and disability undermine their self-esteem and morale.

Social phobias usually develop slowly without obvious precipitant. Less commonly, an embarrassing incident appears to set off the disturbance. Often initial symptoms arise in the climate of heightened social awareness and sensitivity of early adolescence. The disorder tends to be chronic with fluctuating symptoms. It is associated with varying degrees of disability, depending, in part, on the number and importance of situations feared. In varying degrees the phobic person's social activity is restricted, and fears of public speaking or eating may threaten his or her career. It is often at this point that the social phobic seeks treatment.

Simple phobias usually develop without obvious reason, but some begin in association with frightening incidents. Once they have persisted into adulthood, such phobias follow a steady course. Because they are localized there are few symptoms apart from contact with the feared object and little disability. Most persons simply avoid what they fear and put up with certain restrictions on their activities. When, as adults, simple phobics present themselves for treatment, their fears have often been present for decades. Then, changing circumstances may make them intolerable (e.g., a city dweller with a fear of snakes moves to the country) or they may hear that treatment is available.

## Complications

The most common complications of phobic disorders are depression and alcohol or sedative drug dependence. More than half of agoraphobics experience at least one episode of depression over the course of their illness (Noyes et al., in press). Whereas some develop depression in response to severe symptoms, others show a vulnerability to distressing events (e.g., death in the family). Agoraphobic symptoms are severer during episodes of depression, causing some patients to seek psychiatric treatment. The frequency with which depression occurs in social or simple phobias is unknown.

A substantial minority of agoraphobics and social phobics abuse, or become dependent on, alcohol or sedative drugs, including benzodiazepines. Many claim to have used these substances to reduce their anxiety in feared situations only to find themselves increasingly dependent on them. Recent surveys of alcoholic populations indicate that a third to a half suffer from agoraphobia or social phobia (Smail et al., 1984). In the majority, phobic symptoms precede the onset of pathologic drinking, suggesting that these disorders play a part in the development of alcohol dependence. This suggests that a subgroup of alcoholics have primary phobic disorders.

## Differential Diagnosis

The differential diagnosis of phobic disorders includes anxiety disorders, affective disorders, and obsessive-compulsive disorder. In these disorders, phobias are relatively minor features. Also, they tend to appear after the onset of the primary disorder rather than before. Panic disorder is especially difficult to distinguish from agoraphobia; indeed, many regard the latter as a complication of panic disorder. Both suffer from panic attacks, and close questioning will elicit agoraphobic symptoms in many patients with panic disorder. The diagnosis of agoraphobia is reserved, however, for patients who avoid phobic situations.

Phobic symptoms are common in persons with obsessive-compulsive disorder. Obses-

sive phobias have an intrusive quality about them and involve the imagined consequences of contact with the feared object (Marks, 1969). These consequences usually involve contamination or harm to oneself or others and arise in the sufferer's mind, despite his efforts to resist them. The clinical picture is dominated by obsessions and compulsions.

Phobic symptoms are also common in depression. In fact, the overlap in these conditions has caused some to regard agoraphobia as a form of depression (Schapira, Kerr, Roth, 1970). When disabling phobias exist before the development of an affective disorder, the depression should be considered secondary. Phobic symptoms that arise in the context of a depressive episode generally disappear when the depression is successfully treated. Phobias that are part of a depressive syndrome have a mood-congruent quality (e.g., fears of failure and loss of love).

## Treatment

### Management

The treatment of most agoraphobic and social phobic patients involves a combination of pharmacotherapy and behavior therapy. Research is still needed to determine which of these modes is most effective for which patients. For the present, they appear to complement each other. Drug therapy blocks panic attacks, while behavior therapy reduces phobic avoidance. Also, compliance with behavior therapy improves with the use of medication. Clinics that specialize in the treatment of these conditions usually combine these techniques, using groups and lay therapists for maximum efficiency (Chambless and Goldstein, 1982).

The management principles outlined for anxiety disorders apply to phobic disorders as well. Most important, phobic patients must expose themselves to the object of their fears in order to overcome them. Successful treatment also depends on the patients' becoming more confident and self-reliant. Education is important in this regard, and books for patients, such as those by Isaac Marks (*Living with Fear*, 1979) and Stewart Agras (*Panic: Facing Fears, Phobias, and Anxiety*, 1985) provide helpful suggestions for coping with symptoms as well as for understanding phobic disorders and their treatment. Emotional support is also important, and this often comes from meeting and sharing experiences with other phobic persons. Agoraphobia self-help groups that provide opportunities for this kind of sharing now exist in many communities.

### Pharmacotherapy

Both agoraphobia and social phobia are responsive to drug therapy; simple phobias are not. The same tricyclic antidepressants and monoamine oxidase inhibitors that are effective in blocking panic attacks are effective in treating phobic disturbances (Noyes, 1983). Despite their effectiveness, several factors limit their usefulness. First, sensitivity to side effects limits the compliance of some patients. In some studies, drop out rates have been as high as 20 per cent because of overstimulation, jitteriness, irritability, and insomnia on low doses of imipramine. Second, when the drugs are discontinued, most patients relapse.

For the present the drug of choice for agoraphobia is imipramine. Of the tricyclic compounds it has been most widely studied, although a somewhat better tolerated drug, desipramine, is probably equally effective. Phenelzine, a monoamine oxidase inhibitor, may be more effective, especially for social phobia, but is associated with dietary restrictions and a higher risk of adverse reactions. Details concerning the administration of these drugs are given under treatment of anxiety disorders.

### Behavior Therapy

Behavior therapy is a systematic method of exposing persons to phobic situations until they lose their fear of them. Phobias were among the first psychiatric disorders to respond to these methods when they were introduced. Systematic desensitization is probably the most widely used technique. According to this method, patients are trained to eliminate anxiety by means of muscle relaxation. Then, while relaxed, they imagine scenes from a hierarchy of fear-provoking situations ranging from neutral to terrifying. As each is imagined without fear, the patient moves to the next, until the most anxiety-provoking is imagined in relative comfort. What has occurred in imagination

then generalizes to actual situations. This technique is effective for specific phobias but has limited value for agoraphobia and social phobia (Emmelkamp, 1982).

The most effective technique for agoraphobia is exposure in vivo, or flooding (Mathews et al., 1981). In contrast to systematic desensitization, flooding is based on the principle of sudden confrontation in real life. With therapist encouragement, patients go into crowded stores or travel distances until the intense anxiety associated with this confrontation subsides. Prolonged exposure (i.e., several hours) to the most disturbing situations is most effective. When exposure is done in groups, patients support one another and therapist time is conserved. Most patients can be successfully treated in 1 to 20 sessions. Followup studies have demonstrated that the benefits of behavior therapy are lasting (Munby and Johnston, 1980).

### Psychotherapy

Since the introduction of the behavior therapies more than two decades ago, these techniques have replaced psychotherapy in the treatment of phobias. Beginning with the study of Gelder and Wolff (1967), a series of controlled investigations have demonstrated that desensitization is more effective than psychotherapy. Since then, intensive psychotherapy has been reserved for phobic patients with troublesome interpersonal problems. Of course, supportive psychotherapy may be useful in restoring morale and self-confidence. Marital or family counseling may also be important when disturbed marital or family interactions are contributing to symptoms.

Two principles that are important for effective psychotherapy of phobic patients apply to any treatment approach. The first was recognized by Freud, who observed that no progress occurs in treatment until patients are persuaded to confront feared situations. This principle is embodied in the behavior therapies but applies to pharmacologic treatments as well. Drugs may reduce anxiety symptoms, but without exposure to feared situations, phobic symptoms remain. A second principle was identified by Andrews (1966), who observed that phobic patients are dependent and avoid difficult situations. He observed that the successful therapist initially responds to demands for protection and guidance but subsequently uses his influence to persuade patients to confront fear-producing stimuli.

### Cognitive Therapy

Cognitive therapies for phobic disorders can be divided into procedures that modify irrational beliefs, such as rational emotive therapy, and procedures that are designed to modify internal dialogue, such as self-instructional training (Emmelkamp, 1982). Cognitive restructuring involves a rational analysis of phobic behaviors, followed by attempts to modify internal sentences as feared situations are imagined. Self-instructional training assists patients to substitute positive self-statements for fear-producing ones.

Paradoxical intention is a technique designed to reduce symptoms by attempting to increase them. With this procedure, patients are asked to try to realize their worst fears. If they fear fainting or having a heart attack, then, when symptoms of faintness or palpitations appear, they attempt to faint or have an attack. When this effort fails the fear disappears. A reversal of attitude toward symptoms appears to be the essential ingredient in this technique. Few studies have examined its effectiveness.

### Social Skills Training

Many agoraphobics find it difficult to assert themselves or express their feelings adequately. Regardless of how this is interpreted, assertiveness training may produce not only more direct expression, but also less phobic avoidance. This training involves discussion of social situations in which patients have behaved timidly. Alternative behaviors are considered, and training is undertaken through therapist modeling and rehearsal.

Social skills training is a promising technique for social phobics. If the anxiety experienced by these patients is due to ineffectiveness in social situations, then their discomfort may be overcome by learning to initiate conversation and handle themselves in social settings. Social skills training involves an element of exposure to social situations, and this may account for some of its benefit. To date, the results of behavioral treatment of social phobics have been rather modest.

# POSTTRAUMATIC STRESS DISORDER

## Definition

Posttraumatic stress disorder is a disturbance resulting from an emotionally traumatic event. Characteristic features include re-experiencing of the event, hyperalertness toward and detachment from the individual's surroundings, and anxiety as well as phobic symptoms.

A. Existence of a recognizable stressor that would evoke significant symptoms in most persons.

B. Re-experiencing of the trauma, as evidenced by at least one of the following:
  1. Recurrent and intrusive recollections of the event
  2. Recurrent dreams of the event
  3. Sudden acting or feeling as if the traumatic event were recurring

C. Numbing of responsiveness to or reduced involvement with the external world, as shown by at least one of the following:
  1. Diminished interest in important activities
  2. Feeling of detachment or estrangement from others
  3. Constricted affect

D. At least two of the following symptoms:
  1. Hyperalertness or exaggerated startle response
  2. Sleep disturbance
  3. Guilt about surviving or about behavior required for survival
  4. Memory impairment or trouble concentrating
  5. Avoidance of activities that arouse recollection of the traumatic event
  6. Intensification of symptoms by exposure to events that symbolize or resemble the traumatic event

## Etiology

The stressors associated with posttraumatic stress disorder lie outside the range of normal human experience. They include natural disasters (floods, earthquakes, etc.), accidental man-made disasters (automobile accidents, fires, etc.), and deliberate man-made disasters (death camps, combat experiences, etc.). Although physical injury may be involved, it is the psychological threat of serious injury or death that is responsible for the disorder. The stressor is the necessary but not sufficient cause of the disturbance (Andreasen, 1980).

The preexisting condition of the individual and the nature of the posttraumatic environment are important etiologic determinants. A preexisting psychiatric disturbance may heighten the impact of a traumatic event. Likewise, the availability of social supports after the event may influence the development, severity, and duration of the resulting disorder.

## Clinical Picture

Individuals with posttraumatic stress disorder are distressed by re-experiencing of the traumatic event. Most commonly this takes the form of recurrent dreams or nightmares. Also frequent are intrusive daytime recollections. Patients suffer as well from hyperalertness to their environment. Typically, they are irritable, startle easily, and have difficulty falling asleep. On the other hand, they feel emotionally detached or estranged from their surroundings. Anxiety and phobic symptoms are likewise common. Phobic anxiety and avoidance may generalize from the immediate circumstances to more general reminders of the overwhelming experience.

## Course and Complications

Posttraumatic stress disorder usually begins within hours or days of a causal event but may be delayed for months, or even years. The resulting disturbance may be acute or chronic. Most cases are acute, lasting for less than 6 months. Those lasting longer have a less favorable prognosis. Depression and alcohol dependence are serious complications of this disorder.

## Treatment

A variety of treatment measures designed to prevent chronicity or to control symptoms that have become chronic may be useful, although there have been few controlled studies. Supportive psychotherapy soon after the onset may induce an emotional catharsis or abreaction of the traumatic event. This may be facilitated by the use of hypnosis or sodium amobarbital. Benzodiazepines may provide prompt short-term reduction of symptoms, and tricyclic antidepressants and monoamine oxidase inhibitors may be useful for long-term control. Behavioral techniques, including relaxation training and desensitization, may also be useful in certain cases.

## REFERENCES

Agras S, Chapin HN, Oliveau DC: The natural history of phobia. Arch Gen Psychiatry 26:315–317, 1972.

Agras S, Sylvester D, Oliveau D: The epidemiology of common fears and phobia. Compr Psychiatry 10:151–156, 1969.

American Psychiatric Association Task Force on Nomenclature and Statistics: Diagnostic and Statistical Manual of Mental Disorders, ed 3. Washington, DC, American Psychiatric Association, 1980.

Amies PL, Gelder MG, Shaw PM: Social phobia: A comparative clinical study. Br J Psychiatry 142:174–179, 1983.

Anderson DJ, Noyes R Jr, Crowe RR: Panic disorder and generalized anxiety disorder: A comparison. Am J Psychiatry 141:572–575, 1984.

Andreasen NC: Post-traumatic stress disorder, in Kaplan HI, Freedman AN, Sadock BJ (eds): Comprehensive Textbook of Psychiatry, ed 3. Baltimore, Williams & Wilkins, 1980, p 1517.

Andrews G, Tennant C: Life events, stress and psychiatric illness. Psychol Med 8:545–549, 1978.

Andrews JDW: Psychotherapy of phobias. Psychol Bull 66:455–480, 1966.

Beck AT, Emery G: Anxiety Disorders and Phobias, A Cognitive Perspective. New York, Basic Books, 1985.

Benson H: The Relaxation Response. New York, William Morrow, 1975.

Chambless DL, Goldstein AJ: Agoraphobia: Multiple Perspectives on Theory and Treatment. New York, John Wiley, 1982.

Clancy J, Noyes R Jr, Hoenk PR, Slymen D: Secondary depression in anxiety neurosis. J Nerv Ment Dis 160:846–850, 1978.

Coryell W, Noyes R Jr, Clancy J: Excess mortality in panic disorder, a comparison with primary unipolar depression. Arch Gen Psychiatry 39:701–703, 1982.

Coryell W, Noyes R Jr, Clancy J: Panic disorder and primary unipolar depression: A comparison of background and outcome. J Affective Disord 5:311–317, 1983.

Crowe RR, Noyes R Jr, Pauls DL, Slymen D: A family study of panic disorder. Arch Gen Psychiatry 40:1065–1069, 1983.

Dietch JT: Diagnosis of organic anxiety disorders. Psychosomatics 22:661–669, 1981.

Emmelkamp PMG: Phobic and Obsessive-Compulsive Disorders: Theory, Research, and Practice. New York, Plenum, 1982.

Frankl VE: Paradoxical intention: A logo therapeutic technique. Am J Psychother 14:520–535, 1960.

Gelder MG, Wolff HH: Desensitization and psychotherapy in the treatment of phobic states: A controlled inquiry. Br J Psychiatry 113:53–73, 1967.

Gittleman R, Klein DF: Relationship between separation anxiety and panic and agoraphobic disorders. Psychopathology 17:56–65, 1984 (suppl 1).

Goldberg RJ: Anxiety reduction by self-regulation: Theory, practice, and evaluation. Ann Intern Med 96:483–487, 1982.

Goldstein AJ, Chambless DLA: A reanalysis of agoraphobia. Behav Ther 9:47–59, 1978.

Greer S: The prognosis of anxiety states, in Lader MD (ed): Studies in Anxiety. London, Royal Medico-Psychological Association, 1969, pp 151–157.

Guttmacher LB, Murphy DL, Insel TR: Pharmacologic models of anxiety. Compr Psychiatry 24:312–326, 1983.

Hoehn-Saric R: Neurotransmitters in anxiety. Arch Gen Psychiatry 39:735–742, 1982.

Kedward HB, Cooper B: Neurotic disorders in urban practice: A 3-year follow-up. J Coll Gen Pract 12:148–163, 1966.

Kerr TA, Roth M, Schapira K, Gurney C: The assessment and prediction of outcome in affective disorders. Br J Psychiatry 121:167–174, 1972.

Klein DF, Gorman JM: Panic disorders and mitral prolapse. J Clin Psychiatry Monograph 2:14–17, 1984.

Lader M: The peripheral and central rate of the catecholamines in the mechanisms of anxiety, in Klein DF, Gittelman-Klein R (eds): Progress in Psychiatric Drug Treatment, vol 2. New York, Brunner/Mazel, 1976, pp 557–569.

Liebowitz MR, Gorman JM, Fyer AJ, Levitt M, Dillon D, Levy G, Appleby IL, Anderson S, Palij M, Davies SO, Klein DF: Lactate provocation of panic attacks. II. Biochemical and physiological findings. Arch Gen Psychiatry, 42:709–715, 1985.

Marks IM, Lader M: Anxiety states (anxiety neurosis): A review. J Nerv Ment Dis 156:3–18, 1973.

Marks IM: Fears and Phobias. New York, Academic, 1969.

Marks IM: The classification of phobic disorders. Br J Psychiatry 116:377–386, 1970.

Mathews AM, Gelder MG, Johnston DW: Agoraphobia: Nature and Treatment. New York, Guilford, 1981.

Munby M, Johnston DW: Agoraphobia: The long-term follow-up of behavioural treatment. Br J Psychiatry 137:418–427, 1980.

Myers JK, Weissman MM, Tischler GL, Holzer CE, Leaf PJ, Orvaschel H, Anthony JC, Boyd VH, Burke JD, Kramer M, Stoltzman R: Six-month prevalence of psychiatric disorders in three communities: 1980–1982. Arch Gen Psychiatry, 41:959–967, 1984.

Noyes R Jr: Beta-blocking drugs and anxiety. Psychosomatics 23:155–170, 1982.

Noyes R Jr: Anxiety, phobic and obsessional disorders, in Hippius H, Winokur G (eds): Psychopharmacology I: Pt 2. Clinical Psychopharmacology. Princeton, NJ, Excerpta Medica, 1983, pp 203–230.

Noyes R Jr, Anderson DJ, Clancy J, Crowe RR, Slymen DJ, Ghoneim M, Hinrichs J: Diazepam and propranolol in panic disorder and agoraphobia. Arch Gen Psychiatry 41:287–292, 1984.

Noyes R Jr, Clancy J, Hoenk PR, Slymen DJ: Physical illness in anxiety neurosis. Compr Psychiatry 19:407–413, 1978.

Noyes R Jr, Clancy J, Hoenk PR, Slymen DJ: The prognosis of anxiety neurosis. Arch Gen Psychiatry 37:173–178, 1980.

Noyes R Jr, Crowe RR, Harris EL, Hamra BJ, McChesney CM, Chaudhry DR: Relationship between panic disorder and agoraphobia: A family study. Arch Gen Psychiatry, in press.

Redmond DE Jr: New and old evidence for the involvement of a brain norepinephrine system in anxiety, in Fann WE, Karachan I, Porkorny AD (eds): Phenomenology and Treatment of Anxiety. New York, Spectrum, 1979, pp 153–203.

Rickels K, Case WG, Diamond L: Relapse after short-term drug therapy in neurotic outpatients. Int Pharmacopsychiatry 15:186–192, 1980.

Roth M, Mountjoy C: States of anxiety in late life: Prevalence of anxiety and related emotional disorders in the elderly, in Burrows GD, Daviss B (eds): Handbook of Studies on Anxiety. Amsterdam, Elsevier/North Holland, 1980, pp 194–215.

Roth M, Mountjoy CQ: The distinction between anxiety states and depressive disorders, in Paykel ES (ed): Handbook of Affective Disorders. New York, Guilford, 1982, pp 70–92.

Rutter M, Tizard J, Whitmore K: Education, Health and Behavior, London, Longmans, 1970.

Schapira K, Kerr TA, Roth M: Phobias and affective illness. Br J Psychiatry 117:25–32, 1970.

Schopf J: Withdrawal phenomena after long-term administration of benzodiazepines, a review of recent investigations. Pharmacopsychiatria 16:1–8, 1983.

Sheehan DV, Ballenger J, Jacobson G: Treatment of endogenous anxiety with phobic, hysterical, and hypochondriacal symptoms. Arch Gen Psychiatry 37:51–59, 1980.

Sims A: Factors predictive of outcome in neurosis. Br J Psychiatry 127:54–62, 1975.

Smail P, Stockwell T, Canter S, Hodgson R: Alcohol dependence and phobic anxiety states. I. A prevalence study. Br J Psychiatry 144:53–57, 1984.

Spielberger CD: Anxiety and Behavior. New York, Academic, 1966, pp 3–20.

Torgersen S: Genetic factors in anxiety disorders. Arch Gen Psychiatry 40:1085–1089, 1983.

Uhde TW, Boulenger J, Vittone BJ: Historical and modern concepts of anxiety: A focus on adrenergic function, in Ballenger JC (ed): Biology of Agoraphobia. Washington, DC, American Psychiatric Association, 1984, pp 1–26.

Wheeler EO, White PD, Ried EW, Cohen ME: Neurocirculatory asthenia (anxiety neurosis, effort syndrome, neuroasthenia). JAMA 142:878–889, 1950.

Woodruff RA Jr, Guze SB, Clayton PJ: Anxiety neurosis among psychiatric outpatients. Compr Psychiatry 13:165–170, 1972.

Zitrin CM, Klein DF, Woerner MG, Ross DC: Treatment of phobias. I. Comparison of imipramine hydrochloride and placebo. Arch Gen Psychiatry 40:125–138, 1983.

# chapter 11

# ANOREXIA NERVOSA AND BULIMIA

by Elke D. Eckert, M.D.
James E. Mitchell, M.D.

Anorexia nervosa and bulimia are common, potentially serious disorders that primarily affect young females. Both disorders are characterized by peculiar attitudes and behaviors directed toward eating and weight accompanied by intense fear of weight gain. Anorexia nervosa is further characterized by obsessive pursuit of extreme thinness leading to emaciation, disturbance of body image, and, in females, amenorrhea.

The cardinal feature of bulimia is eating binges: powerful and intractible urges to consume large amounts of food over a short time. Usually, this is followed by either self-induced vomiting or ingestion of laxatives

**TABLE 11–1** Comparison of Essential Clinical Features of Anorexia Nervosa and Bulimia

| Essential Features for Anorexia Nervosa | Essential Features for Bulimia |
| --- | --- |
| Intense fear of weight gain | Intense fear of weight gain |
| Peculiar food handling | Peculiar food handling, including, specifically, recurrent binge-eating |
| Severe self-inflicted behaviors directed toward weight loss | Severe self-inflicted behaviors directed toward weight loss* (e.g., vomiting, laxative or diuretic abuse) |
| Significant weight loss below normal range | Weight maintenance in normal range† |
| Refusal to gain weight to a minimal normal for age and height | |
| Disturbance of body image | |
| Amenorrhea in women | |

Adapted from American Psychiatric Association: Diagnostic and Statistical Manual of Mental Disorders, ed 3 (DSM-III). Washington, DC, American Psychiatric Association, 1980.
* Although not required for the diagnosis according to DSM-III, these behaviors are invariably present.
† A minority of bulimics are above normal and some are below normal weight range.

in an attempt to prevent weight gain. However, bulimia does not produce the emaciation, which accompanies anorexia nervosa.

Although anorexia nervosa and bulimia are described separately in this chapter, there are no clear boundaries between the two conditions. Not only can the one frequently develop from the other, but also all the diagnostic features of bulimia, excepting only normal weight, may be present in anorexia nervosa (Table 11–1).

## ANOREXIA NERVOSA

### Etiology and Pathogenesis

The etiology of anorexia nervosa is unknown, although hypotheses abound that involve various psychological, sociocultural, neuroendocrine, and hypothalamic factors. Psychological theories have centered mostly on phobias and psychodynamic interpretations. One view is that anorexia nervosa can be seen as an eating or weight phobia; regardless of the initial stimulus for dieting, eating or weight gain begins to generate severe anxiety, while failure to eat or weight loss serves to avoid anxiety (Brady and Rieger, 1972). Crisp (1970) has postulated that a weight phobia springs from an avoidance response to the sexual and social demands of puberty. Bruch (1962) described early false learning experiences as causing disturbance in body image, disturbance in perception, and, in turn, lack of recognition of hunger, fatigue, and weakness. Sociocultural theories have pointed to a shift in cultural standards for feminine beauty toward thinness (Garner, Garfinkel, Schwartz, Thompson, 1980). This cultural ideal may indirectly contribute to the development of anorexia nervosa, particularly among vulnerable adolescents, who equate weight control and thinness with beauty and success. Some investigators have described family interactional patterns that they regard as related to the development and maintenance of the disorder. For example, Minuchin et al. (1975) identified dysfunctional characteristics in families of anorectics (enmeshment, overprotection, lack of conflict resolution, and rigidity) that they saw as supporting the anorectic symptoms.

Other theories have been biologic. Based on the observation that amenorrhea and disturbed hypothalamic thermoregulation are independent of emaciation in anorexia nervosa, Russell (1965) proposed that hypothalamic dysfunction contributes to the disorder. Barry and Klawans (1976) proposed that increased dopaminergic activity may account for major signs and symptoms of anorexia nervosa, specifically, anorexia, hyperactivity, decreased libido, and a morbid fear of becoming fat.

Newer evidence suggests that anorexia nervosa may be an atypical affective disorder occurring in an adolescent female at a time in her life when body image issues are important. Several findings support this view. Two controlled family studies have shown an increased incidence of primary affective disorder in the families of anorectics compared with families of controls (Winokur, March, Mendels, 1980; Gershon et al., 1983). Also, followup of anorectics suggests an increased risk for affective disorder (Cantwell, Sturzenberger, Burroughs, Salkin, Green, 1977). Biologic markers associated with primary affective disorders, such as elevated plasma cortisol levels, dexamethasone nonsuppression, low urine 3-methoxy-4-hydroxyphenylglycol levels, impaired growth hormone response to provocative stimuli, and an abnormal thyroid-stimulating hormone response to thyrotropin-releasing hormone also are found in anorectics, although the abnormalities appear reversible with weight gain (Halmi, Dekirmenjian, Davis, Casper, Goldberg, 1978; Gross, Lake, Ebert, Hegler, Kopin, 1979; Gerner and Gwirtsman, 1981; Sherman and Halmi, 1977; Casper and Frohman, 1982).

### Editor's Note

*Neuroendocrine alterations in anorexia nervosa and bulimia are common (Brown, GM et al. (eds.), Neuroendocrinology and Psychiatric Disorder, Raven Press, New York, 1984; Brown GM: Endocrine alterations in anorexia nervosa. In Darby PL, Garfinkel PE, Garner DM, and Coscine DV (eds.) Anorexia Nervosa: Recent Developments in Research. New York, Alan R. Liss, Inc., 1983) and controversy on the pathogenesis of these changes continues. Many of these changes relate directly to weight loss. These include alterations in TSH response to TRH, in resting gonadotropin levels and LH responses to provocative stimuli. Other hypothalamic disturbances, such as plasma growth hormone, T3, and reverse T3, directly relate to caloric restriction since they respond rapidly to food (carbohydrate) intake before significant weight changes can occur. Some changes appear to be independent of body weight and diet intake. These include an increased cortisol production rate, an immature pattern of LH, and possibly a decrease in norepinephrine in the cerebrospinal fluid (Kaye WH, Ebert MH, Raligh M, Lake R: Abnormalities in CNS monoamine metabolism in anorexia nervosa. Arch Gen Psychiatry 41:350–354, 1984). Factors such as amount of exercise (relating to a high incidence of amenorrhea in runners and ballet dancers. [Frisch RE, Wyshak G, Vincet L: Delayed menarche and amenorrhea in ballet dancers. N Engl J Med 303:17–19, 1980; Warren MP: The effects of exercise on pubertal progression and reproductive function in girls. J Clin Endocrinol Metab 51:1150–1157, 1980]) and emotional distress (perhaps relating to the elevated cortisol production rate) probably play a role. The possibility of an underlying hypothalamic abnormality remains.*

The role of heredity in anorexia nervosa also is unclear. Increased anorexia nervosa among family members of anorectic patients has been reported in several large series. For example, Theander (1970) found a morbidity risk of anorexia nervosa among sisters of anorectic probands to be 6.6 per cent. Twin studies have been largely limited to case reports. About 50 per cent of monozygotic twin sets reported have been concordant for anorexia nervosa, but biased selection and the small numbers reported do not permit conclusions. A recent study of twins with anorexia nervosa, the largest to date, involved 34 twin pair and one set of triplets (Holland, Hall, Murray, Russell, Crisp, 1984). In this study, anorexia nervosa was more likely to affect both members of the twin pair if they were monozygotic. In discordant pairs, the affected twin had a higher rate of perinatal complications. The affected twin in the discordant pairs was also more likely to have reached menarche later and to be the less dominant twin.

In the absence of controlled studies, the etiologic factors are speculative. It is likely that a complex chain of events interact to precipitate the disorder.

## Epidemiology

Anorexia nervosa has historically seemed an uncommon illness. The incidence and prevalence in the general population have not been determined. In 1973, however, three separate psychiatric case registers in Scotland, England, and northeastern United States supported a low annual incidence of about one case per 100,000 population (Kendall, Hall, Hailey, Babigian, 1973). Recent evidence suggests that the incidence of an-

orexia nervosa is increasing. One study indicates that the incidence nearly doubled from 1960 to 1976 (Jones, Fox, Babigian, Hutton, 1980).

Recent prevalence studies indicate anorexia nervosa to be a common disorder in the age-group at risk: 12 to 30 years. In 1976, Crisp et al. surveyed nine populations of high school girls in England. The prevalence was one severe case in 200 girls, and in those age 16 or older, the prevalence was even higher—one severe case in every 100 girls. Crisp et al. (1976) and other authors have reported anorexia nervosa to be more prevalent in the higher socioeconomic classes, but no controlled studies support this hypothesis.

Anorexia nervosa occurs predominantly in females. Only 4 per cent to 10 per cent of cases are males (Crisp and Burns, 1983). Clinically, except for amenorrhea, male anorectics are remarkably similar to the females. Anorexia nervosa appears to be uncommon in poorly developed countries, and it is seldom seen among blacks in the United States. It is overrepresented in females in certain occupations, such as models and ballerinas, who must rigorously control their body shape (Frisch, Wyskak, Vincent, 1980; Garner et al., 1980).

## Clinical Picture

The essential clinical features of anorexia nervosa, and a comparison with the features of bulimia, are listed in Table 11–1. Anorexia nervosa typically begins with a simple diet adopted in response to concern about real or imagined overweight. At first, high-calorie foods are eliminated. Then other foods are systematically curtailed as negative attitudes toward food develop. As weight loss progresses, disgust about eating and intense fear about being obese begin to outweigh hunger. The term anorexia is a misnomer because true loss of appetite is uncommon until late in the illness. Weight loss progresses until the patient becomes emaciated. The anorectic is typically unaware of her extreme thinness; instead, she continues to feel fat and loses more weight.

Attempts to assess body image disturbance, or the anorectic's failure to recognize her starved body as being too thin or to regard herself as normal, or even overweight, in the face of increasing cachexia, have relied on visual size estimation devices. Using these devices, various investigators have confirmed that anorectics overestimate the width of body parts, but there are wide individual variations among anorectics in their body size estimates (Casper, Halmi, Goldberg, Eckert, Davis, 1979; Button, Fransella, Slade, 1977; Slade and Russell, 1973). Compared with anorectics who more accurately estimate the size of body parts, those who are relatively inaccurate have been found to be more likely to fail to acknowledge their illness, to vomit, to be more severely malnourished, to gain less weight during treatment, and to have failed to gain weight during previous hospitalizations (Casper et al., 1979; Button et al., 1977). Although body size overestimation is significant in a subgroup of anorexia nervosa, it cannot be considered unique to this population, since some studies have found no significant mean differences between anorectics and control groups (Casper et al., 1979; Button et al., 1977).

Anorectics exhibit odd behavior around food. They hide food all over the house. During mealtimes they deviously dispose of food. They cut food into tiny pieces or spend much time arranging food on their plates. Confrontation about these behaviors is often met with denial. Yet anorectics think constantly about food, often collect recipes, and engage in elaborate food preparation for others. Approximately 50 per cent begin to gorge themselves with food (binge-eating, or bulimia), up to 40 per cent induce vomiting, and many begin using laxatives and diuretics in an attempt to reduce weight (Casper, Eckert, Halmi, Goldberg, Davis, 1980; Garfinkel, Moldofsky, Garner, 1980). They may also become hyperactive and engage in strenuous ritualistic exercises to control weight.

Attempts to delineate subgroups have recently focused on clinical differences between anorectics who binge-eat and those who do not. In two large recent surveys, bulimic anorectic patients were characterized by self-induced vomiting and by abuse of laxatives and diuretics (Casper et al., 1980; Garfinkel et al., 1980). They displayed impulsive behaviors, for example, alcohol abuse, stealing, and suicide attempts. They were more extroverted but manifested greater anxiety, guilt, depression, and interpersonal sensitivity and had more somatic complaints than did anorectics who exclusively dieted to lose weight. In one study a high frequency of obesity was found in mothers of the bulimic anorectics (Garfinkel et al., 1980). The delineation of these subgroups extends to the families. The incidence of alcoholism and drug abuse disorders is higher in families of bulimic anorectics than in families of nonbulimic anorectics (Eckert, Goldberg, Halmi, Casper, Davis, 1979a; Strober, Salkin, Burroughs, Morrell, 1982). The bulimic subgroup of anorexia nervosa remarkably shares characteristics with the bulimia syndrome described later. Possibly these two populations form a single group within the eating disorders.

Obsessive-compulsive behavior and anxiety and depression are frequently apparent among anorectics. Depressive symptoms include crying spells, sleep disturbance, social withdrawal, low self-esteem, and suicide attempts. Delayed psychosexual development and poor social and sexual adjustment have been described.

## Clinical Course

Onset of anorexia nervosa occurs from prepuberty to young adulthood, generally between ages 10 and 30. Most commonly, the disorder begins between ages 13 and 20 and the mean age onset is age 16 (Theander, 1970; Halmi, 1974). Although rare cases outside this range are described, they must be scrutinized to rule out other psychiatric or organic disorders simulating anorexia nervosa.

Some investigators find no distinct premorbid personality, whereas others describe a typical case as well behaved, perfectionistic, obsessional, introverted, and shy.

Onset of dieting has been associated with precipitating events, such as moving to a new school, or a traumatic event involving dating or peer relations, but often no specific reason is apparent.

Anorexia nervosa has a variable course and outcome. The course varies from spontaneous recovery without treatment to gradual or rapid deterioration, resulting in death. There may be lasting recovery after one episode of weight loss, or a fluctuating pattern of illness marked by remissions and exacerbations over many years. Although the short-term response of anorectics to well-organized hospital treatment programs is good, there is no consistent data concerning the effect of treatment on long-term outcome.

No followup study done has been free of methodological problems involving, primarily, sampling biases, inconsistent followup intervals, and different outcome measurement (Hsu, 1980; Cantwell et al., 1977; Dally, 1969; Morgan and Russell, 1975; Theander, 1970; Kay and Schapira, 1965; Schwartz and Thompson, 1981; Halmi, Brodland, Rigas, 1975). Full recovery occurs in half the anorectics, usually within 5 years. Others have persistent difficulties in maintaining weight, eating patterns, menses, and social, sexual, and psychological adjustment. A significant number remain amenorrheic despite a return to normal weight. Body weight remains persistently below 75 per cent of normal in up to 25 per cent. Obesity develops in less than 8 per cent. Although weight may be normal at followup, abnormal eating behavior may persist; one half still practice dietary restriction and avoid high-calorie foods, and binge-eating, or compulsive overeating, vomiting, and laxative abuse are common. In one study, half the anorectics had unipolar affective disorder at followup (Cantwell et al., 1977). Other common psychiatric problems at followup are obsessive-compulsive symptoms, social phobias, drug dependency, and stealing. Several studies indicate that psychiatric symptoms are more common and severe in anorectics who, at followup, have low weight and abnormal eating behavior or are preoccupied with food and weight.

The most consistent favorable prognostic feature is early-age onset and the most consistent unfavorable ones are late-age onset and more previous hospitalizations (Theander, 1970; Halmi et al., 1975; Morgan and Russell, 1975). Poorer outcome has also been associated with greater length of illness, the presence of bulimia, vomiting and laxative abuse, overestimation of body size, disturbed family relationships, more physical complaints, and symptoms of neuroticism, depression, and obsessionality.

The illness carries a considerable mortality. The usual causes of death are starvation and electrolyte disturbance, but suicide is also a contributor. Although most studies report a death rate of less than 10 per cent, several report a rate greater than 15 per cent. Two studies with the longest period of followup report the highest death rates (Halmi et al., 1975; Theander, 1983). The most notable of these, a Scandinavian study conducted over 22 years, found an 18 per cent mortality (Theander, 1983). The suicide rate was 5 per cent. Most studies report suicide rates of around 1 per cent.

## Medical Findings

Amenorrhea is invariably present and may begin before, concurrently with, or after the onset of dieting (Falk and Halmi, 1982). Other common physical findings are hypotension, hypothermia, bradycardia, dry skin, and lanugo. Less common features are hair loss, petechiae, peripheral edema, carotenemic skin, and swollen salivary glands.

Medical abnormalities and complications noted in anorexia nervosa, and a comparison with those noted in bulimia, are given in Table 11–2. Most investigators believe that starvation and associated disordered eating behaviors produce most, if not all, of the abnormalities, but the data, especially in the neuroendocrine area, are still inconclusive. One notable finding in emaciated anorectics is the "immaturity" in the pattern of luteinizing hormone (LH) functioning, resembling that of prepubertal girls. After weight gain the LH pattern usually returns to normal, but some anorectics continue to have an immature pattern. In one study those patients who continued to have abnormal eating patterns also continued to have an immature LH secretory pattern (Katz, Boyar, Roffway, Hellman, Weiner, 1977).

## Differential Diagnosis

The major confounding diagnosis is bulimia. The unclear boundaries between anorexia nervosa and bulimia are indicated by the fact that one frequently develops from the other and by the overlap in their essential features (Table 11–1). Although binge-eating occurs both in bulimia and in anorexia nervosa, bulimic patients generally maintain weight within a normal range and do not show extreme pursuit of thinness. Body image disturbance has not yet been systematically assessed in bulimics. Amenorrhea is a variable feature of bulimia.

**TABLE 11–2**   Medical Abnormalities and Complications of Anorexia Nervosa and Bulimia

| System | Anorexia Nervosa | Bulimia |
|---|---|---|
| Hematologic | Leukopenia; thrombocytopenia; bone marrow hypocellularity; granulocyte killing rate decreased | |
| Renal | Elevated BUN (dehydration); decreased glomerular filtration rate; partial diabetes insipidus | Elevated BUN (dehydration) |
| Metabolism | Hypercholesterolemia; elevated carotene levels; low plasma zinc levels; abnormal liver function tests | |
| Gastrointestinal | Altered gastric emptying; low gastric secretion; salivary gland swelling; elevated amylase levels; superior mesenteric artery syndrome | Salivary gland swelling; elevated amylase levels |
| Cardiovascular | ECG abnormalities; arrhythmias, bradycardia; altered circulatory dynamics; hypotension; edema | |
| Dental | Caries; perimyolysis | Caries; perimyolysis |
| Fluid and electrolyte | Dehydration; alkalosis; hypochloremia; hypokalemia | Dehydration; alkalosis; hypochloremia; hypokalemia |
| Central nervous system | EEG abnormality; CAT scan abnormality | EEG abnormality |
| Gonadal steroids | Low LH, FSH; impaired response to LHRH; immature LH pattern; low urinary gonadotropins; low urinary estrogens; abnormal estrogen metabolism; low testosterone (in males) | |
| Thyroid | Low $T_3$, high $rT_3$; impaired TRH responsiveness | Impaired TRH responsiveness |
| Growth hormone | Elevated basal; pathologic responsiveness to provocative stimuli | Pathologic responsiveness to provocative stimuli |
| Glucose | Abnormal glucose tolerance test; fasting hypoglycemia | |
| Adrenal | Elevated cortisol levels; change in cortisol metabolism, secretion; Dexamethasone nonsuppression positive | Dexamethasone nonsuppression positive |

These abnormalities are not necessarily seen in every patient, and many are seen in only a minority (Mitchell, 1984).

Anorexia nervosa must be differentiated from peculiar eating behavior and weight loss, which can occur in several other disorders. In general, the differentiation can readily be made on the basis of positive criteria of anorexia nervosa, such as fear of becoming obese and pursuit of thinness, which are absent in the other disorders.

Weight loss is common in depressive disorders but is generally severer in anorexia nervosa. Whereas depressed patients are aware of a loss of appetite, anorectics generally have a normal appetite, which they may deny. Anorectics, in contrast to depressives, are preoccupied with food. Agitation can be seen in depressive disorders, but it differs from the ritualistic activity of an anorectic.

Weight loss and peculiar eating behavior are sometimes seen in schizophrenics, usually on the basis of delusions. However, the delusions of schizophrenics differ in content and are not concerned with caloric content or fear of weight gain.

It is important to ascertain medical conditions that accompany or simulate anorexia nervosa. Lesions of the pituitary or the hypothalamus may be accompanied by appetite disturbance and weight loss. In general, starvation, resulting from causes other than anorexia nervosa, is associated with inactivity and apathy and not with the intense fear of weight gain, body image distortion, alertness, and hyperactivity seen in anorectics (Casper and Davis, 1977).

## Treatment

There is no agreement about the best treatment. Treatment currently involves a combination of medical management, nutritional rehabilitation often using behavioral techniques, reeducative personal therapy, family therapy, and, sometimes, pharmacotherapy. The immediate aim of treatment during the acute anorectic phase is to correct dehydration and electrolyte imbalance and restore the nutritional state to normal. Starvation itself can lead to many problems, including depression, sleep disturbance, preoccupation with food, and irritability, and improvement in the patient's psychological state will occur with nutritional rehabilitation (Morgan and Russell, 1975; Eckert, Goldberg, Halmi, Casper, Davis, 1982). Treatment is done most efficiently in a structured hospital treatment program. Because many anorectic patients do not acknowledge that a problem exists, it is essential to obtain the family's support so that firm treatments can be effected. Those patients who are less severely ill, are not vomiting or using laxatives, and have family that will cooperate with prescribed treatment may respond to outpatient treatment.

It is advisable to prescribe a structured diet, gradually increasing calories to avoid stomach dilatation and circulation overload. Close observation during and after meals will minimize surreptitious mealtime behavior, such as hiding food and vomiting.

Behavioral contingencies after an operant conditioning paradigm probably increase the rate of weight gain (Agras and Kraemer, 1983). A typical positive reinforcement dependent on weight gain is opportunity for increased physical and social activity, including visitors, while negative reinforcements for failure to gain weight are bed rest, isolation, and tube feeding. However, a randomized controlled treatment study did not demonstrate a clear advantage, expressed as weight gain, for behavior therapy (Eckert et al., 1979b).

Although there is no proven pharmacologic treatment for anorexia nervosa, drugs

may be useful adjuncts. Antidepressant drugs may be useful because of the presence of depressive symptoms, although insufficient data are available in this area. One controlled double-blind study of hospitalized anorectics did not find amitriptyline to decrease depression, although it had a marginal effect on increasing the rate of weight gain (Halmi, Eckert, La Du, Cohen, 1986). In the same controlled study, cyproheptadine, an antihistamine and serotonin antagonist, was found to decrease depression and increase the rate of weight gain in the nonbulimic subgroup of anorexia nervosa. The usefulness of drugs such as metoclopramide to enhance gastric emptying and improve the gastrointestinal symptoms of patients with anorexia nervosa is unclear (Saleh and Lebwohl, 1980). Lithium is contraindicated for patients who vomit or abuse laxatives or diuretics because of the potential for lithium toxicity. The usefulness of antipsychotic medication is unproven.

No information is available about drugs affecting the long-term course of the disorder. However, anorectics who remain depressed after nutritional rehabilitation may benefit from antidepressants.

Psychoanalytically oriented therapy is not effective in treating anorexia nervosa (Bruch, 1970). Individual psychotherapy should aim at correcting cognitive errors of thinking, promoting independence, accepting responsibilities, improving psychosocial skill deficits, and promoting a positive self-concept.

Counseling of family members is a necessary component of an effective treatment program. This involves educating the family about the disorder, assessing the family's impact on maintaining the disorder, and assisting in methods to promote normal functioning of the patient.

## BULIMIA

### Definition

Bulimia denotes a symptom, binge-eating, or the behavioral syndrome described in the *Diagnostic and Statistical Manual of Mental Disorders* (DSM-III; American Psychiatric Association, 1980). The syndrome's most essential feature is binge-eating. Although invariably present, behaviors directed toward weight loss, including vomiting and laxative abuse, are currently not required for diagnosis. Bulimia nervosa, described in England by Russell (1979), overlaps with bulimia. The chief difference is that bulimia nervosa requires either self-induced vomiting or laxative abuse. Other terms used to describe clinical syndromes similar to bulimia include bulimarexia and the dietary chaos syndrome. This chapter defines bulimia as the DSM-III syndrome.

## Etiology and Pathogenesis

Little is known concerning the causes of bulimia. As with anorexia nervosa, sociocultural preoccupation with thinness is commonly implicated. A relationship between obesity, dietary restraint, and binge-eating has been suggested (Wardle and Beinart, 1981). This suggestion is supported by evidence showing that many patients who develop bulimia are overweight during adolescence, before the onset of the disorder, and that binges frequently begin during a period of dieting (Fairburn and Cooper, 1982; Pyle, Mitchell, Eckert, 1981). Some patients also retrospectively link the onset of bulimia with traumatic events, particularly experience of separation or loss (Pyle et al., 1981).

A relationship between affective disorder and bulimia has been suggested. Several findings support this view. Many bulimic patients are depressed, improve with antidepressants, show dexamethasone nonsuppression, and have strong family histories of affective disorder (Hudson, Laffer, Pope, 1982; Gwirtsman, Roy-Byrne, Yager, Gerner, 1983; Pope, Hudson, Jonas, Yurgelon-Todd, 1983; Walsh et al., 1982).

A predisposition to chemical abuse has been described (Pyle et al., 1981; Hatsukami et al., 1982). Bulimic patients, and their families, have been described as being at high risk for abuse of alcohol and other drugs. This is particularly interesting when one considers that there are many behavioral similarities between drug abuse and bulimia, including preoccupation with the substance, loss of control over the use of the substance, the secretive nature of the behavior, and the social isolation that accompanies and results from the behavior.

Once binge-eating has started, it tends to be maintained by several factors. Binge-eating may be used to alleviate dysphoric states (Casper et al., 1980). Depression has been shown to encourage voluntary dieters to overeat and gain weight (Herman and Polivy, 1980). Also, once started, binge-eating may become autonomous.

## Epidemiology

Although the prevalence of bulimia in the general population is unknown, it appears to be a common problem. Estimates of the prevalence of binge-eating and associated syndromes depend on how such cases are defined. Recent questionnaire surveys, mostly in college populations, indicate that episodes of binge-eating occur in 25 per cent to 80 per cent of women and in 40 per cent to 60 per cent of men, a rate so high that it suggests binge-eating is usually not of clinical concern (Halmi, Falk, Schwartz, 1981; Pyle et al., 1983; Pope, Hudson, Yurgelon-Todd, 1984; Cooper and Fairburn, 1983). Eight per cent to 20 per cent of women and 1 per cent to 6 per cent of men endorse responses on questionnaires suggesting a diagnosis of bulimia syndrome, but the frequency of bulimic behavior is low. Only 1 per cent to 2 per cent of women and somewhat less men in college populations acknowledge binge-eating and self-induced vomiting or laxative abuse as frequently as do bulimic patients identified through psychiatric clinics—that is, on at least a weekly basis.

## Clinical Picture

In clinic populations most bulimic patients are female. At presentation they average several years older than anorexia nervosa patients, the majority being between 20 and 30 years old (Pyle et al., 1981; Fairburn and Cooper, 1984; Russell, 1979).

The essential clinical features of bulimia are given in Table 11–1. Most bulimics are of normal weight. There is an intense fear of weight gain coupled with concern about body weight and shape. A desire to lose weight is not invariably present; some patients are content to maintain their current weight. Unlike the typical patient with anorexia nervosa, bulimic patients complain of loss of control over their eating.

Binge-eating, which usually occurs in isolation, is considered the hallmark of bulimia. Patients may eat 5000 or more calories within a few hours (Mitchell, Pyle, Eckert, 1981). Binge foods usually consist of high-calorie carbohydrate or fat-containing foods that the patients usually exclude from their regular diets because they are perceived as being "fattening." Bulimic patients have grossly disturbed eating habits in which regular meals are seldom eaten, and attempts at dietary restriction are interspersed with episodes of binge-eating, followed usually by self-induced vomiting or laxative abuse. Usually vomiting is induced by stimulating the gag reflex with the fingers or an object such as a toothbrush. Occasionally, emesis-inducing drugs are used. Some patients abuse laxatives on a regular basis; others take large amounts only in response to having overeaten. Other frequently reported behaviors include diuretic abuse and chewing food and spitting it out without swallowing it.

Anxiety and depression, with prominent expressions of guilt, worthlessness, and, sometimes, suicidal thoughts, are frequent. Mood tends to parallel control over eating; the less the control, the lower the mood (Russell, 1979). Some have diffuse difficulty controlling their impulses; they may abuse alcohol or drugs or they may steal (Pyle et al., 1981; Russell, 1979). Stealing often consists of shoplifting food.

## Clinical Course

Onset of bulimia generally occurs during adolescence or the young adult years, with a mean age onset for binge-eating of 18 years (Pyle et al., 1981; Fairburn and Cooper, 1982). The onset of vomiting occurs on average 1 year after onset of binge-eating (Fairburn and Cooper, 1982).

Premorbid characteristics vary. In general, bulimic patients are more outgoing, socially competent, and sexually experienced than anorexia nervosa patients.

Little is known about the longitudinal course of bulimia. A history suggesting episodes of anorexia nervosa before bulimia becomes manifest is found in a significant minority (Pyle et al., 1981; Fairburn and Cooper, 1984). The typical bulimic has been symptomatic for 3 to 6 years before seeking treatment, and the usual patttern is that the frequency of abnormal behaviors has increased over that period of time (Fairburn and Cooper, 1982, 1984; Pyle et al., 1981). Many patients lose weight when they first become bulimic; however, as the disorder progresses, they tend to gain weight, possibly because of increasing intensity and frequency of binge-eating episodes (Russell, 1979).

## Physical Findings

Most bulimics menstruate regularly, but some menstruate irregularly or are amenorrheic (Fairburn and Cooper, 1982, 1984). Medical abnormalities and complications noted in bulimia, and a comparison with those noted in anorexia nervosa, are given in Table 11–2. The most serious problem is fluid and electrolyte abnormalities, which are found in approximately 50 per cent of patients. Such abnormalities result from variable combinations of vomiting and laxative or diuretic abuse (Mitchell, Pyle, Eckert, Hatsukami, Lentz, 1983). A medical complication of particular concern is gastric dilatation after binge-eating, which can result in gastric perforation and death. Fortunately, this occurs infrequently. The pathogenesis of salivary gland swelling, usually involving the parotid glands, is unclear. Elevated serum amylase levels are presumably related to the parotid gland changes. Problems of dentition are probably related to exposure of dental surfaces to acidic gastric contents during vomiting.

## Differential Diagnosis

The differential diagnosis between bulimia and anorexia nervosa is discussed in the section on anorexia nervosa. Differentiation must be made from common overeating, which involves neither the massive caloric intake nor the loss of control associated with binge-eating. Overeating resembling binge-eating can also occur in certain organic states, such as the Kleine-Levine syndrome, tumors of the hypothalamus, and Klüver-Bucy–like syndromes.

## Treatment

There is considerable uncertainty about how to best manage bulimia. Available reports favor two general approaches: pharmacologic and psychotherapeutic. The pharmacologic treatment of bulimia has been based on two types of agents: anticonvulsants and antidepressants. A controlled study using phenytoin reports benefit to some patients, but the findings are difficult to interpret because of the study design (Wermuth, Davis, Hollister, Stunkard, 1977). Recently, placebo-controlled double-blind studies indicate that antidepressants (imipramine, amitriptyline, desipramine, phenelzine) may be helpful for patients with bulimia (Pope et al., 1983; Walsh et al., 1984; Hughes, Wells, Cunningham, 1984; Mitchell and Groat, 1984). It is unclear whether the antidepressants exert their therapeutic effect by improving mood or through a primary effect on eating behavior.

Many authorities have suggested psychotherapeutic approaches, particularly cognitive and behavioral approaches designed to modify the behavior and attitudes characteristic of the condition using both individual and group format (Fairburn, 1981; Pyle, Mitchell, Eckert, Hatsukami, Goff, 1984). Such treatment usually includes educating patients about the nature of their problem and its medical consequences, self-monitoring techniques to increase patients' awareness of their eating patterns, contracting and goal setting to change eating behavior, manipulation of the behavioral antecedents and consequences of bulimic behavior, problem-solving and adaptive-skills training, and cognitive restructuring procedures. Although such approaches seem effective in the short term, long-term effects are not known.

## REFERENCES

Agras WS, Kraemer HC: The treatment of anorexia nervosa: Do different treatments have different outcomes? Psychiatric Ann 13:928, 1983.

American Psychiatric Association: Diagnostic and Statistical Manual of Mental Disorders. Washington, DC, American Psychiatric Association, 1980.

Barry BC, Klawans HL: On the role of dopamine in the pathophysiology of anorexia nervosa. J Neural Transm 38:107, 1976.

Brady JP, Rieger W: Behavioral treatment of anorexia nervosa, in Proceedings of the International Symposium on Behavior Modification. New York, Appleton-Century-Crofts, 1972.

Bruch H: Perceptual and conceptual disturbances in anorexia nervosa. Psychosom Med 24:187, 1962.

Bruch H: Psychotherapy in primary anorexia nervosa. J Nerv Ment Dis 150:51, 1970.

Button EJ, Fransella F, Slade PD: A reappraisal of body perception disturbance in anorexia nervosa. Psychol Med 7:235, 1977.

Cantwell DP, Sturzenberger S, Burroughs J, Salkin B, Green JK: Anorexia nervosa—an affective disorder? Arch Gen Psychiatry 34:1087, 1977.

Casper RC, Davis JM: On the course of anorexia nervosa. Am J Psychiatry 134:974, 1977.

Casper RC, Eckert ED, Halmi KA, Goldberg SC, Davis JM: Bulimia: Its incidence and clinical importance in patients with anorexia nervosa. Arch Gen Psychiatry 37:1030, 1980.

Casper RC, Frohman LA: Delayed TSH response in anorexia nervosa following injection of thyrotropin-releasing hormone (TRH). Psychoneuroendocrinology 7:59, 1982.

Casper RC, Halmi KA, Goldberg SC, Eckert ED, Davis JM: Disturbances in body image estimation as related to other characteristics and outcome in anorexia nervosa. Br J Psychiatry 134:60, 1979.

Cooper PJ, Fairburn CG: Binge-eating and self-induced vomiting in the community: A preliminary study. Br J Psychiatry 142:139, 1983.

Crisp AH: Anorexia nervosa: "Feeding disorder," "nervous malnutrition," or "weight phobia"? World Rev Nutr Diet 12:452, 1970.

Crisp AH, Burns T: The clinical presentation of anorexia nervosa in males. Int J Eat Disord 2:5, 1983.

Crisp AH, Palmer RL, Kalucy RS: How common is anorexia nervosa? A prevalence study. Br J Psychiatry 128:549, 1976.

Dally PJ: Anorexia nervosa. New York, Grune & Stratton, 1969.

Eckert ED, Goldberg SC, Halmi KA, Casper RC, Davis JM: Alcoholism in anorexia nervosa, in Pickens RW, Heston LL (eds): Psychiatric Factors in Drug Abuse. New York, Grune & Stratton, 1979a.

Eckert ED, Goldberg SC, Halmi KA, Casper RC, Davis JM: Behavior therapy in anorexia nervosa. Br J Psychiatry 134:55, 1979b.

Eckert ED, Goldberg SC, Halmi KA, Casper RC, Davis JM: Depression in anorexia nervosa. Psychol Med 12:115, 1982.

Fairburn CG: A cognitive behavioral approach to the management of bulimia. Psychol Med 11:707, 1981.

Fairburn CG, Cooper PJ: Self-induced vomiting and bulimia nervosa: An undetected problem. Br Med J 284:1153, 1982.

Fairburn CG, Cooper PJ: The clinical features of bulimia nervosa. Br J Psychiatry 144:238, 1984.

Falk JR, Halmi KA: Amenorrhea in anorexia nervosa: Examination of the critical body weight hypothesis. Biol Psychiatry 17:799, 1982.

Frisch RE, Wyshak G, Vincent L: Delayed menarche and amenorrhea in ballet dancers. N Engl J Med 303:17, 1980.

Garfinkel PE, Moldofsky H, Garner DM: The heterogeneity of anorexia nervosa: Bulimia as a distinct subgroup. Arch Gen Psychiatry 37:1036, 1980.

Garner DM, Garfinkel PE, Schwartz D, Thompson M: Cultural expectation of thinness in women. Psychol Rep 47:483, 1980.

Gerner RH, Gwirtsman HE: Abnormalities of dexamethasone suppression test and urinary MHPG in anorexia nervosa. Am J Psychiatry 138:650, 1981.

Gershon ES, Hamovit JR, Schreiber JL, Dibble ED, Kaye W, Nurnberger JI, Andersen A, Ebert M: Anorexia nervosa and major affective disorders associated in families: A preliminary report, in Guze SB, Earls FJ, Barrett JE (eds): Childhood Psychopathology and Development. New York, Raven Press, 1983.

Gross HA, Lake CR, Ebert MH, Hegler MG, Kopin IJ: Catecholamine metabolism in primary anorexia nervosa. J Clin Endocrinol Metab 49:805, 1979.

Gwirtsman HE, Roy-Byrne P, Yager J, Gerner RH: Neuroendocrine abnormalities in bulimia. Am J Psychiatry 140:559, 1983.

Halmi KA: Anorexia nervosa: Demographic and clinical features in 94 cases. Psychosom Med 36:18, 1974.

Halmi KA, Brodland G, Rigas C: A follow-up study of 79 patients with anorexia nervosa: An evaluation of prognostic factors and diagnostic criteria. Life Hist Rev Psychopathol 4:2990, 1975.

Halmi KA, Dekirmenjian H, Davis JM, Casper R, Goldberg S: Catecholamine metabolism in anorexia nervosa. Arch Gen Psychiatry 35:458, 1978.

Halmi KA, Eckert ED, La Du TJ, Cohen J: Anorexia nervosa: Treatment efficacy of cyproheptadine and amitriptyline. Arch Gen Psychiatry 43:177, 1986.

Halmi KA, Falk JR, Schwartz E: Binge-eating and vomiting: A survey of a college population. Psychol Med 11:697, 1981.

Hatsukami D, Owen P, Pyle R, et al: Similarities and differences on the MMPI between women with bulimia and women with alcohol or drug abuse problems. Addict Behav 7:435, 1982.

Herman CP, Polivy J: Restrained eating in obesity, in Stunkard AJ (ed): Obesity. Philadelphia, WB Saunders Company, 1980.

Holland AJ, Hall A, Murray RM, Russell GFM, Crisp AH: Anorexia nervosa: A study of 34 twin pairs and one set of triplets. Br J Psychiatry 14:414, 1984.

Hsu LKG: Outcome of anorexia nervosa. Arch Gen Psychiatry 37:1041, 1980.

Hudson JI, Laffer PS, Pope HG Jr: Bulimia related to affective disorder by family history and response to dexamethasone suppression test. Am J Psychiatry 139:685, 1982.

Hughes PL, Wells LA, Cunningham JC: A controlled trial using desipramine for bulimia. Presented at the 137th Annual Meeting, American Psychiatric Association, Los Angeles, May 1984.

Jones DJ, Fox MM, Babigian HM, Hutton HE: Epidemiology of anorexia nervosa in Monroe County, New York: 1960–1976. Psychosom Med 42:551, 1980.

Katz JL, Boyar RM, Roffway H, Hellman L, Weiner H: LHRH responsiveness in anorexia nervosa: Intactness despite prepubertal circadian LH pattern. Psychosom Med 39:241, 1977.

Kay DWK, Schapira K: The prognosis in anorexia nervosa, in Meyer JE, Feldman H (eds): Symposium on Anorexia Nervosa. Stuttgart, Thieme Verlag, 1965.

Kendall RE, Hall DJ, Hailey A, Babigian HM: The epidemiology of anorexia nervosa. Psychol Med 3:200, 1973.

Minuchin S, Baker L, Rosman BL, Liebman R, Milman L, Todd T: A conceptual model of psychosomatic illness in children. Arch Gen Psychiatry 32:1031, 1975.

Mitchell JE: Medical complications of anorexia nervosa and bulimia. Psychiatr Med 1:229, 1984.

Mitchell JE, Groat R: A placebo-controlled, double-blind trial of amitriptyline in bulimia. J Clin Psychopharmacol 4:186, 1984.

Mitchell JE, Pyle RL, Eckert ED: Frequency and duration of binge-eating episodes in patients with bulimia. Am J Psychiatry 138:835, 1981.

Mitchell JE, Pyle RL, Eckert ED, Hatsukami D, Lentz R: Electrolyte and other physiological abnormalities in patients with bulimia. Psychol Med 13:273, 1983.

Morgan HG, Russell GF: Value of family background in clinical features as predictors of long-term outcome in anorexia nervosa. Psychol Med 5:355, 1975.

Pope HG Jr, Hudson JI, Jonas JM, Yurgelon-Todd D: Bulimia treated with imipramine: A placebo-controlled, double-blind study. Am J Psychiatry 140:554, 1983.

Pope HG Jr, Hudson JI, Yurgelon-Todd D: Anorexia nervosa and bulimia among 300 suburban women shoppers. Am J Psychiatry 141:292, 1984.

Pyle RL, Mitchell JE, Eckert ED: Bulimia: A report of 34 cases. J Clin Psychiatry 42:60, 1981.

Pyle RL, Mitchell JE, Eckert ED, Halvorson PA, Neuman PA, Goff GM: The incidence of bulimia in freshman college students. Int J Eat Disord 2:75, 1983.

Pyle RL, Mitchell JE, Eckert ED, Hatsukami DK, Goff G: The interruption of bulimic behaviors: A review of three treatment programs. Psychiatr Clin North Am 7:275, 1984.

Russell G: Bulimia nervosa: An ominous variant of anorexia nervosa. Psychol Med 9:429, 1979.

Russell GFM: Metabolic aspects of anorexia nervosa. Proc R Soc Med 58:811, 1965.

Saleh JW, Lebwohl P: Metoclopromide—induced gastric emptying in patients with anorexia nervosa. Am J Gastroenterol 74:127, 1980.

Schwartz DM, Thompson MG: Do anorectics get well? Current research and future needs. Am J Psychiatry 138:319, 1981.

Sherman BM, Halmi KA: The effect of nutritional rehabilitation on hypothalamic-pituitary function in anorexia nervosa, in Vigersky RA (ed): Anorexia Nervosa. New York, Raven Press, 1977.

Slade PD, Russell GFM: Experimental investigations of bodily perception in anorexia nervosa and obesity. Psychother Psychosom 22:259, 1973.

Strober M, Salkin B, Burroughs J, Morrell W: Validity of the bulimic-restricter distinction in anorexia nervosa. J Nerv Ment Dis 170:345, 1982.

Theander S: Anorexia nervosa. Acta Psychiatr Scand [Suppl] 214, pp. 1–194, 1970.

Theander S: Research on outcome and prognosis of anorexia nervosa and results from a Swedish long-term study. Int J Eat Disord 12:167, 1983.

Walsh BT, Stewart JW, Roose SP, Carino JS, Gladis M, Glassman AH: A double-blind study of phenelzine in bulimia. Presented at the 137th Annual Meeting, American Psychiatric Association, Los Angeles, May 1984.

Walsh BT, Stewart JW, Wright L, Harrigan W, Roose SP, Glassman AH: Treatment of bulimia with monoamine oxidase inhibitors. Am J Psychiatry 139:1629, 1982.

Wardle J, Beinart H: Binge-eating: A theoretical review, Br J Clin Psychol 20:97, 1981.

Wermuth BM, Davis KL, Hollister LE, Stunkard AJ: Phenytoin treatment of the binge-eating syndrome. Am J Psychiatry 134:1249, 1977.

Winokur A, March V, Mendels J: Primary affective disorder in relatives of patients with anorexia nervosa. Am J Psychiatry 130:695, 1980.

# chapter 12

# PARANOID DISORDERS

*by* Raymond R. Crowe, M.D.

## DEFINITION

If any psychiatric illness with delusions is considered to be a paranoid disorder, then these disorders are among the most common conditions in psychiatry (Freedman and Schwab, 1978). For example, 48 per cent of manic and 33 per cent of bipolar depressives are delusional (Winokur, Clayton, Reich, 1969), and practically all schizophrenics experience delusions at some time during the course of their illness. Therefore, if the concept of a paranoid disorder is to have any validity as a diagnostically pure group of patients, it must be defined by paranoid delusions in the absence of other psychiatric illness that might account for the delusional thinking.

Although the term *paranoia* dates from the time of Hippocrates, Kahlbaum (1863) was the first to use it to designate a diagnostically separate group of disorders that remained so over their course (Lewis, 1970; Tanna, 1974). Kraepelin (1921) further developed the concept of paranoia as a chronic and unremitting system of delusions that were distinguished from schizophrenia by the absence of hallucinations and other psychotic features. These ideas were incorporated into the first diagnostic manual (DSM-I) of the American Psychiatric Association (1952), and paranoid reactions were defined as illnesses with persistent persecutory or grandiose delusions, ordinarily without hallucinations, and with emotional responses and behavior consistent with the ideas held.

Subtypes included paranoia, a chronic disorder characterized by an intricate and complex delusional system, and paranoid state, usually of shorter duration and lacking the systematization of paranoia. These concepts of paranoid disorders and their subtypes have been preserved in all their essential features by DSM-II (1968) and DMS-III (1980).

DSM-III describes the essential features of paranoid disorders as persistent persecutory delusions or delusional jealousy, not caused by another mental disorder, and includes the subtypes of paranoia, acute paranoid disorder, and shared paranoid disorder. A diagnosis of paranoia requires a stable persecutory delusional system of at least 6 months' duration. Acute paranoid disorder is a paranoid disorder of less than 6 months' duration. In shared paranoid disorder the delusional system develops as a result of a close relationship with another person or persons who have an established disorder with persecutory delusions. This condition is commonly known as folie à deux. Such persons are probably not truly delusional, but passively accept the delusional beliefs of the more dominant member of the relationship. Atypical paranoid disorder refers to individuals who do not fit into any of the other subtypes.

One way in which DSM-III departs from the older nomenclature is by using the criterion of chronicity to subtype the paranoid disorders rather than systematization of the delusion. This difference may be more apparent than real for, as we shall see, chronicity is strongly correlated with systematization. Thus paranoia and acute paranoid disorder of DSM-III are similar to paranoia and paranoid state of the older nomenclature.

International Classification of Diseases (ICD)-9 classifies most paranoid disorders under "paranoid states" and includes four types. Simple paranoid states are those in which "delusions, especially of being influenced, persecuted, or treated in some special way, are the main symptom." They may be acute or chronic. Paranoia is a "chronic psychosis in which logically constructed systematized delusions have developed gradually without concomitant hallucinations." When hallucinations are prominent, the disorder is classified as a paraphrenia, the third subtype. Shared paranoid disorder is similar to the DSM-III concept. A category is provided for other specified paranoid states; acute paranoid disorders are classified outside the paranoid states.

## EPIDEMIOLOGY

Paranoid disorders have always been considerd uncommon illnesses, but until recently little was known of their epidemiology. Demographic reports from the United States and other countries have now provided a reasonably complete picture of the epidemiology of these conditions (Table 12–1; Kendler, 1982).

The annual incidence ranges from 0.7 to 3.0 new cases per 100,000 population per year. This rate accounts for 1.3 per cent of all first admissions to mental hospitals and 3.9 per cent of first admissions for nonor-

### TABLE 12–1   Epidemiology of Paranoid Disorders

| | |
|---|---|
| Incidence* | 0.7–1.3 |
| Prevalence* | 24–30 |
| Percent of first admissions* | 1.3 |
| Mean age of onset† | 39 |
| Sex ratio (F/M) | 1.18 |

The figures for incidence, prevalence, and sex ratio represent cases per 100,000 population.
* From Kendler, 1982.
† From Retterstol, 1966.

ganic psychoses. Moreover, the incidence appears to have been stable from 1932 to 1952, with a small decrease since 1952 owing to an increase in the number of first admissions for other illnesses. Thus there seems to have been little change recently in the incidence of new cases.

Prevalence refers to the number of active and inactive cases in the population at any given time. For the paranoid disorders, it is approximately 24 to 30 cases per 100,000 population, which substantiates clinical impressions that these are indeed uncommon conditions. Thus, for every case of paranoid disorder, there are approximately 30 cases of schizophrenia and 150 of affective disorder (assuming a prevalence of 1 per cent for schizophrenia and 5 per cent for affective disorder; Goodwin and Guze, 1979). These figures show how much more likely a delusional patient is to have one of the more common psychoses than a paranoid disorder.

Paranoid disorders are most likely to appear in mid-life. The peak age of onset and the age at first admission both occur in the fourth to fifth decade and range from the teens into senescence (Winokur, 1977; Kendler, 1982). The sexes are nearly equally affected, although most studies have found a small excess of females, about 55 per cent of first admissions being women.

## ETIOLOGY

Because paranoid disorders are uncommon, and because schizophrenia and depression can both present with paranoid delusions, the question arises whether paranoid disorders represent a separate group of illnesses or simply atypical forms of these more common ones. This question is important because of the obvious treatment implications, and several lines of evidence converge to provide a reasonably consistent answer.

Epidemiologic findings suggest that paranoid disorders are unrelated to either affective disorder or schizophrenia (Kendler, 1980). Paranoid disorders are far less prevalent than either of the other two. They begin at a later time in life than schizophrenia, and the sex ratio is closer to unity than that of the affective disorders, with their prominent excess of females. Although these findings are suggestive, they by no means prove the case for a diagnostically separate condition.

The familial findings are more convincing. If paranoid disorders were a form of either schizophrenia or affective disorder, the incidence of these latter conditions should be increased in the families of paranoid disorders, but this has not been found (Kolle, 1931; Debray, 1985; Winokur, 1977; Kendler and Hays, 1981). Familial rates of schizophrenia range from 0.6 per cent to 1.7 per cent, and those of affective disorder, from 1.1 per cent to 5.0 per cent. Both are within the population expectation for their respective prevalences. Morever, reanalysis of data from a large adoption study of schizophrenia did not find a higher rate of paranoid disorders in the biologic relatives of schizophrenic adoptees than in other groups of relatives (adoptive relatives of the same adoptees and biologic and adoptive relatives of control adoptees) (Kendler, 1981).

### Editor's Comment

*Two recent studies address the question of whether delusional disorder (paranoia) breeds true in families. Patients with delusional disorder were more likely to have family members who were considered suspicious, secretive, jealous, showed delusions, or had some kind of paranoid disorder more frequently than controls. The family members of paranoid schizophrenics as opposed to delusional disorder patients were less likely to have family members showing these characteristics (Winokur G: Familial psychopathology in delusional disorder. Comp Psychiatry 26:241–248, 1985). Another study showed that paranoid personality disorder was more common in relatives of delusional disorder patients than in relatives of controls or schizophrenics (Kendler K, Masterson C, Davis K: Psychiatric illness in first-degree relatives of patients with paranoid psychosis, schizophrenia, and medical illness. Br J Psychiatry 147:524–531, 1985). These findings clearly suggest that delusional disorder is a separate illness from either schizophrenia or paranoid schizophrenia; also, they provide a clue as to what is transmitted intrafamilially.*

Followup studies of paranoid disorders range in length of followup from a few months to 20 years and indicate that the diagnosis of paranoid disorder tends to remain stable over time (Kendler, 1980). If they were a form of affective disorder or schizophrenia, this length of observation should allow sufficient time for the correct diagnosis to declare itself. However, 78 per cent to 93 per cent of paranoid disorder patients retained the same diagnosis, only 3 per cent to 22 per cent developing schizophrenia and less than 6 per cent developing affective disorder.

These observations indicate that Kahlbaum's original concept of paranoid disorders as uncommon but distinct entities was correct. They appear to form a chronologically stable group of disorders that are biologically distinct from the other psychoses.

## CLINICAL PICTURE

The hallmark of the paranoid disorders is the delusional system. This consists of a unique set of false ideas that are rigidly adhered to despite all contradictory evidence. The uniqueness of the delusion distinguishes these patients from persons with idiosyncratic ideas shared by a larger social group, such as a religious cult. The fixed quality of the delusion also separates them from nondelusional persons with unusual ideas. A third feature of delusions is that facts are reinterpreted to fit the delusion, rather than the delusion being modified to fit the facts.

The delusions of paranoid disorders are usually systematized and encapsulated to varying degrees. The first term refers to the ramifications of the delusional system being connected by a common theme. Encapsulation refers to thought processes outside the delusional system remaining unaffected.

The content of the delusions usually centers around themes of persecution or jealousy, but limiting paranoid disorders to these two delusions, as in DSM-III, is probably too restrictive, for erotic and grandiose themes occur in these disorders as well. Perhaps the best criterion for a paranoid delusion should be that the delusion be "possible," as proposed by Winokur (1977). Delusions that are possible, however implausible, would be compatible with a diagnosis of paranoid disorder, while patently impossible and bizarre delusions would not.

Many paranoid disorders have hallucinations that are not sufficiently prominent to justify a diagnosis of schizophrenia. Some would exclude any patient with hallucinations (Winokur, 1977), whereas others would include them as long as the hallucinations are not prominent (Kendler, 1980). At the present time it seems reasonable to consider infrequent hallucinations to be a symptom of delusional disorders.

Retterstol's study provides an invaluable source of information on the clinical picture of paranoid disorders (1966). More than 300 patients with non-affective paranoid psychoses were rediagnosed at followup (2 to 18 years later) independently of their presenting symptoms. Two diagnoses are particularly relevant because they overlap, to a large extent, with the DMS-III subtypes of paranoia and acute paranoid disorder. The 26 "paranoiac psychosis" were so diagnosed because of well-systematized delusions, and 88 per cent had been ill longer than 6 months at admission, making them comparable to the DSM-III subtype of paranoia. The 57 "paranoid disorders" were diagnosed on the basis of less systematized delusions than the paranoiacs. Because they were more acute—54 per cent ill less than 6 months at admission—they are comparable with DSM-III acute paranoid disorders.

Most of the delusional themes were accounted for by persecution and jealousy, but paranoia and acute paranoid disorder differed strikingly with respect to these two delusions (Table 12–2). The findings indicate that paranoia is primarily a delusional jealousy, whereas acute paranoid disorder is a persecutory illness. Hallucinations, which were almost exclusively auditory, occurred in only 4 per cent of the paranoias but were present in a quarter of the acute paranoid disorders.

The affect is usually well preserved in paranoid disorders, and emotional contact was good in 94 per cent of Retterstol's cases. Thus the emotional response is usually appropriate to the delusional belief, and the

mood is often depressed. In fact, the presence of depression on admission militated strongly against the development of schizophrenia at followup.

Psychomotor activity was normal in both subtypes. When abnormal, it usually reflected agitation and restlessness. None had psychomotor retardation.

When a thought disorder is present, it is not prominent and does not affect communication as the thought disorder of schizophrenia does. Winokur (1977) found loquatiousness and circumstantiality in 30 per cent of his cases. When this occurs, it usually accompanies descriptions of the delusional system.

Munro (1982) suggested five subtypes of paranoia based on the delusional theme: erotomania, pathologic jealousy, monosymptomatic hypochondriacal psychosis, litigious paranoia, and megalomania. To this list must be added the persecutory delusions of the more acute paranoid disorders. Several of the more common of these delusional themes are illustrated by case vignettes.

Persecutory delusions may develop insidiously from a situation in which some degree of suspicion is justified. As the illness develops the bounds of reason are exceeded, and simple suspiciousness is replaced by a delusional system. In time the system becomes increasingly elaborate as more details are incorporated into it. The following case illustrates this development, as well as the preservation of affect leading the patient to act on the delusion.

### Some Illustrative Cases

### CASE HISTORY 1. PERSECUTORY DELUSIONAL DISORDER

A 22-year-old single man, who lived on a farm with his parents, was brought to the hospital because of increasing suspiciousness of a neighbor. There had been long-standing friction between the patient's family and the neighbor, but over the preceding 3 weeks the patient had become convinced that the neighbor was involved in a grain and beef theft ring (which was indeed operating in the area) and informed the Federal Bureau of Investigation of his suspicions. He became convinced that his house was bugged and that some apples his father bought were poison because they had been purchased from a friend of the neighbor. He was hospitalized when he began sleeping with a gun for self-protection. On interview he was cooperative, although suspicious at times. The affect was appropriate to the

**TABLE 12–2** Predominant Delusion

| | Paranoia (%) N = 26 | Acute Paranoid Disorder (%) N = 57 |
|---|---|---|
| Reference | 8 | 11 |
| Persecution | 12 | 79 |
| Hypochondriasis | 3 | 4 |
| Jealousy | 54 | 2 |
| Sex | 8 | 0 |
| Grandeur | 15 | 2 |
| Other | 0 | 2 |

Data adapted from Retterstol, 1966. Paranoia is used instead of paranoiac, and acute paranoid disorder, instead of paranoid in the reference.

delusional system. The speech was circumstantial and, at times, tangential when discussing the delusion. Over a 1-month hospitalization, the delusion cleared rapidly, and at discharge he had gained complete insight into the irrationality of his former beliefs. However, his suspiciousness toward the neighbor remained.

## Editor's Comment

*A. Meyer suggested the following stages in the development of paranoid symptomatology (Muncie W: Psychobiology in Psychiatry, CV Mosby, St. Louis, 1939). Meyer's stages started with (1) "a rigid makeup with a tendency to pride and self-contained haughtiness, mistrust and disdain," (2) "appearance of affectively charged dominant notions, as autochthonous ideas or revelation which illuminates all the brooding questioning in a manner to leave no need for further check," (3) "an irresistible need for working over the material for evidence to support the dominant notion. That it will support it is a foregone conclusion." (4) "Systematization of a sort that is so tightly knit that it remains logically correct if the original dominant notion be admitted." (5) "When the present has been ransacked for proofs and systematized, the attention is turned to the past with a re-examination of the past experiences in the light of newer certainty. There result misinterpretations of past events and retrospective falsification. . ."*

*No psychiatrist has ever done a better job describing the march of circumstances in delusional disorder.*

## CASE HISTORY 2. JEALOUS PARANOID DISORDER

Paranoid disorder with jealous delusions is referred to as conjugal paranoia. Such patients become convinced that their spouses are unfaithful, and they become preoccupied with proving the infidelity and extracting a confession. Of all the paranoid disorders, these patients spend the greatest amount of time attempting to verify their suspicions (Shepherd, 1961).

A 22-year-old college student was brought to the hospital for threatening his wife with a hammer. She first became aware of his jealousy on their honeymoon, 3 years earlier, when he accused her of infidelity because she was not home on one occasion when he returned. Over the ensuing 3 years he often nagged her for confessions of past affairs. His bullying led to frequent arguments of such intensity that the police were once called. During the year before his admission, his suspicions had intensified to the point that he accused her of having affairs after work whenever she was not home as promptly as he expected. He called her at work to check on her, set traps around the house, inspected

her underwear, and even examined a vaginal smear under a microscope. He often kept her awake all night attempting to extract a confession of infidelity. His deteriorating school performance was blamed on his wife for the anguish she was causing him. He was hospitalized after the incident with the hammer and viewed the admission as an attempt by his wife and the doctors to "railroad" him and threatened to "even the score." On admission he was antagonistic and threatening, with a superior attitude. Although the speech was pressured, it was coherent. The affect was intense but appropriate to his suspicions. After his admission he became calmer, but the delusion remained unchanged during a 1-month hospitalization. He was discharged to another hospital, and his wife separated from him and obtained a divorce.

## Editor's Comment

*Clinicians have noted that patients with delusional jealousy will lose most of the pressure and need to add interpretations and delusions when they are divorced. They will get along in the community in a satisfactory manner and appear ordinary though they will continue to be delusional about the past. On re-marriage they will have a recrudescence of their jealous delusions, this time attached to the new spouse.*

Erotic paranoids have delusions of secret suitors, and they interpret ordinary comments and gestures from the delusional suitor as concealed messages proclaiming their love. The "suitor" is often a prominent person with whom the patient has had some dealings. When their overtures are not reciprocated, such patients only become more convinced of the other's love for them, which, for various reasons, cannot be returned openly. Eventually, they may feel jilted and attempt to avenge themselves against their former "lover." This type of paranoid disorder is also known as eroto-

**TABLE 12–3  Course of Paranoid Disorders**

|  | Paranoia | Acute Paranoid Disorder |
|---|---|---|
| Mean age of onset | 44 | 37 |
| Acute onset (%) | 67 | 93 |
| Six-month duration (%) | 88 | 54 |
| Predominant delusion | Jealous | Persecutory |
| Remission (%) | 54 | 90 |
| Relapse (%) (of those remitting) | 7 | 41 |

See Table 12–2 footnote.

mania and as DeClerambault's syndrome (Hollender and Callahan, 1975; Seeman, 1978).

## CASE HISTORY 3. EROTIC PARANOID DISORDER

A 46-year-old farm wife, who had been unhappily married for 15 years, fell in love with an itinerant evangelist conducting tent meetings in her town. Convinced that her love was secretly reciprocated, she neglected her housework to spend hours writing him unanswered letters. In her letters she asked him not to reply if he loved her, as it would cause a scandal in the community. She then interpreted his lack of response as proof of his love. The only abnormality noted on admission to the hospital was the erotic delusion, which failed to clear over a 3-week hospitalization. She was discharged home unimproved.

Grandiose paranoids believe themselves to be persons of special importance. Common delusions of this genre include those of inventions and discoveries, as well as delusions of being an important part of an organization such as the Central Intelligence Agency. They can describe their delusions with such enthusiasm and loquatiousness that they may initially appear manic.

## CASE HISTORY 4. GRANDIOSE DELUSIONAL DISORDER

A 56-year-old businessman developed diabetes 4 years before admission. Shortly thereafter, he developed his own treatment for the disease, which consisted of replacing sugar lost in the urine with a diet rich in sugar. He began publishing materials on his new treatment and advertised courses in it over the radio. Because he charged a nominal fee for these, he was arrested on charges of mail fraud and hospitalized for a court-ordered psychiatric examination. On admission he was cooperative and discussed his ideas with considerable loquatiousness and circumstantiality. His affect was appropriate to the ideas discussed. The delusional system remained fixed over a 3-week hospitalization, and he was discharged unimproved.

Paranoid disorders with solitary hypochondriacal delusions have been termed monosymptomatic hypochondriacal psychosis (Munro, 1980). Such patients have disfigurement and infestation. They were infrequent in Retterstol's (1966) series, accounting for 3 per cent to 4 per cent of his hospitalized paranoid disorders.

Litigious paranoids are primarily persecutory patients who become preoccupied with righting imagined wrongs that have been perpetrated against them.

## COURSE

Paranoia and acute paranoid disorder differ with respect to their onset, course, and prognosis. Therefore, they need to be taken up separately when considering the natural history of the paranoid disorders (Retterstol, 1966).

Paranoia is an illness of the middle aged, beginning at an average age of 44 years and ranging in age of onset from the 20s into late life. The onset is relatively acute in two thirds of cases and insidious in the remainder. By definition, this illness is more chronic than acute paranoid disorder, and 88 per cent of Retterstol's cases had been ill longer than 6 months, 61 per cent longer than 1 year. Despite their chronicity, half had recovered without relapse on followup 2 to 18 years later. The remainder followed an unremitting course. The predominant delusion disappeared completely in 53 per cent, improved in 10 per cent, and remainded unchanged in 31 per cent. The remainder evolved into unsystematized delusions.

The acute paranoid disorders began at a slightly earlier age of 37 years and ranged from adolescence into late life. On admission 80 per cent had been ill less than a year and 54 per cent, less than 6 months. An acute onset was noted in 93 per cent. The subsequent course was one of complete and lasting remission in 53 per cent, remission with relapse in 37 per cent, and chronicity in only 10 per cent. Those who relapsed usually did so in the first year after discharge.

Another aspect of the course is the outcome of the predominant delusion. In this regard the prognosis was best for delusions of reference and persecution, with 72 per cent to 87 per cent resolving, hypochondriasis 80 per cent, and eroticism 70 per cent. The worst prognosis occurred with delusions of grandeur and jealousy; only 46 per cent and 57 per cent resolving, respectively. Although 11 of 18 jealous paranoias were recovered from the delusion, few were willing to admit that they had been ill (Retterstol, 1967). To a large extent, the outcome of the delusion reflects the outcome of the type of paranoid disorder that the delusion usually occurs in.

A good index of social outcome is work status, and here the prognosis was excellent. Eight-four per cent of the paranoias were, at most, briefly incapacitated from work during their course, and the same percentage was self-supporting at last contact. The outcome of the acute paranoid disorders was almost identical, the respective rates being 79 per cent and 77 per cent.

These findings provide the basis for some optimism about the prognosis of paranoid disorders. While not all investigators have found the prognosis to be as favorable, Retterstol's conclusions are based on personal assessments and must be considered the most reliable. Based on his findings, more than half of all paranoid disorders can be expected to remit eventually, although relapses are not uncommon.

## DIFFERENTIAL DIAGNOSIS

Because paranoid disorders are so uncommon, the possibility that a delusional illness is caused by some other condition must always be kept in mind. A large number of causes are possible; these include organic brain syndromes, affective disorders, schizophrenia, and schizophreniform disorder (Manschreck and Petri, 1978).

Three organic brain syndromes can present with delusions. Delirium is characterized by a fluctuating state of consciousness, and the delusions are likewise evanescent and rapidly changing, while those of paranoid disorders remain relatively fixed for the duration of the illness. In addition, the cognitive symptoms of delirium (e.g., disorientation and memory impairment) are absent in paranoid disorders.

Dementia may be accompanied by delusions and should be suspected in an elderly paranoid patient. Suspiciousness and delusional thinking can be more prominent than the cognitive impairment of the dementia, but the latter can usually be uncovered by a careful mental status examination. In questionable cases, psychometric testing for organicity may lead to the correct diagnosis. Organic delusional syndromes present a greater diagnostic problem because of the absence of the cognitive impairment of delirium and dementia. For this reason a careful medical history, with particular attention to the drug history, should be obtained. Medical conditions that can present with delusions include neurologic (limbic epilepsy and other diseases of the limbic system, Huntington's chorea, presenile dementia), metabolic (lupus, Wilson's disease, porphyria, pernicious anemia), endocrine (Addison's disease, hypoparathyroidism), and infectious (neurosyphilis) diseases. Paranoid symptoms are associated with a variety of commonly abused drugs. These include alcohol, amphetamines, marijuana, and sympathomimetics (phenylpropanolamine). Among prescription drugs, paranoid symptoms occur with steroids and L-dopa.

Delusions are often the initial psychotic symptoms of schizophrenia. This diagnosis should be suspected whenever the delusionals tend toward the bizarre, when the affect is blunted or inappropriate, or when a thought disorder is prominent. If the correct diagnosis is schizophrenia, this will usually become apparent with the passage of time.

Affective disorder should be suspected whenever the delusional content is depressive or expansive, when a preexisting affective illness is present, or when the family history is positive for one.

Paranoid personality disorder presents a diagnostic problem when the suspiciousness becomes so pronounced that it resembles a delusion. However, these disorders never become truly delusional and are distinguished in this way from paranoid disorders.

## LABORATORY EXAMINATIONS

Several laboratory examinations are useful in ruling out other diseases that can present as a paranoid disorder. Neuropsychological tests demonstrating organic brain damage raise the possibility of a dementia or an organic delusional syndrome. A positive drug screen for amphetamine or other substances known to cause delusions raises the possibility of a drug-induced organic delusional syndrome. The dexamethasone suppression test has not been investigated in paranoid disorders, but nonsuppression should suggest a delusional depression.

## TREATMENT

Because paranoid disorders are psychotic illnesses it would seem reasonable to treat them with antipsychotic medication. Unfortunately, there are no controlled trials to support this practice. Kendler (1980) reviewed four open trials of antipsychotics, totaling 51 patients, and all four reported improvement on the drug. Mooney (1965) reported a favorable response to antipsychotics in delusional jealousies. If spontaneous improvement in paranoid disorders were uncommon, one might view these reports with more optimism. But in an illness with this high a spontaneous remission rate, controlled trials are essential before deciding that a drug works. However, until such data are available, a trial of antipsychotics in these patients seems appropriate.

## REFERENCES

American Psychiatric Association: Diagnostic and Statistical Manual of Mental Disorders. Washington, DC, American Psychiatric Association, 1952.

American Psychiatric Association: Diagnostic and Statistical Manual of Mental Disorders, ed 2 (DSM-II). Washington, DC, American Psychiatric Association, 1968.

American Psychiatric Association: Diagnostic and Statistical Manual of Mental Disorders, ed 3 (DSM-III). Washington, DC, American Psychiatric Association, 1980.

Debray Q: A genetic study of chronic delusions. Neuropsychobiology 1:313–321, 1985.

Freedman R, Schwab PJ: Paranoid symptoms in patients on a general hospital psychiatric unit: Implications for diagnosis and treatment. Arch Gen Psychiatry 35:387–390, 1978.

Goodwin DW, Guze SB: Psychiatric Diagnosis. New York, Oxford University Press, 1979.

Hollender MH, Callahan AS: Erotomania or deClerambault syndrome. Arch Gen Psychiatry 32:1574–1576, 1975.

Kahlbaum K: Die Gruppirung der Psychischen Krankheiten. Danzig, Kafemann, 1863.

Kendler KS: The nosologic validity of paranoia (simple delusional disorder): A review. Arch Gen Psychiatry 37:699–707, 1980.

Kendler KS: Demography of paranoid psychosis (delusional disorder): A review and comparison with schizophrenia and affective illness. Arch Gen Psychiatry 39:890–902, 1982.

Kendler KS, Hays P: Paranoid psychosis (delusional disorder) and schizophrenia: A family history study. Arch Gen Psychiatry 38:547–551, 1981.

Kendler KS, Gruenberg AM, Strauss JS: An independent analysis of the Copenhagen sample of the Danish adoption study of schizophrenia. Arch Gen Psychiatry 38:985–987, 1981.

Kolle K: Die Primare Verruckheit (Primary Paranoia). Leipzig, East Germany, Thieme, 1931.

Kraepelin E: Manic-depressive Insanity and Paranoia, (trans) Barclay RM. Edinburgh, E.S. Livingstone, 1921.

Lewis A: Paranoia and paranoid: A historical perspective. Psychol Med 1:2–12, 1970.

Manschreck TC, Petri M: The parnoid syndrome. Lancet 2:251–253, 1978.

Mooney HB: Pathologic jealousy and psychochemotherapy. Br J Psychiatry 111:1023–1042, 1965.

Munro A: Monosymptomatic hypochondriacal psychosis. Br J Hosp Med 24:34–38, 1980.

Munro A: Paranoia revisited. Br J Psychiatry 141:344–349, 1982.

Retterstol N: Paranoid and Paranoiac Psychoses. Springfield, IL, Charles C Thomas, 1966.

Retterstol N: Jealousy-paranoiac psychoses: A personal follow-up study. Acta Psychiatr Scand 43:75–107, 1967.

Seeman MV: Delusional loving. Arch Gen Psychiatry 35:1265–1267, 1978.

Shepherd M: Morbid jealousy: Some clinical and social aspects of a psychiatric syndrome. J Met Sci 197:687–753, 1961.

Tanna VL: Paranoid states: A selected review. Compr Psychiatry 15:453–470, 1974.

US Department of Health and Human Services: The International Classification of Diseases, 9th rev Clinical Modification (ICD-9 CM). DHHS publ. No. (PHS) 80-1260. Washington, DC, Government Printing Office, 1980.

Winokur G: Delusional disorder (paranoia). Compr Psychiatry 18:511–521, 1977.

Winokur G, Clayton PJ, Reich T: Manic-depressive Illness. St Louis, CV Mosby, 1969.

# chapter 13

# ALCOHOLISM

*by* Barry Liskow, M.D.
Donald W. Goodwin, M.D.

## DEFINITION

Alcoholism has been defined by Keller (1982) as the "repetitive intake of alcoholic beverages to a degree that harms the drinker in health or socially or economically, with indication of inability consistently to control the occasion or amount of drinking." A synonym for alcoholism recommended by the World Health Organization (Edwards, Gross, Keller, Moser, Room, 1977) and the *Diagnostic and Statistical Manual of Mental Disorders*, third edition (DSM-III), is *alcohol dependence.*

DSM-III (American Psychiatric Association, 1980) separates alcoholism into two types: *alcohol abuse* and *alcohol dependence.* The criteria for alcohol abuse is as follows:

A. *Pattern of pathologic alcohol use:* **need for daily use of alcohol for adequate functioning; inability to cut down or stop drinking; repeated efforts to control or reduce excessive drinking by "going on the wagon" (periods of temporary abstinence) or restricting drinking to certain times of the day; binges (remaining intoxicated throughout the day for at least 2 days); occasional consumption of a fifth of spirits (or its equivalent in wine or beer); amnesic periods for events occurring while intoxicated (blackouts); continuation of drinking despite a serious physical disorder that the individual knows is exacerbated by alcohol use; drinking of nonbeverage alcohol.**

B. *Impairment in social or occupational functioning because of alcohol use:* **violence while intoxicated, absence from work, loss of job, legal difficulties (e.g., arrest for intoxicated behavior, traffic accidents while intoxicated), arguments or difficulties with family or friends because of excessive alcohol use.**

C. *Duration of disturbance of at least 1 month.*

The diagnostic criteria for alcohol dependence is identical with two exceptions: to receive a diagnosis of alcohol dependence, the patient must demonstrate either A or B and *tolerance or withdrawal. Tolerance* is defined as a "need for markedly increased amounts of alcohol to achieve the desired effect." *Withdrawal* is defined as the development of alcohol withdrawal (e.g., morning "shakes" and malaise relieved by drinking) after cessation of or reduction in drinking. These definitions pose many problems. For example:

- "Need for daily use of alcohol for adequate functioning" is not characteristic of all alcoholism. Some alcoholics drink amounts that are incompatible with "adequate functioning"; many alcoholics do not drink alcohol daily.
- Many alcoholics never "go on the wagon," or at least not for many years.
- About one third or more of *non*alcoholics have had at least one blackout.
- The minimal number of symptoms to meet the diagnosis are not cited, nor are cutoff points with regard to severity. For example, an individual could receive a diagnosis of alcohol abuse and alcohol dependence if he had experienced a single blackout or missed a single morning from work because of a hangover.
- The diagnosis of alcohol abuse includes "occasional consumption of a fifth of spirits or its equivalent in wine or beer." It is inconceivable that a person could drink this much alcohol on a single occasion without having developed tol-

erance, and therefore be diagnosable as *alcohol dependent*. Malaise is cited as an example of alcohol withdrawal. Even mild hangovers are often characterized by malaise. Finally, "remaining intoxicated throughout the day for at least 2 days" ("characteristic" of alcohol abuse) would probably produce morning shakes in many people, who thus would be "dependent."

In short, the distinction between alcohol abuse and alcohol dependence probably serves no useful purpose. A preferable classification would base the diagnosis of *alcoholism* on psychological, interpersonal, and medical problems resulting from chronic excessive use of alcohol. Alcoholism could then be subdivided into the traditional medical categories of mild, moderate, and severe. The requirement of "duration of disturbance of at least 1 month" is too arbitrary. Many people have had one-time experiences in their lives when they were "impaired" socially because of drinking and have had some of the symptoms listed under pattern of pathologic use. Such episodes may occur in young men when they are in the military and in people who are experiencing an acute situational stress, such as a divorce. After a period of heavy drinking they reduce their drinking to amounts that are compatible with community norms.

## EPIDEMIOLOGY

Epidemiologic studies of alcohol use and abuse are bedeviled by the uncertainties of what to measure and how to measure it. The terms alcoholism, alcohol dependence, alcohol abuse, problem drinking, and drinking problems continue to be used by different researchers in different ways. To further complicate matters, such categories as abstainers and light, medium, and heavy drinkers, referring to quantity and frequency of alcohol use, are defined differently by various investigators. Finally, there is disagreement regarding which effects of alcohol use on a given population should be studied and over what period of time. It is, therefore, surprising that there is as much agreement regarding the scope of alcohol problems as there is.

Three distinct methods of epidemiologic investigation have been used in assessing the extent and effects of alcohol use. These are the estimation of apparent alcohol consumption, collection of data relating to morbidity and mortality from alcohol, and surveys of alcohol use and problems in the general population.

### Apparent Consumption

Apparent per capita consumption of alcohol is calculated by adding up the amount of alcohol sold based on sales and tax data and dividing it by the adult population under consideration. Sales and tax data of various quality exist for the United States back to at least 1850. After being approximately level in the 1940s and 1950s, per capita consumption of alcohol for adults age 14 or over began rising, at first rapidly and recently more slowly, from 2.07 gal of absolute alcohol per year in 1960 to 2.73 gal in 1978. This represents about 1 oz of absolute alcohol per day for every person age 14 or older in the United States, or about 1.5 oz for every drinking person. Such figures are misleading because it is estimated that 11 per cent of adults drink 50 per cent of the alcohol sold (Malin et al., 1982). The figure may also be misleading because it does not consider the amount of illicit (untaxed) alcohol made and consumed each year. Of the alcohol consumed, approximately 50 per cent is from beer, 10 per cent from wine, and 40 per cent from liquor.

In the United States, apparent consumption is highest in the West and lowest in the South, highest in Nevada (where many drinking tourists evidently increase per capita consumption for this state) and lowest in Arkansas. Internationally, consumption of alcohol has been rising since 1950, with the highest consumption in France, Italy, Portugal, Spain, and Switzerland (Brenner, 1982).

### Morbidity and Mortality Attributable to Alcohol

Cirrhosis mortality historically has been used to assess the prevalence of alcoholism. Jellinek developed a formula for calculating the prevalence of alcoholism in a population by extrapolation from the number of deaths caused by cirrhosis in a given year (Jellinek and Keller, 1952). This method was chosen in the belief that population surveys would be futile because people (in the United States at least) would be unwilling to report accurately on their use of alcohol (Keller, 1975). The Jellinek formula was useful because it at least gave an estimate of the prevalence of alcoholism. It was hence widely used, with occasional modification, in the 1950s, despite numerous critics, including Jellinek himself (Keller and Effron, 1955; Jellinek, 1959). Currently, cirrhosis rates are considered important not because of what they reveal about the prevalence of alcoholism, but because of what they reveal about morbidity and mortality related to alcohol.

Cirrhosis death rates rose steadily in the United States from 1950 to 1973, when they peaked at 15.0 deaths per 100,000 population. Between 1973 and 1977 the rate fell steadily to 13.1 per 100,000 (Malin et al., 1982). Schmidt and Popham (1975/76) and Brenner (1975) have hypothesized that cirrhosis death rates, as well as other complications of alcohol abuse, rise when per capita alcohol consumption increases, with a lag of 1 to 2 years. However, the recent fall in cirrhosis mortality has occurred despite a rise in per capita alcohol sales. Although cirrhosis mortality has been dropping among all groups, it remains highest for young urban nonwhite males, whose cirrhosis mortality is ten times that of comparable white male groups (Malin et al., 1982).

Cirrhosis is not the only cause of alcohol-related mortality. Table 13–1 lists the estimated mortality related to alcohol in the United States in 1977 from a variety of causes. The estimate of 61,000 to 95,000 deaths related to alcohol is conservative because it does not include death from other causes to which alcohol contributes, such as cardiomyopathy, gastrointestinal hemorrhage, and pancreatitis.

Morbidity associated with alcohol is also considerable. In the mid-1970s hospital discharges for alcohol-related disorders ranged from 2.5 per cent for short-stay hospitals to 17 per cent for VA hospitals. Alcohol is involved in an estimated 45 per cent of violent crimes, 45 per cent of episodes of marital violence, 40 per cent of suicide attempts, 20 per cent of nonfatal industrial accidents, and 15 per cent of nonfatal traffic accidents. The cost of alcohol-related mortality and morbidity in the United States is estimated at $42 billion per year (Malin et al., 1982; Roizen, 1982; USDHHS, 1981). Although such morbidity and mortality data gathered from various agencies indicate the scope of the alcohol problem, they do not represent the

**TABLE 13–1 Estimated Deaths Related to Alcohol in the United States, 1977 (for Selected Causes)**

| Cause of Death | No. of Deaths | Estimated Percentage Related to Alcohol | Estimated No. Related to Alcohol |
|---|---|---|---|
| *Alcohol as a direct cause* | | | |
| Alcoholism | 5,100 | 100 | 5,100 |
| Alcoholic psychosis | 318 | 100 | 318 |
| Cirrhosis | 30,848 | 41–95 | 12,648–29,306 |
| Total | 36,266 | | 18,066–34,724 |
| *Alcohol as an indirect cause* | | | |
| Accidents | | | |
| Motor vehicle | 49,510 | 30–50 | 14,853–24,755 |
| Falls | 13,773 | 44.4 | 6,115 |
| Fires | 6,357 | 25.9 | 1,646 |
| Other | 30,455 | 11.1 | 3,381 |
| Homicides | 19,968 | 49–70 | 9,784–13,978 |
| Suicides | 28,681 | 25–37 | 7,170–10,612 |
| Total | 148,744 | | 42,949–60,487 |
| Total for direct and indirect causes | 185,010 | | 61,015–95,211 |

Adapted from Malin H, Coakley J, Klaeber C, et al: An epidemiologic perspective on alcohol use and abuse in the United States, in Alcohol Consumption and Related Problems. NIAAA Alcohol and Health Monograph No. 1, DHMS Pub. No. (ADM) 82-1190. Washington, DC, Government Printing Office, 1982, p 129.

full spectrum of such problems. Many people who drink and have problems from alcohol do not appear in such agency data. Population surveys are needed for a more complete picture of alcohol problems.

## Population Surveys

General population surveys of drinking practices and problems began in earnest in the United States in the 1960s (Cahalan, 1970) and have been conducted regularly since the early 1970s. Between 1970 and 1979 nine national surveys funded by the National Institute of Alcohol Abuse and Alcoholism (NIAAA) and two by the Department of Health, Education, and Welfare (HEW) were conducted based on probability samples of the noninstitutionalized civilian adult population and ranged from 1,071 to 22,842 persons per survey (Clark and Midank, 1982). These surveys probably seriously underestimate alcohol consumption. Apparent consumption data, based on sales and tax data, consistently have indicated that 50 per cent to 75 per cent of the alcohol consumed in the United States is unaccounted for when consumption is extrapolated from nationwide general population surveys (Malin et al., 1982). This may be due to a number of factors, including (a) alcohol use may be consciously, or unconsciously, underreported by those surveyed; (b) heavy drinkers may not be easily available for surveys that are generally done in households; (c) questionnaires and interview techniques may be inadequate; and (d) population groups, such as hospitalized patients, prisoners, and military personnel, that may contain large numbers of heavy drinkers are often excluded from population surveys. Despite these problems and the incomparability of the survey methods, enough information from each is available to make comparisons among them and with earlier studies. Such comparisons allow an assessment of the trends in alcohol consumption and alcohol problems across time and in different segments of the U.S. population. The findings of these surveys include (Malin et al., 1982; Clark and Midank, 1982; USDHHS, 1981; Johnson et al., 1977):

1.  Self-reported alcohol consumption for U.S. adults remained unchanged in the 1960s and 1970s, and this was true for the subgroups of men, women, blacks, and adolescents (10th to 12th graders). Approximately 33 per cent of adults reported abstention, 33 per cent light drinking (averaging 0.01 to 0.21 oz of absolute alcohol per day over 1 year), 24 per cent moderate drinking (0.22 to 0.99 oz absolute alcohol per day) and 9 per cent heavier drinking (1.0 or more oz of absolute alcohol per day).

2.  Female abstainers outnumbered male abstainers, 40 per cent to 25 per cent, while male heavier drinkers outnumbered female heavier drinkers, 14 per cent to 4 per cent. Heavier drinking peaked in males at ages 21 to 34, with 19 per cent of that age-group drinking heavily, and in females at ages 35 to 49, with 8 per cent reporting heavier drinking. For both men and women, heavier drinking percentages declined progressively after these peak ages.

3.  Blacks abstained at a higher rate than whites, but among black drinkers the percentage of heavier drinkers is comparable to that among white drinkers.

4.  Those who report their country of origin as Spain, Poland, Ireland, Germany, or England had the greatest proportion of heavier drinkers (10.4 per cent to 13.0 per cent). Those of Chinese or Jewish origin had the smallest proportion of heavier drinkers (0 per cent to 1.9 per cent). Those of American Indian descent, contrary to popular notion, had a modest percentage of heavier drinkers (5.8 per cent) and the highest proportion of abstainers (51.9 per cent) of any group investigated, although they had the highest percentage of drinking problems of any group.

5.  Problems associated with drinking varied widely among surveys that tended to emphasize different problems. For example, psychological dependence, defined as drinking to alter mood, occurred in 49 per cent of males surveyed in 1967 (Cahalan, 1970), whereas dependence, defined as three or more symptoms (e.g., tremors after drinking, sneaking drinks, morning drinking) in the year before interview occurred in 6 per cent of male and 2 per cent of female drinkers surveyed in 1979 (Clark and Midank, 1982). Social consequences, defined as problems with one's job, the law, or one's spouse in the 12 months before interview, occurred in 9 per cent of male and 5 per cent of female drinkers in 1979. As was true for

the amounts of alcohol consumed, most problems were highest among young males aged 18 to 24 and declined with age. Regardless of how problems were defined, there was a positive correlation between the presence and number of problems and the average amount of alcohol consumed.

There are no nationwide epidemiologic surveys that begin from the premise that alcoholism is a specific illness, separable from abusive drinking or problem drinking. However, such surveys have been conducted with more limited population groups. Various definitions of alcohol dependence have been used in these more limited surveys, although most require the presence of impaired social functioning because of alcohol, pathologic use of alcohol, and symptoms of tolerance or withdrawal because of alcohol. Considering the various definitions that have been used, agreement on the prevalence of the disorder is good. For example, in 1972 Hagnell and Tunving investigated the total adult population of Lunby, Sweden (2617 persons), and reported a lifetime prevalence for alcoholism of 10.3 per cent for men and less than 1.0 per cent for women. Winokur and Tsuang (1978) interviewed 541 first-degree relatives of individuals who had been hospitalized at the University of Iowa for appendectomies and herniorrhaphies and found a lifetime prevalence for alcoholism of 6.7 per cent for men and 0.4 per cent for females. Weissman, Myers, and Harding (1980) systematically selected 1095 households and randomly selected one member from each household for a longitudinal survey of mental health problems in the community. Of this original group, 510 were interviewed 8 to 9 years later and assigned psychiatric diagnoses. The point prevalence of alcoholism in this population of 510 was 3.6 per cent for men and 1.7 per cent for women and the lifetime prevalence was 10.1 per cent for men and 4.1 per cent for women.

Boyd et al. (1983) looked at the data collected from these 510 subjects and diagnosed alcoholism, using seven definitions of the illness (research diagnostic criteria, DSM-III alcohol abuse criteria, DSM-III alcohol dependence criteria, Feighner criteria, National Council of Alcoholism criteria, Jellinek's definition of gamma alcoholism, and definitions of alcohol dependence syndrome from the International Classification of Diseases [ICD]-9). Although not an ideal study because not all of the criteria for each definition could be extracted from the original data, the current prevalence of alcoholism based on these seven definitions ranged from 1.6 per cent to 2.4 per cent and the lifetime prevalence ranged from 3.1 per cent to 6.3 per cent of the total population (breakdown between men and women not given).

These studies, therefore, although differing in their operational definitions of alcoholism, are in agreement that the lifetime prevalence of alcoholism for men is between 5 per cent and 10 per cent and for women, between 0.4 per cent and 4.0 per cent.

In summary, although epidemiologic studies disagree about what should be measured and how to measure it, there is good agreement that the majority of adults in the United States drink, that a large minority of these drinkers have trouble at some time because of their drinking, and that those who do have trouble tend to be young males who drink a lot but who drink less as they grow older. The percentages of those who abstain, those who drink without problems, and those who drink with problems have remained stable in the United States since the 1970s. Although cirrhosis mortality rates have declined since the mid-1970s, the overall morbidity and mortality of alcoholism continues to be a tremendous drain on the human and financial resources of the United States. This morbidity and mortality is greatest among the 5 per cent to 10 per cent of males and the 0.4 per cent to 4.0 per cent of females who are diagnosable as alcohol dependent at some time in their lives, but it is not exclusive to them.

## CLINICAL PICTURE

The clinical presentation of the alcohol-dependent patient is contingent on when in the course of his illness he presents. There are no pathognomonic signs or symptoms of alcohol abuse or dependence. Early in the course of the illness there may be no physical or laboratory signs of the condition. Often indications of an alcohol problem can be gained only through a careful social and medical history. Specific inquiry regarding marital conflict, absenteeism from work or school, job losses, accidents, and legal difficulties should be made; such problems occur more commonly in alcoholics than in nonalcoholics. Patients who indicate that they have such problems should be asked about the relationship of alcohol to the problems and about specific drinking practices. Not infrequently, the alcoholic will deny or rationalize the relationship of alcohol to his problems and will underreport the quantity of alcohol consumed. If willing to admit to problem drinking, the early alcoholic may report sneaking drinks, hiding alcohol, feeling comfortable only with other drinkers, experiencing guilt associated with drinking, and attempting to control drinking by using alcohol only at specified times (Goodwin, 1984).

Medical complaints early in the course of alcoholism include anorexia, morning nausea and vomiting, gastroesophageal reflux, diarrhea, palpitations, insomnia, amenorrhea, impotence, and polyuria (Holt, Skinner, Israel, 1981). Psychiatric and neurologic complaints may include irritability, nervousness, blackouts (memory lapses), and subjectively poor memory (Holt et al., 1981).

### Editor's Comment

*Recent reports (Saunders JB, Beevers DG, Paton A: Alcohol-induced hypertension. Lancet 2:653–656, 1981; Taylor JR, Combs-Orme T: Alcohol and strokes in young adults. Am J Psychiatry 142:1, 1985; Taylor JR, Combs-Orme T, Anderson D, et al.: Alcohol, hypertension, and stroke. Alcoholism: Clinical and Experimental Research 8:283–286, 1984; Kornhuber HH, Lisson G, Suschka-Sauermann L: Alcohol and obesity: A new look at high blood pressure and stroke: An epidemiological study in preventive neurology. Eur Arch Psychiatr Neurol Sci 234:357–362, 1985) have stressed the positive association between alcohol consumption and hypertension and between alcohol use and stroke. Psychiatrists should be careful to record blood pressure regularly, and internists should be careful to elicit information about drinking habits. Even the prospective study of medical students by Thomas and Greenstreet (Thomas CB, Greenstreet RL: Psychobiological characteristics in youth as predictors of five disease states: Suicide, mental illness, hypertension, coronary heart disease, and tumor. Johns Hopkins Med J 132:16–43, 1973) found a positive association between frequency of drinking and an outcome in hypertension 25 years later.*

As alcoholism progresses, physical signs may begin to appear, such as an alcohol odor on the breath, careless grooming and hygiene, signs of intoxication (ataxia, slurred speech), multiple contusions, hepatomegaly (Holt et al., 1981), and certain facial features, including rhinophyma and persistent erythema, with or without telangiectasias (Young, 1974). Later in the course, signs of chronic liver disease may appear, including jaundice, ascites, palmar erythema, spider angiomata, purpura, abdominal varices, testicular atrophy, gynecomastia, and Dupuytren's contractures (Korsten and Leiber, 1982). Associated symptoms of liver, pancreatic, and other chronic gastrointestinal disturbances may be reported, including abdominal pain, food intolerance, hematemesis, melena, weight loss, weakness, and fatigue (Mezey, 1982).

Neurologic and psychiatric signs and symptoms may occur in later-stage alcoholism and include withdrawal syndromes (seizures, hallucinations, delusions, delirium), psychotic syndromes (paranoia, hallucinations, and delusions in a clear sensorium), peripheral neuropathy (usually in the lower extremities, bilateral, symmetrical, and sensorimotor in type), and cognitive deficits (ranging from minor memory problems to dementia and the amnestic syndrome) (Sellers and Kalant, 1976; Mardsden, 1977; Goodwin and Hill, 1975; Schuckit, 1979).

Uncommonly, myopathy may occur acutely with muscle pain and swelling or chronically with progressive weakness and atrophy (Rubin, 1977). Also, rarely, cardiomyopathy may occur with signs and symptoms of congestive heart failure (Demakis et al., 1974).

Traumatic injuries, such as rib and thoracic fractures (Israel et al., 1980) and subdural hematomas (Gallbraith et al., 1976), are frequently associated with alcoholism.

Two miscellaneous signs that have been linked to alcoholism are painless parotid gland enlargement (Duggan and Rothball, 1957) and premature arcus senilis (Ewing and Rouse, 1980).

As these progressive signs and symptoms indicate, late-stage alcoholism is often easy to diagnose because of the multiplicity of its manifestations. Early phases of the disease may be marked by subtle or no physical or laboratory signs and often require of the physician a high index of suspicion, coupled with a sensitive and thorough approach to history taking.

*Illustrative Case*

## CASE HISTORY

J.W., a 35-year-old plant foreman, arrived at his physician's office with chief complaints of 3 weeks of intermittent epigastric pain, anorexia with a 5-lb (2.3-kg) weight loss, and nausea and vomiting. He related that these symptoms were worse in the morning and improved as the day progressed. He indicated that he was not too worried by the symptoms but had come at the urging of his supervisor, who was concerned because of his frequent absences from work.

He denied all other gastrointestinal symptoms, and review of systems was negative except for numerous "colds" in the past year, causing frequent work absence. Physical examination was within normal limits.

When questioned about his drinking practices, he said that he drank "no more than anyone else." When asked to elaborate, he stated that he went to a local tavern with fellow employees after work for "a few beers" and drank "a six pack or two on the weekends while watching football on TV." When asked about drinking at other times, he replied, "That's all. Why do you keep badgering me about my drinking?" He was then asked if others badgered him; he answered, "Yes, my wife—she thinks everybody drinks too much. Just because I was arrested for driving under the influence last year . . . but I'm here for my stomach, Doc. Can you help me?" He was scheduled for routine laboratory tests and an upper gastrointestinal series and was asked to return in 1 week.

J.W. may or may not be an alcoholic, but the pattern of his symptoms and his responses to questions about his drinking habits should raise his physician's index of suspicion.

## LABORATORY

As is true of signs and symptoms, there are no pathognomonic laboratory measures that can be used to diagnose alcoholism. There are a number of laboratory findings, however, that, when present, should increase the physician's index of suspicion that alcohol may be a problem. These tests, in approximate order of their usefulness, include:

1. *Blood alcohol level.* The National Council on Alcoholism includes among its criteria for diagnosing alcoholism a blood alcohol level greater than 300 mg/dl at any time or a level greater than 100 mg/dl recorded during a routine clinical examination (NCA,

1972). It has also been noted that a blood alcohol level of more than 150 mg/dl in a patient not obviously intoxicated is strong evidence of significant tolerance to alcohol, and hence potentially of alcoholism (Holt et al., 1981). Blood alcohol levels may be obtained either by direct measurement of blood levels or by estimation from the amount of alcohol in expired air using a Breathalyzer. A new method for estimating the amount of alcohol consumed over a specific period of time involves placing a patch, which has been specially treated to react chemically with alcohol excreted in sweat, on the skin and then removing it several days to a week later and analyzing it for amount of alcohol excreted (Phillips, Vandervoort, Becker, 1978). The reliability and usefulness of this method is yet to be determined.

2. *Mean corpuscular volume (MCV).* Macrocytosis, as indicated by an elevation of the MCV (commonly reported as part of a complete blood count), has been reported to occur in 40 per cent to 95 per cent of actively drinking alcoholics. Although in one third of alcoholics such MCV elevations are associated with signs of folate deficiency, including hypersegmented neutrophils and anemia, in most this is not the case, and folate supplementation does not reverse the macrocytosis if drinking continues (Wu, Chanarin, Levi, 1974). The cause of the elevation is unknown, and it is more marked in alcoholics who smoke. MCV returns to normal 2 to 4 months after alcohol ingestion ceases (Colman and Herbert, 1980).

3. *Gamma glutamyl transpeptidase (GGTP), serum aspartate aminotransferase (SGOT), serum alanine aminotransferase (SGPT).* Elevations in these liver enzymes frequently occur in alcoholics. GGTP has been reported to be raised in 75 per cent of alcoholics without clinical evidence of liver disease, and this finding is considered by some to be the earliest laboratory sign of heavy alcohol use (Holt et al., 1981). It has also been reported, however, that even in conjunction with other laboratory measures, it has been able to classify correctly only 36 per cent of alcoholics, although it is able to classify 94 per cent of nonalcoholics (Eckardt et al., 1981).

SGOT and SGPT are raised in liver damage from a variety of causes. SGOT has been reported elevated in 30 per cent to 75 per cent of inpatient alcoholics and SGPT, in approximately 50 per cent of such alcoholics (Holt et al., 1981). Various rules relating SGOT to SGPT have been formulated to differentiate alcoholic from nonalcoholic liver disease. A ratio of SGOT-SGPT greater than 1 with SGOT plus SGPT less than 300 to indicate alcohol liver disease was applied to patients with liver disease and correctly identified 90 per cent of patients with alcoholic liver disease and 77 per cent of patients with nonalcoholic liver disease (Ryback et al., 1982).

4. *Chest x-ray.* In one study, 28.9 per cent of alcoholics had evidence of rib or vertebral fractures or both on routine chest x-rays, compared with 1.3 per cent of an age-matched group of social drinkers (Israel et al., 1980).

5. *Uric acid.* Uric acid levels have been reported to be elevated in heavy drinkers and to return to normal several days after alcohol ingestion ceases (Holt et al., 1981).

6. The following routine laboratory tests have been reported to be abnormal in alcohol abusers (Holt et al., 1981): *elevated* (above control levels)—HDL–cholesterol (elevated in 50 per cent to 80 per cent of alcoholics except those with severe liver disease, in whom it is low or normal) and lactic acid dehydrogenase (LDH); *depressed* (below control levels)—LDL–cholesterol, BUN, leukocytes, red blood cells, and thrombocytes; *elevated or depressed*—plasma glucose and serum iron.

Attempts have been made to distinguish alcoholics from nonalcoholics with a battery of common laboratory tests subjected to complex mathematical manipulations. Eckardt et al. (1981) carried out a quadratic multiple discriminant analysis on 24 common laboratory tests and compared 121 alcoholic males with 130 nonalcoholic males. The analysis correctly classified 100 per cent of the nonalcoholics and 98 per cent of the alcoholics. Ryback et al. (1982), using the same procedure, reported similar success in distinguishing among nonalcoholics without liver disease, alcoholics with presumed mild liver involvement, alcoholics with liver disease, and nonalcoholics with liver disease. These results appear promising, but the method must be tested in diverse normal and medically ill groups and in diverse settings before its usefulness can be adequately assessed.

There have also been attempts to find a laboratory test that would be specific for alcoholism, a biochemical marker for the disease. The ratio of plasma $\alpha$-amino-$n$-butyric acid to leucine was proposed as such a marker (Shaw, Lue, Lieber, 1978) until it was shown to be elevated in nonalcoholic patients with liver disease (Dienstag et al., 1978). An abnormal transferrin has recently been reported as an indicator of prolonged alcohol consumption (5 to 11 days of 0.6 gm/ kg daily) unaffected by liver disease (Stibler, Borg, Allgulander, 1979). Another potential marker, salsolinol, a condensation product of acetaldehyde and dopamine, has been reported to be markedly elevated in the urine of alcoholic patients admitted for detoxification compared with controls (Collins et al., 1979). The significance of this finding has been weakened by the report that there are substantial amounts of salsolinol in a wide variety of alcoholic beverages (Duncan and Smythe, 1982). Other potential markers will undoubtedly be proposed, and all will require testing in alcoholic, normal, and nonalcoholic medical patients in a variety of settings before their value as biologic markers can be validly asserted.

All laboratory tests may be normal early in the course of alcoholism. However, not infrequently, MCV, GGTP, SGOT, and uric acid will be mildly elevated and blood alcohol levels markedly elevated in a clinically nonintoxicated patient. As alcoholism progresses, many laboratory tests are apt to be abnormal, reflecting the chronic effects of alcohol on a number of organ systems. There are promising approaches that may eventually allow the diagnosis of alcoholism at an early stage by the complex analysis of currently available laboratory tests. In addition, active research is under way to discover the elusive biochemical marker for alcoholism that may allow early detection of alcoholism or, possibly, identification of those at risk for developing the disease.

## CLINICAL COURSE

Understanding the clinical course of any disease requires longitudinal investigations of individuals with that illness. The clinical course of alcoholism is obscured by a dearth of such longitudinal studies and a lack of agreement on the definition of the illness.

The studies that have been done have investigated a subset of patients with alcohol problems, for example, felons (Goodwin, Crane, Guze, 1971), public hospital inpatients (Vaillant, 1983), private clinic outpatients (Hyman, 1976), and college students (Vaillant, 1983). Despite the limitations of these studies, there are enough of them to provide a reasonable idea of the various clinical courses alcoholism can take.

Historically, the first modern attempt to delineate the course of alcoholism was undertaken by Jellinek (1952). He analyzed questionnaires from 2000 Alcoholics Anonymous members, and from their responses he postulated that alcoholism is a progressive disease in which 43 distinct symptoms occur in more or less definite order (Table 13–2). He grouped the symptoms into three phases: *prodromal*, the first symptom of which is blackouts; *crucial*, the first symptom of which is loss of control; and *chronic*, the first symptom of which is binge drinking. In a later work Jellinek (1960) introduced the

### TABLE 13–2 Jellinek's Phases of Alcohol Addiction

*Prodromal phase*
  1. Blackouts
  2. Surreptitious drinking
  3. Preoccupation with alcohol
  4. Gulping drinks
  5. Guilt feelings regarding drinking behavior
  6. Avoiding reference to alcohol in conversation
  7. Increasing frequency of blackouts

*Crucial phase*
  8. Loss of control over amount drunk once drinking starts
  9. Rationalizing drinking behavior to self and others
  10. Social pressure from others to moderate or stop drinking
  11. Grandiose behavior as a compensation for loss of self-esteem
  12. Marked aggressive behavior
  13. Persistent remorse regarding drinking
  14. Periods of total abstinence
  15. Changing the pattern of drinking in an attempt to control problems from drinking
  16. Dropping friends usually before being dropped
  17. Quitting jobs often in anticipation of being fired
  18. Behavior becomes alcohol centered
  19. Loss of outside interests not related to alcohol
  20. Reinterpretation of interpersonal relations to allow continued drinking
  21. Marked self-pity
  22. Geographic escape, either contemplated or actual
  23. Family changes; individual becomes either more withdrawn or markedly increases outside activities
  24. Unreasonable resentments toward others
  25. Protecting supply of alcohol, including hiding alcohol
  26. Neglect of proper nutrition
  27. First alcohol-related hospitalization
  28. Decreasing sexual drive
  29. Alcoholic conjugal jealousy
  30. Regular morning drinking

*Chronic phase*
  31. Prolonged intoxication lasting for several days (binges, "benders")
  32. Marked ethical deterioration
  33. Impairment of cognitive functions
  34. Alcoholic psychoses
  35. Drinking with persons far below one's social level
  36. Drinking nonbeverage alcohol (e.g., aftershave, mouthwash, hair tonic)
  37. Loss of alcohol tolerance
  38. Persistent indefinable fears
  39. Tremors
  40. Psychomotor inhibition in the absence of alcohol
  41. Obsessive drinking
  42. Vague religious desires
  43. Failure of the rationalization system as the alcoholic admits defeat

Adapted from Jellinek EM: Phases of alcohol addiction. Q J Stud Alcoholism 13:673–684, 1952.

concept that there are five types of drinking patterns and complications, which he labeled alpha, beta, gamma, delta, and epsilon. He suggested that gamma (characterized by tolerance, craving, and loss of control) and delta (characterized by tolerance, craving, and inability to abstain) represented true diseases that followed most closely his 43 symptoms' progression. In Jellinek's view, once the disease of alcoholism was established, usually when an individual was in his early or mid 20s, its course was inexorable, with chronic progression over 20 to 30 years, ending at any stage in death or abstinence. Many studies then followed, some supporting in part, some seriously questioning Jellinek's conclusions and methodology (Trice and Wahl, 1958; Park and Whitehead, 1973; Paredas et al., 1973; Clark, 1976; Pattison, Sobell MB, Sobel LC, 1977; Goodwin, Crane, Guze, 1969).

One of the first studies to challenge Jellinek's hypothesis of an inexorable progression of alcoholism was Lemere's 1953 study, in which he asked his patients about the drinking histories of their deceased relatives who had had alcohol problems. He thus collected information on 500 presumed alcohol abusers and found that 28 per cent increased their alcohol use before death; 10 per cent decreased alcohol use substantially, with 3 per cent of the total sample returning to social drinking; 29 per cent did not change their alcohol consumption; approximately 20 per cent stopped drinking because they were too ill to drink; and approximately 10 per cent achieved abstinence. Because of lack of treatment resources available, Lemere concluded that these results, with approximately 20 per cent of those with alcohol problems becoming abstinent or reducing their drinking, represented the natural history of untreated alcoholism.

In 1968 Drew observed that first admissions for alcoholism increased steadily from ages 25 to 55 but that the predicted prevalence of alcoholism of those 40 and over, based on these admission figures, was consistently more than the actual prevalence figures for this age-group. He did not believe that the literature supported the conclusion that this decreased prevalence was due to treatment effectiveness or to mortality and suggested that the decreased prevalence indicated that alcoholism is a self-limiting disease mainly of young and middle-aged individuals.

Vaillant (1983) reviewed 10 major followup studies of alcohol abusers, each of which followed patients for 7 years or longer. The studies had different methodologies and followed different subgroups of alcohol patients (Table 13–3). As Vaillant points out, these methodologically disparate studies are remarkably similar in indicating that approximately 2 per cent to 3 per cent of alcoholics become abstinent each year and 1 per cent return to asymptomatic ("controlled") drinking. The approximations hold for samples of both treated alcoholics (e.g., Vaillant, 1983; Voetglin and Broz, 1949) and untreated alcoholics (e.g., Goodwin et al., 1971; Ojesjo, 1981). These studies, therefore, partially support Davis's hypothesis that alcoholism is, for some, a self-limiting disorder. However, as is pointed out in studies by Vaillant (1983) and Pokorny, Kanas, and Overall (1981), the more numerous and severer the symptoms of alcoholism, the closer the clinical picture is to Jellinek's stages and the more alcoholism appears to be a progressive disease, ending in abstinence, serious morbidity, or death. Such conclusions, however, may be tautological; the more serious and intense the symptoms, the more serious and numerous the effects (many of which are also symptoms) unless halted by abstinence.

There have been further attempts to determine whether the 2 per cent to 3 per cent abstinence rate per year and the 1 per cent annual rate of return to social drinking are due to spontaneous remission or to treatment. As Emrick (1974, 1975) points out, in his review of the treatment outcome literature, most treatment studies have major methodological flaws, such as inadequate controls, failure to control for premorbid variables, and inadequate followup periods. However, he concludes from his review that improvement rates at 6 months and longer are positively correlated with the amount of treatment. Conversely, several well-done studies since Emrick's review conclude that treatment does little to change the natural course of alcoholism (Orford and Edwards, 1977; Ojesjo, 1981; Vaillant, 1980, 1983). The current evidence, therefore, appears to indicate that spontaneous remission, abstinence, and return to asymptomatic drinking

### TABLE 13–3 Long-term Followup Studies of Alcohol Abuse

| Study and Nature of Sample | Length of Followup (yr) | Size of Original Sample | No. of Survivors Followed | Outcome for Survivors (%) | | |
|---|---|---|---|---|---|---|
| | | | | ABSTINENT | ASYMPTOMATIC DRINKERS | STILL ALCOHOLIC |
| Voetglin and Broz, 1949<br>Private inpatient; ages 30–50 | 10 | ? | 104 | 22* | | 78 |
| Myerson and Mayer, 1966<br>Skid row; ages 40–60 | 10 | 101 | 80 | 22* | | 78 |
| Sundby, 1967<br>Clinic; all classes; ages 30–55 | 20–35 | 1722 | 632 | 64* | | 36 |
| Goodwin, Crane, Guze, 1971<br>Felons; ages 20–35 | 8 | c. 111 | 93 | 8 | 33 | 59 |
| Lundquist, 1973<br>Inpatient; ages 30–55 | 9 | 200 | 155 | 37* | | 63 |
| Bratfos, 1974<br>Inpatient; ages 30–60 | 10 | 1179 | 412 | 13 | 0 | 87 |
| Hyman, 1976<br>Private outpatient clinic; ages 30–55 | 15 | 54 | 26 | 19 | 19 | 62 |
| Vaillant, 1983<br>Inpatient; public clinic; ages 30–50 | 8 | 106 | 71 | 39 | 6 | 55 |
| Ojesjo, 1981<br>Community; age 46 | 15 | 96 | 71 | 32* | | 68 |
| Vaillant, 1983<br>Community; ages 20–40 | 20 ± 10 | 120 | 102 | 34 | 20 | 46 |

Adapted from Vaillant G: The Natural History of Alcoholism. Cambridge, MA, Harvard University Press, 1983, pp 124–125.
* Study did not distinguish abstinent from asymptomatic drinker.

rates are equivalent for treated and untreated alcoholics. Several investigators (Pattison, 1981; Sells, 1981) have suggested that therapy appears ineffective because all patients are expected to respond to the same treatment. They suggest that patients should be matched to the treatments best suited to them. Although this approach is logical, the method for matching patients to treatments has not been established and the theory that such matching would be advantageous awaits verification.

It should be emphasized that the rate of improvement noted earlier applies to patients who are probably diagnosable as being alcohol dependent. Many patients with alcohol problems, especially those in their teens and 20s, return to social drinking and abstinence at much higher rates. For example, Fillmore (1975), in her 20-year followup of college students, found that only 30 per cent of 31 individuals who had been problem drinkers in college were still having problems with alcohol at followup.

All alcoholics, including those who become abstinent or return to social drinking, are likely to experience significant medical and psychosocial morbidity from their illness. On average, the alcoholic's first hospitalization for alcohol-related causes occurs 10 to 15 years after the onset of heavy drinking for males and 5 years after the onset for females (Glatt, 1961, 1967). The studies referred to thus far concern the natural history of alcoholism in males. There are far fewer studies in women, and what studies there are (Glatt, 1961; Gomberg, 1976; Winokur and Clayton, 1968; Liban and Smart, 1980; Ashley et al., 1977; Dahlgren, 1978; Wilsnack, 1982) indicate that women begin problem drinking later than men; have a more rapid development of symptoms, with onset of physical complications at an earlier age; have more psychiatric disability, especially affective disorder; have a worse prognosis; and respond equally well to treatment.

The medical complications that lead alcoholics to hospitalizations are manifold and encompass both acute and chronic problems. Acute effects directly linked to alcohol include overdose (which may lead to coma) and withdrawal (which may lead to delirium), gastritis, hepatitis, pancreatitis, macrocytic anemia, and thrombocytopenia. Chronic effects solidly linked to alcohol are numerous and include various organic mental disorders (including amnestic disorder, i.e., Wernicke-Korsakoff's disease), peripheral neuropathy, chronic pancreatitis, cirrhosis, cardiomyopathy, and myopathy (Schuckit, 1979). Another type of disorder recently described (Jones et al., 1973) is the fetal alcohol syndrome, diagnosed by specific developmental abnormalities, including dysmorphic facial features and central nervous system abnormalities, occurring in infants born to alcoholic mothers. Other illnesses not commonly associated with alcohol abuse may also be linked. D'Alonzo and Pell (1968) studied 922 employees of a large corporation who were known or suspected alcoholics and matched them with nonalcoholic employees for age, sex, income, and geographic location. They found hypertension definitely linked to alcoholism, and peptic ulcer, asthma, diabetes mellitus, gout, and cerebrovascular disease possibly linked.

Alcoholism is also associated with the psychiatric illnesses of depression, antisocial personality, and drug abuse. Alcoholics often become depressed, especially after drinking heavily for several weeks. The depression usually clears within 3 to 10 days after drinking ceases. However, approximately 5 per cent of hospitalized male and 20 per cent of hospitalized female alcoholics have an independent diagnosis of affective disorder (Schuckit, 1979). Antisocial symptoms are frequently found in alcoholics both before and after the onset of their alcoholism. Some of these patients have an independent diagnosis of antisocial personality (approximately 20 per cent of inpatient male and 5 per cent of inpatient female alcoholics). In some, antisocial behavior is a consequence of heavy drinking, and in others, it is unclear which came first (Schuckit, 1973). Drug abuse, especially opiate abuse, is also strongly associated with alcohol abuse, and it is estimated that 20 per cent of drug abusers also abuse alcohol (Freed, 1973).

The alcoholic also experiences much psychosocial morbidity. Given that alcoholism is diagnosed in part by its psychosocial con-

sequences, it is somewhat difficult and arbitrary to separate psychosocial complications from symptoms of alcoholism. It is worth emphasizing that job difficulties and loss; marital tensions, separations, and divorces; and arrests for traffic offenses, disturbing the peace, and criminal behavior are all strongly associated with alcoholism (Taylor and Helzer, 1983).

Not only does a diagnosis of alcoholism carry a significant risk of various complications, but it is also strongly associated with increased mortality, especially in younger alcoholics (Costello and Schneider, 1974; Pell and D'Alonzo, 1973; Schmidt and deLint, 1972). At any age, death rates in alcoholics are two to four times higher than those expected from age-matched controls. Alcohol use and probably abuse are strongly associated with violent deaths, including suicide, accidents, and homicide. Alcoholism is strongly associated with death from cirrohosis and, in conjunction with cigarette smoking, with cancer of the oropharynx and esophagus. Moderately increased morbidity, 1.5 to 3.0 times that expected, in alcoholics from cardiovascular disease and infectious disease has also been reported (Vaillant, 1983; Taylor and Helzer, 1983). These various causes lead to an average age of death of 55 to 60 for alcoholics (Schuckit, 1979). Also of note is the finding of Vaillant (1983) that offering intense, readily available treatment to alcoholics does not lower their mortality rate, and the finding of Pell and D'Alonzo (1973) that the mortality rate of recovered alcoholics is not significantly different from that of alcoholics who continue to drink.

An overall view of the natural history of alcoholism reveals that an alcoholic's first drink occurs at age 17 (for men) or age 19 (for women); problem drinking begins at age 28 to 33 for men and 5 years later for women; first hospitalization for drinking problems occurs in men and women at about age 40; and death at age 55 to 60 for both men and women (Glatt, 1959; Schuckit, 1979; Taylor and Helzer, 1983). There are many exceptions to this timing, as there are to the onset, order, and occurrence of specific signs and symptoms of alcoholism. The severest alcoholic spends much of his time sober (Ludwig, 1972) with concomitant decreases at such times in alcohol-related problems. The disease appears to fit the pattern of a chronic relapsing illness, with periods of remission and exacerbation. Some alcoholics appear to have permanent remissions either spontaneously, through internal resolve, or with the help of various factors in their environment. Others continue a pattern of intermittent but not worsening problems, and still others inexorably deteriorate with increasingly severe, debilitating, and often fatal alcohol-related problems. A continuing challenge to those working in the field of alcoholism is to identify the patients with the more benign course and determine what factors lead to such a course and to identify those with a more malignant course and determine what interventions and treatments are effective for them.

## DIFFERENTIAL DIAGNOSIS

Chronic excessive use of alcohol produces a wide range of psychiatric symptoms that, in various combinations, can mimic other psychiatric disorders. *Therefore, while a person is drinking heavily and during the withdrawal period, it is difficult to determine whether he suffers from a psychiatric condition other than alcoholism.*

The diagnosis of alcoholism itself is relatively easy. However, many alcoholics also use other drugs, and it may be difficult to determine which symptoms are produced by alcohol and which by barbiturates, amphetamines, and so on. If a patient has been drinking heavily and not eating, he may become hypoglycemic (Freinkel and Arky, 1966), and this condition may produce symptoms resembling those seen in withdrawal.

The two psychiatric conditions most commonly associated with alcoholism are primary affective disorder and sociopathy (Goodwin, 1982). Female alcoholics apparently suffer more often from primary affective disorder than do male alcoholics (Schuckit, Pitts, Reich, King, Winokur, 1969). The diagnosis of primary affective disorder usually can be made by past history or by observing the patient during long periods of abstinence. According to one study, about one third of patients with manic-depressive illness drink more while depressed and another third drink less (Cassidy, Flanagan, Spellman, Cohen, 1957). Studies indicate that small amounts of alcohol administered to a depressed patient relieve depressive symptoms, but large amounts worsen depression (Mayfield, Coleman, 1968).

Many sociopaths drink to excess, although how many would be considered "alcoholic" is uncertain. A followup study of convicted felons, about half of whom had alcohol problems, indicates that sociopathic drinkers have a higher "spontaneous" remission rate than do nonsociopathic alcoholics (Goodwin et al., 1971). When sociopaths reduce their drinking, their criminal activities are correspondingly reduced.

Various personality disorders have been associated with alcoholism, particularly those in which "dependency" is a feature. The consensus at present is that alcoholism is not connected with a particular constellation of personality traits. Longitudinal studies help little in predicting what types of individuals are particularly susceptible to alcoholism (McCord and McCord, 1962).

## ETIOLOGY

Most adults in Western countries drink alcohol. About 1 in 12 to 1 in 15 have serious problems from drinking. There is no scientifically acceptable explanation why some develop problems and most do not. Although the cause of alcoholism is unknown, a number of risk factors have been identified.

1. *Family history.* Alcoholism runs in families. Four times as many children of alcoholics become alcoholic as do children of nonalcoholics. There is evidence that they become alcoholic whether they are raised by their alcoholic parents or not. Whether "hereditary" or not, alcoholism in the family is probably the strongest predictor of alcoholism occurring in particular individuals.

2. *Sex.* More men are alcoholic than women. The difference is about three to one.

3. *Age.* Alcoholism in men usually develops in the twenties and thirties. In women it often develops later. People of either sex over 65 rarely become alcoholic.

4. Alcoholism is unevenly distributed geographically and among people of different occupations, racial backgrounds, nationality, income, and religion (see section on Epidemiology).

5.   A childhood history of attention deficit disorder or conduct disorder apparently increases a child's risk of becoming alcoholic, particularly if there is alcoholism in the family.

In recent years the familial nature of alcoholism has been intensively studied. Many family studies have been conducted in Western countries, and all show much higher rates of alcoholism among the relatives of alcoholics than in the general population. Children are usually raised by the same individuals who provide their genes, and nature-nurture studies have attempted to separate genetic from environmental influences. Among these are twin, genetic marker, and adoption studies.

There have been four twin studies of alcoholism. A Swedish study found that identical twins were concordant for alcoholism more often than were fraternal twins (Kaij, 1960). The severer the alcoholism, the greater the discrepancy between concordance rates in identical vs. fraternal twins.

Another study, in Finland, found that identical twins were more concordant for quantity and frequency of drinking but not for adverse consequences of drinking (Partanen, Bruun Markkanen, 1966). There was a trend for younger identical twins to be more concordant for adverse consequences.

In 1972 Loehlin analyzed questionnaire data from 850 like-sex twins in the United States (unpublished data). His findings were consistent with a genetic factor in drinking behavior. Jonsson and Nilsson (1968) reported findings also based on questionnaire data from 7500 twin pairs in Sweden. Monozygotic twins were more concordant with regard to quantity of alcohol consumed but not with regard to adverse consequences. The results resemble those of the Finnish study.

These studies point to genetic control of drinking behavior, but the evidence for a genetic determinant of alcoholism is inconsistent. Other twin studies (Vessell, Page, Passananti, 1971) indicate genetic control over the metabolism of alcohol, but varying rates of metabolism probably have no relevance to alcoholism (Reed, 1977).

Establishment of a relationship between a known inherited biologic trait and a familial disease would also suggest that the latter was genetic. More than a score of genetic marker studies relevant to alcoholism have

been published (Goodwin, 1982). Almost without exception, whenever a report of an association between a marker and alcoholism is followed by attempts to replicate the finding, the findings are contradictory.

Among markers studied have been color blindness, blood groups, genetically determined proteins, and finger ridge count. The observation (Cruz-Coke and Varela, 1966) that alcoholics are likely to be color blind has been confirmed in several studies, but apparently the color blindness is reversible, perhaps caused by malnutrition or toxic effects.

A third approach to separating "nature" from "nurture" is to study individuals separated from their biologic relatives soon after birth and raised by nonrelative foster parents. Beginning in 1970 a group from Washington University in St. Louis initiated a series of adoption studies in Denmark, supported by the NIAAA and intended to investigate further the possibility that alcoholism, in part, has genetic roots (Goodwin, 1979). The studies involved interviewing four groups of subjects.

The first group consisted of sons of alcoholics (average age, 30 years) raised by nonalcoholic foster parents. The second group consisted of sons of alcoholics (average age, 33 years) raised by their alcoholic biologic parents. The third and fourth groups consisted, respectively, of daughters of alcoholics (average age, 37 years) raised by nonalcoholic foster parents and daughters of alcoholics (average age, 32 years) raised by their alcoholic biologic parents. Paired with each group was a control group matched for age and, in the adopted samples, circumstances of adoption. All adoptees were separated from their biologic parents in the first few weeks of life and adopted by nonrelatives. The interviews were conducted by Danish psychiatrists "blind" to the overall purpose of the study and the identity of the interviewees, that is, whether they were children of alcoholics or controls. The results were as follows:

1.   Sons of alcoholics were about four times more likely to be alcoholic than were sons of nonalcoholics, whether raised by nonalcoholic foster parents or by their own biologic parents. Sons of alcoholics raised by foster parents also were more likely to be divorced than were controls. Otherwise, sons of alcoholics and nonalcoholics did not

differ with regard to a wide range of variables: depression, anxiety neurosis, personality disorders, criminality, drug abuse, or "heavy drinking" (defined as drinking daily and, on occasion, large amounts but without adverse consequences).

2.  Sons raised by their alcoholic parents differed from nonadopted controls only with regard to alcoholism, defined by operational criteria.

3.  Of the adopted daughters of alcoholics, 2 per cent were alcoholic and 2 per cent more had serious problems from drinking. In the adopted control group, 4 per cent were alcoholic. Of the nonadopted daughters, 3 per cent were alcoholic and 2 per cent were problem drinkers.

Between 0.1 per cent and 1.0 per cent of Danish women are alcoholic. Thus, in both the proband and the control groups, a higher than expected prevalence of alcoholism was found. Nothing was known about the biologic parents of the controls other than that they did not have a hospital diagnosis of alcoholism (the alcoholic parents of the probands were identified because they had been hospitalized with this diagnosis). Possibly some of the biologic parents of the alcoholic controls were alcoholic. However, this could not be demonstrated one way or the other, and the findings from the daughter adoption study are inconclusive.

In both the adopted and the nonadopted daughter groups there were low rates of heavy drinking. About 8 per cent of the female subjects were heavy drinkers, compared with nearly 40 per cent of the male subjects. Therefore, of women who met the criteria for heavy drinking, a substantial number developed problems from drinking that were serious enough to require treatment.

Again, as with the male adoptees, the adopted-out daughters of alcoholics and controls did not differ with regard to other variables, such as depression and drug abuse. There has been speculation, based on family studies, that female relatives of alcoholics are apt to be depressed, whereas male relatives are likely to suffer alcoholism (Winokur and Clayton, 1968). Indeed, 30 per cent of the daughters raised by alcoholics had been treated for depression by age 32, compared with about 5 per cent of

the controls. Apparently, growing up with an alcoholic parent increases the risk of depression in women but not in men, a susceptibility that does not exist if the daughters are raised by nonalcoholic foster parents. This does not deny the possibility of a genetic predisposition to depression in female relatives of alcoholics, since many genetic disorders require an environmental "trigger" to become clinically apparent.

Summarizing the results of the Danish studies:

•  Children of alcoholics are particularly vulnerable to alcoholism whether raised by their alcoholic parents or by nonalcoholic foster parents.

•  The vulnerability is specific for alcoholism and does not involve increased risk for other psychopathology, including abuse of other substances.

•  Alcoholism is *not* on a continuum with "heavy drinking," or even "problem drinking" (defined as heavy drinking that results in problems but does not justify the term alcoholism as operationally defined in these studies).

•  More definitive conclusions could be drawn from studies of the sons of alcoholics than from studies of the daughters because the female control adoptees also had a higher rate of alcoholism than would be anticipated from the estimated prevalence in the general population. In general, heavy drinking was far less common in the women than in the men, but of those women who did drink heavily, a high percentage become alcoholic. As for an overlap between depression and alcoholism in the family histories, daughters of alcoholics raised by their alcoholic parents were more subject to depression than were controls, but this was not true of daughters raised by nonalcoholic foster parents. This suggests that in women, environment may be more important in producing depression than in producing alcoholism.

Four other adoption studies have been conducted, two of them subsequent to the Danish studies. In the early 1940s Roe (1944) obtained information about 49 foster children in the 20- to 40-year age-group, 22 of normal parentage and 27 with a biologic parent described as a "heavy drinker." Neither group had adult drinking problems. Roe concluded that there was no evidence of hereditary influences on drinking.

This conclusion can be questioned on several grounds. First, the sample was small. There were only 21 men of "alcoholic" parentage and 11 of normal parentage. Second, the biologic parents of the probands were described as "heavy drinkers," but it is not clear how many were alcoholic. Most had a history of antisocial behavior; none had been treated. All of the biologic parents of the proband group in the Danish study received a hospital diagnosis of alcoholism, at a time when the diagnosis was seldom used in Denmark.

In 1972 Schuckit, Goodwin, and Winokur also studied a group of individuals who were reared apart from their biologic parents who had either a biologic parent or a "surrogate" parent with a drinking problem. The subjects were significantly more likely to have a drinking problem if a biologic parent was considered alcoholic than if a surrogate parent was alcoholic.

More recently, Bohman (1978) studied 2000 adoptees born between 1930 and 1949. He inspected official registers in Sweden for notations about alcohol abuse and criminal offenses in the adoptees and their biologic and adoptic parents. There was a significant correlation between registrations for abuse of alcohol among biologic parents and their adopted sons. Registered criminality in the biologic parents did not predict criminality or alcoholism in the adopted sons.

Cadoret and Gath (1978) studied 84 adult adoptees (18 years or older) separated at birth from their biologic relatives and having no further contact with them. Alcoholism occurred more frequently in adoptees whose biologic background included alcoholism than it did in other adoptees. Alcoholism did not correlate with any other biologic parental diagnosis.

The results of the four studies were similar to those found in the Danish adoption studies: alcoholism in the biologic parents predicted alcoholism in their male offspring raised by unrelated adoptive parents but did not predict other psychiatric illness.

## Editor's Comment

*A recent paper (Cadoret R, O'Gorman T, Troughton E, Heywood E: Alcoholism and antisocial personality, interrelationships, genetic and environmental factors. Arch Gen Psychiatry 42:161–167, 1985) presents an adoption study that shows a genetic effect operative in female alcohol abuse. The odds of a female adoptee being alcoholic given that a biologic parent was alcoholic is 8.5 times greater than if the biologic parent was not alcoholic. This is a highly significant association.*

## Familial Alcoholism

Studies reviewed here suggest that "familial alcoholism" may be a useful diagnostic category—at least for research purposes—to separate alcoholics into familial vs. nonfamilial types. They also indicate that familial alcoholism should include four features:

1. *A family history of alcoholism.* If an alcoholic reports having one close relative who is alcoholic, he often reports having two or more.

2. *Early onset of alcoholism.* The sons of alcoholics in the Danish study were alcoholic by their late 20s. Alcoholism may begin in early life, but usually male alcoholics are in their mid or late 30s before they are identified as alcoholics. In the Finnish twin study younger identical twins were concordant for alcoholism more often than older twins. Jones (1972) reports that younger alcoholics have alcoholic relatives more often than do older alcoholics.

3. *Severe symptoms, requiring treatment at an early age.* The alcoholic biologic fathers in the Danish studies were identified because they were diagnosed in a Danish hospital. As noted, many Danish hospitals avoid the diagnosis of alcoholism when another diagnosis is available, e.g., a personality disorder. Therefore, it can safely be assumed that the alcoholic parents were severely alcoholic, and this may explain why their offspring were so clearly alcoholic at a young age. In the study of Kaij (1960) the concordance rate for alcoholism in identical twins rose as a function of the severity of the alcoholism. Another study (Jones, 1972) reported that "essential" alcoholism is associated with a family history of alcoholism more often than is "reactive" alcoholism. Essential alcoholism is defined as alcoholism that apparently is unrelated to external events (as "endogenous" depression is often contrasted with "reactive" depression); it connotes severity as well as lack of other psychopathology. Amark (1953) noted that periodic (severe) alcoholics have a family history of alcoholism more often than do less severe alcoholics.

4. *Absence of other conspicuous psychopathology.* This was found in both the Danish studies and the Bohman study.

If alcoholism in some individuals is influenced by heredity, what is inherited? No one knows, but one kind of reaction to alcohol is definitely inherited. Millions of persons have unpleasant reactions to small amounts of alcohol. These may take the form of dizziness, nausea, or headaches. Adverse reactions to alcohol have been most studied in Orientals. About two thirds of Orientals develop a flush of the skin and have palpitations and other unpleasant effects after drinking a small amount of alcohol. Oriental babies given small amounts of alcohol also develop a flush. The basis for the flush unquestionably is genetic. This response apparently can be blocked by antihistamine drugs, for reasons as yet unknown.

There is some evidence that a higher proportion of women than men have adverse reactions to small amounts of alcohol. The alcoholism rate in the Orient is lower than in Western countries, and this is usually attributed to culture. Women have a lower rate of alcoholism than men, and this also has been ascribed to culture. Culture may indeed be important in both instances, but obviously, in Orientals, and perhaps in women, another factor contributing to the low alcoholism rate may be physiologic and, presumably, genetic in nature. Many people, in short, are born *protected* against becoming alcoholic. Conversely, those who become alcoholic are born *un*protected.

Does this mean that children of alcoholics are vulnerable to alcoholism only because they lack an inborn intolerance for alcohol? The answer to this question is complex. People differ in their response to alcohol in other ways than having varying degrees of intolerance for alcohol. Some people become more euphoric from alcohol than others.

There are many theories—psychological and biochemical—for the differential effects of alcohol. Space does not permit exploration of all the theories, but one has stimulated a good deal of recent research and is summarized here.

## The Alkaloid Theory of Alcoholism

In 1970 two groups independently reported that central biogenic monoamines and aldehyde metabolites of the amines and alcohol form condensation products in the presence of alcohol (Cohen and Collins, 1970; Davis and Walsh, 1970). These products, generically called TIQs (after tetrahydroisoquinolone), structurally resemble morphinelike alkaloids. TIQs, some believe, play an important role in alcoholism, possibly by acting as "false" transmitters.

The two studies led to a large amount of research. It was found that infusion of TIQs into the lateral ventricle of the rat brain resulted in increased ethanol preference. TIQs were found in urine and cerebrospinal fluid of alcoholics in higher concentration than in nonalcoholics (Sjoquist, Borg, Kvande, 1981). TIQs were reported to bind opiate receptors (Greenwald, Fertel, Wong, Scharz, Bianchine, 1978), and alcohol was reported to inhibit binding of "endogenous opioids" to delta opiate receptors (Hiller, Angel, Simon, 1981). Considerable work is in progress on the relationship of alcohol and opiates.

From a treatment standpoint, the most intriguing alcohol–opiate work concerns effects of the potent opiate antagonist naloxone. Naloxone inhibits withdrawal convulsions in ethanol-dependent mice (Blum, Futterman, Wallace, Schwertner, 1977) and blocks subcortical seizure activity produced by ethanol in monkeys (Triana, Frances, Stokes, 1980). In two studies naloxone reduced alcohol-induced coma in humans (Mackenzie, 1979). In one study naloxone prevented psychomotor impairment induced by small doses of alcohol in normal volunteers (Jeffcoate, Herbert, Cullen, Hastings, Walder, 1979).

These experiments should be viewed with caution. There are studies showing no effect on alcohol intoxication from naloxone, and it is possible that naloxone has pharmacologic actions unrelated to opiate receptor blockade. Nevertheless, reports that naloxone antagonizes alcohol effects have therapeutic implications. Many people experience adverse effects or little euphoria from alcohol, and alcohol blockers could be useful in the treatment of alcoholism by "protecting" the physiologically vulnerable individual.

## TREATMENT

The treatment of alcoholism and the management of alcohol withdrawal symptoms present separate problems.

In the absence of serious medical complications, the alcohol withdrawal syndrome is usually transient and self-limiting; the patient recovers within several days regardless of treatment (Victor and Adams, 1953). Insomnia and irritability may persist for longer periods (Gerard, Saenger, Wile, 1962).

Treatment of withdrawal is symptomatic and prophylactic. Agitation and tremulousness can be relieved with a variety of drugs, including barbiturates, paraldehyde, chloral hydrate, the phenothiazines, and the benzodiazepines. The benzodiazepines currently are considered the drugs of choice for withdrawal. They have little, if any, synergistic action with alcohol and, compared with barbiturates and paraldehyde, relatively little abuse potential. They can be administered parenterally to intoxicated patients without apparent risk and continued orally during the withdrawal period. There is some evidence that mortality is increased when the phenothiazines are used, reportedly from hypotension or hepatic encephalopathy.

Administration of large doses of vitamins—particularly the B viatmins—is obligatory, given the role of these vitamins in preventing peripheral neuropathy and the Wernicke-Korsakoff syndrome. The B vitamins are water soluble, and there is no apparent danger in administering them in large doses.

Unless the patient is dehydrated because of vomiting or diarrhea, there is no reason to administer fluids parenterally. Contrary to common belief, alcoholics usually are not dehydrated; actually, they may be overhydrated from consumption of large volumes of fluid (Ogata, Mendelson, Mello, 1968). During the early stages of withdrawal, hyperventilation may cause respiratory alkalosis, and this, together with hypomagnesemia, has been reported to produce withdrawal seizures (Mendelson, 1970).

If the patient develops delirium, he should be considered dangerous to himself and others, and protective measures should be taken. Ordinarily, tranquilizers calm the patient sufficiently to control agitation, and restraints are unnecessary. Administration of intravenous barbiturates or diazepam may be needed to control severe agitation. Most important, if delirium occurs, further exploration should be conducted to rule out serious medical illness missed in the original examination. When a patient is delirious, an attendant should always be present. It is sometimes helpful to have a friend or relative present.

The treatment of alcoholism should not begin until withdrawal symptoms subside. Treatment has two goals: (1) sobriety and (2) amelioration of psychiatric conditions associated with alcoholism. A small minority of alcoholics are eventually able to drink in moderation, but for several months after a heavy drinking bout, total abstinence is desirable for two reasons. First, the physician must follow the patient, sober, for a considerable period to diagnose a coexistent psychiatric problem. Second, it is important for the patient to learn that he can cope with ordinary life problems without alcohol. Most relapses occur within 6 months of discharge from the hospital; they become less and less frequent after that (Glatt, 1959).

For many patients, disulfiram (Antabuse) is helpful in maintaining abstinence. By inhibiting aldehyde dehydrogenase, the drug leads to an accumulation of acetaldehyde if alcohol is consumed. Acetaldehyde is highly toxic and causes nausea and hypotension. The latter condition leads to shock and may be fatal. In recent years, however, Antabuse has been prescribed in a lower dosage (250 mg) than was used previously, and no deaths from its use have been reported for a number of years. One study indicates that the dose is irrelevant; the deterrent effect is psychological and not dose dependent (Fuller and Williford, 1980).

When Antabuse is discontinued after administration for several days or weeks, the deterrent effect still lasts for a 3- to 5-day period, since the drug takes that long to be excreted. Thus it may be useful to give patients Antabuse during office visits at 3- to 4-day intervals early in the treatment program.

Until recently, it was recommended that patients be given Antabuse for several days and then be challenged with alcohol to demonstrate the unpleasant effects that follow. This procedure was not always satisfactory because some patients showed no adverse effects after considerable amounts of alcohol were consumed and other patients became very ill after drinking small amounts of alcohol. At present, the alcohol challenge test is considered optional. The principal disadvantage of Antabuse is not that patients drink while taking the drug, but that they stop taking the drug after a brief period. This, again, is a good reason to give the drug on frequent office visits during the early crucial period of treatment.

A wide variety of procedures, both psychological and somatic, have been tried in the treatment of alcoholism. None has proved to be definitely superior to others (Blum and Blum, 1969). There is no evidence that intensive psychotherapy helps most alcoholics. Nor are tranquilizers or antidepressants usually effective in maintaining abstinence or controlled drinking (Goodwin, 1982). Aversive conditioning techniques have been tried with such agents as apomorphine and emetine to produce vomiting, succinylcholine to produce apnea, and electrical stimulation to produce pain. The controlled trials required to show that these procedures are effective have not been conducted, but a high rate of success has been reported for the apomorphine treatment in motivated patients (Goodwin, 1981). Although the number of alcoholics who benefit from participation in Alcoholics Anonymous is unknown, most clinicians agree that alcoholics should be encouraged to attend AA meetings on a trial basis.

In two double-blind studies, lithium carbonate was found to be superior to a placebo in reducing drinking in depressed alcoholics (Kline, Wren, Cooper, Varga, Canal, 1974; Merry, Reynolds, Bailey, Coppen, 1976). The dropout rate was high in both studies. Other studies are currently under way to test the efficacy of lithium for alcoholism.

Relapses are characteristic of alcoholism, and physicians treating alcoholics should avoid anger or excessive pessimism when such relapses occur. Alcoholics see nonpsychiatric physicians as often as they see psychiatrists (probably more often), and there is evidence that general practitioners and internists are sometimes more helpful (Gerard and Saenger, 1966). This may be particularly true when the therapeutic approach is warm but authoritarian, with little stress on "insight" or "understanding." Because the cause of alcoholism is unknown, "understanding," in fact, means acceptance of a particular theory. This may provide temporary comfort but probably seldom provides lasting benefit.

## REFERENCES

Amark C: A study in alcoholism: Clinical, social-psychiatric and genetic investigations. Acta Psychiatr Neurol Scand [Suppl] 70:94–96, 1953.

American Psychiatric Association: Diagnostic and Statistical Manual of Mental Disorders, ed 3. Washington, DC, American Psychiatric Association, 1980.

Ashley MJ, Olin JW, le Reiche WM, et al: Morbidity in alcoholics. Arch Int Med 137:883–887, 1977.

Blum EM, Blum RH: Alcoholism. San Francisco, Jossey-Bass, 1969.

Blum K, Futterman S, Wallace JE, Schwertner HA: Naloxone-induced inhibition of ethanol dependence in mice. Nature 265:49–52, 1977.

Bohman M: Genetic aspects of alcoholism and criminality. Arch Gen Psychiatry 35:269–276, 1978.

Boyd JH, Weissman MM, Thompson WD, et al.: Different definitions of alcoholism. I. Impact of seven definitions on prevalence rates in a community survey. Am J Psychiatry 140:1309–1313, 1983.

Bratfos O: The Course of Alcoholism: Drinking, Social Adjustment and Health. Oslo, Universitet Forlaget, 1974.

Brenner MH: Trends in alcohol consumption and associated illnesses. Some effects of economic changes. Am J Public Health 65:1279–1292, 1975.

Brenner MH: International trends in alcohol consumption and related pathologies, in Alcohol Consumption and Related Problems. NIAAA Alcohol and Health Monograph No. 1 DHMS Pub. No. (ADM) 82-1190. Washington, DC, Government Printing Office, 1982, pp 157–176.

Cadoret R, Gath A: Inheritance of alcoholism in adoptees. Br J Psychiatry 132:252–258, 1978.

Cahalan D: Problem Drinkers. San Francisco, Jossey-Bass, 1970.

Cassidy WL, Flanagan NB, Spellman M, Cohen ME: Clinical observations in manic-depressive disease. JAMA 164:1535–1546, 1957.

Clark WB: Loss of control, heavy drinking and drinking problems in a longitudinal study. J Stud Alcohol 37:1256–1290, 1976.

Clark WB, Midank L: Alcohol use and alcohol problems among U.S. adults: Results of the 1979 national survey, in Alcohol Consumption and Related Problems. NIAAA Alcohol and Health Monograph No. 1 DHMS Pub. No. (ADM) 82-1190. Washington, DC, Government Printing Office, 1982, pp 3–52.

Cohen G, Collins M: Alkaloids from catecholamines in adrenal tissue: Possible role in alcoholism. Science 167:1749–1750, 1970.

Collins MA, Nijm WP, Borge GR, et al: Dopamine related tetrahydroisoquinolines: Significant urinary excretion by alcoholics after alcohol consumption. Science 206:1184–1186, 1979.

Colman N, Herbert V: Hematologic complication of alcoholism: Overview. Semin Hematol 17:164–176, 1980.

Costello RM, Schneider SL: Mortality in an alcoholic cohort. Int J Addict 9:355–363, 1974.

Cruz-Coke R, Varela A: Inheritance of alcoholism. Lancet 2:1282–1283, 1966.

Dahlgren L: Female alcoholics. III. Development and pattern of problem drinking. Acta Psychiatr Scand 57:325–334, 1978.

D'Alonzo C, Pell S: Cardiovascular disease among problem drinkers. J Occup Med 10:344–350, 1968.

Davis VE, Walsh MJ: Alcohol, amines and alkaloids: A possible biochemical basis for alcohol addiction. Science 167:1005–1007, 1970.

Demakis JG, Proskey A, Rahimtoola SM, et al: The natural course of alcoholic cardiomyopathy. Ann Intern Med 80:293–297, 1974.

Dienstag JL, Carter EA, Wards JR, et al: Plasma alpha amino-$n$-butyric acid to leucine (A/L) ratio: Nonspecificity as a marker for alcoholism. Gastroenterology 75:561–565, 1978.

Drew LR: Alcoholism as a self limiting disease. Q J Stud Alcohol 29:956–967, 1968.

Duggan JJ, Rothball LN: Asymptomatic enlargement of the parotid glands. N Engl J Med 257:1262–1267, 1957.

Duncan MW, Smythe GA: Salsolinol and dopamine in alcoholic beverages. Lancet 1:904–906, 1982.

Eckardt MJ, Ryback RS, Rawlings RR, et al: Biochemical diagnosis of alcoholism: A test of the discriminating capabilities of gamma-glutamyl transpeptidase and mean corpuscular volume. JAMA 246:2707–2710, 1981.

Edwards G, Gross MM, Keller M, Moser J, Room R (eds): Alcohol related disabilities. WHO Offset Publ. No. 32. Geneva, World Health Organization, 1977.

Emrick CD: A review of psychologically oriented treatment of alcoholism. I. The use and interrelationship of outcome criteria and drinking behavior following treatment. Q J Stud Alcohol 35:523–549, 1974.

Emrick CD: A review of psychologically oriented treatment of alcoholism. II. The relative effectiveness of different treatment approaches and the effectiveness of treatment versus no treatment. J Stud Alcohol 36:88–109, 1975.

Ewing JA, Rouse BA: Corneal arcus as a sign of possible alcoholism. Alcohol Clin Exp Res 4:104, 1980.

Fillmore KM: Relationship between specific drinking problems in early adulthood and middle age: An exploratory 20 year follow up study. Q J Stud Alcohol 36:882–907, 1975.

Freed EX: Drug abuse by alcoholics: A review. Int J Addict 8:451–473, 1973.

Freinkel N, Arky RA: Effects of alcohol on carbohydrate metabolism in man. Psychosom Med 28:551–563, 1966.

Fuller RK, Williford WO: Life-table analysis of abstinence in a study evaluating the efficacy of disulfiram. Alcoholism 4:298, 1980.

Gallbraith S, Murray WR, Patel AR, et al: The relationship between alcohol and head injury and its effect on the conscious level. Br J Surg 63:128–130, 1976.

Gerard D, Saenger G, Wile R: The abstinent alcoholic. Arch Gen Psychiatry 6:83–95, 1962.

Gerard DL, Saenger G: Out-patient Treatment of Alcoholism. Toronto, University of Toronto Press, 1966.

Glatt MM: An alcoholic unit in a mental hospital. Lancet 2:397–398, 1959.

Glatt MM: Drinking habits of English (middle-class) alcoholics. Acta Psychiatr Scand 37:88–113, 1961.

Glatt MM: Complications of alcoholism in the social sphere. Br J Addict 62:35–44, 1967.

Gomberg E: Alcoholism in women, in Kissin B, Begleiter H (eds): Biology of Alcoholism, Vol 4. New York, Plenum Press, 1976, pp 117–166.

Goodwin DW: Alcoholism and heredity. Arch Gen Psychiatry 36:57–61, 1979.

Goodwin DW: Alcoholism: The Facts. New York, Oxford University Press, 1981.

Goodwin DW: Alcoholism and affective disorders, in Alcoholism and Clinical Psychiatry, NY Academy of Medicine. New York, Plenum Press, 1982.

Goodwin DW: Alcoholism, in Goodwin DW, Guze SB (eds): Psychiatric Diagnosis. New York, Oxford University Press, 1984, pp 147–178.

Goodwin DW, Crane JB, Guze SB: Alcoholic "blackouts": A review and clinical study of 100 alcoholics. Am J Psychiatry 126:191–198, 1969.

Goodwin DW, Crane JB, Guze SB: Felons who drink: An 8-year follow-up. Q J Stud Alcohol 32:136–147, 1971.

Goodwin DW, Hill SY: Chronic effects of alcohol and other psychoactive drugs on intellect, learning and memory, in Rankin G (ed): Alcohol, Drugs, and Brain Damage. Toronto, Addiction Research Foundation, 1975, pp 55–69.

Greenwald JE, Fertel RH, Wong LK, Scharz RD, Bianchine JR: Salsolinol and tetrahydropapaveroline bind opiate receptors in the rat brain. Fed Proc 37:379, 1978.

Hagnell O, Tunving K: Prevalence and nature of alcoholism in a total population. Soc Psychiatry 7:190–201, 1972.

Hiller JM, Angel LM, Simon EJ: Multiple opiate receptors: Alcohol selectively inhibits binding to delta receptors. Science 214:468–470, 1981.

Holt S, Skinner HA, Israel Y: Early identification of alcohol abuse. II. Clinical and laboratory indicators. Can Med Assoc J 124:1279–1295, 1981.

Hyman MM: Alcoholics 15 years later. Ann NY Acad Sci 273:613–623, 1976.

Israel Y, Orrego H, Host S, et al: Identification of alcohol abuse: Thoracic fractures on routine chest-xray as indicators of alcoholism. Alcohol Clin Exp Res 4:420–422, 1980.

Jeffcoate WJ, Herbert M, Cullen MH, Hastings AG, Walder CP: Prevention of effects of alcohol intoxication by naloxone. Lancet 2:1157–1158, 1979.

Jellinek EM: Phases of alcohol addiction. Q J Stud Alcohol 13:673–684, 1952.

Jellinek EM: Estimating the prevalence of alcoholism: Modified values in the Jellinek formula and an alternate approach. Q J Stud Alcohol 20:261–269, 1959.

Jellinek EM: The Disease Concept of Alcoholism. New Haven, CT, Hillhouse Press, 1960.

Jellinek EM, Keller M: Rates of alcoholism in the United States of America, 1940-1948. Q J Stud Alcohol 13:49–59, 1952.

Johnson P, Armor D, Polish S, et al: U.S. Adult Drinking Practices: Time Trends, Social Correlates, and Sex Roles. Draft report prepared for the National Institute on Alcohol Abuse and Alcoholism under Contract No. (ADM) 281-76-0020. Santa Monica, CA, Rand Corporation, 1977.

Jones KL, Smith DW, Ulleland CN, et al: Patterns of malformation in offspring of chronic alcoholic mothers. Lancet 1:1267–1271, 1973.

Jones RW: Alcoholism among relatives of alcoholic patients. Q J Stud Alcohol 33:810–815, 1972.

Jonsson E, Nilsson T: Alkoholkonsumption ho s monozygota och dizygota tvillingar Nord Hyg Tidskr 49:21–25, 1968.

Kaij L: Studies on the etiology and sequels of abuse of alcohol. Thesis, University of Lund, Sweden, 1960.

Kaij L, Dock J: Grandsons of alcoholics. Arch Gen Psychiatry 32:1379–1381, 1975.

Keller M: Problems of epidemiology in alcohol problems. Q J Stud Alcohol 36:1442–1451, 1975.

Keller M: On defining alcoholism: With comment on

some other relevant works, in Gomberg E (ed): Alcohol, Science and Society Revisited. Ann Arbor, University of Michigan Press, 1982.

Keller M, Effron V: The prevalence of alcoholism. Q J Stud Alcohol 16:619–644, 1955.

Kline NS, Wren JC, Cooper TB, Varga E, Canal O: Evaluations of lithium therapy in chronic and periodic alcoholism. Am J Med Sci 268:15–22, 1974.

Korsten MA, Leiber CS: Liver and pancreas, in Pattison EM, Kaufman E (eds): Encyclopedia Handbook of Alcoholism. New York, Gardner Press, 1982, pp 225–244.

Lemere F: What happens to alcoholics? Am J Psychiatry 109:674–676, 1953.

Liban C, Smart RG: Generational and other differences between males and females in problem drinking and its treatment. Drug Alcohol Depend 5:207–221, 1980.

Ludwig AM: On and off the wagon: Reasons for drinking and abstaining by alcoholics. Q J Stud Alcohol 33:91–96, 1972.

Lundquist GAR: Alcohol dependence. Acta Psychiatr Scand 49:332–340, 1973.

McCord W, McCord J: A longitudinal study of the personality of alcoholics, in Pittman D, Snyder C (eds): Society, Culture and Drinking Patterns. New York, Wiley, 1962.

Mackenzie AL: Naloxone in alcohol intoxication. Lancet 1:733–735, 1979.

Malin H, Coakley J, Klaeber C, et al: An epidemiologic perspective on alcohol use and abuse in the United States, in Alcohol Consumption and Related Problems. NIAAA Alcohol and Health Monograph No. 1 DHMS Pub. No. (ADM) 82-1190. Washington, DC, Government Printing Office, 1982, pp 99–153.

Mardsden CD: Neurological disorders induced by alcohol, in Edwards G, Grant M (eds): Alcoholism: New Knowledge and New Responses. Baltimore, University Park Press, 1977, pp 189–197.

Mayfield D, Coleman L: Alcohol use and affective disorder. Dis Nervous System 29:467–474, 1968.

Mendelson JH: Biologic concomitants of alcoholism. N Engl J Med 283:24–32, 1970.

Merry J, Reynolds CM, Bailey J, Coppen A: Prophylactic treatment of alcoholism by lithium carbonate. Lancet 2:481–482, 1976.

Mezey E: Effects of alcohol on the gastrointestinal tract, in Pattison EM, Kaufman E (eds): Encyclopedia Handbook of Alcoholism. New York, Gardner Press, 1982, pp 245–254.

Myerson DJ, Mayer J: Origins, treatment and destiny of skid row alcoholic men. N Engl J Med 275:419–424, 1966.

National Council on Alcoholism, Criteria Committee: Criteria for the diagnosis of alcoholism. Am J Psychiatry 129:127–135, 1972.

Ogata M, Mendelson J, Mello N: Electrolytes and osmolality in alcoholics during experimentally induced intoxication. Psychosomatic Med 30:463–488, 1968.

Ojesjo L: Long-term outcome in alcohol abuse and alcoholism among males in the Lundley general population, Sweden. Br J Addict 76:391–400, 1981.

Orford J, Edwards G: Alcoholism. New York, Oxford University Press, 1977.

Paredes A, Hood W, Seymour H, et al: Loss of control in alcoholism: An investigation of the hypothesis with experimental findings. Quart J Stud Alc 34:1146–1161, 1973.

Park P, Whitehead PC: Developmental sequence and dimensions of alcoholism. Q J Stud Alcohol 34:887–904, 1973.

Partanen J, Bruun K, Markkanen T: Inheritance of Drinking Behavior: A Study on Intelligence, Personality, and Use of Alcohol of Adult Twins. Helinski, Finnish Foundation for Alcohol Studies, 1966, pp 14–159.

Pattison EM: Differential diagnosis of the alcoholism syndrome: Clinical implications of empirical research, in Gotheil E, McLellan AT, Druley KA (eds): Matching Patient Needs and Treatment Methods in Alcoholism and Drug Abuse. Springfield, IL, Charles C Thomas, 1981, pp 3–31.

Pattison EM, Sobell MB, Sobell LC: Emerging Concepts of Alcohol Dependence. New York, Springer, 1977.

Pell S, D'Alonzo CA: A five-year mortality study of alcoholics. J Occup Med 15:120–125, 1973.

Phillips M, Vandervoort RE, Becker CE: A sweat test for alcohol consumption, in Sexias FA (ed): Currents in Alcoholism, vol 3. New York, Grune & Stratton, 1978, pp 504–514.

Pokorny AD, Kanas T, Overall J: Order of appearance of alcoholic symptoms. Alcohol Clin Exp Res 5:216–220, 1981.

Reed TE: Three heritable responses to alcohol in a heterogeneous randomly mated mouse strain—inferences for humans. Rutgers Univ Cent Alcohol Stud 38:618–632, 1977.

Roe A: The adult adjustment of children of alcoholic parents raised in foster homes. Q J Stud Alcohol 5:378–393, 1944.

Roizen J: Estimating alcohol involvement in serious events, in Alcohol Consumption and Related Problems. NIAAA Alcohol and Health Monograph No. 1 DHMS Pub. No. (ADM) 82-1190. Washington, DC, Government Printing Office, 1982, pp 179–219.

Rubin E: Alcoholic myopathy in heart and skeletal muscle. N Engl J Med 301:28–33, 1977.

Ryback RS, Eckardt MJ, Feisher, et al: Biochemical and hematologic correlates of alcoholism and liver disease. JAMA 248:2261–2265, 1982.

Schmidt W, deLint J: Causes of death of alcoholics. Q J Stud Alcohol 33:171–185, 1972.

Schmidt W, Popham R: Heavy alcohol consumption and physical health problems. A review of the epidemiological evidence. Drug Alcohol Depend 1:27–50, 1975/76.

Schuckit M: Alcoholism and sociopathy—diagnostic confusion. Q J Stud Alcohol 34:157–164, 1973.

Schuckit M, Pitts FN Jr, Reich T, King LJ, Winokur O: Alcoholism. Arch Environ Health 18:301–306, 1969.

Schuckit MA: Drug and Alcohol Abuse. New York, Plenum Press, 1979.

Schuckit MA, Goodwin DW, Winokur G: A half-sibling study of alcoholism. Am J Psychiatry 128:1132–1136, 1972.

Sellers EM, Kalant H: Alcohol intoxication and withdrawal. N Engl J Med 294:757–762, 1976.

Sells SB: Matching clients to treatment: Problems, preliminary results, and remaining tasks, in Gotheil E, McLellan AT, Druley KA (eds): Matching Patient Needs and Treatment Methods in Alcoholism and Drub Abuse. Springfield, IL, Charles C Thomas, 1981, pp 33–50.

Shaw S, Lue SL, Lieber CS: Biochemical tests for the detection of alcoholism: Comparison of plasma alpha amino-n-butyric acid with other valuable tests. Alcohol Clin Exp Res 2:3–8, 1978.

Sjoquist B, Borg S, Kvande H: Catecholamine derived compounds in urine and cerebrospinal fluid from alcoholics during and after long-standing intoxication. Subst Alcohol Actions Misuse, 2:63–72, 1981.

Sjoquist B, Borg S, Kvande H: Salsolinol and methylated salsolinol in urine and cerebrospinal fluid from healthy volunteers. Subst Alcohol Actions Misuse, 2:73–77, 1981.

Stibler H, Borg S, Allgulander C: Clinical significance of abnormal heterogeneity of transferrin in relation to alcohol consumption. Acta Med Scand 206:275–282, 1979.

Sundby P: Alcoholism and Mortality. Oslo, Universitets Forlaget, 1967.

Taylor JR, Helzer JE: The natural history of alcoholism, in Kissin B, Begleiter H (eds): The Biology of Alcoholism, vol 6. New York, Plenum Press, 1983, pp 17–65.

Triana E, Frances RJ, Stokes PE: The relationship between endorphins and alcohol-induced subcortical activity. Am J Psychiatry 137:491–496, 1980.

Trice HM, Wahl JR: A rank order analysis of the symptoms of alcoholism. Q J Stud Alcohol 19:636–648, 1958.

U. S. Department of Health and Human Services, De Luna JR (ed): Fourth Special Report to the U.S. Congress on Alcohol and Health. DHHS Pub. No. (ADM) 81-1080. Washington, DC, Government Printing Office, 1981.

Vaillant G: The doctor's dilelmma, In Edwards GE, Grant M (eds): Alcoholism, Treatment and Transition. London, Croom Helm, 1980.

Vaillant G: The Natural History of Alcoholism. Cambridge, MA, Harvard University Press, 1983.

Vessell ES, Page JF, Passananti GT: Genetic and environmental factors affecting ethanol metabolism in man. Clin Pharmacol Ther 12:192–194, 1971.

Victor M, Adams RD: The effects of alcohol on the nervous system, in Merritt H, Hare C (eds): Metabolic and Toxic Diseases of the Nervous System. Baltimore, Williams & Wilkins, 1953.

Voetglin WL, Broz WR: The conditioned reflex treatment of chronic alcoholism. X. An analysis of 3125 admissions over a period of ten and a half years. Ann Intern Med 30:580–597, 1949.

Weissman MM, Myers JK, Harding PS: Prevalence and psychiatric heterogeneity of alcoholism in a United States urban community. Q J Stud Alcohol 41:672–681, 1980.

Wilsnack SC: Alcohol abuse and alcoholism in women, in Pattison EM, Kaufman E (eds): Encyclopedia Handbook of Alcoholism. New York, Gardner Press, 1982, pp 718–735.

Winokur G, Clayton P: Family history studies. IV. Comparison of male and female alcoholics. Q J Stud Alcohol 29:885–891, 1968.

Winokur G, Tsuang M: Expectancy of alcoholism in a midwestern population. Q J Stud Alcohol 39:1964–1967, 1978.

Wu A, Chanarin I, Levi AJ: Macrocytosis of chronic alcoholism. Lancet 1:829–830, 1974.

Young AW: Cutaneous stigmata of alcoholism. Alcohol Health Res World, Summer:24–28, 1974.

# chapter 14

# DRUG ABUSE

*by* Joseph Westermeyer, M.D., Ph.D.

## DEFINITION

Diagnostic criteria for drug abuse, according to the *Diagnostic and Statistical Manual of Mental Disorders*, third edition (DSM-III; American Psychiatric Association, 1980), are:

A. **A pattern of pathologic drug use (i.e., inability to reduce or cease using; intoxication throughout the day; daily or frequent use)**
B. **Impairment of social or occupational functioning in association with drug use (i.e., fights, loss of friends, absence from work or school, job loss or school suspension, legal difficulties)**
C. **Duration of drug use over at least 1 month**

Pharmacologic issues also must be considered in the diagnosis. Sedative abuse, for instance, usually involves 600 mg or more of secobarbital, or 60 mg or more of diazepam. Clinical judgment still must be applied regardless of dosage, however; for example, mixed drug abuse, mental retardation, organic brain syndrome, other psychiatric conditions, or extreme youth or old age may lead to drug-related problems at lower doses. Even relatively mild psychoactive compounds, such as caffeine, can lead to disabling symptoms in sensitive patients or in large doses. Episodes of opioid or cocaine overdose, amphetamine delusional disorder, phencyclidine delirium, or cannabis delusional disorder also exemplify other types of pathologic drug use.

Drug dependence is a special category of drug abuse. It involves the presence of either tolerance to the drug or withdrawal on stopping use. With tolerance, the patient must consume markedly increased amounts of the drug to achieve the desired effect, or there is markedly diminished effect with regular use of the same amount. If tolerance is present, sudden drug withdrawal results in abstinence symptoms. Different drugs produce different withdrawal symptoms:

- *Opioids:* lacrimation, rhinorrhea, mydriasis, piloerection, sweating, diarrhea, yawning, mild hypertension, tachycardia, fever, insomnia
- *Sedatives:* nausea, vomiting, malaise, weakness, tachycardia, sweating, hypertension, anxiety, depressed mood or irritability, orthostatic hypotension, coarse tremor, convulsions
- *Amphetamines:* fatigue, disturbed sleep, increased dreaming
- *Tobacco:* craving, irritability, anxiety, difficulty concentrating

Onset of abstinence symptoms after the last dose varies with the drug's duration of action. Withdrawal can begin in 4 to 6 hours with short-acting drugs (e.g., sodium amytal, heroin, morphine), in 8 to 16 hours with intermediate-acting drugs (e.g., opium, methadone, phenobarbital), or in a few to several days with long-acting drugs (e.g., ethchlorvynol, diazepam).

DSM-III includes the diagnosis of tobacco dependence but not tobacco abuse. The former diagnosis is made if the tobacco withdrawal syndrome occurs on cessation, if serious attempts to stop or reduce use have been unsuccessful, or if use continues despite a serious tobacco-related physical disorder (e.g., emphysema, coronary artery disease, Berger's disease of leg arteries). By contrast, there are diagnoses of abuse owing to phencyclidine and cocaine but no diagnoses of dependence.

Other drug-related conditions include hallucinogen hallucinosis, hallucinogen or cannabis delusional disorder, and hallucinogen affective disorder. Substance-related amnestic disorder and organic affective syndrome are additional diagnostic categories that may be associated with drug use. Depending on duration and pattern of drug use, these diagnoses may or may not be accompanied by the diagnosis of drug abuse.

Cannabis does not have a distinct withdrawal syndrome, but chronic heavy users do experience a need for markedly increased doses to achieve the desired effect or markedly diminished effect from regular doses. Lack of abstinence symptoms may be due to storage of active cannabis fractions (such as tetrahydrocannabinal) in body fat stores, with gradual excretion over days or weeks.

## ETIOLOGY AND PATHOGENESIS

Other than excessive or problematic drug use as a final common pathway, there is no one cause of drug abuse. Rather, it is multifactorial in its etiology. The public health model of agent (i.e., drug), host (i.e., the individual), and environment (i.e., society) has proved useful in conceptualizing the complex causes of drug abuse.

### Host Factors

#### Family-Genetic Influences

Like many other psychiatric disorders, drug abuse tends to recur within the same family, suggesting that genetic factors may play a role in drug abuse. Offspring of heavy tobacco smokers are considerably more apt to become tobacco dependent than the general population (Sarvik, Cullen, Gritz, Vogl, West, 1977; Krasnagor, 1979). Opium-dependent persons in Asia show a higher rate of opium dependence among their siblings and relatives than does the general population (Westermeyer, 1974). Similarly, drug-dependent persons in the United States often have alcoholic relatives, as well as depressed or manic relatives. Thus far, adoptive and twin studies have not established the extent to which family prevalence is due to genetics or environment.

### Neurotransmitters

Specific opiate receptors exist in several areas of the brain, including the limbic system. Endogenous morphinelike substances, called endorphins, have been shown to exist in several mammalian species. Opioid drugs probably interact with this system directly, thereby replacing endogenous or host rewards (e.g., from food, social approval, sex, exercise) with exogenous or drug rewards. The same mechanism may also operate for other drugs. For example, condensation products of alcohol metabolism with dopamine include tetrahydroisoquinolines (TIQs), which are also intermediary products of morphine in opium poppy (Simon, 1980).

Benzodiazepine receptors in the brain have also been demonstrated. These probably play a role in sedative abuse. Like other biologic systems, these may be influenced by genetic as well as environmental factors.

Elucidation of these neurotransmitters and their locus of action in the brain has contributed much to current thinking regarding drug abuse. It has helped us to understand why drug-dependent persons often ignore other personal and social needs to seek drug-induced effects. As the drug-abusing person becomes increasingly reliant on drugs as a means of functioning and enjoying life, other means for enhancing life diminish. Consequently, the drug-dependent person pays less attention to food, exercise, work, recreation, friends, and family.

### Psychological Variables

Psychological and personality variations usually accompany drug abuse, although it is difficult to ascertain the extent to which these are primary and etiologic, or secondary to drug abuse. Factors that initially lead a person to start drug use may change over time, so that the original causes may be replaced by different or altered factors, which govern continued or increased drug use (Gottheil et al., 1983). Most clinicians and researchers agree that no one personality type predates drug abuse, although those with chronic pain, anxiety, depression, impulsiveness, or antisocial attitudes appear to be at greater risk. Personality characteristics of drug abusers, perhaps as much acquired as primary, typically include hostile dependence; suppression of emotion, anxiety, or anger in interpersonal relationships; low frustration tolerance; limited flexibility and adaptiveness; and low self-esteem.

Several theories regarding host psychology, difficult to test in either laboratory or clinical settings, remain popular but still unproven. The anxiety reduction theory states that some people take drugs initially to reduce tension, especially in social settings. The field dependent theory holds that drug abusers rely more on external, rather than internal, cues in making decisions and adjusting to life, and thus are vulnerable to exogenous drug administration as a means for modifying or controlling internal emotional or physiologic states. The career addict hypothesis suggests that many drug-dependent persons cease their career of abusing drugs later in life, as they "mature out" of a need to rely on drugs.

## Agent or Drug Factors

### Pharmacologic Considerations

The pharmacologic properties of drugs affect their propensity to be abused. Opioids and sedatives produce rapid, albeit temporary, relief of anxiety, fear, and insomnia. Stimulants similarly relieve boredom, somnolence, anergy, and fatigue. Drugs that alter perceptions may aid in blocking out undesirable thoughts or feelings. Physiologic symptoms relieved by drugs of potential abuse include pain, nausea, vomiting, cramps, diarrhea, and cough.

For abusive purposes, drugs with more rapid onset of action and briefer actions (e.g., heroin, amytal) are preferred over more delayed, longer-acting drugs (e.g., methadone, phenobarbital).

Mode of administration also governs the rate of drug effect, and thereby the liability for drug abuse. Intravenous injecting, smoking, and snuffing produce quicker drug effect than subcutaneous injection or ingestion.

Tolerance and withdrawal phenomena contribute to drug abuse syndromes. Tolerance relates to the need for increasing doses to have the same effect; it is particularly characteristic of opioids and sedatives but also has been observed with stimulants, cannabis, and tobacco. Cessation of drug use in the tolerant individual precipitates withdrawal, a morbid state that usually persists for some days to weeks, depending on the drug, in its acute phase. Subclinical abstinence symptoms can continue for months in the chronic phase of withdrawal. These chronic abnormalities, best described for opioid drugs, consist of altered sleep patterns, vital signs, and endocrine functions, which may persist for up to a year. Anxiety symptoms, panic attacks, irritability, suspiciousness, low pain tolerance, depressive symptoms, and sometimes manic symptoms may persist for several weeks to several months after a return to abstinence. Stimulant withdrawal tends to be marked by fatigue, hyperphagia, bradycardia, and somnolence. Sedative and opioid withdrawal are accompanied by weakness, anorexia, tachycardia, agitation, and insomnia. Irritability, social withdrawal, and remorse may occur with either category of drug. In the chronic stages of drug dependence, drug usage is often continued more to avoid the withdrawal syndrome than to obtain the acute effects of the drug (Martin and Jasinsky, 1969; Wikler, 1961).

### Host-Agent and Environment-Agent Considerations

Host factors may interact with drug factors in various ways. Insomniac, anxious, rageful, or chronic pain patients may seek relief of their symptoms in opioids and sedatives. Bored or depressed individuals may seek relief in stimulant drugs. Those seeking a pharmacologic "time out" from their ordinary cognitions may enjoy the effect of hallucinogens. Antisocial persons may find enjoyment in the deviant social role afforded by illicit drug use.

As availability of a drug increases in the environment, the prevalence of its use tends to increase as well (Hughes, Barker, Crawford, Jaffee, 1972). Availability of licit drugs (e.g., tobacco) may be governed by such factors as distance between sales outlets, hours of sale, and restrictions on sale to minors. Prohibition of a substance by law usually leads to decreased availability, but this is not inevitably true. In the case of prescribed drugs, availability may be largely due to prescribing habits among physicians. The greatly increased use of benzodiazepines in the late 1960s and 1970s, and their waning use in the 1980s, has hinged on physician prescribing practices. The same has also been true of amphetamine prescribing, which was prevalent during the 1950s and 1960s in many countries, including the United States (Smart, 1980).

Cost of drugs of abuse also influence their use. As the price increases, drug use tends to decrease, even if availability is held constant. This is one argument for drug prohibition laws, which often increase the cost of drugs considerably (because they are illicit) but may not greatly reduce availability. Both price and availability affect society-drug interactions.

## Environmental or Social Factors

### Social Traditions Regarding Drugs of Abuse

Cultures that effectively prohibit or preferentially ignore certain drugs have little or no problems with them. For example, alcohol abuse is uncommon in certain Muslim nations that forbid beverage alcohol for religious reasons. Certain Middle Eastern countries have economy problems with widespread importation of khat, a stimulant that is somewhat stronger than caffeine but weaker than the amphetamines. Because khat must be consumed within 24 hours of being harvested from a bush, its distribution of use is limited to the rapidity of accessible commercial transportation. Currently raised only around the Red Sea, it has reached England by way of jet aircraft, and recently even North America.

Patterns of use for a particular drug determine the likelihood that the drug will be associated with abuse. Problematic use is more apt to attend nonritual use, in which some (but not all) adolescents are introduced to the drug by slightly older adolescents, away from family, in a surreptitious fashion, with intoxication as a goal. Use without abuse is more apt to occur when all children or adolescents in the society are introduced to the drug experience in a family-sponsored, multigenerational, socially approved setting, with ritual feasting and celebration.

A dilemma in today's world is that only one or a few drugs can be thus woven into the fabric of a society. Families cannot enculturate (and thereby "immunize") their offspring against all drugs to which they will probably be exposed. In general, cultures approve a few mild intoxicants (e.g., tobacco, caffeine drinks, betel-areca) and perhaps one stronger intoxicant (e.g., alcohol, peyote, cannabis) but not the more addicting or potentially psychopathologic drugs (e.g., heroin, amphetamine, phencyclidine).

### Drug Laws

Antidrug laws began to appear several hundred years ago. Even before the 19th century, the Aztecs, Chinese emperors, and several European kingdoms enacted legislation regarding alcohol, tobacco, and opium. Antidrug legislation accelerated in the 18th century during a time when many new drugs, as well as new routes of administration, were spreading around the world, following the newly established international trade routes of the time. We are still in the midst of this period of drug diffusion as modified drugs (e.g., cocaine from coca, heroin from opium) and new manufactured drugs (e.g., synthetic opioids, sedatives, hallucinogens) spread rapidly from one part of the world to another.

Regulations governing or prohibiting drug use have been most successful in countries with strong centralized power, including both rightist and leftist police states. They have been weakest in the democratic and socialist countries, which rely heavily on citizen support for law enforcement. Legislation alone, without other social interventions, can exacerbate drug problems by driving the drug user into a criminal subculture.

## EPIDEMIOLOGY

### Methods of Study

Epidemiologic assessment is a key step in measuring the extent of drug abuse in the population and in observing the results of treatment and prevention efforts over time. Self report, blood and urine tests, withdrawal signs, and autopsy studies have been used as measures. Sampling methods have ranged from door-to-door surveys to studies of special populations (e.g., students, medical patients, arrested persons in jail).

One special technique used for drug abuse epidemiology is the capture-recapture technique. For example, the number of diagnosed cases may be measured (e.g., those admitted to a treatment program, say 100 over a period of time). Then the number of drug abuse cases surfacing to another facility is measured (e.g., deaths in a morgue or arrests by the police). If any 1 person out of 10 deaths, or arrests, was previously known to the treatment facility, then an estimate of 1000 drug abuse persons in the community would be made. Other factors that must be considered in this technique include duration of time and ingress into or egress from the community.

Another special method has been a registry, most often used for opioid abusers. One central agency collects data on opioid abusers admitted from treatment or rehabilitation, seeking help at social agencies, arrested, convicted for opioid possession, dead from an opioid-related cause, and so forth.

Complications of drug abuse have also been used. These include antibodies against serum hepatitis as epidemiologic indicators (from parenteral injection) and overdose deaths from opioids and sedatives. Because many non-drug factors can influence such data, they tend to have a low stability, and thus a poor reliability over time.

## Rates of Drug Abuse

Rates of drug abuse in the United States often fluctuate widely over time and from place to place. Several opioid "epidemics" have occurred in the 20th century, especially during and after war actions. An amphetamine "epidemic" occurred in the late 1950s and early 1960s. Tobacco dependence has increased progressively over the past century, first among men and more recently among women. Cannabis abuse increased markedly during the late 1960s and did not begin to decline until the early 1980s. Cocaine abuse and dependence continued at stable levels during the 1970s and then increased dramatically in the early 1980s. Al-

though sedatives are largely obtained from physicians by prescription, attention has been increasingly focused on excessive use. During a recent 12-month period, pharmacists filled 85 million prescriptions for diazepam alone.

## Demographic Characteristics

Men generally engage in drug abuse more frequently than women, although there are exceptions. Betel-areca dependence in parts of Asia and sedative abuse in North America and in Europe have occurred predominantly among women. In recent years the rates of tobacco and alcohol dependence have been increasing more among American women than among men.

Since World War II, drug abuse has begun to affect teenagers to a considerable extent; it formerly began primarily in adulthood. There has been an especially dramatic upsurge in the use of heroin, cannabis, tobacco, volatile hydrocarbons, and hallucinogens among youths. Cocaine, amphetamine, and sedative abuse still tend to begin later. Elderly people have shown increased rates of alcohol and sedative abuse, often in association with death of a marital partner, isolation from friends and family in old-age residences, major depression, chronic pain, and disabling medical conditions (Cohen, 1981).

Socioeconomic variables affect the availability and type of drugs used. For example, successful athletes and entertainers have had both the money for and access to such drugs as cocaine and heroin. This has also been true of many smugglers bringing drugs into the United States. Because of the poor interdiction of drugs by law enforcement officers, even students have been able to afford cannabis, stimulants, and sedatives.

Medical workers are especially liable to abuse of prescription drugs. Out of 10 substance-abusing physicians, 1 is usually abusing drugs only. The remaining 9 are abusing alcohol primarily, while abusing other drugs to offset the effects of alcohol. Drug-dependent physicians have preferred the synthetic opioids in recent years, perhaps because these drugs have been incorrectly touted as less addicting than the opium-based drugs (e.g., morphine). Nurses, pharmacists, and dentists show similar patterns. Among younger health professionals, drug abuse with illicit, or "street," drugs has appeared in recent years.

## PATHOLOGY

Pathologic consequences from drug abuse varies widely with the drug, dosage, and duration of use. Route of administration is also an important consideration.

## Opioids

Although opioid drugs differ considerably in dosage and duration of action, the maximal potency of the stronger opioid drugs (e.g., morphine, heroin, fentanyl, methadone) is similar. Weaker opioids (e.g., codeine, propoxyphene) cannot equal them, even in large dosage. Some opioids, such as pentazocine, have mixed agonist-antagonist effects. In order to ameliorate the antagonist effects, drug abusers may take such drugs with antihistamines. The recently popular "Ts and blues" among opioid dependents consist of Talwin along with an antihistamine in a blue capsule.

Opioids can relieve pain, anxiety, cough, and diarrhea. Especially in the naive user, they produce nausea and vomiting. Although acute doses may relieve social and sexual inhibition, chronic use leads, paradoxically, to social withdrawal and decreased libido. Tolerance to analgesia begins within a few days, so that opioids are excellent for acute, severe pain but poor choices for chronic or recurrent pain.

Acute effects include meiosis or pinpoint pupils (which occurs with most but not all opioids), constipation, hypotension, lethargy, coma, and possibly death by respiratory depression. The withdrawal syndrome, beginning 4 to 12 hours after the last dose (depending on the drug), consists of agitation, piloerection, dilated pupils, muscle aches, and abdominal cramps. A subclinical withdrawal syndrome, consisting of sleep disturbance, irritability, vital sign fluctuations, and autonomic system lability, may persist for several months in tolerant individuals (Wikler, 1961; Jaffee, 1980).

## Sedatives

Sedatives include the benzodiazepines, barbiturates, glutethimide, methaqualone, chloral hydrate, paraldehyde, and ethchlorvynol. Although they show cross tolerance with alcohol, they are synthetic and chemically dissimilar to each other. Sedatives with shorter half-lives tend to be more readily abused. Longer-acting sedatives allow a safer, stabler withdrawal regimen.

Sedative drugs are more apt to be abused by those presenting to physicians with insomnia, palpitations, tachycardia, headache, epigastric burning, or similar psychophysiologic symptoms of anxiety. Much sedative abuse in the United States is iatrogenic. Careful psychiatric assessment and careful monitoring of sedative prescribing are key strategies in reducing sedative abuse.

Duration of action and margin of safety differ widely among the sedatives. Like the opioids and alcohol, they can produce tolerance if taken chronically in increasing doses. Acute effects include incoordination, dysarthria, lethargy, somnolence, coma, and death by respiratory depression. The withdrawal syndrome consists variably of tachycardia, fever, hypertension, headache, agitation, tremor, seizure, confusion, delusions, and hallucinations. Onset of withdrawal can occur within several hours after the last dose in the case of short-acting barbiturates, or several days with the long-acting diazepines (Smith and Wesson, 1971; Maletzky and Klotter, 1976).

## Amphetamines and Similar Drugs

Amphetamines (including methylphenidate) are often abused by night workers, those doing prolonged repetitive work (e.g., truck drivers), or chronically dysthymic individuals. Formerly obtained primarily from physicians, most amphetamines today come from illegal sources.

Amphetamines facilitate the release of noradrenalin, thereby increasing pulse, blood pressure, metabolic rate, and sometimes temperature. Stimulant effects on the central nervous system include mydriasis, tachycardia, elevated mood, heightened self-confidence, alertness, and wakefulness with a decrease in rapid-eye-movement (REM) sleep.

Tolerance and increased daily doses occur in chronic users. Confusion, panic, and paranoia may ensue, and a psychotic state similar to schizophrenia or mania can persist for days, weeks, or months. Hyperthermia, arrhythmias, convulsions, and cerebrovascular accidents accompany overdose. A withdrawal consists of lethargy and increased REM sleep. Depression often appears after withdrawal; this may be a withdrawal effect, the emergence of a primary depression, or a combination of both (Ellinwood, 1967).

## Cocaine

Like amphetamine abuse, cocaine abuse is apt to ensue in the user who is bored, fatigued, or depressed. Because the half-life is short compared with other drugs of abuse, the user may snort, smoke, or inject drugs several times an hour to obtain the drug effect. Under such circumstances the cost of a cocaine habit mounts readily. The heavy user may become financially destitute or enter an illegal occupation (e.g., drug smuggling or selling, burglary, prostitution) to obtain the drug (Cohen, 1981).

One form of cocaine is hydrochloride, taken by injection or snorting. The paste form, used for smoking, involves an extraction from coca leaves, using kerosene and sulfuric acid. Cocaine potentiates catecholamine effect by interfering with reuptake. Its effects are similar to those of amphetamine but with a half-life persisting over minutes rather than hours. Certain complications resemble those of amphetamine abuse, such as paranoia, hallucinations, and hypertension.

## Cannabis

Although numerous psychoactive compounds exist in cannabis, most of its effect appears to be caused by delta-9-tetrahydrocannabinal. Potency of cannabis preparation varies with proximity to the equator, climate, plant species, parts of the plant consumed, and procedures to increase potency (e.g., hashish). It may be consumed by eating or smoking. Effect persists for a few to several hours, depending on dose, tolerance, and pattern of use.

Many people can consume small amounts of cannabis at infrequent intervals (i.e., weekly or monthly) without ill effect. Vulnerable individuals may experience hallucinations, delusions, or confusion at low doses. With chronic, heavy use, the percentage of impaired users probably increases.

Intoxication involves aspects of both stimulation and depression, sympathetic and parasympathetic manifestations, including dry mouth, increased appetite, tachycardia, injected conjunctivae, and relaxation. At lower doses coordination for simple tasks is not impaired; with higher doses balance and complex tasks become increasingly impeded. Minutes may be perceived as hours. This may contribute to the enhanced sexual enjoyment reported by some. Short-term memory loss leads to disjointed thinking, with consequent silliness, social withdrawal, or panic.

Some tolerance occurs with chronic use, but a distinct withdrawal syndrome has not been described. Because tetrahydrocannabinal is stored in fat, chronic users may demonstrate cannabis effect and excrete the drug for days after the last use (Jaffee, 1980).

## Tobacco

Whether consumed by smoking, snuffing, or chewing, tobacco's psychoactive effect is largely due to nicotine. Like cocaine, the half-life of nicotine is brief (less than an hour). Many carcinogens also coexist in tobacco. Nicotine, which mimics the effects of acetylcholine, acts as a mild stimulant. Although smoking produces almost instantaneous effect, absorption after oral ingestion is slow. Effects include increased heart rate, gastric atony, and peripheral vasoconstriction. Large doses may cause nausea, emesis, and convulsions. Withdrawal effects include bradycardia, irritability, and increased appetite.

Heavy smokers maintain plasma nicotine levels by smoking tobacco about every half hour. Tobacco consumption in dependent persons may be linked to such biologic events as waking up, eating, and bowel movements. Other smoking reinforcers may be more social in nature (e.g., meeting with friends, sexual encounters). If the nicotine content in a cigarette is decreased, dependent smokers adjust by increasing their inhalations.

As a mild intoxicant, with few or mild effects on cognition, mood, and coordination, tobacco seldom produces acute problems. However, it can be a health hazard, sometimes producing catastrophic damage, such as heart disease and lung cancer. Health complications increase markedly after 20 pack-years of smoking (i.e., one pack per day per year over 20 years). Although tobacco dependence is notoriously difficult to reverse permanently, physician recommendations to cease tobacco use are effective (Russel, 1971).

## Caffeine

In low doses, caffeine reduces fatigue and enhances mental activity, while causing some tachycardia, vasodilatation, and diuresis. It produces these effects by stimulating catecholamine release (Bellet, Roman, DeCastro, Kim, Kershbaum, 1969). Higher doses (i.e., more than 600 mg per day) may produce excitement, agitation, headache, irritability, and insomnia. Withdrawal symptoms in high-dose users can include fatigue and somnolence (Driesbach and Pfeiffer, 1943; Greden, 1981). Caffeine is present in many common beverages, including coffee, tea, cocoa, colas, and other soft drinks. It is also present in many over-the-counter and prescription drugs taken for pain, appetite suppression, and the common cold.

## Volatile Hydrocarbons

Volatile hydrocarbons have the same psychotoxic effects as alcohol but with a shorter half-life, often less than an hour. Because they are available, inexpensive, and short-acting, special populations, such as prisoners and children, sniff them. Aerosols, glue, cleaning and industrial solvents, and paint thinners can produce hepatic, renal, hematologic, or neurologic damage, depending on the chemical, pattern of use, and individual propensity. Early symptoms, which may come to the attention of a pediatrician or psychiatrist, are irritability, declining academic or occupational perform-

ance, memory loss, and personality change. Health students and professionals have sometimes abused anesthetic agents, especially nitrous oxide. Amyl nitrate use for sexual enhancement has led to chronic abuse, especially in recent years (Easson, 1962; Lowry, 1979; Prockop, 1977).

## Phencyclidine

Phencyclidine (PCP) is a versatile drug; it may be ingested, snuffed, smoked, or injected. Its effects are variable, so that it may produce relaxation or panic, hypotension or hypertension, decreased reflexes or status epilepticus. In general, it potentiates adrenergic effects. Impurities from illicit production may cause anticholinergic effects. Body image distortions, agitation, and hallucinations are common in PCP users coming to clinical attention. Vertical or horizontal nystagmus, muscle rigidity, and dystonic reactions are clues to the diagnosis. Half-life is relatively short, but after effects can continue over hours or a few days. Acute and chronic users may present to emergency rooms with various psychiatric syndromes, from panic attack, to mania, to schizophreniform psychosis, to delirium (Cohen, 1981).

## Hallucinogens

Hallucinogens include natural substances (e.g., peyote, morning glory seeds) and synthetic compounds (e.g., D-lysergic acid, or LSD). Altered perceptual states are produced; panic, hallucinations, and delusions may occur. Although the half-life of these drugs is only a few hours, psychic effects may persist for 6 to 12 hours. Hallucinosis may continue for a few to several days in unusual cases. In vulnerable individuals, mania or schizophreniform pyschosis may ensue. Physical manifestations are few except when anticholinergic properties are present (Cohen, 1981).

## CLINICAL PICTURE

### The Great Imitator

The clinical picture depends on the drug, duration of abuse, route of administration, nutrition, associated medical and psychiatric problems, social and economic impairment. Impairment may be minimal, with only mild signs or symptoms, or so severe that signs and symptoms irrefutably support the diagnosis. Patients may hide, alter, or accurately describe the drug use and its associated problems, depending on their openness, wish for help, and extent of discomfort. A key factor is the clinician's comfort and skill in aiding patients to relate their history. A nonjudgmental attitude toward patients is also critical. Clinical skill, as well as judgment, in managing drug abuse cases requires supervised clinical training. Without training and experience, the clinician is not likely to perceive the clinical picture accurately.

Substance abuse has been called the Great Imitator of our time for good reason. It may present with medical, psychiatric, or surgical pictures. Drug abusers are found in medical settings more frequently than expected from their number in the population. Drug-related problems are proportionately more common among inpatients than among outpatients. Patients may present quite early in their course or in severely advanced stages. The problem may be acute or chronic, life threatening or minor, readily discerned or vague and difficult to define (Dupont, Goldstein, O'Donnell, 1979).

## Data Collection

Drug abuse patients usually seek clinical help because of some coercive force, either external (e.g., family, work supervisor) or internal (e.g., malaise, depression). An important step in management involves delineating this coercive force. Complicating this process is the patient's frequent lack of awareness regarding the relationship between the current problem and the drug use. Another obstacle is the patient's tendency to blame others for the current problems rather than to take responsibility for the problem.

Because drug abuse may present with various surgical, medical, or psychiatric problems, the clinician will want to inquire routinely about each patient's use of drugs. In order to rule drug abuse in or out, the physician must know each patient's drug use type (if present), duration, dose, pattern,

and route of administration. Most drug-abusing patients do not volunteer symptoms indicative of depression, anxiety, panic, or psychosis; specific inquiry is necessary.

Formal mental status often reveals unsuspected deficits in orientation, memory, or cognition. Physical examination can demonstrate evidence of parenteral injection (e.g., venous tracks, skin popping scars), chronic smoking (e.g., rales and rhonchi), malnutrition, infectious diseases, and traumatic sequelae. Neurologic findings (e.g., ataxia, dysarthria, pupillary changes), autonomic signs (e.g., flushing, perspiration, piloerection), and vital sign abnormalities (e.g., tachycardia, hypertension) provide valuable clues. See Table 14–1 for signs associated with various drugs.

## Analysis of Findings

Acute drug-related problems are generally related to pharmacologic actions of the drug itself, or the route of administration. Problems include intoxication, overdose, withdrawal, and such medical emergencies as agitated delirium, malignant hyperthermia, and anaphylaxis. This is the opposite of many other disorders in which early manifestations are subjective and historical, while objective biomedical signs appear in later stages. On the contrary, the initial problems associated with chronic use tend to result from psychosocial complications. These may be elicited by a careful history but are not evident on physical examination. Socioeconomic deterioration, increasing family alienation and social withdrawal, progressive (rather than static) sociopathy, and legal problems should raise the index of suspicion for drug abuse.

Special clinical pictures depend on the drug and the setting. Amotivational syndromes and decline in grades are seen among adolescents in schools. Families report anger, oppositional behavior, and personality change. Monday morning absenteeism and injuries occur in the workplace. Family members and friends may observe social withdrawal or secretive behavior. Nurses or physicians may note drug-seeking behaviors, with symptomatic complaints out of proportion to physical or laboratory findings.

## CLINICAL COURSE

The typical course of untreated, chronic drug abuse is deterioration over a period of years, often with periods of relative stabilization or brief improvement followed by further deterioration. Acute problems associated with recent drug abuse may cause the disorder to be self-limiting, if the consequences motivate the user to moderate or cease drug usage. However, spontaneous abstinence from drugs occurs infrequently among those with recurrent episodes of drug abuse or with chronic drug dependence. Death or lifelong disability may complicate the picture even before drug dependence is established (Vaillant 1970, 1973).

Duration of course, like the clinical picture, varies with the drug, route of administration, and various host and environmental factors. Other things being equal, routes with rapid drug onset (i.e., injection, smoking, snuffing) hasten the morbid course over slower routes of administration (e.g., ingestion, chewing). Drugs with shorter half-lives (e.g., heroin, amytal, cocaine) lead to a more rapid course than those with longer half-lives (e.g., opium, diazepam, amphetamine). More potent drugs (e.g., morphine, methadone) hasten and increase the morbid effects over weaker drugs in the same category (e.g., codeine, propoxyphene). Some drugs usually produce medical complications (e.g., tobacco) or neuropsychiatric complications (e.g., phencyclidine) as their first manifestation, whereas others are more apt initially to produce psychosocial consequences (e.g., sedatives, opioids). Despite these differences, most drug-dependent patients present for treatment within 3 years of initiating their drug abuse, although some individuals may go as long as 10 years without treatment.

Age at onset influences the course, so that opioid dependence beginning at age 15 affects the patient's life course different from opioid dependence beginning at age 35. Younger individuals have not yet had the opportunity to complete their education, learn an occupation, become employed, marry, have children, or otherwise establish some social competency. Older drug abusers coming to treatment usually have more biomedical problems and social isolation, whereas younger drug abusers gradually experience more legal, occupational, and marital problems. At times, women show a more rapid progression than men, but this is not always so (Wilsnack, 1982).

Individual differences also exist. In one survey of opioid-dependent subjects, I encountered one subject who presented initially for treatment after 3 months of dependence and another who presented for his first treatment experience after 45 years of dependence. Despite these extremes, it was unusual for most opioid-dependent subjects to have their first treatment before 1 year or after 10 years of opioid dependence.

Tables 14–2 through 14–6 describe arbitrary phases in the course of drug abuse. Course progression is not always as consistent as shown in the tables, however. A patient may show early changes in some areas along with more advanced changes in other areas.

Treatment usually, but not always, alters the natural course of drug abuse. In general, treatment earlier in the course tends to be more effective and less costly. Later treatment, especially after occupational loss and alienation from family, is less apt to be effective. Even in advanced cases, however, treatment often reduces the patient's morbidity and may set the stage for eventual recovery.

Acute phases of recovery, from medical, psychiatric, or social crises, usually take place over several weeks. Later recovery from autonomic instability, remorse, and social isolation occurs over several months. Psychological well-being, social fulfillment, and occupational stability may require a few to several years. Brief but increasingly less frequent return to drug abuse often persists during the early months of recovery. Although pharmacologic factors greatly influence the pretreatment course, the posttreatment relapse rates for heroin, alcohol, and tobacco (in the absence of ongoing outpatient treatment) are remarkably similar, as shown in Figure 14–1 (Hunt, Barnett, Branch, 1971).

## LABORATORY FINDINGS

Laboratory tests for drug abuse are of two kinds. One set of tests involves direct assessment of drugs or drug action in the body, such as drug levels in body fluids or administration of an antagonist to precipi-

**TABLE 14–1    Drug Signs**

| | INTOXICATION | | | | | | OVERDOSE | | | | | | WITHDRAWAL | | | |
|---|---|---|---|---|---|---|---|---|---|---|---|---|---|---|---|---|
| | Alcohol | Stimulants | Sedatives | Opiates | Hallucinogens | Phencyclidine | Alcohol | Stimulants | Sedatives | Opiates | Hallucinogens | Phencyclidine | Alcohol | Stimulants | Sedatives | Opiates |
| **Vital Signs** | | | | | | | | | | | | | | | | |
| Circulatory collapse | | | | | | | ● | | ● | ● | ● | | ● | | ● | ● |
| Hypertension | | ● | | | | ● | | ● | | | ● | ● | ● | | ● | |
| Hyperthermia | | ● | | | ● | | | ● | | | ● | | ● | | ● | |
| Orthostatic hypotension | | | | | | | ● | | ● | ● | | | ● | | ● | |
| Respiration, slow and shallow | | | | | | | ● | | ● | ● | | | | | | |
| Tachycardia | | ● | | | ● | ● | ● | ● | | | ● | ● | ● | | ● | ● |
| **Appearance, Behavior, Mental Status** | | | | | | | | | | | | | | | | |
| Affect, labile | ● | ● | ● | ● | ● | ● | ● | ● | ● | ● | ● | ● | ● | ● | ● | ● |
| Comprehension, slow | ● | | ● | ● | ● | ● | ● | | ● | ● | ● | ● | ● | | ● | ● |
| Delirium | ● | ● | ● | | | ● | ● | ● | ● | ● | ● | ● | ● | | ● | |
| Delusions | ● | ● | ● | ● | | ● | ● | ● | ● | ● | ● | ● | ● | | ● | |
| Depressed mood | ● | | ● | | | | ● | | ● | | | | ● | ● | ● | ● |
| Euphoria | ● | ● | ● | ● | ● | ● | | | | | | | | | | |
| Hostile, assaultive | ● | ● | ● | | | | | ● | | | ● | ● | ● | | ● | ● |
| Irritability | ● | ● | ● | | | ● | | ● | | | ● | ● | ● | ● | ● | ● |
| Lethargy | ● | | ● | ● | | | ● | | ● | ● | | | | ● | | |
| Memory, poor | ● | | ● | ● | | ● | ● | | ● | ● | | | ● | | ● | ● |
| Restlessness | | ● | | | ● | ● | ● | ● | ● | ● | ● | ● | ● | | ● | ● |
| Skin picking | | ● | | ● | | | | ● | | | | | ● | | ● | |
| Suspiciousness | | ● | | | ● | ● | | ● | | | ● | ● | ● | ● | ● | |
| Sweating | | | | | | | | ● | | | | | ● | | ● | ● |
| Talkativeness | ● | ● | ● | ● | | | | ● | | | | | | | | |
| Vomiting | ● | | | ● | | ● | ● | ● | ● | ● | ● | ● | ● | | ● | ● |
| Yawning | | | ● | | | | | | | | | | | | | ● |

Adapted from Westermeyer J: Primer on Chemical Dependency: A Clinical Guide to Alcohol and Drug Problems. Baltimore, Williams & Wilkins, 1976.

TABLE 14–1   (*continued*)

| | INTOXICATION | | | | | | OVERDOSE | | | | | | WITHDRAWAL | | | |
| --- | --- | --- | --- | --- | --- | --- | --- | --- | --- | --- | --- | --- | --- | --- | --- | --- |
| | ALCOHOL | STIMULANTS | SEDATIVES | OPIATES | HALLUCINOGENS | PHENCYCLIDINE | ALCOHOL | STIMULANTS | SEDATIVES | OPIATES | HALLUCINOGENS | PHENCYCLIDINE | ALCOHOL | STIMULANTS | SEDATIVES | OPIATES |
| **Eyes, Ears, Nose, and Throat** | | | | | | | | | | | | | | | | |
| Coryza | | | | | | | | | | | | | | | | ● |
| Lacrimation | | | | | | | | | | | | | | | | |
| Mouth, dry | | ● | | ● | | | | ● | | ● | | | | | | |
| Nystagmus | ● | | ● | | | ● | ● | | ● | | | ● | ● | | | |
| Pupils, dilated | | ● | | | | | ● | ● | ● | ● | ● | ● | | | | ● |
| Pupils, pinpoint | | | | ● | | | | | | ● | | | | | | |
| Rhinorrhea | | | | | | | | | | | | | ● | | | |
| **Neurological Examination** | | | | | | | | | | | | | | | | |
| Analgesia to pinprick | ● | | ● | ● | | ● | ● | ● | ● | ● | | ● | | | | |
| Coma | | | | | | | ● | | ● | ● | | ● | | | | |
| Convulsions | | | ● | | | | ● | ● | ● | ● | ● | ● | ● | ● | | ● |
| Dysmetria | ● | | ● | ● | | ● | ● | | ● | ● | | | | | | |
| Facial grimacing | | | | | | ● | | ● | | | | | | | | |
| Hypotonia | ● | | ● | ● | | | ● | | ● | ● | | | | ● | | |
| Muscle spasms (rigidity) | | | | | | ● | | ● | | | | ● | ● | | ● | ● |
| Reflexes, hyperactive | | ● | | | | ● | | ● | | ● | | ● | ● | | ● | ● |
| Speech, slurred | ● | | ● | ● | | ● | ● | | ● | ● | | | | | | |
| Stare, blank | ● | | ● | ● | ● | ● | ● | ● | ● | ● | | ● | | | | |
| Tremor | ● | ● | ● | | | | | ● | | | | ● | ● | | ● | ● |
| **Skin** | | | | | | | | | | | | | | | | |
| Flushing | ● | | ● | ● | | | ● | ● | | ● | ● | | ● | | ● | |
| Piloerection (gooseflesh) | | | | | | | | | | | | | | | | ● |

**TABLE 14–2    Phases of Chemical Dependency: Behavioral Factors**

| Characteristic | Early Phase: Problematic Usage | Middle Phase: Chronic Dependence, Addiction | Late Phase: Deterioration |
|---|---|---|---|
| Drug usage | Increasing amounts and frequency of use | "Titer" or "binge" usage; attempts at abstinence | Continuous usage; uses "substitute" intoxicants |
| Control over usage | Begins attempts to decrease amounts or frequency of use | Begins to lose control (takes more than intended or for a longer period than intended) | Loses control most of the time |
| Drug-related behavior | Seeks occasions to use; chooses friends who use heavily; may begin to be secretive about usage | Increased need to use at specific times and places; develops ingenuity at obtaining, paying for, hiding, and using drug | Compulsive usage, despite many problems associated with usage and decreased enjoyment from drug or alcohol; plans daily activities around usage |
| Drug effects on behavior | Episodic intoxication, dysarthria, emotional lability; attempts to hide drug or alcohol effects from others | Impairment between intoxication episodes: trite expressions and "non sequiturs" prevail in conversation; fatigue; decreased productivity | Poor grooming, disheveled dress; lack of interest in appearance; unconcern with opinions of others |

tate withdrawal (e.g., naloxone for opiate dependence). Another set of tests involves indirect biochemical, physiologic, and psychological tests to assess the extent of impairment produced by drugs. These tests augment but cannot substitute for a thorough history, psychiatric interview, mental status, and physical examination. Another important assessment technique is the "test of time," in which the individual is observed and reassessed over time in order to determine the severity of the condition.

Many drugs of abuse can be found in urine for 12 to 48 hours after the last dose, and sometimes longer in the case of chronic use (e.g., cannabis). Qualitative urine tests are useful for screening in high-risk situations, such as emergency rooms, orthopedic

**TABLE 14–3    Phases of Chemical Dependency: Psychologic Factors**

| Characteristic | Early Phase: Problematic Usage | Middle Phase: Chronic Dependence, Addiction | Late Phase: Deterioration |
|---|---|---|---|
| Motivation | Uses to enjoy, build up confidence, relieve insomnia, anxiety, etc.; use becomes increasingly important | Uses to feel normal; use is as important as family, friends, work | Enjoys usage less, but cannot stop; use becomes the central element of person's life |
| Emotional concomitants | Mood swings related to usage: anger, remorse, anxiety; shamed or anxious regarding usage; feels weak, remorseful | Personality change, increasing emotional lability; ambivalent about usage; feels guilty, resentful, inadequate, inferior | Erratic, suspicious, often apathetic; defensive regarding usage; feels alone, deserted |
| Cognitive processes | Obsesses regarding next usage; reduced interests and ambition; focuses thoughts and conversation on chemical usage | Increasing self-pity, deteriorating self-image; self-deception regarding usage and its effects; loses sense of time | Confused, projects own problems onto others; unable to conceptualize current status objectively |
| Judgment, insight | Begins to exercise poor judgment; still able to extricate self from most problems; episodic insight and concern with drug or alcohol usage | Large proportion of decisions lead to problems; problem solving increasingly ineffective; avoids being insightful, although capable of insight | Extremely poor judgment in most matters; unable to solve own problems; is not insightful even during abstinent intervals |

TABLE 14–4    Phases of Chemical Dependency: Social Factors

| Characteristic | Early Phase: Problematic Usage | Middle Phase: Chronic Dependence, Addiction | Late Phase: Deterioration |
|---|---|---|---|
| Interpersonal relationships | Changes associates, from abstainers and moderate users to heavy users | Alienates others by arguing, embarrassing, taking advantage; breaks promises, lies | Manipulates others to obtain drug or alcohol; compensatory bragging |
| Family | Argues with family over usage; spends less time at home; neglects family emotionally | Abuses family by lying, stealing, or fighting; spends most of time away from home | Alienated from family; lives away from family |
| Employment | "Monday morning" absenteeism; conflict with boss | Decreased job efficiency; changes jobs often or is fired; decreasing job prestige; holds jobs for shorter periods | Day labor; unemployed, on relief or social welfare |
| Residence | Stable residence; lives with others | Begins moving from place to place; loses roommates, family members | Lower socioeconomic neighborhood; lives alone |
| School* | Decreasing grades; complaints from teachers | Suspension from school; school dropout | Requires special educational and rehabilitation facilities |
| Legal effects | May have legal problems; driving while intoxicated, disorderly, assault | Usually has legal problems and large attorney fees; may be litigious | Defaults on contractual obligations; may be imprisoned for property offenses, manslaughter |
| Finances | Spends family funds on drug or alcohol; may take extra job to support habit; may become extravagant | Spends $\frac{1}{4}$ to $\frac{1}{2}$ of annual income on drug or alcohol; heavily in debt, bankruptcy | Spends most of income on drugs or alcohol; destitute |
| Social affiliations | Discontinues social activities not involving usage (e.g., church, hobby, theater, sports) | Drops formal group affiliations (e.g., union, guild, club); begins short-lived companionship with chemically dependent persons | Becomes an involuntary client of social institutions |

* For chemically dependent persons of school age.

and psychiatric hospital admissions, and certain target groups (e.g., trauma victims, brittle diabetics, treatment failures). Quantitative blood measures are usually required only for special instances, such as management of overdose or forensic evaluation. Naloxone challenge, specific for the diagnosis of opioid dependence, consists of administering parenteral naloxone and observing for the opioid withdrawal syndrome.

The second group of laboratory tests can aid in assessing the severity of the drug abuse problem. Acute intoxication or recent withdrawal may produce abnormalities on the electroencephalogram, which can suggest specific drug effects to the experienced electroencephalographer. Biochemical tests for renal and hepatic function reflect drug-related tissue damage to these organs. Vitamin levels (e.g., carotene or folic acid), serum iron, and serum protein can reveal nutritional neglect. With chronic drug abuse, many patients experience mild to moderate endocrine dysfunctions reflected in thyroid tests, electrolyte disturbances, hematologic abnormalities, hyperglycemia or hypoglycemia, and an abnormal dexamethasone suppression test. Chronic smoking produces physiologic changes in respiratory dead space, vital capacity, rate of timed expiration, and blood gases. Parenteral injection can give rise to positive blood cultures, an elevated sedimentation rate, high white blood cell count, and an increased gamma globulin fraction in the serum protein. Depending on the psychiatric picture, abnormalities may occur on personality tests (e.g., the Minnesota Multiphasic Personality Inventory), intelligence tests (e.g., Wechsler Intelligence Scales), and organicity tests (e.g., Bender-Gestalt). Secondary traumatic injuries (from fights or falls) may show up as healing fractures on x-ray of the ribs or extremities.

**TABLE 14–5   Phases of Chemical Dependency: Biomedical Factors**

| Characteristic | Early Phase: Problematic Usage | Middle Phase: Chronic Dependence, Addiction | Late Phase: Deterioration |
|---|---|---|---|
| Pharmacology | Tolerance increases; larger doses used to relax, relieve insomnia or other symptoms | Withdrawal effects; blackout (for alcohol); morning or daytime usage to alleviate withdrawal | Decreased tolerance (early onset of intoxication or blackout); delirium tremens or withdrawal seizure (with alochol or sedatives) |
| Common health problems | Injuries: vehicular or industrial, accidents, falls, burns | Infections: respiratory, urogenital, skin; injuries; accidental overdosage; suicide attempts | Parenteral users: septicemia, pulmonary edema, endocarditis; alcoholics: cirrhosis, pancreatitis, myocarditis; violence: injuries, homicide, suicide; nutritional problems: vitamin, protein, mineral deficiency |
| Sexual effects | May initially enhance sexual function | Sexual problems: impotence, frigidity, promiscuity or extramarital liaisons, venereal disease | Difficulty obtaining sexual partner; purchase of sexual services; loss of interest in sex; prostitution to obtain funds for drug |
| Common symptoms | Insomnia, boredom, chronic anxiety, headache, palpitation, tachycardia, flatulence, belching, cramps, epigastric distress, irritability, puffy face or extremities | Sweating, apprehension, decreased libido, visual disturbances, myalgia, malaise, obesity, diarrhea, weight change (loss or gain), memory lapses, weak, fatigues easily, "dry heaves," depression, panic, fears | Bad taste, impotence, halitosis, cachexia, persistent abdominal pain, seizures |

**TABLE 14–6   Phases of Chemical Dependency: Treatment Approaches**

| Characteristic | Early Phase: Problematic Usage | Middle Phase: Chronic Dependence, Addiction | Late Phase: Deterioration |
|---|---|---|---|
| Prognosis without treatment | Some spontaneously improve, some progress to later stages (percentages unknown) | Small percentage (<10%) spontaneously improve; most progress to later stage | Virtually no spontaneous improvement; a few "plateau"; most deteriorate rapidly |
| Most effective treatment modalities | Self-help groups; marital, family therapy; selective use of pharmacotherapy for 1–2 years (e.g., antidepressants, Antabuse); partial hospitalization (e.g., day only, evening only, weekend only) | Initial residential treatment: hospital unit, therapeutic community, halfway house, followed by some outpatient treatment methods as in "early phase" | Long-term residential treatment: special long-term units, nursing home, quarterway house, followed by "middle" and "early" treatment methods in selected cases |
| Prognosis with treatment | Optimal: 60%–80% "significantly improved" at 1 year posttreatment | Fairly good: 40%–60% "significantly improved" at 1 year posttreatment | Poor: 10%–20% improved at 1 year; high mortality and morbidity rate in remainder |
| Cooperation with treatment | Willing to undertake a prolonged period of abstinence, see physician regularly, follow treatment recommendations | Does not enter treatment unless pressured by family, employer, court, friends, physician | Will not undertake abstinence voluntarily; must be coerced by society (e.g., incarceration, legal commitment into treatment) |

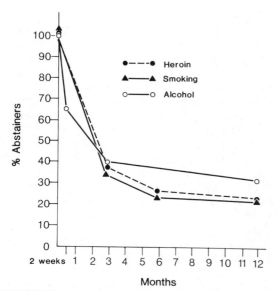

**FIGURE 14–1.** Relapse Rate Over Time for Heroin, Smoking, and Alcohol. From: Hunt, W.A., Barnett, L.W., Branch, L.G.: Relapse rates in addiction programs. *J. Clin. Psychol.* 27:455–456, 1971.

Response to treatment can be assessed by following both the first category of tests (e.g., direct drug measures) and the second cateogory (e.g., tests of impairment), especially when these have previously been abnormal.

## DIFFERENTIAL DIAGNOSIS

Differentiating drug abuse from other psychiatric disorder is often difficult. Substance abuse and psychiatric disorder coexist in one quarter to one third of psychiatric patients and in about the same proportion of substance abuse patients. Drug abuse may develop as an attempt at self-treatment for a preexisting disorder (e.g., stimulant abuse for depression, sedative abuse for anxiety or mania). Or secondary psychiatric disturbances (e.g., reactive depression, panic disorder) may appear in the later stages of drug abuse. Secondary sociopathy may attend the disinhibiting effects of certain drugs. Hostile-dependent behavior is a common secondary behavioral manifestation that clears with successful recovery.

Drug effects may mimic psychiatric disorder. For example, caffeine, cocaine, or amphetamine intoxication can produce symptoms like those of anxiety or mania (Greden, 1974). Withdrawal from these drugs may resemble depression or, less often, paranoia. Acute cannabis, PCP, or hallucinogen intoxication may present clinically as acute schizophreniform psychosis, manic psychosis, or organic delirium.

Drugs may also precipitate psychiatric syndromes, which persist well beyond the drug effect in the body. Acute or chronic use of cocaine, amphetamine, cannabis, PCP, or the hallucinogens may bring about a lengthy illness that is indistinguishable from schizophrenia or bipolar illness. In some cases the disorder (once successfully treated) does not recur. In other cases the disorder may recur even without subsequent drug abuse, as in this case:

A 19-year-old college student became acutely and floridly psychotic after her first use of hashish. She failed to respond to high doses of neuroleptics prescribed over several weeks but did recover with a course of electroconvulsive therapy and subsequent neuroleptic treatment. A discharge diagnosis of schizoaffective schizophrenia was made. Over the subsequent year her medication was reduced without incident. She later completed graduate school, worked for a few years, and married. Within weeks after the birth of her third child, at age 31, she developed insomnia, racing thoughts, euphoric mood, grandiose plans, and poor judgment (but without hallucinations or delusions). Neuroleptics (in low doses) along with lithium, prescribed on an outpatient basis, led to resolution of her symptoms over several weeks.

In this case it appears that drug abuse may have precipitated as well as exacerbated her first episode. The second episode, without drug abuse, was milder and responded more readily to treatment. Her course suggests that hashish alone did not produce her first illness, but rather precipitated the illness in a person with a premorbid potential for affective disorder.

Drug effect from opioids, sedatives, stimulants, cannabis, PCP and the hallucinogens, and the volatile hydrocarbons may produce an organic brain syndrome, with confusion and delirium. Chronic organic brain syndrome is less common but can occur. Sedative and opioid abusers may also demonstrate it, probably from recurrent hypoxia secondary to respiratory depression. Certain volatile hydrocarbons can, with chronic use, produce dementia pictures similar to those of alcohol. The milder, although dependency-producing, drugs—such as caffeine and tobacco—do not directly produce chronic brain syndromes, but they may indirectly do so as a result of secondary medical complications (e.g., hypertension).

## TREATMENT

### Drug-Related Emergencies

Intoxication is managed simply by observing and protecting the individual until the drug is metabolized or excreted. It is important to ensure that the patient does not injure self or others while the drug is being metabolized or excreted. Involuntary hospitalization may be necessary for 2 or 3 days during this phase.

Overdose is managed on medical or psychiatric units, depending on the nature of the problem and the type of drug involved. Specific antidotes are available for two drug types liable to abuse: opioids and anticholinergics. Naloxone for opioid overdose and physostigmine for anticholinergic overdose share two common features: first, dosage must be individualized for each patient; second, repeated doses at 2- to 3-hour intervals are necessary, since their duration of action is considerably shorter than many drugs of abuse (particularly when taken in large doses). Gastric lavage and administration of activated charcoal remain cornerstones in the treatment of most drug overdoses. Rarely, dialysis may be necessary for sedative overdose; very high blood levels, rapidly progressing stupor, and depression of vital signs constitute indications for dialysis. Acidification of the urine hastens the excretion of PCP and amphetamines, while alkalinization aids excretion of some barbiturates (Bourne, 1976).

Withdrawal treatment hastens recovery, reduces mortality, and can aid in establishing the doctor-patient relationship. It may also induce the suffering patient, still ambivalent about giving up drug dependence, to enter treatment. Opioid and sedative withdrawal are managed by using one or another drug that is cross-tolerant with the drug being abused. Some clinicians use tricyclic drugs for stimulant withdrawal. The first step consists of administering enough drug to make the patient comfortable, even to the point of mild intoxication. For patients in severe withdrawal, most clinicians prefer to administer the first dose intravenously, since oral ingestion or subcutaneous injection of the drug may not be well absorbed. The half-life of the drug used should be at least as long as the drug being abused, and preferably longer (e.g., phenobarbital for seconal dependence, methadone for heroin dependence). Otherwise, the patient will be in and out of withdrawal, frequent doses will be necessary, and the withdrawal will be stormy. For barbiturate withdrawal, some clinicians prefer to administer a shorter-acting drug initially in case the patient requires respiratory assistance with the stabilizing dose. It is important to remember that 30 mg of phenobarbital is equivalent to 100 mg of seconal and pentobarbital. Duration of the withdrawal is shorter for short-acting drugs and longer for longer-acting drugs. For short-acting drugs, such as amytal or heroin, 5- to 10-day withdrawal regimens are adequate for resolution of acute symptoms. Intermediate-acting drugs, such as seconal and opium, require 10 to 20 days, depending on the degree of dependence and the patient's medical condition. Longer withdrawal regimens, lasting for several weeks to a few months, may be needed for the long-acting drugs, such as diazepam and ethchlorvynol. Doses should be administered on a routine basis rather than as requested by the patient. For example, a 20 per cent daily reduction would cover a 5-day withdrawal, or 10 per cent daily for a 10-day withdrawal. Patients should understand that some mild insomnia or discomfort may still occur. Patients should be dissuaded from seeking sedatives, analgesics, antiemetics, and other symptomatic drugs, since these may mask underlying medical or psychiatric disorders that should be identified and managed appropriately.

Common medical complications associated with drug abuse should be considered early during patient assessment. These include nutritional abnormalities, acute and chronic infections, and occult trauma.

Referral to special drug treatment programs may be necessary if those providing early medical care do not have resources for further treatment. Patients commonly view such a referral as a rejection by the physician. This can be avoided by making an appointment for the patient in a few weeks or months after the referral. If the patient is dissatisfied with or no longer working with the referral resource, the followup appointment provides an opportunity to assess this and consider other alternatives with the patient.

## Treatment Modalities

Modalities for treatment of drug abuse are numerous and include the following (Lowinson and Ruiz, 1981; Patterson, 1974):

- *Residential:* general hospital units, special residential facilities, halfway houses, therapeutic communities
- *Psychotherapies and sociotherapies:* individual, couples, family, and group; verbal aversion; contingency contracting; social skills learning; day, evening, or weekend programs
- *Self help:* Narcotics Anonymous (primarily for illicit drug abusers), Alcoholics Anonymous (primarily for abusers of prescribed or licit drugs, as well as alcohol), Alanon (for relatives of drug abusers)
- *Pharmacotherapies:* methadone (for opioid-dependent patients who have failed other modalities), tricyclic medication (especially for amphetamine- or cocaine-dependent patients and those with persistent depressive symptoms)
- *Somatotherapies:* electrical or chemical aversion, electroacupuncture

If major psychiatric problems persist beyond a few to several days, they will probably not resolve spontaneously. Continuation of major depression, schizophreniform psychosis, mania, and other major disorders beyond 2 weeks almost always calls for specific treatment rather than expectant observation. If the patient responds rapidly and completely to low doses of medication, a lengthy course of medication may not be needed.

Minor or less disabling psychiatric syndromes are common in the early weeks of recovery. These include adjustment reactions, generalized anxiety, and panic disorder. If these are decreasing in severity and becoming less frequent, specific treatment may not be necessary. On the other hand, increasing, severe, or disabling symptoms generally require psychiatric treatment.

## Treatment Goals, Outcome, and Efficacy

Treatment of drug abuse may be aimed at total abstention, reduction of drug use, or removal of problematic aspects from continued drug use. Generally, abstention, temporary or permanent, is the explicit goal. Still, many favorable outcomes from treatment involve reduction in associated problems or in amounts of drug used despite continued or episodic use. Assessment of treatment outcome must take into account these diverse goals of treatment.

Treatment success is related to many factors besides treatment modalities. Patients who are doing better at the end of 1- and 2-year followup studies show the following characteristics (Hunt and Azrin, 1973; Senay, 1983; Westermeyer, 1976):

- Occupied as employees or students
- Living with their families
- Come earlier rather than later to treatment
- Collaborate with treatment recommendations
- Their families are involved in treatment
- Outpatient treatment or self-help activities on a regular basis over 1 or more years
- Receive pharmacotherapies, especially when other modalities have been ineffective

Acute management alone tends to have limited efficacy. This is also true of residential treatment alone with outpatient aftercare. Under such circumstances the rate of abstinence 1 year after discharge is low, usually round 0 per cent to 15 per cent. With aftercare, the rate of abstinence can range up to 80 per cent under optimal conditions, although rates half that are more common. Because those abstinent and doing well at the end of 1 year have good outcomes in most cases, the first year of outpatient care is most critical (McClellan et al., 1982).

Cost benefit from treatment must also be considered. Effective treatment over an adequate period of time is expensive. For unemployed or destitute patients, society must provide the care, and society must be assured that its funds are well spent. Ethical considerations also intrude. For example, methadone maintenance is the most cost-effective modality in many cases of opioid dependence (Dole and Nyswander, 1965; Newman and Whitehill, 1979), but most clinicians believe that other treatment alternatives should be available for such patients.

## REFERENCES

American Psychiatric Association: Diagnostic and Statistical Manual of Mental Disorders, ed 3. Washington, DC, American Psychiatric Association, 1980.

Bellet S, Roman L, DeCastro O, Kim KD, Kershbaum A: Effect of coffee ingestion on catecholamine release. Metabolism 18:288, 1969.

Bourne P (ed): Acute Drug Abuse Emergencies: A Treatment Manual. New York, Academic Press, 1976.

Cohen S: The Substance Abuse Problems. New York, Haworth Press, 1981.

Dole VP, Nyswander ME: A medical treatment of diacetylmorphine (heroin) addiction. JAMA 193:646–650, 1965.

Dreisbach RH, Pfeiffer C: Caffeine-withdrawal headache. J Lab Clin Med 28:1212, 1943.

Dupont R, Goldstein A, O'Donnell J (eds): Handbook on Drug Abuse. Washington, DC, National Institute on Drug Abuse, 1979.

Easson W: Gasoline addiction in children. Pediatrics 29:250, 1962.

Ellinwood E: Amphetamine psychosis. I. Description of the individuals and process. J Nerv Ment Dis 144:273–283, 1967.

Gottheil E et al (eds): Etiological Aspects of Alcohol and Drug Abuse. Springfield, IL, Charles C Thomas, 1983.

Greden JF: Anxiety or caffeinism: A diagnostic dilemma. Am J Psychiatry 131:1089, 1974.

Greden JF: Caffeinism and caffeine withdrawal, in Lowinson JH, Ruiz P (eds): Substance Abuse: Clinical Problems and Perspectives. Baltimore, Williams and Wilkins, 1981, pp 274–286.

Hughes PH, Barker NW, Crawford GA, Jaffee H: The natural history of a heroin epidemic. Am J Public Health 62:995–1001, 1972.

Hunt GM, Azrin NH: A community-reenforcement approach to alcoholism. Behav Res Ther 11:91–104, 1973.

Hunt WA, Barnett LW, Branch LG: Relapse rates in addiction programs. J Clin Psychol 27:455–456, 1971.

Jaffee JH: Drug addiction and drug abuse, in Gilman AG, Goodman LS, Gilman A (eds): The Pharmacological Basis of Therapeutics, ed 6. New York, Macmillan, 1980, pp 284–324.

Krasnagor NA (ed): The Behavioral Aspects of Smoking. NIDA Research Monograph 26. Washington, DC, Government Printing Office, 1979.

Lowinson JH, Ruiz P (eds): Substance Abuse: Clinical Problems and Perspectives. Baltimore/London, Williams and Wilkins, 1981.

Lowry TP: The volatile nitrites as sexual drugs: A user survey. J Sex Educ Ther 1:8, 1979.

Maletzky BM, Klotter J: Addiction to diazepam. Int J Addict 11:95–115, 1976.

Martin WR, Jasinski DR: Physiological parameters of morphine dependence in man: Tolerance, early abstinence, protracted abstinence. J Psychiatr Res 7:9–17, 1969.

McClellan AT et al: Is treatment for substance abuse effective? JAMA 247:1423–1428, 1982.

Newman RG, Whitehill WB: Double-blind comparison of methadone and placebo maintenance treatments of narcotic addicts in Hong Kong. Lancet ii:485–488, 1979.

Patterson MA: Electro-acupuncture in alcohol and drug addictions. Clin Med 81:9–13, 1974.

Prockop L: Multifocal nervous system damage from volatile hydrocarbon inhalation. J Occup Med 19:139, 1977.

Russell MAH: Cigarette smoking: Natural history of a dependence disorder. Br J Med Psychol 44:1, 1971.

Sarvik ME, Cullen JW, Gritz E, Vogl TM, West LJ (eds): Research on Smoking Behavior. NIDA Research Monograph 17. Washington, DC, Government Printing Office, 1977.

Senay EC: Substance Abuse Disorders in Clinical Practice. Littleton, MA, John Wright, 1983.

Simon EJ: Opiate receptors and their implications for drug abuse, in Lettieri DJ, Sayers M, Pearson HW (eds): Theories on Drug Abuse, Selected Contemporary Perspectives. NIDA Research Monograph 30, 303–308. Washington, DC, Government Printing Office, 1980.

Smart RG: An availability-proneness theory of illicit drug abuse, in Theories on Drug Abuse, selected Contemporary Perspectives. Lettieri DJ, Sayers M, Pearson HW. NIDA Research Monograph 30. Washington, DC, Government Printing Office, March 1980.

Smith DE, Wesson DR: Phenobarbital technique for treatment of barbiturate dependence. Arch Gen Psychiatry 24:56–60, 1971.

Vaillant GE: The natural history of narcotic drug addiction. Semin Psychiatry 2:486–498, 1970.

Vaillant GE: A 20-year follow-up of New York narcotic addicts. Gen Arch Psychiatry 19:237–241, 1973.

Westermeyer J: Opium smoking in Laos: A survey of 40 addicts. Am J Psychiatry 13:165–170, 1974.

Westermeyer J: Primer on Chemical Dependency: A Clinical Guide to Alcohol and Drug Problems. Baltimore, Williams and Wilkins, 1976.

Wikler A: On the nature of addiction and habituation. Br J Addict 57:73–79, 1961.

Wilsnack SC: Alcohol abuse and alcoholism in women, in Pattison E, Kaufman E (eds): Encyclopedic Handbook of Alcoholism. New York, Gardner Press, 1982, Chap 57.

World Health Organization: Review of general population surveys of drug abuse. WHO Offset Publication No. 52, 1980.

# chapter 15

# ANTISOCIAL PERSONALITY

*by* Remi Cadoret, M.D.

## DEFINITION

Antisocial personality (sociopathy or sociopathic personality) is a chronic condition that manifests itself before age 15 and continues throughout adult life. It is characterized by repeated disturbances in interpersonal and social relations, such as aggressivity, various derelictions of social responsibility, and criminal activity.

## ETIOLOGY

Sociopathy, like many psychiatric conditions, runs in families. Studies of families of convicted felons (most of whom have antisocial personalities) show higher numbers of relatives with antisocial personality or alcoholism than are found in the general population (Guze et al., 1967; Cloninger and Guze, 1973; Robins, 1966). As with other familial conditions, hereditary factors are usually confounded with environmental factors so that the relative importance of each factor is difficult to assess. Adoption studies offer a way of studying separately the effects of heredity and environment. Adoptees, separated at birth from biologic parents and placed with nonrelatives, bring to their adoptive environments a set of unrelated genes. In addition, the adoptive environments provide a varied spectrum of different conditions. Despite careful screening,

many adoptive families have family members with psychiatric problems, such as depression, alcoholism, or antisocial behavior, so that the effect of these conditions can be assessed on adoptees from a variety of biologic backgrounds. A number of adoption studies have shown that children of convicted felons, of parents with antisocial types of behavior, are more likely to be diagnosed as antisocial personality even though separated at birth from biologic parents (Cadoret, 1978; Crowe, 1972, 1974; Schulsinger, 1972). Adoption studies of criminal behavior have also shown that adopted-away offspring of convicted criminals are more likely themselves to be convicted of crimes (Bohman et al., 1982; Cloninger et al., 1982; Mednick, Gabrielli, Hutchings, 1984). These studies are consistent with a genetic factor in criminal behavior and indirectly suggest that antisocial behavior traits may be the common transmitted features.

As noted earlier, family studies of antisocials have found relationships to alcoholism. Adoption studies have helped to elucidate this important relationship. Figure 15–1 shows, for an adoption sample, the relationship of biologic backgrounds of alcohol problems and antisocial behavior and adult adoptee alcohol abuse and antisocial personality. There appears to be some specificity of inheritance, with the biologic parent's alcohol problem predicting alcohol

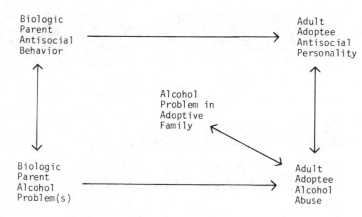

FIGURE 15–1. Inter-relationship of biologic and environmental factors in adult antisocial personality and alcohol abuse in males.

Key: Arrows indicate significant correlations of factors. If factors are not connected by arrows, their correlations are not significant.

abuse in adult offspring (but not antisocial personality), while the biologic parent's antisocial behavior predicts antisocial personality in their separated-at-birth offspring (but not alcohol abuse). The environmental factor of having an individual in the adoptive family with alcohol problems increases the chance of adoptee alcoholism as well. Environmental factors such as psychiatric disturbance in adoptive family members have proved important in predicting *adolescent* antisocial behavior (Cadoret, 1985; Cadoret, Cain, Crowe, 1983) but not as important in adult antisocial personality. The diagram (Figure 15–1) shows the strong correlation usually found between antisocial personality and alcohol abuse in adults (right-hand vertical arrow). The left-hand vertical arrow shows the correlation found in this particular sample of biologic parents and represents both a combination of selective mating (tendency for individuals with alcohol problems to mate with antisocials) and the simultaneous occurrence of antisocial behavior and alcohol abuse in one biologic parent. The independent genetic transmission of alcoholism and antisocial personality shown in Figure 15–1 is confirmed by family and population studies (Vaillant, 1983; Cloninger and Reich, 1983).

## EPIDEMIOLOGY

The incidence of antisocial personality is difficult to determine, since most population studies have used other definitions than those in the *Diagnostic and Statistical Manual of Mental Disorders*, third edition (DSM-III; American Psychiatric Association, 1980), for personality disorder. Depending on the study, anywhere from 0.1 per cent to 10 per cent of civilian populations have personality disorders (Ekblad, 1950; Hagnell, 1966; Sjogren, 1948). Figures from the United States suggest a value of about 3 per cent for antisocial personality (Cloninger and Reich, 1983). As with alcoholism, many more men than women are affected, and family studies generally show a sex ratio of male-female antisocials from 3:1 to 8:1 (Guze, Wolfgram, McKinney, 1968; Guze, Goodwin, Crane, 1970; Winokur, Reich, Rimmer, 1970).

Antisocials often come from families with marked social disturbances, such as parental desertion, separation and divorce, alcohol and drug abuse, and criminality; families of antisocials are more likely to be of low socioeconomic status (Robins, 1966; Cowie, Cowie, Slater, 1968; Guze et al., 1967).

## CLINICAL PICTURE

The description of antisocial personality is organized around the DSM-III criteria, which are presented in Table 15–1. The clinical picture of antisocial personality varies to a certain degree, depending on the age at which the person is seen, since the quality of problems that adolescents or young adults can get into is sometimes different from those seen in older individuals. However, all of the problems may be characterized by repeated disturbances in interper-

**TABLE 15–1   DSM-III Diagnostic Criteria for Antisocial Personality Disorder**

A.   Current age at least 18.

B.   Onset before age 15 as indicated by a history of three or more of the following before that age:
1.   Truancy (positive if it amounted to at least 5 days per year for at least 2 years, not including the last year of school)
2.   Expulsion or suspension from school for misbehavior
3.   Delinquency (arrested or referred to juvenile court because of behavior)
4.   Running away from home overnight at least twice while living in parental or parental surrogate home
5.   Persistent lying
6.   Repeated sexual intercourse in a casual relationship
7.   Repeated drunkenness or substance abuse
8.   Thefts
9.   Vandalism
10.  School grades below expectations in relation to estimated or known IQ (may have resulted in repeating a year)
11.  Chronic violations of rules at home and/or at school (other than truancy)
12.  Initiation of fights

C.   At least four of the following manifestations of the disorder since age 18:
1.   Inability to sustain consistent work behavior, as indicated by any of the following: (a) too frequent job changes (e.g., three or more jobs in 5 years not accounted for by nature of job or economic or seasonal fluctuation); (b) significant unemployment (e.g., 6 months or more in 5 years when expected to work); (c) serious absenteeism from work (e.g., average 3 or more days of lateness or absence per month); (d) walking off several jobs without other jobs in sight. (*Note:* Similar behavior in an academic setting during the last few years of school may substitute for this criterion in individuals who by reason of their age or circumstances have not had an opportunity to demonstrate occupational adjustment.)
2.   Lack of ability to function as a responsible parent as evidenced by one or more of the following: (a) child's malnutrition; (b) child's illness resulting from lack of minimal hygiene standards; (c) failure to obtain medical care for a seriously ill child; (d) child's dependence on neighbors or nonresident relatives for food or shelter; (e) failure to arrange for a caretaker for a child under 6 when parent is away from home; (f) repeated squandering, on personal items, of money required for household necessities
3.   Failure to accept social norms with respect to lawful behavior, as indicated by any of the following: repeated thefts, illegal occupation (pimping, prostitution, fencing, selling drugs), multiple arrests, a felony conviction
4.   Inability to maintain enduring attachment to a sexual partner as indicated by two or more divorces and/or separations (whether legally married or not), desertion of spouse, promiscuity (10 or more sexual partners within 1 year)
5.   Irritability and aggressiveness as indicated by repeated physical fights or assault (not required by one's job or to defend someone or oneself), including spouse or child beating
6.   Failure to honor financial obligations, as indicated by repeated defaulting on debts, failure to provide child support, failure to support other dependents on a regular basis
7.   Failure to plan ahead, or impulsivity, as indicated by traveling from place to place without a prearranged job or clear goal for the period of travel or clear idea about when the travel would terminate, or lack of a fixed address for a month or more
8.   Disregard for the truth as indicated by repeated lying, use of aliases, "conning" others for personal profit
9.   Recklessness, as indicated by driving while intoxicated or recurrent speeding

D.   A pattern of continuous antisocial behavior in which the rights of others are violated, with no intervening period of at least 5 years without antisocial behavior between age 15 and the present time (except when the individual was bedridden or confined in a hospital or penal institution).

E.   Antisocial behavior is not due to either severe mental retardation, schizophrenia, or manic episodes.

From American Psychiatric Association: Diagnostic and Statistical Manual of Mental Disorders, ed. 3. Washington, DC, American Psychiatric Association, 1980.

sonal and social relationships. The disturbance characteristically starts before age 15, and types of behavioral problems met with in this life period are shown in Table 15–2. As might be expected, since minors spend most of their waking time in school situations, a good deal of antisocial behaviors occurs in school. Truancy and consequences of truancy, such as school suspension and expulsion and poor school performance, are common, as can be seen from Table 15–2. Aggressiveness toward other individuals, especially toward authority figures, such as teachers, can also figure into school difficulties. School problems often lead to dropping out, and it is an un-

**TABLE 15–2    Disturbed Behavior Before Age 15 in Antisocial Personality**

| Behavior | Persons with Adult Diagnosis of Antisocial Personality Who Demonstrated This Behavior (%) |
| --- | --- |
| Truancy | 33 |
| School expulsion | — |
| Delinquency | — |
| Running away | 34 |
| Persistent lying | 45 |
| Casual sex (premarital) | 45 |
| Alcohol or other substance abuse | 50 |
| Thefts | 30 |
| Vandalism | — |
| Poor school work | — |
| Chronic violation of home or school rules (stay out late) | 32 |
| Initiation of fights | |
|   Aggressive toward relatives | 32 |
|   Aggressive toward authority figures | 28 |

Data from Robins LN: Deviant Children Grown Up. Baltimore, Williams & Wilkins, 1966. Reprinted with permission from Cadoret RJ, King LJ: Psychiatry in Primary Care, ed 2. St. Louis, C.V. Mosby, 1983.

usual antisocial who has finished high school. Antisocials who do graduate high school usually are indifferent scholars who do not achieve their academic potential. Many young antisocials while truant from school will seek the company of others of similar interests, especially older adolescents, and engage with them in alcohol and other substance abuse, casual sex, thefts, and vandalism. If these behaviors are blatant enough and the individuals are detected in them, the adolescents will come to the attention of the police and be charged with delinquency. Misbehaviors are not confined to the school or the outside world, but occur in the home as well, where antisocials are often aggressive toward parents and get into much difficulty by chronically violating rules, such as staying out when they are supposed to be home, not doing chores, stealing money and other items from the home to support such activities as drug habits, and frequently lying. Lying is done sometimes to escape the consequences of misbehavior or to cover up their tracks; or again, lying sometimes occurs as a form of self-aggrandizement, as, for example, when an adolescent boasts about having had contact with famous people. The young antisocial causes further problems at home and at school by his association with other children of bad reputation and by his impulsive and reckless behavior. Many antisocials also have difficulty getting along with peers and are frequently disliked, especially because of their aggressivity, their thieving and bullying, and their bad language. One of the early behaviors in adolescent antisocial girls is casual sex, with its concomitant increased risk of illegitimate pregnancy and venereal diseases. Alcohol and drug abuse also lead to early medical complications in some cases, such as accidents, so that antisocials are more often seen in an emergency department than in an office for counseling. Investigators, such as Lee Robins, have shown that there is a strong correlation between the total number of these early adolescent behaviors and the later diagnosis in adult life of antisocial personality. For example, she has shown that if an individual has 10 or more of the types of behavior shown in Table 15–2, then there is a 43 per cent chance that the individual will receive a diagnosis of antisocial personality as an adult. If two or less of these behaviors are present, then there is only a 4 per cent chance of such an adult diagnosis.

DSM-III diagnostic criteria for antisocial personality require that after age 18, a number of antisocial behaviors shown in Table 15–1 be present. The frequency of these be-

**TABLE 15–3**  Diagnostic Disturbed Behavior in Adult Antisocials

| Area of Behavior | Antisocials with This Behavior (%) | Controls (%) |
|---|---|---|
| 1. Poor work record | | |
| Too frequent job changes (longest job held less than 2 years) | 26 | 1 |
| Median number of employers in 10-year period | 6.4 | 2.6 |
| Significant unemployment (ever unemployed in past 10 years) | 78 | 23 |
| Median duration of unemployment in months | 19 | 3 |
| Serious work absenteeism | — | — |
| Leaving job without another job to go to | — | — |
| 2. Lack of ability to function responsibly as a parent | | |
| Cited for child neglect | 7 | 0 |
| Placed children | 20 | 0 |
| 3. Serious breaking of law | | |
| Nontraffic arrests | 94 | 17 |
| Arrest for major crime of those ever arrested | 73 | 13 |
| Conviction rate for nontraffic offenses | 80 | 0 |
| 4. Inability to maintain enduring attachment to sexual partner | | |
| Unfaithful | 28 | 4 |
| Two or more divorces in those who remarry | 54 | 12 |
| Ever divorced | 78 | 20 |
| Promiscuity | 56 | 12 |
| Desertion | 22 | 4 |
| 5. Aggressiveness | | |
| Physical cruelty to spouse or children | 12 | 5 |
| Combative behavior reason for hospitalization if ever in hospital | 5 | 0 |
| 6. Failure to honor financial obligations | | |
| Derogatory credit report of those with credit record | 57 | 13 |
| Current debt | 14 | 2 |
| Nonsupport | 22 | 10 |
| 7. Failure to plan ahead—impulsivity | 67 | — |
| 8. Disregard for truth | | |
| Pathologic lying | 17 | — |
| Use of alias | 8 | — |
| 9. Recklessness | — | — |

Data from Robins LN: Deviant Children Grown Up. Baltimore, Williams & Wilkins, 1966. Reprinted with permission from Cadoret RJ, King LJ: Psychiatry in Primary Care, ed 2. St. Louis, C.V. Mosby, 1983.

haviors in adult antisocials is compared with normal controls in Table 15–3. Some type of difficulty with work occurs in a high percentage of antisocial individuals, and such problems can be brought out by a carefully obtained job history, with attention to a careful chronological order of jobs held, so that hiatuses in the job record can be detected. Reasons for leaving work should also be routinely sought as part of the job history. Typical antisocial job histories are characterized by frequent changes of job, punctuated by episodes of unemployment. Reasons for leaving jobs are, characteristically, impulsive quitting because of fights or disagreements with people in authority,

being fired for incompetency, fighting on the job, or coming in late or being absent without sufficient reason. Because of these types of job difficulties, antisocials frequently cross the white collar–blue collar line in a downward direction. As can be seen in Table 15–3, a high percentage of antisocials show frequent job changes, significant unemployment, and longer periods of unemployment. Job difficulty contributes to financial instability and increasing dependency of such individuals on state and federal funds. One important clinical feature of antisocial job performance was pointed out a number of years ago by Lee Robins, who showed that the length of time a job could be held appeared to be related to the amount of supervision. Solo jobs (such as a truck driver or a serviceman working by himself) were associated with longer periods of employment. In contrast, highly supervised positions (such as clerks in stores or factory workers) were not held as long.

Inability to function as a responsible parent leads to such problems as child neglect and children being removed from the home for abuse or neglect. In part, this difficulty in parenting is probably associated with other behaviors of antisocials that occur in clinically significant numbers of patients. These behaviors are not specifically cited in the DSM-III criteria and are presented separately in Table 15–4. Because antisocials often marry spouses with behavior difficulties, such as unfaithfulness, excessive drinking, or child neglect, the home of the antisocial is more likely to show a resultant chaotic environment. The chaotic home environment may also contribute to the high rate of behavior problems in children (item 3 in Table 15-4), and more children of antisocials are held back in school and themselves show antisocial behaviors, such as truancy, running away from home, stealing. All of these factors, then—poor choice of spouses and difficulty with children—are associated with inability to function responsibly as a parent.

Illegal behavior is an extremely common feature of antisocial adult behavior, as can be seen from Table 15–3, where the number of arrests for major crime is quite high, as well as high conviction rates for nontraffic offenses. In convicted felons, antisocial personality is probably the most common psychiatric diagnosis. Brushes with the law and the consequences, such as incarceration, lead to further disturbance of the antisocial's family and increased financial dependency of all concerned.

Inability to maintain an enduring attachment to a sexual partner, as manifested by a high divorce rate, unfaithfulness, and promiscuity, is prominent in antisocial behavior, as indicated in Table 15–3. Other antisocial characteristics also contribute to the high divorce rate, such as interpersonal aggressiveness, as shown in physical fighting. Impulsivity, which is present in adolescence and persists through adulthood, also plays a significant role in marital and family problems. In the Robins study, 67 per cent of antisocials showed sudden, poorly thought out moves from one city to another, elopements from hospital, and unprovoked desertion of their spouses and children. Such behaviors can contribute significantly to social disruption and lead to divorces.

Irritability and aggressiveness are frequent features of the antisocial. Physical cruelty to spouse and children and physical fighting are two of the biggest reasons for placing the antisocial in the hospital. This increasing combativeness manifests itself in many situations. For example, antisocials who are alcoholic are much more likely to be arrested for disturbing the peace or for fighting in public than primary alcoholics (Cadoret, Troughton, Widmer, 1984).

Failure to honor financial obligations is part of the picture of social dereliction of duties and manifests itself by poor credit ratings, many debts, and, in those who are separated or divorced, failure to provide child support.

Failure to plan ahead, or impulsivity, occurs in a high proportion of antisocials and leads to vagrancy and wanderlust. In Robins's study of antisocials at least 60 per cent had spent a period of several months hitchhiking around the country with no financial support or employment in prospect. Such individuals occasionally will push drugs or take temporary jobs requiring little skills to support their wanderlust. Marked impulsivity seems to have a poor prognosis for antisocials, since Robins reported that individuals with this characteristic early in life seemed to have severer problems later with their antisocial behavior.

Disregard for the truth, such as pathologic lying or using an alias, occurs in a significant number of individuals. Many times the lies serve a useful purpose of "conning" someone else, and individuals who are extremely verbal can sometimes put up convincing arguments or rationalizations for their behavior. Frequently, conning procedures are used by antisocials in getting drugs from physicians by either reporting nonexistent physical symptoms or exaggerating ones that might be present. Hence the importance for knowing one's patients and realizing that antisocial individuals are likely to indulge in this type of activity should lead a physician to question requests for tranquilizers, narcotics, and other such medications from antisocials.

**TABLE 15–4** Nondiagnostic Areas of Behavioral Disturbance in Antisocials

| Area of Behavior | Antisocials (%) | Controls (%) |
|---|---|---|
| 1. Financial dependency | | |
|     Received welfare funds | 45 | 2 |
|     Financial or work assistance | 63 | 8 |
| 2. Behavior problems in spouse | | |
|     Desertion or unfaithfulness | 28 | 6 |
|     Drinking to excess | 28 | 5 |
|     Neglect of home or child | 23 | 7 |
|     Arrests | 21 | 7 |
|     Solution to problem spouse | | |
|       Divorce and remarry another problem spouse | 42 | 13 |
|       Divorce | 84 | 36 |
| 3. High rate of behavior problems in children | | |
|     Held back in school | 30 | 15 |
|     Truant | 16 | 0 |
|     Runaway | 14 | 0 |
|     Stealing | 11 | 0 |
|     High school graduations of sons 18 and older | 9 | 69 |
| 4. Difficulties in armed forces (men) | | |
|     Reason for rejection | | |
|       Criminal record | 41 | 0 |
|       Physical incapacity | 37 | 24 |
|     Problems in service (of those who served) | | |
|       Dishonorable discharge | 23 | 0 |
|       AWOL | 40 | 3 |
|       Punishments | 37 | 3 |
|       Court-martial | 23 | 0 |
| 5. Alcohol and drug use | | |
|     Social and medical problems associated with alcohol use | | |
|       Any ever | 62 | 7 |
|       Arrests | 42 | 3 |
|       Fired from job | 13 | 1 |
|     Drug addition ever | 10 | 0 |
| 6. Poor socialization | | |
|     No contact with living siblings or parents | 27 | 0 |
|     No contact with neighbors | 75 | 33 |
|     Lack of planned social contacts | 51 | 7 |
|     No organizational memberships | 69 | 31 |
| 7. Increased psychiatric treatment and hospitalization | | |
|     Mental hospital | 21 | 1 |
|     Any psychiatric attention | 50 | 20 |
|     Reason for hospitalization* | | |
|       Alcohol | 18 | 0 |
|       Drugs | 14 | 0 |
|       Depressed or suicidal | 18 | 100† |
|       Dangerous to others | 14 | 0 |
|       Prostitution (women only) | 25 | 0 |
| 8. Suicidal behavior—suicide attempts | 11 | — |
| 9. Unusual emotional response—lack of guilt at interview | 40 | — |

Data from Robins LN: Deviant Children Grown Up. Baltimore, Williams & Wilkins, 1966. Reprinted with permission from Cadoret RJ, King LJ: Psychiatry in Primary Care, ed 2. St. Louis, C.V. Mosby, 1983.

* Reason for hospitalization (for those hospitalized).
† Reflects depression of the one control subject that had been hospitalized.

Recklessness is also a large feature of antisocial life, especially in late adolescence, and leads to arrests for speeding and public intoxication and involves the antisocial in accidents where they are likely to come in contact with physicians or other health care professionals.

All of these behaviors may be detected by taking good histories from the patient or, better still, from reliable informants. It is necessary in obtaining the history to obtain a chronological accounting of behaviors in all of these different areas so that important hiatuses can be noted and periods of time when embarrassing situations occurred that the patient does not wish to report can be detected (e.g., time done in prison).

As noted earlier, many other behaviors occur in antisocials more frequently than in individuals without these characteristics that may bring the individual in contact with physicians. These "nondiagnostic" behaviors appear in Table 15–4 and include financial dependency, marrying a spouse with significant behavior problems, and having chaotic families with high rates of behavior problems in children. Table 15–4 presents a number of additional behaviors that are important because they cause the antisocial to have contact with physicians. The first of these is difficulties in the armed forces. Many antisocials are rejected from service for a criminal record. Those who do serve have a disproportionate number of problems both in the service and when they are discharged. A high proportion during service get into difficulty with absent-without-leaves and other punishments, including court-martial. A significant proportion eventually receive a less than honorable discharge. In the service, antisocials are likely to come in contact with physicians in trying to get drugs or in trying to get out of their service obligations by playing the sick role. Once these individuals are discharged from active duty, they request more veteran's benefits, such as treatment or pensions, than do non-antisocial individuals. Thus VA hospitals are more likely to contain individuals with this type of history and personality.

An important part of antisocial behavior that frequently brings antisocials in contact with health care professionals is their abuse of alcohol and drugs. Antisocials characteristically start such drug abuse much earlier in life than individuals who are primary alcoholics. It is not unusual to find alcoholic antisocials using alcohol regularly in grade school and early high school. In addition to alcohol, a large part of substance abuse is the use of illicit street drugs. One study of alcoholic antisocials who had been admitted for detoxification found that such individuals were much more likely to have significant illicit street drug abuse than were primary alcoholics admitted to the same unit (Cadoret et al., 1984). High amounts of alcohol and drug use are associated with many and early complications so that, in general, antisocial alcoholics are usually admitted to detoxification centers at an earlier age than primary alcoholics. Alcohol and drug use also contributes significantly to difficulty in holding jobs and to performing criminal acts to supply the money necessary for heavy drug and alcohol use. In Robins's study of antisocials, alcohol accounted for most of the hospitalizations, largely because of the aggressive behavior that was associated with drinking. In the Guze and Cantwell study (1965) of convicted felons, alcoholic antisocials showed a much higher rate of recidivism than those who were not alcoholic. Thus the use of drugs and alcohol is an important complication of antisocial personality.

Antisocial individuals show higher rates of psychiatric treatment and hospitalization, as indicated in Table 15–4. The reasons for hospitalization are frequently associated with alcohol and drugs. Depression and suicidal behavior are also important features of antisocial behavior that result in hospitalization. In general, suicide attempts far outweigh completed suicide, as evidenced in the Robins study. Other studies agree in suggesting that completed suicide in antisocials is probably relatively low (Pokorny, 1960; Robins, Murphy, Wilkinson, 1950; Tuckman and Youngman, 1965). A number of studies have shown that there is a high incidence of antisocial personality among individuals who come to hospital emergency departments with attempted suicide. These studies (Batchelor, 1954; James, Derham, Scott-Orr, 1963) indicate that between 20 per cent and 25 per cent of suicide attempters seen in hospital emergency departments are antisocial personalities. Suicide attempts in antisocials were more likely to be medically nonserious, in contrast to primary depressives, whose attempts were more likely to be medically serious. As one might expect, a high proportion of antisocials' attempts were regarded as impulsive and were often closely associated in time with a socially upsetting situation, such as a personal fight with a spouse or lover or the threat of being arrested and put in prison or a mental hospital. One study suggested that the most common motive for the suicide attempt was bad feelings for a person about whom there was considerable ambivalence, so that the suicide attempt often represented a way of revenge to the antisocial individual. In only a few cases were the suicidal motives manipulative, in the sense that they were designed to change others' behavior. Many antisocials do suffer from feelings of guilt, especially in the presence of a depressive syndrome, although a goodly proportion of antisocials are reported as being cold and affectionless and not feeling guilt. For example, a recent study of 35 antisocial persons treated in an outpatient clinic showed that 22 of them had a secondary depression with marked self-deprecatory and guilt feelings. Indeed, secondary depression is probably one of the principal reasons for antisocials coming to physicians for treatment. Such individuals can also make suicide attempts.

One other area of disturbance brings antisocial individuals in contact with physicians. A high proportion of antisocial individuals show a large number of neurotic or somatic symptoms. These symptoms are shown in Table 15–5, where it can be seen that anxiety and gastrointestinal symptoms are rather high in frequency. Likewise, "neurologic" symptoms, such as blurred vision or even episodes of blindness and paralysis, including trances and amnesia, occur with significantly greater frequency in antisocial individuals. In the Robins series, 5 per cent of hospitalizations were for amnesia. The presence of large numbers of

**TABLE 15–5**  Somatic "Nonsociopathic" Symptoms in Adult Antisocials

| | Antisocials (%) | Controls with No Disease (%) |
|---|---|---|
| 1. Average number of symptoms | 7.8 | 2.6 |
| 2. High level of neurotic or somatic symptoms (>9 symptoms and/or disabling symptoms) | 37 | — |
| 3. Neurologic symptoms | | |
| Blurred vision | 17 | 3 |
| Episode of blindness | 8 | 0 |
| Paralysis | 7 | 1 |
| Trouble walking | 7 | 1 |
| Trances | 7 | 0 |
| Amnesia | 7 | 0 |
| 4. Anxiety symptoms | | |
| Anxiety attacks | 22 | 0 |
| Dizzy spells | 30 | 5 |
| Dyspnea | 30 | 12 |
| Palpitations | 30 | 10 |
| "Nervous" | 47 | 15 |
| Chest pain | 29 | 7 |
| Anxiety in crowds | 15 | 0 |
| 5. Other somatic symptoms | | |
| Weakness | 20 | 4 |
| Nausea | 32 | 9 |
| Vomiting | 22 | 8 |
| Abdominal pain | 28 | 8 |
| Bowel trouble | 28 | 8 |
| Insomnia | 30 | 12 |
| Fatigue | 22 | 10 |
| Anorexia | 12 | 5 |
| Back pain | 45 | 31 |

Data from Robins LN: Deviant Children Grown Up. Baltimore, Williams & Wilkins, 1966. Reprinted with permission from Cadoret RJ, King LJ: Psychiatry in Primary Care, ed 2. St. Louis, C.V. Mosby, 1983.

such somatic or neurotic symptoms in some antisocials but not in others has raised the question of heterogeneity in antisocial personality.

Heterogeneity has long been described in sociopathy. Karpman (1947) distinguished primary and secondary psychopaths. Secondary psychopaths "act out" in antisocial and aggressive ways as a result of inner conflict and, as part of the clinical picture, often show guilt, anxiety, depression, remorse, paranoia, or other psychoneurotic symptoms. In contrast to this, primary psychopaths usually show a low level of anxiety, with little evidence of guilt. Primary psychopaths have been shown to be impulsive, undersocialized, aggressive, and lacking anxiety or other forms of subjective distress (Jenkins, 1966; Quay, 1964a, 1964b; Peterson, Quay, Tiffany, 1961). Prison populations that are high in proportion of sociopaths as defined in this chapter have shown evidence of these two types of antisocials (Blackburn, 1971; Hare, 1975). One study of primary and secondary sociopaths used scales derived from the Minnesota Multiphasic Personality Inventory and showed that secondary psychopaths had high levels for depression, tension, body symptoms, autistic thinking, and anxiety, in contrast to primary psychopaths, who had high levels of extraversion, impulsivity, aggression, suspicion, and psychopathic deviation (Blackburn, 1973). Evidence for two such groupings of sociopathics was also described in a study where alcoholic sociopaths were divided on the basis of low and high numbers of depressive symptoms (Whitters et al., 1984). Those with high numbers of depressive symptoms had larger numbers of manic, panic, schizophrenic, and somatic symptoms. These differences are shown in Table 15–6. One additional clinical difference of practical importance was the high rate of drug abuse in those antisocials with a high number of depressive symptoms. Although heterogeneity may be present, it is not recognized by DSM-III.

## PATHOLOGY

There is no known basic pathology process causing antisocial personality such as is found in a disease like Huntington's chorea. While, for example, abnormalities of electroencephalography or autonomic nervous system reactivity have been described more frequently in antisocial populations, many antisocials still do not show such abnormalities. Any basic structural, biochemical, or functional abnormality eludes us at present.

## CLINICAL COURSE

In general, antisocial behavior seems to decrease as individuals grow older, although the condition is a chronic one, with one or more disturbed areas of behavior usually present. In the Robins series, approximately 40 per cent improved later in life, with the median age of improvement being 35 years. The best predictor for remission in the series was the diagnosis of the father: 3 per cent of children from antisocial fathers remitted contrasted with 26

TABLE 15–6    Clinical Differences Between Antisocial Alcoholics with High and Low Number of Depressive Symptoms

|  | Low Depressive Symptoms (%) N = 46 | High Depressive Symptoms (%) N = 48 |
|---|---|---|
| Any drug abuse/dependence diagnosis | 37.0 | 70.0* |
| Average number of manic symptoms | .83 | 3.9† |
| Average number of panic symptoms | 1.7 | 3.8* |
| Average number of schizophrenic symptoms | 1.2 | 2.9† |
| Average number of somatic symptoms | 1.0 | 2.1‡ |

Data from Whitters A, Troughton E, Cadoret RJ, et al.: Evidence for clinical heterogeneity in antisocial alocholics. Compr Psychiatry 25:158–164, 1984.
* Significant 1.0% level.
† Significant 0.1% level.
‡ Significant 5.0% level.

percent of children who improved whose fathers were not diagnosed antisocial. Other series (Maddocks, 1970) also report chronicity with a tendency for improvement later in life. In this latter series, those who had *not* improved were more likely to be alcoholic and to exhibit marked hypochondriacal symptoms. Although a certain amount of improvement seems to occur, especially regarding brushes with the law, many of these individuals are pathetically socially isolated. Some idea of this social isolation, which is little appreciated, can be seen in Table 15–4. Antisocials tend to stay by themselves, to have little contact with neighbors, to have few friends, and to be isolated, even from blood relatives and in-laws. When improvement later in life does occur, it is difficult to know how much can be attributed to treatment.

Vaillant's longitudinal study of alcoholics has shown that by the fifth decade of life, individuals diagnosed as sociopaths were *more* likely to be abstinent than were primary alcoholics (Vaillant, 1983). This suggests that improvement in psychopathology might be more likely to occur with older antisocials, since sociopathy is generally considered an unfavorable prognostic sign in the treatment of alcoholism (Gibbs and Flanagan, 1977).

## DIFFERENTIAL DIAGNOSIS

Differentiation of antisocial personality from other psychiatric conditions is based mostly on long-term history rather than on a cross-sectional view of symptoms. Difficulty beginning in childhood or adolescence and continuing through adult life is the rule for antisocial personality, whereas most other psychiatric conditions have a more episodic course and a later onset. Psychiatric conditions that must be distinguished from the antisocial are as follows:

1. *Major depression.* Depressed individuals may act in self-destructive ways. Some of these self-destructive ways may involve criminal activity and resemble the kinds of behaviors done by antisocials, such as drug or alcohol abuse, sexual promiscuity, difficulties with discipline, recklessness (including reckless driving), neglect of work, and other derelictions of social responsibilities. As with other psychiatric conditions, the major feature distinguishing antisocial from primary depression is the time course, with antisocial behavior starting before age 15, as well as being more chronic. Depression generally starts later than age 15 and is more likely to be episodic with intervals of relatively good functioning. An antisocial individual may also suffer from major depression during his lifetime; if this is the case, then the diagnosis of antisocial personality with secondary depression can be made.

2. *Manic illness.* The distinguishing feature of manic illness, like that in depression, is the periodicity of mania and its onset usually in the late teens or early 20s, with relatively good functioning up to the point of onset. During manic episodes behavior of antisocial flavor can occur, such as overspending, misusing credit cards, recklessness, financial irresponsibility, sexual promiscuity, and argumentativeness.

3. *Schizophrenia.* A number of children with conduct disorder or antisocial behavior turn out later in life to be schizophrenic (Robins, 1966). As shown in Table 15–6, antisocial individuals tend to complain more of psychiatric symptoms, including schizophrenic-type symptoms. This makes a differential diagnosis rather difficult at times. If symptoms and a course diagnostic of schizophrenia are present, then this condition should be diagnosed and treated. It should be kept in mind, however, that antisocial individuals frequently indulge in drug abuse and that this may be presenting as a schizophrenic-like picture in an antisocial individual. Hospital admission to a controlled environment in which drugs are not available might help to differentiate the situation from schizophrenia.

4. *Neuroses.* Classic obsessions and compulsions seem to be uncommon in antisocial individuals, although, as indicated in Table 15–5, a number of anxiety symptoms do occur and may raise the question of generalized anxiety, phobic disorder, or panic disorder. Again, phobic, panic, or generalized anxiety disorders usually do not have a preexisting antisocial history. If an antisocial history is present along with anxiety attacks, then it is reasonable to assume that the anxiety is part of the antisocial picture and treat it accordingly. Similar considerations should hold for symptoms of hysteria that, as indicated in Table 15–5, occur in antisocial individuals and raise the question of so-

matiform disorder, conversion disorder, or other dissociative disorders.

5. *Mental Retardation.* Most definitions of antisocial personality, including that in DSM-III, eliminate individuals who are severely mentally retarded (see exclusion E in DSM-III diagnostic criteria, Table 15–1). However, a number of individuals with mild, or even moderate, retardation show considerable antisocial behavior. If these meet criteria for antisocial personality, then this condition may be diagnosed.

6. *Other personality diagnoses.* Sometimes differentiation of antisocial personality from other personality diagnoses may be difficult. This is especially true when distinguishing between passive-aggressive personality disorder and antisocials. Many individuals with passive-aggressive personality disorder manifest derelictions of social responsibility as part of their resistance, expressed through such mechanisms as procrastination, stubbornness, dawdling, intentional inefficiency, or "forgetfulness." The dependency of these individuals, including financial dependency, also smacks of antisocial personality. If features of antisocial and passive-aggressive personality disorder are clearly present, then the diagnosis of mixed personality disorder can be made.

The DSM-III borderline personality can also be confused with the antisocial. Impulsivity, self-destructive behaviors, such as gambling and substance abuse, temper outbursts, suicidal attempts, and gestures are characteristics that borderlines share with antisocials. The early onset in antisocials and their more criminal activity should help to make the distinction.

7. *Alcohol and drug abuse/dependency.* Diagnosis of these conditions should arouse suspicion of an underlying antisocial personality.

8. *Miscellaneous conditions,* such as factitious disorders or malingering, should raise the question of whether an underlying antisocial personality is present.

## TREATMENT

Treatment of antisocial personalities is generally difficult owing to a number of factors. First, antisocial behaviors are embedded in a social matrix of bad company and other adverse environmental factors, which tends to enmesh the antisocial and encourage antisocial behavior. Second, the length of time that these antisocial behaviors have been practiced and reinforced makes change difficult. Third, antisocial individuals seldom volunteer for treatment, hence their motivation for change is usually low. Physicians probably find that their major contact with antisocials is in such areas as emergency departments, where antisocials appear with impulsive suicide attempts, for treatment of injuries received in fights, or for treatment of drinking or drug-related problems, such as medical complications of their substance abuse. Many antisocials are brought to the attention of a physician when they are expelled from school and are creating a great deal of difficulty at home with discipline problems. No matter where the contact is made, the treating professional is impressed with the magnitude of the problems that beset antisocials and wonder where to begin management.

In dealing with antisocials, three questions must be raised: (1) What behaviors are involved in the present problems that bring the person to attention? (2) What is the patient's insight into his or her responsibility to affect changes in this area? (3) Most important, how motivated is the patient to try to make changes? Motivation to change is especially important, since most antisocials appear at professionals' doorsteps only under considerable social pressure from spouse, family, friends, or the police. Superficially, some appear to be motivated and elect treatment rather than some alternative, such as going to jail. Sometimes it is possible to arrange that social pressure be continued on the antisocial, thus assuring a certain amount of motivation, for example, by putting the individual on probation and requiring her or him to report for treatment regularly or go to jail for failure to comply. In the case of marital problems, separation from a spouse could be maintained as a means of applying pressure on the antisocial to change his behavior, with the reward for efforts to change being living again with the spouse. With a specific problem behavior in mind, then, and some motivation on the patient's part to change, some approach to treatment of antisocial behavior is possible. This rather limited problem-oriented approach does not deal with all difficulties, but at least it allows, in many cases, more realistic goals to be set. It also may be less likely to lead therapists to expect too much and result in the often-quoted conclusion that response to treatment aimed at antisocial behavior is so bad that any treatment is an exercise in futility.

In describing treatment, discrete areas of disturbed behavior in antisocials, as shown in Tables 15–3 and 15–4, are considered, and some therapeutic approaches that might be tried for each of these areas are indicated. Some treatments may require elaborate settings, such as in an institution where such measures as token economies might be used. Other treatment methods, such as medication, group psychotherapy, family or marital counseling, could be used in outpatient settings.

Antisocial behavior that leads to trouble with the law (Table 15–3, area 3) has long been a prime target for treatment. Most of the studies that describe effects of treatment on criminals have dealt with incarcerated individuals, so that some cooperation with treatment was enforced. The treatments used in such settings include individual or group psychotherapy, therapeutic communities, and behavioral psychotherapies, such as token economies. The use of these techniques has been detailed in some reports (LeVine and Bornstein, 1972). The physician faces the problem of finding an institution or treatment for a particular individual, since many public institutions may require a court commitment, thus limiting those admitted to antisocials with usually severe behavior problems. In some instances, patients and their families are also required to go the route of contact with a juvenile court. Many institutions limit intake to certain age-groups, and there are few facilities, other than jails or hospitals, for adult antisocial individuals. In many communities, group homes or halfway houses are available for younger adolescents. Such facilities are usually organized along therapeutic community lines and are characterized by the setting of behavioral limits. In some communities, hospitals maintain live-in, long-term facilities where antisocial individuals may be exposed to controlled environments. Halfway houses, group homes, and long-term hospitalizations in therapeutic community situations can be useful not only for types of behavior leading to crime, but also in situations where individuals

come from chaotic homes in which discipline was absent or, at best, inconsistent.

One important factor in the therapy for antisocial behavior is the setting of behavioral limits. Institutionalization of some type is often the best way to achieve this. Outpatient management can be attempted, however, when parents or guardians are willing and able to try to set limits and carry out consistent discipline. Discipline appears to be an important ingredient of treatment. Robins's studies have shown that antisocial individuals often come from homes in which discipline is poor, inconsistent, or nonexistent. Craft (1965) has reported that in institutional settings, rigid discipline seems to result in greater improvements in incarcerated antisocials. Providing a disciplined environment can be done in family conferences, where the antisocial and the parents or guardians meet together and set up agreements or contracts as to which behaviors are to be changed, which behaviors are to be expected, and what rewards are to be obtained if change occurs and is maintained.

Aggressivity (Table 15–3, area 5), a cardinal manifestation of antisocial behavior, may be dealt with in a number of ways. Medications, such as phenytoin (Dilantin) and major tranquilizers, have been recommended, but there are no studies that show their efficacy. One study, however, has shown that maintenance lithium carbonate reduced the number of physical assaults in incarcerated individuals with severe personality disorders (Sheard et al., 1976). Thus a trial on lithium might be attempted for some individuals. Propranolol has recently been used with some success in children and adolescents who show rage and aggressive outbursts (Williams et al., 1982). Most of these individuals also have some significant organic brain dysfunction, such as cerebral palsy, moderate to severe mental retardation, or a seizure disorder. The value of propranolol for aggressive outbursts in antisocials is unknown. In behavior problems where impulsivity is a factor, some type of individual psychotherapy might encourage the antisocial person to consider and try other responses to situations that might otherwise end with violence. For example, an antisocial and his spouse may receive marital counseling to help guide them around the situations that would ordinarily call forth aggression. Because alcohol or other drug abuse is often associated with aggressivity, it is important to assess this factor. Having the individual stop drinking may be sufficient to ameliorate significant aggression. Treatment of the alcohol problem in antisocials can involve administration of drugs, such as disulfiram, and antisocial individuals can certainly be referred to alcoholism treatment units for treatment and management of their alcohol problems if they see this as a contributing factor to their difficulties in life.

At one time, as a means of treatment or punishment, many antisocials were required to enlist in the armed forces (Table 15–4, area 4). Recent law now specifies that "antisocial attitudes and behavior" are reason for psychiatric rejection. Although some antisocial individuals may benefit from the discipline of the armed forces, the rate of significant behavior problems in the armed forces and subsequent problems after discharge would make armed forces service a poor general method of treatment.

Somatic symptoms (Table 15–5) frequently bring an antisocial in contact with a physician. Selecting the appropriate medication for specific conditions that might be causing such symptoms is important. Thus, for crippling anxiety attacks, usual medical methods of approach might include the use of propranolol, tricyclic antidepressants, or even monoamine oxidase inhibitors. There is no evidence that antisocials fail to respond to psychotropic drugs so that when somatic symptoms of depression, such as fatigue or sleeplessness, occur, antidepressants may be prescribed perhaps with a bit more caution, realizing that antisocials may be more likely to abuse medication or mix it with other substances, such as illicit drugs or alcohol. Medications directed against specific somatic problems may be helpful to the individual antisocial and enable him or her to make a better general adjustment.

Suicide attempts (Table 15–4, area 8) are fairly common in antisocial individuals and are one of the main reasons for antisocials being seen by physicians in emergency departments. The suicidal motive is often a wish to take revenge on some significant other person. In some cases, marital or family therapy may help to uncover frictions and teach the patient to deal with frustration and anger in ways other than suicide attempts. One-to-one psychotherapy could be attempted with such individuals in order to point out alternative behaviors to suicide attempts, and training aimed at postponing impulsive activity, which is frequently associated with suicide attempts, could be given.

A poor work record (Table 15–3, area 1) and consequent financial dependency (Table 15–4, area 1), hallmarks of antisocial history, can be attacked in a number of ways. In properly motivated individuals, job training might be offered through such agencies as vocational rehabilitation. Intelligent sociopaths could be sent back to complete the schooling necessary for higher-level jobs. Job training should take into account the antisocial's interests and abilities. Job training could make the antisocial more competitive in the job market and help to reduce financial dependency.

Lack of ability to function responsibly as a parent (Table 15–3, area 2) and concomitant problems, such as inability to maintain enduring attachment to a sexual partner (Table 15–3, area 4), behavior problems in one's spouse (Table 15–4, area 2), and high rate of behavior problems in children (Table 15–4, area 3) might be handled in marriage and family counseling that deals with specific problems arising in the marriage or family relationships.

In many antisocials' lives one of the most important factors affecting their social behavior is alcohol (and other substance) abuse (Table 15–4, area 5). Substance abuse enters into all kinds of problems: family, job, and crime. One of the most positive changes that can be made in the antisocial life-style is to stop substance abuse. Antisocials can benefit from programs aimed at alcohol and drug abuse and should be encouraged to try such approaches to sobriety as Alcoholics Anonymous.

Treatment goals are often limited. Whatever the goals, the chance of achieving success will be greater if they are agreed on in advance by all parties concerned. Sometimes changes in one target area (e.g., stopping substance abuse) will be reflected by large gains in other areas (e.g., acting more responsibly as a parent).

## REFERENCES

American Psychiatric Association: Diagnostic and Statistical Manual of Mental Disorders, ed 3. Washington, DC, American Psychiatric Association, 1980.

Batchelor IRC: Psychopathic states and attempted suicide. Br Med J 1:1342–1347, 1954.

Blackburn R: Personality types among abnormal homicides. Br J Criminol 11:14–31, 1971.

Blackburn R: An empirical classification of psychopathic personality. Br J Psychol 127:456–460, 1973.

Bohman M, Cloninger CR, Sigvardsson S, et al: Predisposition to petty criminality in Swedish adoptees. I. Genetic and environmental heterogeneity. Arch Gen Psychiatry 39:1233–1241, 1982.

Cadoret RJ: Psychopathology in adopted-away offspring of biologic parents with antisocial behavior. Arch Gen Psychiatry 35:176–184, 1978.

Cadoret RJ: Genes, environment and their interaction in the development of psychopathology, in Sakai T, Tsuboi T (eds): Genetic Aspects of Human Behavior. Tokyo, Igaku-Shoin Ltd, 1985.

Cadoret RJ, Cain CA, Crowe RR: Evidence for gene-environment interaction in development of adolescent antisocial behavior. Behav Genet 13:301–310, 1983.

Cadoret R, Troughton E, Widmer R: Clinical differences between antisocial and primary alcoholics. Compr Psychiatry 25:1–8, 1984.

Cloninger CR, Guze SB: Psychiatric illness in the families of female criminals: A study of 288 first-degree relatives. Br J Psychol 122:697–703, 1973.

Cloninger CR, Reich T: Genetic heterogeneity in alcoholism and sociopathy, in Kety SS, Rowland LP, Sidman RL, Matthysse SW (eds): Genetics of Neurological and Psychiatric Disorders. New York, Raven Press, 1983, pp 145–166.

Cloninger CR, Sigvardsson S, Bohman M, et al: Predisposition to petty criminality in Swedish adoptees. II. Cross-fostering analysis of gene-environment interaction. Arch Gen Psychiatry 39:1242–1247, 1982.

Cowie J, Cowie V, Slater E: Delinquency in Girls. London, Humanities Press, 1968.

Craft M: Ten Studies into Psychopathic Personality. Bristol, England, J Wright & Sons, 1965.

Crowe RR: The adopted offspring of women criminal offenders. Arch Gen Psychiatry 27:600–603, 1972.

Crowe RR: An adoption study of antisocial personality. Arch Gen Psychiatry 31:785–791, 1974.

Ekblad M: A psychiatric and sociological study of a series of Swedish naval conscripts, in Stromgren E (ed): Statistical and Genetical Population Studies Within Psychiatry: Methods and Principal Results. Paris, Congres Internationale de Psychiatrie, 1950.

Gibbs SE, Flanagan J: Prognostic indicators of alcoholism treatment outcome. Int J Addict 12:1097–1141, 1977.

Guze SB, Cantwell DP: Alcoholism and criminal recidivism: A study of 116 parolees. Am J Psychiatry 122:436–439, 1965.

Guze SB, Wolfgram ED, McKinney JK, et al: Psychiatric illness in the families of convicted criminals. A study of 519 first-degree relatives. Dis Nerv Syst 28:651–659, 1967.

Guze SB, Wolfgram ED, McKinney JK: Delinquency, social maladjustment and crime: The role of alcoholism (a study of first-degree relatives of convicted criminals). Dis Nerv Syst 29:238–243, 1968.

Guze SB, Goodwin DW, Crane JB: Criminal recidivism and psychiatric illness. Am J Psychiatry 127:832–835, 1970.

Hagnell O: A Prospective Study of the Incidence of Mental Disorder. Stockholm, Svenska Boknorloget Norstedts-Bonnias, 1966.

Hare RD: Psychophysiological studies of psychopathy, in Fowles DC (ed): Clinical Applications of Psychophysiology. New York, Columbia University Press, 1975, pp 77–105.

James IP, Derham SP, Scott-Orr DV: Attempted suicide--a study of 100 patients referred to a general hospital. Med J Aust 6:375–380, 1963.

Jenkins RL: Psychiatric syndromes in children and their relation to family background. Am J Orthopsychiatry 36:450–457, 1966.

Karpman B: Passive parasitic psychopathy: Toward the personality structure and psychogenesis of idiopathic psychopathy. Psychoanal Rev 34:102–118, 198–222, 1947.

LeVine WR, Bornstein PE: Is the sociopath treatable? The contribution of psychiatry to a legal dilemma. Wash Univ Law Q 693–711, 1972.

Maddocks PD: A five-year follow-up of untreated psychopaths. Br J Psychol 116:511–515, 1970.

Mednick SA, Gabrielli WF, Hutchings B: Genetic influences in criminal convictions: Evidence from an adoption cohort. Science 224:891–894, 1984.

Peterson DR, Quay HC, Tiffany TL: Personality factors related to juvenile delinquency. Child Dev 32:355–372, 1961.

Pokorny AD: Characteristics of 44 patients who subsequently committed suicide. Arch Gen Psychiatry 2:314–323, 1960.

Quay HC: Dimensions of personality in delinquent boys as inferred from the factor analysis of case history data. Child Dev 35:479–484, 1964a.

Quay HC: Personality dimensions in delinquent males as inferred from the factor analysis of behavior rating. J Res Crime Delinquency 1:33–37, 1964b.

Robins E, Murphy G, Wilkinson R Jr: Some clinical considerations in the prevention of suicide based on a study of 134 successful suicides. Am J Public Health 49:888–899, 1950.

Robins LN: Deviant Children Grown Up. Baltimore, Williams & Wilkins, 1966.

Schulsinger F: Psychopathy, heredity, and environment. Int J Ment Health 1:190–206, 1972.

Sheard MH, Marini JL, Bridges CI, et al: The effect of lithium on impulsive aggressive behavior in man. Am J Psychiatry 133:1409–1413, 1976.

Sjogren T: Genetic, statistical and psychiatric investigations of a West Swedish population. Acta Psychiatr Neurol Scand 1948 Munksgaard, Copenhagen pp 102. [Suppl 52].

Tuckman J, Youngman W: Suicide and criminality. J Forensic Sci 10:104–107, 1965.

Vaillant GE: The Natural History of Alcoholism. Cambridge, MA, Harvard University Press, 1983.

Whitters A, Troughton E, Cadoret RJ, et al: Evidence for clinical heterogeneity in antisocial alcoholics. Compr Psychiatry 25:158–164, 1984.

Williams DT, Mehl R, Yudofsky S, et al: The effect of propranolol on uncontrolled rage outbursts in children and adolescents with organic brain dysfunction. J Am Acad Child Psychiatry 21:129–135, 1982.

Winokur G, Reich T, Rimmer J: Alcoholism. III. Diagnosis and familial psychiatric illness in 259 alcoholic probands. Arch Gen Psychiatry 23:104–111, 1970.

# chapter 16

# SEXUAL DISORDERS

*by* Gene G. Abel, M.D.
Joanne-L. Rouleau, Ph.D.

Sexual disorders include three major categories: (1) psychosexual dysfunctions that interfere with an individual's attempts to perform various sexual behaviors; (2) paraphilic disorders, interest in sexual behaviors that are outside the range of what our culture considers appropriate; and (3) gender identity disorders, a problem with the individual's self-concept as male or female.

## PSYCHOSEXUAL DYSFUNCTIONS

### Definition

Accurate definitions are essential to any science, since they allow communication between individuals dealing with similar problems, improve our understanding of the etiology and psychopathology of disorders, assist in the selection of appropriate treatment in the prediction of an individual's behavior in specific situations, and suggest the prognosis of these conditions with or without treatment (Heiman and Lo Piccolo, 1983; Jevitch, 1984; Lo Piccolo and Hogan, 1978). The current system of classifying sexual dysfunctions is by typology. Typologies, however, have a number of shortcomings because (a) borderline cases frequently do not fit into the classification system; (b) an individual may fit into multiple categories of classification; (c) it is difficult to quantify the disorders once categorized; and (d) professionals sometimes fail to appreciate that sexual behavior usually results from cultural and social interactions, learning histories, and biologic functioning.

The current standard of classification is the *Diagnostic and Statistical Manual of Mental Disorders,* third edition (DSM-III), of the American Psychiatric Association, which attempts to categorize sexual dysfunctions according to the stages of the sexual arousal cycle (Sharpe, Kuriansky, O'Connor, 1976). A variety of shortcomings have been reported with this classification system. Many investigators have asked for a more detailed elaboration of the descriptions of sexual dysfunctions. For example, erection dysfunctions categorized by the current system do not specify whether (a) the erection difficulty occurs during intercourse, nonintercourse, or both; (b) the dysfunction is primary, i.e., the patient has never been able to obtain or maintain an erection, or secondary, i.e., the patient has functioned previously but cannot function presently; (c) the erection difficulty is continuous or intermittent; and (d) the individual's erection difficulty is complete or partial. Graber and Kline-Graber (1981) have appropriately suggested that additional subcategories be added to each DSM-III classification code to qualify sexual dysfunctions along these

**TABLE 16–1**   Categorization of Sexual Dysfunctions

| Sexual Dysfunction | Diagnostic Criteria |
| --- | --- |
| Inhibited sexual desire (302.71) | Persistent and pervasive inhibition of sexual desire. The judgement of inhibition is made by the clinician's taking into account factors that affect sexual desire such as age, sex, health, intensity and frequency of sexual desire, and the context of the individual's life. |
| Inhibited sexual excitement (302.72) | Recurrent and persistent inhibition of sexual excitement during sexual activity, manifested by (1) in males, partial or complete failure to attain or maintain erection until completion of the sexual act or (2) in females, partial or complete failure to attain or maintain the lubrication-swelling response of sexual excitement until completion of the sexual act. Assumes that the individual has been engaging in sexual activity that is adequate in focus, intensity, and duration. |
| Inhibited female orgasm (302.73) | Recurrent and persistent inhibition of the female orgasm as manifested by a delay in or absence of orgasm following a normal sexual excitement phase during sexual activity that is judged by the clinician to be adequate in focus, intensity, and duration. The disturbance is not caused exclusively by organic factors (e.g., physical disorder or medication) and is not due to another Axis 1 disorder. |
| Inhibited male orgasm (302.74) | Recurrent and persistent inhibition of the male orgasm as manifested by a delay in or absence of ejaculation following an adequate phase of sexual excitement. |
| Premature ejaculation (302.75) | Ejaculation occurs before the individual wishes it, because of recurrent and persistent absence of reasonable voluntary control of ejaculation and orgasm during sexual activity. The judgement of reasonable control is made by the clinician's taking into account factors that affect duration of the excitement phase, such as age, novelty of the sexual partner, and the frequency and duration of coitus. |
| Functional dyspareunia (302.76) | Coitus is associated with recurrent and persistent genital pain, in either the male or the female. |
| Functional vaginismus (306.51) | There is a history of recurrent and persistent involuntary spasm of the musculature of the outer third of the vagina that interferes with coitus. |
| Atypical psychosexual dysfunction (302.70) | Sexual dysfunction symptoms not otherwise classified. |

From American Psychiatric Association: Diagnostic and Statistical Manual of Mental Disorders, ed 3. Washington, DC, American Psychiatric Association, 1980.

lines. Table 16–1 lists the eight DSM-III categories of sexual dysfunction. In each case, it is assumed that the symptoms are not the result of another significant psychiatric disorder and are not caused exclusively by organic factors. Unfortunately, at present, the diagnostic ability to determine whether sexual symptoms are exclusively psychological or exclusively organic in etiology, or a combination of both, is lacking.

A possible explanation for this diagnostic dilemma is that sexual behavior frequently results from the interaction of multiple factors. For example, assume that a male diabetic has developed a neuropathy that now affects his genitourinary system and interferes with erections. After this erectile dysfunction has occurred a number of times, it would be quite understandable for a normal male to consult his physician, who will inform him that diabetics may develop a neuropathy that affects their ability to obtain an erection. This information, coupled with the patient's own experience of erection difficulty, may magnify his concerns and prompt even more fears about his sexual performance. These newfound concerns cause him to be more anxious, to "spectator" or observe his own performance, which in turn leads to further performance anxiety, inhibiting his performance further. As a consequence, he begins to withdraw from his partner. Less and less communication and physical contact result until, from a purely psychological basis, further erection difficulties develop.

The shortcoming with DSM-III is the lack of more specific and comprehensive classification codes that would enable the clinician to delineate and determine the level of organic or psychological factors contributing to the patient's sexual dysfunction. Given these significant limitations, it is best to categorize by describing the various sexual dysfunctions and to await further diagnostic developments in an etiologic system of classification.

## Prevalence

The prevalence of sexual dysfunctions is difficult to determine because (a) sexual behavior is an intimate, personal aspect of our lives that we are reluctant to discuss with others; (b) surveys of large populations are usually conducted by researchers with minimal relationship with the subject, thus inhibiting him or her from revealing the presence of sexual dysfunctions; and (c) representative samples of the general population are difficult to obtain because a percentage of possible subjects will refuse to participate. Those who refuse may be individuals who are uncomfortable talking about sexuality and are more inhibited than those who accept participation. As a result, the studied populations represent more well-adjusted individuals, who presumably would have fewer sexual dysfunctions.

Frank, Anderson, and Rubenstein (1978) conducted a unique study of 100 couples reporting themselves as happily married. None was in treatment for sexual dysfunction or seeking same. The incidence of sexual dysfunctions in the males was 40 per

**TABLE 16–2  Sexual Dysfunctions in "Normal Couples"**

| Sexual Dysfunctions | Frequency | |
|---|---|---|
| | FEMALES (%) | MALES (%) |
| All sexual dysfunctions | 63 | 40 |
| Inhibited sexual desire | 35 | 16 |
| Inhibited sexual excitement | 48 | 7 |
| Inhibited orgasm | 61 | 4 |
| Premature orgasm/ejaculation | 11 | 36 |

cent and in the females, 63 per cent. The primary difficulties for the males (Table 16–2) were premature ejaculation and a lack of sexual interest, while females reported a high incidence of inhibited sexual desire and sexual excitement, and nonorgasm. These data from an upper-middle socioeconomic class may not be representative of the general population, but they do reflect the high incidence of sexual dysfunctions in couples who do not perceive themselves as specifically in need of therapy.

Table 16–3 shows the results of a similar study of consecutive referrals to an outpatient gynecologic clinic (Levine and Yost, 1976). In this population of predominantly lower socioeconomic black females, the incidence of specific sexual dysfunction was reported considerably less frequently than inhibited sexual desire and inhibited sexual excitement. A comparison of Tables 16–2 and 16–3 demonstrates the tremendous impact of sample selection on the reported incidence of sexual dysfunctions. At present, no recent representative cross-sectional sample population has been examined regarding the prevalence of sexual dysfunction in the general population.

## Etiology

Determining the etiology of sexual dysfunctions demands a valid, reliable system of differential diagnosis applied to a repre-

**TABLE 16–3  Sexual Dysfunctions in Females Attending a Gynecology Clinic**

| Sexual Dysfunction | Frequency (%) |
|---|---|
| Inhibited sexual desire | 12 |
| Inhibited sexual excitement | 12 |
| Inhibited orgasm | 5 |
| Dyspareunia | 2 |
| Vaginismus | 0 |

sentative sample with sexual dysfunctions. Current etiologic studies either fail to appreciate the sample biases of their populations or, if a disease process is present in a patient with sexual dysfunction, the diagnostician assumes that the dysfunction results from the disease. Abel, Becker, Cunningham-Rathner, Mittelman, and Primack (1982) examined a group of diabetic males with erectile impotence. Using the most valid means of separating organic from psychogenic erection difficulties (nocturnal penile tumescence monitoring), it was discovered that 30 per cent of the subjects experienced impotence of psychogenic origin unrelated to their diabetes, demonstrating that the diagnostician should be cautious in assuming that the disease process is the source of the sexual problem. Diabetic males, like nondiabetic males, may have emotional reactions leading to impotence.

Segraves, Schoenberg, Zarins, Camic, and Knopf (1981), in a study that used clearer criteria for organic vs. psychogenic erection difficulties (nocturnal penile tumescence monitoring was not required), determined the etiology of the erectile dysfunctions in 93 males referred either to a sex clinic or to a urologist. Many patients referred to a urologist were diagnosed as having organic etiologies of their sex dysfunctions (30.8 per cent), whereas the presence of organic disease in those referred to a sex clinic was infrequent (4.7 per cent). If individuals are referred to an endocrinologist, it is likely that a high incidence of endocrinologic disease will be found (Sparks, White, Connolly, 1980). If referred to a medical outpatient clinic, patients are found to have a high incidence of medically related disease (Slag et al., 1983), and if referred to a sex clinic, patients are found to have a high incidence of psychogenic erectile dysfunctions (Segraves et al., 1981). Once the importance of the sample population is appreciated, the marked variance in the incidence of organic vs. psychogenic etiologies reported by investigators becomes easier to understand. At present, a clinician can expect that patients referred to a sex clinic will have a low incidence of organic erection difficulties (5 per cent). Patients seen in a medical or surgical clinic will have a higher incidence of organically caused erectile difficulties (40 per cent to 50 per cent) (Frank et al., 1978).

Less is known about the etiology of sexual dysfunction in females because valid diagnostic procedures to discriminate between organic and psychogenic etiologies have not been developed.

## Clinical Course

Because sexual behavior results from an interaction of our cultural training, biologic function, and psychological state, it is not surprising that the clinical course of sexual dysfunctions is highly varied. When sexual dysfunctions develop, they are likely to disappear spontaneously or they become resistant to common home remedies. Collins et al. (1981), for example, studied 200 males with erectile impotence and found that 13 per cent had the dysfunction less than 6 months, 24 per cent 6 to 12 months, 29 per cent 1 to 2 years, 22 per cent 3 to 5 years, and 12 per cent longer than 5 years. Clinically, acute sexual symptoms either resolve themselves or the dysfunctions persist chronically.

It is also apparent that an isolated sexual dysfunction by itself is rather unusual. Table 16–1 lists the various sexual symptoms in a group of nonorganically impaired males seeking sexual dysfunction treatment (Rouleau, Abel, Mittelman, Becker, Cunningham-Rathner, 1984). These data reflect the percentage of occurrence of various sexual dysfunctions. Earlier clinical reports about sexual dysfunctions categorized patients in broad diagnostic categories, such as impotence, frigidity, or erection problems. However, broad classification and the lack of a detailed history conceal the variety of sexual symptoms present in most patients.

Not only do patients present with multiple sexual symptoms, but in discrete etiologic categories, there also appears to be a sequence in which these symptoms develop. In nonorganically impaired males, the sequence is premature ejaculation, followed by the episodic inability to achieve a full erection, increased incidence of partial or incomplete erections, loss of erection, loss of sexual desire, retarded ejaculation, and decreased ejaculate. In a group of male diabetics with erectile difficulties, the sequence also begins with premature ejaculation but is followed by partial erections, loss of erections, inability to achieve a full erection, loss of sexual desire, and decreased ejaculate (Rouleau et al., 1984).

The interaction between the various sexual dysfunctions is beginning to be identified. Inhibited sexual desire in males or females appears in two clinical forms. In a small percentage of individuals, the loss of sexual desire is the patient's first symptom and is often followed by the development of either erectile dysfunction in males or excitement and orgasmic dysfunction in females. More commonly, however, erectile dysfunction is the first symptom observed in males (excitement or orgasmic dysfunction in females) that leads to an increased avoidance of sexual relationships based on the belief that they are no longer able to function sexually. Removed from sexual interactions, they begin to change their cognitions that support active participation in sexual activities and they develop a loss of desire. As a result, their low sexual desire matches their functional capacity. Although their partners may be displeased with decreased frequency of sex, the patients themselves suffer less depression and lowered self-esteem because their desire equals their performance.

The clinical course of inhibited sexual excitement appears to run differently in females and males. In females, increased sexual experience is likely to reduce the incidence of sexual symptoms. In males, increased sexual experience may also reduce the incidence of sexual symptoms as he learns to adapt to new partners. In many cases, however, males will attempt home remedies or will seek new partners with the expectation of resolving their erection difficulty. These attempts tend to aggravate, rather than resolve, their erectile difficulties, resulting in more inhibited sexual excitement.

Inhibited female orgasm either persists throughout a woman's lifetime or, more commonly, there is steady improvement in her sexual functioning and reduction of her inhibited orgasms as she becomes more experienced at self-stimulation and teaches others how to stimulate her. Inhibited orgasm in the male is a more difficult problem than in the female. The symptom does not result from a lack of experience, but from a more deeply rooted, chronic fear of sexual functioning. Its subsequent course is more resistant to increased knowledge about sexual stimulation.

Premature ejaculation in the male is a relatively common problem, occurring early in patients' sexual lives. It may also follow chronic erectile impotence. In some cases the symptom spontaneously resolves itself as the patient increases the frequency of his sexual encounters. In a large percentage of males, however, it persists throughout their sexual lives if untreated.

The remaining sexual dysfunctions have a varied course.

## Assessment

Assessment should lead the clinician toward an accurate diagnosis, an appreciation of etiology (or etiologies), and therefore the most appropriate treatment intervention. (Lo Piccolo and Hogan [1978] have recently reviewed the assessment of sexual dysfunctions.) To meet these various goals, assessment should include a detailed history of the development of the sexual dysfunction symptoms, the patient's current functioning (and that of his or her partner), and an understanding of the attitudes or cognitions that have led to or maintain the current symptoms, the intrapsychic dynamics and defenses of the patient that may impede treatment, the interpersonal communications and interactions of the patient and his or her partner, the presence or absence of other significant psychiatric diagnoses, and the evaluation of the patient's biologic functioning.

The clinical interview is the most commonly used (and frequently misused) means of assessing sexual disorders. The following are typical deficits of clinical interviews:

- The interviewer fails to evaluate the patient's functioning in nonintercourse sexual activites (masturbation, oral sex, fondling, or while observing or reading erotica), and as a result, valuable diagnostic information is missed.
- Interviewers fail to ask about all possible sexual dysfunctions. Patients are not knowledgeable about the interrelationship between sexual symptoms and tend to report only those symptoms that are problematic for them.
- The clinician ignores the sexual functioning of the patient's partner (Kilman, 1978). Because sexual functioning requires interacting with a partner, the partner's attitudes, feelings, and

behaviors directly affect the patient's difficulties. Information about the patient's partner is essential.

The means of ensuring consistency and completeness in the clinical interview is to follow a standard, semistructured interview. Lo Piccolo and Heiman (1978) provide an excellent example of appropriate interviewing.

Paper-and-pencil testing provides a second means of qualifying and quantifying the patient's sexual difficulties. Although a number of such instruments are available, those by Derogatis (1976) and Lo Piccolo and Steger (1974) appear to be the most helpful, since each is applicable to both the patient and the sexual partner.

Laboratory assessment is used predominantly to separate psychogenic from organic sexual dysfunctions. Standard laboratory testing to rule out organic disease has included general measures of health (SMA-25), assessment for diabetes (3-hour glucose tolerance test), measures to evaluate hypothyroidism and hyperthyroidism, hormonal studies (plasma testosterone, plasma luteinizing hormone, and serum follicle-stimulating hormone to differentiate subcategories of hypogonadism), and serum prolactin. In addition, a number of noninvasive diagnostic techniques are used to differentiate various organic deficits (Jevitch, 1984).

The current standard for separating organic from psychogenic erection difficulties involves nocturnal penile tumescence (NPT) monitoring. This assessment methodology is based on the observation that males without erection difficulties or those having psychogenic erection difficulties obtained full erection four to six times a night during rapid-eye-movement (REM) sleep. Individuals with organic disease (excluding patients with spinal cord injuries), by contrast, fail to get full erections during the night. NPT monitoring involves measuring the patient's tumescence during sleep. A limitation of this procedure is that fullness of an erection (100 per cent penile circumference) does not necessarily mean rigidity of the penis, sufficient for penetration (Wasserman, Pollack, Spielman, Weitzman, 1980). To overcome this limitation during REM erections, a technician directly observes and quantifies the degree of rigidity the sleeping patient has obtained.

Viraq, Viraq, Lajingte, and Frydman (1982) have developed a noninvasive measure of penile rigidity. Simultaneous, direct measurement of intracavernous penile pressure with the noninvasive, mechanical measure of rigidity shows an exceedingly high correlation between actual pressure and the rigidity measure. The rigidity measurement device allows exact quantification of penile rigidity during REM sleep and therefore assists markedly in separating organic from psychogenic erection difficulties, since the extent of penile rigidity reflects the patient's ability to perform sexually. Other techniques, such as measurement of penile blood flow (Wagner, Hilsted, Jensen, 1981), show promise in assisting in the determination of differential diagnosis, but the validity of all new diagnostic methods must be determined.

### Differential Diagnosis

The differential diagnosis of sexual dysfunctions is a complex process. If a laboratory test was found positive with only one category of sexual dysfunction (with a high specificity and high sensitivity), differential diagnosis would be accurate (Galen and Gambino, 1975). At present, our diagnostic methods are inefficient at discriminating between organic and psychogenic erectile difficulties. A clinical diagnosis of neuropathy in impotent individuals is assumed to be the cause of their erectile difficulties. Such false assumptions are based on abnormal vascular, hormonal, neurologic, or psychological findings without consideration of the sensitivity, specificity, or efficiency of these diagnostic methods (Galen and Gambino, 1975).

To investigate this dilemma, Rouleau et al. (1984) compared the prevalence of various sexual symptoms in diabetic males who complained of sexual problems with that of such symptoms in males with similar complaints whose extensive medical evaluations failed to reveal organic disease. The literature indicates specific symptoms that discriminate organic (in this case, diabetes) from nonorganic impotence. A lack of morning erections, impotence during nonintercourse sexual activities, sustained sexual drive, and the presence of emotional stress temporarily related to symptom onset are all reported to be useful in such discrimination.

**TABLE 16–4**  Prevalence of Sexual Symptoms in Diabetics vs. Nondiabetics

| | Disease | | |
|---|---|---|---|
| Sexual Symptoms | DIABETES (%) N = 171 | NONE (%) N = 92 | Significance |
| 1. Continuous (not intermittent) impotence | 67.7 | 42.9 | .001 |
| 2. No morning erection | 52.2 | 44.0 | NS |
| 3. Retarded ejaculation | 16.6 | 23.9 | NS |
| 4. Impotence during nonintercourse sex | 85.9 | 48.9 | .001 |
| 5. Decreased ejaculation | 40.3 | 26.1 | .05 |
| 6. No premature ejaculation | 65.6 | 53.8 | NS |
| 7. Failure to achieve erection | 56.0 | 77.2 | .001 |
| 8. Slow (longer than 1 month) onset of problem | 71.2 | 70.3 | NS |
| 9. Sustained sex drive | 77.8 | 72.5 | NS |
| 10. No emotional stress at onset | 69.9 | 57.1 | NS |
| 11. Sex problem not partner specific | 90.6 | 74.5 | .01 |
| 12. Decreased sensitivity to pain in T-10 area | 12.9 | 8.8 | NS |
| 13. No climax during intercourse | 16.7 | 10.3 | NS |
| 14. Loss of erection | 50.3 | 73.9 | .001 |
| 15. Retrograde ejaculation | 13.0 | 7.6 | NS |
| 16. Partial erection | 91.0 | 79.1 | .05 |
| 17. No climax with any type stimulation | 19.1 | 8.8 | NS |
| 18. No loss of desire | 77.6 | 72.8 | NS |

NS, not significant.

An examination of Table 16–4, however, indicates a high prevalence of most of these symptoms in both diabetic and nondiabetic males complaining of sexual disorders. Some symptoms listed in Table 16–4 do reliably discriminate between organic and psychogenic etiologies (sexual symptoms 1, 4, and 11). Other symptoms not reported by the literature to discriminate between the groups are, nevertheless, significantly more prevalent in one group or the other (sexual symptoms 5, 7, 14, and 16).

To further validate which of these symptoms could discriminate organic from psychogenic erectile difficulties in diabetics, Abel et al. (1982) examined 60 males with diabetes, all of whom complained of erectile impotence. Using NPT monitoring, the accepted standard for discriminating organic from psychogenic erectile difficulties, these subjects were divided into three groups: (1) those who clearly had an organic impotence, (2) those who clearly did not, and (3) those with only partial organic impairment or in whom the diagnosis was unclear. Twenty-nine per cent were found to have organically caused impotence; however, 29 per cent were found to have psychogenic impotence, irrespective of their concomitant diabetes.

Using these two discrete groups, the sexual symptoms outlined in Table 16–4 were then reevaluated to determine their sensitivity, specificity, and efficiency in discriminating organic from psychogenic impotence. The seven most efficient sexual symptoms were identified. Summary scores derived from these seven symptoms produced an overall efficiency of 88 per cent, a sensitivity of 100 per cent, and a specificity of 76 per cent. Those with psychogenic erection difficulties responded negatively to a total of three or less of the following statements: (1) Every time I try to get an erection, it is less than a full erection; (2) I never wake up in the morning or during the night with a full erection; (3) It frequently or always takes me longer to reach ejaculation than it used to; (4) During oral sex or masturbation, I always get less than a full erection; (5) The amount I ejaculate is frequently or always less than it used to be; (6) I rarely or never ejaculate prematurely; and (7) I frequently or always fail to get a full erection.

These results show that symptoms assumed to be of diagnostic value in some cases are valuable, while in other cases they are not. Only when homogeneous samples of impotent males are extensively studied, and their symptoms investigated for sensitivity and specificity, will it be possible to construct a valid diagnostic system. At present, such assessment is lacking in the differential diagnosis of most types of erectile dysfunctions and has not even been attempted with the other dysfunctions of males and females.

A second methodology for improving the differential diagnosis of various sexual symptoms is to identify the most likely causative agent, remove it, and reinstate it while evaluating the effect on the patient's sexual symptom (Barlow, Hayes, Nelson, 1984). A common cause of erectile dysfunction in males presenting to outpatient medical clinics is assumed to be medication (25 per cent) (Slag et al., 1983). Substantiation of whether a drug is the causative agent would involve discontinuing the drug (and subsequently recording NPT measurements) and then reinstating it (with subsequent NPT monitoring). Results of such experimental manipulation should demonstrate evidence of organic impotence while the medication is discontinued.

Unfortunately, a more common strategy is to discontinue the drug and then evaluate the patient's reported sexual functioning. The belief here is that if the patient begins to function without the medication, the medication would be the causative agent. The problem with such a methodology is that many patients are highly responsive to the suggestions of their physician, and if their erectile difficulties are of psychogenic origin, they may also improve temporarily when the medication is discontinued. False conclusions could also be reached if the patient fails to function after the medication is discontinued because he has both an organic (medication) and a psychogenic etiology. Removal of the drug may eliminate that element but not the psychogenic factors. Successful treatment demands that both factors be dealt with. Use of NPT monitoring or the newer measure of rigidity during the night would clarify such difficult diagnostic matters, but only a few studies report the use of such a methodology.

At present, insufficient data have been gathered to determine the sensitivity, specificity, and efficiency of the diagnostic procedures. Appropriate designs are not being used to indicate and validate where suspected etiologic agents are truly responsible for various sexual dysfunctions. Until further studies are completed, one must rely on the limited validity of clinical lore in available textbooks.

## Treatment

Before the 1970s, treatment of sexual dysfunction was limited in its effectiveness. Using the psychodynamic model predominantly, most sexual dysfunctions were believed to be caused by either an unresolved Oedipus complex or castration anxiety (in males) and penis envy (in females). In the late 1960s and early 1970s, treatment approaches that focused directly on correcting various sexual symptoms emerged. Direct treatment was effective, brief, and cost-efficient. Although the specific components of treatment responsible for treatment gains have not been determined, most of the direct treatment approaches include:

- Sex education to clarify the sexual myths commonly held by the patient and his partner
- Anxiety reduction techniques (including systematic desensitization and in vivo desensitization)
- Sensory and cognitive therapy changes (treatments incorporating sensate focus and cognitive restructuring)
- Behavioral change that alters the antecedents and consequences of a couple's sexual interactions (so as to reduce the likelihood of dysfunctions recurring)
- Marital therapy to improve a couple's communications
- Psychodynamic treatment to reduce noncompliance with treatment interventions resulting from personality factors
- Medical interventions specifically designed to correct biologically caused deficits or excesses that interfere with functioning.

Although a number of treatment centers have reported outcome results, only a few have conducted controlled studies evaluating treatment effectiveness. In evaluating treatment outcome, one must view the subsample of sexual dysfunction patients cautiously. Segraves et al. (1981) examined two groups of males with erectile difficulties—one group was referred to a urologist and the other was referred to a sexual dysfunction clinic. Treatment was declined by 70.4 per cent of the patients entering treatment through urology, while only 39 per cent of those entering treatment through a sexual dysfunction clinic declined. Treatment of those referred through urology was exceedingly difficult, with only 4 per cent of treatment cases considered successful. Conversely, treatment was successful in 24 per cent of cases referred through a sexual dysfunction clinic.

Kilman (1978) has reviewed a number of the methodological difficulties in evaluating treatment outcome with sexually dysfunctional patients. His review indicates that, at present, no study of treatment outcome has overcome the many methodological limitations.

Heiman and Lo Piccolo (1983) have completed the most methodologically sound assessment of treatment intervention. In the treatment of 69 couples, 30.4 per cent of the male partners complained of premature ejaculation, 27.5 per cent complained of erectile failure; 36.2 per cent of the females complained of primary orgasmic dysfunction, and 23.2 per cent complained of secondary orgasmic dysfunction. Before and after measures using clinical interviews of the couples as well as paper-and-pencil tests revealed that significant improvement occurred in males complaining of premature ejaculation and in females complaining of primary orgasmic dysfunction. Poorer results occurred in females treated for secondary orgasmic dysfunction, and the poorest results occurred in males complaining of erectile failure. Despite various methodological limitations (32 per cent of subjects failed to complete a 3-month followup and 59.4 per cent failed to complete a 12-month followup), the treatment outcome was successful. The authors concluded that the high failure rate of males with erectile dysfunction may have resulted because of a high percentage of male subjects having organic etiologies and because males with erectile dysfunction had frequently disassociated themselves from their sexual partners.

Other authors have reported treatment effectiveness with various sexual dysfunctions; these are uncontrolled studies with methodological limitations, precluding accurate interpretation of the results. More controlled studies are needed before treatment effectiveness can be determined.

## PARAPHILIAS

### Definition

All of us are sexually interested in specific objects and specific acts. Some categories of sexual object choice (such as 4-year-old children) and sexual activities (e.g., rape) are either inappropriate within our cultural context or are so dangerous and harmful to the victim that they have been categorized as psychiatric disorders known as paraphilias. In Table 16–5 the various categories of paraphilia and their criteria for diagnosis are listed. The current DSM-III classification indicates that in order to be classified as a paraphilia, specific images or acts must be necessary for sexual excitement. In the majority of paraphilic acts, however, the individual can function successfully without the use of paraphilic images or acts in order to attain a genital experience with his partner. Although a few paraphiliacs must use paraphilic fantasies or acts to attain orgasm, they constitute a small percentage of the total number of individuals committing a small percentage of deviant sexual behaviors.

More than 50 per cent of paraphiliacs develop their unusual arousal pattern before age 18, with more than 50 per cent of homosexual pedophiles developing their arousal by age 15, 50 per cent of exhibitionists by age 16, 51 per cent of rapists by age 18, and 50 per cent of heterosexual pedophiles by age 20 (Abel, Rouleau, Cunningham-Rathner, 1985).

### Prevalence

Accurate information regarding the prevalence of paraphilias is not available because sexual behavior is considered a private interest and is not readily discussed with others, especially when it is considered deviant behavior. Discussion of one's paraphilic interests or acts may lead to arrest, conviction, and incarceration, which intensifies the difficulty of getting accurate information regarding the prevalence of paraphilias. Data gathered from a large number of outpatient paraphiliacs suggest that, in terms of victimizations, the acts of the highest incidence are those of frottage (women being touched by men for sexual purposes), exhibitionism, and child molestation. Criminal justice records are poor reflections of the incidence of various paraphilias because (a) some paraphilic acts considered by the police to be of minor consequence are unreported; (b) paraphilic acts that offend the general decency of our culture are more likely to be reported,

**TABLE 16–5** Categorization of Paraphilias

| Paraphilia | Diagnostic Criteria |
|---|---|
| Zoophilia (302.10) | The act or fantasy of engaging in sexual activity with animals is a repeatedly preferred method of achieving sexual excitement. |
| Pedophilia (302.20) | The act or fantasy of engaging in sexual activity with prepubertal children is a repeatedly preferred method of achieving sexual excitement. |
| Transvestism (302.30) | Recurrent and persistent cross-dressing by a heterosexual. Use of cross-dressing for the purpose of sexual excitement, at least initially in the course of the disorder. Intense frustration when the cross-dressing is interfered with. |
| Exhibitionism (302.40) | Repetitive acts of exposing the genitals to an unsuspecting stranger for the purpose of achieving sexual excitement, with no attempt to further sexual activity with the stranger. |
| Fetishism (302.81) | The use of nonliving objects is a repeatedly preferred method of achieving sexual excitement. The fetishes are not limited to articles of female clothing used in cross-dressing or to objects designed to be used for the purpose of sexual stimulation. |
| Voyeurism (302.82) | The individual repeatedly observes unsuspecting people who are naked, in the act of disrobing, or engaging in sexual activity, and no sexual activity with the observed people is sought. The observing is the repeatedly preferred method of achieving sexual excitement. |
| Sexual masochism (302.83) | Either a preferred or exclusive mode of producing sexual excitement is to be humiliated, bound, beaten, or otherwise made to suffer, or the individual has intentionally participated in an activity in which he or she was physically harmed or his or her life was threatened, in order to produce sexual excitement. |
| Sexual sadism (302.84) | One of the following: (1) on a nonconsenting partner, the individual has repeatedly intentionally inflicted psychological or physical suffering in order to produce sexual excitement; (2) with a consenting partner, the repeatedly preferred mode of achieving sexual excitement combines humiliation with simulated or mildly injurious bodily suffering; (3) on a consenting partner, bodily injury that is extensive, permanent, or possibly mortal is inflicted in order to achieve sexual excitement. |
| Atypical paraphilia (302.90) | Paraphilias not otherwise categorized. |

From American Psychiatric Association: Diagnostic and Statistical Manual of Mental Disorders, ed 3. Washington, DC, American Psychiatric Association, 1980.

and thus form the basis for statistical information from the criminal justice system; and (c) during the course of the criminal dispositions of sex offense crimes, plea bargaining conceals the true frequencies of various paraphilias.

## Etiology

A number of theories have been postulated to explain the etiology of deviant sexual arousal, but the social learning theory model appears to best encompass what is known about the development of behavior with regard to these specific sexual disorders. Bandura (1973) describes the initiators or instigators of the behavior and the factors that maintain it. The early developmental years encompass a variety of exploratory sexual behaviors for most males and females. Some of these early sexual behaviors are instigated by watching others perform them (modeling) either in vivo (as in cases of incest) or through the mass media. Other deviant sexual behaviors are expressions of actual experiences that the perpetrator has had in the past; a young boy who is molested by an adult male may carry out similar behavior when he becomes an adult. Finally, some deviant behavior is normal exploratory sexual behavior practiced by adolescents as they attempt to experience sexual behavior for the first time. Because of their lack of knowledge, or misinformation, they sometimes carry out highly inappropriate behavior.

Maintenance of the paraphilic behavior depends on its consequences to the offender. If the paraphiliac leaves the scene and avoids arrest, he not only fails to suffer the negative consequences of his actions, but also fails to see the consequences of his behavior on his victim. A major contributor to the maintenance of paraphilic behavior is the paraphiliac's use of his memories or fantasies of the deviant experience during masturbation (Abel and Blanchard, 1974). If the paraphiliac recalls and relives his deviant experience(s) during masturbation, the fantasies or images recalled become associated with the positive experience of orgasm. Through classical conditioning, these fantasies subsequently become more and more erotic as thousands of repeated pairings occur over time. Such reinforcement is more likely to occur in paraphiliacs who have not experienced nonparaphilic sexual experiences. Because of this selective recall, paraphilic images become more erotic as they are associated with orgasm, while nonparaphilic experiences, which are not used, become less powerful. In this manner a few paraphilic experiences recalled numerous times during orgasm serve as a reinforced pairing of paraphilic images with orgasm. Once this process becomes firmly entrenched, paraphilic behavior is more likely to occur and a chronic, recurring condition ensues.

The learning histories of some individuals make them more likely to commit paraphilic acts. The developmentally delayed are especially at risk to carry out paraphilic behavior if they fail to receive appropriate sex education. Not knowing exactly how to provide sex education to the developmentally delayed, society frequently attempts to conceal sexual knowledge and information from this group. As a result, the individual is more likely to initiate sexual behavior that may be inappropriate within our cultural context.

Some paraphilic acts reflect poor impulse control resulting from other Axis 1 conditions, such as schizophrenia. Treatment of the underlying disorder frequently leads to effective control of the paraphilic behavior, although some individuals develop an organic brain syndrome or schizophrenia and have a concomitant second diagnosis of paraphilia.

A final category of individuals commits a variety of antisocial acts, including some described as paraphilia. Individuals with antisocial personalities may commit child molestation simply to gratify their immediate need for a sexual outlet. Most of these individuals fail to have a true paraphilia, that is, a repetitive urge for sexual involvement with culturally prohibited objects or behaviors. As with the other conditions, however, some antisocials have a secondary diagnosis of paraphilia.

## Clinical Course

The behavior of most paraphiliacs follows a recurrent cycle. Urges to participate in paraphilic behavior usually develop during adolescence. As the paraphiliac asks others about his fantasies, or acts on these urges, he learns that they are inappropriate. He attempts to develop internal controls to inhibit his interest. Lacking the knowledge that the use of paraphilic fantasies during masturbation will intensify his interest and lead to a stronger desire to commit the acts, he inadvertently pairs and associates his paraphilic fantasies with orgasm. His paraphilic arousal becomes strengthened during the course of these learning trials, and as time passes, his control breaks down, and he acts (once or a number of times) until orgasm is attained or until the negative consequences of commission of the acts outweigh the expected benefits.

Immediately postarrest, there is frequently a cessation of interest in the deviant act or behavior in acute situations, which, unfortunately, gives the paraphiliac a false impression that the arrest experience has eradicated the problem. In actuality, this can be an exceedingly dangerous time for the offender, since marked reduction of the fantasies is misinterpreted as a cure, and he is more likely to place himself in situations where recommission of the act is probable.

As negative consequences follow expression of his paraphilic interests or the patient's internal analysis of the impropriety of his behavior becomes more powerful, he temporarily curtails his urges. As time passes, however, and the memory of these negative consequences weakens, his control breaks down and the cycle repeats itself.

Cognitive distortions serve an especially important role in the maintenance of paraphilic behavior. Paraphiliacs are raised in a culture that prohibits the commission of deviant sexual behavior. However, as the paraphiliac repeatedly carries out an inappropriate behavior, he must balance his commission of the behavior with his cognitions or attitudes about its appropriateness.

When marked disparity exists between the paraphiliac's behavior and his perception of that behavior as inappropriate, anxiety and depression are likely to follow. To protect against these negative emotional responses, the paraphiliac alters his cognitions. Exhibitionists, for example, conclude that exposing their genitals is actually an enjoyable sexual experience for the victim. The victim's laughter or confusion on seeing his penis is interpreted as sexual interest. Individuals who molest children will interpret their behavior as nonharmful to the child unless physical violence occurs. When the child does not refuse to participate in the act or report the crime, the paraphiliac interprets this as an expression of the child's desire to participate in the behavior. Incest offenders likewise falsely believe that if their adult sexual partners are cold and distant from them, it is better to be sexual with their own children than become involved with extramarital sex. Indeed, it appears that all paraphiliacs develop cognitive distortions that support or justify their continued involvement in the paraphilic behavior.

Table 16–6 reflects the typical lifetime course of various paraphilias. As can be seen, the majority of paraphilic arousal patterns begin during adolescence and start to decrease in frequency in the late 30s and early 40s. Paraphilic arousal patterns that can be enjoyed without a sexual partner tend to be more persistent. These acts (transvestism, fetishism, and voyeurism) can persist longer than other paraphilias.

## Assessment

Assessment of paraphiliacs requires (a) evaluation to quantify the presence or absence of arousal to paraphilic stimuli; (b) clarification of behavioral excesses or deficits that are closely correlated with deviant sexual behavior (cognitive distortion, deficits of sexual knowledge, insufficient social and assertive skills, and inadequate arousal to nondeviant stimuli); and (c) factors less closely associated with paraphilic arousal and yet reported as contributors to the expression of paraphilic behavior (anxiety, deficit coping skills/time management). Assessment includes the clinical interview, paper-and-pencil tests, and, more recently, psychophysiologic laboratory measurements.

**TABLE 16–6   Lifetime Course of Paraphilias**

| Paraphilia | Clinical Course |
|---|---|
| Zoophilia | Onset at early age, usually ceases during late teens. |
| Pedophilia | Onset at early age, suppressed for 5 to 10 years, or onset at early age and continues throughout adolescence. In both situations, pedophilic acts peak in the late 20s and early 30s and decrease in frequency by age 40, although behavior may continue into the 90s. |
| Transvestism | Onset at early age with continuation throughout adulthood. |
| Exhibitionism | Onset at early age with gradual reduction during the 40s, but behavior may continue through the 80s. |
| Fetishism | Onset at early age, continuation throughout adulthood. |
| Voyeurism | Onset at early age, with reduction of symptoms by late 30s. |
| Sexual masochism | Onset at early age, fluctuating course throughout adulthood if compliant sexual partner permits. |
| Sexual sadism | Onset in early life, fluctuating course throughout adulthood. |
| Atypical paraphilia | The majority have an early onset, with reduction in frequency of paraphilic acts by age 40. |

### Clinical Interview

Paraphiliacs are often under coercion to participate in assessment and treatment as a result of a recent arrest. Frequently, the paraphiliac fears that accurate reporting of the extent of his sexual crime may put him at greater risk for incarceration. Consequently, the paraphiliac is reluctant to reveal the scope, intensity, and frequency of his paraphilic interest. Without this information the clinician is severely limited in defining the paraphiliac's treatment needs. This major difficulty with valid reporting explains the marked discrepancies between the reports of deviant sexual behavior by the paraphiliac when confidentiality is protected and when confidentiality is not protected (Abel, Mittelman, Becker, Cunningham-Rathner, Lucas, 1983).

Abel describes various steps the clinician can take to obtain a more accurate clinical history (Abel, 1985). A common error is failure to assess the multiplicity of categories of paraphilic behavior in which the offender may be involved. Unless questioned about each paraphilia specifically, paraphiliacs are unlikely to reveal their complete arousal patterns. A structured interview should explore each paraphilic category and include the patient's age at the time of onset of each paraphilia, the frequency of paraphilic acts, the number of victims, the amount of force used during the commission of the act(s), the extent of present control over paraphilic arousal, the amount of masturbatory fantasies that involve paraphilic behaviors, and a rating or comparison of the relative arousal of each of the various paraphilic interests. Interviews should incorporate developmental milestones that help the offender to identify the chronology of his history.

Particular attention should be paid to the behavioral antecedents and consequences of the paraphiliac's use of deviant fantasies or commission of deviant acts because these factors strongly affect maintenance of the arousal. Appropriate therapy can then be devised to reduce the frequency of these antecedents, and negative consequences can be arranged to follow use of deviant fantasies or acts.

### Paper-and-Pencil Test

A number of paper-and-pencil tests have been specifically developed for use with paraphiliacs to outline reporting of the extent of deviant interests by various paraphilic categories, measures of cognitive distortions associated with child molestation and incest (Abel et al., 1984), measurement of appropriate social skills (Barlow, Abel, Blanchard, Bristow, Young, 1977), and assertiveness and various measures of anxiety and sexual knowledge. Each of these tests helps to quantify various aspects contributing to paraphilic behavior.

### Laboratory Measures

The greatest advancement in the assessment of paraphilias has been in the area of psychophysiologic assessment. Kurt Freund's pioneering work in the measurement of sexual arousal using the penile transducer (Freund, 1963) has contributed immensely to the subsequent quantification of deviant interests. This measurement procedure involves the paraphiliac wearing a penile transducer (that quantifies penile circumference) while listening to or looking at depictions of paraphilic and nonparaphilic stimuli. Using this technology, it has been possible to qualify and quantify an individual's interest in virtually every category of paraphilic arousal. Quantification of interests in child molestation, sadism, rape, masochism, exhibitionism have been substantiated (Abel, Rouleau, Cunningham-Rathner, 1985). This scientific advancement has provided the clinician, for the first time, with a means of quantifying treatment needs before, during, and after therapy by repeated objective measures of deviant interest.

Various limitations exist that interfere with the validity of psychophysiologic assessment. The greatest limitation is that some offenders are able to suppress their erection responses to deviant stimuli and, subsequently, present false negative responses. Various methods to identify attempts at faking have been developed (Laws and Holman, 1978). Because it is now possible to identify paraphilic arousal beyond the awareness of the offender, the clinician must obtain informed consent before such measurement and be aware of the ethical dilemmas involved in the productive use of such measures to identify the paraphiliac's treatment needs.

A new psychophysiologic assessment involves quantification of deviant interests on the basis of pupillometry (Abel, Lucas, Mittelman, Becker, 1983). During 4 to 7 seconds after a paraphilic stimulus is presented, a paraphiliac will develop greater pupil dilatation to those stimuli to which he is aroused. This methodology is even less under the control of the paraphilic, which means that ethical, legal, and therapeutic issues may be even more problematic than with erection measurement. Quantification of arousal, however, is the cornerstone of assessment-treatment; thus, these issues must be resolved.

## Differential Diagnosis

Differentiation of paraphilic behavior resulting from schizophrenia or organic disease is relatively straightforward because of the clinical presentation of the organic brain syndrome or schizophrenia and because the expression of paraphilic behavior resulting from these two conditions is usually different from the expression of deviant behavior by paraphiliacs. The individual with an organic brain syndrome does not have a history of early interest in paraphilic behaviors, since expression of paraphilic behavior follows the development of the organic brain syndrome. Paraphilia resulting from poor control associated with schizophrenia is likewise unusual in its presentation. The schizophrenic develops idiosyncratic interpretations of the meaning of his behavior and frequently openly admits his involvement for reasons idiosyncratic to him. The true paraphiliac, on the other hand, attempts to conceal his deviant behavior.

Developmentally delayed individuals whose paraphilic behavior is more a reflection of their limited intellectual functioning and limited sex education can also be identified by the existence of the primary diagnosis.

One of the most difficult differential diagnostic problems is evaluating whether deviant sexual behavior by adolescents is caused by a true paraphilic interest (which usually develops during adolescence) or whether it is an exploratory behavior devoid of an underlying paraphilic interest. Abel, Mittelman, Becker, Cunningham-Rathner, and Lucas (1983) report preliminary data on the penile tumescence monitoring of adolescent sex offenders to assist in this differential diagnosis. Results indicate that the same psychophysiologic assessment used with adults can be effectively used with adolescents to assist in the differential diagnosis.

## Treatment

Treatment of the paraphilias was of limited value until the advent of more direct, behavioral interventions of the early 1970s. Instead of exploring the possible early developmental factors and interpersonal conflicts that may lead to the patient's earliest interest in paraphilic behavior, the behavioral approach deals with the directly observable behavioral excesses and behavior deficits of the paraphiliac. With the development of psychophysiologic assessment, laboratory evaluation allows direct observation of the patient's excessive interest in deviant stimuli and possible deficits of nondeviant arousal. The ability to quantify the patient's sexual interest has made possible the development of various treatment interventions to reduce excessive deviant arousal and increase arousal to nondeviant stimuli (Abel and Blanchard, 1976; Abel, Blanchard, Becker, 1976; Abel, Barlow, Blanchard, Guild, 1977; Abel, Blanchard, Becker, 1978; Abel, Blanchard, Barlow, 1981; Abel, Blanchard, Becker, Djenderedjian, 1981; Abel, Becker, Blanchard, Flanagan, 1981; Abel, Becker, Murphy, Flanagan, 1981). Extensive details about these treatments to reduce deviant arousal (masturbatory satiation, covert sensitization) or generate arousal to nondeviant themes (masturbatory conditioning) have been reported (Abel and Blanchard, 1974).

Treatment has also been developed to:

- Increase or expand the paraphiliac's social skills so that he is able to communicate more effectively with potential adult partners (social skills training) (Abel et al., 1976)
- Expand the paraphiliac's assertive skills so that he can better express his needs, request behavior change, or express positive or negative feelings toward others
- Restructure the faulty cognitions that the paraphiliac uses to justify his behavior
- Improve the paraphiliac's sexual knowledge so that he is better able to interact with adult partners
- Reduce the anxiety and stress that are frequently antecedents to paraphilic behavior
- Improve daily living skills and reduce unstruc-

tured time that is more likely to lead to paraphilic behavior

- Treat drug or alcohol abuse that has been associated with paraphilic behavior (Abel et al., 1984; Abel et al., 1976; Barlow, Abel, Blanchard, Bristow, Young, 1977; Abel et al., 1978; Abel, Becker, Skinner, 1980; Abel, Rouleau, Cunningham-Rathner, 1985).

Treatment programs developed to treat less aggressive paraphilic behavior can also be applied to more dangerous crimes, such as sadistic assaults, rape, and child molestation.

A number of factors make it difficult to evaluate the effectiveness of treatment programs for sex offenders.

1. The health care system has historically ignored this major health problem by failing to develop appropriate treatment modalities for sex offenders. Only a few centers have developed assessment-treatment programs, since incarceration has traditionally been the method of intervention.

2. When a paraphiliac offends, the act is frequently classified as a felony, which makes his behavior particularly dangerous for him to report. However, because treatment outcome is measured by reoffenses, the collection of accurate data on reoffenses requires extreme confidentiality between the paraphiliac and the individual who is evaluating the reoffense. Unfortunately, most treatment programs are conducted within the criminal justice system (within prison or parole or by a therapist who is required to report reoffenses to authorities). As a result, traditional reporting methods are of questionable validity.

3. Sex crimes are frequently episodic in nature. Exhibitionists, for example, may have a burst of exposure behavior, with 30 to 40 exposures within 1 week, which is then followed by cessation of the behavior for 3 months. This natural variability in the expression of the offense makes the determination of treatment more difficult. Some paraphilic behaviors have seasonal variation. Frottage, exhibitionism, and child molestation, for example, are more likely to occur in the summer months, when lighter clothing is worn by potential victims of frottage, less restraining clothing is worn by exhibitionists, and children are frequently left outdoors unattended.

4. Many attempts to evaluate treatment effectiveness have used subject samples that are exceedingly small or heterogeneous. Comparison of recidivism rates for high-frequency crimes (frottage, exhibitionism, voyeurism) with recidivism rates for low-frequency crimes (rape) ignores the frequency of the crimes. Proper outcome studies, therefore, require homogeneity of paraphilic categories.

Only two studies in the literature approach moderate standards of appropriate design to evaluate treatment effectiveness. The first of these, by Doshay (1943), involved the treatment of 256 juvenile sex offenders treated in the late 1930s and early 1940s. The principal component of the treatment was generating guilt in the adolescent offender by mobilizing the general guilt and shame inherent to his culture regarding his sex crime. The adolescent sex offenders (some of whom did not have paraphilias that would meet the current DSM-III classification) were brought together with their parent(s) for an open discussion of the boy's deviant behavior that led to his arrest.

Recidivism was determined by a 6-year followup that examined the records of various bureaus, agencies, courts, and schools in the city (New York) where the study was completed. Recidivism rates showed that in the 108 boys who had committed sex offenses exclusively, only 2 reoffended for sex crimes before reaching adulthood and none recommitted sex crimes as adults. Of the 148 adolescent offenders who had committed sex offenses in addition to other kinds of nonsexual crimes, 14 recommitted sex offenses as adults. This surprisingly low frequency of reoffense (according to arrest records) suggests that this rather simple treatment intervention might be highly effective with adolescent sex offenders.

The second study, conducted by Abel et al. (1984), is a multicomponent behavioral treatment of 194 child molesters seen on an outpatient basis for 30 weeks, with numerous behavioral assessments before, during, and after treatment and followup at 6- and 12-month intervals. Unique to this study was that data were gathered from the offenders under a Certificate of Confidentiality from the federal government, which protected the confidentiality of the offender's self-report. Treatment success rates were 99 per cent immediately post-treatment, 90 per cent 6 months post-treatment, and 82 per cent 12 months post-treatment. Final 12-month followup of all treated subjects is currently in progress, but these tentative results once again show that behavioral treatment for sex offenders can be effective.

A number of reports of the use of medroxyprogesterone acetate (Depo-Provera), which reduces the effectiveness of the offender's circulating testosterone, indicates that reduction of the paraphiliac's sexual drive can also be a valuable adjunct to treatment to help the paraphiliac gain control of his deviant arousal. Berlin and Meinecke (1981) report a 35 per cent success rate for a group of 20 paraphiliacs. These results must be tempered by the fact that of the eight offenders who discontinued medication, seven reoffended, suggesting that compliance with the treatment regimen and sustained use of Depo-Provera is necessary to reduce recidivism.

## GENDER IDENTITY DISORDERS

How an individual represents himself or herself sexually to others depends on a variety of factors. Most obvious to others is an individual's gender motor behavior (Barlow, Abel, Blanchard, Bristow, Young, 1977), since, in most cultures, there are stereotypic ways in which individuals present themselves as either male or female. By examining the cultural norms, it is possible to rate any individual as having gender motor behavior that is masculine, neutral, or feminine. A less conspicuous element of how patients represent themselves is their sexual attraction to members of the same biologic sex, the opposite biologic sex, or to both. These preferences lead to the diagnosis of homosexual interests, heterosexual interests, or bisexual interests. Even more difficult to discern is how each patient conceptualizes his or her sexual identity as either male or female.

Since the mid-1970s, research in transsexualism has markedly increased in response to the growing number of patients seeking sex reassignment surgery. Table 16–7 lists the diagnostic criteria for the gender identity disorders classified as transsexualism, in which an individual's sexual identity is opposite to that of his or her biologic sex.

## Definition

A transsexual is a cross dresser who wishes to live and be accepted as a member of the sex opposite to his or her own biologic sex, with the prototypical complaint of being a female trapped in a male body or vice versa (Stoller, 1968).

## Prevalence

Edgerton (1984) reported that, in 1979, an undocumented estimate of the number of adult Americans having had hormonal and surgical sex reassignment ranged from 3000 to 6000 individuals, and that an estimated 30,000 to 60,000 Americans see themselves as being candidates for sex reassignment.

Since the mid-1970s the number of demands for psychological, hormonal, and surgical therapy for sex reassignment has increased. More than 40 centers in the western hemisphere offer surgical sex reassignment (Edgerton, 1984).

Early estimates (Green, 1974) revealed that in the United States, females who wanted to become and live as males were only one third to one sixth as common in number as their male counterparts; that is, only one female wanted to become male for every three to six males who wanted to become female. However, as surgical techniques for phallic construction have improved, the number of female-to-male transsexuals has increased significantly (Hester, Hill, Jurkiewicz, 1978; McCraw et al., 1976). At the Virginia Gender Clinic, for example, equal numbers of males and females request sex reassignment (Edgerton, 1984).

## Etiology

An etiologic pattern in male-to-female and in female-to-male transsexuals can be observed from a series of events commonly present in feminine boys and masculine girls (Green, 1974). The following events are frequently reported in feminine boys:

- Mothers of feminine boys see their infant sons as being unusually attractive.
- The mother's time commitment toward her son is considerable.

**TABLE 16–7   Categorization of Gender Identity Disorders**

| Gender Identity Disorder | Diagnostic Criteria |
| --- | --- |
| Transsexualism (302.5x) | Sense of discomfort and inappropriateness about one's anatomical sex. Wish to be rid of one's own genitals and to live as a member of the other sex. The disturbance has been continuous (not limited to periods of stress) for at least two years. Absence of physical intersex or genetic abnormality. |
| Gender identity disorder of childhod (302.60) | *For females:* Strongly and persistently stated desire to be a boy, or insistence that she is a boy (not merely a desire for any perceived cultural advantages from being a boy). Persistent repudiation of female anatomical structures as manifested by at least one of the following repeated assertions: (1) that she will grow up to become a man (not merely in that role), (2) that she is biologically unable to become pregnant, (3) that she will not develop breasts, (4) that she has no vagina, (5) that she has, or will grow, a penis. Onset of the disturbance before puberty.<br>*For males:* Strongly and persistently stated desire to be a girl, or insistence that he is a girl. Either (1) or (2): (1) persistent repudiation of male anatomical structures, as manifested by at least one of the following repeated assertions: (a) that he will grow up to become a woman (not merely in that role), (b) that his penis or testes are disgusting or will disappear or (c) that it would be better not to have a penis or testes. (2) Preoccupation with female stereotypical activities as manifested by a preference for either cross-dressing or simulating female attire, or by a compelling desire to participate in the games and pastimes of girls. Onset of the disturbance before puberty. |
| Atypical gender identity disorder (302.85) | Gender identity disorders not otherwise classified. |

From American Psychiatric Association: Diagnostic and Statistical Manual of Mental Disorders, ed 3. Washington, DC, American Psychiatric Association, 1980.

- As the child begins exploring his environment, many colorful accessories belonging to his mother are used by the child as objects for play.
- The child's feminine behaviors are first seen as being charming or cute.
- As the boy matures, his father is a less significant person than his mother.
- Like the mother, the father first sees his son's feminine behavior as being funny, cute, or neutral.
- Girls are primarily available for the boy's early peer relationships.
- The father finds that his son has no interest or little interest in father-son rough and tumble play.
- During the first years of school, earlier feminine skills socialization is an obstacle to same-sex peer companionships.
- The mother continues to respond positively to the boy's interest in improvising feminine modes of dress and his attentiveness to her clothing and grooming.
- Emotional distances increase between the father and son.
- Traditionally feminine displays of affection reveal the boy's increasing identification with females.
- Adults outside the family (often schoolteachers) will repeatedly call the boy's feminine behaviors to the attention of the mother.

Events frequently reported in masculine girls are essentially the counterparts of the same series of events reported in feminine boys. Masculinity, or "tomboyishness," in girls is much more common than femininity, or "sissiness," in boys. Because many girls experience a tomboy state at an early age and later become feminine, the earliest stage is less noticeable to adults and seldom leads masculine girls to treatment. If a female child is given a male derivative name and has a stable, warm father and an unpleasant or emotionally distant mother, and if rough and tumble play are reinforced, she can be expected to identify more with males.

## Clinical Course

Striving for full acceptance by society as a member of the opposite biologic sex, adult transsexuals seek medical help. Typically, they request hormone therapy to bring the body anatomically and hormonally closer to that of the opposite sex. They plead for sex reassignment surgery and seek a birth certificate designating their new status.

Group studies related to male-to-female transsexuals showed them as being (a) less stable and more psychologically disturbed than their female counterparts (Hunt, Carr, Hampson, 1981), (b) less informed about sexuality and having a lower sex drive (Derogatis, Meyer, Boland, 1981), (c) psychologically stabilized once they live out and enact a cross gender role and identity (Langevin, Paitich, Steiner, 1977), and (d) stabler after hormonal treatment and surgical sex reassignment (Edgerton, 1984).

Group studies related to female-to-male transsexuals showed them as being (a) lacking in significant psychopathology and evidence of reality impairment (Derogatis et al., 1981), (b) healthier than their male counterparts (McCauley and Ehrhardt, 1977), and (c) as a group, similar to a control group enacting more stereotypical gender roles and identities (Strassberg, Roback, Cunningham, McKee, Larson, 1979).

## Differential Diagnosis

The major diagnostic dilemma with individuals complaining of a sexual identity disorder is to rule out schizophrenia, effeminate homosexuality (those who believe that sex reassignment surgery might make them more appealing sexual partners), and transvestism (those whose cross dressing has continued over time and who now believe that sex change surgery would be a natural extension of their transvestism).

Minimal sexual arousal and wearing clothing of the opposite sex in public are essential criteria for the diagnosis of transsexualism (Stoller, 1968). Additional criteria include self-concept as being a member of the opposite biologic sex during sexual relations and the refusal to permit manipulation or stimulation of genitals by sex partners. The preceding two criteria clearly differentiate transsexualism from transvestism; the latter criterion differentiates transsexualism from homosexuality. Furthermore, male and female transsexuals deny any interest in homosexuality and report a cross gender orientation from earliest memory.

## Assessment

### Feminine Boys and Masculine Girls

In his study, Green (1974) compared a population of feminine boys, masculine boys, and typical girls. The groups were comparable for age, IQ, ethnic background, and extent of their fathers' formal education. The standard tests given to the subjects were the It-Scale for Children, Draw-a-Person Test, Family-Doll Preference Test (Green, 1971a), and the Parent and Activity Preference Test (Green, 1971b). When both biologic parents were available, they were tested with their child with the Family Communication Test.

According to Green, the overall psychological results supported the subjective impressions obtained from clinical interviews. For example, one of the most striking observations was the degree of similarity between feminine boys and girls. With this more objective way to collect data (test situations), feminine boys did not emerge as a "third sex."

### Adult Transsexuals

As reported by Lothstein (1984), over the past 30 years, 41 studies have been published on the psychological testing of transsexuals in which 699 self-labeled transsexuals have been evaluated. A summary of these studies shows that 80 per cent focused on male-to-female transsexuals.

The most commonly used tests are the Minnesota Multiphasic Personality Inventory, the Draw-a-Person Test, and several cognition tests or intellectual functioning tests (mainly the Wechsler Adult Intelligence Scale).

Contrary to the assessment of feminine

boys and masculine girls, the assessment of adult transsexuals was not designed to evaluate their psychological treatment needs. Rather, it was designed to be used as a predictor of success of surgical reassignment.

As pointed out by Lothstein (1984), a considerable amount of psychological information has been obtained about transsexuals without providing a real understanding of the phenomenon itself. More psychological forms of testing should be used with transsexuals in order to provide a profile of psychological characteristics of transsexualism, a description of their treatment needs, and a means of evaluating their treatment needs and treatment outcome.

A newer method of assessing transsexuals involves direct measurement of sexual responses while presenting various stimuli depicting the subject as heterosexual, homosexual, lesbian, or as a transvestite. Using the penile transducer, Abel, Blanchard, Barlow, and Mavissakalian (1975) described the assessment of a male seeking sex reassignment surgery. Contrary to the subject's self-report, the psychophysiologic erection responses demonstrated his major arousal pattern to be that of masochism, including themes of being changed into a female against his will. Cunningham-Rathner and Abel (1984) described a similar psychophysiologic assessment of a female-to-male transsexual using the vaginal photoplethysmograph, a device that measures female sexual arousal by quantifying vaginal engorgement in biologic females while concomitantly presenting various sexual stimuli. Standards for such psychophysiologic measurement have not been established, but these preliminary studies suggest that objective psychophysiologic assessment can be an important adjunct to traditional clinical interviews and paper-and-pencil testing for potential transsexuals.

## Treatment

At the Gender Identity Treatment Program at UCLA, many approaches to treatment of feminine boys and masculine girls have been developed (Green, 1974). Three specific strategies of intervention have been used: (1) individual sessions with the patient and separate sessions with his parent(s); (2) group sessions with several patients, with the patient's mother, and with the patient's father; and (3) introducing parents to specific aspects of behavior in their child that would be systematically reinforced or extinguished at home. The aims of these clinical interventions are to:

- Develop a relationship of trust and affection between a patient and the therapist of the sex opposite to that of the patient
- Inform the child of the impossibility of changing his or her sex
- Demonstrate to the child the positive aspects of participating in some of the activities engaged in by same-sex peers and promote comfort in such activity
- Teach parents how they may be fostering sexual identity conflicts in their child
- Make the parents aware of the importance of consistent disapproval of opposite-sex behaviors performed by the child and consistent approval of appropriate behaviors
- Increase the same-sex parent's involvement in the child's life.

Regarding the treatment of adult transsexuals, as psychiatrists and psychologists, what meaningful alternative help (other than surgical sex reassignment) have we been able to offer to the transsexual patient? Clinical interviews and psychological testing of transsexuals seem to target exclusively the narrow issue of predicted success of sex reassignment surgery. However, recent developments raise some question about this approach, since reports are appearing that describe patients so dissatisfied with sex reassignment surgery that they discard their biologic gender role despite the physical irreversibility of the surgery (Van Putten and Fawzy, 1976).

A few reports now suggest that behavioral procedures are effective in changing gender identity in some patients. Barlow, Reynolds, and Agras (1973) have reported the first successful change of gender identity in a diagnosed transsexual using a behavioral approach. Six years later, Barlow, Abel, and Blanchard (1979) reported a followup study on this case; two additional cases are also presented. In the first study, with a 17-year-old male transsexual, gender-specific motor behavior, appropriate sex-role social behavior, cognitive sexual activity, and sexual arousal patterns were defined, measured, and sequentially modified. In the 6 years post-treatment, the patient remained "completely sexually reoriented," denied desire for sex reassignment surgery, and reported masturbation approximately four times a week to heterosexual fantasies. His memories of treatment were fuzzy, but he recalled this period as an unhappy time in his life.

After the successful treatment of this patient, Barlow et al. (1979) described two additional cases using a similar therapeutic package. In the first case, sweeping changes in gender identity, sex-role behavior, and sexual arousal patterns were observed. In the second case, rigid feminine gender identity was given up, but the patient chose to retain homosexual interests and behavior. Social adaptation was satisfactory.

Most amazingly, Barlow, Abel, and Blanchard (1977) also report that successful "treatment" in a conservatively diagnosed 21-year-old male transsexual was observed by faith healing. Objective and independent measurement was obtained before and after the patient's religious experience. Although the authors mentioned that additional followup is necessary in this case to confirm the stability of the measures, it cannot be denied that this patient, who was clearly diagnosed as a transsexual by the most conservative criteria, assumed a long-lasting masculine gender identity in a remarkably short period after his reported exorcism.

Successful data on behavioral treatment of female-to-male transsexualism have not as yet been reported.

Readers who are interested in the recommended procedure leading to sex reassignment surgery are referred to the *Standards of Care*, developed and available from The Harry Benjamin International Gender Dysphoria Association, Inc., 900 Welch Road, Suite 402, Stanford, California 94304.

## CONCLUSION

The evaluation and treatment of sexual disorders is a relatively new field of endeavor for medicine. The late arrival of the sexual disorders into the medical sphere appears to result from the cultural prohibition against discussing sexuality. Paradoxically, this is one of the principal factors that contribute to the development and maintenance of sexual dysfunctions and paraphilias. Secrecy and concealment about one's sexuality contribute to the patient's reluctance to seek help with his sexual dysfunction or unusual sexual preferences. Medicine must take the lead toward the open discussion of sexual disorders with patients so that they can be helped to proceed with a healthier and more fulfilling sexual life.

## REFERENCES

Abel GG: A clinical evaluation of possible sex offenders, in The Incest Offender, the Victim, the Family: New Treatment Approaches. White Plains, NY, Mental Health Assoc of Westchester County, 1985.

Abel GG, Barlow DH, Blanchard EB, Guild D: The components of rapists' sexual arousal. Arch Gen Psychiat 34:895–903, 1977.

Abel GG, Becker JV, Blanchard EB, Flanagan B: The behavioral assessment of rapists, in Hays R, Roberts TK, Solway K (eds): Violence and the Violent Individual. New York, Spectrum, 1981, pp 221–230.

Abel GG, Becker JV, Cunningham-Rathner J, Mittelman M, Primack M: Differential diagnosis of impotence in diabetics: The validity of sexual symptomatology. J Neuro Uroly 1:57–69, 1982.

Abel GG, Becker JV, Cunningham-Rathner J, Mittelman M, Rouleau JL, Kaplan M, Reich J: Treatment of Child Molesters. Atlanta, Department of Psychiatry, Emory University, School of Medicine, 1984.

Abel GG, Becker JV, Murphy WD, Flanagan B: Identifying dangerous child molesters, in Stuart R (ed): Violent Behavior Social Learning Approaches to Prediction, Management, and Treatment. New York, Brunner Mazel, 1981, pp 117–137.

Abel GG, Becker JV, Skinner LJ: Aggressive behavior and sex. Psychiatr Clin North Am 3:1, 133–151 1980.

Abel GG, Becker JV, Skinner LJ: Treatment of the violent sex offender, in Roth LH (ed): Clinical Treatment of the Violent Person. Crime and Delinquency Issues: A Monograph Series. National Institute of Mental Health, DHHS Publication N. (ADM) 85–1425, 1985.

Abel GG, Blanchard EB: The role of fantasy in the treatment of sexual deviation. Arch Gen Psychiatry 30:467–475, 1974.

Abel GG, Blanchard EB: The measurement and generation of sexual arousal in male sexual deviates, in Hersen M, Eisler R, Miller PM (eds): Progress in Behavior Modification, vol 2. New York, Academic Press, 1976, pp 99–136.

Abel GG, Blanchard EB, Barlow DH: Measurement of sexual arousal in several paraphilias: The effect of stimulus modality, instructional set and stimulus content on the objective. Behav Res Ther 19:25–33, 1981.

Abel GG, Blanchard EB, Barlow DH, Mavissakalian M: Identifying specific erotic cues in sexual deviation by audiotaped description. J Appl Behav Anal 8:247–260, 1975.

Abel GG, Blanchard EB, Becker JV: Psychological treatment for rapists, in Brodsky S, Walker M (eds): Sexual Assault. Toronto, Lexington Books, 1976, pp 99–116.

Abel GG, Blanchard EB, Becker JV: An integrated treatment program for rapists, in Rada R (ed): Clinical Aspects of the Rapists. New York, Grune & Stratton, 1978, pp 161–214.

Abel GG, Blanchard EB, Becker JV, Djenderedjian A: Differentiating sexual aggressives with penile measures. Crim Just Behav 5:315–332, 1978.

Abel GG, Blanchard EB, Becker JV, Djenderedjian A: Two methods of measuring penile response. Behav Ther 12:320–328, 1981.

Abel GG, Cunningham-Rathner J, Becker JV, McHugh J: Motivating sex offenders for treatment with feedback from their psychophysiologic assessment. Paper presented at the World Congress of Behavior Therapy, Washington, DC, December 1983.

Abel GG, Lucas L, Mittelman MS, Becker JV: Pupillometry to determine the sexual preferences of paraphiliacs. Paper presented at the World Congress of Behavior Therapy, Washington, DC, December 1983.

Abel GG, Mittelman MS, Becker JV, Cunningham-Rathner J, Lucas L: The characteristics of men who molest young children. Paper presented at the World Congress of Behavior Therapy, Washington, DC, December 1983.

Abel GG, Rouleau JL, Cunningham-Rathner J: Sexually aggressive behavior, in Curran W, McGarry AL, Shah SA (eds): Modern Legal Psychiatry and Psychology. Philadelphia, FA Davis, 1985.

Bandura A: Aggression: A Social Learning Analysis. Englewood Cliffs, NJ, Prentice-Hall, 1973.

Barlow DH, Abel GG, Blanchard EB: Gender identity change in a transsexual: An exorcism. Arch Sex Behav 6:387–395, 1977.

Barlow DH, Abel GG, Blanchard EB: Gender identity change in transsexuals: Follow-up and replications. Arch Gen Psychiatry 36:1001–1007, 1979.

Barlow DH, Abel GG, Blanchard EB, Bristow A, Young LA: Heterosocial skills checklist for males. Behav Ther 8:229–239, 1977.

Barlow DH, Hayes SC, Nelson RO: The Scientist Practitioner: Research and Accountability in Clinical and Educational Settings. New York, Pergamon Press, 1984.

Barlow DH, Reynolds EH, Agras WS: Gender identity change in a transsexual. Arch Gen Psychiatry 28:569–579, 1973.

Berlin F, Meinecke C: Treatment of sex offenders with antiandrogenic medication: Conceptualization, review of treatment modalities. Am J Psychiatry 138:601–607, 1981.

Collins WE, McKendry SBR, Silverman M, Krul LE, Collins JP, Irvine AH: Multidisciplinary survey of erectile impotence. Can Med Assoc J 28:1393–1399, 1981.

Cunningham-Rathner J, Abel GG: Psychophysiologic measurements of sexual arousal in females, in Fisher M, Fishkin R, Jacobs J (eds): Sexual Arousal. Springfield, IL, Charles C Thomas, 1984, pp 70–87.

Derogatis LR: Psychological assessment of sexual disorders, in Meyer J (ed): Clinical Management of Sexual Disorders. Baltimore, Williams and Wilkins, 1976.

Derogatis LR, Meyer M, Boland P: A psychological profile of the transsexual. II. The female. J Nerv Men Dis 169:157–168, 1981.

Doshay LJ: The Boy Sex Offender and His Later Career. New York, Grune & Stratton, 1943.

Edgerton MT: The role of surgery in the treatment of transsexualism. Ann Plast Surg 13:6, 1984.

Fleming M, Cohen D, Salt P, Jones D, Jenkins S: A study of pre- and post-surgical transsexuals: MMPI characteristics. Arch Sex Behav 10:161–169, 1981.

Frank E, Anderson C, Rubenstein D: Frequency of sexual dysfunction in "normal couples". N Engl J Med 229:111–115, 1978.

Freund K: A laboratory method for diagnosing predominance of homo and hetero erotic interest in the male. Behav Res Ther 1:85–93, 1963.

Galen RS, Gambino SR: Beyond Normality: The Predictive Value and Efficiency of Medical Diagnosis. New York, John Wiley & Sons, 1975.

Graber B, Kline-Graber G: Research criteria for male erectile failure. J Sex Marital Ther 7:37–48, 1981.

Green R: Family-Doll Preference Test. Copyright 1971, Richard Green, M.D., 1971a.

Green R: Parent and Activity Preference Test. Copyright 1971, Richard Green, M.D., 1971b.

Green R: Sexual Identity Conflicts in Children and Adults. New York, Basic Books, 1974.

Heiman JR, Lo Piccolo J: Clinical outcome of sex therapy. Arch Gen Psychiatry 40:443–449, 1983.

Hester TR, Hill HL, Jurkiewicz MJ: One-stage reconstruction of the penis. Br J Plast Surg 31:279, 1978.

Hunt D, Carr J, Hampson J: Cognitive correlates of biologic sex and gender identity in transsexualism. Arch Sex Behav 10:66–75, 1981.

Jevitch M: Vascular non-invasive diagnosis, in Chane RJ, Siloky MB, Goldstein I (eds): Male Sexual Dysfunction. Boston, Little, Brown, 1984, pp 139–164.

Kilman PR: The treatment of primary and secondary orgasmic dysfunction: A methodological review of the literature since 1970. J Sex Marital Ther 4:155–162, 1978.

Langevin R, Paitich D, Steiner B: The clinical profile of male transsexuals living as females vs. those living as males. Arch Sex Behav 6:143–154, 1977.

Laws DR, Holman ML: Sexual response faking by pedophiles. Crim Just Behav 5:343–356, 1978.

Levine SB, Yost MA Jr: Frequency of sexual dysfunction in a general gynecological clinic: An epidemiological approach. Arch Sex Behav 5:229–238, 1976.

Lo Piccolo L, Heiman J: Sexual assessment and history interview, in Lo Piccolo J, Lo Piccolo L (eds): Handbook of Sex Therapy. New York, Plenum Press, 1978, pp 103–113.

Lo Piccolo J, Hogan DR: Sexual dysfunction, in Lo Piccolo J, Lo Piccolo L (eds): Handbook of Sex Therapy. New York, Plenum Press, 1978, pp 199–203.

Lo Piccolo J, Steger JC: The sexual interaction inventory: A new instrument for the assessment of sexual dysfunction. Arch Sex Behav 3:585–595, 1974.

Lothstein LM: Psychological testing with transsexuals: A 30-year review. J Person Assess 48:5, 1984.

McCauley E, Ehrhardt A: Role expectations and definitions: A comparison of female transsexuals and lesbians. J Homosex 3:137–147, 1977.

McCraw J, Massey F, Shanklin K, Horton C: Vaginal reconstruction using gracilis myocutaneous flaps. Plast Reconstr Surg 58:176, 1976.

Rouleau JL, Abel GG, Mittelman MS, Becker JV, Cunningham-Rathner J: Sexual symptoms specific to diabetes. Paper presented at the World Meeting of Impotence, Paris, June 1984.

Segraves RT, Schoenberg HW, Zarins CK, Camic P, Knopf J: Characteristics of erectile dysfunction as a function of the medical care system entry point. Psychosom Med 43:227–234, 1981.

Sharpe LJ, Kuriansky JB, O'Connor JF: A preliminary classification of human functional sexual disorders. J Sex Marital Ther 2:106–114, 1976.

Slag MF, Morley JE, Elson MK, Dace LT, Nelson CJ, Nelson AE, Kinlaw WB, Beyer HS, Nuttal FQ, Shafer RB: Impotence in medical clinic outpatients. JAMA 249:1736–1740, 1983.

Sparks RF, White RA, Connolly PB: Impotence is not always psychogenic: Newer insights into hypothalamic-pituitary-gonadal dysfunction. JAMA 243:750–755, 1980.

Strassberg D, Roback H, Cunningham J, McKee E, Larson P: Psychopathology of self-identified female-to-male transsexuals, homosexuals, and heterosexuals. Arch Sex Behav 8:491–496, 1979.

Stoller R: Sex and Gender: On the Development of Masculinity and Femininity. New York, Science House, 1968.

Van Putten T, Fawzy FI: Sex conversion surgery in a man with severe gender dysphoria: A tragic outcome. Arch Gen Psychiatry 33:751–754, 1976.

Viraq R, Viraq H, Lajingte L, Frydman D: A new device to measure rigidity of the penis. Paper presented at the Third International Conference on Corpus Cavernosum Revascularization, Copenhagen, August 1982.

Wagner B, Hilsted J, Jensen SB: Diabetes mellitus and erectile failure, in Wagner G, Green R (eds): Impotence. New York, Plenum Press, 1981, pp 51–61.

Wasserman MD, Pollack CP, Spielman AJ, Weitzman ED: Theoretical and technical problems in the measurement of nocturnal penile tumescence for the differential diagnosis of impotence. Psychosom Med 42:575, 1980.

# chapter 17

# SPECIAL AND UNUSUAL PSYCHIATRIC SYNDROMES

*by* Henry A. Nasrallah, M.D.

## INTRODUCTION

Several psychiatric syndromes are unusual, exotic, uncommon, or otherwise hard to classify. Many of these disorders have been described in case reports or reviews over the past 100 years, and most have not been integrated into any classification system except perhaps for that of Leonhard, which includes the area of atypical psychosis (Fish, 1964). This chapter reviews those special psychiatric syndromes and includes an attempt to address, whenever possible, their etiology, epidemiology, clinical manifestations, differential diagnosis, laboratory findings, clinical course, and treatment.

## CLASSIFICATION

Although most of the unusual psychiatric disorders described here are regarded as "syndromes," many are, in fact, merely an unusual or clinically "dramatic" symptom, embedded within a clinically recognizable psychiatric or neurologic illness. For example, Capgras's syndrome, or the "delusion of doubles," is occasionally seen in schizophrenia and bears a high degree of resemblance (and pathogenesis?) to the neurologic syndromes of reduplicative phenomenon and prosopagnosia. Various authors have subclassified the unusual psychiatric disorders using such descriptive or arbitrary terms as situation-specific behaviors, culture-bound syndromes, atypical psychoses, idiopathic syndromes, collective psychoses, unclassifiable syndromes, and exotic syndromes.

This chapter approaches these special psychiatric conditions as either unusual symptoms of well-known psychiatric disorders or, where appropriate, freestanding syndromes that may be grouped with clinically established disorders. They are presented alphabetically.

## UNUSUAL PSYCHIATRIC SYMPTOMS

### Autoscopy

The term autoscopy was first coined by Schilder (1950), and it literally means "seeing one's own self." Critchley (1950) defined it as "delusional dislocation of the body image into the visual sphere." Lippman (1953) defined it as "hallucinations of physical duality." Lukianowicz (1958), who wrote the best review of the subject, defined autoscopy as a "complex psychosensorial hallucinatory perception of one's own body image, projected into the external visual space." The cases reported describe seeing a mirror image of themselves wearing the same clothes and mimicking every movement as if in a mirror.

Autoscopy is uncommon. It has been described by famous literary figures, including Aristotle, Goethe, de Maupassant, Shelley, and Poe, some of whom are believed to have had autoscopic experiences.

As with other hallucinatory phenomena, the cause of autoscopy is unknown. However, a strong association between autoscopic phenomena and two neurologic conditions (temporal lobe epilepsy and migraine) supports the notion of an organic etiology. Irritative lesions in the temporo-parieto-occipital areas have been suggested by several investigators, in contrast to the (untestable) psychodynamic hypothesis that attributes autoscopy to wish fulfillment and narcissistic archetypal thinking. Autoscopy is occasionally seen in schizophrenia or depression, but the possibility that epilepsy or migraine may be present in such patients has not been studied. The actual autoscopic experience may be preceded by a brief sensory aura and, frequently, depersonalization. No relationship with age, gender, intelligence, or family history of psychosis has been found. The most frequent emotional reaction is sadness, as well as amazement or bewilderment and sometimes satisfaction. The experience lasts for a few seconds and may occur once or repeatedly. The majority of autoscopic phenomena occur at dusk and seldom during daytime.

Seeing one's double may occasionally occur in "normal" subjects, usually as part of hypnagogic or hypnopompic sleep phenomena (Lukianowicz, 1958).

A special form of autoscopy is the "Doppelganger," which involves the fear of disintegration or imminent death and sometimes active suicide intent (Maack and Mullen, 1983).

There is no specific therapy for autoscopy. However, symptomatic treatment of the coexisting disorder (epilepsy, migraine, depression) is frequently indicated and helpful.

## Capgras's Delusion

In 1923, Capgras and Reboul-lachaud reported the "illusion des sosies," which refers to the delusional negation of identity of familiar persons. Later, two similar types of delusions were described: the syndrome of Fregoli (Courbon and Fail, 1927) and the syndrome of intermetamorphosis (Courbon and Tusques, 1927). All three are variants of the "delusion of doubles," in which a (usually psychotic) patient misidentifies a relative or a friend as having been replaced by a double with close resemblance to the familiar person. Levy-Valensi (1939) called it "the syndrome of Capgras," even though it was first described in 1883 by Magnan and in 1913 by Bessiere.

The delusion of Capgras is an uncommon manifestation of psychosis, usually schizophrenia, but is also present in mania and depression with psychotic features (Enoch and Trethowan, 1979) and in dementia (Goldfarb and Weiner, 1977). The Germans regarded Capgras as a symptom, but the French saw it as a syndrome.

Clinically, most patients have prominent paranoid features, and many experience feelings of depersonalization or derealization. Some authors believe that Capgras may represent a delusional evolution of the phenomena of depersonalization and derealization (Christodoulou, 1977), and all tend to occur more in females.

Although Capgras's delusion usually involves close relatives, such as spouses, parents, or siblings, I have treated a chronic schizophrenic patient who not only misidentified his mother as an imposter, but also would misidentify some objects in the hospital room, such as chair, table, or heating pipes as those in his own home, which is probably déjà vu.

The etiology of Capgras remains unknown. The trend in the literature over the past decade, however, has shifted from a psychodynamic formulation (e.g., intense ambivalent feelings toward the delusional object) to a more organic etiology. There are strong similarities between Capgras and certain phenomena that occur during the epileptic aura, such as false memories of familiarity (déjà vu and déjà vecu) or nonfamiliarity (jamais vu). Weston and Whitlock (1971) first reported the Capgras delusion in a patient with head injury and no psychiatric history, which pointed to an organic etiology. Hay et al. (1974) reported a case in which Capgras's delusion was precipitated by electroconvulsive therapy (ECT) on two separate occasions in a 57-year-old patient with schizophrenia-like symptoms.

Some authors (Hayman and Abrams, 1977) have suggested that prosopagnosia (the neurologic deficit in recognition of faces) may underlie Capgras's delusion. However, specific testing of patients with Capgras's delusions did not show impairment in face recognition (Synodinov, Christodoulou, Tzavaras, 1977).

More recently, the similarities between Capgras and the neurologic disorder of reduplicative paramnesia have been suggested as evidence that Capgras may be a form of reduplicative paramnesia, which is usually associated with bilateral frontal and left hemisphere pathology (Alexander, Stuss, Benson, 1979).

The possibility of a genetic or familial basis for Capgras was raised in a report of Capgras's delusion in a brother and a sister who were living apart (Pulman, Dupon, Ananth, 1983) and in two brothers who lived together (Moskowitz, 1975). No systematic genetic studies of Capgras have been conducted.

The treatment of Capgras's delusion is accomplished through the treatment of the primary psychiatric illness it occurs with, such as schizophrenia or affective disorder. The delusion tends to recur with subsequent psychotic relapses and responds well to pharmacotherapy.

## Clérambault's Delusion

Also known as "pure erotomania" and "Psychose passionelle," this delusion was named after Clérambault (1942), who studied it extensively. It is basically a delusion by a woman, usually one who is married, that a man (either famous or of higher social status than her husband) is in love with her. This delusional love affair becomes the central purpose of existence for the patient, and all events are interpreted as related to the "affair." For example, the patient may believe that her lover directs many customers to her husband's store so that she would become rich, or that gifts from the husband are believed to be indirect gifts from the lover.

The delusion usually develops suddenly and "explosively" and is frequently encountered as part of paranoid schizophrenia or paranoid disorder or organic psychosis. Although Kraepelin distinguished erotomania from schizophrenia and labeled it "paranoiac megalomania," followup studies showed an evolution into chronic schizophrenia. Hallucinations and disinhibited behavior (erotic or assaultive) may occur with Clérambault's delusion, which is probably a variant of the schneiderian symptom of being influenced by an external source.

John Hinckley, who attempted to assassinate President Reagan in 1981, was found to have a delusional attachment to a movie star, and his assassination attempt was admittedly part of his efforts to "impress" the movie star. Although more common in females, erotomania have been reported in males as well (Taylor, Mahendra, Gunn, 1983).

Treatment of this delusion is accomplished through treatment of the underlying disorder, such as schizophrenia (Ellis and Mellsop, 1985). However, the delusion may either persist and not respond to pharmacotherapy or remit spontaneously.

## Cotard's Delusion

In 1880 the French psychiatrist Cotard described several patients who suffered from what he called "delire de negation," which is a nihilistic delusion of having lost everything, including not only their possessions, but also their internal organs, such as heart, intestines, flesh, and blood, and being essentially reduced to nothing. Many subsequent authors have regarded Cotard's delusion as basically a symptom that occurs in various psychiatric disorders, such as psychotic depression, the depressive phase of bipolar affective disorder, schizophrenia, and confusional states, as well as in neurologic conditions, such as epilepsy, general paresis, and encephalitis.

The risk of suicide in such patients is high, although they may, paradoxically, believe that they are already dead or nonexistent.

Cotard's delusion has become more uncommon over the recent past, possibly because it may have represented a severe end stage in psychiatric disorders, which is no longer encountered because of early recognition and treatment (Leger, Destruhault, Blanchinet, Person, Vallat, 1969).

Treatment of Cotard's delusion usually occurs promptly with the treatment of the underlying disorder, whether by pharmacotherapy or ECT. Severely depressed patients with this nihilistic delusion, who frequently refuse food or drink, are best managed by ECT.

## Fregoli's Delusion

Fregoli's delusion, a variant of Capgras's delusion, is the false identification of strangers as familiar persons. It is seen as a delusion of "hyperidentification," while Capgras is a delusion of hypoidentification.

## Glossolalia

Glossolalia is defined as speech in "unknown or imaginary language," or as "unintelligible jargon." It is frequently observed in psychiatrically well people of certain religious sects during periods of religious fervor and is regarded as evidence of being touched by the Holy Spirit, and "speaking in tongues" as a form of communication with God. Psychiatrically, it may represent a dissociative or hypnoid state secondary to intense religious excitement, but it is also encountered in temporal lobe seizures, aphasia, toxic states, and multiple personality (Ludwig, 1980).

Glossolalia may be similar to the word salad of chronic disorganized schizophrenia, which is an extreme form of neologistic speech. Although both are unintelligible, there is more "babbling" and a delirious quality in glossolalia.

## Intermetamorphosis

Intermetamorphosis is an uncommon variant of Capgras's delusion in which the patient perceives that an individual has been transformed both psychologically and physically into another person. In addition to schizophrenia, organic brain disorders, especially epilepsy, are usually associated with this symptom.

## Lycanthropy

Lycanthropy is a form of psychosis in which the patient has delusions of being a wild animal, usually a wolf. It was mentioned in the Bible (the book of Daniel) as afflicting the Babylonian king Nebuchadnezzar for 7 years, in which he behaved like a wild animal.

The delusion of being a wild animal is uncommon in the developed countries but still occurs frequently in underdeveloped countries (Surawicz and Banta, 1975). The species involved in delusional transformation into an animal also include elephants, crocodiles, sharks, eagles, snakes, lions, leopards and buffalos. In some patients, bestiality or other deviations are exhibited as part of the illness and may in fact precede the illness (Rosenstock and Vincent, 1977).

Symptoms of the illness include delusions of being a wolf, visual hallucinations of facial or body changes (metamorphosis), intense sexual and aggressive urges, obsessive need to frequent woods or graveyards, and bizarre and disinhibited behavior.

Delusions of lycanthropy are most commonly manifested as part of a schizophrenic illness, bipolar disorder, dissociative states, hallucinogenic drug-induced psychosis, and organic brain syndromes. Psychomotor epilepsy frequently may be involved in lycanthropy, and many cases have been reported that have a history of seizures or amnestic episodes (Summers, 1966).

Treatment of lycanthropy delusion is best accomplished through the treatment of the underlying illness.

## Mummification

The term mummification was first used by Gorer (1965) to describe a condition in which a bereaved person preserves the home in exactly the same manner that the deceased left it. Queen Victoria, a famous example, preserved Prince Albert's room exactly as it was when he died and even had his clothes laid out and his shaving water brought in for several years.

Mummification is regarded as a symptom of a pathologic grief reaction in which the bereaved transforms the deceased's home into the equivalent of a "shrine" and metaphorically preserves or "mummifies" the deceased. In its extreme form the bereaved may actually keep the body at home and make crude attempts to preserve it, such as by spraying it with disinfectant or stuffing newspapers in orifices or eyesockets to prevent the maggots from spreading (Gardner and Pritchard, 1977). In such extreme cases the deceased is literally and not just metaphorically "mummified," and the bereaved live with the dead.

This symptom may occur as part of a psychotic illness or as part of a severe personality disorder (such as avoidant or schizotypal) or in one member of a socially isolated mutually dependent couple with a symbiotic relationship.

Mummification should be considered against a wide variety of cultural variations in mourning and grief. In some cultures the dead are eaten before or after cremation, or they are exhumed and reburied after the remains are examined. Sometimes the skull or bones are kept at home.

In developed countries the decline in the rituals of mourning and grief has led to an increase in pathologic grief reaction. Mummification is an extreme form of atypical grief, and treatment involves psychotherapy to work through the grief and to accept the permanent loss, as well as somatic treatment of any underlying psychosis, depression, or anxiety.

## The Othello Delusion

The Othello delusion is the delusion of spouse infidelity, also called "morbid jealousy," "sexual jealousy," and "psychotic jealousy." This delusion may be seen in psychotic disorders, such as schizophrenia and bipolar illness, and in epilepsy, alcoholism, and dementia. However, it frequently presents as the central symptom of a pure paranoid disorder, in which case it is also labeled "conjugal paranoia."

The symptom is not uncommon. It usually afflicts middle-aged males with no previous history of psychiatric illness but who may have obsessional, rigid, or suspicious paranoid traits and frequently a positive family history of paranoia. The delusion of spouse infidelity may appear suddenly and crystallizes to include all past and present events involving the spouse as "evidence" of her infidelity. The patient may hire detectives to follow his wife, or he may check her underwear for seminal stains. Sometimes the patient may increase his sexual demands on his wife or he may experience impotence, and the reaction of the spouse would be seen as "confirming" her infidelity (Enoch and Trethowan, 1979). The patient frequently experiences irritability, depression, and impaired functioning. Suicidal/homicidal tendencies may appear in some cases.

Treatment of the Othello delusion occurring in the context of another psychiatric illness is best done through treatment of the primary illness. The pure forms may be hard to treat and may not respond completely to somatic therapy. In some cases only separation, divorce, or death of the spouse result in remission of the delusion.

## Possession

In the delusion of possession, patients (and occasionally relatives or friends) strongly believe that their behavior, thoughts, emotions, and will are possessed by another spirit, often claimed to be that of the devil. It is most commonly a product of schneiderian first-rank delusions, including passivity, influence, thought insertion, and withdrawal, which are attributed to satanic origin because of the cultural or situational background of the patient. Sometimes the possessing spirit is believed to be that of a dead relative or friend or a notorious historical person (Napoleon, Hitler, etc.).

In addition to schizophrenia, possession may also be manifested in dissociative states, multiple personality, or even as an explanation for obsessions and compulsions (Crapanzano, 1977).

Osterreich (1930) suggested two types of possession: lucid possession, in which the subject is aware of his or her self but is also aware of a spirit within, and somnambulistic possession, in which the subject loses consciousness of his or her self while a "force" appears to take control of the body. The subject would then claim amnesia for the episode. Because both forms bear a strong resemblance to multiple personality, some cases of possession may quite possibly be a variant of multiple personality.

Yap (1960) found underlying organic disease in several patients with possession, including phthisis, amphetamine intoxication, epilepsy, and febrile illness. Psychiatric disorders in Yap's series included mainly schizophrenia, hysteria, and depression.

The course of the possession state varies with the underlying neuropsychiatric illness and usually responds to the treatment of the primary disorder.

## Pseudocyesis

Pseudocyesis, or false pregnancy, is an uncommon psychiatric condition, with about 104 cases (96 per cent female) reported over the past 45 years (Cohen, 1982). It has been described as far back as 300 B.C., but the term was coined from Greek by Good (1823).

In addition to a firm conviction of being pregnant despite medical evidence to the contrary, the delusion of pseudocyesis may include one or more of the following in that order: amenorrhea, abdominal enlargement, breast changes, sensations of fetal movements, gastrointestinal symptoms (nausea, vomiting, increased appetite, weight gain), cervical softening, and uterine enlargement (Bivin and Klinger, 1937).

Psychological (Fried, Rakoff, Schopbach, 1951), mechanical (Murray and Abraham, 1978), and endocrinologic (Brown and Barglow, 1971) etiologic factors have been postulated for pseudocyesis in women. Pseudocyesis occurs in animals as well (Moulton, 1942), and this has led to neuroendocrine models for the development of the condition in humans, including alterations in hypothalamic–pituitary–ovarian function, gonadotropin release, and prolactin secretion (Brown and Barglow, 1971).

Pseudocyesis in males is extremely uncommon (Evans and Seely, 1984), and in most cases reported the patient was psychotic. In one case the patient was later found to have a kidney tumor and the delusion of pregnancy ceased when the patient found the cause of his abdominal symptoms.

It is quite likely that somatic factors in a psychotic patient, such as prolactin secretion and lactation after neuroleptic treatmet (Cramer, 1971) and ileus and intestinal dilation with anticholinergic side effects of neuroleptics, antidepressants, or other drugs (Evans, Rogers, Peiper, 1979), may combine with the wish to be pregnant or may trigger a delusion of being pregnant to produce the symptom of pseudocyesis in females.

Pseudocyesis is managed by the treatment of the underlying psychiatric disorder (usually a psychosis), along with psychotherapy to address the emotional needs of the patient as indicated.

## UNUSUAL PSYCHIATRIC SYNDROMES

### Collective Psychosis

The old psychiatric literature contains many references to reports of "psychic epidemics" or what may be labeled as "collective psychoses," which occurred in Europe between 1000 and 1600. According to Arieti and Meth (1959), these syndromes probably represented manifestations of fanaticism of members of religious sects, such as the Flagellants, who tried to atone for their sins during the plague epidemics in the 13th and 14th centuries, the Palamites, who tried to touch the umbilicus with their heads to see the glory of the divinity, and the Adamites, who walked naked.

Ferrio (1948) is the main source for many of these medieval epidemics. He reports about people gathering near churches, singing and dancing continuously for many days and nights until they collapsed or experienced seizures. The label St. Vitus's dance originated from such events because some of the patients were treated in a chapel dedicated to St. Vitus.

Zilboorg and Henry (1941) described epidemics in 15th-century Italy, such as tarantism, when many people had excitement and convulsions, allegedly because of being bitten by a spider (*Lycosa tarentula*).

Another important collective psychosis involved lycanthropy (see earlier discussion), in which groups of people believed themselves to be transformed into animals (especially wolves), and many committed crimes in that state. According to Ferrio (1948), one French Judge in the 16th century condemned to death about 600 persons suffering from lycanthrophy! Other collective epidemics involved nuns who would suddenly abandon their convents and act in a hysterical or bizarre manner, such as mewing like cats.

It is sometimes thought that ignorance, superstition, or religious fanaticism contributed to such collective syndromes, which are believed to be psychotic, dissociative, or hypnotic states. The mass suicide by more than 1000 followers of the Rev. James Jones at Guyana in 1978 is poignant evidence that such events still occur. Many religious cults in the United States and in other countries have been known to act in unusual or bizarre ways. A spectrum of psychopathology may be represented in some but not all followers of such cults and may have played a role in their choice of cult membership (Galanter, 1982).

Treatment, if sought, should be on an individual basis, with somatic or psychotherapeutic modalities, as indicated.

## Culture-bound "Exotic" Syndromes

Several well-known behavioral syndromes have been observed in various cultures around the world. These include disorders that are similar to psychiatric illnesses observed in the Western world, but sometimes the syndromes are quite different and clearly related to primitive cultural beliefs or traditions. In some cultures, delusions and hallucinations, which are regarded as the core of the psychosis in the West, are accepted as normative during certain trance states and do not require treatment.

Arieti and Meth (1959) judiciously point to possible organic etiologies for many mental disorders in tropical and subtropical regions, which may account for some "exotic" syndromes that are not seen in other world regions. Psychiatric symptoms may result from such diseases as malaria (confusion, excitement, stupor), trypanosomiasis (delusions, hallucinations, manic, and schizophrenic symptoms), ascariasis (confusional states, epilepsy), syphilis, pellagra, and kwashiorkor, as well as from intoxication with such substances as cannabis, peyote, mescal cohoba, and mushrooms.

### Latah

As reviewed by Yap (1952), latah occurs mainly in Malayan middle-aged women and consists of repeating or imitating gestures and acts of other people, even if it results in

harm to the self, and uttering obscenities that the individual never used before. The apparent echopraxia, echolalia, and coprolalia suggest a possible neurologic etiology or involvement.

In other parts of the world, such as Africa, the latah syndrome may involve additional symptoms, such as climbing dangerous cliffs without regard for personal safety, suggesting impairment in judgment and insight.

A similarity between latah and posthypnotic behavior was noted by Murphy (1973), who regarded it as a cultural trance state that incorporates elements of Malaysian culture and mythology.

Syndromes similar to latah but occurring in different regions have been described, including miryachit (Siberia), inu (northern Japan), bah-tschi (Siam), Yuan (Burma), mali-mali (Philippines), ramaninjana (Madagascar), misala (Nyasaland), and banga (Congo). Many authors in the past used to regard Gilles de la Tourette's syndrome as a variant of latah.

### Amok

Amok, a Malayan word meaning "to engage furiously in battle," describes a syndrome consisting of a sudden, unprovoked outburst of wild rage that causes the affected person to run madly about armed with a deadly weapon, attacking, maiming, or killing indiscriminately any human or animal he encounters until he is overpowered or killed (Westermeyer, 1972). This senseless and savage homicidal spree (an average of 10 victims, according to Westermeyer) is usually preceded by a period of mild depression and preoccupation. After the attack the patient has complete amnesia.

Amok used to be described as occurring exclusively in Malayan men but has been described in other cultures as well. The incidence of the condition dropped significantly after the British took over the administration of government and has now become uncommon.

The etiology of the disorder is unknown but has been thought to be a reaction to humiliation or frustration, chronic painful physical disease, or an acute toxic or febrile illness. At the present time it is seen mainly in chronically psychotic or confused patients. Treatment depends on the underlying condition of the patient.

## Koro

Koro, an acute anxiety reaction with sudden onset in Malayan or southern Chinese men, consists of the fear that the penis will disappear into the abdomen and that death will ensue. To prevent this, the patient grips his penis firmly, and when he gets tired, his wife, relatives, and friends help him. The Chinese have a special wooden clasp constructed for this purpose. At times, fellatio practiced immediately by the wife can stop the phobia (Arieti and Meth, 1959). If untreated, koro may last for up to several weeks.

Linton (1956) reported a female equivalent of koro in Southeast Asia, in which a woman believes that her breasts and vulval labia are shrinking.

The etiology of koro is unknown, but Kraepelin mentions that shrinkage of the penis is a hypochondriacal delusion of the depressed state of manic-depressive psychosis. A possible organic etiology is also suggested by reports of koro after amphetamine intoxication (Dow and Silver, 1973) and with a frontotemporal brain tumor (Lapierre, 1972). Yap (1965) regards koro as a depersonalization syndrome and discusses various physical or psychological precipitants. He treated 19 cases with convulsive therapy and got recovery in the majority of his patients, but about half remained prone to anxiety. The amphetamine-induced case responded completely to diazepam and reassurance. Koro may be treated as a phobia or an anxiety disorder.

## Whitigo

Whitigo is a type of psychosis restricted to certain North American Indians, who believe that they may be transformed into a whitigo, a giant monster that eats flesh. It is similar to lycanthropy and possession states. Teicher (1961) conducted the most comprehensive review of the subject.

## Piblokto

Piblokto, also referred to as "Arctic hysteria," usually afflicts Eskimo women. It is characterized by attacks lasting for 1 to 2 hours, during which the woman screams and tears off her clothing, runs wildly or throws herself on the snow, and may imitate the sounds of animals. There is usually amnesia after the attack.

Piblokto is probably a dissociative state and is but one of many hysterical conditions (conversion symptoms, pseudoseizures) that have been described in Eskimo women (Ackerknecht, 1948).

## Voodoo

Voodoo is a delusion of possession that afflicts many patients from North American black ghettos, who present with organic or psychological symptoms. Wintrob (1970) reported that 10 per cent of psychiatric male patients in a Liberian psychiatric center had delusions of possession by "manny water."

The voodoo cult is widespread in Haiti, and its rituals are known to produce trance states, with many symptoms of convulsions, excitement, and opisthotonos. There is widespread belief that one can be involuntarily possessed by evil spirits, and many organic psychiatric symptoms are blamed on voodoo, thus delaying treatment (Prince, 1968).

Sudden voodoo deaths (also known as thanatomania) have been reported but not verified (Golden, 1977). Although emotional causes of sudden death are known (Dimsdale, 1977), the zombie state of voodoo, in which a person is "hexed" to die and then reappears after burial, has recently been attributed to a poison that produces a reversible comatose state.

## Couvade Syndrome

In several cultures an expectant father retires to bed during his wive's labor, simulating labor pains, and receives attention like a woman in labor. The couvade syndrome is a psychiatric disorder that strongly resembles the couvade ritual but is not done consciously as a ritual. It refers to a cluster of symptoms that expectant fathers may manifest that resemble those of a pregnant woman or a woman in labor.

The syndrome of couvade (the French word *couver* means to hatch) is not uncommon and is believed to affect 10 per cent of expectant fathers (Enoch and Trethowan, 1979), and perhaps even 20 per cent (Bogren, 1983). It usually starts around the end of the first trimester, reaches a crescendo around parturition, and then stops. The symptoms are mostly gastrointestinal (indigestion, vague abdominal pain, nausea, vomiting, constipation, diarrhea, and cravings). In severe cases a swelling of the abdomen (reminiscent of pseudocyesis) may appear, which more than a century ago was shown to subside under anesthesia but returns afterward (Simpson, 1872).

The largest study of the couvade syndrome was by Trethowan (1965), in which 327 expectant fathers were found to have significantly more anorexia, nausea, vomiting, and toothache compared with 221 controls.

The etiology of the couvade syndrome is unknown but is usually attributed to unconscious psychological factors, including identification with and envy of the wife's childbearing capacity. It has recently been suggested, however, that couvade may be a somatic expression of an anxiety disorder.

The couvade syndrome generally is self-limiting, and treatment is seldom sought or needed.

## Folie à Deux

Also known as double insanity, folie à deux was first described by Lasegue and Falret in 1877. It is characterized by psychotic symptoms, usually paranoid delusions, that are shared by two or more persons who are either living together or intimately associated with one another.

A subclassification of folie à deux into the following forms was suggested by De Montyel in 1881 (Enoch and Trethowan, 1979):

**Folie Imposee.** In folie imposee the patient suffering from psychosis is dominant, and the other is passive and less intelligent. When separated, the passive partner abandons the delusions. This is the most common form of the syndrome.

**Folie Simultanee.** Folie simultanee occurs simultaneously but independently in two persons in close association who are genetically predisposed to psychosis. There is no dominant partner, and separation does not improve either patient.

**Folie Communiquee.** In folie communiquee one of two genetically predisposed individuals develops delusions similar to that of the other, who had become psychotic earlier. Later, the two will have different delusions. Separation helps neither.

**Folie Induite.** In folie induite a patient "enriches" his delusions with those of another patient in the same hospital.

The elderly are reported to be particularly vulnerable to folie à deux (McNeil, Verwoerdt, Peak, 1972). The "recipients" of psychosis frequently suffer from physical disabilities (e.g., deafness, stroke, alcoholism).

Gregory (1959) reported 11 cases of folie à deux in spouses, which may suggest some kind of assortative mating. In one case a married couple developed folie à deux while both were taking methylphenidate (Spensley, 1972), suggesting a combination of organic and social causes.

Folie à trois and folie à quatre have been reported (Kamal, 1965). Also, reports of shared psychosis in families (folie à famille or folie à plusieurs) of seven, eight (Tseng, 1969), and even twelve persons (Waltzer, 1963) have been reported. Folie à deux in families is more common in a close pair who sleep in the same bed, such as sisters, or in a mother and child.

The causes of folie a deux are unknown, but frequently it is attributed to the dynamics of persons in a symbiotic relationship where the submissive partner with a low self-concept identifies with the aggressor (the dominant partner). It has also been regarded as a type of "transference" phenomenon because of the strong emotional involvement. Nonpsychological factors that also predispose to the development of folie à deux include low intelligence, dementia, and a genetic predisposition to schizophrenia (Soni and Rockley, 1974).

Treatment includes pharmacotherapy or ECT for the psychosis, as well as psychotherapy (especially for the passive partner). Separation of the partners is sometimes but not always helpful. McNeil et al. (1972) emphasize the poor prognosis of folie à deux in the aged population.

## Ganser's Syndrome

Also known as "hysterical pseudodementia," Ganser's syndrome is a "hysterical twilight state." The German psychiatrist Ganser (1898) described the syndrome as being characterized by approximate answers or "talking past the point" (Vorbeireden). For example, if asked how much two plus two was, the Ganser patient would say "five."

Thus the patient would give wrong but approximate answers and appears to have understood the sense of the question. The patient usually manifests temporal and spacial disorientation and may not appear confused. Other symptoms frequently found in such patients include low intelligence, anxiety, and hysterical conversion symptoms, such as amnesia, analgesia, incontinence, and pseudoseizures. Sometimes psychotic symptoms such as auditory hallucinations are involved.

The differential diagnosis of Ganser's syndrome includes schizophrenia, mania, epileptic twilight state, toxic organic confusion, and malingering. In the *Diagnostic and Statistical Manual of Mental Disorders*, third edition (DSM-III), Ganser's syndrome is classified as factitious illness with psychological symptoms. However, the literature on this subject has frequently confused Ganser's syndrome with malingering, which involves deliberate falsification. Ganser's patients may appear to have an ulterior motive for faking an illness, such as to avoid the draft or jail. It is generally accepted that Ganser's syndrome is a dissociative state that may be superimposed on a psychotic or organic psychiatric illness (Goldin and MacDonald, 1955). As with many other dissociative states, the etiology of Ganser's syndrome is unknown. While some authors regard it as a regressive state (Ingraham and Moriarty, 1967), others take the position that the diagnosis of Ganser's syndrome should be restricted to patients with previous cerebral trauma or who develop the symptoms in the course of a psychotic illness (Whitlock, 1967). Carbon monoxide encephalopathy presenting as Ganser's syndrome lends further support for possible organic factors in some cases of Ganser's syndrome (McEvoy and Campbell, 1977).

Ganser's syndrome is usually self-limiting and short-lived, as in other dissociative states. Psychotic features during the illness may be treated with pharmacotherapy, and supportive reality-oriented psychotherapy may be useful.

## Gilles de la Tourette's Syndrome

Tourette's syndrome (TS) was first described in 1885. It is characterized by onset in childhood, various tics and stereotyped movements, compulsive motor outbursts, forced utterance of obscenities (coprolalia) or various barking and grunting sounds (vocal tics), and, sometimes, the repetition of words or phrases immediately after hearing them (palilalia). Symptoms are sometimes triggered or worsened by stress or fatigue. Before its current recognition as a neurologic disorder, probably with familial transmission (Kidd, Prusoff, Cohen, 1980), TS was regarded as a diabolical "possession state" in the Middle Ages or as a bizarre psychosis, such as lycanthropy, latah, or myriachit.

The differential diagnoses include the various tics of childhood, Sydenham's chorea, Wilson's disease, Huntington's chorea, postencephalitic disorder, and other degenerative central nervous system diseases.

TS is three times more common in boys than in girls. Parents tend to show more than expected frequency of paranoid and dominant traits (Shapiro, Shapiro, Wayne, 1972).

The etiology of TS is believed to be related to increased brain catecholamine activity, particularly that of dopamine, as evidenced by the response of the symptoms to dopaminergic antagonists (Friel, 1973). Attempts to explain TS in psychodynamic terms (Morphew and Sim, 1969) were systematically refuted by Shapiro et al. (1972), who showed organicity and neurologic symptoms in the majority of cases and documented the absence of hostility, hypochondriasis, and neurotic traits.

TS has been precipitated by stimulant therapy given for the treatment of attention-deficit disorder, which not only confirms the neurochemical basis of the illness, but also suggests that TS may first present as hyperactivity or attention-deficit disorder and that clinical evaluation of tics and other TS symptoms in children and their families should precede stimulant therapy in children (Lowe et al., 1982).

Treatment of TS was generally inadequate until neuroleptics, especially haloperidol, were found to be effective in reducing most symptoms. However, side effects of haloperidol, as well as the natural course of waxing and waning of symptoms in TS, may complicate and frustrate treatment efforts. Other treatments found to be effective include chlorimipramine in TS patients with prominent obsessive features (Yaryura-Tobias, 1977), behavior therapy (Doleys and Kurtz, 1974), and psychosurgery in treatment-resistant cases (Beckers, 1973).

## Munchausen's Syndrome

Although Munchausen's syndrome of "hospital addiction" is one of the most recently described of the unusual psychiatric disorders (Asher, 1951), it has become widely known among psychiatrists and in the medical community at large.

The DSM-III nomenclature for this syndrome is factitious disorder with physical symptoms, but its original name (after the notorious fictional character of a German adventurer) is still widely used. Patients with this disorder spend their entire lives trying to get admitted to hospitals by successfully fabricating serious medical signs and symptoms that prompt physicians to admit them for evaluation and treatment. The presentation is usually dramatic, but the actual symptoms are characteristically vague, elusive, and inconsistent and may involve one or more organ systems, such as abdominal pain, nausea, vomiting, hemoptysis, pains and aches, blackouts, rashes, and fever of unknown origin. The patients use risky and devious methods to simulate medical symptoms, such as ingesting anticoagulants to produce bleeding, ingesting toxins to simulate fever, and infecting their skin to produce abscesses.

Munchausen's patients usually possess an exceptional knowledge of medical jargon and procedures as well as hospital routine. When the physician workup comes out with normal results, they fabricate new symptoms (Hall, 1977) and frequently resort to pathologic lying (pseudologia fantastica) to substantiate their stories. They frequently (and eagerly) undergo exploratory laparaotomies or other invasive procedures and may have "gridiron" abdomens, reflecting the evidence of many previous successes of convincing well-intentioned surgeons to operate. Patients frequently insist on receiving analgesics for their symptoms and may become belligerent if their "pain" is not medicated.

When finally confronted with their schemes, Munchausen's patients vehemently deny the charges or indignantly discharge themselves from the hospital against medical advice, only to seek admission at the nearest unsuspecting hospital. They often crisscross the country, and even continents, to find hospitals that are unfamiliar with them or their modus operandi. Increased awareness of this disorder and its impact on hospital finances has led many medical centers to share information and create a "black list" of suspected Munchausen's patients. Such patients usually resist psychiatric referrals or hospitalizations.

Onset of Munchausen's syndrome is usually in young adulthood, often after hospitalization for a true physical illness. Patients are later misdiagnosed as having hypochondriasis or somatoform disorder. Nearly all eventually have a criminal record. In the United States most patients are males around 40 years of age; in Germany they tend to be females around 30 years of age with a nursing background (Linneke, 1971).

The psychopathology of Munchausen's syndrome is believed to be much severer than simple malingering, although both involve conscious simulation of illness. It is believed to involve masochistic tendencies, impaired relationships with others, a background of cold or sadistic parents, and close relatives in the medical profession. In some cases chronic illness or placement in institutions during childhood has been noted (Ford, 1973).

Effective treatment is not yet established. Patients tend to be poorly motivated for psychological treatments, and no successful somatic treatment has yet been found. Behavior modification has occasionally produced good outcome (Yassa, 1978). Stone (1977) cited three prognostically favorable features: depressive symptoms, borderline functioning, and minimal antisocial traits.

## Puerperal Psychoses

Puerperal psychoses, which, as the name suggests, occur at the termination of pregnancy, have been recognized for thousands of years. Despite the apparent association with parturition as a trigger, the etiologic factors of puerperal psychoses remain obscure.

The most controversial issue in puerperal psychoses is whether they constitute a separate set of psychopathologic entities or are basically the same as other psychoses. The most common clinical symptoms in puerperal psychoses are those consistent with affective disorders and schizophrenia. Clinical studies, however, have found many differences in symptoms between puerperal psychoses and other psychoses, such as less frequent systematized or persecutory delusions, auditory hallucinations, and flat affect and more frequent elation, lability of mood, rambling speech, flight of ideas, distractibility, euphoria, and excessive activity (Brockington, Winokur, Dean, 1982). There is a noticeable deficit of paranoid psychoses in cases of puerperal psychoses. Also, there does not seem to be a relationship between puerperal psychoses and mild "postpartum blues."

The incidence of puerperal psychoses ranges from 0.8 to 2.5 cases per 1000 deliveries in various studies. Primiparous women seem to be at higher risk, according to Kendell, Rennie, Clarke, and Dean (1981), who calculated a risk of 2.6/1000 for the first vs. 1.4/1000 for subsequent confinements. The rate for black women is twice that of white women (Paffenberger, 1964) and is twice as high in unmarried females (Tetlow, 1955). A higher incidence of dystocia, prematurity, and cesarean sections has also been reported.

There is evidence of a genetic component in puerperal psychoses. Reich and Winokur (1970) found a high proportion (41×) of relatives with puerperal episodes. Prothroe (1969) found affective psychosis and schizophrenia to breed true in families of puerperal psychoses, and Thuwe (1974) reviewed 10 studies over the previous 60 years and found hereditary factors in 22 per cent to 65 per cent of the samples reported.

However, Kadrmas, Winokur, and Crowe (1979) found severer psychotic (schneiderian) symptoms in puerperal mania with less likelihood of recurrences and less positive family history than in a control group of manics, suggesting that puerperal mania may be a different type of bipolar illness than nonpuerperal mania.

Psychosocial factors for the development of postpartum disorders include feeling rejected or unloved by the husband, an undesired pregnancy, past history of postpartum illness, single or separated status, marital turmoil, and unplanned pregnancy (Braverman and Roux, 1978).

Although there is a high level of suspicion that the sudden and drastic change in various hormone levels after delivery may contribute to puerperal psychoses, there is no conclusive evidence in this regard. There are reports of a decrease in breast-feeding luteinizing hormone and progesterone and higher levels of prolactin and estrogen (George, Copland, Wilson, 1980; Smith, 1975) as well as circulating corticosteroids (Tuimala, Kauppila, Ronnberg, Jouppila, Haapalahti, 1976), which may be implicated in the pathophysiology of puerperal psychoses.

The treatment of puerperal psychoses is similar to that of other psychoses, with antipsychotics, lithium, antidepressants, and ECT. Before the introduction of somatic treatments, puerperal psychoses persisted for several months and mortality was high (10 per cent to 25 per cent), mostly from exhaustion. The proper treatment nowadays also includes psychosocial intervention and preventive planning for future episodes.

## SUMMARY

Many unusual psychiatric symptoms or syndromes are probably of organic/neurologic etiology. They tend to occur in the context of such disorders as schizophrenia, dissociative states, temporal lobe epilepsy, and brain injury. Many unusual psychiatric disorders need further systematic epidemiologic, clinical, pathophysiologic therapeutic, and outcome research studies to further elucidate their role in psychiatry.

## REFERENCES

Ackerknecht BH: Medicine and disease among Eskimos. Ciba Symp 10:916, 1948.
Alexander MP, Stuss DT, Benson DF: Capgras syndrome: A reduplicative phenomenon. Neurology 29:334, 1979
Arieti S, Meth JM: Rare, unclassifiable, collective and exotic psychotic syndromes, in Arieti S (ed): American Handbook of Psychiatry. New York, Basic Books, 1959.
Asher R: Munchausen's syndrome. Lancet 1:339, 1951.
Beckers W: Five cases of Gilles de la Tourette disease based on personal observations. Arch Psychiatr Nervenkr 217:169, 1973.
Bivin GD, Klinger MP; Pseudocyesis. Bloomington, IN, Principia Press, 1937.
Bogren LY: Couvade. Acta Psychiatr Scand 68:55, 1983.
Braverman J, Roux JF: Screening for the patient at risk for postpartum depression. Obstet Gynecol 52:731, 1978.

Brockington IF, Winokur G, Dean C: Puerperal psychosis, in Brockington IF, Kumar R (eds): Motherhood and Mental Illness. New York, Grune & Stratton, 1982, pp 37–69.

Brown E, Barglow P: Pseudocyesis: A paradigm for psychophysiological interactions. Arch Gen Psychiatry 24:221, 1971.

Capgras J, Reboul-lachaud J: L'illusion des sosies dans un delire systematique chronique. Bull Soc Clin Med Ment 2:6, 1923.

Christodoulou GN: The syndrome of Capgras. Br J Psychiatry 130:556, 1977.

Clérambault GG: Ouvre Psychiatrique, Paris, Presses Universitaires, 1942.

Cohen LMA: A current perspective of pseudocyesis. Am J Psychiatry 139:1140, 1982.

Courbon P, Fail G: Syndrome "d'illusion de Fregoli" et schizophrenie. Bull Soc Clin Med Ment 15:121, 1927.

Courbon P, Tusques J: Illusion d'intermetamorphose et de charme. Ann Med Psychol 90:401, 1927.

Cramer B: Delusions of pregnancy in a girl with drug-induced lactation. Am J Psychiatry 127:960, 1971.

Crapanzano V: Introduction, in Crapanzano V, Garrison V (eds): Case Studies in Spirit Possession. New York, Wiley, 1977.

Critchley M: The body-image in neurology. Lancet 1:335, 1950.

De la Tourette G: Etude sur une affection nerveuse, caracterise par de l'incoordination motorice accompagnee d'echolalie et de coprolalie. Arch Neurol 9:158, 1885.

Dimsdale JE: Emotional causes of sudden death. Am J Psychiatry 134:1425, 1977.

Doleys DM, Kurtz PA: A behavioral treatment program for Gilles de la Tourette syndrome. Psychol Rep 35:43, 1974.

Dow TW, Silver D: A drug-induced koro syndrome. J Fla Med Assoc 60:32, 1973.

Ellis P, Mellsop G: DeClerambault's syndrome—a nosological entity? Br J Psychiatry 146:90–95, 1985.

Enoch MD, Trethowan WH: Uncommon psychiatric syndromes. Bristol, England, John Wright Sons, 1979.

Evans DL, Rogers TF, Peiper SC: Intestinal dilatation associated with phenothiazine therapy: A case report and literature review. Am J Psychiatry 136:970, 1979.

Evans DL, Seely TJ: Pseudocyesis in the male. J Nerv Ment Dis 172:37, 1984.

Ferrio C: La Psiche e i Nervi. Turin, Utet, 1948.

Fish F: A guide to the Leonhard classification of chronic schizophrenia. Psychiatr Q 38:438, 1964.

Ford CV: The Munchausen syndrome: A report of four new cases and a review of psychodynamic considerations. Psychiatry Med 4:31, 1973.

Fried PH, Rakoff AE, Schopbach RR, et al: Pseudocyesis: A psychosomatic study of gynecology. JAMA 145:1329, 1951.

Friel PB: Familial incidence of Gilles de la Tourette's disease, with observations on aetiology and treatment. Br J Psychiatry 122:655, 1973.

Galanter M: Charismatic religious cults and psychiatry: An overview. Am J Psychiatry 139:1539, 1982.

Ganser SJM: Uber einen eigenartigen hysterischen Dammerzustand. Arch Psychiatr Nervenkr 38:633, 1898.

Gardner A, Pritchard M: Mourning, mummification and living with the dead. Br J Psychiatry 130:23, 1977.

George AJ, Copland JRM, Wilson KCM: Prolactin secretion and the postpartum blues syndrome. Br J Psychiatry 70:102, 1980.

Golden KM: Voodoo in Africa and the United States. Am J Psychiatry 134:1361, 1977.

Goldfarb AI, Weiner MB: The Capgras syndrome as an adaptational maneuver in old age. Am J Psychiatry 134:1434, 1977.

Goldin S, MacDonald JE: The Ganser state. J Ment Sci 101:267, 1955.

Good JM: Physiological system of nosology with corrected and simplified nomenclature. Boston, Wells & Lilly, 1823.

Gorer G: Death, Grief and Mourning in Contemporary Britain. London, Cresset Press, 1965.

Gregory I: Husbands and wives admitted to mental hospital. J Ment Sci 105:457, 1959.

Hall MS: Factitious contributions to a staphylococcuse sepsis. Conn Med 41:353, 1977.

Hay G, Jolly D, Jones, R: A case of the Capgras syndrome in association with pseudo-hyperparathyroidism. Acta Psychiatr Scand 50:73–77, 1974.

Hayman MA, Abrams R: Capgras' syndrome and cerebral dysfunction. Br J Psychiatry 130:68, 1977.

Ingraham MR, Moriarty DM: A contribution to the understanding of Ganser's syndrome. Compr Psychiatry 8:35, 1967.

Kadrmas A, Winokur G, Crowe R: Postpartum mania. Br J Psychiatry 135:551, 1979.

Kamal A: Folie a cinq: A clinical study. Br J Psychiatry 111:583, 1965.

Kendell RE, Rennie D, Clarke JA, Dean C: The social and obstetric correlates of psychiatric admissions in the puerperium. Psychol Med 11:341, 1981.

Kidd KK, Prusoff BA, Cohen DJ: Familial pattern of Gilles de la Tourette syndrome. Arch Gen Psychiatry 37:1336, 1980.

Lapierre YD: Koro in a French Canadian. Can Psychiatr Assoc J 17:333, 1972.

Lasegue C, Falret J: La folie à deux ou folie communiquee. Ann Med Psychol 18:321, 1877.

Leger JM, Destruhault J, Blanchinet J, Person A, Vallat JN: Peut-on parler de formes intermittentes du syndrome de Cotard? Role de la therapeutique actvelle dans l'evolution de ce syndrome. Ann Med Psychol (Paris) 2:545, 1969.

Levy-Valensi J: L'illusion des sosie. Gazette des Hospitaux, 10 July, 1939.

Linneke P: Beitrag zum Munchausen syndrome. Z Aertzl Fortbild 14:707, 1971.

Linton R: Culture and Mental Disorders. Springfield, IL, Charles C Thomas, 1956.

Lippman CW: Hallucinations of physical duality in migraine. J Nerv Ment Dis 117:345, 1953.

Lowe TL, Cohen DJ, Detlor J, et al: Stimulant medications precipitate Tourette's syndrome. JAMA 247:1729, 1982.

Ludwig A: Principles of Clinical Psychiatry. New York, Free Press, 1980.

Lukianowicz N: Autoscopic phenomena. Arch Neurol Psychiatry 80:199, 1958.

Maack LH, Mullen PE: The Doppelganger, disintegration and death: A case report. Psychol Med 13:651, 1983.

McEvoy J, Campbell T: Ganser-like signs in carbon monoxide encephalopathy. Am J Psychiatry 134:1448, 1977.

McNeil JN, Verwoerdt A, Peak A: Folie à deux in the aged: Review and case report of role reversal. J Am Geriatr Soc 20:316, 1972.

Morphew JA, Sim M: Gilles de la Tourette's syndrome: A clinical and psychopathological study. Br J Med Psychol 42:293, 1969.

Moskowitz JA: Capgras syndrome in male siblings. Am J Psychiatry 132:86, 1975.

Moulton R: The psychosomatic implication of pseudocyesis. Psychosom Med 4:376, 1942.

Murphy HBM: History and the evolution of syndromes: The striking case of latah and amok, in Hammen M, Salzinger K, Hutton S (eds): Psychopathology: Contributions from the Social, Behavioral and Biological Sciences. New York, John Wiley & Sons, 1973.

Murray JL, Abraham GE: Pseudocyesis: A review. Obstet Gynecol 51:627, 1978.

Osterreich TK: Possession: Demoniacal and Other. New York, Richard R. Smith, 1930.

Paffenberger RS: Epidemiological aspects of postpartum mental illness. Br J Prev Soc Med 18:189, 1964.

Prince R: Trance and Possession States. Montreal, RM Bucke Memorial Society, 1968.

Prothroe C: Puerperal psychoses: A long term study 1927–1961. Br J Psychiatry 115:9, 1969.

Pulman J, Dupon D, Ananth J: Capgras syndrome in siblings. Can J Psychiatry 28:301, 1983.

Reich T, Winokur G: Postpartum psychoses in patients with manic depressive disease. J Nerve Ment Dis 151:60, 1970.

Rosenstock HA, Vincent KR: A case of lycanthropy. Am J Psychiatry 134:1147, 1977.

Schilder P: The Image and Appearance of the Human Body. New York, International University Press, 1950.

Shapiro AK, Shapiro E, Wayne H: Birth, developmental and family histories and demographic information in Tourette syndrome. J Nerv Ment Dis 155:335, 1972.

Simpson J: Clinical Lectures on Diseases of Women. Edinburgh, Blach, 1872.

Smith SL: Mood and the menstrual cycle, in Sachar EJ (ed): Topics in Psychoneuroendocrinology. New York, Grune & Stratton, 1975, pp 19–58.

Soni SD, Rockley GJ: Socio-clinical substrates of folie à deux. Br J Psychiatry 125:230, 1974.

Spensley J: Folie à deux with methylphenidate psychosis. J Nerv Ment Dis 155:788, 1972.

Stone, M: Factitious illness, psychological findings and treatment recommendations. Bull Menninger Clinic 41:239–254, 1977.

Summers M: The Werewolf. New York, University Books, 1966.

Surawicz F, Banta R: Lycanthropy revisited. Can Psychiatr Assoc J 20:537, 1975.

Synodinov C, Christodoulou GN, Tzavaras A: Capgras' syndrome and prosopagnosia. Br J Psychiatry 132:413, 1977.

Taylor P, Mahendra B, Gunn J: Erotomania in males. Psychol Med 13:645, 1983.

Teicher M: Windigo psychosis: A study of a relationship between belief and behavior among the Indians of Northeastern Canada. Proc Am Ethnol Soc 11:1, 1961.

Tetlow C: Psychoses of childbearing. J Ment Sci 101:629, 1955.

Thuwe I: Genetic factors in puerperal psychosis. Br J Psychiatry 125:378, 1974.

Trethowan WH: The Couvade Syndrome. Brit J Psychiatry 111:57–66, 1965.

Tseng WS: A paranoid family in Taiwan. A dynamic study of folie a famille. Arch Gen Psychiatry 21:55, 1969.

Tuimala R, Kauppila A, Ronnberg L, Jouppila R, Haapalahti J: The effects of labor on ACTH and cortisol levels in amniotic fluid and maternal blood. Br J Obstet Gynecol 83:707, 1976.

Waltzer M: A psychotic family—folie a douze. J Nerv Ment Dis 137:67, 1963.

Westermeyer JA: Comparison of amok and other homicide in Laos. Am J Psychiatry 129:79, 1972.

Weston MJ, Whitlock FA: The Capgras syndrome following head injury. Br J Psychiatry 119:25, 1971.

Whitlock FA: The Ganser's syndrome. Br J Psychiatry 113:19, 1967.

Wintrob RM: Mammy water: Folk beliefs and psychotic elaborations in Liberia. Can Psychiatr Assoc J 15:143, 1970.

Yap PM: The latah reaction: Its pathodynamics and nosological position. J Ment Sci 98:515, 1952.

Yap PM: The possession syndrome: A comparison of Hong Kong and French findings. J Ment Sci 106:114, 1960.

Yap PM: Koro: A culture-bound depersonalization syndrome. Br J Psychiatry 111:43, 1965.

Yaryura-Tobias JA: Gilles de la Tourette syndrome: A new clinico-therapeutic approach. Progr Neuropsychopharmacol 1:335, 1977.

Yassa R: Munchausen's syndrome: A successfully treated case. Psychosomatics 19:242, 1978.

Zilboorg G, Henry GW: A History of Medical Psychology. New York, WW Norton, 1941, p 266.

# SYNDROMES— CHILD PSYCHIATRY

UNIT

II

# chapter 18

# CONDUCT DISORDERS AND HYPERACTIVITY

*by* Mark A. Stewart, M.D.

Conduct disorders are some of the more serious and chronic handicaps that afflict children and their parents. Such disorders disrupt families and classrooms and bring unhappiness to the children themselves. They are relatively common, affecting 5 per cent to 10 per cent of boys and 1 per cent to 3 per cent of girls (Rutter, Tizard, Whitmore, 1970; Rutter, Cox, Tupling, Berger, Yule, 1975). Furthermore, the outcome can be poor; in a proportion of cases, the children develop alcoholism or antisocial personality as adults.

Children with conduct disorders pose a hard challenge for psychiatrists and pediatricians. Their difficulties do not fit the medical model easily; there are not well-proven treatments; and the problems are usually complicated by misery in the home. On the other hand, many of the affected children are eager to learn healthier behavior; there are promising behavioral, cognitive, and drug treatments; and the prognosis is surprisingly good. Moreover, clinical and laboratory studies suggest that the disorders are partly biologic in origin.

This chapter begins with a brief discussion of how conduct disorders should be classified and then focuses on one type, the aggressive, which is the most common among children referred to a psychiatrist.

Other types are described as well as possible, given the limits of the available data. Finally, the controversial symptom of hyperactivity is discussed.

## CLASSIFICATION OF CONDUCT DISORDERS

Rutter, Shaffer, and Sturge (1976) gave the following definition of conduct disorders:

Disorders mainly involving aggressive and destructive behavior and disorders involving delinquency. [This category] should be used for abnormal behavior which gives rise to social disapproval but which is not part of any other psychiatric condition. To be included, the behavior—as judged by its frequency, severity and type of associations with other symptoms—must be abnormal in its context. Disturbances of conduct are distinguished from an adjustment reaction by a longer duration and by a lack of close relationship in time and content to some stress. They differ from a personality disorder by the absence of deeply engrained maladaptive patterns of behavior present from adolescence or earlier.

In this broad definition, there is already a hint of how conduct disorders should be subdivided, that is, by parting children who are primarily aggressive from those who are primarily delinquent or antisocial. Alternative solutions are to divide children with these disorders into socialized and unsocialized, or aggressive and nonaggressive, or those whose misbehavior is confrontive and those whose misbehavior is not. It is unlikely that experts in this field will agree on one of these alternatives in the near future, but the findings to date support a division into children whose main problem is aggressiveness, those who are primarily antisocial, and those who have a combination of aggressiveness and antisocial behavior.

The evidence favoring this approach comes first from factor analysis of the symptoms of children attending psychiatric clinics. Several of these studies, particularly those of Achenbach (1978) and Achenbach and Edelbrock (1979), show that aggressive and antisocial behaviors are relatively independent of each other. More support comes from a prospective study of developing delinquency (West and Farrington, 1973, 1977), which showed that the aggressive boys in a community and the delinquents overlap to an extent, but that they are not identical.

Age bedevils the classification of conduct disorders. In Hewitt and Jenkins's (1946) pioneering study, the mean age of socialized delinquents was 13.6 years, while that of the unsocialized aggressives was 10.9 years. (The former was defined by going with a bad crowd, gang activities, stealing, truancy, and running away from home, while the latter corresponds to aggressive conduct disorder.) This difference in age raises the possibility that some boys would qualify as "unsocialized aggressive" in childhood but become "socialized delinquents" as adolescents. In fact, this was observed on a small scale in a 4-year followup of boys with aggressive conduct disorder by August, Stewart, and Holmes (1983), and it is common clinical experience that the clinical picture of aggressive boys changes subtly as they grow older. This change has been demonstrated in the factor analytic studies of Achenbach (1978), Achenbach and Edelbrock (1979), and Arnold and Smeltzer (1974), which show a shift with increasing age from physical aggression to threats and other forms of verbal aggression. Furthermore, a prospective study in which 369 8-year-old children were followed to age 20 (Pulkkinen, 1983a) shows the broadening of an aggressive

child's repertoire of obnoxious behavior as he or she becomes an adolescent. Aggressiveness is a persistent theme, but by age 14, roaming the streets, smoking, drinking, and sexuality have been added. Findings such as these imply a need for different diagnostic criteria for aggressive conduct disorder in the three eras of preschool, grade school, and high school.

Something also must be said of the *Diagnostic and Statistical Manual of Mental Disorders*, third edition (DSM-III), classification of conduct disorders. In their preamble, the authors of this section admit that their system is controversial. Although no grounds are given for the comment, the main drawback is clearly that the validity of the distinction between socialized and undersocialized has not been established. Nor are there ways to measure this dimension that have proved to be reliable and effective. On the other hand, there is no great objection to the separation of aggressive and nonaggressive, except the principle that a positive definition is better than a negative one. Following this guide, the latter category, nonaggressive, should be called antisocial or delinquent.

## AGGRESSIVE CONDUCT DISORDER

### Definition

Hewitt and Jenkins (1946) were the first to separate aggressive conduct disorder from the other behavioral and emotional problems of children who were attending a psychiatric clinic; they named it the "unsocialized aggressive" behavior syndrome. More recently, the official name has been "undersocialized conduct disorder of aggressive type," but "aggressive conduct disorder" carries less theoretical baggage. Hewitt and Jenkins's definition, which was derived from a form of factor analysis, consisted of physical attacks, fighting, cruelty, disobedience, and destructiveness. Recently, Stewart and deBlois (1985) applied discriminant analysis to the behavioral symptoms of children with aggressive conduct disorder and with other diagnoses, excluding autism, more than mild retardation, organic disorders, and psychosis. The combination of aggressiveness, antisocial behavior, and egocentricity served to separate the groups efficiently. Noncompliance did not contribute to the discriminant function, no doubt because it was a common symptom in both groups. The set of symptoms that best separated boys and girls with aggressive conduct disorder from those with other diagnoses is shown in Table 18–1.

A full set of diagnostic criteria include the following:

• Onset is no later than the first year of school and duration is at least a year.
• Aggressive symptoms are relatively stable throughout childhood and adolescence.
• An affected child should have four or more of the eight symptoms shown in Table 18–1, and among these should be "fights" or "quarrelsomeness" or both. To be counted, the symptoms should clearly disrupt the child's home and classroom, as well as damage his or her relations with other children. Also, the symptoms should be reported by both parents and teachers, and both sources should rate them as serious.
• The symptoms are not explained by another primary diagnosis, such as autism, depression, brain syndrome, or schizophrenia.

The first two requirements are justified in the course of this chapter; the requirement of two sources, parents and teachers, rests on the evidence that misbehavior that is observed in school as well as at home is more likely to persist (Mitchell and Rosa, 1981; Schachar, Rutter, Smith, 1981).

## Prevalence

Aggressive conduct disorder is a relatively common problem, judging from field studies done in England and New Zealand. There are no data that bear specifically on the rates of aggressive conduct disorder in large populations, but Schachar et al. (1981) found that 2.5 per cent of boys aged 10 to 11 in a semirural part of England were "pervasively unsociable." The definition of this term was based on three items: "fights with other children," "not liked by other children," and "tends to do things on his own." McGee, Williams, and Silva (1984) used a similar definition and found that 2.2 per cent of 7-year-old boys in a mixed urban and rural sample were judged aggressive by both parents and teachers.

Boys with this disorder account for a third or more of admissions to child psychiatry clinics, at least in the United States. In such clinics, the ratio of boys to girls with aggressive conduct disorder is about 4:1 (Stewart, deBlois, Meardon, Cummings, 1980b), and the same sex ratio probably prevails among the general population (Rutter, Tizard, Whitmore, 1970).

## Origins

### Social Factors

The failure of parents to provide their children with love, consistent and reasonable discipline, a stable home, and an example of good behavior has long been held to cause antisocial behavior. This seems only common sense. Explaining why fighting other children was his only pleasure, Maxim Gorky (1913) wrote: "I warned Mother that

**TABLE 18–1** Symptoms Separating Children with Aggressive Conduct Disorder from Those with Other Diagnoses

| Symptoms | Boys | | Girls | |
|---|---|---|---|---|
| | With Aggressive Conduct Disorder (%) (N = 64) | With Other Diagnoses (%) (N = 48) | With Aggressive Conduct Disorder (%) (N = 17) | With Other Diagnoses (%) (N = 36) |
| Fights | 94 | 16 | 94 | 19 |
| Quarrelsome | 98 | 21 | 100 | 28 |
| Steals outside the home | 31 | 6 | 29 | 8 |
| Attacks adults | 41 | 4 | 12 | 8 |
| Undue need for attention | 88 | 40 | 76 | 44 |
| Lies | 52 | 15 | 88 | 28 |
| Problem sharing | 59 | 17 | 65 | 17 |
| Extreme competitiveness | 67 | 32 | 88 | 31 |

if she didn't stop beating me I would bite her hand and run away into the fields to freeze. . . . That living, throbbing gamut of feelings called love slowly faded in me and in its place there flared up, more and more often, smoldering blue fires of ill will against everyone."

Several large and well-controlled studies have shown that such factors in the home are closely associated with the development of aggressiveness and delinquency. For example, McCord, McCord, and Howard (1961) found that the parents of aggressive boys, when compared with those of normal boys, were more often rejecting, punitive, and threatening; inconsistent in discipline and poor supervisors; socially deviant; and in conflict with each other. Similarly, McCord, McCord, and Howard (1963) found that the severity of these factors was least in the homes of boys who were normal, intermediate in the homes of aggressive boys, and greatest in the homes of boys who were both aggressive and delinquent. Farrington (1978) found a similar progression of severity in the homes of normal boys, nonviolent delinquents, and violent delinquents. Thus the emotional poverty of homes seems to be related to the severity of boys' misbehavior, but so far, no factor has been found that is peculiar to aggressiveness or to delinquency.

Two obvious questions are whether a boy's early behavior elicits the rejection and inconsistent discipline or vice versa, and whether another variable, such as personality disorder in a parent, is responsible for both the boy's misbehavior and the poor environment. Although there are no firm answers to such questions, it is more than likely that such variables as the father's being antisocial or alcoholic and the mother's being depressed or dull do affect the interactions in the family, and that there is a continuing interaction between the boy's obnoxious behavior and the parents' limited ability to deal with it.

To study this issue at a more molecular level, Patterson and his colleagues (Patterson and Cobb, 1973; Patterson, 1980) have sent observers into the homes of aggressive boys and controls to count and record specific interactions between family members. Their central finding is that there are repeated cycles of negative interactions between the boy and his mother and, to a lesser extent, between the boy and his siblings. An interaction might start with a critical comment by the mother, for example, and there follows an escalating exchange, which ends in a particularly aversive behavior by the boy, such as hitting or threatening. An important element in these exchanges is that mothers of aggressive boys tend to be dysphoric and lack self-confidence. The end result of such upbringing is that the child is out of control and a high level of tension exists in the family.

The idea that aggressive or antisocial behavior is learned by example also has the appeal of common sense. The fact that aggressive and antisocial boys tend to resemble their natural fathers adds to the appeal (West and Farrington, 1973; Stewart, deBlois, Cummings, 1980a). However, example is not enough to explain a further observation, that such boys may resemble their fathers when the fathers are long gone from the home (Robins, 1966; Stewart and deBlois, 1983a & b). It seems worth mentioning here that aggressive conduct disorder in boys is associated with both wife abuse and child abuse in the family (Stewart and deBlois, 1981; Behar and Stewart, 1982).

### Biologic Factors

It has been known at least since the turn of the century that children can have a change in personality and become aggressive and antisocial as a result of physical illness or injury, whether neurologic or systemic (Still, 1902). This lesson was drilled home by the epidemic of encephalitis in western Europe and the United States in the early 1920s. Nowadays such personality changes are uncommon, but organic factors, such as congenital brain damage and temporal lobe epilepsy, may still be associated with aggressiveness and antisocial behavior. However, the epidemiologic study of Rutter, Graham, and Yule (1970) shows that such factors only account for about 1 per cent of children with conduct disorders.

Assuming that virtually all antisocial men have had conduct disorder in their boyhood (Robins, 1978), and assuming that specific genetic influences play a part in the origin of criminality and alcoholism (Christiansen, 1977; Cadoret, Cain, Grove, 1980; Mednick, Gabrielli, Hutchings, 1984), it seems reasonable to expect that future studies will uncover genetic determinants of conduct disorders. Meanwhile, there is no direct evidence, but the reader may well feel that the clinical picture and natural history of aggressive conduct disorder suggest biologic as well as social origins. There is little doubt that social factors maintain or enhance the disorder, but there are no data to show that they can cause it in a child who lacks a biologic predisposition.

## Clinical Picture

The following description is based on the reports of parents, teachers, and the children themselves and on the observations of nurses working on a child psychiatry ward. Affected children are loud, obtrusive, "handsy," and given to teasing, besides being physically aggressive (Hewitt and Jenkins, 1946; Stewart et al., 1980a; Behar and Stewart, 1982). They want to be the center of attention; they must win and will cheat or break up a game rather than lose. They are willful and resent directions, tend to be insensitive to the feelings and needs of others, and seldom admit to being sorry for misbehavior. They are prone to tantrums, in which they throw or break things. Cruelty to animals or young children and destructiveness are also common.

As West and Farrington (1977) have observed, aggressiveness is often associated with delinquent behavior. This seems to be true of boys with aggressive conduct disorder but not of girls (Stewart et al., 1980a), for the former tend to be involved in lying, stealing, vandalism, and fire setting. Affected girls, on the other hand, tend to be precociously interested in sex. Both boys and girls with aggressive conduct disorder tend to have more difficult temperamental traits than do corresponding children with other diagnoses. These traits, which include impulsivity, low tolerance for frustration, impatience, and easy excitability are present whether or not the child is hyperactive (Stewart, Cummings, Singer, deBlois, 1981).

Children with aggressive conduct disorder can be divided into those who are involved in specific antisocial behavior, such as stealing, vandalism, and fire setting, and those who are not. Preliminary research suggests that the less antisocial are more likely to respond to behavioral and cognitive treatment (Stewart and Behar, 1983).

## Associated Problems

Beside these essential symptoms, there are several intriguing correlates of aggressive conduct disorder (Table 18–2). The most obvious to the outside observer is the combination of overactivity and inattentiveness, which occurs in about 80 per cent of affected boys and 50 per cent of girls (Stewart et al., 1981; Stewart and Behar, 1983). As far as the aggressive children themselves are concerned, the most hurtful is rejection by their peers (Coie and Kupersmidt, 1983; Dodge, 1983). This rejection does not necessarily imply lack of popularity, but a study by Milich and Landau (1984) suggests that aggressive boys who are also withdrawn have the highest risk of being both unpopular and rejected.

Boys and girls with aggressive conduct disorder tend to be chronically sad and lacking in self-esteem (Stewart et al., 1980a), and this state can become so severe that a child meets the criteria for a major depressive disorder (Puig-Antich, 1982). Another potentially serious correlate is the liability to repeated accidental injury, which affects about 30 per cent of boys with aggressive conduct disorder and a lesser proportion of girls (Mellinger and Manheimer, 1967; Bijur, Stewart-Brown, Golding, Butler, Rush, 1983).

Aggressive conduct disorder is associated with cognitive handicaps as well as behavioral and emotional handicaps. When children with this disorder are compared with children who have other diagnoses, and autistic, "organic," and more than mildly retarded children are excluded from both groups, the former have lower IQs than the latter (Behar and Stewart, 1982). Similarly, McGee et al. (1984) found that aggressive boys in the general population had lower IQs than boys who were neither aggressive nor hyperactive. In both instances, however, it was the boys who were hyperactive as well as aggressive that accounted for the

**TABLE 18–2   Clinical Correlates of Aggressive Conduct Disorder**

Hyperactive and inattentive
Rejected by peers
Low mood
Repeated accidental injury
Lower than average IQ
Speech, language, and reading problems

difference. Among the patients with aggressive conduct disorder, there was a 9-point gap in verbal IQ between the hyperactive and normally active boys but no difference in performance IQ (Stewart and Behar, 1983). In McGee et al.'s field sample, both verbal and performance IQs were 6 points lower for the hyperactive and aggressive boys than for the purely aggressive, and there was a similar difference between the former group and the nondeviant boys on verbal IQ but not on performance IQ. These findings echo the results of Huesmann and Yarmel's (1983) work on the intellectual competence of aggressive men.

Boys with aggressive conduct disorder tend to have speech defects and delayed language development (Behar and Stewart, 1982), but again, the problems are characteristic of those who are hyperactive. McGee et al. (1984) also found that aggressive and hyperactive boys had difficulties learning to read. Thirty-six per cent of this group had specific reading retardation; the proportions in the purely aggressive and the nondeviant were 19 per cent and 7 per cent, respectively. Lastly, Camp (1977) has shown that the performance of aggressive boys on academic tasks is hampered by their inability to direct themselves with internal speech.

The age, sex, and social class of patients with aggressive conduct disorder generally have little effect on their clinical picture (Behar and Stewart, 1984). However, there are a few interesting differences by age and sex. Children who were seen in a psychiatric clinic between the ages of 3 and 10 were more likely than those who were older to have antisocial fathers. They also had an earlier age of onset. The older children more often were adopted and had fathers who were free of psychiatric disorder. Moreover, they came from larger sibships and had lower birth ranks. Girls were less likely than boys to be referred for physical fighting, less often had set fires, but had more often injured themselves, more often had frequent physical complaints, and tended to live in a home with a stepfather. The only obvious difference related to social class was that children from poorer families had more often been abused.

There are two intriguing hints in these findings. First, the frequent physical complaints of the girls, and possibly their harming themselves, seem to fit Robins's (1966) observation that aggressive, antisocial girls are liable to develop somatization disorder in adult life. Second, the differences between children who presented early and late raise the possibility that there are two tracks to developing aggressive conduct disorder: one in which the problem is transmitted from father to son and another that may be associated with lack of supervision.

### Family Background

When boys with aggressive conduct disorder who were attending a psychiatric clinic were compared with boys with other diagnoses, excluding autism, organic disorders, and more than mild retardation, significant differences appeared in the prevalence of psychiatric disorder among their immediate relatives. Most obviously, boys with aggressive conduct disorder more often had biologic fathers who were antisocial, but the fathers also had a significantly higher rate of psychiatric disorder in general (Stewart et al., 1980b). There was no such clear-cut difference between the mothers of boys with conduct disorder and those of boys with other diagnoses, but there were trends for the former to have a higher rate of neurotic disorders and somatization disorder. In a separate study, Twito and Stewart (1982) found that 20 per cent of the full brothers and 10 per cent of the half brothers of boys with aggressive conduct disorder had the disorder themselves. Interestingly, the full and half brothers had, on the average, spent the same length of time growing up with the probands. Finally, Jary and Stewart (1985) studied the legal parents of a series of boys with aggressive conduct disorder who had been adopted and found that the prevalence of alcoholism and antisocial behavior among the adoptive parents was significantly less than that of the natural parents of a group of boys with aggressive conduct disorder who were not adopted. In fact, there was virtually no such disorder among the adoptive parents. This finding suggests that being raised by an antisocial father is not a necessary condition for a boy to develop aggressive conduct disorder.

### Clinical Course

### Age of Onset

Parents usually date the first signs of aggressive conduct disorder as between the child's first and fifth birthdays (Behar and Stewart, 1982; August and Stewart, 1982), these signs being overactivity, hitting and biting, getting into things, daring, and willfulness. Whether such reports are valid is not yet proven, but circumstantial evidence suggests that they are. The age of first admission to a clinic is significantly correlated with the reported age of onset, as one would expect (Behar and Stewart, 1984). Earlier "reported" onset is also associated with more psychopathology in the parents (Behar and Stewart, 1984; Stewart, Copeland, deBlois, submitted) and poorer outcome of the disorder (Kelso and Stewart, in press). Also, several epidemiologic studies (e.g., Crowther, Bond, Rolf, 1981) have shown that aggressiveness is a relatively common problem among preschool children, and that such problems tend to persist (Richman, Stevenson, Graham, 1982).

## Outcome

The outcome of conduct disorders in general is quite well established, but little work has been done on the fate of children who specifically have aggressive conduct disorder. Over the short run, say, up to 10 years after having been identified, a quarter to a half of children who have a conduct disorder persist in being antisocial (Warren, 1965; Graham and Rutter, 1973). The results of longer-term followup studies are much the same. In four separate samples, Robins and her colleagues have studied the degree to which antisocial behavior of childhood persists into adult life (Robins, 1966; Robins, 1978; Robins and Ratcliff, 1979). The proportions of highly antisocial children who developed into equally antisocial adults varied from 23 per cent to 41 per cent, and of those who became free of psychiatric disorder, from 17 per cent to 28 per cent.

Morris, Escoll, and Wexler (1956) published the first followup of a group of children who had been treated for "aggressive behavior disorder." At age 18, roughly 8 years after their admission, 23 per cent were well, 18 per cent were schizophrenic (a diagnosis of schizophrenia from that era has to be taken with reservation), 18 per cent had court records, and the remaining 41 per cent were described as "never adjusted" or "borderline." August et al. (1983) followed a group of boys who had aggressive conduct disorder and were hyperactive, comparing

them with boys who were purely hyperactive; both groups had been recruited from a psychiatric clinic. Eleven of thirty boys (37 per cent) who had been diagnosed as having aggressive conduct disorder still had conduct problems after 4 years; eight had the aggressive type and three, a nonaggressive type. None of the purely hyperactive had developed a conduct disorder.

There is a larger body of data on the history of aggressive children in general and of those who have attended psychiatric clinics. The findings are remarkably consistent. Aggressiveness in childhood predicts heavy drinking among adolescent boys (Kellam, Ensminger, Simon, 1980; Pulkkinen, 1983b) and alcoholism in men (Jones, 1968; Nylander, 1979). It also predicts delinquency among adolescent boys (Kellam et al. 1980; Pulkkinen, 1983a; West and Farrington, 1973) and criminality or antisocial personality among men (Robins, 1966; Nylander, 1979). The well-proven stability of aggressiveness further implies that this trait is likely to persist through adolescence and into adult life, although showing itself in different forms (Olweus, 1979; Huesmann, Eron, Lefkowitz, Walder, 1983).

In a scholarly review, Loeber (1982) has shown that the main predictors of outcome for children with conduct disorder are the frequency, severity, and variety of antisocial behavior in childhood; the occurrence of such behavior both at home and at school; and the age of onset. The more antisocial the child and the earlier the onset, the greater the likelihood of the problem persisting. Recent work by Kelso and Stewart (in press) on factors that predict the outcome of boys with aggressive conduct disorder showed that "child variables" were more powerful predictors than were "family variables." The salient characteristics of the boys were the number of symptoms of conduct disorder, the age of onset, fire setting, quarrelsomeness, and having several accidental injuries before age 6. All of these variables predicted the persistence of aggressive conduct disorder. The important family variables were the prevalence of alcoholism or antisocial personality among immediate relatives and the number of times that the mother had been married. A higher prevalence of deviant behavior among relatives predicted persistence of the conduct disorder, while the mothers having been married more than once made it less likely that the problem would persist. The explanation of the last factor is that the child's home improved when his antisocial father was divorced by the mother and she married a healthy man.

## Laboratory Findings

Many researchers are now exploring the field of laboratory findings. None of the possible leads is well established, but they all seem worth pursuing.

Mattsson, Schalling, Olweus, Low, and Svensson (1980) found that levels of plasma testosterone in male recidivist delinquents tended to be higher than those in normal high school boys, and that the more violent delinquents tended to have higher levels than the less violent. Among the controls, levels of testosterone were significantly correlated with self-reported aggression (Olweus, Mattsson, Schalling, Low, 1980). These findings are consistent with the data from several studies on violent, antisocial men (e.g., Kreuz and Rose, 1972).

Rogeness, Hernandez, Macedo, and Mitchell (1982) measured a number of biochemical variables in boys with aggressive conduct disorder, with socialized conduct disorder, and with no psychiatric disorder. The boys in the first group had lower activities of dopamine-$\beta$-hydroxylase (D$\beta$H) in plasma than those in the other groups. The same researchers (Rogeness et al., 1984) also showed that among boys on a child psychiatric ward, low activities of this enzyme in plasma were associated with the diagnosis of aggressive conduct disorder. Studies on disturbed adults have shown varying correlates of low plasma D$\beta$H activity, but there is evidence (Major et al., 1980) suggesting an association with antisocial tendencies.

On the positive side, Virkkunen and Penttinen (1984) have reported that serum cholesterol levels in boys with aggressive conduct disorder and attention deficits were significantly lower than those of boys with only attention deficits. This result fits Virkkunen's earlier work on criminal men, in which he has shown differences between the violent and nonviolent in glucose tolerance, insulin release, and serum cholesterol (Virkkunen, 1983a, 1983b).

How these disparate biochemical findings are related to aggressive behavior is still unclear, but if they are confirmed, they would enhance the validity of aggressive conduct disorder. It would be wrong not to mention the original biologic correlate, abnormal electroencephalographic (EEG) tracings. This once exciting line of research has been severely criticized, for example by Harris (1978), for lack of specificity in the supposed correlates of the EEG abnormalities, failure to classify subjects rigorously, and having inadequate controls. However, the greater sensitivity and specificity of computerized EEGs and the new sophistication of psychiatric diagnosis are likely to revive interest in this field.

## Differential Diagnosis

The possibilities for differential diagnosis are listed in Table 18–3. In addition, there are three conditions that may be associated with aggressive conduct disorder: secondary depression, alcohol abuse, and somatization disorder. The first of these is common among children and adolescents with aggressive conduct disorder, and such depressions can be severe enough to raise the possibility of suicide. It is worth remembering that the rare suicides among children under age 14 are associated with the diagnosis of conduct disorder (Shaffer, 1974).

As mentioned earlier, aggressive conduct disorder usually declares itself in the first few years of life. When behavior problems such as aggressiveness, willfulness, and irritability start in middle childhood or later, depression or a beginning dementia may be the explanation. Both of these disorders tend to be associated with a decline in school performance, but the dementia would also be marked by a progressive impairment of intelligence, speech and language skills,

**TABLE 18–3    Differential Diagnosis of Aggressive Conduct Disorder**

Primary depression
Dementia
Autism
Schizoid personality
Intermittent explosive disorder
"Pure hyperactivity"

and social behavior. Dementias in children are so uncommon that it is relatively easy to overlook the diagnosis, a mistake that could be tragic (Rivinus, Jamison, Graham, 1975).

Some young autistic children are aggressive and willful, but there should be no difficulty in seeing that these behavior problems are secondary to the more serious illness. Schizoid children are also liable to outbursts of violent behavior, but they are not habitually aggressive and disobedient, and again, the primary diagnosis should be obvious. The definition of intermittent explosive disorder is incompatible with the diagnosis of aggressive conduct disorder; children with the former behave normally for stretches of time, whereas those with the latter consistently misbehave.

Lastly, there are children who have mild signs of conduct disorder but are obviously hyperactive and inattentive. If such a child seems to be noncompliant from not attending to directions rather than willfully ignoring them, and if there is little in the way of aggressive behavior, he or she does not belong in the category of aggressive conduct disorder.

## Treatment

### General Principles

Aggressive conduct disorder is a broad syndrome within which there is variation from child to child and from one age to another in a given child. The targets and methods of treatment vary accordingly, although the common targets are aggressiveness, resistance to authority, and impulsivity. The specific targets may also vary from home to school, particularly the relative emphasis on cognitive problems.

The first moves are generally to teach parents how to deal with misbehavior and to make sure that the classroom teachers are skilled in this field. At this stage, one also has to make sure that a child's learning problems, if any, are getting proper attention in school. If such conservative management is not enough, the program should be enlarged to include training in social skills and impulse control, consideration of placing the child in a special class, and an investigation of the parents' mental state. The latter commonly uncovers a chronic low-grade depression in the mother, which is an ob-

stacle to her practicing more positive ways of managing the child's behavior. Such a mother needs supportive psychotherapy and possibly even drug treatment. If this second round fails to deal with the problems, the next step should be to admit the child to a short-stay inpatient unit for more intensive psychological treatment and possibly for trials of drug treatment.

Ideally, the training in behavior management for both parents and teachers is carried out in the child's natural setting. This practice has far more impact than discussions carried out in the physician's office. An alternative way of helping is to assemble a group of parents whose children have similar problems and to have regular, focused problem-solving sessions with them.

Again, ideally, there is a division of labor that makes the most economic use of the physician's time and that of his professional colleagues. In my unit, nurses work with parents in their homes, specialized teachers work with the children in their own schools, and social workers attend to the social and emotional needs of the parents. The physicians meets at regular intervals with the children and their parents in order to monitor progress.

The most common forms of treatment, in the United States at least, are family therapy, behavior management, and individual psychotherapy. The first and third of these are important adjuncts, but they do not deal directly with the child's problems. Nor is there a body of evidence to support the effectiveness of either method on its own or of the two in combination. Indeed, when either one is used as the sole treatment, the child's misbehavior may actually worsen because of the attention given to it.

Training parents and teachers in scientific ways of shaping behavior has been pioneered by Patterson (1974a, 1974b) and is now widely accepted as a way of dealing with the behavior problems of children and adolescents. The data that support this approach, however, are modest, and skeptics can point to the lack of long-term followups. My experience is that after a year, many parents tire of planning the discipline of their children. To keep such a program going requires constant support and advice for the parents.

The systematic shaping of a child's behavior through the use of reinforcements is a form of external control, while the aim is to steer the child to governing his or her own behavior in healthy ways. Thus the ideal is a program that gradually turns the responsibility for monitoring the rewarding behavior over to the child. Such programs are in common use but have not been researched adequately.

Over the past decade, two new treatments have emerged: training in social skills and in impulse control. Their virtues are that they are aimed directly at the child's main problems and that, at least in theory, they will teach him or her healthier behavior and greater self-control. For example, social skills training would include the substitution of verbal self-assertion for hitting and screaming, and the cognitive work would include coaching on how to handle frustration calmly. The drawback of such approaches is that they depend for success on the child's ability to learn the skills and on his or her interest in doing so. There seem to be some children who do not want to learn, and there may be some who cannot learn. Still, many children seem to benefit from this kind of training. Unfortunately, it is too early to tell whether the method is effective over the long run.

The behavior of some children with aggressive conduct disorder is so far out of control that drug treatment seems vital if they are to lead a near normal life. The possibilities at the time of writing are propranolol, lithium, drugs that block the uptake of serotonin into brain cells, antipsychotics, and stimulants. Of these, the last class should not be used for the treatment of conduct disorders because there is no convincing evidence that they influence aggressive and antisocial behavior when given in therapeutic doses. Weighing heavily against the use of antipsychotics are the risk that the child will develop tardive dyskinesia (Gualtieri, Quade, Hicks, Mayo, Schroeder, 1984) and their interference with cognitive functions (Werry and Aman, 1975; Breuning and Davidson, 1981).

Several case reports that appeared in the late 1970s suggested that propranolol calmed the aggressiveness and agitation of patients suffering from brain syndromes. Yudofsky, Williams, and Gorman (1981) reported that they had successfully treated the violent behavior of three adults and one adolescent who had definite brain damage with doses of propranolol ranging from 320 to 520 mg per day. Following this report, Williams, Mehl, Yudofsky, Adams, and Roseman (1982) described their experience in treating 30 children and adolescents who had uncontrolled aggressive outbursts associated with brain dysfunction. At followup, which ranged from 2 to 30 months, 10 of the 30 patients were markedly improved, 14 were moderately improved, and 6 had not changed. Side effects were transitory and reversible; they included sleepiness, lack of energy, hypotension, slowing of the pulse, depression, and asthma. Over the past two years, the staff of the University of Iowa's Division of Child Psychiatry have treated 16 aggressive children with propranolol (Kuperman, personal communication). The children had all proved resistant to psychologic treatments but were not necessarily brain damaged. Ten of the sixteen responded well to the drug at an average dose of about 140 mg per day. How propranolol reduces aggression is not known.

The reader should be warned that propranolol may impair memory. Soloman et al. (1983) found that middle-aged men being treated for hypertension with this drug or methyldopa had significant deficits in remembering. Clearly this finding cannot be extrapolated directly to the treatment of children, but it is something to bear in mind.

The treatment of aggressive children with lithium has been reviewed by Campbell, Cohen, and Small (1982). The studies reported so far are on a small scale and not particularly rigorous, but it seems that lithium is worth trying in intractable cases. For example, Siassi (1982) found a significant drop in the rate of outbursts among 17 children who were treated with relatively high doses of lithium over a 3-month period.

The most rational treatment for aggression, but one that has barely been explored, is to give drugs that will raise the ambient level of serotonin in the brain. This statement is based on a number of animal studies that show that low levels of serotonin in the brain stem are associated with aggression (e.g., Valzelli and Garattini, 1972) and similar findings in the spinal fluid of adult men (Brown, Goodwin, Ballenger, Goyer, Major, 1979; Linnoila et al., 1983). Although there have been reports from the United Kingdom that drugs such as trazodone (a serotonin uptake inhibitor) are effective in reducing aggression in elderly patients, no study on this approach to children has been published to my knowledge.

## ANTISOCIAL OR DELINQUENT CONDUCT DISORDER

### Definition

There is no accepted definition of antisocial or delinquent conduct disorder, but straightforward clinical studies and those that have applied factor analysis to the symptoms of disturbed children and adolescents show a dimension of delinquent behavior that includes the items in Table 18–4. In the present context, the word delinquent is used in a general, rather than legal, sense, unless otherwise specified.

The description of this broad disorder is, to some extent, the other side of the coin of aggressive conduct disorder. The findings that many children with aggressive conduct disorder are also specifically antisocial and that aggressiveness in childhood tends to be followed by delinquent behavior in adolescence have already been mentioned. It would be tidier to present material under the headings of a primarily aggressive disorder, a primarily antisocial disorder, and a combination of the two, but the necessary data are lacking. The best that can be done is to deal with the combination but emphasize aggressiveness first and delinquency second.

Age helps to sharpen the distinction. It has already been pointed out that aggressive behaviors begin early in life and are remarkably persistent over time. On the other hand, antisocial behaviors, such as lying and stealing, may begin early but are not

**TABLE 18–4  Common Delinquent Symptoms Among Adolescent Boys Attending a Clinic**

Poor schoolwork
Lies to get out of trouble
Steals at home
Steals outside the home
Tells tall stories
Delinquent friends
Defies authority
Runs away from home
Truant
Drinks often and heavily
Vandalism

usually stable until ages 10 to 12 (Gersten, Langner, Eisenberg, Simcha-Fagan, McCarthy, 1976). More importantly, the incidence of legal delinquency is relatively low until age 13, when it begins to increase rapidly.

An aspect of the problem that is confusing to the clinician and the medically oriented researcher is the commonness of both legal and self-reported delinquent behavior among adolescents. For example, in the urban, working class community where West and Farrington (1973) studied the development of delinquency, 21 per cent of the male youths were convicted as juveniles (i.e., before age 17) and 31 per cent had been convicted by age 19. It is difficult to apply the disease model to something so common. Granted, one could study the small and more deviant group (9 per cent) who were recidivists, but the one-time delinquents could actually be separated from the nondelinquents on a wide range of behaviors and background factors. The recidivists simply had these characteristics to a greater degree.

### Etiology

From the statistics in the preceding paragraph, it follows, in all likelihood, that the origins of delinquency are several and that they vary from one individual to another. Serious study of this subject in the United States began with the founding of the Juvenile Psychopathic Institute at Chicago, in 1909. William Healy and Augusta Bronner started their pioneering studies on delinquents there and continued them later in Boston. Although Healy and Bronner (1936) recognized the influence of broken homes, poverty, and parental deviance, they were very much aware of differences in personality between delinquent boys and their nondelinquent siblings. Table 18–5 summarizes the differences that they found between 105 delinquents and 105 controls who were siblings of the same sex and nearest in age to them.

These early investigators saw the differences in personality, behavior, and attitudes as stemming from the frustration of the delinquents' need for the love and guidance of their parents. Thus the lack of a healthy relationship between parent and child was

**TABLE 18–5**  Differences in Behavior Between 105 Official Delinquents and 105 Sibling Controls

|  | Number with Symptoms | |
|---|---|---|
|  | DELINQUENTS | CONTROLS |
| Hyperactive and/or aggressive | 46 | 0 |
| Truant | 60 | 0 |
| Dislikes school | 40 | 4 |
| Feels inferior | 38 | 4 |
| Wets the bed | 22 | 4 |
| Poor school achievement | 20 | 5 |
| Nervous habits | 44 | 24 |

From Healy W, Bronner AF: New Light on Delinquency and Its Treatment. New Haven, Conn., Yale University Press, 1936. All differences are significant at the 1 per cent level or better, based on $\chi^2$ test with Yates' correction.

seen as the prime cause of delinquency; social misery also played a part.

The findings of Healy and Bronner have been confirmed repeatedly. Delinquency and aggressiveness have been found to be associated with parental rejection, broken homes, and broader social variables, such as poverty and overcrowding. The broken home has been refined by Rutter (1971) to the more specific event of conflict between the parents, which, among boys at least, is clearly associated with the development of behavior problems.

Another likely cause of antisocial and aggressive behavior, mentioned earlier, is the poor example set by deviant parents. Delinquent boys, as well as aggressive boys, commonly have alcoholic or criminal fathers and mothers. However, the relationship of delinquency to parental behavior is complicated by the finding that a father's criminality can be associated with delinquency in his son even when the father's conviction occurred before the son's birth (Osborn and West, 1979), thus suggesting a genetic influence.

A point about parental deviance that has been made by Robins (1966) is that the antisocial personality of the father may be the prime cause of most of the miserable aspects of the child's home. Such fathers usually have poor work records and are irresponsible with money, thus explaining the poverty and hardship of the home. They tend to be violent, hence wife and child abuse are common. Neighbors and relatives disapprove of the father, so the family is socially isolated. And so on. Given the chain of consequences that flow from a father's criminality, or a mother's, it comes as no surprise that delinquency is highly concentrated among "multiple-problem families," that is, those whose poverty, squalor, and disorganization bring them into frequent contact with social agencies.

As was pointed out in the section on the origins of aggressive conduct disorder, finding that certain factors in the home, for example harsh and inconsistent discipline, are associated with delinquency cannot be taken as evidence of causation. It does seem likely that there are frustrating interactions between a child and his or her parents that occur early in a child's life and that create lasting conflict between the parents and the child, and that this conflict can lead to antisocial behavior. But it also seems likely that these environmental variables will affect only children who are predisposed from genetic influences or, less commonly, from those of acquired biologic factors, such as perinatal stress. There is beginning evidence from studies of adoptees (such as that of Cadoret, Cain, and Crowe [1983]) that specific genetic factors interact with environmental factors to produce antisocial behavior among adolescents as well as adults.

## Epidemiology

Because the prevalence of antisocial conduct disorder among adolescents is not known, this section is based on the statistics of official delinquency. Data from the work of West and Farrington (1973, 1977) are presented, since the United Kingdom is representative of Western societies. Presumably the rates in the United States, Canada, and other Western countries are similar.

West and Farrington tracked the development of delinquency among 411 boys living in an urban working class district, following them from age 8 to 20 and beyond. Twenty-one per cent of the boys were convicted as juveniles, and by age 20, the rate had climbed to 31 per cent. The national figure for the prevalence of juvenile delinquency in the United Kingdom is somewhat lower, 15 per cent, reflecting the tendency for rates to be lower among middle-class boys and among those who are living in rural or semirural areas. Among West and Farrington's subjects, 9 per cent were recidivists as juveniles, that is, before their 17th birthday.

The incidence of convictions was very low before age 13 but then climbed rapidly. The greatest change took place from 13 to 14, in which year the incidence rose from 5 per cent to 10 per cent. The rate then climbed slowly to a maximum of 14 per cent at age 18, after which it declined.

Crimes of dishonesty were by far the most common offense, both among juveniles and young adults. Among the former, they accounted for 88 per cent and among the latter, for 76 per cent of offenses. Among the juveniles, aggressive crimes accounted for 7 per cent of the total; damage to property, 3 per cent; and sex offenses, 2 per cent. In this population, which was studied during the 1960s and 1970s, drug offenses were not observed.

Most offenses by juveniles involved one or two companions, but gang crimes were unusual. A clear correlation was observed between the number of juvenile convictions and convictions as a young adult. Also, chil-dren who were convicted between ages 10 and 12 tended to have a higher rate of convictions as adults. For example, their rate of conviction was three times the rate of those juveniles who were first convicted at ages 17 to 19.

## Clinical Picture

This section is based almost entirely on the findings of West and Farrington (1977), which include a superb description of the delinquent way of life. To begin with, delinquent boys tend to be aggressive (Table 18–6). West and Farrington rated every boy in their sample on the number of fights they reported having in the previous 3 years, the number of fights that they had started, the number of days on which they had carried a weapon, and the number of days on which they had used a weapon. Each item was rated on a 1-to-4 scale, and those boys who had a score of 10 or more were classed as aggressive. The resulting breakdown was as follows: 46 per cent of the 101 boys who were convicted of an offense as a juvenile or as a young adult were among those classed as aggressive, while 58 per cent of the 79 most aggressive boys were delinquent. Vandalism or destructiveness was associated with both aggressiveness and delinquency. Roughly half of the boys who had been involved in such behavior were aggressive and half were delinquent.

Delinquents were also significantly overrepresented among the boys who drank frequently (almost every night in a given week), those who had a large weekly consumption (20 or more pints of beer), those who habitually drank a large amount at one sitting (6 or more pints of beer in an evening), and, finally, among those who be-

TABLE 18–6  Overlap of Aggressiveness and Delinquency

|  | No. of Nondelinquents (%) N = 278 | No. of Delinquents (%) N = 101 |
|---|---|---|
| Involved in 10 or more fights in past 3 years (n = 71) | 32  (11.5) | 39  (38.5) |
| Started 2 or more fights in past 3 years (n = 96) | 43  (15.5) | 53  (53.0) |
| Used weapon to injure someone in past 3 years (n = 61) | 29  (10.4) | 32  (32.0) |

From West DJ, Farrington DP: The Delinquent Way of Life. London, Heinemann, 1977.

came violent while drinking. The association of delinquency with problem drinking was even more obvious for those who were recidivists, a finding that was true of almost all aspects of the delinquent life-style. Regular smoking and starting to smoke at 13 years of age or younger were significantly associated with delinquency, as was the use of prohibited drugs.

British juvenile delinquents less often drove than their nondelinquent counterparts, but despite this, they had more drinking and driving offenses and more driving offenses in general and were more often disqualified from driving. The delinquents did not gamble more often than nondelinquents, but they were more often heavy gamblers. Other characteristic leisure activities were hanging around in the street looking for girls or spending time in coffee bars and discotheques. They went out more often in the evening than the nondelinquents and were less likely to attend evening classes or other forms of self-improvement. Group activities were common in the whole sample of boys; 86 per cent went out regularly in a group of four or more friends. However, there was only one delinquent boy among the 55 boys who did not go out in groups.

Throughout the period of the study, juvenile delinquents were more likely than nondelinquents to have a relationship with a girl. They were younger when they first had intercourse, more often had six or more partners, and more often had intercourse one or more times a week. Putting this information together, the proportion of delinquents among the sexually active boys was much greater than that among the sexually inactive.

Beginning with the work of Healy and Bronner, many investigators have noted the poor relationships between delinquent boys and their parents and other authority figures. In West and Farrington's study, juvenile delinquents were significantly overrepresented among those who had troubled relationships with their parents, and this was particularly true of recidivists. The attitudes toward authority were sampled in a questionnaire, and the delinquents' characteristic responses were to reject school and view the police with hostility and suspicion.

The delinquents were carefree with their money. Compared with nondelinquents, they spent more than they earned, they spent more on nonessentials, they less often had savings, and they more often ran up debts. They had jobs with lower status—a phenomenon related to their poor attainment in school—their work histories were erratic, they had casual attitudes toward work, and they got into more difficulties with bosses because of their rebelliousness.

Finally, the delinquents were more often scarred from accidents or fights, they made up two thirds of the small number of boys who were tattooed, and, curiously, they were less likely to wear glasses. The first of these observations fits well with the results of a study by Lewis and Shanok (1977) on the medical histories of delinquents compared with nondelinquents. These authors found that delinquents had more often been to a hospital for an accident or an injury, particularly in the age ranges of 0 to 4 and 14 to 16.

In summary, the boys who had been convicted, usually for theft, burglary, or "borrowing" a car, had a specific life-style that separated them from their nondeviant comrades (Table 18–7). This antisocial quality permeated almost every aspect of their lives, and its intensity was directly related to the degree of their delinquency. An interesting sidelight is that aggressive boys who had not been convicted were likely to share this life-style. The reader will no doubt recognize this portrait of delinquent boys as a more detailed version of the definition of antisocial personality in DSM-III.

One gap in the clinical description of delinquents is the lack of information on their habitual mood. At least two studies (How-

---

**TABLE 18–7    The Delinquent Way of Life**

Fighting
Vandalism
Drinking heavily and often
Smoking early and regularly
Driving offenses
Heavy gambling
Hanging around on the street
Early and promiscuous sexuality
Rebellious attitude toward parents, teachers, and police
Irresponsible with money
Poor job history
Accident prone
Chronic low mood
Scarred and tattooed

ard, 1981; Kashani et al., 1980a) show that delinquents who are confined to a detention center or reform school are often clinically depressed. It would be reasonable to attribute this to their loss of freedom, especially since a significant number of young people commit suicide in jail, but for Howard's finding that persistent offenders tended to be more depressed than those who were committed to a reform school for the first time and his finding that depression scores were strongly correlated with the degree of antisocial tendency and aggressiveness.

A more serious gap in knowledge of the clinical aspects of delinquency is that there are no large-scale comparisons of male and female offenders. The impression given by research on special samples, such as delinquents referred to psychiatric clinics, is that there are no great differences (Lukianowicz, 1972; Kashani, Husain, Robins, Reid, Wooderson, 1980b). There is an intriguing hint in the latter group's work that delinquent girls may be duller than the boys, although they come from families of higher socioeconomic status. Furthermore, Offord et al. (1978, 1979) have shown differences in the family backgrounds of delinquent boys and girls. For example, the delinquent boys more often had alcoholic fathers than their matched controls (42 per cent vs. 23 per cent), but there was no such difference for the girls. On the other hand, only 33 per cent of the delinquent girls were living with their original parents compared with 52 per cent of the boys, a trend at the $P < 0.1$ level.

## Clinical Course

### Age of Onset

Three sets of data bear on the question of when antisocial conduct disorder begins: the statistics on the incidence of official or self-reported delinquency, the predictors of delinquency, and the findings on aggressive conduct disorder.

In West and Farrington's (1977) sample, 22 per cent of the delinquents had been convicted before age 13, and this group had a particularly poor prognosis. Evidence of an earlier onset for some boys comes from the finding that teachers' ratings of boys' behavior in middle childhood are quite efficient predictors of delinquency. Craig and Glick (1963, 1968) and West and Farrington (1973) have reported that disobedience and disruptiveness in grade school foretell antisocial behavior in adolescence or official delinquency. Similarly, Kellam et al. (1980) and Pulkkinen (1983b) have found that teachers' ratings of boys' aggressiveness in the early grades predict delinquency and problem drinking. Finally, the earlier section on aggressive conduct disorder argued a connection between misbehavior that starts at ages 2 to 4 and later delinquency.

### Outcome

The fate of juvenile delinquents, at least those who come from blue-collar families, has been well defined by Osborn and West (1980) and by West (1982). Forty-four per cent in their sample of 82 delinquents, or 9 per cent of the whole sample of boys, became persisting recidivists; that is, they had been convicted at least twice for offenses committed before their 19th birthday and at least once in the next 5 years. These men continued to show many of the antisocial tendencies that were described earlier under Clinical Picture, in contrast to temporary recidivists, who were defined as having two or more convictions before age 19 but none in the next 5 years. The latter apparently became much less antisocial in their late teens and early 20s and could hardly be distinguished from the nondelinquents.

Childhood characteristics that predicted long-term recidivism included a teacher's rating the boy's behavior in grade school as very poor; the father's having been convicted of a crime as an adult twice or more before the boy was 10; and the mother's having been convicted as an adult, or a sibling convicted as a juvenile or adult before the boy was 10. Of 397 boys in the sample, 35 qualified on two or three of these items, and in this group, 26 (74 per cent) were persistent recidivists. A later event that also predicted this poor outcome was being convicted before age 13. And at age 18, the temporary recidivists had had fewer convictions, were less involved in the delinquent life-style, and less often came from criminal families than the persisting recidivists.

To sum up, the outcome for antisocial and delinquent boys, and probably for girls too, is a function of the age at which their misbehavior starts, the variety of the antisocial behaviors, and their frequency. The extent of deviance among the parents and siblings is also an important factor.

## Differential Diagnosis

Researchers have persistently tried to subgroup juvenile delinquents on a clinical basis. One durable classification has been to divide them into psychopathic, neurotic, and subcultural groups (Quay, 1964). A weakness of this approach is that the degree of antisocial behavior has not been controlled. In fact, the groups seem to vary more along this dimension than on some basic personality trait. For example, Genshaft (1980) gave the Minnesota Multiphasic Personality Inventory to 57 adolescent boys who had all been convicted of many offenses. She divided them into the three groups, using a questionnaire that was developed by Quay and his colleagues for this purpose. The main result was that the neurotic group had the highest scores on the psychopathic-deviate, depression, and psychasthenia scales. In other words, the boys in the three groups resembled one another in describing themselves as antisocial, but those in the most antisocial group were more likely to report symptoms of anxiety and depression. It is more conservative to conclude that the most antisocial delinquents have significant affective symptoms than to say that delinquents can be divided into three groups on the basis of their personalities.

As far as I know, no study has been published in which a large, unselected sample of juvenile delinquents have been examined systematically and given psychiatric diagnoses. Therefore, the most that can be said at this point is that delinquents are prone to abuse alcohol and other drugs as part of their life-style; that they may suffer from depression and anxiety, either of which may reach clinical levels; and that some will be aggressive and others not.

## Treatment

As yet, there are no specific treatments for delinquent behavior, but cognitive training may help to arouse a sense of guilt over theft and other delinquencies (Chandler, 1973; Chandler, Greenspan, Barenboim, 1974;

Stewart and Ashby, 1981). Such training would be aimed at increasing a boy's awareness of the feelings of others and the effects of his behavior on them.

Society may invoke probation or detention when a boy has been convicted, the aim being to reform the already delinquent and deter those who are at risk. However, there is evidence that conviction makes the behavior of a delinquent worse. West and Farrington (1977) matched 53 of their subjects who had been convicted between ages 14 and 18 with 53 who had not been convicted on the extent of self-reported delinquency at age 14. The former had significantly more self-reported delinquency than the latter at age 18; the rate of the first group had climbed over the 4 years, while that of the second group had dropped. When the groups were matched on further variables (IQ, family size and income, and parental deviance), the difference between the convicted and the nonconvicted increased. Lastly, it was possible to link the deterioration of behavior to the period immediately after the conviction. There is also evidence that confining delinquents to a "training school" is a mistake. More than 80 per cent of boys discharged from such schools in England were reconvicted within 2 years, and even boys who were sent to "community homes" committed more offenses than those who were returned to their own homes (Smith, 1984).

Such findings have prompted drastic changes in parts of the United States and the United Kingdom. For example, juvenile courts have been abolished in Scotland for all except the most serious offenses. Instead, offenders appear before panels of responsible lay people. Correspondingly, in a number of communities in the United States, offenders are diverted from the juvenile courts to people who are especially interested in youth for their informal supervison. Whether such a caring approach will have any long-term benefit remains to be seen. On the other hand, it seems likely that the punitive approach simply makes matters worse.

To close this section on a positive note, at least one one event seems to improve the course of a delinquent's life. Moving away from the urban area in which a delinquent had grown up clearly lessened his risk of reconviction (Osborn, 1980).

## ATYPICAL CONDUCT DISORDERS

Until more is known about conduct disorders, particularly their natural history, a number of children attending psychiatric clinics will have to be given the vague diagnosis of atypical conduct disorder. Some will not fully match the description of either of the specific syndromes. Others will have the necessary sets of symptoms but an unusual presenting problem that raises doubt over the diagnosis. An example from my experience was an adolescent girl who was constantly occupied with sexual fantasies and talk but whose behavior otherwise corresponded to aggressive conduct disorder.

Another group of children who are best given this label apparently misbehave only in the home or only in school; they are "situational cases." Whatever the explanation, such children have a better outcome than those whose misbehavior is "pervasive" (Mitchell and Rosa, 1981). For this reason, and because either aggressive or antisocial conduct disorder is a serious, although not malignant, diagnosis, it is worth repeating that these diagnoses should not be made unless there is evidence that the misbehavior is seen in different settings.

Lastly, some patients present with what seem to be equal parts of depression and antisocial behavior, both of which date from a major stress. Most of these are adolescent girls and they have often attempted suicide. The stresses tend to be events such as parental divorce or moving from the home in which the child has grown up. These cases look different from the specific conduct disorders, but whether they have a different outcome remains a question.

## HYPERACTIVITY

In the minds of many clinicians and researchers in the United States and Canada, hyperactivity still denotes a common behavioral syndrome. In all likelihood, this idea is wrong, but even when it is proven wrong beyond doubt, the term hyperactivity may survive as a euphemism for conduct disorder because this diagnosis is widely held to be ominous, despite findings to the contrary.

The data now available support the existence of three groups of children who are unusually active and inattentive. First, there are children who are constantly and severely overactive and who only attend to a stimulus for seconds at a time. These children often have clear-cut brain dysfunction, and they are commonly retarded. The second type is the child who has aggressive conduct disorder as well as symptoms of hyperactivity and distractibility. Third, some children with moderate degrees of hyperactivity and distractibility are not clearly retarded or brain damaged and do not have conduct disorder. Children in this latter group typically have learning problems.

It is convenient to call children in the first group hyperkinetic. They are relatively uncommon; Rutter et al. (1970a) found a rate of 1 in 1000 among the general population of 10- and 11-year-olds and 4 per cent among children who had epilepsy or definite brain damage (Rutter et al., 1970b). Ounsted (1955) and Ingram (1956) were among the first to describe the clinical picture. Typical features were extreme overactivity and distractibility, unpredictable outbursts of aggression, tantrums, impulsivity, a tendency to mouth objects, emotional lability, lack of a sense of danger, and general disinhibition. Both authors also mention that the affected children tended not to show normal affection toward parents and siblings, suggesting that some of their subjects were autistic. In fact, Rutter, Greenfield, and Lockyer (1967) found that almost half of a series of 50 autistic children were hyperkinetic when they were first seen at an average age of 6 years. In the same paper, Rutter and his colleagues reported data on a 5- to 15-year followup of the autistic children and their controls who were matched on IQ. At followup, the once hyperkinetic children who were older than 13 tended to have become less active than normal, while the younger ones were still overactive. Only 14 per cent of the older children remained hyperkinetic.

Both Ounsted and Ingram reported that a significant proportion of children showed immediate improvement when they were given amphetamine. My experience with prescribing stimulants for such children has been less positive, and I believe that propranolol is a more promising drug for hyperkinetic children.

The intimate association of the two symptoms, aggressiveness and hyperactivity, has already been mentioned. Seventy-five per cent of boys with aggressive conduct disorder are hyperactive and 50 per cent of girls (Stewart et al., 1981). The differences between hyperactive and normally active boys with aggressive conduct disorder are interesting. Stewart and Behar (1983) found that the former were more likely to have speech and language problems and that they had lower verbal IQs. Similar differences have been found in an epidemiologic study by McGee et al. (1984). These authors found that aggressive and hyperactive boys scored lower on both the verbal and the performance scales of IQ tests than boys who were only aggressive. They also had significantly lower skills in reading and spelling. This association of hyperactivity with cognitive problems suggests that some boys with aggressive conduct disorder have subtle brain dysfunction.

Loney, Kramer, and Millich (1981) followed up more than 110 hyperactive boys who were seen in a child psychiatry clinic. Their social adjustment and school achievement at age 16 depended much more on their original level of aggressiveness than it did on whether or not they were hyperactive. In fact, the level of activity was a weak predictor of school achievement only, whereas aggressiveness accounted for most of the variance in social behavior and whether or not they were delinquent.

The remaining "pure hyperactive" children are an ill-defined group. They have generally been referred to psychiatric clinics for hyperactivity or poor performance in school and have been diagnosed by staff as having a learning disability. Characteristically, they have relatively low IQs and a high rate of specific problems with reading and arithmetic but a low rate of behavioral and emotional symptoms (Stewart et al., 1981). A further study by August and Stewart (1982) was aimed specifically at finding differences between such boys and those who were hyperactive but also had aggressive conduct disorder. Boys with brain damage, an IQ less than 55, or a psychosis were excluded from both groups. The findings were similar to those of the earlier study. The purely hyperactive had lower verbal IQs and a higher rate of learning problems. Moreover, their IQs were more widely dispersed, and a similar trend appeared in their parents' educational attainment and level of

occupation. Their fathers had less psychopathology than those of the boys with aggressive conduct disorder. August et al. (1983) carried out a 4-year followup of the two groups of boys. Those who were originally diagnosed as purely hyperactive continued to be inattentive and impulsive at followup but showed few aggressive or antisocial behaviors. The hyperactive boys who were originally diagnosed as having aggressive conduct disorder also continued to have problems with attention and impulsivity but in addition tended to be aggressive, noncompliant, egocentric, and antisocial. Some of them were beginning to abuse alcohol. Thus the differences between the two groups persisted over time.

There is a clinical impression, hard to validate, that purely hyperactive boys are motivated to carry out school tasks but lack the physical wherewithal to concentrate and apply themselves to getting the work done. On the other hand, hyperactive boys with aggressive conduct disorder have the means but lack the motivation for doing schoolwork, particularly written work. This impression tends to support the advisability of treating purely hyperactive children with stimulants, but not those with conduct disorder.

Putting aside this speculation, a conservative approach to treating hyperactivity and inattentiveness when they are significantly affecting the child's performance in school is to give behavioral approaches a thorough trial first and only when these fail, prescribe stimulants. Competent teachers can usually shape children to concentrate longer and persist at their work. This would be particularly true in classes for children with learning disabilities, mild retardation, or behavior problems. When attention and application are improved, hyperactivity tends to diminish for the simple reason that concentrating on an assignment is not compatible with being out of seat or bothering a neighbor.

When behavioral approaches do not work, one can rely on stimulant drugs to improve attention and performance, but this approach must be guided by some important findings. Unfortunately, there are abysmally few data on dose–response curves for these drugs, but the first rule is to start at a low level and stay in a narrow range. From the work of Sprague and Sleator (1977) and

Brown and Sleator (1979), it seems that the therapeutic range is between 0.1 and 0.3 mg of methylphenidate per kg of body weight per day. Beyond these levels, the drug may actually worsen behavior and school performance. Also, it is well recognized now (Rapoport, 1983) that even therapeutic levels may reduce responsiveness and participation in class and lower a child's mood. The drug's prime effect is to increase concentration on schoolwork; there is little effect in less structured situations (Ellis, Witt, Reynolds, Sprague, 1974). A corollary is that the drug should not be used to control behavior at home in the evenings and on weekends. Parents and teachers also have to accept that the drug will not change the rate at which a child learns (Rie et al., 1976a, 1976b), nor will it remedy any specific learning disabilities (Gittelman-Klein and Klein, 1976). And finally, the parents and child should be under no illusion that the drug will have a lasting effect. It is clear from the work of Weiss, Kruger, Danielson, and Elman (1975) that treatment with stimulant drugs has no effect on the long-range outcome for hyperactive children.

Despite these reservations, there are still children who seem to need short-term treatment with a stimulant and benefit from it in some general way. The question of whether behavioral treatments can accomplish as much or more as treatment with stimulant drugs is still not settled, but to some extent, it is a theoretical rather than a practical issue. The quality of schools and teachers set limits to what can be done with behavioral approaches. The ability and willingness of parents to learn the necessary techniques also set limits, and so do the intelligence, motivation, and physical makeup of the child.

## Some Illustrative Cases

### CASE HISTORY 1

A is a 12-year-old boy, the older of two boys living with their parents. His presenting problems are that he is disruptive in school, a discipline problem at home, and quite aggressive. In addition, he is said to be unduly active.

The parents report that the patient has been a discipline problem almost from the word go. He has also been accident prone. He was first examined for behavior problems when he went to kindergarten and at that time was put on a minor tranquilizer. At age 8 he was started on methylphenidate (Ri-

talin), and his parents believe that he is unmanageable without this drug.

He is difficult at home; when frustrated, he cries, sulks, and throws things; he does not accept limits; the parents continually yell at him and occasionally spank him; he fights a lot with his younger brother; he has a hard time sitting still; he needs to be the center of attention; he lies to get out of trouble, and he has been involved in some stealing. Similar behaviors occur at school, and he is reported to get into many fights there.

Past psychological tests have shown him to have a full-scale IQ of 90. He is the natural child of his mother but has never known his father. The mother reports being nervous but has never had any treatment. The biologic father is said to have had a bad temper, but nothing else is known about him.

On the ward, A has responded well to firm limits and the threat of time out. On one or two occasions he has lied, but there has been no stealing. He has once been destructive. He is constantly on the move, and he is not able to entertain himself. He seems impatient and has low tolerance for frustration. He reports being unpopular at home and nervous. He teases the other children here and plays roughly.

Diagnosis: aggressive conduct disorder.

### CASE HISTORY 2

B is an 11-year-old boy whose presenting problem is that he lit paper darts and threw them on the porch of a neighboring house.

For the past 5 years the parents have found B difficult to discipline, they have observed him stealing frequently, both from stores and within the household, he has lied a lot and been quite destructive. On the other hand, there have been no problems with aggressiveness, nor has he been impulsive, irritable, given to tantrums, or unable to handle frustration. He has set a number of fires, including one that severely damaged two rooms of the parents' rented house.

B was abandoned by his natural parents and adopted by his mother when he was 11 months old. His history since then has been one of good health and normal development. The mother divorced her first husband when the patient was 3 years old, then lived in a commune, and a few years ago married her present husband. Neither parent has a history of psychiatric treatment, but the mother is quite depressed at present. The father has a history of alcohol and drug abuse and may have had an antisocial tendency as well.

B has no major behavior problems on the ward. He does tease the other children and may have instigated trouble among them. On the other hand, he is helpful to the other children. In the classroom, his reading and math achievement levels are far beyond his present grade placement.

Diagnosis: antisocial conduct disorder.

## CASE HISTORY 3

C is a 15-year-old boy who has been living with his adoptive father and mother for the past few years. The presenting problem is that C has been involved in more and more antisocial behavior, fights a lot with other children, and has been suspended from school.

C was previously admitted to this unit at age 7, when he and his younger brother were reported to be unmanageable by the grandmother, who was then taking care of them. The older sister and two younger brothers had grown up in a miserably deprived home with the natural parents, had been cared for later by two abusive uncles, and finally ended up with the grandmother, who treated them severely. C and his immediately younger brother were separately admitted to this unit because of their behavior problems. From here, C went to a group home and was then adopted.

C's recent history has been marked by serious noncompliance, stealing from family members and neighbors, pathologic lying, taking revenge on neighbors by destroying their things, fighting with peers, and poor school performance. In the past year, he has done essentially no work in school and he has been quite disruptive in the classroom. He has never been truant, but he has run away from home several times, twice overnight. He has a poor relationship with his adoptive mother. Finally, he wets the bed often. The natural father is probably an antisocial personality. As far as we know, the sister and the two brothers are doing well. All three of them have been in foster care.

The physical examination revealed that C carries a tattoo on his right arm. At interview he was cheerful, loud, boastful, and distractible. He admitted his shoplifting exploits and had a cynical view of his behavior and its effect on others. Past testing showed him to be in the borderline range of IQ (full scale 77) and to have low school achievement levels.

On the ward, he is aggressive, boastful, noncompliant, loud and silly, and manipulative. He incites rebellion among the little children and domineers them. He boasts of his prowess in martial arts and in lock picking. Generally, his behavior is intolerable.

Diagnosis: aggressive and antisocial conduct disorder

## REFERENCES

Achenbach TM: The child behavior profile. I. Boys aged 6–11. J Consul Clin Psychol 46:478, 1978.

Achenbach TM, Edelbrock CS: The child behavior profile. II. Boys aged 12–16 and girls aged 6–11 and 12–16. J Consul Clin Psychol 47:223, 1979.

Arnold LE, Smeltzer DJ: Behavior checklist factor analysis for children and adolescents. Arch Gen Psychiatry 30:799, 1974.

August GJ, Stewart MA: Is there a syndrome of pure hyperactivity? Br J Psychiatry 140:305, 1982.

August GJ, Stewart MA, Holmes CS: A four-year follow-up of hyperactive boys with and without conduct disorder. Br J Psychiatry 143:192, 1983.

Behar D, Stewart MA: Aggressive conduct disorder of children: The clinical history and direct observations. Acta Psychiatr Scand 65:210, 1982.

Behar D, Stewart MA: Aggressive conduct disorder: The influence of social class, sex and age on the clinical picture. J Child Psychol Psychiatry 24:119, 1984.

Bijur P, Stewart-Brown S, Golding J, Butler NR, Rush D: Behavioral correlates of severe accidental injuries in children birth to five. Pediatr Res 17:93A, 1983.

Breuning SE, Davidson NA: Effects of psychotropic drugs on intelligence test performance of institutionalized mentally retarded adults. Am J Ment Defic 85:575, 1981.

Brown GL, Goodwin FK, Ballenger JC, Goyer PF, Major LF: Aggression in humans correlates with cerebrospinal fluid amine metabolite. Psychiatr Res 1:139, 1979.

Brown RT, Sleator EK: Methylphenidate in hyperkinetic children: Differences in dose effects on impulsive behavior. Pediatrics 64:408, 1979.

Cadoret RJ, Cain CA, Grove WM: Development of alcoholism in adoptees raised apart from alcoholic biologic relatives. Arch Gen Psychiatry 37:561, 1980.

Cadoret RJ, Cain CA, Crowe RR: Evidence for gene-environmental interaction in the development of adolescent antisocial behavior. Behav Genet 13:301, 1983.

Camp BW: Verbal mediation in young aggressive boys. J Abnorm Psychol 86:145, 1977.

Campbell M, Cohen I, Small AM: Drugs in aggressive behavior. J Am Acad Child Psychiatry 21:107, 1982.

Chandler MJ: Egocentrism and antisocial behavior: The assessment and training of social perspective-taking skills. Develop Psychol 9:326, 1973.

Chandler, MJ, Greenspan S, Barenboim C: Assessment and training of role-taking and referential communication skills in institutionalized emotionally disturbed children. Develop Psychol 10:546, 1974.

Christiansen KO: A preliminary study of criminality among twins, in Mednick S, Christiansen KO (eds): Biosocial Bases of Criminal Behavior. New York, Gardner Press, 1977.

Coie JD, Kupersmidt JB: A behavioral analysis of emerging social status in boys' groups. Child Develop 54:1400, 1983.

Craig MM, Glick SJ: Ten years' experience with the Glueck Social Prediction Table. Crime Delinq 9:149, 1963.

Craig MM, Glick SJ: School behavior related to later delinquency and non-delinquency. Criminology 5:17, 1968.

Crowther JH, Bond LA, Rolf JE: The incidence, prevalence, and severity of behavior disorders among preschool-aged children in day care. J Abnor Child Psychol 9:23, 1981.

Dodge KA: Behavioral antecedents of peer social status. Child Develop 54:1386, 1983.

Ellis MJ, Witt PA, Reynolds R, Sprague RL: Methylphenidate and the activity of hyperactives in the informal setting. Child Develop 45:217, 1974.

Farrington DP: The family backgrounds of aggressive youths, in Hersov LA, Shaffer D (eds): Aggression and Antisocial Behavior in Childhood and Adolescence. Oxford, Pergamon, 1978.

Genshaft JL: Personality characteristics of delinquent subtypes. J Abnorm Child Psychol 8:279, 1980.

Gersten JC, Langner TS, Eisenberg JG, Simcha-Fagan O, McCarthy ED: Stability and change in types of behavioral disturbance of children and adolescents. J Abnorm Child Psychol 4:111, 1976.

Gittelman-Klein R, Klein DF: Methylphenidate effects in learning disabilities. Arch Gen Psychiatry 33:655, 1976.

Gorky M: (Translater: Ronald Wilks) My Childhood. Baltimore, Penguin Books, 1966.

Graham P, Rutter M: Psychiatric disorder in the young adolescent: A follow-up study. Proc R Soc Med 66:58, 1973.

Gualtieri CT, Quade D, Hicks RE, Mayo JP, Schroeder SR: Tardive dyskinesia and other clinical consequences of neuroleptic treatment in children and adolescents. Am J Psychiatry 141:20, 1984.

Harris R: Relationship between EEG abnormality and aggressive and antisocial behaviour—A critical appraisal, in Hersov LA, Berger M, Shaffer D (eds): Aggression and Antisocial Behavior in Childhood and Adolescence. Oxford, Pergamon, 1978.

Healy W, Bronner AF: New Light on Delinquency and Its Treatment. New Haven, CT, Yale University Press, 1936.

Hewitt L, Jenkins RL: Fundamental Patterns of Maladjustment. Springfield, IL, State of Illinois, 1946.

Howard J: The expression and possible origins of depression in male adolescent delinquents. Aust NZ J Psychiatry 15:11, 1981.

Huesmann LR, Eron LD, Lefkowitz MM, Walder LO: The stability of aggression over time and generations. Paper presented at the Society for Research on Child Development Meeting, Detroit, April 1983.

Huesmann R, Yarmel PW: Intellectual competence and aggression. Paper presented at the meeting of the American Psychological Association, Anaheim, Calif, August 1983.

Ingram TTS: A characteristic form of overactive behaviour in brain damaged children. J Ment Sci 102:550, 1956.

Jary ML, Stewart MA: Psychiatric disorder in the parents of adopted children with aggressive conduct disorder. Neuropsychobiology 13:7, 1985.

Jones MC: Personality correlates and antecedents of drinking patterns in adult males. J Consul Clin Psychol 32:2, 1968.

Kashani JH, Manning GW, McKnew DH, Cytryn L, Simonds JF, Wooderson PC: Depression among incarcerated delinquents. Psychiatr Res 3:185, 1980a.

Kashani JH, Husain A, Robins AJ, Reid JC, Wooderson PC: Patterns of delinquency in girls and boys. J Am Acad Child Psychiatry 19:300, 1980b.

Kellam SG, Ensminger ME, Simon MB: Mental health in first grade and teenage drug, alcohol and cigarette use. Drug Alcohol Depend 5:273, 1980.

Kelso J, Stewart MA: Factors which predict the persistence of aggressive conduct disorder. J Child Psychol Psychiatry, in press.

Kreuz LE, Rose RM: Assessment of aggressive behavior and plasma testosterone in a young criminal population. Psychosom Med 34:321, 1972.

Kuperman S: Use of propranolol in decreasing aggressive outbursts in children. Personal communication.

Lewis DO, Shanok SS: Medical histories of delinquent and non-delinquent children: An epidemiological study. Am J Psychiatry 134:1020, 1977.

Linnoila M, Virkkunen M, Scheinin M, Nuutila A, Rimon R, Goodwin FK: Low cerebrospinal fluid 5-hydroxyindoleacetic acid concentration differentiates impulsive from nonimpulsive violent behavior. Life Sci 33:2609, 1983.

Loeber R: The stability of antisocial and delinquent child behavior: A review. Child Develop 53:1431, 1982.

Loney J, Kramer J, Milich R: The hyperkinetic child grows up, in Gadow K, Loney J (eds): Psychosocial Aspects of Drug Treatment for Hyperactivity. Boulder, Colo, Westview Press, 1981.

Lukianowicz N: Juvenile offenders. Acta Psychiatr Scand 48:423, 1972.

McCord W, McCord J, Howard A: Familial correlates of aggression in nondelinquent male children. J Abnorm Soc Psychol 62:79, 1961.

McCord J, McCord W, Howard A: Family interaction as antecedent to the direction of male aggressiveness. J Abnorm Soc Psychol 66:239, 1963.

McGee R, Williams S, Silva PA: Behavioral and developmental characteristics of aggressive hyperactive and aggressive-hyperactive boys. J Am Acad Child Psychiatry 23:270, 1984.

Major LF, Lerner P, Goodwin FK, Ballenger JC, Brown GL, Lovenberg W: Dopamine β-Hydroxylase in CSF. Arch Gen Psychiatry 37:308, 1980.

Mattsson A, Schalling D, Olweus D, Low H, Svensson J: Plasma testosterone, aggressive behavior, and personality dimensions in young male delinquents. J Am Acad Child Psychiatry 19:476, 1980.

Mednick SA, Gabrielli WF Jr, Hutchings B: Genetic influences in criminal convictions: Evidence from an adoption cohort. Science 224:891, 1984.

Mellinger GD, Manheimer DI: An exposure-coping model of accident liability among children. J Health Soc Behav 8:96, 1967.

Milich R, Landau S: A comparison of the social status and social behavior of aggressive and aggressive/withdrawn boys. J Abnorm Child Psychol 12:277, 1984.

Mitchell S, Rosa P: Boyhood behaviour problems as precursors of criminality: A fifteen-year follow-up study. J Child Psychol Psychiat 22:10, 1981.

Morris HH Jr, Escoll PJ, Wexler R: Aggressive behavior disorders of childhood: A follow-up study. Am J Psychiatry 112:991, 1956.

Nylander I: A 20-year prospective follow-up study of 2164 cases at the child guidance clinics in Stockholm. Acta Paediatr Scand [Suppl] 276:1, 1979.

Offord DR, Allen N, Abrams N: Parental psychiatric illness, broken homes, and delinquency. J Am Acad Child Psychiatry 17:224, 1978.

Offord DR, Abrams N, Allen N, Poushinsky M: Broken homes, parental psychiatric illness, and female delinquency. Am J Orthopsychiatry 49:252, 1979.

Olweus D: Stability of aggressive reaction patterns in males: A review. Psychol Bull 86:852, 1979.

Olweus D, Mattsson A, Schalling D, Low H: Testosterone, aggression, physical, and personality dimensions in normal adolescent males. Psychosom Med 42:253, 1980.

Osborn SG: Moving home, leaving London and delinquent trends. Br J Criminol 20:54, 1980.

Osborn SG, West DJ: Conviction records of fathers and sons compared. Br J Criminol 19:120, 1979.

Osborn SG, West DJ: Do young delinquents really reform? J Adolesc 3:99, 1980.

Ounsted C: The hyperkinetic syndrome in epileptic children. Lancet 2:302, 1955.

Patterson GR, Cobb JA: Stimulus control for classes of noxious behavior, in Knutson JF (ed): The Control of Aggression: Implications from Basic Research. Chicago, Aldine, 1973.

Patterson GR: Retraining of aggressive boys by their parents. Can Psychiatr Assoc J 19:142, 1974a.

Patterson GR: Interventions for boys with conduct problems: Multiple settings, treatments, and criteria. J Consul Clin Psychol 42:471, 1974b.

Patterson GR: Mothers: The Unacknowledged Victims. Chicago, University of Chicago Press, 1980.

Puig-Antich J: Major depression and conduct disorder in pre-puberty. J Am Acad Child Psychiatry 21:118, 1982.

Pulkkinen L: Finland: The search for alternatives to aggression, in Goldstein AP, Segall MH (eds): Aggression in Global Perspective. New York, Pergamon, 1983a.

Pulkkinen L: Youthful smoking and drinking in a longitudinal perspective. J Youth Adolesc 12:253, 1983b.

Quay HC: Dimensions of personality in delinquent boys as inferred from the factor analysis of case history data. Child Develop 35:479, 1964.

Rapoport JL: The use of drugs: Trends in research, in Rutter M (ed): Developmental Neuropsychiatry, New York, Guildford, 1983.

Richman N, Stevenson J, Graham PJ: Pre-school to School: A Behavioral Study. London, Academic Press, 1982.

Rie HE, Rie ED, Stewart S, Ambuel JP: Effects of Ritalin on underachieving children: A replication. Am J Orthopsychiatry 46:313, 1976a.

Rie HE, Rie ED, Stewart S: Effects of methylphenidate on underachieving children. J Consult Clin Psychiatry 44:250, 1976b.

Rivinus TM, Jamison DL, Graham PJ: Childhood organic neurological disease presenting as psychiatric disorder. Arch Dis Childhood 50:115, 1975.

Robins LN: Deviant Children Grown Up. Baltimore, Williams & Wilkins, 1966.

Robins LN: Sturdy childhood predictors of adult antisocial behaviour: Replications from longitudinal studies. Psychol Med 8:611, 1978.

Robins LN, Ratcliff KS: Risk factors in the continuation of childhood antisocial behavior into adulthood. Int J Ment Health 7:96, 1979.

Rogeness GA, Hernandez JM, Macedo CA, Mitchell EL: Biochemical differences in children with conduct disorder socialized and undersocialized. Am J Psychiatry 139:307, 1982.

Rogeness GA, Hernandez JM, Macedo CA, Mitchell EL, Amrung SA, Harris WR: Clinical characteristics of emotionally disturbed boys with very low activities of dopamine-β-hydroxylase. J Am Acad Child Psychiatry 23:203, 1984.

Rutter M: Parent-child separation: Psychological effects on the children. J Child Psychol Psychiatry 12:233, 1971.

Rutter M, Cox A, Tupling C, Berger M, Yule W: Attainment and adjustment in two geographical areas. I. The prevalence of psychiatric disorder. Br J Psychiatry 126: 493, 1975.

Rutter M, Graham P, Yule W: A Neuropsychiatric Study in Childhood. London, Heinemann, 1970.

Rutter M, Greenfeld D, Lockyer L: A five to fifteen year follow-up study of infantile psychosis. II. Social and behavioural outcome. Br J Psychiatry 113:1183, 1967.

Rutter M, Shaffer D, Sturge C: A Guide to a Multi-Axial Classification Scheme for Psychiatric Disorders in Childhood and Adolescence. London, Institute of Psychiatry, 1976.

Rutter M, Tizard J, Whitmore K: Education, Health and Behavior. London, Longmans, 1970.

Schachar R, Rutter M, Smith A: The characteristics of situationally and pervasively hyperactive children: Implications for syndrome definition. J Child Psychol Psychiatry 22:375, 1981.

Shaffer D: Suicide in childhood and early adolescence. J Child Psychol Psychiatry 15:275, 1974.

Siassi I: Lithium treatment of impulsive behavior in children. J Clin Psychiatry 43:482, 1982.

Smith R: "Schools for criminals." Br Med J 288:706, 1984.

Solomon S, Hotchkiss E, Saravay SM, Bayer C, Ramsey P, Blum RS: Impairment of memory function by antihypertensive medication. Arch Gen Psychiatry 40:1109, 1983.

Sprague RL, Sleator EK: Methylphenidate in hyperkinetic children: Differences in dose effects on learning and social behavior. Science 198:1274, 1977.

Stewart MA, Ashby HB: Treatment of hyperactive, aggressive, and antisocial children, in Kratochwill TR (ed): Advances in School Psychology. Hillsdale, NJ, Lawrence Erlbaum, 1981.

Stewart MA, Behar D: Subtypes of aggressive conduct disorder. Acta Psychiatr Scand 68:178, 1983.

Stewart MA, Copeland L, deBlois CS: Age of onset of aggressive conduct disorder. Submitted for publication.

Stewart MA, Cummings C, Singer S, deBlois CS: The overlap between hyperactive and unsocialized aggressive children. J Child Psychol Psychiatry 22:35, 1981.

Stewart MA, deBlois CS: Wife abuse among families attending a child psychiatry clinic. J Am Acad Child Psychiatry 20:845, 1981.

Stewart MA, deBlois CS: Father-son resemblances in aggressive and antisocial behaviour. Br J Psychiatry 142:78, 1983a.

Stewart MA, deBlois CS: Father-son resemblances in aggressive and antisocial behavior. Br J Psychiatry 143:310, 1983b.

Stewart MA, deBlois CS: Diagnostic criteria for aggressive conduct disorder. Psychopathology 18:11, 1985.

Stewart MA, deBlois CS, Cummings C: Psychiatric disorder in the parents of hyperactive boys and those with conduct disorder. J Child Psychol Pyschiatry 21:283, 1980a.

Stewart MA, deBlois CS, Meardon J, Cummings C: Aggressive conduct disorder of children—the clinical picture. J Nerv Ment Dis 168:604, 1980b.

Still GF: Some abnormal physical conditions in children. Lancet 1:1008, 1902.

Twito TJ, Stewart MA: A half-sibling study of aggressive conduct disorder. Neuropsychobiology 8:144, 1982.

Valzelli L, Garattini S: Biochemical and behavioural changes induced by isolation in rats. Neuropharmacology 11:17, 1972.

Virkkunen M: Insulin secretion during the glucose tolerance test in antisocial personality. Br J Psychiatry 142:598, 1983a.

Virkkunen M: Serum cholesterol levels in homicidal offenders. Neuropsychobiology 10:65, 1983b.

Virkkunen M, Penttinen H: Serum cholesterol in aggressive conduct disorder: A preliminary study. Biol Psychiatr 19:435, 1984.

Warren W: A study of adolescent psychiatric in-patients and the outcome six or more years later. II. The follow-up study. J Child Psychol Psychiatry 6:141, 1965.

Weiss G, Kruger E, Danielson U, Elman M: Effect of long-term treatment of hyperactive children with methylphenidate. Can Med Assoc J 112:159, 1975.

Werry JS, Aman MG: Methylphenidate and haloperidol in children. Arch Gen Psychiatry 32:790, 1975.

West DJ: Delinquency: Its Roots, Careers and Prospects. Cambridge, Mass, Harvard University Press, 1982.

West DJ, Farrington DP: Who Become Delinquent? London, Heinemann, 1973.

West DJ, Farrington DP: The Delinquent Way of Life. London, Heinemann, 1977.

Williams DT, Mehl R, Yudofsky S, Adams D, Roseman B: The effect of propranolol on uncontrolled rage outbursts in children and adolescents with organic brain dysfunction. J Am Acad Child Psychiatry 21:129, 1982.

Yudofsky S, Williams D, Gorman J: Propranolol in the treatment of range and violent behavior in patients with chronic brain syndromes. Am J Psychiatry 138:218, 1981.

# chapter 19

# MAJOR AFFECTIVE DISORDERS IN CHILDREN AND ADOLESCENTS

*by* Barry D. Garfinkel, M.D.

## INTRODUCTION

The investigation and understanding of child and adolescent affective disorders have historically been hampered by a series of theoretical misconceptions. Psychoanalytic theory originally stressed that children could not experience depression because they had not completely progressed through and resolved the oedipal conflict (Mendelson, 1972). It was postulated that only after childhood and the complete resolution of the oedipal conflict, a superego or conscience results, allowing for the capacity to experience guilt and remorse (Rie, 1966). Because guilt, self-blame, and remorse were among the central feelings said to characterize adult depression, it was assumed that children could not have depression without a fully formed superego (Rochlin, 1959; Sandler and Joffe, 1965). Many empirical reports, as well as substantial clinical experience derived from interviews with depressed children, indicated that self-blame, remorse, guilt, and low self-esteem all indeed occur at younger ages. Despite

the incongruity between psychoanalytic theory and actual clinical observation, theory continued to dominate psychodynamic psychiatric perspectives on childhood affective disorders.

The second major hurdle in understanding child and adolescent affective disorders was the concept that developmental stages altered the presentation of clinical symptoms so that totally different symptoms were expressed at different ages (Bemporad and Wilson, 1978). It was postulated that particular symptoms were only observed in children with major affective disorder. Such concepts as "depressive equivalents" (Malmquist, 1971) and "masked depression" (Glaser, 1967; Cytryn and McKnew, 1972) became terms that described vastly divergent behaviors that were assumed to be expressions of an underlying depression. These terms made depression incomprehensible from direct patient interview and observation. Depression became a diagnosis that was discernible only by clinicians who were astute enough to identify underlying affective states. From encopresis and enuresis to promiscuity and drug abuse, vastly discrepant behaviors were viewed as manifestations of affective disorders in children and adolescents (Frommer, 1968).

With regard to childhood, a specific developmental stage that was thought to influence the expression of depression was infancy. Spitz (1946) coined the term anaclitic depression, and Bowlby (1973, 1980) described concepts concerning attachment and loss. Although these terms describe marked behavioral and, at times, physiologic responses to grieving, mourning, or loss, it is impossible to discern a unique relationship to affective disorders. These concepts and the conditions that they describe are not representative of affective disorders, and thus, on the basis of their presumed presence, it cannot be assumed that an underlying affective disorder exists other than grief and mourning (Carlson and Cantwell, 1980b).

Adolescence has been characterized by specific stages of development associated with concerns about identity, relationships, and communication (Erikson, 1950), all of which have been theorized to influence the expression of depression at this age. Early adolescents have been described as normally reflecting low self-esteem, guilt, remorse, and a poor self-concept (Anthony and Scott, 1960). Identity concerns, fearfulness, multiple somatic complaints, dysphoria, and irritability have been identified (Blos, 1962). Worries of a pervasive nature have been described, reflecting thoughts of pessimism and ineffectuality. It has been concluded, however, that these observations have not been systematically derived and do not represent normal characteristics of this stage of development, but in fact may represent clinically derived symptoms. Similarly, these symptoms alone do *not* satisfy the criteria for the presence of an affective disorder (McConville, Boag, Purohit, 1973).

Research has suggested that the identification of symptoms during a clinical interview with a child may depend on specialized interview techniques, and that the interview process may be more difficult to conduct. At each stage of development, consideration should be given to the fact that without exception the adult criteria for major affective disorder can be identified in children and adolescents. Numerous studies (Poznanski and Zrull, 1970; Puig-Antich et al., 1978; Chambers and Puig-Antich,

1982; Carlson and Cantwell, 1981) have identified the presence of symptoms, in children and in adolescents, that are equivalent to those found in adults, and it has been shown that the adult criteria can be applied satisfactorily for child and adolescent affective disorders. Concepts concerning separation (Harlow and Harlow, 1965; Bowlby, 1973; Spitz, 1946) and developmental models do not describe affective disorders in children, but demonstrate the developing individual's response to attachment, grief, and mourning in response to breaks in the attachment to a significant figure in the child's life (Bowlby, 1980). The proper conclusion derived from these studies is that stages of development may be associated with some of the features resembling the criteria of affective disorders. There is, however, no stage of development that has either as its primary characteristics or in the routine reaction to stresses associated with that stage the manifestation of sufficient criteria to fulfill the diagnosis of an affective disorder.

## DEFINITION

In the past 15 years, it has been demonstrated that symptoms constituting the adult criteria for affective disorders have been observed in children and adolescents (Annell, 1971). Because children and adolescents do not easily or accurately verbalize their affective states, these symptoms are harder to recognize. A number of classification systems showing little overlap with the diagnostic criteria for affective disorder in children and adolescents have been unsuccessfully proposed. In general, the earlier diagnostic systems incorporated two conceptual errors: first, the criteria were far too broad, and second, the diagnosis was determined by developmental stage rather than by clinical presentation.

The Weinberg et al. (1973) criteria are an example of a major effort at a systematic classification system that was far too inclusive. The original classification system was based on the Feighner et al. (1972) criteria adapted for children. A study by Carlson and Cantwell (1981) comparing the Weinberg criteria with that of the *Diagnostic and Statistical Manual of Mental Disorders*, third edition (DSM-III), showed that most children who met DSM-III criteria for depression also met Weinberg criteria. Many more children were diagnosed by Weinberg criteria as being depressed; however, approximately 40 per cent of them did not meet the DSM-III criteria for depression. Most of these children had behavioral, conduct, and attention-deficit disorders.

Another example of an exceptionally broad concept of depression was held by Frommer (1968). The approach postulated three types of depressed children: enuretic, pure, and phobic. Enuretic depressed children were characterized by immaturity, developmental delays, and learning disabilities, as well as conduct disorder forms of behavioral problems. The pure depressives were characterized by profound periods of sadness, irritability, crying, anger, hostility, suicidal ideation, and sleep disturbances. Antisocial and anxiety symptoms were not commonly observed in such children. The phobic depressives were seen as being severely depressed, with multiple somatic symptoms, lack of energy, and feelings of anxiety. The latter group was predominantly female, with a young age of onset and without a family history of significant psychiatric disorders. The other two groups had an approximately equal representation of boys and girls and a significant family history for psychiatric disorders. The three subtypes of depression were thought to respond to different pharmacologic and behavioral forms of treatment.

Two other descriptive classifications of depression are worth noting—those by Malmquist (1971) and McConville et al. (1973). Malmquist (1971) suggested five types of depression: the first group are those depressions resulting from an organic etiology, the second group resulting from severe deprivation, and the three remaining types related to three stages of development: toddler, primary school age, and adolescence. These forms of depression confounded three independent features: etiology, developmental stage, and analytic theory. For example, a child of a certain age, because of the intrafamilial relationships and the real and symbolic past experiences, appears depressed in a unique way. This classification reinforced the notion that development altered the causation as well as the presentation of depressive symptomatology. It was thought impossible to separate the stage of development from the acute disorder, since maturation not only altered symptom presentation, but also influenced the psychosocial etiology of an affective disorder.

McConville et al. (1973) established a classification system based on cognitive development, repeated loss, and interpersonal relationships. They linked development to three types of depression. Early childhood depression (ages 6 to 8 years) was said to be characterized by dysphoria, guilt, and low self-esteem. The second type of depression was thought to occur in children between ages 8 and 11 and was primarily characterized by significant low self-esteem and cognitive changes, such as guilt, self-reproach, pessimism, preoccupation with failure, and helplessness. In this stage, feelings of worthlessness were thought to be derived from repeated loss. The third type of childhood depression was theorized to occur in children older than 11 and was typified by significant feelings of guilt and self-blame.

Cytryn and co-workers (1972, 1980) postulated a classification system based on developmental stage, the time course of the disorder, and the patient's family history. The three types that were observed were acute, chronic, and "masked" (Glaser 1967). Acute depression was said to be associated with a good premorbid adjustment, minimal family history of psychiatric disorders, and a brief duration of the affective disorder. The chronic type was said to be associated with significant preexisting psychopathology and a family history for psychiatric disorders. The "masked" depression group, on reexamination, was predominantly a group of conduct-disordered children (Cytryn et al., 1980).

The classification that most professionals have adopted for children is the same as that for adults. Poznanski, Krahenbuhl, and Zrull (1976), Puig-Antich et al. (1978), and Carlson and Cantwell (1980a) have all demonstrated that affective disorders in prepubertal children are best conceptualized and defined according to a schema that includes all of the diagnostic criteria observed in adults. To date, not every adult form of affective disorder has been systematically observed in children. The greatest number of children have been placed in one of four categories: major depression, bipolar disorder, dysthymia, or adjustment disorder

TABLE 19–1    Affective Disorders in Children and Adolescents

A. Primary affective disorders in children and adolescents
   1. Chronic unremitting
      a. Dysthymia (habitual pattern resembling a chronic characterological depression)
   2. Multiple recurrent episodes
      a. Unipolar depression
      b. Bipolar disorder (manic and depressive episodes)
      c. Manic episodes
   3. Acute single episode
      a. Major depressive disorder
      b. Adjustment disorder with depressed mood (an environmental precipitant present or duration too short to be a major depressive disorder, i.e., reactive type of depression)
B. Secondary affective disorders
   1. Physical etiology: medication usage (e.g., steroids, reserpine) and endocrine disorder (e.g., hypothyroidism)
   2. Other psychiatric disorder present: e.g., attention-deficit disorder, conduct disorder, eating disorder (anorexia nervosa)

with depressed mood. It is not known whether schizoaffective disorder or cyclothymic disorder will be systematically documented in children. These disorders may be viewed as occurring as one acute episode, as recurrent episodic disorders, or as chronic unremitting states (see Table 19–1). It is important to determine the time course, as well as the primary or secondary nature, of the affective disorder. Any physical or psychiatric condition that predates the affective disorder determines that it would be a secondary affective disorder.

## ETIOLOGY AND PATHOGENESIS

There are four major explanations that contribute to our understanding of the etiology of affective disorders in children and adolescents. These models do not represent mutually exclusive formulations, but in effect describe interactive factors that predispose an individual to a specific affective disorder. The disorder itself represents a final common pathway through which all or many of these factors exert their influence (Akiskal and McKinney, 1975). Because major affective disorders have been studied much more extensively in children, this condition will be used as a model for understanding these etiologic factors. The four main models are (1) reinforcement, (2) cognition, (3) life stresses, and (4) genetic/biochemical factors (Lewinsohn and Hoberman, 1982).

The first model, behavioral reinforcement (Lewinsohn, 1979), assumes that depression results from and is augmented by limited social reinforcement. This may include a poor living situation with an actual insufficiency of positive reinforcers, fewer social skills that elicit less positive reinforcement from the child's environment, or a punishing and aversive environment that creates a deficiency in reinforcements in life situations. These three circumstances would decrease the frequency and impact of the positive reinforcers with which the child has contact. This model does not explain why the child originally is lacking in the social skills that create opportunities for positive reinforcement. Also, all children exposed to these circumstances do not develop an affective disorder. Similarly, this is a purely psychosocial model, which would imply that with the correction of the reinforcement situation, depression would invariably go away. Increasing positive reinforcement is one component of an intervention program of therapy, but in itself, it is not always sufficient in the treatment of major affective disorder. Pleasant interactions, positive responses from others, and the avoidance of punishing and unpleasant experiences generally enhance the medical treatment of depression. Positive experiences for children include enjoyable games, competition in sports, and the pursuit of skill development.

The second model assumes that depression is a result of negative cognition that the child has concerning himself or herself, the world, or his or her personal future (Beck, 1970). Cognitive patterns occur that lead to a selective and negative view of current and past events. At times, it appears that the child "rewrites history" to support a negative self-perception. Self-control is deficient in depressed individuals, with inadequate self-monitoring, self-evaluation, and self-reinforcement. These tasks are always used to further depreciate the individual and support a pessimistic view of oneself and the world. "Learned helplessness," a concept developed in laboratory animals, is an aspect of this overall model in which features of depression occur when an organism experiences that it has no control over reinforcers from its environment (Seligman and Maier, 1967). A balance between the locus of control of internal and external events is also a function of this model, with individuals feeling controlled both by others and external events creating a greater sense of inadequacy and failure. For depressed individuals, internal control and responsibility are assumed when something negative occurs, whereas external factors are thought to create positive events. Longitudinal studies have not indicated that these cognitive styles predate the onset of depression, but rather that they are probably a consequence of depression and may perpetuate depression once it occurs. After the remission of depression, these cognitive symptoms disappear, and the individual returns to a more optimistic and positive cognitive style (Lewinsohn and Hoberman, 1982).

The life stress, or third model, has two major theoretical orientations. The first is psychoanalytic, with the original Freudian model (1917) emphasizing the symbolic or metaphorical loss of a significant, highly valued person or thing that results in depression. The lost object was ambivalently regarded, and the negative feelings that were formerly directed to the lost object are subsequently internalized and self-directed. According to this theory, all losses, irrespective of how trivial they may appear to objective scrutiny, can be a cause of a major depression because of the personalized significance with which the lost object was regarded.

The other life stress model, proposed by Graham (1974) and Lefkowitz and Burton (1978), indicates that childhood depression is a consequence of actual environmental stress and loss, primarily based within the family. This model does not take into account individual variability and the fact that depression is not asssociated with signifi-

cant stress or loss in all families. Clearer distinction between major affective disorder and mourning or grief must be established. These three theoretical models do not adequately explain individual vulnerability, onset, morbidity, or the recurrent and episodic course of a specific affective disorder.

The fourth model proposes a genetic predisposition that alters the neurochemical regulation of mood. For affective disorders, the concordance rates for monozygous twins is approximately 76 per cent and for dizygotic twins, 19 per cent. Monozygous twins reared apart had a concordance rate of 67 per cent (Tsuang, 1978). Welner et al. (1977), Tsuang (1978), Kuyler et al. (1980), and Cantwell and Baker (1983) established a strong genetic predisposition for psychiatric disorders in children of parents with affective disorder. Welner et al.'s study showed that children of depressed mothers had more symptoms of an affective disorder than did children of normal mothers. The family history of affective disorder in parents is associated with a much greater likelihood of affective disorder in the children (Puig-Antich et al., 1978; McKnew and Cytryn, 1979). Although no definitive neurochemical pathway has been established, there is some evidence to suggest that monoamine metabolism in children may be altered (Kashani et al., 1981).

In general, a final common pathway exists for childhood depression, with multiple determinants that include social, genetic, environmental, life events, and neurochemical factors all interacting to create the clinical condition of major affective disorder (Akiskal and McKinney, 1975). Subsequent study of children with affective disorder must determine what psychological, biologic, and social abnormalities are a consequence of the depression and which factors predate the clinical disorder, as well as how these factors interact with one another. Similarly, it will be important to establish the permanence of these features after the remission of the acute illness. Depression alters family life, school performance, skill attainment, and the internal subjective view the child has about himself. Because affective disorders have such a profound impact on the individual, it is not surprising that multiple psychosocial factors that reflect these effects have been identified.

## EPIDEMIOLOGY

The studies of specific clinical samples of children for affective disorders have been influenced by the unique qualities defining the subjects and the criteria by which affective disorder was diagnosed. In general, the criteria for affective disorder have been varied and there are few studies using DSM-III criteria. The studies can be divided into two broad categories: those investigating the prevalence of this disorder in a normal population and those identifying its specific representation in a clinical sample of children. Rutter, Tizard, and Whitmore (1970), in the Isle of Wight Study, found 1.4 cases per 1000 children. Nissen (1971), in Germany, observed severe depression in 1.8 per cent of the 6000 children he studied. Kashani and Simonds (1979), in the United States, found that 1.9 per cent of 103 children had major affective disorder. Kashani et al. (1983), in New Zealand, demonstrated a rate of 1.8 per cent for major affective disorder in 641 9-year-old children. Another 2.5 per cent met criteria for minor affective disorder.

In various clinical samples of both inpatient and outpatient psychiatrically treated children, studies have demonstrated that between 13.7 per cent and 58 per cent of the patients had a major affective disorder (Bauersfeld, 1972; McConville et al., 1973; Weinberg et al., 1973; Pearce, 1977; Carlson and Cantwell, 1981).

The risk for major depression increases with age, and there is a threefold greater likelihood of depression being identified at age 14 than at age 10 (Rutter et al., 1970). It is also significant that children showed a higher rate of minor depressive disorder, whereas adults consistently are found to have a greater proportion of major affective disorder (Kashani et al., 1983). In general, children with affective disorders are recognized as being in need of help more often by parents than by teachers. This is in contrast to recognizing conduct disorders in children, which are readily identified by teachers.

Kupferman and Stewart (1979) demonstrated a major affective disorder rate of 13 per cent for girls seen in their clinic and 5 per cent for boys. Weinberg et al. (1973), Poznanski and Zrull (1970), and Kashani et al. (1981) found more boys than girls to be affected. In a comprehensive report by Ka-

shani et al. (1983), similarly, there was a higher rate for boys in the nonreferred sample. This finding is in contrast to the female predominance in adults.

## CLINICAL PICTURE

In describing major affective disorders of children and adolescents, four main disorders are commonly observed. They include major depression with or without psychotic features, bipolar affective disorder, dysthymia, and adjustment disorder with depressed mood. Kovacs, Feinberg, Crouse-Novak, Paulavskas, and Finkelstein (1984) studied 65 children who met criteria for major depression, dysthymic disorder, and adjustment disorder with depressed mood. It was shown that these three disorders had a similar age of onset and that the adjustment disorder had episodes of shortest duration (25 weeks ± 18 weeks), with a peak recovery occurring at 6 to 9 months after diagnosis; the dysthymic disorder lasted for approximately 3 years (± 68 weeks) and maximal recovery rate was 89 per cent at 6 years. The major depression lasted for 32 weeks (± 28 weeks), which was not significantly different from the adjustment disorder, with the maximal recovery rate approximately 1½ years from onset. The dysthymic disorder was also the purest illness, being least likely to be associated with other common childhood psychiatric disorders. Anxiety disorder and other psychiatric diagnoses were most frequently associated with the other two diagnoses. In general, dysthymic disorder is a more chronic, severer disorder, with the potential for other affective disorders developing subsequently. Both dysthymic disorder and major depressive disorder showed a high rate of recurrence, with dysthymic children showing a high rate of major depressive disorder occurring within the first 5 years after the onset of the dysthmia. However, children originally diagnosed with major depressive disorder do not show the later development of dysthymic disorder.

Major depression is characterized by the symptoms listed in Table 19–2. This disorder has been well established in both children and adolescents. It may be associated with psychotic features, as documented by Puig-Antich et al. (1978) and Carlson and

**TABLE 19–2  Symptom Clusters of Depressive States in Children and Adolescents**

Dysphoria or anhedonia (loss of interest or pleasure in usual activities)
  Tearfulness
  Sadness*
  Irritability*
  Sulkiness
Cognitive change—conscience
  Low self-esteem
  Guilt/remorse*
  Helplessness/hopelessness
  Self-reproach*
  Suicidal ideation
Cognitive change—psychomotor
  Psychomotor retardation/agitation*
  Loss of energy/fatigue*
  Restlessness
  Decreased concentration*
  Loss of interest
  Aggressivity*
Vegetative
  Sleep disturbance*
  Somatic complaints*
  Appetite change*
  Weight loss/gain*

Either dysphoria or anhedonia and at least 4 of the remaining symptoms must be present nearly every day for at least a two week duration while interfering with everyday functioning.
* Found in DSM-III.

Cantwell (1979, 1980a). Other disorders, such as learning disabilities, attention-deficit disorder, conduct disorder, and anorexia, may also be recognized. The somatic complaints of affective disorder children have long been recognized, with pediatricians and surgeons acknowledging that somatic complaints without organic etiology result most often from an affective disorder (Weinberg, 1970).

Bipolar affective disorder has been recognized and well documented in both children and adolescents (Strober and Carlson, 1982; Strober, Green, Carlson, 1981; Feinstein and Wolpert, 1973; Thompson and Schindler, 1976; Weinberg and Brumback, 1976). The cyclic nature of mood swings are much more difficult to document in children than in adults. The younger the child, the less prominent are typically manic features such as elation and grandiosity (Strober and Carlson, 1982). Marked increase in psychomotor activity is the most readily observable and consistently noted symptom. Manic or hypomanic children are most often confused with hyperactive children. The bipolar symptoms in children are sufficiently different from those in adults to raise questions concerning a different phenotypic expression of the same adult genotype (Lowe and Cohen, 1980).

Children and adolescents with bipolar affective disorder have family histories positive for affective disorder. The cyclothymic or extroverted personality is not commonly observed in children and adolescents with this disorder. Strober and Carlson (1982) showed that 20 per cent of the hospitalized early adolescents with major depressive disorder later developed bipolar affective disorder. Those children who developed bipolar affective disorder, when compared with the other children with major depressive disorder, had the following characteristics: more rapid onset of depression, greater psychomotor retardation, psychotic features, family history of bipolar disorder or stronger family history of affective disorder, and a manic or hypomanic response to antidepressant medication. In general, the bipolar patients appeared more severely affected than the unipolar depressed adolescents. Carlson, Davenport, and Jamison (1977), however, were unable to demonstrate that adolescent-onset bipolar disorder had a worse prognosis than adult-onset bipolar disorder.

## CLINICAL COURSE

Two prospective studies have examined the clinical outcome of a clinic sample of children with major affective disorder. On followup, Poznanski et al. (1976) demonstrated that during adolescence, approximately $6\frac{1}{2}$ years later, the children had almost a 50 per cent chance of being depressed, and that the depression was indistinguishable from other adult forms of affective disorder. Herjanic, Hudson, and Kotloff (1976) followed 20 children with a clinical diagnosis of depression. Those children who met specific systematic criteria for depression had some form of an affective disorder at followup, whereas those who were simply given various clinical diagnoses at the time of discharge were less likely to have a psychiatric diagnosis on followup, and if diagnosed had diagnoses other than depression.

Two European studies should also be noted because of their opposite findings. Nissen (1971) followed 105 severely depressed children and adolescents and found that they had a poor prognosis, unrelated to the type of depression they had. Dahl (1971) showed that on followup of a large Danish sample of child psychiatric patients, few developed major affective disorder.

In the Chess, Thomas, and Hassibi (1983) longitudinal study of 133 children, 6 were diagnosed as having an affective disorder, 2 with primary affective disorder, with an early severe onset and a recurrent course. Four had secondary affective disorder, also with early onset, but for these children, the primary diagnoses were varied and precipitating events were also noted. There was a tendency for recurrence and a chronic history in this group of young people as well.

Retrospective studies of adults with major affective disorder have revealed that in childhood, there was marked family disruption, discord, and parental neglect. Parents were viewed as having high rates of psychiatric disorders (Perris, 1968; Jacobson, Fasman, DiMascio, 1975; Raskin, 1977; Orvaschel, Mednick, Schulsinger, Rock, 1979). In general, these adults did not have a psychiatric disorder during their childhood. Furthermore, only a small proportion of adult affective disorders have their onset during the prepubertal years. It can be con-

cluded that affective disorders whose onset is in the childhood and adolescent years may be severer and more chronic, with a worse prognosis.

## LABORATORY FINDINGS

A child can be evaluated for depression using standardized and reliable techniques (Kazdin, 1981). The diagnosis is based on five methods of clinical investigation (Table 19–3). They include (1) structured interviews, (2) rating scales (self-report, parent, and clinician), (3) personality inventories, (4) neuroendocrinologic investigation, and (5) clinical pharmacologic trials (i.e., a trial of medication with a positive response being weak support for the clinical diagnosis). Chambers, Puig-Antich, and Tabrizi (1978) have demonstrated the utility of the Kiddie-SADS (schizophrenia affective diagnosis schedule). This structured interview has successfully identified children with major depression, according to Research Diagnostic Criteria (Endicott and Spitzer, 1978), and who had a favorable response to antidepressant medication. The Diagnostic Interview for Children and Adolescents (DICA)

---

**TABLE 19–3  Laboratory Investigation of Major Affective Disorders in Children and Adolescents**

I.  Structured interviews with children
    a.  Diagnostic Interview for Children and Adolescents (DICA) (Herjanic, 1975)
    b.  Diagnostic Interview Schedule for Children (DISC) (Costello, 1984)
    c.  Kiddie-SADS (E and L) (Puig-Antich, 1978)
    d.  Interview Schedule for Children (SCI) (Kovacs, 1978)
II.  Structured interviews with parents
    a.  Diagnostic Interview for Children and Adolescents—Parent (DICA-P)
    b.  Diagnostic Interview Schedule for Children—Parent (DISC-P)
    c.  Kiddie-SADS (Puig-Antich, 1978)
III.  Rating scales
    a.  Children's Depression Rating Scale (CDRS) (Poznanski et al., 1979)
    b.  Children's Depression Scale (CDS) (Lang and Tisher, 1978)
    c.  Children's Depression Inventory (CDI) (Kovacs and Beck, 1978)
    d.  SCDI (Carlson and Cantwell, 1979)
    e.  Montgomery-Asberg (1979)
    f.  Child Behavioral Checklist (Achenbach, 1979)
    g.  Birelson (1981)
    h.  Teacher Affect Rating Scale (TARS) (Petti, 1981)
    i.  Bellevue Index of Depression (Petti, 1981)
    j.  Peer Nomination Inventory (PNID) (Lefkowitz and Terri, 1981)
IV.  Neuroendocrine
    a.  Cortisol—dexamethasone suppression test (Carroll, 1982)
    b.  Growth hormone—clonidine or ITT challenge (Puig-Antich et al., 1984)
V.  Psychometric tests
    a.  Minnesota Multiphasic Personality Inventory
    b.  Personality Inventory for Children (Wirt et al., 1977)

(Herjanic, Herjanic, Brown, Wheatt, 1975; Reich et al., 1982) was developed as a structured interview for parent and child. It systematically reviews specific DSM-III criteria. The Interview Schedule for Children (ISC) was developed by Kovacs (1978) and includes both a parent and a child interview for depression. The DISC and DISC-P were developed at the National Institute for Mental Health and are a children's version of the adult DIS (diagnostic interview schedule) interview (Brent et al., 1984).

The Children's Depression Inventory (CDI) (Kovacs and Beck, 1977) is a simple self-report method of identifying depression in children between ages 7 and 17 and is somewhat effective. The Short Children's Depression Inventory (SCDI) (Carlson and Cantwell, 1979) is a modification of the CDI. Birelson (1981) developed an 18-item self-rating scale, which is a reliable instrument and is strongly associated with the clinical diagnosis. The Children's Depression Scale (CDS) (Lang and Tisher, 1978), a 48-item card-sorting task, addresses symptoms that are most-to-least like the patient. All of these techniques have both a high false positive and a false negative error rate but are found to compliment a structured interview.

The Children's Depression Rating Scale (CDRS) was developed by Poznanski, Cook, and Carroll (1979) to be used after an interview by clinicians to assess the child according to items similar to those in the Hamilton Rating Scale for Adults (Hamilton, 1960). The Montgomery-Asberg Depression Rating Scale (1979) has also been used by clinicians after an interview with children and adolescents. Parent rating of children by the Personality Inventory for Children (Wirt, Lachar, Klinedinst, Seat, 1977) may also be useful in detecting depression.

During the past 10 years, scientists using the dexamethasone suppression test (DST) have studied the presence of cortisol hypersecretion in adult depression (Brown, Goodwin, Ballenger, Goyu, Major, 1979; Carroll, 1982; Carroll et al., 1981; Meltzer et al., 1982). Carroll, Curtis, and Mendels (1976) found that depressed individuals responded to dexamethasone in one of two ways: they showed either a normal 24-hour cortisol suppression or a morning cortisol suppression followed by elevated cortisol levels in the afternoon and evening. Few studies have examined cortisol hypersecre-

tion in childhood affective disorders. Puig-Antich et al. (1979a) found evidence for adrenocortical hyperactivity in depression, but this study was limited to four subjects. On followup of 20 depressed children, 20 per cent were found to be hypersecretors (Puig-Antich, 1980). Poznanski, Carroll, Banegar, Cook, and Grossman (1982) examined 18 outpatient children, 6 to 12 years of age, and reported DST sensitivity and specificity that were similar to those in adult studies. Weller, Weller, and Fristad (1983) found that 70 per cent of 20 hospitalized depressed children were nonsuppressors. In contrast, Geller, Rogol, and Knitter (1983) found a low sensitivity of 17 per cent in their sample of depressed 6- to 12-year-old children. Extein, Rosenberg, Pottash, and Gold (1982) compared post-dexamethasone cortisol levels for 15 depressed and 12 nondepressed postpubertal patients. This study reported a sensitivity of 53 per cent and a specificity of 92 per cent. Similarly, Robbins, Alessi, Yanchyshyn, and Colfer (1982), in a study of 9 children and adolescents, reported a DST sensitivity of 50 per cent and a specificity of 100 per cent. Klee and Garfinkel (1984) demonstrated a 40 per cent sensitivity and a 92 per cent specificity for 33 inpatient children and adolescents. These preliminary studies involving both prepubertal and postpubertal children and adolescents have demonstrated a range for sensitivity and specificity comparable to that of adult patients. Puig-Antich et al. (1984) also studied growth hormone in response to insulin-induced hypoglycemia. Major depression in children was associated with a hyposecretion of growth hormone. In contrast, sleep studies, as reviewed by Puig-Antich (1980), have not revealed significant findings for children with affective disorder.

## DIFFERENTIAL DIAGNOSIS

There are six major diagnoses that are often confused with major affective disorders in children and adolescents. They are attention-deficit disorder, conduct disorder, anxiety disorders—especially school phobia or school refusal—eating disorders, substance abuse, and early stages of schizophrenia. Other organic syndromes that have affective disorder symptoms as part of their clinical presentation are endocrinopathies (e.g., hyperthyroidism, hypothyroidism, hypercalcemia), viral infections (e.g., infectious mononucleosis, infectious hepatitis, cytomegalovirus, and respiratory syncitial virus), and severe chronic illness (e.g., cystic fibrosis, inflammatory bowel disease, rheumatoid arthritis, and diabetes mellitus).

Attention-deficit disorder may resemble depression in children because these youngsters exhibit increased psychomotor activity, difficulty concentrating, mood lability and may have some of the vegetative symptoms, especially sleep disturbance. Attention-deficit disorder children also have a high rate of depressive spectrum disease in their families, presenting with family psychopathology similar to that of depressed children (Cantwell, 1972). The low self-esteem in attention-deficit disorder children is secondary to school failure and is not a primary feature of the cognitive state and self-perceptions of the attention-deficit disorder syndrome. Attention-deficit disorder children most resemble children with dysthymic disorder because both disorders are chronic. In contrast, the main differentiating feature of major affective disorder is its episodic nature, with completely euthymic and symptom-free periods between episodes. Attention-deficit disorder is a chronic, unremitting, and continuous disorder of childhood, with onset in the preschool years. Further research will be necessary to provide more differentiating features.

Conduct disorders in children and adolescents have for many years been confused with major affective disorders. Antisocial and delinquent behavior has often been interpreted as a "depressive equivalent" and as covering over, or "masking," an underlying depression (Cytryn et al., 1980). Antisocial behaviors have often obscured hypomanic and manic behaviors in bipolar disorder adolescents. Lying, running away, promiscuity, drug overdoses, school truancy, gambling, and other aggressive or antisocial behaviors have been frequent methods by which young people have expressed themselves when significantly depressed or elated. Poor impulse control and immature judgment have resulted in a high rate of these behaviors occurring in depressed youngsters. Puig-Antich (1982) and Carlson and Cantwell (1980a) demonstrated that one third of all conduct disorder children met the criteria for major affective disorder. If the criteria for affective disorder are not satisfied, these behaviors would likely represent an unsocialized, nonaggressive conduct disorder. Conduct disorder children without an affective disorder exhibit an uninterrupted, continuous progression of more serious misbehavior, a disregard for others and their property. In affective disorder children with disturbing behavior the behavior is directed more toward themselves than to others.

The studies by Hershberg, Carlson, Cantwell, and Strober (1982) and by Bernstein and Garfinkel (1986) indicate that many children and adolescents who refuse to attend school are actually depressed. These depressed individuals also have symptoms of anxiety disorders but meet the criteria for major affective disorder as well. In the school-refusing population, affective disorder and anxiety disorders overlap to a large extent, especially in the older, more chronic school refuser. Children with severe anxiety disorders and school refusal have many of the symptoms of depression as well as family histories positive for anxiety and affective disorders. In general, anxiety disorders are frequently confused with affective disorders, and only with precise, systematic interviews is one able to differentiate these two disorders.

Recent research indicates that a number of patients with anorexia nervosa may have a major affective disorder, and that anorexia symptoms may be simply vegetative symptoms of the depression (Cantwell, Sturzenberger, Burroughs, Salkin, Green, 1977). Related to this are the clinical observations that treatment with tricyclic antidepressants and monoamine oxidase inhibitors has been efficacious in some patients with eating disorders. To differentiate between a primary eating disorder and undereating or overeating associated with an affective disorder, one looks for chronic symptoms rather than episodic symptoms; the absence of a family history for affective disorder and the preoccupation with food and body size predominate over affective symptoms.

Dysphoria and other primary symptoms of depression have long been recognized as early features of the onset of schizophrenia in adolescents. A disorder of thought process, severe social isolation, first-rank characteristics of schizophrenia and bizarre thoughts or behaviors distinguish the early schizophrenic adolescent from the depressed adolescent.

Alcoholism and substance abuse have also been associated with affective disorders. Depressed children and adolescents may use street drugs or alcohol in an effort to self-medicate themselves and treat their depression. Unfortunately, when the depressed individual chronically uses alcohol in this manner, dependency may develop. The affective symptoms predominating at the time of the *onset* of alcohol or drug use are the best way to differentiate between these two disorders.

## SUICIDE IN CHILDREN AND ADOLESCENTS

Self-destructive behavior in children and adolescents is under greater scientific scrutiny than ever before. No other fatal medical condition has increased to the same extent as suicide in children and adolescents. Each year in the United States approximately 5000 young persons 24 years old and younger commit suicide (Frederick, 1978; Holinger, 1982). It has become the third leading cause of death for this age-group, exceeded only by motor vehicle accidents and homicide (Holinger, 1978). Since 1960, completed suicide has increased more than 200 per cent for young people between ages 10 and 24 (Holinger, 1978). Furthermore, research has shown that for every one completed suicide, there are approximately 30 to 40 attempts (Weissman, 1974; Wexler, Weissman, Kasl, 1978). In adolescents, there may be as many as 50 to 100 suicide attempts for every young person who commits suicide (Otto, 1966).

Epidemiologic findings reflect an underestimate of the true occurrence of the problem, with current government statistics underreporting the extent of suicide by 10 to 15 per cent and incompletely documenting the problem below age 10 (Garfinkel and Golombek, 1983). Most, if not all, suicides in children 10 years of age or younger are recorded as accidental deaths because suicide is not recorded in government statistics below this age. In other words, our understanding, knowledge, and description of suicidal children and adolescents may in fact be based on a smaller and more incomplete data set than actually exists.

The unique features of completed suicide in children and adolescents not only distinguish it from suicide in adults, but also provide specific characteristics that allow clinicians to identify the young individual at risk for self-destructive behavior. Suicide below the age of 10 does occur but is uncommon. Suicide increases rapidly to peak by ages 18, 19, and 20, the late teenage years, followed by a plateau that occurs for the remainder of the early young adult years, 20 through 24 (Holinger, 1978; Garfinkel and Golombek, 1983). The age at greatest risk is the time during which adolescents are leaving high school, going off to college, or seeking employment for the first time, a time when there is a natural ending of the family and community-based support systems that provide guidance, direction, and problem resolution when serious psychiatric disorders arise. Two thirds of all suicides occur in the 20 to 24-age-group, appearing during the late teenage years and early young adult years; 30 per cent occur in the middle teen years (16 to 19 years); approximately 8 per cent of all youthful suicide occurs in children younger than 15 years.

Suicide appears to depend on maturation (Weininger, 1979). Various factors reflecting cognitive development must be present, such as judgment, abstract reasoning, formulation of a suicide plan, self-blame, and the age at risk for the onset of significant depression. Young people who commit suicide are not only reacting to a seriously depressed mood and the impulse to end their suffering. They must also have sufficient cognitive abilities to determine which of their actions will likely be fatal (Schneidman, 1976; Garfinkel, Froese, Hood, 1982). To this extent, various investigators have studied the role of intelligence and academic achievement as they influence the suicide rate and have demonstrated that the number of suicides is greater in students doing well at school and for students attending more prestigious schools and universities (Rook, 1959; Hawton, Crowle, Simkin, Bancroft, 1978). The question persists whether there are more environmental stressors and expectations placed on students at the schools with the highest standards, or whether brighter students are more prone to feelings of failure, depression, and self-criticism. Similarly, individuals who are intelligent are more able to plan on not being rescued. There is no evidence to date that suggests that the better universities studied provide fewer support systems, are more stressful, and are more alienating than less prestigious institutions. More intelligent youngsters can conceptualize what is lethal and what is not and will likely succeed on the first attempt. The identification of a successful plan is a critical factor that is both intelligence and age dependent and explains the steep increase in the suicide rate according to age.

For every girl who completes suicide, four boys succeed (Garfinkel and Golombek, 1983). This gender difference has only been observed for completed suicide, whereas suicide attempts occur three times more often in girls than in boys. If cultural and societal factors create these gender differences, it would appear that with the changing role of women in North America from the mid-1970's onward, one would expect a trend toward an equalization of the completed and attempt rates for both sexes. This has not occurred. What was observed from 1975 onward was a significant trend for girls and young women to use methods of self-destruction that were more similar to those that males were using (firearms, carbon monoxide, and jumping from buildings) (Garfinkel and Golombek, 1983). When males experience depression, there is a much greater internal perception of the irreversibility and irrevocable nature of their sense of failure and pessimism. The observed higher rate of suicide attempts for females indicates that the self-destructive action is probably undertaken ambivalently, with only a limited amount of resolve.

Suicide is much more common in Caucasian young people than in black youth (Murphy and Robins, 1967). Similarly, the number of Protestant children and adolescents committing suicide is disproportionate to the number of Catholics and Jews committing suicide (Lukianowicz, 1968) and attempting suicide (Garfinkel and Golombek, 1983). Some authors suggest that religious taboos and strongly supportive families may be factors that create a lower suicide rate.

Completed suicide is unevenly distributed throughout the country and is much more common in urban centers than in rural settings (Mintz, 1970). Some regions and states have a suicide rate that is two to three times higher than in other areas (e.g., Ne-

vada, Alaska) (Liberakis and Hoenig, 1978; Frederick, 1978). Areas with a high Native American population have high suicide rates, with studies indicating that the suicide rate among Native Americans is 10 times higher than that in the Caucasian American population (Dizmang et al., 1974).

Young people who commit suicide have a much lower unemployment rate than the youthful population in general (Garfinkel and Golombek, 1983). Completed suicide is much more common in college students, high school students, and young people pursuing gainful employment. Socioeconomic factors also play a role in suicide for children and adolescents, with middle- to upper-middle-class youth having a higher rate of suicide than do children of lower socioeconomic groups.

Completed suicide in young people appears to be related to a family history of alcoholism, substance abuse, and major affective disorder (Murphy, 1983). A definite family pattern emerges, with suicide occurring in specific families. Both suicide and suicide attempts occurred more frequently in the families of young people who attempted suicide than in a comparison group. These families also had more substance abuse and affective disorder. Family breakdown was much more common, with most suicidal young people coming from single-parent families or having experienced placement in foster care, group homes, and institutions. Whether the effect of the family is a result of modeling, a genetic predisposition, or a breakdown of the support provided by adults is not clear at this time; however, it is likely that all three interact. There is a strong association between suicide and psychiatric disorders that have a known genetic predisposition (such as depression, anxiety, and alcoholism). For example, it is not uncommon to find completed suicide in two or three first-degree family members from two generations in a family of a child who committed or attempted suicide.

Child and adolescent suicide does not occur randomly throughout the year (Sanborn, Sanborn, and Cimbolie, 1973; Eastwood and Peacocke, 1976). Just as recent research has indicated that serious psychiatric disorders occur at peak times, so the same may be said of suicide in children and adolescents. For this age-group, suicide occurs much more often in the late fall, winter, and early spring. These findings are in contrast to adults, who commit suicide most often in the late spring. Self-destructive behavior in youth most often occurs in the afternoon and evening hours, unlike adult suicides, which occur primarily in the early morning hours, before dawn (Garfinkel et al., 1982).

In North America, completed suicide is primarily a function of firearm use. Forty-five per cent to 55 per cent of all completed suicide in young people is attributed to firearms (Boyd, 1983). The second most common method is hanging, followed by drug overdoses. Carbon monoxide poisoning, jumping from high places, jumping in front of moving vehicles, and drowning are the next most common methods. The choice of specific methods is determined by many factors, including sex, age, demographic factors (e.g., urban vs. rural, geographic location, race, socioeconomic status), and psychopathology (Garfinkel and Golombek, 1983). It is apparent from these findings that a major means of prevention may be to curtail the availability of the various methods of self-destruction for specific risk groups. Figure 19–1 is a schematic depiction of the vulnerable individual undergoing stress, not using help from others, and having a method of injury readily available. This figure represents the key temperamental and psychosocial elements determining suicidal behavior.

## Suicide Attempts

A failed suicide or suicide attempt occurs when the individual is fully intent on dying as a result of the self-inflicted injury but for some unforeseen circumstance was prevented from doing so; a suicide gesture is self-inflicted injury with no intention of dying as a result of the injury; the action is primarily "a cry for help." Because there are many more attempts and suicide gestures than there are completed suicides, it is important to distinguish those failed suicides from less lethal behavior. In general, all attempts must be taken seriously, and a complete psychiatric workup is often necessary. It has been demonstrated that 1 out of 10 individuals who attempt suicide will ultimately succeed (Otto, 1971; Dahlgren, 1977). Our followup research indicated that when suicide attempters were compared with medically and surgically ill children and adolescents, they had a higher mortality rate despite the fact that the nonsuicidal group was significantly physically ill (Garfinkel et al., 1982). A severe suicide attempt is commonly preceded by symptoms of depression, hostility, nihilism, and self-depreciation. Young people who make serious attempts are often those with a clinical depression in combination with a large amount of rage, hostility, and impulsivity.

It is often possible to identify specific

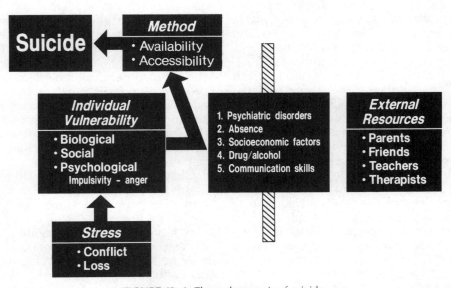

**FIGURE 19–1.** The pathogenesis of suicide.

crises, precipitants, and environmental stressors that led to the suicide attempt (Garfinkel et al., 1982). Most often conflict with parents, nonspecific conflict within the family, or conflict between boyfriend and girlfriend precedes the attempt. Surprisingly, 1 in 10 suicide attempts have been related to problems at school. It is often difficult to determine just how stressful a particular event is, since adolescents may view such occurrences idiosyncratically. An apparently nontraumatic event may become overwhelming to a young person because she or he is already overburdened with a preexisting depression. The stress may be related to the depression, result from it, or be coincidental in time. Nevertheless, at that particular time, the individual is exquisitely sensitive to that event and cannot cope with the feelings and thoughts generated by it. Often the environmental stressor or precipitant has been identified as a "loss" (Stanley and Barter, 1978). The loss may be based in reality, such as losing one's girlfriend, or peer status; or the loss may be internal and not readily recognized, such as loss of self-esteem, reputation, or sense of worth. It is during the adolescent years of development that private, closely guarded personal perceptions of oneself can be painfully destroyed by life's events, and this can intensify an already existing mood disorder. For example, a varsity basketball star who was forced to miss a season because of a knee injury committed suicide. It is possible that he was experiencing a major depression previously, with the injury further affecting his mood and representing the "straw that broke the camel's back." The athlete perceived loss of self-esteem when he could not play on the team.

Unlike completed suicides, suicide attempts most often result from overdoses, with approximately 90 per cent of all attempts in the child and adolescent age-group attributed to this method. As shown in Table 19–4, household analgesics, benzodiazepines, and barbiturates are the most common medications used in such attempts (Garfinkel et al., 1982).

Suicidal individuals often talk about a desire to die or say that they would be better off dead. The psychiatrist working with depressed and suicidal children must be able to determine the mental status of the individual and the severity of the attempt. Some

**TABLE 19–4** Drugs Used by Children and Adolescents in Suicide Attempt

| Attempts by ingestion N = 532* | (%) |
|---|---|
| Analgesics | 36.8 |
| Benzodiazepines | 23.7 |
| Barbiturates | 18.6 |
| Phenothiazines | 5.6 |
| Solvents/Inhalants | 5.5 |
| Street drugs (LSD, speed, opiates) | 5.1 |
| Antibiotics | 4.5 |
| Patent medicines | 3.9 |
| Antihistamines | 3.6 |
| Bizarre ingestion (perfume, soap, etc.) | 3.4 |
| Hypnotics | 3.4 |
| Anticonvulsants | 2.4 |
| Alcohol | 2.3 |
| Antidepressants | 2.1 |
| Other | 3.2 |
| Unknown | 3.0 |

* 144 patients used two drugs.

warning before the self-destructive behavior occurs is often recognized only after the event. In young people, it may take the form of giving away a prized possession or giving inappropriate advice (Connell, 1972).

A severe attempt has the following characteristics: (1) the amount of planning associated with the attempt; (2) the timing and the isolation of the actions, with no one nearby; (3) the method chosen (hanging, jumping, etc., are severer than wrist slashing or drug overdoses); (4) leaving of a suicide note; (5) a family history of suicide; and (6) symptoms of depression (Garfinkel et al., 1982). Of all the features that identify severe suicidal behavior in children and adolescents, one of the strongest predictors of a serious attempt is the family history of suicide (Dabbagh, 1977). In our 1982 study, completed suicide occurred only in the families of those young people who attempted suicide, and not in a matched control group and suicide attempts were six times more common in the attempters' families compared with the families of the control group of children.

## TREATMENT

The literature on the pharmacologic management of affective disorders in children has only recently reflected systematic scientifically controlled studies. This literature is reviewed in Tables 19–5 and 19–6 as to

**TABLE 19–5    Tricyclic Antidepressant Use in Children and Adolescents**

| Author (yr) | No. in Study | Drug | Daily Dosage | Duration of Drug Trial | Use of Placebo | Double Blind | Diagnosis | Assessment Procedures | Improvement | Side Effects |
|---|---|---|---|---|---|---|---|---|---|---|
| Lucas (1965) | 14 | Amitriptyline | 30–50 mg | 42 days | Yes | Yes | Mixed | Clinical rating | 60% | Sedation |
| Frommer (1967) | 32 | Phenelzine, chlordiazepoxide, phenobarbitane | 30 mg 20 mg 60 mg | 14+ days | Yes | Yes | Affective/depression | Clinical impression | 88%—combination of phenelzine and chlordiazepoxide | NR |
| Annell (1969) | 8 | Amitriptyline and/or lithium carbonate | 30 mg 300 mg 600 mg | Varied | No | No | Affective/manic depression | Parent, teacher, and clinician's impression | 100% | NR |
| Ling (1970) | 10 | Amitriptyline or imipramine | Varied | Varied | No | No | Depression | Clinical impression | 70%–90% | NR |
| Frommer (1971) | 200 | Amitriptyline | NR | NR | No | No | Affective/depression | Clinical impression | 67% | NR |
| Kuhn and Kuhn (1971) | 100 | Imipramine, desmethylimipramine, clomipramine, opipramol | NR | NR | No | No | Affective/phasic, chronic depression | NR | 76% | Nausea, vomiting, dizziness, headaches, gastric upset |
| Stack (1971) | 116 | Opipramol, amitriptyline, imipramine | 50 mg 2–5 mg 10 mg | 28–730 days | No | No | Affective/depression (preschool) | NR | Imipramine especially effective | Drowsiness; fatigue with opipramol and amitriptyline |
| Stack (1971) | 75 | Nortriptyline, amitriptyline, opipramol, phenelzine | 30 mg 2–25 mg 50–150 mg NR | NR | No | No | Affective/depression (school-age) | NR | 80% | Drowsiness; fatigue with opipramol and amitriptyline |
| Stack (1971) | 64 | Phenelzine | NR | NR | No | No | Affective/phobic obsession with depressive states | NR | 94% | NR |

| Study | N | Drug | Dose | Duration | | | Type | Assessment | Response | Side effects |
|---|---|---|---|---|---|---|---|---|---|---|
| Stack (1971) | 150 | Nortriptyline, imipramine | 75 mg | NR | No | No | Affective/mixed depression | NR | 67% | NR |
| Stack (1971) | 85 | Opipramol, amitriptyline | 100–150 mg 75 mg | NR | No | No | Affective/depression-related psychosis | NR | 57% | Drowsiness; fatigue with opipramol and amitriptyline NR |
| Polvan and Cebiroglu (1971) | 29 | Pyrithioxin and amitriptyline, or nortriptyline and levomepromazine | According to age and weight | 56 days | No | No | Affective/depression | NR | 90% | NR |
| Petti and Campbell (1975) | 1 | Imipramine | 75 mg | 20 days | No | No | Affective/manic depression | Clinical impression, EEG | Seizures occurred; IMI discontinued | Extensive seizures |
| Brumback et al. (1977) | 19 | Imipramine or amitriptyline | 25–125 mg | 28 days | No | No | Affective/depression | Clinical impression | 95% | NR |
| Puig-Antich et al. (1978) | 8 | Imipramine | 3–5 mg/kg | 42–56 days | No | No | Affective/depression | RDC CPRS | 75% | (Elicited in interview) nausea, constipation, somnolence, tachycardia, anorexia |
| Puig-Antich et al. (1979b) | 6 7 | Imipramine | 4 mg/kg | 35 days | No Yes Crossover | Yes Yes | Affective/manic depression | Kiddie-SADS, RDC | Plasma levels indicated good response | NR |
| Kupfer et al. (1979) | 12 | Imipramine | 4.3 mg/kg | 21 days | No | No | Affective/depression | EEG, sleep observation, clinical assessment | REM suppression | Sleep disturbance |
| Pallmeyer and Petti (1979) | 2 | Imipramine | 3.5–5 mg/kg | 51 days | No | No | Affective/depression | CBI | Anger and hostility increased with IMI | Hostility, anger |

*Table continued on following page.*

**TABLE 19–5** (continued)

| Author (yr) | No. in Study | Drug | Daily Dosage | Duration of Drug Trial | Use of Placebo | Double Blind | Diagnosis | Assessment Procedures | Improvement | Side Effects |
|---|---|---|---|---|---|---|---|---|---|---|
| Kashani et al. (1980) | 1 | Amitriptyline | 1.5 mg/kg | 28 days | Yes | Yes | Affective/depression | Clinical impression | Hypomanic reaction (dose reduced) | Hypomanic |
| Petti et al. (1980) | 1 | Imipramine | 5 mg/kg | 40 days | No | No | Affective/depression | CBI, SoSAD | Behavioral symptoms improved | NR |
| Petti and Unis (1981) | 1 | Imipramine | 5 mg/kg | 7 days | Yes | No | Affective/depression, borderline psychosis | Clinical, and parent assessment, PALS-C | Marked improvement | NR |
| Staton et al. (1981) | 11 | Amitriptyline, desipramine | 1.1–3.5 mg/kg 3.4 mg/kg | 90–100 days | No | No | Affective/depression | CDRS, CDI, WISC-R | 100% | NR |
| Weller et al. (1982) | 11 | Imipramine | 5 mg/kg | 20 days | No | No | Affective/major depression | Plasma IMI levels, CGI rating scales | 100% | Minimal—tachycardia, syncope, diaphoresis |
| Conners and Petti (1983) | 21 | Imipramine | 5 mg/kg | 53–202 days | No | No | Affective/depression | BID, CBI | 66% | NR |
| Geller et al. (1983) | 12 | Nortriptyline | | 172 days | No | No | Affective/depression | RDC, CDI | 75% | Minimal |

NR, not reported; RDC, Research Diagnostic Criteria; CPRS, Children's Psychiatric Rating Scale; Kiddie-SADS, Schedule for Affective Disorders and Schizophrenia for School Aged Children; CBI, Children's Behavior Inventory; SoSAD, Scale of School Age Depression; CDRS, Children's Depression Rating Scale; CDI, Children's Depression Inventory.

**TABLE 19–6** Lithium Use in Children and Adolescents

| Author (yr) | No. in Study | Drug | Daily Dosage | Duration of Drug Trial | Use of Placebo | Double Blind | Diagnosis | Assessment Procedures | Improvement | Side Effects |
|---|---|---|---|---|---|---|---|---|---|---|
| Berg et al. (1974) | 1 | (Amitriptyline) lithium carbonate | 2400 mg/ 1 mEq/l | 365 days | No | No | Affective/bipolar, manic-depressive psychosis | Clinical impressions | Caused switch from depression to hypomania | NR |

| Study | N | Medication | Dose | Duration | | | Diagnosis | Assessment | Outcome | Side effects |
|---|---|---|---|---|---|---|---|---|---|---|
| Sovner (1975) | 1 | (Haloperidol, mesoridazine) lithium carbonate | 2400 mg/1 mEq/l | 18+ days | No | No | Affective/manic depression | WAIS, Bender-Gestalt Test | Dramatic improvement | NR |
| Warneke (1975) | 1 | (Haloperidol, doxepin) lithium carbonate | 1800 mg/1.2 mEq/l | 21 days | No | No | Affective/manic depression | Clinical impression | Marked improvement | NR |
| Horowitz (1977) | 8 | Lithium carbonate | 1500–2400 mg/0.5–1.2 mEq/l | 14–90 days | No | No | Affective/manic depression | Clinical impression | Marked improvement | NR |
| White and O'Shanick (1977) | 1 | (Haloperidol) lithium carbonate | 1200 mg/1 mEq/l | 42 days | No | No | Affective/manic depression | Clinical impression | Marked improvement | NR |
| Brumback and Weinberg (1977) | 6 | Lithium carbonate | 30–40 mg/kg/0.6–1.2 mEq/l | 5–110 days | No | No | Affective manic/depression | Clinical impression | 33% | Nausea, anxiety, increased depression, EEG abnormalities |
| DeLong (1978) | 4 | Lithium carbonate | 450–1200 mg | 80–1000 days | Yes | Yes | Affective/manic depression | Conner's PSQ | Behaviorally effective | Minimal hand tremors, increased urination, blunted motivation |
| Engstrom et al. (1978) | 1 | Lithium carbonate | 2100–2400 mg/1.0–1.5 mEq/l | 14+ days | No | No | Affective/manic depression | Clinical impression | Marked improvement | NR |
| Davis (1979) | 4 | Lithium carbonate | 0.8–1.0 mEq/l serum level | 180 days | No | No | Affective/manic depression | Parental symptom assessment | Marked improvement | NR |
| Mayo et al. (1979) | 1 | Lithium carbonate | NR | 730 days | No | No | Affective bipolar manic depression | RDC, CGI, CPRS | Substantial decrease in stress events during treatment | NA |

NR, not reported; WAIS, Wechsler Adult Intelligence Scale; Conner's PSQ, Conner's Parent Symptom Questionnaire; RDC, Research Diagnostic Criteria; CGI, Clinical Global Impression Scale; CPRS, Children's Psychiatric Rating Scale; NA, not applicable.

methodology, design and controls of the research, the instruments of evaluating improvement, the degree of improvement, duration of treatment, and side effects. There have been 35 published reports describing tricyclic antidepressant and lithium carbonate treatment of childhood major affective disorders. In general, the methodology is limited to 17 case reports in which no experimental control was implemented. Characteristically, these studies did not have a placebo phase, patient or clinician blindness, or objective review of therapeutic response. In most of these 17 studies, the diagnostic criteria for inclusion in the study were not presented. The duration of treatment recorded in the studies is also a significant factor, with six studies not recording length of treatment, five studies for 1 to 3 weeks, and only eight studies using tricyclic antidepressants for longer than 4 weeks.

There were only seven double-blind studies. After excluding Frommer's (1967) study, because of diagnostic imprecision, the remaining six double-blind studies included 14 children receiving imipramine, 1 child receiving amitriptyline, and 4 receiving lithium carbonate. Puig-Antich et al. (1979b) conducted a crossed double-blind study with a placebo phase. This study accounted for seven patients. Kashani, Hodges, and Shekim (1980) and Petti and Unis (1981) each had one patient who was in a double-blind placebo-controlled crossover study.

Clinical improvement was measured in 12 studies by nonspecific clinician judgment alone, in 7 by an unspecified method, and in 9 by a combination of rating scales, clinical judgment, and serial psychometric tests. With these limitations in mind, the reported efficacy for tricyclic antidepressants and monoamine oxidase inhibitors was between 57 per cent and 100 per cent, with a mean of 85 per cent. Puig-Antich et al. (1979b) and Weller, Weller, Preskorn, and Glotzbach (1982) have correlated serum levels of desmethylimipramine and imipramine with therapeutic efficacy and have unequivocally demonstrated that only with levels within the 150 to 250 ng/ml range will a positive therapeutic response be observed.

Side effects observed were hypomania and aggression (Berg et al., 1974; Pallmeyer and Petti, 1979; Kashani et al., 1980) and rapid-eye-movement suppression (Kupfer, Cable, Kane, Petti, Conners, 1979). Puig-Antich et al. (1978) have documented cardiac arrhythmias as a function of tricyclic antidepressant dosage. Monitoring for electrocardiographic abnormalities when one exceeds 3.5 mg/kg is mandatory, since first degree heart block is common beyond this dosage.

## Psychotherapy of Major Affective Disorders in Children and Adolescents

The major principles for managing and treating affective disorders in children and adolescents are similar to those for adults (Lewinsohn, 1979). The literature supports combination treatment as the most efficacious management (i.e., psychotherapy in combination with medication). Individual therapy or drugs alone are less effective in adults. Consideration must be given to the age of the child, cognitive development, and verbal skill attainment before psychotherapy is provided. Psychotherapy need not be entirely verbal, but may rely on activity or play as well. Concurrent family therapy is often provided to families of depressed children. Such therapy should include child management techniques. The overall goal is to teach children how to increase pleasant experiences and decrease negative reinforcement (Ross, 1981).

Behavioral and cognitive behavioral therapy for affective disorders in children and adolescents reflects the underlying behavioral principles assumed to affect the cognitive and perceptual state of the individual. These include graduated task assignment with cognitive rehearsal, assertiveness training, and role playing (Leon, Kendall, Garber, 1980). Children also benefit from a psychoeducational approach (Lewinsohn, 1979). Therapy for children is time limited, with sufficient direction, control, and encouragement to undertake new activities, enabling skill attainment and positive reinforcement. However, little empirical work has been conducted as to the nature and efficacy of cognitive-behavioral therapy for depression in children and adolescents.

# REFERENCES

Achenback TM, Edelbrock CS: The child behavior profile: II. Boys aged 12–16 and girls aged 6–11 and 12–16. J Consult Clin Psychol 47:223–233, 1979.

Akiskal HS, McKinney WT Jr: Overview of recent research in depression. Arch Gen Psychiatry 32:285–305, 1975.

Annell AL: Manic-depressive illness in children and effect of treatment with lithium carbonate. Acta Paedopsychiatrica (Basel) 36:292–301, 1969.

Annell AL (ed): Depressive States in Childhood and Adolescence. New York, Halsted Press, 1971.

Anthony J, Scott P: Manic depressive psychosis in childhood. J Child Psychol Psychiatry 1:52–72, 1960.

Bauersfeld KH: Diagnosis and treatment of depressive conditions at a school psychiatric center, in Annell AL (ed): Depressive States in Childhood and Adolescence. Stockholm, Almquist & Wiksell, 1972.

Beck AT: Cognitive therapy: Nature and relation to behavior therapy. Behav Ther 7:184–200, 1970.

Bemporad JR, Wilson A: A developmental approach to depression in childhood and adolescence. J Am Acad Psychoanal 6:325–352, 1978.

Berg I, Hullin R, et al: Bipolar manic depressive psychoses in early adolescence: A case report. Br J Psychiatry 125:416–417, 1974.

Bernstein GA, Garfinkel BD: School phobia: The overlap of affective and anxiety disorders. J Am Acad Child Psychiatry 25:235–241, 1986.

Birleson P: The validity of depressive disorder in childhood and the development of a self-rating scale: A research report. J Child Psychol Psychiatry 22:73–88, 1981.

Blos P: The Psychology of Adolescence—A Psychoanalytic Interpretation. Glencoe, NY, Free Press of Glencoe, 1962.

Bowlby J: Separation: Attachment and Loss, Vol. 2. New York, Basic Books, 1973.

Bowlby J: Attachment and loss, vol. 3. Loss: Sadness and Depression. London, Hogarth Press and the Institute of Psychoanalysis, 1980.

Boyd JH: The increasing rate of suicide by firearms. N Engl J Med 308:872–874, 1983.

Brent DA, Kalas R, Edelbrock C, Costello AJ, Dulkan MK, Connover N: Nosologic correlates of the severity of suicidal ideation in children and adolescents. Paper presented at the Annual Meeting of the American Academy of Child Psychiatry, Toronto, 1984.

Brown GL, Goodwin FK, Ballenger JC, Goyu PF, Major LF: Aggression in humans: Correlates with cerebrospinal fluid amine metabolites. Psychiatry Res 1:131–139, 1979.

Brumback RA, et al: Depression in children referred to an educational diagnostic center: Diagnosis and treatment and analysis of criteria and literature review. Dis Nerv Syst 38:529–535, 1977.

Brumback RA, Staton RD: Depression-induced neurologic dysfunction [letter]. N Engl J Med 10:305:642.

Brumback RA, Weinberg WA: Mania in childhood: II therapeutic trial of lithium carbonate and further description of manic-depressive illness in children. Am J Dis Child 131:112–126, 1977.

Cantwell DP, Baker L: Parental psychiatric illness and psychiatric disorder in at-risk children. Paper presented at the 30th Annual Meeting of the American Academy of Child Psychiatry, San Francisco, October 26–30, 1983.

Cantwell DP: Psychiatric illness in the families of hyperactive children. Arch Gen Psychiatry 27:414–417, 1972.

Cantwell DP, Carlson G: Problems and prospects in the study of childhood depression. J Nerv Ment Dis 167:522–529, 1979.

Cantwell D, Sturzenberger S, Burroughs J, Salkin B, Green J: Anorexia nervosa: An affective disorder. Arch Gen Psychiatry 34:1087–1091, 1977.

Carlson GA, Davenport YB, Jamison K: A comparison of outcome in adolescent and late onset bipolar manic-depressive illness. Am J Psychiatry 134:919–922, 1977.

Carlson GA, Cantwell DP: A survey of depressive symptoms in a child and adolescent psychiatric population: Interview data. J Am Acad Child Psychiatry 18:587–599, 1979.

Carlson GA, Cantwell DP: A survey of depressive symptoms, syndrome and disorder in a child psychiatric population. J Child Psychol Psychiatry 21:19–25, 1980a.

Carlson GA, Cantwell DP: Unmasking masked depression in children and adolescents. Am J Psychiatry 137:445–449, 1980b.

Carlson GA, Cantwell DP: Diagnosis of childhood depression—A comparison of Weinberg and DSM-III criteria. J Am Acad Child Psychiatry 21:247–250, 1981.

Carroll BJ: Use of the dexamethasone suppression test in depression. J Clin Psychiatry 43:44–48, 1982.

Carroll BJ, Curtis GC, Mendels J: Neuroendocrine regulation in depression. II. Discrimination of depressed from nondepressed patients. Arch Gen Psychiatry 33:1051–1058, 1976.

Carroll BJ, Feinberg M, Greden JF, et al: A specific laboratory test for the diagnosis of melancholia. Arch Gen Psychiatry 38:15–22, 1981.

Chambers WJ, Puig-Antich J: Psychiatric symptoms in prepubertal major depressive disorder. Arch Gen Psychiatry 39:921–927, 1982.

Chambers W, Puig-Antich J, Tabrizi MA: The ongoing development of the Kiddie-SADS. Paper presented at the 25th Annual meeting of the American Academy of Child Psychiatry, San Diego, 1978.

Chess S, Thomas A, Hassibi M: Depression in childhood and adolescence: A prospective study of six cases. J Nerv Ment Dis 171:411–420, 1983.

Connell HM: Depression in childhood. Child Psychiatry Hum Dev 4:70–85, 1972.

Cytryn L, McKnew DH Jr: Proposed classification of childhood depression. Am J Psychiatry 129:149–155, 1972.

Cytryn L, McKnew DH Jr, Bunney WE Jr: Diagnosis of depression in children: A reassessment. Am J Psychiatry 137:22–25, 1980.

Dabbagh F: Family suicide. Br J Psychiatry 130:159–161, 1977.

Dahl V: A follow-up study of a child psychiatric clientele with special regard to manic depressive psychosis, in Annell AL (ed): Depressive States in Childhood and Adolescence. Stockholm, Almquist & Wiksell, 1971, pp 534–541.

Dahlgren KG: Attempted suicides—35 years afterward. Suicide Life Threat Behav 7:75–79, 1977.

Davis RE: Manic-depressive variant syndrome of childhood: A preliminary report. Am J Psychiatry 136:702–705, 1979.

DeLong GR: Lithium carbonate treatment of select behavior disorders in suggesting manic-depressive illness. J Pediatrics 93:689–694, 1978.

Dizmang LH, Watson J, May PA, et al: Adolescent suicide at an Indian reservation. Am J Orthopsychiatry 44:43–49, 1974.

Eastwood MR, Peacocke J: Seasonal patterns of suicide, depression and electroconvulsive therapy. Br J Psychiatry 129:472–475, 1976.

Endicott J, Spitzer RL: A diagnostic interview: The schedule for affective disorders and schizophrenia. Arch Gen Psychiatry 35:837–844, 1978.

Engstrom FW, Robbins DR, May JG: Manic-depressive illness in adolescence. J Am Acad Child Psychiatry 17:514–520, 1978.

Erikson EH: Childhood and Society. New York, WW Norton, 1950.

Extein I, Rosenberg G, Pottash ALC, Gold MS: Preliminary data on the dexamethasone suppression test in depressed adolescents. Am J Psychiatry 139:1617–1618, 1982.

Feighner JP, Robins E, Guze SB, et al: Diagnostic criteria for use in psychiatric research. Arch Gen Psychiatry 26:57–63, 1972.

Feinstein SC, Wolpert EA: Juvenile manic-depressive illness clinical and therapeutic considerations. J Am Acad Child Psychiatry 12:123–136, 1973.

Frederick C: Current trends in suicidal behavior in the United States. Am J Psychother 32:169–200, 1978.

Freud S: Mourning and melancholia, in Gaylin W (ed): The Meaning of Despair: Psychoanalytic Contributions to the Understanding of Depression. New York, Science House, 1968.

Frommer EA: Treatment of childhood with antidepressant drugs. Br Med J 1:729–732, 1967.

Frommer EA: Depressive illness in childhood, in Coppens A, Walk A (eds): Recent Developments in Affective Disorders. Ashford, Kent, Headley Bros, 1968, pp 117–136.

Frommer EA: Indications for antidepressant treatment with special reference to depressed preschool children, in Annell AL (ed): Depressive States in Childhood and Adolescence. Stockholm, Almquist & Wiskell, 1971.

Garfinkel BD, Froese AM, Hood J: Suicide attempts in children and adolescents. Am J Psychiatry 139:1257–1261, 1982.

Garfinkel BD, Golombek H: Suicidal behavior in adolescence, in Golombek H, Garfinkel BD (eds): The Adolescent and Mood Disturbance. New York, International University Press, 1983.

Geller B, Rogol AA, Knitter EF: Preliminary data on the dexamethasone suppression test in children with major depressive disorder. Am J Psychiatry 140:620–622, 1983.

Glaser K: Masked depression in children and adolescents. Am J Psychother 21:565–574, 1967.

Graham P: Depression in prepubertal children. Dev Med Child Neurol 136:1203–1205, 1974.

Hamilton M: A rating scale for depression. J Neurol Neurosurg Psychiatry 23:56–62, 1960.

Harlow HF, Harlow MIC: The affectional systems, in Schrier AM, Harlow HF, Stollnitz F (eds): Behavior of Nonhuman Primates. New York, Academic Press, 1965.

Hawton K, Crowle J, Simkin S, Bancroft J: Attempted suicide and suicide among Oxford University students. Br J Psychiatry 132:506–509, 1978.

Herjanic B, Herjanic M, Brown F, Wheatt T: Are children reliable reporters? J Assoc Child Psychol 3:41–48, 1975.

Herjanic B, Hudson R, Kotloff K: Does interviewing harm children? Res Commun Psychol Psychiatr Behav 1:523–531, 1976.

Herjanic B, Reich W: Development of a structured psychiatric interview for children: Agreement between child and parent on individual symptoms. J Abnorm Child Psychol 10:307–324, 1982.

Hershberg SG, Carlson GA, Cantwell DP, Strober M: Anxiety and depressive disorders in psychiatrically disturbed children. J Clin Psychiatry 43:358–361, 1982.

Holinger PC: Adolescent suicide: An epidemiologic study of recent trends. Am J Psychiatry 135:754–756, 1978.

Holinger PC, Offer D: Prediction of adolescent suicide: A population model. Am J Psychiatry 139:302–307, 1982.

Horowitz HA: Lithium and the treatment of adolescent manic-depressive illness. Dis Nerv Syst 38:480–483, 1977.

Jacobson S, Fasman J, DiMascio A: Deprivation in the childhood of depressed women. J Nerv Ment Dis 166:5–14, 1975.

Johnson GFS, Leeman MM: Ancestral secondary cases on paternal and maternal sides of bipolar affective illness. Br J Psychiatry 133:68–72, 1978.

Kashani JH, Hodges KK, Shekim WO: Hypomanic reaction to amitriptyline in a depressed child. Psychosomatics 21:867–872, 1980.

Kashani JH, Husain A, Shekim WO, et al: Current perspectives on childhood depression: An overview. Am J Psychiatry 135:143–153, 1981.

Kashani JH, McGee RO, Clarkson SE, Anderson JC, Walton LA, Williams S, Silva PA, Robins AJ, Cytryn L, McKnew DH: Depression in a sample of 9-year-old children. Arch Gen Psychiatry 40:1217–1223, 1983.

Kashani JH, Simonds JF: The incidence of depression in children. Am J Psychiatry 136:1203–1205, 1979.

Kazdin AE: Assessment techniques for childhood depression: A critical appraisal. J Am Acad Child Psychiatry 20:358–375, 1981.

Klee SH, Garfinkel BD: Identification of depression in children and adolescents: The role of the DST. J Am Acad Child Psychiatry 4:410–415, 1984.

Kovacs M, Beck AT: Maladaptive cognitive structures in depression. Am J Psychiatry 135:525–533, 1978.

Kovacs M: Interview Schedule for Children (ISC). Unpublished document. Pittsburgh, University of Pittsburgh, 1978.

Kovacs M: Rating scales to assess depression in school age children. Acta Paedopsychiatr 46:305–315, 1981.

Kovacs M, Beck AT: An empirical clinical approach toward a definition of childhood depression, in Schulterbrandt JG (ed): Depression in Childhood: Diagnosis, Treatment and Conceptual Models. New York, Raven Press, 1977, pp 1–25.

Kovacs M, Feinberg TL, Crouse-Novak MA, Paulavskas SL, Finkelstein R: Depressive disorders in childhood. Arch Gen Psychiatry 41:229–237, 1984.

Kuhn V, Kuhn R: Drug therapy for depression in children: Indications and methods, in Depressive States in Childhood and Adolescence, Proc. 4th U.E.P. Congress. Stockholm, Almquist & Wiskell, 1971, pp 455–459.

Kuhn V, Kuhn R: Drug therapy for depression in children. Indications and methods, in Annell AL (ed): Depressive States in Childhood and Adolescence. Stockholm, Almquist & Wiskell, 1972, pp 455–459.

Kupfer DJ, Cable P, Kane J, Petti T, Conners CK: Imipramine and EEG sleep in children with depressive symptoms. Psychopharmacology 60:117–123, 1979.

Kupferman S, Stewart MA: The diagnosis of depression in children. J Affect Disord 1:117–123, 1979.

Kuyler PL, Rosenthal L, Igel G, et al: Psychopathology among children of manic-depressive illness. Biol Psychiatry 15:589–597, 1980.

Lang M, Tisher M: Children's Depression Scale. Victoria, Australia, Australian Council for Educational Research, 1978.

Lefkowitz MM, Burton N: Childhood depression: A critique of the concept. Psychol Bull 85:716–726, 1978.

Lefkowitz M, Monroe M, Tesiny EP: Assessment of childhood depression. J Consult Clin Psychol 48:43–50, 1980.

Lefkowitz MM, Tesiny EP: Assessment of childhood depression. J Consult Clin Psychol 48:43–50, 1980.

Leon GR, Kendall PC, Garber J: Depression in children: Parent, teacher and child perspectives. J Abnorm Child Psychol. 8:221–235, 1980.

Lewinsohn PM: Depression: A social learning perspective. Paper presented at Western Psychiatric Institute and Clinic, Pittsburgh, 1979.

Lewinsohn PM, Hoberman H: Depression, in Bellack AS, Hersen M, Kazdin AE (eds): International Handbook of Behavior Modification and Therapy. New York, Plenum Press, 1982, pp 397–431.

Liberakis EA, Hoenig J: Recording of suicide in Newfoundland. Psychiatr J Univ Ottawa 3:254–259, 1978.

Ling W, Oftdahl G, Weinberg W: Depressive illness in childhood presenting as severe headache. Am J Dis Child 120:122–124, 1970.

Lowe TL, Cohen DJ: Mania in childhood and adolescence, in Belmaker RH, van Preag HM (eds): Mania—an Evolving Concept. New York, Spectrum Publications, 1980, pp 111–117.

Lucas AR, Lockett HJ, Grimm F: Amitriptyline in childhood depressions. Dis Nerv Syst 26:105–110, 1965.

Lukianowicz N: Attempted suicide in children. Acta Psychiatr Scand 44:415–435, 1968.

Malmquist C: Depression in childhood and adolescence. Pts I and II. N Engl J Med 284:887–955, 1971.

Mayo JA: Marital therapy with manic-depressive patients treated with lithium. Comp Psychiatry 20:419–426, 1979.

McConville BJ, Boag LC, Purohit AP: Three types of childhoood depression. Can J Psychiatry 18:133–138, 1973.

McKnew DH, Cytryn L: Urinary metabolites in chronically depressed children. J Am Acad Child Psychiatry 18:608–615, 1979.

Meltzer HY, Fang VS, Tricou BJ, et al: Effect of dexamethasone on plasma prolactin and cortisol levels in psychiatric patients. Am J Psychiatry 139:763–768, 1982.

Mendelson M: Psychoanalytic Concepts of Depression, ed 2. New York, Spectrum Publications, 1972.

Mintz RS: Prevalence of persons in the city of Los Angeles who have attempted suicide: A pilot study. Bull Suicidal 7:9–16, 1970.

Montgomery SA, Asberg M: A new depression scale disagreed to be sensitive to change. Br J Psychiatry 134:382–389, 1979.

Murphy GE: Problems in studying suicide. Psychiatr Dev 4:339–350, 1983.

Murphy GE, Robins E: Social factors in suicide. JAMA 199:303–308, 1967.

Nissen G: Symptomatik und prognose depressive vertimmungszwstande in Kindes und Jungendelter, in Arnell A (ed): Depressive States in Childhood and Adolescence. Stockholm, Almquist & Wiksell, 1971, pp 517–524.

Orvaschel H, Mednick S, Schulsinger F, Rock D: The children of psychiatrically disturbed parents: Differences as a function of the sex of the sick parent. Arch Gen Psychiatry 36:691–695, 1979.

Otto U: Suicide attempts made by children. Acta Psychiatr Scand 55:64–72, 1966.

Otto U: Suicidal attempts in childhood and adolescence—today and after 10 years. A follow-up study, in Annell AL (ed): Depressive States in Childhood and Adolescence. Stockholm, Almquist & Wiskell, 1971, pp 357–366.

Pallmeyer T, Petti TA: Effects of imipramine on aggression and dejection in depressed children. Am J Psychiatry 136:1472–1473, 1979.

Pearce J: Depressive disorder in childhood. J Child Psychol Psychiatry 18:79–82, 1977.

Perris C: The course of depressive psychoses. Acta Psychiatr Scand 44:238–248, 1968.

Perris C: Abnormality on paternal and maternal sides: Observations in bipolar (manic-depressive) and unipolar depressive psychoses. Br J Psychiatry 118:207–210, 1971.

Petti TA, Campbell M: Imipramine and seizures. Am J Psychiatry 132:538–540, 1975.

Petti TA, Bornstein M, Delameter A, Conners CK: Evaluation and multimodality treatment of a depressed prepubertal girl. J Am Acad Child Psychiatry 19:690–702, 1980.

Petti, TA, Conners CK: Changes in behavioral ratings of depressed children treated with imipramine. J Am Acad Child Psychiatry 22:355–360, 1983.

Petti TA, Unis A: Imipramine treatment of borderline children's case reports with a controlled study. Am J Psychiatry 134:516–518, 1981.

Polvan O, Cebiroglu R: Treatment with psychopharmacologic agents in childhood depressions, in Annell AL (ed): Depressive States in Childhood and Adolescence. Stockholm, Almquist & Wiskell, 1971.

Poznanski E, Krahenbuhl V, Zrull J: Childhood depression. J Am Acad Child Psychiatry 15:491–501, 1976.

Poznanski E, Zrull J: Childhood depression: Clinical characteristics of overtly depressed children. Arch Gen Psychiatry 23:8–15, 1970.

Poznanski EO, Carroll BJ, Banegar MC, Cook SC, Grossman JA: The dexamethasone suppression test in prepubertal depressed children. Am J Psychiatry 139:321–324, 1982.

Poznanski EO, Cook SC, Carroll BJ: A depression rating scale for children. Pediatrics 64:442–450, 1979.

Puig-Antich J, Blau S, Marx N: A pilot open trial of imipramine in prepubertal depressive illness (proceedings). Psychopharmacol Bull 14:40–42, 1978.

Puig-Antich J: Affective disorders in childhood: A review and perspective. Psychiatr Clin North Am 3:403–424, 1980.

Puig-Antich J: Major depression and conduct disorder in prepuberty. J Am Acad Child Psychiatry 21:118–123, 1982.

Puig-Antich J, Blau S, Marx N, et al: Prepubertal major depressive disorder: Pilot study. J Am Acad Child Psychiatry 17:695–707, 1978.

Puig-Antich J, Chambers W, Halpern F, Hanlon C, Sachar EJ: Cortisol hypersecretion in prepubertal depressive illness: A preliminary report. Psychoneuroendocrinology 4:191–197, 1979a.

Puig-Antich J, Gittleman R: Depression in childhood and adolescence, in Paykel ES (ed): Handbook of Affective Disorders. London, Churchill Livingstone, 1980.

Puig-Antich J, Novecenko H, Davies M, et al: Growth hormone secretion in prepubertal children with major depression. I. Final report on response to insulin-induced hypoglycemia during a depressive episode. Arch Gen Psychiatry 41:455–460, 1984.

Puig-Antich J, Perel JM, Lupatkin W, Chambers WJ, Shea C, Tabrizi MA, Stiller RL: Plasma levels of imipramine (IMI) and desmethylimipramine (DMI) and clinical response in prepubertal major depressive disorders. J Am Acad Child Psychiatry 18:616–627, 1979b.

Raskin A: Depression in children: Fact or fallacy, in Schulterbrandt JG, Raskin A (eds): Depression in Childhood: Diagnosis, Treatment, and Conceptual Models. New York, Raven Press, 1977, pp 141–146.

Reich W, Herjanic B, Welner Z, et al: Development of a structured interview for children: Agreement on diagnosis comparing child and parent interviews. J Abnorm Child Psychol 10:325–336, 1982.

Rie HE: Depression in childhood: A survey of some pertinent contributors. J Am Acad Child Psychiatry 5:653–685, 1966.

Robbins DR, Alessi NE, Yanchyshyn GW, Colfer MV: Preliminary report on the dexamethasone suppression test in adolescents. Am J Psychiatry 139:942–943, 1982.

Rochlin G: The loss complex. J Am Psychoanal Assoc 7:299–316, 1959.

Rook A: Student suicides. Br Med J 1:599–603, 1959.

Ross AO: Child behavior therapy: Principles, procedures, and empirical basis. New York, Wiley, 1981.

Rutter M, Tizard J, Whitmore K: Education, Health and Behavior. London, Longman, 1970.

Sanborn DE, Sanborn CJ, Cimbolie P: Two years of suicide: A study of adolescent suicide, in NH Child Psychiatry and Human Development, 1973, pp 234–242.

Sandler J, Joffe WG: Notes on childhood depression. Int J Psychoanal 46:88–96, 1965.

Schaffer D: Suicide in childhood and early adolescence. J Child Psychol Psychiatry 15:275–291, 1974.

Schneidman ES: Suicide among the gifted, in Schneidman ES (ed): Suicidology: Contemporary Developments. New York, Grune & Stratton, 1976.

Seligman M, Maier S: Failure to escape traumatic shock. J Exp Psychol 74:1–9, 1967.

Sovner R: The diagnosis and treatment of manic-depressive illness in childhood and adolescence. Psych Opinion 12:37–42, 1975.

Spitz RA: Anaclitic depression. Psychoanal Study Child 11:313–342, 1946.

Stack JJ: Chemotherapy in childhood depression, in Depressive States in Childhood and Adolescence. Proc.

4th U.E.P. Congress. Stockholm, Almquist & Wiksell, 1971, pp 460–466.

Stanley EJ, Barter JT: Adolescent suicidal behavior. Am J Orthopsychiatry 132:180–185, 1978.

Strain PS, Hill AD: Social interaction, in Wehrman P (ed): Recreation Programming for Developmentally Disabled Persons. Baltimore, University Park Press, 1979.

Strober M, Carlson GA: Bipolar illness in adolescents with major depression. Arch Gen Psychiatry 39:349–355, 1982.

Strober M, Green J, Carlson GA: Reliability of psychiatric diagnosis in adolescents: Interrater agreement using DSM-III. Arch Gen Psychiatry 38:141–145, 1981.

Strober M, Salkin B, Burroughs J, Morrell W: Validity of the bulimia-restricter distinction in anorexia nervosa: Parental personality characteristics and family psychiatric morbidity. J Nerv Ment Dis 170:345–351, 1982.

Thompson RJ, Schindler FH: Embryonic mania. Child Psychiatry Hum Dev 6:149–154, 1976.

Tsuang MT: Genetic counseling for psychiatric patients and their families. Am J Psychiatry 135:1465–1475, 1978.

Warneke L: A case of manic-depressive illness in childhood. Can Psychiatry Assoc J 20:195–200, 1975.

Weinberg S: Suicidal intent in adolescence: A hypothesis about the role of physical illness. J Pediatr 77:579–586, 1970.

Weinberg WA, Brumback RA: Mania in childhood. Am J Dis Child 130:380–385, 1976.

Weinberg WA, Rutman J, Sullivan L, et al: Depression in children referred to an educational diagnostic center: Diagnosis and treatment. J Pediatr 83:1065–1072, 1973.

Weininger O: Young children's concept of dying and dead. Psychol Rep 44:395–407, 1979.

Weissman MM: The epidemiology of suicide attempts, 1960–1971. Arch Gen Psychiatry 30:737–746, 1974.

Weller EB, Weller RA, Fristad M: Dexamethasone suppression test in prepubertal depressed children. Paper presented at the American Psychiatric Association Meeting, New York, May 1983.

Weller EB, Weller RA, Fristad MA, et al: Dexamethasone suppression test in prepubertal depressed children. Am J Psychiatry 141:290–291, 1984.

Weller EB, Welner A, McCrary H, et al: Psychopathology in children of inpatients with depression: A controlled study. J Nerv Ment Dis 164:408–413, 1977.

Weller EB, Weller RA, Preskorn SH, Glotzbach R: Steady state plasma imipramine levels in prepubertal depressed children. Am J Psychiatry 139:506–508, 1982.

Welner A, Welner A, McCray MD, et al: Psychopathology in children of inpatients with depression: A controlled study. J Nerv Ment Dis 164:408–413, 1977.

Wexler L, Weissman MM, Kasl SV: Suicide attempts 1970–1975: Updating a United States study and comparisons with international trends. Br J Psychiatry 132:180–185, 1978.

White JH, O'Shanick G: Juvenile manic-depressive illness. Am J Psychiatry 134:1035–1036, 1977.

Wirt RD, Lachar D, Klinedinst JK, Seat PD: Multidimensional Description of Child Personality Manual for the Personality Inventory for Children. Los Angeles, Western Psychological Services, 1977.

# chapter 20

# INFANTILE AUTISM AND SCHIZOPHRENIA IN CHILDHOOD

*by* Luke Y. Tsai, M.D.

## INFANTILE AUTISM

### Definition

The term autism was first used by Kanner in 1943 to describe a group of 11 children with a previously unrecognized syndrome. He noted a number of characteristic features in these children, such as an inability to develop relationships with people, extreme aloofness, a delay in speech development, noncommunicative use of speech after it develops, a lack of imagination, insistence on preserving sameness, and repeated simple patterns of play activity. He described these children as having "autistic disturbance of affective contact" (Kanner, 1943). In 1944, he adopted the term early infantile autism and called attention to the fact that its symptoms were already evident in infancy. During the next decade, clinicians in the United States and Europe reported cases with similar features (Despert, 1951; Van Krevelen, 1952; Bakwin, 1954). There was considerable controversy over the definition of the syndrome, however, because the name—autism—was ill-chosen. It led to confusion with Bleuler's (1911) use of the same term to describe schizophrenia in adults. This confusion led many clinicians to use childhood schizophrenia (Bender, 1956), autism, borderline psychosis (Ekstein and Wallerstein, 1954), and symbiotic psychosis (Mahler, 1952) as interchangeable diagnoses. Each label had its roots in a particular view of the nature and causation of autism.

In an attempt to clarify the confusion, Eisenberg and Kanner (1956) reduced the essential symptoms to just two: extreme self-isolation and preoccupation with the preservation of sameness. The peculiar abnormality of language was considered to be secondary to the disturbance of human relatedness, and hence not essential. They also expanded the age of onset to the first 2 years of life. Their efforts, however, were sometimes taken as a license to ignore age of onset as a necessary diagnostic criterion or to change the criteria altogether (Rutter, 1978). For example, disorders beginning in early infancy were grouped together with psychoses emerging in later childhood or adolescence (Vrono, 1974); Schain and Yannet (1960) omitted preservation of sameness from their criteria; Creak et al. (1961) used nine diagnostic points to encompass all forms of childhood psychoses, including Kanner's infantile autism, within a single diagnosis (schizophrenic syndrome of childhood); and Ornitz and Ritvo (1968) emphasized disturbances of perception as a primary symptom that was not included by Kanner. It was apparent that the confusion over the boundaries of infantile autism continued.

To clarify the diagnostic confusion, Rutter (1968) reviewed the literature and critically analyzed the existing empirical evidence. When this knowledge is summarized, four essential characteristics of autism stand out: (1) a lack of social interest and responsiveness; (2) impaired language, ranging from absence of speech to peculiar speech patterns; (3) bizarre motor behavior, ranging from rigid and limited play patterns to more complex ritualistic and compulsive behavior; and (4) early onset, before 30 months of age. These are the general characteristics on which there is the greatest consensus and that have enjoyed considerable popularity.

In 1978, the Professional Advisory Board of the National Society for Children and Adults with Autism (NSAC) further formulated a "Definition of the Syndrome of Autism" (Ritvo and Freeman, 1978). The NSAC scheme views autism as a behaviorally defined syndrome with essential features typically manifested before 30 months of age. The essential features are (a) disturbances of developmental rates and sequences; (b) disturbances of responses to sensory stimuli; (c) disturbances of speech, language, cognition, and nonverbal communication; and (d) disturbances of the capacity to relate appropriately to people, events, and objects. This definition obviously is based on work by Kanner, Rutter, and, particularly, Ornitz and Ritvo. Nonetheless, the NSAC scheme, as well as the definitions of Kanner (1943) and Rutter (1968), paved the way for two sets of criteria that are now being used widely by clinicians all over the world: the International Classification of Disease, 9th revision, Clinical Modification (ICD-9-CM) (USDHHS, 1980) and the *Diagnostic and Statistical Manual of Mental Disorders*, third edition (DSM-III) (APA, 1980).

Although the ICD-9-CM and the DSM-III have a similar definition of infantile autism, there are apparent differences in the two concepts of autism. In ICD-9-CM, infantile autism is classified as a subtype of the "psychoses with origin specific to childhood,"

whereas the DSM-III system views autism as a developmental disorder and has classified it as a subtype of the "pervasive developmental disorders." I and many other workers adopt the definition and diagnostic criteria set out by the DSM-III for several reasons. First, there is now strong evidence that children with a disorder as described by Kanner bear little relationship to the psychotic disorders of adult life. Second, it is now clear that the core clinical disturbance of this disorder affects many basic areas of psychosocial development at the same time. Third, only the DSM-III system provides a set of necessary, sufficient, and supposedly operational diagnostic criteria.

The DSM-III defines the essential features of infantile autism as "a lack of responsiveness to other people (autism), gross impairment in communicative skills, and bizarre responses to various aspects of the environment, all developing within the first 30 months of age" (APA, 1980, p. 87). The following are the DSM-III criteria for infantile autism (APA, 1980, pp. 89–90):

A. **Onset before 30 months of age**
B. **Pervasive lack of responsiveness to other people (autism)**
C. **Gross deficits in language development**
D. **If speech is present, peculiar speech patterns, such as immediate and delayed echolalia, metaphorical language, pronominal reversal**
E. **Bizarre responses to various aspects of the environment, e.g., resistance to change, peculiar interest in or attachments to animate or inanimate objects**
F. **Absence of delusions, hallucinations, loosening of associations, and incoherence as in schizophrenia**

These appear to be taken largely from Rutter's study (1968), which found these criteria to be present in all or nearly all autistic children. Many additional specific features have not been included in the diagnostic criteria simply because they are unevenly distributed. At the present time, the DSM-III definition and diagnostic criteria for infantile autism must be seen as "arbitrary conventions, limited by current knowledge, and arrived at by many compromises" (Fish and Ritvo, 1979, p. 262). They will not satisfy everyone, and no doubt they will be revised when it is known which symptoms in autism are primary and which are secondary, or when the causal mechanisms are clearly understood.

# Etiology

## Organic Factors

### Genetic Factors

Some genetic syndromes have been associated with some cases of autism. In a study of 64 patients with a diagnosis of autism, 14 were found to have phenylketonuria (Knoblock and Pasamanick, 1975). Autism has also been reported sporadically in association with fragile X syndrome (Brown et al., 1982; Levitas et al., 1983). Several studies have shown that about 2 per cent of the siblings of autistic children suffer from the same condition (Rutter, 1967; Tsai, Stewart, August, 1981; Minton, Campbell, Green, Jennings, Samit, 1982). When this estimated sibling incidence is compared with the general population risk of 4.5 per 10,000 (Lotter, 1966), the rate of autism in siblings is 50 times higher. Folstein and Rutter (1977) studied 21 same-sex autistic twin pairs and found that 4 of the 11 (36 per cent) monozygotic twin pairs were concordant for autism, as compared with none of 10 dizygotic twins. Discordance was usually associated with definite or suggestive evidence of organic brain dysfunction in the affected twin. They suggested that autism may arise on the basis of a combination of genetic predisposition and biologic impairment. This view is in accordance with Spence's (1976) suggestion that the nature of the causal mechanism of autism would most likely involve a complex genetic mechanism, such as polygenic or multifactorial inheritance. Recently, Ritvo (1983) reported that there are 281 families enrolled in the UCLA Registry for Genetic Studies in Autism. They include (by parental report) 22 sets of monozygotic twins, all concordant for autism; 18 sets of dizygotic twins, 2 sets of whom are concordant for autism; 46 sets of non-twin siblings concordant for autism; 6 families with three autistic siblings; 20 families with autistic cousins; five parents who have an autistic brother. Based on his preliminary findings, Ritvo suggests that a subgroup of autistics may develop this syndrome by way of a recessive gene transmission. Ritvo's suggestion, however, is based on a highly selected group of autistic patients and their family members. Nonetheless, there is reasonable evidence for speculating that in a subgroup of autistic individuals, genetic factors may play a contributory role.

### Neurologic and Congenital Factors

Results of studies show that many autistic children suffer from organic brain disorders, ranging from 30 per cent to 100 per cent, depending on whether the children were selected from psychiatric or pediatric-neurologic cohorts (Fish and Ritvo, 1979). A wide variety of neurologic disorders have been reported: cerebral palsy, congenital rubella, toxoplasmosis, tuberous sclerosis, cytomegalovirus infection, lead encephalopathy, meningitis, encephalitis, severe brain hemorrhage, many types of epilepsy, and others. Because many of these neurologic or congenital disorders derived from unfavorable prenatal, perinatal, and neonatal complications, several studies have examined the obstetric histories of autistic children. Certain prenatal and perinatal complications, such as breech delivery, the presence of amniotic meconium, low birth weight, and elevated serum bilirubin, are more common in autistic children as compared with controls (Lotter, 1967; Finegan and Quarrington, 1979; Gillberg and Gillberg, 1983). Because of the lack of uniformity in both the diagnostic criteria for autism and in the selection of obstetric complications, these findings should be received with caution. Werry (1979), in a review of this subject, suggested that "autism is, in some cases, one of the possible expressions of severe congenital or perinatal brain damage" (p. 59).

Neurologic abnormalities, such as hypotonia or hypertonia, disturbance of body schema, clumsiness, choreiform movements, pathologic reflexes, myoclonic jerking, drooling, abnormal posture and gait, dystonic posturing of hands and fingers, tremor, ankle clonus, emotional facial paralysis, and strabismus, have been reported in 30 per cent to 75 per cent of several series of autistic patients (Gittelman and Birch, 1967; DeMyer et al., 1973; Tsai et al., 1981). These are all signs of dysfunction in the basal ganglia, particularly the neostriatum, and closely related structures of the mesial aspect of the frontal lobe or limbic system (Schwab and England, 1968; Damasio and Maurer, 1978). Based on the analogy to signs and conditions seen in adults with certain forms of brain damage, Damasio and Maurer (1978) proposed that autism results from dysfunction in a system of bilateral central nervous system structures that include the ring of mesolimbic cortex located in the mesial frontal and temporal lobes, the neostriatum, and the anterior and medial nuclear groups of the thalamus. They suggested that such dysfunction might involve macroscopic or microscopic cerebral changes consequent to a variety of causes, such as perinatal viral infection, insult to the periventricular watershed area, or genetically determined neurochemical abnormalities. This hypothesis is plausible, but it needs to be verified.

### Neuroanatomical Factors

Little neuropathologic information has been reported on autistic individuals. Systematic autopsy studies of neuropathology are lacking because autistics appear to have normal longevity. The few isolated autopsy reports published to date are inconclusive (Ritvo, 1983). Hauser, DeLong, and Rosman (1975), using pneumoencephalography, demonstrated a regional enlargement of the left temporal horn of the lateral ventricle in 15 out of 18 highly selected autistic children. Recently, several computed tomographic (CT) scan studies have demonstrated evidence of ventricular enlargement and cerebral atrophy in otherwise clinically indistinguishable subgroups of autistic children (Damasio, Maurer, Damasio, Chu, 1980; Caparulo et al., 1981; Campbell et al., 1982; Gillberg and Svendsen, 1983; Rosenbloom et al., 1984). These findings appear to be nonspecific as to their cause and relationship to autistic symptomatology. In another study, Hier, LeMay, and Rosenberger (1979) reported a reverse pattern of hemispheric asymmetry of the parieto-occipital region in CT scans of some autistic children, but subsequent studies have not been able to confirm the finding (Damasio et al., 1980; Caparulo et al., 1981; Tsai, Jacoby, Stewart, Beisler, 1982a). The newer imaging neuroradiologic technique nuclear magnetic resonance (NMR) may provide superior anatomical diagnosis, superior in resolution to that of the CT scan. It is expected that the use of NMR will significantly improve the anatomical investigation of autism. The availability data to date suggest that an analysis of a reasonably large sample of autistic children may reveal subgroups with various combinations of structural features.

### Neurophysiologic Factors

Electroencephalographic (EEG) studies of autistic children suggest that a significant proportion (usually about 50 per cent) have EEG abnormalities (DeMyer et al., 1973; Small, 1975; Waldo et al., 1978; Tsai and Tsai, 1984), although a minority have reported a lower incidence of EEG abnormalities (Ritvo, Ornitz, Walter, Hanley, 1970; Kolvin et al., 1971). In general, these abnormalities tend to involve bilateral brain hemispheres (Tsai and Tsai, 1984) and are characterized by focal or diffused spike, slow wave, or slow dysrhythmic patterns. The type of abnormality does not seem to be specific. Two studies (Hutt, Hutt, Lee, Ounsted, 1965; Kolvin et al., 1971) reported unusually low-voltage EEGs, interpreted as suggestive of chronic hyperarousal. The finding was not confirmed in two other studies (Hermelin and O'Conner, 1968; Creak and Pampiglione, 1969) when stimulus conditions were monitored.

The sleep EEG studies in autistic children (Ornitz, 1965; Tanguay, Ornitz, Forsythe, Ritvo, 1976) have found that the eye movements of autistics were more like those of normal infants than like those of age-matched controls, a finding suggestive of immaturity. Maturational deviation has also been indicated in several auditory evoked-response (AER) studies of autistic children (Student and Sohmer, 1978; Skoff, Mirsky, Turner, 1980; Fein, Skoff, Mirsky, 1981; Tanguay, Edwards, Buchwald, Schwafel, Allen, 1982; Gillberg, Rosenhall, Johansson, 1983). These studies begin to suggest maturational deviation in a subgroup of autistics as compared with normal children.

Lelord, Laffont, Jusseaume, and Stephant (1973) coupled sound and light inputs to measure the coupling effects on the AER in both autistic and normal children. They noted that the AER was stable and regular in normals but irregular and variable in autistic subjects, that the amplitude of the AER was smaller in the autistics than in the normals, and that the normals, but not the autistics, showed an increase in amplitude and a diminution in variability of the AER. They suggested that these findings may indicate a defective integration between the visual and auditory pathways in autistic children.

It appears that definitely different AER patterns are being observed in a subgroup of autistic children; however, the correlation between AER results and clinical symptoms has not yet been consistently established.

A number of studies have attempted to explore the etiologic role of the vestibular system in autistic children because the vestibular system is believed to be intimately involved with self-monitoring functions. Ritvo et al. (1969) noted a decrease in duration of nystagmus after vestibular stimulation by rotation or by caloric irrigation in autistic children, as compared with the controls. Ornitz, Brown, Mason, and Putnam (1974) demonstrated that this finding is not dependent on visual fixation, but rather reflects a pathophysiologic interaction of the visual and vestibular systems. These findings appear to indicate physiologic disturbance, possibly involving the central connections of the vestibular system in some autistic children.

Disturbances in autonomic function have been observed in some autistic children. Hutt, Forrest, and Richer (1975) noted significantly more arrhythmia in autistics than in normals when the children's heart rates were recorded in a variety of situations. Bernal and Miller (1970) noted an inadequate galvanic skin response to both auditory and visual stimuli in some autistic children. At the moment, the etiologic role of the autonomic system in autism is unclear.

### Biochemical Factors

Recent biochemical studies in autism have centered on indoleamines (serotonin), catecholamines, enzymes, and other biomedical measures. One well-established finding is that approximately one third of autistic subjects have a hyperserotonemia (reviewed by Young, Kavanagh, Anderson, Shaywitz, Cohen, 1982). Campbell et al. (1975) had demonstrated that the blood serotonin levels were significantly higher in autistic children who remained ill as compared with those of the autistic children who were in remission or partial remission. Whether this relationship reflects a primary disturbance in brain serotonin metabolism or a secondary response to behavioral consequences of autism is not clear. Furthermore, these findings are also commonly noted in children with other types of childhood psychiatric disorders.

Cohen, Caparulo, Shaywitz, and Bowers (1977) reported that autistic children did not differ from other diagnostic groups in cerebrospinal fluid (CSF) levels of homovanillic acid (HVA, the principal dopamine metabolite). However, the more severely impaired autistic children, especially those with greater locomotor activity and severer stereotypies, tended to have higher CSF HVA levels. Campbell (1977) reported that neuroleptics, dopamine receptor-blocking agents, modulated several systems involving the motor system (e.g., hyperactivity, stereotypies, aggression, and self-injury) and made autistic children more compliant and receptive to special education procedures. On the other hand, dopamine agonists, such as stimulants, cause a worsening of preexisting stereotypies, aggression, and hyperactivity in autistic children (Young et al., 1982). It appears that the dopaminergic system may be a potentially high-yield research area.

Lake, Ziegler, and Murphy (1977) reported an elevated plasma norepinephrine (NE) level in autistic children. Young et al. (1981), however, found a normal range of CSF and plasma 3-methoxy-4-hydroxyphenylglycol (MHPG, the principal brain metabolite of NE) in autistic patients. On the other hand, Young, Cohen, Caparulo, Brown, and Maas (1979) also found that the urinary free catecholamines and MHPG were decreased in five autistic boys, as compared with nine normal boys, a finding that suggests a reduction in noradrenergic activity in autistic children. As it is believed that the catecholamine and indoleamine systems may be in dynamic balance and that disturbances in one or both systems may well be involved in adult schizophrenia, it is well worth pursuing the studies of catecholamine in autism.

### Other Biomedical Factors

A number of other abnormal biomedical measures in autistics have been reported. In one study, Sankar (1971) reported significantly lower blood adenosine triphosphatase activity in assays of red blood cells from autistic children. In another study, Katz and Liebman (1970) found an elevated CSF creatine phosphokinase (CPK) activity in some autistic children, as well as in children with a meningitis, a finding suggesting that autistic children with an increased CSF CPK activity may represent a subgroup of children whose autism is due to brain insult from infection (Piggott, 1979). Immunologic studies suggest that there may be an immunologic system deficiency in some autistic children (review by Piggott, 1979). On the whole, the significance of these findings is far from clear, but these studies merit further exploration.

### Psychogenic Factors

Kanner's (1943) original descriptions of autism, as well as a number of subsequent reports by other workers, had suggested that parents of autistic children were highly intelligent, were preoccupied with abstractions, had limited interest in people, and were emotionally cold. Some studies reported findings of disturbances in family dynamics (Reiser, 1963, I and II), unconscious parental hostility and rejection (Bettelheim, 1967), parental perplexity (Meyers and Goldfarb, 1961), and lack of parent–child communicative clarity (Goldfarb, Levy, Meyers, 1972). These investigators had suggested that autism might be a response to these parental personality characteristics, to deviant parent–child interactions, or to severe early stress of various kinds. However, findings that support these psychogenic hypotheses have come from samples that did not make any distinction between autism and schizophrenia in childhood, from projective tests, and from selected family observations. Similar techniques and other well-controlled studies have produced largely negative findings (Ornitz and Ritvo, 1976).

A number of studies had suggested that autistic children tended to come from upper socioeconomic families (reviewed by Tsai,

Stewart, Faust, Shook, 1982b). The finding has not been confirmed by other investigators (see Table 20–1). Furthermore, several recent studies have shown that selection bias accounts largely for the previous notion of social class bias in autism (Schopler, Andrews, Strupp, 1979; Wing, 1980; Tsai et al., 1982b). Thus there are good grounds for concluding that no psychological or social factors can cause infantile autism.

### Summary of Etiology

So far, no specific cause or causes have been identified. This may be due to the possibility that infantile autism is a behavioral syndrome that may include several different but distinct conditions. If this is the case, it is anticipated that future studies will determine a range of biologic etiologies for the subgroups making up the autistic syndrome.

## Epidemiology

The first detailed epidemiologic study of infantile autism was conducted by Lotter (1966), who investigated all the 78,000 children, 8 to 10 years of age, in Middlesex County, England. All children were screened by means of a questionnaire completed by teachers or other relevant professional staff. Lotter found 15 children who were definitely autistic and 17 who were probably autistic. Hence the prevalence of autism was 2.0 or 4.5 per 10,000 children in this age range, depending on how rigorous are the diagnostic criteria that one chooses.

Brask (1970) carried out a survey in Aarhus County, Denmark. She examined the case notes of all children aged 2 to 14 years

**TABLE 20–1** Social Class Distribution in Studies of Autistic Children

| Author | No. of Subjects | Social Class (%) | | |
| --- | --- | --- | --- | --- |
| | | I & II | III | IV & V |
| Kanner (1943) | 11 | 91 | 9 | 0 |
| Creak & Ini (1960) | 102 | 59 | 31 | 9 |
| Lotter (1967) | 32 | 44 | 41 | 13 |
| Rutter & Lockyer (1967) | 63 | 56 | 41 | 3 |
| Ritvo et al. (1971) | 74 | 36 | 15 | 49 |
| Campbell et al. (1978a) | 99 | 31 | 13 | 56 |
| Schopler et al. (1979) | 264 | 22 | 17 | 61 |
| Tsai et al. (1982b) | 102 | 21 | 18 | 61 |

I & II, upper class; III, middle class; IV & V, lower class.

who were in psychiatric hospitals, mental retardation services, and pediatric wards. She screened approximately 1500 children out of a total population of approximately 46,000 in the chosen age range. She found the age-specific prevalence of autism to be 4.3 per 10,000.

Treffert (1970) surveyed 280 children aged 3 to 11 who had been given a diagnosis of "childhood schizophrenia" by the special services in the state of Wisconsin. Treffert found 69 cases who fit the definition of classic early infantile autism (Group A) and 158 cases who fit into Group B, that is, children who had some features of classic infantile autism and had an onset later in childhood. Thus the age-specific prevalence for Group A was 0.8; for Group B, 1.7; for Group A and B combined, 2.5 per 10,000.

Wing, Yeates, Brierley, and Gould (1976), using case-note inspection and interview, surveyed 854 children aged 5 to 14 in Camberwell, England. The children were identified by referring to records of both the education authority and individual agencies concerned. Wing and her associates identified five children with the "nuclear autistic syndrome (Group A)" and seven children with the "non-nuclear autistic syndrome (Group B)." Thus the age-specific prevalence for Group A was 2.0; for Group B, 2.8; for Group A and B combined, 4.8 per 10,000.

Several Japanese studies concerning the epidemiology of infantile autism have been conducted. The studies have reported that the prevalence ranges from 0.9 to 5.6 per 10,000 children (reviewed by Hoshino, Kumashiro, Yshima, Tachibana, Watanake, 1982).

In a total population study concerning autism and other childhood psychoses in the region of Gothenburg, Sweden, Gillberg (1984) found that an estimated 2 children in every 10,000 born in the years 1961 through 1976 fulfilled Rutter's (1978) diagnostic criteria for infantile autism.

The prevalence of infantile autism in these reports have not concurred because of differences in the diagnostic criteria and epidemiologic techniques. Surveys that counted diagnosed cases only or that relied on local authority records tended to produce much lower prevalence rates for autism than the studies in which a total population of children was screened. At the moment, the DSM-III suggests a prevalence of two to four cases per 10,000.

It is not clear whether prevalence rates of autism in cities differ from those in rural districts. Treffert (1970) reported that there was no statistically significant difference between the rural and urban prevalence rates. Hoshino et al. (1982), however, reported the prevalence rates of the cities were significantly higher than those of the rural districts. Further studies should be pursued to delineate the relationship between autism and geographical factors.

All studies of infantile autism have shown a predominance of boys over girls. Ratios from three to four boys to one girl have consistently been reported (see Table 20–2). In addition, several recent studies have found that autistic girls tend to suffer a greater degree of morbidity; that is, a greater proportion of the autistic females are more often severely impaired than are autistic males (Lotter, 1974; Tsai et al., 1981; Wing, 1981; Lord, Schopler, Revick; 1982). The findings indicate that there are significant sex differences in the occurrence and severity of autism.

TABLE 20–2   Sex Ratio of Autism

| Author | No. of Autistic Children | | | Male/Female Ratio |
|---|---|---|---|---|
| | Total | Male | Female | |
| Lotter (1966) | 32 | 23 | 9 | 2.6:1 |
| Rutter and Lockyer (1967) | 63 | 51 | 12 | 4.3:1 |
| Ritvo et al. (1971) | 74 | 76* | 24* | 3.2:1 |
| DeMyer et al. (1973) | 120 | 85 | 35 | 2.4:1 |
| Campbell et al. (1978a) | 105 | 80 | 25 | 3.2:1 |
| Schopler et al. (1979) | 264 | 201 | 63 | 3.2:1 |
| Tsai et al. (1981) | 102 | 78 | 24 | 3.3:1 |

* Percentage.

## Clinical Features

### Age at Onset

The syndrome originally described by Kanner (1943) began shortly after birth. Subsequent observations by other workers, however, have found that in perhaps one third of the autistic children, parents reported a clinical picture indistinguishable from Kanner's original autism, which arose after a period of apparently normal development (up to 2 years of age). Whether early development in these children had been truly normal in all aspects is hard to decide. Some subtle signs might indeed occur during the first 2 years of life, but these may be forgotten, overlooked, or denied because of parental memory difficulty, anxiety, or lack of knowledge of normal child development.

A few investigators have reported the onset of typically autistic behavior beginning in the 3rd to 5th year of life. In Rutter and Lockyer's (1967) series of 63 autistic children, four had an onset between the ages of 3 and $5\frac{1}{2}$ years. Lotter (1966) found similar histories among the autistic children identified in his survey: 3 out of 32 children with a "setback in development" occurred between 3 and $4\frac{1}{2}$ years. Little is known about these cases in terms of etiology and outcome. Until researchers begin to show evidence that clearly distinguishes autism beginning before 30 months of age from autism beginning after 30 months of age, the diagnosis of infantile autism should be made solely on clinical grounds.

### Pervasive Lack of Responsiveness to Other People

In infancy, autistic babies tend to avoid eye contact and demonstrate little conventional interest in the human voice. They do not assume an anticipatory posture or put up their arms to be picked up in the way that normal children do. They are indifferent to affection and seldom show facial responsiveness. As a result, parents often suspect that the child is deaf. In the more intelligent autistics, lack of social responsiveness may not be obvious until well into the 2nd year of life.

In early childhood, autistic children continue to show deviation in eye contact, but they may enjoy a tickle or may passively accept physical contact, such as lap sitting. They do not develop attachment behavior and there is a relative failure to bond. They generally do not follow their parents about the house. The majority of them do not show normal separation or stranger anxiety. Adults usually are treated as interchangeable, so that they may approach a stranger almost as readily as they do their parents. There is a lack of interest in being with or playing with other children, or they may even actively avoid other children.

In middle childhood, greater awareness of the attachment to parents and other familiar adults may develop. However, serious social difficulties continue. They show a disinterest in playing group games, and there is an inability to form peer relationships. Some of the least handicapped may become passively involved in other children's games or physical play. This apparent sociability is superficial.

As autistic children grow older, they may become affectionate and friendly with their parents and siblings. They seldom initiate social contacts, however, and show an apparent lack of positive interest in people. Some of the less severely impaired autistics may have a desire for friendships. But a lack of response to other people's interests and emotions, as well as a lack of appreciation of humor, often results in the autistic youngster's saying or doing socially inappropriate things that usually prevent the development of friendships.

### Problem of Communication

#### Impairment in Nonverbal Communication

Autistic infants show their needs through crying and screaming. In early childhood, they may develop the concrete gesture of pulling adults by the hand to the object that is wanted. This is often done without a socially appropriate facial expression. Nodding and shaking of the head are seldom seen either as a substitute for or as an accompaniment of speech. They usually use toys for sensory stimuli rather than for their proper purpose or for imaginative play. They generally do not participate in imitative games. They are less likely than other, normal children to copy or follow their parents' activity.

In middle and late childhood, they use gestures infrequently, even when they understand other people's gestures fairly well. Wing (1971) found that the frequency of using gestures changed little with increasing age, although comprehension of gestures tended to improve. A small number of autistic children do develop the stage of imitative play, but this tends to be stereotyped and repetitive actions of their own experience.

Generally speaking, autistic children are able to show their emotions of joy, fear, or anger, but they tend to show only the extreme of emotions. Facial expressions that ordinarily reinforce meaning are usually absent. Some autistics appear wooden and expressionless much of the time.

### Impairment of the Understanding of Speech

Comprehension of speech is impaired to a varying degree. Severely retarded autistics may never develop any awareness of the meaning of speech. Children who are less severely impaired may follow simple instructions if given in an immediate present context or with the aid of gestures. When impairment is mild, only the comprehension of subtle or abstract meanings may be affected. Humor and idiomatic expressions can be confusing for even the brightest autistic person.

### Impairment in Speech Development

The majority of autistics have an impaired amount or pattern of babble in their 1st year. Nearly half of Kanner's subjects (Eisenberg and Kanner, 1956) were still mute by age 5 (and remained so). About half of autistics remain mute all their lives (Ricks and Wing, 1976). When speech has developed, it usually exhibits many abnormalities. Meaningless, immediate echolalia and delayed repetition of stereotyped phrases may be the only kind of speech that is acquired in some autistics. Other autistics may develop appropriate use of phrases copied from others. This is often accompanied by pronoun reversal in the early stages of language development. When echolalia is extreme, distorted syntax and fragmented speech patterns result.

Often the mechanical production of speech is impaired. The speech may be like that of a robot, characterized by a monotonous, flat delivery with little lability, change of emphasis, or emotional expression. Problems of pronunciation are common in young autistics, but these tend to diminish with increasing age. There may be a marked contrast between clearly enunciated echolalic speech and poorly pronounced spontaneous speech. There may be chanting or singsong speech, with odd prolongation of sounds, syllables, and words. A question-like intonation may be used for propositional statements. Odd respiratory rhythms may produce staccato speech in some autistics.

Immature and abnormal grammatical constructions are often in autistics' spontaneous speech. Words and phrases may be used idiosyncratically, or phrases may be telegraphic and distorted. Words of similar sound or related meaning may be muddled. They may label objects by their use or else coin words of their own. Prepositions, conjunctions, and pronouns often are dropped from phrases or used incorrectly.

When functional speech develops, it tends not to be used in the usual way for social communication. Usually autistics rely on stereotyped phrases and repetition when they talk. Their speech almost always fails to convey subtle emotion. They are generally poor in talking about anything outside the immediate situation. They tend to talk excessively about their special interests, and the same pieces of information tend to recur whenever the same subject is raised. The most advanced autistics may be able to exchange concrete pieces of information that interest them, but once the conversation departs from this level, they become lost and may withdraw from social contact. In general, the ordinary to-and-fro chatter of a reciprocal interaction is lacking. Thus they give the impression of talking "to" someone rather than "with" someone.

## Bizarre Responses to the Environment

Autistic children's bizarre responses to the environment may take several forms. All of the items of behavior mentioned in this section are common in autistics, but a single child seldom shows all the features at one time.

### Resistance to Change

Autistic children are disturbed by some changes in the familiar environment, and catastrophic reactions may follow even a minor change of everyday routine. The behavior is twice as common in retarded autistics as in autistics with normal intelligence (Bartak and Rutter, 1976). Almost all autistic children show a resistance to learning or practicing a new activity.

### Ritualistic or Compulsive Behaviors

In childhood, ritualistic or compulsive behaviors usually involve rigid routines or stereotyped, repetitive motor acts, such as hand clapping or finger mannerisms (twisting, flicking movements carried out near the face). In adolescence, some of these behaviors may develop into obsessional symptoms, with compulsive touching and the like. Ritualistic or compulsive behaviors are more often displayed by normally intelligent autistics than by retarded autistics (Bartak and Rutter, 1976).

### Abnormal Attachments

Many autistics develop intense attachments to odd objects, such as a pipe cleaner or a little rock. The child will carry the object at all times and protest or throw tantrums if it is removed. However, if the object is not eventually returned to the child, he or she frequently becomes attached to a new object.

### Fascination with Sensory Experiences

There may be a fascination with lights, patterns, sounds, spinning objects, and tactile sensations. Objects often are manipulated without regard for their usual functions. Thus young autistics may perseveratively line up, stack, or twirl objects. There may be a perseverative preoccupation with certain features of objects, such as their texture, taste, smell, color, or shape. Older autistic children with functional speech may be absorbed in certain topics, such as sports or television programs. They ask stereotyped and repeated questions on these subjects, to which specific answers must be given.

### Abnormal Responses to Sensory Experiences

There is often either an underresponsiveness or an overresponsiveness to sensory stimuli, such as sound, light, pain, temperature, tactile, taste, and smell. Thus they may be suspected of being deaf, short-sighted, or blind. An autistic child may ac-

tively avoid gentle physical contact, but the same child may react with intense pleasure to rough games of tickling, being swung around, and bouncing up and down. Some autistic children may follow extreme food fads.

### Disturbance of Motility

The typical motor milestones may be delayed but are often within normal range. Young autistic children usually have difficulties with motor imitation, especially when they have to learn by watching and the movements have to be reversed in direction. Many young autistic children are markedly overactive but tend to become underactive in adolescence.

The autistic child often displays grimacing, hand flapping or twisting, toe walking, body rocking and swaying, and head rolling or banging. These movements do not appear to be involuntary. In some cases they may appear intermittently, whereas in other cases they are continuously present. They are usually interrupted by episodes of immobility and odd posturing with head bowed, arms flexed at the elbow, and hands drooping at the wrist. These movements are often exacerbated by excitement or during absorption in some sensory experience, such as watching a spinning toy.

### Intelligence and Cognitive Deficits

Autistic children are seen to be mostly retarded (review by Rutter, 1978). About 40 per cent to 60 per cent of autistic children have an IQ below 50; only 20 per cent to 30 per cent have an IQ of 70 or more (see Table 20–3). Because a significant number of autistic children in every series were either without functional speech or untestable, the validity of testing intelligence in autistic children is questionable. Several observations argue against the notion that autism masks the intellectual potential of autistic children. First, Hingtgen and Churchill (1971) showed that low IQ scores are not a function of poor motivation because even when motivation was greatly increased through operant techniques, intellectual performance still remained well below normal. Second, both short-term (Alpern and Kimberlin, 1970) and long-term studies (Lockyer and Rutter, 1969) have shown that autistic children who failed to score on IQ tests do so because they are severely retarded, not because of an un-

**Table 20–3  IQ Distributions in Studies of Autistic Children**

| | IQ Distribution (%) | | |
| --- | --- | --- | --- |
| | 50 or Below | 51–70 | Over 70 |
| Ritvo and Freeman (1978) | 60 | 20 | 20 |
| Tsai (1983) | 54 | 24 | 22 |
| Rutter and Lockyer (1967) | 43 | 29 | 29 |
| APA | 40 | 30 | 30 |

APA, American Psychiatric Association.

willingness to attempt the tasks. Third, a number of autistics had major improvements in autism during the followup period, but there was no change in IQ (Lockyer and Rutter, 1969). Fourth, followup studies have shown that retardation present at the time of initial diagnosis tends to persist (reviewed by Werry, 1979).

Although both low-IQ and high-IQ autistic children are similar in terms of the main symptomatologies associated with autism, the low-IQ autistics show a more severely impaired social development and are more likely to display deviant social responses, such as touching or smelling people, stereotypies, and self-injury (Bartak and Rutter, 1976). A third of mentally retarded autistic youngsters develop a seizure disorder; this condition is less prevalent in those of normal intelligence (Rutter, 1978). The prognosis is both worse and different for low-IQ autistics (Rutter, 1970). As the difference in outcome according to IQ is so marked, it is essential to obtain an accurate assessment of intelligence during the initial evaluation of every autistic child.

Earlier studies (Eisenberg and Kanner, 1956; Creak et al., 1961) suggested that the retardation accompanying autism is differentiated from general retardation by islets of normal or near-normal intellectual function, revealed particularly on performance tests or in special abilities of the idiot savant kind. Rutter and Lockyer (1967) noted that, in contrast to a clinic control group matched for IQ, autistic children were generally superior on the subtests requiring manipulative or visuospatial skills or immediate memory, while they did poorly on tasks demanding symbolic or abstract thought and sequential logic. Other studies have shown that cognition in autistic children is impaired, most particularly in capacity for imitation, comprehension of spoken words and gestures, flexibility, inventiveness, rule

formation and application, and information utilization. The impairment is both severer and more extensive than in nonautistic children of comparable IQ (reviewed by Werry, 1979). On the other hand, mentally retarded autistic children tend to have a wider cognitive deficit that involves general difficulties in sequencing and feature extraction, whereas in the normally intelligent autistic children, the deficits mainly affect verbal and coding skills (Rutter, 1977).

### Other Associated Features

The mood of autistic children often is labile; crying or screaming may be unexplained or inconsolable; laughing and giggling may occur for no obvious reason. Real dangers, such as moving vehicles or heights, may not be appreciated by a young autistic child, but the same child may be terrified of harmless objects or situations, such as a stuffed animal or visiting a relative's house. Peculiar habits, such as hair pulling or biting parts of the body, are sometimes present, particularly in mentally retarded autistic children. Lack of dizziness after spinning has often been observed, and some autistic children love to spin themselves for long periods.

### Clinical Course and Prognosis

The general picture is of a disorder with a chronic course. Although social, conceptual, linguistic, and obsessive difficulties frequently persist, they do so in forms that are rather different from those shown in early years. One well-established finding is that autistic children almost never develop a thought disorder with delusions and hallucinations, as one sees in psychotic adults. Only a few well-diagnosed autistic children have been reported to develop schizophrenia during followup periods (Dahl, 1976;

Petty, Ornitz, Michelman, Zimmerman, 1984). However, a recent study (Howells and Guirguis, 1984) has demonstrated that whether an autistic child develops schizophrenia in adulthood may depend on which set of diagnostic criteria is used.

A small number of autistic children (7 out of 64 cases) in Rutter and Lockyer's (1967) study showed a progressive deterioration in adolescence, characterized by a general intellectual decline. Between 7 per cent and 28 per cent of autistic children who had shown no clinical evidence of neurologic disorder in early childhood developed seizures for the first time in adolescence or early adult life. The seizures are usually major in type but tend to occur infrequently (Rutter, 1977).

During adolescence, hyperactivity is often replaced by marked underactivity and lack of initiative and drive; some autistics may have increased anxiety and tension; there may be inappropriate sexual curiosity that may lead to socially embarrassing behavior, such as masturbation in public or self-exposure.

In a recent extensive review of followup studies of psychotic children, Lotter (1978) found that only 8 out of a total of 25 studies could be used for final analysis. The eight studies were more nearly comparable in methodology and in dealing with children, most of whom appeared to meet the main diagnostic criteria for infantile autism. These studies, however, only followed the autistics up to the age of about 30 years. Based on the eight studies, between 5 per cent and 17 per cent of the autistic children were found to have a good outcome as assessed from a judgment of overall social adjustment; that is, they had a normal or near-normal social life and demonstrated satisfactory functioning at school or work. But even those with a good adjustment generally have continuing difficulties in relationships and some oddities of behavior. Between one in six and a quarter of the autistics had an intermediate outcome; that is, they had some degree of independence and only minor problems in behavior, but they still needed supervision and could not hold a job. Between 61 per cent and 74 per cent had a generally poor outcome, remaining severely handicapped and unable to lead any kind of independent life.

Between 39 per cent and 74 per cent of the autistics were placed in institutions. Obviously, placement depends on age and on local patterns of available services. The effect of age in institutional placement is evident in the study of Rutter and Lockyer (1967): at the first followup, 44 per cent were so placed; the proportion had risen to 54 per cent 6 years later.

Three factors were consistently found to be related to outcome: IQ, the presence or absence of speech, and the severity of the disorder. IQ alone predicts best only those with poor outcome. A high nonverbal score with no subsequent language is of no predictive value, whereas if language subsequently does develop, the nonverbal score is a useful guide to later general IQ scores (Rutter, 1970). Thus some combination of speech and IQ may be a more useful predictor than either would be separately.

One additional factor, work–school status, was found to be the best predictor of academic or work performance at followup (DeMyer et al., 1973). Using simple observation criteria of common school-related skills, each child was rated on a 5-point scale (normal, borderline, educable, trainable, subtrainable) when he or she was first seen. Similar ratings were made at followup, with the addition of items involving postschool training and employment. For all their subjects (120 autistics and 26 nonpsychotic subnormals), prediction on the 5-point scale was correct for more than half (55 per cent) and within one step in 89 per cent of cases.

Four other variables have been reported to be significantly associated with outcome, but the correlations are less strong than the variables already described. These are (1) amount of time spent in school, (2) rating of social maturity, (3) rating of social behavior, and (4) developmental milestones.

Conflicting findings have been reported on a number of variables in terms of their relation with outcome. These are sex, brain dysfunction or damge, and the category "untestable" child. It is worth noting, however, that it has been consistently pointed out that there are few girls among the autistics with the best outcome.

Factors that were unrelated to outcome included birth weight, perinatal complications, age of onset, history of a period of normal development before onset, late development of seizures, social class, broken home, family mental illness, and type of treatment.

## Differential Diagnosis

*Childhood-onset pervasive developmental disorder* is a DSM-III subtype of pervasive developmental disorder (PDD). The main and associate features, as described in the DSM-III, are similar to those of infantile autism. The major difference is age of onset. For childhood-onset PDD, the age at onset is defined as "after 30 months of age and before 12 years" (APA, 1980, p. 91). As already discussed in the section on age at onset, it is absurd to only use "age at onset" to divide a disorder into subtypes. Because little is known about this newly created disorder, and because there are findings that age at onset, as well as a history of a period of normal development before onset, is unrelated to the outcome of autism, it is reasonable to speculate that childhood-onset PDD may be just a subtype of infantile autism.

*Autistic psychopathy* is a syndrome described by Asperger (1944) as an abnormal personality trait that is not evident until the 3rd year of life. The main features are a lack of social intuition, leading to naive and tactless behavior and difficulty with social relationships; a normal intelligence but with poor coordination and visuospatial perception; and obsessive preoccupation or circumscribed interest patterns, such as astronomy. It remains uncertain whether the syndrome is distinct from autism (Rutter, 1977) because the picture described by Asperger can be seen in some adults who were clearly classic autistics as children but who have made progress in language and other skills (Wing, 1976).

*Disintegrative psychoses* are a group of childhood disorders that roughly fits Heller's account of dementia infantilis (Heller, 1954): a progressive intellectual deterioration with, ultimately, the appearance of neurologic signs. In these conditions, development usually appears normal or near-normal up to the age of 3 or 4 years, at which time there is a profound regression and behavioral disintegration. There is a loss of speech and language, social skills, and interest in objects. Interpersonal relationships are impaired. There is development of stereotypies and mannerisms. Sometimes these disorders develop after some clear-cut organic brain disease. More often there are no clinical signs of neurologic damage, but the subsequent course and postmortem studies often reveal some kind of organic cortical degeneration (Rutter, 1977). Neither the etiology nor the clinical picture in this group of disorders is uniform. Furthermore, the patterns of symptomatology differ in crucial aspects from infantile autism.

In *schizoid disorder of childhood,* the essential feature is a defect in the capacity to form social relationships. Children with this disorder have no close friends of similar age other than a relative or a similarly socially isolated child. They do not appear distressed by their isolation, however, and show little desire for social involvement. Nevertheless, the language development of such children is relatively normal, and there is an absence of bizarre responses to the environment, as seen in autistic children.

Children with a *developmental language disorder, receptive type,* may show some autistic behavior, especially before age 5 (Wing, 1969). They may develop disturbances in relating and social responses, but they do not manifest the perceptual disturbances (e.g., sensory hyperreactivity or hyporeactivity) that are characteristic of autistic children (Ornitz and Ritvo, 1976). They are much more likely to be able to relate to others by nonverbal gestures and expressions. When they do acquire speech, they also demonstrate communicative intent and emotion, characteristics that are not present in verbal autistic children. Furthermore, children with a receptive language disorder have some imaginative play, which is markedly deficient in autistic children (Bartak, Rutter, Cox, 1975).

In *general mental retardation,* there are often behavioral abnormalities similar to those seen in infantile autism. Wing (1975) found that about one quarter of the severely retarded children in one area of London demonstrated a lack of affect, resistance to change, stereotypies, and bizarre responses to sensory input, but few could be called classically autistic. Furthermore, in general mental retardation, there are generalized delays in development across many areas. Some children, especially those with Down's syndrome, are quite sociable and can communicate in gesture and mime. Moreover, there are studies in which autistic children were found to be different from matched groups of mental retardates. The autistic children made less use of meaning in their memory processes, were impaired in their use of concepts, and were limited in their abilities of coding and categorizing

(Schopler, 1966; Hermelin and O'Connor, 1970).

Children with a *congenital peripheral blindness* or *partial sightedness* may be associated with self-stimulation and stereotyped movements like those seen in autism. Blind children, however, usually develop an interest in their environment and do not have disturbances in relating with other people.

Although *psychosocial deprivation* is commonly mentioned as a possible cause of autism, no data from systematic studies have yet been presented to support such a view. On the other hand, there are children who had been deprived over several years, resulting in severe retardation of all aspects of development, who then made rapid strides in development when they were rescued and put in a caring and stimulating environment. They showed no evidence of autism (Wing, 1976). Thus careful history taking and observation of a rapid response to improvement in the stimulating environment should differentiate this condition from autism.

In *elective mutism*, the child refuses to speak in almost all social situations, despite the ability to comprehend spoken language and to speak. The child may communicate by gestures, nodding or shaking the head, or, in some cases, by monosyllabic or short, monotone utterances. The same child may talk normally at home with family members. Autistic children retain their characteristic language abnormalities in all situations. In any case, the whole pattern of behavior is markedly different in the two conditions.

The differences between *schizophrenia in childhood* and infantile autism are discussed in greater detail later in the chapter. Briefly, there are two well-established findings that should help to differentiate the two conditions. First, there are delusions, hallucinations, and loosening of associations or incoherence in schizophrenia occurring in childhood, but not in infantile autism. Second, there is an increased incidence of schizophrenia in the families of children with schizophrenia, but not of children with infantile autism.

## Treatment

As it has become clear that autism is a pervasive developmental disorder, it is not surprising that individual, as well as group, psychotherapy has been used less and less. Emphasis has now been placed on treatment to promote the autistic child's more normal social and linguistic developments and on minimizing the child's maladaptive behaviors (e.g., hyperactivity, stereotypies, self-injury, aggressiveness), which interfere with or are incompatible with the child's functioning and learning. There has been an increasing focus on treating preschool autistic children through special education programs in highly structured environments and on working closely with the family members of autistic children to help them cope better with the problems faced at home.

Extensive research in behavior therapy since the 1960s has shown that many autistic children can be taught special skills in the areas of social adaptation and cognitive and motor skills (Frankel, Tymchuk, Simmons, 1976). Their maladaptive behavior can also be ameliorated significantly. Lovaas, Schreibment, and Koegel (1976) have reviewed the principles involved in behavior therapy with autistic children. A few points are emphasized here. First, behavior therapy programs should be designed for individual children because autistic children vary greatly in their handicaps and family circumstances. Some treatment approaches that work in certain cases may not work in others. Second, autistic children are handicapped in generalizing from one situation to another, so that the skills they have learned in a hospital or school tend not to transfer to the home or other settings (Lovaas, Koegel, Simmons, Long, 1973). It is crucial in treatment to plan the approach specifically to ensure that the changes of the child's clinical state are being carefully monitored, that the problems in each setting are dealt with, and that steps are taken to encourage generalization of behavior changes. Third, because one of the treatment goals is to promote the child's social development, long-term residential treatment is a definite drawback. A home–community-based approach, which trains parents and local special education teachers to carry out behavior therapies, has been instrumental in achieving maximum results (Hemsley et al., 1978).

Pharmacotherapy does not alter the natural history or course of autism. It may be helpful, however, in controlling specific symptoms, such as hyperactivity, with-drawal, stereotypies, self-injury, aggres-siveness, and sleep disorders. This subject has recently been reviewed by Campbell, Anderson, Deutsch, and Green (1984). Low-potency neuroleptics, such as chlorproma-zine, have little, if any, therapeutic effect be-cause they yield excessive sedation, even at low doses. On the other hand, haloperidol, a high-potency neuroleptic, has demon-strated both short-term and long-term effi-cacy in 40 young autistic children (ages 2.6 to 7.2 years) in doses ranging from 0.5 to 4.0 mg per day (Campbell et al., 1978b). At these dosages, haloperidol was significantly superior to a placebo in reducing symptoms of withdrawal and stereotypies in those chil-dren who were 4.5 to 7.2 years of age. The combination of haloperidol and contingent reinforcement was found to be most effec-tive in facilitating the acquisition of imitative speech. Long-term studies of haloperidol by Campbell et al. (1983a) have shown that the effect remains from 6 months to $2\frac{1}{2}$ years. At optimal doses, no untoward effects were noted. Above optimal doses or during dose regulation, excessive sedation was most common, followed by acute dystonic reac-tion. All drug-related movements ceased anywhere from 16 days to 9 months later (Campbell, Grega, Green, Bennett, 1983b). Campbell et al. recommend that the dosage increments be gradual and made on a reg-ular basis. The emergence of untoward ef-fects may necessitate dosage reduction or administration of diphenhydramine (Ben-adryl). Furthermore, about every 6 months the haloperidol should be discontinued in order to determine whether the child needs further drug treatment.

Recently, fenfluramine (an antiseroto-nergic anorectic) has been reported to be beneficial in terms of decreasing abnormal behavioral symptoms and raising IQs in a sample of 15 autistics, ages 2 to 18 years (Ritvo, Freeman, Geller, Yuwiler, 1983). Poor appetite, weight loss, and lethargy were reported in a few cases. So far, some feel that fenfluramine appears to be a prom-ising drug, but this notion merits further critical investigation.

So far no single treatment modality can alter the course of autism. To achieve sig-nificant goals of treatment of autistic chil-dren, comprehensive treatment programs, which include behavior modification and special education in a highly structured en-vironment, are required. Pharmacotherapy may frequently be useful to control behav-iors that are not responsive to behavior modification and special education tech-niques.

## SCHIZOPHRENIA IN CHILDHOOD

### Definition

The term schizophrenic syndrome of childhood, or its synonym, childhood schiz-ophrenia, has a different meaning than the term schizophrenia in childhood. The for-mer is a term proposed by the British Work-ing Party (Creak et al., 1961) to apply to a wide spectrum of patients, including autis-tics, schizophrenics, disintegrative psychot-ics, and other childhood psychotics. The lat-ter is a term to be applied to children only if clear schizophrenic symptoms, as found in adult schizophrenia, are present. Thus it is clear that data derived from the studies that use childhood schizophrenia diagnostic criteria (most of these studies were con-ducted before 1970) are not very meaningful because they failed to make any distinction between autism and schizophrenia in child-hood.

For the purpose of this chapter, the defi-nition and diagnostic criteria for schizo-phrenia in childhood are the same as those described in the DSM-III for adult schizo-phrenia (which is described in detail in Chapter 6). There are at least two good rea-sons to do so. First, there is now convincing evidence supporting the view that infantile autism and schizophrenia in childhood are two distinct disorders (Rutter, 1978). Sec-ond, it is clear that schizophrenia, as de-scribed in adults, can begin in childhood (Kolvin, 1971; Vrono, 1974). Although stud-ies of schizophrenia in childhood based on the DSM-III criteria are increasing, they are still uncommon.

### Etiology

Because schizophrenia in childhood is so similar symptomatically, genetically, and epidemiologically to the adult form, readers are referred to current theories of this dis-order described in Chapter 6. Suffice it to say that most of the theories are now centering on biochemical or neuropathophysiologic abnormalities of genetic origin, triggered in some instances by psychological stress.

## Epidemiology

The true incidence of schizophrenia in childhood is uncertain. Population studies have suggested that the prevalence may be less than 1 per 1000 (reviewed by Werry, 1979). Kydd and Werry (1982) reviewed schizophrenic children admitted as inpatients to a child psychiatric unit in Auckland, New Zealand. They found only 15 cases over a period of 10 years (the at-risk population served by the unit was approximately 130,000). On the other hand, Makita (1966) found that only 3 of the 32 schizophrenics in his study had an onset before age 13 (2 at age 10 and 1 at 11 years). Similar findings have been reported by Loranger's (1984) study of the age at first treatment of 100 males and 100 females with a DSM-III diagnosis of schizophrenia. Loranger found that 18 per cent of male and 11 per cent of female schizophrenics were first treated under 15 years of age.

Kydd and Werry (1982) noted a nearly equal sex ratio (i.e., eight boys and seven girls), and Eggers (1978) found a slight female preponderance (i.e., 25 boys and 32 girls) in their respective samples. However, as far as schizophrenic children under 10 years of age are concerned, Kydd and Werry's study, like that of Kolvin (i.e., ratio of 2.7:1) (1971), showed a preponderance of boys. It appears that the age of the child may determine the sex ratio in schizophrenia occurring in childhood.

Although Kydd and Werry (1982) found that the social class distribution of the schizophrenic children's families resembles that of the base population, schizophrenic children probably tend to come from lower social class families, just as adult schizophrenics do (Kolvin et al., 1971; Rutter, 1972).

Parents of schizophrenic children often do have psychopathology (e.g., isolation, introversion, neurosis, aggressiveness, suicide, affective disorder) and an increased family prevalence of schizophrenia (Kolvin et al., 1971; Eggers, 1978; Kydd and Werry, 1982).

## Clinical Features

The age at onset is most often during the pre-adolescent or adolescent period, but the onset may be as early as 7 years and, rarely, even before that (Rutter, 1977). Eggers (1978) noted that in the schizophrenic children who had manifested the disorder in or before the 10th year of life, the acute course was less frequent than the chronic. Conversely, in patients with age of onset in the prepubertal phase, the acute type was seen more frequently than the chronic type. On the whole, about two thirds of the schizophrenic children had experienced a gradual development of symptoms (Kolvin et al., 1971; Kydd and Werry, 1982). Eggers (1978) noted that in slightly more than half the cases (55 per cent), the manifestation of the schizophrenia was preceded by prodromal features, characterized by depressive mood and delusions. The risk of suicide increases during the prodromal phase. On the other hand, Kolvin et al. (1971) observed that almost 90 per cent of schizophrenic children had been shy, different, withdrawn, sensitive, or timid before their psychosis developed. Eggers (1978), however, reported that the early development in slightly half the schizophrenic children was unremarkable, and that slightly more than half the schizophrenic children had a fair-to-good adaptive functioning before the first presentation of the disorder. Nevertheless, obvious psychological precipitating factors (e.g., change to a new school, brief hospitalization, death of a close relative, a disturbed parental relationship) were present in about half the cases (Kolvin et al., 1971; Kydd and Werry, 1982).

Schizophrenic children, although less studied, would appear to be mostly of dull-normal intelligence (Werry, 1979). They probably tend to exhibit a substantial excess of perinatal, developmental, soft neurologic, and EEG abnormalities, as compared with normal children (Werry, 1979). Goldfarb's work, and that of Kolvin (reviewed by Werry, 1979), suggests that while speech and language difficulties can also be associated with schizophrenia in children, they are more variable, more bizarre, and less related to fundamental defects of the comprehension of language so characteristic of autism.

The symptomatology may be determined

by the stage of development. Generally speaking, the clinical picture in younger schizophrenic children is similar to that of hebephrenic schizophrenia in adults. It is characterized by an increasing loss of contact with reality, diminishing of interests, disturbed motility (e.g., stereotypies, peculiar mannerisms, grimacings, bizarre posture), echolalia, neologism, disintegration of speech, moodiness, excessive anxiety, and blunting of affect. Some children become compulsively disinhibited and destructive, defecate or masturbate openly, or injure themselves. Delusions and hallucinations are uncommon in younger children. The delusional symptoms in younger children often appear in the form of irrational and diffuse fears, or even cosmic threats (e.g., "the sun won't come out again"). Delusion of loss of identity or of being poisoned may also, although seldom, be observed.

Schizophrenia in later childhood and prepubertal phase is characterized by more persistent, abstract, and systematized delusions and hallucinations. In general, ideas of reference are the most frequent among the delusions (Eggers, 1978), and the most frequent type of hallucinations are auditory. Nearly half the patients with auditory hallucinations also had bodily or visual hallucinations (Kolvin et al., 1971). Disorders of thought association and thought blocking were present in three fifths of schizophrenic patients, with an age at onset in later childhood (Kolvin et al., 1971). Eggers (1978) noted that 65 per cent of the patients in the study were preoccupied by problems connected with death. During their illness, 25 per cent of the cases expressed death thoughts, 15 per cent had suicidal intentions without autoaggressive actions, 20 per cent attempted suicide, and 5 per cent committed suicide. The average time between onset of the disorder and attempted suicide was 8.5 years.

## Course and Prognosis

As already mentioned, studies conducted before 1970 are not very meaningful in terms of data on course and prognosis because they made no distinction between groups. Most of the recent work, however, has centered on autistic children. There are few well-documented, long-term outcome stud-

ies of schizophrenia in childhood that are based on criteria similar to that of the DSM-III. Eggers (1978) reported a followup study of 57 clearly diagnosed schizophrenic children, aged 7 to 13 years at initial evaluation. At an average of 15 years after onset of the disorder, 20 per cent were rated to be in complete remission, while another 30 per cent had made a very good or good-to-satisfying social adaptation. Recently, Kydd and Werry (1982) reported a followup study of ten schizophrenic children, aged 6 to 15 years at first presentation, diagnosed according to the DSM-III criteria. The followup interval ranged from 1 to 9 years, with a mean of 4.6 and a median of 5. Forty per cent of the cases were found to be in remission at followup, and deterioration after the active phase of the illness occurred in only four cases. The authors felt that the outcome in schizophrenic children may be more favorable than generally assumed. They also cautioned that better results possibly reflect the brief followup interval, as well as the small sample sizes.

On the whole, the best predictors of favorable outcome are later age at onset, a good premorbid adaptive functioning, an above-average intelligence, and the presence of precipitating factors. Factors that are unrelated to outcome include family history of psychiatric disorders, socioeconomic status and intactness of the family, frequency of psychotic episodes, occurrence of cyclothymic phase and prodromal episodes, and patterns of psychopathologic symptoms.

## Treatment

There is an obvious lack of data about the effect of antipsychotic medication on schizophrenic children. Nonetheless, there is a suggestion that different forms of schizophrenia in children may respond differently to drugs, and when the age at onset is before 15 years of age, prognosis with drug treatment tends to be poor (Werry, 1982). Winsberg and Yepes (1978) hold that when antipsychotics are used in children, they are useful for behavioral management through sedating effects but are not really controlling the disorder. Kydd and Werry (1982) noted that acute positive symptoms (delusions, hallucinations, thought disorder) seem to respond better to the neuroleptics, but negative symptoms (withdrawal, blunting of affect) less so. They suggest that it may be that the effect of the antipsychotics in well-defined schizophrenic children is the same as in adults.

Although medical therapy for schizophrenia in childhood is the goal and there are indications that pharmacotherapies may prove effective, present intervention must continue to include supportive and symptomatic therapeutic measures, such as behavior therapy, special education, structured programs, and even residential treatment.

## REFERENCES

Alpern GD, Kimberlin CC: Short intelligence test ranging from infancy levels through childhood levels for use with the retarded. Am J Ment Deficiency 75:65–71, 1970.

American Psychiatric Association: Diagnostic and Statistical Manual of Mental Disorders, ed 3. Washington, DC, American Psychiatric Association, 1980.

Asperger H: Die autistischen psychopathen im kindesalter. Arch Psychiatr Nervenkr 117:76–136, 1944.

Bakwin H: Early infantile autism. Pediatrics 45:492–497, 1954.

Bartak L, Rutter M: Differences between mentally retarded and normally intelligent autistic children. J Autism Child Schizo 6:109–120, 1976.

Bartak L, Rutter M, Cox A: A comparative study of infantile autism and specific developmental receptive language disorder. I. The children. Br J Psychiatry 126:127–145, 1975.

Bender L: Schizophrenia in childhood—its recognition, description, and treatment. Am J Orthopsychiatry 26:499–506, 1956.

Bernal ME, Miller WH: Electrodermal and cardiac responses of schizophrenic children to sensory stimuli. Psychophysiology 7:155–168, 1970.

Bettelheim B: The Empty Fortress—Infantile Autism and the Birth of the Self. New York, Free Press, 1967.

Bleuler E: Dementia Praecox Oder Gruppe der Schizophrenien. Deutiche, 1911; Trans J. Zinkin. New York, International University Press, 1950.

Brask BH: A prevalence investigation of childhood psychoses, in the 16th Scandinavian Congress of Psychiatry, Aarhus, Denmark, 1970.

Brown WT, Jenkins EC, Friedman E, Brooks J, Wisniewski K, Raguthu S, French J: Autism is associated with the fragile-X syndrome. J Autism Dev Disord 12:303–308, 1982.

Campbell M: Treatment of childhood and adolescent schizophrenia, in Wiener JM (ed): Psychopharmacology in Childhood and Adolescence. New York, Basic Books, 1977, pp 101–118.

Campbell M, Anderson LT, Deutsch SI, Green WH: Psychopharmacological treatment of children with the syndrome of autism. Ped Ann 13:309–316, 1984.

Campbell M, Anderson LT, Meier M, Cohen IL, Small AM, Samit C, Sachar EJ: A comparison of haloperidol and behavior therapy and their interaction in autistic

children. J Am Acad Child Psychiatry 17:640–655, 1978b.

Campbell M, Friedman E, Green WH, Collins PJ, Small AM, Breuer H: Blood serotonin in schizophrenic children. Int Pharmacopsychiatry 10:213–221, 1975.

Campbell M, Grega DM, Green WH, Bennett WG: Neuroleptic-induced dyskinesia in children. Clin Neuropharmacol 6:207–222, 1983b.

Campbell M, Hardesty AS, Burdock EI: Demographic and perinatal profile of 105 autistic children: A preliminary report. Psychopharmacol Bull 14:36–39, 1978a.

Campbell M, Perry R, Bennett WG, Small AM, Green WH, Grega D, Schwartz V, Anderson L: Long-term therapeutic efficacy and drug-related abnormal movements: A prospective study of haloperidol in autistic children. Psychopharmacol Bull 19:80–83, 1983a.

Campbell M, Rosenbloom S, Perry R, George AE, Kricheff II, Anderson L, Small AM, Jennings SJ: Computerized axial tomography in young autistic children. Am J Psychiatry 139:510–512, 1982.

Caparulo BK, Cohen DJ, Rothman SL, Young G, Katz JD, Shaywitz SE, Shaywitz BA: Computed tomographic brain scanning in children with developmental neuropsychiatric disorders. J Am Acad Child Psychiatry 20:338–357, 1981.

Cohen DJ, Caparulo BK, Shaywitz BA, Bowers MB Jr: Dopamine and serotonin metabolism in neuropsychiatrically disturbed children: CSF homovanillic acid and 5-hydroxyindoleacetic acid. Arch Gen Psychiatry 34:545–550, 1977.

Creak M, Cameron K, Cowie V, Ini S, MacKeith R, Mitchell G, O'Gorman G, Orford F, Rogers W, Shapiro A, Stone F, Stroh G, Yudkin S: Schizophrenic syndrome in childhood. Br Med J 2:889–890, 1961.

Creak M, Ini, S: Families of psychotic children. J Child Psychol Psychiatry 1:156–175, 1960.

Creak M, Pampiglione G: Clinical and EEG studies on a group of 35 psychotic children. Dev Med Child Neurol 11:218–227, 1969.

Dahl V: A follow-up study of a child psychiatric clientele with special regard to the diagnosis of psychosis. Acta Psychiatr Scand 54:106–112, 1976.

Damasio AR, Maurer RG: A neurological model for childhood autism. Arch Neurol 35:777–786, 1978.

Damasio H, Maurer RG, Damasio AR, Chu HC: Computerized tomographic scan findings in patients with autistic behavior. Arch Neurol 37:504–510, 1980.

DeMyer M, Barton S, DeMyer W, Norton J, Allen J, Steele R: Prognosis in autism: A follow-up study. J Autism Child Schizo 3:199–246, 1973.

Despert JL: Some considerations relating to the genesis of autistic behavior in children. Am J Orthopsychiatry 21:335–350, 1951.

Eggers C: Course and Prognosis of childhood schizophrenia. J Autism Child Schizo 8:21–36, 1978.

Eisenberg L, Kanner L: Early infantile autism 1943–55. Am J Orthopsychiatry 26:556–566, 1956.

Ekstein R, Wallerstein J: Observations on the psychology of borderline and psychotic children. Psychoanalytic Study of the Child, vol 9. New York, International University Press, 1954.

Fein D, Skoff B, Mirsky AF: Clinical correlates of brainstem dysfunction in autistic children. J Autism Dev Disord 11:303–315, 1981.

Finegan JA, Quarrington B: Pre-, peri-, and neonatal factors and infantile autism. J Child Psychol Psychiatry 20:119–128, 1979.

Fish B, Ritvo ER: Psychoses of childhood, in Noshpitz JD (ed): Basic Handbook of Child Psychiatry. New York, Basic Books, 1979.

Folstein S, Rutter M: Infantile autism: A genetic study of 21 twin pairs. J Child Psychol Psychiatry 18:297–321, 1977.

Frankel F, Tymchuk AJ, Simmons JQ III: Operant analysis and intervention with autistic children: Implications of current research, in Ritvo ER (ed): Autism: Diagnosis, Current Research and Management. New York, Spectrum, 1976.

Gillberg C: Infantile autism and other childhood psychoses in a Swedish urban region: Epidemiological aspects. J Child Psychol Psychiatry 25:35–43, 1984.

Gillberg C, Gillberg IC: Infantile autism: A total population study of reduced optimality in the pre-, peri-, and neonatal period. J Autism Dev Disord 13:153–166, 1983.

Gillberg C, Rosenhall U, Johansson E: Auditory brainstem responses in childhood psychosis. J Autism Dev Disord 13:181–195, 1983.

Gillberg C, Svendsen P: Childhood psychosis and computed tomographic brain scan findings. J Autism Dev Disord 13:19–32, 1983.

Gittelman M, Birch G: Childhood schizophrenia: Intellect, neurologic status, perinatal risk, prognosis and family pathology. Arch Gen Psychiatry 17:16–25, 1967.

Goldfarb W, Levy DM, Meyers DI: The mother speaks to her schizophrenic child: Language in childhood schizophrenia. Psychiatry 35:217–226, 1972.

Hauser SL, DeLong GR, Rosman NP: Pneumographic findings in the infantile autism syndrome: A correlation with temporal lobe disease. Brain 98:667–688, 1975.

Heller T: Dementia infantilis, 1930; trans Hulse WC. J Neur Ment Dis 119:471–477, 1954.

Hemsley R, Howlin P, Berger M, Hersov L, Holbrook D, Rutter M, Yule W: Treating autistic children in a family context, in Rutter M, Schopler E (eds): Autism: A Reappraisal of Concepts and Treatment. New York, Plenum Press, 1978.

Hermelin B, O'Connor N: Measures of the occipital alpha rhythm in normal, subnormal and autistic children. Br J Psychiatry 114:603–610, 1968.

Hermelin B, O'Connor N: Psychological Experiments with Autistic Children. Oxford, Pergamon Press, 1970.

Hier DE, LeMay M, Rosenberger PB: Autism and unfavorable left-right asymmetrics of the brain. J Autism Dev Disord 9:153–159, 1979.

Hingtgen JN, Churchill DW: Differential effects of behaviour modification in four mute autistic boys, in Churchill DW, Alpern CD, DeMyer M (eds): Infantile Autism. Springfield, IL, Charles C Thomas, 1971.

Hoshino Y, Kumashiro H, Yshima Y, Tachibana R, Watanake M: The epidemiological study of autism in Fukushima-Ken. Folia Psychiatr Neurol Jpn 36:115–124, 1982.

Howells JG, Guirguis WR: Childhood schizophrenia 20 years later. Arch Gen Psychiatry 41:123–128, 1984.

Hutt C, Forrest SJ, Richer J: Cardiac arrhythmia and behavior in autistic children. Acta Psychiatr Scand 51:361–372, 1975.

Hutt S, Hutt C, Lee D, Ounsted C: A behavioral and electroencephalographic study of autistic children. J Psychiatr Res 3:181–197, 1965.

Kanner L: Autistic disturbances of affective contact. Nervous Child 2:217–250, 1943.

Katz RM, Liebman W: Creatine phosphokinase activity in central nervous system disorders and infections. Am J Dis Child 120:543–546, 1970.

Knoblock H, Pasamanick B: Some etiologic and prognostic factors in early infantile autism and psychosis. Pediatrics 55:182–191, 1975.

Kolvin I: Psychoses in childhood—a comparative study, in Rutter M (ed): Infantile Autism: Concepts, Characteristics and Treatment. London, Churchill Livingstone, 1971.

Kolvin I, Ounsted C, Humphrey M, et al: Six studies in the childhood psychoses. Br J Psychiatry 118:381–419, 1971.

Kydd RR, Werry JS: Schizophrenia in children under 16 years. J Autism Dev Disord 12:343–357, 1982.

Lake CR, Ziegler MG, Murphy DL: Increased norepinephrine levels and decreased DBH in primary autism. Arch Gen Psychiatry 35:553–556, 1977.

Lelord G, Laffont F, Jusseaume P, Stephant JL: Comparative study of conditioning of averaged evoked responses by coupling sound and light in normal and autistic children. Psychophysiology 10:415–425, 1973.

Levitas A, Hagerman RJ, Braden M, Rimland B, McBogg P, Matus I: Autism and the fragile X syndrome. J Dev Behav Ped 4:151–158, 1983.

Lockyer L, Rutter M: A five to fifteen year follow-up study of infantile psychosis. III. Psychological aspects. Br J Psychiatry 115:865–882, 1969.

Loranger AW: Sex difference in age at onset of schizophrenia. Arch Gen Psychiatry 41:157–161, 1984.

Lord C, Schopler E, Revicki D: Sex differences in autism. J Autism Dev Disord 12:317–329, 1982.

Lotter V: Epidemiology of autistic conditions in young children. I. Prevalence. Soc Psychiatry 1:124–137, 1966.

Lotter V: Epidemiology of autistic conditions in young children. II. Some characteristics of the parents and children. Social Psychiatry 1:163–173, 1967.

Lotter V: Factors related to outcome in autistic children. J Autism Child Schizo 4:263–277, 1974.

Lotter V: Follow-up studies, in Rutter M, Schopler E (eds): Autism: A reappraisal of concepts and treatment. New York, Plenum Press, 1978, pp 475–495.

Lovaas OI, Koegel R, Simmons JQ, Long JS: Some generalizations and follow-up measures on autistic children in behavior therapy. J Appl Behav Anal 6:131–166, 1973.

Lovaas OI, Schreibment L, Koegel RL: A behavior modification approach to the treatment of autistic children, in Schopler E, Reichler RJ (eds): Psychopathology and Child Development. New York, Plenum Press, 1976.

Mahler M: On child psychosis and schizophrenia. Autistic and symbiotic psychoses. Psychoanalytic Study of the Child, vol 7. New York, International University Press, 1952.

Makita K: The age of onset of childhood schizophrenia. Folia Psychiatr Neurol Jpn 20:111–121, 1966.

Meyers D, Goldfarb W: Studies of perplexity in mothers of schizophrenic children. Am J Orthopsychiatry 3:551–564, 1961.

Minton J, Campbell M, Green WH, Jennings S, Samit C: Cognitive assessment of siblings of autistic children. J Am Acad Child Psychiatry 3:256–261, 1982.

Ornitz EM: Dreaming sleep in autistic twins. Arch Gen Psychiatry 12:77–79, 1965.

Ornitz EM, Brown MB, Mason A, Putnam NH: Effect

of visual input on vestibular nystagmus in autistic children. Arch Gen Psychiatry 31:369–375, 1974.

Ornitz EM, Ritvo ER: Perceptual inconstancy in early infantile autism. Arch Gen Psychiatry 18:76–98, 1968.

Ornitz EM, Ritvo ER: The syndrome of autism: A critical review. Am J Psychiatry 133:609–621, 1976.

Petty LK, Ornitz EM, Michelman JD, Zimmerman EG: Autistic children who become schizophrenic. Arch Gen Psychiatry 41:129–135, 1984.

Piggott LR: Overview of selected basic research in autism. J Autism Dev Disord 9:199–218, 1979.

Reiser DE: Psychosis of infancy and early childhood, as manifested by children with atypical development. I. N Engl J Med 269:790–798, 1963a.

Reiser DE: Psychosis of infancy and early childhood, as manifested by children with atypical development. II. N Engl J Med 269:844–850, 1963b.

Ricks DM, Wing L: Language, communication and the use of symbols, in Wing L (ed): Early Childhood Autism. Oxford, Pergamon Press, 93–134, 1976.

Ritvo ER: The syndrome of autism: A medical model. Integrative Psychiatry 1:101–109, 1983.

Ritvo ER, Cantwell D, Johnson E, Clements M, Benbrook F, Slagle S, Kelly P, Ritz M: Social class factors in autism. J Autism Child Schizo 1:297–310, 1971.

Ritvo ER, Freeman BJ: Current research in the syndrome of autism: Introduction—The National Society for Autistic Children's definition of the syndrome of autism. J Am Acad Child Psychiatry 17:565–575, 1978.

Ritvo ER, Freeman BJ, Geller E, Yuwiler A: Effects of fenfluramine on 14 outpatients with the syndrome of autism. J Am Acad Child Psychiatry 22:549–558, 1983.

Ritvo ER, Ornitz EM, Eviatar A, Markham CH, Brown MB, Mason A: Decreased postrotatory nystagmus in early infantile autism. Neurology 19:653–658, 1969.

Ritvo ER, Ornitz EM, Walter RD, Hanley J: Correlation of psychiatric diagnoses and EEG findings: A double-blind study of 184 hospitalized children. Am J Psychiatry 126:988–996, 1970.

Rosenbloom S, Campbell M, George AE, Kricheff II, Taleporos E, Anderson L, Reuben RN, Korein J: High resolution CT scanning in infantile autism: A quantitative approach. J Am Acad Child Psychiatry 1:72–77, 1984.

Rutter M: Psychotic disorders in early childhood. Br J Psychiatry, Special Publication No. I:133–158, 1967.

Rutter M: Concepts of autism: A review of research. J Child Psychol Psychiatry 9:1–25, 1968.

Rutter M: Autistic children: Infancy to adulthood. Semin Psychiatry 2:435–450, 1970.

Rutter M: Childhood schizophrenia reconsidered. J Autism Child Schizo 2:315–337, 1972.

Rutter M: Infantile autism and other child psychoses, in Rutter M, Henson L (eds): Child Psychiatry: Modern Approach. Oxford, Blackwell, 1977, pp 717–747.

Rutter M: Diagnosis and definition, in Rutter M, Schopler E (eds): Autism—A Reappraisal of Concepts and Treatment. New York and London, Plenum Press, 1978.

Rutter M, Lockyer L: A five to fifteen year follow-up study of infantile psychosis. I. Description of sample. Br J Psychiatry 113:1169–1182, 1967.

Sankar DV: Studies on blood platelets, blood enzymes, and leukocyte chromosome breakage in childhood schizophrenia. Behav Neuropsychiatry 2:2–10, 1971.

Schain RJ, Yannet H: Infantile autism: An analysis of 50 cases and a consideration of certain relevant neurophysiologic concepts. J Pediatr 57:560–567, 1960.

Schopler E: Visual versus tactual receptor preference in normal and schizophrenic children. J Abnorm Psychol 71:108–114, 1966.

Schopler E, Andrews CE, Strupp K: Do autistic children come from upper-middle-class parents? J Autism Dev Disord 9:139–152, 1979.

Schwab R, England AC: Parkinson syndromes due to various specific causes, in Vinken PJ, Bruyn GW (eds): Handbook of Clinical Neurology: Disorders of Basal Ganglia, vol 6. Amsterdam, North Holland, 1968.

Skoff B, Mirsky AF, Turner D: Prolonged brainstem transmission time in autism. Psychiatry Res 2:157–166, 1980.

Small JG: EEG and neurophysiological studies of early infantile autism. Biol Psychiatry 10:385–397, 1975.

Spence MA: Genetic studies, in Ritvo R (ed): Autism: Diagnosis, Current Research and Management. New York, Halstead/Wiley, 1976, pp 169–174.

Student M, Sohmer H: Evidence from auditory nerve and brainstem evoked responses for an organic brain lesion in children with autistic traits. J Autism Child Schizo 8:13–20, 1978.

Tanguay PE, Edwards RM, Buchwald J, Schwafel J, Allen V: Auditory brainstem evoked responses in autistic children. Arch Gen Psychiatry 39:174–180, 1982.

Tanguay PE, Ornitz EM, Forsythe AB, Ritvo ER: Rapid eye movement (REM) activity in normal and autistic children during REM sleep. J Autism Child Schizo 6:275–288, 1976.

Treffert DA: Epidemiology of infantile autism. Arch Gen Psychiatry 22:431–438, 1970.

Tsai LY: The relationship of handedness to the cognitive, language and visuo-spatial skills of autistic patients. Br J Psychiatry 142:156–162, 1983.

Tsai LY, Jacoby CG, Stewart MA, Beisler JA: Unfavourable left-right asymmetries of the brain and autism: A question of methodology. Br J Psychiatry 140:312–319, 1982a.

Tsai LY, Stewart MA, August G: Implication of sex differences in the familial transmission of infantile autism. J Autism Dev Disord 11:165–173, 1981.

Tsai LY, Stewart MA, Faust M, Shook S: Social class distribution of fathers of the children enrolled in the Iowa Autism Program. J Autism Dev Disord 12:211–221, 1982b.

Tsai LY, Tsai MC: Using EEG diagnosis to subtype autistic syndrome. Proceedings, 1984 International Conference of the National Society for Children and Adults with Autism. San Antonio, Texas, July.

US Department of Health and Human Services: International Classification of Disease—9th Revision—Clinical Modification. Washington, DC, US Department of Health and Human Services, 1980.

Van Krevelen DA: Early infantile autism. Acta Paedopsychiatr 91:81–97, 1952.

Vrono M: Schizophrenia in childhood and adolescence. Int J Ment Health 2:7–116, 1974.

Waldo MC, Cohen DJ, Caparulo BK, Young G, Prichard JW, Shaywitz BA: EEG profiles of neuropsychiatrically disturbed children. J Am Acad Child Psychiatry 17:656–670, 1978.

Werry JS: The childhood psychoses, in Quay HC, Werry JS (eds): Psychopathological Disorders of Childhood, ed 2. New York, John Wiley & Sons, 1979.

Werry JS: An overview of pediatric psychopharmacology. J Am Acad Child Psychiatry 21:3–9, 1982.

Wing L: The handicaps of autistic children—a comparative study. J Child Psychol Psychiatry 10:1–40, 1969.

Wing L: Perceptual and language development in autistic children: A comparative study, in Rutter M (ed): Infantile Autism: Concepts, Characteristics and Treatment. London, Churchill Livingstone, 1971, pp 173–197.

Wing L: A study of language impairments in severely retarded children, in O'Conner N (ed): Language, Cognitive Deficits and Retardation. London, Butterworths, 1975, pp 87–112.

Wing L: Diagnosis, clinical description and prognosis, in Wing L (ed): Early Childhood Autism. Oxford, Pergamon Press, 1976, pp 15–64.

Wing L: Childhood autism and social class: A question of selection. Br J Psychiatry 137:410–417, 1980.

Wing L: Sex ratios in early childhood autism and related conditions. Psychiatry Res 5:129–137, 1981.

Wing L, Yeates SR, Brierley LM, Gould J: The prevalence of early childhood autism: Comparison of administrative and epidemiological studies. Psychol Med 6:89–100, 1976.

Winsberg BG, Yepes LE: Antipsychotics (major tranquilizers, neuroleptics), in Werry JS (ed): Pediatric Psychopharmacology: The Use of Behavior Modifying Drugs in Children. New York, Brunner/Mazel, 1978, pp 234–273.

Young JG, Cohen DJ, Caparulo BK, Brown SL, Maas JW: Decreased 24-hour urinary MHPG in childhood autism. Am J Psychiatry 136:1055–1057, 1979.

Young JG, Cohen DJ, Kavanagh ME, Landis HD, Shaywitz BA, Maas JW: Cerebrospinal fluid, plasma, and urinary MHPG in children. Life Sci 28:2837–2845, 1981.

Young JG, Kavanagh ME, Anderson GM, Shaywitz BA, Cohen DJ: Clinical neurochemistry of autism and associated disorders. J Autism Dev Disord 12:147–165, 1982.

*chapter 21*

# EMOTIONAL DISORDERS IN CHILDREN

*by* Susan E. Folstein, M.D.

Emotional disorder is a broad term that subsumes a variety of childhood conditions in which the major complaint is some abnormality of emotions or feelings. In rare cases, these symptoms are part of distinctly delineated psychiatric syndromes or neurotic disorders that have clear diagnostic criteria and fairly specific treatments. In other cases, the emotional symptoms are given expression in particular abnormal behaviors, such as school refusal and elective mutism; these problems have a variety of causes, but the behavior itself is usually the focus of treatment. However, the vast majority of children who are referred to psychiatrists because of emotional problems are suffering from a mixture of emotional symptoms that do not fit into any precise syndrome or category (see Table 21–1). The emotional complaints are like normal emotions except in their severity and duration. The causes of distress are various and the treatment must be tailored for each individual patient. This most common category of emotional disorder is considered first.

## NONSPECIFIC EMOTIONAL DISORDER

### Definition

As already mentioned, most children who suffer from emotional symptoms have the same emotions as normal children, but their severity, persistence, and prominence in the child's life make them cause for concern. Many attempts have been made to define and subdivide the condition of emotional disorder more precisely but without success. The symptoms of anxiety, misery, and somatic complaints tend to overlap, and when psychiatrists are asked to make specific diagnoses (such as anxiety disorder or somatoform disorder) from case summaries, they can seldom agree (Mattison, Cantwell, Russell, Will, 1979; Rutter and Shaffer, 1980).

The general category of emotional disorder is, however, a reliable designation on which psychiatrists can agree, and epidemiologic studies have demonstrated its validity (Hewitt and Jenkins, 1946; Rutter, Tizard, and Whitmore, 1970b; Rutter and Hersov, 1976). Unlike other childhood psychiatric conditions, emotional disorder affects girls as frequently as boys (Rutter et. al., 1970b; McGee, Silva, Williams, 1984), intelligence and school performance are usually normal (Rutter et al., 1970b), and the prognosis for recovery is good (Rutter, Tizard, Yule, Graham, and Whitmore, 1976b). Another validating factor for the diagnosis in children is that if psychiatric disorder persists or recurs in adult life, the adult diagnosis is also likely to be some neurotic or emotional condition (Pritchard and Graham, 1966).

**TABLE 21–1  Features of Emotional Disorders in Children**

| | Prevalence in Children | Sex Ratio M:F | Changes at Adolescence | Prognosis for Adult Outcome | Treatment | Etiology/Pathogenesis |
|---|---|---|---|---|---|---|
| Nonspecific emotional disorder | 2%–5% of school children | Approx. 1:1 | Increases in girls with emotional complaints. Recovery of about ½ the cases diagnosed at age 10. | Most recover. Those that persist have diagnosis of anxiety and depression. | Psychotherapy | Small families, eldest children; ?overprotective parents |
| School refusal | About 3% of clinic series | 1:1 | Incidence increases. Early onset cases resolve. | Cases with adolescent onset have poor prognosis for school and social adjustment. | Return to school; then treatment for primary diagnosis | Separation anxiety; ?overprotective parents; depression in adolescents |
| Elective mutism | 2/3300 7-year-olds | Approx. 1:1 | Most improve | Not investigated | Psychotherapy, family counseling | Abnormality of development and personality |
| Phobias | 5% of clinic series | 1:1 | More males recover than females, leading to preponderance of female cases. | Good. Those that persist respond well to treatment. | Behavior therapy | Social learning; ?persistence of developmentally appropriate fears |
| Conversion hysteria | 4%–8% of pediatric referrals to child psychiatry | Approx. 1:1 | Not known | All males and most females recover. Severely symptomatic females may persist. | Combined psychological and behavioral treatment | Not known |
| Obsessive compulsive neuroses | Uncommon; 0.5%–2% of clinic series | 3–4:1 | Most cases persist; some new cases. | Most cases persist. | "Exposure and response prevention"; chlorimipramine | Probably genetic |
| Tourette's syndrome | Up to 1:2000 school-aged children | 3–4:1 | Symptoms may worsen. Some cases become manifest. | Most cases persist but may remit somewhat. | Haloperidol or clonidine | Probably genetic. Family history of obsessive compulsive neurosis, tics, attention deficits |

## Prevalence

Prevalence varies with circumstance. According to a study by Rutter, Cox, Tupling, Berger, and Yule (1975), urban children are more likely to suffer from emotional disorder than are rural children. They found the prevalence of emotional disorder among 10- to 11-year-olds to be about 1.6 per cent on the Isle of Wight, an island of farms and small villages, and about 3.2 per cent in a working-class section of London. Brain damage is also associated with increased prevalence. The rate of emotional disorder among brain-damaged children on the Isle of Wight was 11 per cent (Rutter, Graham, and Yule, 1970a).

The prevalence in a particular population remains about the same throughout childhood, with boys and girls equally likely to be affected. In adolescence, however, the prevalence in girls appears to increase. The 10- and 11-year-olds from the Isle of Wight were followed at age 14. If only those cases were included that were detected by parent and teacher screening questionnaires, the prevalence rate and sex ratio remained the same as when subjects were studied at age 10. In the unselected control group (not detected by screening), however, a large number of girls complained of sufficiently severe and persistent emotional symptoms to receive a diagnosis. For the most part, these children did not appear to be functionally incapacitated, and thus the importance of the symptoms was not clear (Rutter and Hersov, 1976).

## Causes and Predisposing Factors

The causes of emotional disorder in children are varied and not always easy to discern. There is no particular association with overcrowding or family discord, as there is in conduct disorder, but there seem to be certain predisposing factors. For example, there is some evidence to suggest that the emotionally disturbed child tends to be the only or the oldest child in the family, to have few separations from his or her family, and to be overprotected (Hersov, 1976a; Breit, 1982). Children with brain damage are more likely to suffer from many types of psychiatric symptoms, including emotional disorder.

Recent studies of children of patients with major affective disorder have showed an increased prevalence not only of depressive disorder in the children, but also of a variety of conditions falling under the category of emotional disorder (Cytryn, McKnew, Bartko, Lamour, Hamovitt, 1982). It is not yet clear whether these emotional disorders represent early manifestations of inherited affective disorder or are the result of abnormalities of the home environment provided by a psychiatrically ill parent (Zahn-Waxler, McKnew, Cummings, Davenport, Radke-Yarrow, 1984; Emery, Weintraub, Neale, 1982; Davenport, Zahn-Waxler, Adland, Mayfield, 1984; Weissman et al., 1984; Kuyler, Rosenthal, Igel, Dunner, Fieve, 1980; Billings and Moos, 1983; Conners, Himmelhoch, Goyette, Ulrich, Neil, 1979). Followup studies of the children diagnosed as having emotional disorders are necessary to clarify this issue.

Similar studies of the families of children with emotional disorder are needed to investigate whether parental depression is an important etiologic factor in emotional disorder generally.

## Clinical Features

Patients with emotional disorder usually complain of anxiety, fear, misery, or bodily complaints, and a mixture of these symptoms is often present.

Anxiety has been defined as an unpleasant emotion that has the quality of fear, dread, or alarm (Lader, 1972); the patient feels that there is some vague impending danger when in reality there is no danger, or the fear is out of proportion to any actual danger. Anxiety may be diffuse or related to a specific situation, in which case it is usually called fear or phobia. Children are not able to describe anxiety very clearly and do not answer questionnaires in the same way as adults with anxiety (e.g., Stone, Rawley, Keller, 1965). Its presence must often be inferred from facial expression, nervous behavior in particular situations, or the complaint that "it just feels bad."

Misery is a downcast, unhappy feeling that may be associated with withdrawal or loss of confidence. It is common in child psychiatric populations (seen in up to half the patients) but is accompanied by other features of depressive disorder in only 15 per cent (Carlson and Cantwell, 1979; Hershberg, Carlson, Cantwell, Strober, 1982) and is more responsive to situational changes than depression.

Common bodily complaints in children are headaches and stomachaches. They can usually be distinguished from physical disease by their vague and variable description and their occurrence in the context of some situation that the child wishes to avoid.

Fears, worries, and a certain amount of misery are, of course, part of the human condition, even among normal children. The content of normal fears varies with age. Very young children are commonly fearful of strangers or of being dropped; 4- to 5-year-olds tend to worry about abandonment, the dark, monsters, and ghosts; older children worry more about real problems, such as schoolwork, and have fears about real dangers, including death (LaPouse and Monk, 1959, 1964). Social circumstance also influences the rate and content of children's worries. For example, Orton (1982) found that children in the 1930s worried more about having enough money than did children of the same age in the 1970s. Urban children seem to worry more than rural children. Not only do urban children have a higher rate of emotional problems severe enough to qualify as disorder, but normal urban children also seem to have more emotional symptoms than do rural children (Rutter, 1973).

The symptoms that trouble emotionally disturbed children, then, do seem similar to normal, understandable emotions. They become cause for concern and for psychiatric intervention when they appear to persist beyond developmentally appropriate times or are severe or prolonged enough to cause suffering or interfere with the child's function with the family, at school, or with peers. The differential diagnosis can be complex, and the important features of the case are not always immediately obvious. It is most important to be sure that the patient is not suffering from a major affective disorder. A case example illustrates these issues more clearly.

## CASE HISTORY

Melvin, age 10, was referred because of worrying about his preoccupation with sexual thoughts and his fear of death and of sleeping in his own room.

Several months before referral, a neighbor whom Melvin visited regularly was shot by a burglar. Melvin's parents decided not to take him to the funeral and avoided discussion of the murder at home. At about the same time, Melvin's class at school was receiving a series of sex education lectures. After these events, Melvin began to worry that his parents might die. He was fearful at night and had begun sleeping with his father, the mother moving to the couch. He was also preoccupied with sexual words and focused on parts of ordinary words, such as cockroach and pussycat. He was afraid that he might molest a 6-year-old neighbor.

Melvin, a conscientious boy, was always anxious to do what was right and enjoyed church activities. He did well in school, was active in sports, and had friends. There had been no previous psychiatric disorder.

He had three siblings, all of whom were older than he by 6 to 15 years. They had always been fond and protective of Melvin. His parents had a stable 30-year marriage. They were conservative in their views and were uncomfortable when discussing Melvin's symptoms. The mother was a fearful, anxious person who would drive the car only short distances and preferred to avoid crowded places.

At the initial interview, Melvin was a boy with early pubertal features who was miserable and anxious. He was preoccupied with obsessional sexual thoughts, which he saw as wrong, and tried to drive them out of his mind. On close questioning, there was no evidence of compulsions or symptoms of major affective disorder. He did not initially connect his symptoms to his neighbor's death.

Melvin was diagnosed as having an emotional disorder, but it took several weeks to be certain that he did not have early features of obsessive compulsive disorder or a major depressive illness. Once these disorders were ruled out, the treatment plan rested on a formulation that took into account his conscientious temperament, the conservative family setting in which feelings were not discussed, and the stressful events that had occurred just before onset. These issues were addressed in weekly psychotherapy with Melvin and in separate sessions with his parents. Discussion first focused on his sexual feelings and approaching puberty and how these normal events and sensations could be compatible with his moral and religious beliefs. After several months of weekly psychotherapy, Melvin was able to discuss his feelings about his neighbor and the sudden, frightening nature of his death. He was gradually able to relate his presenting symptoms to these events and feelings. During treatment, which continued for about 2 years, his fears and preoccupations gradually subsided. There has been no recurrence 3 years after onset.

## Treatment

Because each emotional disorder occurs in a child with particular features in unique environmental circumstances, treatment must be tailored to the individual patient. Sometimes parents can be reassured that the symptoms are normal at that child's age. If treatment is indicated, some form of psychotherapy and work with parents and school is often beneficial.

Most children with nonspecific emotional disorder recover eventually even without treatment (Rutter et al., 1976b; Hersov, 1976a). There is, therefore, some question about whether treatment is needed at all. Most treating psychiatrists have strong clinical impressions that children with emotional disorders improve with treatment; however, investigations into the efficacy of psychotherapy are fraught with methodological problems, and it has been difficult to demonstrate the benefits statistically.

In their review of a large number of studies of psychotherapy in children, Wright and Moelis (1976) found that most studies in which measurements were made only at the end of the treatment period demonstrated little or no difference between treated and nontreated groups. Only those studies that did second comparisons some months after treatment ended found clear benefits to the treated group. This finding suggests that the children and their families do benefit from treatment in the long run, perhaps as they begin to consider for themselves some of the issues raised in therapy and to incorporate some of the ideas into their own thoughts and behavior. In any case, while there is some hope of reducing the severity or duration of a child's suffering, treatment is certainly justified.

## Prognosis

As stated earlier, the prognosis for children with nonspecific emotional disorder is generally good (Michael, Morris, Soroker, 1954; Robins, 1966; Gorsten, Langner, Eisenberg, Simcha-Fagan, McCarthy, 1976). One study of those children who did continue to have psychiatric problems in adult life showed that these patients continued to suffer from emotional problems, such as minor depression, anxiety disorder, or other neuroses, and none had antisocial behavior (Pritchard and Graham, 1966). Patients with emotional disorders during adolescence were most likely to have persisting problems (Gorsten et al., 1976).

## BEHAVIORS THAT MAY BE ASSOCIATED WITH EMOTIONAL DISORDER

School refusal and elective mutism are abnormal behaviors of childhood that are usually accompanied by emotional symptoms. Specific abnormal behaviors almost always have a variety of causes and seldom constitute specific diagnostic entities (McHugh and Slavney, 1983). School refusal and elective mutism are given separate discussion because it is the behaviors themselves that have social consequences and that usually become the focus of treatment.

### School Refusal

#### Definition

When a child persistently misses school with the knowledge of his or her parents because of fear of going to school or of leaving the mother, the behavior is called school refusal. This behavior was distinguished from truancy (nonattendance at school without parental knowledge) by Broadwin in 1932 and was later labeled "school phobia" by Johnson, Falstein, Szurek, and Svendsen (1941).

#### Prevalence

School refusal occurs with equal frequency in girls and boys (Baker and Wills, 1979), although severe cases requiring hospital treatment are more likely to involve boys (Hersov, 1960b). There are peaks in prevalence at the age of first school attendance, at age 11 (Chazan, 1962), and at adolescence (Hersov, 1976b).

#### Causes and Predisposing Factors

Nonattendance at school has a variety of causes, and the precipitating factors differ at each age of increased prevalence. In the youngest group, anxiety over the first prolonged period of separation from the mother is most common; at age 11, the precipitating factor is often a change of school; in adolescence, there is often an association with affective disorder or other psychiatric conditions that begin in adolescence. Shaffer (1974) reported four adolescent suicides who had presented as school refusers. Tisher (1983) also reported depressive symptoms in adolescent school refusers but interpreted the symptoms as understandable and felt that, as in younger children with school refusal, the family relationships were the most important factor.

The relationship between school refusers and their families has been considered crucial by most investigators. Compared with the parents of truants and other, unselected child psychiatric patients, the parents of school refusers are more often described as overprotective, have been less often separated from their children, and have a high prevalence of neurotic and affective illness (Hersov, 1960a; Eisenberg, 1959; Berg and McGuire, 1974). Eight of Hersov's sample of 50 children had elderly parents. It is not clear to what extent these parental features differ from those of other neurotic children, and parental characteristics and behaviors do not entirely explain why adolescent patients refuse to go to school (Berg, Butler, Fairbairn, McGuire, 1981; Berg and McGuire, 1971, 1974). Because of the association in adolescents of school refusal with severer psychiatric disorders, family factors may be less important in these cases.

### Clinical Features

School refusal is a behavior, not a diagnosis, but most school refusers are given psychiatric diagnoses of anxiety or depression (Hersov, 1960a). Excluding adolescents, who may constitute a separate group, school refusers usually do not manifest severe anxiety or depression except during the morning, when it is time to get ready for school. At this time they become anxious and fearful, may complain of physical symptoms, may become panic-stricken, and may often physically resist being taken to school. These symptoms begin insidiously and, if the parents give in, may become so severe that the parents become afraid to insist that the child attend school. Refusal may go on for weeks to years in the face of "persuasion, entreaty, recrimination, and punishment" (Hersov, 1976b). Development, IQ, and school performance of school refusers are usually normal, but social adjustment is commonly poor (Hersov, 1960b).

### Treatment

Most investigators and clinicians agree that the first step in treatment is to return the child to school (Rodriguez, Rodriguez, Eisenberg, 1959; Eisenberg, 1959; Kennedy, 1971). This requires firm handling of both the child and the parents, as well as careful arrangements with schoolteachers and administrators. In severe, persistent cases, an inpatient admission may be required in order to effect a return to school. Adolescents in particular should be carefully screened for signs of serious affective disorder.

Simultaneously with and after return to school, some type of family counseling and psychotherapy is indicated, as family relationships are almost always disturbed. (However, there are no controlled studies.) Greenbaum (1964) dissents from the prevailing view that the child be returned to school first, pointing out that once the child is back in school, it is difficult to keep the family in therapy long enough to resolve the family problems.

### Prognosis

The prognosis for return to school is usually good. In one study, 90 per cent of children under age 11 had returned to school (Rodriguez et al., 1959). In adolescents, the likelihood of return to school is only 60 per cent (Berg, 1970). The prognosis for a satisfactory social adjustment is not as good, however (Weiss and Burke, 1967; Warren, 1965; Berg, 1970). Many school refusers go on to have difficulties in severing ties with their families, excessive dependency on their spouses, agoraphobia, and dropping out of school at higher levels (Berg, Marks, McGuire, Lipsedge, 1974).

## Elective Mutism

Elective mutism is an uncommon behavior in which talking is persistently confined to a familiar situation or a small group of intimates. It was first described and so named by Tramer (1934).

### Prevalence

Although transient refusal to speak at school is common, persistent elective mutism is uncommon, seen in only 2 of 3000 7-year-olds in one British survey of schoolchildren (Fundudis, Kolvin, Garside, 1979). The sex ratio in a case series reported by Kolvin and Fundudis (1981) was about equal (11 boys and 13 girls), while in Wright's series (1968), girls predominated (7:17).

## Causes and Predisposing Factors

Unlike most other children with emotional disorders, children with elective mutism have developmental abnormalities more often than do controls. In the series reported by Kolvin and Fundudis (1981), the children walked a bit late, spoke significantly later, 42 per cent were enuretic, and, at the time of evaluation, half had immaturities of speech. Wright (1968) reports similar findings. Kolvin reported no excess of perinatal complications, although three of his cases had epileptiform electroencephalograms (EEGs) and three more had EEGs described as "immature." Others had tics, hyperactive behavior, obsessions, or faints in addition to mutism. The mean IQ was 85, and 76 per cent had IQs under 100.

There is a high prevalence of personality disorders among the parents of electively mute children. In 14 of 24 families reported by Kolvin and Fundudis, at least one parent had neurosis, depressive disorder, or "a markedly unusual personality" (usually shy or aggressive). Two siblings in the sample had seen physicians on account of excessive shyness, and two others were mentally handicapped. In Wright's series of 24 cases from 21 families, in 16 families at least one parent had some obvious psychological abnormality, and shyness was particularly common. There were three pairs of mute siblings in his series. Brown and Lloyd (1975) reported that in their sample, more than half the children had an extremely shy parent compared with 5 per cent in the control group. Many authors believe that parental psychiatric disorder, with its associated abnormal parenting, is the explanation for elective mutism. It seems plausible that, in children, the combination of predisposing personality traits of extreme shyness and stubbornness (see later), psychiatrically handicapped parents, and the stress of school or social situations could lead to refusal to speak. The meaning of occasional familial aggregation is not clear.

## Clinical Features

Elective mutism develops insidiously in shy children, becoming more noticeable when they begin school. Like children with other emotional disorders, these children are described as shy, sensitive, and fearful in their temperaments, and very attached to their mothers. Children with mutism differ, however, in being commonly described as stubborn and controlling, using their refusal to speak as a way of controlling their families and teachers (Wright, 1968; Kolvin and Fundudis, 1981).

## Treatment

There is no generally accepted treatment for elective mutism and no research into treatment methods. Because of the rarity of the disorder, it may be difficult to assemble enough cases for a treatment trial.

Most patients are treated with intensive psychotherapy, during which the therapist first develops a caring relationship with the child and then combines behavioral methods with insight into the child's personality and relationships. Wright (1968) describes his treatment approach in this way: he first indicates to the child his acceptance of the problem, showing concern and sympathy, and says that he knows that the child wishes to speak. He then begins to reward the child for nodding and other nonverbal responses and encourages speech, explaining that the first words will be the most difficult but then speech will become easier. Once the child speaks in the treatment session, the focus is turned to speech in school. Finally, attention is given to the often-unpleasant controlling relationship of the child to his or her family.

## Prognosis

In Kolvin's series of 24 cases, the prognosis was better for younger children. Eleven of 24 improved, although only three markedly, and all but one of those who had improved did so by age 10. More girls than boys had a satisfactory recovery, and the prognosis was best when there were no parental personality problems. Wright reported a somewhat better outcome, with 15 of his 25 cases having an extremely good outcome. In his series, the children with low IQs did somewhat worse.

## EMOTIONAL SYMPTOMS IN NEUROTIC DISORDERS

In rare cases, the symptoms of children with emotional problems take on a stereotyped, syndromal quality and can be recognized as belonging to distinct psychiatric disorders, such as phobia, conversion hysteria, obsessive compulsive neurosis, tics, and Gilles de la Tourette's syndrome. These disorders are more clearly delineated than nonspecific emotional disorders, and the symptoms seem to fall outside the range of normal human experience. Without treatment, such conditions have a much worse prognosis than nonspecific emotional disorders, and they often persist into adult life. Because of the psychoanalytic view that they are based on unconscious, unresolved conflicts concerning sexual and aggressive impulses, these disorders are traditionally called neuroses.

## Phobias

A phobia is an irrational, involuntary fear that is inappropriate to the actual danger of the feared object or situation.

Transient fears and phobias are extremely common among young children, and most are easily handled by parents. About a third of 2- to 4-year-olds have transient phobias of animals, insects, monsters, and the dark (DuPont, 1983). These are seldom a cause for concern or treatment and gradually subside. A smaller number (about 10 per cent to 15 per cent) of normal 6- to 8-year-olds have transient phobias, most commonly of storms, heights, and other situations that may be associated with physical danger.

Transient isolated phobias of animals and other exogenous phobias are about equally common in boys and girls and become unusual by age 10. Adolescents may have transient fears of social situations, such as fear of blushing, eating in restaurants, going to parties (Marks and Gelders, 1966). These are more common in girls.

When phobias persist long after they are developmentally common and are associated with significant anxiety and functional limitations, they become a cause for psychiatric referral and a diagnosis of phobic disorder or neurosis.

### Prevalence

The prevalence of phobic disorder is much lower than transient, developmentally appropriate fears, representing 5 per cent of the 10-year-olds on the Isle of Wight who were given a psychiatric diagnosis, and thus less than 1 per cent of all children studied (Rutter et al., 1970b). Most of these children also had other emotional symptoms, and there were equal numbers of boys and girls. However, of those children with phobias that persist to adult life (almost all "exogenous," i.e., of animals, elevators, etc.), most are girls (MacFarlane, Allen, Honzik, 1954; Abe and Masui, 1981). In one series of adults with phobias, all animal phobias had been present since childhood (Sheehan, Sheehan, Minichiello, 1981).

### Causes

It is not clear how or why phobias arise in children, but according to social learning theory, the fear is a learned maladaptive response. Clear precipitants (such as a dog bite or being accidentally locked in) are not usually elicited, but children often have the same phobias as their mothers, which suggests a learned response (DuPont, 1983). Another possibility is that particular phobias are normal and even adaptive at certain developmental stages but occasionally persist beyond their usefulness. The features of family functioning and family history of this child psychiatric disorder have apparently not been studied.

### Clinical Features

When faced with the feared object or situation, or even the possibility of it, terrifying feelings of fear and impending doom arise in phobic patients. Adults say that they become afraid they will lose control or do something humiliating; children just say it feels bad. These feelings lead the patient to avoid the feared object or situation and avoid places where there is any possibility that the object or situation may be encountered.

Diagnosis is not difficult when phobia of an object or situation is the only symptom. Phobias can, however, be a part of other psychiatric disorders and be accompanied by more generalized anxiety and timidity, in which case the diagnosis and treatment should reflect the predominant syndrome.

### Treatment

For isolated phobias, the treatment of choice is some form of behavior therapy. Miller, Barrett, and Hampe (1974) distill this treatment into four essential features: (1) the establishment of a helping relationship with the patient and family, (2) clarification of the stimulus, (3) desensitization to the stimulus, and (4) confrontation of the patient with the stimulus. This requires careful delineation of what aspect of the object or situation elicits the fear and the planning of a systematic schedule of the behavior modification. Parents should be involved so that practice can be carried out at home. With children, it appears that in vivo desensitization is more effective than simulation of the fear-provoking situation (Ultee, Griffioen, Schellekens, 1982), perhaps because children cannot adequately reproduce the situation mentally.

Although there are no published series of phobias in children (but see Marks, 1974), the outcome of treatment is usually good in isolated phobias, even if they are long-standing. More complex phobias, especially agoraphobia, which is not seen in children, probably have a different etiology, and treatment is more difficult (Marks and Gelder, 1966). When phobias are accompanied by other emotional symptoms or disorders, treatment plans should include behavioral therapy, but in combination with other forms of treatment.

## Conversion Hysteria

The definition of conversion hysteria is the same for children as for adults. Patients with conversion hysteria present with physical symptoms that appear to have no medical explanation and do not follow the usual patterns of medical disorder. On further investigation, the symptoms appear to be serving some psychological purpose, and patients are often described as indifferent to the disability caused by the symptoms. "Conversion" refers to a proposed psychological mechanism of converting unbearable anxiety into somatic manifestations. One symptom usually predominates, although patients often complain of many symptoms.

### Prevalence

There are few studies of hysteria in childhood and no current prevalence estimates. Most cases come to attention through referral from pediatricians. Robins and O'Neal (1953) found 41 children with a diagnosis of hysteria or some related disorder among 1029 pediatric inpatients who were given a psychiatric diagnosis. When children with mental retardation were excluded, the 41

children with hysteria or hypochondriasis accounted for about 8 per cent of the cases referred to psychiatry. Rock (1971) reported that conversion reactions accounted for 3.6 per cent of pediatric referrals to the child psychiatric service. Most published case collections report rather more males than are seen in adult populations, but females still predominate in most series. The age of onset can be as early as 5 years (Robins and O'Neal, 1953).

### Causes

It is usually presumed that children with conversion symptoms have discovered that the "sick role" can somehow be used to their advantage, for example, to stop their parents' quarreling (Creak, 1969), to forestall return to an unhappy school situation (Dubowitz and Hersov, 1976), or to relieve them of some unwanted responsibility. Family difficulties are presumed to play a role, but no formal studies of this hypothesis have been reported. The case reports in the literature nearly always state that parents cooperated with treatment, suggesting that parental collusion is not an important feature. It is possible, however, that unrealistic parental expectations of the child, or other parental attitudes that cause the child to be fearful, may play a role.

### Clinical Features

Mildred Creak (1938) defined three subtypes of conversion symptoms commonly seen in children. The first is "true" conversion hysteria, in which the physical symptom has no organic basis; the second is a hysterical prolongation of organically based disease; and the third, clear organic disease, in which nervous or psychological symptoms accompany and modify the manifestations of the disease. The latter subtype is not usually included within the diagnostic category, but conversion hysteria may be part of the differential diagnosis.

Diagnosis of conversion hysteria can be extremely difficult. On the one hand, children with vague physical symptoms frequently turn out to have a diagnosable physical disorder, the treatment to which may be delayed by making a psychiatric diagnosis (Caplan, 1970; Dubowitz and Hersov, 1976; Rinvinus, Jamison, Graham, 1975). On the other hand, continuing to perform tests and procedures on patients with true conversion symptoms not only delays appropriate psychiatric treatment, but also makes it more difficult and increases the risk of iatrogenic injury from tests, procedures, and surgery (Creak, 1969; Rock, 1971).

In the study of Robins and O'Neal (1953), 23 patients were reexamined from 2 to 17 years after a hospital diagnosis of conversion hysteria. It was possible, in retrospect, to distinguish to some extent between true hysterical conversions and symptoms that later were found to be caused by a medical condition. Of the 23 patients examined at followup, only 4 were currently suffering from conversion symptoms. They were all women and had initially complained of many symptoms. At followup, they continued to show hysterical symptoms and were considered the most severely disabled of the 23 patients examined. An additional eight patients (five males and three females) had mild anxiety neuroses at followup but were not hysterical, and they were considered mildly disabled or not disabled by their symptoms. Four of these persons probably had organic symptoms that were prolonged or colored by their anxious temperamental features and would be classified into Creak's second and third groups. Most of the remaining 11 (four males and seven females) had probably been suffering from misdiagnosed physical conditions. The "true" conversions were distinguished not so much by the type of symptoms at their initial childhood presentation as by their multiplicity.

Rinvinus et al. (1975) described 12 children with neurologic conditions who were initially given psychiatric diagnoses. Only two were called hysteria, but a further four were described as having anxiety or emotional disorders. The authors propose that the clinical features that distinguished this group from true conversion hysteria were the complaints of deterioration of school performance and disturbances of posture and gait. However, there was no control group, and the same features, especially disturbances of posture and gait, were common complaints in the patients of Robins and O'Neal, who had hysteria or anxiety neuroses at followup.

Dubowitz and Hersov (1976) described five children with hysterical prolongation of symptoms caused by an acute, but resolving illness. These children would fit Creak's second subtype. It was possible in each case to elicit a history of injury or illness that clearly brought on the symptoms. The confusion arose when the symptoms, usually a disturbance of gait, did not subside. In each case, it was possible to find psychological reasons for the child to wish to continue in the sick role. Treatment was seriously delayed by the physicians' confusion and by continued tests, procedures, and somatic treatments.

### Treatment

Treatment of conversion symptoms consists of several steps. First, a clear diagnosis must be made based on the history and a careful examination. Second, the physicians caring for the child must agree that all tests and somatic treatment be stopped. Third, the parents must be given an explanation of the nature of the symptoms and their cooperation gained for treatment. And finally, the child must be reassured that he or she will recover and gradually be encouraged and rewarded for improved physical and psychological functioning. It is best not to confront the child specifically with the opinion that the symptoms are not organically based. During the treatment, aspects of the home and school environment that may have encouraged the child to take on a sick role should be explored.

### Prognosis

The short-term outcome of hysterical symptoms is good if treatment is promptly instituted, but it is less good if symptoms have persisted for a long time. Because the sex ratio for conversion hysteria changes with age from slight female preponderance to almost exclusively female, it appears that the prognosis is especially good for boys. In Robins and O'Neal's study, only 4 of the 12 persons with psychiatric diagnoses at followup had hysteria.

## Obsessive-Compulsive Neurosis

### Definition

An obsession is an unwanted repetitive thought that intrudes itself into consciousness and is seen by the patient as senseless or foolish. A compulsion is a repeated act carried out in response to the obsessional thought. There are three essential characteristics of obsessional symptoms (Lewis, 1938): (1) the experience of an inner compelling force, (2) internal resistance to it, and (3) the retention of insight.

### Prevalence

Obsessive compulsive neurosis is a severe but, fortunately, uncommon condition in both children and adults, accounting for about 1 per cent of childhood psychiatric referrals. In children, it is more common in boys than in girls by 2 to 4:1 (Judd, 1965; Adams, 1973; Hollingsworth, Tanguay, Grossman, Pabst, 1980; Rapoport et al., 1981). Intelligence and development are normal, and above-average IQs are often reported.

### Cause

The cause is not yet clear, but there is probably a strong genetic component. Hollingsworth et al. (1980) reports 22 of 34 parents with psychiatric illness, half with obsessive compulsive neurosis. Judd (1965) reports a family history of psychiatric disorder, often obsessive compulsive neurosis in four of five families. In nine childhood cases reported by Rapoport, no parents were affected, but more than half the sibs had psychiatric diagnoses. Her sample was assembled in an unusual way, which may have selected for normal parents. Reports of twins suggest an excess of monozygotic concordant pairs (Elkins, Rapoport, Lipsky, 1980).

### Clinical Features

Symptoms can begin at any time from early life on. The onset is most often acute, with some definable precipitating event. About 20 per cent of adult cases give histories of first symptoms before age 10, and one of three, by age 15. The most common obsessional thoughts focus on fears of contamination with feces, dirt, or germs; fears of doing something wrong, such as stealing; or fear of potential danger. These thoughts persist, despite attempts to force them from consciousness, resulting in increasing amounts of tension and anxiety, which is relieved temporarily by the compulsive activity. Washing rituals, ritualistic touching sequences to ward off trouble, or complex bedtime routines are common compulsions. Most children do not go on to have any other

psychiatric disorder, although some appear depressed, mostly secondary to their inability to control their behavior. Obsessions and compulsions are sometimes seen in patients with anorexia nervosa, severe depression, or schizophrenia, and they wax and wane with the symptoms of the primary condition.

### Treatment

Many treatments have been tried over the years—psychotherapy, neurosurgery, behavior therapy (Bolton, Collins, Steinberg, 1983), and pharmacotherapy. Treatments are somewhat difficult to evaluate because symptoms wax and wane in the untreated state. Psychotherapy, however, does not appear to have any long-term benefit, and neurosurgery is helpful but ethically unsatisfactory.

Marks and his colleagues have considerable research experience with behavioral treatments in adults. They report that repeated forced exposure to the object of obsessional thoughts (e.g., touching trash cans), along with prevention of the compulsive response, is of great benefit if clear rituals are present and the patient is not depressed (Marks, Stern, Mawson, Cobb, McDonald, 1980). They recommend chlorimipramine for obsessive compulsive patients not meeting those criteria. Several studies have demonstrated the benefit of chlorimipramine compared with other types of treatment and compared with other antidepressant medications in adults (Marks et al., 1980; Insel et al., 1983). The one study of chlorimipramine in children (Rapoport et al., 1980) did not demonstrate any benefit over the untreated group. However, further studies are needed. Because of the essential similarity of obsessive compulsive neurosis at all ages, it seems reasonable to expect that the same treatments would work for children and adults.

### Prognosis

The outcome for children with obsessive compulsive neurosis varies, but it is generally persistent without treatment (Ross, 1964). Hollingsworth et al. (1980) reported that only 3 of 10 cases in their series were without symptoms at followup, although most were somewhat improved. Warren (1965) reported that only 6 of 15 were normal to near-normal at followup, but none of these cases had received modern pharmacologic or behavioral treatments.

## Tics and Gilles de la Tourette's Syndrome

### Definition

Tics are rapid, rhythmic, stereotyped motor movements (motor tics) or vocalizations (vocal tics). Although motor and vocal tics are extremely varied, a particular patient will show a characteristic stereotyped pattern, at least in the short run.

Transient tics are common in children; around 10 per cent to 15 per cent of children aged 6 to 12 have them (LaPouse and Monk, 1964). The most common ones are eye blinking, nose puckering, grimacing, and squinting. Common vocal tics are throat clearing, coughing, and humming (Cohen, Leckman, Shaywitz, 1983). Transient tics last for weeks to months and usually disappear but may be replaced by other tics over a series of years. The tendency to transient tics appears to be familial and is probably more common in boys.

Tics that persist unchanged over years are called chronic tics, and when there are a number of tics, chronic multiple tics. These syndromes fade into one another, and the latter fades into the Gilles de la Tourette's syndrome (TS). TS is defined by the presence of chronic, frequent, complex, multiple, changing motor and vocal tics, often including coprolalia (explosive utterance of foul language). There are usually attentional deficits. Forty per cent of patients with TS also suffer from obsessions and compulsions.

### Prevalence

The prevalence of TS may be as high as 1:2000 (Cohen et al., 1983), with symptoms beginning usually between ages 2 and 15. Boys are much more likely to be affected than girls.

### Causes and Predisposing Features

In all varieties—or perhaps severities—of tics there is clearly a familial aggregation. (For reviews, see Paul, Kruger, Leckman, Cohen, Kidd, 1984; Comings and Comings, 1984). Not only are other TS patients found in the families, but also chronic and transient tics, attention-deficit disorders, and obsessive compulsive disorder. The data are possibly compatible with mendelian transmission of some trait or predisposition to all these conditions, with unknown factors modifying penetrance, particularly in girls. Polygenic, sex-dependent threshold models have also been suggested (Cohen et al., 1983). Male-to-male transmission is the most frequent phenotypic pattern, so that X-linkage can be ruled out.

A considerable body of research has focused on possible neurochemical mechanisms in TS. Probably there are such abnormalities, but the nature of these is not clear. Based on the response to haloperidol, abnormalities of the dopaminergic system have been suggested. However, serotonergic, cholinergic, and noradrenergic systems have all been implicated by various investigations (Cohen et al., 1983). Noradrenergic abnormalities are suggested by the clinical response to clonidine, but measurements of transmitter metabolites have not supported direct noradrenergic involvement (Leckman et al., 1983).

### Clinical Features

In severe chronic multiple tics and TS, the type of tics varies from patient to patient. Symptoms change over time in content and wax and wane in severity. TS is a lifelong condition, although longitudinal experience suggests that symptoms are worst during adolescence. Many exotic motor and vocal tics have been described (Cohen et al., 1983). In addition to simple motor and vocal tics, complex movements like hopping, clapping, and kissing are seen. It becomes difficult to distinguish these from compulsions, and more elaborate compulsive behaviors also occur. For example, patients may feel compelled to rebutton their shirts many times "to get it right." Examples of complex verbal tics are exclamations ("wow," "shit," "you said it") and complex rude sentences (e.g., "You're a fat, boring doctor.").

In addition to tics and compulsive behaviors, many young patients are also diagnosed as having attention-deficit disorder, either before or after the onset of tics. It has been suggested that methylphenidate may precipitate tics. If so, it is probably more likely to occur in susceptible individuals.

The rate of familial aggregation of tics is equally prominent for TS patients who were and were not treated with stimulants before the onset of tics (Comings and Comings, 1984).

When manifestations are severe, many secondary academic and social handicaps and symptoms appear. Family problems are common because of embarrassment, concern for the child's social adjustment, and worry over school performance. After a time, parents may begin to wonder whether the child could control his symptoms if he wanted to. Symptoms may nearly disappear for long periods and may vary according to the situation. Some patients can suppress tics when at school or in the doctor's office.

### Treatment

Although some improvement is sometimes seen with behavioral techniques (Azrin, Nunn, Frantz, 1980; Cohen and Marks, 1977), haloperidol is, to date, the most effective treatment for tics (Shapiro, Shapiro, Wayne, 1973). Most patients respond at low doses (sometimes less than 1 mg per day). Higher doses often do not yield any additional benefit and result in debilitating side effects (Bruun, 1984). Some clinicians have recently advocated using clonidine before trying haloperidol (Cohen et al., 1983) because, although improvement is not seen in as large a percentage of cases as haloperidol (60 per cent vs. 80 per cent), the side effects are fewer and less debilitating. In addition, attention deficits may be improved with clonidine. Pimozide has recently been used successfully but is also fraught with dangerous side effects (Shapiro and Shapiro, 1984).

Because of the difficulties with chronic pharmacologic treatment, mild cases are better left unmedicated. Family education and therapy can often help the patient and family appreciate the nature and course of the disorder and feel less in need of complete symptom suppression.

In severely afflicted patients, counseling and understanding are also an important part of treatment. Patients become overwhelmed by the bizarre and unpleasant content of their vocal and motor tics and compulsions and begin to wonder "what's me and what's Tourette's." Before undertaking the treatment of a TS patient, more detailed reading of the references is suggested.

## REFERENCES

Abe K, Masui T: Age-sex trends of phobic and anxiety symptoms in adolescents. Br J Psychiatry 138:297–302, 1981.

Adams PL: Obsessive Children: A Sociopsychiatric Study. London, Butterworth, 1973.

Azrin NH, Nunn RG, Frantz SE: Habit reversal vs. negative practice treatment of nervous tics. Behav Ther 2:169–178, 1980.

Baker H, Wills U: School phobic children at work. Br J Psychiatry 135:561–564, 1979.

Berg I: A follow-up study of school phobic adolescents admitted to an in-patient unit. J Child Psychol Psychiatry 11:37–47, 1970.

Berg I, Butler A, Fairbairn I, McGuire R: The parents of school phobic adolescents—A preliminary investigation of family life variables. Psychol Med 11:79–83, 1981.

Berg I, Marks I, McGuire R, Lipsedge M: School phobia and agoraphobia. Psychol Med 4:428–434, 1974.

Berg I, McGuire R: Are school phobic adolescents overdependent? Br J Psychiatry 119:167–168, 1971.

Berg I, McGuire R: Are mothers of school phobic adolescents overprotective? Br J Psychiatry 124:10–13, 1974.

Billings AG, Moos RH: Comparisons of children of depressed and nondepressed parents: A social-environmental perspective. J Abnorm Child Psychol 11:463–486, 1983.

Bolton D, Collins S, Steinberg D: The treatment of obsessive-compulsive disorder in adolescence. A report of fifteen cases. Br J Psychiatry 142:456–464, 1983.

Breit M: Separation anxiety in mothers of latency-age fearful children. J Abnorm Child Psychol 10:135–144, 1982.

Broadwin IT: A contribution to the study of truancy. Am J Orthopsychiatry 2:253–259, 1932.

Brown JB, Lloyd H: A controlled study of children not speaking at school. J Assoc Workers Maladjusted Child 3:49–53, 1975.

Bruun RD: Gilles de la Tourette's syndrome: An overview of clinical experience. J Am Acad Child Psychiatry 23:126–133, 1984.

Caplan HL: Hysterical conversion symptoms in childhood. Unpublished M. Phil. Thesis, University of London, 1970.

Carlson GA, Cantwell DP: A survey of depressive symptoms in a child and adolescent psychiatric population: Interview data. J Am Acad Child Psychiatry 18:587–599, 1979.

Chazan M: School phobia. Br J Educ Psychol 34:292–304, 1962.

Cohen D, Leckman JF, Shaywitz BA: Tourette's Syndrome: Assessment and treatment, in Shaffer D, Ehrhardt AA, Greenhill L (eds): Diagnosis and Treatment in Pediatric Psychiatry. New York, MacMillan Free Press, 1983.

Cohen D, Marks FM: Gilles de la Tourette's syndrome treated by operant conditioning. Br J Psychiatry 130:315, 1977.

Comings DE, Comings BG: Tourette's syndrome and attention deficit disorder with hyperactivity: Are they genetically related? J Am Acad Child Psychiatry 23:138–146, 1984.

Conners CK, Himmelhoch J, Goyette CH, Ulrich R, Neil JF: Children of parents with affective illness. J Am Acad Child Psychiatry 18:600–608, 1979.

Creak M: Hysteria in childhood. Br J Child Dis 35:85–95, 1938.

Creak M: Hysteria in childhood. Acta Paedopsychiatr 36:269–274, 1969.

Cytryn L, McKnew DH, Bartko JJ, Lamour M, Hamovitt J: Offspring of patients with affective disorders. II. J Am Acad Child Psychiatry 21:389–391, 1982.

Davenport YB, Zahn-Waxler C, Adland ML, Mayfield A: Early child rearing practices in families with a manic-depressive parent. Am J Psychiatry 141:230–235, 1984.

Dubowitz V, Hersov L: Management of children with non-organic (hysterical) disorders of motor function. Dev Med Child Neurol 18:358–368, 1976.

DuPont RL: Phobias in children. J Pediatr 102:999–1002, 1983.

Eisenberg L: The pediatric management of school phobia. J Pediatr 55:758–766, 1959.

Elkins R, Rapoport JL, Lipsky A: Obsessive-compulsive disorder of childhood and adolescence. A neuro-biological viewpoint. J Am Acad Child Psychiatry 19:511–524, 1980.

Emery R, Weintraub S, Neale JF: Effects of marital discord on the school behavior of children of schizophrenic, affectively disordered, and normal parents. J Abnorm Child Psychol 10:215–228, 1982.

Fundudis T, Kolvin I, Garside RF: Speech Retarded and Deaf Children: Their Psychological Development. London, Academic Press, 1979.

Gorsten JC, Langner TS, Eisenberg JG, Simcha-Fagan O, McCarthy ED: Stability and change in types of behavior disturbance in children and adolescents. J Abnorm Child Psychol 4:111–127, 1976.

Greenbaum RS: Treatment of school phobias: Theory and practice. Am J Psychother 18:616–633, 1964.

Hershberg SG, Carlson GA, Cantwell DP, Strober M: Anxiety and depressive disorders in psychiatrically disturbed children. J Clin Psychiatry 43:358–361, 1982.

Hersov LA: Persistent non-attendance at school. J Child Psychol Psychiatry 1:130–136, 1960a.

Hersov LA: Refusal to go to school. J Child Psychol Psychiatry 1:137–145, 1960b.

Hersov LA: Emotional disorders, in Rutter M, Hersov L (eds): Child Psychiatry: Modern Approaches. Oxford, Blackwell, 1976a, pp 428–454.

Hersov LA: School refusal, in Rutter M, Hersov L (eds): Child Psychiatry: Modern Approaches. Oxford, Blackwell, 1976b, pp 455–486.

Hewitt LE, Jenkins RL: Fundamental Patterns of Maladjustment: The Dynamics of their Origins; A Statistical Analysis Based upon Five Hundred Case Records of Children Examined at the Michigan Child Guidance Institute. Springfield, IL, 1946.

Hollingsworth CE, Tanguay PE, Grossman L, Pabst P: Long-term outcome of obsessive-compulsive disorder in childhood. J Am Acad Child Psychiatry 19:134–144, 1980.

Insel TR, Murphy DL, Cohen RM, Alterman I, Kilts C, Linnoila M: Obsessive-compulsive disorder. A double blind trial of chlorimipramine and clorgyline. Arch Gen Psychiatry 40:605–612, 1983.

Johnson AM, Falstein EI, Szurek SA, Svendsen M: School phobia. Am J Orthopsychiatry 11:702–711, 1941.

Judd L: Obsessive-compulsive neurosis in children. Arch Gen Psychiatry 12:136–143, 1965.

Kennedy WA: A behaviouristic community-oriented approach to school phobia and other disorders, in Richard HC (ed): Behavioural Intervention in Human Problems. Oxford, Pergamon Press, 1971.

Kolvin I, Fundudis T: Elective mute children: Psychological development and background factors. J Child Psychol Psychiatry 22:219–232, 1981.

Kuyler PL, Rosenthal L, Igel G, Dunner DL, Fieve RR: Psychopathology among children of manic-depressive patients. Biol Psychiatry 15:589–597, 1980.

Lader M: The nature of anxiety. Br J Psychiatry 121:481–491, 1972.

LaPouse R, Monk M: Behavior deviations in a representative sample of children: Variation by sex, age, race, social class and family size. Am J Orthopsychiatry 34:436–446, 1964.

LaPouse R, Monk MA: Fears and worries in a representative sample of children. Am J Orthopsychiatry 29:803–818, 1959.

Leckman JF, Deltor J, Harcherick DF, Young JG, Anderson GU, Shaywitz BA, Cohen DJ: Acute and chronic clonidine treatment with Tourette's syndrome: A preliminary report on clinical response and effect on plasma and urinary catecholamine metabolites, growth hormone, and blood pressure. J Am Acad Child Psychiatry 22:433–440, 1983.

Lewis A: Problems of obsessional illness. Proc R Soc Med 29:4060–4064, 1938.

MacFarlane JW, Allen L, Honzik MR: A Developmental Study of the Behavior Problems of Normal Children Between 21 Months and 14 Years. Berkeley, University of California Press, 1954.

Marks I: Research in neurosis: A selective review. II. Treatment. Psychol Med 4:89–100, 1974.

Marks I, Gelder M: Different ages of onset in varieties of phobia. Am J Psychiatry 123:218–221, 1966.

Marks IM, Stern RS, Mawson D, Cobb J, McDonald R: Chlorimipramine and exposure for obsessive-compulsive rituals. I. Br J Psychiatry 136:1–25, 1980.

Mattison R, Cantwell DP, Russell AT, Will L: A comparison of DSM-II and DSM-III in the diagnosis of child psychiatric disorders. II. Interrater agreement. Arch Gen Psychiatry 36:1217–1222, 1979.

McGee R, Silva PA, Williams S: Behavior problems in a population of seven-year-old children: Prevalence, stability and types of disorder—A research report. J Child Psychol Psychiatry 25:251–259, 1984.

McHugh PR, Slavney P: The Perspectives of Psychiatry. Baltimore, Johns Hopkins University Press, 1983.

Michael CM, Morris DP, Soroker E: Followup studies of shy withdrawn children. I. Evaluation of later adjustment. Am J Orthopsychiatry 24:743–754, 1954.

Miller LC, Barrett CL, Hampe E: Phobias of childhood in a prescientific era, in Davids A (ed): Child Personality and Psychopathology: Current Topics. New York, John Wiley & Sons, 1974.

Orton GL: A comparative study of children's worries. J Psychol 110:153–162, 1982.

Paul DL, Kruger SD, Leckman JF, Cohen DS, Kidd KK: The risk of Tourette's syndrome and chronic multiple tics among relatives of Tourette's syndrome patients obtained by direct interview. J Am Acad Child Psychiatry 23:134–137, 1984.

Pritchard M, Graham P: An investigation of a group of patients who have attended both the child and adult departments of the same psychiatric hospital. Br J Psychiatry 112:603–612, 1966.

Rapoport J, Elkins R, Langer DH, Sceery W, Buchsbaum MS, Gillin JC, Murphy DL, Zahn TP, Lake R,

Ludlow C, Mendelson W: Childhood obsessive-compulsive disorder. Am J Psychiatry 138:1545–1554, 1981.

Rapoport J, Elkins R, Mikkelsen E: Clinical controlled trial of chlorimipramine in adolescents with obsessive-compulsive disorder. Psychopharmacol Bull 16:61–63, 1980.

Rinvinus TM, Jamison DL, Graham PJ: Childhood organic neurological disease presenting as psychiatric disorder. Arch Dis Child 50:115–119, 1975.

Robins E, O'Neal P: Clinical features of hysteria in children with a note on prognosis. A 2- to 17-year follow-up study of 41 patients. Nervous Child 10:246–271, 1953.

Robins LN: Deviant Children Grown Up. Baltimore, Williams & Wilkins, 1966.

Rock NL: Conversion reactions in childhood: A clinical study on childhood neuroses. J Am Acad Child Psychiatry 10:65–93, 1971.

Rodriguez A, Rodriguez M, Eisenberg L: The outcome of school phobia: A follow-up study based on 41 cases. Am J Psychiatry 116:540–544, 1959.

Ross J: A follow up of obsessional illness presenting in childhood and adolescence. DPM diss., University of London, 1964.

Rutter M: Why are London children so disturbed? Proc R Soc Med 66:1221–1225, 1973.

Rutter M, Cox A, Tupling C, Berger M, Yule M: Attainment and adjustment in two geographical areas. I. The prevalence of psychiatric disorder. Br J Psychiatry 126:493–509, 1975.

Rutter M, Graham PJ, Chadwick O, Yule W: Adolescent turmoil: Fact or fiction? J Child Psychol Psychiatry 17:35–56, 1976a.

Rutter M, Graham P, Yule W: A neuropsychiatric study in childhood. Clin Dev Med, Nos. 35/36. Philadelphia, JB Lippincott, 1970a.

Rutter M, Hersov L: Child Psychiatry: Modern Approaches. Oxford, Blackwell, 1976.

Rutter M, Shaffer D: DSM III: A step forward or back? J Am Acad Child Psychiatry 19:371–394, 1980.

Rutter M, Tizard J, Whitmore K: Education, Health and Behavior. London, Longman, 1970b.

Rutter M, Tizard J, Yule W, Graham P, Whitmore K: Research report: Isle of Wight Studies, 1964–1974. Psychol Med 6:313–332, 1976b.

Shaffer D: Suicide in children and early adolescents. J Child Psychol Psychiatry 15:275–291, 1974.

Shapiro AK, Shapiro E: Controlled study of pimozide vs. placebo in Tourette's syndrome, J Am Acad Child Psychiatry 2:161–173, 1984.

Shapiro AK, Shapiro E, Wayne HL: Treatment of Tourette's syndrome with haloperidol: Review of 34 cases. Arch Gen Psychiatry 28:92–97, 1973.

Sheehan DV, Sheehan KE, Minichiello WE: Age of onset of phobic disorders: A re-evaluation. Compr Psychiatry 22:544–553, 1981.

Stone F, Rawley V, Keller E: Clinical anxiety and the children's manifest anxiety scale. J Clin Psychol 21:409–412, 1965.

Tisher M: School refusal: A depressive equivalent, in Cantwell DP, Carlson GA (eds): Affective disorders in Children and Adolescence: An update. New York, Spectrum Publications, 1983, pp. 129–144.

Tramer M: Selective mutism of children. Kinderpsychiatrie 1:30–35, 1934.

Ultee CA, Griffioen D, Schellekens J: The reduction of anxiety in children: A comparison of the effects of "systematic desensitization in vitro" and "systematic desensitization in vivo." Behav Res Ther 20:61–70, 1982.

Warren W: A study of adolescent psychiatric in-patients and the outcome six or more years later. II. The follow-up study. J Child Psychol Psychiatry 6:141–160, 1965.

Weiss M, Burke GB: A five-ten year follow-up of hospitalized school phobic children and adolescents. Am J Orthopsychiatry 37:294–295, 1967.

Weissman MM, Prusoff BA, Gammon GD, Menkangas KR, Leckman JF, Kidd KK: Psychopathology in the children (ages 6–18) of depressed and normal parents. J Am Acad Child Psychiatry 23:78–84, 1984.

Wright DM, Moelis I: The outcome of individual child psychotherapy: Increments at follow-up. J Child Psychol Psychiatry 17:275–285, 1976.

Wright HL: A clinical study of children who refuse to talk. J Am Acad Child Psychiatry 7:603–617, 1968.

Zahn-Waxler C, McKnew DH, Cummings EM, Davenport YB, Radke-Yarrow M: Problem behaviors and peer interactions of young children with a manic depressive parent. Am J Psychiatry 14:236–240, 1984.

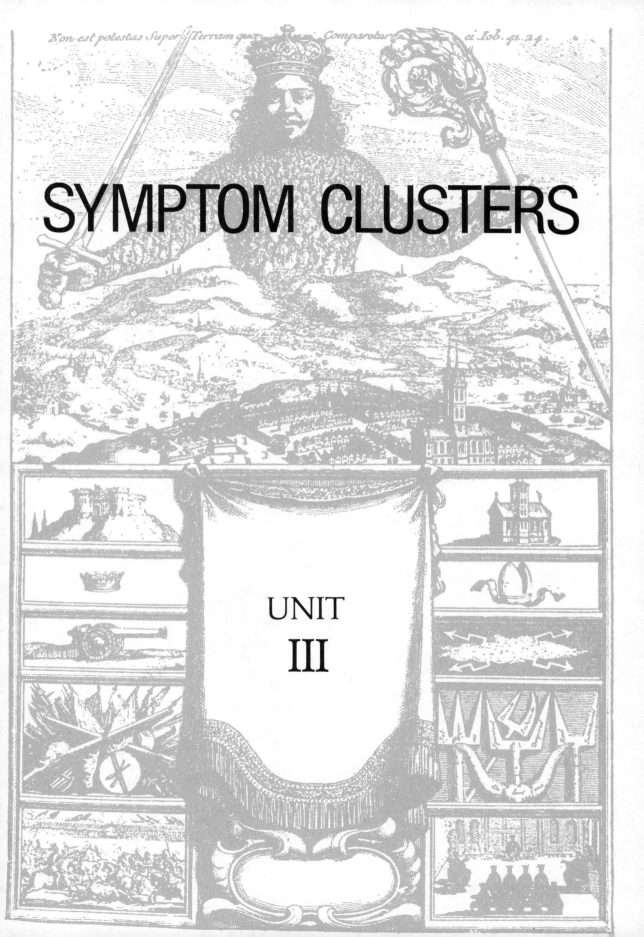

# SYMPTOM CLUSTERS

UNIT
III

# chapter 22

# DIAGNOSIS IN PSYCHIATRY AND THE MENTAL STATUS EXAMINATION

*by* Hagop Souren Akiskal, M.D.

This chapter is devoted to the science and art of eliciting the specific signs and symptoms of psychiatric disorders. The systematic perusal of these manifestations during the psychiatric interview constitutes the mental status examination, which can be viewed as analogous to physical examinations in other branches of medicine (Kraepelin, 1904).

Consider, as an example of this process, the mental status examination of a 26-year-old single, Caucasian engineering student who was brought to the hospital because he had locked himself in his apartment for a week and refused to speak to anyone. When asked about his reasons for this behavior, he stated that he was afraid other people would hear the "voices emanating from my sinuses." The patient looked disheveled and had a frightened facial expression. Despite the psychotic content of his verbalizations, associations were grossly intact. The voices that were of the greatest concern to the patient argued in the third person

about whether or not he was a "fag." During the interview, he walked to a mirror and began to examine his facial features; his explanation was that he needed to see whether he was "transforming into a female," as the voices implied. At one point he became hostile and threatened to take legal action against a surgeon who had "implanted an electronics device" into his sinuses during an operation for deviated nasal septum 8 months previously; he added that his thoughts had been "implanted from outside." All of these manifestations occurred in clear consciousness, without evidence of disorientation or memory disturbances.

To arrive at a diagnostic formulation, the examiner considers the signs and symptoms observed during the mental status examination in combination with information obtained from the psychiatric history. In this case, the diagnosis of paranoid schizophrenia was suggested by lifelong traits of seclusiveness, suspiciousness, and litigiousness; the absence of a history of substance abuse;

and persistence of this clinical picture for longer than 6 months in the absence of major affective symptoms. Laboratory studies (e.g., negative urinary drug screen for stimulants and a normal sleep-deprived electroencephalogram [EEG]) were used to rule out, respectively, the possibility of amphetamine psychosis or complex partial (temporal lobe) seizures as the basis for his presenting complaints. The presence of a positive family history for schizophrenia in a paternal cousin provided further support for a schizophrenic diagnosis.

Thus the diagnostic process in psychiatry is analogous to that used in other branches of medicine: personal history, family history, examination, and laboratory tests constitute the essential steps. Because the raw data of psychopathology are often subjective and may elude precise characterization, the examination is of particular importance in psychiatry. Accurate description is difficult to obtain without careful and skillful probing during face-to-face interview. The faithful description of subjective experiences in psychiatry, known as *phenomenology*, was perfected by the German psychiatrist Karl Jaspers (1963). His approach differs from that of Freudian psychodynamics, which concerns itself with the unconscious meaning and interpretation of symptoms. In contrast to the Freudians, who focused on the *content* of psychopathology—which derived meaningfully from life situations—Jaspers believed that phenomenology, by its emphasis on the *form* of psychopathologic experiences, would eventually disclose "primary" or so-called first-rank symptoms, which are closest to the neurophysiologic substrate of the illness, and which would therefore carry the greatest diagnostic weight. For instance, in the case of the young student, the fact that he heard voices arguing about him in the third person is more important diagnostically than what these voices said about him (that he was homosexual).

A detailed mental status examination constitutes an area of psychiatric expertise, but in briefer format, it is an essential tool for all physicians. A brief mental status examination should be performed as part of the routine physical examination on all patients. When indicated, this should be followed by a more detailed mental examination.

## THE IMPORTANCE OF SIGNS AND SYMPTOMS IN PSYCHIATRY

Precision in the use of clinical terms to describe signs and symptoms is essential in all branches of medicine, promoting professional communication and preparing the ground for differential diagnostic workup. Imagine, for instance, what would happen if a patient with hemoptysis was erroneously described as having hematemesis. This would certainly confuse one's colleagues as to the medical status of the patient and could lead to an inappropriate series of diagnostic procedures. One can cite many other examples, such as jaundice vs. pallor, ascites vs. obesity, a functional vs. an aortic stenosis murmur, which can all lead to difficulties in differentiation. In brief, genuine difficulties in eliciting, describing, and differentiating the myriad of signs and symptoms that characterize diseases occur in all branches of medicine. Psychiatry is certainly not immune to such difficulties, but the belief—regrettably voiced by some medical educators—that differential diagnosis in psychiatry is haphazard and unproductive is both unfounded and dangerous. This attitude can lead to patients with "functional" complaints being labeled as "crocks," without appropriate diagnostic evaluation. They may be viewed as having "imaginary" somatic complaints that waste the physician's time. The potential dangers of this attitude can be seen in a study in the *Annals of Internal Medicine* (Murphy, 1975), which reported that the majority of a sample of completed suicides in St. Louis were seen by physicians within six months before their deaths; not only was the depressive nature of their ailment missed, but sedatives, in lethal quantities, were prescribed for their complaints of disordered sleep.

Although physicians typically spend many years mastering the art and science of physical diagnosis, little attention is given in medical education to the mental status examination. Many physicians are unaware that there exist systematic rules—analogous to those used in physical diagnosis—for use in assessing mental status. Moreover, it is seldom recognized that the failure to distinguish, for instance, whether a patient on reserpine is "sedated" or "depressed" can be as grave as the failure to distinguish between dyspepsia and angina: just as angina can be the prelude to myocardial infarction, reserpine-triggered depression can be the prelude to jumping out the hospital window.

The mental status examination is not just common sense or an expression of humane attitudes that assist the physician in empathizing with the patient while probing his inner experiences. Good judgment in complex human situations (an uncommon form of common sense) and an approach that considers the patient in his totality are not the sole prerogative of psychiatry: they are important in all branches of medicine. These attitudes merely set the stage for the practice of the clinical principles that constitute the body of scientific knowledge in any field. In psychiatry, there are established rules in the use of phenomenologic terms to arrive at diagnostic formulations that are the product of nearly 200 years of systematic clinical observation (Hamilton, 1974; Wing, Cooper, Sartorius, 1974).

## SPECIAL PROBLEMS IN PSYCHIATRIC PHENOMENOLOGY

Admittedly, there are many difficulties in the application of psychiatric terms and concepts. These fall into several categories.

1. Many psychiatric phenomena are subjective and do not easily lend themselves to objective description. For instance, when a patient describes herself as being "transformed into a pig" while looking in the mirror, her verbal report is the only evidence for the occurrence of this experience. It is important to report such symptoms—in the patient's exact words—to decide whether the incident described above is indicative of incipient schizophrenia (psychotic depersonalization in which the self changes) or primary mood disorder (a depressive delusion that one is as ugly and dirty as a pig). This patient, who had no family or personal history of mental illness, suffered from a psychotic major depressive episode. She also saw herself in a coffin and heard voices commanding her to cut her throat with a butcher knife. She recovered fully with a course of electroconvulsive therapy (ECT).

2. The concepts used in psychiatry are not readily susceptible to the same types of external validation that are used in other branches of medicine (e.g., laboratory data). Psychiatrists heavily rely on family history, pharmacologic response, and prospective course in validating diagnostic decisions made during cross-sectional examination. For instance, in the case described earlier, the response to ECT and the full recovery from the psychotic episode strongly favor the affective diagnosis. The past decade has witnessed considerable momentum in attempting to link psychopathologic events with biologic correlates (Akiskal and Webb, 1978). Although no single biologic finding has yet been accepted universally as an unambiguous marker for a specific psychiatric syndrome, several sleep laboratory and neuroendocrine indices can now be used—along with more traditional approaches—in elucidating diagnostic dilemmas (Carroll, 1982; Kupfer and Thase, 1983; Akiskal and Lemmi, 1983).

3. Mental health professionals themselves have, at times, been imprecise in the use of psychopathologic terms and concepts. This situation, however, has improved with the advent of modern pharmacotherapy and biologic psychiatry, in which syndrome-specific treatments, like lithium carbonate, dictated precise diagnostic evaluation.

Being awarded a doctorate in medicine does not automatically confer to the recipient the art of communication. Given the life-and-death nature of their endeavor, medical students—perhaps more than any other group of professional students—should endeavor to develop the proper habits of precise expression.

## RECORDING SIGNS AND SYMPTOMS IN PSYCHIATRY

Signs refer to the clinician's observations of the patient. Symptoms, on the other hand, represent the subjective complaints of the patient based on his verbal report. For instance, agitation is a sign, based on the observation of motor restlessness, pacing, pulling one's hair, and so on. Auditory hallucination is a symptom that must be based on patient report. Signs assume major significance when the patient is mute, stuporous, confused, or reluctant to talk.

Whenever feasible, one should try to corroborate symptoms with other observations. There are several ways to accomplish this.

- *Recording overt behavior that is consistent with the symptom.* For instance, does the patient who reports hearing voices appear preoccupied—perhaps mumbling to himself in an attempt to answer the voices? More serious, the patient may obey the commands given by voices. Likewise, the presence of a delusion can be inferred from behavior that results from it. For instance, a patient who believes himself to be persecuted by the Mafia may decide to move to another town.

- *Recording historical data consistent with the symptoms.* Often patients' reports suggest corollary data that can be confirmed or refuted by other information obtained from patient or significant others. For instance, in the case of a patient who reports loss of ability to derive pleasure from life (anhedonia), one may question his wife as follows: Does he indulge in his hobbies? Does he engage in sexual activities that he previously enjoyed? For the patient who complains of loss of appetite, one might inquire whether he had lost weight or whether his clothes are large on him.

- *Recording other subjective experiences correlated with the symptom.* In some situations this is indeed the best validation. For instance, the avowal of homosexual orientation or preoccupation can be assessed in terms of masturbatory fantasies. In this instance, it is known that homosexual masturbatory fantasies may be more valid indicators of homosexuality than, say, incidental same-sex activity.

- *Physiologic monitoring.* In some situations a precise physiologic measure can be recorded to substantiate a symptom. The subjective complaint of insomnia, for instance, can be measured with all-night sleep polygraphy. This is important because many complaints of insomnia are vague. Neurophysiologic evaluations in sleep laboratories have indeed found that some "insomniacs" actually sleep as long and consistently as people without sleep complaints.

A cardinal rule in recording psychopathologic phenomena is to distinguish clearly those phenomena that are based on history, direct observation, or patient report from inferences that one may derive from such phenomena. For instance, the student should avoid describing a patient who says "Everybody hates me" as engaging in "massive projection." The patient's actual report appears in quotes in the mental status proper, while the inference of "projection" (if made plausible by other evidence) is best reserved

for psychodynamic formulation. Thus the mental status examination should be free from speculation: it should be a record of the patient's mental condition as described by him and as observed by the clinician.

Aristotle said that some phenomena, such as colors, can only be defined by pointing at them. This is also true of many manifestations of psychopathology that can be learned only in reference to actual patients. Hence the definitions offered in the following sections are merely a guide for a more intensive patient-based study. Moreover, this is not an exhaustive list of approaches and terms used in mental status examinations. As differential diagnosis of signs and symptoms is discussed throughout part of this book, there is a selective focus on those concepts that have special diagnostic significance and that appear to be particularly problematic for beginning students.

## CONDUCT OF THE MENTAL EXAMINATION

The areas covered in the mental status examination are summarized in Table 22–1. Although flexibility is necessary to allow for special circumstances presented by individual patients, a complete psychiatric examination should generally cover all of these areas and is conventionally written up (if not conducted) in the order outlined.

Patients' presenting problems generally dictate the types of questions asked and the length and depth of interview. Research clinicians often conduct extensive structured interviews using specific probes for a standardized assessment of individual signs and symptoms. Practicing clinicians have traditionally conducted more or less unstructured interviews that provide for flexibility to tailor questions to the particular situation of the individual patient. Current experience indicates that when major mental illness is suspected, much can be gained by combining the virtues of these two approaches in a semistructured format. This way one would conduct a full examination to inquire about areas that an unstructured interview could easily miss, while at the same time providing flexibility to follow the patient's leads and to frame the questions as best understood by that patient. When conducting an interview, beginning stu-

TABLE 22–1  Mental Status Examination Outline

Appearance and behavior
  Attire, grooming, appears stated age?, posture, facial expression, eye contact
Attitude toward interviewer
  Friendly, cooperative, seductive, ambivalent, hostile
Psychomotor activity
  Normal, retarded, accelerated, agitated, catatonic symptoms
Affect and mood (emotional state)
  Euthymic, irritable, anxious, labile, inappropriate, blunted or flat, depressed, elated
Speech and thinking
  *Process or form*: Coherent, circumstantial, pressure of speech, flight of ideas, derailment
    (loose associations)
  *Content*: Phobias, obsessions, compulsions, delusions
  *Specific speech disorders*: Echolalia, perseveration, mutism, aphonia, aphasia
Perceptual disturbances
  Illusions, hallucinations, depersonalization, derealization
Orientation
  Time, place, person, situation
Attention (concentration) and memory
  Digits forward and backward, serial 7, street address, recall of three objects, amnesia
Intelligence
  Abstraction, vocabulary, global clinical impression of IQ
Reliability, judgment, and insight

dents should have available for quick reference an outline of the mental status examination, as well as the specific signs and symptoms most relevant to the differential diagnosis at hand. A pocket copy of the "mini-DSM-III" (*Diagnostic and Statistical Manual of Mental Disorders*, third edition [1980]) is useful for this purpose; another useful guide is Goodwin and Guze's *Psychiatric Diagnosis* (1984).

It is not necessary to conduct all parts of the interview with the same depth on all patients. For instance, one need not directly check the orientation, vocabulary, and calculating ability of a moderately anxious young university professor who appears to be in good contact. Nor is it necessary to inquire extensively about bizarre psychotic experience when interviewing a diabetic patient who presents with the chief complaint of difficulty in attaining erections. Experience teaches one when such shortcuts can be made. Sometimes omission of a given area is necessary out of consideration for the patient, who may be unwilling or too uncomfortable to talk about certain topics; if the omitted area is of major significance for differential diagnosis, one should endeavor to obtain collateral information from significant others and return to questioning the patient at a later time, using a more indirect approach. There are situations in which one should conduct the mental status in multiple brief encounters, as in the case of extremely disturbed, violent, psychotic, or semistuporous patients, attempting to glean the optimum amount of information necessary for a tentative diagnosis.

## AREAS OF THE MENTAL STATUS

The mental status typically begins with a statement about the setting in which the examination was conducted (e.g., inpatient or outpatient, private or public institution) and the purpose for which it was done (e.g., initial evaluation for outpatient treatment, disability determination, consultation for another psychiatrist). It typically follows a careful review of all existing records, and proceeds with the areas described below.

### Appearance and Behavior

Although this is the first section of the mental examination, relevant data are gathered throughout the interview process. Attire, posture, facial expression, and the level of grooming are described in such a way that the person reading the narration can visualize the patient's physical appearance at the time of the examination. It is important to note any obvious physical signs or deformities that point toward medical disease. The chronically ill and those experiencing great suffering may look older than stated age; by contrast, hypomanic, histrionic, and hebephrenic individuals may look younger. Poor eye contact may indicate shame, embarrassment, anxiety, social phobia, or paranoia. In some cases, little will be revealed in this section beyond the fact that the patient's physical appearance was unremarkable compared with other individuals of same age, educational level, and socioeconomic status. In other instances, the general observation may provide important clues about the patient's personality, mood, thought, awareness of social conventions, and ability to function adequately within society.

## Attitude Toward the Interviewer

The patient's attitude toward the interviewer is often evident without specific inquiry, simply by ongoing observing of the patient throughout the interview. Some patients relate easily, are open and cooperative, and reveal plenty of information without much probing. Others may be reticent, guarded, or even suspicious—too embarrassed, unwilling, or frightened to share personal experiences. Some may be overtly hostile, perhaps attempting to embarrass or humiliate the examiner; in the extreme, the patient may be uncommunicative or even openly belligerent. Some patients are obsequious, trying to flatter the examiner, emphasizing how competent he is compared with all previous doctors, who "do not seem to care." Others may display *ambivalence*, a term that refers to the simultaneous presence of incompatible emotions (positive and negative). Some patients may be overtly seductive. Clinical experience teaches the student how to interview these different kinds of patients.

## Psychomotor Activity

Psychomotor activity refers to physical activity as it relates to psychological functioning. A patient who displays *psychomotor agitation* moves around constantly, cannot sit still, and often shows pressure to talk. One may observe hand wringing, shuffling of feet, crossing and uncrossing of knees, picking on scabs, scratching, nail biting, hair twisting, and even hair pulling. One must contrast this purposeless physical restless-

ness with the more patterned *psychomotor acceleration*, in which the patient is extremely "busy," engages in many activities, talks incessantly by jumping from topic to topic, and experiences rapid thought progression. In the extreme, both agitation and acceleration may lead to frenzied activity that can be debilitating. In fact, before the availability of electroconvulsive and neuroleptic treatments, some of these patients died of sheer exhaustion. In other patients, one observes *psychomotor retardation*, in which there is a general slowing of movement, speech, and thought progression. Here, the patient may sit in a slumped, often frozen posture; speech is slow, monosyllabic, and of low pitch, accompanied by few gestures; and facial expression is either sad or blank. For such patients, talking may seem to be an effort, and latency of response to questions is typically prolonged. In some conditions, such as mixed states of affective psychosis, psychomotor agitation and retardation can be simultaneously present (i.e., physical restlessness with mental slowing). Abnormal psychomotor activity on repeated examination is usually indicative of a major psychiatric disorder. Quantitative rating of psychomotor function is now possible through the use of a reliable scale recently developed by Widlöcher (1983) and his team at the Salpêtrière in France. Attempts are also under way to develop physiologic measures of speech pause time and abnormalities of facial expression of emotions (Greden and Carroll, 1981).

Other forms of psychomotor disturbances that occur in psychotic states include *posturing, stereotyped movements, mannerisms, negativism* (doing the opposite of what is requested), *echopraxia* (imitating the movements of another person), and *waxy flexibility* (maintaining certain awkward positions despite apparent discomfort). In the extreme, such manifestations may progress to stupor, which represents an extreme degree of psychomotor retardation and mutism combined. The condition is sometimes observed on the battlefront or in civilian catastrophes, where the victim may be "paralyzed by fear." In the absence of such history, medical contributions should be excluded by EEG, computed tomography scan, lumbar puncture, and other laboratory tests. Once this is done, intravenous amytal may help in differentiating depressive from schizophrenic stupor; the schizophrenic patient will momentarily come out of his state of hypokinesia and express delusional thoughts, for example, that he dare not move because his weight "would tilt the balance of the earth and bring the end of the world." The two conditions can be distinguished clinically by the presence of incontinence, catalepsy (increased muscle tension), and expressionless facies, all of which are more suggestive of catatonic schizophrenia than of depression.

## Affect and Mood

Affect is the prevailing emotional tone during the interview, as observed by the clinician. One must describe whether the patient exhibits an appropriate range of affect, which varies with the theme of the conversation and may include fear, sadness, and joy. In the case of marked disparity between affect and thought content, one speaks of *inappropriate* or *incongruent affect*. Other commonly observed disturbances of affect include *tension* (or inability to relax), *panic* (a crescendo increase in fear), *anger* (a predominantly argumentative or hostile stance), lability (rapid shifts from happiness to sadness, often accompanied by giggling, laughing, or, conversely, sobbing and weeping), and *blunting* or *flattening* (minimal display of emotion, with little variation in facial expression). In addition to the observed disturbances of affect, the clinician must also record the mood or subjective feeling state reported by the patient over the preceding several days or weeks. The most common moods reported by patients are *depression* (i.e., feeling in "low spirits" or "down in the dumps") and *anxiety*, a feeling of apprehension whose source remains undefined. When *irritability* is the prevailing mood, the patient may report having a "short fuse." In *euphoria*, the mood is one of extreme happiness and jubilation that is not justified by objective circumstances. These self-reports will not necessarily coincide with the observed affect. For instance, some patients may have a gloomy, downcast expression yet vigorously deny experiencing depressed mood; conversely, patients who do not show prominent signs of emotional distress may report a pervasive gloom. Such lack of concordance between subjective report of mood and observable affect and behavior is not uncommon in both normal and psychopathologic states (Lader and Marks, 1971). In the absence of specific disturbance in affect or mood, the patient is described as *euthymic*.

## Speech and Thought

One describes the patient's verbal communication and its pathology. Thought form (or thought process) refers to how ideas are put together in an observed sample of speech, and in what sequence and speed. A patient exhibiting no abnormality in the formal aspect of thought is said to have coherent thought that is clear, logical, and easy to follow and understand. In *circumstantiality*, there is a tendency to answer questions in terms of long-winded details. In *pressure of speech*, the patient seems to be compelled to talk, while in *flight of ideas*, thoughts actually race ahead of the patient's ability to communicate them; he skips from one idea or theme to another, and ideas may be connected by rhymes or puns (*clang association*), as shown in this address made by a patient to the psychiatrist in chief during the morning round:

"Let me part soon—to the moon—moonshine is for lovers—the cure for lovers' heart—the lure of poets—the doors of perception—a magnificent conception—on! on! Let me conquer the moon."

This form of thought is most characteristic of mania and tends to be *overinclusive*, with difficulty in excluding irrelevant, extraneous details from the association. In the extreme, it may be hard to draw the line between manic flight of ideas and schizophrenic *derailment* (literally, "off the track"), in which it is impossible for the observer to glean any logical sequence from the patient's speech. Patients with this degree of *loosening of associations* sometimes invent new words that have private meanings (*neologisms*). Associative slippage may also manifest in general vagueness of thinking, which is not grossly incoherent but conveys little information, even though many words may have been used. This disturbance, known as *poverty of thought*, is a major diagnostic sign of schizophrenia when known organic mental disorders have been ruled out (Andreasen,

1979b). Here is a sample from a letter a high school student wrote to the psychiatrist to explain why he was in the hospital:

I often contemplate. It is a general stance of the world. It is a tendency which varies from time to time. It defines things more than others. It is in the nature of habit. This is what I would like to say to explain everything that happened.

Bleuler (1950) coined the term *autism* to refer to the self-absorption that he believed characterized schizophrenic thought, feeling, and behavior. Thinking that is governed by inner drives and a "private logic" is therefore known as autistic thinking; *dereistic* thinking is a synonym for it. Current evidence indicates that such thinking may actually reflect, in some cases, measurable neurologic deficits (Andreasen, 1984).

*Echolalia*, most commonly observed in catatonia, is the irrelevant, sometimes playful, repeating of words used by the interviewer (e.g., "What day is today?" "Today.") In *perseveration*, also seen in catatonia, as well as in chronic organic mental disorders, the patient adheres to the same concept or words and appears unable to proceed to others. *Thought block* refers to the sudden arrest of thought in the middle of a sentence, often followed, after a momentary pause, with a new and unrelated thought. When mild, this experience may be caused by exhaustion, anxiety, or depression; severer degrees are seen in schizophrenia, where they may be the observable counterpart of the subjective experience of thought withdrawal. *Mutism* consists of the loss of speech and can be intentional or hysterical in origin and limited to interactions with certain people (elective mutism), or involuntary, as part of catatonia or midline lesions of the brain. In *aphasia*, owing to dominant temporal lobe lesions, the patient has a specific memory disorder for words and language; even when unable to talk, the patient usually attempts to communicate by other methods. In *dysphonia*, the patient loses his voice and cannot raise it beyond a whisper, which, in the extreme, can proceed to *aphonia*; here, in contrast with mutism, one can observe lip movements or nonverbal attempts to communicate. Unless based on laryngeal pathology or excessive abuse of vocal cords (as seen in voluble manics), these deficits in phonation are almost always hysterical in origin, representing, for example, a com-

promise in an adolescent who feels conflicted between lying and telling her parents the truth about sexual behavior of which they would strongly disapprove.

The most important abnormalities of thought content include *obsessions* (repetitive ideas, images, or impulses that enter the patient's mind involuntarily and cannot be shaken off), *compulsions* (irresistible urges to engage in apparently meaningless motor acts), *phobias* (irrational fears), and *delusions* (false beliefs that are unshakable and idiosyncratic to the individual). Two obsessions that cause immense torment to patients include the idea that one might harm or kill loved ones and the thought of killing oneself. Although the former type of obsession does not ordinarily lead to taking action, suicidal obsessions can be followed by self-destructive acts. Therefore, the clinician should always inquire about suicidal ideation; the notion that one thereby inadvertently "puts thoughts into the patient's head" is unfounded.

The beliefs of a delusional patient cannot be undone by logical arguments to the contrary. Furthermore, the idiosyncratic nature of these beliefs means that they are not shared by members of the same culture or subculture. For instance, the belief that one is sexually "voodooed" and will not regain one's potency until the spell is lifted is not necessarily delusional; neither are beliefs in unusual health practices and folk remedies. The decision of whether one is dealing with culturally accepted phenomenon must be based on a thorough knowledge of a given culture or subculture. To complicate matters, in cultures where voodoo and witchcraft are part of daily life, delusions may sometimes represent pathologic elaborations of such beliefs. The definitive test is whether an unusual belief is shared by members of the patient's subculture. Delusions must also be differentiated from *overvalued ideas*, which are fanatically maintained notions, such as the superiority of one sex, nation, or race over others, and, not uncommonly, occur in individuals who have been termed fanatical psychopaths (Schneider, 1958).

Delusions are categorized as primary or secondary. Primary delusions cannot be understood in terms of other psychological processes. The most common examples of these are represented by Schneider's first-rank symptoms (1959), which consist of externally imposed influences in the spheres of thought (*thought insertion*), emotion, and somatic function (*passivity feelings*), as well as experiences of *thought withdrawal* and *thought broadcasting;* hence they are also known as *delusions of control,* or *delusions of influence.* Primary delusions may arise in the setting of what is termed delusional mood in which the patient is gradually losing his grasp of reality: neutral percepts may suddenly acquire special personal or revelatory significance of delusional proportion (e.g., a red car being seen as an indicator of imminent invasion by communist forces). This two-stage phenomenon, known as *delusional perception,* is also considered a first-rank symptom. Although one or two schneiderian symptoms may be seen in severely psychotic affective—especially manic—patients (Clayton, Pitts, Winokur, 1965; Carlson and Goodwin, 1973; Taylor, Gaztanaga, Abrams, 1974), the presence of a large number of such symptoms usually point toward schizophrenia (Mellor, 1970; Andreasen and Akiskal, 1983), provided that amphetamine psychosis, complex partial (temporal lobe) seizures, and alcoholic hallucinosis are excluded.

Secondary delusions derive from other psychopathologic experiences and occur in a variety of psychiatric disorders. Delusions may be secondary to:

- *Hallucinations*—the patient hears the voice of his deceased mother and concludes that he must be dead too.

- *Other delusions*—the patient, believing that he is being persecuted by others, may decide that he must be the messiah.

- *Impaired memory*—a patient with general paresis of the insane who, unable to remember where she had placed her purse, repeatedly called the police to report that her neighbors were robbing her.

- *Morbid affective states*—These are sometimes referred to as affective delusions and arise from the prevailing mood—usually depression—and the associated guilt, low self-esteem, and insecurity (Akiskal and Puzantian, 1979). They can take the form of *delusions of guilt* or *sinfulness* (the belief that one has committed an unpardonable act), *delusions of jealousy* (false belief in infidelity of spouse or lover), *hypochondriacal or somatic delusions* (i.e., delusions of ill-health), *nihilistic delusions* (the belief that parts of one's body are missing), and *delusions of poverty* (the belief that one has lost all means and family members will starve).

Other secondary delusions include *delusions of reference* (the idea that one is being observed, talked about, laughed at, etc.), *erotomania* (in which the patient believes that a famous person is in love with him or her), and *grandiose delusions* (belief that one has unusual talents or powers, or that one has the identity of a famous person). Although erotomania and grandiose delusions often arise in the setting of expansive mood, one can usually find clinical evidence for underlying low self-esteem or depression. Delusions of reference can occur in affective, schizophrenic, as well as organic psychoses. In *delusions of assistance,* the patient believes himself to be the object of benevolence from others or supernatural powers; for example, a manic woman, who had run away from her ex-husband's harassment, stated that chariots were being sent to transport her and her children to heaven. In the more common *persecutory delusions,* the patient believes himself or herself to be the target of malevolent action; this may be due to the conviction that one is somehow guilty and deserves punishment, or it may result from a grandiose self-concept; in other cases, the patient may be projecting his hostile impulses on his presumed persecutors.

## Perceptual Disturbances

The simplest form of perceptual aberration is represented by an *illusion,* often in the visual sphere, in which real stimuli are mistaken for something else (e.g., a belt for a snake in a dimly lit room). Such misinterpretation can be secondary to exhaustion, anxiety, altered states of consciousness, delirium, or a functional psychosis. *Hallucination,* a more serious perceptual disturbance, consists of a perception without external stimulus (Esquirol, 1965) (e.g., hearing voices when nobody is around, seeing things that are not there, or perceiving unusual odors and tastes). In *synesthesia,* observed in psychedelic intoxication, the perceptual disturbances are in more than one sensory modality, and the subject "hears" colors, "smells" music, and so on. For example, Baudelaire, the French poet whose drug experimentation was well known, wrote about the color of vowels: *"A noir, E blanc, I rouge, U vert, O bleu."*

*Auditory hallucinations* are classified as either elementary (noises) or complete (voices or words). They are commonly reported by schizophrenic patients but also occur in organic mental disorders and drug intoxication or withdrawal. Some patients in the initial stages of a psychotic breakdown report hearing their own thoughts spoken aloud (*écho de pensée*); at a later stage, voices lose their connection with the person and appear to be coming from outside, making a running commentary on the patient's behavior or arguing about him in the third person. These are all special categories of hallucinatory phenomena included in Schneider's list of first-rank symptoms (1959). They occur in a variety of psychotic disorders, but when they are extremely pronounced or continuous, they suggest schizophrenia. Schneiderian hallucinations are considered to be mood-incongruent, in that they have no plausible link to the patient's state of mood. Hallucinations can also be mood-congruent; these are observed in the affective psychoses, in which voices typically make derogatory statements about the patient, usually in the second person ("You are a jerk"), or give self-destructive commands ("Slit your throat"). Perceptual disturbances that occur in affective illness tend to be transient and typically occur at the depth or height of an affective episode or during the unstable neurophysiologic transition (mixed state) from depression to mania. They can also be secondary to the exhaustion, dehydration, or superimposed drug or alcohol abuse that often complicates affective disorders; these complications explain in part why mood-incongruent psychotic experiences are occasionally seen in otherwise classic affective psychoses (Akiskal and Puzantian, 1979).

*Visual hallucinations* are most characteristic of organic mental disorders, especially acute delirious states. Sometimes they are lilliputian (less than life-size); they may coexist with auditory hallucinations and can be frightening. Visual phenomena associated with psychedelic drugs can be pleasant or frightening, depending on mental set. Visual hallucinations are not characteristic of schizophrenia but can occur in normal grief (visions of a dead relative), in depressive psychoses (e.g., seeing oneself in one's casket), and in brief reactive psychoses observed in abnormal personalities. *Hypnagogic hallucinations* are visual experiences that occur in twilight state between sleep and wakefulness, especially when falling asleep. Although their occasional occurrence is normal, repeated experiences, especially when associated with sleep paralysis and sudden loss of muscle tone under emotional arousal (cataplexy) are cardinal manifestations of narcolepsy, representing rapid eye movement intrusions into consciousness. Other circumstances that can provoke visual hallucinosis include sensory deprivation (e.g., after cataract surgery), delirium, and other organic mental disorders. Histrionic personalities may give flamboyant accounts of "perceiving" objects or events that fit their fantasies. All of these manifestations must be distinguished from *dysmegalopsia*, in which objects may seem to get larger or closer (*macropsia*) or smaller and recede into space (*micropsia*), which are special forms of illusory phenomena that occur in retinal detachment, disorders of accommodation, posterior temporal lesions, and psychedelic drug intoxication. Finally, psychedelic drugs can produce impression of extremely vivid colors with geometric patterns (*kaleidoscopic hallucinations*).

*Olfactory hallucinations* may be difficult to distinguish from illusions. For example, a woman with low self-esteem might be preoccupied with vaginal odor and might misinterpret neutral gestures made by other people as indicative of olfactory disgust. In complex partial seizures of temporal lobe origin, hallucinations of burning paint or rubber present as auras.

*Haptic hallucinations* (hallucinations of touch) are usually experienced as insects crawling on one's skin (known as *formication*) and characteristically occur in cocaine intoxication, amphetamine psychosis, and delirium tremens owing to alcohol or sedative-hypnotic withdrawal. In schizophrenic disorders, they may take such bizarre forms as orgasms produced by invisible objects or creatures. *Tactile hallucinations* must be distinguished from extreme tactile sensitivity (*hyperesthesia*) and diminished sensitivity (*hypesthesia*), both of which can occur in peripheral nerve disease as well as in hysterical conditions.

*Vestibular hallucinations* (e.g., those of flying) are most commonly seen in organic states, such as delirium tremens and LSD psychosis, and may result in serious injuries when, for example, the subject attempts to fly off a roof. In *hallucinations of presence*, most commonly reported by schizophrenic, histrionic, or delirious patients, the subject senses the presence of another person or creature who remains invisible. In *extracampine hallucinations*, the patient sees objects outside the sensory field (e.g., behind his head), whereas in *autoscopy*, the patient visualizes himself projected into space. The latter phenomenon, which can occur in organic, hysterical, depressive, and schizophrenic conditions, is also known as Döppelganger, or seeing one's double, and is skillfully portrayed in Dostoevski's novel "The Double."

Other perceptual disturbances that cannot be easily classified into specific sensory modalities include *depersonalization* (the uncanny feeling that one has changed), *derealization* (the feeling that the environment has changed), *déjà vu* (a sense of familiarity with a new perception), and *déjà entendu* (the feeling that a new auditory perception has been experienced before). As isolated findings, these can occur in normal people who are anxious, tired, or sleepy, but repeated experiences along these lines indicate the following differential diagnosis (Roth, 1959): complex partial seizures, panic disorder, schizophreniform disorder, hysterical dissociation, and psychedelic intoxication.

## Orientation

In this section, the clinician records whether the patient knows who he is (orientation to person), where he is (orientation to place), why he is there and with whom he is interacting (orientation to situation), and what date and time of day it is (orientation to time). One who is orientated in all spheres is considered to have a *clear sensorium*. Patients with affective and schizophrenic psychoses are not typically disoriented (although, because of apathy, they may fail to keep track of daily routines), whereas patients who suffer from organic mental disorders are characteristically disoriented. In acute brain disease, patients often show remarkable fluctuation in orientation depending on time of day, with worsening disorientation at night. With in-

creasing severity of brain impairment, the patient is totally confused as to orientation, and his sensorium may be *clouded* at all times to such an extent that he may lapse into an *organic stupor*.

## Attention (Concentration) and Memory

The patient who shows deficits in attention or concentration is, in the extreme, unable to filter relevant from irrelevant stimuli as they pertain to the interview material, and thus may be easily distracted by the TV, telephone, and other background stimuli. A patient with milder disorder may be able to achieve the attention required for a successful interview but may complain that his mind is "not working." Care must be taken to distinguish between deficits in attention, which are involuntary, and lack of cooperation; an example of the latter would be a patient who whistles instead of answering questions posed to him. Attention and concentration are usually tested by digits forward and digits backward ("Can you repeat 7248 forward? Can you repeat it backward?"). A related test is serial sevens (i.e., subtracting 7 from 100 and from each successive remainder); in using this test, the observer needs to make some allowance for educational background.

Deficits in memory are conveniently grouped into four kinds: (1) immediate, when the patient cannot even register things he has just been told; (2) short-term, when he cannot retain information for 5 minutes or so; (3) recent, when he is unable to recall the events of the past months or years; and (4) long-term, or remote, when he is unable to recollect what took place many years ago. Deficits in immediate recall suggest serious acute brain impairment or stupor. Less severe brain insults tend to spare registration but can lead to deficits in short-term memory, which can be assessed by asking the patient to remember a street address or three unrelated items (e.g., "17, yellow, chair") in 5 to 7 minutes, after making sure that the patient fully understands the items to be remembered. Recent memory is most likely to be compromised by chronic organic impairment; its intactness can be tested by asking the patient about verifiable recent events in his life or current events. Remote memory is usually spared in the early course of dementing diseases, but at later stages, it may be impaired to such an extent that the patient may not recognize his own children. This is best tested by asking about several past historical events that someone with the patient's social background and intelligence can reasonably be expected to be familiar with.

Disturbances in attention, concentration, and memory are most characteristic of organic mental disorders, yet schizophreniform and acute affective psychoses may also exhibit reversible abnormalities in these functions. Although it is customary to use the term pseudodementia to refer to this phenomenon, it appears that reversible neurophysiologic derangements underlying these psychotic illnesses may well be responsible for the observed cognitive deficits (McHugh and Slavney, 1983). Memory disturbances can sometimes result from a combination of organic insults (e.g., head trauma) and emotional causes (e.g., hysterical dissociation) that could lead to amnesia for events before (retrograde) or after (anterograde) the injury. In general, the more psychogenic in origin, the more circumscribed the amnesia is, and the more organic, the more global. Retrograde amnesia for autobiographic events for variable periods is also common after a course of electroconvulsive therapy.

### Intelligence

Intelligence can be indirectly inferred from the patient's overall intellectual performance during the mental status examination. If deficits are grossly apparent, historical information should be used to decide whether they have always been present (intellectual subnormality) or developed after a certain age (intellectual impairment). Intelligence is commonly assessed by testing for abstracting ability. To do this, one inquires about similarities, going from simpler comparisons ("How are an airplane and a car alike?") to more difficult ones ("A painting and a poem?") The examiner must also pay special attention to the patient's vocabulary. Vocabulary and performance on similarities testing depend not only on the patient's intellectual capacity, but also on his age, social background, and educational level. For instance, the presence of a good

vocabulary and abstracting ability, despite a third-grade education, indicates above-average intelligence. If vocabulary and abstracting ability are poor, allowance should be made for social deprivation. In the absence of such factors, and especially if the patient has a college education, the examiner must consider the possibility of intellectual impairment owing to an organic mental disorder.

### Reliability, Judgment, and Insight

Every mental status examination should have a statement regarding the extent to which the patient's report of his experiences and behavior is to be considered reliable. This assessment is largely based on an estimate of the patient's intellectual ability, honesty, attention to detail, and motivation. Sociopathic and histrionic individuals are notoriously unreliable. *Retrospective falsification*, commonly observed in such patients, consists of distortion of real past experiences to conform with present emotional needs; at other times, they may lie to avoid personal responsibilities. A related type of unreliability is *pseudologia fantastica*, expansive storytelling such that the individual is unable to discern which of his statements are true and which are false. Psychotic patients and those with organic mental disorders also tend to be unreliable informants; here one sometimes observes *confabulation*, a spontaneous fabrication of responses to fill in memory gaps.

*Judgment* refers to the patient's ability to evaluate the proper course of action in difficult situations and is traditionally tested by asking what one would do if one were the first to observe smoke in a movie theater. The patient's history will often give clues as to whether he generally has good or poor judgment. Disturbances in judgment can be circumscribed to one or more areas (e.g., money, attire, sexual conduct), leaving other areas, like maternal role, intact. *Insight* pertains to a more complex form of judgment regarding the patient's awareness of his emotional state, its causes, its severity, and its impact on significant others. Psychotic patients, especially manics, notoriously lack insight and are often unaware of the painful consequences of their spending sprees and sexual promiscuity, which explains in part their frequent lack of co-operation with treatment regimens.

## COMMON ERRORS IN MENTAL STATUS EXAMINATION

Eugen Bleuler's work on schizophrenia (1950) continues to exert a major influence in the description and differential diagnosis of schizophrenic manifestations. Bleuler believed that disturbances in associations, affect, ambivalence, and autism characterized this group of disorders. His ideas were, unfortunately, accepted before being empirically tested, leading to much confusion in mental status evaluations. This is particularly true for disturbance in affect and associations. Recent work, as exemplified by Andreasen (1979a, 1979b), has provided a fresh empirical perspective in regard to these two areas. This section examines affective and thinking disturbances in light of recent experience.

### Disturbances in Affect

The examiner must distinguish between flat and depressed affect, which occur in disorders that seldom intersect (i.e., chronic schizophrenia vs. primary affective illness). Shallow, blunted, and flat affect refer to increasing degrees of emotional impoverishment—often accompanied by a subjective feeling that one cannot experience emotions, a classical disturbance of schizophrenia. By contrast, depression is a painful affect, what William James termed a psychical neuralgia. Many depressed patients also experience anhedonia, best described by Shakespeare: "How weary, stale, flat, and unprofitable/Seem to me all the uses of this world" (Hamlet, Act I, Scene II). Diagnostic difficulties arise in severe depression, where the anhedonia may progress to a pervasive sense of emptiness, often accompanied by the inability to cry; such patients may feel "dead inside" and see the world around them as lifeless. Differentiation can be accomplished as follows. First, the facial expression of the chronic schizophrenic is typically vacuous, whereas that of the depressive is one of pain, gloom, and dejection. Second, the schizophrenic tends to produce, in the observer, a cold feeling and

an inability to empathize (the so-called praecox feeling), whereas the depressive's dejection and pain is usually communicated in such a way that the interviewer can empathize with him. Admittedly, this is a subjective criterion, but it is quite useful in the hands of experienced clinicians.

Labile affect (which changes quickly, often from one extreme to the other) must be distinguished from incongruent affect (which is inappropriate to the thought content or the context). Labile and incongruent affects should both be differentiated from *affective incontinence*, in which the patient laughs or cries for long periods with little or no provocation. Lability is encountered in personality disorders (such as hysteria); in mixed states of manic-depressive illness, where there are rapid shifts from elation to irritability to depression; and in acute organic brain disease, where the affect can quickly change from anxiety to terror to panic. Inappropriate affect (e.g., laughing while relating the gory details of a natural disaster) should raise the suspicion of schizophrenia. Emotional incontinence suggests organic states, such as arteriosclerotic dementia and multiple sclerosis.

Euphoria and elation, although characteristic of manic states, can also occur in organic mental disorders, such as general paresis of the insane and multiple sclerosis. The euphoria seen in mania has a warmth that is communicated to the observer (although manics are not infrequently irritable, hostile, and obnoxious). A type of euphoria characteristic of chronic schizophrenia and frontal lobe lesions, known as *Witzelsucht*, consists of the patient relating silly jokes.

*La belle indifference* should be differentiated from *apathy*. In the former condition—seen in hysterical conversion reactions—the patient exhibits lack of concern or even smiles in the face of reported disability. Apathy, on the other hand, seen in many chronic psychiatric patients because of the overall hopelessness of their situation, is a feeling akin to demoralization.

### Disturbances in Thinking

Unfortunately, "thought disorder" is often used rather loosely to refer to both formal thought disorder as well as delusional content. For the sake of clarity, the unqualified use of "thought disorder" should be discarded. Even the term formal thought disorder covers too wide a territory. It should always be made clear whether one is referring to derailment, or loose associations, flight of ideas, or circumstantiality. The presence of a delusion cannot be considered evidence of underlying formal thought disorder because, as noted previously, delusions can be secondary to affective, perceptual, and memory disturbances.

Derailment refers to a disorder in associations whereby different thoughts are dissociated, disconnected, or rambling. If mild, it leaves the impression of vagueness; if the patient makes no sense at all, it is referred to as *word salad*. The phrase loose associations is used for an intermediate degree of severity, wherein one finds fragmented thoughts that do not seem to follow Aristotelian logic but may nevertheless have an inner, private (autistic) logic of their own. The incoherence that one observes in the thinking of organic patients is qualitatively different from the loose associations of the schizophrenic in that it lacks symbolism and autistic quality; however, in severe cases of schizophrenia, this distinction may be difficult to make. *Vorbeireden*, or talking past the point, should also be differentiated from incoherence. In vorbeireden, which occurs in the Ganser syndrome, the patient gives obvious indication that he has understood the question yet deliberately provides "approximate" answers. For instance, a patient examined in 1977, when asked who the president was, replied, "Jerry Carter," and when asked who was president before him, he replied, "Jimmy Ford."*

It is often erroneously assumed that inability to abstract on testing of similarities or proverbs (i.e., *concrete thinking*) has major diagnostic importance in schizophrenia. There is little scientific rationale for this belief. Concreteness correlates best with poor intellectual endowment, cultural impoverishment, and organic brain disease. Because all three of these factors not infrequently coexist with schizophrenia, to that extent schizophrenics will have impaired ability in abstraction. The major value of testing abstraction in schizophrenia lies in the patient's tendency to give highly idiosyncratic and bizarre answers to proverb and similarities testing.

Pressure of speech, usually seen in agitated depression, refers to patients who feel pressured to talk and usually cannot be stopped. Flight of ideas, a major diagnostic sign of mania, refers to a type of overproductivity wherein the patient skips from one idea or theme to another, sometimes through rhyming or punning, but without totally abandoning logic. Pressure of speech and flight of ideas should be both distinguished from loose associations that do not follow Aristotelian logic. Circumstantiality is the unnecessary elaboration of detail and is seen in dullards (borderline IQ), pedantic obsessionals, and hysterics, but in severe degree, it may be difficult to differentiate from schizophrenic looseness.

The term paranoid is often used incorrectly to refer to suspiciousness or persecutory beliefs. Paranoid actually means delusional and should be restricted as a generic term for disorders characterized by prominent delusional formation (e.g., paranoid schizophrenia and paranoid states). Paranoid schizophrenia is a schizophrenic subtype in which delusions—not always persecutory in nature—occur in abundance. In paranoid states, usually one delusional theme predominates, with no evidence of schizophrenic formal thought disorder. For example, in conjugal paranoia, a man believes that his wife is having an affair and interprets all her behavior along those lines.

Delusions can be graded on the basis of their plausibility. For instance, the false belief that one's spouse is unfaithful is nevertheless a believable idea. The false belief that one's spouse is having multiple affairs simultaneously, although delusional, is not impossible. However, the belief that one's spouse is having an affair with a creature with green tentacles is patently absurd; such bizarre delusions are the hallmark of schizophrenia, although they can also sometimes be associated with organic mental disorders.

---

*The Ganser syndrome seen among prisoners is best understood in terms of conscious and unconscious reasons for appearing psychotic or demented; hence it is also referred to as "hysterical pseudodementia." To complicate matters, adolescent schizophrenic patients may find approximate answers amusing and may respond to an entire interview with a series of approximate answers; such patients may therefore *appear* to exhibit hysterical pseudodementia, but in reality, they have a "hysterical pseudopseudodementia."

## SUMMARY

The mental status examination represents the portion of the psychiatric interview that is devoted to a systematic elicitation of psychopathologic signs and symptoms that are important in diagnostic formulation. Consequently, it is essential that descriptive terms be used precisely and consistently. This will not only facilitate professional communication, but will also enhance the chances of formulating differential diagnosis in a cogent way, setting the stage for rational therapy.

Dr. Armen Djenderedjian provided valuable criticism on an earlier version of this chapter.

## *REFERENCES*

Akiskal HS, Lemmi H: Clinical, neuroendocrine, and sleep EEG diagnosis of "unusual" affective presentations: A practical review. Psychiatr Clin North Am 6:69–83, 1983.

Akiskal HS, Puzantian VR: Psychotic forms of depression and mania. Psychiatr Clin North Am 2:419–439, 1979.

Akiskal HS, Webb WL: Psychiatric Diagnosis: Exploration of Biological Predictors. New York, Spectrum Publications, 1978.

Andreasen NC: Affective flattening and the criteria for schizophrenia. Am J Psychiatry 136:944–947, 1979a.

Andreasen NC: The clinical assessment of thought, language, and communication disorders. Arch Gen Psychiatry 36:1315–1330, 1979b.

Andreasen NC: The Broken Brain. New York, Harper & Row, 1984.

Andreasen NC, Akiskal HS: The specificity of bleulerian and schneiderian symptoms: A critical re-evaluation. Psychiatr Clin North Am 6:41–54, 1983.

Bleuler E: Dementia Praecox, or the Group of Schizophrenias, trans Zinkin J. New York, International Universities Press, 1950.

Carlson G, Goodwin F: The stages of mania. Arch Gen Psychiatry 28:221–288, 1973.

Carroll J: Use of the dexamethasone suppression test in depression. J Clin Psychiatry 43:44–48, 1982.

Clayton PJ, Pitts FN, Winokur G: Affective disorder. V. Mania. Compr Psychiatry 6:313–322, 1965.

Esquirol JE: Mental Maladies: A Treatise on Insanity. New York, Hafner Publishing Co, 1965.

Greden J, Carroll B: Psychomotor functioning in affective disorders: An overview of new monitoring techniques. Am J Psychiatry 11:1441–1448, 1981.

Goodwin DW, Guze SB: Psychiatric Diagnosis. New York, Oxford University Press, 1984.

Hamilton M (ed): Fish's Clinical Psychopathology: Signs and Symptoms in Psychiatry. Bristol, John Wright & Sons, 1974.

James W: Varieties of Religious Experience. Glasgow, William Collins & Sons, 1982.

Jaspers K: General Psychopathology, trans Hoenig J, Hamilton MW. Manchester, University Press, 1963.

Kraepelin E: Lectures on Clinical Psychiatry. London, Balliere, Tindall & Cox, 1904.

Kupfer DJ, Thase ME: The use of the sleep laboratory in the diagnosis of affective disorders. Psychiatr Clin North Am 6:3–21, 1983.

Lader M, Marks IM: Clinical Anxiety. New York, Grune & Stratton, 1971.

McHugh PR, Slavney PR: The Perspective of Psychiatry. Baltimore, Johns Hopkins University Press, 1983.

Mellor CS: First rank symptoms of schizophrenia. Br J Psychiatry 117:15–23, 1970.

Murphy GE: The physician's responsibility for suicide. Ann Intern Med 82:301–309, 1975.

Quick Reference to Diagnostic Criteria from DSM-III. Washington, DC, American Psychiatric Press, 1980.

Roth M: The phobic anxiety-depersonalization syndrome. Proc R Soc Med 52:587–595, 1959.

Schneider K: Psychopathic Personalities, trans Hamilton MW. London, Cassell, 1958.

Schneider K: Clinical Psychopathology, trans Hamilton MW. New York, Grune & Stratton, 1959.

Taylor MA, Gaztanaga P, Abrams R: Manic-depressive illness and acute schizophrenia: A clinical, family history and treatment response study. Am J Psychiatry 131:678–682, 1974.

Widlöcher DJ: Psychomotor retardation: Clinical, theoretical, and psychometric aspects. Psychiatr Clin North Am 6:27–40, 1983.

Wing JK, Cooper JE, Sartorius N: The Measurement and Classification of Psychiatric Symptoms. Cambridge, Cambridge University Press, 1974.

# chapter 23

# MOOD DISTURBANCES

*by* Hagop Souren Akiskal, M.D.

## AFFECTS AND MOODS

Disturbances in the sphere of affect and mood—especially depressive manifestations—are among the most common signs and symptoms prompting medical consultation, both in psychiatry and in general medical practice. This is not surprising given the fact that, from an evolutionary point of view, affective arousal serves essential communication functions. Affect is something that moves us to appraise, for instance, whether another person is content, dissatisfied, or in danger. Affect refers to that aspect of emotion that is expressed through facial expression, vocal inflection, words, gestures, posture, and so on, whereas mood denotes more enduring emotional expressions. Joy, sadness, fear, and anger are the basic affects, and their expression tells us how an individual feels at any given moment.

An individual's affective "tone" is thus the barometer of his or her inward emotional well-being. Each individual has a characteristic pattern of basal affective oscillations that defines his temperament. For instance, some people are minimally touched by adversity or reward and tend to remain placid. In contrast, others are easily moved to tears by sad or happy circumstances, and still others are more prone to fear, worry, or anger. Normally, oscillations in

affective tone are relatively minor, tend to resonate with day-to-day events, and do not interfere with functioning. We speak of affective disturbances when the amplitude and duration of affective change are beyond adaptive demands and lead to impaired function. Affective disturbances may manifest in extreme variability of affect, when with no obvious provocation, the individual alternates between normal mood and depression, elation, or both; examples are *cyclothymic disorder*, in which the individual exhibits highs and lows, and *dysthymic disorder*, in which the individual exhibits an intermittent pattern of low periods. Both disorders typically begin in adolescence and tend to persist throughout adulthood. In other types of mood disorders, disturbances in the form of extreme sadness or elation persist in the absence of any obvious circumstances that would justify them. Such sustained pathologic moods are characteristic of what DSM-III (*Diagnostic and Statistical Manual of Mental Disorders*, third edition [1980]) terms *manic* and *major depressive disorders*.

Major depressive disorder most commonly runs its course in single or recurrent attacks with intervening periods of relatively normal mood (unipolar illness); less commonly, it alternates as well with manic periods (bipolar illness). Although some patients seem to experience manic attacks only, history of mild depression will usually be obtained from significant others; such patients should therefore be classified as bipolar. When the elated periods are mild and transient or hypomanic, the illness is spoken of as bipolar II; when full-blown mania is seen, it is considered bipolar I.

In its pathologic expression, angry affect is not elaborated into a distinct psychopathologic disorder and is generic to a wide variety of psychiatric disorders. Fear, on the other hand, in its pathologic expression known as anxiety, is seen not only secondary to many psychiatric conditions, but also elaborated into a spectrum of anxiety disorders. Because DSM-III limits the rubric of mood disorder to conditions characterized by elation and depression, the discussion of anxiety and anger in this chapter is only to the extent they represent manifestations of these conditions.

The primary aim of this chapter is to describe the signs and symptoms of disturbed affect and mood in such detail as to permit their differentiation from normal affective states and the manifestations of other psychiatric disorders.

## THE DEPRESSIVE SYNDROME

As in other medical conditions, signs and symptoms of depression tend to cluster together in the form of a syndrome described since antiquity; an excellent review is provided by Lewis (1934). Multiple etiologic factors—some genetic, others environmental—can give rise to the final common pathway of depression (Akiskal and McKinney, 1973). One group of causative factors that should always be considered in the etiology of depression, especially in patients over the age of 40, is somatic disease or drugs used in their treatment (see Table 23–1). It is not always clear, however, that such diseases are sufficient causes of depression. Typically, not more than 15 per cent of those with one of the conditions listed in the table will suffer from clinical depression. Further, eliminating the offending physical condition (e.g., reserpine) does not necessarily cure the depression. Indeed, those who succumb to depression secondary to reserpine and other medical factors seem to have past personal or familial history for depression. Thus some form of underlying predisposi-

**TABLE 23–1   Medical Conditions and Pharmacologic Agents Commonly Associated with Onset of Depression**

Medical Conditions
  Hypothyroidism
  Cushing's disease
  Systemic lupus erythematosus
  Avitaminosis
  Cancer (especially abdominal)
  Tuberculosis
  Influenza; viral pneumonia
  Infectious mononucleosis
  General paresis (tertiary syphilis)
  Cerebral tumor
  Head trauma
  Complex partial seizures (temporal lobe epilepsy)
  Stroke
  Parkinson's disease
  Multiple sclerosis
  Alzheimer's disease
  Sleep apnea

Pharmacologic Agents
  Reserpine, alphamethyldopa, other
    antihypertensives
  Anticancer chemotherapy
  Corticosteroids, oral contraceptives
  Cimetidine, indomethacin
  Phenothiazines, other classes of neuroleptics
  Anticholinesterase insecticides
  Alcohol, barbiturates
  Stimulant withdrawal
  Psychedelics (?)

tion, often of genetic nature, seems to be required, especially for recurrent mood disorders. However, the prognosis of the depressive syndrome may vary, depending on whether or not it is superimposed on a medical or a nonaffective psychiatric disorder, such as panic disorder, sociopathy, or schizophrenia (Robins and Guze, 1972). These secondary depressions tend to have somewhat atypical clinical features owing to the underlying disorder and often linger for many months (and sometimes years) beyond the usual duration of the depressive syndrome. It is in the syndrome occurring as a primary mood disorder that one observes the most typical manifestations of depressive illness, and whereas the course of secondary depressions is generally dictated by the underlying disorder, many primary depressions tend to recur on the basis of an inherent biologic periodicity.

The depressive syndrome is characterized by disturbances in four areas: mood, vegetative, psychomotor, and cognitive.

## Mood Change

The mood disturbance is usually considered the sine qua non of the syndrome and may manifest itself either in painful arousal or loss of the capacity for pleasurable experiences (anhedonia).

The painful arousal can take the form of depression, irritability, or anxiety and, in the extreme, is indescribably agonizing. The irritability and anxiety are often qualitatively different from their "neurotic" counterparts and take the form of severe inner turmoil and groundless apprehensions. In the full-blown form of the malady, the sustained nature of the dysphoric mood does not permit distraction even for a moment. The psychic pain of depression is so agonizing that patients often describe it as being beyond ordinary physical pain. William James (1902), a sufferer of the malady, referred to his depression as "psychical neuralgia." Suicide often represents an attempt to find deliverance from such tormenting psychic pain. Other patients, suffering from a milder form of the malady and typically seen in primary care settings, deny experiencing such mental pain and instead complain of physical agony in the form of, for example, headache, epigastric pain, and precordial distress, in the absence of any evidence of somatic pathology. Such conditions have been described as *depressio sine depressione*, or *masked depression* (Kielholz, Poldinger, Adams, 1982). In these situations, the physician can corroborate the presence of mood change by the depressed affect in the facial expression, the voice, and the patient's overall appearance.

Paradoxically, this heightened perception of pain is often accompanied by an inability to experience normal sadness and grief, as well as joy and pleasure. Thus anhedonia, the loss of the ability to experience pleasure, is a special instance of a more generalized inability to experience normal emotions. Patients exhibiting this disturbance often lose the capacity to cry—an ability that may return as the depression is lifting.

During the clinical interview, it is not enough to inquire whether the patient has lost the sense of pleasure; the clinician must document that the patient has given up previously enjoyed pastimes. In the extreme, patients may complain that they have lost all feeling for their children, who once were a source of joy. The impact of the loss of emotional experience can be so pervasive that patients may give up values and beliefs that had previously given meaning to their lives. This is well described by Tolstoy in his autobiographical *My Confessions* (1887), in which he describes how his bouts of depression later in life led to "spiritual crises." The depressive's inability to experience normal emotions is different from the blunting seen in schizophrenia in that the loss of emotions is itself experienced as painful; that is, the depressive suffers immensely from his inability to experience emotions.

## Vegetative Disturbances

The ancients believed that depression was a somatic illness and ascribed it to black bile, hence the term melancholia, from the Greek word for this substance. Indeed, the mood change in depressive illness is accompanied by several physiologic disturbances that implicate limbic-diencephalic dysfunction (Akiskal and McKinney, 1973). These include changes in libido and menstruation, appetite and sleep, as well as other circadian rhythms. DSM-III now uses the term melancholia for a special cluster of depressive symptomatology that includes marked vegetative and psychomotor disturbances, anhedonia, and self-reproach; these manifestations persist autonomously, showing no reactivity to psychosocial contingencies. It replaces the term endogenous depression, which carried the connotation of lack of precipitation, a notion not supported by current evidence. The melancholic cluster is generally believed to predict response to tricyclic antidepressants and electroconvulsive therapy.

Although decreased sexual desire occurs in both men and women, women are more likely to complain of infrequent menses or cessation of menses. Their unwillingness to participate in sex often leads to marital conflict. Therapists may mistakenly ascribe the depression to the marital conflict, leading to unnecessarily zealous psychotherapeutic attention to the marital situation and a prolongation of the depressive agony. Decrease or loss of libido in men often results in erectile failure, which may prompt endocrinologic or urologic consultation. Again, depression may be ascribed to the sexual dysfunction rather than the reverse, and definitive treatment is often delayed because of the physician's focus on the sexual complaint.

Disturbed appetite and sleep have been described since Hippocrates' classic case (Adams, 1939):

> In Thesus a woman, of a melancholic turn of mind . . . became affected with loss of sleep, aversion to food . . . frights . . . despondency . . . pains frequent, great and continued.

Most characteristically, there is a diminution in sleep and appetite, but not uncommonly, one may see an increase or, in rare cases, an alternation between them. Weight gain may be due to overeating, decreased activity, or both. Weight changes secondary to depression can have serious consequences. Inanition, especially in the elderly, can lead to malnutrition and electrolyte disturbances that represent medical emergencies, often requiring electroconvulsive therapy. Weight gain in middle-aged patients, on the other hand, may aggravate preexisting diabetes, hypertension, or coronary artery disease. In younger patients, especially women, weight problems may conform to a bulimic pattern. This is sometimes the expression of the depressive phase of a bipolar disorder with infrequent hypomanic periods (bipolar II disorder) and may benefit from specific therapies available for this disorder.

Like appetite, sleep may be increased or decreased. Insomnia is one of the major manifestations of depressive illness and is characterized more by multiple awakenings, especially in the early hours of the morning, than by difficulty falling asleep. This was described in "Waking up in the Blue," a verse by the American poet Robert Lowell, who had a documented history of bipolar swings (Hamilton, 1982). The "light" sleep of the depressive is a reflection of the painful arousal and prolongs the agony of the patient. Deep stages of sleep (3 and 4) are either decreased or deficient. The understandable attempt to drown the sorrow in alcohol, as the poet Lowell did, may initially have some success but ultimately leads to an aggravation of the insomnia. The same applies to sedative-hypnotic drugs, which are often prescribed by the busy medical practitioner who has not spent adequate time to diagnose the depressive condition. (Sedatives, including alcohol, although ef-fective in reducing the number of awakenings in the short-term, are not effective in the long run because of a further diminution of stage 3 and 4 sleep.)

Young depressives, especially those with bipolar tendencies, typically complain of hypersomnia, sleeping as long as 15 hours a day. Obviously, such patients will have difficulty getting up in the morning; this may lead to their being labeled lazy. Whether suffering from insomnia or hypersomnia, nearly two thirds of melancholic patients exhibit a shortening of rapid eye movement (REM) latency, the period from the onset of sleep to the first REM period (Kupfer and Thase, 1983). This abnormality is seen throughout the depressive episode and, in recurrent depressives, may be seen in relatively euthymic periods as well (Akiskal, 1983a). Other REM abnormalities include longer REM periods and increased density of eye movements in the first half of the night. These abnormalities in REM sleep are rather specific to primary depressive disorders in that they do not occur in most schizophrenic, anxious, and personality-disordered subjects. Figure 23–1 contrasts the sleep electroencephalogram (EEG) of a major depressive with insomnia to that of a normal control.

Other circadian abnormalities in depression include feeling worse in the morning, periodicity of episodes, and seasonal precipitation (Wehr and Goodwin, 1983). The last two abnormalities are most commonly associated with bipolar II disorder. As with other vegetative abnormalities, these, too,

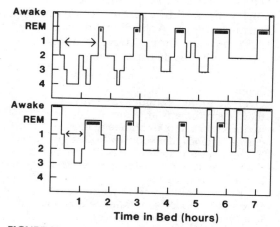

**FIGURE 23–1.** Comparison of sleep in normal (top) and depressed (bottom) subject.

point to the limbic-diencephalic dysfunction as the pathophysiologic substrate of the illness. Abnormal response to the dexamethasone suppression test (DST) (i.e., early escape from suppression of elevated plasma cortisol on overnight dexamethasone), seen in 50 per cent of melancholic patients (Carroll et al., 1981), can be considered another indirect indicator of disturbed midbrain function.

In summary, vegetative dysfunction in depressive illness has lent itself to laboratory evaluation that has opened windows into the midbrain origins of the disorder. The sleep EEG and neuroendocrine abnormalities in depression, irrespective of their etiologic significance, are among the most replicated biologic findings in all of psychiatry and herald psychiatry's new momentum as a medical specialty.

## Psychomotor Disturbances

Depressed patients exhibit characteristic abnormalities in the execution of motor functions in relation to psychological tasks. Although agitation (pressured speech, restlessness, wringing of hands, and, in the extreme, pulling of one's hair) is the more commonly described abnormality, it is less specific to the illness than retardation (slowing of psychomotor activity). Indeed, psychophysiologic studies have demonstrated that such slowing often co-exists with the agitation (Greden and Carroll, 1981). Psychomotor retardation underlies many of the psychiatric deficits seen in depression and is considered the best predictor of response to tricyclic antidepressants (Nelson and Charney, 1981). According to Widlöcher (1983), psychomotor slowing is manifested by the following disturbances:

- Paucity of spontaneous movements
- Slumped posture with downcast gaze
- Overwhelming fatigue—patients complain that "everything is an effort"
- Reduced flow and amplitude of speech and increased latency of responses—often giving rise to monosyllabic speech
- Subjective feeling that time is passing slowly or has actually stopped
- Poor concentration and forgetfulness
- Painful rumination—or thinking that dwells on few (usually unpleasant) topics
- Indecisiveness—inability to make simple decisions

DSM-III places greater emphasis on the more easily measurable objective or physical aspects of retardation. For the patient, however, the subjective sense of slowing is often the more pervasive and disabling aspect of retardation. This more "psychological" dimension of retardation is not always easy to elicit from patients and only those with unusually good premorbid verbal skills can provide reliable descriptions.

### CASE HISTORY 1

A 47-year-old moderately depressed physics professor gave the following self-report: I am weary with a "leaden" feeling. Manual dexterity is diminished—writing legibly seems like an impossible task. What is most disabling, however, is a kind of staring or stoppage of mental functions. . . . . I have great difficulty with the retention of facts and especially words. Recall is sluggish, frustrating. The brain feels "muddled"—thought processes slowed and confused. My mind simply "cuts off" at times—often in mid-sentence or mid-thought. Yet it seems to dwell on painful subjects. I think about how inadequate I am—and I cannot get rid of that idea, it keeps on coming back. In the morning I feel literally paralyzed with inadequacy and indecision—I cannot even decide which necktie to wear—or whether to wear one at all. I seem to lack any sense of direction or purpose. I have such an inertia—I cannot assert myself, I cannot fight. I do not seem to have any will at all.

It is because of such psychomotor deficits that depressed patients are often unable to continue to work, or do so with much diminished efficiency; the household is typically disorganized; and students fail their classes or drop courses. In the elderly, the slowing of mental functions can be so pronounced that the patient may appear "demented" because of memory difficulties, disorientation, and confusion. This clinical picture is known as *depressive pseudodementia* (Roth, 1976) and often responds dramatically to a course of electroconvulsive therapy. Although appropriate neurologic evaluation may sometimes be necessary before instituting such therapy, the differentiation of pseudodementia from dementia can often be accomplished on primarily clinical grounds (Table 23–2). In some instances, a therapeutic trial with a heterocyclic antidepressant that possesses minimal side effects may be the only way to arrive at a differential diagnosis.

In young depressives, especially bipolars, psychomotor slowing may in the extreme

**TABLE 23–2  Clinical Features Useful in Differential Diagnosis of Depressive Pseudodementia from Primary Dementia**

|  | Pseudodemented Depression | Primary Dementia |
|---|---|---|
| Onset | Acute | Insidious |
| Past affective episodes | Common | Uncharacteristic |
| Self-reproach | Yes | Uncharacteristic |
| Diurnality | Worse in A.M. | Worse at night |
| Memory deficit | Recent = remote | Recent > remote |
| Responses | "Don't know" | Near miss |
| Reaction to failure | Tend to give up | Catastrophic reaction |
| Practice effects | Can be coached | Consistently poor |

manifest stupor—the patient is unable to participate even in basic biologic functions like feeding himself. History is the most reliable way to distinguish depressive stupor from its hysterical and schizophrenic counterparts. Again, electroconvulsive therapy is often lifesaving in such cases, but somatic causes of stupor (e.g., metabolic, neurologic) must first be ruled out by appropriate clinical and laboratory evaluation.

## Cognitive Disturbances

The term cognitive refers to such things as memory, thinking processes, and thought content. In depression, abnormalities in these areas are often secondary to psychomotor disturbances and, for this reason, were described under that heading. In addition to difficulties in concentration and memory, the depressive exhibits a characteristic thought abnormality consisting of negative evaluations of the self, the world, and the future (Beck, 1967). Clinically, these are manifested as:

• Ideas of deprivation and loss
• Low self-esteem and self-confidence
• Self-reproach and pathologic guilt
• Helplessness, hopelessness, and pessimism
• Recurrent thoughts of death and suicide

The essential characteristic of the depressive's thinking is that he or she views everything in an extremely negative, gloomy light. The self-accusations are typically unjustified or grotesquely blown out of proportion, as in the case of a woman who was tormented by guilt because on one occasion 20 years previously, she permitted someone other than her fiancé to kiss her on the lips. Some of these symptoms verge on the delusional. For instance, a world famous artist

presented to his physician with the complaint that he was "nothing." In what is termed *psychotic depression*, negative thinking acquires grossly delusional proportions, being maintained with such conviction that they are not amenable to change by evidence to the contrary. Thus severely depressed patients may manifest delusions of worthlessness and sinfulness, reference, and persecution. They believe that they are being singled out for their past transgressions and that everyone is aware of these grievous errors. Persecutory ideation in depression is often prosecutory and derives from belief in the necessity of punishment for such transgressions. Other depressives believe that they have lost all their means and that their children will starve (delusions of poverty), or that they harbor an occult and "shameful" illness, such as cancer or syphilis (delusions of ill health), or that parts of their bodies are missing (nihilistic delusions). A minority of depressives may have fleeting auditory or visual hallucinations with extremely unpleasant content along the lines of their delusions (e.g., accusatory voices or seeing themselves in coffins or graveyards). All of these psychotic experiences are considered mood-congruent in the sense that they are understandable in light of the prevailing pathologic mood.

Given the fact that the depressive typically finds himself locked in the private hell of his negative thoughts, it is not surprising that 15 per cent of untreated patients give up hope that they will ever be free of such torments, and kill themselves. However, they do not do this at the depth of their melancholia. I once asked such a patient if she was contemplating suicide, to which she replied, "Doctor, I am already dead. I have no existence." Such a patient is unlikely to undertake suicidal action. It is when psycho-motor activity is improving either sponta-neously or with antidepressants—yet mood and thinking are still dark—that the patient is most likely to have the requisite energy to commit the suicidal act.

## THE DISTINCTION BETWEEN GRIEF AND MELANCHOLIA

Depression in its full-blown form is sharply demarcated from the "blues" (Ak-iskal, 1983a). The patient and his family will tell the doctor that the depressed state rep-resents a break from his or her usual self. The sustained nature of the mood disturb-ance, the often disabling characteristic signs and symptoms in vegetative, psychomotor, and cognitive areas, the tendency for recur-rence (especially in a periodic and seasonal fashion) and, in many cases, the presence of "loaded" (three consecutive generations) family histories for the same type of illness serve to distinguish this clinical disorder from the ordinary disappointments that are part of the fabric of human existence.

It is in deciding whether a given patient is suffering from ordinary grief or has pro-gressed to clinical depression that the doctor will encounter the greatest difficulty. Since bereaved individuals manifest many de-pressive symptoms within the first year (Clayton, Herjanic, Murphy, Woodruff, 1974), how does one decide whether grief has progressed to melancholia, as it does in 2 to 5 per cent of such individuals? Clayton and associates have suggested the following criteria as a guideline:

- Preoccupation with suicidal ideation does not occur in normal grief except in some men dur-ing the first month or so of bereavement.

- Marked psychomotor retardation is not ob-served in normal grief.

- Although bereaved individuals sometimes ex-perience guilt about having *omitted* to offer cer-tain services that may have saved the life of the deceased loved one, they typically do not ex-perience guilt of commission.

- Mummification, which refers to maintaining the belongings of the deceased person exactly as they were before his or her death, is abnor-mal and indicates the possibility of psycho-pathology.

- Severe anniversary reaction should alert the cli-nician to the possibility of psychopathology.

Although dexamethasone suppression test and REM latency findings have not been systematically studied in this context, they might also assist, especially when extremely deviant values are obtained, in the differ-ential diagnostic process. The following vi-gnette (taken from Akiskal and Lemmi, 1983) on the joint use of clinical and biologic indices in the differential diagnosis of affec-tive syndromes illustrates the features of pathologic grief.

### CASE HISTORY 2

A 75-year-old widow was brought by her daugh-ter because of severe insomnia and loss of interest in daily routines after her husband's death 1 year ago. She had been agitated for the first 2 or 3 months and thereafter "sank into total inactivity—not want-ing to get out of bed, not wanting to do anything, not wanting to go out." According to her daughter, she was married at 21, had four children, and had been a housewife until her husband's death from a heart attack. Past psychiatric history was negative; premorbid adjustment had been characterized by compulsive traits.

During the interview, she was dressed in black, appeared moderately slowed, and sobbed inter-mittently, saying, "I search everywhere for him—I don't find him." When asked about life, she said, "Everything I see is black." Although she expressed no interest in food, she did not seem to have lost an appreciable amount of weight. Her DST was 18 μg/dl. The patient declined psychiatric care, stating that she "preferred to join her husband rather than get well." She was too religious to commit suicide, but by refusing treatment, she felt that she would "pine away—find relief in death and reunion."

## THE DISTINCTION BETWEEN ANXIETY AND DEPRESSIVE STATES

Anxiety is a common symptom of de-pressive illness, and depression is a com-mon complication of anxiety states. Sepa-rating these two alternatives on strictly clinical grounds is not always easy. System-atic studies by Roth and Mountjoy (1982) have shown that early-morning awakening, psychomotor retardation, self-reproach, hopelessness, and suicidal ideation repre-sent the most solid clinical markers of depression in this differential diagnosis. On followup of depressed patients, these manifestations tend to remit, whereas patients with anxiety states continue to exhibit a spectrum of signs and symptoms consisting of marked tension, phobias, panic attacks, vasomotor instability, feelings of unreality, perceptual distortions, as well as paranoid and hypochondriacal ideas. A predominance of such anxiety features antedating the present bout of illness suggests the diagnosis of an anxiety disorder. It must be kept in mind, however, that anxiety disorders seldom make their first appearance after age 40. Therefore, it is best to consider a patient who presents with marked anxiety features for the first time after age 40 as suffering from major depression and treat him accordingly (Watts, 1966):

## CASE HISTORY 3

A 52-year-old married teacher with unremarkable previous psychiatric history was referred by his internist to "rule out sleep apnea." Over the previous 3 weeks, he had begun to awaken several times at night, gasping for air and sweating, with palpitations and intense fear. There was no special dream recall. History revealed that a colleague, to whom the patient was not particularly close, had recently suffered a severe coronary attack and underwent bypass surgery. Additional complaints of the patient included early-morning awakening, feeling tired in the morning, and tension, irritability, and apprehension throughout the day, rendering classroom teaching difficult. Appetite and libido were unchanged. The patient denied subjective depression. During psychiatric interview, his face expressed worry and gloom, and he was visibly agitated; he was tormented by the fear that he might die suddenly, although he could not say from what. Family history was unremarkable. The patient had not responded to a 3-week trial of diazepam, 20 mg/day. After drug washout, polysomnographic evaluation ruled out sleep apnea while demonstrating a REM latency of 38 minutes, middle and terminal insomnia with a sleep efficiency of 64 per cent. Within 15 days, the patient showed a dramatic response to trazodone, 300 mg/day.

Such agitated patients represent variants of unipolar depression and, in former classifications, were termed involutional melancholics.

Currently, the differential diagnosis of anxiety and depressive states is not fully resolved. Although recurrent (especially retarded) major depressive illness is most certainly a distinct disorder from anxiety states, at least some forms of depression may share

a common diathesis with panic disorder (Leckman et al., 1983). Emerging biologic markers may contribute to the resolution of this nosologic problem:

• Sleep EEG studies indicate that short REM latency is uncharacteristic of anxiety states, even when complicated by depression (Akiskal et al., 1984). Furthermore, arecoline challenge shortens the REM latency in depression but not in anxiety states (Dube et al., in press).

• DST findings are generally negative in anxiety states (Curtis et al., 1982).

• Basal forearm blood flow is elevated in anxiety but not depressive states (Kelly and Walter, 1969).

• Intravenous lactate infusion tends to elicit a panic attack predominantly in those patients who have had previous history of such attacks (Pitts and McClure, 1967).

A final consideration in discussing the relationship between anxiety and depressive states is what have been termed *atypical depressions* (Davidson, Miller, Turnbull, Sullivan, 1982). As originally described in the British literature, these were mild, fluctuating outpatient depressions (which sometimes reached full syndromal depth), seen mostly in young women referred from the cardiology service, where they had been seen because of manifestations of autonomic nervous system overactivity. Against this background of somatic anxiety symptoms, which often led to phobias, these patients suffered from initial insomnia (yet slept deeply and too long once they fell asleep), daytime fatigue and lethargy, overeating, and feeling worse in the evening. Current experience supports the British suggestions that monoamine oxidase inhibitors (MAOIs) are more likely to be effective in such patients. Furthermore, Liebowitz et al. (1984) have shown that response to MAOIs is most likely in those atypical patients who give a history of panic attacks. It would therefore appear that atypical depression, as defined earlier, is in effect atypical panic disorder, presenting with or complicated by depressive symptoms. To compound matters, atypical depressions without the anxiety component seem to represent a heterogeneous group of disorders that range from mild hypothyroidism to mild bipolar disorder, both of which manifest with extreme lethargy, hypersomnia, and overeating (Akiskal et al., 1984).

## THE HETEROGENEITY OF DYSTHYMIC DISORDERS

As defined in DSM-III, dysthymia refers to chronic, typically mild, and fluctuating depressions of at least 2 years' duration. Except for the requirement of chronicity, this group of patients is similar to what, in former classifications, was termed neurotic depression. This is a heterogeneous grouping that subsumes several nosologically unrelated categories (Akiskal, 1983b). Most patients manifesting low-grade depressive mood swings are not suffering from primary mood disorder; their gloom is secondary to other psychiatric conditions, such as anxiety disorders, anorexia nervosa, or ego-dystonic homosexuality, hysteria, sociopathy, and their variants. In a special subgroup, however, low-grade depression represents the residual phase of incompletely remitted primary major depressions; such residuals are most commonly seen in late-onset unipolar illness (>40 years).

There is also an early-onset dysthymic pattern termed subaffective dysthymia. It begins insidiously in teenage years in the absence of other psychiatric disorders and pursues an intermittent course. If major depressions are superimposed, the patient returns to the low-grade intermittent baseline on recovery. Such patients tend to be introverted, self-denigrating, and masochistic. They are habitually brooding, anhedonic, and hypersomnolent, suffer from psychomotor inertia, and tend to feel worse in the morning. REM latency is reduced to less than 70 minutes, and family history can be positive for bipolar disorder. For this reason, such patients may respond to tricyclic antidepressants with hypomanic episodes. In brief, this form of dysthymia appears to be a true subaffective disorder (i.e., an attenuated clinical expression of primary mood disorder) or, more specifically, cyclothymia minus spontaneous hypomania. The vignette that follows is a self-description given by a 34-year-old nurse of her "depressive self"; it exemplifies the concept of dysthymia as a true subaffective disorder distinct from primary character pathology.

## CASE HISTORY 4

Suffering is so much part of me that it defines my personality. This is manifested by a profound sense of inadequacy which is almost physical. I feel as though a stone is suspended from a long chain inside me dangling over a dark bottomless well. I sense the futility of effort—though not where work is concerned which, over the years, has been the major principle of my life. It is a personal isolation. It has never been possible for me to describe to anyone the overwhelming sadness that almost paralyzes me in the mornings. I have never timed the periods of depression as they seem to come and go irregularly. My appetite is usually unchanged, but I sleep more, sometimes 15 hours per day.

These black periods have been my share in life for as long as I can remember. I have never taken medication for them. Onset is insidious but return to normal mood can come on suddenly, like the snapping of a light switch, and I will be well for a week or so, and, if I am lucky, for several weeks.

My mother suffered a mood disorder. I remember days when she would cry for no reason—when I would come home from school to find her still huddled in bed. My aunt said she was "lazy." And then I remember her becoming hyperactive, grandiose, expansive. Her father also suffered periods of depression. So it would seem almost by destiny that I have been sentenced to a life of suffering. My major question is why I have been denied the highs that my mother enjoyed so much—even though at such times she gave hell to my father.

This is one of the unresolved questions in the riddle of the mood disorders—why some of the relatives of bipolar individuals suffer from depressive episodes alone and from depressive "personality" developments, as in the case of this patient. As described in a subsequent section of this chapter, in reality such patients are pseudo-unipolar in the sense that they are at risk for pharmacologically induced hypomanic periods.

## THE MANIC SYNDROME

As with the depressive syndrome, mania manifests in disturbances in mood, vegetative, psychomotor, and cognitive functions. Kraepelin's description (1921) remains the classic in this area. A more recent monograph is that by Winokur, Clayton, and Reich (1969). Clinical manifestations in mania are often, although not always, opposite in direction from those seen in depression. Mild degrees of mania (hypomania) can be useful in business, leadership roles, and the arts (Akiskal, 1983c). A powerful literary portrayal of hypomania is provided by Bellow's *Herzog* (1964). Many creative people have had such elevated periods, often reaching clinical proportions (Andreasen and Canter, 1975). For instance, Van Gogh, who painted almost 200 masterpieces in his Arles period before committing suicide in 1890, wrote the following description in his letters to his brother Theo (1927): "Ideas for my work are coming to me in swarms . . . continued fever to work . . . an extraordinary feverish energy . . . terrible lucidity." In the case of Van Gogh, who suffered from extreme lows and highs, the unstable mood appeared based on an epileptic disorder (Blumer, 1984). Although mania can be symptomatic of several medical conditions or precipitated by catecholaminergic drugs (Krauthammer and Klerman, 1978), the syndrome most typically develops in those with the familial manic-depressive diathesis. (Symptomatic manias are listed in Table 23–3.) One of many reasons that mania is considered an illness is that it often leads to personal disaster and tragedy, as it did in the case of Van Gogh. Fortunately, current treatments can often attenuate manic mood swings with no appreciable effect on creativity, which may even be enhanced, thanks to freedom from incapaci-

**TABLE 23–3    Medical Conditions and Drugs Commonly Associated with Onset of Mania**

Medical Conditions
  Thyrotoxicosis
  Systemic lupus erythematosus
  Rheumatic chorea
  Influenza
  St. Louis encephalitis
  General paresis (tertiary syphilis)
  Huntington's chorea
  Multiple sclerosis
  Diencephalic and third ventricular tumors
  Complex partial seizures (temporal lobe epilepsy)
  Stroke
  Head trauma

Drugs
  Corticosteroids
  Levodopa
  Bromocriptine
  Amphetamines
  Methylphenidate
  Cocaine
  Monoamine oxidase inhibitors
  Heterocyclic antidepressants

tating mood swings (Schou, 1979). This is not universal, however, and each patient who derives benefits from hypomanic bursts should be considered individually.

## Mood Change

The mood in mania is classically one of elation, euphoria, and jubilation, often associated with laughing, punning, and gesturing. The mood is not stable, and momentary tearfulness is not uncommon. Also, for many patients, the high is so excessive that it is dysphoric. When crossed, the patient can become extremely irritable and hostile. Thus lability is as much a feature of the manic's mood as the mood elevation.

## Vegetative Disturbances

The cardinal sign here is decreased amount of sleep, the patient needing only a few hours of sleep and feeling energetic on awakening. Some patients may go without sleep for 48 hours at a time and feel even more energetic.

There does not seem to be a primary disturbance of appetite as such, but weight loss may occur because of increased activity and inattention to nutritional needs. The sexual appetite is increased and may lead to much sexual indiscretion. Married women with previously unblemished sexual histories may associate with men below their social station. Men may overindulge in alcohol and women—frequenting bars and prostitutes on whom they squander their savings. The sexual adventures of manic patients characteristically result in marital disasters and multiple separations or divorces.

## Psychomotor Disturbances

Increased psychomotor activity, the hallmark of mania, is characterized by increased energy and activity level and by rapid and pressured speech. These are coupled with a subjective sense of physical well-being known as eutonia and by flight of ideas; thinking and perception are unusually sharp—even creative. Sometimes the patient speaks with such pressure that it is difficult to follow his associations; termed *clang associations,* these are often based on rhyming or chance perceptions and flow with great rapidity (see Chapter 22, on mental status).

The manic patient is typically impulsive, disinhibited, and meddlesome. He is intrusive in his increased involvement with people, leading to much friction with colleagues, friends, and family. He is distractible and quickly moves not only from one thought to another, but also from one person to another, showing heightened interest in every new activity that strikes his fancy. He is indefatigable and engages in various and sundry activities, in which he usually displays poor social judgment. Examples include preaching or dancing in the streets; abuse of long-distance calling; buying new cars, hundreds of records, expensive jewelry, or other unnecessary items; engaging in risky business ventures; gambling; and sudden trips. Obviously, these pursuits can lead to personal and financial ruin. In severe mania, known as *delirious mania,* frenzied physical activity continues unabated, leading to a medical emergency requiring daily electroconvulsive therapy.

## Cognitive Disturbances

The manic has an inflated self-esteem and a grandiose sense of confidence and achievements. Underneath this facade, however, the patient sometimes has a painful recognition that these positive self-concepts do not represent reality. Such insight,

if present at all, is, unfortunately, transient. Indeed, manic patients are notoriously refractory to self-examination and insight. As a result, manic delusions are often maintained with extraordinary fervor. These include delusions of exceptional mental and physical fitness; exceptional talent; wealth, aristocratic ancestry, or other grandiose identity; assistance (i.e., well-placed people or supernatural powers are assisting in their endeavors); or reference and persecution (i.e., enemies are observing them or following them out of malignant jealousy).

## THE DISTINCTION BETWEEN BIPOLAR AND SCHIZOPHRENIC PSYCHOSES

As in depressive psychoses, fleeting auditory or visual hallucinations involving the mood-congruent themes mentioned earlier can be seen in a sizable minority of manic patients. Furthermore, severely ill manic patients can exhibit such a degree of psychotic disorganization that mood-incongruent symptoms pervade the clinical picture, and cross-sectionally, it may prove difficult to distinguish them from schizophrenic patients. They may even exhibit isolated schneiderian symptoms, although this is typically fleeting and occurs at the height or depth of affective psychosis (Carlson and Goodwin, 1973). Thinking may be so rapid that it may appear "loosened," but unlike schizophrenia, this will be in the setting of expansive and elated affect. By contrast, the severely retarded bipolar depressive, whose affect may superficially seem flat, will al-

**TABLE 23–4    Clinical Features Distinguishing Bipolar from Schizophrenic Psychoses**

|  | Bipolar Disorder | Schizophrenia |
|---|---|---|
| Cross-sectional |  |  |
| Affect | "Infectious" | "Praecox feeling" |
| Thought | Accelerated or retarded | Poverty of content and bizarre |
| Autism | Uncharacteristic | Characteristic |
| Hallucinations | Fleeting | Intermittent or continuous |
| Schneiderian symptoms | Few ($\leq 2$) | Numerous |
| Longitudinal |  |  |
| Premorbid | Cyclothymic | Schizotypal |
| Intermorbid | Tempestuous, "supernormal" | Withdrawn or low functioning |
| Course | Biphasic | Fluctuating, downhill |

A fuller description is available in Andreasen and Akiskal (1983).

most never exhibit major fragmentation of thought. The clinician should therefore consider the clustering of symptoms—rather than individual symptoms—in the differential diagnosis of affective and schizophrenic psychoses. Because the two psychotic conditions entail radically different pharmacologic treatments on a long-term basis, this differential diagnosis (Table 23–4) is of major clinical import.

In the past, many bipolar patients, especially those with prominent manic features at onset, were considered "acute schizophrenics" or "schizoaffective schizophrenics" (Cooper et al., 1972). This often resulted from exclusive reliance on the cross-sectional clinical picture. Although modern treatments tend to keep many schizophrenics out of the hospital, the illness still pursues a downhill course; by contrast, the intermorbid periods in bipolar illness may be normal or even "supernormal," although over time, some social impairment may come from the accumulation of divorces, financial catastrophes, and ruined careers. Genetic studies tend to separate the two disorders; e.g., discordance in identical twins for schizophrenia and bipolar illness is never due to the presence of the other disorder. Laboratory markers have not yet been systematically applied in the two disorders in the clinical setting; it is of clinical interest, however, that thyroid-stimulating hormone (TSH) blunting in response to thyrotropin-releasing hormone (TRH) challenge is almost never positive in schizophrenia, at least not in chronic schizophrenia (Loosen and Prange, 1982). This means that a blunted TSH response would essentially rule out schizophrenia.

Schizoaffective (or cycloid) psychosis refers to an uncommon form of recurrent psychosis with full affective and schizophrenic symptoms during each episode (Perris, 1974). Such a diagnosis should not be considered in an affective psychosis where mood-incongruent psychotic features (e.g., schneiderian and bleulerian symptoms) can be explained on the basis of one of the following: (a) affective psychosis superimposed on mental retardation, giving rise to extremely hyperactive and bizarre manic behavior; (b) affective psychosis complicated by concurrent medical or neurologic diseases, substance abuse or withdrawal, giving rise to numerous schneiderian symptoms; (c) mixed episodes of bipolar illness, which are notorious for signs and symptoms of psychotic disorganization.

Although mixed features (i.e., crying while manic) commonly occur in the course of bipolar disorder, mixed states with the full complement of depressive and manic syndromes are relatively uncommon, occurring in perhaps 10 to 15 per cent of bipolar patients (Himmelhoch et al., 1976) and exhibiting the following signs and symptoms: crying, euphoria, racing thoughts, grandiosity, hypersexuality, suicidal ideation, irritability-anger, psychomotor agitation, severe insomnia, persecutory delusions, auditory hallucinations, and confusion. Such an episode, if it is the patient's first psychotic break, can be extremely difficult to characterize diagnostically unless it is immediately followed by more typical retarded depressive or manic episodes, or family history is positive for bipolar illness. The following vignette (reprinted from Akiskal and Puzantian, 1979) exemplifies these points.

### CASE HISTORY 5

A 19-year-old boy was admitted to a state psychiatric facility because of social withdrawal, insomnia, severe headaches, and the obsession of sticking a knife into his heart in order to punish himself for rape fantasies. While in the hospital, he heard the devil's voice telling him that he should hang himself before a misfortune killed his entire family. His mood was extremely labile; his mental status shifted to an irritable-cantankerous mood; he expressed thoughts of cutting someone's cheeks with a knife (which he eventually did); he entered women's lavatories and said he could "seduce all of them at once"; he started communicating with God (but he wouldn't say how) and expressed the idea that his biologic father was Jesus Christ. At this juncture, he was physically accelerated, spoke constantly, did not experience any need for sleep, flirted with the nurses, joked with everybody, and danced naked in front of other patients "to aid in a campaign to help the poor." On full remission on lithium carbonate, he expressed great guilt over his aggressive behavior during the intermediate mixed state of transition from depression into mania; as a matter of fact, he donated all of his savings to aid his victim in recovering from cosmetic surgery.

A subacute mixed state (i.e., one without psychotic features) can be confused with a severe anxiety state. Accurate diagnosis is essential, as mixed states tend to be notoriously refractory to antidepressants as well as neuroleptics, and lithium may work too slowly; electroconvulsive therapy is usually the more definitive treatment.

## HYPOMANIA AND ITS DIAGNOSTIC SIGNIFICANCE

Setting the threshold for clinically significant hypomania is not only important for differentiating normal merriment and creative moods from illness, but also for diagnosing bipolar II disorder. The following criteria, developed at the University of Tennessee Mood Clinic (Akiskal, 1983a), may assist in setting the clinical threshold for hypomania:

- It is often dysphoric in its drivenness.
- It is labile, i.e., the elation is unstable and easily alternates with irritability and anger.
- It may lead to substance abuse as a means to control the experienced high.
- It tends to impair social judgment.
- It is preceded or followed by retarded depression, typically with abrupt transition.
- It often springs from familial background of bipolar disorder.

Hypomania is a recurrent condition forming part of several overlapping bipolar affective subtypes (Fig. 23–2) of which bipolar II disorder is the most common. Bipolar II patients who seek psychiatric help are usually women in their twenties and thirties who have suffered recurrent bouts of retarded depression. Because their highs are short-lived and typically not perceived as disruptive—indeed, the patient often finds them enjoyable—these individuals seldom present for help during such periods. The illness usually begins in the mid or late teens

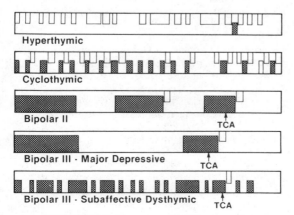

**Hyperthymic**

**Cyclothymic**

**Bipolar II**    TCA

**Bipolar III - Major Depressive**    TCA

**Bipolar III - Subaffective Dysthymic**    TCA

**FIGURE 23–2.** The spectrum of hypomania.

and leads to much interpersonal chaos. This facet of the illness can so impress the clinician that he may embark on a long-term psychotherapeutic endeavor, when in reality the tempestuous biography represents a complication of the recurrent mood disorder. It is therefore critical to document hypomanic swings in such patients in order to bring them the benefit of lithium carbonate. Another reason why accurate early diagnosis is important here lies in the fact that the continued use of tricyclic drugs (TCA) in such patients may not only precipitate hypomanic periods, but also tends to lead to increased cycling* in the long term (Kukopulos et al., 1983). The vignette that follows describes the subtle nature of the hypomanic periods in bipolar II patients and the ease of its induction by antidepressant drugs.

### CASE HISTORY 6

A 26-year-old medical secretary who was separated from her third husband presented for outpatient psychiatric care with the chief complaint of "lack of hope, joy, meaning, and focus in life." She said she lacked the energy and motivation to take care of daily routines and slept 12 to 14 hours nightly. She said she would rather die than go through another divorce. She could not concentrate at work, and her typing speed had deteriorated. Since her teens she had had numerous similar periods that lasted from 2 to 12 weeks. These episodes often terminated abruptly, at which time she felt such an "intense relief and joy that I would sleep with the first man who happened to be around." It is this behavior that has led to repeated marital conflict and intermittent psychotherapy with little tangible benefit. On further questioning, she revealed that during the sudden recovery period, which lasted for four to five days, she sometimes felt no need for sleep, felt such "ecstasy from being alive again that I would cry," and had to drink whiskey to be able to "calm down my mind and body galloping with new life." Her husbands and numerous lovers were often irritated by her increased zeal, which led to new sexual misadventures. Family history revealed that a maternal uncle who had never received psychiatric help but who was known to be an alcoholic had hanged himself in his early 40s. An older sister had been treated for "mild depressions." Their mother had been periodically treated for excited psychotic states that had been labeled

---

* Cycles refer to the period from the onset of one episode to that of a subsequent one. In so-called rapid-cycling patients, who often come from the rank of bipolar II disorder, cycle frequency increases to at least four per year (Dunner, 1979).

"paranoid schizophrenia," but little evidence could be found to substantiate that diagnosis; she had been married five times, indulged in much gambling, and associated with people in art circles. Given that the mother's illness suggested mania, and given the abundance of historical evidence for hypomanic episodes in the patient, lithium carbonate was recommended. The patient refused to consider this treatment. Ten days later she was seen in the emergency department in an accelerated state and complained that she had not slept for two nights; she also revealed that she had been taking her sister's "tranquilizer," which turned out to be imipramine tablets.

Cyclothymic disorder often presents clinically in a similar fashion, except that the depressive periods are shorter, lasting for three to ten days rather than for weeks, and are not of full syndromal depth. These rapid and tempestuous mood swings render the differential diagnosis from personality disorder even more problematic. Table 23–5 summarizes the main features of cyclothymia that need to be taken into account in such differential diagnosis.

In still another variant of the bipolar spectrum known as bipolar III, the patient suffers from early-onset repeated bouts of retarded depression—which can be either major episodes or intermittent minor depressions with the pattern of subaffective dysthymia as described earlier—but without evidence for spontaneous hypomanic periods; the bipolar tendency in these patients becomes manifest on pharmacologic challenge with antidepressants. Family history is often positive for frank bipolar ill-ness. These pseudounipolar patients, who are sometimes referred to as unipolar II, represent either a less penetrant genetic form of bipolar disorder or simply the earliest depressive beginnings of bipolar disorder. The question then becomes, can one predict which depressives will eventually switch into bipolar disorder? The following clinical features have been found useful in this regard in prospective followup studies (Strober and Carlson, 1982; Akiskal et al., 1983):

• Onset before age 25
• Psychotic depression in a teenager
• Abrupt onset
• Postpartum onset
• Hypersomnic-retarded depression
• Pharmacologic mobilization of hypomania
• Bipolar family history
• Loaded (especially three consecutive generations) family history for mood disorder

This section on the milder end of the bipolar spectrum would be incomplete without mentioning chronically or intermittently hypomanic individuals termed hypomanic personality, or hyperthymic disorder (Akiskal, 1983c). This condition is characterized by intermittent subsyndromal hypomanic features with infrequent intervening euthymia (Fig. 23–2). They are typically short sleepers (four to six hours per night) and are high achievers. Although irritability is often seen in these patients, depression as such is extremely uncommon; in other words, hyperthymia is cyclothymia with the minimum amount of depression, characterized

**TABLE 23–5  Clinical Features of Cyclothymic Disorder**

General Characteristics
  Onset before 21 years
  Short cycles (days), which are recurrent in an irregular fashion, with infrequent euthymia
  May not attain full syndrome for depression and hypomania during any one cycle, but entire range of affective symptoms occur at various times
  Abrupt and unpredictable mood change, often unrelated to external circumstances

Subjective Symptoms
  Lethargy alternating with eutonia
  Pessimism and brooding alternating with optimism and carefree attitudes
  Mental confusion and apathy alternating with sharpened and creative thinking
  Shaky self-esteem alternating between low self-confidence and grandiose overconfidence

Behavioral Signs
  Hypersomnia alternating with decreased need for sleep
  Introverted self-absorption alternating with uninhibited people-seeking
  Decreased verbal output alternating with talkativeness
  Unexplained tearfulness alternating with excessive punning and jocularity
  Marked unevenness in quantity and quality of productivity (unusual working hours)

Modified from Akiskal et al. (1979).

by excessive use of denial, and given their successes in leadership positions or business, such individuals seldom, if ever, present for psychiatric treatment. However, they can be seen in sleep disorders centers where they seek help because of sleep difficulty.

## MOOD DISORDER IN DIFFERENT CLINICAL SETTINGS

This chapter has presented the manifold clinical picture of mood disorders that embrace a broad range of somatic, psychomotor, emotional, and cognitive manifestations, as well as certain personality disturbances representing complications of the illness. For this reason, the differential diagnosis of affective signs and symptoms interfaces with the "blues," bereavement reactions, anxiety states, primary character disorders, substance use disorders, schizophrenia, and dementia. Furthermore, depending on clinical setting, one set of manifestations may dominate the clinical presentation. Common examples include the following:

- Primary care–somatic complaints and substance abuse
- Sleep disorders center–insomnia and hypersomnia
- Urology–impotence
- Neurology–memory disturbances
- Emergency department–psychosis
- Educational counseling–scholastic failure
- Psychology and social work–marital problems
- Psychoanalysis–character pathology
- Courts–violence and murder
- City morgue–suicide

As primary mood disorders are eminently treatable disorders—and because the complications of untreated depression or mania can be extremely serious—all physicians, as well as mental health professionals, should be competent in determining whether a given set of affectively tinged signs or symptoms are due to a primary mood disorder. The clinician should always inquire:

- Are unexplained somatic complaints and substance abuse alternative expressions of a primary mood disorder?
- Are insomnia and hypersomnia part of an affective syndrome, acute or chronic?
- Did depression precede the impotence?
- Are memory disturbances secondary to a reversible melancholia?
- Despite "schizophrenic" coloring, is the psychosis one phase of a recurrent bipolar disorder?

- Is school failure in a teenager or a young adult caused by a retarded depression heralding the onset of a bipolar disorder?
- Are marital problems secondary to depression, cyclothymia, or frank bipolar disorder in one or both spouses?
- What appears to be borderline character pathology—is it due to a cyclothymic or related temperament?
- Was the violent act committed during a psychotic depression or manic excitement?

It is necessary to inquire along these lines because it is obviously too late to do so in the city morgue.

These are serious clinical issues and necessitate a systematic approach to determine the affective basis of a patient's presenting complaints in different settings (Akiskal and Cassano, 1983):

- To elicit other clinical features of the affective syndrome under consideration
- To document history of more typical major affective episodes in the past
- To assess if the presenting complaints recur in a periodic or cyclic fashion
- To substantiate good social functioning between periods of illness
- To obtain positive family history for mood disorder and construct a family pedigree
- To document an unequivocal therapeutic response to thymoleptic drugs or electroconvulsive therapy

In summary, the physician or mental health worker who engages in a systematic differential diagnosis of affective disturbances, will soon find that many clinical enigmas will be solved in favor of a primary affective diagnosis. Because primary affective illness is the most common and treatable of the serious psychiatric disorders, the practitioner is statistically admonished to err on the side of such diagnosis.

### REFERENCES

Adams F (ed. and trans.): The Genuine Works of Hippocrates. Baltimore, Williams & Wilkins, 1939.

Akiskal HS: Diagnosis and classification of affective disorders: New insights from clinical and laboratory approaches. Psychiatric Developments 1:123–160, 1983a.

Akiskal HS: Dysthymic disorder: Psychopathology of proposed chronic depressive subtypes. Am J Psychiatry 140:11–20, 1983b.

Akiskal HS: The bipolar spectrum: New concepts in classification and diagnosis in Grinspoon L (ed): Psychiatry Update: The American Psychiatric Association Annual Review, Vol. II. Washington, DC: American Psychiatric Press, Inc, 271–292, 1983c.

Akiskal HS, Cassano GB: The impact of therapeutic advances in widening the nosologic boundaries of affective disorders: Clinical and research implications. Pharmacopsychiatria 16:111–118, 1983.

Akiskal HS, Khani MK, Scott–Strauss A: Cyclothymic temperamental disorders. Psychiatr Clin North Am 2:527–554, 1979.

Akiskal HS, Lemmi H: Clinical neuroendocrine, and sleep EEG diagnosis of "unusual" affective presentations: A practical review. Psychiatr Clin North Am 6:69–83, 1983.

Akiskal HS, Lemmi H, Dickson H, King D, Yerevanian BI, Van Valkenburg C: Chronic depressions: Part 2. Sleep EEG differentiation of primary dysthymic disorders from anxious depressions. J Affect Disord 6:287–297, 1984.

Akiskal HS, McKinney WT Jr: Depressive disorders: Towards a unified hypothesis. Science 182:20–28, 1973.

Akiskal HS, Puzantian VR: Psychotic forms of depression and mania. Psychiatr Clin North Am 2:419–439, 1979.

Akiskal HS, Walker PW, Puzantian VR, King D, Rosenthal TL, Dranon M: Bipolar outcome in the course of depressive illness: Phenomenologic, familial and pharmacologic predictors. J Affect Disord 5:115–128, 1983.

Andreasen NC, Akiskal HS: The specificity of bleulerian and schneiderian symptoms: A critical re-evaluation. Psychiatr Clin North Am 6:41–54, 1983.

Andreasen NC, Canter A: "Genius and Insanity" Revisited: Psychiatric Symptoms and Family History in Creative Writers, in Wirt RD, Winokur G, Roft M (eds): Life History in Psychopathology, vol 4. Minneapolis, University of Minnesota Press, 1975, pp 187–214.

Beck AT: Depression: Causes and Treatment. Philadelphia, University of Pennsylvania Press, 1967.

Bellow S: Herzog. New York, Viking Press, 1964.

Blumer DB (ed): Psychiatric Aspects of Epilepsy. Washington, DC, American Psychiatric Press, 1984.

Carlson G, Goodwin F: The stages of mania. Arch Gen Psychiatry 28:221–288, 1973.

Carroll BJ, Feinberg M, Greden JF, Tarika J, et al: A specific laboratory test for the diagnosis of melancholia. Arch Gen Psychiatry 38:15–22, 1981.

Clayton PJ, Herjanic M, Murphy GE, Woodruff R: Mourning and depression: Their similarities and differences. J Can Psychiatr Assoc 19:309–312, 1974.

Cooper JE, Kendell RE, Gurland BJ, Sharpe L, Copeland JRM, Simon R: Psychiatric Diagnosis in New York and London. London, Oxford University Press, 1972.

Curtis GC, Cameron OG, Nesse RM: The dexamethasone suppression test in panic disorder and agoraphobia. Am J Psychiatry 139:1043–1046, 1982.

Davidson JRT, Miller RD, Turnbull CD, Sullivan JL: Atypical depression. Arch Gen Psychiatry 39:527–534, 1982.

DSM-III: Diagnostic and statistical manual of mental disorders, ed 3. Washington, DC, American Psychiatric Press, 1980.

Dube S, Kumar N, Ettedgui E, et al: Cholinergic REM-induction response: Separation of anxiety and depression. Biol Psychiatry, 1985 (in press).

Dunner D: Rapid cycling bipolar manic depressive illness. Psychiatr Clin North Am 2:461–467, 1979.

Greden J, Carroll B: Psychomotor functioning in affective disorders: An overview of new monitoring techniques. Am J Psychiatry 11:1441–1448, 1981.

Hamilton I: Robert Lowell—A biography. New York, Random House, 1982.

Himmelhoch JM, Mulla D, Neil JF, et al: Incidence and significance of mixed affective states in a bipolar population. Arch Gen Psychiatry 33:1062–1066, 1976.

James W: The Varieties of Religious Experience (lectures). Edinburgh, Scotland, 1902.

Kelly D, Walter CJS: A clinical and physiological relationship between anxiety and depression. Br J Psychiatry 115:401–406, 1969.

Kielholz, Poldinger, Adams C (eds): Masked depression. Köln-Lövenich, Deutscher Arzte-Verlag Gmb, 1982.

Kraepelin E: Manic-depressive insanity and paranoia. Edinburgh, E & S Livingstone, 1921.

Krauthammer C, Klerman GL: Secondary mania: Manic syndromes associated with antecedent physical illness or drugs. Arch Gen Psychiatry 35:1333–1339, 1978.

Kukopulos A, Caliari B, Tundo A, et al: Rapid cyclers, temperament, and antidepressants. Compr Psychiatry 24:249–258, 1983.

Kupfer DJ, Thase ME: The use of the sleep laboratory in the diagnosis of affective disorders. Psychiatr Clin North Am 6:3–21, 1983.

Leckman JF, Weissman MM, Merikangas KR, et al: Panic disorder and major depression. Arch Gen Psychiatry 40:1055–1060, 1983.

Lewis A: Melancholia: A clinical survey of depressive states. J Ment Sci 80:277–378, 1934.

Liebowitz MR, Quitkin FM, Stewart JW, et al: Phenelzine vs imipramine in atypical depression. Arch Gen Psychiatry 41:669–680, 1984.

Loosen PT, Prange AJ: Serum thyrotropin response to thryotropin-releasing hormone in psychiatric patients: A review. Am J Psychiatry 139:405–416, 1982.

Nelson JC, Charney DS: The symptoms of major depressive illness. Am J Psychiatry 138:1–13, 1981.

Perris C: A study of cycloid psychoses. Acta Psychiatr Scand [Suppl] 253, 1974.

Pitts FN, McClure JN: Lactate metabolism in anxiety neurosis. N Engl J Med 277:1329–1336, 1967.

Robins E, Guze SB: Classification of affective disorders: The primary-secondary, the endogenous-reactive, and the neurotic-psychotic concepts, in Williams TA, Katz DM, Shield JA (eds): Recent advances in the psychobiology of the depressive illnesses. Washington, DC, Government Printing Office, 1972, pp 283–292.

Roth M: The psychiatric disorders of later life. Psychiatr Ann 6:417–444, 1976.

Roth M, Mountjoy Q: The distinction between anxiety states and depressive disorders, in Paykel ES (ed): Handbook of Affective Disorders. New York, Guilford Press, 1982, pp 70–92.

Schou M: Artistic productivity and lithium prophylaxis in manic-depressive illness. Br J Psychiatry 135:97–103. 1979.

Strober M, Carlson G: Clinical, genetic and psychopharmacologic predictors of bipolar illness in adolescents with major depression. Arch Gen Psychiatry 39:549–555, 1982.

Tolstoy L: My Confessions. New York, Crowell, 1887.

Van Gogh V: The Letters of Van Gogh to His Brother 1872–1886: With a Memoir by His Sister-in-Law—J. vanGogh-Bonger. London, Constable & Co, Ltd; Boston and New York, Houghton-Mifflin, 1927.

Watts CAH: Depressive Disorders in the Community. Bristol, John Wright & Sons, 1966.

Wehr TA, Goodwin FK: Circadian Rhythms in Psychiatry. Pacific Grove, Calif, Boxwood Press, 1983.

Widlöcher DJ: Psychomotor retardation: Clinical, theoretical, and psychometric aspects. Psychiatr Clin North Am 6:27–40, 1983.

Winokur G, Clayton P, Reich T: Manic-Depressive Illness. St. Louis, C.V. Mosby, 1969.

# chapter 24

# ANXIETY SYMPTOMS

*by* Charles Van Valkenburg, M.D.

Panic attacks are spells of intense anxiety, which usually have a sudden and unexpected onset and which last from a few minutes to an hour or two. Anxiety can be so intense that patients describe it as worse than the worst anxiety they could possibly have, a transcendental, unreal experience. Even those who have survived hundreds of panic attacks are often unable to console themselves with this fact, nor to believe that this particular attack will not be the one that kills them. Many who have previously visited emergency departments without satisfaction for the same symptoms feel compelled to do so again. They feel that something horrible is about to happen, that they are doomed. The world around them seems to be changed, menacing. They fear that they will lose control of their bodies, perhaps urinating and defecating in front of everyone, perhaps running screaming and naked, or killing babies. They feel that they are losing their mind, going crazy. They may feel that their bodies have become distorted, that they are no longer theirs, or that they are floating outside their bodies. They feel their hearts pounding and have the sensation of not being able to get air, despite their breathing as rapidly as possible. Sometimes breathing seems to be choked off by a lump or constriction in their throats. The chest feels heavy, uncomfortable, painful. There are waves of numbness or tingling in the arms or legs or around the mouth. They

feel dizzy, unsteady, as if they will faint, weakened, tense, tremulous, possibly with hot or cold flashes, and drenching perspiration. Sometimes they feel the need to urinate or defecate.

The panic attack is not a distinct illness, but a syndrome, like fever, that can result from many causes. Before a diagnosis of panic disorder can be made in a patient who has panic attacks, all possible medical causes and then all possible psychiatric causes for the syndrome must first be ruled out.

Patients who experience panic attacks typically have gone to primary care specialists before seeing psychiatrists. Most of those who have medical illnesses have been diagnosed and treated, and only those whose illness is thought to be "functional" or not organic are referred to psychiatrists. As panic disorder increasingly is the topic of articles in the popular press and television shows, an increasing number of patients are contacting psychiatrists directly, without having had an adequate medical evaluation. Psychiatrists are therefore becoming primary-care physicians, who must be able to determine which cases they can treat and which need to be referred to another specialist.

The differential diagnosis of panic attack syndromes is made first by considering and ruling out the physical illnesses that can result in panic syndromes and then by considering each of the other mental illnesses, all of which can be associated with panic attacks.

# ORGANIC ANXIETY SYNDROMES

Apart from the feeling of anxiety or panic itself, depersonalization, or derealization, most of the symptoms of the panic attack are physical. Until medical assessments have indicated the contrary, many patients with panic attacks believe that they have physical illness. This is not initially an implausible assumption, since there are common physical illnesses that cause such symptoms. Before categorizing attacks as "functional" (not organic), it must first be determined whether a physical illness is causing all or some of the patient's anxiety symptoms.

## Myocardial Infarction

The predominant symptom of a heart attack is crushing chest pain. Shortness of breath and a choking or smothering sensation, palpitations, heavy perspiration, and a feeling of impending death are commonly associated. Some heart attack patients who recover report out-of-body experiences and other forms of depersonalization or derealization. Many patients with myocardial infarction will have had previous episodes of similar symptoms.

Fortunately, it is now possible to diagnose heart attack with a good degree of certainty. An electrocardiogram (EKG) can often establish the diagnosis in a few minutes, and tests for cardiac enzymes in the blood can make the diagnosis certain. Thus, by the time the first episode of symptoms has been assessed, it should be clear whether or not there has been a heart attack. Seen in the acute phase, a heart attack can be recognized by most clinicians and even untrained persons. In panic disorder, chest pain is often reported as a concomitant symptom, but it is rarely the chief complaint; it is of a less severe quality than the pain of a myocardial infarction. The affect of a heart attack patient is one of obvious physical pain, which is easy to discriminate from an anxious affect.

## Angina Pectoris

Angina pectoris is characterized by episodes of chest pain or discomfort, heart palpitations, shortness of breath or trouble breathing, and, understandably, anxiety (Bass et al., 1983; Thompson et al., 1982). The episodes are often brought on by physical exertion or typical anxiety-producing stimuli, or they can appear to be spontaneous. Although there is general agreement that the symptoms of angina pectoris are caused by intermittent restrictions of blood flow to the heart muscle, this is often difficult to prove in individual cases; laboratory tests will not necessarily differentiate angina from panic. An EKG stress test, in which the patient exercises increasingly strenuously while an EKG is recorded, can sometimes clearly establish the diagnosis but often cannot. Injecting dye into the left atrium and recording its passage through the coronary arteries will sometimes show narrowing of the arteries, but the degree of narrowing correlates poorly with the severity of symptoms. Spasm of the coronary arteries, thought to be the proximate cause of the pain, is difficult to document.

Later age of onset, presence of cardiac risk factors, such as heavy smoking or hypertension, and a preponderance of chest pain over other symptoms favor a diagnosis of angina over panic disorder, whereas overanxious behavior and milder chest pain favor a diagnosis of anxiety disorder. The symptomatic overlap of these two syndromes is considerable. As both are relatively common, an individual patient might have both diseases.

The ability of the cardiologist to diagnose angina pectoris correctly is not, at present, demonstrably superior to the ability of the psychiatrist to diagnose panic attacks. Therefore, the possibility of a panic disorder cannot be dismissed solely because of a possibly uncertain diagnosis of angina. Sedatives, beta blockers, and relaxation have been used to treat both angina and panic attacks, but the use of antidepressants or nitroglycerin to treat one syndrome may exacerbate the other. In this particular area, ongoing consultation between psychiatrist and cardiologist is required, and treatment plans must be specifically tailored to each individual patient.

## Hyperdynamic Beta Adrenergic State

Increased sensitivity of the circulatory system to the beta catecholamines isoproterenol and epinepherine, or elevated levels of these amines in the system, is thought to cause hyperkinetic heart syndrome. The symptoms of this disorder are not distinctly different from those of panic; indeed, some authorities consider that panic disorder is caused by a hyperdynamic beta adrenergic state (Charney, Heninger, Redmond, 1983), and some laboratory evidence supports this view. Except in extreme cases, where there is left ventricular hypertrophy or a prominent murmur, there seems no sure way to discriminate these two syndromes clinically, nor even to demonstrate that they are not the same illness. Hyperdynamic beta adrenergic state responds to beta blockers, such as propranolol; in many cases, the diagnosis is based on symptomatic improvement on these drugs. Panic disorder can also respond to beta blockers, although generally less well than to antidepressants or benzodiazepines.

## Mitral Valve Prolapse Syndrome

When mitral valve prolapse syndrome is symptomatic, its symptoms are often identical to those of panic attacks. But most cases of mitral valve prolapse are asymptomatic, and there is considerable disagreement among cardiologists as to whether the asymptomatic condition is even a disorder, or merely an incidental finding of echocardiography.

There are at least two forms of mitral valve prolapse syndrome. In one form, the mitral valve itself is abnormal, thickened and myxomatous, such as is seen in Marfan's syndrome. Such patients often deteriorate. Most of the reported negative sequelae of mitral valve prolapse syndrome, such as unexpected sudden deaths, are accounted for by these myxomatous forms. Paradoxically, these patients are relatively unlikely to be troubled by the panic, anxiety, and cardiovascular symptoms.

Patients whose mitral valves appear anatomically normal but who show dynamic or functional prolapse are the patients who are most likely to complain of symptoms. Circulating catecholamines or other modula-tors associated with anxiety may be the cause of functional prolapse. Inhalation of amyl nitrite will exacerbate mitral valve prolapse, and chronic hyperthyroidism appears to cause permanent mitral valve prolapse. But in most cases, the cause is unknown.

Although mitral valve prolapse can be documented by echocardiography, there is disagreement among cardiologists as to the proper diagnostic criteria. Some diagnose it on echo evidence alone, whereas others won't make the diagnosis unless there is also a midsystolic murmur or click or moderately severe incapacitation. Most seem to agree that the treatment of choice for symptomatic mitral valve prolapse is beta blockade. Mitral valve prolapse does not seem to affect symptoms or treatment response of panic disorder. Both conditions are heritable, but in families that have both, they may be inherited independently of each other.

Since patients with panic disorder or agoraphobia are at high risk of mitral valve prolapse as well, the psychiatrist evaluating panic attacks should listen to the patient's heart for a midsystolic murmur or click, ideally with the patient squatting or performing a Valsalva maneuver to accentuate the sounds. It is less clear whether an echocardiogram should be ordered. The test is noninvasive and can be done relatively inexpensively. Those who believe that prophylactic antibiotics are indicated and that beta blockers are a good treatment may prove to be right. And many patients, after having been told for years that their symptoms are "all in the head" are vastly pleased and relieved finally to have some objective evidence of more honorable heart disease. The best course is probably to explain all this to the patient and then let him or her decide whether to have echocardiography. In those already diagnosed as having mitral valve prolapse syndrome, apart from the question of antibacterial prophylaxis, no deviation from the usual treatment for panic disorder appears indicated.

## Cardiac Dysrhythmias

Cardiac dysrhythmias can cause palpitations, chest pain or discomfort, dizziness, breathing difficulty, syncope, and anxiety. Panic disorder is often associated with cardiac dysrhythmias, including premature ventricular contractions. Not all dysrhythmias cause subjective symptoms, and not all symptoms in dysrhythmia patients coincide with documentable dysrhythmias. Paroxysmal atrial tachycardia (PAT) can particularly be mistaken for a panic attack. Pulse rates in panic attacks are sometimes normal (Barr et al., 1982–83) and seldom exceed 120, in contradistinction to the pulse rate of 200 that might occur in PAT. Fortunately, most dysrhythmias can be well documented and characterized by EKG. EKG dysrhythmias can be identified by most physicians, and those who need help can consult a cardiologist or a computer. The absence of dysrhythmia on a single EKG does not rule out the condition, particularly if no symptoms are present at the time of the EKG. But if clinically significant dysrhythmias are found, they must be dealt with. First, it must be determined whether the patient's anxiety symptoms are primarily caused by dysrhythmia and would be better treated with cardiospecific drugs. Second, the effects of antipanic drugs on heart rhythm must be taken into account. Most tricyclic antidepressant drugs exert quinidine-like antiarrhythmic effects but exacerbate ventricular dysrhythmias. Propranolol and other beta blockers used to treat anxiety symptoms affect various dysrhythmias differently. Monoamine oxidase inhibitors are less predictable, whereas benzodiazepines have little effect on heart rhythm.

Important cardiac dysrhythmias may not be present when an EKG is done. They can sometimes be documented by having the patient wear a portable EKG monitor for 24 hours. The patient should keep a record of any symptoms that occur, so it can be determined whether the subjective symptoms coincide with dysrhythmias. Some EKG monitors allow the patient to mark the record electronically when a symptom occurs, making interpretation more precise. In interpreting the results of portable EKG monitoring, it should be remembered that panic disorder patients have more dysrhythmias, particularly premature ventricular contractions, than is usual in asymptomatic persons.

This is another area in which a dialogue between psychiatrist and cardiologist is required. Panic attacks cannot be dismissed as trivial and not worth the risk of treating in the presence of a mild heart condition, but neither should the heart be made worse. Tricyclics' quinidine-like antiarrhythmic effects might help the patient with atrial dysrhythmia, but potentially dangerous additive effects might occur if the psychiatrist prescribes imipramine and the cardiologist prescribes quinidine without consulting each other.

## Hyperthyroidism

Like panic disorder, hyperthyroidism is associated with both chronic and acute episodic anxiety (Pringuet et al., 1982). Symptoms include anxiety, palpitations, perspiration, hot skin, tachycardia, hyperreflexia, diarrhea, weight loss, heat intolerance, proptosis, and lid lag. Severe degrees of chronic hyperthyroidism are easily recognized by clinical signs. Earlier or milder illness can usually be discriminated from primary panic disorder by serum $T_3$ and $T_4$ levels. Chronic hyperthyroidism can lead to mitral valve prolapse syndrome, which persists after the thyroid disease is controlled.

## Hypoparathyroidism

The symptoms of hypoparathyroidism are variable (Denko, 1962). Anxiety is the predominant symptom in 20 per cent of cases. Other typical symptoms include paresthesias, muscle tension and cramps, spasm, and tetany. The most common cause of the syndrome is removal of parathyroid glands during thyroidectomy. Diagnosis is suggested by low serum calcium and high phosphate levels and confirmed by parathormone assay. A low serum calcium level of any etiology can cause the same symptoms and requires immediate treatment.

## Pheochromocytoma

Pheochromocytoma is uncommon but dangerous and treatable, so it must always be borne in mind as a diagnostic possibility (Bravo and Gifford, 1984). Half of pheochromocytoma patients have acute attacks, with typical anxiety symptoms, headache, and flushing. Blood pressure is almost always high during these episodes and usually between them as well. The diagnosis can be established by measuring urinary metanephrine, catecholamines, or vanillylmandelic acid or plasma catecholamines. A single urine sample can be used instead of a 24-hour collection.

## Reactive Hypoglycemia

Reactive hypoglycemia is rare but fashionable. Patients who think that they have hypoglycemia are considerably more likely to be experiencing panic attacks, even if a "hypoglycemia clinic" has told them otherwise. The diagnosis of hypoglycemia is difficult to establish, requiring a glucose tolerance test for the reactive type and a 72-hour fast with frequent blood glucose levels for the insulinoma type. The syndrome is easily ruled out if a normal blood glucose level is obtained during the acute attack.

## Pulmonary Emboli

Small bits of clotted blood or debris that are released into the bloodstream usually come to rest in the lung. If a large enough area of blood flow is interrupted, impaired respiration results in shortness of breath, hyperventilation, and acute anxiety.

Listening to the lungs will sometimes suggest this diagnosis, but in many cases of pulmonary embolism, there are no physical findings. A chest x-ray is often of little help. Arterial blood gas analysis might show decreased oxygen. Lung scan and pulmonary arteriogram can establish the diagnosis definitively. Recurrent pulmonary emboli are expected mainly in individuals with predisposing conditions, such as phlebitis or intravenous drug use.

## Asthma

Like panic disorder, asthma is characterized by episodic attacks of cardiopulmonary symptoms and anxiety. Anxiety can play a part in the precipitation and continuation of asthma attacks, and anxiolytics have been effectively used in the treatment of asthma. Asthma is easily differentiated from panic by listening to the chest, which should be clear during a panic attack. Although the diagnosis and treatment of asthma take prec-

edence over that of panic disorder, management of anxiety has long been an appropriate part of the treatment of asthma. Theophylline, used to treat asthma, can cause or exacerbate panic anxiety.

## Seizure Disorders

In seizure disorders characterized by grand mal convulsions, the primary illness is obvious, but it is important to remember that seizure disorders can cause any psychiatric symptom, particularly any anxiety symptom.

Some temporal lobe seizures do not progress to generalized convulsions, but present with episodes of anxiety, anger, or other affects. Williams (1956) found fearfulness to be the predominant emotion in 61 per cent of patients with partial complex seizures. The diagnosis can usually be established by electroencephalography (EEG), particularly if nasopharyngeal leads are used with provocative stimuli and hyperventilation. Additional cases can be detected by continuously monitored EEG and by characteristic EEG changes after partial complex seizures. Although often easy to establish, this disorder can be difficult to rule out, since the most complete workups still leave an estimated 5 per cent to 10 per cent of cases undocumented. An extensive seizure workup is generally not indicated in patients with panic unless there has been a head injury or symptoms strongly suggestive of partial complex seizures.

## Transient Ischemic Attacks

Transient ischemic attacks (TIAs) include transient neurologic signs that are similar to those seen in stroke. Anxiety is often part of these episodes and may be manifest in discrete episodes or attacks for weeks or months before other symptoms begin to occur. The attacks are caused by episodes of arterial insufficiency, most often in the internal carotid artery. Basilar artery insufficiency is also likely to cause anxiety symptoms. Patients with TIAs require prophylaxis with anticoagulant drugs. Stroke is a frequent outcome.

## Combined Systemic Disease (Posterolateral Sclerosis)

Combined systemic disease, a vitamin $B_{12}$ deficiency syndrome, can present as panic. It frequently causes anxiety, paresthesias, weakness, hyperreflexia, and numerous "soft" symptoms easily misdiagnosed as anxiety or hypochondriacal disorder. In cases where associated pernicious anemia is severe, compensatory hyperventilation may occur. Documentation of low serum $B_{12}$ with impaired absorption or of pernicious anemia establishes the diagnosis, but mental symptoms can occur without anemia. Posterorlateral spinal tract degeneration occurs progressively, and the primary neurologic nature of the illness eventually becomes clear. It is important to make the diagnosis early, before extensive neurologic damage occurs.

## Huntington's Chorea

In a minority of cases, panic anxiety symptoms predominate in the prodromal phase of this illness, before choreiform movements and flaccid paralysis begin. Antisocial personality change, suspiciousness, aggressiveness, and labile mood are the typical prodrome of this illness. Panic and anxiety symptoms might respond to antipsychotic or antianxiety drugs.

## Intoxications

### Caffeine and the Methylxanthines

Caffeine is a commonly consumed stimulant, and too much of it will provoke anxiety symptoms (Eaton et al., 1984). While lower dosages of caffeine usually cause acceleration and euphoria, higher doses cause hyperalertness, hypervigilance, motor tension and tremors, gastrointestinal distress, and anxiety. The *Diagnostic and Statistical Manual of Mental Disorders*, third edition (DSM-III) (American Psychiatric Association, 1980) descriptions of generalized anxiety disorder and caffeine intoxication are almost identical. In dosages of around 700 mg, about seven cups of coffee, caffeine will provoke panic attacks in most persons susceptible to panic disorder and in some persons without prior panic attacks. Diagnostic evaluation of panic attacks must assess the possibility of caffeine intoxication. Caffeine appears to bind to the same brain receptor sites as the benzodiazepines but to exert opposite effects. Caffeine, theophylline, theobromine, and related methylxanthines are found in coffee, tea, cola and many other carbonated drinks, yerba mate, guarana, and other drinks derived from various plant leaves or berries and in many medications, particularly analgesic combinations, diet pills, and nonprescription stimulants, Theophylline, the methylxanthine that predominates in tea, is prescribed by physicians for a variety of respiratory diseases and can cause the same generalized and panic anxiety as caffeine.

Most patients with panic disorder have already learned to avoid caffeine. Patients who complain of anxiety and report heavy caffeine consumption should be advised to decrease or discontinue the caffeine before other treatments are considered.

### Amphetamines, Cocaine, Sympathomimetic Abuse

Persons who use amphetamines or cocaine expect to become euphoric, energetic, confident, and accelerated. But they often become agitated, anxious, or panicky, particularly after higher dosages or prolonged use. The anxiety can become so severe that abusers will take heroin to counteract it. Because the anxiety is caused by acute toxicity, it is easy to recognize and diagnose: elevated blood pressure with slowed pulse, headache, dizziness, confusion, and aggressiveness suggest sympathomimetic abuse, and blood or urine toxicology confirms it. Apart from illicitly obtained cocaine and amphetamine, there are many amphetamine-like compounds that can cause the same anxiety syndromes. These include the so-called non-amphetamine prescription diet pills, nonprescription diet pills or "counterfeit" amphetamines containing phenylpropanolamine, or decongestants containing ephedrine or pseudoephedrine.

### Yohimbine

Yohimbine produces panic anxiety so reliably that it has been useful in experimental anxiety research. In lower doses, it has long been used as a stimulant. It was prescribed for many years as a sexual stimulant and has recently been sold as "legal cocaine," or

**TABLE 24–1** **Physical Illnesses with Symptoms Resembling Those of Panic Disorder**

| | |
|---|---|
| Cardiac | Malnutrition |
|   Myocardial infarction |   Low weight |
|   Angina pectoris |   Chronic vitamin deficiency |
|   Paradoxical atrial tachycardia | Neurologic |
|   Cardiac dysrhythmia |   Grand mal seizure disorder |
|   Anemia |   Partial complex seizures |
|   Mitral insufficiency |   Transient ischemic attacks |
| Pulmonary |   Cerebrovascular insufficiency |
|   Pulmonary emboli |   Tumor or third ventricle, or other brain tumor |
|   Asthma |   Cerebral syphilis |
| Endocrine |   Encephalitis |
|   Hyperthyroidism |   Postencephalitic disorders |
|   Hypoparathyroidism |   Multiple sclerosis |
|   Hypoglycemia |   Meniere's disease |
|   Pheochromocytoma |   Subclavian steal syndrome |
|   Cushing's disease |   Posttraumatic cerebral syndrome, postconcussive |
|   Diabetes mellitus |     snydrome |
|   Pancreatic carcinoma |   Wilson's disease |
|   Hypopituitarism |   Huntington's chorea |
|   Eosinophilic pituitary adenoma |   Combined system disease (posterolateral sclerosis) |
|   Thyroiditis |   Myasthenia gravis |
|   Addison's disease | Drug-induced Intoxications |
| Infections |   Caffeine, theophylline |
|   Malaria |   Amphetamine |
|   Viral pneumonia |   Ephedrine, pseudoephedrine, |
|   Mononucleosis |     phenylpropanolamine |
|   Viral hepatitis |   Cocaine |
|   Rheumatic fever |   Yohimbine |
|   Tuberculosis |   Khat |
|   Bacteremia |   Cannabis |
|   Viremia |   LSD, psychotomimetic drugs, hallucinogens |
| Collagen Vascular | Withdrawal States |
|   Systemic lupus erythematosus |   Alcohol |
|   Rheumatoid arthritis |   Sedative-hypnotic |
|   Polyarteritis nodosa |   Beta blocker |
|   Temporal arteritis |   Antidepressant |
| Metabolic | Non-drug Toxicities |
|   Hypocalcemia, reactive, insulinoma, or decreased |   Arsenic, mercury, lead, other heavy metal |
|     food intake |   Carbon disulfide |

"yocaine." Intoxicated persons will show more evidence of overstimulation and irritability than is typical of spontaneous panic states, and those who have knowingly consumed the drug will probably report this when they seek emergency treatment. Few persons who have had yohimbine-induced panic are willing to try the drug again. Pharmacologically, yohimbine is an alpha-adrenergic blocker. It selectively blocks alpha$_2$ autoreceptors at lower dosages, but at higher dosages, it blocks alpha$_1$ receptors as well.

### Khat

Khat is yet another botannical stimulant. More popular in North Africa than elsewhere, its stimulant effects are described as intermediate between caffeine and amphet-

amine. Like other botannical stimulants, it produces extreme anxiety in higher doses.

### Amyl Nitrite

Amyl nitrite is used medically as a short-acting vasodilator and is abused primarily as a sexual stimulant, for prolonging and intensifying arousal, erection, and orgasm. Echocardiographists use amyl nitrite diagnostically to provoke an increased degree of mitral valve prolapse in susceptible patients. Panic anxiety can also be brought on briefly by the drug. Patients with panic disorder who have tried amyl nitrite typically report that they did so only once, and that it nearly killed them. Amyl nitrite-induced panic symptoms are of short duration. Isobutyl nitrite produces similar symptoms.

## SEDATIVE WITHDRAWAL

Sedative and hypnotic drugs (e.g., benzodiazepines, barbiturates, meprobamate, methaqualone, chloral hydrate, paraldehyde, ethchlorvynol, and glutethamide) are prescribed to relieve anxiety and sleeplessness, but their discontinuation causes rebound anxiety. The severity of this rebound depends on the dosage and duration of previous consumption and the rapidity with which the effect of the drug is lost. The central nervous system activity of these drugs can be much longer or shorter than their serum half-lives, but in general, the intermediate- (4 to 6 hours) and shorter-acting sedatives produce severer rebound anxiety, ranging from hyperalertness, motor tension, muscle aches, agitation, anxiety, insomnia, hyperactive reflexes and startle response, postural hypotension, tremulousness, nausea, vomiting, and abdominal cramps to convulsions and delirium in severe withdrawal. Panic and generalized anxiety occur in mild withdrawal. Intermediate-acting barbiturates are particularly likely to cause life-threatening withdrawal, but fortunately, these drugs are now seldom prescribed. Benzodiazepine withdrawal can be severe after prolonged use of diazepam in dosages of 80 to 100 mg per day or equivalent amounts of other benzodiazepines. Non–life-threatening but severe rebound anxiety can occur after use for a few weeks of even recommended dosages of benzodiazepines. Older benzodiazepines, like diazepam and chlordiazepoxide, have long-lasting metabolites that tend to attenuate the abstinence syndrome. Lorazepam has no such active metabolites, and rebound anxiety and withdrawal symptoms from it have been severer. Some physicians have been prescribing high dosages of alprazolam, 6 to 20 mg per day, for panic attacks, and severe rebound anxiety, and even convulsions, within a day of discontinuation has resulted. Many patients, particularly those already prone to anxiety, have reported distressing rebound anxiety the day after a single bedtime dose of short-acting benzodiazepine hypnotic. Patients with panic disorder, who typically have insomnia, often cannot tolerate these shortest-acting hypnotics because of increased panic symptoms the next day.

### Sedative Abuse

Some patients with panic symptoms have them only because of withdrawal from addictive sedative drugs. These patients cannot be objectively identified except by their drug-abusing behavior, which they often try to conceal or disguise. They report and often demonstrate extreme anxiety states. Sometimes they can be identified by complaints of muscle aches or vomiting, which are uncommon in panic disorder but common in sedative withdrawal. What can be done to treat these patients remains a matter of considerable disagreement. Physicians must be constantly on guard not to create or maintain illicit addictions.

### Alcoholism

Alcohol, in the short term, usually reduces anxiety, while in the long term, it usually increases it. Alcoholic beverages not only produce the usual rebound anxiety after the initial antianxiety effect wears off, but also cause more general physiologic distress because of the toxicity of ethanol and of the methanol or higher alcohol congeners that typically accompany beverage ethanol.

Regular excessive alcohol consumption clearly increases anxiety. In most patients who have both alcohol abuse and panic attacks, the alcohol is the primary problem, and alcohol withdrawal is the principal cause of their panic symptoms. But anxiety disorders also seem to predispose certain persons to alcoholism. Alcohol abstainers with panic or agoraphobic disorders are more likely than others to have immediate relatives who are alcoholic. The best way to determine whether alcoholism or panic is etiologically primary in a patient who has both disorders is to ask which began first. If panic attacks first occurred during the period of withdrawal after heavy drinking and have since predominantly occurred in association with alcohol or sedative withdrawal, it is best to diagnose and treat the patient's primary alcoholism. Such patients' panic attacks usually cease within several weeks of alcohol withdrawal, and antipanic drugs will not be needed.

If a patient has panic disorder that has clearly preceded and probably caused secondary alcohol abuse and dependence but is still drinking heavily, it is again necessary to treat the alcoholism first and to consider antipanic maintenance therapy only if panic attacks persist after all other alcohol withdrawal symptoms have resolved. Prescribing potentially addictive antipanic drugs to these patients poses an obvious risk, although sometimes no other treatment will help. Sedatives potentiate the effects of alcohol and might increase the risk of alcoholic relapse. Patients who were formerly alcoholics are more likely than others to become addicted to sedative drugs. On the other hand, unabated panic attacks increase the risk of alcoholic relapse, and panic disorder itself can be a disabling illness, one that cannot be dismissed as negligible compared with alcohol or drug abuse. There is no uniform answer: each patient must be treated as an individual.

When interviewed adequately, many patients with primary panic disorder report past heavy drinking that, at the time, met the diagnostic criteria for alcohol abuse or dependence. Often they report having decided that their drinking was making their anxiety worse and having stopped drinking without difficulty. Such patients also present a dilemma, one that less conscientious physicians avoid by not adequately asking about alcohol to begin with. Although tricyclic antidepressants, monoamine oxidase inhibitors, and trazodone are probably preferable first antipanic choices for these patients, many of them seem able to use alprazolam and other benzodiazepines properly, when they are appropriately informed of the risks of addiction and when prescriptions are monitored carefully. But any evidence that these patients are increasing their own dosages over what is deemed appropriate, such as by seeking renewals of prescriptions before they should be needed, reporting lost or stolen medication, or evidence that other drugs or alcohol are being used to augment intoxication, or that other physicians are also being asked for prescriptions must be responded to immediately.

## PANIC ATTACKS IN MENTAL DISORDERS

Even within the domain of illnesses with predominantly mental and behavioral symptoms, panic disorder is a diagnosis of exclusion that is made only when panic attacks cannot be attributed to another mental syndrome. Because psychiatric disorders are not mutually exclusive, a person with another mental illness could have panic disorder as well. But panic attacks that occur in the course of other mental illnesses are usually considered a secondary manifestation of the principal illness. Establishing the presence of panic attacks in other illnesses is important in diagnostic assessment; panic often has a bearing on treatment response, course, and outcome of mental illness.

### Schizophrenia

Panic attacks are frequently seen in schizophrenia, particularly early in the course of the illness. The associated symptoms may be different from the cardiopulmonary and autonomic symptoms that characterize the attacks in primary panic disorder. The mental symptoms of these panic attacks can include fearfulness, tension, agitation or immobility, disorganized thinking, dilated pupils, extreme insecurity and suspiciousness, delusions of reference and persecution, and auditory hallucinations, often with derogatory accusative content, such as voices accusing the patient of homosexuality or prostitution. It is not clear whether schizophrenia with panic attacks is different from other schizophrenia. Cardiopulmonary panic attacks in an acute psychotic syndrome, when some symptoms suggest a diagnosis of schizophrenia but the full chronic syndrome has not yet emerged, might suggest a diagnosis other than schizophrenia. Both panic attacks and psychotic symptoms are seen transiently in patients variously classified as having hysterical or somatoform or factitious states, in malingerers who are consciously feigning mental illness, in the so-called borderline disorders, reactive psychoses, bouffées délirantes, and similar syndromes, which do not typically progress to chronic schizophrenia. When panic attacks occur in schizophrenia, they should be treated differently from those in a primary anxiety disorder; monoamine oxidase inhibitor and tricyclic antidepressant medications, which are often effective in primary anxiety disorders, are more likely to make schizophrenic psychosis worse. Antipsychotic medications will probably be most effective in relieving episodes of schizophrenic panic.

## Manic Disorder

Panic attacks can occur as part of manic-depressive disease, in either the manic or the depressed phase. In milder manic disorders, the predominant cheerful affect and euphoric mood are quite different from the decidedly dysphoric affect of extreme anxiety states. In severer manic states with psychosis and dysphoric affect, panic symptoms can also occur. These panic attacks are best treated with antimanic or antipsychotic drugs. The antidepressants used in typical panic disorder usually increase the severity of mania, while benzodiazepines and other sedative-hypnotic drugs usually have little effect.

## Depressive Disorder

Roughly half the patients with primary panic disorder develop episodes of major depression, and almost all are bothered by some degree of depressed mood. Episodic or chronic depression is a frequent symptom of panic disorder, particularly of severer cases, which have poorer outcome and treatment response. Conversely, panic attacks occur in about one unipolar depressive episode out of six. It is often not clear which is the primary illness when panic disorder or major depression has been preceded by some symptoms of the other syndrome. When panic and depression begin at the same time, agitated depression must first be considered. Agitated depressions are more likely to occur in older patients. Typical symptoms include severe insomnia, fidgeting, pacing, restlessness, inability to hold still, worrying, extreme guilt feelings, and delusions, often around themes of hypochondriasis, guilt, or persecution. Memory can be impaired enough to lead to a misdiagnosis of dementia. The syndrome usually responds well to electroconvulsive therapy.

When depression and panic attacks occur without overt agitation, anxious depression is diagnosed. Tricyclic antidepressants, which are quite effective in relieving either depression or panic disorder alone, are consistently less effective in treating anxious depression. Monoamine oxidase inhibitors help some of these patients well, others not at all.

Patients who, in addition to panic or severe anxiety and depression, also have marked hostility, somatization, or "hysteroid" features respond surprisingly well to antidepressant medication. These depressions improve well on tricyclic antidepressants or monoamine oxidase inhibitors. Benzodiazepines sometimes make them worse.

## Somatization Disorder

Hysteria has been recognized since antiquity as a disorder that mimicked other disorders. Sheehan and Sheehan (1982) have traced the history of our current concept of panic disorder back to Egyptian and Greek writings on hysteria. Much of psychiatry still believes that anxiety disorders and hysteria are pretty much the same thing. Many neurologists, on the other hand, can see little difference between hysterical conversion symptoms and malingering. An influential study by Slater (1965) demonstrated that many patients with single apparent hysterical conversion (pseudoneurologic) symptoms were found to have organic disease at followup, and that many had died of these diseases. At the same time, panic disorder was being established as a distinct illness (Klein, 1964; Feighner et al., 1972), a more limited concept of hysteria was developing, based on Briquet's (1859) model of a highly positive review of systems: as these patients told it, about anything that could go wrong had gone wrong. No medical illnesses could be found to adequately explain the symptoms. Panic attacks were among the original diagnostic criteria, but these patients seemed different from panic disorder patients without excessive somatization in that they had more male alcoholic or antisocial male relatives (Cloninger, Reich, Guze, 1975). Hysteroid patients seem more likely to abuse medication but respond well to monoamine oxidase inhibitor drugs (Liebowitz and Klein, 1979). Thus it seems important to distinguish patients with panic disorder from those with somatization disorder. Unfortunately, the symptomatology of the two conditions overlaps considerably:

somatizers are so likely to express anxiety that anxiety symptoms are included in the Feighner et al. (1972) and DSM-III (1980) somatization criteria, while investigators reporting on patients they consider to have anxiety states (Roth et al., 1972; Sheehan and Sheehan, 1982) have noted high prevalences of somatic complaints. The practical treatment application is that monoamine oxidase inhibitors should increasingly be favored over addictive sedative drugs as the number of symptoms suggestive of somatization disorder increases.

### Hypochondriasis

Hypochondriasis, or morbid fear of illness, despite DSM-III categorization, is an anxiety state and because of that has numerous anxiety symptoms. Patients with this disorder, as opposed to those with somatization disorders, often are reluctant to take any and all drugs.

### Mimicry

Mimicry abounds in nature, whenever there is advantage to be had by an animal's appearing to be something it is not. Viceroy butterflys physically resemble nauseous monarchs; some birds feign injury to draw predators away from their nest; nonvenomous hognose snakes behave like rattlesnakes; and baby cuckoos physically and behaviorally mimic chicks of the species whose nests they parasitize. Humans feign mental illness. Even the biblical David once did so to escape possible execution: "And David . . . was much afraid of Achish the King of Gath. So he changed his behavior before them, and feigned himself mad in their hands, and made marks on the doors of the gate, and let his spittle run down his beard" (1 Samuel 21:12–13). In more modern times, human individuals and cultures altruistically provide care and sustenance to the physically and mentally ill. Some patients exploit this altruism by reporting or appearing to manifest illness. These mimics might variously be diagnosed as malingerers or factitious illness (Munchausen's syndrome), or as "borderlines." (The distinction between malingering and factitious illness is that in the former, there is an obvious goal [e.g., to avoid military], whereas

in the latter, this is not apparent.) It is the nature of this disorder to imitate other disorders. Clinicians must try to identify such individuals as best they can, particularly before prescribing potentially dangerous drugs, ordering hazardous diagnostic procedures, performing surgeries, or directing society to pay expensive hospitalization or disability benefits. Unfortunately, identifying deceivers by symptoms alone is often difficult. It remains impossible to prove that a person does not have panic attacks. Panic disorder is one of the easier psychiatric diseases to feign: most of the symptoms and signs can be duplicated by voluntary hyperventilation, and a consistently anxious affect between attacks is not necessary to the diagnosis. As panic disorder is increasingly discussed in the popular press, more mimics are "catching" this illness.

Because the distinction between panic and "factitious" panic often cannot be made with any certainty, the clinician must constantly keep both possibilities in mind when treating patients who complain of panic attacks. Treatment should always be conservative.

### Phobic Disorders

Simple phobias are common. A person with a simple phobic disorder will experience mild to extreme panic anxiety in certain situations. Simple phobias include fears of common animals, of high places, of being confined in a small place, of darkness. Panic anxiety that occurs only in specific phobic situations is properly classified as caused by phobic rather than panic disorder. Mild simple phobias generally require no treatment. Severe phobias respond poorly to medication but well to behavioral psychotherapy; in primary panic disorder, the opposite is true. Simple phobias are common in patients with panic disorder. A patient with spontaneous panic attacks as well as phobia is therefore properly diagnosed as having panic disorder and treated initially with antipanic medication.

### Agoraphobia

Most cases of agoraphobia are thought to result from panic disorder, as the patient increasingly avoids situations in which a panic attack would be particularly inconvenient or embarrassing, or from which escape would be difficult. The current convention is to classify these patients as having "agoraphobia with panic attacks," rather than panic disorder with agoraphobia. This potentially disabling complication of panic disorder should be preventable by early vigorous treatment with antipanic medications. In agoraphobia of longer duration, some patients require behavioral therapy to resume normal activities outside the home, while others accomplish this on their own once panic attacks end.

## REFERENCES

Adams RD: Neurological manifestations of chronic pulmonary insufficiency. N Engl J Med 257:579–590, 1957.

American Psychiatric Association: Diagnostic and Statistical Manual of Mental Disorders, ed 3. Washington, DC, American Psychiatric Association, 1980.

Ames F: The hyperventilation syndrome. J Ment Sci 101:466–525, 1955.

Avery TL: Seven cases of frontal tumor with psychiatric presentation. Br J Psychiatry 119:19–23, 1971.

Banks T, Shugoli GI: Confirmatory physical findings in angina pectoris. JAMA 200:1031–1035, 1967.

Barr TC, et al: Ambulatory heart rate changes during panic attacks. J Psychiatr Res 17:261–266, 1982–83.

Bass C, et al: Unexplained breathlessness and psychiatric morbidity in patients with normal and abnormal coronary arteries. [letter] Lancet 1:1282, 1983.

Beard GM: Neurasthenia or nervous exhaustion. Boston Med Surg J 3:217, 1869.

Bingley T: Mental symptoms in temporal lobe epilepsy. Acta Psychiatr Neurol 33:1–151, 1958 (suppl 120).

Blustein JE, Seeman MV: Brain tumors presenting as functional psychiatric disturbances. Can Psychiatr Assoc J 17:55–63, 1972.

Bowen RC, Kohout J: The relationship between agoraphobia and primary affective disorders. Can J Psychiatry 24:317–322, 1979.

Braestrup C, Nielsen M: Anxiety. Lancet 2:1030–1034, 1982.

Bravo EL, Gifford KW: Pheochromocytoma: Diagnosis, localization and management. N Engl J Med 311: 1298–1303, 1984.

Briquet P: Traité clinique et thérapeutique a l'hysterie. Paris, J.B. Balliere et Fils, 1859.

Brown RP, Sweeney J, Loutsch E, Kocsis J, Frances A: Involutional melancholia revisited. Am J Psychiatry 141:24–28, 1984.

Cassidy WL, Flanigan NB, Spellman M, et al: Clinical observations in manic depressive disease: A quantitative study of one hundred manic depressive patients and fifty medically sick controls. JAMA 164:1535–1546, 1957.

Charney DS, Heninger GR, Redmond DE Jr: Yohimbine induced anxiety and increased noradrenergic function in humans: Effects of diazepam and clonidine. Life Sci 40:19–29, 1983.

Charney DS, Heninger GR, Sternberg DE: Assessment of alpha-2 adrenergic autoreceptor function in humans: Effects of oral yohimbine. Life Sci 30:2033–2041, 1982.

Clancey J, Noyes R, Hoenk PR, et al: Secondary depression in anxiety neurosis. J Nerv Ment Dis 166:846–850, 1978.

Cloninger CR, Martin RL, Clayton P, et al: A blind follow-up and family study of anxiety neurosis: Preliminary analysis of the St. Louis 500, in Klein DF, Rabkin J (eds): Anxiety: New Research and Changing Concepts. New York, Raven Press, 1981, pp 137–148.

Cloninger CR, Reich T, Guze SB: The multifactorial model of disease transmission. III. Familial relationship between sociopathy and hysteria (Briquet's syndrome). Br J Psychiatry 127:23–32, 1975.

DaCosta JM: On irritable heart, a clinical form of functional cardiac disorder and its consequences. Am J Med Sci 61:17, 1871.

Davis JM: Minor tranquilizers, sedatives, and hypnotics, in Kaplin HI, Freedman AM, Sadock BJ (eds): Comprehensive Textbook of Psychiatry. Baltimore, Williams & Wilkins, 1980, pp 2316–2333.

Davis JM: Antidepressant drugs, in Kaplan HI, Freedman AM, Sadock BJ (eds): Comprehensive Textbook of Psychiatry. Baltimore, Williams & Wilkins, 1980b, pp 2290–2316.

Denko JD, Kaelbling R: The psychiatric aspects of hypoparathyroidism. Acta Psychiatr Scand 38:1–70, 1962 (suppl 164).

Denny-Brown D: Disability arising from closed-head injuries. JAMA 127:429–436, 1945.

Derogatis LR, Lipman RS, Covi L, et al: Factorial invariance of symptom dimensions in anxious and depressive neuroses. Arch Gen Psychiatry 27:659–665, 1972.

Donnelly EF, Murphy DL, Goodwin FK: Primary affective disorders: Anxiety in unipolar and bipolar depressed groups. J Clin Psychol 34:621–623, 1978.

Eaton WW, et al: Consumption of coffee or tea and symptoms of anxiety. Am J Public health 74:66–68, 1984.

Ettigi PG, Brown GM: Brain disorders associated with endocrine dysfunction. Psychiatr Clin North Am 1:117–135, 1978.

Feighner JP, Robins E, Guze S, et al: Diagnostic criteria for use in psychiatric research. Arch Gen Psychiatry 26:57–63, 1972.

Ferrer M: Mistaken psychiatric referral of occult serious cardiovascular disease. Arch Gen Psychiatry 18:112–113, 1968.

Freud S: The justification for detaching from neurasthenia a particular syndrome: The anxiety-neurosis (1894), in Jones E (ed): Collected Papers. New York, Basic Books, 1959, p 80.

Frohlich ED, Tarazi RC, Dustan HP: Hyperdynamic beta-adrenergic circulatory state. Arch Intern Med 123:1–7, 1969.

Gawin FH, Markoff RA: Panic anxiety after abrupt discontinuation of amitriptyline. Am J Psychiatry 138:117–118, 1981.

Gurney C, Roth M, Garside RF, et al: Studies in the classification of affective disorders: The relationship between anxiety states and depressive illness. Br J Psychiatry 121:162–166, 1972.

Guze SB: The diagnosis of hysteria: What are we trying to do? Am J Psychiatry 124:491–498, 1967.

Guze SB, Perley MJ: Observations on the natural history of hysteria. Am J Psychiatry 119:960–965, 1963.

Guze SB, Woodruff RA, Clayton PJ: Hysteria and antisocial behavior: Further evidence of an association. Am J Psychiatry 127:957–960, 1971.

Hamilton M: Symptoms and assessment of depression, in Paykel ES (ed): Handbook of Affective Disorders. New York, Guilford Press, 1982, pp 3–11.

Harper M, Roth M: Temporal lobe epilepsy and the phobic anxiety-depersonalization syndrome. Compr Psychiatry 3:129–151, 1962.

Hollister LE, Overall JE, Shelton J, et al: Drug therapy of depression: Amitriptyline, perphenzine, and their combination in different syndromes. Arch Gen Psychiatry 17:486–493, 1967.

Holmberg G, Gershon S: Autonomic and psychiatric effects of yohimbine hydrocloride. Psychopharmacologia 2:93–106, 1961.

James WE, Mefferd RB, Kimball I: Early signs of Huntington's chorea. Dis Nerv Syst 30:556–559, 1969.

Johnstone EC, Owens DGC, Firth CD, et al: Neurotic illness and its response to anxiolytic and antidepressant treatment. Psychol Med 10:321–328, 1980.

Kaplan NM, Kramer NJ, Holland BO, et al: Single-voided urine metanephrine assays in screening for pheochromocytoma. Arch Intern Med 137:190–193, 1977.

Kerr TA, Roth M, Schapira K, et al: The assessment and prediction of outcome in affective disorders. Br J Psychiatry 121:167–174, 1972.

Klein DF: Delineation of two drug-responsive anxiety syndromes. Psychopharmacologia 5:397–408, 1964.

Klein DF: Anxiety reconceptualized, in Klein DF, Raskin J (eds): Anxiety: New Research and Changing Concepts. New York, Raven Press, 1981, pp 235–263.

Koranyi EK: Morbidity and rate of undiagnosed physical illness in a psychiatric clinic population. Arch Gen Psychiatry 36:414–419, 1979.

Lader M, Sartorius N: Anxiety in patients with hysterical coversion symptoms. J Neurol Neurosurg Psychiatry 31:490–495, 1968.

Leckman JF, Weissman MM, Merikangas KR, et al: Panic disorder increases risk of major depression, alcoholism, panic, and phobic disorders in affectively ill families. Arch Gen Psychiatry 40:1055–1060, 1983.

Levine R: Hypoglycemia. JAMA 230:462–463, 1974.

Lewis AJ: Melancholia, a clinical survey of depressive states. J Ment Sci 80:277–378, 1934.

Lewis AJ: Melancholia: A prognostic study. J Ment Sci 82:488–558, 1936.

Liebowitz MR, Klein DF: Hysteroid dysphoria. Psychiatr Clin North Am 2:555–575, 1979.

Lipman RS: Differentiating anxiety and depression in anxiety disorders: Use of rating scales. Psychopharmacol Bull 18:69–77, 1982.

Lishman WA: Endocrine disorders and metabolic disorders, in Organic Psychiatry. London, Blackwell, 1978.

Lynch JJ, Paskewitz DA, Gimbel KS, et al: Psychological aspects of cardiac arrhythmia. Am Heart J 93:645–657, 1977.

Mackenzie TB, Popkin MK: Organic anxiety syndrome. Am J Psychiatry 140:342–344, 1983.

Marks I, Lader M: Anxiety States (Anxiety Neurosis): A Review. J Nerv Ment Dis 150:3–18, 1973.

Marks IM, Gray S, Cohen D, et al: Imipramine and brief therapist-aided exposure in agoraphobics having self-exposure homework. Arch Gen Psychiatry 40:153–162, 1983.

Mersky H, Woodforde JM: Psychiatric sequellae of minor head injury. Brain 95:521–528, 1972.

Modlin HC: Post accident anxiety syndrome: Psychosocial aspects. Am J Psychiatry 123:1008–1012, 1967.

Mountjoy CQ, Roth M: Studies in the relationship between depressive disorders and anxiety states. J Affect Disord 4:149–161, 1982.

Mountjoy CQ, Roth M, Garside RF, et al: A clinical trial of phenelzine in anxiety depressive and phobic neuroses. Br J Psychiatry 131:486–492, 1977.

Munjack DJ, Moss HB: Affective disorder and alcoholism in families of agoraphobics. Arch Gen Psychiatry 38:869–871, 1981.

Noyes R, Clancy J, Hoenk PR, et al: The prognosis of anxiety neurosis. Arch Gen Psychiatry 37:173–178, 1980.

O'Connor JF, Musher DM: Central nervous involvement in systemic lupus erythematosus. Arch Neurol 14:157–164, 1966.

Overall JE, Hollister LE, Johnson M, et al: Nosology of depression and differential response to drugs. JAMA 195:946–948, 1966.

Overall JE, Rhoades MH: Use of the Hamilton Rating Scale for classification of depressive disorders. Compr Psychiatry 23:370–376, 1982.

Paykel ES: Classification of depressed patients: A cluster analysis derived grouping. Br J Psychiatry 118:275–288, 1971.

Paykel ES: Depressive typologies and response to amitriptyline. Br J Psychiatry 120:147–156, 1972.

Paykel ES, Parker RR, Penrose RJJ, et al: Depressive classification and prediction of response to phenelzine. Br J Psychiatry 134:572–581, 1979.

Pringuet G, et al: Death; anxiety in thyrotoxicosis. Ann Med Psychol (Paris) 140:753–768, 1982.

Prusoff B, Klerman GL: Differentiating depressed from anxious neurotic outpatients: Use of discriminant function analysis for separation of neurotic affective states. Arch Gen Psychiatry 30:302–309, 1974.

Prusoff BA, Paykel ES: Typological prediction of response to amitriptyline: A replication study. Int Pharmacopsychiatry 12:153–159, 1977.

Raskin A, Schulterbrandt JG, Reatig N, et al: Depression subtypes and response to phenelzine, diazepam, and a placebo. Arch Gen Psychiatry 30:66–75, 1974.

Reilly EL, Wilson WP: Mental symptoms in hyperparathyroidism. Dis Nerv Syst 26:361–363, 1965.

Ross AT, Reitan RM: Intellectual and affective functions in multiple sclerosis. Arch Neurol Psychiatry 73:663–677, 1955.

Roth M: The phobic anxiety-depersonalization syndrome. Proc R Soc Med 52:587–595, 1959.

Roth M, Gurney C, Garside RF, et al: Studies in the classification of affective disorders: The relationship between anxiety states and depressive illness. Br J Psychiatry 121:147–161, 1972.

Roth M, Mountjoy CQ: The distinction between anxiety states and depressive disorders, in Paykel ES (ed): Handbook of Affective Disorders. New York, Guilford Press, 1982, pp 70–92.

Schapira K, Roth M, Kerr TA, et al: The prognosis of affective disorders: The differentiation of anxiety states from depressive illness. Br J Psychiatry 121:175–181, 1972

Scheinberg P, Rice-Simons RA: The treatment of recurring cerebral ischemia. Geriatrics 19:887–893, 1964.

Schwab JJ: Psychiatric illnesses produced by infection. Hosp Med 5:98–108, 1969.

Sheehan DV, Ballenger J, Jacobsen G: Treatment of endogenous anxiety with phobic, hysterical and hypochondriacal symptoms. Arch Gen Psychiatry 37:51–59, 1980.

Sheehan DV, Sheehan KH: The classification of anxiety and hysterical states. I. Historical review and empirical delineation. J Clin Psychopharmacol 2:235–244, 1982.

Shulman R: Psychiatric aspects of pernicious anemia: A prospective study. Br Med J 3:266–269, 1967.

Slater E: Diagnosis of "hysteria." Br Med J 1:1395–1399, 1965.

Soffer A: Regatine and benadine in the diagnoses of pheochromocytoma. Med Clin North Am 38:375–384, 1954.

Strain JJ, et al: Anxiety and panic attacks in the medically ill. Psychiatr Clin North Am 39:333–350, 1981.

Thompson D, et al: Anxiety in coronary patients. Int Rehabil Med 4:161–164, 1982.

Tyrer P, Candy J, Kelly D: A study of the clinical effects of phenelzine and placebo in the treatment of phobic anxiety. Psychopharmacologia 32:237–254, 1973.

VanValkenburg C, Akiskal H, Puzantian V, et al: Anxious depressions: Clinical, family history, and naturalistic outcome comparisons with panic and major depressive disorders. J Affect Disord 6:67–82, 1984.

Weil AA: Ictal emotions ocurring in temporal lobe dysfunction. Arch Neurol 1:101–111, 1959.

Wernicke K: Allgemeine Z Psychiatrie 51:1020–1021, 1895.

Williams D: The structure of emotions reflected in epileptic experiences. Brain 79:29–67, 1956.

Wilson-Barnett J: Anxiety in hospitalized patients. R. Soc Health J 101:118–122, 1981.

Winokur G, Holemon E: Chronic anxiety neurosis: Clinical and sexual aspects. Acta Psychiatr Scand 39:384–412, 1963.

Woodruff RA, Guze SB, Clayton PJ: Anxiety neurosis among psychiatric outpatients. Compr Psychiatry 13:165–170, 1972.

Zitrin CM, Klein DF, Woerner MG: Behavior therapy, supportive therapy, imipramine and phobias. Arch Gen Psychiatry 35:307–316, 1978.

Zitrin CM, Klein DF, Woerner MG: Treatment of agoraphobia with group exposure in vivo and imipramine. Arch Gen Psychiatry 37:63–72, 1980.

## SUGGESTED ADDITIONAL READING

Dietch JT: Diagnosis of organic anxiety disorders. Psychosomatics 22:661–669, 1981.

Hall RC (ed): Psychiatric Presentations of Medical Illness: Somatopsychic Disorders. New York, Spectrum Publications, 1980.

Hall RCW, Popkin MK, Devaul R, et al: Physical illness presenting as psychiatric disease. Arch Gen Psychiatry 35:1315–1329, 1978.

Strain JJ, et al: Anxiety and panic attacks in the medically ill. Psychiatr Clin North Am 4:333–350, 1981.

Wilson-Barnett J: Anxiety in hospitalized patients. R Soc Health J 101:118–122, 1981.

# chapter 25

# THOUGHT DISORDER

*by* Nancy C. Andreasen, M.D., Ph.D.

The term thought disorder is confusing to medical students, residents, and senior clinicians alike. The confusion arises because the term thought disorder has no universally agreed on definition, although some consensus has begun to emerge. Some clinicians use the term broadly to refer to such varied phenomena as disorganized speech, confusion, delusions, and even hallucinations. Others restrict the definition to a much narrower concept, sometimes referred to as "formal thought disorder," or disorganized speech that is presumed to reflect disorganized thinking.

## DEFINITION

Kraepelin and other great clinicians of the late 19th and early 20th centuries frequently described abnormalities in language and cognition among the patients whom they observed (Kraepelin, 1919). The concept of thought disorder derives principally from Bleuler, who defined it in terms of the association psychology that prevailed during his era and believed that it occurred only in schizophrenia (Bleuler, 1950):

Certain symptoms of schizophrenia are present in every case and at every period of the illness even though, as with every other disease symptom, they must have attained a certain degree of intensity before they can be recognized with any certainty. . . . For example, the peculiar

association disturbance is always present, but not each and every aspect of it. . . . Besides these specific or permanent symptoms, we can find a host of other, more accessory manifestations such as delusions, hallucinations, or catatonic symptoms. . . . As far as we know, the fundamental symptoms are characteristic of schizophrenia, while the accessory symptoms may also appear in other types of illness. (Bleuler, 1950)

It is not clear precisely what Bleuler means by "association disturbance," but he appears to be referring to many types of confused thinking, which are usually expressed in confused speech.

Bleuler's ideas have been influential in modern psychiatry. Until recently, thought disorder was considered to be the pathognomonic symptom of schizophrenia. During past decades, clinicians and psychologists have developed many methods for assessing this important symptom, including the use of proverb interpretation, IQ testing, perceptual tests such as the Rorschach and thematic apperception tests, and even physiologic measures of attention, such as eye tracking (Goldstein, 1944; Kasanin, 1944; Chapman and McGhie, 1962; Cromwell and Dokeckie, 1968; Cameron, 1939; Payne and Friedlander, 1962; Harrow, Tucker, Adler, 1965; Wynne and Singer, 1965; Andreasen, 1977; Holtzman, 1983). Thought disorder is sometimes used as loosely equivalent to cognitive disorder, and cognition is an extremely broad concept.

In a clinical setting, it is probably useful

to simplify the concept somewhat. In his classic text on psychopathology, Frank Fish has outlined a logical system for categorizing abnormalities in cognition that is quite useful (Fish, 1962). He suggests dividing the abnormalities into four main groups: disorders of perception, disorders of content of thought, disorders of process of thought, and disorders of form of thought. At its broadest, thought disorder is sometimes used to refer to all of these. At its narrowest, it refers only to formal thought disorder, or disorders in process of thought.

*Perceptual disorders* are abnormalities in perceptual experiences. The most common perceptual abnormalities seen in psychiatric patients are hallucinations of various types. Hearing voices that are not really there, seeing forms that in fact do not exist, or experiencing a sensation of bugs crawling on one's skin when one is not infested are all types of perceptual disorders.

*Disorders in content of thought* are abnormalities in beliefs and in interpretation of experiences. The most common seen in psychiatric patients are delusions of various types. Typical delusions include beliefs that messages are being given over the radio or TV about the person, that people are conspiring against the person and trying to harm her, or that a person has some type of special or unusual ability.

*Disorders in the process of thought* involve abnormalities in the way ideas and language are formulated before they are expressed. Unlike hallucinations or delusions, which are usually determined to be present because the patient describes them, thought process disorders are usually inferred by observing what the patient says or does and only occasionally by self-report. One common manifestation of thought process disorder is pressured speech, in which the patient tends to speak loudly, intensely, and rapidly. Another common clinical manifestation is blocking, in which the patient stops suddenly in the middle of a sentence because he has lost his train of thought for some reason. Disordered thought processes may also be reflected by impaired attention, poor memory, or difficulty in formulating abstract concepts. These aspects of impaired thinking are assessed through observing the patient or through using simple mental status tests, such as serial sevens or memory tests.

*Disorders in the form of thought*, or formal thought disorder, are abnormalities in the way thought is expressed in language, whether it be in speech or in writing. Clinically, this abnormality appears in various types of disorganized speech that are given a variety of names (defined in more detail later), such as incoherence, tangentiality, and derailment (loose associations). This type of thought disorder is assessed simply by listening to the patient talk or by looking at his writing. The clinician observes the patient's verbal output and determines whether it is well connected and well organized and seems to make sense or whether it seems disconnected, disorganized, and bizarre.

The boundaries between these four types of cognitive abnormalities are not always clear. For example, when a patient feels a crawling sensation and then interprets it as caused by an infestation of parasites living in his bed, is that a delusion, a hallucination, or both? (Probably both.) When a patient speaks rapidly, skips from topic to topic, makes little sense, and admits that his thoughts seem to be occurring too rapidly to control, is that a disorder of thought process or thought form? (Again, probably both.) Further, some patients may clearly display all four classes of cognitive abnormality, while others display only one or two. The four types may, in theory, be mutually exclusive as definitions or classes, but they are not mutually exclusive as symptoms in actual patients.

Other chapters in this book focus in more detail on the first two types of cognitive abnormality, disorders in perception (hallucinations) and disorders in content of thought (delusions). Described in this chapter are some common clinical manifestations of the last two types of cognitive abnormalities, disorders in process of thought (dyslogias) and disorders in form of thought (dysphasias).

## BOUNDARIES OF THOUGHT DISORDER

Don't people who are otherwise normal sometimes speak in a disorganized manner? Doesn't everyone occasionally experience blocking or a rapid flood of ideas? How does one draw the line between normal thinking and thought disorder?

The following passage from James Joyce's last novel, *Finnegan's Wake*, illustrates the problem in an extreme case:

Oh, by the way, yes another thing occurs to me. You let me tell you, with the utmost politeness, were ordinarily designed, your birth wrong was, to fall in with the Plan, as out nationals should, as all nationalists must, and do a certain office (what, I will not tell you) in a certain holy office (nor will I say where) during certain agonizing office hours from such a year to such an hour on such and such a date at so and so much a week (which, may I remind, were just a gulp for you, failing in which you might have taken the scales off boilers like any boskp of Yorek) and do your little two bit and thus earn from the nation true thanks, right here in our place of burden, your bourne of travel and ville of tares. (Joyce, 1939)

Joyce is using language in an idiosyncratic and confusing way, relying on punning, word play, and allusions. When this sample of speech was given to a group of clinicians to read blindly for severity of thought disorder and diagnosis, 95 per cent of the clinicians thought it displayed thought disorder and 48 per cent diagnosed its author as having schizophrenia (Andreasen, Tsuang, Canter, 1974).

This result indicates that even clinicians are not clear on the boundaries of abnormal thinking, particularly when they must look at examples out of context and cannot rely on important clinical cues, such as the appearance of the individual, his manner of speech, the presence or absence of other symptoms, and past history. The boundaries of thought disorder are particularly blurred when language is used creatively, when it is used pedantically, or when it is used poorly because of low intelligence or inadequate education.

The difference between the creative use of language and thought disorder is largely a matter of intent and control rather than in the nature of the language actually produced. Writers depend on unusual associations to find fresh imagery, and they enjoy playing with words and ideas, which may seem to represent loose associations or derailment. But writers and other creative individuals usually have their cognition under control, and they have a method in their madness. Because of this, an organization can usually be seen in the apparent disorganization, and the result is said to be "cre-

ative" or "original." On the other hand, patients who are psychotic are usually out of control, and their language and thinking are therefore perceived as disorganized rather than disciplined and as bizarre rather than creative.

Pedantic use of language may also resemble thought disorder. Verbose, pedantic, empty language is a hazard of some occupations, such as politics, administration, philosophy, the ministry, and some sciences. People in these occupations tend to speak verbosely, with excessive use of obscure or overabstract terminology, and to say little. Patients suffering from psychosis may have a similar problem, which is referred to as "poverty of content of speech." Again, drawing the line between a "normal thought disorder" manifested by a government employee speaking bureaucratese and a psychotic patient depends heavily on contextual cues. Is the speaker in control? Can the speaker moderate his style if requested to be more specific or more concise? Can the speaker do better on another topic? Does the speaker have any other significant symptoms?

Finally, people who are mentally dull or uneducated may also show some characteristics that are similar to those of patients with relatively severe psychopathology. The mentally handicapped or uneducated may be excessively concrete, may be unable to speak clearly and fluently in reply to a question, may use words idiosyncratically because they do not understand what they mean, or may use poor grammar. Unlike the creative individual or the bureaucrat, these individuals do not have conscious control and cannot shift their language patterns on request. In this instance, the clinician must evaluate their language and thinking in terms of norms adjusted for their intellectual and educational level. He must take into account information concerning number of years of schooling, level of performance, and intelligence testing.

Thus thought disorder is probably not a phenomenon discontinuous from normality, but on a continuum with it. It may occur occasionally in the speech of normal people, particularly when they are fatigued or disinhibited, and it may occur more frequently in the conscious productions of artists. Whenever the clinician recognizes that he is reading or listening to unusual language and thinking, he must always evaluate it in terms of its context. He must ask questions such as the following: Is the abnormality under conscious control? Can it be varied and reversed to normal through prompting or a change of subject? Does the patient have other symptoms? What is the patient's educational and intellectual background? Usually, intelligent use of context will help the clinician to distinguish between normal thought disorder and thought disorder that has a pathologic significance.

## COMMON TYPES OF THOUGHT DISORDER

Thought disorder is a heterogeneous phenomenon. During the past 50 years, clinicians have described many manifestations of thought disorder, such as derailment, incoherence, tangentiality, and poverty of speech. The many subtypes have also been a source of confusion, since they tend to be referred to through the global term thought disorder. During recent years, efforts have been made to define the various subtypes more carefully and precisely and examine the relationship of the various subtypes to clinical diagnosis.

One approach has been to subdivide types of thought disorder into two main groups: negative and positive thought disorders. This distinction has been useful because some evidence suggests that negative thought disorders are more common in schizophrenia and indicate a somewhat poorer prognosis, whereas positive thought disorders occur in both mania and schizophrenia and have a better outcome.

### Negative Thought Disorders

#### Poverty of Speech

In poverty of speech, the *amount* of spontaneous speech is restricted, so that replies to questions tend to be brief, concrete, and unelaborated. Unprompted additional information is seldom provided. For example, in answer to the question, "How many children do you have?" the patient replies, "Two. A girl and a boy. The girl is thirteen and the boy, ten." "Two" is all that is required to answer the question, and the rest of the reply is additional information. Replies may be monosyllabic, and some questions may be left unanswered. When confronted with this speech pattern, the interviewer may frequently find himself prompting the patient in order to encourage elaboration of replies. To elicit this finding, the examiner must allow the patient adequate time to answer and elaborate the answer.

#### Example

*Interviewer:* Do you think there'a a lot of corruption in government?
*Patient:* Yeah, seems to be.
*Interviewer:* Do you think Haldeman and Ehrlichman and Mitchell have been fairly treated?
*Patient:* I don't know.
*Interviewer:* Were you working at all before you came to the hospital?
*Patient:* No.
*Interviewer:* What kinds of jobs have you had in the past?
*Patient:* Oh, some janitor jobs, painting.
*Interviewer:* What kind of work do you do?
*Patient:* I don't.
*Interviewer:* How far did you go in school?
*Patient:* Eleventh grade.
*Interviewer:* How old are you?
*Patient:* Eighteen.

### Poverty of Content of Speech

Although replies are long enough so that speech is adequate in amount, they convey little information. Language tends to be vague, often overabstract or overconcrete, repetitive, and stereotyped. The interviewer may recognize this finding by observing that the patient has spoken at some length but has not given adequate information to answer the question. Alternatively, the patient may provide enough information, but require many words to do so, so that a lengthy reply can be summarized in a sentence or two. Sometimes the interviewer may characterize the speech as "empty philosophizing."

#### Example

*Interviewer:* Ok. Why is it, do you think, that people believe in God?
*Patient:* Well, first of all because, he uh ly, he are the person that, is their personal savior. He walks with me and talks with me. And uh, the understanding that I

have, um, a lot of people, they don't really uh know they own personal self. Because, uh, they ain't, they all, just don't know they personal self. They don't, know that he uh, seemed like to me, a lot of em don't understand that he walks and talks with them. And uh, show them their way to go. I understand also that every man and every lady, is just not pointed in the same direction. Some are pointed different. They goes in their different ways. The way that uh, Jesus Christ wanted 'em to go. Me myself I am pointed in the ways of uh, knowing right from wrong and doing it. I can't do no more, or no less, than that.

### Blocking

Blocking is interruption of a train of speech before a thought or idea has been completed. After a period of silence, which may last from a few seconds to minutes, the person indicates that he cannot recall what he had been saying or meant to say. Blocking should only be judged to be present either if a person voluntarily describes losing his thought or if, on questioning by the interviewer, the person indicates that that was his reason for pausing.

### Perseveration

Perseveration is persistent repetition of words, ideas, or subjects so that, once a patient begins a particular subject or uses a particular word, he continually returns to it in the process of speaking.

#### Examples

*Patient:* I think I'll put on my hat, my hat, my hat.
*Interviewer:* Tell me what you are like, what kind of person you are.
*Patient:* I'm from Marshalltown, Iowa. That's sixty miles northwest, northeast of Des Moines, Iowa. And I'm married at the present time. I'm thirty-six years old. My wife is thirty-five. She lives in Garwin, Iowa. That's fifteen miles southeast of Marshalltown, Iowa. I'm getting a divorce at the present time. And I am presently in a mental institution in Iowa City, Iowa, which is a hundred miles southeast of Marshalltown, Iowa.

## Positive Thought Disorders

### Derailment

Derailment (loose associations, flight of ideas) is a pattern of spontaneous speech in which the ideas slip off the track onto another one that is clearly but obliquely related or one that is completely unrelated. Things may be said in juxtaposition that lack a meaningful relationship, or the patient may shift idiosyncratically from one frame of reference to another. At times, there may be a vague connection between the ideas, and at others, none will be apparent. This pattern of speech is often characterized as sounding disjointed. Perhaps the most common manifestation of this disorder is a slow, steady slippage, with no single derailment being particularly severe, so that the speaker gets further and further off the track with each derailment without showing any awareness that his reply no longer has any connection with the question that was asked. This abnormality is often characterized by lack of cohesion between clauses and sentences and by unclear pronoun references.

Although less severe derailments (i.e., those in which the relationship between juxtaposed ideas is oblique) have sometimes been referred to as tangentiality or as flight of ideas when in the context of mania, such distinctions are not recommended because they tend to be unreliable. Flight of ideas is a derailment that occurs rapidly in the context of pressured speech. Tangentiality has been defined herein as a different phenomenon, in that it occurs as the immediate response to a question.

#### Example

*Interviewer:* Did you enjoy doing that?
*Patient:* Um-hm. Oh hey—well—I, I—oh— I really enjoyed some communities I tried it, and the next day when I'd be going out you know, um I took control like uh, I put, um, bleach on my hair in, in California. My roommate was from Chicago and she was going to the junior college. And we lived in the YWCA so she wanted to put it, um, peroxide on my hair, and she did, and I got up and looked at the mirror and tears came to my eyes. Now do you understand it, I was fully aware of what was going on but why couldn't I why the tears? I can't understand that, can you?

Interviewer: No.

Patient: Have you experienced anything like it?

Interviewer: You just must be an emotional person that's all.

Patient: Well, not very much I mean, what if I were dead? It's funeral age. Well I um? Now I had my toenails, uh, operated on. They're uh, um got infected and I wasn't able to do it but they won't let me at my tools. Well.

## Incoherence

Incoherence (word salad, jargon aphasia, schizophasia, paragrammatism) is a pattern of speech that is essentially incomprehensible at times. The incoherence is due to several mechanisms, which may sometimes occur simultaneously. Sometimes portions of coherent sentences may be observed in the middle of a sentence that is incoherent as a whole. Sometimes the disturbance appears to be at a semantic level, so that words are substituted in a phrase or sentence so that the meaning seems to be distorted or destroyed; the word choice may seem totally random or may appear to have some oblique connection with the context. Sometimes "cementing words" (coordinating and subordinating conjunctions such as "and," "although"; adjectival pronouns such as "the," "a," and "an") are deleted.

Incoherence is often accompanied by derailment. It differs from derailment in that in incoherence, the abnormality occurs *within* the level of the sentence or clause, which contains words or phrases that are joined incoherently. The abnormality in derailment involves unclear or confusing connections between larger units, such as sentences or clauses.

This type of language disorder is relatively uncommon. When it occurs, it tends to be severe or extreme, and mild forms are quite uncommon. It may sound quite similar to a Wernicke's aphasia or jargon aphasia, and in these cases, the disorder should only be called incoherence (thereby implying a psychiatric disorder as opposed to a neurologic disorder) when history and laboratory data exclude the possibility of a known organic etiology and formal testing for aphasia is negative.

### Examples

Interviewer: Why do you think people believe in God?

Patient: Um, because making a do in life. Isn't none of that stuff about evolution guiding isn't true any more now. It all happened a long time ago. It happened in eons and eons and stuff they wouldn't believe in him. The time that Jesus Christ people believe in their thing people believed in, Jehovah God that they didn't believe in Jesus Christ that much.

Interviewer: Um, what do you think about current political issues, like the energy crisis?

Patient: They're destroying too many cattle and oil just to make soap. If we need soap when you can jump into a pool of water, and then when you go to buy your gasoline, my folks always thought they should, get pop but the best thing to get is motor oil, and, money. May, may as well go there and, trade in some, pop caps and, uh, tires, and tractors to grup, car garages, so they can pull cars away from wrecks, is what I believed in. So I didn't go there to get no more pop when my folks said it. I just went there to get a ice cream cone, and some pop, in cans, or we can go over there and get a cigarette. And it was the largest thing you do to get cigarettes 'cause then you could trade off, what you owned, and go for something new, it was sentimental, and that's the only thing I needed was something sentimental, and there wasn't anything else more sentimental than that, except for knick-knacks and most knick-knacks, these cost thirty to forty dollars to get, a good billfold, or a little stand to put on your desk.

## Tangentiality

Tangentiality is replying to a question in an oblique, tangential, or even irrelevant manner. The reply may be related to the question in some distant way. Or the reply may be unrelated and seem totally irrelevant. In the past, tangentiality has been used as roughly equivalent to loose associations or derailment. The concept of tangentiality has been partially redefined so that it refers only to replies to questions and not to transitions in spontaneous speech.

### Example

Interviewer: What city are you from?

Patient: Well, that's a hard question to answer because my parents . . . I was born in Iowa, but I know that I'm white instead of black so apparently I came from the North somewhere and I don't know where, you know. I really don't know where my ancestors came from. So I don't know whether I'm Irish or French or Scandinavian or I don't believe I'm Polish but I think I'm—I think I might be German or Welsh. I'm not but that's all speculation and that that's one thing that I would like to know and is my ancestors you know where did I originate? But I never took the time to find out the answer to that question.

## Illogicality

Illogicality is a pattern of speech in which conclusions are reached that do not follow logically. Illogicality may take the form of non sequiturs (= it does not follow), in which the patient makes a logical inference between two clauses that is unwarranted or illogical. It may take the form of faulty inductive inferences. Or, it may take the form of reaching conclusions based on the faulty premise without any actual delusional thinking.

### Example

Patient: Parents are the people that raise you. Any thing that raises you can be a parent. Parents can be anything, material, vegetable, or mineral, that has taught you something. Parents would be the world of things that are alive, that are there. Rocks, a person can look at a rock and learn something from it, so it could be a parent.

## Clanging

Clanging is a pattern of speech in which sounds, rather than meaningful relationships, appear to govern word choice, so that the intelligibility of the speech is impaired and redundant words are introduced. In addition to rhyming relationships, this pattern of speech may also include punning associations, so that a word similar in sound brings in a new thought.

### Example

Patient: I'm not trying to make noise. I'm trying to make sense. If you can make sense out of nonsense, well, have fun. I'm trying to make sense out of sense. I'm not making sense (cents) anymore. I have to make dollars.

## Neologisms

A neologism is a completely new word or phrase whose derivation cannot be understood. Sometimes the term neologism has also been used to mean a word that has been incorrectly built up but with origins that are understandable as being caused by a misuse of the accepted methods of word formation. For purposes of clarity, these should be referred to as word approximations. Neologisms are uncommon.

### Example

Patient: I go so angry I picked up a dish and threw it at the geshinker. . . . So I sort of bawked the whole thing up.

## Pressured Speech

Pressured speech is an increase in the amount of spontaneous speech as compared with what is considered ordinary or socially customary. The patient talks rapidly and is difficult to interrupt. Some sentences may be left uncompleted because of eagerness to get on to a new idea. Simple questions that could be answered in only a few words or sentences are answered at great length, so that the answer takes minutes rather than seconds and indeed may not stop at all if the speaker is not interrupted. Even when interrupted, the speaker often continues to talk. Speech tends to be loud and emphatic. Sometimes patients with severe pressure will talk without any social stimulation and even though no one is listening. When patients are receiving phenothiazines or lithium, their speech is often slowed down by medication, and then it can be judged only on the basis of amount, volume, and social appropriateness. If a quantitative measure is applied to the rate of speech, then a rate greater than 150 words per minute is usually considered rapid or pressured. The disorder may be accompanied by derailment, tangentiality, or incoherence, but it is distinct from them.

## Distractible Speech

During the course of a discussion or interview, the patient stops talking in the middle of a sentence or idea and changes the subject in response to a nearby stimulus, such as an object on a desk or the interviewer's clothing or appearance.

*Example*

*Patient:* Then I left San Francisco and moved to . . . where did you get that tie? It looks like it's left over from the fifties. I like the warm weather in San Diego. Is that a conch shell on your desk? Have you ever gone scuba diving?

## Diagnostic and Prognostic Significance of Thought Disorder

Bleuler, the psychiatrist responsible for introducing the term schizophrenia, believed that thought disorder occurred only in schizophrenia. Recently, however, Bleuler's beliefs about the specificity of thought disorder have been questioned. A number of investigators have observed that thought disorder may occur in other diagnostic groups, such as manic patients, and that abnormalities in speech and thinking also occur in normal people. Also, it has been observed that not all schizophrenic patients display thought disorder, thereby raising additional questions about its diagnostic specificity.

After the above definitions were developed, they were applied to consecutive admissions to Iowa Psychiatric Hospital (Andreasen, 1979b, 1979c). The frequency with which various types of thought disorder could be found in various diagnostic groups was then determined. The results are shown in Table 25–1.

As this table indicates, manics have a great deal of formal thought disorder. Pressured speech, as might be expected, is their most prominent symptom, but they also have high rates of derailment, tangentiality, incoherence, and loss of goal. Incoherence does not occur with great frequency, but the frequency is equal to that found in schizophrenia. On the other hand, schizophrenic patients tend to have relatively more negative thought disorder than do the manics, but they also have relatively high rates of some types of positive thought disorder. Depressive patients have little thought disorder. The most prominent types are poverty of speech, poverty of content of speech, and circumstantiality.

These data have been replicated in several subsequent investigations (Andreasen, Hoffman, Grove, 1984). They confirm the fact that thought disorder is not pathognomonic of any particular type of psychosis. When thought disorder is divided into subtypes, such as positive vs. negative, it may have somewhat more diagnostic significance. In particular, negative thought disorder, in the absence of a full affective syndrome, is highly suggestive of schizophrenia. These results also indicate the uility of subdividing thought disorder into various clinical subtypes.

Followup studies have also been conducted in order to determine the prognostic significance of thought disorder (Andreasen et al., 1984). When manics are evaluated 6

**TABLE 25–1 Frequency of Types of Thought Disorder**

| | Manics (N = 32) | | Depressives (N = 36) | | Schizophrenics (N = 45) | |
|---|---|---|---|---|---|---|
| | N | % | N | % | N | % |
| Negative thought disorder | | | | | | |
| Poverty of speech | 2 | 6 | 8 | 22 | 13 | 29 |
| Poverty of content of speech | 6 | 19 | 6 | 17 | 18 | 40 |
| Blocking | 1 | 3 | 2 | 6 | 2 | 4 |
| Perseveration | 11 | 34 | 2 | 6 | 11 | 24 |
| Positive thought disorder | | | | | | |
| Derailment | 18 | 56 | 5 | 14 | 25 | 56 |
| Incoherence | 5 | 16 | 0 | 0 | 7 | 16 |
| Tangentiality | 11 | 34 | 9 | 25 | 16 | 36 |
| Illogicality | 8 | 25 | 0 | 0 | 12 | 27 |
| Clanging | 3 | 9 | 0 | 0 | 0 | 0 |
| Neologisms | 1 | 3 | 0 | 0 | 1 | 2 |
| Pressured speech | 23 | 72 | 2 | 6 | 12 | 27 |
| Distractible speech | 10 | 31 | 0 | 0 | 1 | 2 |

months after their index evaluation, most clinical manifestations of thought disorder (such as derailment or pressured speech) have fallen to normal levels. Thus manic thought disorder, although transiently as severe as that occurring in schizophrenia, tends to be reversible.

On the other hand, the thought disorder observed in schizophrenic patients is somewhat more complex. Negative thought disorders persist 6 months later, and even worsen. On the other hand, positive thought disorders tend to diminish somewhat. When types of thought disorder are correlated with other measures of outcome, such as ability to work or to relate in normal social settings, then negative thought disorder is found to be a powerful predictor of outcome. Patients who had prominent negative thought disorder at index evaluation tended to perform poorly on measures of social functioning 6 months later. Thus thought disorder, and particularly the type of thought disorder, has considerable clinical and prognostic significance.

## REFERENCES

Andreasen NC: The reliability and validity of proverb interpretation to assess mental states. Compr Psychiatry 18:465–472, 1977.

Andreasen NC: Scale for the Assessment of Thought, Language, and Communication. Iowa City, University of Iowa, 1979a.

Andreasen NC: The clinical assessment of thought, language, and communication disorders. I. The definition of terms and evaluation of their reliability. Arch Gen Psychiatry 36:1315–1321, 1979b.

Andreasen NC: The clinical assessment of thought, language, and communication disorders. II. Diagnostic significance. Arch Gen Psychiatry 36:1325–1330, 1979c.

Andreasen NC, Hoffman RE, Grove WM: Mapping abnormalities in language and cognition, in Alpert M (ed): Controversies in Schizophrenia. New York, Guilford Press, 1985, pp. 199–226.

Andreasen NC, Tsuang MT, Canter A: The significance of thought disorder in diagnostic evaluations. Compr Psychiatry 15:27–34, 1974.

Bleuler E: Dementia Praecox or the Group of Schizophrenias, trans Zinkin J. New York, International Universities Press, 1950.

Cameron N: Deterioration and regression in schizophrenic thinking. J Abnorm Soc Psychol 34:265–270, 1939.

Chapman J, McGhie A: A comparative study of disordered attention in schizophrenia. J Ment Sci 108:487–500, 1962.

Cromwell RL, Dokeckie PR: Schizophrenic language: A disattention interpretation, in Rosenberg S, Koplin JH (eds): Developments in Applied Psycholinguistic Research. New York, Macmillan, 1968.

Fish FJ: Schizophrenia. Bristol, England, Bright, 1962.

Goldstein K: Methodological approach to the study of schizophrenic thought disorder, in Kasanin JS (ed): Language and Thought in Schizophrenia. Los Angeles, University of California Press, 1944.

Harrow N, Tucker GH, Adler D: Concrete and idiosyncratic thinking in acute schizophrenic patients. Arch Gen Psychiatry 12:443–450, 1965.

Holtzman PS: Smooth pursuit eye movements in psychopathology. Schizophr Bull 9:33–72, 1983.

Joyce J: Finnegan's Wake. New York, Viking Press, 1939.

Kasanin JS: The disturbance of conceptual thinking in schizophrenia, in Kasanin JS (ed): Language and Thought in Schizophrenia. Los Angeles, University of California Press, 1944.

Kraepelin E: Dementia Praecox and Paraphrenia, trans Barkley RM. Edinburgh, E & S Livingstone, 1919.

Payne RW, Friedlander D: A short battery of simple tests for measuring overinclusive thinking. J Ment Sci 108:362–367, 1962.

Wynne LC, Singer NT: Thought disorder and family relations of schizophrenics. Arch Gen Psychiatry 12:187–221, 1965.

# chapter 26

# PHENOMENOLOGY OF COARSE BRAIN DISEASE

*by* Richard Abrams, M.D.
Michael Alan Taylor, M.D.
Frederick Sierles, M.D.

## INTRODUCTION

Behavioral neurology has played an increasingly important role in recent years in the examination of psychiatric patients (Pincus and Tucker, 1978; Taylor, 1981), and the mental status examination is no longer complete without a behavioral neurologic assessment. The quality of this assessment is a function of the examiner's ability to observe, elicit, and describe the diverse manifestations of cerebral dysfunction, and the aim of this chapter is to provide such expertise. The individual manifestations of cerebral dysfunction are described and catalogued, and specific bedside testing techniques are presented. The differential diagnostic implication of each feature is considered, as well as the syndromal importance of grouped features.

Studies since the 1970s have demonstrated a substantial prevalence of electroencephalographic, neuropsychological, and radiographic abnormalities among patients suffering from the major "functional" psychoses, and it behooves the modern psychiatric practitioner to be able to integrate the clinical manifestation of these abnormalities into the diagnosis and prognosis.

## LANGUAGE FUNCTIONS

Assessment of language is an extension of the thought process and content section of the traditional mental status examination. Language functions include spontaneous speech, naming, reading, and writing. Language functions are, by definition, primarily served by the dominant hemisphere, but the affective components of speech (called prosody) are subserved by the nondominant hemisphere (Benson, 1979; Ross, 1981).

The function of *speech* localizes primarily to the perisylvian areas of the frontal, temporal, and parietal lobes of the dominant (for words and word usage and not the affectivity of speech) hemisphere. In the dominant hemisphere, this includes Broca's area, the frontal cortex deep to Broca's area, the supplementary motor cortex, the arcuate fasciculus connecting Broca's area to Wernicke's area, Wernicke's area and adjacent temporal lobe structures, and the supramarginal gyrus of the parietal lobe (Geschwind, 1965, 1974a,b; Golden, 1978; Benson, 1979; Heilman and Valenstein, 1979).

*Fluency of speech* is a function of Broca's area, the frontal cortex deep to it, and the supplementary motor cortex. Speech fluency can be grossly estimated by simply listening to the extent, continuity, and fluidity of the patient's utterances. A standardized, sensitive test of general verbal fluency should also be administered by asking the patient to name as many animals as he can (or words beginning with a specific letter) as fast as he can. If expressive language function is normal, the patient can name 20 to 30 animals (or 20 to 30 "alliterated" words) in 60 seconds (Pincus and Tucker, 1978; Golden, 1978; Heilman and Valenstein, 1979; Benson, 1979). Abnormalities of speech fluency include Broca's aphasia, transcortical motor aphasia, and mixed aphasias (Geschwind, 1974a,b; Golden, 1978; Benson, 1979).

*Broca's (motor) aphasia* results from damage to the left posteroinferior region of the frontal lobe (Broca's area). Although patients with Broca's aphasia may have some comprehension and thinking deficits, they often understand spoken language reasonably well. Characteristically, however, they are unable to express themselves fluently and are occasionally mute. Most can speak but struggle to get the words out. Their speech is often dysarthric, with labored utterances or mispronounced syllables (e.g., "Messodist Epistopal" for "Methodist Episcopal"). Their sentences are most commonly missing small words, such as "the," "to," or "a." Speech without these small words is termed telegraphic (e.g., "don't write, send money").

Because of the extent of brain tissue damage associated with most diseases producing Broca's aphasia, problems not directly related to spoken language often accompany it (Wheeler and Reitan, 1962; Geschwind, 1974a,b; Benson, 1979). These abnormalities include ideokinetic dyspraxia of the ipsilateral hand (sympathetic dyspraxia), buccolingual dyspraxia (the patient may have trouble puffing out his cheeks, whistling, or blowing out a match), weakness or paralysis of the contralateral extremity, and dysgraphia of the ipsilateral (and sometimes the contralateral) hand.

*Transcortical motor aphasia* results from damage to the frontal lobe deep to Broca's area. In this type of aphasia, the patient manifests a paucity of speech. Speech is labored, as with Broca's aphasia, but not telegraphic. Comprehension and thinking may also be affected.

Sometimes a mild motor aphasia is not immediately recognized unless the examiner routinely tests for it by having all patients repeat sentences or phrases containing small words (e.g., "The Polish pope now lives in the Vatican," "No ifs, ands, or buts") or phrases that are difficult to pronounce (e.g., "Methodist Episcopal," "Massachusetts Avenue"). Repetitive language also involves decoding and phonemic expression, so dysfunction in posterior language areas must be ruled out if a patient has difficulty repeating sentences.

*Auditory comprehension* and *linkage of words to visual images* are a function of (a) the posterior two thirds of the superior temporal gyrus, encompassing the transverse auditory gyrus of Heschl (the medial third of the superior temporal gyrus) and Wernicke's area (the posterior third), and (b) the angular gyrus. Dysfunctions in these regions or in tracts such as the arcuate fasciculus connecting Wernicke's area to Broca's area can produce Wernicke's aphasia, impaired auditory comprehension, dysnomia, and conduction aphasia.

*Wernicke's (receptive) aphasia* is the product of a lesion in or near Wernicke's area. It is characterized by fluent, jargon-filled speech, paraphasic utterances, loss of word complexity, phonemic problems, and impaired comprehension of the speech of others. Syntax appears intact, but the content is often meaningless. Writing is usually aphasic. A synonym for jargon aphasia is driveling speech.

The poor *auditory comprehension* of a Wernicke's aphasia patient may be immediately apparent in his inappropriate responses to simple requests. It may have to be elicited, however, by presenting to the patient requests of gradually increasing complexity; a patient who responds properly to a simple request (e.g., "Please sit down") may be unable to respond to one that is more complex (e.g., "Show me all the pictures that contain white or black or red"). On occasion, a lesion of the middle third of the superior temporal gyrus will produce a solitary defect of auditory comprehension. Here the patient's speech is fluent, clear, and understandable, but the patient has grossly impaired comprehension of the speech of others.

The patient with *dysnomia* (or anomia) has difficulty naming objects. The examiner first asks the patient to name a series of common objects (e.g., a pen, a wristwatch, a tie, a light switch, and a thermostat) commensurate with the patient's level of education. The examiner also asks the patient to point to various items that the examiner names (e.g., "Point to your belt," "Show me a button"). Dysnomia can be the product of a dominant temporal or dominant parietal lesion.

A recent study (Faber et al., 1983) demonstrated that patients with schizophrenia and formal thought disorder and neurologic patients with posterior aphasia exhibited elements of aphasic speech with equal frequency. Both groups had fluent speech and speech with reduced content or meaning (fewer nouns and more pronouns). The schizophrenics, however, were able to use multisyllabic words (e.g., "military industrial complex"), whereas the posterior aphasics did not use such words and tended to exhibit auditory comprehension deficits. Reading and writing are other language functions associated with the dominant temporoparietal region (Critchley, 1953; Luria, 1973; Geschwind, 1974; Seamon, 1974; Benson, 1979; Heilman and Valenstein, 1979). To test reading, the patient is asked to read several words and sentences. He should also be asked to demonstrate reading comprehension by reading a sentence and then doing what it says to do (e.g., "Touch your left hand to your right ear"). Impaired reading ability is called dyslexia; when the disability is profound, it is called alexia.

Writing is tested by asking the patient to write a sentence. The patient should be instructed to write in script, rather than print, because testing of cursive writing may permit detection of a subtle dysgraphia that otherwise would not be noticed. The examiner also evaluates what is written for letter construction, syntax, and word usage. Recent studies of regional blood flow during spontaneous speech have revealed changes in the perisylvian regions of the nondominant hemisphere. During speech, activity in these regions mirrors changes in homologous regions of the dominant hemisphere serving the functions of prosody and emotional gesturing (expressing meaning through tonal modulation) (Seamon, 1974; Heilman and Valenstein, 1979; Benson, 1979; Ross, 1981). Patients with normal dominant hemispheric functioning and lesions in the nondominant hemisphere manifest normal spontaneity, clarity, and comprehension of speech but exhibit impairments of range, modulation, and melody of voice, of gesturing with speech, or of comprehension of the emotional tone of the speech of others. These abnormalities are analogous to aphasic disturbances owing to dominant hemisphere dysfunction. For example, in an anterior (e.g., frontal) prosodic disturbance, there is impaired spontaneous emotionality and gesturing with speech; in posterior (e.g., temporal) prosodic disturbance, there is impaired comprehension of the prosody and speech gesturing of others. The assessment of language-related functions of the nondominant hemisphere include:

- Observations of the patient's range, modulation, and melody of voice; the spontaneity of his speech gestures and their ability to convey the feeling associated with what he is saying
- The patient's ability to repeat a sentence with the same affective quality as the examiner. The examiner presents statements in a happy, sad, angry, or surprised voice, and the patient is requested to repeat these statements the same way
- The patient's ability to comprehend (rather than just mimic) the emotions of others. To test this ability, the examiner, standing behind the patient, speaks in sentences with varying affective tones but devoid of emotionally laden words. The patient is then asked to state whether the sentence was spoken with an"angry, sad, happy, indifferent or surprised tone." This is analogous to the assessment of the comprehension of speech
- The patient's ability to comprehend emotional gesturing. The examiner faces the patient and mimes a facial expression to convey one of the above-mentioned moods. The patient is then asked to describe the mood portrayed. If he is unable to do this, he is given the possible choices and asked to choose which one is correct.

Sometimes dysprosodia can be distinguished from emotional blunting by the patient's stating that he experiences moods normally but is unable to convey them and is troubled by this problem. Also, emotional blunting is, by definition, associated with other affective incompetence (e.g., avolition), whereas dysprosodia can be, and often is, a solitary affective dysfunction.

## MEMORY

Modern cognitive psychologists generally describe three phases of memory storage after stimulus input:

1. *Sensory memory store* (short-term store, echoic or iconic memory), which can hold two to three items and which decays in 1 to 2 seconds if not attended to. This is not tested clinically.

2. *Short-term store* (primary memory, working memory), which requires attention to have been paid to the stimulus. This store holds seven to eight items, decays in less than 20 seconds if not further processed (e.g., by rehearsal), and is interfered with by interpolated material. The short-term store is tested for by assessing digit span, assuming concentration ability to be intact.

3. *Long-term store* (secondary memory) is achieved only with rehearsal of the contents of the short-term store and becomes permanent after a variable consolidation period lasting from 30 seconds to 20 minutes. Long-term store is tested for by determining the extent of recall for recently learned material.

Two procedures may be used to assess memory functions: digit span and paired-associate learning. *Digit span* is a test of reproduction or immediate recall. The examiner asks the patient to repeat series of random numbers presented 1 second apart, starting with a sequence of three digits and increasing the length by one digit each time, to a total of seven digits, if the preceding sequence is correctly reproduced. A normal person can repeat six to eight digits forward and four to five backward; inability to repeat at least five digits forward and three digits backward indicates substantial impairment of short-term store.

*Paired-associate learning* is a test of retention. The examiner reads to the patient a list of 10 word pairs (from the Wechsler Memory Scale), presented at 1-second intervals. When the examiner is finished, he goes back and presents the first word of each pair, requesting the patient to respond with the second word. Six of the pairs are easy to recall (e.g., baby-cries) and four are difficult (e.g., school-grocery). If the patient cannot reproduce all 10 correct responses after three separate presentations of the list, his immediate recall (short-term store) is too impaired to proceed with the retention portion of the test. If all 10 are reproduced correctly within three trials, the examiner returns in five minutes to test for the number of half pairs correctly recalled in response to the first word of each pair. A normal person can produce five to six of the easy items and three to four of the hard ones. Inability to recall at least four easy items and two hard ones indicates substantial impairment of retention (long-term store). This procedure requires an intact retrieval mechanism to be valid—this is the mechanism that is impaired in retrograde amnesia and that is assessed by asking the patient to recall various items from the remote past (e.g., the names of presidents from several years ago). If such remote recall is impaired, the retrieval mechanism is at fault and tests of retention are invalid.

## TEMPORAL LOBE FUNCTIONS

Language and memory assessment, in part, tests temporal lobe function. Temporal lobe dysfunction can also be expressed in a variety of psychomotor symptoms, although discharges in other areas of the brain (e.g., centrencephalon) can also produce psychomotor features.

Some patients without temporal lobe epilepsy nevertheless have temporal lobe lesions. Patients with stroke, head injury, viral disease (particularly herpes), vascular malformations, and degenerative disease involving the temporal lobes can present with delusions, hallucinations (particularly auditory and panoramic visual), and mood disturbances. Patients with posterior (temporoparietal) aphasia and those with formal thought disorder share many of the same elements of language dysfunction. There is a strong association between temporal lobe dysfunction and psychopathology. In the absence of a classic epileptic picture and course, a temporal lobe etiology in the differential diagnosis of a psychotic patient must nevertheless be considered (Davidson and Bagley, 1969; Hayman and Abrams, 1977; Pincus and Tucker, 1978; Heilman and Valenstein, 1979; Taylor, 1981; Benson and Blumer, 1982; Koella and Trimble, 1982).

Disturbances in language and memory are most commonly observed in psychiatric patients with temporal lobe dysfunction. Bilateral involvement is typically associated with dementia. When the dysfunction is in the dominant temporal lobe, euphoria, auditory hallucinations (often "complete" voices), formal thought disorder, and primary delusional ideas are the likely psychopathology. These clinical phenomena are associated with such cognitive deficits as decreased learning and retention of verbal material (read or heard), poor speech comprehension, and poor reading comprehension. When the dysfunction is in the nondominant temporal lobe, dysphoria, irritability, depression, and inappropriate emotional expression (aprosodia) are the likely psychopathology. These clinical phenomena are associated with such cognitive deficits as decreased recognition and recall of visual and environmental sounds, amusia (loss of ability to repeat musical sounds), poor visual memory, decreased auditory discrimination and comprehension of tonal patterns, and decreased ability to learn and recognize nonsense figures and geometric shapes (Pincus and Tucker, 1978; Golden, 1978; Heilman and Valenstein, 1979; Cummings, 1982).

## FRONTAL LOBE FUNCTIONS

The frontal lobes constitute 25 per cent of adult brain weight. The portion of the frontal lobes rostral to the motor areas has executive function over other cortical areas and is considered by many to be the association cortex for the limbic system. Frontal lobe dysfunction (either intrinsic or secondary to limbic system dysfunction) adversely affects performance on tasks designed to test other cortical areas, and the clinician must be especially careful in trying to diagnose the locus of a lesion in the presence of frontal lobe dysfunction (Luria, 1973; Golden, 1978; Pincus and Tucker, 1978; Heilman and Valenstein, 1979).

Motor behavior and expressive language are regulated by frontal lobe systems. Additional frontal lobe functions should also be assessed, beginning with an evaluation of the patient's ability to concentrate or attend to a task. This is reliably and readily done by asking the patient to subtract sevens serially from 100. Assuming adequate calculating ability, the patient should be able to produce at least six accurate sequential subtractions in a row. Another useful test of concentration is to have the patient spell the word "earth" backward (Spear and Green, 1966; Luria, 1973; Folstein, Folstein, McHugh, 1975; Golden, 1978).

Reasoning and thinking abilities should also be assessed as part of the frontal lobe evaluation, as well as other dominant hemisphere functioning. Proverb interpretation is a widely used mental status strategy for assessing thinking, but responses to proverbs do not correlate well with deficits in abstract thinking (Andreasen, 1977), and fewer than 22 per cent of non–brain-damaged adults fully understand them (Matarazzo, 1972). Because thinking is also not a monolithic function, no single test spans the various cognitive processes subsumed under that rubric. A clinical assessment of "thinking," however, can be obtained by specifically assessing a patient's comprehension, concept formation, and reasoning. The extent of this assessment will be determined by the individual clinical situation.

Some of the non-proverb items from the comprehension subtest of the Wechsler Adult Intelligence Scale (WAIS) (Matarazzo, 1972; Lezak, 1983, pp 259–262) can be used to clinically assess a patient's comprehension. Sample questions are (a) Why do we wash clothes? (b) Why does a train have an engine? (c) Why should we keep away from bad company?

Encouragement and asking the patient to elaborate his answer may be needed to obtain the patient's best performance.

*Verbal concept formation* (abstract thinking ability) can be tested by items drawn from the similarities subtest of the WAIS. The examiner should begin with a pair of moderate difficulty ("In what way are air and water alike?"). If the patient correctly identifies them as "elements," no further testing is required. If a concrete response is produced (e.g., "Air is dry and water is wet"), the examiner should provide the correct answer and proceed to a second pair of somewhat less difficulty (ax-saw). If the response is again inadequate, the procedure is repeated once more with an easy pair (orange–banana); failure on this item demonstrates substantial impairment of verbal concept formation (ability to abstract). To test verbal reasoning, the patient is asked to listen to a statement and then tell the examiner what is "foolish" about the statement. Some examples are: (1) A man had flu twice: the first time it killed him, but the second time he got well quickly; (2) in the year 1980, many more women than men got married in the United States.

Other tests of frontal lobe function include orientation to time, place, and person (Luria, 1973; Golden, 1978); assessing the patient's ability to recognize the right side of space or the right side of his body (Dimascio, Dimascio, Chui, 1980); and testing for active perception (Luria, 1973; Ratcliff, 1979). Orientation is tested in the manner that is familiar to those experienced in the mental status examination. Neglect of the right side of space may result in the patient's reading only the left side of printed material (e.g., he reads "MGW" as "MG"), shaving only the left side of his face, or bumping into objects only to his right (Dimascio et al., 1980). Active perception, that is, the ability to "mentally" rotate an item in space, is a nondominant hemisphere function and is tested by asking the patient to identify a picture of an object (e.g., a baby, a hat) presented in a sideways or upside down position. The patient should be able to identify the rotated object without tilting his head.

Frontal lobe dysfunction can also be expressed in behavioral change. Two major frontal lobe syndromes have been described: the *convexity syndrome* and the *orbitomedial syndrome* (Luria, 1969, 1973; Hecaen and Albert, 1975; Heilman and Valenstein, 1979, pp. 360–412). The convexity syndrome, related to lesions within or near the lateral surface of the frontal lobes, is characterized by "negative symptoms." These patients are apathetic, indifferent to their surroundings, and emotionally unresponsive. They appear to have lost all drive and ambition. Loss of social graces is common, and they frequently appear disheveled and dirty. Their movements are slow and reduced in frequency (motor inertia). Occasionally, they may remain in positions for prolonged periods (catalepsy) and may posture. A slight flexion at the waist, knees, and elbows is a typical body position of such patients. They occasionally move with a floppy, shuffling gait, progressively picking up steam only to slow gradually to a halt (glissando/deglissando gait). Unlike patients with Parkinson's disease, muscle tone is decreased and "pill-rolling" is not present. These patients have difficulty attending to tasks but do respond to irrelevant, intense stimuli.

If the convexity syndrome is due to dominant hemisphere pathology, it is also associated with a deficit in language and in verbal thinking. Impoverished thinking (vague and without detail) is almost always present; verbal fluency is significantly impaired; speech is often stereotyped with perseverative and verbigerated utterances; and Broca's or transcortical aphasia may be present. Most frontal lobe, cognitive, and soft neurologic signs can be observed in these patients, who may also be dyspraxic (gait, bucco-linguo-facial, or ideo-motor dyspraxias) and incontinent of urine.

A second frontal lobe syndrome is associated with dysfunction in the orbitomedial areas of the frontal lobes. Some patients may be asthenic and easily fatigued, bland, akinetic, aphonic, withdrawn, and fearful. They may have diminished wakefulness, with clouding of consciousness and even stupor. Others may have an intense affect, expressing euphoria, irritability, or extreme lability of affect, with rapid mood shifts and mixed or cycling mood states. *Witzelsucht* (a fatuous jocularity) is common. These affectively intense patients are hyperactive and overresponsive to stimuli. They rapidly terminate one incomplete goal-directed behavior only to start another and may appear frenetic as they run from one activity to another, never completing a task. These patients lose their inhibitions and may become reckless. They are impulsive and may engage in buying sprees or other high-risk behaviors. They lack foresight, cannot make decisions, are unable to persevere, and have uncontrollable and often irrelevant associations. They are strongly stimulus bound, distractible, intrusive, and importunate. They will interrupt conversations and mimic the examiner's movements and comments. These are the patients who, despite repeated injunctions, continually enter a room in which a group of people are in conference or pull fire alarms or change channels continually on television sets, simply as a function of the visual stimulus. These patients may have uncontrollable, often fantastic, confabulations, and when prevented from doing as they please, they may have violent outbursts.

The obvious similarity in behaviors between patients with orbitomedial syndrome and those with bipolar affective disorder requires particular care in the differential diagnostic evaluation. Neurologic findings (particularly soft signs), the shallowness of affect, a prolonged and insidious onset, a chronic non-episodic course, a negative family history for affective disorder, and localized computed tomography scan and electroencephalographic abnormalities all suggest coarse brain disease.

## PARIETAL LOBE FUNCTIONS

Touch, pain, and temperature senses are represented in primary cortex in the posterior central gyrus, located in the anterior portion of the parietal lobe contralateral to the side of the body on which the sensation is being tested. Proprioception, stereognosis, and graphesthesis are functions represented in the contralateral parietal lobe, just caudal to the posterior central gyrus (Critchley, 1953; Luria, 1973).

The *nondominant parietal lobe* coordinates motor, sensory, and spatial perception. Its functions include the awareness of one's body in space, the recognition of faces, and the ability to copy the outline of simple objects (Critchley, 1953; Luria, 1973; Golden, 1978; Heilman and Valenstein, 1979).

The *dominant parietal lobe* coordinates visual and language functions, including reading (lexic function), writing (graphic function), and parietal lobe language functions. Two other parietal lobe functions, kinesthetic praxis and ideokinetic (ideomotor) praxis, have also been discussed (Critchley, 1953; Luria, 1973; Golden, 1978: Heilman and Valenstein, 1979). Others include finger gnosis, calculating, right-left orientation, symbolic categorization, graphesthesis, and stereognosis.

The examiner tests finger gnosis (Neilsen, 1938; Critchley, 1953) by pointing to (without touching) each of the patient's fingers and asking him to name them. Inability to do this suggests finger agnosia or dysnomia. The examiner may then assign a number to all 10 fingers. When the patient has learned the numbering system, he should be instructed to interlock his fingers (as if in prayer) and then rotate his wrists so that the interlocking fingers face the patient. If the patient is then able to identify his fingers by number, finger gnosis is intact.

The patient's ability to compute simple mathematical problems is assessed by asking him to perform, on paper, several calculations in which he is asked to "carry" one or two digits (Critchley, 1953; Luria, 1973; Golden, 1978; Pincus and Tucker, 1978; Heilman and Valenstein, 1979). The way the patient writes the problem may reveal dysfunctions other than dominant parietal dysfunction. For example, if the patient miscalculates and also transcribes the numbers in a rotated alignment, he is making an error of visuomotor coordination, revealing parietal dysfunction. If he perseverates numbers rather than miscalculating, his dysfunction is likely to be frontal. Single-digit computations (e.g., 4 + 4, 5 × 3) should not be used because they are likely to be overlearned, rote responses.

Right-left orientation (Neilsen, 1938; Critchley, 1953; Luria, 1973) is tested by asking the patient to perform several tasks, each of which require that he tell left from right while crossing his body midline. For example, he is told, "Touch your left hand to your right ear"; "Touch your right hand to your right knee . . . left elbow"; "Touch your right hand to your right knee."

Another dominant parietal lobe function is symbolic categorization (Critchley, 1953; Luria, 1973), which can be tested by asking the patient to identify relationships between members of a family. For example, the patient can be asked: "What would be the relationship to you of your brother's father?" Symbolic categorization requires that the patient make a mental diagram in order to answer the question correctly.

Just as in the assessment of kinesthetic praxis, the evaluation of graphesthesis and stereognosis tests both the parietal lobe contralateral to the hand being tested and the connections between the two hemispheres (Critchley, 1953; Luria, 1973; Golden, 1978; Pincus and Tucker, 1978; Heilman and Valenstein, 1979). The examiner tests graphesthesis by tracing numbers, one at a time, on the patient's palms while the patient's eyes are closed. If the patient experiences difficulty in identifying the number, and if his ability to read numbers is intact, the error is called agraphesthesia and might be due to dysfunction of the contralateral parietal lobe or the interhemispheric connections, such as the corpus callosum. After the test of graphesthesis on the hand ipsilateral to the patient's dominant hemisphere, the other hand should be tested. If the patient manifests graphesthesia on the latter hand, the abnormality is likely in the contralateral parietal lobe.

The examiner tests stereognosis by placing objects (e.g., key, button, paper clip), one at a time, in the patient's hands while the patient's eyes are closed. After each placement, the patient is asked to "feel it with your fingers and then name it." If the patient experiences difficulty in the presence of intact naming ability, he is manifesting astereognosis, which might be due to dysfunction of the contralateral parietal lobe or the interhemispheric connections, such as the corpus callosum, if errors are primarily lateralized to the nonpreferred hand.

Previously discussed functions of the nondominant parietal lobe included constructional praxis, dressing praxis, kinesthetic praxis (of the contralateral hand), graphesthesis (of the contralateral hand), and stereognosis (of the contralateral hand) (Critchley, 1953; Luria, 1973; Golden, 1978; Pincus and Tucker, 1978; Heilman and Valenstein, 1979). Additional functions can be characterized as the abilities to recognize or be aware of one's self and environment. Abnormalities include nonrecognition of (a) serious medical disability (anosognosia), (b) the left side of space, and (c) familiar faces (prosopagnosia). These abnormalities, when present, are often so obvious that the examiner's questions are usually required only to reaffirm and elaborate on his impression of the existence of such a disability. Anosognosia (Critchley, 1953; Weinstein and Kahn, 1955; Luria, 1973; Golden, 1978; Pincus and Tucker, 1978; Heilman and Valenstein, 1979) is nonrecognition of a serious medical disability. For example, in Babinski's agnosia, a patient with hemiparalysis will attempt to get out of bed and walk despite evidence of paralysis from repeated failures to walk and instructions not to walk from staff and visitors. It is also possible that other phenomena routinely described as "denial" are actually the product of posterior nondominant hemisphere dysfunction. Prosopagnosia (Critchley, 1953; Luria, 1973; Meadows, 1974) is nonrecognition of faces familiar to the patient. It is sometimes diagnosed when the patient accuses one or more familiar people, usually a family member, of being an impostor (i.e., Capgras' syndrome) (Hayman and Abrams, 1977; Alexander, Struss, Benson, 1979). Some recent evidence suggests that prosopagnosia extends to the nonrecognition of other, nonfacial visual stimuli and that lesions are often bilateral.

A related phenomenon is called the Fregoli syndrome (Christodoulou, 1976), or delusional hyperidentification. Here, the patient mistakenly thinks that people who are not well known to him are familiar (e.g., the other person is a friend or a relative or a famous person), despite the lack of resemblance. For example, a patient in a psychiatric ward was convinced that Charlton Heston and Marilyn Monroe had been admitted to his ward.

Another related phenomenon is reduplicative paramnesia (Critchley, 1953; Weinstein and Kahn, 1955; Luria, 1973), in which a patient with nondominant parietal dysfunction insists that a duplicate of a person or place exists elsewhere. For example, a white woman on a psychiatric service had the delusion that she had a twin sister who was black. This patient also manifested Capgras' syndrome, thinking that her husband was an impostor sent to spy on her.

Some patients with intact left-right orientation pay no attention to the left side of their bodies or to objects in their left visual field. Such left spatial nonrecognition is a product of nondominant parietal lobe dysfunction (Critchley, 1953; Weinstein and Kahn, 1955; Luria, 1973; Golden, 1978; Pincus and Tucker, 1978; Heilman and Valenstein, 1979) and may reveal itself in a number of ways, including not shaving the left side of one's face, bumping into objects on the left, or reading only the right side of printed materials. East-west orientation (Critchley, 1953; Luria, 1973) is also a function of the nondominant parietal lobe. The examiner assesses this function by drawing two crossed lines to represent the directions on an imaginary map. He then asks the patient to identify which portions of the map would be north, south, east, and west.

Occasionally, a patient with normal global orientation, who can select the correct answer when given a series of choices about their location, is unable to state spontaneously where he is. When asked to do so, he will make a series of wild guesses. For example, a patient on a psychiatric ward is unable to answer correctly the question, "Where are we now?" Instead, he answers in rapid succession, "At the McDonalds," "At the railway station," "In a high-rise building." This wild guessing is called paragnosia and is often associated with lesions in the nondominant parietal lobe (Critchley, 1953; Luria, 1973).

Parietal lobe dysfunction can be associated with significant psychopathology (e.g., delusional ideas, experiences of alienation), which can lead to misdiagnoses and inappropriate treatment for a "functional" disorder (Critchley, 1953; Luria, 1973; Heilman and Valenstein, 1979). Two general patterns of symptoms have been observed. Lesions of the dominant parietal lobe usually are associated with disorders of language (dyslexia, word-finding problems, conduction aphasia), problems with calculation, dyspraxias (ideomotor, kinesthetic), difficulties in spatially related abstraction, and contralateral sensory (agraphesthesia, astereognosis) and motor (hypotonia, posturing, paucity of movement) deficits. The best-known dominant parietal syndrome is Gerstmann's syndrome (dysgraphia, dyscalculia, right-left disorientation, finger agnosia) (Neilsen, 1938), said to result from a lesion in the posteroinferior aspect (angular gyrus) of the dominant parietal lobe. The validity of the syndrome has been questioned by some authors, however, and it has been reported in more than 20 per cent of chronic psychiatric patients (Birkett, 1967).

Lesions of the nondominant parietal lobe are associated with profound (occasionally delusional) denial of illness (anosognosia), left-sided spatial neglect, constructional difficulties, dressing dyspraxia, and contralateral sensory and motor deficits. Capgras' syndrome and the first-rank symptom of experience of alienation (body parts or thoughts not belonging to the self) all have been described in patients with nondominant parietal lesions. One patient, observing his own left arm, thought that there was another person in bed with him. He complained about this to his relatives, who in turn complained to the chief of the department of neurology that overcrowding at the hospital had gone too far! These patients also may have difficulty orienting themselves in their environment. They complain that things look "confused" or "jumbled." They cannot find their way along previously familiar routes and can no longer drive a car because they lose track of the other vehicles around them. They may complain that their bodies are somehow different, that an arm or leg feels heavy, bigger than usual or that they are not always sure of the location of an arm or leg.

## OCCIPITAL LOBE FUNCTIONS

Other than in the testing of primary occipital cortical functions, such as visual fields or color vision, it is difficult to test separately for right and left hemispheric occipital lobe functioning, and errors on tests for occipital cortical functioning cannot readily be lateralized (Pincus and Tucker, 1978; Golden, 1978; Heilman and Valenstein, 1979). A gross test of occipital lobe associational cortex requires the patient to identify a simple picture overlaid by a distracting background (Luria, 1973). The patient is shown a drawing and asked to name it. If he cannot do so, and his capacity to name objects is intact, he may have occipital lobe dysfunction.

## SOFT NEUROLOGIC SIGNS

Soft neurologic signs are clinical features that indicate brain dysfunction but that cannot be definitely localized within the brain. When present, these signs are well correlated with psychiatric illnesses and other behavior disorders (Ben-Yishay, Diller, Gerstman, Haas, 1968; Pincus and Tucker, 1978; Cox and Ludwig, 1979; Taylor, 1981; Nasrallah, Tippin, McCalley-Whitters, 1983).

The examiner tests the palmar-mental reflex by repeatedly scratching the base of the patient's thumb. If the lower lip and jaw move slightly downward, and if this response does not extinguish with repetition (50 per cent of the population will exhibit this feature but will quickly lose it with repeated stimulation), the patient has manifested a palmar-mental reflex. The examiner tests the grasp reflex by pressing his fingers into the palm of one or both of the patient's hands. If the patient's hand grasps the examiner's fingers despite instructions to the contrary, a grasp reflex is present. The snout (rooting) reflex is tested when the examiner strokes the corner of the subject's mouth. If the patient's lips purse and the lips or head moves toward the stroking, the patient has a snout reflex. Adventitious motor overflow is tested by asking the patient to tap rapidly and repeatedly with one hand on his knee or on a table. If he also taps or moves the other hand, he has shown adventitious motor overflow. Each hand should be tested separately.

Double simultaneous discrimination is tested with the patient's eyes closed. The examiner simultaneously lightly brushes one of his fingers across one of the patient's cheeks and another finger across the back of one of the patient's hands, using identical pressure. He asks the patient where he feels the touch. With impaired double simultaneous discrimination, the touch on the hands is usually not perceived. Occasionally, only stimuli on one side of the body are extinguished, suggesting contralateral dysfunction. Some patients with large parietal lobe lesions (usually on the right) locate the stimuli outside their body parts. The phenomena of motor impersistence and *gegenhalten* are also thought by some to be soft neurologic signs.

## REFERENCES

Alexander MP, Struss DT, Benson DF: Capgras syndrome: A reduplicative phenomena. Neurology 29:334–339, 1979.

Andreasen NC: Reliability and validity of proverb interpretation to assess mental status. Compr Psychiatry 18:465–472, 1977.

Benson DF: Aphasia, Alexia and Agraphia. Clinical Neurology and Neurosurgery Monographs. Edinburgh, Churchill Livingstone, 1979.

Benson DF, Blumer D: Psychiatric manifestations of epilepsy, in Benson DF, Blumer D (eds): Psychiatric Aspects of Neurologic Disease, vol 2. New York, Gruen & Stratton, 1982, pp 25–47.

Ben-Yishay Y, Diller L, Gerstman L, Haas A: The relationship between impersistence, intellectual function and outcome of rehabilitation in patients with left hemiplegia. Neurology 18:852–861, 1968.

Birkett DP: Gerstmann's syndrome. Br J Psychiatry 113:801, 1967.

Christodoulou GN: Delusional hyper-identifications of the Fregoli type. Organic pathogenetic contributors. Acta Psychiatr Scand 54:305–314, 1976.

Cox SM, Ludwig AM: Neurological soft signs and psychopathology. I. Findings in schizophrenia. J Nerv Ment Dis 167:161–165, 1979.

Critchley M: The Parietal Lobes. New York, Hafner Press, 1953.

Cummings JL: Cortical dementias, in Benson DF, Blumer D (eds): Psychiatric Aspects of Neurologic Disease, vol 2. New York, Grune & Stratton, 1982, pp 93–121.

Davidson K, Bagley CR: Schizophrenia-like psychoses associated with organic disorders of the central nervous system: A review of the literature, in Current Problems in Neuropsychiatry. Br J Psychiatry Special Publication No. 4:113–184, 1969.

Dimascio AR, Dimascio H, Chui HC: Neglect following damage to frontal lobe or basal ganglia. Neuropsychologia 18:123–132, 1980.

Faber R, Abrams R, Taylor MA, Kasprisin A, Morris C, Weisz R: Formal thought disorder and aphasia: Comparison of schizophrenic patients with formal thought disorder and neurologically impaired patients with aphasia. Am J Psychiatry 140:1348–1351, 1983.

Folstein MF, Folstein SW, McHugh PR: "Mini-Mental State": A practical method of grading the cognitive state of patients for the clinician. J Psychol Res 12:189–198, 1975.

Geschwind N: Disconnection syndromes in animals and man. Part I. Brain 88:237–294, 1965; Part II. Brain 88:585–644, 1965.

Geschwind N: The anatomical basis of hemisphere differentiation, in Diamond SJ, Beaumont JG (eds): Hemisphere Function in the Human Brain. New York, Halstead Press, 1974a, pp 7–24.

Geschwind N: Selected Papers on Language and the Brain. Boston, Reidel, 1974b.

Golden C, Hammeke T, Purisch A: Diagnostic validity of a standardized neuropsychological battery from Luria's neuropsychological tests. J Consult Clin Psychol 48:1258–1265, 1978.

Golden CJ: Diagnosis and Rehabilitation in Clinical Neuropsychology. Springfield, Il, CC Thomas, 1978.

Hayman M, Abrams R: Capgras' syndrome and cerebral dysfunction. Br J Psychiatr 130:68–71, 1977.

Hecaen H, Albert ML: Disorder of mental functioning related to frontal lobe pathology, in Benson DF, Blumer D (eds): Psychiatric Aspects of Neurologic Disease, vol 1. New York, Grune & Stratton, 1975, pp 137–169.

Heilman KM, Valenstein E (eds): Clinical Neuropsychology. New York, Oxford University Press, 1979.

Koella WP, Trimble MR (eds): Temporal Lobe Epilepsy, Mania and Schizophrenia and the Limbic System, Advances in Biological Psychiatry, vol 1982. Basil, S. Kruger, 1982.

Lezak MD: Neuropsychological Assessment, ed 3. New York, Oxford University Press, 1983, pp 414–474.

Luria AR: Frontal lobe syndromes, in Vinken PJ, Bruyn GW (eds): Handbook of Clinical Neurology, vol 2, Localization in Clinical Neurology. New York, Elsevier-North Holland, 1969, pp 725–775.

Luria AR: The Working Brain: An Introduction to Neuropsychology, trans Hough B. New York, Basic Books, 1973.

Matarazzo J: Wechsler's Measurement and Appraisal of Adult Intelligence, New York, Oxford University Press, 1972.

Meadows J: The anatomical basis of prosopagnosia. J Neurol Neurosurg Psychiatry 37:489–501, 1974.

Nasrallah HA, Tippin J, McCalley-Whitters M: Neuropsychological soft signs in manic patients, a comparison with schizophrenics and control groups. J Affect Disord 5:45–50, 1983.

Neilsen J: Gerstmann's syndrome: Finger agnosia, agraphia, comparison of right and left and acalculia. Arch Neurol Psychiatry 39:536–560, 1938.

Pincus JH, Tucker GJ: Behavioral Neurology, ed 2. New York, Oxford University Press, 1978.

Ratcliff G: Spatial thought, mental rotation and the right cerebral hemisphere. Neuropsychologia 17:49–54, 1979.

Ross ED: The aprosodias: Functional anatomic organization of the affective components of language in the right hemisphere. Arch Neurol 38:562–569, 1981.

Seamon JG: Coding and retrieval processes and the hemispheres of the brain, in Diamond SJ, Beaumont JG (eds): Hemisphere Function in the Human Brain. New York, Halstead Press, 1974, pp 184–203.

Spear FG, Green R: Inability to concentrate. Br J Psychiatry 112:913–915, 1966.

Taylor MA: The Neuropsychiatric Mental Status Examination. New York, SP Medical and Scientific Books, 1981.

Weinstein EA, Kahn RL: Denial of Illness: Symbolic and Physiological Aspects. Springfield, Il, CC Thomas, 1955.

Wheeler L, Reitan RM: Presence and laterality of brain damage predicted from responses to a short aphasia screening test. Percept Mot Skills 15:783–799, 1962.

# chapter 27

# MOTOR BEHAVIOR

*by* Michael Alan Taylor, M.D.

## MOTOR BEHAVIORS AND THE MENTAL STATUS EXAMINATION

Systematic observation of motor behavior has long been recognized as an essential procedure in diagnosing psychiatric patients. The identification of motor retardation and hyperactivity, manifestations of melancholia and mania, respectively, are well-known examples of the predictive value of accurately assessing a patient's movements. Abnormalities in motor behavior are more variable and often subtler than these two global phenomena. An awareness of the full range of motor abnormalities associated with psychiatric disorder, an expertise in how to elicit those phenomena that are not readily apparent, and a knowledge of the diagnostic implications of each provide the clinician with a powerful diagnostic tool. With this in mind, these motor behaviors, and their assessment and relationship to psychiatric syndromes, are reviewed in this chapter.

Motor behavior is initially observed on meeting the patient. Observations of motor behavior should include an assessment of gait, abnormal movements, frequency of movement, rhythm, coordination, and speed. Walking with the patient to the examining room is an excellent opportunity to begin observing these behaviors. The wide-based, or ataxic, gait of the alcoholic, the hesitant gait of the Huntington's patient, the stooped shuffle of the patient with frontal lobe disease, the manneristic hopping and tiptoe gaits of the catatonic are but a few of the unusual motor behaviors that can be observed while walking with the patient to the office.

One of the more common motor disturbances seen in seriously ill patients is agitation. Agitation, or an increase in the frequency of non–goal-directed motor behavior, is usually the expression of an intense mood and can reflect anxiety, sadness, anger, or euphoria. Pacing, hand wringing, head rubbing, constant shifting of body position, playing with one's fingers, and picking at bed sheets are all examples of agitation.

Because of chronic ingestion of neuroleptics, many psychiatric patients exhibit constant jerky finger movements, foot tapping, pelvic thrusts, and repetitive oral movements, such as lip smacking or moving the tongue in and out of the mouth. These movements are manifestations of a coarse brain disorder and have been given the global term tardive dyskinesia (Crane, 1973). Although tardive dyskinesia typically exacerbates with stress, it is also frequently observed in patients who are calm. It should not be confused with agitation.

Adventitious motor overflow comprises small, uncontrollable, jerky hand, head, and shoulder movements (e.g., chorea), which must also be distinguished from agitation.

433

Motor overflow can be observed as the patient walks toward the examining room. Patients with chorea often exhibit sudden involuntary hand movements, which they try to cover up by transforming the movement into a socially accepted action (e.g., smoothing hair, fixing a tie). Adventitious motor overflow can be tested by asking the patient to hold both arms straight out in front of him for 20 seconds, during which choreiform jerks may appear. Adventitious motor overflow, unlike agitation, is not an expression of an intense mood and can be observed in calm individuals (Quitkin, Rifkin, Klein, 1976; Paulson and Gottlieb, 1968).

Global, usually goal-oriented activities of psychiatric patients are often abnormal. The extremes of these activity changes are termed hyperactivity and hypoactivity. A patient who is engaged in too many things at the same time, who talks to several people, one after the other, who goes from one place to another in quick succession is said to be hyperactive. The patient who does nothing, who sits for long periods in a chair, seldom moving or responding to surrounding events is said to be hypoactive. In its extreme form, hyperactivity appears as frantic, constant, impulsive, and incomplete multiple activities that may appear non-goal directed. It is invariably associated with an intense excitement state, in which the patient is constantly talking and often shouting. Extreme importunate and intrusive behavior and intense irritability or euphoria are usually present (Taylor, 1981). Before the availability of electroconvulsive treatment, patients experiencing extreme excitement were reported occasionally to suffer cardiovascular collapse and even death (Derby, 1933). Extreme hyperactivity or excitement is most frequently observed in individuals who satisfy modern diagnostic criteria for mania (Taylor and Abrams, 1973; Carlson and Goodwin, 1973).

Extreme hypoactivity is termed stupor. A stuporous patient may stay motionless for hours, staring fixedly or following the examiner about the room with his eyes yet being mute and unresponsive to verbal comments and even to painful stimuli (general analgesia) (Kahlbaum, 1973). When associated with coarse brain disease, particularly of the brainstem, the syndrome is termed akinetic mutism (McCusker, Rudick, Honch, Griggs, 1982). When coarse brain disease cannot be demonstrated, such stuporous patients most frequently satisfy diagnostic criteria for affective disorder (Kraepelin, 1976; Abrams and Taylor, 1976; Taylor and Abrams, 1977). Stupor is also a feature of catatonia.

## CATATONIA

Catatonia has long been recognized as a syndrome rather than a specific disease process (Hearst, Munoz, Tuason, 1971; Abrams and Taylor, 1976). It is characterized by specific motor behaviors and by periods of extreme hyperactivity and hypoactivity. Studies (Abrams and Taylor, 1976; Taylor and Abrams, 1977; Morrison, 1973) show that 25 per cent to 50 per cent of individuals who exhibit catatonic features have affective disorder and that about 20 per cent of patients with bipolar affective disorder exhibit one or more catatonic features (Taylor and Abrams, 1977). Those patients who have catatonia as part of their affective disease are indistinguishable from affectively disordered patients without catatonia in their demographic characteristics, psychopathology, and treatment response and in the prevalence and pattern of psychiatric illness in their first-degree relatives (Taylor and Abrams, 1977; Morrison, 1974; Kirby, 1913; Bonner and Kent, 1936). Although 5 per cent to 10 per cent of catatonics satisfy criteria for the diagnosis of schizophrenia, catatonia generally has a favorable treatment response (Taylor and Abrams, 1977).

The traditional catatonic features are shown in Table 27–1. Mutism and stupor, although characteristic of catatonia, are not pathognomonic. Other motor behaviors should be present, and most patients have three or more features (Taylor and Abrams, 1977). There appears to be no relationship among any one feature or number of features and any one diagnosis or response to treatment (Taylor and Abrams, 1977). Thus the presence of one or two features has as much diagnostic and treatment significance as the presence of seven or eight features. Three features—mutism, negativism, and stupor—occur together more frequently than by chance (Abrams, Taylor, Stolurow, 1979) and correspond to the clinical syndrome of negativistic stupor (i.e., akinetic mutism or coma vigil secondary to frontal lobe damage)

**TABLE 27–1    Classic Catatonic Features**

| Feature | Description |
| --- | --- |
| Mutism | State of verbal unresponsiveness. It is not always associated with immobility. |
| Stupor | Extreme hypoactivity, in which the patient is mute, immobile, and unresponsive to severe painful stimuli. |
| Catalepsy | Maintenance of postures for long periods. Includes facial postures, such as a masklike, expressionless face, grimacing, schnauzkrampf (lips in an exaggerated pucker), and body postures, such as psychological pillow (patient lying in bed with his head elevated as if on a pillow), lying in a jackknifed position, sitting with upper and lower portions of body twisted at right angles, holding arms above the head or raised in prayerlike manner, and holding fingers and hands in odd positions. |
| Waxy flexibility | Initial resistance patient offers before allowing himself to be postured, similar to that of a bending candle. |
| Mannerisms | Odd purposeful movements, such as hopping instead of walking, walking on tiptoe, saluting passersby, or exaggerations or stilted caricatures of mundane movements. |
| Stereotypy | Often striking, non–goal-directed, repetitive motor behavior. The repetition of phrases and sentences in an automatic fashion, similar to a scratched record, termed verbigeration, is a verbal stereotypy. |
| Gegenhalten (negativism) | Patient resisting examiner's manipulations, light or vigorous, with strength equal to that applied, as if bound to the stimulus of the examiner's actions. |
| Echophenomena | Includes *echolalia*, in which the patient constantly repeats the examiner's utterances, and *echopraxia*, in which the patient spontaneously copies the examiner's movements or is unable to refrain from copying the examiner's test movements despite instructions to the contrary. |
| Automatic obedience | Includes *Mitgehen* ("going with"), in which the patient, despite instructions to the contrary, permits the examiner's light pressure to move his limbs into a new position (posture), which is then maintained by the patient despite instructions to the contrary; *Mitmachen* ("making with"), in which the patient cooperates to light pressure by the examiner despite instructions to the contrary, followed by a slow return to his previous position; and acquiescing to such demands as "stick your tongue out, I want to jab it with a pin." |
| Ambitendency | The patient appears motorically "stuck" in an indecisive, hesitant movement, resulting from the examiner verbally contradicting his own strong nonverbal signal, such as offering his hand as if to shake hands, while stating, "Don't shake my hand, I don't want you to shake it." |

(Pincus and Tucker, 1978; Benson, 1975; Hecaen and Albert, 1975), third ventricle tumors (Slater and Roth, 1969), or lesions of the reticular activating system and caudal hypothalamus (Solomon, 1975). Mutism, stereotypy, catalepsy, and automatic obedience also occur together more frequently than by chance (Abrams et al., 1979), correspond to the classic description of catatonia (Kahlbaum, 1973), and are associated with the diagnosis of mania (Abrams and Taylor, 1976; Taylor and Abrams, 1977; Abrams et al., 1979). Luria (1973) described several patients with catatonia-like symptoms after frontal lobe injury. Dogs with ablated frontal lobes also demonstrate many catatonic features (Pavlov, 1949; Anoklin, 1949). This relationship between frontal lobe lesions and catatonia-like behaviors is not surprising, since the frontal lobe is intimately involved in the regulation of motor activity (Luria, 1973). The frontal lobe signs of pathologic inertia (difficulty initiating motor acts or stopping them once started) and stimulus bound behavior (motor response to stimuli despite instructions to the contrary) may underlie all catatonic features.

Specific procedures to elicit catatonic signs are seldom part of the routine mental status examination. The examiner should, however, always test for catatonia when the following behaviors are observed: odd gaits inconsistent with known neurologic disease (e.g., tiptoe walking, hopping), standing in one place for prolonged periods, holding the arms up as if carrying something, shifting position when the examiner shifts position, repeating most of the examiner's questions before answering, responding to most of the examiner's questions with the same question (e.g., *Examiner:* How old are you? *Patient:* How old are *you?*), making odd hand or finger movements that are not typically dyskinetic, performing inconspicuous repetitive actions (e.g., making a series of clicking sounds before or after speaking, tapping or automatically touching objects while walking about), mutism, psychomotor retardation, speech that becomes progressively less voluble until it becomes a nonunderstandable mumble (prosectic speech).

Patients displaying one or more of these features while conversing with the examiner may allow themselves to be placed in odd postures; may be unable to resist the examiner moving his arms, despite instructions to the contrary; or may be unable to resist shaking the examiner's proffered hand, despite instructions to the contrary (automatic obedience). Some patients with catatonic features will automatically obey the examiner's request to stick their tongues out, despite being told that they will be jabbed with a sharp needle.

Patients with classic catatonic features are often misdiagnosed because of the false expectation that they must be mute and immobile. In fact, most patients with catatonic features speak and move about (Abrams and Taylor, 1976; Taylor and Abrams, 1977; Morrison, 1973; Kirby, 1913; Bonner and Kent, 1936; Kahlbaum, 1973). Because motor behavior is regulated by frontal lobe systems (Luria, 1973; Heilman and Valenstein, 1979), motor abnormalities, including the catatonic syndrome, severe hyperactivity, and stupor may reflect coarse frontal lobe disease. Table 27–2 lists some additional motor signs of frontal lobe dysfunction.

## FRONTAL LOBE MOTOR SIGNS AND BEHAVIORS

Patients with lesions within or near the lateral surface of the frontal lobes (convexity syndrome) (Luria, 1969, 1973; Hecaen and Albert, 1975; Heilman and Valenstein, 1979, pp. 360–412) often exhibit movements that are slow and reduced in frequency (motor inertia). Occasionally, they may remain in positions for prolonged periods (catalepsy) and may posture. A slight flexion at the waist, knees, and elbows is a typical body position of these patients. They occasionally move with a floppy, shuffling gait, progressively picking up steam only to slow gradually to a stop (glissando/deglissando gait). Unlike patients with Parkinson's disease, muscle tone is decreased and "pill-rolling" is not present. They may tend to walk close to walls (just touching them), rather than in the middle of the hallway, and may even follow architectural contours rather than take a direct route across open space. Most frontal lobe cognitive and soft neurologic signs can be observed in these patients, who may also be dyspraxic (gait, bucco-linguofacial, or ideomotor dyspraxias) and incontinent of urine.

A second frontal lobe syndrome is associated with dysfunction in the orbitomedial areas of the frontal lobes (orbitomedial syndrome). Some patients may be asthenic and

**Table 27–2   Frontal Lobe Motor Signs**

| Sign | Description |
|---|---|
| Motor impersistence | Inability to sustain simple motor tasks (e.g., making a fist, holding out an arm) for 20 seconds despite adequate sensory function and motor strength. If present only when eyes closed, may reflect parietal lobe dysfunction. |
| Motor perseveration | Unnecessary repetitions or maintenance of a simple movement. |
| Motor inertia | Inability or difficulty in starting or stopping a simple movement. |
| Poor rapid sequential fine movement | Inability to tap each finger, one at a time (little finger, ring finger, middle finger, forefinger, thumb), rapidly and in sequence. |
| Adventitious motor overflow | Choreiform movements and extraneous movements in body parts not involved in a specific movement (e.g., protruding the tongue while writing). |

easily fatigued, akinetic, and aphonic. They may have diminished wakefulness, be in an oneiroid (dreamlike, clouded) state or even stuporous. Some affectively intense patients are hyperactive and overresponsive to stimuli. They rapidly terminate one incomplete goal-directed behavior only to start another and may appear frenetic as they run about from one activity to another, never completing a task. They are strongly stimulus bound, distractible, intrusive, and importunate. They interrupt conversations and mimic the examiner's movements and comments. Such patients, despite repeated injunctions, continually enter a room in which a group of people are in conference or pull fire alarms or change channels continually on television sets simply because they see them. These patients may have uncontrollable, often fantastic confabulations, and when prevented from doing as they please, they may have violent outbursts.

## PARIETAL LOBE MOTOR SIGNS AND BEHAVIOR

Parietal lobe dysfunction is also associated with disorders in movement (Critchley, 1953; Luria, 1973; Heilman and Valenstein, 1979). Lesions of the dominant parietal lobe usually are associated with dyspraxias (ideomotor, kinesthetic) and motor (hypotonia, posturing, paucity of movement) deficits. Lesions of the nondominant parietal lobe are associated with constructional difficulties, dressing dyspraxia, and contralateral motor deficits. Table 27–3 lists some motor signs of parietal lobe dysfunction.

Other common motor symptoms of nervous system dysfunction include clumsiness or weakness of the extremities, tremors and involuntary movements, change in speech and difficulty in swallowing, loss of balance, symptoms of convulsive disorder, and paralysis.

**Table 27–3    Dyspraxias Associated with Parietal Lobe Dysfunction**

| Dyspraxia | Description |
| --- | --- |
| Ideomotor | Inability to perform simple motor tasks on command (e.g., demonstrate the use of a key, a hammer, scissors) despite understanding the task and having adequate motor strength and sensory function. Patient's attempts can range from awkwardness and lack of coordination to grossly nonfunctional movements and using body part as object (e.g., extending index finger as the key rather than using the index finger and thumb to turn the imaginary key). Ideomotor dyspraxia generally suggests dominant parietal lobe dysfunction. When it occurs in the nonpreferred hand only, it may indicate a disconnection syndrome. |
| Kinesthetic | Inability to position one's hands, arms, and legs on command or inability to copy the examiner's movements despite adequate understanding of the tasks, motor strength, and sensory function. Patient's attempts may be inaccurate or simply aborted as he seems unable to know what to do with his body to achieve the required positioning. Suggests dysfunction in the parietal lobe contralateral to the affected side. |
| Constructional | Inability to copy the outline of simple shapes despite adequate understanding of the task, motor strength, and sensory function. Patient's attempts may range from some distortion and rotation of the copy to total loss of its gestalt. Constructional difficulties generally suggest nondominant hemisphere dysfunction. When the performance with the nonpreferred hand is better than that of the preferred hand, the dysfunction may be in the dominant hemisphere or corpus callosum. |
| Dressing | Inability to dress oneself despite adequate understanding of the task, motor strength, and sensory function. Patient's attempts may range from putting clothing (e.g., robe) on backwards or upside down to being totally unable to maneuver the garment and his body into the proper positions for dressing. Suggests nondominant hemisphere dysfunction. |

## SPEECH

Motor speech functions localize primarily to Broca's area in the dominant hemisphere, the frontal cortex deep to Broca's area, and the supplementary motor cortex. The process of speech is a form of motor behavior always assessed in the mental status examination (Heilman and Valenstein, 1979).

Although the rate of speech may reflect cultural patterns, severe deviations can be readily observed. For example, slow or hesitant speech is characteristic of depression, altered states of consciousness, and certain coarse brain diseases in which the ability to select or express the proper words is defective (Benson, 1975, 1979; Roth, 1959; Levin and Switzer, 1962). Rapid speech is characteristic of anxiety states. When rapid speech is also pressured, it is a cardinal sign of mania (Taylor, 1981; Kraepelin, 1976).

The rhythm of speech is often disrupted in central nervous system disease. Scanning speech (in which word sounds are stretched, producing a slow, sliding cadence) is typical of multiple sclerosis (Levin and Switzer, 1962); mumble, hesitant speech is often heard in patients with Huntington's chorea (McHugh and Folstein, 1975); whereas staccato (i.e., abrupt, clipped) speech (both fast and slow) is often a sign of psychomotor epilepsy (Blumer, 1975).

## SPONTANEOUS ABNORMAL MOVEMENTS

Abnormal movements have long been recognized as a feature of mental disorder. Nineteenth- and early twentieth-century writers (Kraepelin, 1971; Bleuler, 1950; Hammond, 1973) have richly described patients with such hyperkinetic phenomena as rocking, twisting truncal movements, ballistic arm movements, athetoid finger and hand movements, shaking, nodding, facial twitching, forehead wrinkling, grimacing and pouting movements, stereotyped biting and chewing, clicking, flicking and licking of the tongue, rubbing, picking, kneading, tapping, grasping, and pulling behaviors. Patients were said to be uncoordinated, stiff, and fragmented in their movements with a loss of normal smooth-transition movements. Continuous grimacing and twisting of facial features and making snorting, gutteral, and clicking sounds were also thought to be common. Kraepelin believed that choreiform movements of the face and fingers were common in dementia praecox, and he (Kraepelin, 1971) and Bleuler (1950) each described dementia praecox patients to exhibit tremor, adiadochokinesia, ataxia (the cerebellar form of dementia praecox), grand mal seizures, transient paralysis after apoplectiform seizures, and wavering movements. The prevalence of these behaviors then and now is unknown but is probably highest among schizophrenics and the chronically ill (Kraepelin, 1971; Bleuler, 1950). In a given patient, these behaviors do not appear to change in character or frequency over time, although they appear to increase in frequency during stress and decrease in frequency during sleep (Jones, 1965; Yarden and Discipio, 1971). The high prevalence of these behaviors in patients in the pre-psychotropic drug era probably reflected the inclusion of patients with coarse brain disease among psychiatric patients, whereas the prevalence of these behaviors today reflects drug-induced dysfunction, as well as diagnostic heterogeneity.

## DRUG-INDUCED ABNORMAL MOVEMENTS

Virtually all psychotropic agents exert some influence on motor function (Goldman, 1961). Cyclic antidepressants and lithium salts have been associated with extrapyramidal syndromes (Jefferson, Greist, Ackerman, 1983; Baldessarini, 1980) and produce persistent, fine, and rapid tremors and coordination difficulties that can impair fine motor performance. Coarse tremors, ataxia, and myoclonus can occur after ingestion of toxic amounts of these compounds. Monoamine oxidase inhibitors may induce agitation. Anxiolytics, in large doses, can also induce ataxia, tremors, and myoclonus (Cohen, Pickar, Murphy, 1980). Neuroleptics, however, clearly have the most profound effect on motor behavior (Delay and Deniker, 1968).

Neuroleptics differ widely in potency and capacity to effect motor function. For example, the piperazine phenothiazines are 10 to 30 times as potent in inducing extrapyramidal signs as are other classes of phenothiazines (DiMascio, 1970; Domino, 1968). Parkinsonism is a common manifestation of this potency. Bradykinesia (i.e., decreased frequency of movement), the earliest and most common feature of this syndrome (Ayd, 1961; Haase and Janssen, 1965), is characterized by a bland, expressionless face, slow initiation of motor activity, loss of secondary movements (such as arm swing, which gives the patient a stiff, frozen appearance), and micrographia (handwriting becomes small and choppy). Bradykinesia is associated with muscle weakness and fatigue; muscle rigidity of the neck, trunk, and extremities; and cogwheeling (a delayed sign in which the examiner, as he flexes and extends the patient's arm at the elbow, feels the arm move in short, stop-and-go arcs, as if periodically stopped by the gears of a wheel). Also observed are postural difficulties, including a flexed posture and deficits in righting responses; a shuffling, propulsive gait; tremor at rest and during voluntary actions; pill-rolling at rest (uncommon in drug-induced states), and a fine perioral tremor (the rabbit syndrome) (Ayd, 1961; Schwab and England, 1968; Villeneuve, 1972). Drug-induced Parkinsonism usually begins within a few days of drug administration and seldom occurs for the first time after 3 months of treatment. Depending on the neuroleptic administered and the dose used, upward of 50 per cent of patients may be affected (Ayd, 1961). The very young, the very old, and women may be most susceptible (Ayd, 1961; Duvoism, 1968).

Drug-induced acute dystonias, sudden muscle spasms, usually begin within the first few days of neuroleptic treatment. They are dramatic, frightening to the patient, often painful, and may recur over several days before they are controlled. Young patients are most vulnerable to these reactions, which commonly include cramps and spasms of the muscles of the face, jaw, neck, throat, and tongue. Oculogyric crisis, blepharospasm, respiratory stridor with cyanosis, torticollis, and opisthotonos can occur, as well as slow, writhing movements of the extremities. Acute dyskinesias without severe muscle spasm can also occur early in treatment. These include tongue protrusion, lip smacking, chewing movements, blinking, athetosis of the fingers and toes, shoulder shrugging, and myoclonic movements of the head, neck, and extremities. The incidence of dystonias rises with the increased usage of high-potency neuroleptics (Ayd, 1961; Crane and Naranjo, 1971; Delay and Deniker, 1968).

Akathesia is a state of motor restlessness in which the patient is unable to sit, stand, or be still. It is usually associated with a subjective feeling of jitteriness and tension and may be mistaken for a spontaneous panic attack or an exacerbation of psychoses. Akathesia usually does not begin until several days of drug administration and continues to increase in incidence during the first several months of treatment. Its severity and duration is variable and its medical relationship to other drug-induced movements is unknown. Risk factors are unknown. The incidence is about 20 per cent (Ayd, 1961; Goldman, 1961).

Tardive dyskinesia, characterized by an extraordinary variety of abnormal movements, results from prolonged exposure to neuroleptics. Its onset is usually after many months or years of dosage and may become manifested only after dose reduction or termination of drug administration. Thirty per cent to 50 per cent of patients exposed to prolonged neuroleptic treatments may be affected. Causing factors have not been established, although elderly men, women, and patients with preexisting coarse brain conditions may be more vulnerable. Features of tardive dyskinesia include the buccolinguomasticatory syndrome (vermicular movements of the tongue on the floor of the mouth, protruding, twisting and curling tongue movements combined with pouting, sucking, and movements and bulging of the cheeks), choreiform and movements of the extremities (particularly the fingers), ballistic arm movements, gait and postural (lordosis, rocking and swaying, shifting of weight, struggling, pelvic thrusting, and rotary movements), grunting vocalizations, respiratory dyskinesias and chest heaving resulting in stridor and cyanosis, dysphagias, and symptoms exacerbate with stress and decrease with sleep or rest. Many patients seem unaware of their abnormal movement. Some appear to have associated cognitive impairment. Tardive dyskinesia appears to be irreversible (APA Task Force, 1980).

Drug-induced abnormal movements are strikingly similar to the spontaneous abnormal movements reported in patients during the pre-psychotropic drug era. Other than by history, there is no reliable way of discriminating the two phenomena.

## REFERENCES

Abrams R, Taylor MA: Catatonia: A prospective clinical study. Arch Gen Psychiatry 33:579–581, 1976.

Abrams R, Taylor MA, Stolurow KAC: Catatonia and mania: Patterns of cerebral dysfunction. Biol Psychiatry 14:111–117, 1979.

Anoklin PK: Problems in higher nervous activity. Izd. Akad. Med. Nauk USSR Moscow, 1949; cited in Luria AR: The Working Brain. New York, Basic Books, 1973, pp 89–90.

APA Task Force on Late Neurological Effects of Antipsychotic Drugs: American Psychiatric Association Task Force Report No. 18, Tardive Dyskinesia. Washington DC, American Psychiatric Association, 1980.

Ayd FJ Jr: A survey of drug-induced extrapyramidal reactions. JAMA 175:1054–1060, 1961.

Baldessarini RJ: Drugs and the treatment of psychiatric disorders, in Gilman AG, Goodman LS, Gilman A (eds): Goodman and Gilman's The Pharmacological Basis of Therapeutics, ed 6. New York, Macmillan, 1980, pp 391–447.

Benson DF: Disorders of verbal expression, in Benson DF, Blumer D (eds): Psychiatric Aspects of Neurologic Disease, vol 1. New York, Grune & Stratton, 1975, pp 121–136.

Benson F: Aphasia, alexia and agoraphobia. Clinical Neurology and Neurosurgery Monographs. Edinburgh, Churchill Livingstone, 1979.

Bleuler E: Dementia Praecox or the Group of Schizophrenias, trans Zinkin J. New York, International Universities Press, 1950.

Blumer D: Temporal lobe epilepsy, in Benson DF, Blumer D (eds): Psychiatric Aspects of Neurological Disease, vol 1. New York, Grune & Stratton, 1975, pp 171–198.

Bonner CA, Kent GH: Overlapping symptoms in catatonic excitement and manic excitement. Am J Psychiatry 92:1311–1322, 1936.

Carlson GA, Goodwin FK: The stages of mania. Arch Gen Psychiatry 28:221–228, 1973.

Cohen RM, Pickar D, Murphy DL: Myoclonus-associated hypomania during MAO-inhibitor treatment. Am J Psychiatry 137:105–106, 1980.

Crane GE: Persistent dyskinesia. Br J Psychiatry 122:395–405, 1973.

Crane GE, Naranjo ER: Motor disorders induced by neuroleptics. Arch Gen Psychiatry 24:179–184, 1971.

Critchley M: The Parietal Lobes. New York, Hafner Press, 1953.

Delay J, Deniker P: Drug-induced extrapyramidal syndromes, in Vinken PJ, Bruyn GW (eds): Handbook of Clinical Neurology, vol 6, Disease of the Basal Ganglia. Amsterdam, North-Holland, 1968, pp 248–266.

Derby IM: Manic-depressive "exhaustion" deaths. Psychiatr Q 7:436–449, 1933.

DiMascio A: Classification and overview of psychotropic drugs, in DiMascio A, Shader RI (eds): Clinical Handbook of Psychopharmacology. New York, Academic Press, 1970, pp 3–15.

Domino EE: Substituted phenothiazine antipsychotics, in Efron D (ed): Psychopharmacology: A Review of Progress 1957–1967. Washington, DC, US Public Health Service Publ. No. 1836, 1968, pp 1045–1056.

Duvoism RC: Neurological reactions to psychotropic drugs, in Efron D (ed): Psychopharmacology: A Review of Progress 1957–1967, Washington, DC, US Public Health Service Publ. No. 1836, 1968, pp 561–573.

Goldman D: Parkinsonism and related phenomena from administration of drugs: Their production and control under clinical conditions and possible relation to therapeutic effect. Rev Can Biol 20:549–560, 1961.

Haase HJ, Janssen PAH: The Action of Neuroleptic Drugs. Amsterdam, North-Holland, 1965.

Hammond WA: A Treatise on Insanity in Its Medical Relations, 1883. Mental Illness and Social Policy. The American Experience. New York, Arno Press, 1973.

Hearst ED, Munoz RA, Tuason VB: Catatonia: Its diagnostic validity. Dis Nerv Syst 32:453–456, 1971.

Hecaen H, Albert ML: Disorders of mental functioning related to frontal lobe pathology, in Benson DF, Blumer D (eds): Psychiatric Aspects of Neurologic Disease, vol 1. New York, Grune & Stratton, 1975, pp 137–149.

Heilman KM, Valenstein E (eds): Clinical Neuropsychology. New York, Oxford University Press, 1979.

Jefferson JW, Greist JH, Ackerman DL: Lithium Encyclopedia for Clinical Practice. Washington, DC, American Psychiatric Press, 1983, pp 186–192.

Jones IH: Observations on schizophrenic stereotypies. Compr Psychiatry 6:323–335, 1965.

Kahlbaum KL: Catatonia, trans Levy Y, Prider T. Baltimore, The Johns Hopkins University Press, 1973.

Kirby GH: The catatonic syndrome and its relation to manic-depressive insanity. J Nerv Ment Dis 40:694–704, 1913.

Kraepelin E: Dementia Praecox and Paraphrenia. Facsimile 1919 Edition, trans Barclay RM, Robertson GM. Huntington, NY, Robert E. Krieger, 1971.

Kraepelin E: Manic-Depressive Insanity and Paranoia. New York, Arno Press, 1976.

Levin N, Switzer M: Voice and Speech Disorders: Medical Aspects. Springfield, Il, CC Thomas, 1962.

Luria AR: Frontal lobe syndromes, in Vinken PJ, Bruyn GW (eds): Handbook of Clinical Neurology, vol 2. New York, Elsevier-North Holland, 1969, pp 725–775.

Luria AR: The Working Brain. New York, Basic Books, 1973, pp 89, 187–225.

McCusker EA, Rudick RA, Honch GW, Griggs RC: Recovery from the "locked-in" syndrome. Arch Neurol 39:145–147, 1982.

McHugh PR, Folstein MF: Psychiatric syndromes of Huntington's chorea. A clinical and phenomenological study, in Benson DF, Blumer D (eds): Psychiatric Aspects of Neurologic Disease, vol 1. New York, Grune & Stratton, 1975, pp 267–286.

Morrison JR: Catatonia: Retarded and excited types. Arch Gen Psychiatry 28:39–41, 1973.

Morrison JR: Catatonia: Prediction of outcome. Compr Psychiatry 15:317–324, 1974.

Paulson G, Gottlieb G: Developmental reflexes: The reappearance of foetal and neonatal reflexes in aged patients. Brain 91:37–52, 1968.

Pavlov IP: Complete Collected Works, vols 1–3, Izd. Akad. Med Nauk USSR, Moscow and Leningrad, 1949; cited in Luria AR: The Working Brain. New York, Basic Books, 1973, pp 89–90.

Pincus JH, Tucker GJ: Behavioral Neurology, ed 2. New York, Oxford University Press, 1978, pp 131–132.

Quitkin F, Rifkin A, Klein DF: Neurologic soft signs in schizophrenia and character disorders: Organicity in schizophrenia with premorbid asociality and emotionally unstable character disorders. Arch Gen Psychiatry 33:845–853, 1976.

Roth M: The phenomenology of depressive states. Can Psychiatr Assoc J 4:532–553, 1959.

Schwab RS, England AC: Parkinson syndromes due to various causes, in Vinken PJ, Bruyn GW (eds): Handbook of Clinical Neurology, vol 6, Disease of the Basal Ganglia. Amsterdam, North-Holland, 1968, pp 227–247.

Slater E, Roth M: Clinical Psychiatry. Baltimore, Williams & Wilkins, 1969, p 498.

Solomon S: Clinical neurology and pathophysiology, in Freedman AM, Kaplan HI, Sadock BJ (eds): Comprehensive Textbook of Psychiatry, vol 1, ed 2. Baltimore, Williams & Wilkins, 1975, p 250.

Spitzka EC: Insanity: Its Classification, Diagnosis and Treatment, 1887. Mental Illness and Social Policy. The American Experience. New York, Arno Press, 1973.

Taylor MA: The Neuropsychiatric Mental Status Examination. New York, SP Medical and Scientific Books, 1981.

Taylor MA, Abrams R: The phenomenology of mania: A new look at some old patients. Arch Gen Psychiatry 29:520–522, 1973.

Taylor MA, Abrams R: The prevalence and importance of catatonia in the manic phase of manic-depressive illness. Arch Gen Psychiatry 34:1223–1225, 1977.

Villeneuve A: The rabbit syndrome: A peculiar extrapyramidal reaction. Can Psychiatr Assoc J 17:2:SS69, 1972 (suppl).

Yarden PE, Discipio WJ: Abnormal movements and prognosis in schizophrenia. Am J Psychiatry 128:317–323, 1971.

# chapter 28

# PERSONALITY DISORDERS

*by* Bruce Pfohl, M.D.

## DEFINITION

Personality traits are defined in the *Diagnostic and Statistical Manual of Mental Disorders*, third edition (DSM-III), as "enduring patterns of perceiving, relating to, and thinking about the environment and oneself . . . [which] . . . are exhibited in a wide range of important social and personal contexts." A personality disorder (PD) exists when personality traits form a syndrome that results in distress or disability. There is a tendency for researchers who emphasize biologic and genetic influences on behavior to use the term character disorder and for those who emphasize learned aspects of behavior to use the term personality disorder.

## AXES, CATEGORIES, AND CLUSTERS

DSM-III defines five separate axes for coding psychiatric conditions. Axis I includes syndromes such as depression, schizophrenia, alcoholism, and mental retardation. Personality disorders and traits are coded under Axis II. Axis III covers physical disorders that are relevant to the understanding or management of psychiatric conditions. Axis IV provides a coding for severity of psychosocial stressors, and Axis V codes highest level of "adaptive functioning" in the past year. There are several justifications for providing a separate axis for personality

disorder. Taken individually, none are convincing. For example, the personality disorders are noted frequently to coexist with Axis I disorders. The use of a separate axis reminds the clinician that a patient with depression or panic disorder may also have personality features that cause distress or complicate treatment. However, the same argument could be raised in favor of creating a separate axis for substance abuse or sexual dysfunction. It is also argued that Axis II disorders are generally lifelong illnesses that affect many aspects of behavior, whereas Axis I disorders are episodic or circumscribed. However, Axis I disorders, such as somatization disorder and obsessive-compulsive disorder, are also lifelong disorders that affect many aspects of behavior. Cyclothymic disorder was considered a personality disorder in DSM-II but was moved to the affective disorder section of DSM-III, since data suggest that it is a variant of affective disorder. Schizotypal personality disorder is placed in Axis II, despite data suggesting that it may share a familial and genetic association with schizophrenia.

It is still unclear whether personality disorder is best conceptualized as a series of continuous dimensions or as discrete categories. DSM-III uses discrete categories, thus implying that personality traits tend to cluster in certain specific combinations rather than varying independently (orthogonally) from individual to individual. This may be true for patients with personality disorders even if it is not true for individuals with no mental illness. The choice of categories over dimensions has two advantages. Most clinicians have been trained to think in categories, and researchers can use the categories to define supposedly homogeneous groups for comparative studies. Even so, DSM-III does mention that the clinician may wish to rate relevant personality traits under Axis II even if no personality disorder is present.

Specific criteria are presented for 11 personality disorders plus a category labeled "atypical or mixed." With few exceptions, the 11 disorders are not mutually exclusive.

DSM-III organizes the 11 personality disorders into three clusters, as indicated in Table 28–1. The assignment of disorders to clusters is intuitive rather than empirical. Available data suggest that the distinction between clusters is blurred. For example, there is considerable diagnostic overlap between schizotypal, borderline, and avoidant personality disorders despite the fact that the three disorders fall into three separate clusters.

## RELIABILITY, VALIDITY, AND OVERLAP

The criteria for the 11 disorders were created by a committee, based on clinical experience and a minimum of data. The criteria are not strictly behavioral. The level of inference necessary to rate Axis II criteria is often higher than that required for rating Axis I criteria. This probably accounts for the relatively low interrater reliability of Axis II diagnoses. Kappa, a statistic that approaches 1.0 as interrater diagnostic agreement approaches perfection, was only 0.56

**TABLE 28–1   Personality Clusters Defined by DSM-III**

Cluster 1 (Odd or Eccentric)
| Paranoid | Schizotypal |
| Schizoid | |

Cluster 2 (Dramatic, Emotional, or Erratic)
| Histrionic | Narcissistic |
| Antisocial | Borderline |

Cluster 3 (Anxious or Fearful)
| Avoidant | Dependent |
| Compulsive | Passive-aggressive |

for presence or absence of any personality disorder during the DSM-III field trials (Spitzer, Forman, Nee, 1979). This compares with kappas of 0.69 for affective disorders and 0.81 for schizophrenia. The kappas for individual personality disorders appear to be rather low when the criteria are applied in the context of a typical clinical evaluation, although antisocial personality may be an exception (Mellsop, Varghese, Joshua, Hicks, 1982). It appears that reliability can be greatly improved through the use of a structured interview for personality disorder (Baron, Asnis, Gruen, 1981; Pfohl et al., 1986; Stangl, Pfohl, Zimmerman, Bowers, 1985).

The concept of personality disorder is based on the assumption that personality, or at least personality disorders, is stable over time. Although the diagnosis of antisocial personality has been stable over time, the temporal reliability of the other DSM-III personality disorders is still not established. There is reason for concern, since at least one study using a structured interview to assess International Classification of Diseases (ICD)-9 personality disorders found stability with respect to presence or absence of personality disorder but not with respect to specific personality disorder when patients were reassessed after a mean of 3 years (Tyrer, Strauss, Cicchetti, 1983b). Another report found fair stability over time for the diagnosis of borderline personality disorder (Pope, Jonas, Hudson, Cohen, Gunderson, 1983).

Table 28–2 indicates another problem with the DSM-III personality disorders. The table displays the results from the assessment of 131 individuals (primarily inpatients) who were assessed using the Structured Interview for DSM-III Personality Disorders (Pfohl, Stangl, Zimmerman, 1982). Sixty-seven (51 per cent) of the patients met criteria for at least one personality disorder. Of the 67 with at least one personality disorder, 36 (54 per cent) received two or more personality diagnoses. The 54 per cent figure was obtained despite DSM-III's exclusion of a diagnosis of passive-aggressive personality disorder if any other personality disorder is present. A similar high rate of multiple personality diagnoses has been confirmed by other investigators (Mellsop et al., 1982). It is interesting that a study using systematic categorical assess-

**TABLE 28–2   Cross-Tabulation of Patients with Personality Disorder Who Met Criteria for Other Personality Disorders**

| | Paranoid | Schizoid | Schizotypal | Histrionic | Narcissistic | Antisocial | Borderline | Avoidant | Dependent | Compulsive | Passive-aggressive |
|---|---|---|---|---|---|---|---|---|---|---|---|
| Paranoid | 1 | 0 | 0 | 0 | 0 | 0 | 0 | 0 | 0 | 0 | 0 |
| Schizoid | | 1 | 0 | 0 | 0 | 0 | 0 | 0 | 0 | 0 | 0 |
| Schizotypal | | | 12 | 4 | 1 | 1 | 6 | 7 | 0 | 2 | 6 |
| Histrionic | | | | 30 | 4 | 3 | 20 | 4 | 5 | 3 | 9 |
| Narcissistic | | | | | 5 | 0 | 4 | 1 | 0 | 1 | 1 |
| Antisocial | | | | | | 5 | 4 | 1 | 0 | 0 | 3 |
| Borderline | | | | | | | 29 | 7 | 2 | 2 | 12 |
| Avoidant | | | | | | | | 15 | 3 | 2 | 5 |
| Dependent | | | | | | | | | 17 | 1 | 3 |
| Compulsive | | | | | | | | | | 7 | 3 |
| Passive-aggressive* | | | | | | | | | | | 18 |

Based on a sample of 131 patients who received a structured interview.

* Ignores exclusive criteria.

ment of personality done almost two decades ago also pointed out a tendency for clinicians to ignore other personality diagnoses once one personality diagnosis was made (Lazare, Klerman, Armor, 1966).

The main diagonal of Table 28–2 indicates the number of patients who received each diagnosis. The rows and columns indicate the number of patients with each diagnosis who simultaneously met criteria for each of the other personality diagnoses. The tremendous overlap between borderline and histrionic personality disorder has been reported elsewhere (Pope et al., 1983). The overlap between narcissistic and borderline personality disorder is not surprising, given the criteria and theoretical concepts that they have in common (Akhtar and Thomson, 1982). Diagnostic overlap is also noted by several studies that use non–DSM-III criteria for borderline personality disorder. These studies use the Gunderson-Singer criteria for borderline (Gunderson and Singer, 1975), which are assessed by the Diagnostic Interview for Borderlines (DIB). The DIB criteria show considerable overlap with the DSM-III criteria for borderline (Loranger, Oldham, Russakoff, Susman, 1984). Akiskal (1981) reported 15 of 100 DIB borderline patients met criteria for Briquet's hysteria (somatization disorder) and 13 per cent met criteria for antisocial personality. These findings are supported by my own data (Table 28–2) and by Pope et al. (1983). Although borderline males may sometimes meet criteria for antisocial personality and borderline females may sometimes meet criteria for somatization disorder, it does not appear that either of these two diagnoses adequately capture the majority of patients identified by DSM-III borderline personality disorder.

Table 28–2 also indicates that more than half of the schizotypal patients also meet criteria for borderline and avoidant disorders. The accumulated evidence suggests that about half of schizotypal patients meet criteria for borderline personality disorder (Spitzer et al., 1979; Gunderson, Siever, Spaulding, 1983), but that the vast majority of DIB or DSM-III borderline patients do not meet criteria for schizotypal disorder (Akiskal, 1981; Pope et al., 1983). DSM-III does not allow the diagnosis of passive-aggressive personality disorder if other personality disorders are present. If passive-aggressive personality disorder were diagnosed even when other personality disorders are present, the frequency of diagnosis jumps from 3 to 18, as indicated in Table 28–2. It is clear that passive-aggressive behavior is common to many personality disorders. Table 28–2 indicates that few patients meet criteria for paranoid or schizoid personality disorder. Many of the patients who would fit the historical concept of schizoid personality disorder appear to be diagnosed instead as schizotypal or avoidant by DSM-III criteria. Because of the overlap of some diagnoses and the rarity of others, future editions of DSM may define a smaller number of personality disorders.

## COEXISTING AXIS I DISORDERS

Associations between Axis I and Axis II disorders have been examined by looking at the frequency with which they coexist in the same patient, as well as by examining that rate at which they coexist in different members of the same family. Tyrer, Casey, and Gall (1983a) have suggested that patients who were previously diagnosed with such labels as atypical depression or atypical anxiety disorder are often better categorized as patients who have an Axis I disorder in combination with a personality disorder.

The most frequent Axis I disorders to be examined in this regard are affective disorder and schizophrenia. A number of studies suggest that patients with depression frequently meet criteria for additional Axis II disorders. Studies using both DSM-III and non–DSM-III approaches to personality diagnoses suggest that the coexisting personality disorder may significantly influence response to treatment for the depression. A study of 78 nonpsychotic inpatients with major depression conducted by me and my colleagues found that 41 (53 per cent) met criteria for at least one DSM-III personality disorder, based on a structured interview (Pfohl et al., 1984). The most common personality diagnoses were borderline, histrionic, dependent, and avoidant. The patients with a concurrent personality disorder were much more likely to have first-degree relatives with alcoholism and much less likely to respond to antidepressant medication than were patients with depression only. A chart review study that applied DSM-III Axis II criteria less systematically also concluded that coexisting personality disorder predicts worse outcome for depression (Charney, Nelson, Quinlan, 1981). Lazare and Klerman (1968) studied a consecutive series of 35 depressed female inpatients and measured the frequency of hysterical personality disorder using some criteria that only roughly resembled the DSM-III criteria for histrionic personality disorder. They found that 15 (43 per cent) met their criteria for hysterical personality.

Those depressives with histrionic personality disorder were more likely to have alcoholic fathers and tended to respond more poorly to electroconvulsive therapy.

Tyrer, Alexander, Cicchetti, Cohen, and Remington (1979) used a structured interview to diagnose a series of neurotic depressive patients according to the ICD-9 classification of personality disorders. They found that one third of the depressives also met criteria for an ICD-9 personality disorder. Anancastic (compulsive) was the most common disorder, although passive dependent and schizoid personality disorders were also present in substantial numbers of depressives. They found that the presence of any concurrent personality disorder predicted a worse response to a trial of phenelzine (Tyrer et al., 1983a).

Although patients with depression plus personality disorder appear to do worse than patients with depression alone, patients with depression plus personality disorder may do better on followup than patients with personality disorder alone. At least that was the finding of two studies examining patients with borderline disorder (Pope et al., 1983; Cole et al., 1984). This finding may relate to the concept of subaffective dysthymia proposed by Akiskal and co-workers (1980, 1983). Akiskal has used response to antidepressant medications and electroencephalographic (EEG) studies to support his suggestion that patients with personality problems may fall into two types: those with chronic low-grade affective disorder predisposing to personality problems (subaffective dysthymia) and those with underlying personality problems leading to depression (character spectrum disorder). The former group responds well to tricyclic antidepressants. To date, there are no studies proving that this distinction can be made before treatment in a typical clinical setting.

The majority of studies of personality disorder and depression use various dimensional measures of personality based on self-report. A review of studies published before 1970 suggests that depressed patients are more likely to have premorbid personalities characterized by rigidity, compulsiveness, and dependency (Chodoff, 1972). A recurrent problem in the research on depression and personality disorder is the possibility that the depressive state is contaminating the personality trait measurement (Hirschfeld et al., 1983a; Liebowitz, Stallone, Dunner, Fieve, 1979b; Lumry, Gottesman, Tuason, 1982). One large study is available that attempts to avoid this bias by comparing 134 females who had recovered from depression with 272 female relatives who had never been depressed (Hirschfeld et al., 1983b). The recovered depressives were more introverted, submissive, passive, and dependent. Several studies suggest that depressed patients who score in the abnormal range on dimensional measures of personality have a worse outcome for the depression (Kerr, Schapira, Roth, Garside, 1970; Kerr, Roth, Schapira, Gurney, 1972; Weissman, Prusoff, Klerman, 1978).

Several studies are available that look at personality features in patients with anxiety. Roth, Gurney, Garside, and Kerr (1972) compared 62 depressed patients with 68 anxiety state patients. Most of the latter group (86 per cent) had panic attacks. Many had agoraphobia. Patients in the anxiety state group were much more likely than those in the depressed group to have personality disorder. The anxiety disorder patients were also twice as likely to have first-degree relatives with personality disorder. Personality was assessed in the patients using several dimensional instruments. The anxiety state patients were significantly worse than the depressives on measures of dependence, lack of confidence, hysterical traits, and hypersensitivity. Measures of solitariness and obsessional traits did not separate the two groups. Tyrer et al. (1983a) also found the rate of ICD-9 personality disorder seen in 94 patients with anxiety neurosis (48 per cent) to be higher than that seen in 144 patients with depressive neurosis (30 per cent). The most common ICD-9 personality disorder among the anxiety neurotics was passive-dependent disorder (26 per cent). Other studies using dimensional measure of personality find many more similarities than dissimilarities between anxious and depressed patients (Derogatis, Lipman, Covi, Rickels, 1972; Murray and Blackburn, 1974).

Obsessive-compulsive disorder is listed with the anxiety disorders in DSM-III. Available data support clinical experience that patients with obsessive-compulsive disorder frequently also meet criteria for compulsive personality disorder (Tyrer et al., 1983a; Black, 1974).

The study of premorbid personality in schizophrenics is difficult, since the illness usually exhibits an insidious onset. Zigler, Glick, and March (1979) used chart review information from family interviews to rate the premorbid social functioning of 92 schizophrenics and found them much less "socially competent" than depressed and neurotic control groups. A prospective study of children of schizophrenic mothers found that children who later developed schizophrenia were more likely to have premorbid personality features such as defective emotional rapport and formal cognitive disturbance (Parnas, Schulsinger, Schulsinger, Mednick, Teasdale, 1982). Another chart review study of 51 hebephrenic schizophrenics found that 18 (35 per cent) appeared to have some type of premorbid personality disorder (Pfohl and Winokur, 1983). Eleven of these met criteria approximating DSM-III schizoid personality disorder. It would be a mistake to assume the converse, that patients with schizoid personality who lack social competence are at high risk for developing schizophrenia. Historically, borderline personality patients were considered at high risk for schizophrenia (Stone, 1979), but this is not supported by any of the followup studies using criteria similar to DSM-III for borderline personality disorder (Werble, 1970; Carpenter and Gunderson, 1977; Pope et al., 1983).

Few studies are currently available that examine patients with a specific personality disorder to see what Axis I disorders might coexist. Pope et al. (1983) examined the charts of 33 inpatients who met DSM-III criteria for borderline personality disorder and found that 16 (48 per cent) met criteria for major affective disorder, including 3 cases that also had a history of mania. Baxter, Edell, Gerner, Fairbanks, and Gwirtsman (1984) found that 52 per cent of 27 borderline inpatients also met criteria for major depression. A similar association has been reported elsewhere (Akiskal, 1981; Carroll et al., 1981b). A weak association between borderline personality and somatization disorder was noted earlier. A substantial number of borderline patients also appear to meet criteria for substance abuse (Akiskal, 1981; Andrulonis et al., 1981; Pope et al., 1983). Nace, Saxon, and Shore (1983) reported that 13 per cent of 94 alcoholic inpatients also met criteria for DIB borderline personality disorder. Numerous studies suggest that many patients with antisocial personality also frequently met criteria for depression and alcoholism (see Chapters 5 and 13). Epidemiologic studies of personality disorder are clearly needed, since patients with multiple disorders are likely to be overrepresented in both clinic and hospital populations.

## ETIOLOGY

### Psychosocial Factors

Psychoanalytic theory regarding personality disorder is difficult to summarize because of a lack of systematic development and a wide diversity of opinion (Auchincloss and Michels, 1983). Even so, several of the DSM-III personality disorders have historical roots in the psychoanalytic trichotomy of personality types of oral, anal, and phallic character types. Fixation at the oral stage was said to result in a personality characterized by demanding and dependent behavior, which is captured, to some degree, by the DSM-III dependent and passive-aggressive personality disorder. Fixation at the anal stage led to a personality type that is similar to the DSM-III compulsive personality disorder (Pollak, 1979). Fixation at the phallic stage led to lack of capacity for intimate relationships and shallowness, which relates to DSM-III histrionic personality (Lazare, 1971). Lazare et al. (1966) investigated the various traits that were traditionally considered characteristic of each of the three personality types, using a self-report instrument that they constructed. Using a factor analysis, they found that three factors could be derived that corresponded to oral (dependent), obsessive (anal), and hysterical (phallic) personality patterns. Attempts to replicate this factor structure in other patient populations have generally supported the original finding (Lazare, Klerman, Armor, 1970; Paykel and Prusoff, 1973; Torgersen and Psychol, 1980).

Freud (1963) defined the anal character type as typified by such traits as obstinacy (stubborn, rigid, overconscientious), parsimony (stingy with time and money), and orderliness (perfectionistic, lives by strict routine). The concept clearly has much in common with the DSM-III compulsive personality. The term anal was used, since the disorder was said to arise from conflicts with parents during the anal stage of psychosexual development. Too early toilet training and too harsh punishment for failure to control the bowels as the parents wished predisposed toward this personality type. Freud even allowed for the possibility that a genetic predisposition characterized by excessive sensitivity to erotic stimulation in the anal area might also play a role in the pathogenesis of this disorder. A number of studies have attempted to validate empirically the connection between toilet training and anal (compulsive) personality. Pollak (1979) reviews more than a dozen studies that attempt to assess independently anal character and childhood experience with toilet training. Some studies make use of direct interview of the patient's mother. Pollak concludes that the connection between toilet training and so-called anal personality is not supported by the facts.

Those patients who were called borderline by analytic writers in the past would probably fall into several DSM-III Axis II categories, including schizoid, schizotypal, and borderline. Different authors have clearly used the term in different ways. Analytically, the borderline patient was considered to have a fragile ego (Stone, 1979). Rather than representing a particular type of personality, borderlines were seen as having a fragile personality organization that could break down. Thus psychotic experiences might result from stress or even psychoanalysis. Conceptually, borderline personality disorder is supposed to be a much severer personality disorder than histrionic personality disorder, despite the diagnostic overlap noted earlier. This overlap may be due to the failure of the DSM-III criteria for histrionic personality disorder to discriminate out the classic higher-functioning type of hysterical patient who is said to function well except for an inability to handle social and sexual intimacy (Lazare, 1971).

Analytic theories of etiology of borderline personality encompass seeming opposites from overprotective mothering (Levy, 1943; Masterson, 1976) to neglectful mothering (Guntrip, 1969; Gunderson and Englund, 1981). Some empirical studies are available that lend support to these explanations. Gunderson, Kerr, and Woods (1980) abstracted family interview information from borderline patients and a like number of "neurotics" and paranoid schizophrenics. The diagnostic criteria for borderline were close to those in DSM-III. Blind ratings of more than 72 family characteristics showed families of borderline to be distinguishable by "the rigid tightness of the marital bond to the exclusion of the attention, support or protection of the children." The authors acknowledge methodological problems. Similar results, however, were obtained by Frank and Paris (1981), who used Gunderson's DIB criteria to identify borderline patients, which were compared with neurotic patients and normal controls. All subjects were female. On a systematic self-report scale, the borderline women recalled less approval and more disinterest from their fathers in response to those childhood behaviors that could be described as moves toward independence (autonomy). Paternal response to dependent behavior and maternal response to either type of behavior did not separate borderlines from other groups. Soloff and Millward (1983) present some empirical support for the presence of overinvolved mothers and underinvolved fathers in borderline PD.

Studies such as these that investigate parenting behavior as it relates to personality diagnoses are few in number and hardly definitive. Even so, they do represent a willingness to investigate empirically what has too long been buried in layers of theory without recourse to scientific hypothesis testing. Future studies will need to take a number of issues into account, including retrospective falsification of reports of past behavior, the impact of the child's personality on the parents' behavior, and the possibility of genetic factors that might influence both parenting style and personality disorder in the offspring. Because the concordance rate for personality disorder among identical twins is not 100 per cent, it makes sense to give some attention to psychosocial factors. What those psychosocial factors are or how much of the variance they might explain is not known.

## Genetic Factors

The same questions about nature and nurture that surround research into Axis I dis-

orders also apply to Axis II. Twin studies and adoption studies are the most useful research designs for separating out the effects of environment and heredity. With a few exceptions, these designs have not been applied to DSM-III personality disorders. Several studies have examined the relative contribution of nature vs. nurture, using dimensional measures of personality in series of twins and siblings. Virtually all of them find that genetic factors explain a substantial portion of the variance for personality, including such dimensions as extroversion, neuroticism and anxiety, "capacity to mobilize," and approach-withdrawal (Rutter, Korn, Birch, 1963; Young, Fenton, Lader, 1971; Fuller and Thompson, 1978; Lochlin, 1982; Cattell, Vaughan, Schuerger, Rao, 1982). An association between blood group antigens and personality dimensions has been reported by several investigators as support for the presence of genetic factors (Angst and Maurer-Groeli, 1974; Eysenck, 1977, 1982; Jogawar, 1984).

Twin study methodology has been applied to the Lazare et al. (1970) measure of oral (dependency), obsessive, and hysterical traits, described earlier. Torgersen and Psychol (1980) examined correlations for these traits in a series of 50 monozygotic twins and 49 dizygotic twins. Some of the twins were identified by the fact that they had been previously hospitalized for a neurotic illness. Correlations between monozygotic female cotwins were above 0.5 for all three traits. Correlations for dizygotic female cotwins was low for oral and hysterical traits; the heritability index reached statistical significance only for the latter. Correlations between female dizygotic cotwins on obsessive traits was high (0.42), suggesting that a common childhood environment was influential in determining obsessionality in female cotwins. Correlations between monozygotic male cotwins was high only in the case of oral traits. The heritability of this trait was statistically significant. The correlation for hysterical traits among male dyzygotic cotwins was sufficiently high (0.47), suggesting that a common childhood environment played an important role in this trait.

To what extent the dimensions examined in these studies represent components of DSM-III Axis II disorders is not clear; nor is it clear whether these dimensions might be measuring symptoms of Axis I disorders. It is also possible that the hereditability estimates based on meaurement of personality traits in normal individuals is not applicable to the more pathologic levels of traits seen in individuals labeled as having personality disorder. For example, in the general population, parents' Wechsler Adult Intelligence Scale IQ scores show a significant correlation with their children's IQ scores. However, in a sample of parents and children where 20 per cent of the children have Down's syndrome, there would be a poor correlation between parents' and children's IQ scores. This results from the fact that risk for Down's syndrome is not correlated with parental IQ.

A number of twin and adoption studies examine personality factors that may be genetically associated with schizophrenia in a family member. Before DSM-III, Kety, Rosenthal, Wender, and Schulsinger (1971) suggested that schizophrenia may be genetically related to a spectrum of personality disorders. Later, DSM-III criteria for both paranoid and schizotypal personality disorder were retrospectively applied to the Kety et al. data. Schizotypal personality was found in 11 (10.5 per cent) of 105 biologic relatives of schizophrenics, 0 of 48 adoptive relatives, and 2 (1.5 per cent) of 138 controls (Kendler, Gruenberg, Strauss, 1981). Paranoid personality disorder was found in 4 (3.8 per cent) of 105 biologic relatives, in 1 of the adoptive relatives, and in none of the control relatives (Kendler and Gruenberg, 1982). The data were subsequently reanalyzed by applying DSM-III criteria for schizophrenia to the probands (Kendler and Gruenberg, 1984). Similar results for both schizotypal and paranoid personality disorder were again obtained. In addition, biologic relatives of adoptees with schizophrenia were at higher risk for schizotypal personality than were relatives of adoptees with nonschizophrenic psychoses (14.3 per cent vs. 0 per cent).

Torgersen and Psychol (1984) studied a series of monozygotic and dizygotic twins in which at least one cotwin had either schizotypal personality or borderline personality, or both. Seven of 25 monozygotic twins vs. 1 of 34 dizygotic twins were concordant for schizotypal personality. This suggests that genetics are involved in the etiology of schizotypal disorder. Because the only concordant cases among 10 cotwins with borderline personality were among dizygotic twins, a genetic link was not supported for borderline personality. None of the cotwins had schizophrenia. Affective disorder was equally common in both cotwins and controls. The authors of this study concur with Gunderson et al. (1983) in finding that psychotic-like symptoms in the definition of schizotypal personality did not contribute much to the identification of illness in relatives. Specifically, soft perceptual distortions, magical thinking, and derealization did not help to identify the genetic association in most cases. In contrast, social isolation, odd appearance, and constricted affect were characteristic of the affected relatives. The description of relatives of schizophrenics suggests that some might meet criteria for avoidant personality disorder; however, no studies are currently available that examine for this disorder.

As noted in Chapter 15, antisocial personality disorder has been the subject of several adoption studies (Schulsinger, 1972; Crowe, 1974), which all confirm a strong genetic factor in the etiology.

## FAMILIAL ASSOCIATIONS

Although adoption and twin studies can sort out familial from genetic factors in the etiology of personality disorder, such studies are not available for most of the DSM-III personality disorders. Even so, there is a growing number of studies examining the rates of Axis I and Axis II disorders in families of patients with personality disorder. A familial association of this type can result from the transmission of a relevant genetic factor. Another possibility is that the psychiatric illness diagnosed in one family member contributes to a family environment that predisposes to psychiatric illness in other family members.

There are now several studies that examine the rate of Axis I disorders in first-degree relatives of borderlines using some type of control group. Loranger, Oldham, and Tulis (1982) used a chart review to study first-degree relatives of 83 borderline patients, 100 schizophrenics, and 100 bipolar patients. Morbidity risk for major depression among relatives of borderline patients (6 per cent) differed significantly from that seen in relatives of schizophrenics (2 per cent) but was similar to that seen in relatives of bipolar patients (7 per cent). Morbidity risk for schizophrenia was 0 per cent, 3 per cent, and 0.3 per cent among relatives of borderline, schizophrenic, and bipolar patients, respectively. Using rather broad family history criteria for diagnosing borderline personality, the morbidity risk for borderline personality was 12 per cent among first-degree relatives of borderline patients and less than 2 per cent in the other two groups. Pope et al. (1983) also found that borderline personality tended to run in families. In addition, both histrionic and antisocial personality disorder were common among first-degree relatives of borderline probands.

The familial link between borderline personality and affective disorder described in the Loranger et al. (1982) study is still not clearly established. Soloff and Millward (1983) reported that families of borderlines were more likely to have depression than were families of schizophrenics, but interpretation of this study is confounded by several methodological problems. Pope et al. (1983) found the prevalence for major affective disorder among relatives of borderline patients (6 per cent) to be no different than that found among relatives of bipolar patients (8 per cent) yet significantly higher than that found among relatives of schizophrenic patients (0.6 per cent). However, when borderline probands without a concurrent major depression were examined separately, no familial association with affective disorder was observed. This suggests the possibility that there are two types of borderlines: one type that is related to affective disorder and one that is not. Despite the lack of clarity regarding affective disorders, these studies and several others form a strong consensus that there is no association between borderline personality disorder and schizophrenia (Akiskal, 1981; Andrulonis et al., 1981; Stone, 1979).

Several studies suggest that many borderline patients have first-degree relatives with alcoholism or substance abuse (Andrulonis et al., 1981; Akiskal, 1981; Soloff and Millward, 1983; Pope et al., 1983). However, none have demonstrated that alcoholism is significantly more common among relatives of borderlines than among relatives of other psychiatric patients. While this question awaits more data, it is reasonable to ask whether the putative familial link between borderline personality and alcoholism might actually be explained by the frequent coexistence of borderline personality with either depression or alcoholism in the proband. The study by Pope et al. (1983) suggests that coexisting depression does not explain such an association. Pope et al. found alcoholism to be about equally common among first-degree relatives of borderline probands and with borderline probands without a concurrent depression. Even after discarding all probands who had ever met criteria for alcoholism or antisocial personality, Pfohl et al. (1984) found that first-degree relatives of patients with personality disorder (mostly borderline) plus depression were three times more likely to suffer from alcoholism than were relatives of depressed patients with no personality disorder. This suggests the interesting possibility that the familial association between depression and alcoholism is actually explained by the frequent coexistence of depression with personality disorder. Perhaps the risk of alcoholism is only increased among relatives of patients with both depression and personality disorder and not among relatives of patients with depression alone.

Several studies using criteria roughly similar to DSM-III compulsive personality find that compulsive personality tends to run in families and to be more frequent in families of patients with obsessive-compulsive disorder (Lewis, 1936; Hays, 1972).

## BIOCHEMICAL ABNORMALITIES

Low platelet monoamine oxidase (MAO) activity has been reported in patients with schizophrenia (Buchsbaum, Coursey, Murphy, 1976; Wyatt, Steven, Murphy, 1979) and affective disorder (Murphy and Weiss, 1972), although the literature is not unanimous (Reveley, Glover, Sandler, Coppen, 1981). Baron, Levitt, and Perlman (1980) measured platelet MAO activity in a series of random nonpatient volunteers. Structured diagnostic interviews were given to 13 individuals who scored two standard deviations below the mean and 15 individuals who scored two standard deviations above the mean on platelet MAO activity. Nine (69 per cent) of the low platelet MAO individuals met criteria for schizotypal personality disorder. None of the high platelet MAO individuals met criteria. This study has not been replicated, although others have reported an association between platelet MAO activity and personality traits, such as extroversion and attention seeking (Murphy et al., 1977; Perris et al., 1981; Gattaz and Beckman, 1981; Abou-Saleh, 1983). More recently, Baron, Asnis, Gruen, and Levitt (1983) have examined plasma amine oxidase (PAO) activity in relatives of schizophrenics. They report a decrease in PAO activity in both schizophrenics and relatives with schizotypal personality. These studies serve to strengthen evidence for a link between schizophrenia and schizotypal personality.

Cerebrospinal fluid (CSF) 5-hydroxyindoleacetic acid (5-HIAA), a metabolite of serotonin, has been reported to be unchanged in schizophrenia and low in patients with affective disorders (Banki and Arato, 1983). It has also been reported to be low in suicide attempters with or without major depression (Traskman, Asberg, Bertilsson, Sjostrand, 1981). Brown et al. (1982) examined CSF 5-HIAA in a series of 12 patients with borderline personality who had no history of affective disorder or alcoholism. They found CSF 5-HIAA negatively correlated with several measures of aggression and past history of suicide attempts. Banki and Arato (1983) examined CSF 5-HIAA in 45 women inpatients whose diagnoses included alcohol dependence, depression, and schizophrenia. CSF 5-HIAA levels were not correlated with diagnosis but were inversely correlated with the personality trait validity. Patients with high validity have high energy and may lack caution. The presence of a personality trait that cuts across several diagnoses does give some support to the concept of multiaxial diagnosis.

The failure of patients with depression to suppress serum cortisol in response to the overnight dexamethasone suppression test (DST) has been widely reported (Carroll et al., 1981; Schlesser, Winokur, Sherman, 1979). Pfohl et al. (1984) found that depressed patients with a concurrent personality disorder were significantly less likely to be DST nonsuppressors than were patients with depression alone. Several authors report high rates of DST nonsuppression in borderline patients (Carroll et al., 1981; Sternbach, Fleming, Extein, Pottash, Gold, 1983; Baxter et al., 1984). However, others do not (Soloff, Anselm, Nathan, 1982; Pfohl et al., 1984). It appears that patients with borderline personality combined with depression are the ones most likely to be nonsuppressors (Baxter et al., 1984). Banki and Arato (1983) looked for and failed to find any association between the DST and several personality dimensions.

Smooth pursuit eye movement (SPEM) has been found to be abnormal in more than half of all schizophrenic patients (Holzman et al., 1974; Shagass, Amadeo, Overton, 1974; Latham, Holzman, Manschreck, 1981). SPEM is usually assessed by some type of device that measures eye movement while the subject tracks the course of a swinging pendulum. SPEM has been shown to be abnormal in relatives of schizophrenics (Holzman et al., 1974) and is clearly an inherited trait (Holzman et al., 1980; Iacono and Lykken, 1979). SPEM is apparently also abnormal in some patients with affective disorder (Levin, Lopton, Holzman, 1981). Siever et al. (1982) compared nonpatient college students with poor SPEM scores (low-accuracy trackers) with students who scored in the normal range. They found that the low-accuracy trackers could be differentiated on several traits, including social introversion, poor self-concept, fewer heterosexual contacts, and higher scores on the psychopathic and schizophrenia scales of the Minnesota Multiphasic Personality Inventory (MMPI). They also noted no correlation between SPEM and platelet MAO activity. They speculated that SPEM may be an index of the ability to inhibit "neuronal noise" when focusing on a task.

Electroencephalographic abnormalities have been reported in antisocial personality for many years. The reported abnormalities are most often slow wave activity (Ellingson, 1954; Hare, 1970). More recently, Snyder and Pitts (1984) have reported on a series of 37 borderlines who met DSM-III criteria. Cases with antisocial personality were excluded, as were cases with other Axis I diagnoses, such as depression or recent alcoholism or drug abuse. Cases were compared with 31 males with dysthymic disorder. Fourteen (38 per cent) of the borderline patients had at least marginal EEG abnormalities. Half of these were definitely abnormal. Only 19 per cent of the dysthymic patients had EEG abnormalities—all were only marginal. Slow wave activity was the most common abnormality. Some authors have suggested that some borderline patients might actually be manifesting characterological changes associated with minimal brain dysfunction (Andrulonis et al., 1981). Akiskal (1981) has reported decreased rapid-eye-movement latency in the EEG sleep pattern of a sample of borderline patients who were not acutely depressed. More recently, Siegel, Waldo, Mizner, Adler, and Freedman (1984) have reported that abnormalities in auditory evoked responses, as measured by summation of multiple EEG records, might also correlate with certain personality traits, such as the hypochondriasis, hysteria, and psychoasthenia, and schizophrenia scales of the MMPI.

Many of the laboratory abnormalities await replication. Many need to be reexamined in light of the full range of DSM-III Axis II criteria. Although the findings are not yet ready for application to clinical diagnosis of personality disorder, it is likely that these or similar biologic tests may play a role in personality evaluation in future years.

## DIFFERENTIAL DIAGNOSIS

Personality diagnoses should generally be considered only after a careful differential diagnosis of Axis I. An appreciation for Axis I problems allows the clinician to consider whether current or past examples of behavior reflect the patient's usual personality. Personality assessment becomes particularly difficult if the patient is currently suffering from an episode of major depression or the effects of some acute crises, such as an adjustment disorder. Interviewing a knowledgeable informant or simply having repeated contact with the patient over time can help sort out these issues. In the case of schizophrenia, no personality diagnosis is made unless the personality disorder clearly preceded the onset of schizophrenia. In the case of Axis I disorders, which are often chronic, such as dysthymia and agoraphobia, a concurrent personality disorder is usually diagnosed if criteria are met.

A common error in the use of Axis II is to use the category of "mixed personality disorder" when criteria for multiple personality disorders are present. Sometimes the "mixed" category is used because the clinician does not have the time or interest to sort out which personality disorders are present. Both uses of this term are incorrect, according to DSM-III. If patients meet criteria for several personality disorders, then all should be noted on Axis II, except when specific exclusion criteria are given. As noted earlier, many clinicians stop with the first personality disorder that seems to fit the patient. This leads to a situation in which differences in Axis II diagnoses become a function of the clinician's favorite disorder rather than any true distinction between patients. In cases where limitations in time or information prevent precise determination of the patient's diagnoses, it is preferable to simply describe the traits or behaviors in a short narrative description rather than to use automatically the term mixed personality disorder.

Medical students and residents often have difficulty deciding what questions to ask to assess Axis II. The following questions are designed to screen for major personality problems. If the answer to a question is positive, the patient should be encouraged to elaborate or provide examples. Ideally, a knowledgeable informant should be asked many of the same questions about the patient if a personality disorder is suspected.

### Social Interaction

Some people enjoy being the center of attention. Others prefer not to be noticed. How would you describe yourself? Can you think of any time that you did something risky or outrageous just to get noticed? Have you taken chances out of sheer boredom? Have you found that it is better not to let people get to know you too well? (*Remember to ask for elaboration or examples whenever the patient answers affirmatively.*)

### Confidence

What is your usual level of self-confidence? Do you ever pretend to be something that you are not just to impress people? Do you find that your opinions keep changing so much that you are not sure what you believe anymore? Have you worried that others criticize you behind your back? Are your feelings easily hurt?

### Irritability

What does it take to get you very angry? What are you like when you are angry? Do you let people know? Do you break things? Hit people? What kind of things make you jealous?

### Compulsivity

Are you perfectionistic? Do you often worry about details—want everything arranged just so? Do you get so caught up in your work that you have little time for friends or leisure activities?

### Friendships

Do you have any close friends in whom you confide? Describe who they are. What do you admire about them? Do you dislike anything about them? Can you describe any situations in which friends let you down or betrayed you?

### Dependency

When you have an important decision to make, is there someone you rely on to tell you what to do? Examples? Have you ever been physically or emotionally abused by someone that you depended on? Tell me about that.

### Manipulation

If you are upset with someone, are you more likely to tell them or keep it bottled up inside? Can you think of situations in which you got even with someone by "forgetting" to do something they wanted you to do? . . . by dawdling or pretending to make mistakes? Can you describe any situations in which you decided that misleading people was necessary to get something important?

If the answers to these questions indicate problems, the specific criteria for Axis II disorders should be reviewed. It may then be necessary to return to the patient or a knowledgeable informant to clarify specific points required by the criteria.

## PSYCHOPHARMACOLOGIC TREATMENT

The majority of patients with personality disorder probably never seek treatment. Many patients with schizotypal or compulsive personality, for example, are probably content with their life-style. Personality disorder is, by definition, a lifelong pattern of behavior. If an individual with personality disorder does seek treatment, the first step must be to investigate whether a more acute Axis I disorder, such as major depression, might not be responsible. As noted earlier, Axis I disorders are often more resistant to treatment when accompanied by a personality disorder (Kerr, Schapira, Roth, Gar-

side, 1970; Weissman et al., 1978; Tyrer et al., 1983a; Carroll et al., 1981; Pope et al., 1983; Pfohl et al., 1984). On the other hand, patients with personality disorder plus an Axis I disorder appear to have greater potential for improvement than do patients with personality disorder alone (Akiskal et al., 1980; Pope et al., 1983; Cole et al., 1984). If a patient displays an Axis I disorder, such as major depression, panic disorder, agoraphobia, or so-called brief reactive psychosis, then the pharmacologic treatment generally recommended for those disorders should generally be considered.

The majority of drug treatment studies of personality disorder involve either borderline or antisocial personality. Antisocial personality is considered in Chapter 15. Because many borderline patients have a history of drug abuse, such agents as amphetamines, barbiturates, and benzodiazepines should be avoided. Because suicide attempts also are common, it may be necessary to give prescriptions for shorter durations with weekly refills or admit the patient to the hospital for a drug trial. Several reports suggest that tricyclic antidepressants (Cole et al., 1984; Pope et al., 1983) or lithium (Rifkin et al., 1972) can be effective in stabilizing mood and behavior in borderlines. Many of the responders appear to have diagnosable affective disorder on Axis I. Low-dose neuroleptics have also been found to be efficacious in some studies (Brinkely et al., 1979; Leone, 1982). Before making the decision to put any patient on long-term neuroleptics, there should be clear evidence that significant symptoms recur if the medication is withdrawn or replaced with some other medication that is less likely to cause tardive dyskinesia. Ellison and Adler (1984) have recently reviewed pharmacologic approaches to borderline personality and related personality disorders.

The operational criteria provided for Axis II in DSM-III make drug treatment trials for specific personality disorders feasible. If different personality disorders are found to respond differentially to pharmacologic agents, a much needed validation of the various disorders will have been provided. Given the frequency with which Axis I disorders appear to complicate the personality disorder presentation, this may not be easy to accomplish.

The issues and controversies surrounding the psychotherapy of personality disorders are the same as the issues and controversies surrounding psychotherapy in general. Opinions range from those who believe that personality disorders are the main indication for psychoanalysis (Auchincloss and Michels, 1983) to those who believe that psychotherapy can make some personality disorders worse (Stone, 1979). A review of psychotherapeutic approaches to personality disorder is provided by Frosch (1983).

Patients with borderline, histrionic, antisocial, and passive-aggressive traits may be particularly likely to evoke frustration and anger in the therapist. Such irritation often results when the therapist becomes the victim of the manipulation and rapid shifts from overidealization to devaluation that characterize many personality disorders. The patients are frequently unaware of how their own behavior contributes to their problems.

It is often necessary to establish clear ground rules. The therapist may need to set up guidelines to limit telephone calls to the home or office. The skilled therapist learns simultaneously to reassure the patient that he or she will continue to be available but that this availability has certain constraints and limits that both patient and therapist must observe. Although the therapist may become angry with the patient, it is seldom appropriate to communicate this anger directly to the patient. On the other hand, it may be productive to point out specific behaviors and ask the patient to consider what types of reactions such behavior may be eliciting from those around them. It may be possible for the patient to recognize certain problem behaviors and rehearse alternatives.

Although certain schools of thought regarding psychotherapy support the notion that basic personality structure can be changed, the genetic and biochemical data cited earlier suggest that there are probably severe limitations to what psychotherapy can accomplish. The DSM-III criteria for personality disorder provide a new approach to assessing personality that is only now being applied to psychotherapy research. At present, most therapists specializing in psychotherapy, as well as most therapists specializing in psychopharmacology, seem to agree that the personality disorders are among the most resistant psychiatric disorders to treat. Certainly these disorders cause sufficient problems for both patients and those around them to justify a great deal of further research.

## REFERENCES

Abou-Saleh MT: Platelet MAO, personality and response to lithium prophylaxis. J Affect Disord 5:55–65, 1983.

Akhtar S, Thomson JA: Overview: Narcissistic personality disorder. Am J Psychiatry 139:12–20, 1982.

Akiskal HS: Subaffective disorders: Dysthymic, cyclothymic, and bipolar II disorders in the borderline realm. Psychiatr Clin North Am 4:25–46, 1981.

Akiskal HS: Dysthymic disorder: Psychopathology of proposed chronic depressive subtypes. Am J Psychiatry 140:11–20, 1983.

Akiskal HS, Rosenthal TL, Haykal RF, Lemmi H, Rosenthal RH, Scott-Strauss A: Characterological depressions: Clinical and sleep EEG findings separating "subaffective dysthymias" from "character spectrum disorders." Arch Gen Psychiatry 37:777–783, 1980.

Andrulonis PA, Glueck BC, Stroebel CF, Vogel NG, Shapiro AL, Aldridge DM: Organic brain dysfunction and the borderline syndrome. Psychiatr Clin North Am 4:47–66, 1981.

Angst J, Maurer-Groeli YA: Blutgruppen und personlichkeit. Arch Psychiatr Nervenkr 218:291–300, 1974.

Auchincloss EL, Michels R: Psychoanalytic theory of character, in Frosch JP (ed): Current Perspectives on Personality Disorders. Washington, DC, American Psychiatric Press, 1983.

Banki CM, Arato M: Relationship between cerebrospinal fluid amine metabolites, neuroendocrine findings and personality dimensions (Marke-Nyman scale factors) in psychiatric patients. Acta Psychiatr Scand 67:272–280, 1983.

Baron M, Asnis L, Gruen R: The schedule for schizotypal personalities (SSP): A diagnostic interview for schizotypal features. Psychiatry Res 4:213–228, 1981.

Baron M, Asnis L, Gruen R, Levitt M: Plasma amine oxidase and genetic vulnerability to schizophrenia. Arch Gen Psychiatry 40:275–279, 1983.

Baron M, Levitt M, Perlman R: Low platelet monamine oxidase activity: A possible biochemical correlate of borderline schizophrenia. Psychiatry Res 3:329–335, 1980.

Baxter L, Edell W, Gerner R, Fairbanks, L, Gwirtsman H: Dexamethasone suppression test and Axis I diagnoses of inpatients with DSM-III borderline personality disorder. Clin Psychiatry 45:150–153, 1984.

Black A: The natural history of obsessional neurosis, in Beech HR (ed): Obsessional States. London, Methuen, 1974.

Brinkely JR, Breitman BD, Friedel RO: Low-dose neuroleptic regimens in the treatment of borderline patients. Arch Gen Psychiatry 36:319–329, 1979.

Brown GL, Ebert MH, Goyer PF, Jimerson DC, Klein WJ, Bunney WE, Goodwin FS: Aggression, suicide and serotonin: Relationships to CSF amine metabolites. Am J Psychiatry 139:741–746, 1982.

Buchsbaum MS, Coursey RD, Murphy DL: The biochemical high-risk paradigm: Behavioral and familial correlates of low platelet monoamine oxidase activity. Science 194:339, 1976.

Carpenter WT, Gunderson JG: Five-year follow-up comparison of borderline and schizophrenic patients. Compr Psychiatry 18:567–571, 1977.

Carroll BJ, Feinberg M, Greden JF, et al: A specific laboratory test for the diagnosis of melancholia. Arch Gen Psych 38:15–22, 1981.

Carroll BJ, Greden JF, Feinberg M, et al: Neuroendocrine evaluation of depression in borderline patients. Psychiatr Clin North Am 4:89–99, 1982.

Cattell RB, Vaughan DS, Schuerger JM, Rao DC: Heritabilities by the multiple abstract variance analysis (MAVA) model and objective test measures of personality traits. Behav Genet 12:361–378, 1982.

Charney DS, Nelson JC, Quinlan DM: Personality traits and disorder in depression. Am J Psychiatry 138:1601–1604, 1981.

Chodoff P: The depressive personality. Arch Gen Psychiatry 27:666–672, 1972.

Cole JO, Salomon M, Gunderson J, Sunderland P, Simmonds P: Drug therapy in borderline patients. Compr Psychiatry 25:249–254, 1984.

Crowe R: An adoption study of antisocial personality. Arch Gen Psychiatry 31:785–791, 1974.

Derogatis LR, Lipman RS, Covi L, Rickels K: Factorial invariance of symptom dimensions in anxious and depressive neuroses. Arch Gen Psychiatry 27:659–665, 1972.

Ellingson RL: Incidence of EEG abnormality among patients with mental disorders of apparently nonorganic origin: A critical review. Am J Psychiatry 111:263–275, 1954.

Ellison JM, Adler DA: Psycholpharmacologic approaches to borderline syndromes. Comprehensive Psychiatry 25:255–262, 1984.

Eysenck HJ: National differences in personality as related to ABO blood group polymorphism. Psychol Rep 41:1257–1258, 1977.

Eysenck HJ: The biological basis of cross-cultural differences in personality: Blood group antigens. Psychol Rep 51:531–540, 1982.

Frank H, Paris J: Recollections of family experience in borderline patients. Arch Gen Psychiatry 38:1031–1034, 1981.

Frosch JP: The psychosocial treatment of personality disorders. In: Frosch JP (ed.) Current perspectives on personality disorders. American Psychiatric Press, Inc., Washington, DC, 1983.

Freud S: Character and anal eroticism, in Rieff P (ed): Collected Papers, vol 10. New York, Collier, 1963.

Fuller JL, Thompson WR: Foundations of Behavioral Genetics, St. Louis, C.V. Mosby, 1978.

Gattaz WF, Beckman H: Platelet MAO activity and personality characteristics. Acta Psychiatr Scand 63:479–485, 1981.

Gunderson JG, Englund DW: Characterizing the families of borderlines: A review of the literature. Psychiatr Clin North Am 4:159–168, 1981.

Gunderson JG, Kerr J, Woods D: The families of borderlines. Arch Gen Psychiatry 37:27–33, 1980.

Gunderson JG, Siever LJ, Spaulding E: The search for a schizotype. Arch Gen Psychiatry 40:15–22, 1983.

Gunderson JG, Singer MT: Defining borderline patients: An overview. Am J Psychiatry 132:1–10, 1975.

Guntrip H: Schizoid phenomena, object relations, and the self. New York, International Universities Press, 1969.

Hare RD: Psychopathy—theory and research. John Wiley, New York, 1970.

Hays P: Determination of the obsessional personality. Am J Psychiatry 129:217–219, 1972.

Hirschfeld RMA, Klerman GL, Clayton PJ, Keller MB: Personality and depression, Arch Gen Psychiatry 40:993–998, 1983b.

Hirschfeld RMA, Klerman GL, Clayton PJ, Keller MB, MacDonald-Scott MA, Larkin BH: Assessing personality: Effects of the depressive state on trait measurement. Am J Psychiatry 40:695–699, 1983a.

Holzman PS, Kringlen E, Levy DL, et al: Deviant eye tracking in twins discordant for psychosis: A replication. Arch Gen Psychiatry 37:626–631, 1980.

Holzman PS, Proctor LR, Levy DL, et al: Eye-tracking dysfunctions in schizophrenic patients and their relatives. Arch Gen Psychiatry 31:143–151, 1974.

Iacono WG, Lykken DT: Eye tracking and psychopathology: New procedures applied to a sample of normal monozygotic twins. Arch Gen Psychiatry 36:1361–1369, 1979.

Jogawar VV: Personality correlates of human blood groups. Personality and Individual Differences 4:215–216, 1984.

Kendler KS, Gruenberg AM: Genetic relationship between paranoid personality disorder and the "schizophrenic spectrum" disorders. Am J Psychiatry 139:1185–1186, 1982.

Kendler KS, Gruenberg AM: An independent analysis of the Danish adoption study of schizophrenia. VI. The relationship between psychiatric disorders as defined by DSM-III in relatives and adoptees. Arch Gen Psychiatry 41:555–564, 1984.

Kendler KS, Gruenberg AM, Strauss JS: An independent analysis of the Copenhagen sample of the Danish adoption study of schizophrenia. II. Relationship between schizotypal personality disorder and schizophrenia. Arch Gen Psychiatry 38:982–984, 1981.

Kerr TA, Roth M, Schapira K, Gurney C: The assessment and prediction of outcome in affective disorders. Br J Psychiatry 121:167–174, 1972.

Kerr TA, Schapira K, Roth M, Garside RF: The relationship between the Maudsley Personality Inventory and the course of affective disorders. Br J Psychiatry 116:11–19, 1970.

Kety SS, Rosenthal D, Wender PH, Schulsinger F: Mental illness in the biologic and adoptive families of adopted schizophrenics. Am J Psychiatry 128:302–306, 1971.

Koenigsberg HW, Kernberg OF, Schomer J: Diagnosing borderline conditions in an outpatient setting. Arch Gen Psychiatry 40:49–53, 1983.

Latham C, Holzman PS, Manschreck TC, Tole J: Optokinetic nystagmus and pursuit eye movements in schizophrenia. Arch Gen Psychiatry 38:997–1003, 1981.

Lazare A: The hysterical character in psychoanalytic theory. Arch Gen Psychiatry 25:131–137, 1971.

Lazare A, Klerman GL: Hysteria and depression: The frequency and significance of hysterical personality features in hospitalized depressed women. Am J Psychiatry 124:48–56, 1968.

Lazare A, Klerman G, Armor DJ: Oral, obsessive and hysterical personality patterns. Arch Gen Psychiatry 14:624–630, 1966.

Lazare A, Klerman G, Armor DJ: Oral, obsessive and hysterical personality patterns: Replication of factor analysis in an independent sample. J Psychol Res 7:275–279, 1970.

Leone NF: Response of borderline patients to loxapine and chlorpromazine. J Clinical Psychiatry 43:148–150, 1982.

Levin S, Lopton RB, Holzman PS: Pursuit eye movements in psychopathology: Effects of target characteristics. Biol Psychiatry 16:255–267, 1981.

Levy DM: Maternal Overprotection. New York, Columbia University Press, 1943.

Lewis A: Problems of obsessional illness. Proc R Soc Med 29:325–336, 1936.

Liebowitz MR, Klein DF: Hysteroid dysphoria. Psychiatr Clin North Am 2:555–575, 1979a.

Liebowitz MR, Stallone F, Dunner DL, Fieve RF: Personality features of patients with primary affective disorder. Acta Psychiatr Scand 60:214–224, 1979b.

Lochlin JC: Are personality traits differentially heritable? Behav Genet 12:417–428, 1982.

Loranger AW, Oldham JM, Russakoff LM, Susman V: Structured interviews for borderline personality disorder. Arch Gen Psychiatry 41:565–568, 1984.

Loranger AW, Oldham JM, Tulis EH: Familial transmission of DSM-III borderline personality disorder. Arch Gen Psychiatry 39:795–799, 1982.

Lumry AE, Gottesman II, Tuason VB: MMPI state dependency during the course of bipolar psychosis. Psychiatry Res 7:59–67, 1982.

Masterson J: Psychotherapy of the borderline adult. New York, Brunner/Mazel, 1976.

Mellsop G, Varghese F, Joshua S, Hicks A: The reliability of Axis II of DSM-III. Am J Psychiatry 139:1360–1361, 1982.

Murphy DL, Belmaker RH, Buchsbaum MS, Bartin NF, Ciarnell R, Wyatt RJ: Biogenic amine-related enzymes and personality variations in normals. Psychol Med 7:149–157, 1977.

Murphy DL, Weiss R: Reduced monamine oxidase in blood platelets from bipolar depressed patients. Am J Psychiatry 128:35–41, 1972.

Murray LG, Blackburn IM: Personality differences in patients with depressive illness and anxiety neurosis. Acta Psychiatr Scand 50:183–191, 1974.

Nace EP, Saxon JJ, Shore N: A comparison of borderline and nonborderline alcoholic patients. Arch Gen Psychiatry 40:54–56, 1983.

Parnas J, Schulsinger F, Schulsinger H, Mednick SA, Teasdale TW: Behavioral precursors of schizophrenia spectrum. Arch Gen Psychiatry 39:658–664, 1982.

Paykel ES, Prusoff BA: Relationships between personality dimensions: Neuroticism and extraversion against obsessive, hysterical and oral personality. Br J Soc Clin Psychol 12:309–318, 1973.

Perris C, Jacobsson L, von Knorring L, Oreland L, Perris H, Ross SB: Enzymes related to biogenic amine metabolism and personality characteristics in depressed patients. Acta Psychiatr Scand 63:477–484, 1981.

Pfohl B, Coryell W, Zimmerman M, Stangl D: DSM-III personality disorders: Diagnostic overlap and internal consistency of individual DSM-III criteria. Compr Psychiatry 27:21–34, 1986.

Pfohl B, Stangl D, Zimmerman M: The Structured Interview for DSM-III Personality disorders (SIDP). Dept of Psychiatry, University of Iowa, Iowa City, Iowa, 1982.

Pfohl B, Stangl D, Zimmerman M: Increasing Axis II reliability (letter). Am J Psychiatry 140:271–272, 1983.

Pfohl B, Stangl D, Zimmerman M: The implication of DSM-III personality disorders for patient with major depression. J Affect Disord 7:309–319, 1984.

Pfohl B, Winokur G: The micropsychopathology of hebephrenic/catatonic schizophrenia. J Nerv Mental Dis 171:296–300, 1983.

Pollak JM: Obsessive-compulsive personality: A review. Psychol Bull 86:225–241, 1979.

Pope HG, Jonas J, Hudson J, Cohen B, Gunderson J: The validity of DSM-III borderline personality disorder. Arch Gen Psychiatry 40:23–30, 1983.

Reveley MA, Glover V, Sandler M, Coppen A: Increased platelet monoamine oxidase activity in affective disorders. Psychopharmacology 73:257–260, 1981.

Rifkin A, Quitkin F, Carrillo C, Blumberg AG, Klein DF, Oaks G: Lithium carbonate in emotionally unstable character disorder. Arch Gen Psychiatry 27:519–523, 1972.

Roth M, Gurney C, Garside R, Kerr T: Studies in the classification of affective disorders: The relationship between anxiety states and depressive illness. Br J Psychiatry 121:147–161, 1972.

Rutter M, Korn S, Birch HG: Genetic and environmental factors in the development of "primary reaction patterns." Br J Soc Clin Psychol 2:161–178, 1963.

Schlesser MA, Winokur G, Sherman BM: Genetic subtypes of unipolar primary depressive illness distinguished by hypothalamic-pituitary-adrenal axis activity. Lancet 1:739–741, 1979.

Schulsinger F: Psychopathy: Heredity and environment. Int J Ment Health 1:190–206, 1972.

Shagass C, Amadeo M, Overton DA: Eye tracking performance in psychiatric patients. Biol Psychiatry 9:245–260, 1974.

Siegel C, Waldo M, Mizner G, Adler LE, Freedman R: Deficits in sensory gating in schizophrenia patients and their relatives: Evidence obtained with auditory evoked responses. Arch Gen Psychiatry 41:607–612, 1984.

Siever LJ, Haier RJ, Coursey RD, Sostek AJ, Murphy DL, Holzman PS, Buchsbaum MS: Smooth pursuit eye tracking impairment: Relation to other "markers" of schizophrenia and psychologic correlates. Arch Gen Psychiatry 39:1001–1005, 1982.

Snyder S, Pitts WM: Electroencephalography of DSM-III borderline personality disorder. Acta Psychiatr Scand 69:129–134, 1984.

Soloff PH, Anselm G, Nathan RS: The dexamethasone suppression test in patients with borderline personality disorders. Am J Psychiatry 139:1621–1623, 1982.

Soloff PH, Millward JW: Developmental histories of borderline patients. Compr Psychiatry 24:574–588, 1983.

Soloff PH, Millward JW: Psychiatric disorders in the families of borderline patients. Arch Gen Psychiatry 40:37–44, 1983.

Spitzer RL, Endicott J, Gibbon M: Crossing the border into borderline personality and borderline schizophrenia. Arch Gen Psychiatry 36:17–24, 1979.

Spitzer RL, Forman JBW, Nee J: DSM-III field trials. I. Initial interrater diagnostic reliability. Am J Psychiatry 136:815–817, 1979.

Stangl D, Pfohl B, Zimmerman M, Bowers W: A structured interview for DSM-III personality disorders. Arch Gen Psychiatry 42:591–596, 1985.

Sternbach HA, Fleming J, Extein I, Pottash ALC, Gold MS: The dexamethasone suppression test and thyrotropin-releasing hormone tests in depressed borderline patients. Psychoneuroendocrinology, 8:459–462, 1983.

Stone MH: Contemporary shift of the borderline concept from subschizophrenic disorder to a subaffective disorder. Psychiatr Clin North Am 2:577–593, 1979.

Torgersen S, Psychol C: The oral, obsessive and hysterical personality syndromes: A study of hereditary and environmental factors by means of the twin method. Arch Gen Psychiatry 37:1272–1277, 1980.

Torgersen S, Psychol C: Genetic and nosological aspects of schizotypal and borderline personality disorders: A twin study. Arch Gen Psychiatry 41:546–554, 1984.

Traskman L, Asberg M, Bertilsson L, Sjostrand L: Monamine metabolites in cerebrospinal fluid and suicidal behavior. Arch Gen Psychiatry 38:631–637, 1981.

Tyrer P, Alexander MS, Cicchetti D, Cohen MS, Remington M: Reliability of a schedule for rating personality disorders. Br J Psychiatry 135:168–174, 1979.

Tyrer P, Casey P, Gall J: Relationship between neurosis and personality disorder. Br J Psychiatry 142:404–408, 1983a.

Tyrer P, Strauss J, Cicchetti D: Temporal reliability of personality in psychiatric patients. Psychol Med 13:393–398, 1983b.

Van Valkenburg C, Lowry M, Winokur G, Cadoret R: Depression spectrum disease versus pure depressive disease. J Nerv Ment Dis 165:341–347, 1977.

Weissman MM, Prusoff BA, Klerman GL: Personality and the prediction of long-term outcome of depression. Am J Psychiatry 135:797–800, 1978.

Werble B: Second follow-up study of borderline patients. Arch Gen Psychiatry 23:3–7, 1970.

Winokur G: Depression spectrum disease: Description and family study. Compr Psychiatry 13:3–8, 1972.

Wyatt RJ, Steven GP, Murphy DL: Platelet monoamine oxidase activity in schizophrenia: A review of the data. Am J Psychiatry 136:377–385, 1979.

Yerevanian BI, Akiskal HS: "Neurotic," characterological, and dysthymic depressions. Psychiatr Clin North Am 2:595–617, 1979.

Young JPR, Fenton GW, Lader MH: The inheritance of neurotic traits: A twin study of the Middlesex Hospital Questionnaire. Br J Psychiatry 119:393–398, 1971.

Zigler E, Glick M, March A: Premorbid social competence and outcome among schizophrenics and nonschizophrenic patients. J Nerv Ment Dis 167:478–483, 1979.

Zimmerman M: The Positive and Negative Impact (PANI) Life Events Interview. Dept of Psychiatry, University of Iowa, Iowa City, Iowa, 1982.

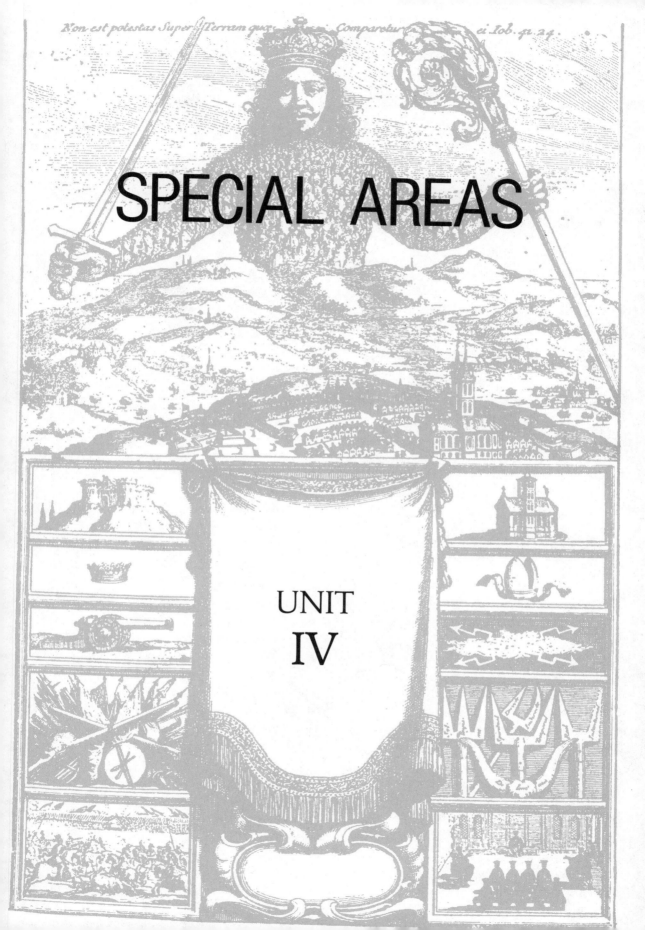

SPECIAL AREAS

UNIT
IV

# chapter 29

# THE NEUROBIOLOGIC BASIS OF PSYCHIATRIC ILLNESSES

*by* Fritz A. Henn, Ph.D., M.D.

One of the central debates in psychiatry since the 1960s involves the question of nature vs. nurture. Initially, this was a debate between those who held the view that behavior was the result of social and environmental influences and those who believed that behavior was programmed into the genetic makeup of an individual. The rise of modern neurosciences, which has as a principal tenet the view that all behavior is a result of brain function, appeared to support the latter view. More knowledge about the adaptability and plasticity of the nervous system has made it clear that the debate is fruitless. Brain clearly directs behavioral responses, but brain is also modified by environmental forces. Thus, regardless of one's bias, a clear understanding of brain structure and function is necessary to dissect the factors that lead to the behavioral malfunctions we call psychiatric syndromes. Our current biochemical theories of psychiatric illnesses are undoubtedly gross simplifications. A complete neurobiologic understanding requires precise specification of the nature of the genetic susceptibility, how this is acted on by environmental influences, and the alterations in the pathways controlling the behavior. Thus, in this chapter, we begin by looking at the neurobiologic foundations on which subsequent biochemical theories will be built; then the theories of specific illnesses are reviewed.

## ORGANIZATIONAL ANATOMY

The brain, as the interpreter of the outside world and director of the musculoskeletal system, sits at the midpoint between the input of a variety of receptors bringing sensory information in and the output of a variety of tracts directing voluntary and involuntary responses to that information. Malfunctions in the analysis of the input lead to psychiatric symptomatology. Unfortunately, although we are beginning to have some understanding of how sensory information comes into the central nervous system (CNS) and how instructions flow out, we know relatively little about where and how they are analyzed. The brain (Fig. 29–

461

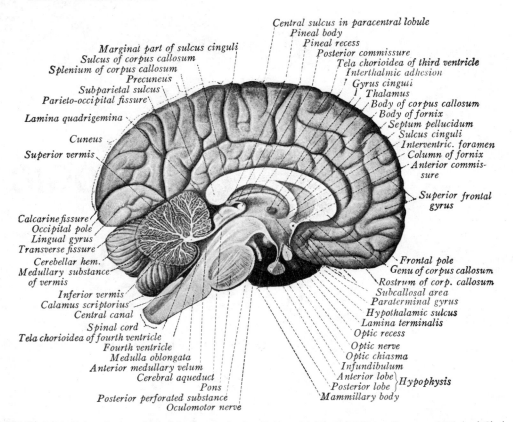

Central sulcus in paracentral lobule
Pineal body
Pineal recess
Posterior commissure
Tela chorioidea of third ventricle
Interthalmic adhesion
Gyrus cinguli
Thalamus
Body of corpus callosum
Body of fornix
Septum pellucidum
Sulcus cinguli
Interventric. foramen
Column of fornix
Anterior commissure

Marginal part of sulcus cinguli
Sulcus of corpus callosum
Splenium of corpus callosum
Precuneus
Subparietal sulcus
Parieto-occipital fissure
Lamina quadrigemina
Cuneus
Superior vermis

Superior frontal gyrus

Calcarine fissure
Occipital pole
Lingual gyrus
Transverse fissure
Cerebellar hem.
Medullary substance of vermis
Inferior vermis
Calamus scriptorius
Central canal
Spinal cord
Tela chorioidea of fourth ventricle
Fourth ventricle
Medulla oblongata
Anterior medullary velum
Cerebral aqueduct
Pons
Posterior perforated substance
Oculomotor nerve

Frontal pole
Genu of corpus callosum
Rostrum of corp. callosum
Subcallosal area
Paraterminal gyrus
Hypothalamic sulcus
Lamina terminalis
Optic recess
Optic nerve
Optic chiasma
Infundibulum
Anterior lobe
Posterior lobe } Hypophysis
Mammillary body

**FIGURE 29–1.** Medial sagittal section of the human brain. (Sobotta-McMurrich.) (From Ransom, S.W. and Clark, S.L.: The Anatomy of the Nervous System: Its Development and Function. Philadelphia, W. B. Saunders Company, 1959.)

1) monitors information coming in through the spinal cord and cranial nerves. The brain stem, a region comprising the medulla, the pons, and the midbrain, receives sensory input and relays it. Several collections of cells called nuclei in this region serve as the relay stations to higher centers. Among these are the neurons, using the monoamine transmitters that are of such interest in psychiatry. The cerebellum lies rostral and is important in regulating fine motor movement. Continuing upward from the midbrain leads to the diencephalon and the basal ganglia. The latter, consisting of caudate nucleus, putamen, and globus pallidus, are also involved in coordinating fine motor movements. These areas may be involved in behavioral responses as well. Many of the nuclei in the midbrain, using monoamines, appear to be adjuncts to the main information-carrying pathways and may serve as modulators. The main relay stations for information from the periphery

is in the diencephalon. Here the thalamus contains a host of important relay nuclei related to sensation and movement. The hypothalamus integrates autonomic function and endocrine responses regulating homeostasis. Capping the CNS is the cerebral cortex, consisting of four lobes: frontal, parietal, temporal, and occipital. These structures are concerned with the integration of perceptual and motor functions, cognition, and elements of affect. Recent studies of language have clarified the role that the neocortex probably plays in integrating emotional responses with cognitive, perceptual, and motor functions. Heilman et al. (1975), among others, has shown that just as the comprehension of speech is localized in the left hemisphere, the comprehension of emotional gesturing and inflections in speech are localized in the right hemisphere. The new data complement our earlier understanding of the anatomical substrates of emotion, which arose from the work of

Papez (1937). If the neocortex interprets and integrates emotions, it has been postulated that the limbic structures are the anatomical sites for their generation.

The idea of a limbic lobe was initially put forth by Broca to indicate the older cortical structures, which form a border (limbus) around the brain stem. These structures include the cingulate gyrus, fornix, septal nuclei, stria terminalis, amygdala, lateral striae, olfactory tubercle, medial striae, and hippocampus (Fig. 29–1). In 1937, Papez published "A Proposed Mechanism of Emotion." In this contribution, Papez attempted to define the anatomical basis for a connection between higher cortical centers and the hypothalamus. He believed that the hypothalamus had a central role in the production of emotion and that since emotions were part of consciousness, they must also be connected to higher cortical centers. He proposed a pathway that received cortical input by way of the cingulate gyrus. The cortical input was sent to the hippocampus, which processed the information, and relayed it through the fornix, to the mammillary bodies of the hypothalamus. It could then be sent back through the thalamus to the cingulate gyrus. The circuit is potentially a closed loop, allowing for the possibility of reverberatory activity. The theory was initially put forth with minimal hard evidence, but subsequent lesion studies have provided some support. Even today, however, we do not have convincing proof of these ideas. As we approach the fiftieth anniversary of Papez's contribution, it remains, nevertheless, the central hypothesis around which to structure an understanding of the anatomical localization of emotion.

In humans, bilateral temporal lobectomy results in a total loss of affect and emotional response. These studies interrupt the tracts connecting cortex to hypothalamus and so are consistent with the ideas of Papez. Modern neuroanatomy has provided evidence of extensive connections between the hippocampus and the neocortex and has demonstrated the relationship of other structures, such as the amygdala, the septum, the nucleus accumbens, and the subiculum. However, these details have not led to a much more refined picture than the notion that the neocortex receives and processes information, selecting those inputs that are significant. The material is relayed to structures in the limbic lobe and processed. The resulting emotions lead to motor and endocrine responses that are integrated when the information is passed to the hypothalamus. What we do now appreciate is the complexity of the responses that the hypothalamus can induce. This structure has a variety of peptides that may not only act as releasing factors for hormones, but may also have a direct action on CNS receptors. Peptide neurotransmission and neuromodulation on brain sites unrelated to endocrine function vastly broaden the range of responses of the CNS to limbic stimulation. Although we have only the most general clues as to how the limbic circuitry may be involved with specific psychiatric syndromes, this material does provide a starting point for attempts to relate symptoms to anatomy. Such localizations may ultimately help us to define more precise points of neurochemical attack on psychiatric illnesses.

## CNS CELLS—STRUCTURE AND FUNCTION

The unique properties of brain must arise from the particular cellular constituents that make it up. On the surface, the cellular composition of nervous tissue is surprisingly simple. It consists of neurons and glial cells. The remarkable complexity of output comes from the variety of neurons, their large numbers ($10^7$), the patterns of connections, and the mechanisms that modify output on the basis of experience. Any given neuron can receive thousands of inputs through its dendrites and send out thousands of outputs through branches from its axons.

Neurons contain the usual constituents found in cells; a nucleus (usually large), nucleoli, smooth and rough endoplasmic reticulum, golgi complex, and mitochondria. What makes the cell unique is (1) its ability to transmit an electrical signal without decrement over relatively long distances—a property caused by the electrically active membrane—and (2) a mechanism to signal its neighbor. Signaling is usually accomplished through a specialized structure called the synapse. This structure is an area of specialized contact formed by the presynaptic terminal of one neuron and the specialized receptive area, the postsynaptic membrane region, of the second. Not surprisingly, the areas of contact are the regions implicated in the action of most psychopharmacologically active drugs, for by altering the nature of the communication between neurons, one most selectively can alter the behavioral output of the system.

In general, neuronal structure consists of a cell body or soma, a series of branched dendrites, an axon, and a region of presynaptic terminals (Fig. 29–2). The cell body is often large and the patterns of dendritic branches are varied. In general, there are multipolar cells with dendrites coming from all portions of the soma, bipolar cells with information coming in from one direction and flowing out through the axon in another, and unipolar cells with a short-fused axon that splits after leaving the soma. Larger cells with long axons often have them wrapped in a myelin sheath. This structure, formed by the oligodendroglia, acts as an insulator and is important to achieve high-speed conduction. The end of the axon that branches and forms regions of presynaptic fibers ends with little knoblike structures that form part of the synapse. These struc-

tures contain many mitochondria and dense granules, which can be viewed in the electron microscope. It is this region that must be examined in more detail, for most theories of biologic alterations in psychiatric disease suggest that it is at the point of transmission of information from one cell to another that alterations occur.

When one neuron signals another, the process begins with information going out through the axon. This occurs when the membrane is depolarized. All cells have a potential difference across their plasma membrane, the size of which is a function of the differences between the ion composition inside and outside and the resistance of the membrane itself. What is unique about neurons is that when they are depolarized sufficiently, they do not simply follow the imposed depolarization, but undergo a spontaneous, rapid, self-limited depolarization that carries the membrane potential from the negative values usually seen to positive values of up to 30 mV. Then the potential returns to its initial value—this is the action potential and the electrical sig-

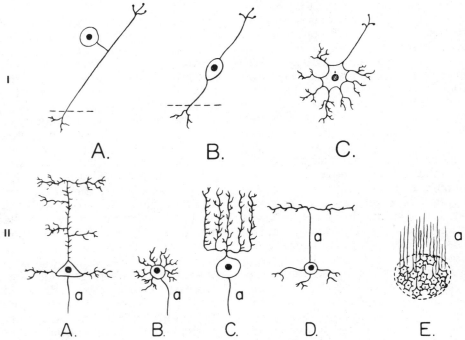

**FIGURE 29–2.** I, Morphologic types of neurons. The unipolar (pseudobipolar) neuron (A) is typical of all dorsal root ganglia and general sensory ganglia associated with cranial nerves. The bipolar neuron (B) occurs in the cranial nerves for special senses. The multipolar neurons differ widely in shape; the motoneuron type is shown here (C).

II, Various representative configurations of multipolar neurons. A, pyramidal cell. B, stellate cell. C, Purkinje cell. D, granule cell. E, a nucleus of multipolar cells (dendrites have been omitted for clarity). The small letter a indicates axon. (Modified from Patton et al.: Introduction to Basic Neurology, by kind permission of the authors and publisher.)

nal moves down the axon membrane to the presynaptic region. If a strong enough signal arrives at the presynaptic region, it causes the release of a transmitter substance. These substances are stored in the dense granules and are released in response to the action potential. The basis for the action potential is the transient opening of ion channels. Similarly, in the presynaptic area, ion channels are opened as a consequence of depolarization. However, here the important ion to enter is $Ca^{++}$, which is central to the release of the transmitter. As the action potential arrives, $Ca^{++}$ permeability goes up and, subsequently, the transmitter is released. The transmitter diffuses through the region of the synaptic clef and reacts with a specific receptor of the postsynaptic membrane. This reaction often sets in motion a change in permeability that depolarizes the subsequent neuron. The transmitter is quickly removed from the synaptic region by reuptake into cells or metabolic destruction. It is the elements of this process—synthesis and degradation of transmitter, release, reuptake and receptor activity—that are altered by most psychoactive drugs. We will consider the processes for several transmitters that appear to be related to psychiatric conditions.

First, a general word about transmitters. These substances include several classes of compounds: amines, amino acids, and peptides. Until recently it appeared that transmitter candidates all acted to transmit information from one cell to an adjacent cell. Now complications have developed: compounds do clearly carry out this transmission role, but they may also act as modulators in a variety of settings. These latter functions are still incompletely understood but may prove vital to an understanding of the pathophysiology of psychiatric diseases. In addition, such a role may be central to the action of a majority of CNS peptides. Such a modulating role may involve action on a variety of sites, not only communication with the next neuron.

## THE NEUROTRANSMITTERS

### Norepinephrine

The catecholamines dopamine, norepinephrine, and epinephrine constitute the most studied class of neurotransmitters.

Early studies showed that epinephrine and norepinephrine play a crucial role in the body's response to stress. This, plus an ability to measure and fairly early on an ability to localize these compounds histochemically, resulted in a great deal of information that provided the building blocks for several theories involving these compounds in the pathophysiology of psychiatric diseases.

### Norepinephrine System Anatomy

The localization of norepinephrine neurons became possible with the discovery that formaldehyde reacted in situ with the catecholamines to produce a highly fluorescent product. This allowed Dahlstrom and Fuxe (1965) to begin mapping the CNS neurons containing norepinephrine. Subsequent advances using gloxylic acid and immunocytochemical techniques have refined the available mapping techniques. Basically, the norepinephrine system consists of two clusters of cell bodies sending widespread innervation throughout the CNS. The largest collection of cells is in the locus ceruleus, a small nucleus consisting of a few thousand neurons located around the midline at the base of the pons. This nucleus takes its name from the blue color, owing to pigmented neurons, seen in primates and humans. Outflow from the locus goes along five major tracts and results in widespread innervation. Three tracts ascend to the cortical regions, following the major blood vessels and fascicular routes. These include (1) the central tegmental tract, (2) the central dorsal gray longitudinal fasciculus tracts, and (3) the ventral tegmental-medial forebrain tract. These pathways provide innervation to the thalamus and the hypothalamus as well as a relatively diffuse and even innervation of cortical areas. Another major outflow goes through the superior cerebellar peduncle to innervate the cerebellar cortex, while the final outflow pathway descends through the mesencephalon to the spinal cord. The other source of norepinephrine neurons is the lateral tegmental group. These cells are more diffuse than those located in the locus ceruleus. They are scattered throughout the lateral tegmental fields. The outflow from these cells mingles with the tracts from the locus. A major outflow goes to the spinal cord and another innervates the areas of the limbic system.

The fine structure of the anatomical innervation may provide an important clue to the functions of this system. There is a general pattern of innervation. The branches move into the cortical area by going through myelinated tracts up to cortical areas; then the axons form a characteristic T-shaped branch, with fine branches running parallel to the surface of the molecular layer. From these fine branches, nerve terminals come off at regular intervals. Studies suggest that not all of these presynaptic boutons make contact with a postsynaptic membrane. Thus the fine structure points to a system that, at one level at least, is ideally structured to modulate the function of a wide

area of cortex. This is not a system designed to deliver information from one nucleus directly to another (Descarries, Watkins, Lapierre, 1977). The study of central norepinephrine pathways suggest that, at least in some instances, the transmitter acts to inhibit firing by way of a slow, hyperpolarizing response, which results in increased membrane resistance. The mechanism that appears responsible for this operates through the second messenger system by way of cyclic adenosine monophosphate (cAMP) formation. Pharmacologic studies suggest that a beta-adrenergic receptor mediates the response.

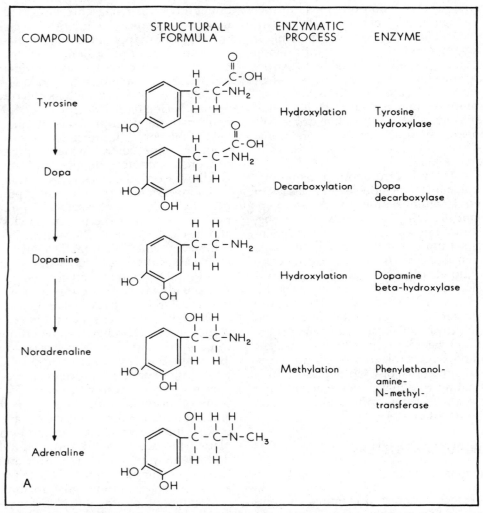

**FIGURE 29–3A.** The sequential synthesis of the catecholamines. (From Gardiner, E.: Fundamentals of Neurology. Philadelphia, W. B. Saunders Company, 1975.)

## Metabolism

All of the catecholamines are derived from the amino acid tyrosine. The biosynthetic pathway is shown in Fig. 29–3A. The first enzyme in the pathway is tyrosine hydroxylase, first described by Underfriend in 1966. This enzyme is specific to catecholamine-containing neurons in the CNS and the peripheral nervous system. It also controls the rate-limiting step in the synthesis of these compounds. The enzyme exhibits a high degree of stereospecificity, requires oxygen, $Fe^{++}$, and a tetrahydropteridine cofactor, probably tetrahydrobiopterin. The Km of the enzyme is in the range of $10^{-5}$, while other enzymes in the biosynthetic pathway are 100- to 1000-fold more active. The next enzyme in this pathway is aromatic amino acid decarboxylase. The decarboxylase is not specific for DOPA, nor is its distribution restricted to nerve cells. It is an active non-specific decarboxylase that takes DOPA and converts it into dopamine. Inhibition of this enzyme has little effect on the concentration of norepinephrine available in tissue. The final enzyme used in the synthesis of norepinephrine is dopamine-β-hydroxylase. This enzyme is only present in adrenergic

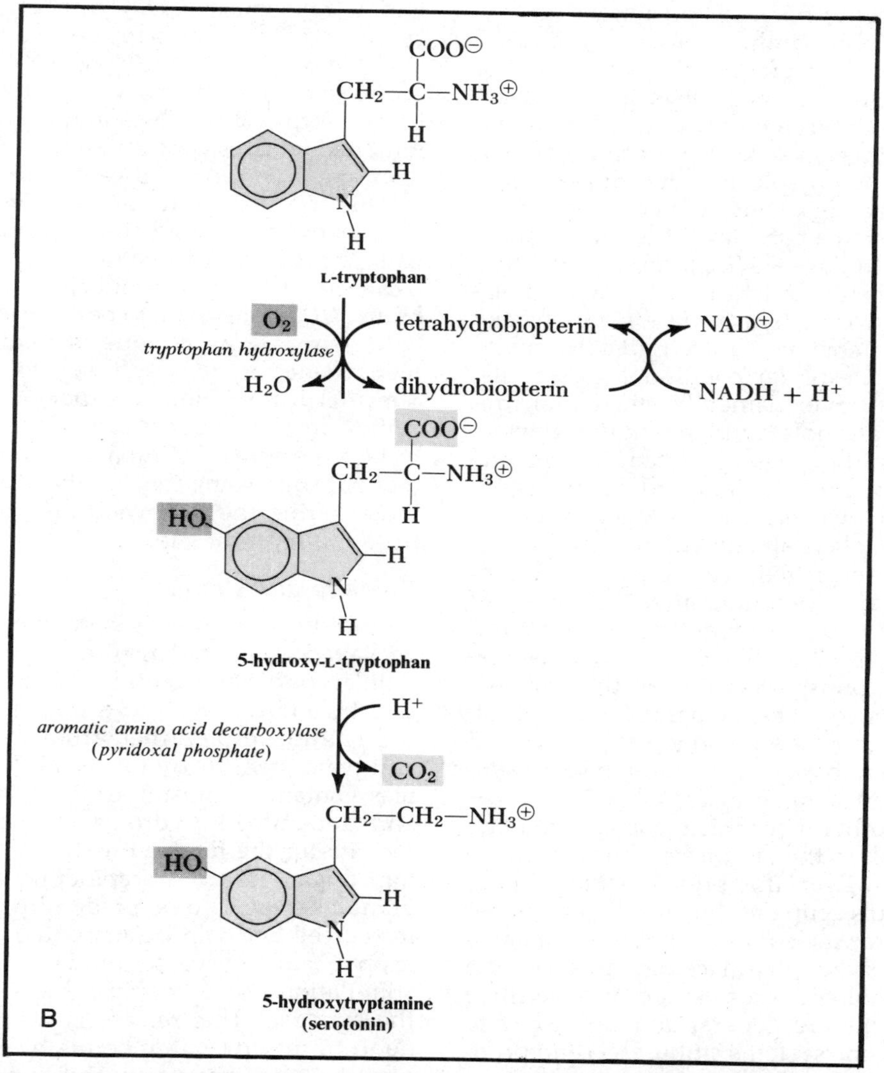

FIGURE 29–3B. *Continued.* The formation of serotonin from tryptophan. (From McGilvery, R.W.: Biochemistry: A Functional Approach. Philadelphia, W. B. Saunders Company, 1983.)

neurons but does not have a high degree of specificity. It will oxidize almost any phenylethylamine to the corresponding phenylethanolamine. The final enzyme that should be mentioned is phenylethanolamine-*N*-methyl transferase. This enzyme converts norepinephrine to epinephrine in the adrenal medulla and probably in the CNS as well.

The regulation of the synthesis of norepinephrine is complex and under a variety of controls. As mentioned, tyrosine hydroxylase is the rate-limiting enzyme. For example, when sympathetic nerves are repetitively stimulated, there is a marked increase in the synthesis of norepinephrine. The opposite effect is noted when tissues are exposed to monoamine oxidase inhibitors, compounds that prevent the breakdown of catecholamines and result in increased tissue levels of these compounds. This is evidence that a feedback loop controls the synthesis of norepinephrine. The studies aimed at defining this control mechanism have demonstrated a complex set of phenomena. Initially, studies on sympathetic nerve stimulation demonstrated that no new molecules of tyrosine hydroxylase were formed; rather, the enzyme showed greater activity per molecule under conditions of stimulation. This was explained by the demonstration that catechols could inhibit the enzyme; thus when they were depleted, the enzyme was no longer inhibited and synthesis increased. However, end product inhibition did not explain all the changes seen. The enzyme appears to have altered affinities for cofactors and inhibitors after the period of active neuronal depolarization. Such alteration may be due to allosteric changes mediated by phosphorylation of the enzyme. This action could be mediated by way of calcium influx or cAMP and provides a second mechanism to regulate norepinephrine synthesis. If prolonged neuronal activity takes place, another mechanism comes into play. This involves the synthesis of new enzyme molecules. Even this brief consideration of the controls acting at the level of a rate-controlling enzyme suggests that this is an area in which both pharmacologic intervention and physiologic error can occur. The three mechanisms are general and can apply to most enzyme systems studied: (1) end product inhibition, (2) allosteric alteration of activity (e.g., phosphorylation), and (3) new

synthesis of enzyme. The signals for such regulatory steps can be varied as well. For example, hormonal signals can trigger such responses, as can signals from other neuromodulators. Thus the complexity and subtlety of the controls that regulate CNS activity can begin to be seen.

The breakdown of a neurotransmitter is another important step in controlling its activity. In general, the activity of released neurotransmitters is a function of how much is at an active receptor site. Thus the transport and metabolism of the transmitter directly affect its activity. The two enzymes that degrade the catecholamines are monoamine oxidase (MAO) and catechol-*O*-methyltransferase (COMT). The MAO enzymes oxidize amines to their corresponding aldehydes, while COMT adds a methyl group to the ring hydroxyl. There appear to be two forms of MAO, A and B. MAO A is inhibited by clorgyline and has a preference for norepinephrine and serotonin. MAO B is inhibited by deprenyl and prefers β-phenylethylamine as a substrate. Dopamine is equally metabolized by both forms. MAO is localized to the outer mitochondrial membrane. COMT appears to be, at least in part, extraneuronal and requires *S*-adenosinemethionine, a methyl donor, to function. Short-term inhibition of either of these enzymes does not appear to potentiate the effects of peripheral sympathetic nerve stimulation, suggesting that another mechanism must control the removal of the transmitter from the receptor site.

### Release and Uptake

Once norepinephrine is synthesized, it is packaged and stored in granules. These subcellular particles occur in all tissues with catecholamines and serve to sequester the compounds, protect them from metabolism, and have them ready for release. The granules contain adenosine triphosphate (ATP) and dopamine-β-hydroxylase and may be the site for the final synthetic step converting dopamine to norepinephrine. These granules appear to be predominantly made in the cell body and transported down the axon to the nerve terminus. After nerve stimulation, norepinephrine is released at the synapse. This release is $Ca^{++}$ dependent. In the adrenal, it occurs by way of exocytosis, the contents of the granule being released as the granule fuses with the plasma membrane. It is unlikely that this occurs, at least exclusively, in the CNS. First, there is evidence that newly snythesized transmitters are preferentially released, and second, it is unlikely that the rate of synthesis of the granule proteins and ATP is sufficient to have them released with each nerve impulse. What is clear is that the permeability changes caused by the nerve impulse results in increased $Ca^{++}$ influx and release of norepinephrine into the synaptic clef.

After the transmitter is released, it reacts with the appropriate postsynaptic receptor. This action triggers the response in the postsynaptic cell. It is terminated by removal of the transmitter from the area of the membrane receptors. In the case of the catecholamines, the removal is accomplished by a high-affinity uptake system. This mechanism controls the immediate level of activity of norepinephrine at the receptor site. Iversen (1971) described a high-affinity uptake system with Kms in the range of $10^{-8}$ M. Although other cells in the CNS, notably glia, can transport catecholamines, their transport systems do not have the high affinity noted for the presynaptic system. Thus, after release, the transmitter is taken back up into the presynaptic neuron, where it can be stored in the storage granules and reused again. While this happens to a portion of the transmitter, some is metabolized. Not only does the norepinephrine neuron have sites for reuptake, but there are also presynaptic receptors, thought to be $\alpha_2$-receptors, that regulate the rate of release. High levels of extracellular norepinephrine acting on these presynaptic receptors inhibit the release of more transmitter. An alternative control that does not involve presynaptic receptors uses prostaglandin E. This mechanism appears to limit the availability of $CA^{++}$, and thus inhibit the release of norepinephrine.

## Dopamine

The first neurotransmitter candidate to be formed in the biosynthetic reactions detailed earlier is dopamine. This catecholamine does not have a peripheral system, such as the sympathetic nervous system; however, it is well defined because of its distinct role in the fine control of movement. It also is the transmitter implicated in psychotic processes owing to the pharmacology of the antipsychotic drugs.

### Dopamine System Anatomy

The anatomy of the dopamine system is somewhat different than that of the adrenergic system. It involves discrete pathways and many more cells than the norepinephrine system. In general, there are three main projections of dopamine neurons and four minor systems. The major pathways include two long projections. First is the nigrostriatal pathway, linking the cells of the substantia nigra with those of the caudate and the putamen. This pathway, well known because of its role in Parkinson's disease, plays a role in the control of fine motor movements and has been well studied. The second pathway, now receiving more study because of its proposed role in psychotic illness, involves the projections of cells in the ventral tegmental area to limbic and cortical areas. These are referred to as the mesolimbic and the mesocortical projections. The final major pathway is the tuberohypophysial system, which has cells in the arcuate and periventricular nuclei projecting into the intermediate lobe of the pituitary. This short pathway plays a role in prolactin release.

The minor pathways are either short, such as the tuberohypophysial pathway, or intrinsic to certain structures. The two intrinsic pathways include retinal cells linking the outer and inner plexiform layers and a group of cells in the olfactory bulb, linking mitral cells from separate glomeruli. The short pathways involve cells in the dorsal posterior hypothalamus projecting to the dorsal anterior hypothalamus and septal nuceli and a group of cells around the dorsal motor nucleus of the vagal nerve.

### Metabolism

The metabolism of dopamine has been detailed under the discussion of norepinephrine. The biosynthesis takes place through tyrosine hydroxylase and the degradation, through MAO and COMT. The controls outlined earlier play a role in dopamine regulation. The major antipsychotic drugs all interact with the dopamine system as either blockers or antagonists. Thus they cause increased dopamine synthesis. Chronic treatment results in differences in response between the long tracts for atypical drugs, such as thioridazine. The nigrostriatal tract appears not to go into depolarization block when atypical neuroleptics are used. Thus the increased rate of dopamine synthesis and release continues in cells of the substantia nigra. This results in a partial reversal of the dopamine blockage in this pathway. Thus less in the way of motor side effects is seen with these drugs.

### Release and Uptake

The production and storage of dopamine is similar to that of norepinepherine. It is stored in granules and released in response to neuronal activity. The uptake system is also similar, having a high-affinity system located on the presynaptic membrane. The story of dopamine postsynaptic effects are not as clear, however. It is usually stated that dopamine is an inhibitory transmitter. However, the electro-physiological data are ambiguous.

## Serotonin

Serotonin (5-hydroxytryptamine, 5-HT) was first isolated by investigators as a possible hypertensive agent. It was a potent agent for the contraction of smooth muscle and only later was it identified in the CNS. After the isolation of the hallucinogen LSD, it was found that serotonin and LSD apparently interacted at the same receptor in smooth muscle. This, plus the finding that reserpine depleted serotonin, soon led to a number of theories about its action in a variety of mental illnesses. Although some of these theories, such as those concerning psychotic illness, have faded, others, such as those concerned with affective disorders, are still very much under consideration.

### Serotonin Cell Anatomy in the CNS

Although 5-HT was shown to form fluorescent condensation products when reacted with formaldehyde vapors, it has been more difficult to get detailed anatomical data about this system. This is due to the short lifetime of the fluorescence and the inability to measure the nerve terminals using this technique. By applying immunocytochemical techniques, a fairly good picture of the anatomy has emerged. In general, 5-HT–containing neurons lie in clusters around the midline of the pons and upper brain stem. These midline, or raphe, nuclei lie in nine distinct groups. In general, the lower or caudal nuclei project down to the medulla and the spinal cord, while the upper groups project to the limbic and cortical areas. The terminal fields of these neurons are diffuse and relatively formless. The fine structure of the 5-HT system has been the subject of a great deal of discussion. Descarries et al. (1975) have pointed out that the boutons of the 5-HT, as well as norepinephrine neurons, have widespread, relatively even distribution. Most important, the presynaptic boutons do not appear always to make contact with the postsynaptic membrane. This type of anatomy gives rise to the possibility that the 5-HT is functioning as a modulating system, regulating information flow in other transmitter systems.

### Metabolism

Peripherally serotonin is predominantly found in cells, such as mast cells; however, peripheral serotonin cannot cross the blood–brain barrier. In the CNS synthesis takes place in neurons. Tryptophan, another amino acid, is the precursor for 5-HT. The level of tryptophan intake in the diet controls the rate of serotonin synthesis in brain. Tryptophan is hydroxylated by the enzyme tryptophan decarboxyhydroxylase and then decarboxylated to form 5-HT. The rate-limiting step appears to be the hydroxylation, but this seems to be controlled by the amount of tryptophan available. In other words, the enzyme does not appear to be saturated under normal conditions. The decarboxylase is not the same general enzyme discussed under norepinephrine metabolism. Although its function is similar and the same enzyme operates peripherally, the CNS appears to have two separate and distinct decarboxylases. The synthesis of serotonin can be blocked with p-chlorophenylalanine, an inhibitor of tryptophan hydroxylase. This drug combines irreversibly with the enzyme, and the synthesis of more serotonin requires the synthesis of new enzyme molecules. The breakdown of 5-HT proceeds through MAO and the further oxidation of the aldehyde produced to form 5-hydroxyindoleacetic acid (5-HIAA). The control of serotonin synthesis does not appear to involve end product inhibition. It may involve some feedback relating neuronal impulse flow to tryptophan hydroxylase activity; however, the nature of these controls is not clear.

### Release and Uptake

Serotonin is stored in granules in nerve endings, just as the catecholamines. Release also appears to be $CA^{++}$ dependent. The reuptake systems of serotonin are similar to those described for the catecholamines. The high-affinity uptake system is specific for serotonin and has been postulated to be the site of action of some antidepressant drugs. The drugs chlorimipramine and zimelidine are relatively specific inhibitors of 5-HT high-affinity transport systems.

### Pineal

The pineal gland, situated at the base of the brain outside the blood–brain barrier, is rich in serotonin. Here 5-HT may serve as a precursor for the synthesis of melatonin. Both melatonin and serotonin are under the control of environmental light, which entrains them in a cyclic daily rhythm. As such, melatonin is a marker of circadian rhythms, an area of active investigation in affective disorders. The control of melatonin is regulated directly by noradrenergic beta receptors, coupled to a second messenger system.

## Acetylcholine

Acetylcholine (ACh) was the first neurotransmitter described and identified. It is used at the neuromuscular junction and by the parasympathetic nervous system. The exact nature of its central pathways has been difficult to determine, however, and although the study of this system's molecular details is fairly advanced, the system's functional aspects are by no means complete.

### Anatomy

The distribution of cholinergic neurons is widespread centrally. There are two groups of projecting nuclei as well as several sites in which cholinergic cells act as interneurons. Two areas of importance for psychiatry in which ACh neurons act as interneurons include the nucleus accumbens and the striatum. The cells in the basilar portion of the forebrain, especially the basal nucleus of Mynert, are also of increasing interest, having been implicated in dementias of the Alzheimer type. The fine structure of ACh systems suggest that many of the cells do project directly to a postsynaptic surface. Several features of ACh suggest that this compound might also have a hormonal role, as suggested earlier for the other amines. Among these is the stimulation of phosphate into phosphoinositol, the ability to release catecholamines, and a possible role in $Na^+$ transport in corneal epithelium.

### Metabolism

The synthesis of acetylcholine looks simple. It is a reaction in which acetylcoenzyme A (acetyl-CoA) and choline are joined to form ACh. The enzyme catalyzing this reaction is choline acetyltransferase. The two substrates appear to be common metabolities. Acetyl-CoA is the principal metabolite formed from the degradation of sugars or fats, while choline is a central constituent of lipids. It turns out that glucose is the most preferred substrate for the formation of acetyl-CoA in the brain, while choline is not synthesized at all in the brain. Thus the choline must either be transported into the CNS or come from phospholipids, such as phosphatidylcholine. This lipid is one of the main constituents of cell membranes; thus the synthesis of ACh is intimately tied to the metabolism of principal cell constituents, glucose and phospholipid. The degradation of ACh is carried out by esterases, the most specific of which is acetylcholine esterase. Unlike the catecholamines and amino acid transmitters, ACh is not taken up to terminate its action after presynpatic release; rather, it is hydrolyzed. Acetylcholine esterase is well equipped to carry out the function, being one of the most rapid and efficient enzymes known. It is at this site that irreversible organophosphorous inhibitors bind. This binding results in the fatal build-up of ACh seen when these compounds were used as nerve gases. In addition to this enzyme, there are nonspecific esterases, known as butyrylcholinesterases, which are less specific for ACh and not localized to neurons. They may, in fact, be associated with glial membranes and probably serve as a safety factor to ensure the destruction of all free ACh.

### Storage, Release, and Uptake

Studies on the neuromuscular junction, the work of Katz (1966) and his colleagues, demonstrated the quantal release of ACh. When ACh vesicles were discovered, an obvious interpretation was that the contents of a vesicle constituted a quanta of neurotransmitter. This interpretation has been challenged in the CNS on the following grounds: (a) it is clear that newly synthesized ACh is preferentially released; (b) in large axons of Aplysia, the injection of acetylcholinesterase inhibits release of ACh, suggesting that free, not bound, ACh is released; (c) the speed of CNS transmission appears too fast for exocytotic release of vesicles to provide transmitter for each firing. Other facts in the discussion of the role of vesicles in transmitter release are the synapses, such as those using amino acids, which do not have vesicular storage. These fire as efficiently as those systems that do have storage granules. The release of ACh is a $Ca^{++}$-mediated process. There is no high-affinity uptake system for ACh; rather, as mentioned earlier, the action of this transmitter is terminated by hydrolysis. There is, however, a high-affinity transport process to transport choline, one of the products of the hydrolysis. Choline is taken back up into the presynaptic neuron, where it is a valuable precursor for the resynthesis of ACh. The reuptake process is saturable and energy dependent, as are those described for the monoamines. The choline uptake system appears to be localized to regions of cholinergic innervation.

## Receptors

An area of exploding research is the detailed analysis of the receptors for transmitters. This development is due, in part, to the ability to identify, measure, and pharmacologically analyze receptors through simple binding studies. In principle, all that is needed is a ligand that binds with high affinity to the receptor of interest. This compound can then be radioactively labeled and used to measure the receptor. The ease with which these measurements are obtained has led to an ever-increasing amount of receptor research. What must be kept in mind is that each receptor defined by binding studies should demonstrate saturability, specificity, and a correlation of pharmacologic and functional effects with the binding affinity of a series of biologically active ligands. These studies, plus more traditional pharmacologic studies, have led to the definition of multiple receptor subtypes shown in Table 29–1.

The isolation of receptors is actively being pursued by many laboratories. To date, because of the extraordinary density of receptors for ACh in the electric organ of the eel, the greatest progress has been made with the nicotinic ACh receptor. This receptor has been purified and reconstituted in phospholipid vesicles. Among the reasons for such effort at isolating receptors is the possibility of making antibodies to them. This has also been accomplished with the ACh receptor. When these antibodies are injected into a healthy animal, myasthenia gravis symptoms appear, providing further clues to the pathophysiology of the disease. This is one example of how a detailed knowledge of a receptor may help to uncover the details of neuropathology for a variety of illnesses.

## Amino Acid Transmitters

Although the amino acids are not as directly involved in the theories of psychiatric illnesses as the transmitters discussed thus far, they probably constitute the workhorses of both excitatory and inhibitory transmission. Dysfunction of these systems may not be compatible with life; nonetheless, subtle changes in the transmission of these systems may play an important role in the control of mood and emotion. This is hinted at by the actions of the benzodiazepines, which probably affect the gamma-aminobutyric acid (GABA) system, which will be discussed when anxiety disorders are considered. The principal excitatory amino acids are glutamic acid and aspartic acid, while the sulfur-containing amino acids are also being considered as reasonable neurotransmitter candidates. The predominant inhibitory amino acids are GABA and glycine, with taurine being somewhat of a mystery candidate.

From the standpoint of neurotransmission, GABA is the most studied amino acid. This compound was found to be a major constituent of the CNS more than 30 years ago. A problem with attempts to define its

**TABLE 29-1    Receptor Subtypes in CNN**

| | |
|---|---|
| **Norepinephrine** | |
| alpha 1 | Postsynaptic localization; seen primarily in heart and brain; antagonist—prazosin |
| alpha 2 | Primarily presynaptic; seen in GI tract and brain; antagonist—clonidine |
| beta 1 | Linked to adenylate cyclase; seen in heart, fat cells, and brain; antagonist—practolol |
| beta 2 | Linked to adenylate cyclase; seen in lung, blood vessels, and brain; antagonist—(IPS—339) |
| **Dopaminergic** | |
| D-1 | Linked to adenylate cyclase; found in brain; antagonist—bromocriptine |
| D-2 | Not linked to adenylate cyclase; found in brain; antagonist—spiroperidol |
| **Serotonergic** | |
| 5-HT-1 | Regulated by guanine nucleotides; found in brain; labeled by 5-HT; antagonist—LSD |
| 5-HT-2 | Labeled by spiroperidol |
| **Cholinergic** | |
| Muscarine benzilate (QNB) | All labeled by quinuclidinyl |
| $M_1$ | Seen in striatum, sympathetic ganglia; selective antagonist—pirenzipine |
| $M_2$ | Seen in cerebellum and heart; inhibits adenylate cyclase |
| Nicotinic | Very high-affinity antagonist and bungarotoxin; seen at neuromuscular junction |
| **Opiate** | |
| mu | Mediates analgesia, morphine; selective |
| delta | Enkephalin-selective; seen in limbic region |
| kappa | Dynorphin sensitive—deep layers of cerebral cortex |
| epsilon | Beta endorphin selective |
| **Adenosine** | |
| $A_1$ | Labeled by $^3$(H) cyclohexyadenosine; inhibits adenylate cyclase |
| $A_2$ | Labeled by $5^1$-N($^3$H) ethylcarboxamide adenosine |
| **Histamine** | |
| $H_1$ | Mediates bronchoconstriction; agonist—2 methylhistamine |
| $H_2$ | Mediates gastric secretion; antagonist—cimetidine |

anatomical distribution is its almost ubiquitous distribution wherever neurons or nerve endings exist in the CNS. There is a gradient in the density of GABA between various cellular areas of the CNS, with the highest concentration found in the substantia nigra and globus pallidus and the lowest, in the cerebellar cortex. The ratio between the concentration in these regions is less than 3, whereas the ratio between the cerebellar concentration, the area of cells with the lowest GABA concentrations, and regions of pure white matter exceeds 7. Any attempt to define GABA pathways suffers from an embarrassment of riches. It is safe to say that GABA plays a role in most CNS systems. One of the best ways to localize GABA is to examine the localization of glutamic acid decarboxylase (GAD), using immunocytochemical methods. This enzyme constitutes the biosynthetic pathway for the synthesis of GABA. Two forms of the enzyme exist—one primarily localized to GABAergic neurons and the other found in heart, glia, and kidney. These enzymes exhibit a differential sensitivity to $Cl^-$ ion, with the neuronal enzyme showing inhibition to the ion. The two forms of GAD are also immunologically distinct.

The synthesis of GABA takes place primarily in nerve endings. Although GABA does not appear to be stored in vesicles, it is estimated that high concentrations of GABA are maintained in the synapse; these have been calculated to be in the range of 100 mM. There is some evidence that GAD undergoes feedback inhibition; this must therefore take place at relatively high product concentrations. The cofactor used by the enzyme, pyridoxyl-5-phosphate, may be the other site of synthesis regulation. The enzyme may only be one third saturated under some in vivo conditions.

The degradation of GABA involves two enzymes that form a shunt pathway into the Krebs cycle. GABA transaminase (GABA-T) transfers an amine group from GABA to α-oxyglutamate–forming succinic semialdehyde. This can be further metabolized by a dehydrogenase to succinic acid, which then follows along the Krebs cycle. Its significance, metabolically, is unclear. For our purposes, it is important to note that GABA-T is widely distributed and rapidly metabolizes GABA. When released, GABA is rapidly taken up by high-affinity transport systems located both in the presynaptic neuron and on adjacent glial cells.

On release, GABA acts on a postsynaptic receptor that appears to be coupled to the $Cl^-$ ion channel, thus inhibiting firing. This molecular receptor complex appears to be the site of action of the benzodiazepines, which act to increase the affinity of the GABA receptor for GABA. Bicuculline acts as an antagonist of the GABA receptor, while picrotoxin is a specific antagonist of the $Cl^-$ ion channel.

The two other amino acids that appear to have inhibitory actions on neurons are glycine, which appears to act specifically on spinal cord neurons and taurine, a sulfur containing amino acid. Glycine has a high-affinity uptake system and asymmetric distribution and mimics the inhibitory transmitter's actions on neurons in the spinal cord. Strychnine is a glycine antagonist. Taurine is found in high concentrations in mammalian brain; it has high-affinity uptake systems, is released in a $Ca^{++}$-dependent process, and acts iontophoretically to inhibit neurons. This amino acid is crucial for the maintenance of photoreceptors, and the absence of taurine in the diet of kittens will cause photoreceptor degeneration. Because few drugs affect taurine, little is known about the CNS role this amino acid plays.

On the excitatory side of the spectrum, glutamate and aspartate appear as likely neurotransmitter candidates. Disassociating the metabolic pools of these amino acids from the putative transmitter pools has been difficult. The use of lesions in cerebellum and hippocampus supports the idea that glutamate is an excitatory neurotransmitter.

Glutamate has a high and asymmetric concentration in the CNS; possesses a high-affinity uptake system found in both neurons and glia, shows $CA^{++}$-dependent release, and its biosynthesis is under feedback control. These are all properties that would be expected of a neurotransmitter.

## NEUROPEPTIDES

The most rapidly emerging area of study in the neurosciences is that of peptides. To date, nearly 50 peptides have been proposed to be in the brain. Of these, at least 33 shown in Table 29–2 have been identified in mammalian neurons. Such a vast addition to the chemical messengers present in the CNS increases greatly the complexity of

**TABLE 29–2    Neuropeptides**

Pituitary peptides
  Corticotropin (ACTH)
  Growth hormone (GH)
  Lipotropin
  α-Melanocyte-stimulating hormone (alpha-MSH; three forms)
  Oxytocin
  Vasopressin
Hypothalamic-releasing hormones
  Corticotropin-releasing factor (CRF)
  Luteinizing hormone-releasing factor (LHRH)
  Somatostatin
  Thyrotropin-releasing hormone (TRH)
Circulating hormones
  Angiotensin
  Calcitonin
  Glucagon
  Insulin
Gut hormones
  Cholecystokinin (CCK)
  Gastrin
  Motilin
  Pancreatic polypeptide (PP)
  Secretin
  Substance P
  Vasoactive intestinal polypeptide (VIP)
Opioid peptides
  Dynorphin
  β-endorphin (three forms)
  Met-enkephalin
  Leu-enkephalin
  Kyotorphin
Miscellaneous peptides
  Bombesin
  Bradykinin
  Carnosine
  Neuropeptide Y
  Neurotensin
  Proctolin
  Substance K

interactions possible. Several general features should be mentioned; first, there is probably no "typical" action for all peptides. True, they have been proposed to serve a modulatory role and to act over greater distances and with a slower time course than normal transmitters. Undoubtedly some do, just as ACh, norepinephrine, and 5-HT may play such a modulatory role. An example of such an action is the role of luteinizing hormone-releasing hormone in the sympathetic ganglia of bullfrogs. This peptide probably exists in the same neurons as ACh but acts over much greater distances and has a much longer time course (Jan, Jan, Kuffler, 1980).

Other peptides, such as substance P, appear to act as classic synaptic neurotransmitters. In one respect, most larger peptides do share two unique properties for chemical messengers in the brain.

1. They are synthesized by way of the protein synthetic machinery of the cell, transcribed from DNA to messenger RNA, an energy- and time-consuming process.

2. The active portions are finally formed by the cleavage of larger peptides or prohormones, which usually contain a family of neuroactive peptides that are liberated by the action of cleavage enzymes.

These two features may at times operate together, since prohormones can give rise to multiple active peptides. The sequential release of peptides from a single precursor may govern a particular type of behavior. Many peptides are colocalized with other transmitters. Colocalization does not imply corelease, and in fact, it may be that the peptide is released only under certain conditions. For example, after a certain level of excitation is reached, peptides may be coreleased and alter the response to the classic transmitter.

An example of the multiple peptides of one family coming from one precursor is the story of pro-opiomelanocortin. This prohormone, identified and characterized from pituitary tissue, gives rise to the three forms of melanocyte-stimulating hormone, adrenocorticotropin hormone, and three forms of β-endorphin. Of particular interest is that various forms of β-endorphin are found in different proportions in different parts of the brain. For example, in the anterior pituitary, the full-length 1-31 amino acid form of β-endorphin predominates, while in the intermediate lobe, the shorter forms 1-26 and 1-27 β-endorphins constitute the major forms. This suggests that particular attention should be paid to the cleavage enzymes and the cleavage conditions, for they may alter the functions performed by the peptides.

A final example of how a family of peptides produced by closely related genes can regulate complex behavior comes from studies of the egg-laying behavior of *Aplysia*. This process, which involves a series of specific stereotypical behaviors, is induced by the extract of a group of cells known as bag cells. Actions in the bag cells and atrial gland of the animal appear to control this behavioral pattern, and it turns out that a related gene family differentially expressed in these tissues generates the peptides that control this behavior. Egg-laying hormone (ELH), a 36-amino-acid peptide, and α-BCP (bag cell peptide) are made in bag cells, while two closely related peptides, A and B, are made in the atrial gland. These peptides cause long-lasting activity in the CNS of *Aplysia*, which corresponds to the behavioral time course and results in egg laying. The genes encoding for these peptides appear to be different but are 90 per cent homologous, and the peptides are quite different. These differences in structure are accomplished through selective cleavage of the precursor protein, in this case directed by the genes involved. ELH and α-BCP act together but in different ways. ELH causes long-lasting (hours) effects, while α-BCP causes effects that last for minutes. By coming from a common precursor, long- and short-term effects appear to be coordinated. Thus it may be that specific behavioral sequences are partially programmed into the peptide patterns produced in related families of genes. It is not known whether such a behavioral control exists in mammals, but it is probable that it does and that it can be modified by other factors acting on the CNS.

## Summary

It is hoped that this overview of neurosciences will remind the student of psychiatry of both the promise of the biologic revolution and the incompleteness of our knowledge. Nervous system function can be regulated in a variety of ways. Some have been used by earlier workers to explain brain function; others await integration into our understanding of the CNS. Subtle dysfunctions of the brain that are represented by psychiatric illnesses are probably due to a breakdown of regulatory mechanisms. By finding ways to modulate the balance between competing neuronal systems, we hope to create a new generation of drugs that will help us to control psychiatric illness with fewer side effects and more precision.

## AFFECTIVE DISORDERS

In considering the biochemical theories of affective disorders, two major lines of research must be considered: the first involves the monoamine hypothesis and the second involves neuroendocrine studies. The serious study of amines began in 1958, when Strom-Olsen and Weil-Malherbe reported on the catecholamine content of the urine of depressed and manic patients. They found an increase in catecholamines in mania and a decrease in catecholamines during depression. This discovery was the start of an extensive investigation of blood, urine, and cerebrospinal fluid (CSF) of depressed patients, leading to the formalization of the catecholamine hypothesis in the mid-1960s. The initial theory put forth by numerous investigators, including Prange (1964), Schildkraut (1965), and Bunney and Davis (1965), suggested that there was a functional deficit of norepinephrine at synapses in depression and an excess in mania. Although some of the original impetus for this theory was from metabolic studies, the strongest support came from pharmacology.

Four drugs having an effect on mood disorders were brought into use in the 1950s; lithium salts, reserpine, monoamine oxidase inhibitors, and tricyclic antidepressants. Lithium salts were described by Cade in 1948 (see Cade, 1970) and were investigated heavily in the late 1950s. Reserpine was isolated in 1952 and used to treat both hypertension and psychosis. Although it was soon displaced from the psychiatrist's armamentarium, internists found that up to 15 per cent of people treated for high blood pressure developed clinically severe depression. With the advent of iproniazid to treat tubercular patients, reports began to come

back from the sanatoriums of inappropriately high spirits and increased energy and sexual drive among the patients. This drug was soon shown to be a monoamine oxidase inhibitor. Finally, in the late fifties, imipramine was discovered and the era of effective antidepressant treatment was well under way. For each of these drugs, some connection to monoamines was found. For example, lithium is effective against mania and appears to inhibit the release of monoamines to some extent. Reserpine causes depletion of the monoamines chronically, and chronic usage can lead to depression. Iproniazid was shown to be an effective treatment for depression, and as an MAO inhibitor, it raises the concentration of amines. Finally, the tricyclic antidepressants were shown to be effective uptake inhibitors of the amines. Thus considerable support came from early pharmacologic studies, suggesting that functional decreases in monoamines could be correlated with depression, whereas functional increases in these compounds led to mania.

One problem with these studies is that they do not define which monoamines are causing changes in mood. Most drug effects can be shown to involve 5-HT, norepinephrine, and dopamine. Detailed pharmacologic and metabolic studies have not resolved the issue of the relative importance of these compounds in affective disorders. Two factors have complicated the studies. First, most drugs lack specificity and act on a number of systems. Second, the metabolites measured may not reflect the state of the relevant amine at the areas of important synaptic contact. For example, it is possible that only 10 per cent of the norepinephrine synapses matter. Thus, when 3-methoxy-4-hydroxyphenylglycol (MHPG), the main norepinephrine metabolite, is measured in urine, probably about half comes from the peripheral nervous system, and changes in the central metabolite would be lost in the normal variance of the system. Another problem that cannot be controlled for is the possibility of biochemical (genetic) heterogeneity among affective disorders.

A summary of the physiologic data for depression produces somewhat inconsistent results. Looking at norepinephrine, urine studies in general have shown decreased MHPG in series of bipolar depressed patients (Schildkraut, 1982) and no real differences in MHPG levels of unipolar depressed patients and controls. Because of the variability in the results and limitations of MHPG as a marker of central norepinephrine levels, these results have been less than conclusive. MHPG does appear to be increased in mania, and while not decreased in all studies of depression, it may have a bimodal distribution. In fact, one series of studies suggest that those patients with low urinary MHPG respond better to drugs operating on the norepinephrine system, while those with normal MHPG do better with drugs active on the 5-HT system. In looking at 5-HT, Coppen (1967) and his colleagues have consistently reported that the 5-HT metabolite 5-HIAA is decreased in the urine of a subgroup of depressed patients. Measurements on CSF have provided similar results. The serotonin metabolite 5-HIAA definitely appears to have a bimodal distribution, with a subgroup of depressives having lower 5-HIAA levels. Thus urine metabolite studies suggest heterogeneity, rather than supporting one amine as causative of depression. Studies of the enzymes involved in amine metabolism have also been inconclusive. Analyses of postmortem material from suicide victims have also been carried out. These studies showed lower 5-HIAA levels in suicide brains, but no other striking findings emerged. In an effort to make sense of these data, depressions have been divided into a series of biochemically defined subgroups: those involving low norepinephrine, showing decreased MHPG, and those with normal MHPG and by inference, low 5-HT. These divisions led to specific therapeutic recommendations. Those patients who had low MHPG should be more responsive to drugs acting on norepinephrine uptake, such as imipramine, whereas the normal MHPG group should be responsive to drugs with mixed or 5-HT activity, such as amitriptyline. These predictions have some support in the literature but have generally not been clinically useful. In part, this could be predicted, since antidepressants probably do not work by acting on uptake systems, as assumed in these formulations.

Precursor loading is also an approach that continues to be studied. This was first attempted by Pare and Sandler in 1959 using L-DOPA to increase dopamine and norepinephrine. Coppen, Shaw, Herzberg, and Maggs (1967) reported that tryptophan in high doses was an effective antidepressant for women. Currently, tyrosine is being suggested as a possible antidepressant. In general, the data suggest that substrate loading of the norepinephrine system is activating and that such loading of the 5-HT system helps to induce sleep, but neither approach results in clinically uniform antidepressant activity.

Thus, taken together, the physiologic data strongly suggest that amines are involved in depressive illness and that a unitary amine hypothesis is insufficient to account for the data. In other words, the general association between amine levels and mood appears to allow an understanding of the general biology of depression, but when a closer examination is made and the details are examined, no particular theory appears to hold up.

By examining the pharmacologic data, an analogous conclusion can be reached. The initial data suggested that all effective treatments for depression raised the concentration of amines. MAO inhibitors certainly operate this way by inhibiting the degradation of amines. The tricyclics are thought to inhibit reuptake of amines, and this is consistent. A closer look, however, poses the same problems seen with the physiologic studies. Tricyclics have widely varying ability to inhibit the uptake of norepinephrine and 5-HT, yet they are about equally effective in clinical situations if given in adequate dosage. Furthermore, their ability to inhibit amine reuptake is a rapid process, effective essentially as soon as effective concentrations are reached. Yet, clinically, these drugs sometimes take weeks to take effect. An even greater challenge to the reuptake theory is presented by newer antidepressants. Mianserin and trazodone are effective antidepressants, yet they do not block the reuptake of either norepinephrine or 5-HT at clinically useful dosages. Thus the pharmacologic theories have had to undergo considerable revision.

New theories have been proposed that relate to receptor sensitivity changes. As mentioned earlier, a receptor is the mechanism by which a chemical transmitter signals its target cell. Receptors can undergo a variety of changes, analogous to those seen by enzymes, that alter the efficacy with which they translate a transmitter's message. For example, they can undergo conformational changes in response to the binding of small molecules that alter the affinity of their ligand, or the cell can change the absolute number of receptors in response to external conditions. These changes in functional receptors result in either up regulation or down regulation at the point of transmitter action. When antidepressant medications are given, the CNS receptors respond by down regulating. This was initially noted for β-adrenergic receptors. All known treatments for depression, including electroconvulsive shock, result in the down regulation of beta receptors. This down regulation takes place over the same time course as the behavioral change caused by these medications. Thus one newer theory of antidepressant drug activity suggests that these compounds act to down regulate beta receptors. Another receptor that has been proposed to play a role in antidepressant action is the alpha₂ receptor. These receptors sit on the presynaptic membrane and regulate the release of norepinephrine. When these receptors are stimulated, they inhibit the release of norepinephrine, forming a feedback loop to control adrenergic activity. There is evidence from basic and clinical studies that these receptors are down regulated by antidepressants, thus allowing increased norepinephrine release.

The other neurotransmitter system discussed in depression, the 5-HT system, has also generated several receptor theories. Basically, data from antidepressant effects and CSF studies of 5-HIAA, the major metabolite of 5-HT, suggest that the efficacy of 5-HT is decreased in depression. This is at variance with a variety of animal data reported primarily by Aprison and Hingtgen (1981). They show that many animal studies are consistent with the idea that an effective excess of serotonin causes behavioral depression. The injection of 5-HT causes a decrease in activity and decreased performance in a variety of operant conditioning paradigms. To resolve this apparent paradox, they have proposed that in some people who are susceptible to depression, the level of 5-HT is lower. As a result, less 5-HT is released and the postsynaptic receptor becomes supersensitive, or is up regulated. When a stress occurs that releases 5-HT, the system is overly sensitive. In this way, modest, or even low, 5-HT causes increased behavioral consequences. The authors suggest that such diverse drugs as amitriptyline, mianserin, and iprindole act by blocking postsynaptic 5-HT receptors; in other words, they are receptor antagonists, thus preventing the consequences of increased receptor activation after release of 5-HT.

The result of all these pharmacologic studies has been a shift from the presynaptic neuron to the receptor field in theorizing about depression. Perhaps most important, a clear recognition that 5-HT and norepinephrine systems are related and in balance in the CNS is emerging (Janowsky et al., 1982). Thus no single transmitter can account for the changes seen in a complex behavioral phenomena such as depression. That the CNS is a complex interacting system with regard to mood is also seen looking at neuroendocrine variables. Norepinephrine inhibits the action of corticotropin-releasing factor and adrenocorticotropin. Thus it is no surprise that hypersecretion is seen in depressive states. This hypersecretion has become the basis of a laboratory test in which the potent corticosteroid dexamethasone is given and cortisol values are measured, usually at three intervals over the next 24 hours. In depressive states, there is an escape from the normal suppression seen after dexamethasone. In other words, continued cortisol is released. This test initially appeared to be relatively specific for depression; however, escape from dexamethasone suppression of cortisol production can be seen in a variety of other conditions, including conditions that involve decreased food intake. This test is a useful clinical correlate to the depressive state, and a reversion to normal suppression may be a good biochemical index of remission from depression. The levels of circulating cortisol in the blood of some depressives can reach levels seen in Cushing's disease. This is reminiscent of the levels of cortisol seen in a primate when it loses a dominance struggle. After this occurs, the animal is socially isolated and withdrawn, features often seen in human depression, and its cortisol levels go up. Thus it may be that cortisol secretion is a response to any stressor, and for humans, depression is such a stressor. Therefore, the question is whether cortisol secretion is a result of other more basic sites of pathology or a reflection of the pathology of depression directly.

A summary of the biochemical theories of affective disorders would not be complete without mention of the ACh system. Janowsky, El-Yousef, Davis, and Sekerke (1972) have proposed that depression results from an imbalance between cholinergic and adrenergic systems. The data include the ability of physostigmine, an ACh agonist, to alleviate temporarily the symptoms of mania. Thus affective states involve all of the neurotransmitter systems most studied. It will then be no surprise that a variety of biochemical defects have been proposed as markers of affective disorders. Unfortunately, none have been reliably reproduced in independent laboratories.

There has been enormous effort and some progress in understanding affective disorders since the 1950s. However, a clear concept of the anatomy, physiology, and biochemistry of such disorders has not yet occurred. This challenge for the new generation of biologic psychiatrists will undoubtedly involve coordination of the actions of various transmitter substances.

## ALZHEIMER'S DEMENTIA

Until recently, little could be said about the biochemical concomitants of senile or presenile dementia. However, with the emergence of Alzheimer's dementia as one of the major problems in an increasingly aging population, more effort has gone into its study and results are constantly being brought forth. An intriguing story is emerging that may put together many of the diverse findings in senile dementia of the Alzheimer's type (SDAT). Pathologically, the disease is characterized by widespread neuritic amyloid plaques and neurofibrillary tangles. These are the signs of damaged and dying neurons in this disorder. Early investigations showed that the degree of dementia is correlated with the number of plaques found. These plaques and tangles are widespread over the cortical surface and, until recently, did not appear to offer any clues concerning localization of a specific defect. Recent postmortem studies suggest that memory loss may be correlated specifically with pathology in the subiculum of the hippocampus. This is the outflow connecting the hippocampus with the cortex and hypothalamus (Hyman et al., 1985). The careful measurement of enzyme levels in dementia by several groups in the mid-70s suggested that there is a marked decrease in acetylcholine in SDAT. Choline acetyl transferase was found to be decreased by more than 50 per cent in autopsy samples of patients with SDAT, suggesting that cholinergic neurons might be involved in the disease. Parallel to this work, researchers began to examine the physiology of the basal forebrain. It was discovered that the area is heavily cholinergic and responds to rewards and higher order behaviors. The area was also found to project into the cortical region. Autopsy studies of SDAT patients revealed almost total loss of nucleus basalis cells (Whitehouse et al., 1982). This particular nucleus in the basal forebrain is cholinergic and has a variety of cortical projections. Even more suggestive lesion studies of primates using a potent neurotoxin results in loss of ACh in the cortex. Could the slow loss of cholinergic neurons from the nucleus basalis result in plaques and tangles and account for the pathology seen in SDAT? It is possible, but some other facts have recently emerged that must be integrated into the story. First, other transmitter systems are also involved. The noradrenergic system has clear evidence of cell loss and lowered transmitter levels (Perry et al., 1981). In addition, recent suggestions point to diminished 5-HT function as well (Bowden et al., 1983). This correlates with measures of cell loss or volume loss in patients with SDAT. It is found that brains from patients who suffered from this disorder can have decreases corresponding to 25 per cent of volume, while ACh neurons probably account for no more than 10 per cent of the total volume of the CNS. Somatostatin is also found to be decreased in postmortem brain samples and may be more decreased in temporal lobes than in frontal lobes. Thus the disease appears in its ultimate expression to be much more complex than a single-transmitter, single-nucleus problem.

The central issue, of course, is the question of etiology. What kills the basal forebrain neurons? One possibility is an infective agent. Both a slow virus and a proteinaceous factor, called prion, have been proposed, but neither has been demonstrated. In addition, considerable work, including family history studies, and an association between SDAT and Down's syndrome support a genetic factor. Thus an infective agent may act on genetically susceptible targets. The answers to these questions and an understanding of the etiology of Alzheimer's disease may well come from studies using the techniques of molecular neurobiology. Recent studies using these techniques have pointed to a unique enzyme defect and these powerful techniques should help in finding the infectious agent should this be the cause.

## SCHIZOPHRENIA

Although the forms of schizophrenia are varied and the core concept has been elusive, the two major biochemical theories have been remarkably consistent. The initial idea was that some toxin might be involved. This originated from observations on hallucinogens and very early on was incorporated into the methylation hypothesis of Osmond and Smythies (1952). This hypothesis suggested that aberrant metabolic pathways might produce a toxin that caused the schizophrenic illness. This concept arose from the observation that methylated forms of catecholamine metabolites are hallucinogens. Unfortunately, hallucinogens do not mimic the psychotic symptoms seen in schizophrenia with any close correspondence, nor has a naturally occurring toxin been isolated, despite the analysis of many gallons of schizophrenic urine and blood. For these reasons, methylation theories have recently received less attention.

The second biochemical theory of schizophrenia, the dopamine hypothesis, arose somewhat later. The principal lines of support came from a study of toxic psychosis, namely, amphetamine psychosis, and from the pharmacology of anitpsychotic drugs. This theory, the dopamine hypothesis of schizophrenia, has been of enormous value in directing research efforts and in understanding the pharmacology of antipsychotic drugs.

The dopamine theory of schizophrenia suggests that the illness is a result of the functional overactivity of DA at certain CNS synapses. Historically, the evidence on which this hypothesis is based began to appear in the late 1950s. Connell (1958) provided a careful review of amphetamine psychosis and noted that this condition could result in a paranoid psychosis with a clear sensorium. When the patient was first seen, this was difficult to distinguish from typical paranoid schizophrenia unless a history of drug ingestion was obtained. Thus it was felt that perhaps the action of amphetamine might be analogous to what spontaneously happens in schizophrenia. This rationale suggested that an understanding of the action of amphetamine action centrally would give some clues to the CNS abnormalities in schizophrenia. Amphetamine was shown to act at both norepinephrine and DA synapses in a variety of ways. Because both amphetamine and norepinephrine have stereoisometric forms, while DA does not, it should be possible to distinguish the site of action centrally. One example of how this distinction is used involved a study of the ability of amphetamine to block the reuptake of catecholamines. The $l$ amphetamine isomer is the more potent norepinephrine inhibitor, while the $d$ and $l$ forms block DA reuptake about equally well. This suggests that if the isomers of amphetamine are equally effective, the action is on the DA system. Angrist, Shopsin, and Gershon (1971) used this type of analysis to examine the potency of $d$ or $l$ isomers of amphetamine in causing a paranoid psychosis. They found that $d$ or $l$ amphetamines were about equally potent in causing paranoid psychosis, leading to the conclusion that dopamine systems were probably involved in the production of this psychosis and, by implication, involved in schizophrenia.

The greatest thrust for investigations into the biochemical basis of schizophrenia began with the discovery of antipsychotic drugs. These compounds were introduced in the late 1950s. Delay and Deniker (1957), who discovered the activity of chlorpromazine, coined the word neuroleptic to emphasize the similar actions of two drugs, reserpine and chlorpromazine. These drugs had effects on motor functions and psychosis. The motor effects were analogous to the symptoms seen in Parkinsonism, so studies of this disorder had implications for schizophrenia. In 1960, Ehringer and Hornykiewicz were able to demonstrate that in autopsy samples from patients with Parkinsonism, DA was almost entirely depleted from the striatum. Because it was well known that reserpine depleted amines centrally, the fact that DA was depleted in Parkinsonism and neuroleptics caused Parkinsonlike symptoms pointed to the possibility that neuroleptic drugs worked by depleting DA. Studies on chlorpromazine and haloperidol soon showed they did not deplete DA levels; thus alternative actions were sought. Carlsson and Lindqvist (1963) examined the effect of these drugs on the accumulation of catecholamine metabolites. Increased levels of metabolites were found, and the authors postulated that this could occur if the drugs in some way block the DA signal and caused increased synthesis, followed by increased degradation of these compounds. This was the first suggestion that DA blockade was a mechanism of action for neuroleptics. This work and the studies on amphetamine psychosis led to the formulation of the DA hypothesis by Van Rossen (1966), which, simply stated, suggests that schizophrenia is associated with an overactivity of DA synapses.

There has been enormous support of the idea that neuroleptic drugs act through the blockage of central DA receptors. The ability of these drugs to antagonize DA has been demonstrated in receptor studies, biochemical studies, electrophysiologic studies, and behavioral studies, leaving little doubt that this is the mechanism of action of these compounds. Some of the strongest support for this idea came from biochemical studies. Kebabian and Greengard (1971) described a DA-sensitive adenylate cyclase in striatal tissue. This is a specific enzyme and turned out to be sensitive to inhibition by a variety of neuroleptics. Unfortunately, when carefully measured, this inhibition did not correlate with the clinical potency of these compounds. Butyrophenones, potent drugs clinically proved to be weak inhibitors of the DA, stimulated adenylate cyclase. This discrepancy between the potency of drug dosages used to treat psychosis and inhibit the production of cAMP was resolved by the finding of multiple DA receptors. This concept was initially suggested from studies of DA turnover and supported by electrophysiologic studies. With the advent of receptor binding studies, it was directly demonstrated. The direct measurement of DA receptors began when Seeman and co-workers developed a binding assay using butyrophenones as ligands (1975). Subsequent work with other ligands has identified at least two DA receptors—$D_1$, which stimulates adenylate cyclase, and $D_2$, which does not and appears to be the receptor responsible for antipsychotic and motor effects. The correlation of $D_2$ sites as measured by butyrophenone binding with the clinical potency of these drugs is excellent.

The pharmacologic evidence established the site of action of antipsychotic drugs, but the question that remains is whether DA overactivity is etiotogically involved in the production of schizophrenia. For that, pharmacology will not do and evidence of DA overactivity must be looked for. One approach is to look at the metabolites of DA in CSF. If overproduction occurs, then perhaps an increased level of DA metabolites would be found. Multiple laboratories have done this study, and the results do not support increased metabolite levels; rather, there is a tendency for lowered levels of HVA, the principal DA metabolite. Another way to look at DA activity is to recall that prolactin release is, in part, regulated by DA. Thus several studies have attempted to find a difference between schizophrenic patients and controls in serum prolactin levels. Careful studies (Meltzer et al., 1981) have not demonstrated such a difference. A final way to examine this question is an examination of postmortem tissue of schizophrenic patients and controls. Studies of enzymatic activity are incomplete and difficult but have not resulted in any significant differences. Recently, however, a direct measurement of binding receptors has resulted in interesting data. In a variety of laboratories, postmortem binding studies have suggested that in both caudate and mesolimbic tissue, there are more receptors in the tissue from schizophrenic patients than in that from controls. The problem with these studies is that most of the patients had been on neuroleptic drugs before their deaths. The drugs appear to cause a supersensitivity reaction owing to prolonged DA blockade. Studies in animals support the idea that chronic neuroleptic use increases the number of DA receptors. Thus the role of increased DA is only partially supported by these studies.

What does DA blockage do in schizophrenia? Clearly, the drugs do not cure the illness. In fact, they only suppress one set of symptoms: the frankly psychotic symp-

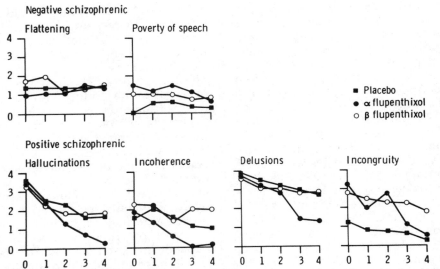

**FIGURE 29–4.** Changes in positive and negative schizophrenic symptoms on α- and β-flupenthixol and placebo. (From Henn, F., and Nasrallah, H.E.: Schizophrenia as a Brain Disease. Oxford, Oxford University Press, 1982.)

toms that are not unique to schizophrenia. These are primarily symptoms such as hallucinations and delusions. The other group of symptoms that are an intrinsic part of the illness include the negative symptoms, such as lack of pleasure (anhedonia), lack of motivation, flat affect, and poverty of speech. These are unaffected, as shown by a summary of Crow et al.'s data (1982) in Fig. 29–4. This dichotomy has prompted the suggestion that schizophrenia may consist of two main types: one in which psychotic features dominate and are responsive to neuroleptics and one in which negative symptoms are dominant, in which neuroleptics are not helpful. If this were to be the case, only the former type of patients would be expected to have DA overactivity.

In summary, it appears that all antipsychotic drugs used to date act by way of blockage of the dopamine system. This system appears central in the expression of psychotic symptoms such as hallucinations and delusions. The drugs are effective in suppressing these symptoms regardless of their cause, working well in psychotic forms of mania, depression, and organic brain syndromes, as well as in schizophrenic conditions. Thus it appears that dopamine overactivity is a final common pathway for psychotic processes, regardless of their origin. The evidence for DA overactivity playing an etiologic role in schizophrenia rests

on the postmortem findings of increased DA receptor levels in schizophrenics opposed to controls. These findings, while suggestive, are less than conclusive because of the possible contribution of supersensitivity reactions and the fact that most patients sampled were end-stage patients. Thus it appears that a clear biochemical explanation of the schizophrenic illnesses is still lacking.

## ANXIETY DISORDERS

One of the real difficulties in getting detailed biochemical information on various psychopathologic states has been the difficulty in finding valid models to study these conditions. The ability to induce psychopathologic states in patients under controlled conditions would be a real advantage. For only one condition has the possibility of laboratory-controlled study readily existed. This is the study of panic attacks. Pitts and McClure (1967) showed that if patients with a diagnosis of panic attacks were infused with sodium lactate, a large proportion (>90 per cent) would experience typical panic attacks. This has been replicated numerous times and is accepted as a provocative research test for panic attacks with susceptible individuals. The mechanism behind lactate induction has not been fully explained. Pitts and McClure felt

$Ca^{++}$ chelation played a role in the phenomena and showed that the addition of $Ca^{++}$ to the infusion mixture prevented the effect of lactate infusion. Adequate treatment of panic attacks with MAOIs or tricyclic antidepressants also prevents the initiation of panic attacks in susceptible individuals.

These findings suggest that drugs that act on the catecholamines can prevent anxiety attacks. Further studies with adrenergic agents showed that both isoproterenol, a beta agonist, and yohimbine, an $alpha_2$ antagonist could induce anxiety in patients. Thus the involvement of the adrenergic system has been postulated. This is not surprising; a basic description of the effects of stress include increases in blood pressure, heart rate, and plasma cortisol levels, all part of the activation of the peripheral sympathetic system, which uses norepinephrine. Questions of the origin of central anxiety and the role of peripheral factors have been debated without definite conclusions. The problem is, can sensing of the peripheral features of anxiety, such as muscle tension, mediate the central perception of anxiety? Does lactate act peripherally or centrally? These questions have not been completely resolved. However, it is clear that there are central centers that mediate anxiety. Two basic models have come about through animal studies.

The first central pathway implicated in anxiety was the adrenergic pathway. Recently, this system has been refined by Redmond and Huang (1979) to involve the $alpha_2$ adrenergic system as critical for the central expression of anxiety. Recall the central norepinephrine system is widely distributed and ideally situated to modulate a variety of CNS functions. More specifically, the locus ceruleus neurons may act to focus and enhance sensory stimulation. When signaled by this system, the organism reacts with an alarm state, which, if inappropriately activated, could result in pathologic anxiety. Redmond has recently shown that if the $alpha_2$ receptor is blocked in monkeys, causing increased norepinephrine release, an alarm state results. This is correlated with increased MHPG, a sign of increased norepinephrine activity. Very recently, similar studies have been carried out in humans, and it has been shown in several centers that the $alpha_2$ agonist clonidine is effective in alleviating panic attacks induced by lactate; therefore, one would predict that this drug would also protect susceptible patients against panic attacks. It appears that the $alpha_2$ system must mediate some of the effects of lactate-induced panic attacks and perhaps is the site of action for MAOI and tricyclics in this disorder.

There is another central system for anxiety, however, but this system may not be related to the pathophysiology of panic attacks. This system has been elucidated through the pharmacology of the benzodiazepines. These compounds, with diazepam as a typical example, constitute the largest-selling drug group in the world. They clearly have some antianxiety properties but are not as effective against panic attacks as drugs that act on the amine system. The drugs all show four distinct activities. They are anxiolytic, sedative, cause muscle relaxation, and act as anticonvulsants. The interest in how these drugs work has been intense, and early electrophysiologic studies suggest that they work by way of an interaction with the GABA system. It was not until the demonstration of benzodiazepine receptors in 1977 that the localization and mechanistic study of their action advanced. It is now clear that this receptor is part of a multiprotein complex involving the GABA receptor, $Cl^-$ channel protein, and the benzodiazepine receptor. The binding affinities of this receptor suggest that the drug effects of these compounds occur through the receptor. The antianxiety action of these compounds is not on the alarm or vigilance system, which appears to be mediated by the $alpha_2$ system, but rather works to reduce anxiety or fear in conflict situations.

Recently, the development of benzodiazepine antagonists such as carboline-3 carboxylic acid ethyl ester (beta-CCE) have allowed the development of another model of anxiety (Insel et al., 1984). This compound causes anxiety in primates, which also involves increases in blood pressure and heart rate without obvious increases in norepinephrine release. Cortisol is released after beta-CCE administration. These effects can be prevented by diazepam or clonidine. Thus it appears the benzodiazepine receptor is involved in an anxiety-controlling system that interacts with but is distinct from the adrenergic system. A clarification of the relationship between lactate-induced panic, generalized anxiety treated by benzodiazepines, and the alpha$_2$ system in the locus ceruleus is the next task for biologic psychiatrists who are interested in anxiety.

## REFERENCES

Angrist B, Shopsin B, Gershon S: The comparative psychomimetic effects of stereoisomers of amphetamine. Nature 234:152–154, 1971.

Aprison MH, Hingtgen JN: Hypersensitive serotonin receptors: A new hypothesis for one subgroup of unipolar depression derived from an animal model, in Haber B, Gabay S, Alivisatos S, Issidorides M (eds): Serotonin–Current Aspects of Neurochemistry and Function. New York, Plenum Press, 1981, pp 627–656.

Bowden DM, Allen SJ, Benton JS, Goodhardt MJ, Haan EA, Palmer AM, Sims NR, Smith CCT, Spillane JA, Esiri MM, Neary D, Snowdon JS, Wilcock GK, Davison AN: Biochemical assessment of serotonergic and cholinergic dysfunction and cerebral atrophy in Alzheimer's disease. J Neurochem 41:266–272, 1983.

Bunney WE Jr, Davis M: Norepinephrine in depressive reactions. Arch Gen Psychiatry 13:483–494, 1965.

Cade JFJ: The story of lithium, in Ayd F, Blackwell B (eds): Discoveries in Biological Psychiatry. Philadelphia, JB Lippincott, 1970, pp 218–229.

Carlsson A, Lindqvist M: Effect of chlorpromazine or haloperidol on formation of 3 methyoxytyramine and normetanephrine in mouse brain. Acta Pharmacol 20:140–144, 1963.

Connell PH: Amphetamine Psychosis. London, Chapman & Hall, 1958.

Coppen A, Shaw DM, Herzberg B, Maggs R: Tryptophan in the treatment of depression. Lancet 2:1178–1180, 1967.

Coppen A: Depressed states and indolealkylamines. Adv Pharmacol 6:283–291, 1968.

Coyle J, Snyder SH: Catecholamine uptake by synaptosomes in homogenates of rat brain: Stereo-specificity in different areas. J Pharmacol Exp Ther 170:221–231, 1969.

Crow TJ, Cross AJ, Johnstone, Eve, Owen F: Two syndromes in schizophrenia and their pathogenesis, in Henn F, Nasrallah H (eds): Schizophrenia as a Brain Disease. New York, Oxford University Press, 1982, pp 196–234.

Dahlstrom A, Fuxe K: Evidence for the existence of monoamine containing neurons in the central nervous system—A demonstration of monoamines in cell bodies on brain stem neurons. Acta Physiol Scand 62:232:1, 1965 (suppl).

Delay J, Deniker P: Caracteristiques psychophsiologiques des medicaments neuroleptiques, in Garattini S, Ghetti V (eds): The Psycotropic Drugs. Amsterdam, Elsevier, 1957, pp 485–501.

Descarries L, Watkins K, Lapierre Y: Noradrenergic axon terminals in the cerebral cortex of rat. III. Topometric structural analysis. Brain Res 133:197–222, 1977.

Descarries L, Beandet A, Watkins KC: Serotonin nerve terminals in adult rat neocortex. Brain Res 100:563–588, 1975.

Ehringer H, Hornykiewicz O: Distribution of noradrenaline and dopamine in the human brain and their behavior in diseases of the extrapyramidal system. Klin Wschr 38:1236–1239, 1960.

Heilman KM, Scholes R, Watson RT: Auditory affective agnosia—Disturbed comprehension of affective speech. J Neurol Neurosurg Psychol 38:69–72, 1975.

Hyman BT, Van Hoesen GW, Damasio AR, Barnes CL: Alzheimer's disease: Cell-specific pathology isolates the hippocampal formation. Science 225:1168–1170, 1985.

Insel T, Ninan P, Aloi J, Jimerson DC, Skolnick P, Paul S: A benzodiazepine receptor mediated model of anxiety. Arch Gen Psychiatry 41:741–750, 1984.

Iverson L: Role of transmitter uptake mechanisms in synaptic neurotransmission. Br J Pharmacol 41:571–591, 1971.

Jan YN, Jan LY, Kuffler SW: Further evidence for peptidergic transmission in sympathetic ganglia. Proc Natl Acad Sci USA 77:5008–5012, 1980.

Janowsky A, Okada F, Manier DH, Applegate CD, Sulser F, Steranka LR: Role of serotenergic input in the regulation of the beta-adrenergic receptor-coupled adenylate cyclase system. Science 218:900–901, 1982.

Janowsky D, El-Yousef K, Davis M, Sekerke HJ: A cholinergic-adrenergic hypothesis of mania and depression. Lancet 2:632–635, 1972.

Katz B: Nerve Muscle and Synapse. New York, McGraw-Hill, 1966.

Kebabian J, Greengard P: Dopamine sensitive adenyl cyclase: Possible role in synaptic transmission. Science 174:1346–1349, 1971.

Meltzer HY, Busch D, Fang US: Hormones, dopamine receptors and schizophrenia. Psychoneuroendocrinology 6:17–36, 1981.

Nadi SN, Nurnberger JI Jr, Gershon EG: Muscarinic cholinergic receptors on skin fibroblasts in familial affective disorder. N Engl J Med 311:225–230, 1984.

Osmond H, Smythies JR: Schizophrenia: A new approach. J Ment Sci 98:309–315, 1952.

Papez JW: A proposed mechanism of emotion. Arch Neurol Psychol 38:725–743, 1937.

Pare CMB, Sandler MJ: A clinical and biochemical study of a trial of iproniazid in the treatment of depression. J Neurol Neurosurg Psychol 22:247–251, 1959.

Perry EK, Blessed G, Tomlinson BE, Perry RH, Crow TJ, Cross AJ, Dockray GJ, Dimaline R, Arregiu A: Neurochemical activities in the human temporal lobe related to aging and Alzheimer-type changes. Neurobiol Aging 2:251–256, 1981.

Pitts FN Jr, McClure JN Jr: Lactate metabolism in anxiety neurosis. N Engl J Med 277:1328–1336, 1967.

Prange AJ: The pharmacology and biochemistry of depression. Dis Nerv Syst 25:217–221, 1964.

Redmond DE, Huang YH: New evidence for a locus coeruleus-norepinephrine connection with anxiety. Life Sci 25:2149–2162, 1979.

Schildkraut JJ: The biochemical discrimination of subtype of depressive disorders: An outline of our studies on norepinephrine metabolism and psychoactive drugs in endogenous depression since 1976. Pharmakopsychiatry 15:121–127, 1982.

Schildkraut J: Catecholamine hypothesis of affective disorders. Am J Psychiatry 122:509–522, 1965.

Seeman PM, Chaw-Wong M, Tedesco J, Wong K: Brain receptors for antipsychotic drugs and dopamine: Direct loading assays. Proc Natl Acad Sci USA 72:4376–4380, 1975.

Strom-Olsen R, Weil-Malherbe H: Humoral changes in manic-depressive psychosis with particular reference to the excretion of catecholamines in urine. J Ment Sci 104:696–704, 1964.

Underfriend, S: Biosynthesis of the sympathetic neurotransmitter, norepinephrine. Harvey Lectures 60, pp 57–83, New York, Academic Press, 1966.

Van Rossen JM: The significance of dopamine receptor blockage for the mechanism of action of neuroleptic drugs. Arch Int Pharmacodyn Ther 160:492–494, 1966.

Whitehouse PJ, Price DL, Struble RG, Clark AW, Coyle JT, DeLong MR: Alzheimer's disease and senile dementia: Loss of neurons in the basal forebrain. Science 215:1237–1239, 1982.

## SUGGESTED READINGS

Copper JR, Bloom FE, Roth RH: The Biochemical Basis of Neuropharmacology. New York, Oxford University Press, 1982.

Kandel ER, Schwartz JH: Principles of Neural Science. New York, Elsevier/North-Holland, 1981.

# chapter 30

# GENETICS OF PSYCHIATRIC DISORDERS

*by* John I. Nurnberger, Jr., M.D., Ph.D.
Lynn R. Goldin, Ph.D.
Elliot S. Gershon, M.D.

## INTRODUCTION

Major psychiatric disorders, like many other medical conditions, appear to result partially from inherited predisposition. This may be surprising if one regards these disorders as fundamentally behavioral and conceives of human behavior as the product of psychologically motivated acts of free will. However, it would seem more in line with present evidence to take the view that in psychiatric disorder, we are dealing with a primary brain dysfunction that, like those of other organ systems, results from abnormal microanatomy and physiology. The state of the brain is a substrate for behavior, and the range of behaviors possible is constricted by the condition of the substrate. The behavior of a person suffering an epileptic fit, harboring a brain tumor, intoxicated with a psychoactive drug, or undergoing a manic episode is behavior that is constrained by physical or chemical abnormalities—it is often behavior that may be regarded as stereotyped. In this sense, it is quite meaningful to think of the heritability of disorders that are manifested primarily in disordered human behavior.

What is the nature of the evidence that suggests heritability? What disorders are inherited? Is the genetic predisposition general or related to specific disorders? What is the mode of transmission? How does one apply this knowledge to the clinical situation? These questions are dealt with in this chapter.

Different strategies may be used to elucidate the genetics of a condition. Twin, family, and adoption studies are used to provide evidence for or against heritability, to ascertain the mode of transmission, to illuminate the spectrum of conditions that may result from a single genetic anomaly, and to permit a quantitative assessment of risk in relatives. Biologic marker studies are used to give evidence about the nature of pathophysiologic processes or as tools in clinical genetic counseling. Biologic markers may be incorporated into twin, family, or adoption studies. They may also be tested in so-called high-risk studies that include offspring or other relatives of patients who are known empirically to have an increased chance of developing the disorder.

### Twin Studies

A common initial strategy for assessing the genetic contribution to a disorder is the twin study. Identical (monozygotic, or MZ) twins have 100 per cent identity of parental genes; fraternal (dizygotic, or DZ) twins, as other siblings, have 50 per cent identity of parental genes. A trait that is under genetic control, therefore, should be more similar (or "concordant") in identical than in fraternal twins. The assumption is made that MZ and DZ pairs share environmental influences to the same extent. It may be argued that identical twins actually have more similar environments than do fraternal twins. This argument has been considered in detail by Kendler (1983), who argues that differential environments do not account for much of the MZ–DZ differences in concordance for psychiatric disorders. A more definitive but difficult demonstration of genetic influence may be made on the basis of concordance in identical twins raised apart.

A comparison of the MZ and DZ twin concordance provides a broad estimate of heritability. Several functions have been suggested to quantitate heritability from the two types of twin data: an example is Holzinger's index (1929):

$$\text{Heritability} = \frac{[\% \text{ MZ Concordance} - \% \text{ DZ Concordance}]}{[100 - \% \text{ DZ Concordance}]}.$$

Gottesman and Carey (1983), however, have argued that one may obtain a statistically more meaningful estimate of heritability by combining twin data with epidemiologic data on disease prevalence in the general population.

A deviation from 100 per cent concordance in MZ twins implies a contribution of environmental influences to the onset of the condition. In the case of a single major gene, such a deviation is termed variable penetrance.

The ratio between MZ concordance and DZ concordance may give supplementary information about the mode of inheritance. For a single gene trait, the ratio should be 2 to 4, whereas for traits requiring more than one locus, the ratio may be considerably larger. A ratio of less than 2 may result from significant environmental factors (although certain genetic conditions, such as heterogeneous illness with a high population prevalence, can produce this as well).

There are alternate methods of calculating twin concordance. One may use pairwise concordance in which the concordance for the sample is calculated directly, or probandwise concordance, in which each ill person is considered a proband regardless of twin relationship (this results in pairs with both members ill being counted twice). It is more appropriate to use the pairwise measure if the study consists of a random sample of twins from the population. Because psychiatric twin studies are not generally done in this way (inclusion of a given twin pair in the calculations being based on the presence of illness in at least one twin), probandwise calculations are preferable. Both types of calculation are commonly used in the literature.

Twins may also be used in the assessment of putative biologic markers. A common strategy is the comparison of illness-concordant vs. illness-discordant MZ twins with regard to the measurement being considered. This strategy is useful in separating genetic from environmental influences on the biologic marker being tested, but it is not a useful demonstration that the marker is associated with inheritance of illness (see discussion in Gershon and Goldin, submitted).

## Adoption Studies

An adoption study may be performed in several ways. In one method, a group of index probands are identified who have the condition to be studied and who also happen to be adopted. A control group of adoptees without the illness is chosen. One then studies the adoptive and the biologic families of both groups. If the genetic hypothesis is correct, one sees an increased incidence of illness only in the biologic relatives of the index probands. The critical comparison is biologic relatives of index probands vs. biologic relatives of controls (the comparison of biologic vs. adoptive relatives is not meaningful because of selective factors in the adoption process). Variations on this strategy include (1) the study of adopted-away children of ill parents compared with adopted-away children of well parents and (2) the cross-fostering study—children of ill biologic parents raised by well adoptive parents compared with children of well biologic parents raised by ill adoptive parents. These strategies have been discussed at greater length by Rosenthal (1974).

For obvious reasons, these studies are difficult to carry out. The most successful adoption studies have been performed in the Scandinavian countries, where central registers of adoption and psychiatric hospitalization make identification of probands and relatives more straightforward.

Adoption studies offer no data regarding the mode of transmission of an illness. However, they do provide most definitive evidence that a prenatal or perinatal factor is at work. An adopted-away child sharing illness with his biologic parents is a relatively convincing argument for inheritance. One might still argue, however, that events in uterine life or in early infancy predispose a person to the illness in question, such as the possibility that a virus (e.g., a "slow virus") may be causing the illness.

A possible bias in adoption studies is demographic or other unknown stratification in placing infants. That is, adoption agencies may tend to place babies with adoptive parents who are, in terms of exposure to nongenetic risk factors, similar to their biologic parents. The effects of such a bias may be considerable (Clerget-Darpoux et al., unpublished results).

## Family Studies

Family studies are typically done by beginning with a patient having the illness under consideration (the proband) and examining that person's blood relatives. A family history study is done without direct examination of relatives; in disorders in which there may be subtle manifestations and concealment because of social stigma, family history alone is likely to be inadequate (Gershon and Guroff, 1984).

Family studies may be used to assess whether individual disorders share a genetic vulnerability. If alcoholism and affective illness are related, for instance, then relatives of depressed probands ought to show an increased incidence of alcoholism and vice versa. Genetically related disorders are often referred to as part of a spectrum.

In the study of psychiatric disorders, as in the study of other disorders with variable age of onset, estimates of the prevalence of illness in relatives must be corrected for the proportion of the age of risk that each rela-

tive has yet to live through. Age correction is done by a variation of the following method: an age of onset table is constructed from figures pertinent to the population being studied. The total number of relatives studied who are in a particular age decade is then multiplied by the percentage of ill people in the population who first became ill by that decade of their lives; the product is called the bezugziffer. The sum of bezugziffers represents the number of relatives actually at risk for the disorder. This number is then used as the denominator and the number of ill relatives is used as the numerator; the quotient is termed the morbid risk.

Family study data may be used to compute empirical risk figures for use in genetic counseling. Examples of such risk figures are given later in Table 30–6 and discussed in the appropriate section of this chapter.

Data from family studies may also be analyzed to detect mode of transmission. One may consider classes of relatives (for instance, a comparison of siblings of probands to offspring of probands to test for dominance effects). A more powerful approach is to examine the segregation of illness in families in terms of various genetic models and attempt to identify the most likely mode of transmission.

Elston and Stewart (1971) developed a likelihood approach for testing single-locus hypotheses in pedigree data. Briefly, one compares the likelihood of the observed familial data under various subhypotheses of the general model. This method is effective for ruling out possible modes of single-locus transmission.

Reich, James, and Morris (1972) extended the multifactorial model proposed originally by Falconer (1965). This model assumes a large number of underlying liability factors that are normally distributed. The underlying factors can either be modeled as a polygenic mechanism or by a single major locus. A threshold point on the liability scale determines the expression of illness. Multiple threshold points can be added to account for illness of varying severity. A greater number of liability factors is associated with more transmission of illness. This model can test whether the transmission of different diagnostic entities fits a single dimension of liability factors, whether transmission is affected by sex, and whether single locus is more likely than multifactorial transmission.

Morton and MacLean (1974) and Lalouel and Morton (1981) developed a likelihood method to test both a major locus and a polygenic hypothesis under the same model (mixed model). This method is considered to be the most powerful way of testing genetic hypotheses (see Lalouel, Rao, Morton, Elston, 1983).

## High-Risk Studies

In a typical high-risk study, offspring of patients with an illness are studied. The offspring should, ideally, just be entering the age of risk, although studies have been done even in infants. One may make two types of comparisons: (1) immediate results may be obtained by comparing offspring of patients to offspring of controls; (2) a long-term result may be obtained by comparing offspring of patients who then become ill with those who do not. Both strategies are robust. The second has the added advantage of testing the ability of a pathophysiologic hypothesis to predict illness that has not yet occurred.

There are special statistical considerations in the choice of variables to be studied in a high-risk design; problems of possible heterogeneity are compounded by the fact that only some of the offspring will in fact carry genetic vulnerability for the illness. These considerations are detailed in a manuscript submitted for publication (Goldin et al.). One must essentially choose variables that show large mean differences between patients and controls (e.g., a two-standard deviation difference in means) if one is to have a reasonable chance of differentiating vulnerable high-risk offspring from controls.

## Studies of Biological Markers

Two basic strategies can be used to identify specific genetic components causing susceptibility to an illness. The first strategy is to study linkage or association relationships of known genetic loci (such as ABO blood types) to these illnesses both at the population level and within families of affected individuals. Various statistical methods are available to analyze these relationships in order to detect loci that are either directly or indirectly involved in disease susceptibility. The second strategy is to identify a biologic trait that is correlated with susceptibility to a particular illness. This may be, for example, an enzyme, a neurotransmitter, or a receptor protein that is measured in psychiatric patients and controls. If a variant of such a trait can be shown to be associated with an illness in a population and to be genetically transmitted with the illness in families, then the trait may represent a specific genetic susceptibility component (although other genetic and environmental components may exist).

Both strategies are important for identifying traits that are determined susceptibility components. The first strategy identifies traits determined by single loci, whereas the second strategy identifies traits in which the underlying genetics are usually unknown. The first strategy may be pursued without any hypothesis as to the etiology of the condition while the second follows upon a pathophysiologic hypothesis.

### Linkage and Association

Studies of populations of patients having both common and uncommon diseases have revealed associations of certain diseases with genetic marker phenotypes. For instance, blood group O has been consistently shown to be associated with an increased risk for duodenal ulcers (Mourant, Kopac, Domaniewska-Sobczak, 1978). The genetic traits most commonly studied are ABO blood types and HLA types. HLA (human leukocyte antigen) consists of several loci on chromosome 6 that code for antigens on leukocytes and other immune function parameters. There are a large number of alleles at each locus.

The association of a genetic marker trait (such as an HLA antigen or an ABO blood type) with a disease is tested by comparing the frequency of the trait in populations of patients vs. controls. This is shown by the $2 \times 2$ table below.

|  |  | Marker Trait | |
| --- | --- | --- | --- |
|  |  | Present | Absent |
| Disease Trait | Present | a | b |
|  | Absent | c | d |

In this table, a, b, c, and d are the numbers of individuals falling into each category. The most commonly used measure of association is the relative risk (R) given below, which describes the increased risk for an individual to have the disease when he has the marker trait:

$$R = \frac{a\,d}{b\,c}$$

The significance of an association can be determined by a chi-square statistic from the $2 \times 2$ table.

There are several explanations for the existence of an association between a genetic marker trait, such as HLA, and a disease. First, the marker trait itself may play a role in disease susceptibility. This is likely to be true in the case of ankylosing spondylitis, in which 90 per cent of patients with the disease have HLA B27 and only 10 per cent of controls have B27 (Thomson, 1980). Second, a gene closely linked to the marker trait may cause susceptibility. In general, if a disease susceptibility gene is chromosomally linked to a marker locus, then there should be no association between alleles at the two loci in the population unless there is some disequilibrium between them. Disequilibrium refers to the case in which particular allele combinations of the two loci occur in individuals more frequently than expected by chance. Disequilibrium can be caused by natural selection for certain allelic combinations, recent admixture of populations, or chance genetic drift. Last, such an association may be an artifact resulting from population stratification.

Loci that are situated close to one another on the same chromosome do not assort independently and are said to be linked. However, rearrangement of alleles between pairs of homologous chromosomes by crossing over (recombination) occurs during meiosis so that alleles at linked loci are not always transmitted together. The further apart two loci are situated, the more chances they have to recombine in this way. The distance between two loci is expressed as the percentage of recombination ($\theta$) between them.

The lod score method developed by Morton (1955) is a means of testing the hypothesis of linkage between two loci when the mode of transmission for each locus is known. The underlying assumptions are that (a) the parameters (gene frequency and genotypic penetrances) for the disease locus

and marker locus are known; (b) there is no population association between the disease locus and marker locus; (c) mating is random. Under these assumptions, one compares the probability of observing the pattern of segregation of the two traits in a family if there is linkage with the probability of observing the same pattern if there is no linkage. The probability of linkage is expressed as a function of the recombination fraction ($\theta$), where $\theta$ is some value between 0 and $\frac{1}{2}$. The probability of no linkage is the probability that two loci are segregating independently (i.e., $\theta = \frac{1}{2}$). This odds ratio is expressed by a statistic called the lod score (or log of the odds ratio) and is defined as follows:

$$\text{lod score} = \log_{10}\left|\frac{\begin{array}{c}\text{probability of observing}\\ \text{a family for } \theta < \frac{1}{2}\end{array}}{\begin{array}{c}\text{probability of observing}\\ \text{a family for } \theta = \frac{1}{2}\end{array}}\right|$$

A lod score of 1.0 means that linkage is 10 times more likely than no linkage. The lod scores for small families can be done by hand (see Levitan and Montagu, 1971) or by using tables in simple cases. For larger or more complex families, a widely available computer program, LIPED (Ott, 1974), performs the calculations. In practice, for each family, the lod score is evaluated for several values for $\theta$. Because the scores are in $\log_{10}$ units, they can be summed across families. If linkage is true, the best estimate of $\theta$ is that value of $\theta$ which results in the highest lod score.

Linkage can also be tested by collecting a sample of affected sib pairs. If a marker locus is linked to a disease locus, then affected pairs of siblings will have the same phenotype at the marker locus more often than expected by chance. Because only affected sibs are used, this method is especially useful for disease susceptibility loci that are thought to have low penetrance. Although general in theory, this method has been mainly developed to apply to problems of detecting linkage to the HLA loci (Suarez, 1978). Because there is so much polymorphism in the HLA region, each parental chromosome has a different set of HLA alleles (or haplotype). Thus it is usually possible to determine whether affected sib pairs share exactly 2, 1, or 0 haplotypes identical by descent (IBD) at the marker locus. If there is no linkage, then the proportion of affected sib pairs sharing 2, 1, and 0 haplotypes is $\frac{1}{4}$, $\frac{1}{2}$ and $\frac{1}{4}$, respectively. If linkage is present, then this distribution is skewed so that more than 25 per cent of affected sib pairs have identical haplotypes. The simple hypothesis of linkage can be tested by comparing the observed IBD distribution in a sample of independent affected sib pairs with that expected when there is no linkage.

Recombinant DNA technology may be used to examine the genetic material directly, rather than assessing protein products. In this strategy, a recombinant DNA "probe" is used to isolate a particular DNA region. The same region from many individuals may then by examined by gel chromatography. Differences in the base pair composition (polymorphisms) will be evidenced as different length nucleotide chain fragments on the gel after "cutting" with specific restriction endonucleases. One may then look for associations (if one picked the probe following a specific pathophysiologic hypothesis) or linkages (if one examined a random series of probes in a "brute force" technique). The latter technique was recently responsible for a major breakthrough in the form of a linkage marker for Huntington's disease on chromosome 4 (Gusella et al., 1983).

### Etiologic Markers

Starting with observations about the illness itself, one may pursue a systematic strategy of assessing potential genetic markers. First, the characteristic should distinguish patients and controls (as with most biologic characteristics, one expects some overlap between the groups—some patients may not have the marker because of heterogeneity and some normals may have it because of incomplete penetrance of the illness). The characteristic should be independent of the activity of the illness—detectable in well-state manic-depressives, for instance, or non-drinking alcoholics. It should, of course, be demonstrably not an effect of the treatment for the condition or a persistent effect of an episode of illness. There must be some evidence of the genetic determination of the characteristic, such as twin or family studies. Finally, the characteristic should segregate with the illness within families (ill relatives of a patient with

the marker should have the abnormality significantly more often than do well relatives). Thus, while heterogeneity may be present within the whole population of ill persons, it is unlikely to be present within individual pedigrees. This strategy is discussed at greater length by Rieder and Gershon (1978).

Another strategy has been designated the "biochemical high risk" design by Buchsbaum, Coursey, and Murphy (1976). In this strategy, a biologic characteristic is studied in an unselected population, and those on the high and low ends are compared clinically. In this way, groups of related clinical conditions may be assessed by reference to a common biologic substrate. This strategy has been criticized, however (Cloninger, Lavis, Rice, Reich, 1981), for a lack of robustness in the analysis of conditions with heterogeneous etiologies.

## AFFECTIVE DISORDERS

### Twin Studies

The clear difference between MZ and DZ concordance in numerous twin studies of affective illness over a 50-year period argues strongly for heritability of affective illness (Gershon et al., 1976, 1977, 1981) (Table 30–1). Price (1968) has reviewed 12 cases of MZ twins raised apart in which at least one twin had affective disorder. In that series, eight pairs (67 per cent) were concordant. Although this is similar to findings for MZ twins raised together, one must note the study's lack of systematic sampling for twins raised apart.

### Adoption Studies

Mendelwicz and Rainer (1977) reported on a study of bipolar adoptees. They found affective disorder in 31 per cent of the biologic parents of these probands compared with 2 per cent in biologic parents of normal adoptees. The morbid risk in biologic parents was comparable to the risk these investigators found in the parents of non-adopted bipolars (26 per cent).

Schulsinger, Kety, Rosenthal, and Wender (1979) and Kety (1979) reported preliminary data on an adoption study of suicide.

**TABLE 30–1**   Concordance Rates for Affective Illness in Monozygotic and Dizygotic Twins*

| Study | Monozygotic Twins | | Dizygotic Twins | |
|---|---|---|---|---|
| | CONCORDANT PAIRS/ TOTAL PAIRS | CONCORDANCE (%) | CONCORDANT PAIRS/ TOTAL PAIRS | CONCORDANCE (%) |
| Luxenberger (1930) | 3/4 | 75.0 | 0/13 | 0.0 |
| Rosanoff et al. (1935) | 16/23 | 69.6 | 11/67 | 16.4 |
| Slater (1953) | 4/7 | 57.1 | 4/17 | 23.5 |
| Kallman (1954) | 25/27 | 92.6 | 13/55 | 23.6 |
| Harvald and Hauge (1965) | 10/15 | 66.7 | 2/40 | 5.0 |
| Allen et al. (1974) | 5/15 | 33.3 | 0/34 | 0.0 |
| Bertelsen (1979) | 32/55 | 58.3 | 9/52 | 17.3 |
| Totals | 95/146 | 65.0 | 39/278 | 14.0 |

* Data not corrected for age. Diagnoses include both bipolar and unipolar illness.

The biologic relatives of 71 adopted persons with affective disorder had a disproportionate number of suicides (3.9 per cent) in comparison with adoptive relatives of these persons (0.6 per cent) or with adoptive relatives of control adoptees (0.3 per cent and 0.6 per cent, respectively). The difference between biologic relatives of affective patients and biologic relatives of controls is statistically significant at the .01 level. Nonpsychiatric suicide, defined as suicide with no preceding psychiatric hospitalization, also appeared to be genetically transmitted in this Danish adoption study. Whether this entity is independent of affective disorders is not clear from the published data.

Von Knorring, Cloninger, Bohman, and Sigvardsson (1983) report an adoption study from Sweden that included 56 probands with affective disorder and matched adopted and nonadopted controls. The proband diagnoses (following Perris's classification system) were BP, or cycloid (similar to schizoaffective), 5; UP and other psychotic depression, 11; nonpsychotic depression, 40. Probands and relatives were diagnosed through medical records. The investigators found no general concordance of psychopathology between biologic parents and adoptees.

The negative Swedish study should not be seen as a failure to replicate the Danish adoption study. Suicide, the key outcome variable in the Danish study, could be entirely missed in the Swedish study. Furthermore, because subjects were not directly examined, untreated psychiatric disorders and disorders treated privately or under nonpsychiatric guise could be missed. For example, none of eight parents of adoptees with psychotic depression showed any affective disorder. Even though this is similar to the parents of control adoptees in this study, it is far less than observed in any family study in which relatives are examined directly. Nonetheless, this study does cast some doubt on the genetic transmissibility of non-bipolar major depression.

## Family Studies

The familial concentration of affective disorders is evident in the case-controlled studies of Gershon et al. (1982, 1975) and Weissman et al. (1984). Relatives of bipolar and unipolar patients have higher prevalence of bipolar and unipolar disorder than is found in relatives of controls. Major depression (unipolar disorder) is the most frequent affective disorder in families of both unipolar and bipolar patients, which, like the twin data, implies overlap in the familial causes of both forms of disorder (Table 30–2).

The actual figures for morbid risk reported by different investigations are not consistent with one another; on the contrary, a severalfold difference in reported rates is found in comparing the family studies in Table 30–2. It appears that there is no "true" morbid risk, since morbid risk estimates vary for many demonstrable reasons, including cultural factors (nationality, urban or rural residence), age cohort, diagnostic criteria, and procedure for obtaining information (where direct interview of all relatives plus information from four relatives gives maximal estimated prevalences) (Gershon, 1984; Gershon et al., 1982; Weissman and Myers, 1978; Coryell, Winokur, Andreasen, 1981; Winokur, 1972; Andreasen et

**TABLE 30–2**  Lifetime Prevalence of Affective Illness in First-Degree Relatives of Patients and Controls

| | Number At Risk | Morbid Risk% | |
|---|---|---|---|
| | | Bipolar | Unipolar |
| *Bipolar Probands* | | | |
| Perris (1966) | 627 | 10.2 | 0.5 |
| Winokur and Clayton (1967) | 167 | 10.2 | 20.4 |
| Goetzl et al. (1974) | 212 | 2.8 | 13.7 |
| Helzer and Winokur (1974) | 151 | 4.6 | 10.6 |
| Mendlewicz and Rainer (1974) | 606 | 17.7 | 22.4 |
| James and Chapman (1975) | 239 | 6.4 | 13.2 |
| Gershon et al. (1975) | 341 | 3.8 | 8.7 |
| Smeraldi et al. (1977) | 172 | 5.8 | 7.1 |
| Johnson and Leeman (1977) | 126 | 15.5 | 19.8 |
| Pettersen (1977) | 472 | 3.6 | 7.2 |
| Angst et al. (1979, 1980) | 401 | 2.5 | 7.0 |
| Taylor et al. (1980) | 601 | 4.8 | 4.2 |
| Gershon et al. (1981, 1982) | 598 (572)[1] | 8.0 | 14.9 |
| *Unipolar Probands* | | | |
| Perris (1966) | 684 | 0.3 | 6.4 |
| Gershon et al. (1975) | 96 | 2.1 | 14.2 |
| Smeraldi et al. (1977) | 185 | 0.6 | 8.0 |
| Angst et al. (1979, 1980) | 766 | 0.1 | 5.9 |
| Taylor et al. (1980) | 96 | 4.1 | 8.3 |
| Weissman et al. (1984) (Severe) | 242 (234) | 2.1 | 17.5 |
| Weissman et al. (1984) (Mild) | 414 (396) | 3.4 | 16.7 |
| Gershon et al. (1981, 1982) | 138 (133) | 2.9 | 16.6 |
| *Normal Probands* | | | |
| Gershon et al. (1975) | 518 (411) | 0.2 | 0.7 |
| Weissman et al. (1984) | 442 (427) | 1.8 | 5.6 |
| Gershon et al. (1981, 1982) | 217 (208) | 0.5 | 5.8 |

[1] Number at risk (corrected for age) for bipolar illness appears first in at-risk column; in parenthesis is number at risk for unipolar illness when this is available separately.

al., 1977; Thompson et al., 1982; Orvaschel et al., 1982; Mendlewicz et al., 1975; Gershon and Guroff, 1984; Weissman et al., 1984).

Reliable, reproducible estimates can be achieved with careful attention to procedure and diagnostic criteria in comparable populations. Weissman et al. (1984) in New Haven, Connecticut, and our group in Bethesda, Maryland, with close coordination between centers, found remarkably similar morbid risks for major affective disorders.

Several conclusions may be drawn. First, morbid risk in affective disorders is not meaningful without a control group, such as a case-control series done simultaneously with a study of patients with affective illness. Similarly, without specifying the status of known variables that affect morbid risk (see above), estimates are not comparable. Second, recent U.S. urban morbid risk estimates are higher than earlier and foreign

studies. For example, we found higher morbid risks of major depression in relatives of normal control subjects and in relatives of patients in the United States (Bethesda) as opposed to those in Israel (Jerusalem), using the same criteria and procedures, and a similar difference when relatives of Jewish patients only were compared with each other in the two countries.

One possible interpretation is that there is an excess morbid risk for major depression of 2 per cent to 5 per cent associated with being a young or middle-aged urban American, perhaps because of the culture of our time; this may obscure studies in noncultural causes of affective disorder. The age cohort effect (the apparent rise in incidence of depression over the past several generations, see Gershon et al., 1982; Klerman et al., 1985; Gershon et al. submitted), in particular, confounds attempts at genetic analysis of multigenerational data.

## Mode of Transmission

The multiple threshold multifactorial model of Reich et al. (1972) has been applied to prevalences of affective illness in first-degree relatives (Gershon et al., 1976, 1982). The key question this model tests is whether there is shared or independent transmission of several disease entities under multifactorial inheritance. This model fit three of the four data sets to which is has been applied, including our own recent data in which the greatest transmissible vulnerability is found in schizoaffective (S-A) disorder, followed by bipolar and then unipolar disorders (Table 30–3).

The biologic implications of the fit of the multifactorial model are that the BP vulnerability includes all of the UP genetic vulnerability, plus transmissible factors that may be genetic or environmental. A similar statement can be made for S-A as compared with BP, in the data of Gershon et al. (1982). In other words, the model predicts that there are vulnerability factors shared by all three diagnoses, and that there is more biologic abnormality to be found in BP and S-A patients than in UP patients.

However, no analyses have yet been reported in which the age cohort effect (noted earlier) is considered separately from multifactorial transmission, such as by "normalizing" prevalences in groups of relatives according to an age-sex cohort function. We have also not tested the hypothesis of multifactorial transmission in a computational framework (such as that of Lalouel and Morton [1981]), in which the relative likelihood of the nested single-locus, multifactorial, and mixed models can be tested. Single-locus models have been rejected in most data sets in which they have been tested (see review in Nurnberger and Gershon, 1984) but not in the recent analysis of O'Rourke, McGuffin, and Reich (1983).

## Spectrum Disorders

The clinical genetic spectrum of affective disorders can be constructed by comparing the prevalence of illnesses in relatives of patients with the prevalence in relatives of controls.

### Schizoaffective Disorder

We refer here to patients with episodic as opposed to chronic periods of schizophreniform psychosis along with affective symptoms, and patients with some episodes that appear schizophrenic and some that appear affective in nature, again episodic over the

**TABLE 30–3**   Recent Genetic Analyses of Family Study and Pedigree Data in Affective Disorders

| Authors | Type of Analysis | Results |
|---|---|---|
| Bucher & Elston (1981) and Bucher et al. (1981) | Pedigree analysis on 1969–1971 U.S. data (model of Elston and Stewart [1971] for single locus inheritance) | Not autosomal or X-chromosome transmission |
| Smeraldi et al. (1981) | Segregation analysis | Could not distinguish single locus from polygenic transmission |
| Goldin et al. (1983) | Pedigree analysis of 1981 U.S. data (model of Elston and Stewart [1971]) | Not autosomal or X-chromosome transmission in data set as a whole or in various subsets |
| Crowe et al. (1981) | Pedigree analysis of one UP family | Single gene not more likely than environmental transmission |
| Van Eeerdewegh et al. (1980) | X-chromosome multiple threshold model of prevalences in relatives | X-chromosome transmission excluded in 2/3 data sets |
| Gershon et al. (1981, 1982) | Autosomal multifactorial multiple threshold model of prevalences in relatives (Reich et al. [1972]) | Multifactorial inheritance with thresholds of liability defined by diagnosis fit 3 of 4 data sets analyzed |

lifetime. Most studies of first-degree relatives of patients with schizoaffective illness have shown more affective illness (particularly bipolar illness) and (to a lesser extent) schizophrenia in the relatives than schizoaffective illness (see review by Angst, Felder, and Lohmeyer, 1979).

Although schizoaffective probands tend to have a high frequency of affective illness in relatives (and a low incidence of schizoaffective illness), the twin studies present a different picture. McCabe (1975) reviewed and combined the twin data of Kringlen (1967); Essen-Möller (1963); Tienari (1963); Fischer, Harvald, and Hauge (1969); and Cohen, Allen, Pollin, and Hrubec (1972). Thirteen out of 44 MZ twins vs. 1 out of 45 same-sex DZ twins were concordant for type of illness. The twin studies thus show that the form of psychosis appears to be genetically transmitted, but this does not appear true in the family studies. Where the MZ twin concordance appears so much greater than the concordance among first-degree relatives, the data may be reflecting a complex (e.g., multifactorial) form of inheritance. The phenomenon may be produced by interaction among several loci, since MZ twins will be identical by descent at all loci, but the chances of two siblings (for example) being identical by descent at a given locus is one half. The probability of being identical by descent at n loci is therefore $0.5^n$, which becomes a vanishingly small number as the number of loci involved increases. An example of this type of inheritance appears to be found in the visual evoked response (Dustman and Beck, 1965).

As applied to schizoaffective disorder, this speculation suggests specific genetic factors that cause the psychosis to have a schizoaffective expression, since there is a high MZ twin concordance. But these factors in turn are superimposed on the genetic diathesis for affective illness, since this is the most common disorder found in relatives of schizoaffective patients.

## Anorexia Nervosa

Cantwell, Sturzenberger, Burroughs, Salkin, and Green (1977) reported in a family history study of anorectics that an excess of affective disorder was present in relatives. In a family study, Winokur, March, and Mendels (1980) investigated 25 anorectic women and 192 of their first- and second-degree relatives. A group of 25 age-matched women with no history of anorexia or depression were used as controls. Of the relatives of the anorectics, 17.7 per cent had unipolar illness and 4.7 per cent had bipolar illness (not age corrected). The corresponding figures for controls' relatives were 9.2 per cent and 0.6 per cent. The difference in total incidence of affective illness was significant, suggesting a genetic relationship between the two disorders.

Gershon et al. (1983) have had similar findings, including a modest amount of anorexia in relatives of anorectics (2 per cent) and as much affective disorder as in relatives of bipolars (8.3 per cent bipolar and 13.3 per cent unipolar). In relatives of bipolars, however, there is little anorexia (0.6 per cent). There is only a modest amount of twin data. Schepank (1981) found 6/8 MZ twin pairs to be concordant for anorexia compared with 0/5 DZ twin pairs. It appears that anorexia has a unique familial vulnerability factor, possibly genetic, which is superimposed on a genetic tendency to bipolar and unipolar affective disorder. This appears to be similar to the findings in schizoaffective disorder.

## Other Diagnoses

Cyclothymic personality has been reviewed as a separate entity by Akiskal et al. (1977, 1979). Evidence from family studies (Gershon et al., 1982, 1975, 1981) suggests that it may be related to bipolar affective disorder. Hyperactive syndrome of childhood or attention-deficit disorder (Dyson and Barcai, 1970) and agoraphobia and anxiety disorder have also been hypothesized to be related to affective illness, but we did not find these disorders to aggregate in relatives of BP patients. "Nonpsychiatric suicide" may belong in the clinical spectrum as noted earlier.

## Biological Markers

### Linkage and Association Studies

Studies of the association of marker locus phenotypes with affective disorders have mainly centered on the ABO and HLA loci (Goldin et al., 1983). Results from the ABO studies are conflicting. A few studies found a higher frequency of type O in manic-depressive patients than in controls (Mendlewicz, Massart-Guiot, Wilmotte, Fleiss, 1974; Parker, Theillie, Spielberger, 1961; Rinieris, Stefanis, Lykouras, Varsou, 1979). Other studies have found an increased frequency of type A (Flemenbau and Larson, 1976) and type B (Beckman, Cedergren, Perris, Strandman, 1978) in patients. Still other studies have found no differences (James, Carroll, Haines, Smouse, 1979; Tanna and Winokur, 1968). There has also been some interest in the HLA locus. One of the first studies by Shapiro et al. (1976, 1977) reported a significantly increased frequency of HLA BW16 in patients. This finding generated some excitement but, unfortunately, could not be replicated.

Linkage of bipolar illness to markers on the X chromosome has been supported in some studies but not in others (see review in van Eerdewegh, Gershon, and van Eerdewegh, 1980). Risch and Baron (1982) have reanalyzed all of the published X chromosome data incorporating age of onset and concluded that there is heterogeneity of the illness so that in a proportion of families, illness is segregating at a gene linked to the CB locus of the X chromosome. This interpretation is controversial (Gershon, 1980), since most of the families favoring linkage are from one group of investigators and most of the families favoring nonlinkage are from another group of investigators. This issue may be resolved in the near future with the use of DNA polymorphisms in the CB region of the X chromosome (Siniscalco, Szabo, Filippi, Finaldi, 1982). If enough polymorphisms can be identified, *all* families will be informative for X chromosome linkage.

There has recently been considerable interest in the relationship of a possible susceptibility gene for affective disorders to the HLA region.

Smeraldi and co-workers in Italy (1978, 1981) found that pairs of siblings, both of whom had a major affective disorder (UP or BP), shared HLA haplotypes more often than would be expected by chance.

Weitkamp et al. (1981) reported data from 21 sibships (six pairs were part of a single large multigenerational pedigree) from UP and BP families. The distribution of HLA haplotypes in the overall sample did not deviate from random. However, a subset of sib pairs, in which there were only two affected sibs in the sibship (as opposed to three or more affected), did share more HLA types than expected from chance. However, we have pointed out (Goldin, Clerget-Darpoux, Gershon, 1982) that this subdivision of the data is not theoretically justified because it does not correspond to any specific genetic hypothesis.

We and others have not been able to demonstrate a relationship of HLA to major affective disorder (Goldin et al., 1982; Targum, Gershon, van Eerdewegh, Rogentine, 1979; Suarez and Croughan, 1982; Suarez and Reich, 1984). In addition, both our data and that of Suarez are inconsistent with Weitkamp's predictions of increased haplotype sharing in sibships with only two affected sibs. In summary, linkage of a susceptibility locus for affective disorder to HLA has not been consistently supported.

## Etiologic Markers

Stable characteristics that have been examined in the hope of identifying a marker (Table 30–4) include measures related to neurotransmitter chemistry: monoamine metabolism (enzymes and metabolites); cholinergic pharmacologic response, plasma and CSF GABA, and $^3$H-imipramine binding (which is related to serotonin transport); indices of cation transport and a brain protein variant (Pc 1 Duarte). Neurotransmitter receptors on peripheral cells have recently been investigated in genetic studies of affective disorder, including the fibroblast muscarinic cholinergic receptor, the lymphoblast beta receptor, and the platelet alpha$_2$ adrenoceptor.

Platelet alpha$_2$ adrenoceptor density appears to be heritable and associated with illness but has not been studied in a clinical genetic paradigm (Kafka et al., 1980; Propping and Friedl, 1983). Beta receptor density on lymphoblasts is reduced in bipolar patients in the work of Wright, Condon, Hampson, Crichton, and Steel (1984), but only a few ill relatives have been studied. These also had decreased density, whereas well relatives did not. Interpretation of this work is rendered difficult by the fact that the lymphoblast (a virally transformed cell that is viable in tissue culture) retains only a small fraction of the beta receptors detectable in the lymphocyte from which it is derived (Ebstein, Steinitz, Mintzer, Lipshitz, Stessman, unpublished).

**TABLE 30–4  Current Status of Proposed Genetic Vulnerability Markers for Affective Illness**

| Finding | Patients Differ from Controls | State Independent | Heritable | Segregates with Illness | References |
|---|---|---|---|---|---|
| **Enzymes of Monoamine Metabolism** | | | | | |
| Plasma DBH | No | Yes | Yes–single locus | No | |
| Erythrocyte COMT | No | Yes | Yes–single locus | No | Gershon et al. (1980) |
| Platelet MAO | Yes | Yes | Yes–single locus | No | Rice et al. (1984) |
| **Monoamine and Amino Acid Metabolites** | | | | | |
| CSF 5HIAA | Yes | Yes | Possibly | Unknown | van Praag, de Haan (1980) |
| | | | | | Sedvall et al. (1980) |
| Plasma GABA | Yes | Yes | Possibly | No data | Berrettini et al. (1982, 1983) |
| **Membrane Transport** | | | | | |
| Lithium erythrocyte | Yes (most studies) | Possible | Yes | Possibly | Dorus et al. (1979, 1983) |
| Plasma ratio | | | | | Nurnberger et al. (1983) |
| Platelet ³H-Imipramine | Yes | No | Possibly | No data | Berrettini et al. (1982) |
| | | | | | Paul et al. (in press) |
| | | | | | Mellerup et al. (1982) |
| | | | | | Langer et al. (1982) |
| | | | | | Suranyi-Cadotte et al. (1982) |
| | | | | | Friedl & Propping (in press) |
| **CNS Protein Polymorphism** | | | | | |
| Duarte PCl brain protein | Yes | Presumably | Yes–single locus | No data | Comings (1979) |
| **Muscarinic Cholinergic Studies** | | | | | |
| Early induction of REM | Yes | Yes | Possibly | No data | Sitaram et al. (1980) |
| Sleep by arecoline | | | | | Nurnberger et al. (1983c, 1982b) |
| Muscarinic agonist | | | | | |
| Fibroblast muscarinic | Yes | Yes | Yes | Possibly | Nadi et al. (1984) |
| Receptor density | | | | | |

Review and additional references in Gershon (1982; 1983); Gershon et al. (1977; 1982); and Nurnberger & Gershon (1984).
DBH—Dopamine β-hydroxylase; COMT—Erythrocyte catechol-O-methyltransferase; MAO—Platelet monoamine oxidase; CSF-5HIAA—Cerebrospinal fluid 5-hydroxyindoleacetic acid; REM—Rapid eye movement; GABA—γ-aminobutyric acid.

Two areas of investigation, lithium ion (Li) transport and muscarinic pharmacogenetic and receptor density studies, are of great current interest as vulnerability markers. Dorus et al. (1979, 1983) recently found that if erythrocyte plasma Li ratio and affective illness are considered as a single trait, no combination of single-locus and multifactorial inheritance could describe this trait, but that if the psychiatric criterion was changed to "ever hospitalized," a single-locus genetic model would fit. These data, however, have a modest number of ill relatives evaluated for Li transport, and no probands evaluated, so they cannot be accepted as a demonstration of segregation of Li transport with illness in pedigrees.

Waters, Thakkar, and Lapierre (1983), studying 73 individuals from 12 affective disorder families, found no segregation of affective illness with inhibition of lithium efflux by phloretin, which is thought to measure the same Na–Li countertransport system as the Li erythrocyte-plasma ratio. Egeland, Frazer, and Kidd found no segregation of Li erythrocyte-plasma ratio with affective illness in a large Amish pedigree (Egeland, 1984).

A cholinergic hypothesis of affective disorders was advanced by Janowsky, El-Yousef, and Davis (1972). Sitaram, Nurnberger, Gershon, and Gillin (1980, 1982) demonstrated that ill and well-state affective disorder patients were more sensitive to muscarinic cholinergic induction of rapid-eye-movement (REM) sleep than normal controls. Recently, Sitaram, Dube, Jones, Bell, Gurevich, and Gershon (1984) found that in families of 10 patients with increased REM induction sensitivity, there was a significant association in the relatives between history of affective illness and REM induction. This suggests segregation of illness with muscarinic sensitivity in the central nervous system. Nadi, Nurnberger, and Gershon (1984), directly measuring muscarinic receptor density on cultured fibroblasts, found increased density in patients and ill relatives, as compared with well relatives and normal controls. However, the receptor charcteristics reported were not able to be reproduced in subsequent studies in the same laboratory (Gershon, Nadi, Nurnberger, Berrettini, 1985) and other laboratories (Kelsoe et al., 1985; Lenox, Hitzemann, Richelson, Kelsoe, 1985).

## SCHIZOPHRENIA

### Twin Studies

Table 30–5 shows concordance rates for schizophrenia in MZ and DZ twins. Inouye (1972) has reported on nine pairs of MZ twins with schizophrenia reared apart during infancy. Three of nine (33 per cent) were concordant using a "strict" definition and 6/9 (67 per cent concordance), using a "broad" definition. The twin studies of schizophrenia were recently reviewed by Kendler (1983). Using probandwise concordance, he found that estimates of heritability were fairly consistent and averaged about 70 per cent. Kendler and Robinette (1983), studying the medical records of 15,924 pairs of twins in the National Academy of Sciences–National Research Council Twin Registry, found greater heritability for schizophrenia than for hypertension, diabetes, ischemic heart disease, ulcers, or chronic obstructive pulmonary disease.

### Adoption Studies

The adoption study methodology was first applied to schizophrenia by Heston (1966), who found more schizophrenia in the adopted-away offspring of schizophrenic women than in control adoptees. A series of large, systematic studies were carried out by Kety et al. (1968, 1975, 1978) and Rosenthal, Wender, Kety, Welner, and Schulsinger (1971), who made use of adoption and psychiatric hospitalization registries in Denmark. In the later studies, subjects were directly interviewed. In all studies, adoptees were separated from their biologic parents at an early age and adopted by non-relatives. In the original study design (Kety et al., 1968, 1975, 1978), it was found that there was more schizophrenia and schizophrenia spectrum disorders in the biologic relatives of schizophrenic adoptees than in the biologic relatives of psychiatrically normal adoptees. The prevalences of psychiatric illnesses in the adoptive relatives of the two groups were small and comparable.

In a second type of study (Rosenthal et al., 1971), the frequency of schizophrenia spectrum disorders was found to be higher in adopted-away offspring of schizophrenic

**TABLE 30–5  Twin Studies of Schizophrenia**

| Study | "Strict" Schizophrenia | | | "Broad" Schizophrenia | | |
|---|---|---|---|---|---|---|
| | MZ Con* | Same sex DZ Con* | Heritability† | MZ Con* | DZ Con* | Heritability† |
| Luxenberger, 1928 | 10/17  59% | 0/13  0% | .59 | 13/17  76% | 0/13  0% | .76 |
| Rosanoff et al., 1934 | 18/41  44% | 5/53  9% | .38 | 25/41  61% | 7/53  13% | .55 |
| Essen Möller, 1941 | 1/7  14% | 2/24  8% | .06 | 5/7  71% | 4/24  17% | .65 |
| Kallmann, 1946 | | | | 120/174  69% | 34/296  11% | .65 |
| Slater, 1953 | | | | 23/37  65% | 8/58  14% | .59 |
| Inouye, 1963 | | | | 33/55  60% | 2/11  18% | .51 |
| Tienari, 1975 | 3/20  15% | 3/42  7.5% | .08 | | | |
| Kringlen, 1966 | 14/50  28% | 6/94  6% | .24 | 19/50  38% | 13/94  14% | .28 |
| Fischer et al., 1969 | 5/21  24% | 4/41  10% | .16 | 10/21  48% | 8/41  19% | .36 |
| Gottesman and Shields, 1972 | 8/20  40% | 3/31  10% | .33 | 11/22  50% | 3/33  9% | .45 |
| Kendler and Robinette, 1983 | | | | 30/164  18% | 9/268  3% | .15 |
| | 59/176  33% | 23/298  8% | .27 | 289/588  49% | 78/891  9% | .44 |

If multiple publications have resulted from the same data, only the most definitive is included.
* Pairwise concordance figures, in general following the interpretation of Fischer et al., 1969.
† $\dfrac{(MZ-DZ)}{(1-DZ)}$

parents than in the adopted-away offspring of normal parents. All of these studies have been criticized for the selection of subjects, validity of diagnoses, and validity of comparisons (Lidz, Blatt, Cook, 1981; Lidz and Blatt, 1983). This area has proved to be controversial, with comments written back and forth in the literature (Grove, 1983; Kety, 1983). However, the application of DSM-III (*Diagnostic and Statistical Manual of Mental Disorders*, third edition) criteria to subjects who were directly interviewed in these studies has confirmed the essential results; that is, biologic relatives of schizophrenics who have not shared the same environment have a significantly higher prevalence of schizophrenia and schizophrenic spectrum disorders than do biologic relatives of comparable control groups (Kendler, Gruenberg, Strauss, 1981a; Lowing, Mirsky, Pereira, 1983).

## Family Studies

Numerous studies have examined the rates of schizophrenia in various classes of relatives of schizophrenics. Gottesman and Shields (1982) have summarized the family data collected in Europe and Scandinavia. They have pooled these studies because the populations are relatively homogeneous and the definition of schizophrenia is comparable. Pooling the data also results in large sample sizes in most categories. They summarize the risk for schizophrenia to be 5.6 per cent in parents, 10.1 per cent in siblings, and 12.8 per cent in children. The low rate in parents is thought to be a result of selection for mental health in individuals who marry and have children. The rate in siblings is probably not different from that in children because the children are not classified with respect to the disease status of the second parent. In fact, the risk for children of two schizophrenic parents is 46.3 per cent.

Several family studies have also been carried out recently in the United States. As part of a large study in Iowa, Tsuang, Winokur, and Crowe (1980) found that 5.5 per cent of first-degree relatives of 200 schizophrenic probands were diagnosed as schizophrenic either by direct interview or by family history information. The corresponding rate in relatives of hospitalized controls

was 0.6 per cent. In a small study (128 relatives of 30 probands), Abrams and Taylor (1983) found only 1.6 per cent of first-degree relatives affected. This is an extremely low rate. However, only 55 per cent of relatives were personally interviewed and no control population was studied. Guze, Cloninger, Martin, and Clayton (1983) found that in ill relatives of 44 patients, 8.1 per cent were diagnosed as schizophrenic. The corresponding rate in relatives of other psychiatric patients was 1.7 per cent. It is hard to compare the familial risks for schizophrenia among these studies, since the diagnostic criteria vary. This stresses the necessity for each investigator to study a control population. None of these studies separates data on parents (who are expected to have lower rates) from that of sibs and offspring. Nonetheless, the rate of 8.1 per cent in the Guze et al. (1983) study corresponds fairly well to the rate of roughly 10 per cent in the pooled European data. However, the Tsuang et al. (1980) and Abrams and Taylor (1983) studies find much lower rates of illness. It is important for family studies to present these data in ways that allow application of any of the commonly used diagnostic systems.

## Mode of Transmission

Almost every possible genetic mechanism has been proposed at one time or another to explain the familial transmission of schizophrenia. However, recent studies have systematically tested these hypotheses, using current analytic methods. Elston, Namboodiri, Spence, and Rainer (1978) applied pedigree analysis methods to Kallmann's family data and rejected single major locus inheritance. Debray, Caillard, and Stewart (1979) and Stewart, Debray and Caillard (1980) examined the relative likelihoods of several genetic models in a sample of 25 large French pedigrees. Although some models had lower likelihoods than others, it was not possible to distinguish models involving one, two, or four loci. Statistical testing of hypotheses was not performed, but the results suggest specific models to examine in future studies. Carter and Chung (1980) located records of all individuals hospitalized for schizophrenia in 1942 in Hawaii. They then ascertained all relatives of these individuals who had been hospitalized for schizophrenia and applied Morton's mixed model of analysis (Morton and MacLean, 1974) to their sample. Both a major locus and a polygenic hypothesis were compatible with the data.

Tsuang et al. (1982, 1983) rejected major locus transmission of schizophrenia in families of 200 probands collected in Iowa. They also rejected a multifactorial multiple-threshold model when various spectrum disorders were included as "mild" illness.

A series of three studies have reanalyzed twin and family study data collected in Europe. The European data were used because of the greater clinical homogeneity of the studies. O'Rourke, Gottesman, Suarez, Rice, and Reich (1982) examined the limits of familial prevalences and twin concordance rates based on a general single-locus model. They concluded that the majority of studies fell outside the expected limits, making a unitary single-locus etiology unlikely. Rao, Morton, Gottesman, and Lew (1981) and McGue, Gottesman, and Rao (1983) have estimated genetic and environmental variance components under a multifactorial liability threshold model using pooled familial and twin prevalence rates. In both analyses, the genetic heritability was 70 per cent and the cultural heritability was 20 per cent. Assortative mating and environment unique to twins were also found to be significant components.

From these analyses, one can conclude that the heritable component of schizophrenia is large but not consistent with a unitary single-locus hypothesis. This does not exclude the possibility that single, identifiable loci lead to susceptibility, but it suggests that there is no homogeneous single locus for schizophrenia.

## Spectrum Disorders

In Table 30–5, one may observe the following: in studies in which a "broad" and a "strict" definition of schizophrenia is used, the broad definition consistently results in a greater heritability estimate. This suggests that, in fact, a spectrum of genetically related disorders does exist for schizophrenia. Kety and co-workers have referred to cases of "borderline schizophrenia" and "uncertain schizophrenia" in relatives of schizophrenic probands. This work

was used to create the DSM-III category of schizotypal personality. Baron, Gruen, Asnis, and Kane (1983) have recently reported on an association between schizophrenia and schizotypal personality disorder in families of schizophrenic probands (schizotypal personality disorder in the parents was associated with an excess risk of schizophrenia in the siblings).

## Biological Markers

### Association and Linkage

Numerous studies have compared ABO types in schizophrenic and control populations. A few early studies reported a higher frequency of type A in schizophrenics (reviewed in Mendlewicz et al., 1974). However, this association has not been consistently present. In a study of about 800 patients in Greece, Rinieris Stefanis, Lykouras, and Varsou (1982) found no differences between schizophrenics and controls. Gc types have also been reported to be associated with schizophrenia, but different alleles have been found to be significant in different studies (Böök, Wetterberg, Modrzewska, 1978; Pahina, Roberts, McLeish, 1982; Lange, 1982).

There have been approximately 17 independent studies of HLA types in schizophrenics since the mid-1970s. Although no specific antigen has been associated with schizophrenia, some trends have been seen. McGuffin, Farmer, and Yonace (1981) and Ivanyi, Droes, Schreuder, D'Amaro, and van Rood (1983) have compiled data on paranoid patients from several studies and have shown that overall, there is significant association with HLA A9. We have pooled all the available data from the literature and find that the overall relative risk of A9 is about 1.25 in all patients and 1.61 for paranoid patients. Both of these risks are significantly different from 1.0. These results suggest that the HLA region plays a small but significant role in susceptibility to schizophrenia.

Two studies have examined linkage of the HLA region to a susceptibility locus for schizophrenia. Turner (1979) studied possible linkage to a series of markers, including HLA, in six informative pedigrees with chronic schizophrenia and six pedigrees that were classified as having atypical psychoses. There was positive evidence for linkage of HLA to the six chronic schizophrenia pedigrees but not to the six atypical psychoses pedigrees. The diagnostic methods used in the study (i.e., the definition of schizophrenia spectrum, the differentiation of atypical families, and diagnosing individuals on the basis of family constellation) do not strictly correspond to those used by other investigators, and it is therefore difficult to interpret the results.

McGuffin, Festenstein, and Murray (1983) have studied linkage of HLA and other genetic markers to schizophrenia in 12 multiplex families. They found no evidence for linkage to HLA, no matter which spectrum disorders were included as being related to chronic schizophrenia.

It does not appear that any genetic marker locus is consistently linked to a gene causing susceptibility to schizophrenia. However, as reviewed earlier, the mode of transmission of schizophrenia is not well defined and does not appear to be caused by a general single locus. The finding of association with HLA A9 deserves further testing.

### Etiologic Markers

Among the multiplicity of neurochemical, neuroanatomical, and neurophysiologic theories of the etiology of schizophrenia, few have been tested using genetic methodologies. A hypothesis of considerable heuristic value since the 1960s has been the idea of dopaminergic overfunction in the CNS. Much data has accumulated on the presence of low platelet monoamine oxidase (MAO) in some schizophrenic patients (see, for instance, Wyatt, Potkin, Murphy [1979]). Platelet MAO is under genetic control, and the mode of inheritance appears to be codominant (Goldin et al., 1982; Rice, McGuffin, Goldin, Shaskan, Gershon, 1984). Wyatt et al. (1973) showed concordance of MAO activity in MZ twins discordant for schizophrenia, and Reveley, Reveley, Clifford, and Murray (1983) reported similar data. Recently, Baron, Levitt, Gruen, Kane, and Asnis (1984) reported segregation of MAO activity with illness in schizophrenic families. However, a major problem in continuing to study this variable in schizophrenic patients is that it has become clear that neuroleptics lower platelet MAO activity (DeLisi, Wise, Bridge, Potkin, Wyatt, 1981; Chojnacki et al., 1981). Because almost all schizophrenics are today treated with neuroleptics at some point during their illness, it will be necessary to circumvent or control for this effect in some way. One possibility is to test MAO in a high-risk group and do followup studies.

Another finding in the dopamine system that is promising is the increase in spiroperidol binding in autopsy specimens of schizophrenic brain (Owen et al., 1978). This finding may not be simply a neuroleptic effect (Crow et al., 1980). However, it will need to be tied to a more accessible marker to be investigated genetically. Dopamine receptors in peripheral cells have been investigated. LeFur et al. (1980) originally reported success in measuring dopamine receptors on lymphocytes, and Bondy et al. (1984) have reported an association between schizophrenic illness and increased numbers of those receptors (as measured by $^3$H spiroperone binding). Dopamine receptors are not present on cultured fibroblasts (Berrettini et al., 1983). Amphetamine response (Schulz et al., 1981) and apomorphine response (Jeste et al., 1983) have been explored as a way of subtyping schizophrenic patients, but genetic studies remain to be done.

Other monoamine-related findings include elevation of 5-hydroxyindoleacetic acid (5-HIAA) and homovanillic acid (HVA) in CSF of schizophrenics with a positive family history of that illness. However, these measurements show similar concordances in MZ and DZ twins, and therefore may not be significantly influenced by genetic factors (Sedvall et al., 1980; Sedvall and Oxenstierna, 1981). Increased $\alpha$-adrenoceptor binding in platelets has been reported by Kafka et al. (1980). Recently, Propping and Friedl (1983) reported heritability of a similar measure. They used yohimbine rather than dihydroergocryptine as ligand. No pedigree studies have been done. Rotman, Zemishlany, Munitz, and Wijsenbeck (1982) reported abnormal platelet serotonin uptake in schizophrenic patients and some of their relatives, but cosegregation of illness with the abnormality was not demonstrated.

The neuroanatomy of schizophrenia has been an area of renewed interest since the advent of new technologies for investigating brain conformation and gross activity. Computerized tomography has consistently shown increased ventricular size in some schizophrenics (Johnstone et al., 1976; Weinberger et al., 1979). This can be found in untreated individuals suffering their first psychotic break (Weinberger et al., 1982). A study of schizophrenics and their siblings, however, did not demonstrate familial concordance in ventricular size (Weinberger et al., 1981). A recent twin study (Reveley, Reveley, Murray, 1984) found increased ventricular size only in schizophrenics without a family history of the illness, and these authors hypothesized that some environmental factor, such as birth complications, probably was responsible for increased ventricular size in some schizophrenic patients. However, another study (DeLisi et al., 1986) did find both familial and illness effects on ventricular size in schizophrenic siblings. A potential difficulty with ventricular size as a potential etiologic marker for schizophrenia is that it is found in a number of bipolar affective patients as well (Nasrallah, Jacoby, McCalley-Whitters, 1982). It is likely that this represents a nonspecific outcome with multiple possible etiologies.

Positron emission tomography (PET) has shown decreased activity in the frontal lobes of some schizophrenic patients (Buchsbaum et al., 1982), confirming previous studies of cerebral blood flow (Ingvar, 1980). A recent study, however, on patients assessed early in their course of illness, and, for the most part, never medicated, did not confirm this "hypofrontality" hypothesis (Sheppard et al., 1983). These "acute" schizophrenics may not have the same course as patients followed for a longer time, but it does raise the question of effects of neuroleptics and disease state in the "hypofrontality" findings. DeLisi et al. (1986) did not find a relationship between hypofrontality in schizophrenics and a family history of schizophrenia.

Attentional measures have been reported abnormal in schizophrenics and in several studies of high risk-offspring (a continuous performance task deficit shown by Rutschmann, Cornblatt, and Erlenmeyer-Kimling, [1977] and a smaller auditory evoked-potential augmentation in a study by Brecher and Begleiter [1983]). Saitoh et al. (1984) reported evoked potential augmentation to be abnormal in schizophrenic patients and their well siblings.

Holzman et al. (1977, 1984) have reported extensive investigations of another psychophysiologic abnormality in schizophrenic patients—defects in smooth pursuit eye movements. This defect appears to be

present in well relatives also (suggesting that this may be a necessary but not sufficient cause of illness); it is also present in some manic-depressive patients.

A convincing demonstration of a genetic vulnerability marker for a significant proportion of schizophrenic patients has yet to be made.

## ALCOHOLISM

### Twin Studies

Twin studies have examined heritability of both drinking behavior in normal twins and alcohol abuse in twins ascertained through an alcoholic member. Large surveys of normal twins in Finland found significant heritability for frequency of drinking and total consumption (reviewed in Murray et al., 1983). In a study of a sample of normal twin pairs in England, it was found that 40 per cent of the total variance of weekly alcohol consumption was due to additive genetic factors and 28 per cent was due to common familial environments (Murray et al., 1983).

Data from a large twin study of alcohol abuse in Sweden carried out by Kaij have recently been reanalyzed by Gottesman and Carey (1983). In this study, alcohol abuse was defined by criteria of varying severity, including chronic alcoholism, multiple convictions for intoxication, and a single conviction for intoxication. Gottesman and Carey (1983) calculated heritability of the different severities of alcohol abuse, taking into account the population prevalence of these disorders. The heritability of chronic alcoholism itself was 98 per cent. As the definition of alcohol abuse was widened to include convictions for intoxications, the genetic heritability decreased and the cultural heritability increased.

In a study of male twins serving in the U.S. armed forces, MZ twins were recorded to be significantly more concordant than DZ twins for alcohol-related disorders, as ascertained from the records of the Veterans Administration (Hrubec and Omenn, 1981).

In contrast to these studies, preliminary results from a twin study of alcohol abuse in England has shown no heritability of alcoholism. Murray et al. (1983) report that of 56 twin pairs, 21 per cent of MZ twins and 25 per cent of DZ twins were concordant.

The authors suggest several possible reasons for the difference between their results and others. These include potential contamination of the sample with other psychopathology, inclusion of females in the sample, and the fact that not all of the twins have passed through the age of risk. Except for the last study, most of the twin data indicate a high heritability for chronic alcoholism and a smaller, although significant, heritability of drinking patterns.

## Adoption Studies

Two large-scale independent adoption studies of alcoholism have been carried out in the Scandinavian countries. The first series of studies from Denmark were reported by Goodwin and collaborators. They found that adopted-away sons of alcoholics had a significantly greater prevalence of alcoholism that did adopted-away sons of nonalcoholics (18 per cent vs. 5 per cent). However, heavy drinking and other psychopathology were distributed equally between the two groups (Goodwin, Schulsinger, Hermansen, Guze, Winokur, 1973). In another study (Goodwin et al., 1974), the authors found that sons of alcoholics raised by their alcoholic father had a similar rate of alcoholism as their adopted-away brothers and greater rates than in controls. In contrast, these researchers could find no difference in rates of alcoholism between adopted-away daughters of alcoholics and their controls (Goodwin, Schulsinger, Knop, Mednick, Guze, 1977). However, the rate of alcoholism in women is much lower than in men, and large samples would be required to detect a difference.

These basic findings were confirmed in a large sample of Swedish adoptees (Bohman, 1978). Data from this population have been expanded and reanalyzed by Cloninger, Lavis, Rice, and Reich (1981) and Bohman, Sigvardsson, and Cloninger (1981), using a different approach. They applied discriminant analysis techniques to identify those variables about the biologic and adoptive parents that were significant predictors of alcohol abuse in adoptees. On the basis of their results, they proposed that there were two types of alcoholism in males. The more common type was associated with mild alcohol abuse and minimal criminality in either biologic parent, the severity of alcohol abuse in the adoptee being determined by environmental variables of rearing. The less common type was associated with severe alcohol abuse and criminality in the biologic father only, and the resulting abuse in the adoptee did not seem to be affected by the rearing environment. Alcoholic women adoptees in the sample more often had an alcoholic biologic mother, but mild alcoholism in the biologic father was also a significant predictor. The investigators propose that the female alcoholics have the same genetic factors as the more common type of male alcoholic (i.e., associated with mild alcohol abuse and mild criminality in biologic parents). However, there also seems to be an independent maternal transmission, since alcoholic biologic mothers have a higher percentage of alcoholic offspring than do alcoholic fathers. These analyses have made use of much more data than is generally examined in adoption studies. The results with regard to subtypes of alcoholism are provocative and suggest a framework for future research. For example, if a strictly male-transmitted form of alcoholism exists, this should be identifiable in family and biologic studies.

## Family Studies

Most family studies of primary alcoholism find that the prevalence of alcoholism in relatives of probands is severalfold higher than that in the population. Goodwin (1979) summarized the familial prevalences in the European studies and found the rates in the pooled studies to be about 25 per cent in male relatives and 5 per cent to 10 per cent in female relatives. The corresponding population prevalences are 5 per cent to 10 per cent in males and 0.1 per cent to 1 per cent in females. As with other disorders, the prevalences will vary according to diagnostic criteria. For example, in a study in St. Louis, the familial prevalences were 34 per cent in males and 6.4 per cent in females, the population prevalences being 11.4 per cent in males and 2.9 per cent in females (Cloninger, Christiansen, Reich, Gottesman, 1978).

## Mode of Transmission

There have not been many analyses of the mode of transmission of alcoholism, probably because of likely heterogeneity and the association of alcoholism with many other psychiatric disorders. Cloninger et al. (1978) have examined the fit of various multifactorial models to the familial data mentioned earlier. There are two ways to explain the observed sex difference in prevalence of alcoholism. In order to become ill, a female might require either more genetic susceptibility factors or more nonfamilial environmental factors. In the first case, since affected females should have more genetic liability factors than do males, their relatives should have more alcoholism than do relatives of males. In the St. Louis study, the prevalence of alcoholism in relatives was *not* affected by sex of the proband. These data thus support the hypothesis that nonfamilial environmental factors cause the male–female differences (see discussion under Adoption Studies also).

## SPECTRUM DISORDERS

Alcoholism is often found in conjunction with other psychiatric disorders within an individual and within families. Winokur (1972) has hypothesized that depression, alcoholism, and sociopathy occur as a syndrome (depression spectrum disease) in some families. However, this syndrome has not been consistently definable through biologic mechanisms (see discussion in Nurnberger and Gershon, 1984). Cloninger, Reich, and Wetzel (1979) have reviewed data on the overlap of alcoholism and other disorders in families. In a large collaborative study, alcohol abuse was not found to have a higher prevalence in relatives of patients with major affective disorders than in controls (Weissman et al., 1984). However, there does seem to be an association between depression, anxiety, and alcoholism. Leckman, Weissman, Merikangas, Pauls, and Prusoff (1983) have found that relatives of patients with both affective and panic disorders have a greater risk for depression, anxiety, and alcoholism than do relatives of patients with affective disorders alone. Relatives of patients with anxiety disorders have an increased risk for anxiety and alcoholism

(Noyes, Clancy, Crowe, Hoenk, Slymen, 1978). The Swedish adoption data indicates an association between alcohol abuse and antisocial behavior (Cloninger et al., 1981; Bohman, 1978). Biologic studies are likely to be the best tool for defining more subtypes of what appears to be a heterogeneous disorder.

## Biological Markers

### Association and Linkage

Many studies have examined the distribution of red cell antigen types and other genetic markers in populations of alcoholics, although no consistent patterns have emerged (reviewed in Goodwin, 1982). However, HLA types may be associated with the development of liver cirrhosis in alcoholics (e.g., see Saunders et al., 1982; Tait and Mackay, 1982).

### Etiologic Markers

Variants of enzymes of alcohol metabolism, alcohol dehydrogenase (ADH) and aldehyde dehydrogenase (ALDH), have been found to have altered biologic activities (reviewed in Goedde, Agarwal, Harada, 1983). For example, Orientals have both a high rate of an atypical ADH enzyme and a high rate of deficiency of the ALDH type I. Presumably, these differences are related to the increased sensitivity to the adverse effects of alcohol in Orientals. This is an example of a genetic variation that may *protect* against alcoholism.

One problem in attempting to identify biologic susceptibility factors in alcoholics is that differences found could be a result of chronic alcohol abuse. Alcoholics have been found to differ from controls in parameters such as levels of monoamine oxidase (Murphy et al., 1982), resting electroencephalographic (EEG) parameters (Propping, Krüger, Mark, 1981), and levels of acetaldehyde after an ethanol dose (Korsten, Matsuzaki, Feinman, Lieber, 1975). An alternative approach to this problem is to study subjects who are not themselves alcoholic but who are at high risk for developing alcoholism by virtue of having an alcoholic first-degree relative. Schuckit and Rayses (1979) studied sons of alcoholics and sons of controls and found the high-risk subjects to have higher acetaldehyde levels than controls after an ethanol dose. This finding is somewhat controversial because of technical problems (Eriksson, 1980) and nonreplication (Behar et al., 1983). In the same experiment, Schuckit, Parker, and Rossman (1983) found high-risk subjects to have a different prolactin response than controls. More recently, Schuckit (1984) has reported less subjective intoxication and less measurable "body sway" in high-risk subjects compared with controls and after a similar dose of alcohol. Other traits, such as baseline MAO and dopamine-beta-hydroxylase (DBH), did not show any differences (Schuckit et al., 1981, 1982). Pollack et al. (1983) could distinguish high risk and control groups by their EEG patterns after a dose of ethanol.

Although there are no consistent biologic markers that predispose individuals to alcoholism, several promising findings have emerged that deserve further study. The high-risk approach may be the most powerful way to identify these traits.

## ANTISOCIAL PERSONALITY

### Twin Studies

In a large Danish twin series (Cloninger et al., 1978), the probandwise concordance for criminality in male MZ twins was 51.5 per cent and in male DZ twins, 26.2 per cent (corresponding figures for females were 35.3 per cent and 14.3 per cent).

### Adoption Studies

Adoption studies of criminality have provided evidence for important genetic *and* environmental factors in the development of antisocial personality. In the adoption study of Hutchings and Mednick (1975), for instance, both the adoptive and the biologic fathers of antisocial adoptees had an excess of criminal convictions.

Crowe (1974) studied adopted-away children of female criminals. Six of 46 were found to have antisocial personality by research criteria, while 0 of 46 controls received this diagnosis ($p < .01$). No other disorder was significantly increased in the probands. On the other hand, Bohman (1978) did not find an excess of criminality in adopted-away offspring of antisocial or alcoholic parents except among offspring with alcohol abuse themselves. This study was based on criminal or alcohol abuse records in Stockholm. Individual interviews of offspring were not performed. Bohman, Cloninger, and colleagues (Bohman et al., 1982; Cloninger et al., 1982) expanded this observation and demonstrated that in the absence of alcohol abuse, criminality in adopted-away offspring of criminals was likely to involve nonviolent property crime (petty criminality), and that this petty criminality could be best explained as a result of gene-environment interaction. The relative risk of an antisocial outcome in adoptees with criminality in both biologic and adoptive parents was nine times greater than in the population, as compared with a two times increased risk for those with criminal biologic parents alone or one and a half times for those with criminal adoptive parents alone. These authors noted that the threshold for antisocial behavior in women appears to be higher than that in men and that the women who actually do manifest antisocial behavior have a relatively greater genetic predisposition. Environmental influences that were implicated were multiple foster homes (for men) and extensive institutional care (in women).

Cadoret (1981, 1982) also reported independent contributions of genetic predisposition and environmental variables (discontinuous mothering or the presence of a behavioral or psychiatric problem in a sibling or parent) in adoptees who subsequently showed antisocial behavior. There was evidence for a more than additive increase in vulnerability in persons with both genetic and environmental predisposing factors.

### Family Studies and Mode of Transmission

Cloninger, Reich, and Guze (1975) studied 227 first-degree relatives of sociopathic men or women and women with Briquet's syndrome (somatization disorder). The prevalence of Briquet's was increased in female relatives of sociopathic probands, and sociopathy was increased in male relatives of probands with Briquet's. Their data fit a multifactorial model of disease transmission in which the same genetic tendency might be expressed as sociopathy in men or in hysteria (or with a higher threshold) sociopathy in women.

A similar clustering of illnesses was reported in family studies of hyperactive children by Morrison and Stewart (1971) and Cantwell (1972) and in a study of the biologic families of adopted hyperactive children by Morrison and Stewart (1973). These studies also noted an excess of alcoholism in fathers of hyperactive children.

## Biological Markers—The Y Chromosome

Jacobs et al. (1965, 1971) have noted that there is a 20-fold increased prevalence of the XYY karyotype in inmates of security hospitals for mentally disordered individuals who were violent or criminal or both. This karyotype has also been associated with increased height and decreased intelligence.

It has been difficult to evaluate the data that was based on surveys of institutionalized men because of the lack of adequate control groups from the rest of the population. This objection was overcome by a study from Denmark (Witkin et al., 1976) in which the group of men born to women living in Copenhagen between 1944 and 1947 was taken as a starting point. The tallest 15 per cent of that population (4558) were asked to undergo chromosomal analysis, and the results were compared with data from penal records. Of 12 XYY males, 5 had a criminal conviction (41.7 per cent) compared with 9.3 per cent of the 4096 XY males ($p < .01$ by Fisher's exact test). Criminality appeared to be associated with decreased intelligence in the XYY males but not with height. The criminal acts involved in this study were not personally violent. Although the number of probands in the Danish study was quite small, it is the best-controlled assessment of the relationship of the XYY genotype to criminality. It does appear that there is a significantly increased risk of antisocial behavior in a male with this genotype. As for the societal impact of this increased risk, it is small. XYY males represent

0.5 per cent to 3 per cent of the institutionalized population (Shah and Roth, 1974). Other investigators have reported an increased length of the Y chromosome in persons with behavioral disturbance (Dorus, 1980; McConville et al., 1983). These two types of data suggest a possible role for the Y chromosome in the predisposition to socially disruptive behavior.

## PANIC DISORDER AND OTHER ANXIETY DISORDERS

Crowe et al. (1980) reported a 31 per cent risk of panic disorder in relatives of persons with anxiety neurosis. Among relatives personally interviewed, the incidence was 41 per cent. The presence or absence of mitral valve prolapse in the proband did not affect the morbid risk in relatives. Alcoholism was also increased in relatives, but DSM-III major depression was not. In a pedigree study of these same families, Pauls, Bucher, Crowe, and Noyes (1980) concluded that autosomal dominant transmission was likely. Crowe, Noyes, Pauls, and Slymen (1983), in a followup including the data in their earlier study, reported a 25 per cent incidence of definite or probable panic disorder in relatives of patients with panic. No excess of generalized anxiety disorder or major depressive disorder was found. A nonsignificant excess of alcoholism was present. Data were consistent with single-locus or polygenic transmission.

Twenty agoraphobic probands and their families were studied by Harris, Noyes, Crowe, and Chaudhry (1983). An excess of "all-anxiety disorder" (agoraphobia, panic, generalized anxiety, atypical anxiety, social phobia, simple phobia, and obsessive compulsive disorder) and alcoholism, but not affective disorders, was found in relatives of agoraphobic probands.

However, Leckman et al. (1983) have studied probands with depression and panic disorder. Relatives of those persons show an increased risk of depression, anxiety disorder (phobias, panic disorder, and generalized anxiety), and alcoholism. These data are compatible with a partially shared genetic predisposition to panic disorder and depression. Anxiety disorders themselves do clearly seem to be familially aggregated.

## OTHER GENETICALLY TRANSMITTED BEHAVIORAL/COGNITIVE DISORDERS

### Gilles de la Tourette's Syndrome

A rare syndrome of chronic vocal and motor tics, with a waxing and waning course, Gilles de la Tourette's syndrome is well known to be familial. Males are more often affected than females. It appears to be highly concentrated in Ashkenazi Jews, a genetically homogeneous subgroup of Jews that includes nearly all European-origin Jews (Eldridge, Wassman, Nee, Koerber, 1979). Twin and adoption studies have not been performed. Analysis of the distribution of illness in families showed that chronic multiple tics were familially associated with Tourette's syndrome, apparently as a milder form of illness (Pauls, Cohen, Heimbuch, Detlor, Kidd, 1981; Kidd, Prusoff, Cohen, 1980). A sex threshold effect in transmission appears present, with relatives of female probands having more Tourette's and more multiple tics, than do relatives of male probands. A recent analysis of 250 families of Tourette's patients using the model of Lalouel and Morton (1981) concluded that a single semidominant major gene was likely to explain most of the variation in incidence of this condition (Comings, Comings, Devor, Cloninger, 1984).

### Specific Reading Disability

First described as "congenital word blindness" in 1896, the familial nature of this disorder has been known for most of this century. Males are more severely affected. Zerbin-Rudin (1967), in a review, found that MZ concordance was complete but that DZ concordance was 35 per cent. Although not all cases fit a single mode of transmission (DeFries and Decker, 1982), a most convincing demonstration of autosomal dominant inheritance of at least a subtype of this disorder was provided by Smith, Kimberling, Pennington, and Lubs (1983), who found a significant linkage to a chromosomal banding polymorphism on chromosome 15 in a series of pedigrees.

### Male Homosexuality

As reviewed by Pillard, Poumadere, and Caretta (1981), the only large twin study was performed by Kallman more than 30 years earlier. MZ concordance was complete, and DZ concordance was much lower. Later authors have reported discordant MZ twins. The epidemiologic study of Pillard, Poumadere, and Caretta (1982) consists of well-sampled homosexuals and controls and shows that in male, but not female, homosexuals, there is increase of homosexuality in relatives of the same sex.

### Delusional Disorder

Kendler (1980), Kendler et al. (1981), and Kendler and Hays (1981) argued that delusional disorder (paranoid psychosis without other signs and symptoms of schizophrenia) is genetically distinct from affective disorders and schizophrenia. The evidence does suggest that the persons with this uncommon disorder (about one tenth as common as schizophrenia) have fewer schizophrenic relatives than otherwise defined schizophrenic probands.

## GENETIC COUNSELING

Genetic counseling for psychiatric disorders should begin with the following general principles:

- The major psychiatric disorders appear to be inherited.
- The mode of transmission of these disorders is unknown.
- Biologic markers of genetic vulnerability are not sufficiently established to be of clinical use.
- Empirical risk estimates are available and should be used (see Table 30–6).
- A request for genetic counseling should be approached as a problem in short-term psychotherapy.

The most common questions that the psychiatric genetic counselor is asked are probably (a) "What is the chance of my child developing the same disorder that I/my spouse has?" and (b) "What are the chances of my developing the same disorder that my relative has?"

Consider the first of these questions. It is often asked in the context, "Should I have children?" The astute clinician will be aware of the concerns that are evident in this question—issues of self-esteem, competency, feelings of being damaged or impaired.

**TABLE 30–6**

| Illness | Evidence for Heritability | Mode of Transmission | Risk First-Degree Relatives/ Risk General Population | Median Age of Onset |
|---------|--------------------------|----------------------|------------------------------------------------------|---------------------|
| Affective disorder | Twin Family/adoption studies | Multifactorial? | 20–25%/7% | 25–30 |
| Schizophrenia | Twin Family/adoption studies | Multifactorial? | 6–10%/1% | 20–25 |
| Alcoholism | Twin Family/adoption studies | Unknown | 25–35(males)/5–10% 5–10%(females)/1–3% | 25–30 |
| Antisocial personality | Twin Family/adoption studies | Multifactorial? | 15–25% (males)/2–3% 2–11% (females)/0.5% | 15–20 |
| Panic disorder | Family studies | Autosomal Dominant? | 40%/2% | 20–25 |

References are found in the appropriate sections of the text.

These are concerns that should be addressed.

Practical issues regarding child-bearing and child-raising must be dealt with. Suppose the prospective mother has bipolar manic-depressive illness. Will she be able to manage the strains of pregnancy, birth, and dealing with a young child? Can she safely go off medication during pregnancy (lithium appears to increase teratogenic risk; the data for antidepressants and neuroleptics is not as clear). If so, when should medication be restarted (most experts believe that the first trimester is the most dangerous). Most psychotropic agents are passed through breast milk, and therefore, if they are reinstituted after birth, the child should be bottle-fed. It is agreed that puerperium is a time of particular danger for mothers with affective illness.

If the prospective father has major psychiatric disorder, the issues are somewhat different. Psychodynamically, the major difficulty may be the shift in attention of his spouse, who now must devote her mothering energies to the new child rather than to an ill husband. Issues of medication-induced fetal damage do not appear to be a concern here.

If both mother and father have a psychiatric illness, all of the previous issues apply as well as a new concern: the empirical risk of psychiatric illness in the child is then greatly increased, perhaps more than additively. For children of two parents with major affective illness, for instance, the risk is probably between 50 per cent and 75 per cent. There is, in general, no advantage in amniocentesis for such couples because there is no marker to be found.

All this being said, the fact is that most prospective parents are not deterred from starting or enlarging a family by these concerns. Nor should they be. Most psychiatric illnesses are manageable and are likely to become more so. Exceptions might be the instance in which two persons with chronic schizophrenic or schizoaffective illness are prospective parents, or in which the mother has poorly controlled rapid-cycling bipolar illness. The keynote of the discussion with parents concerned about their children developing a psychiatric illness should be in education about the nature of the condition and an inculcation of awareness, where it is indicated, that if such symptoms develop, they should receive early professional attention. This is especially true for the affective disorders, for which early treatment can prevent major disruption of young adulthood.

Empirical risk figures for first-degree relatives are shown in Table 30–6. These are lifetime risks for the development of the indicated condition. In general, offspring of a person with one major psychiatric condition are not at increased risk for other illnesses (exceptions are noted in the Discussion). These figures should be used in conjunction with the population risk figures in the same table. These risk figures are for first-degree relatives: parents, siblings, children; the age of the subject should be taken into account when they are used (see below).

Second-degree relatives have in general a small increase in risk over the general population.

Special cases are (a) dual matings, considered earlier, and (b) identical twins, for whom lifetime risk is quite high (see summaries of twin studies in the individual sections of this chapter).

Consider the second common question posed to the counselor: "My [brother, mother, great aunt, ex-husband, roommate] has schizophrenia. Will I also get it?" The last two examples are included not frivolously. The evidence for viral transmission of schizophrenia has been summarized by Crow (1983), and similar theories of affective illness are extant. One may specify, however, that in general, the epidemiologic evidence for contagion rests on studies among relatives, that is, among persons sharing both genetic *and* environmental factors.* Thus the family study-derived figures, even if they included effects of a viral factor, would still be accurate; the danger of developing major psychiatric disorder by contact alone must be regarded as a hypothesis without evidence.

One should, of course, do a thorough diagnostic evaluation when presented with the second question. It may be that the disorder has already been manifest but has been denied (for instance, the sister of a bipolar patients asks, "Will I become ill?" and under questioning reveals a major depressive episode 5 years previously; the answer is that she appears to be vulnerable to affective illness [Yes, she is ill], but the chances are that it will not be as severe as that of her brother [see Gershon et al., 1982]). Or the son of an alcoholic patient who has already experienced blackouts from drinking—the real question in these and similar cases is "Will my life be like that of (the sick relative)?" and the answer, in general, is "not with treatment."

Sometimes what may have been noted is a minor disorder of a type similar to that of the probands (for instance, cyclothymic or minor depression in the child of a bipolar patient). Here the answer is that we do not know what to expect—the major disorder *may* come, one should know the symptoms, and one should be aware of the difference that early treatment will make.

If the counselor is satisfied that a major disorder does not exist at present, then the question of the subject's age must be addressed (see Table 30–6 for median ages of onset for the various psychiatric disorders). For instance, a 25-year-old male with no history of antisocial behavior is highly unlikely to develop criminality, even if his family tree is loaded with criminals and he has the XYY genotype. However, a 25-year-old male with a bipolar sibling is just at the midpoint of his risk for affective disorder (that is his lifetime risk is $\frac{1}{4}$ [as the first-degree relative of a manic-depressive patient] $\times \frac{1}{2}$ [since he has passed through half of the period of risk] $= \frac{1}{8}$). There is some evidence, although it is equivocal, of concordance in age of onset among relatives (for affective illness, Weissman et al., submitted for publication; for schizophrenia, Abe, 1969). This might confer an additional degree of safety on those well persons who have already passed the age at which their relative became ill.

The general attitude of the clinician in these circumstances should be reassuring but informing: reassuring because the news is usually more good than bad, but informing because, more than others, relatives of those with major psychiatric disorder need to know as much as possible about the signs, symptoms, and treatment of these conditions.

Two further observations on the meaning of inherited disorders for patients may be made. First, there is a widespread misapprehension that genetic illnesses are likely to be untreatable. Such is not the case. The prospects of cure for such illnesses are in the hands of the molecular biologists and may be available within the lifetimes of most of us. But more important, existing treatments for many genetic disorders are efficacious (e.g., dietary therapy for phenylketonuria). Second, the recognition of genetics as an important factor in etiology of these conditions may be a tremendous relief to families who have lived through an era when exaggerated claims were made for psychosocial causation and treatment. No credible evidence exists for specific psychosocial factors in the vulnerability for chronic schizophrenia, bipolar affective disorder, or panic disorder; such factors appear to play a role in antisocial personality and alcoholism, along with genetic factors. Life events may precipitate individual episodes of psychiatric disturbance (see review in Nurnberger, Jimerson, Bunney, 1983a), but it is not clear

---

* An exception is the study of Kazanetz, referred to by Crow, in which Moscow housing complexes were studied and propinquity alone found to be a risk factor for schizophrenic illness. The original report of this study was not available to us.

that they contribute to the vulnerability of a person to develop the disorder at some point during his or her life. There is little evidence that drug abuse precipitates persistent psychiatric syndromes in unpredisposed persons (see review by Propping, 1983), although the possibility cannot be ruled out. For parents to realize that they have not caused a disorder in their children by something they did (other than the decision to have children in itself) may often be liberating.

## DISCUSSION

The points of significance for the clinician are summarized in the foregoing genetic counseling section and in Tables 30–6 and 30–7. What might be addressed at this point is the question, "What is needed in psychiatric genetics?" and the answer is, essentially, "biologic markers." To assert that a disorder is heritable is to assert that an altered DNA produces an altered protein in persons having that disorder. We may make that assertion with regard to the major psychiatric disorders. There appear to be independent genetic vulnerability factors for affective illness, schizophrenia, alcoholism, anxiety, sociopathy, although these diagnostic entities also show some overlap. There are, of course, many persons seeking psychiatric attention who do not fall neatly into one of these categories. What is necessary at this point is to identify the altered proteins that predispose a person to disrupted central nervous functioning. With a more specific biology of genetic vulnerability to psychiatric illness, the diagnostic schemes could be rewritten.

How should such markers be pursued? Perhaps a word is in order about how they should not be pursued. Biologic studies on acutely ill, medicated patients are not likely to be of value unless comparison groups of unmedicated well patients are included. The definition of "unmedicated" may have to be revised from the previously accepted 3 days or 1 or even 2 weeks to months or "never medicated." Of course, acute intake of alcohol or street drugs needs to be considered. Other factors that need to be considered for certain variables (besides the obvious ones of age, sex, and concurrent illnesses) include time of day, time of year, diet, and menstrual status of women.

One may argue that these kinds of restrictions make studies almost impossible to do. We would agree that the difficulties are extreme but would suggest that the field is in a state of maturity now such that it is worth taking the time to design appropriate, although difficult, studies.

Some methods that may get around the difficulties are the following:

1. *Direct examination of DNA using recombinant techniques.* This may be done in lymphocytes or fibroblasts and may start with a pathophysiologic hypothesis or rely on "brute force." Cells from pedigrees with multiple ill persons are desirable for these studies. A functioning molecular genetics laboratory is required, and thus this must be a collaboration between the clinical ge-

**TABLE 30–7**

| Illness | Spectrum Disorders | Putative Vulnerability Markers |
|---|---|---|
| Affective disorder | BP, UP, schizoaffective, anorexia nervosa, bulimia, cyclothymic personality | REM induction; fibroblast muscarinic receptor; lithium ratio? |
| Schizophrenia | Schizotypal personality? | HLA-A$_9$; smooth pursuit eye movements; monoamine-related abnormalities in platelets; cognitive or attentional deficits |
| Alcoholism | — | Aldehyde dehydrogenase intoxication level |
| Antisocial personality | Briquet's syndrome Attention deficit disorder | XYY karyotype |
| Panic disorder | Agoraphobia Generalized anxiety disorder Obsessive compulsive disorder | — |

References are found in the appropriate sections of the text.

netic researcher and the molecular biologist. The effectiveness of these methods has been demonstrated by Kan and Dozy (1978) and Gusella et al. (1983).

2. *Tissue cultures.* Transformed lymphocytes and fibroblasts may be cultured and grown almost indefinitely. They may be grown to sufficient quantity for multiple biologic tests. Because the cells themselves are many passages away from the patient, it is unlikely that illness state or medication status would influence them. Recently, lymphoblasts (Wright et al., 1984) have provided a possible marker in affective illness.

3. *High-risk studies.* Well offspring of patients or siblings of patients face increased risk of illness if they have not yet passed through the age of risk. Such persons are not yet biochemically influenced by the effects of illness or the treatments for it. Schuckit and Rayses (1979) used this method to study acetaldehyde as a marker for alcoholism. Similarly, Rutschman et al. (1977) have identified a psychomotor deficit in offspring of schizophrenics. Appropriate design and statistical considerations must be observed (Goldin et al., submitted). Followup studies of such populations are of value.

4. *Pharmacogenetic studies.* Pharmacologic responses in appropriate populations (well state patients, twins, relatives) may be evaluated, similar to the use of a glucose tolerance test. The cholinergic REM induction test (Sitaram et al., 1980; Nurnberger et al. 1983c) is an example. We have found that an outpatient clinic in which selected patients are periodically asked to go off medication for testing is valuable. Such strategies may also be used to identify subgroups in the "normal" population that may be more sensitive to the effects of psychoactive drugs on a genetic basis (Nurnberger et al., 1982a).

5. *Comparison of familial risks in biologically characterized groups.* Schlesser and co-workers (1979, 1980) have pursued a variant of this strategy in studying familial correlates of the dexamethasone suppression test in affective illness. Reveley et al. (1984) have used this strategy in studying ventricular size in schizophrenia. An essential for such studies, however, is appropriate family study methodology (Gershon and Guroff, 1984).

6. *Epidemiologic studies using biologic markers.* Buchsbaum et al. (1976) applied this approach to demonstrate differences between high MAO and low MAO groups in a college population. Since that time, however, the interpretation of MAO data has become more difficult because of drug and alcohol effects. The strategy is still of value in extending biologic genetic studies from the research institute to the "real world." A more detailed consideration of this and related strategies may be found in Nurnberger et al. (1983a).

7. *Longitudinal followup of individual patients or groups in different mood states and medication states.* VanPraag and deHaan (1980) used this method to separate a group of patients with persistent low 5-HIAA. Suranyi-Cadotte, Wood, Nair, and Schwartz (1982) followed depressed patients with imipramine binding studies to demonstrate that alterations in this parameter were *not* a trait marker of depression.

8. *Preclinical studies.* If a biochemical abnormality predisposes to psychiatric illness in humans, one presumes that the same abnormality might be found in certain animal species. Appropriate animal models of psychiatric illness, however, are difficult to validate. Recently, Suomi (1983) described depressionlike states in monkeys who were unusually sensitive to separation. There is some evidence for a genetic predisposition to such states; they may be associated with dexamethasone nonsuppression; and they respond to imipramine. Biochemical hypotheses, such as increased $D_2$ receptors in schizophrenia (Owen et al., 1978) might be studied by examining inbred rodent populations. The physiologic and neuroanatomical "meaning" of these biochemical abnormalities might then become clearer. In a variant of this strategy, Murphy, McBride, Lumeng, and Li (1982b) have studied a strain of rats bred for alcohol-preferring behavior. These rats showed a difference in serotonin content in several brain areas, and this difference predates the exposure to alcohol.

The types of studies we have been discussing are possible now partly because of methodological advances in the laboratory, but more critically because of methodological advances in the clinic. A generation ago few basic researchers were interested in psychiatric problems. If clinicians could not agree on who had schizophrenia, how was one to inquire into the biology of it? The development of diagnostic criteria, while not eliminating differences of opinion, at least makes it clearer what sort of patients one is studying. A second major step has been the development of rigorous methodologies for making biologic measurements in intact humans. Only by adherence to such constraints may we hope to attract the interest and collaboration of the neurochemist, the molecular geneticist, the psychophysiologist, and others who are essential to the enterprise of translating clinical genetic knowledge into a molecular understanding of brain dysfunction.

## SUMMARY

Data from twin, family, and adoption studies suggest the following: a predisposition to affective illness is inherited—elements of the affective spectrum include bipolar illness, unipolar illness, schizoaffective disorder, cyclothymic personality, and the eating disorders anorexia nervosa and bulimia. Schizophrenia, or at least some forms of it, appears to originate in genetic vulnerability. The spectrum of schizophrenic illness has yet to be fully defined in terms of modern criteria. The development of antisocial personality is strongly influenced by both genetics and the home environment; XYY men are at increased risk for this disorder. Severe forms of alcoholism appear to be strongly heritable. Anxiety disorders are probably also heritable; the anxiety spectrum may include generalized anxiety, panic disorder, agoraphobia, and obsessive-compulsive disorder. Some forms of anxiety disorder may have overlapping vulnerability with depressive disorders.

The mode of transmission of these disorders is not yet clear; biologic markers of genetic vulnerability are not yet available for clinical use. Genetic counseling should be based on empirical risk figures, some of which are presented herein. Strategies for the elucidation and testing of biologic markers are considered.

## REFERENCES

Abe K: The morbidity rate and environmental influence in monozygotic cotwins of schizophrenics. Br J Psychiatry 115:519–531, 1969.

Abrams R, Taylor MA: The genetics of schizophrenia: A reassessment using modern criteria. Am J Psychiatry 140:171–175, 1983.

Akiskal HS, Djenderedjian AH, Rosenthal RH: Cyclothymic disorder: validating criteria for inclusion in the bipolar affective group. Am J Psychiatry 134:1227–1233, 1977.

Akiskal HS, Khan MK, Scott-Strauss A: Cyclothymic temperamental disorders. Psychiatr Clin North Am 2:527–554, 1979.

Allen MG, Cohen S, Pollin W, Greenspan SI: Affective illness in veteran twins. A diagnostic review. Am J Psychiatry 131:1234–1239, 1974.

Angst J, Felder W, Lohmeyer B: Schizoaffective disorders: results of a genetic investigation I. J Affect Disord 1:139–153, 1979.

Angst J, Frey R, Lohmeyer B, et al: Bipolar manic depressive psychoses: results of a genetic investigation. Hum Genet 55:237–254, 1980.

Andreasen N, Endicott J, Spitzer R, et al: The family history method using diagnostic criteria: Reliability and validity. Arch Gen Psychiatry 34:1229–1235, 1977.

Baron M, Gruen R, Asnis L, Kane J: Familial relatedness of schizophrenia and schizotypal states. Am J Psychiatry 140:1437–1442, 1983.

Baron M, Levitt M, Gruen R, Kane J, Asnis L: Platelet monoamine oxidase activity and genetic vulnerability in schizophrenia. Am J Psychiatry 141:836–842, 1984.

Beckman L, Cedergren B, Perris C, Strandman E: Blood groups and affective disorders. Hum Hered 28:48–55, 1978.

Behar D, Berg CJ, Rapoport JL, Nelson W, Linnoila M, Cohen M, Bozevich C, Marshall T: Behavioral and physiological effects of ethanol in high risk and control children. A pilot study. Alcoholism 7:404–410, 1983.

Berrettini WH, Nadi NS, Gershon ES: Absence of specific binding of several putative neuro-transmitters to human fibroblasts. J Recept Res 3:409–421, 1983.

Berrettini WH, Nurnberger JI Jr, Hare T, Gershon ES, Post RM: Plasma and CSF GABA in affective illness. Br J Psychiatry 141:483–488, 1982.

Berrettini WH, Nurnberger JI Jr, Hare TA, Simmons-Alling S, Gershon ES, Post RM: Reduced plasma and CSF GABA in affective illness: Effect of lithium carbonate. Biol Psychiatry 18:185–194, 1983.

Berrettini WH, Nurnberger JI Jr, Post RM, Gershon ES: Platelet $^3$H-imipramine binding in euthymic bipolar patients. Psychiatry Res 7:215–219, 1982.

Bertelsen A: A Danish twin study of manic-depressive disorders, in Schou M, Stromgren E (eds): Origin, Prevention and Treatment of Affective Disorders. London, Academic Press, 1979, pp 227–239.

Bohman M: Some genetic aspects of alcoholism and criminality. Arch Gen Psychiatry 35:269–276, 1978.

Bohman M, Cloninger CR, Sigvardsson S, Von Knorring AL: Predisposition to petty criminality in Swedish adoptees. I. Genetic and environmental heterogeneity. Arch Gen Psychiatry 39:1233–1241, 1982.

Bohman M, Sigvardsson S, Cloninger CR: Maternal inheritance of alcohol abuse. Cross-fostering analysis of adopted women. Arch Gen Psychiatry 38:965–969, 1981.

Bondy B, Ackenheil M, Birzle W, Elbers R, Fröhler M: Catecholamines and their receptors in blood: Evidence for alterations in schizophrenia. Biol Psychiatry 19:1377–1393, 1984.

Böök JA, Wetterberg L, Modrzewska K: Schizophrenia in a North Swedish geographical isolate, 1900–1977. Epidemiology, genetics and biochemistry. Clin Genet 14:373–394, 1978.

Brecher M, Begleiter H: Event-related brain potentials to high-incentive stimuli in unmedicated schizophrenic patients. Biol Psychiatry 18:661–674, 1983.

Bucher KD, Elston RC: The transmission of manic depressive illness. I. Theory, description of the model, and summary of results. J Psychiat Res 16:53–63, 1981.

Bucher KD, Elston RC, Green R, Whybrow P, Helzer J, Reich T, Clayton P, Winokur G: The transmission of manic depressive illness. II. Segregation analysis of three sets of family data. J Psychiatr Res 16:65–78, 1981.

Buchsbaum MS, Coursey RD, Murphy DL: The biochemical high risk paradigm: behavioral and familial correlates of low platelet monoamine oxidase activity. Science 194:339–341, 1976.

Buchsbaum MS, Ingvar DH, Kessler R, Waters RN, Cappelletti J, van Kammen DP, King AC, Johnson JC, Manning RG, Flynn RW, Mann LS, Bunney WEB Jr, Sokoloff L: Cerebral glucography with positron tomography. Use in normal subjects and in patients with schizophrenia. Arch Gen Psychiatry 39:251–259, 1982.

Cadoret RJ, Cain CA: Genetic-environmental interaction in adoption studies of antisocial behavior. Presented at the World Congress of Biological Psychiatry, Stockholm, Sweden, June 1981.

Cadoret RJ: Genotype-environment interaction in antisocial behaviour. Psychol Med 12:235–239, 1982.

Cantwell DP: Psychiatric illness in the families of hyperactive children. Arch Gen Psychiatry 27:414–417, 1972.

Cantwell DP, Sturzenberger S, Burroughs J, Salkin B, Green JK: Anorexia nervosa: an effective disorder. Arch Gen Psychiatry 34:1087–1093, 1977.

Carter CL, Chung CS: Segregation analysis of schizophrenia under a mixed genetic model. Hum Hered 30:350–356, 1980.

Chojnacki M, Kralik P, Allen RH, Ho BT, Schoolar JC, Smith RC: Neuroleptic induced decrease in platelet MAO activity of schizophrenic patients. Am J Psychiatry 138:838–840, 1981.

Cloninger CR, Bohman M, Sigvardsson S: Inheritance of alcohol abuse. Cross-fostering analysis of adopted men. Arch Gen Psychiatry 38:861–868, 1981.

Cloninger CR, Christiansen KD, Reich T, Gottesman II: Implications of sex differences in the prevalences of antisocial personality, alcoholism, and criminality for familial transmission. Arch Gen Psychiatry 35:941–951, 1978.

Cloninger CR, Lavis C, Rice J, Reich T: Strategies for resolution of cultural and biological inheritance, in Gershon ES, Matthyse S, Breakefield XO, Ciaranello RD (eds): Genetic Research Strategies in Psychobiology and Psychiatry. Pacific Grove, CA, Boxwood Press, 1981, pp 319–332.

Cloninger CR, Reich T, Guze SB: The multifactorial model of disease transmission: III. Familial relationship between sociopathy and hysteria (Briquet's syndrome). Br J Psychiatry 127:23–32, 1975.

Cloninger CR, Reich T, Wetzel R: Alcoholism and affective disorders: familial associations and genetic models, in Goodwin DW, Erickson CK (eds): Alcoholism and Affective Disorders. Clinical, Genetic and Biochemical Studies. New York, Spectrum Publications, 1979, pp 57–86.

Cloninger CR, Sigvardsson S, Bohman M, Von-Knorring AL: Predisposition to petty criminality in Swedish adoptees. III. Cross fostering analysis of gene-environment interaction. Arch Gen Psychiatry 39:1242–1253, 1982.

Cohen SM, Allen MG, Pollin W, Hrubec Z: Relationship of schizo-affective psychosis to manic-depressive psychosis and schizophrenia. Arch Gen Psychiatry 26:539–551, 1972.

Comings DE: Pc 1 Duarte, a common polymorphism of a human brain protein, and its relationship to depressive disease and multiple sclerosis. Nature 277:28–32, 1979.

Comings DE, Comings BG, Devor EJ, Cloninger CR: Detection of major gene for Gilles de la Tourette Syndrome. Am J Hum Genet 36:586–600, 1984.

Coryell W, Winokur G, Andreasen N: Effect of case definition on affective disorder rates. Am J Psychiatry 138:1106–1109, 1981.

Crow TJ: Is schizophrenia an infectious disease? Lancet 1:173–175, 1983.

Crow TJ, Cross AJ, Johnstone EC, Longden A, Owen F, Ridley RM: Time course of the antipsychotic effect in schizophrenia and some changes in postmortem brain and their relation to neuroleptic medication. Adv Biochem Pharmacol 24:495–503, 1980.

Crowe RR: An adoption study of antisocial personality. Arch Gen Psychiatry 31:785–791, 1974.

Crowe RR, Namboodiri KK, Ashby HB, Elston RC: Segregation and linkage analysis of a large kindred of unipolar depression. Neuropsychobiology 7:20–25, 1981.

Crowe RR, Noyes R, Pauls DL, Slymen D: A family study of panic disorder. Arch Gen Psychiatry 40:1065–1069, 1983.

Crowe RR, Pauls DL, Slymen DJ, Noyes R: A family study of anxiety neurosis. Morbidity risk in families of patients with and without mitral valve prolapse. Arch Gen Psychiatry 37:77–79, 1980.

Debray Q, Caillard V, Stewart J: Schizophrenia: A study of genetic models. Hum Hered 29:27–36, 1979.

DeFries JC, Decker SN: Genetic aspects of reading disability: a family study, in Malatesha RN, Aaron PG (eds): Reading Disorders: Varieties and Treatments. New York, Academic Press, 1982, pp 255–279.

DeLisi LE, Buchsbaum MS, Dowling-Zimmerman S, Pickar D, et al: Clinical correlates of decreased anteroposterior metabolic gradients in positron emission tomography (PET) of schizophrenic patients. Am J Psychiatry 142:78–81, 1985.

DeLisi LE, Goldin LR, Hamovit JR, Maxwell ME, Kultz D, Gershon ES: A family study of the association of increased ventricular size with schizophrenia. Arch Gen Psychiatry 43:148–153, 1986.

DeLisi LE, Wise CD, Bridge TP, Potkin SG, Wyatt RJ: A probable effect of neuroleptic medication on platelet monoamine oxidase activity. Psychiatry Res 4:95–107, 1981.

Dorus E: Variability in the Y chromosome and variability of human behavior. Arch Gen Psychiatry 37:587–594, 1980.

Dorus E, Cox NJ, Gibbon RD, Shaughnessy R, Pandey GN, Cloninger CR: Lithium ion transport and affective disorders within families of bipolar patients. Arch Gen Psychiatry 40:545–552, 1983.

Dorus E, Pandey GN, Shaughnessey R, Gaviria M, Val E, Eriksen S, Davis JM: Lithium transport across the red cell membrane: a cell membrane abnormality in manic depressive illness. Science 205:932–934, 1979.

Dustman RE, Beck EC: The visually evoked potential

in twins. Electrocephalogr Clin Neurophysiol 19:570–575, 1965.

Dyson WL, Barcai A: Treatment of children of lithium-responding parents. Curr Ther Res 12:286–290, 1970.

Ebstein RP, Steinitz M, Mintzer J, Lipshitz J, Stessman J: Beta-adrenergic-stimulated adenylate cyclase activity in normal EBV-transformed lymphocytes. Unpublished manuscript.

Egeland J, Frazer A, Kidd K: Affective disorders among the Amish. III. Na-Li counterflow and COMT in bipolar pedigrees. Am J Psychiatry 141:1049–1054, 1984.

Eldridge R, Wassman ER, Nee L, Koerber T: Gilles de la Tourette Syndrome, in Goodman RM, Motulsky AG (eds): Genetic Diseases Among Ashkenazi Jews. New York, Raven Press, 1979, pp 171–185.

Elston RC, Namboodiri KK, Spence MA, Rainer JD: A genetic study of schizophrenia pedigrees. II. One locus hypothesis. Neuropsychobiology 4:193–206, 1978.

Elston RC, Stewart J: A general method for the genetic analysis of pedigree data. Hum Hered 21:523–542, 1971.

Eriksson CPJ: Elevated blood acetaldehyde levels in alcoholics and their relatives: A re-evaluation. Science 207:1383–1394, 1980.

Essen-Möller E: Twin research and psychiatry. Acta Psychiatr Scand 39:65–77, 1963.

Essen-Möller E: Psychiatrische untersuchungen an einen serie von zwillingen. Acta Psychiatr Neurol Suppl 23:1–200, 1941.

Falconer DS: The inheritance of liability to certain diseases, estimated from the incidence among relatives. Ann Hum Genet 29:51–76, 1965.

Fischer M, Harvald B, Hauge M: A Danish twin study of schizophrenia. Br J Psychiatry 115:981–990, 1969.

Flemenbau A, Larson JW: ABO-Rh blood groups and psychiatric diagnosis: A critical review. Dis Nerv Sys 37:581–583, 1976.

Foch TT, DeFries JC, McClearn GE, Singer SM: Familial patterns of impairment in reading disability. J Educational Psychol 69:316–329, 1977.

Friedl W, Propping P: $^3$H-imipramine binding in human platelets: A study in normal twins. Psychiatry Res 11:279–285, 1984.

Gershon ES: Nonreplication of linkage to X-chromosome markers in bipolar illness. (Letter.) Arch Gen Psychiatry 37:1200, 1980.

Gershon ES: Inheritance of major psychiatric disorders. Trends Neurosci 5:241–242, 1982.

Gershon ES, Nurnberger JI Jr: Genetics of major psychoses, in Kety SS, Rowland LP, Sidman RL, Matthysse (eds): Genetics of Neurological and Psychiatric Disorders. New York, Raven Press, 1983, pp 121–144.

Gershon ES: What is the familial morbid risk of major depression? (letter) Arch Gen Psychiatry 41:103–105, 1984.

Gershon ES, Baron M, Leckman JF: Genetic models of the transmission of affective disorders. J Psychiatr Res 12:301–317, 1975.

Gershon ES, Bunney WE Jr, Leckman JF, van Eerdewegh M, DeBauche BA: The inheritance of affective disorders: A review of data and of hypotheses. Behav Genet 6:227–261, 1976.

Gershon ES, Goldin LR, Lake CR, Murphy DL, Guroff JJ: Genetics of plasma dopamine-beta-hydroxylase (DBH), erythrocyte catechol-O-methyltransferase (COMT), and platelet monoamine oxidase (MAO) in pedigree of patients with affective disorders, in Usdin E, Sourkes P, Youdim MBH (eds): Enzymes and Neurotransmitters in Mental Disease. London, John Wiley & Sons Ltd, 1980, pp 281–299.

Gershon ES, Goldin LR, Weissman MM, Nurnberger JI Jr: Family and genetic studies of affective disorders in the Eastern United States: A provisional summary, in Perris C, Struwe G, Jansson B (eds): Biological Psychiatry. Amsterdam, Elsevier, 1981, pp 157–162.

Gershon ES, Guroff JJ: Information from relatives: diagnosis of affective disorders. Arch Gen Psychiatry 41:173–180, 1984.

Gershon ES, Hamovit J, Guroff JJ, Dibble ED, Leckman J, Sceery W, Targum SD, Nurnberger JI Jr, Goldin L, Bunney WE Jr: A family study of schizoaffective, bipolar I, bipolar II, unipolar and normal control probands. Arch Gen Psychiatry 39:1157–1167, 1982.

Gershon ES, Hamovit JH, Guroff JJ, Nurnberger JI Jr: Birth cohort changes in manic and depressive disorders in relatives of bipolar and schizoaffective patients. Submitted for publication.

Gershon ES, Hamovit JR, Schreiber JL, Dibble ED, Kaye W, Nurnberger JI Jr, Andersen A, Ebert M: Anorexia nervosa and major affective disorders associated in families: a preliminary report, in Guze SB, Earls FJ, Barrett JE (eds): Childhood Psychopathology and Development. New York, Raven Press, 1983, pp 279–286.

Gershon ES, Mark A, Cohen N, Belizon N, Baron M, Knobe KE: Transmitted factors in the morbidity of affective disorders: A controlled study. J Psychiatr Res 12:283–299, 1975.

Gershon ES, Nadi NS, Nurnberger JI Jr, Berrettini WH: Letter to the editor. N Engl J Med 312:862, 1985.

Gershon ES, Nurnberger JI Jr, Jimerson DC: Sex, plasma prolactin and plasma 3-methoxy-4-hydroxy-phenylglycol (MHPG) predict heritable d-amphetamine excitation in man, in Angrist B, Burrows GD, Lader M, Lingjaerde O, Sedvall G, Wheatley D (eds): Advances in Biosciences: Recent Advances in Neuropsycho-Pharmacology. New York, Pergamon Press, 1981, pp 83–91.

Gershon ES, Targum SD, Kessler LR, Mazure CM, Bunney WE Jr: Genetic studies and biologic strategies in the affective disorders, in Steinberg AG, Bearn AG, Motulsky AG, Childs B (eds): Progress in Medical Genetics, vol 2. Philadelphia, WB Saunders Co, 1977, pp 101–164.

Goedde HW, Agarwal DP, Harada S: The role of alcohol dehydrogenase and aldehyde dehydrogenase isozymes in alcohol metabolism, alcohol sensitivity, and alcoholism, in Isozymes: Current Topics in Biological and Medical Research, vol 8. New York, Alan R. Liss, 1983, pp 175–186.

Goetzl V, Green R, Whybrow P, et al: X-linkage revisited: A further family study of manic depressive illness. Arch Gen Psychiatry 31:665–673, 1974.

Goldin LR, Clerget-Darpoux F, Gershon ES: Relationship of HLA to major affective disorder not supported. Psychiatry Res 7:29–45, 1982.

Goldin LR, Gershon ES, Targum SD, Sparkes RS, McGinniss M: Segregation and linkage analyses in families of patients with bipolar, unipolar and schizoaffective mood disorders. Am J Hum Genet 35:274–287, 1983.

Goldin LR, Nurnberger JI, Gershon ES: The high risk approach in psychiatric genetic research. Submitted for publication.

Goodwin DW: Alcoholism and heredity. A review and hypotheses. Arch Gen Psychiatry 36:57–61, 1979.

Goodwin DW: The genetics of alcoholism, in Usdin E, Hanin I (eds): Biological Markers in Psychiatry and Neurology. Oxford, Pergamon Press, 1982, pp 433–443.

Goodwin DW, Schulsinger F, Hermansen L, Guze SB, Winokur G: Alcohol problems in adoptees raised apart from alcoholic biological parents. Arch Gen Psychiatry 28:238–243, 1973.

Goodwin DW, Schulsinger F, Knop J, Mednick S, Guze SB: Alcoholism and depression in adopted-out daughters of alcoholics. Arch Gen Psychiatry 34:751–755, 1977.

Goodwin DW, Schulsinger F, Moller N, Hermansen L, Winokur G, Guze SB: Drinking problems in adopted and non-adopted sons of alcoholics. Arch Gen Psychiatry 31:164–169, 1974.

Gottesman II, Carey G: Extracting meaning and direction from twin data. Psychiatr Dev 1:35–50, 1983.

Gottesman II, Shields J: Schizophrenia and Genetics: A Twin Study Vantage Point. New York, Academic Press, 1972.

Gottesman II, Shields J: Schizophrenia: The Epigenetic Puzzle. New York, Cambridge University Press, 1982.

Grove WM: Comment on Lidz and associate's critique of the Danish-American studies of the offspring of schizophrenic parents. Am J Psychiatry 140:998–1002, 1983.

Gusella JF, Wexler NS, Conneally PM, Naylor SL, Anderson MA, Tanzi RE, Watkins PC, Ottina K, Wallace MR, Sakaguchi AY, Young AB, Shouldson I, Bonilla E, Martin JB: A polymorphic DNA marker genetically linked to Huntington's disease. Nature 306:234–306, 1983.

Guze SB, Cloninger CR, Martin RL, Clayton PJ: A follow-up and family study of schizophrenia. Arch Gen Psychiatry 40:1273–1276, 1983.

Harris EL, Noyes R, Crowe RR, Chaudhry DR: Family study of agoraphobia. Report of a pilot study. Arch Gen Psychiatry 40:1061–1064, 1983.

Harvald B, Hauge M: Hereditary factors elucidated by twin studies. in Neal JV, Shaw MW, Shull WJ (eds): Genetics and the Epidemiology of Chronic Diseases. Washington, DC, PHS Publication 1163, 1965, pp 61–76.

Helzer JE, Winokur G: A family interview study of male manic-depressives. Arch Gen Psychiatry 31:73–77, 1974.

Heston LL: Psychiatric disorders in foster home reared children of schizophrenic mothers. Br J Psychiatry 112:819–825, 1966.

Holzinger KJ: The relative effect of nature and nurture influences on twin differences. J Educational Psychol 20:241, 1929.

Holzman PS, Kringlen E, Levy DL, Proctor LR, Haberman SJ, Yasillo NJ: Abnormal-pursuit eye movements in schizophrenia. Arch Gen Psychiatry 34:802–805, 1977.

Holzman PS, Solomon CM, Levin S, Waternaux CS: Pursuit eye movement dysfunctions in schizophrenia. Arch Gen Psychiatry 41:136–139, 1984.

Hrubec Z, Omenn GS: Evidence of a genetic predisposition to alcoholic cirrhosis and psychosis. Alcoholism 5:207–215, 1981.

Hutchings B and Mednick SA: Registered criminality in the adoptive and biological parents of registered male criminal adoptees, in Fieve RR, Rosenthal D, Brill H (eds): Genetic Research in Psychiatry. Baltimore, Hopkins, 1975, pp 105–116.

Ingvar DH: Abnormal distribution of cerebral activity in chronic schizophrenia: A neurophysiological interpretation, in Baxter CF, Melnechuk T (eds): Current Perspectives in Schizophrenia Research. New York, Raven Press, 1980, pp 107–125.

Inouye E: Similarity and dissimilarity of schizophrenia in twins. Proceedings Third International Congress of Psychiatry, 1961. Montreal, University of Toronto Press, 1963, pp 524–530.

Inouye E: Monozygotic twins with schizophrenia reared apart in infancy. J Hum Genet 16:182–190, 1972.

Ivanyi P, Droes J, Schreuder GMT, D'Amaro J, van Rood JJ: A search for association of HLA antigens with paranoid schizophrenia. Tissue Antigens 22:186–193, 1983.

Jacobs PA, Brunton M, Melville MM, Brittain RP, McClemont WF: Aggressive behaviour, mental subnormality and the XYY male. Nature 208:1351–1352, 1965.

Jacobs PA, Price WH, Richmond S, Ratcliff RAW: Chromosome surveys in penal institutions and approved schools. J Med Genet 8:49–53, 1971.

James NM, Carroll BJ, Haines RF, Smouse PE: Affective disorders: ABO and HLA, in Mendlewicz J, Shopsin B (eds): Genetic Aspects of Affective Illness. New York, Spectrum Publications, 1979, pp 35–44.

James NM, Chapman CJ: A genetic study of bipolar affective disorder. Br J Psychiatry 126:449–456, 1975.

Janowsky DS, El-Yousef MK, Davis JM: Cholinergic-adrenergic hypothesis of mania and depression. Lancet 2:632, 1972.

Jeste DV, Zalcman S, Weinberger DR, Cutler NR, Bigelow LB, Kleinman JE, Rogol A, Wyatt RJ: Apomorphine response and subtyping of schizophrenia. Prog Neuropsychopharmacol Biol Psychiatry 7:83–88, 1983.

Johnson GFS, Leeman MM: Analysis of familial factors in bipolar affective illness. Arch Gen Psychiatry 34:1074–1083, 1977.

Johnstone EC, Crow TJ, Friter CD, et al: Cerebral ventricular size and cognitive impairment in chronic schizophrenia. Lancet 2:924–926, 1976.

Kafka MS, van Kammen DP, Kleinman JE, Nurnberger JI Jr, Siever LJ, Uhde TW, Polinsky RJ: Alpha-adrenergic receptor function in schizophrenia, affective disorders and some neurological diseases. Commun Psychopharmacol 4:477–486, 1980.

Kallman F: Genetic principles in manic depressive psychosis in Hoch PH, Zubin J (eds): Depression, New York, Grune and Stratton, 1954, pp 1–24.

Kallman FJ: The genetic theory of schizophrenia. An analysis of 691 schizophrenic twin index families. Am J Psychiatry 103:309–322, 1946.

Kan YW, Dozy AM: Polymorphism of DNA sequence adjacent to human beta-globin structural gene: relation to sickle mutation. Proc Natl Acad Sci 75:5631, 1978.

Kelsoe JR, Gillin C, Janowsky DS, Brown JH, Risch SC, Lumkin B: Letter to the editor. N Engl J Med 312:861–862, 1985.

Kendler KS: The nosologic validity of paranoia (simple delusional disorder). A review. Arch Gen Psychiatry 37:699–706, 1980.

Kendler KS: Overview: A current perspective on twin

studies of schizophrenia. Am J Psychiatry 140:1413–1425, 1983.

Kendler KS, Gruenberg AM, Strauss JS: An independent analysis of the Copenhagen sample of the Danish adoption study of schizophrenia. II. The relationship between schizotypal personality disorder and schizophrenia. Arch Gen Psychiatry 38:982–984, 1981a.

Kendler KS, Gruenberg AM, Strauss JS: An independent analysis of the Copenhagen sample of the Danish adoption study of schizophrenia. IV. The relationship between paranoid psychosis (delusional disorder) and the schizophrenia spectrum disorders. Arch Gen Psychiatry 38:985–987, 1981b.

Kendler KS, Hays P: Paranoid psychosis (delusional disorder) and schizophrenia. A family history study. Arch Gen Psychiatry 38:547–551, 1981.

Kendler KS, Robinette RD: Schizophrenia in the National Academy of Sciences—National Research Council Twin Registry: A 16-year update. Am J Psychiatry 140:1551–1563, 1983.

Kety SS: Disorders of the human brain. Sci Am 241:202–218, 1979.

Kety SS: Mental illness in the biological and adoptive relatives of schizophrenic adoptees: findings relevant to genetic and environmental factors in etiology. Am J Psychiatry 140:720–727, 1983.

Kety SS, Rosenthal D, Wender PH, Schulsinger F: The types and prevalence of mental illness in the biological and adoptive families of adopted schizophrenics, in Rosenthal D, Kety SS (eds): The Transmission of Schizophrenia. Oxford, Pergamon Press, 1968, pp 159–166.

Kety SS, Rosenthal D, Wender PH, Schulsinger F, Jacobsen B: Mental illness in the biological and adoptive families of adopted individuals who have become schizophrenic. A preliminary report based upon psychiatric interviews, in Fieve R, Rosenthal D, Brill H (eds): Genetic Research in Psychiatry. Baltimore, Johns Hopkins University Press, 1975, pp 147–165.

Kety SS, Wender PH, Rosenthal D: Genetic relationships within the schizophrenia spectrum: evidence from adoption studies, in Spitzer RL, Klein DF (eds): Critical Issues in Psychiatric Diagnosis. New York, Raven Press, 1978, pp 213–223.

Kidd KK, Prusoff BA, Cohen DJ: The familial pattern of Gilles de la Tourette's Syndrome. Arch Gen Psychiatry 37:1336–1339, 1980.

Klerman GL, Lavori PW, Rice J, et al: Birth-cohort trends in rates of major depressive disorder among relatives of patients with affective disorder. Arch Gen Psychiatry 42:689–693, 1985.

Korsten MA, Matsuzaki S, Feinman L, Lieber CS: High blood acetaldehyde levels after ethanol administration: differences between alcoholic and nonalcoholic subjects. N Engl J Med 292:386–389, 1975.

Kringlen E: Schizophrenia in twins. An epidemiological-clinical study. Psychiatry 29:172–184, 1966.

Kringlen E: Heredity and Environment in the Functional Psychoses. London, Heinemann, 1967.

Lalouel JM, Morton NE: Complex segregation analysis with pointers. Hum Hered 31:312–321, 1981.

Lalouel JM, Rao DC, Morton NE, Elston RC: A unified model for complex segregation analysis. Am J Hum Genet 35:816–826, 1983.

Lange V: Genetic markers for schizophrenic subgroups. Psychiatr Clin 15:133–144, 1982.

Langer SZ, Raisman R, Sechter D, Loo H, Gay C, Zarifian E: Functional relationship between the uptake of serotonin and the $^3$H-imipramine binding site in platelets in the central nervous system. Presented at the Annual Meeting of the American College of Neuropsychopharmacology, San Juan, Puerto Rico, 1982.

Leckman JF, Weissman MM, Merikangas KR, Pauls DL, Prusoff BA: Panic disorders and major depression. Increased risk of depression, alcoholism, panic and phobic disorders in families of depressed probands with panic disorders. Arch Gen Psychiatry 40:1055–1060, 1983.

Le Fur G, Meininger V, Phair T, Gerard A, Baulac M, Uzan A: Decrease in lymphocyte [$^3$H] spiroperidol binding sites in Parkinsonism. Life Sci 27:1587–1591, 1980.

Lenox RH, Hitzemann RJ, Richelson E, Kelsoe JR: Failure to confirm muscarinic receptors on skin fibroblasts. N Engl J Med 312:861, 1985.

Levitan M, Montagu M: A Textbook of Human Genetics. London, Oxford University Press, 1971.

Lidz T, Blatt S: Critique of the Danish-American studies of the biological and adoptive relatives of adoptees who became schizophrenic. Am J Psychiatry 140:426–435, 1983.

Lidz T, Blatt S, Cook B: Critique of the Danish American studies of the adopted away offspring of schizophrenic parents. Am J Psychiatry 138:1063–1068, 1981.

Lowing PA, Mirsky AF, Pereira R: The inheritance of schizophrenic spectrum disorders: a reanalysis of the Danish adoptee study data. Am J Psychiatry 140:1167–1171, 1983.

Luxenberger H: Vorlänfiger bericht über psychiatrische serienuntersuchungen an Zwillengen. Zentralbl Gesamte Neurol Psychiatrie 116:297–326, 1928.

Luxenberger H: Psychiatrisch-neurologische zwillingspathologie. Zentral Diagesamte Neurol Psychiatrie 14:56–57, 145–180, 1930.

McCabe MS: Reactive psychoses. Acta Psychiatr Scand [Suppl] 259:1–33, 1975.

McConville BJ, Soudek D, Sroka H, Cote J, Boag L, Berry J: Length of the Y chromosome and chromosomal variants in inpatient children with psychiatric disorders: two studies. Can J Psychiatry 28:8–13, 1983.

McGue M, Gottesman II, Rao DC: The transmission of schizophrenia under a multifactorial threshold model. Am J Hum Genet 35:1161–1178, 1983.

McGuffin P, Farmer AE, Yonace AH: HLA antigens and subtypes of schizophrenia. Psychiatry Res 5:115–122, 1981.

McGuffin P, Festenstein H, Murray R: A family study of HLA antigens and other genetic markers in schizophrenia. Psychol Med 13:31–43, 1983.

Mellerup ET, Plenge P, Rosenberg R: $^3$H-imipramine binding sites in platelets from psychiatric patients. Psychiatry Res 7:221–227, 1982.

Mendlewicz J, Fleiss J, Cataldo M, et al: Accuracy of the family history method in affective illness: comparison with direct interviews in family studies. Arch Gen Psychiatry 32:309–314, 1975.

Mendlewicz J, Massart-Guiot T, Wilmotte J, Fleiss JL: Blood groups in manic-depressive illness and schizophrenia. Dis Nerv Sys 35:39–41, 1974.

Mendlewicz J, Rainer JD: Morbidity risk and genetic transmission in manic depressive illness. Am J Hum Genet 26:692–701, 1974.

Mendlewicz J, Rainer JD: Adoption study supporting

genetic transmission in manic depressive illness. Nature 268:327–329, 1977.

Morrison JR, Stewart MA: A family study of the hyperactive child syndrome. Biol Psychiatry 3:189–195, 1971.

Morrison JR, Stewart MA: The psychiatric status of the legal families of adopted hyperactive children. Arch Gen Psychiatry 28:888–891, 1973.

Morton NE: Sequential tests for the detection of linkage. Am J Hum Genet 7:277–318, 1955.

Morton NE, MacLean CJ: Analysis of familial resemblance. II. Complex segregation analysis of quantitative traits. Am J Hum Genet 26:489–503, 1974.

Mourant AE, Kopac AC, Domaniewska-Sobczak K: Blood Groups and Disease: A Study of Associations of Diseases with Blood Groups and Other Polymorphisms. Oxford, Oxford University Press, 1978.

Murphy DL, Coursey RD, Haenel T, Aloi J, Buchsbaum MS: Platelet monoamine oxidase as a biological marker in the affective disorders and alcoholism, in Usdin E, Hanin I (eds): Biological Markers in Psychiatry and Neurology. Oxford, Pergamon Press, 1982, pp 123–134.

Murphy JM, McBride WJ, Lumeng L, Li TK: Regional brain levels of monoamines in alcohol-preferring and in non-preferring lines of rats. Pharmacol Biochem Behav 16:145–149, 1982b.

Murray RM, Clifford C, Gurling HMD, Topham A, Clow A, Bernardt M: Current genetic and biological approaches to alcoholism. Psychiatr Dev 1:179–192, 1983.

Nadi NS, Nurnberger JI Jr, Gershon ES: Muscarinic cholinergic receptors on skin fibroblasts in familial affective disorder. N Engl J Med 311:225–230, 1984.

Nasrallah HA, Jacoby CG, McCalley-Whitters M: Structural brain changes in mania and schizophrenia. Presented at the meeting of the American Psychiatric Association (New Research), Toronto, Canada, May 1982.

Noyes R Jr, Clancy J, Crowe R, Hoenk PR, Slymen DJ: The familial prevalence of anxiety neurosis. Arch Gen Psychiatry 35:1057–1059, 1978.

Nurnberger JI Jr, Gershon ES: Genetics of affective disorders, in Post RM, Ballenger J (eds): Neurobiology of Mood Disorders. Baltimore, Williams & Wilkins, 1984, pp 76–101.

Nurnberger JI Jr, Gershon ES, Simmons S, Ebert M, Kessler LR, Dibble ED, Jimerson SS, Brown GM, Gold P, Jimerson DC, Guroff JJ, Storch FI: Behavioral, biochemical and neuroendocrine response to amphetamine in normal twins and "well state" bipolar patients. Psychoneuroendocrinology 7:163–176, 1982a.

Nurnberger JI Jr, Jimerson DC, Bunney WE Jr: A risk factor strategy for investigating affective illness. Biol Psychiatry 18:903–909, 1983a.

Nurnberger JI Jr, Pandey G, Gershon ES, Davis JM: Lithium ratio in psychiatric patients: a caveat. Psychiatry Res 9:201–206, 1983b.

Nurnberger JI Jr, Sitaram N, Gershon ES, Gillin JC: A twin study of cholinergic REM induction. Biol Psychiatry 18:1161–1173, 1983c.

Nurnberger JI Jr, Sitaram N, Jimerson DC, Gillin JC, Simmons-Alling S, Tamminga C, Nadi NS, Gershon ES: Pharmacogenetic studies of muscarinic agonists. Presented at the Annual Meeting of the American College of Neuropsychopharmacology, San Juan, Puerto Rico, December 1982b.

O'Rourke DH, Gottesman II, Suarez BK, Rice J, Reich T: Refutation of the general single locus model for the etiology of schizophrenia. Am J Hum Genet 34:630–649, 1982.

O'Rourke DH, McGuffin P, Reich T: Genetic analysis of manic-depressive illness. Am J Phys Anthropol 62:51–59, 1983.

Orvaschel H, Thompson W, Belanger A, et al: Comparison of the family history method to direct interview: Factors affecting the diagnosis of depression. J Affect Disord 4:49–59, 1982.

Ott J: Estimation of the recombination fraction in human pedigree: Efficient computation of the likelihood for human linkage. Am J Hum Genet 26:588–597, 1974.

Owen F, Cross AJ, Crow TJ, Longden A, Poulter M, Riley EJ: Increased dopamine-receptor sensitivity in schizophrenia. Lancet ii: 223–226, 1978.

Pahina SS, Roberts DF, McLeish L: Group-specific component (Gc) subtypes and schizophrenia. Clin Genet 22:321–326, 1982.

Pandey GN, Sarkadi B, Haas M, Gunn RB, Davis JM, Tosteson DC: Lithium transport pathways in human red blood cells. J Gen Physiol 72:233–247, 1978.

Parker JB, Theillie A, Spielberger DC: Frequency of blood types in an homogenous group of manic-depressive patients. J Ment Sci 107:936–942, 1961.

Pauls DL, Bucher KD, Crowe RR, Noyes R Jr: A genetic study of panic disorder pedigrees. Am J Human Genet 32:639–644, 1980.

Pauls DL, Cohen DJ, Heimbuch R, Detlor J, Kidd KK: Familial pattern and transmission of Gilles de la Tourette Syndrome and multiple tics. Arch Gen Psychiatry 38:1091–1093, 1981.

Perris C: A study of bipolar (manic-depressive) and unipolar recurrent depressive psychoses. Acta Psychiatr Scand [Suppl] 194:15–44, 1966.

Pettersen U: Manic depressive illness: a clinical social and genetic study. Acta Psychiatr Scand [Suppl] 269:1–93, 1977.

Pillard RC, Poumadere J, Caretta RA: Is homosexuality familial? A review, some data, and a suggestion. Arch Sex Behav 10:465–475, 1981.

Pillard RC, Poumadere J, Caretta RA: A family study of sexual orientation. Arch Sex Behav 11:511–520, 1982.

Pollack VE, Volavka J, Goodwin DW, Mednick SA, Gabrielli WF, Knop J, Schulsinger F: The EEG after alcohol administration in men at high risk for alcoholism. Arch Gen Psychiatry 40:857–861, 1983.

Price J: The genetics of depressive behavior, in Coppen A, Walk A (eds): Recent Developments in Affective Disorders. Br J Psychiatry, Special Publication No 2: 37–54, 1968.

Price RA, Kidd KK, Pauls DL, Gershon ES, Prusoff BA, Weissman MA, Goldin LR: Multiple threshold models for the affective disorders: The Yale-NIMH collaborative family study. Presented at the meeting of the American Psychiatric Association, New York City, May 1983.

Propping P: Genetic disorders presenting as "Schizophrenia". Karl Bonhoeffer's early view of the psychoses in the light of medical genetics. Hum Genet 65:1–10, 1983.

Propping P, Friedl W: Genetic control of adrenergic receptors on human platelets. A twin study. Hum Genet 64:105–109, 1983.

Propping P, Krüger J, Mark N: Genetic disposition to

alcoholism. An EEG study in alcoholics and their relatives. Hum Genet 59:51–59, 1981.

Rao DC, Morton NE, Gottesman II, Lew R: Path analysis of qualitative data on pairs of relatives: application to schizophrenia. Hum Hered 31:325–333, 1981.

Reich T, James JW, Morris CA: The use of multiple thresholds in determining the mode of transmission of semi-continuous traits. Ann Hum Genet 36:163–184, 1972.

Reveley MA, Reveley AM, Clifford CA, Murray RM: Genetics of platelet MAO activity in discordant schizophrenia and normal twins. Br J Psychiatry 142:560–565, 1983.

Reveley AM, Reveley MA, Murray RM: Cerebral ventricular enlargement in non genetic schizophrenia: A controlled twin study. Br J Psychiatry 144:89–93, 1984.

Rice J, McGuffin P, Goldin LR, Shaskan EG, Gershon ES: Platelet monoamine oxidase (MAO) activity: evidence for a single major locus. Am J Hum Genet 36:36–43, 1984.

Rice J, Reich T, Andreasen NC, Lavori PW, Endicott J, Clayton PJ, Keller MB, Hirschfeld RMA, Klerman GL: Sex related differences in depression: Familial evidence. Submitted for publication.

Rieder RO, Gershon ES: Genetic strategies in biological psychiatry. Arch Gen Psychiatry 35:866–873, 1978.

Rinieris P, Stefanis C, Lykouras E, Varsou E: Affective disorders and ABO blood types. Acta Psychiatr Scand 60:272–278, 1979.

Rinieris P, Stefanis C, Lykouras E, Varsou E: Subtypes of schizophrenia and ABO blood types. Neuropsychobiology 8:57–59, 1982.

Risch N, Baron M: X-linkage and genetic heterogeneity in bipolar-related major affective illness: re-analysis of linkage data. Ann Hum Genet 46:153–166, 1982.

Rosanoff JA, Handy L, Plesset IR: The etiology of manic-depressive syndromes with special reference to their occurrence in twins. Am J Psychiatry 91:724–762, 1935.

Rosanoff JA, Handy LM, Plesset IR, Brush S: The etiology of so-called schizophrenic psychoses with special reference to their occurrence in twins. Am J Psychiatry 91:247–286, 1934.

Rosenthal D: A program of research on heredity in schizophrenia, in Mednick SA, Schulsinger F, Higgins J, Bell B (eds): Genetics, Environment, and Psychopathology, American Elsevier Publishing Company, Inc., 1974, pp. 19–35.

Rosenthal D, Wender PH, Kety SS, Welner J, Schulsinger F: The adopted-away offspring of schizophrenics. Am J Psychiatry 128:307–311, 1971.

Rotman A, Zemishlany Z, Munitz H, Wijsenbeek H: The active uptake of serotonin by platelets of schizophrenic patients and their families: possibility of a genetic marker. Psychopharmacology 77:171–174, 1982.

Rutschman J, Cornblatt B, Erlenmeyer-Kimling L: Sustained attention in children at risk for schizophrenia. Arch Gen Psychiatry 34:571–575, 1977.

Saitoh O, Shin-Ichi N, Ken-Ichi H, Tomomichi K, Rymar K, Kenji I: Abnormalities in late positive components of event-related potentials may reflect a genetic predisposition to schizophrenia, 1984.

Saunders JB, Wodak AD, Haines A, Powell-Jackson PR, Portmann B, Davis B, Williams R: Accelerated development of alcoholic cirrhosis in patients with HLA B8. Lancet 1:1381–1384, 1982.

Schepank HGF: Anorexia nervosa: Zwillings Kasuistik uber ein seltenes Krankheitsbild, in Heigl-Evers A, Schepank H (eds): Ursprunge Seelisch Bedingter Krankheiten, vol 2. Gottingen: Verlag fur Medizinische Psychologie in Verlag Vandenhoeck und Ruprecht, 1981, pp 705–719.

Schlesser MA, Winokur G, Elston RC: Hypothalamic-pituitary-adrenal axis activity in depressive illness: its relationship to classification. Arch Gen Psychiatry 37:737–743, 1980.

Schlesser MA, Winokur G, Sherman BM: Genetic subtypes of unipolar primary depressive illness distinguished by hypothalmic-pituitary-adrenal axis activity. Lancet 1:739–741, 1979.

Schuckit MA: Body sway: differences after drinking in sons of alcoholics and controls. Clin Neuropharmacol 7:200–201, 1984 (suppl 1).

Schuckit MA, O'Connor DT, Duby J, Vega R, Moss M: Dopamine-beta-hydroxylase activity levels in men at high risk for alcoholism and controls. Biol Psychiatry 16:1067–1075, 1981.

Schuckit MA, Parker DC, Rossman LR: Ethanol-related prolactin responses and risk for alcoholism. Biol Psychiatry 18:1153–1159, 1983.

Schuckit M, Rayses V: Ethanol ingestion: differences in blood acetaldehyde concentrations in relatives of alcoholics and controls. Science 203:54–55, 1979.

Schuckit MA, Shaskan E, Duby J, Vega R, Moss M: Platelet monoamine oxidase activity in relatives of alcoholics. Preliminary study with matched controls. Arch Gen Psychiatry 39:137–140, 1982.

Schulsinger F, Kety SS, Rosenthal D, Wender PH: A family study of suicide, in Schou M, Stromgren E (eds): Origin, Prevention and Treatment of Affective Disorders. London, Academic Press, 1979, pp 277–287.

Schulz SC, van Kammen DP, Rogol AD, Ebert M, Pickar D, Cohen MR, Naber D: Amphetamine increases prolactin but not growth hormone nor beta-endorphin immunoreactivity in schizophrenic patients. Psychopharmacol Bull 17:193–195, 1981.

Sedvall G, Fyro B, Gullberg B, Nyback H, Wiesel F-A, Wode-Helgodt W: Relationships in healthy volunteers between concentrations of monoamine metabolites in cerebrospinal fluid and family history of psychiatric morbidity. Br J Psychiatry 136:366–374, 1980.

Sedvall G, Oxenstierna G: Genetic and environmental influences on central monaminergic mechanisms in man. Abstracts of the World Congress of Biol Psychiatry 1:s344, 1981.

Shah SA, Roth LH: Biological and psychophysiological factors in criminality, in Glaser D (ed): Handbook of Criminology. Rand McNally College Publishing, 1974, pp 101–173.

Shapiro RW, Block E, Rafaelsen OJ, Ryder LP, Svejgaard A: Histocompatibility antigens and manic-depressive disorders. Arch Gen Psychiatry 33:823–825, 1976.

Shapiro RW, Ryder LP, Svejgaard A, Rafaelsen OJ: HLA antigens and manic-depressive disorders: further evidence of an association. Psychol Med 7:387–396, 1977.

Sheppard G, Gruzelier J, Manchanda R, Hirsch SR, Wise R, Frackowiak R, Jones T: 15⁰ Positron emission tomographic scanning in predominantly never-treated acute schizophrenic patients. Lancet 2:1448–1452, 1983.

Siniscalco M, Szabo P, Filippi F, Finaldi A: Combination of old and new strategies for the molecular mapping of the human X-chromosome, in Bonne-Tamir B (ed): Human Genetics Part A: The Unfolding Genome. New York, Alan R. Liss, 1982, pp 103–124.

Sitaram N, Dube S, Jones D, Bell J, Gurevich D, Gershon S: Cholinergic REM-induction response as a state and possible genetic vulnerability marker of depression. Clin Neuropharmacol 7:966–967, 1984 (suppl 1).

Sitaram N, Nurnberger JI Jr, Gershon ES, Gillin JC: Faster cholinergic REM sleep induction in euthymic patients with primary affective illness. Science 208:200–202, 1980.

Sitaram N, Nurnberger JI Jr, Gershon ES, Gillin JC: Cholinergic regulation of mood and REM sleep: potential model and marker of vulnerability to affective disorder. Am J Psychiatry 139:571–576, 1982.

Slater E: Psychotic and neurotic illnesses in twins. Medicall Research Council of Great Britain, Special Report Series, Her Majesty's Stationery Office, London, 1953.

Smeraldi E, Bellodi L: Possible linkage between primary affective disorder, susceptibility locus and HLA haplotypes. Am J Psychiatry 138:1232–1234, 1981.

Smeraldi E, Negri R, Heimbuch RC, Kidd KK: Familial patterns and possible modes of inheritance of primary affective disorder. J Affect Disord 3:173–182, 1981.

Smeraldi E, Negri F, Melica AM: A genetic study of affective disorder. Acta Psychiatr Scand 56:382–398, 1977.

Smeraldi E, Negri F, Melica AM, Scorza-Smeraldi R: HLA system and affective disorders: A sibship genetic study. Tissue Antigens 12:270–274, 1978.

Smith SD, Kimberling WJ, Pennington BF, Lubs HA: Specific reading disability: identification of an inherited form through linkage analysis. Science 219:1345–1347, 1983.

Stewart J, Debray Q, Caillard V: Schizophrenia: the testing of genetic models by pedigree analysis. Am J Hum Genet 32:55–63, 1980.

Suarez BK: The affected sib-pair IBD distribution for HLA linked disease susceptibility loci. Tissue Antigens 12:87–93, 1978.

Suarez BK, Croughan J: Is the major histocompatibility complex linked to genes that increase susceptibility to affective disorders? A critical appraisal. Psychiatry Res 7:19–27, 1982.

Suarez BK, Reich T: HLA and major affective disorders. Arch Gen Psychiatry 41:22–27, 1984.

Suomi S: Models of depression in primates. Psychol Med 13:465–468, 1983.

Suranyi-Cadotte BE, Wood PL, Nair NPV, Schwartz G: Normalization of platelet $^3$H-imipramine binding in depressed patients during remission. Eur J Pharmacol 85:357–358, 1982.

Tait BD, Mackay IR: HLA and alcoholic cirrhosis. Tissue Antigens 19:6–10, 1982.

Tanna VL, Winokur G: A study of association and linkage of ABO blood types and primary affective disorder. Br J Psychiatry 114:1175–1181, 1968.

Targum SD, Gershon ES, van Eerdewegh M, Rogentine N: Human leukocyte antigen system not closely linked to or associated with bipolar manic-depressive illness. Biol Psychiatry 14:615–636, 1979.

Taylor MA, Abrams R, Hayman MA: The classification of affective disorders: a reassessment of the bipolar-unipolar dichotomy. J Affect Dis 2:95–109, 1980.

Thomson G: A review of theoretical aspects of HLA and disease associations. Theor Popul Biol 20:168–208, 1980.

Thompson W, Orvaschel H, Prusoff B, Kidd, KK: An evaluation of the family history method for ascertaining psychiatric disorders. Arch Gen Psychiatry 39:53–58, 1982.

Tienari P: Psychiatric illnesses in identical twins. Acta Psychiatr Scand [Suppl]:171, 1963.

Tienari P: Schizophrenia in Finnish male twins. Br J Psychiatry, Special Publication No. 10:29–35, 1975.

Tsuang MT, Bucher KD, Fleming JA: Testing the monogenic theory of schizophrenia: An application of segregation analysis to blind family study data. Br J Psychiatry 140:595–599, 1982.

Tsuang MT, Bucher KD, Fleming JA: A search for schizophrenic spectrum disorders: An application of a multiple threshold model to blind family study data. Br J Psychiatry 143:572–577, 1983.

Tsuang MT, Winokur G, Crowe RR: Morbidity risks of schizophrenia and affective disorders among first degree relatives and patients with schizophrenia, mania, depression and surgical conditions. Br J Psychiatry 137:497–504, 1980.

Turner WJ: Genetic markers for schizotaxia. Biol Psychiatry 14:177–206, 1979.

van Eerdewegh MM, Gershon ES, van Eerdewegh PM: X-chromosome threshold models of bipolar manic depressive illness. J Psychiatr Res 15:215–238, 1980.

vanPraag HM, deHaan S: Depression vulnerability and 5-hydroxytryptophan prophylaxis. Psychiatry Res 3:75–83, 1980.

von Knorring A-L, Cloninger CR, Bohman M, Sigvardsson A: An adoption study of depressive disorders and substance abuse. Arch Gen Psychiatry 40:943–950, 1983.

Waters B, Thakkar J, Lapierre Y: Erythrocyte lithium transport variables as a marker for manic-depressive disorder. Neuropsychobiology 9:94–98, 1983.

Weinberger D: Presented at the meeting of the American Psychopathological Association, New York, March 1984.

Weinberger DR, DeLisi LE, Neophytides AN, Wyatt RJ: Familial aspects of CT scan abnormalities in chronic schizophrenia patients. Psychiatry Res 4:65–71, 1981.

Weinberger DR, DeLisi LE, Perman GP, Targum S, Wyatt RJ: Computed tomography in schizophreniform disorder and other acute psychiatric disorders. Arch Gen Psychiatry 39:778–783, 1982.

Weinberger DR, Torrey EF, Neophytides AN, Wyatt RJ: Lateral cerebral ventricular enlargement in chronic schizophrenia. Arch Gen Psychiatry 36:735–739, 1979.

Weissman MM, Gershon ES, Kidd KK, Pusoff BA, Leckman JF, Dibble E, Hamovit J, Thompson WD, Pauls DL, Guroff JJ: Psychiatric disorders in the relatives of probands with affective disorder. Arch Gen Psychiatry 41:13–21, 1984.

Weissman MM, Kidd KK, Prusoff BA: Affective illness in relatives of severe and mild nonbipolar depressives and normal controls. Abstracts 2, F514. Third World Congress of Biological Psychiatry, Stockholm, Sweden, July 1981.

Weissman MM, Myers J: Affective disorders in a US urban community. The use of research diagnostic criteria in an epidemiological survey. Arch Gen Psychiatry 35:1304–1311, 1978.

Weissman MM, Wickramaratne P, Merikangas KR, Leckman JF, Prusoff BA, Caruso KA, Kidd KK. Early onset major depression: increased familial loading and specificity. Submitted for publication.

Weitkamp LR, Stancer HC, Persad E, Flood C, Guttormsen S: Depressive disorders and HLA: A gene on chromosome 6 that can affect behavior. N Engl J Med 305:1301–1306, 1981.

Winokur G: Depression spectrum disease: description and familiy study. Compr Psychiatry 13:3–8, 1972.

Winokur G, Clayton P: in Wortis J (ed): Recent Advances in Biological Psychiatry, vol 9. New York, Plenum Press, 1967.

Winokur G, Clayton P, Reich T: Manic Depressive Illness. St. Louis, CV Mosby, 1969.

Winokur G, March V, Mendels J: Primary affective disorder in relatives of patients with anorexia nervosa. Am J Psychiatry 137:695–698, 1980.

Witkin HA, Mednick SA, Schulsinger F, Bakkestrom E, Christiansen FO, Goodenough DR, Hirschhorn K, Lundsteen C, Owen DR, Philip J, Rubin DB, Stocking M: Criminality in XYY and XXY in men. Science 193:547–554, 1976.

Wright AF, Condon JB, Hampson ME, Crichton DN, Steel CM: Beta adrenoceptor binding defects in lymphoblastoid cell lines from manic depressive patients. Proceedings of the 14th Collegium Internationale Neuropsychopharmacology Congress. New York, Raven, 1984, pp 194–195.

Wyatt RJ, Murphy DL, Belmaker R, Cohen S, Donnelly CH, Pollin W: Reduced monoamine oxidase activity in platelets: A possible genetic marker for vulnerability to schizophrenia. Science 173:916–918, 1973.

Wyatt RJ, Potkin SG, Murphy DL: Platelet monoamine oxidase activity in schizophrenia: A review of the data. Am J Psychiatry 136:377–385, 1979.

Zerbin-Rudin E: Congenital word-blindness, in PE Becker (ed): Humangenetik. Stuttgart, Germany, Thieme, 1967. (Bulletin of the Orton Society 17:47–54, 1967.)

# chapter 31

# USE OF THE LABORATORY IN PSYCHIATRY

*by* Ronald L. Martin, M.D.
Sheldon H. Preskorn, M.D.

## INTRODUCTION

The past five decades have seen a significant advance of medicine as a scientific discipline. This advance is attributable, in part, to the development of accurate laboratory procedures. Although the clinical interview and physical examination remain vital aspects of the diagnostic process, *standardized and reliable procedures of assessing physical parameters yielding data of demonstrated validity* (our definition of a useful laboratory procedure) have dramatically improved the precision of diagnosis and treatment. Moreover, they have provided a means of assessing the pathophysiologic bases of many medical disorders. As a result, in many instances, medicine has moved from symptomatically and syndromatically to pathophysiologically, and even pathogenetically, defined disease categories. Such knowledge allows rational rather than purely empirical approaches to treatment and research.

As the other chapters of this book attest, the past three decades have witnessed a reawakening of psychiatry as a scientifically oriented branch of medicine. Although the role of the laboratory in psychiatry is at a more rudimentary stage than in medicine generally, its use is becoming increasingly important.

The laboratory is used in three major ways in psychiatry. The first, and most widely applied, use is in the exclusion of underlying medical, neurologic, or surgical (i.e., "organic") illness in the evaluation of patients presenting psychiatrically. A second use is in monitoring plasma levels of psychotropic drugs. A third, at least potential, use is the identification of biologic markers useful in the diagnosis, treatment, monitoring, and, ultimately, the pathophysiologic understanding of psychiatric disorders. The three sections of this chapter reflect these divisions.

The use of "organic" in this chapter follows the traditional dichotomy between "organic" and "functional" psychiatric disorders, a demarcation that is often convenient, if not truly accurate. It is not implied, however, that "organic" disorders have organic or biologic causes, while "functional" disorders have nonorganic or nonbiologic causes. The less inferential designations of "medical, neurologic, or surgical" vs. "psychiatric" disorder could have been used but would have been cumbersome.

The chapter is purposely broad in scope. The reader is directed to basic texts and laboratory guides for more detailed discussion and data. Information that is available in basic texts is not necessarily referenced.

Whenever possible, reference is made to review articles with more comprehensive bibliographies regarding specific points.

## EXCLUDING UNDERLYING ORGANIC ILLNESS

### Rationale for Electing Laboratory Evaluations

Normal central nervous system (CNS) functioning is intimately dependent on metabolic homeostasis and can be easily disrupted by endogenous and exogenous chemicals. Not surprisingly, psychiatric symptoms may occur in association with many medical illnesses.

Because laboratory evaluations are a major tool in diagnosing medical illnesses, a complete description of the use of the laboratory in excluding underlying organic illness would be encyclopedic. Rather than provide such a review, this section is designed as a guide for deciding when laboratory procedures are indicated and how to proceed generally.

Considering the large numbers of patients consulting a psychiatrist each year, a routine screening battery of laboratory tests would be a misallocation of resources. The yield in detected pathology would not justify such a policy. Thus some rationale for requesting laboratory evaluations must be followed. Such a rationale can be conceptualized with the aid of the following:

1. In general, laboratory tests are indicated in psychiatric patients when there is a reasonable possibility of underlying organic illness.
2. The possibility of organic illness is increased by any of the following: (a) a history of organic illness, (b) the presence of medical as well as psychiatric complaints, (c) abnormalities in the physical examination, (d) aspects of the psychiatric history or mental status examination that are atypical of a purely psychiatric disorder. The latter would include the presence of specific signs or symptoms that often herald organic illness.
3. The morbidity, discomfort, and cost of the contemplated test should be weighed against its potential diagnostic value and the relative probability of organic illness.

4. Tests should be administered as sparingly as possible with less specific but more broadly screening tests done before a more elaborate and specific workup is initiated.
5. Ample use of consultants should be made to prevent the initiation of extensive, yet unneccessary, testing.

The process of assessing the possibility of organic illness deserves amplification. First, a medical history should be obtained. Certain historical information, such as a past history of liver disease or of hypothyroidism, makes certain laboratory tests (unless recent laboratory data is available) virtually mandatory whatever the psychiatric presentation. Enquiry regarding current medications and use of psychoactive substances (especially caffeine, alcohol, drugs of abuse) should also be made. Realizing that an anxious, restless patient with a tachycardia is suffering from caffeinism may prevent unneccessary testing of thyroid functions.

Generally, medical or physical complaints make the probability of organic illness more likely, especially in a patient who typically does not manifest such complaints. Certain psychiatric disorders are typified by somatic complaints in the absence of demonstrable medical illness. Such complaints, in fact, are the essential characteristics of two major disorder categories of the *Diagnostic and Statistical Manual of Mental Disorders*, third edition (DSM-III; American Psychiatric Association, 1980): the somatoform disorders and the factitious disorders.

The somatoform disorders include somatization (hysteria or Briquet's syndrome), conversion, psychogenic pain, and hypochondriacal disorders. Patients with each of these disorders is characterized, in one way or another, by apparently involuntary and unexplained somatic complaints. In the factitious disorders, medical illness is purposely feigned. The severest form of this class of disorders is the chronic factitious disorder with physical symptoms (also known as Munchausen's syndrome). This latter group of patients often make a career of gaining admission to hospitals by mimicking various illnesses. They frequently receive extensive workups, medical treatments, and even surgeries.

While a clinician must be aware of the possibility of a somatoform or factitious disorder to avoid ordering unnecessary tests, he must also be aware of making an error potentially more costly: witholding an indicated laboratory procedure from an organically ill patient because symptoms were attributed to a psychiatric syndrome.

Patients with psychiatric disorders not predominantly characterized by somatic symptoms also may present with medical complaints. Patients with anxiety disorders may have symptoms such as chest pain and palpitations, suggesting heart disease. Depressed patients may present primarily with fatigue, loss of weight, and other "vegetative" signs, suggesting organic illness. In addition, they may have somatic delusions, such as "my heart has stopped beating" or "my blood has turned solid." Schizophrenics may also have somatic delusions, often of a bizarre nature; "half my brain was removed last week in my sleep," "I have been pregnant for the past 12 years." The validity of somatic complaints must be assessed in each instance. This judgment should be based on all sources of information available, including the patient's past history, current presentation, and a physical examination.

Unfortunately, the physical examination is often neglected in psychiatry. Clinicians sometimes opt to order a laboratory evaluation rather than examine a patient. If an organic disorder is being considered, a physical examination is mandatory. This does not necessarily mean that the treating psychiatrist performs the physical evaluation. This will depend on a variety of factors, including the acuteness of the situation, the nature of the therapeutic relationship, and, of utmost importance, the physician's *current* level of competence in performing the indicated examination.

Although details may vary, there is enough consistency within psychiatric syndromes that the appearance of atypical features in either the mental status examination or the history should alert the clinician to the possibility of an underlying organic factor.

For example, schizophrenia is typically characterized by an insidious onset, an absence of disorientation and memory impairment, and auditory rather than visual hallucinations. A patient presenting with a psychosis resembling schizophrenia but with disorientation, profound memory impairment, or reports of visual hallucinations who was known to have been functioning normally 3 days ago has an underlying organic illness until proved otherwise. In the absence of an identified cause, such a case requires laboratory evaluations, including serum electrolytes, blood and urine drug screens, as well as a careful physical examination and medical history. The investigative procedure should continue until an explanation is identified or efforts to detect an organic etiology are exhausted.

Selection of laboratory tests should remain highly individualized, based on the specifics of the particular case. Indications will be affected not only by the particular symptomatic picture, but also by demographic factors. The diagnostic and laboratory approach to an agitated, uncooperative, and disoriented patient would differ if that patient were a 44-year-old, recently divorced, unemployed bartender; a 65-year-old, married Mennonite pastor from a rural community with no history of psychiatric illness; or a 23-year-old youth with a 4-year history of recurrent episodes of psychosis with multiple state hospital admissions.

## Exclusion of Organic Illness in Particular Psychiatric Symptom Clusters

Although the variety of organic illnesses that may present psychiatrically is endless, the CNS has a rather limited repertoire of symptom clusters with which to respond. Thus the same cluster of psychiatric symptoms may be secondary to a number of disparate organic abnormalities or may represent a "functional" psychiatric illness.

The remainder of this section reviews the major symptom clusters into which most organically determined psychiatric syndromes fall. These include (a) impairment in level of consciousness and intellect (delirium and dementia), (b) psychoses, and (c) anxiety and affective disturbances.

### Disturbances in Consciousness and Intellect: Delirium and Dementia

Delirium and dementia lie at the interface of neurology and psychiatry. Which specialist evaluates and treats such patients is often a matter of happenstance and may have little to do with the patient's disorder itself. There may be a tendency for more obvious cases of organic impairment to be preferentially referred to neurologists and those with more of a functional appearance, to psychiatrists.

The diagnosis of these disorders is at two levels. The first consideration is whether the patient with apparent impaired consciousness or intellect is suffering from an organic disorder at all. Dissociative or catatonic syndromes, or the so-called pseudodementia syndrome of depression, can mimic organic disorders. The second consideration regards the identification of specific organic causes.

### Delirium

In patients presenting with acute brain syndromes, the diagnostic process must begin immediately. Any delay increases the risk of irreversible brain damage, other serious complications, or death. Varied clinical pictures are seen in patients with acute organic syndromes. Symptomatic pictures vary from (and often fluctuate between) agitation/hyperactivity to somnolence/lethargy, inattentiveness to hypervigilance, and from total unresponsiveness to moments of lucidity. These symptomatic pictures could be dealt with separately, but for convenience, they will be subsumed here under delirium.

A careful plan of using the laboratory should be instituted in such cases, a subject that has been well reviewed (Plum and Posner, 1980). Electroencephalography (EEG) may be useful. Patients with an organic or metabolic cause of altered consciousness generally show high-voltage slow activity in stupor or low-voltage fast activity in excitement, whereas in functional cases, good background alpha activity with response to visual and auditory stimuli is typical. Unfortunately, the EEG is often not expedient in an emergency situation, and whether or not a particular syndrome is "organic" or not may not be determinable on an EEG basis.

A myriad of specific organic factors are possible. In a recent review (Plum and Posner, 1980), 99 are listed. To focus the diagnostic process, these can be grouped into a number of more general categories. To focus the diagnostic approach, an outline of major headings are presented in Table 31–1. The most common on medical or surgical wards are hypoxia, ischemia, hypoglycemia, and

**Table 31–1   Causes of Delirium**

Deprivation of oxygen, substrate, or metabolic cofactors
Diseases of organs other than brain
Exogenous drugs or toxins
Drug withdrawal
Abnormalities of ionic or acid–base CNS environment
Disordered temperature regulation
Infections or inflammation of CNS
Primary neuronal or glial disorders
Seizures or postictal states
Head injury or concussion
Postoperative or intensive care unit delirium

From Plum F, Posner J: The Diagnosis of Stupor and Coma, ed 3. Philadelphia, FA Davis, 1980.

sedative-hypnotic or other drug intoxication or withdrawal. In most emergency department settings, drug intoxication and withdrawal are the most frequent.

Fortunately, the laboratory evaluations necessary to evaluate these diagnostic possibilities are readily available at most medical facilities, often in the form of screening profiles. As can be seen by reviewing Table 31–1, serum glucose, electrolytes, enzymes, and blood urea nitrogen (BUN) determinations and a complete blood count (CBC) will screen for most of the suspected causes. Adequate evaluation will improve substantially when additional procedures are done as clinically indicated: arterial blood gas analysis, lumbar puncture, serum alcohol determination, and urine drug screening.

Patients with a known psychiatric history present a special problem. A tragic error is to not recognize delirium as an additional syndrome and to attribute changes in the level of consciousness to the preexisting psychiatric disorder. It must be remembered that, if anything, psychiatric patients are at increased risk of delirium. Many will be on psychotropic medications. Toxicity from these medications, either from overdose or from toxic plasma levels on prescribed doses, is not infrequent. Patients on tricyclic antidepressants (TCAs) should be observed for anticholinergic symptoms. Plasma drug levels should be drawn if testing is available. Patients with TCA toxicity may suffer cardiotoxic death (especially if plasma levels are greater than 1000 ng/ml) even as the mental status is clearing. Patients on neuroleptics may be suffering from the neuroleptic malignant syndrome, consisting of stupor or coma, muscle rigidity and fasciculations, and hyperthermia. In patients with this presentation, serum creatinine phosphokinase (CPK) levels may aid in diagnosis, since elevation of this enzyme is a hallmark of this potentially fatal syndrome.

Psychiatric patients may be subject to other factors that place them at increased risk of delirium. Inattention to or neglect of nutritional, hygienic, or medical problems is frequent. Psychotic patients may do unusual things, such as drink excessive amounts of water (e.g., to "flush out" poison believed to have been placed in food), resulting in overhydration and hyponatremia. In such a case, if fluid and electrolyte balance is not promptly restored, agitation and confusion may progress to intractable seizures and death.

Patients with delirium thought to be secondary to alcohol or sedative-hypnotic withdrawal deserve special attention. Abstinence syndromes may be accompanied by hypoglycemia, ketosis, and acid–base, fluid, and electrolyte imbalances. These parameters should be carefully assessed with serum and urine testing. Intravenous glucose can be both diagnostic and lifesaving. In addition, such patients often fall or sustain other traumatic injuries, resulting in intracranial bleeds. If there is a suggestion of such injury, a skull x-ray or cranial computed tomography (CT) scan is indicated.

### Dementia

In delirium, the need for laboratory results is immediate. In dementia, the need is not as acute, so that laboratory procedures that are more protracted are possible. It must be remembered, however, that dementia and delirium may coexist. In fact, demented patients appear to have a lower threshold for becoming delirious. Delirium superimposed on dementia demands the same rapid assessment as delirium itself.

The first diagnostic discrimination, again, is between an actual, or organic, dementia and a dementia-like picture associated with a functional psychiatric illness. Reviews of the clinical, non-laboratory methods of approaching this differentiation are available (e.g., Wells and Duncan, 1980).

Laboratory evaluations will not necessarily offer a definitive answer, at least not early in the course of a dementia. The majority of demented patients will suffer from dementia of the Alzheimer's type (DAT). Chemistries in such patients are generally normal. The EEG is not necessarily abnormal, although some DAT patients will show some diffuse slowing. Cranial tomography (CT) cannot be entirely relied on. In many cases of DAT, cerebral atrophy is not observed. In addition, some intellectually intact elderly will show cerebral atrophy.

The laboratory can be used to evaluate for the presence of specific dementias—dementias occurring in the context of an identifiable organic cause (other than DAT, which is identifiable at autopsy). The battery of laboratory tests recommended (Wells, 1977) is outlined in Table 31–2. This battery, as simple as it is, has identified most specific dementias in several series of patients (Wells, 1978).

The major importance of making as specific a diagnosis as possible in dementia is the possibility of identifying a treatable cause. The battery recommended by Wells screens for the most common treatable dementias—those associated with chronic anemia, neurosyphilis, major organ failure (e.g., hepatic, renal), hypothyroidism, vitamin $B_{12}$ (pernicious anemia, subacute combined lateral sclerosis) or folate deficiency, metastases to lung or brain, and other space-occupying intracranial lesions. Although this battery is sufficient in most cases, additional procedures should be performed as suggested clinically.

Certain specific neurologic disorders may present with dementia and yet not be evident on routine laboratory testing. Some (such as Parkinson's disease and Huntington's disease) are primarily diagnosed on the basis of history and neurologic examination. The laboratory may be of more spe-

**Table 31–2  Laboratory Studies for Dementia in Absence of Specific Indications**

Blood tests:

| | |
|---|---|
| Complete blood count | 12-parameter metabolic screen |
| Serology for syphilis | Serum thyroxine |
| Vitamin $B_{12}$ and folate levels | |

Urinalysis
Chest x-ray
Computerized axial tomography of head

From Wells C: Diagnostic evaluation and treatment in dementia, in Wells C (ed): Dementia. Philadelphia, FA Davis, 1977.

cific value in others. If Wilson's disease (hepatolenticular degeneration) is suspected on the basis of the neurologic examination, hepatic dysfunction, or a Kayser-Fleischer ring, serum should be examined for increased copper and decreased ceruloplasmin, and urine tested for increased copper. If Creutzfeldt-Jakob (subacute spongiform encephalopathy) is suspected, an EEG may be indicated. Periodic biphasic or triphasic slow bursts, often accompanied by characteristic myoclonic jerks of the extremities, is seen in most (90 per cent) cases and is seldom seen in other types of dementia (Wilson, Musella, Short, 1977).

### Psychoses

Patients presenting with psychotic symptoms in the absence of disruption of attention, memory, or orientation represent a somewhat different situation diagnostically. In cases of recent origin, with no prior history of psychosis, the approach would be similar to that outlined for delirium. The assumption would be that, although the sensorium was clear, the psychosis was still attributable to disruption of brain functioning on a metabolic or toxic basis.

Particular attention should be paid to the possibility of a drug intoxication, particularly from hallucinogens and stimulants. Important diagnostic tools are serum and urine drug screens. The accuracy of these screens varies greatly among laboratories. Moreover, they are often sensitive to interference from multiple other substances. Many of the drugs, particularly the hallucinogens, exert their effects at extremely low serum concentrations. Some, such as phencyclidine (PCP), may have a prolonged psychotomimetic effect, even after measurable levels of the drug have disappeared from serum.

Psychoses of a more long-standing nature require a somewhat different diagnostic approach. For such cases, the recommended laboratory approach resembles that for dementia (Table 31–2). It must be remembered, in fact, that dementias may initially present with psychosis rather than with disruptions in intellect.

Careful attention must be paid to the history and physical examination as well as to the initial screening laboratory values in determining additional testing.

### Anxiety and Affective Disturbances

Delirium, dementia, and psychosis are remarkable events. They occur with rarity in the general population, and when they occur, they are rather easily recognizable, as they are discontinuous in the course of the person's life.

Anxiety and affective syndromes are subtler. Minor fluctuations in level of anxiety or mood are part and parcel of everyday life for most people. Even if the degree of disturbance reaches the point that medical attention is sought, anxiety and affective disorders are so commonplace that diagnosis is often made and treatment initiated without careful medical scrutiny.

A number of medical illnesses may present with anxiety and affective symptoms. These diseases can be subsumed under several categories: endocrinopathies; neurologic disease; neoplasms; metabolic, toxic, and hematologic disorders; and chronic systemic disorders.

#### Endocrinopathies

The nervous and endocrine systems are intimately interrelated (Brown and Seggie, 1980; Haskett and Rose, 1981). The control center of the endocrine system, the hypothalamus, is considered part of the limbic system, a functional part of the CNS that is thought to specifically modulate emotions. Anatomically, the hypothalamus is richly innervated by the limbic system. It also receives inputs from the frontal cortex and ascending reticular activating system. The hypothalamus is reactive to many neurotransmitters, including monoamines such as dopamine, norepinephrine, and serotonin—substances implicated in the pathophysiology of schizophrenia and affective disorders.

With such tight interrelationship, it is not so surprising that endocrinologic imbalances have frequent psychiatric effects, particularly on mood. In fact, as reviewed in the second section of this chapter, endocrinologic changes are observed in functional psychiatric illnesses.

The effects of endocrine hormones are so widespread that virtually any endocrinopathy may be nonspecifically associated with affective changes. The association appears to be more direct with disturbances in thyroid hormones and adrenocortical steroids. Psychiatric symptoms are a relatively consistent and striking aspect in the clinical picture in such imbalances. They are often the presenting complaint. In both cases, psychiatric syndromes are associated with both hormone deficiency and excess.

**Thyroid.** Thyroid hormone has perhaps the most general metabolic effect of any of the endocrine hormones. Deficiency in thyroid hormone results in hypometabolism; an excess results in hypermetabolism.

Hypothyroidism (myxedema) may have profound psychiatric effects. These effects vary with the age at onset of the deficiency. Neonatal hypothyroidism, if untreated, results in retardation of physical and mental development (cretinism). This disorder is observed in about 1 of every 5000 births, and measurement of serum or cord thyroxine ($T_4$) or thyroid-stimulating hormone (TSH) is required at birth in most states as a screening procedure.

In older children, failure to continue on growth or development curves should raise suspicion of hypothyroidism, particularly if x-rays reveal failure of expected epiphyseal closures.

In adults, hypothyroidism often presents insidiously with nonspecific symptoms such as lethargy, anergia, and fatigability. If the deficiency state continues, these symptoms, as well as the classic physical signs of myxedema, will progress. Classically, myxedematous patients are apathetic, withdrawn, and psychomotor retarded and show impaired memory and difficulty in concentrating. Profound dysphoria with suicidal thoughts may occur—a picture not unlike melancholic depression. The affective disturbance may reach psychotic proportions, hence "myxedema madness."

Diagnosis, first of all, depends on a careful history and examination for the classic physical signs of myxedema. A profoundly depressed patient with no prior history of such, or of a syndrome in which apathy-lethargy type symptoms predominate over dysphoria, should make one suspicious.

When hypothyroidism is suspected, one should start with the simplest screen available. Increased serum cholesterol, CPK, serum glutamic-oxaloacetic transferase (SGOT), and lactic dehydrogenase (LDH) are often, but not invariably, present and so

are only remotely useful. Recommended thyroid batteries vary from medical center to medical center, often reflecting the availability of assay procedures. Generally, some measure of serum 3,5,3′,5′-tetraiodothyronine (serum $T_4$) or a thyroid radioactive iodine uptake (RAIU) are recommended. Because serum $T_4$ may be affected by alterations in thyroxine binding globulin (TBG), a serum free $T_4$ ($FT_4$) may also be useful. Metabolic indices, such as determination of the basal metabolism rate (BMR), are seldom done today because of their inconvenience and because they are affected by many nonthyroidal factors.

Hypothyroidism with the same psychiatric manifestations may result from lesions of the thyroid itself, the pituitary, or the hypothalamus. Once having determined hypothyroidism by initial testing, it is probably indicated to consult with an internist or endocrinologist for more specific testing. If psychiatric symptoms persist after a euthyroid state is reestablished, the usual treatments for depression should be instituted.

As with hypothyroidism, the psychiatric manifestations of thyroid excess often develop insidiously. Common early symptoms of hyperthyroidism include emotional instability, nervousness, hyperactivity, a fine tremor, loss of weight and strength, and, at times, palpitations. Generally, if the syndrome has developed rapidly, the patient complains of anxiety; if more gradually, depression. Occasionally, a patient may become hyperactive and grandiose such that a maniclike state is observed. Syndromes resembling anxiety or depressive disorders are more common, however.

Again, diagnosis depends, first of all, on a good history and examination of the patient. In addition to the psychiatric symptoms mentioned, hyperthyroid patients characteristically have heat intolerance. On physical examination, they may (if suffering from Grave's disease) demonstrate a characteristic ophthalmopathy (exophthalmos), a diffuse goiter (sometimes accompanied by a bruit), and a dermopathy.

Laboratory evaluation should, again, start with a basic screen (e.g., serum $T_4$, $FT_4$, RAIU). In most cases, evidence of thyroid imbalance indicates consultation from an internist or endocrinologist, depending on the current competence of the psychiatrist in evaluating and treating such disorders.

**Adrenal Cortex.** Both insufficiency and excess in adrenocortical hormones may be associated with psychiatric syndromes of highly variable presentation but with a predominance of affective or anxiety symptoms.

Adrenocortical insufficiency (Addison's disease) most often presents psychiatrically with depressive symptoms, particularly of an apathetic, negativistic nature, and with fatigue and poverty of thought. In extreme cases, a deliriumlike picture can develop with disorientation and memory loss. Addison's disease should be suspected in patients who, at one time, were receiving steroids as a medical treatment. Suspicion should also be raised in cases of depression in which the degree of weakness and lethargy appear to be out of step with the rest of the picture and in which *hypo*tension is notable. Blood pressure changes occur consequent to lowered levels of aldosterone, a mineralocorticoid, which may be affected as well as the glucocorticoids, such as cortisol. A characteristic form of hyperpigmentation (attributable to elevated levels of adrenocorticotropin hormone [ACTH]) is the hallmark of the syndrome. Its absence, however, does not exclude hyperadrenocortisolism. ACTH may not be elevated in syndromes of extra-adrenal origin.

In milder cases, routine laboratory values may be normal, but in advanced stages, hyponatremia, paired with hyperkalemia, may occur. Documentation of adrenal insufficiency is essential and includes 24-hour urine collections for 17-hydroxy and 17-ketosteroids. Plasma cortisol and ACTH levels are also helpful. ACTH stimulation testing can demonstrate whether the insufficiency is associated with adrenal failure or is of hypothalamic–pituitary origin.

Excess levels of cortisol, whether of adrenal or exogenous (iatrogenic) origin, result in the classic picture of Cushing's syndrome. Psychiatrically, patients with hyperadrenocortisolism may present with a syndrome resembling an anxiety or depressive disorder with fatigue and weakness. In some cases, especially with exogenous corticoids, maniclike syndromes may be seen with euphoria, but this is uncommon and generally transient, with depression ensuing. The psychiatric syndrome may progress to include psychotic features. Hypertension is nearly always present. The diagnosis of hypercortisolism should be considered in depressed patients on exogenous steroids. Once the classic physical signs of Cushing's syndrome appear (altered habitus with round facies and truncal obesity, hirsutism and amenorrhea in women, and cutaneous striae), the diagnosis is fairly obvious, but it must be remembered that the psychiatric syndrome may antedate the other signs.

The laboratory diagnosis of Cushing's syndrome hinges on the demonstration of increased cortisol levels. This is most easily demonstrated by high plasma and urinary 17-hydroxycorticoid levels. Individual plasma levels are not especially meaningful because of diurnal variation and the fact that cortisol is released in pulselike, rather than continuous, fashion. The diagnosis can be refined with various modifications of the dexamethasone suppression test (DST), a test that is discussed in detail later in this chapter.

**Pheochromocytoma.** Catecholamine-producing tumors of the adrenal medulla and other chromaffin-staining tissues frequently present with anxiety symptoms or, in more chronic cases, depression. "Physiologic" anxiety symptoms such as tremulousness, sweatiness, heat intolerance, palpitations, and chest pains are particularly common. Labile hypertension is a prominent feature. Diagnosis should be suspected when severe anxiety symptoms present suddenly in someone without such a history, especially if they also have labile hypertension.

Laboratory evaluation, which generally involves the measurement of norepinephrine and epinephrine in 24-hour urine, is problematic. Many dietary factors and concomitant medications can influence the assay. If pheochromocytoma is suspected, consultation with an internist or endocrinologist is indicated. Even if this tumor is not found, better control of the patient's labile hypertension is indicated.

**Parathyroid.** Both hypoparathyroidism and hyperparathyroidism are associated with psychiatric manifestations. The mechanism differs from that of thyroid or adrenocortical dysfunction in that the symptoms appear to be a function of alteration in calcium levels rather than effects of parathormone directly on the CNS. Psychiatric symptoms are rather nonspecific but correlate with the magnitude of deviation in serum calcium. With mild hypocalcemia, anxiety symptoms and paresthesias are common. As hypocalcemia becomes more marked, tetany may occur; at lower levels yet, seizures may occur. Permanent brain damage may occur. With hypercalcemia, depressive symptoms (fatigue, lethargy, or irritability) may be seen at mild elevations (11 to 16 mg/dl). At elevations greater than 16 mg/dl, delirium may be seen.

These syndromes are often detected from serum calcium levels in a routine chemical profile. Hypoparathyroidism (or pseudohypoparathyroidism) should be suspected in patients with tetany or in patients with a history of neck surgery; hyperparathyroidism (or pseudohyperparathyroidism) should be suspected in patients with repeated nephrolithiasis or with the bone disease osteitis fibrosa cystica.

Laboratory evaluation should start with serum calcium determination. Radioimmunoassay (RIA) of parathormone should also be considered. After such basic testing, the diagnostic workup should probably be continued by a consultant. The differential diagnosis gets complicated, considering the possibilities of primary, secondary, "pseudo," and even "pseudopseudo" hypoparathyroidism. A prompt, definitive diagnosis is advisable, considering the potential complications and the fact that some of the "pseudo" cases may be associated with a malignancy.

**Estrogen.** Two syndromes have been postulated as directly or indirectly related to estrogen deficiency: the premenstrual syndrome and the menopausal syndrome. In the premenstrual syndrome, women are reported to have increased anxiety or depressive symptoms, somatic complaints, and behavioral changes during the 7 to 10 days before menses. In the menopausal syndrome, these same symptoms plus hot flushes are reported. A symptomatically similar posthysterectomy syndrome has been proposed as well. Hot flushes do appear to be related to luteinizing hormone (LH) surges. Otherwise, efforts to delineate these syndromes endocrinologically have not, as yet, been successful. Thus laboratory tests have not been found to be useful in delineating these syndromes (Abplanalp, Haskett, Rose, 1980).

**Hypoglycemia.** When of gradual onset and long duration, hypoglycemia is often associated with CNS symptoms such as ap-

athy, dizziness, confusion, and intellectual decline, and is to be considered in the differential diagnosis of dementia. A rapid drop in blood glucose, on the other hand, more often results in anxiety, tremulousness, sweatiness, tachycardia, and palpitations—a syndrome reminiscent of panic disorder. Serum glucose levels below 50 mg/dl are usually necessary for such symptoms to develop. The mechanism is thought to be by way of excessive secretion of epinephrine in response to the fall in blood sugar.

The differential diagnosis of hypoglycemia is broad, ranging from excessive insulin administration by diabetics to various causes of excessive insulin production. When symptoms continue and appear to be temporally related to meals or in response to certain types of foods, yet no organic illness can be identified, postprandial hypoglycemia should be considered. This syndrome has been observed in patients with a history of gastrointestinal surgery.

Because the symptomatic picture of hypoglycemia overlaps with that of panic or anxiety disorders, the diagnosis should be verified by laboratory evaluations before it is accepted. Glucose tolerance tests are difficult to interpret and may have little bearing on the syndrome. The definitive diagnostic procedure is serum glucose determination during a symptomatic attack. Patients with panic disorder will not show a low serum glucose level and may actually show an elevated serum glucose because of the hyperglycemic effects of epinephrine and cortisol.

### Neurologic Disorders

**Parkinsonism.** Affective symptoms may occur in relation to the disease itself. Pathologic changes similar to those seen in the substantia nigra have been observed in the locus ceruleus of parkinsonian patients. Because this locus is the main norepinephrine nucleus in the brain, the affective symptoms may be neurochemically mediated. Affective syndromes may also occur in association with certain treatments, particularly L-dopa. Depressive, as well as maniclike syndromes, sometimes of psychotic proportions, have been reported with L-dopa use. Thus L-dopa plasma levels may be useful in adjusting dosage. Lowering levels into the therapeutic range may alleviate these symptoms. Nonetheless, some patients will develop psychiatric symptoms even within the therapeutic range.

**Huntington's Disease and Wilson's Disease.** Affective syndromes or psychotic syndromes resembling schizophrenia may be the first presentation of these two disorders. Laboratory tests involved in their diagnosis were discussed previously in reference to dementia.

**Multiple Sclerosis.** This disorder may present with personality changes and lability of mood, which, together with the frequent vagueness of the neurologic picture at least early in the course of the disorder, may suggest a psychiatric rather than a neurologic disorder. As yet, there are no definitive laboratory tests to resolve this problem. Accurate diagnosis is often not possible until the disease is more progressed and neurologic signs become more definite.

### Neoplasms

Anxiety and depression in the context of malignancies has been the object of a great deal of recent interest (Petty and Noyes, 1981). A certain amount of depressive symptomatology can be attributed to a reaction to incapacitation, pain, and possibly death. Depression is also associated with irradiation and several of the antineoplastic drugs. Some studies, however, have shown that depression can occur before the detection of the malignancy. This has been reported with pancreatic carcinoma, for example.

An occult malignancy should be suspected in cases of depression in which weight loss and debility outstep the degree of mood or cognitive symptoms. Testing should begin with a routine chemical profile, CBC, chest x-ray, and any tests that are symptomatically or demographically indicated.

### Metabolic and Toxic Disorders.

A wide variety of metabolic illnesses are probably associated with depressive symptoms, if not a full depressive syndrome. Similarly, many drugs appear to induce affective symptoms both in toxic and therapeutic plasma concentration ranges. Laboratory testing in these situations would be indicated according to historical and symptomatic information. One syndrome (acute intermittent porphyria) deserves special mention, as it is often diagnosed only after unnecessary delay.

**Acute Intermittent Porphyria.** Acute intermittent porphyria, associated with an inborn error of heme metabolism, is characterized by acute attacks often precipitated by the ingestion of one of a number of substances, including barbiturates, anticonvulsants, alcohol, and hormones. These attacks can resemble panic attacks. The one feature of such attacks that is not typical of panic attacks is excruciating abdominal pain, which often heralds the onset of an attack. The abdomen is often surprisingly (considering the degree of complaint) soft and nontender, and a confusing admixture of neurologic signs are often present. Thus a somatoform disorder is sometimes suggested. The syndrome may be life-threatening, with the development of hyponatremia (attributable, in part, to vomiting) and with resulting delirium, coma, and seizures. Thus prompt diagnosis is important so that supportive measures are not delayed. Medications such as barbiturates and anticonvulsants, which may aggravate or prolong attacks, are to be avoided.

Diagnosis in a previously unidentified case is made by documenting excessive excretion of heme precursors in urine during an acute attack. Between attacks, the diagnosis can be made by measuring the activity of porphyrin synthesizing enzymes.

### Chronic Systemic Disorders

As with metabolic disorders, depressive symptoms are probably common in the course of many chronic systemic disorders. In most cases, the underlying disorder and need for laboratory testing are evident.

### Systemic Lupus Erythematosus

In the course of systemic lupus erythematosus, the diagnosis generally becomes evident with the occurrence of the typical physical changes in the renal, cardiopulmonary, and musculoskeletal systems and the skin. Early in the course of the illness, complaints may be vague and include anorexia, vomiting, and depression.

Routine laboratory tests may show nonspecific abnormalities, such as anemia, leukopenia, an elevated sedimentation rate (ESR), and mild proteinuria and microscopic hematuria. Given such a picture, a more specific evaluation is indicated and should include determination of autoantibodies (e.g., antinuclear antibodies, or ANA) and perhaps a lupus erythematosus cell test. Definitive diagnosis, especially at early stages, is problematic, and consultation with an internist or rheumatologist may be indicated.

## PLASMA MONITORING OF PSYCHOTROPIC DRUG LEVELS

In medicine, monitoring of plasma concentration levels of certain drugs, such as anticonvulsants and cardiac glycosides, has been useful, especially in instances when the therapeutic range is well established and the therapeutic index (the mean toxic dose divided by the mean therapeutic dose) is low. In such cases, the determination of proper dosage is critical to assure that a patient achieves a therapeutic, rather than a toxic or even lethal, level. Many of the drugs used in psychiatry today, particularly lithium carbonate and the tricyclic antidepressants (TCAs), also have low therapeutic indices.

Understanding of a few pharmacologic principles is necessary for the appreciation of plasma monitoring. Plasma levels reflect the pharmacokinetics (the time course) rather than the pharmacodynamics (the physiologic effects and mechanisms of action) of a given drug and its metabolites. The time course of a drug is a function of its absorption, distribution, metabolism, and excretion, these determining the plasma and brain levels of the drug and its metabolites.

Important pharmacokinetic parameters are plasma half-life and steady-state. The plasma half-life is the time after the administration of a single dose of a drug at which half has been eliminated. After establishing a fixed dose and dosing interval for a drug, steady-state exists when the amount of the drug ingested per dosing interval equals the amount eliminated. At steady-state, an equilibrium exists between drug levels in plasma and the other body compartments. Thus the amount of drug at the effector site (CNS neurons) is in equilibrium with the free concentration in plasma. Generally, steady-state occurs after five half-lives.

Principles of pharmacokinetics and pharmacodynamics are merged in consideration of concentration-response relationships.

"Response" here generally refers to the therapeutic effects of a drug, but it can refer to side effects as well. It is assumed that a critical drug concentration must be achieved at the receptor site before an effect is observed.

### Lithium Carbonate

It is perhaps proper to start with lithium. Lithium's therapeutic effects in treating mania were discovered in 1949, making it the first specifically effective psychotropic drug (Fieve, 1980). Its toxicity and potential lethality were also known, causing it to be banned in the United States until 1970. It was used cautiously but effectively elsewhere.

The plasma concentration of lithium, an alkali metal existing in the body as a cation, is easily measured by atomic absorption or flame emission photometry.

The mean half-life of lithium for healthy adults is 24 hours, ranging from 18 hours in some adolescents to 30-36 hours in the elderly. Thus truly meaningful plasma levels are obtainable after approximately 5 days on a constant dosage. In clinical practice, levels are often determined more frequently during the early phases of treatment, especially if higher plasma levels are sought in an attempt to terminate the manic episode more promptly.

Three- or four-times-a-day dosage regimens are generally followed; a twice-a-day schedule is followed when slow-release formulations are used. With standard preparations, peak concentrations are observed within 2 hours—within 5 hours for the slow-release drug. Plasma samples are best drawn at 10 to 12 hours after the last dose because the elimination curve flattens out after about 8 hours.

Therapeutic effects occur at concentrations between approximately 0.7 and 1.5 mEq/L, with acute side effects occurring in some patients within the therapeutic range but in most at levels above 1.5 mEq/L. Mild side effects include slight polyuria/polydipsia, nausea or diarrhea, mild sedation, and a fine tremor. At higher levels, one sees exacerbation of these effects. With moderate toxicity, generally occurring at levels from 2.0 to 2.5 mEq/L, a coarse tremor may be seen, along with muscle weakness or hyperirritability with fasciculations. At higher levels (greater than 2.5 mEq/L), muscular hypertonicity, hyperactive deep tendon reflexes, and choreiform–athetoid movements may appear. Consciousness may be grossly impaired. With severe toxicity, coma and death may ensue.

This schema of concentration-side effect correlations is merely a general guideline. It is of the utmost importance to observe the patient for signs of toxicity rather than simply monitor drug levels, since there is a great deal of individual variation in sensitivity. Because there is also individual variation in steady-state concentration on the same dosage, plasma monitoring of lithium is invaluable in maintaining a patient within a desired therapeutic range to avoid inadvertent toxicity.

## Antidepressant Drugs

Several antidepressants of the tricyclic type have been studied from the standpoint of plasma concentration (Preskorn and Mac, 1984). Until recently, monitoring of TCA plasma levels was only possible at research centers. Today, with a burgeoning of commercial laboratories offering such assays, they are readily available to many clinicians.

Assays are generally done by chromatographic techniques, with gas chromatography–mass spectrophotometry (GC–MS) the most accurate from the standpoint of sensitivity and specificity. It is also the most expensive and time-consuming. Hence it is used mainly to standardize other less accurate but more convenient assays. Gas chromatography (GC) and high-performance liquid chromatography (HPLC) are reasonably accurate and are the most commonly used techniques (Preskorn and Mac, 1984). Some caution must be taken in the confidence put in an assay. A well-established laboratory is recommended, as large interlaboratory and intralaboratory differences have been noted (Amsterdam, Brunswick, Mendels, 1980).

To date, plasma levels of amitriptyline, nortriptyline, imipramine, and desipramine have been studied most extensively. Of these, therapeutic ranges for nortriptyline and imipramine are the most widely accepted. Laboratories can now measure most of the antidepressants, including new non-

tricyclics such as trazodone, but currently, there is little data to support purported therapeutic ranges.

The mean half-life of the TCAs varies from 17 hours for doxepin to 78 hours for protriptyline (Richardson and Richelson, 1984). For practical purposes, a half-life of 24 to 36 hours is a reasonable approximation for amitriptyline, nortriptyline, imipramine, and desipramine. Thus steady-state levels can be determined after approximately 7 days.

Samples should be drawn 10 to 12 hours after the last dose to ensure being in the elimination phase, rather than the absorption or distribution phase. Hemolysis should be avoided because red blood cells have a higher TCA concentration than plasma.

TCA plasma level monitoring can be useful in several ways: checking compliance, adjusting dosage to achieve a level in the therapeutic range, minimizing the risk of toxicity, and assessing overdose danger (Preskorn and Madakasira, 1981).

It is well known that patients frequently do not take medications as prescribed. An unusually low plasma level on a particular dosage of TCA would alert the physician to the possibility that the patient may not be complying, since there is as much as a 36-fold interindividual variation in metabolism rates of TCAs, such that the patient may simply be a "fast" metabolizer. Failure of the concentration to increase with an increase in dose, however, would strongly suggest noncompliance. Knowledge that the level will be "checked" may encourage compliance.

Unlike many drugs in which linear or sigmoidal relationships exist, a nonlinear concentration-antidepressant response curve has been reported with certain TCAs, particularly nortriptyline. A "therapeutic window" appears to exist in which antidepressant effects occur only between certain minimum and maximum levels (Asberg, Cronholm, Sjogvist, Tuck, 1971). Above the maximum threshold, not only will side effects be more frequent, but the antidepressant effect itself will also be diminished.

In the case of nortriptyline, the antidepressant "therapeutic window" is estimated between 50 and 175 ng/ml; for amitriptyline, a combined concentration of it and its active metabolite nortriptyline, the window is between 150 and 250 ng/ml.

The concentration-response curve for imipramine appears to be linear (Glassman, 1981). The minimum effective level is approximately 150 ng/ml. However, increasing the concentration above 300 ng/ml in nonresponsive patients is not generally recommended because the risks of toxicity progressively outweigh the chances of therapeutic gains as the concentration is increased above this level.

The adverse side effects of TCAs are many. TCAs affect multiple neurotransmitter systems, most of which may have nothing to do with antidepressant effects. Some side effects are mainly a nuisance (e.g., dry mouth) or may even be useful in some patients (e.g., sedation). Others can be incapacitating (e.g., memory impairment) or life-threatening (e.g., cardiotoxicity). Although wide interindividual variations in sensitivity to side effects exist, they are usually dose related. With the wide variation in the metabolism of TCAs, some patients may develop toxic plasma concentrations on routine dosages. Without plasma level determinations, it would not be possible to detect these "slow metabolizers" until signs of toxicity developed.

TCAs have a serious overdose potential, with major CNS and cardiotoxic effects. Both CNS and cardiac toxicities are dose related but are not always correlated with each other. Thus a patient whose mental status is clearing may still have toxic plasma levels and suffer a fatal cardiac arrhythmia. All patients with plasma levels of total TCAs greater than 1000 ng/ml show impaired intracardiac conduction with QRS prolongation. Death from cardiac arrhythmias has occurred at concentrations as low as 500 ng/ml (Preskorn and Irwin, 1982). Clinically, all TCA overdose patients with a QRS longer than 100 msec should be monitored by electrocardiography (EKG). In overdose cases, TCA plasma levels are not a foolproof method of screening for potentially dangerous overdoses, since absorption may not be complete. In addition, prompt assays are seldom available. Monitoring the EKG and other physical signs is still the best method for assessing risk in an overdose patient.

## Neuroleptics

The study of neuroleptic plasma concentration has lagged far behind the study of TCA levels. Knowledge of concentration-response relationships is fragmentary, even with the few neuroleptic drugs that have been studied from this perspective.

As with the TCAs, chromatographic methods of assay are generally used, particularly HPLC and GC (Friedel, 1984). They are fairly accurate and are much less expensive and time-consuming than GC/MS, which is, again, used mainly for standardization.

RIAs have also been used. The method has great potential but requires the development of a specific antibody for each drug assayed (Friedel, 1984). A radioligand dopamine receptor binding displacement assay is also available. This technique measures the amount of parent neuroleptic drug and any of its metabolites that displace a radiolabeled ligand from the dopamine (DA) receptor. Thus, theoretically, the assay may measure the actual antidopaminergic effects of a neuroleptic drug and its metabolites. The relevance of this to the clinical effects of neuroleptic drugs is unproven, however. Pharmacokinetic studies have shown that, at least with the neuroleptics studied, single-dose concentrations predict steady-state levels, which, in the case of most neuroleptics, can be obtained after 1 week on a fixed dose (Yesavage, 1984).

Studies of concentration-response relationships for neuroleptics have been few. Many of the existing studies suffer from serious methodological problems, compromising the applicability of their conclusions. As argued by Van Putten (1984), fixed-dose design would appear to be necessary. Thus far only chlorpromazine, fluphenazine, haloperidol, and thiothixene have been studied in this way. As interpreted by Van Putten, these studies suggest that with the first three of these drugs, a nonlinear, "therapeutic window" concentration-response relationship exists. A linear relationship may exist for thiothixene. Thus, with a refractory patient, it may be possible to continue increasing the dosage of thiothixene, as tolerated in terms of side effects, without worrying about diminution of antipsychotic effects. In contrast, higher dose levels of the other drugs may cause "psychotoxicity" (i.e., aggravation of the psychosis). At best, these data are very preliminary and the usefulness of neuroleptic plasma monitoring is yet to be established.

## DIAGNOSING AND MONITORING PSYCHIATRIC DISORDERS

This use of the laboratory in psychiatry is in its infancy. Yet some exciting leads, if not concrete findings, have been uncovered and knowledge is expanding. The purpose of this section is to review some promising avenues of discovery.

### Neuroendocrine Strategies

The CNS and endocrine systems are so interrelated that, for many purposes, the two can be referred to as one—the neuroendocrine system. Ramifications of this unity are discussed in detail in several excellent reviews, including those of Brown and Seggie (1980) and Haskett and Rose (1981).

Dysfunction in the endocrine component of this system (reviewed earlier) has long been known to result in serious disruption in CNS function (i.e., the production of psychiatric symptoms). It has also been long believed by many that CNS dysfunction is accompanied by changes in endocrine function. Indeed, some changes have been long reported (e.g., hypercortisolemia in melancholic depressions and gonadotropin changes in anorexia nervosa). The changes observed, however, have lacked sufficient specificity to be useful clinically. From a theoretical or research point of view, it is not clear that such changes are related to a process basic to the pathophysiology of the psychiatric disorder, or are merely epiphenomena.

In recent years, some neuroendocrine strategies made possible, in part, by technological advances such as RIA have allowed more exacting assessment of neuroendocrine functioning. Thus subtle alterations in the responsivity of specific neuroendocrine systems to various challenges may be detected. Such alterations may prove useful as biologic markers for certain major psychiatric disorders. With this in mind, various techniques currently in use in clinical and research settings will be reviewed.

### Affective Disorders

#### Dexamethasone Suppression Test

When dexamethasone, a potent synthetic corticosteroid-like compound, is adminis-tered to "normals," adrenocortical secretion of corticosteroids, of which cortisol constitutes 75 per cent to 95 per cent, is temporarily "suppressed." The mechanism is thought to involve a feedback loop, inhibiting the secretion of corticotropin-releasing factor (CRF) from the hypothalamus, which results in a fall in the pituitary secretion of ACTH, which in turn results in a fall in cortisol secretion by the adrenal glands.

The overnight DST test, as standardized by Carroll et al. (1981), involves giving 1 mg of dexamethasone in tablet form at 11 P.M., just before sleep. Plasma levels are then drawn at 8 A.M., 4 P.M., and 11 P.M. the next day. In outpatients, the 4 P.M. level is often the only level obtained. Any serum plasma level greater than 5 μg/dl is defined as nonsuppression. As used in medicine, failure to suppress is considered *possibly* indicative of pathology in the hypothalamic–pituitary–adrenal axis, but because of the multitude of factors that can give false-positive results, it is only viewed as an initial screening procedure.

The DST has been the subject of intensive research and has gained considerable popularity in clinical practice. Yet several questions remain about its usefulness as a diagnostic screening test for affective disorders. Although reasonably sensitive (proportion of true negatives) and specific (proportion of true positives) in selected populations, such as the severely depressed, its diagnostic usefulness diminishes when less severely depressed outpatients or medically ill patients are studied. The American College of Physicians recently assessed the DST as a "diagnostic test of unproven value in the diagnosis and management of depression" (Young and Schwartz, 1984).

Although controversy exists about the utility of the DST as a broad screening test for depression, some have suggested that it may be useful, especially if given in conjunction with other neuroendocrine challenge tests, in subtyping depression, particularly in separating "endogenous" or "melancholic" depressives from the more heterogenous pool of patients with depressive syndromes (Targum, 1983; Feinberg and Carroll, 1984). Another potential role of the DST is in monitoring treatment response and detecting impending relapse in melancholic depressives (Greden et al., 1983).

## Thyroid-Releasing Hormone Stimulation

As reviewed earlier, hypothyroidism is often accompanied by depression. Conversely, most depressed patients are euthyroid, at least by the usual parameters. It has been suggested, however, that subtler dysregulation exists in the form of blunted thyrotropin (TSH) response to thyrotropin-releasing hormone (TRH).

In this test, TRH is administered in the morning after an overnight fast. First, an intravenous line is started and a baseline TSH level is obtained. Then, 500 µg of TRH is infused over 30 seconds. Serial TSH collections are taken 15, 30, and 45 minutes after infusion. An increase in plasma TSH of from 10 to 20 µU/ml above baseline is expected. An increase of less than 7 µU/ml is considered a blunted response (Targum, 1983). In the absence of a primary pituitary disorder, such a blunted response is reported to occur in 25 per cent to 35 per cent of endogenously depressed patients and seldom in others.

The relatively low sensitivity of the TRH stimulation test to endogenous depression, even if it were highly specific, limits its value when used by itself. Some have argued that the test may be more useful when used in conjunction with other neuroendocrine tests, such as the DST (Targum et al., 1982).

## Dopamine Agonist Studies

Preliminary work has been done in studying the effects of DA agonists on plasma levels of various hormones known to be affected by these compounds (Jimerson and Post, 1984). DA and its agonists inhibit the release of prolactin and stimulate the secretion of growth hormone (GH). It has been suggested that certain depressed patients may show increased pituitary sensitivity to DA and its agonists. A dramatic fall in plasma prolactin levels has been observed in depressed patients in comparison with controls. However, GH response did not distinguish depressed from nondepressed patients. This prolactin effect is of theoretical interest, considering the possibility that antidepressant response may be mediated, in part, by dopaminergic mechanisms, as suggested by the presumed mechanism of action of the new antidepressant bupropion.

## Anorexia Nervosa

Anorexia nervosa is a psychiatric disorder virtually always accompanied by endocrine changes (Vande Wiele, 1977; Garfinkel and Garner, 1984). Affected women typically present with breast atrophy and amenorrhea and characteristically show low plasma 17B-estradiol levels and low LH and follicle-stimulating hormone (FSH). Plasma cortisol is usually high or normal, with $T_4$ usually low-normal and FSH high-normal. The relative preservation of pituitary–adrenal and pituitary–thyroid axes differentiates the hypogonadotropism of anorexia nervosa from that seen in panhypopituitarism. Yet some alteration in these axes is observed in response to challenge. In anorexia nervosa, LH and FSH response to luteinizing hormone-releasing hormone (LHRH) infusion is quantitatively normal but delayed, as is FSH response to TRH infusion.

Although these alterations in endocrine function are consistent in anorexia nervosa, it is not clear that these changes are related to the basic pathophysiology of anorexia nervosa or are epiphenomena representing nonspecific responses to starvation, weight loss, or even emotional stresses that precede the lowering of caloric absorption and weight loss. No single explanation is consistent with all of the information. Some patients (perhaps 25 per cent) become amenorrheic and have lowered plasma LH months before any weight loss or *detectable* dieting (Vande Wiele, 1977). Some will begin to menstruate and show rises in LH with weight gain even while they continue to be preoccupied with dieting and retain a distorted body image.

## Neurotransmitter Studies

The pathogenesis and pathophysiology of the major psychiatric disorders remain unknown. Yet suggestive evidence has implicated various neurotransmitters in certain psychiatric disorders: the catecholamines and serotonin in affective disorders and dopamine in schizophrenia. Intensive research efforts are under way to test these postulated neurochemical bases. Conceivably, such efforts may lead to laboratory procedures to aid in the diagnosis of psychiatric disorders in a manner analogous to the use of such tests in medical illnesses.

## Affective Disorders

A durable, if not proven, biochemical hypothesis in psychiatry is that affective disorders result from a deficit (in the case of depression) or an excess (in mania) in certain amine neurotransmitters (Hughes et al., 1985). This "catecholamine" (pertaining primarily to norepinephrine) or "monoamine" (including serotonin as well) hypothesis derived from certain clinical observations. Drugs such as reserpine, which are known to deplete the brain of these monoamines, produce, in some patients, a depressive syndrome. In addition, the first two classes of drugs known to alleviate depression, the monoamine oxidase inhibitors (MAOIs) and the TCAs, are known to increase monoamine availability to the postsynaptic receptor.

Some laboratory findings have supported the monoamine hypothesis. Low urinary levels of the norepinephrine metabolite 3-methoxy-4-hydroxyphenylglycol (MHPG) have been observed in some depressed patients. Another subgroup of depressed patients appear to have low cerebrospinal fluid (CSF) levels of the serotonin metabolite 5-hydroxyindoleacetic acid (5-HIAA). Low levels of these metabolites would suggest a decrease in the synthesis or release of the neurotransmitter.

Based on these findings, it has been suggested that it may be possible to tailor pharmacologic intervention on the basis of whether a patient were norepinephrine-deficient or serotonin-deficient. Presumably, drugs that are relatively selective for enhancing norepinephrine activity (e.g., desipramine and nortriptyline) or serotonin (e.g., trazodone or experimental agents zimelidine or fluoxamine) could be differentially prescribed. Preliminary testing of this strategy has not produced definitive results (Hughes et al., 1985).

Many of the early studies reporting differences in monoamine function were based on measurement of metabolites in peripheral fluids. This approach is problematic. Estimates of the contribution of metabolized brain norepinephrine to urine MHPG range from 30 per cent to 70 per cent. It is also difficult to assess the effects of psychotropic drug treatment (whether at present or in the past) on transmitter release and metabolism as reflected in urine, serum, and even CSF metabolites.

Other, perhaps more direct, laboratory measurements hold promise for the future. A modification of the monoamine hypothesis is that rather than a deficit in the availability of specific monoamines, the pathophysiology of depression involves altered monoamine receptor function. For example, in depression, $\alpha_2$- or $\beta$-adrenergic supersensitivity has been postulated. This supersensitivity would result in attenuated CNS adrenergic function, since $\alpha_2$-adrenergic stimulation inhibits release of norepinephrine from the presynaptic nerve terminal. It appears that antidepressant drugs, as well as nonpharmacologic treatments such as electroconvulsive therapy and rapid-eye-movement sleep deprivation, reduce these supersensitivities.

Supersensitivity in platelet $\alpha_2$- and leukocyte $\beta$-adrenergic receptors has been reported in depressed patients. The advantages of having such biologic markers for depression so readily available in the peripheral blood are obvious. However, these reports are presently preliminary.

## Schizophrenia

The DA hypothesis proposes that DA hyperactivity in the mesolimbic or mesocortical region is involved in the pathogenesis of schizophrenia. This hypothesis has proved to be the most durable biologic hypothesis in psychiatry and perhaps the most stimulating in terms of its heuristic value, leading to a great body of research about the role of DA in the CNS.

As with the monoamine hypothesis of affective disorders, the DA hypothesis was generated from clinical observations. Amphetamine-induced psychoses were noted to resemble closely acute schizophrenic episodes. In addition, a characteristic common to all early antipsychotic drugs was potent DA-blocking effects.

The DA hypothesis has been useful. In addition to the stimulation of basic research, it suggested an effective method of screening drugs for potential antipsychotic effects. The ability of drugs to block DA agonist activity in animals (amphetamine-induced stereotypic behavior in rats and apomorphine-induced vomiting in cats) has resulted in the identification of a number of chemically unrelated classes of neuroleptics in addition to the original reserpine and phenothiazines.

Laboratory studies on schizophrenics have been less supportive of the DA hypothesis, at least as simply formulated (Henn, 1982). DA is known to be a potent inhibitor of prolactin release. Patients on neuroleptics show increased prolactin levels (evidence of DA blockade with such drugs), yet untreated schizophrenics and controls do not differ on this parameter.

Neurotransmitter and enzymatic studies have not consistently shown abnormalities in the DA system (Hughes et al., 1985). Homovanillic acid (HVA), the principal metabolite of CNS DA, has not been shown to be abnormal in schizophrenics, even in CSF. Autopsy studies have also not shown evidence of increased DA activity, as would conceivably be reflected in increased levels of DA and HVA or defects in MAO activity. The search for something to measure peripherally led to the observation of reduced platelet MAO activity in schizophrenic patients. More recent studies have been inconclusive.

DA receptors have also been studied in postmortem brains of schizophrenics. Some investigations have shown increased density of the D-2 DA receptor in schizophrenics compared with controls. However, the confounding effects of long-term neuroleptic exposure have not been adequately accounted for.

In summary, the DA hypothesis has been useful in predicting the psychotomimetic effects of DA agonists and amelioration of psychosis by DA antagonists. Yet laboratory measurements have not demonstrated definitive abnormalities in schizophrenic patients. It has been hypothesized that DA, rather than being related to a core defect in schizophrenia, is related more closely to certain "positive symptoms," such as hallucinations and delusions. This postulate is consistent with the clinical observation that neuroleptics are more effective in treating "positive symptoms" rather than the "negative" or "deficit" symptoms of schizophrenia, such as apathy, social withdrawal, and vague peculiarities in thought and action. If this hypothesis proves correct, it may lead to neurochemical procedures to validate this clinical distinction.

## Visual Imaging Techniques

Thus far, primarily chemical assays have been reviewed. In addition, new areas of inquiry, born of the availability of modern technology, including the computer, make for more precise, critical imaging of the living brain, with visualization of function as well as structure. These procedures include CT, brain electrical activity measurement (BEAM), regional cerebral blood flow (rCBF) measurement, positron emission tomography (PET), and magnetic resonance imaging (MRI).

### Computerized Tomography

Computerized tomography provides visualization of structural abnormalities, such as cerebral atrophy, without requiring invasive techniques, such as pneumoencephalography (Weinberger and Wyatt, 1983; Hughes et al., 1985). Thus study of brain structure in large numbers of psychiatric patients is now possible. Most of the work, to date, has been with dementia and schizophrenia.

Early studies showed increased ventricular size in association with schizophrenia, particularly Type II. Type II schizophrenia has been characterized by chronicity, negative symptoms, neurologic signs, poor premorbid adjustment, poor response to neuroleptics. It is hypothesized that Type II schizophrenia is associated with loss of critical brain cells, whereas Type I is associated with DA hyperactivity. However, ventricular enlargement has not been consistently found. Moreover, several methodological problems need to be resolved (Boronow et al., 1985).

### Brain Electrical Activity Measurement

A topographical look at brain activity can now be obtained through the use of spectral power density analysis of EEG data made possible by modern computer technology (Bunney, Garland, Buchsbaum, 1983; Hughes et al., 1985). Using "event-related potentials" (the preferred term for evoked responses), topographic color maps showing sequential changes in brain activity in relation to a stimulus "event" can be obtained. Thus far, increased slow (delta) wave EEG activity in frontal brain areas has been found in schizophrenics.

### Regional Cerebral Blood Flow

Using radiolabeled tracers, such as [133]Xe and [123]iodoantipyrine, estimates of regional blood flow can be obtained. Thus far, decreased blood flow has been found in frontal regions in schizophrenics and decreased right hemisphere flow in depressed patients.

### Positron Emission Tomography

In PET, various compounds can be labeled with proton-containing radioisotopes, which are injected intravenously. When the proton decays, a positron is emitted and detected regionally by the PET scanner. The localization of the emission identifies the distribution of the radioisotope.

A useful strategy has been to administer labeled 2-deoxyglucose, an analogue of glucose. This compound follows the distribution of glucose, is not metabolized, and accumulates at locations at levels proportional to glucose metabolism at that point. Thus far, patients with schizophrenia have shown decreased glucose metabolism in the frontal cortex. Other potential uses include studies with labeled psychotropic drugs to localize their site of concentration and action. One factor that will probably hamper the widespread clinical use of PET scanning is the necessity of a nearby cyclotron.

### Magnetic Resonance Imaging

Magnetic resonance imaging is based on the reception of radio frequencies emitted by nuclei in an applied magnetic field. Different elements yield different frequencies. Thus different tissues would yield different frequencies, depending on their elemental composition. Thus far, the technique has been useful in differentiating dead or ischemic tissue. Study of psychiatric patients has begun. Potentially, administration of MRI-detectable compounds would allow visualization of brain metabolic activity or the localization of psychotropic drug concentrations.

In summary, with the exception of the CT, only preliminary attempts to use visual imaging techniques have been made. One interesting finding has been evidence for frontal hypoactivity in schizophrenia, as reflected in electrical activity by BEAM, decreased blood flow by rCBF, and decreased glucose utilization by PET. All three of these parameters are known to be highly interrelated and correlated. What hypofrontality means to the pathophysiologic understanding of schizophrenia remains to be seen.

## CONCLUSIONS

The use of the laboratory in psychiatry parallels, in many ways, the state of knowledge in psychiatry. Psychiatric "disorders" are, at best, at the level of discrete clinical disorders (i.e., they meet the criteria of having distinct correlated features and a more or less uniform course and response to treatment). They do not, however, represent discrete disease entities with known pathophysiologic characteristics. With the improved investigative laboratory tools becoming available today, it is reasonable to assume that discrete disease entities will emerge. The resulting pathophysiologically, or even pathogenetically, based classification system may only remotely resemble the diagnostic systems in use today.

## REFERENCES

Abplanalp J, Haskett R, Rose R: The premenstrual syndrome. Psychiatr Clin North Am 3:327–347, 1980.

American Psychiatric Association: Diagnostic and Statistical Manual of Mental Disorders, ed 3. Washington, DC, American Psychiatric Association, 1980.

Amsterdam J, Brunswick D, Mendels J: Reliability of commercially available tricyclic antidepressant levels. J Clin Psychiatry 41:206–207, 1980.

Asberg M, Cronholm B, Sjogvist F, Tuck D: Relationship between plasma level and therapeutic effect of nortriptyline. Br Med J 3:331–334, 1971.

Boronow J, Pickar D, Ninan PT, Roy A, Hommer D, Tinnoila M, Paul S: Atrophy limited to the third ventricle in chronic schizophrenic patients. Arch Gen Psychiatry 42:266–271, 1985.

Brown G, Seggie J: Neuroendocrine mechanisms and their implications for psychiatric research. Psychiatr Clin North Am 3:205–221, 1980.

Bunney W, Garland B, Buchsbaum M: Advances in the use of visual imaging: Techniques in mental illness. Psychiatr Ann 13:420–428, 1983.

Carroll B, Feinberg M, Greden J, Tarika J, Albala A, Haskett R, James N, Kronfol Z, Lohr N, Steiner M, de Vigne J, Young E: A specific laboratory test for the diagnosis of melancholia. Arch Gen Psychiatry 38:15–22, 1981.

Feinberg M, Carroll B: Biological markers for endogenous depression in series and parallel. Biol Psychiatry 19:3–11, 1984.

Fieve R: Lithium therapy, in Kaplin H, Freedman A, Sadock B (eds): Comprehensive Textbook of Psychiatry, ed 3. Baltimore, Williams & Wilkins, 1980, pp 2348–2352.

Friedel R: An overview of neuroleptic plasma levels: Pharmacokinetics and assay methodology. J Clin Psychiatry Monograph 2:8–12, 1984.

Garfinkel P, Garner D: Menstrual disorders and anorexia nervosa. Psychiatr Ann 14:436–441, 1984.

Glassman A: Blood-level measurements of tricyclic drugs as a diagnostic tool. Psychiatr Ann 11:130–136, 1981.

Greden J, Gardner R, King L, Grunhaus L, Carroll B, Kronfol Z: Dexamethasone suppression tests in antidepressant treatment of melancholia: The process of normalization and test-retest reproducibility. Arch Gen Psychiatry 40:493–500, 1983.

Haskett R, Rose R: Neuroendocrine disorders and psychopathology. Psychiatr Clin North Am 4:239–252, 1981.

Henn F: Dopamine: A role in psychosis or schizophrenia, in Henn F, Nasrallah H (eds): Schizophrenia as a Brain Disease. New York, Oxford University Press, 1982, pp 176–195.

Hughes C, Preskorn S, Adams R, Kent T: Neurobiological etiology of schizophrenia and affective disorders, in Cavenar J (ed): Psychiatry. Philadelphia, JB Lippincott, 1985, ch. 64, pp. 1–16.

Jimerson D, Post R: Psychomotor stimulants and dopamine agonists in depression, in Post R, Ballenger J (eds): Neurobiology of Mood Disorders, Baltimore, William & Wilkins, 1984, pp 619–628.

Loosen P, Prange A: Serum thyrotropin-releasing hormone in psychiatric patients: A review. Am J Psychiatry 139:405–416, 1982.

Petty F, Noyes R: Depression secondary to cancer. Biol Psychiatry 16:1203–1220, 1981.

Plum F, Posner J: The Diagnosis of Stupor and Coma, ed 3. Philadelphia, FA Davis, 1980.

Preskorn S, Irwin H: Toxicity of tricyclic antidepressants—kinetics, mechanism, intervention: A review. J Clin Psychiatry 4:151–156, 1982.

Preskorn S, Mac D: The implication of concentration: Response studies of tricyclic antidepressants for psychiatric research and practice. Psychiatr Dev 3:201–222, 1984.

Preskorn S, Madakasira S: Tricyclic antidepressants, clinical use of plasma levels. J Kans Med Soc 82:122–134, 1981.

Richardson J, Richelson E: Antidepressants: A clinical update for medical practitioners. Mayo Clin Proc 59:330–337, 1984.

Rose R, Sachar E: Psychoendocrinology, in Williams R (ed): Textbook of Endocrinology. Philadelphia, WB Saunders, 1981.

Targum SD: Neuroendocrine challenge studies in clinical psychiatry. Psychiatr Ann 13:385–395, 1983.

Targum SD, Sullivan AC, Byrnes SM: Neuroendocrine interrelationships in major depressive disorder. Am J Psychiatry 193:282–286, 1982.

Vande Wiele R: Anorexia nervosa and the hypothalamus. Hosp Pract 12:45–50, 1977.

Van Putten T: Guidelines to the use of plasma levels: A clinical perspective. J Clin Psychiatry Monograph 2:28–32, 1984.

Weinberger D, Wyatt R: Enlarged cerebral ventricles in schizophrenia. Psychiatr Ann 13:412–418, 1983.

Wells C: Diagnostic evaluation and treatment in dementia, in Wells C (ed): Dementia. Philadelphia, FA Davis, 1977.

Wells C: Chronic brain disease: An overview. Am J Psychiatry 135:1–12, 1978.

Wells C, Duncan G: Neurology for Psychiatrists. Philadelphia, FA Davis, 1980.

Wilson W, Musella L, Short M: The electroencephalogram in dementia, in Wells C (ed): Dementia. Philadelphia, FA Davis, 1977.

Yesavage J: Plasma levels as predictors of clinical response and violent behavior. J Clin Psychiatry Monograph 2:14–20, 1984.

Young M, Schwartz J: The dexamethasone test for the detection, diagnosis, and management of depression. Ann Int Med 100:307–308, 1984.

# chapter 32

# EPIDEMIOLOGY OF PSYCHIATRIC ILLNESS

*by* Thomas J. Craig, M.D., M.P.H.

## INTRODUCTION

In this chapter, methodological issues in the epidemiology of mental illness will be discussed.

## DEFINITION

Epidemiology (literally "epi" = upon and "demos" = the people) is the study of the distribution and dynamics of health and illness in space and time in a given population and of the factors that influence this distribution. Thus epidemiology differs from clinical research primarily in its focus on defined populations as the denominator and clinical cases as the numerator from which it calculates rates of illness occurrence.

## APPLICATIONS OF EPIDEMIOLOGY IN PSYCHIATRY

Epidemiologic methods have been applied in four general ways to the study of psychiatric illness:

1. *Descriptive Epidemiology.* Clues to the etiology of psychiatric illness have been sought through the study of the incidence and prevalence rates of disease in the community and the association of variations in those rates with variations in community characteristics (e.g., age, sex, social class). This approach has been most successful where there is a single necessary and sufficient cause of a specific disorder (e.g., pellagra) (Goldberger, Waring, Tanner, 1925).

2. *Analytic Epidemiology.* Once etiologic hypotheses have been identified, they can be tested using a variety of analytic strategies comparing the relative frequency with which persons with a given risk factor (e.g., a positive family history) or set of risk factors for a specific disorder develop that disorder as compared with persons without such a risk factor. In psychiatric epidemiology, descriptive studies have indicated three broad sets of risk factors relative to the etiology of mental illness: genetic, biologic, and psychosocial. To date, the most successful analytic studies have explored the genetic determinants of psychiatric illness. However, since the causes of the most common psychiatric conditions are believed to result from an interaction of a variety of risk factors (as has been demonstrated for many chronic medical conditions, such as coronary artery disease), future advances in this area will

require the use of sophisticated analytic strategies to sort out their relative contributions (Weissman and Klerman, 1978).

3. *Experimental Epidemiology.* Once a suspected etiologic risk factor has been identified, experiments may be carried out in which the investigator artificially manipulates this risk factor while holding all other variables constant. Because of the current state of knowledge regarding risk factors in psychiatry, the use of this experimental approach has, for the most part, been limited to clinical therapeutic trials. However, psychiatric epidemiologists have capitalized on naturally occurring quasi-experimental situations, such as disasters (e.g., the Three Mile Island accident; Bromet, Schulberg, Dunn, 1982), the adoption of children (e.g., the Danish adoption studies of schizophrenia), and the effects of public policy changes on the prevalence of conditions, such as drug abuse (de Alarcon, 1972) and suicide (Brown, 1979), to study the effects of a specific risk factor on the subsequent development of psychiatric illness or condition.

4. *Program Planning and Evaluation.* Descriptive epidemiologic methods have been widely used to estimate the need for mental health services in defined populations (Goodman and Craig, 1982) and determine the extent to which available services are meeting these needs. For example, Regier, Goldberg, and Taube (1978) drew on a wide range of data sources to demonstrate that only 21 per cent of the total estimated population of mentally ill adults in the United States was receiving specialty mental health services, while an equal proportion was receiving no treatment and the remainder were receiving services only from non-mental health sources. Studies such as these have been used to develop more effective and efficient approaches to the delivery of mental health services.

## METHODOLOGICAL ISSUES IN PSYCHIATRIC EPIDEMIOLOGY

A critical understanding of the findings of the epidemiologic studies of psychiatric illness requires an appreciation of the methodological problems inherent in the epidemiologic method.

### PRIMARY MEASUREMENTS

The primary measurements of epidemiology (incidence and prevalence) require a numerator (cases), a denominator (population at risk), and a time frame. (See below)

### Numerator Data

The accurate enumeration of cases requires a specific definition of a case and the detection of all cases in the study population. The problems of case definition are discussed later. In terms of case ascertainment, most studies have used either treatment source information or community surveys to estimate the number of cases present in the population. Both sources have potential drawbacks, which are more serious for those studies using treatment source data only. For example, the use of mental health services is known to be influenced by a variety of demographic variables (including age, sex, race, and, especially, the distance one lives from the treatment facility) as well as characteristics of the facility itself (e.g., number of beds available, accessibility, reputation in the community, admission policies) and public policy (e.g., legislation discouraging the admission of the elderly). Although attempts have been made to establish more comprehensive sources of

$$\text{Incidence} = \frac{\text{number of new cases per unit time}}{\text{average population at risk during time period}}$$

$$\text{Prevalence (point)} = \frac{\text{number of existing cases at one point in time}}{\text{average population at risk at that point in time}}$$

$$\text{Prevalence (period)} = \frac{\text{number of existing cases during a period of time}}{\text{average population at risk during that time period}}$$

treatment data through the use of psychiatric case registers covering all mental health providers in a geographically defined area, the use of these data will seriously underestimate the numerator of incidence and prevalence rates in ways that are not uniformly distributed across different population subgroups. Despite these limitations, treatment source data have been used extensively in psychiatric epidemiology largely because they can be obtained relatively inexpensively (Terris, 1965).

The other major source of numerator data—community survey data—has advantages and disadvantages that mirror those of treatment source data. Surveys are generally much more expensive and time-consuming to carry out. Therefore, most surveys cannot assess the total population to ascertain the total number of cases and must rely on a sampling of the population. In order to ensure that the findings of the survey are representative of the population surveyed, probability sampling techniques must be used in which the investigator can specify the probability that each person in the population will be included in the survey sample. Most surveys include simple or stratified random sampling techniques so that the results of the survey can be extrapolated to the total population. Community surveys also require a method to determine the presence of a psychiatric disorder. Because diagnosis of every respondent by a clinician is prohibitively expensive, most recent surveys have relied on either questionnaires completed by respondents or structured interviews by nonclinician interviewers. In either case, the survey instruments must meet tests of reliability and validity to ensure that those identified as cases would be diagnosed as such if a clinician examined them. The major advantage of the community survey is its ability to ascertain in a relatively unbiased way the proportion of persons in the study population with definable disorders.

In certain circumstances where accurate responses to surveys cannot be assured, other approaches to case ascertainment have been developed. These approaches have been most common for conditions in which admission of the presence of the disorder might be morally (e.g., alcoholism) or legally (e.g., substance abuse) unacceptable to the respondents. For example, an early approach to the determination of the prevalence of alcoholism used social indicators such as the cirrhosis death rate, while more recent studies of drug abuse prevalence have used a variety of social indicators (e.g., drug-involved deaths, rates of hepatitis, arrest data, drug buys, and a Drug Abuse Warning Network involving emergency department visits for drug abuse) as well as direct observation techniques of drug dealing (Hughes, Crawford, Becker, 1971). The latter approaches provide only indirect measures of the true prevalence of the disorder.

## Denominator Data

An estimate of the population at risk is usually obtained from census data. Thus the main problems with these data involve the extent to which the true population size might be underestimated by the census and the proximity in time between the collection of numerator and denominator data. As regards underestimation, for example, young minority men are known to be seriously undercounted in the U.S. census. Thus incidence and prevalence rates based on this denominator will generally tend to be overestimates of the true prevalence of disorder in these subgroups, since numerator data may be more accurately ascertained. These biases are more pronounced when treatment source data are used to estimate the number of cases, since surveys will ascertain both numerator and denominator information directly. However, with survey data, the response rate becomes crucial, since persons who refuse to participate in surveys or who cannot be located are likely to have a higher rate of psychiatric disorder than those who do participate. Thus surveys with response rates less than 70 per cent are generally considered potentially biased toward underestimation of true prevalence.

## Time Perspective

In general, for episodic conditions, Prevalence = Incidence × Duration. For etiologic investigations, incidence rates are more useful than prevalence rates, since factors that affect the duration of the condition but that are unrelated to its cause will be associated with prevalence, whereas only factors causative of the illness will be associated with incidence. However, for rarely occurring disorders, in which the exact time of onset of the illness cannot be accurately ascertained (characteristic of many psychiatric disorders), incidence data may be either impossible or inordinately expensive to collect. To compensate partially for this situation, psychiatric epidemiologic studies have used the concept of lifetime prevalence (i.e., the probability of a respondent ever having experienced a specific condition up to the date of assessment). This risk will be influenced by the proportion of the population who have passed through the age of risk for the disorder as well as by possible biases owing to disorder-associated mortality or an unwillingness to report or failure to recall disorders that had occurred many years earlier (Robins et al., 1984).

## Definition of a Case

The most crucial variable in any epidemiologic study, and the one that accounts for the greatest amount of variation in the findings of psychiatric epidemiology to date, is case definition. To appreciate the variety of approaches to this question it is necessary to consider briefly the concept of normality. Offer describes four approaches to the definition of normality:

1. *Normality as health* conforms most closely to the medical concept of freedom from a diagnosable condition and assumes most persons to be normal unless they demonstrate clearly the signs and symptoms of an illness.

2. *Normality as utopia* assumes that only those who have attained an optimal level of functioning or self-actualization are normal and that the majority of persons have not yet attained this level. Thus the presence of *any* symptomatology or dysfunction would be considered abnormal.

3. *Normality as average* visualizes a statistical normality along a continuum in which the difference between normal and abnormal depends largely on where the line is drawn (the "threshold" concept). Thus norms are established and pathology defined largely by statistical criteria.

4. *Normality as transactional systems*

adopts a general systems theory approach that conceptualizes normal behavior as the end result of interacting systems that change over time. Thus what might be considered normal at one time and age (e.g., uncomplicated grief) might be seen as abnormal when duration or age is different.

Historically, psychiatric epidemiologic studies have used different concepts of normality and, consequently, have obtained different rates of illness occurrence. Studies carried out in Europe and in the United States before World War II tended to adopt the first concept—normality as health. Mental illness was considered to be not a unitary concept, but one in which could be defined discrete, categorically distinct disorders with different etiologies and differing treatments. Cases were defined according to diagnostic criteria current at the time, and rates of illness were calculated separately for these disorders (Lin and Standley, 1962).

In contrast, after World War II, the predominant psychiatric epidemiologic studies in the United States tended to be based on the concepts of normality as utopia or (for the more sociologically based studies) normality as average. Mental disorder was seen as unitary and on a continuum, rather than as a set of diagnostically distinct conditions. In addition, health was defined as the absence of symptoms or functional impairment and was categorized according to intensity or severity of symptomatology or impairment, despite the fact that most of the population is not totally asymptomatic or totally functional at any point in time (Weissman and Klerman, 1978). Thus these studies reported high rates of mental impairment (e.g., the Midtown Manhattan study found only 19 per cent of the population to be free of significant symptoms, while 23 per cent were significantly impaired) (Srole et al., 1962). However, these studies substantially advanced survey methodology in the areas of sampling, instrument development, and statistical analysis but could not generate rates of specific psychiatric disorders.

As noted by Weissman and Klerman (1978), beginning in the 1960s, several events occurred that significantly influenced psychiatric epidemiology. Research strategies in genetic psychiatry—chiefly twin studies, family studies, and adoption and cross-fostering techniques, as well as the development of sophisticated methods of statistical analysis (described in an earlier chapter)—strengthened the evidence for the existence of discrete psychiatric disorders with different patterns of heritability. In addition, advances in the biologic treatment of psychiatric disorders, including the use of electroconvulsive therapies, as well as the development of psychopharmacologic agents with specific clinical effectiveness for specific disorders, supported the concept of specific psychiatric disorders as opposed to the unitary concept of mental illness.

Both of these sets of developments highlighted the need for valid and reliable diagnostic criteria. The epidemiologic observation of markedly different treated prevalence rates for schizophrenia and affective disorders between the United States (where schizophrenia was about one third more prevalent) and the United Kingdom (where the prevalence of affective disorders was several times greater) led to a series of studies (Kramer, 1969; Zubin, 1969) that demonstrated that these differences were largely attributable to the different diagnostic practices of British and American psychiatrists, rather than to differences in the actual prevalence of the two disorders. When structured interviewing techniques and specified diagnostic criteria were used, good reliability among clinicians and researchers could be obtained. Concomitant with the development of reliable diagnostic procedures, criteria were being developed on the basis of research findings that began to improve the validity of diagnoses themselves. These criteria were based on studies involving phenomenological descriptions, family and genetic studies, followup studies, response to treatment, laboratory studies, and correlation with other psychosocial factors. In the United States, the first published, specified criteria for a subset of mental disorders were the Feighner criteria (Feighner et al., 1972). Subsequently, a set of Research Diagnostic Criteria (RDC) were developed (Spitzer et al., 1978). These developments provided impetus for a third revision of the *Diagnostic and Statistical Manual of Mental Disorders* (DSM-III) of the American Psychiatric Association, which became the official U.S. psychiatric nosology in 1980. These criteria were primarily based on the medical concept of normality as health but also included the concept of normality as a

transactional system by including the concept of time (both duration of symptoms and age of onset) into the diagnostic criteria.

The impact of these diagnostic developments on psychiatric epidemiology in the United States has been recent and far-reaching. As noted earlier, most U.S. epidemiologic studies from World War II to the mid-1970s defined illness in terms of symptom frequency or intensity or functional impairment. Dohrenwend et al. (1980) have described these measures as indicators of nonspecific psychological distress or demoralization (Frank, 1973). Although many, if not most, psychiatrically ill individuals will score highly (as "cases") on such instruments, many persons with no diagnosable mental illness will also score in the "case" range. In addition, these measures do not permit the identification of persons with diagnosable conditions (true positive) from those without diagnoses (false positive) or the division of the mentally ill into specific diagnostic categories. Thus these nonspecific measures do not permit the calculation of incidence and prevalence rates by specific diagnoses, a prerequisite for the development or testing of specific etiologic hypotheses.

The first study in the United States that applied these specified diagnostic criteria to a community sample was carried out by Weissman, Myers, and Harding (1978), using the RDC in a pilot study of 500 persons. The interview schedule used for this study required clinical judgments to be made by master's-level clinicians, using the Schedule for Affective Disorders and Schizophrenia (SADS) (Endicott and Spitzer, 1978). This study demonstrated the feasibility of using such an instrument, but the prevalence rates derived from the study were considered tentative owing to the small sample size and the fact that this was a followup of a study begun in 1966 and might not have been representative of the general population because of migration, deaths, or refusals.

After the conclusion of this study, the Division of Biometry and Epidemiology of the National Institute of Mental Health initiated the development of a new instrument, the Diagnostic Interview Schedule (DIS), which could be conducted by lay interviewers, thus permitting its use in large-scale studies (Robins et al., 1984). The DIS was constructed to elicit diagnoses according to Feighner, RDC, and DSM-III criteria for a subset of adult DSM-III diagnoses selected on the basis of prevalence, clinical significance, and scientific validity based on treatment response, family studies, and followup studies (Myers et al., 1984). This instrument was then used in the largest series of community surveys to date—the Epidemiologic Catchment Area (ECA) Study—currently being conducted in five locations (New Haven, Baltimore, St. Louis, Los Angeles, and North Carolina), each site including approximately 3000 community respondents.

Development efforts are also currently under way for the construction of a similar interview schedule for the diagnosis of disorders of childhood and adolescence in anticipation of a similar community survey of this age-group.

## DIAGNOSTIC INSTRUMENTS

As already noted, community surveys using questionnaires or interviews to collect diagnostic information are required to determine the true prevalence and incidence of mental disorder in the general population. Such surveys, to be economically feasible, require that these instruments be usable by lay interviewers. Even given the availability of valid diagnostic criteria such as those provided by DSM-III, the instruments used to gather these data must meet tests of reliability and validity in their construction and administration.

If constructed and administered properly, it would be expected that scores on the instrument would always reflect true differences in the characteristic being measured (e.g., a person reporting symptoms of schizophrenia should "truly" have a schizophrenic diagnosis). However, a number of other factors may cause spurious variations or lack of variations in scores. For example, differences in transient personal factors (e.g., fatigue, mental set), situational factors (e.g., another person present during the interview), administration of the interview (e.g., nonuniform methods of administration), lack of clarity of the instrument (e.g., ambiguous questions or language barrier), mechanical factors (e.g., checking wrong boxes), and factors in the analysis all may

produce invalid data. In addition, the administration of the instrument may be subject to error introduced by some factor that systematically affects the characteristic being measured or the interview process (e.g., sex or race of interviewer and respondent). In order to minimize these spurious sources of variation, instruments must meet tests of validity and reliability.

*Validity* is the extent to which differences in scores reflect true differences in the characteristic that the test measures and the degree to which the instrument measures what is intended.

Measures of validity include:

- *Predictive validity:* the ability to predict a future event by knowledge of the test score (e.g., a diagnosis of depression should predict responsiveness to antidepressant treatment)
- *Concurrent validity:* the ability to predict the presence or absence of an event when compared with a known criterion (e.g., a diagnosis of depression should correlate with biologic measures indicative of depression)
- *Content validity:* a measure of the pertinence of the instrument to the characteristic tested and the extent to which all aspects of the characteristic are tested (e.g., a depression scale should contain symptoms characteristic of depression)
- *Construct validity:* the relation of the score to other related aspects of the condition (e.g., a depression scale should show higher scores in depressed patients than in nondepressed individuals)

*Reliability* is the amount of variation in scores among individuals that is due to inconsistencies in measurement (Helzer et al., 1977). In epidemiologic surveys, reliability is generally tested in terms of:

- *Test-retest reliability:* the same test is administered at different times and the results are correlated. However, if the two tests are repeated too closely in time, there may be a spurious inflation of reliability owing to memory of the earlier test, while if clinical change occurs between administration, the reliability will be artificially lowered.
- *Interrater reliability:* the observation of the same interview by two or more raters, each of whom independently scores the results.

As noted earlier, a major contribution of the post-World War II epidemiologic studies has been the refinement of instrument development so as to permit increasingly valid and reliable assessment of the presence or absence of psychiatric disorders in community respondents.

## Sensitivity and Specificity

In evaluating the utility of an instrument designed to provide diagnostic information, results are compared with a standard criterion to determine the instrument's sensitivity (i.e., ability to detect true positives) and specificity (i.e., ability to detect true negatives) (Earls, 1980a). In the case of psychiatric diagnoses, since no "objective" diagnostic tests are available, the instrument results are usually compared with diagnoses made by experienced clinicians as shown below.

For an instrument to be useful in epidemiologic investigations, it should demonstrate high sensitivity and at least moderately high specificity, since the more crucial characteristic is its ability to detect cases, especially in view of the relatively low prevalence of most specific psychiatric disorders. In this regard, the DIS is one of the first diagnostic instruments used in psychiatric epidemiology to have been exposed to rigorous tests of sensitivity and specificity before its field application. Most earlier studies have merely demonstrated evidence of satisfactory reliability with little attention to validity issues.

However, even in the presence of adequate levels of sensitivity and specificity, the population prevalence of a given condition will have a major influence on the utility of the instrument. For example, if a specific disorder has a 1 per cent "true" prevalence and the interview instrument has a 1 per cent "false" positive rate, then almost half of the identified "cases" will be false positives (Baldessarini, Finkelstein, Arana, 1983). This phenomenon has led some investigators to suggest that epidemiologic studies use a two-stage case-finding procedure in which a highly sensitive (but not specific) screening test be applied to the total sample to identify potential "cases," who would then be diagnosed by experienced clinicians to minimize the tendency to overestimate the true prevalence (Weissman and Klerman, 1978).

## DESCRIPTIVE EPIDEMIOLOGY

### Incidence Studies

Because of the relatively infrequent occurrence of specific psychiatric disorders, their tendency to recurrence, and the difficulty of attempting to date the onset of the illness accurately, large-scale epidemiologic surveys of the incidence of mental disorders

|  | | Clinician Diagnosis | |
|---|---|---|---|
| Instrument | | POSITIVE | NEGATIVE |
| Diagnosis | Positive | TP | FP |
| | Negative | FN | TN |

TP, true positive; TN, true negative; FP, false positive; FN, false negative.

From this analysis, the following dimensions can be generated:

$$\text{Sensitivity} = \frac{TP}{TP + FN} \qquad \text{Specificity} = \frac{TN}{TN + FN}$$

$$\text{Positive Predictive Value} = \frac{TP}{TP + FP} \qquad \text{Negative Predictive Value} = \frac{TN}{TN + FN}$$

$$\text{False Positive Rate} = \frac{FP}{TN + FP} \qquad \text{False Negative Rate} = \frac{FN}{TP + FN}$$

are virtually nonexistent. A few incidence studies have been carried out in small, isolated communities, chiefly in Europe, but the ECA study, which has as one of its goals a followup of previously examined respondents, represents one of the first attempts at determining the incidence of specific disorders in a large, representative sample of a demographically diverse population.

Therefore, most data regarding the incidence of mental disorders have been derived from treatment sources in the form of first admission rates. Because many people suffering from mental illness never receive treatment, incidence rates from these sources will underestimate the true incidence of the disorders.

Attempts have been made to estimate the incidence of those psychiatric illnesses that are more likely to require treatment at some time, such as schizophrenia. Dunham (1965), for example, contended that every schizophrenic is eventually hospitalized. This assertion is no longer true (if it ever was) since the advent of the deinstitutionalization era in the 1960s. Yolles and Kramer (1969) summarized 12 incidence studies of schizophrenia in the United States between 1924 and 1963 that used first admissions to public and private mental health hospital as a criterion and cited average annual incidence rates for schizophrenia per 1000 population aged 15 and over ranging from 0.30 to 1.20. However, the highest rates, especially those in excess of 1.0 per 1000 per year, were cited for nonwhite populations, in which underestimation of the denominator owing to inadequate census enumeration may have spuriously inflated these rates. For these reasons, most descriptive psychiatric epidemiology to date has focused on the prevalence of mental disorders.

## Prevalence Studies

### Adult Mental Illness

As summarized by Plunkett and Gordon (1960) and Lin (1953), surveys of mental illness among the adult general population from the United States, Europe, and Asia, which were carried out before 1950 and used specific diagnostic criteria for case definition, cited prevalence rates of 0.7 per cent to 6.9 per cent for total mental disorders and rates of 0.2 per cent to 1.4 per cent for psy-

choses. In contrast, studies carried out after 1950 using diagnostic criteria yielded total mental illness prevalence rates of 10.9 per cent to 13.8 per cent while those using nondiagnostic criteria of symptom frequency or intensity or functional impairment found total mental illness prevalence rates in excess of 20 per cent. Because of the wide variations in diagnostic criteria or case definition across these studies, it is virtually meaningless to compare these rates except to point out that the more recent community surveys that used diagnostic criteria have suggested that 10 per cent to 15 per cent of the adult general population have met diagnostic criteria for a specific mental illness at any point in time, while those studies using purely symptomatic or functional measures suggest that an additional 10 per cent to 15 per cent of the general population suffer from nonspecific psychological distress (or demoralization). Treated prevalence estimates drawn from the Monroe County Psychiatric Register, which receives reports on virtually all persons receiving psychiatric services within the county from all specialty mental health providers, suggest that about 3 per cent of that population received specialty mental health services during 1973. Regier et al. (1978) used these data to calculate that about one in five persons with a specific psychiatric disorder in the United States is currently receiving specialty psychiatric services. Viewed another way, treated prevalence estimates will underestimate the total rate of psychiatric disorder by about 80 per cent, although this will vary by diagnostic category, with the severer disorders being more likely to receive treatment at any given time.

Because of these factors, rather than cataloging the varying rates of disorder found in earlier studies of treated and untreated prevalence, this chapter describes the prevalence rates reported from the most recent study (the ECA study), which incorporates the superior design features noted earlier and promises to be the "gold standard" against which future estimates of prevalence will be compared. These rates have been recently reported (Myers et al., 1984; Robins et al., 1984) for the first cross-sectional assessments conducted at three of the five study sites (New Haven, Baltimore, and St. Louis). The other two surveys (North Carolina and Los Angeles) are still in the field and, when completed, will add considerably to the findings among minority groups (black and Hispanic) and rural populations. The use of multiple sites for this study is especially advantageous in permitting the study of a broad range of demographic variables in relation to prevalence rates. It also permits replication of the findings using relatively standardized diagnostic criteria in large population samples—a major test of the reliability and robustness of the rates obtained.

### ECA Study Description

Briefly, the ECA study reported on 15 DIS/DSM-III diagnoses without exclusion because of the presence of other diagnoses. At each study site, representative samples were drawn from official Community Mental Health Catchment Areas with populations of 200,000 or more. Probability sampling techniques were used to select the respondent samples, which varied somewhat across sites but were weighted to provide comparable prevalence estimates. The DIS version used in New Haven was an earlier one with slightly different items than used in other sites. However, computer scoring of the results was carried out so as to maximize comparability across sites. Despite these major differences in sampling and interviews, the questions and methods were substantially the same across sites. All sites used lay interviewers, who received a 2-week training program. Adults 18 or older were surveyed at each site with similar completion rates (75 per cent to 80 per cent). At each site, responses were weighted to compensate for special study designs, the fact that only one member of each household was interviewed regardless of household size, and for possible underrepresentation of certain age-sex-race categories owing to differential response rates. In all, more than 3000 respondents were surveyed in each study site. The New Haven survey was conducted in 1980-81, while the other two sites were surveyed in 1981–82.

Despite these major methodological advances, the prevalence rates reported must be recognized as most likely a minimum estimate of both total and specific psychiatric illness in the surveyed populations. First of all, only 15 of the large number of DSM-III diagnostic categories were studied. While these represent the great bulk of common disorders, the exclusion of other diagnostic categories ensures an underestimate of total prevalence of psychiatric illness. Second, the survey results as reported cover only the noninstitutionalized population. Because a substantial proportion of persons with the severer disorders (e.g., schizophrenia and the organic dementing disorders) are chronically institutionalized, they would not enter the study sample. Because the ECA survey also included a representative sample of institutionalized persons not reported as yet, it is anticipated that future reports will address this issue. Third, because 20 per cent to 25 per cent of the samples were nonrespondents, who generally have higher rates of mental disorder, this may contribute to an underestimate of the "true" prevalence. Finally, because some of the disorders examined (especially mania and alcohol/substance abuse/dependence) are notoriously underreported when instruments such as the DIS are used, it is to be anticipated that the rates obtained for these disorders (in the absence of corroborating information from a third party) may represent underestimates. Nevertheless, despite these limitations, the ECA study represents a major advance over earlier epidemiologic approaches.

Table 32–1 presents the 6-month and lifetime prevalence rates for the major DIS/DSM-III disorders reported for the ECA study (Myers et al., 1984; Robins et al., 1984). The 6-month prevalence is a period prevalence that indicates current (or recent) psychopathology, whereas lifetime prevalence indicates current and past history of a diagnosable disorder. The results are presented as a range of lowest to highest rates across the three study sites. In general, rates across study sites were roughly comparable, although St. Louis reported significantly higher rates of alcohol abuse/dependence, while Baltimore had higher rates for total disorder and phobias and lower rates for major depressive episode and dysthmia.

Approximately 15 per cent to 20 per cent of the samples of both sexes reported having a current diagnosable disorder, a rate similar to those reported in recent studies using diagnostic criteria. In addition, however, almost as many additional respondents reported having had a diagnosable condition in the past, resulting in a lifetime prevalence of approximately 25 per cent to 40 per cent.

**Table 32–1  Six-Month and Lifetime Prevalence Rates (ranges) of DIS/DSM-III Disorders in Three ECA Sites, by Sex**

|  | Males (%) | | Females (%) | |
| --- | --- | --- | --- | --- |
|  | Six-Month | Lifetime | Six-Month | Lifetime |
| Any DIS disorder | 15.4–21.1 | 30.6–39.6 | 14.3–23.6 | 25.7–36.7 |
| Substance use disorders |  |  |  |  |
|   Alcohol abuse/dependence | 8.2–10.4 | 19.1–28.9 | 1.0–1.9 | 4.2–4.8 |
|   Drug abuse/dependence | 2.5–3.0 | 6.5–7.4 | 1.2–1.6 | 3.8–5.1 |
| Schizophrenia/schizophreniform disorders | 0.7–0.9 | 1.0–1.2 | 0.4–1.6 | 1.1–2.6 |
| Affective disorders | 2.7–4.6 |  | 6.0–8.3 |  |
|   Manic episode | 0.4–0.8 | 0.8–1.1 | 0.4–0.9 | 0.5–1.3 |
|   Major depressive episode | 1.3–2.2 | 2.3–4.4 | 3.0–4.6 | 4.9–8.7 |
|   Dysthymia | 1.2–2.6 | 1.2–2.6 | 2.9–5.4 | 2.9–5.4 |
| Anxiety/somatoform disorders |  |  |  |  |
|   Agoraphobia | 0.9–3.4 | 1.5–5.2 | 4.2–7.8 | 5.3–12.5 |
|   Simple phobia | 2.3–7.3 | 3.8–14.5 | 6.0–15.7 | 8.5–25.9 |
|   Panic | 0.3–0.8 | 0.6–1.2 | 0.9–1.2 | 1.6–2.1 |
|   Obsessive-compulsive | 0.9–1.9 | 1.1–2.6 | 1.7–2.2 | 2.6–3.3 |
|   Somatization | 0.0–0.0 | 0.0–0.0 | 0.2–0.3 | 0.2–0.3 |
| Personality disorder |  |  |  |  |
|   Antisocial personality | 0.8–2.1 | 3.9–4.9 | 0.3–1.0 | 0.5–1.2 |
| Cognitive impairment |  |  |  |  |
|   Severe | 1.0–1.4 | 1.0–1.4 | 1.1–1.4 | 1.1–1.4 |
|   Mild | 4.0–6.2 |  | 4.1–6.2 |  |

Most disorders, notably substance use disorders, major depressive episodes, schizophrenia and schizophreniform disorders, and phobic and panic disorders, showed a pattern of about one half to two thirds of those with a lifetime history of the disorder reporting a current episode. In contrast, for certain disorders, such as dysthymia, obsessive-compulsive and somatization disorders, and severe cognitive impairment, virtually all respondents reporting the condition in their lifetime were also currently experiencing an episode, suggesting either that these disorders are relatively persistent or that respondents will generally only report their presence during a current episode.

Although males and females reported remarkably similar overall rates of diagnosable disorder (the lone exception being a significantly higher male lifetime prevalence in St. Louis), significantly different rates were observed for specific diagnoses between the sexes. Males tended to have higher rates of alcohol and drug abuse/dependence and antisocial personality, while females tended to show higher rates of major depressive episodes, agoraphobia, simple phobia, and dysthymia. There was a lesser female predominance for somatization, panic, obsessive-compulsive, and schizophrenic disor-

ders, and no sex difference for manic episodes or severe cognitive impairment.

## Disorders of Childhood and Adolescence

Studies of the incidence and prevalence of psychiatric illness among children and adolescents have been rare and have suffered to a great extent from problems similar to those described earlier. There has recently been renewed interest in mounting large-scale surveys of such populations, as evidenced by two recent monographs addressing the topic (Earls, 1980; Purcell, 1980). In particular, there has been a lack of standardized diagnostic criteria for psychiatric disorders of childhood and adolescence. As a result, most epidemiologic studies in this area have relied on symptom and behavioral indices with unknown relevance for clinical diagnosis. In addition, the identification of disordered behavior in children requires information to be gathered from at least three sources—child, parent, and teacher—with often relatively poor concordance. The methodological problems attendant on the study of childhood and adolescent psychopathology have been detailed in the monograph edited by Earls (1980).

Work is currently under way to develop one or more structured interview schedules similar to the DIS for use in large-scale epidemiologic studies similar to those of the ECA study. Orvaschel, Sholmskas, and Weissman (1980) have described the development of several assessment instruments for childhood disorders. However, virtually all epidemiologic studies of childhood disorders to date have used nonspecific measures of behavioral disturbance, rather than specific diagnoses, as dependent variables. Earls (1980) has described three such studies carried out in the United States, two of which arrived at almost identical estimates of behavioral problems—13.5 per cent and 14.0 per cent. Similarly, Graham (1980) summarized findings from studies in six developing countries in Asia and Africa indicating a prevalence of behavioral and emotional problems ranging from 3 per cent to 18 per cent, using a variety of case-finding techniques (questionnaires and interviews).

Interestingly, in contrast to adult studies, which have been chiefly cross-sectional, a number of studies of childhood psychopathology have been longitudinal (Robins, 1980), although they have generally followed small, highly select samples for specific purposes (e.g., study of drug abuse or the development of schizophrenia) rather than determine incidence and prevalence rates of psychiatric disorders in general. Thus the generalizability of their findings to the total population is questionable.

## ANALYTIC EPIDEMIOLOGY

Descriptive epidemiologic studies, such as the ECA study, through their ability to generate prevalence rates of disorders in population subgroups, provide data for the generation of hypotheses related to the etiology of these disorders. Analytic studies can then be carried out to test these hypotheses, using both the data of the descriptive studies as well as data derived from subsequent studies designed specifically to examine these questions.

### Analytic Strategies

In psychiatric epidemiology, two analytic strategies have been generally used: retro-

spective (or case-control) and prospective (or longitudinal). The basic concept of these strategies can be illustrated from the following figure:

| | Retrospective | | |
| | With Disorder | Without Disorder | |
| Prospective | | | Total |
|---|---|---|---|
| With risk factor | a | b | a + b |
| Without risk factor | c | d | c + d |
| Total | a + c | b + d | N |

*Retrospective studies* use as their index the presence or absence of illness and attempt to determine whether a suspected risk factor is more common among those with the disorder than among those without the disorder. Thus, if the rate $a/a + c$ is significantly greater than $b/b + d$, a statistical association is said to exist between the disorder and the risk factor.

Basic assumptions underlying this strategy are (a) the risk factor predated the onset of disease, (b) the controls (without disease) will not subsequently develop the disease, (c) cases (with the disease) are representative of all persons with the disease, and (d) controls (without the disease) give an unbiased estimate of the prevalence of the risk factor among the entire nondiseased population. Unfortunately, these assumptions are rarely fulfilled completely, the major problem being the difficulty in determining the temporal sequence of risk factor and disease. The advantages of this approach are its inexpensiveness and the ability to carry out such studies quickly with smaller samples. With rarely occurring disorders, the retrospective approach may be the only feasible strategy. Because most discrete psychiatric disorders are relatively uncommon, most analytic studies in psychiatric epidemiology have been retrospective.

*Prospective studies* select a population sample before the onset of disease and follow them over time after the presence or absence of the presumed risk factor has been established. The subsequent development of disease is then ascertained either by periodic reexamination or by checking records. The analysis then compares incidence rates of the disease among those with and without the risk factor. If $a/a + b$ is significantly greater than $c/c + d$, a statistically significant association between the risk factor and the disease is said to exist.

The basic assumptions of this strategy are (a) that the initial sample does not include diseased individuals, and (b) followup is complete or nearly so. This strategy permits a direct estimate of the risk of disease given the presence of the risk factor and eliminates the problem of retrospective studies regarding the temporal relationship of risk factor and disease and subjective bias owing to selective memory. However, it is a much more expensive and time-consuming strategy that is inefficient for studying uncommon diseases. (For example, given a lifetime prevalence for schizophrenia of 1 per cent to 2 per cent, a prospective study of 10,000 persons would be expected to yield only 100 to 200 cases.) Also, even modest levels of attrition may seriously bias the results, since persons lost to followup tend to have disproportionately high rates of mental illness. In addition, the followup procedures themselves may influence the rate of disease development. For these reasons, until recently, few prospective studies of psychiatric disorders have been successfully carried out. Even those studies that have been successful in following several hundred persons have failed to yield sufficient numbers of persons with specific diagnosable disorders for detailed analysis. Currently, the most successful prospective studies either have used extremely large sample sizes by virtue of the existence of official records (e.g., adoption records) of sufficient reliability and validity to permit their use or have focused on high-risk populations (e.g., the children of schizophrenics), where the expected incidence rate of disease development is sufficient to permit a manageable long-term followup.

## Multifactorial Causation

Whichever analytic strategy is used, it is generally accepted that most psychiatric disorders are the result of an interaction of a variety of risk factors, including genetic, biologic, and psychosocial variables. Thus the straightforward analysis of the statistical association between a risk factor and a disorder becomes a complex procedure in which sophisticated statistical techniques are required both to control for potentially confounding variables and to identify potentially significant interactions between variables and classes of variables. Although a discussion of these techniques is beyond the scope of this chapter, these procedures result in the need for even larger sample sizes in order to permit statistically meaningful analysis.

Because of this multifactorial causation, the logic of testing hypotheses regarding causal relationships becomes more complex in psychiatric epidemiology when compared with the epidemiology of infectious diseases (Bebbington, 1980). In the latter category, there is usually a *necessary condition* (one that must occur if the disease is to occur; e.g., an infectious agent) and often a *sufficient condition* (one that is always followed by the disease). With the exception of substance abuse, in which the presence of the drug or alcohol is a necessary condition, psychiatric disorders in general have not been shown to have either necessary or sufficient conditions resulting in disease onset. Rather, there appear to be a variety of *contributing conditions* that increase the likelihood of the disease occurrence but do not guarantee it. Thus the task of analytic epidemiology is to determine which sets of contributory conditions become necessary and sufficient conditions for the occurrence of specific diseases.

Evidence relevant to this causal inference include the following:

1. *Concomitant variation*: the assumed causal factor (independent variable) should be associated with the disease (dependent variable) in a way consistent with the hypothesis.
2. *Time sequence*: the cause should precede the effect.
3. Evidence ruling out other possible factors should be present.
4. The statistical association between cause and disorder should be assessed for:
   a. Strength of association (usually by significance testing)
   b. Specificity of association (the extent to which the occurrence of the cause can be used to predict the occurrence of the effect; e.g., some "causes," such as life stress, may nonspecifically increase the risk for several psychiatric disorders in genetically susceptible individuals)
   c. Dose–response relationship (the

risk of developing the disease is related to the degree of exposure to the presumed cause)

    d.   Consistency of the association

5.  Scientific plausibility of the relationship between presumed cause and effect.

## ETIOLOGY OF PSYCHIATRIC DISORDERS

The remainder of this chapter discusses epidemiologic findings relevant to the etiology of psychiatric disorders. Until recently, most analytic strategies examined the association of one or two presumed etiologic conditions with a psychiatric disorder without consideration for the potential multiplicity of other independent variables. Also, in the more psychosocially oriented investigations, the dependent variable was often nonspecific psychological distress rather than a specific disorder. As noted earlier, the most successful investigations into the etiology of mental disorder are those in the area of genetics and the heritability of specific disorders, which are discussed in Chapter 30. This chapter discusses epidemiologic findings in the biologic, demographic, and psychosocial areas.

### Biological Factors

Apart from familial and genetic influences described in Chapter 30, relatively few biologic variables have been shown to have an association with specific psychiatric disorders and only a handful have been studied from an epidemiologic perspective.

Studies such as those by Thomas and Chess (1977) have attempted to define aspects of "temperament" (which may also be an inherited factor) and assess the association between these variables and subsequent psychiatric disorders. Certain qualities of temperament (described as the "difficult child") have been associated with increased risk for later development of nonspecific psychological distress, but no direct linkage to specific diagnosis has yet been made.

Studies of twins discordant for schizophrenia (Pollin, 1972) have shown an increased prevalence of soft neurologic signs and evidence of a less favored intrauterine environment as indicated by lower birth weight, less adequate psychophysiological regulation, and disordered sleep and feeding behavior among the schizophrenic twins, suggesting possible biologic predisposition to the disorder. Several studies of children of schizophrenics have been begun since the 1960s in an attempt to identify prospectively factors that might predict the subsequent development of schizophrenia in these high-risk children (Mednick et al., 1975; Erlenmeyer-Kimling and Cornblatt, 1978; McNeil and Kaij, 1978). Since, except for the Mednick study, few of the children in these studies have passed through the risk period for the onset of schizophrenia, their findings to date must be considered tentative. In addition, variation in diagnostic criteria and in demographic and familial factors across studies make comparisons difficult. However, early results have suggested that the presence of obstetrical complications and deficits of sustained attentional performance tests may be associated with subsequent deviant behavior in these children. Less consistent but still suggestive findings have also been reported for neurologic abnormalities and psychophysiologic functioning as measured by skin conductance, although on the latter variable, Mednick et al. (1975) and Erlenmeyer-Kimling and Cornblatt (1978) found conflicting results. It must also be recognized that, since the great majority of adult schizophrenics do not have a schizophrenic parent, the results of these findings may apply only to a subset of all schizophrenics. Watt (1978) reported premorbid temperamental characteristics of children who subsequently developed adult schizophrenia as consisting of "negativistic, egocentric, unpleasant or antisocial behavior" among boys and "quiet, introverted and egocentric behavior" among girls, suggesting an enduring biologic predisposition (perhaps inherited) that seemed progressive over time. He cited the diathesis-stress model to suggest that this premorbid temperament might interact with stressors to produce adult schizophrenia.

As regards affective disorder, as Prange and Loosen (1983) have pointed out, no biologic risk factors have been identified with significant certainty to justify epidemiologic investigation at this time, although a number of promising candidates have been suggested from clinical studies (e.g., electroencephalographic (EEG) sleep data, neurotransmitters and their metabolites, monoamine oxidase, neuroendocrine variables, and pharmacokinetics such as RBC-lithium transport).

Biologic variables of epidemiologic interest have also not as yet been identified for anxiety disorders (Marks, 1983) or personality disorders (Martin and Guze, 1983), with the exception of antisocial personality, for which clinical research has suggested differences in EEGs (increased prevalence of slow wave activity and a positive-spike phenomenon), lowered cortical arousal, and a learning deficit in which conditioned responses are acquired slowly and extinguished rapidly (Hare, 1970).

## Psychosocial Factors

*Stress* is defined as that state of an organism in which energy is used in continuously dealing with problems over and above the energy required if the problems had been resolved. In recent years, a body of sociological literature has suggested a variety of models through which stressful events might cause physical or mental illness (Dohrenwend and Dohrenwend, 1981). Most of these models postulate that the occurrence of a stressful event interacts with the individual's personal predisposition, coping abilities, and social support such that the individual either masters the stress, seeks help through which the problem is resolved, or develops physical or mental symptoms.

The types of stressful circumstances that may lead to stress in the individual include:

- *Background stressors* inherent in the individual's social position, role, etc.
- *Strain of chronic stressors*, which are enduring problems related to frustrations of daily living, including role conflict, goal/means discrepancies, and perceived inequities or excessive demands
- *Changes in the pace of daily living* owing to the occurrence of life events
- *Traumatic life events*, which are usually single-episode events with overwhelming and long-lasting effects (e.g., posttraumatic stress disorder)

The assessment of the association of stressful events with psychiatric illness has been hampered by differences across studies in the types of events measured and their

quantification. In addition, Brown (1973) has described several potential sources of error in the reporting of events owing to *direct contamination* (i.e., the subject with a psychiatric disorder retrospectively reports more events than a control subject out of an attempt to explain the illness); *indirect contamination*, in which a subject's condition (e.g., the presence of anxiety) may prospectively increase both the tendency to report a life event and the subsequent development of the illness; and *spuriousness*, in which accurate report of life events has been made, but the association with the psychiatric disorder is due to a third factor causing both the life event and the illness. An additional methodological issue has been the need to separate life events that may be either prodromal to the illness or the result of the illness (e.g., job loss) from those that are independent of and antecedent to the illness. Also, as noted by Hirschfeld and Cross (1983), specific causality for a psychiatric disorder must be demonstrated. Finally, Kessler (1979) has presented data suggesting that the impact of the event on the individual rather than the mere fact of the occurrence of a life event may be more crucial to the development of emotional distress. For example, he demonstrated that the impact of similar exposure to life events was significantly greater among lower social class individuals, at least in part owing to the absence of buffering personal resources. Finally, reliability of reporting life events may vary by diagnosis (Neugebauer, 1983) and whether patient self-reports are corroborated by relatives and friends (Yager et al., 1981; Schless and Mendels, 1978).

Most studies of the emotional effect of life events have used nonspecific psychological distress as the dependent variable, rather than specific diagnostic categories. There is considerable evidence that a variety of life events is associated with an increase in this nonspecific distress (Myers, Lindenthal, Pepper, 1972). Two studies (Jacobs and Myers, 1976; Brown and Birley, 1968) have shown that the number of life events reported by schizophrenics before the onset of a psychotic episode was significantly greater than the number reported by controls during a comparable period, but most of these events could be related to patients' mental status. However, Brown and Birley also found that events independent of the patient's psychiatric condition occurred more frequently during the 3 weeks before the onset of psychosis, leading Brown to suggest that life stress may trigger schizophrenic episodes but not be causative of schizophrenia per se. Leff, Hirsch, Garind, Rhode, and Stevens (1973) also reported a high frequency of events just before relapse among schizophrenics receiving neuroleptic treatment.

As regards depressive illness, several studies have suggested that "markedly threatening" life events (Brown, Skain, Harris, Birley, 1973), "exit" events (Jacobs, Prusoff, Paykel, 1974), and "undesirable" events (Paykel et al., 1969) occurred more frequently to persons who subsequently suffered depression than to normal controls or schizophrenic patients. In addition, the occurrence of "undesirable" life events has been associated with relapse in depressed patients (Paykel and Tanner, 1976). The association between severe life events and depression has recently been replicated in geriatric patients (Murphy, 1982). The presence of medical or psychiatric illness has also been associated with increased risk for depression. Brown (1978) has interpreted these data as indicating that life events are causative of subsequent depression, and Paykel (1978) has estimated that 9 per cent to 10 per cent of all exits are followed by depression. However, the presence of these events accounted for a relatively small amount of the variance (1 per cent to 9 per cent) in the onset of depression, suggesting that stress, while contributing as a cause in some depressive disorders, is a relatively weak predictor of depression. A recent report (Kennedy, Thompson, Stancer, Roy, Perrod, 1983) has also suggested a role for life events in the precipitation of mania, while Finlay-Jones and Brown (1981) have suggested that loss events may be causal for depressive disorders, severe danger may be causal for anxiety states, and both types of events may result in mixed anxiety/depressive disorders. However, most of these findings have been based on retrospectively collected data, whereas a recent review of prospective studies of life events and psychological morbidity has concluded that these findings do not seem to show that life events have a substantial causal role in "neurotic illness" (Tennant, 1983).

A specific life event reported to be associated with the onset of psychiatric disorder is childbirth. Several studies using case registers (Nott, 1982) have shown a marked increase in rates of psychoses (primarily affective) during the postpartum period as compared with rates during pregnancy, with little or no difference in rates of other diagnostic categories.

In addition, childhood parental loss through death or separation has been reported to be significantly more common among adult patients with depression than among matched controls (Nelson, 1982; Roy, 1981; Pfohl, Stangl, Tsuang, 1983; Lloyd, 1980), increasing the risk for depression by a factor of 2 or 3. Moreover, because this event has not been found to be associated with nonspecific distress (Tennant et al., 1981), schizophrenia or bipolar disorder (Pfohl et al., 1983), or total mental disorder (Leaf et al., 1984), it may represent a diagnosis-specific risk factor.

Finally, as regards adopted individuals at genetic risk for antisocial behavior, boys seemed to be more vulnerable than girls to adverse family circumstances in the adoptive family (chiefly a psychiatrically ill family member or divorce in the adoptive parents) (Cadoret and Cain, 1980).

*Personal resources*, including both the individual's coping skills and personal behavior as well as family ties, social networks, and support systems, have been hypothesized as providing buffering in time of stress. However, studies of these variables have suffered from difficulties in quantifying these measures and have primarily suggested that deficiency of some of these resources may be related to nonspecific psychological distress. A major obstacle to this research has been the problem of whether a deficiency in personal resources is the cause or the result of psychiatric impairment. Several studies have shown that indices of inadequate personal resources (living alone, unmarried, role dissatisfaction, low social class, absence of friends) are associated with high levels of nonspecific symptomatology (Myers et al., 1975; Warheit, 1979). Aneshensel and Stone (1982) have further suggested that social support may have a direct effect in ameliorating depressive symptoms, not merely acting as a buffer against life stress.

As regards specific diagnostic categories, absence of a close, confiding relationship has been linked to a vulnerability to depression (Murphy, 1982; Brown and Harris, 1978), as has death of one or both parents before age 11 (Brown and Harris, 1978). Also, late antisocial behavior has been associated with being reared in homes broken by divorce or separation (Rutter, 1974).

## Demographic Factors

### Sex

As noted earlier, the overall prevalence of psychiatric disorder as reported in the ECA data reveals no significant difference in rates by sex (Leaf et al., 1984). However, significant sex differences were noted for specific disorders. Thus antisocial personality and alcohol and drug abuse/dependence are significantly more common among men (by M-F ratios of 5:1, 6:1, and 2:1, respectively), while major depressive disorder (1:2) and agoraphobia (1:2.5) and simple phobia (1:2) are more prevalent among women. Schizophrenia, dysthymia, panic disorder, and obsessive-compulsive disorder are slightly more common among women (less than 1:1.5 male-to-female ratios), while no sex predominance was found for manic episodes or cognitive impairment (Robins et al., 1984).

As Weissman and Klerman (1977) have pointed out for depressive disorders, a variety of genetic, biologic, and psychosocial hypotheses have been proposed to explain these differences, but as yet no definitive conclusions have been forthcoming. However, since the ECA findings are based on a community survey, many of the explanations based on differential treatment utilization (e.g., women are more likely to seek psychiatric care, while men tend to enter correctional facilities) are clearly not operative.

### Age

Six-month prevalence data from the ECA study (Myers et al., 1984) show an overall prevalence of mental disorder to be about twice as high for adults less than 45 years of age when compared with those 45 years and older. By specific disorder, affective disorders, substance abuse/dependency, and antisocial personality disorders are disorders of the young, while panic, obsessive-compulsive, and phobic disorders are more evenly distributed across all ages and cognitive impairment shows a linear increase with age, reaching rates of 12 per cent to 18 per cent for mild impairment and 4 per cent to 6 per cent for severe impairment in the age-group 65 and older.

Age of onset among patients with affective disorders is somewhat earlier for bipolar disorders (mean age in late 20s) compared with nonbipolar disorders (mean mid to late 30s) (Hirschfeld and Cross, 1983). Among schizophrenics, Loranger (1984) commented on a significant sex difference in age of onset, with males having an average age at onset about 5 years earlier than females and paranoid patients showing a significantly later age of onset for both sexes than patients with other subtypes of schizophrenia. Again, as with the sex differences, these age variations have been explained as being due to differential patterns of treatment utilization, to different exposure to and impact of stressful circumstances, and to biologic (e.g., hormonal) differences. However, no definitive explanation has yet been established.

### Ethnicity

In general, studies of symptomatology and prevalence of specific psychiatric disorders within a culture have shown little, if any, evidence of major ethnic differences when similar assessment techniques have been applied and social class is controlled (Simon et al., 1973). For example, in the ECA project, Leaf et al. (1984) report no significant differences in total prevalence of psychiatric disorders by race, although Hispanic respondents showed a nonsignificant excess. The lifetime prevalence of major psychiatric disorders at three ECA sites also showed virtually no ethnic differences except for a significant excess of phobic disorders among blacks in Baltimore by a ratio of 2:1 (blacks–non-blacks).

Treated prevalence studies have shown an increase in utilization of mental health services by persons who represent a "critically small" ethnic minority (usually less than 10 per cent of the total population [Rabkin, 1979]), a finding that has been attributed to levels of social support structure.

Eaton (1983) cites evidence that Irish, Croats, Russians, and native-born Israelis have higher risks for schizophrenia (2:1), while Ashkenazic Jews have higher risks for affective disorders and American blacks have higher risks for antisocial personality disorders. Also, studies of isolated populations (e.g., Hutterites and Amish) have suggested extremely low prevalence of schizophrenia (Egeland and Hostetter, 1983) as compared with affective disorders. However, high or low prevalence rates in highly inbred populations may represent a predominantly genetic influence rather than the effect of cultural characteristics.

*Social class* has been defined using indices of occupation, education, and income that are often not well correlated, thus contributing to problems of interpretation. In addition, current social class may be the result of the presence of a psychiatric illness and its effect on social and occupational function, making causal inferences invalid.

Studies of treated prevalence (Faris and Dunham, 1939; Hollingshead and Redlich, 1958) have consistently found an inverse correlation between indices of social class and the overall risk for mental disorder. However, in part, this finding has been a function of the less adequate treatment accorded lower-class patients with resultant prolonged duration of illness. Community surveys have also shown an increased prevalence of psychiatric symptomatology (Craig and Van Natta, 1979) and overall mental disorder (Leaf et al., 1984) in the lower social classes.

In view of these findings, two major theories have evolved to explain the predominance of pathology in the lowest social class: social causation (i.e., stresses, etc. inherent in being a member of the lower social class cause these disorders) vs. social selection or drift (individuals with mental disorders tend to move into lower-class areas as a result of social and vocational impairment).

Perhaps the most thoroughly studied psychiatric disorder with regard to social class influence is schizophrenia, in which the vast majority of studies have shown a relative risk of 3:1 to 10:1 between lowest and highest social class (Dohrenwend and Dohrenwend, 1969). In this condition, evidence from several sources suggests that the major factor is most likely social selection/drift (Wiersma et al., 1983, Wender et al., 1973). Treated incidence studies have shown the lower-class predominance of schizophrenia to be largely a phenomenon of large cities (Kohn, 1972; Goodman, Siegel, Craig, Lin, 1983), which is much less apparent in smaller communities. Also, Eaton and Lasry (1978) had shown evidence for downward social mobility among schizophrenics after the onset of the disorder.

Nonbipolar affective disorders show an inverse association with social class, which is most evident in minor depressive disorders and depressive symptomatology (Craig and Van Natta, 1979). In this case, there are treated incidence data (Goodman et al., 1983) to suggest a possible social causation effect, which is consistent with Brown's (1979) findings regarding social stress. Lower-class individuals appear to be more vulnerable to social stressors, at least in part because of their limited personal resources. In contrast, bipolar disorders have been reported to show a modest positive relationship with social class, with higher rates among professional persons (Hirschfeld and Cross, 1983).

The relationship of social class to anxiety disorders is not well defined. However, lifetime prevalence rates from the ECA study (Robins et al., 1984) show increased prevalence of phobias (both simple and agoraphobia) of about 2:1 magnitude among respondents with lower educational levels, a finding that was also seen for cognitive impairment. However, because the findings were not adjusted for other demographic variables, they must be viewed as tentative. Antisocial personality disorder has been shown to be strongly correlated with lower social status in the few studies that have addressed this issue.

*Occupation* has rarely been linked as a specific risk factor for a specific diagnostic category. Welner et al. (1979) have reported an increased prevalence of primary affective disorder, chiefly depression, among professional women (51 per cent among M.D.s and 32 per cent among Ph.D.s). However, the explanation for this finding is unclear and may suggest a selection phenomenon rather than an etiologic role for occupation. In addition, a form of traumatic dementia has been reported in professional prizefighters (Brody and White, 1982).

Unstable occupational history and unemployment are commonly seen among patients with a variety of psychiatric disorders, especially schizophrenics and those with antisocial personality, but is more likely a result of the effects of the illness than a cause.

*Marital status* has been linked with the

presence of mental illness in a variety of ways. Leaf et al. (1984), using ECA findings, found total mental disorders to be highest among the separated (26.7 per cent) and divorced (25.8 per cent), followed by the never married (21.5 per cent). However, by sex, men's rates were highest among widowed, separated, and divorced (30.4 per cent), while female rates were highest among singles (21.4 per cent). Relationship with spouse, however, showed a strong correlation with prevalence. Those who reported a poor marital relationship had a prevalence rate of 51.2 per cent vs. 20.1 per cent (fairly good relationship) and 12.0 per cent (very good relationship). There was also a linear inverse relationship between reported ability to confide in spouse and overall prevalence of mental disorder.

For specific diagnoses, the risk for schizophrenia is about four times higher among the never married (greater among males) as compared with the married, probably largely owing to the early age of onset and adverse premorbid personality of many schizophrenics, making marriage unlikely (Eaton, 1983). Among the affective disorders, nonbipolar prevalence rates are lower in the married than in the unmarried, consistent with Brown's (1979) findings of a protective effect conferred by a close, confiding relationship. However, no significant relationship has been demonstrated between marital status and bipolar disorders except for the high prevalence of marital conflict seen among these patients (Hirschfeld and Cross, 1983).

## Migration

Rosenthal et al. (1974) report that virtually all treated prevalence studies of migration and schizophrenia reveal increased prevalence rates among migrants, although in many cases, the differences noted are trivial. As with social class, these findings have raised questions as to causation vs. social selection. In summarizing these findings, Rosenthal et al. (1974) present data suggesting that the major factor to be studied is the motivation for migration, a social selection factor. Thus, in most earlier studies, pre-schizophrenics were seen to be more likely to migrate because of adverse economic circumstances in their countries of origin, whereas in Denmark in the 1950s, schizophrenics were only one fifth as likely to migrate as matched controls. Data on migration as a factor in other psychiatric disorders are scanty.

A recent study using DSM-III criteria found a markedly increased rate of migration among bipolar patients and their parents but not among schizophrenic patients, suggesting that earlier studies that found increased migration among schizophrenic patients may have included substantial numbers of bipolar patients misdiagnosed as schizophrenic and accounting for their findings (Pope, Ionescu-Pioggia, Yurgelun-Todd, 1983).

## Season of Birth

A number of studies have found a relative excess of schizophrenic births during the winter and spring months on the order of 5 per cent to 15 per cent (Torrey et al., 1977). In general, this finding has been more striking in countries with more marked seasonal variations, with a few exceptions, and has been reproduced in both hemispheres. A number of hypotheses have been proposed to explain this phenomenon, including nutritional (e.g., first-trimester protein deficiency), environmental (e.g., exposure to pesticides in first trimester), climatologic effects on ovum maturation, genetic (e.g., heat damage or exaggerated resistance to infectious diseases in the prenatal period), infectious (e.g., exposure to infectious agents with seasonal patterns), or reproductive patterns of mothers of schizophrenics. Kinney and Jacobsen (1978) cited evidence for seasonally related prenatal brain injury among patients with low genetic liability to schizophrenia using adoption techniques. Watson et al. (1984) found greater seasonality in years directly following those with high levels of infectious diseases (especially diphtheria, pneumonia, and influenza) in unmarried, but not married, patients, and no association with temperature extremes. They interpreted these data as consistent with prenatal influence chiefly affecting poor outcome patients and suggested that these effects may hold for only a portion of the total schizophrenic population. However, Hare (1970) found a first quarter elevation in birthrate among depressive patients as well as schizophrenic patients (but not other psychiatric disorders), suggesting that the effect of seasonality may be nonspecific for psychosis in general.

## Urbanization

Treated prevalence rates tend to show higher prevalence of most mental disorders in urban as compared with rural areas. However, these findings probably reflect more the greater accessibility of mental health services in urban areas than a real difference in true prevalence (Mueller, 1981). Community surveys in a variety of settings have shown somewhat higher rates of bipolar affective disorder in rural areas and substantially higher rates of neurosis and personality disorder (especially antisocial personality) in urban areas, while schizophrenia showed no urban/rural differences. Rates of depressive symptomatology and nonbipolar depression have been reported from several studies to be higher in urban areas, which Mueller (1981) has suggested may be due to relatively less adequate social support in urban communities.

## Integration of Etiologic Theories

Unfortunately, to date there has been relatively little integration of the findings from genetic, biologic, and psychosocial studies of etiologic factors related to psychiatric illness. As regards schizophrenia, Pollin (1972) proposed a model in which a biologic factor (hyperactivity of the CNS catecholamine system), which may have both genetic or biologic/environmental origins (e.g., prenatal injury), may predispose an individual to react to psychosocial factors (e.g., stressors) with hyperarousal, which, if not moderated by the availability of personal resources and social support, can result in a psychotic episode. Although this approach is intuitively logical, future prospective studies, including structured assessment of all sets of variables (genetic, biologic, and psychosocial), in both high-risk and general population samples are now needed to begin to integrate these theoretical models and to specify their relevance to specific diagnostic entities if psychiatric epidemiology is to achieve its full potential.

## REFERENCES

Aneshensel CS, Stone JD: Stress and depression. Arch Gen Psychiatry 39:1392–1396, 1982.

Baldessarini RJ, Finkelstein S, Arana GW: The predictive power of diagnostic tests and the effect of prevalence of illness. Arch Gen Psychiatry 40:569–573, 1983.

Bebbington P: Causal models and logical inference in epidemiologic psychiatry. Br J Psychiatry 136:317–325, 1980.

Brody JA, White LR: An epidemiologic perspective on senile dementia—Facts and fragments. Psychopharmacol Bull 18:222–224, 1982.

Bromet E, Schulberg HC, Dunn L: Reactions of psychiatric patients to the Three Mile Island Nuclear Accident. Arch Gen Psychiatry 39:725–730, 1982.

Brown GW, Birley JLT: Crises and life changes and the onset of schizophrenia. J Health Soc Behav 9:203–214, 1968.

Brown GW, Harris TO: Social Origins of Depression. London, Tavestock, 1978.

Brown GW, Skain F, Harris TO, Birley JLT: Life events and psychiatric disorder. I. Some Methodological issues. Psychol Med 3:74–87, 1973.

Brown JH: Suicide in Britian: More attempts, fewer deaths, lessons for public policy. Arch Gen Psychiatry 36:1119–1124, 1979.

Cadoret RJ, Cain C: Sex differences in predictors of antisocial behavior in adoptees. Arch Gen Psychiatry 37:1171–1175, 1980.

Craig TJ, Van Natta PA: Effect of demographic variables on symptoms of depression. Arch Gen Psychiatry 36:149–154, 1979.

de Alarcon R: An epidemiological evaluation of a public health measure aimed at reducing the availability of methylamphetamine. Psychol Med 2:293–300, 1972.

Dohrenwend BS, Dohrenwend BP: Social status and psychological disorder. New York, John Wiley & Sons, 1969.

Dohrenwend BS, Dohrenwend BP: Life stress and illness: Formulation of the issues, in Dohrenwend BS, Dohrenwend BP (eds): Stressful Life Events and Their Contexts. Monographs in Psychosocial Epidemiology 2. New York, Prodist, 1981, pp 1–27.

Dohrenwend BS, Dohrenwend BP: Life stress and psychopathology, in Regie DA, Allen G (eds): Risk Factor Research in the Major Mental Disorders. National Institute of Mental Health. DHHS Pub. No. (ADM) 83-1068. Rockville, Md, The Institute, 1983, pp 55–67.

Dohrenwend BP, Shrout PE, Egri G, Mendelsohn FS: Nonspecific psychological distress and other dimensions of psychopathology: Measures for use in the general population: Arch Gen Psychiatry 37:1229–1236, 1980.

Dunham HW: Community and Schizophrenia—An Epidemiological Analysis. Lafayette Clinic Monographs in Psychiatry. Detroit, Mich, Wayne University Press, 1965.

Earls F: Epidemiologic methods for research in child psychiatry, in Earls F (ed): Studies of Children. Monographs in Psychosocial Epidemiology 1. New York, Prodist, 1980a, pp 1–33.

Earls F: Epidemiological child psychiatry: An American perspective, in Purcell EF (ed): Psychopathology of Children and Youth: A Cross-cultural Perspective. New York, Josiah Macy, Jr. Foundation, 1980b, pp 3–27.

Eaton WW: Demographic and social ecologic risk factors for mental disorders, in Regier DA, Allen G (eds): Risk Factor Research in the Major Mental Disorders, National Institute of Mental Health. DHHS Pub. No. (ADM) 83-1068. Rockville, Md, The Institute, 1983, pp 111–129.

Eaton WW, Lasry JC: Mental health and occupational mobility in a group of immigrants. Soc Sci Med 12:53–58, 1978.

Egeland JA, Hostetter AM: Amish study. I. Affective disorders among the Amish, 1976-1980. Am J Psychiatry 140:56–61, 1983.

Endicott J, Spitzer RL: A diagnostic interview: The schedule for affective disorders and schizophrenia. Arch Gen Psychiatry 35:837–844, 1978.

Erlenmeyer-Kimling L, Cornblatt B: Attentional measures in a study of children at high-risk for schizophrenia. J Psychiat Res 14:93–98, 1978.

Faris REL, Dunham HW: Mental Disorders in Urban Areas: An Ecological Study of Schizophrenia and Other Psychoses. Chicago, University of Chicago Press, 1939.

Feighner JP, Robins E, Guze SB, Woodruff RA Jr., Winokur G, Munoz R: Diagnostic criteria for use in psychiatric research. Arch Gen Psychiatry 26:57–63, 1972.

Finlay-Jones R, Brown G: Types of stressful life event and the onset of anxiety and depressive disorders. Psychol Med 11:803–815, 1981.

Frank JD: Persuasion and Healing. Baltimore, John Hopkins University Press, 1973, pp 312–318.

Goldberger J, Waring CH, Tanner WF: Pellagra prevention by diet in institutional inmates. Public Health Rep 38:2361–2368, 1925.

Goodman AB, Craig TJ: A needs assessment strategy for an era of limited resources. Am J Epidemiol 115:624–632, 1982.

Goodman AB, Siegel C, Craig TJ, Lin SP: The relationship between socioeconomic class and prevalence of schizophrenia, alcoholism and affective disorders treated by inpatient care in a suburban area. Am J Psychiatry 140:166–170, 1983.

Graham PJ: Epidemiological approaches to child mental health in developing countries, in Purcell EF (ed): Psychopathology of Children and Youth: A Cross-cultural Perspective. New York, Josiah Macy, Jr. Foundation, 1980, pp 28–45.

Hare RD: Psychopathy: theory and research. New York: John Wiley & Sons, 1970.

Hare EH, Price JS: Mental disorder and season of birth: Comparison of psychosis with neurosis. Br J Psychiatry 115:533–540, 1969.

Helzer JE, Robins LN, Taibleson M, Woodruff RA Jr, Reich T, Wish ED: Reliability of psychiatric diagnosis. Arch Gen Psychiatry 34:129–133, 1977.

Hirschfeld RMA, Cross CK: Psychosocial risk factors for depression, in Regier DA, Allen G (eds): Risk Factor Research in the Major Mental Disorders. National Institute of Mental Health. DHHS Pub. No. (ADM) 131-143. Rockville, Md, The Institute, 1983.

Hollingshead AB, Redlich FC: Social Class and Mental Illness. New York, John Wiley & Sons, 1958.

Hughes PH, Crawford GA, Becker NW: Developing an epidemiologic field team for drug dependence. Arch Gen Psychiatry 24:389–393, 1971.

Jacobs S, Myers J: Recent life events and acute schizophrenic psychosis: A controlled study. J Nerv Ment Dis 162:75–87, 1976.

Jacobs S, Prusoff BA, Paykel ES: Recent life events in schizophrenia and depression. Psychol Med 4:444–453, 1974.

Kennedy S, Thompson R, Stancer HC, Roy A, Perrod E: Life events precipitating mania. Br J Psychiatry 142:398–403, 1983.

Kessler RC: A strategy for studying differential vulnerability to the psychological consequences of stress. J Health Soc Behav 20:100–108, 1979.

Kinney DK, Jacobsen B: Environmental factors in schizophrenia: New adoption study evidence, in Wynne LC, Cromwell RL, Matthysse S (eds): The Nature of Schizophrenia. New York, John Wiley & Sons, 1978.

Kohn MLK: Class, family and schizophrenia: A reformulation. Soc Forces 50:295–304, 1972.

Kramer M: Cross-national study of diagnosis of the mental disorders: Origin of the problem. Am J Psychiatry 125:1–4, 1969 (suppl).

Leaf PJ, Weissman MM, Myers JK, Tischler GL, Holzer CE 3d: Social factors related to psychiatric disorder: The Yale Epidemiologic Catchment Area Study. Soc Psychiatry 19:53–61, 1984.

Leff JP, Hirsch SR, Garind R, Rhode PD, Stevens BC: Life events and maintenance therapy in schizophrenic relapse. Br J Psychiatry 123:659–660, 1973.

Lin T: A study of incidence of mental disorder in Chinese and other cultures. Psychiatry 16:313, 1953.

Lin T-Y, Standley CC: The scope of epidemiology in psychiatry. Geneva, World Health Organization, 1962.

Lloyd C: Life events and depressive disorders reviewed. Arch Gen Psychiatry 37:529–535, 1980.

Loranger AW: Sex difference in age at onset of schizophrenia. Arch Gen Psychiatry 41:157–161, 1984.

Marks I: Risk factors in anxiety disorders, in Regier DA, Allen G (eds): Risk Factor Research in the Major Mental Disorders. Rockville, MD, US Department of Health and Human Services, National Institute of Mental Health, DHFS Pub. No. (ADM) 83-1068, 1983, pp. 81–93.

Martin RL, Guze SB: Risk factors and personality disorders, in Regier DA, Allen G (eds): Risk Factor Research in the Major Mental Disorders. Rockville, MD, US Department of Health and Human Services, National Institute of Mental Health, DHFS Pub. No. (ADM) 83-1068, 1983, pp. 95-107.

McNeil TF, Kij L: Obstetric factors in the development of schizophrenia. Complications in the births of pre-schizophrenics and in reproduction by schizophrenic parents, in Wynne LC, Cromwell RL, Matthysse S (eds): The Nature of Schizophrenia: New Approaches to Research and Treatment. New York, John Wiley & Sons, 1978, pp 401–429.

McNeil TF, Kaij L: Etiologic relevance of comparisons of high-risk and low-risk groups. Acta Psychiatry Scand 59:545–560, 1979.

Mednick SA, Schulsinger H, Schulsinger F: Schizophrenia in children of schizophrenic mothers, in Davids A (ed): Childhood Personality and Psychopathology: Current Topics, Vol. II. New York, John Wiley & Sons, 1975, pp 221–252.

Mueller DP: The current status of urban-rural differences in psychiatric disorder. J Nerv Ment Dis 169:18–27, 1981.

Murphy E: Social origins of depression in old age. Br J Psychiatry 141:135–142, 1982.

Myers JK, Lindenthal JJ, Pepper MP: Life events and mental status: A longitudinal study. J Health Soc Behav 13:398–406, 1972.

Myers JK, Lindenthal JJ, Pepper MP: Life events, social integration and psychiatric symptomatology. J Health Soc Behav 16:421–427, 1975.

Myers JK, Weissman MM, Tischler GL, Holzer CE 3rd, Leaf PJ, Orvaschel H, Anthony JC, Boyd JH, Burre JD Jr, Kramer M, Stoltzman R: Six-month prevalence of psychiatric disorders in three communities: 1980-1982. Arch Gen Psychiatry 41:959–967, 1984.

Nelson G: Parental death during childhood and adult depression: Some additional data. Soc Psychiatry 17:37–42, 1982.

Neugebauer R: Reliability of life-event interviews with outpatient schizophrenics. Arch Gen Psychiatry 40:378–383, 1983.

Nott PN: Psychiatric illness following childbirth in Southampton: A case register study. Psychol Med 12:557–561, 1982.

Orvaschel H, Sholmskas D, Weissman M: Assessing children in psychiatric epidemiologic studies, in Earls F (ed): Studies of Children. Monographs in Psychosocial Epidemiology. New York, Prodist, 1980, pp 84–95.

Paykel ES: Contribution of life events to causation of psychiatric illness. Psychol Med 8:245–254, 1978.

Paykel ES, Tanner J: Life events, depressive relapse and maintenance treatment. Psychol Med 6:481–485, 1976.

Paykel ES, Myers JK, Dieralt MN, Klerman GL, Lindenthal JJ, Pepper MP: Life events and depression: A controlled study. Arch Gen Psychiatry 21:753–760, 1969.

Pfohl B, Stangl D, Tsuang MT: The association between early parental loss and diagnosis in the Iowa 500. Arch Gen Psychiatry 40:965–967, 1983.

Plunkett R, Gordon J: Epidemiology and mental illness. New York, Basic Books, 1960.

Pollin W: The pathogenesis of schizophrenia: Possible relationships between genetic, biochemical, and experiential factors. Arch Gen Psychiatry 27:29–37, 1972.

Pope HG Jr, Ionescu-Pioggia M, Yurgelun-Todd D: Migration and manic-depressive illness. Compr Psychiatry 24:158–165, 1983.

Prange AA Jr, Loosen PT: Somatic findings in affective disorders. Their status as risk factors, in Regier DA, Allen G (eds): Risk factor research in the major mental disorders. Rockville, MD, US Department of Health and Human Services, National Institute of Mental Health, DHFS Pub. No. (ADM) 83-1068, 1983, pp 69–79.

Purcell EF (ed): Psychopathology of Children and Youth: A Cross-cultural Perspective. New York, Josiah Macy, Jr. Foundation, 1980.

Rabkin JG: Ethnic density and psychiatric hospitalization: Hazards of minority status. Am J Psychiatry 136:1562–1566, 1979.

Regier DA, Goldberg ID, Taube CA: The de facto US mental health services system: A public health perspective. Arch Gen Psychiatry 35:685–693, 1978.

Robins LN, Helzer JE, Weissman MM, Orvaschel H, Gruenberg E, Burke JD, Jr, Regier DA: Lifetime prevalence of specific psychiatric disorder in three sites. Arch Gen Psychiatry 41:949–958, 1984.

Robins LN, Helzer JE, Croughan J, Ratcliff, KS: National Institute of Mental Health Diagnostic Interview Schedule. Arch Gen Psychiatry 34:129–133, 1977.

Robins LN: Longitudinal methods in the study of normal and pathological development, in Earls F (ed): Studies of Children: Monographs in Psychosocial Epidemiology, New York, Prodist, 1980, pp 34–83.

Rosenthal D, Goldberg I, Jacobsen B, Wender PH, Kelty SS, Schulsinger F, Eldred CA: Migration, heredity, and schizophrenia. Psychiatry 37:321–339, 1974.

Roy, A: Role of past loss in depression. Arch Gen Psychiatry 38:301–302, 1981.

Rutter M: The Qualities of Mothering: Maternal Deprivation Reassessed. New York: Jason Aronson, 1974.

Schless AP, Mendels J: The value of interviewing family and friends in assessing life stressors. Arch Gen Psychiatry 35:565–567, 1978.

Simon RJ, Fleiss JL, Gurland BJ, Stiller PR, Sharpe L: Depression and schizophrenia in hospitalized black and white mental patients. Arch Gen Psychiatry 28:509–512, 1973.

Spitzer RL, Endicott J, Robins E: Research diagnostic criteria: Rationale and reliability. Arch Gen Psychiatry 35:773–782, 1978.

Srole L, Langner TS, Michael ST, et al: Mental Health in the Metropolis: The Midtown Manhattan Study. New York, McGraw-Hill Book Co., 1962.

Tennant C: Life events and psychological morbidity: The evidence from prospective studies. Psychol Med 13:483–486, 1983.

Tennant C, Smith A, Bebbington P, Hurry J: Parental loss in childhood. Arch Gen Psychiatry 38:309–314, 1981.

Terris M: Use of hospital admissions in epidemiologic studies of mental disease. Arch Gen Psychiatry 12:420–426, 1965.

Thomas A, Chess S: Temperament and Development. New York, Brunner/Mazel, 1977.

Torrey EF, Torrey BB, Peterson MR: Seasonality of schizophrenic births in the United States. Arch Gen Psychiatry 34:1065–1070, 1977.

Warheit GJ: Life events, coping, stress and depressive symptomatology. Am J Psychiatry 136:502–507, 1979.

Watson CG, Keecala T, Tilleskjor C, Jacobs L: Schizophrenic birth seasonality in relation to the incidence of the infectious diseases and temperature extreme. Arch Gen Psychiatry 41:85–90, 1984.

Watt, NF: Patterns of childhood social development in adult schizophrenics. Arch Gen Psychiatry 35:160–165, 1978.

Weissman MM, Klerman GL: Epidemiology of mental disorders: Emerging trends in the United States. Arch Gen Psychiatry 35:705–712, June 1978.

Weissman MM, Klerman GL: Sex differences and the epidemiology of depression. Arch Gen Psychiatry 34:98-111, 1977.

Weissman MM, Myers JK, Harding PS: Psychiatric disorders in a US urban community: 1975-1976. Am J Psychiatry 135:459-462, 1978.

Welner, A, Welner Z, Fishman R: The group of schizoaffective and related psychoses: IV. A family study. Compr. Psychiatry 20:21–26, 1979.

Wender PH, Rosenthal D, Katz SS, Schulsinger F, Welner J: Social class and psychopathology in adopters. Arch Gen Psychiatry 28:318-325, 1973.

Wiersma D, Giel R, DeJong A, Slooff CJ: Social class and schizophrenia in a Dutch cohort. Psychol Med 13:141-150, 1983.

Yager J, Grant I, Sweetwood HL, Gerst M: Life event reports by psychiatric patients, nonpatients and their partners. Arch Gen Psychiatry 38:343-347, 1981.

Yolles SF, Kramer M: Vital statistics, in Bellak and Loeb L (eds): The Schizophrenic Syndrome, New York, Grune and Stratton, 1969.

Zubin J: Cross-national study of diagnosis of the mental disorders: Methodology and planning. Am J Psychiatry 125 (suppl):12-20, 1969.

# chapter 33

# SUICIDE AND ATTEMPTED SUICIDE

*by* George E. Murphy, M.D.

## SUICIDE

### Definition

There is no universally accepted definition for suicide, although such a death must have been self-inflicted. Coroners and medical examiners, both in the United States and the United Kingdom, may require "some actual evidence pointing to the event" before they will rule a self-inflicted death as suicide (Barraclough 1972). In the absence of a suicide note (which is present in no more than one third of cases), the evidence for intent must be inferred. The victim cannot testify. Leaving aside the question of homicide, circumstances often leave little or no doubt as to intent. The victim found hanged, asphyxiated in a closed garage with the automobile ignition on, or dead of a gunshot wound to the head with the personally owned weapon at hand is readily judged a suicide. When the victim is found dead with a sublethal blood level of a psychotropic medication and a high blood level of alcohol, there is more room for question. Was death intentional or an accident? Although circumstances may often be telling, many times there is room for interpretation. Whether by law, custom, or personal preference, coroners and medical examiners' offices commonly operate under a presumption against suicide. In consequence, as many deaths from drug overdose are ruled accidental in a year as are ruled suicide from all causes in the United States.

Using a less inferential definition of suicide, based on the single question, "Did the deceased initiate the events that led to his death?" Ovenstone (1973) concluded that the number of suicide verdicts in Scotland would be increased by one third over the more conventional definition. It is likely that a similar discrepancy exists in the United States. Independent investigators seldom conclude that a death was incorrectly ruled suicide. Nearly all of the error is in the other direction. Ovenstone's definition is rather generally acceptable to physicians but is considered overly broad by many nonmedical coroners involved in the determination of cause of death. Thus official figures almost certainly represent an underestimate of the prevalence of self-destruction. For statistical purposes, suicide is what the medical examiner or coroner ruled to be the cause of death.

### Etiology and Pathogenesis

Robins, Murphy, Wilkinson, Gassner, and Kayes (1959b) and Dorpat and Ripley

(1960) in the United States, Barraclough, Bunch, Nelson, and Sainsbury (1974) in England, Beskow (1979)· in Sweden, and Chynoweth, Tonge, and Armstrong (1980) in Australia have addressed the subject of suicide clinically. All have come to the conclusion that well over 90 per cent of suicides are suffering from a major psychiatric illness at the time of the act. Two psychiatric illnesses account for two thirds or more of the deaths. Affective disorder, depressed phase, accounts for roughly half and chronic alcoholism for about one fourth of the suicides. Smaller contributions are made by schizophrenia, organic brain syndromes and substance abuse. Table 33–1 lists the principal diagnostic findings in these studies. Note that roughly 90 per cent of the suicides were judged by the investigators to be psychiatrically ill and 98 per cent either medically or psychiatrically ill. The fabled "rational" suicide—carefully considered self-destruction undertaken for personal reasons unattended by psychiatric illness—is largely a myth. Although not altogether unheard of, it is among the least likely of the etiologies for this behavior. It must, therefore, be considered that psychiatric illness is a necessary, albeit not a sufficient, cause for suicide. Considering the troubles in the world and the uneven way in which they are distributed, it seems quite remarkable, not that so *many* commit suicide, but that so *few* do. This emphasizes the limited role that personal calamity plays in suicide.

The annual rate of suicide in the United States is currently about 12/100,000 live population. Ranking 11th in frequency among the causes of death, as compiled by the National Center for Health Statistics, suicide accounts for only about 1 per cent of all deaths. At the same time, it ranks second only to bronchogenic carcinoma in potential preventability.

### Affective Disorder

Affective disorder may be primary or it may be secondary to another, preexisting illness. As a primary condition, it is the most common diagnosis made in connection with suicide. As a clinical condition, the syndrome was recognized in 49 per cent of the cases summarized in Table 33–1. It is clearly the most significant precursor of suicide. By itself or in concert with another illness, it has a lethal potential. Suicides with a prior history of a depressive episode were invariably found to be in a depressive episode at the times of their deaths. Thus, depressives do not appear to be at risk of suicide when not depressed.

When a large number of patients diagnosed as suffering from depressive illness is followed over a period of time, a high proportion of those dying in the first few years are suicides. However, when the same group is followed for 10 or more years, suicide accounts for only about 15 per cent of all deaths in the group. This finding has been remarkably constant over a number of

**TABLE 33–1   Clinical Findings from Five Suicide Studies**

|  | Robins N = 134 (%) | Dorpat N = 114 (%) | Barraclough N = 100 (%) | Beskow N = 271 (%) | Chynoweth N = 135 (%) |
|---|---|---|---|---|---|
| Males | 103 (77) | 78 (68) | 53 (53) | 271 (100) | 85 (63) |
| Uncomplicated or primary depression | 54 (40) | 19 (18)* | 64 (64) | 33 (20) | 44 (33) |
| Clinical depression | 63 (47) | 32 (30)* | 80 (80) | 122 (45) | 70 (52) |
| Alcoholism | 31 (23) | 29 (27)* | 15 (15) | 83 (31) | 27 (20) |
| Schizophrenia | 3 (2) | 13 (12)* | 3 (3) | 16 (6) | 5 (3.7) |
| Organic brain syndromes | 5 (4) | 4 (4)* | † | 6 (2) | 6 (5) |
| Mentally ill | 126 (94) | 108 (95)* | 93 (93) | 228 (84) | 118 (87) |
| Mentally or physically ill | 131 (98) | 108 (100)* | 98 (98) | † | 133 (98.5) |
| No illness | 3 (2) | 0 (0) | 1 (1) | 9 (3) | 2 (1.5) |
| Year studied | 5/56–5/57 | 7/57–6/58 | 1966–68 | 1970–71 | 3/73–2/74 |
| Location | U.S. | U.S. | U.K. | Sweden | Australia |
| Year published | 1959, 1981 | 1960 | 1974 | 1979 | 1980 |

\* N = 108 used for these calculations (Dorpat and Ripley, 1960).
† No information.

studies in several countries, leading to the conclusion that the lifetime risk for suicide in affective disorder is about 15 per cent (Guze and Robins, 1970).

What distinguishes those who will die by suicide from those who will not? This question has occupied the attention of a number of investigators, but it remains substantially unanswered. A series of affectively disordered suicides was found to have been married in the same proportion as the general population of like age. They did not appear to have had an unusual amount of illness. In general, they had not experienced an unusual number of life stresses, such as bereavement, disruption of interpersonal relationships, legal or financial troubles, or interpersonal conflict. However, more than twice as many (17 per cent) were living alone, as would be expected in the U.S. adult population (6.9 per cent) (Murphy and Robins, 1967). Social isolation has been cited by others as prodromal to some suicides. Without making unwarranted assumptions, it was impossible to assign motivation for these suicides beyond the misery of the depression.

### Alcoholism

A primary diagnosis of alcoholism was made in about one fourth of the suicides studied. Most of these were men. There are more alcoholic men than women. But in addition, alcoholic men may be more inclined to suicide. In Beskow's (1979) series of Swedish men, 56 per cent of those from the urban area were diagnosed as suffering from habitual or addictive alcoholism.

The duration of alcoholism in our cases (Robins et al., 1959b) was quite long (mean, 20 years). In contrast to the relatively uneventful lives of the affectively disordered suicides, those of the alcoholics were fraught with strife. Half of them had experienced disruption of a close personal relationship within the year preceding the suicide. More strikingly, one third of the group had experienced this loss within 6 weeks or less of their deaths. Most commonly the event was dissolution of a marriage through divorce or acrimonious separation. Other major disruptions included the breakup of nonmarital erotic relationships, estrangement from family, and, occasionally, loss of someone close through death (Murphy and Robins, 1967). There are slightly more than

8 6-week periods in a year, and none but the proximate period contained a disproportionate number of interpersonal disruptions. The temporal distribution of loss events was significantly different from chance ($p < .01$). Nevertheless, it was an unanticipated finding.

To test it, we pursued the same kind of investigation on a further series of 50 alcoholic suicides (Murphy, Armstrong, Hermele, Fischer, Clendenin, 1979). Again, half were found to have experienced a major interpersonal disruption within a year and 26 per cent had experienced this disruption within 6 weeks or less of their suicide. The difference was again significant statistically ($p < .01$). The 26 per cent figure is not significantly different from the earlier 32 per cent. In the absence of contrary findings, it appears likely that disrupted interpersonal relationships constitute an important precipitant for suicide in alcoholics.

Not surprisingly, the alcoholics, as a group, had experienced a considerable number of other crises in the year preceding their deaths. Economic, financial, legal, occupational, and health problems were substantially represented. None was found with the striking frequency of disrupted interpersonal relationships. In an individual case, any one of these factors might appear to trigger the decision of an alcoholic to destroy himself. In the general population, such events usually do not lead to suicide.

It might be expected that depression would regularly accompany alcoholism that eventuates in suicide. However, one fourth of the alcoholics studied did not exhibit a depressive syndrome. The lifetime risk of suicide in alcoholism appears to be about the same as that in the affective disorders, around 15 per cent (Pitts and Winokur, 1966).

### Other Clinical Conditions

Schizophrenia was diagnosed in from 2 per cent to 12 per cent of cases in the five studies cited. The prevalence of schizophrenia is about one tenth that of affective disorders in the general population. Thus schizophrenic suicides are not so often encountered in a consecutive series from the general population. In a *clinical* population, however, whether from a private practice or from a psychiatric hospital, the proportion of schizophrenic suicides is substantial (Morrison, 1982). Owing to the small numbers of such events in any investigator's jurisdiction, the features of schizophrenia that might predict suicide are difficult to determine. As with other psychiatric conditions, the antecedents may be quite varied. A previous suicide attempt, the addition of a depressive syndrome to the schizophrenic state, and the experience of self-destructive command hallucinations are indicators of increased suicidal risk. The lifetime risk of suicide in patients with this diagnosis is, perhaps, around 10 per cent (Bleuler, 1978).

Organic brain syndromes contribute about as often to suicide as does schizophrenia in the general population (Table 33–1). The overall risk they constitute has not been studied. Acute delirium, as well as chronic dementia, is found. An acutely delirious patient may leap from a window to avoid hallucinated terrors. Some patients become severely depressed after a stroke and may then commit suicide. Sometimes the suicidal act can be seen to have been planned; at other times, it appears to have been impulsive.

Among clinical conditions seldom associated with suicide are uncomplicated Briquet's syndrome (hysteria) and antisocial personality. Both contribute significantly to suicide attempts (see later). If complicated by drug or alcohol abuse, some risk may exist. Panic disorder, anxiety state, agoraphobia, and obsessive-compulsive disorder have not been reported in any of the community studies of suicide. However, suicides have been reported among both inpatients and outpatients clinically identified as suffering from anxiety neurosis (Farberow and McEvoy, 1966; Wheeler, White, Reed, Cohen, 1950). A complicating depression would increase the risk.

Among more than 750 suicides clinically studied, no instance of mania has been reported. In theory, it could occur, whether through ill-advised drug experimentation or in response to a grandiose delusion. However, it must be uncommon, indeed. A rapid switch to depression is possible, of course. Then the considerations already described apply.

Personality disorders have been given as primary diagnoses in a proportion of cases in two studies (Dorpat and Ripley, 1960; Beskow, 1979). The lack of stable diagnostic criteria or a defined natural history for these supposed disorders renders the findings questionable. Similar diagnoses are found among suicide attempters. Just what they represent and how they should be handled is conjectural. Suicide is uncommon in the absence of clinical illness. In any event, persons who are not ill are unlikely to be under medical care. Thus they are not part of the clinical problem.

Terminal medical illness (cancer) accounted for 4 per cent of suicides in one series (Robins et al., 1959b; Robins, 1981). In light of the unpleasant nature of terminal cancer, as well as its prevalence, this seems like a rather small proportion. The finding attests to the fact that suicide is not everyone's cup of hemlock. At the same time, it must be borne in mind that patients dying of cancer are almost always under a physicians' care. Their deaths do not automatically become a matter for the medical examiner. The attending physician may exercise both judgment and bias in completing the death certificate. Certainly some suicides among the terminally ill are concealed in this way. The magnitude of that concealment will probably never be known.

### Family History

Psychiatric illness is virtually always an antecedent of suicide. At the same time, such illness is not a sufficient cause. The majority of sufferers from even the major contributors to suicide—affective disorders and alcoholism—do not take their lives. Seemingly, some sort of predisposition or releaser of this behavior must be present as well. One such factor is a family history of suicide or attempted suicide. The data are largely anecdotal. The Hemingway family pedigree is a case in point. Ernest Hemingway's father was a suicide many years before the author took his life. More recently, Ernest's brother, Liecester, did the same. Hemingway not only suffered from affective disorder, but he was also clinically depressed at the time he killed himself. Clinical details are lacking for his father and brother, but the suspicion of a family pedigree of affective disorder is strong. Similar pedigrees are known for other families. A remarkable example has kindly been supplied by Dr. Alex Pokorny (Fig. 33–1, personal communication).

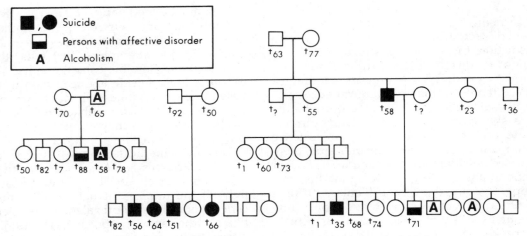

**FIGURE 33–1.** Pedigree of a family with a high incidence of suicide.

## Editor's Comment

*A recent report by Egeland and Sussex from the Amish shows that even in a society where there is no alcohol and drug abuse, no unemployment, no poverty, good social supports, veneration of the elderly, and religious sanctions against suicide, suicide occurs and clusters in pedigrees with unipolar and bipolar affective disorder (Egeland JA, Sussex JN: Suicide and Family Loading for Affective Disorders. JAMA, 254:915–918, 1985).*

A finding from the large Danish adoption study by Schulsinger, Kety, Rosenthal, and Wender (1979) is pertinent. Among 57 adoptee probands who committed suicide, 11 came from natural families containing 12 other suicides. In a matched control sample of equal size, there were two suicides, both in one family. The difference has a probability of 0.06 by Fisher's exact test. Because the psychiatric illnesses that contribute most to suicide are known to be familial, it is of interest that concordance for psychiatric diagnosis between probands and families was small. There were no suicides among adoptive parents. These findings suggest not simply a familial, but possibly a genetic predisposition to suicide, since the history of the biologic families was officially shielded from the probands. Family tradition appears to be ruled out in these cases.

Haberlandt (1967) reviewed the world literature on suicide among twins. Among 51 sets of monozygotic twin pairs with a suicide in one, he found nine concordant for self-destruction. There was no concordant

pair among 98 dizygotic twin pairs. There is a likelihood of bias in the collection of published cases. Those cases confirming a hypothesis are more likely to be published. Thus, although the direction of the trend is likely to be correct, its magnitude is uncertain. Nevertheless, these two studies give some credence to the idea of a small genetic contribution to suicide.

## Method

Firearms currently rank first as a cause of suicidal death in both males and females (Table 33–2). Women employ poisoning somewhat less often than gunshot. Fewer than 10 per cent of men die by overdose. Hanging, strangulation, and suffocation to-

**TABLE 33–2  Proportion of Suicides by Method and Sex, 1980**

|  | Males (%) | Females (%) | Total (%) |
|---|---|---|---|
| Firearms and explosives | 63.6 | 36.0 | 56.4 |
| Poisoning | 6.9 | 29.7 | 12.8 |
| Hanging, strangulation, suffocation | 13.7 | 10.6 | 12.9 |
| Motor vehicle $CO_2$ poisoning | 6.6 | 9.5 | 7.4 |
| Jumping from high places | 2.7 | 4.5 | 3.2 |
| Submersion, drowning | 1.5 | 4.0 | 2.1 |
| Cutting and piercing | 1.5 | 1.5 | 1.5 |
| Other and unspecified | 1.6 | 2.5 | 1.8 |

Source: Statistical Resources Branch, Division of Vital Statistics, National Center for Health Statistics, published and unpublished data for 1980.

gether rank second for men and third for women. (Nearly all of this category is contributed by hanging.) Smaller proportions of both sexes use motor vehicle carbon monoxide asphyxia, jumping from a high place, submersion or drowning, or cutting and piercing. Asphyxiation by domestic gas has been an infrequently used method for many years in the United States. Among persons of both sexes, aged 15 to 19 years, firearms are the most popular method. Sixty-five per cent of male and 56 per cent of female adolescents chose this route in 1980. Determinants of the choice of method are complex and include physical availability, familiarity, psychological acceptability, suggestion or contagion, symbolic, and perhaps other factors.

Poisonings are usually with psychotropic or hypnotic medications. Only seldom nowadays are classic poisons, such as household disinfectants, caustics, or pesticides, used. Agents used in self-poisoning deaths are not detailed in the vital statistics system. Poison control reporting (National Institute on Drug Abuse, 1983) is the only source for this information, and its purposes are different. The data come from 816 hospital emergency departments and 84 medical examiner facilities. A distinction between suicidal and accidental deaths is not made. The emphasis is on identification of specific substances (amitriptyline, for example), rather than on classes of substances (such as antidepressants).

Drug "mentions" (present in unspecified amount) in these reports of deaths have the same status as primary agents, further blurring the picture. Thus "alcohol and other" ingestants are mentioned most often (32 per cent in 1982). Heroin and morphine are listed second, codeine third, and amitriptyline fourth. Such specificity for a single antidepressant ensures that the incidence of deaths from all antidepressants will remain unknown. The fact that amitriptyline ranked sixth among mentions in 1972 and fourth in 1982 only suggests that fatal antidepressant overdoses are increasing. Overdose deaths are not. A more striking trend is seen for secobarbital, which ranked fifth in death mentions in 1977 and eleventh in 1982. It is clear from both this and other evidence that barbiturate overdose deaths are on the wane as the much safer benzodiazepines take over the hypnotic market. How-

ever, all of the figures on modes of suicide are provisional. As many deaths from drug overdose are ruled accidental in a year as are ruled suicide *from all causes* in the United States. There is good reason to be skeptical of the accuracy of the overdose figures.

Hanging, strangulation, and suffocation are available to all, as are jumping from high places, submersion or drowning, and cutting or piercing. The means are readily at hand if there is matching motivation. Unlike the cartoon version, the hanging or strangulation victim typically secures some sort of a loop around the neck and then around a stationary object. He or she then simply relaxes bodily support and dies within minutes of interrupted blood flow to the brain. The means are as simple as a piece of rope, a belt, or even a wire coathanger. There is clearly a significant degree of single-mindedness in this effort.

The use of multiple methods is not uncommon. Ingestion of multiple drugs simultaneously is the most common. Significant alcohol consumption attends 30 per cent to 40 per cent of cases. In addition, some suicides are known to have ingested an overdose of medication before asphyxiation, hanging, drowning, leaping, cutting, or gunshot. All attest to a determination "to do a good job."

Motor vehicle fatalities are seldom investigated as possible suicides. Pokorny, Smith, and Finch (1972) systematically investigated 28 consecutive auto crash fatalities of drivers. In addition to physical autopsy, they performed a "psychological autopsy" (Litman, Curphey, Shneidman, Farberow, Tabachnick, 1963) and an "automobile autopsy." Based on their findings, they concluded that four (14 per cent) of the 28 were suicides. Communication of suicidal intent had been identified in each of these cases. In a larger study, Schmidt, Perlin, Townes, Fisher, and Shaffer (1972) identified only three suicides among 111 single-vehicle fatalities, a rate of 2.7 per cent. The truth probably lies toward the lower end of the range. With about 55,000 motor vehicle fatalities annually in the United States, this would represent around 1000 to 2000 vehicular suicides in a year. It is unlikely that medical examiners and coroners will soon change their investigational procedures to search more diligently for suicides among vehicular fatalities.

## Epidemiology: Demographics

In the United States, men are more than three times as likely as women to take their lives. The age structure of the suicide rate curves differs both between the sexes and between races (see Fig. 33-3). That for white males rises steeply between ages 15 and 24, declines slightly, and then resumes an upward trend throughout the remainder of the life span. A similar early rise in the rate for black males extends to age 34 and then declines and remains fairly flat. White females show a much lower peak around ages 50 to 54 and then a gradual, steady decline. The low suicide rate for black females peaks in the 40- to 44-year age bracket.

The single, the widowed, and the divorced all have higher suicide rates than the married. Socioeconomic status does not appear to play a major role. Suicide rates by occupational group do not differ as much as is commonly believed. A widely quoted publication (Blachly, Osterud, Josslin, 1963) reported high rates for physicians, dentists, and attorneys compared with all males over age 19. The population base was that of a single Western state and the number of cases was small. More recent nationwide studies of physicians' deaths have substantially revised the conclusion for this profession. Among male physicians, the age-specific rates are mildly (1.15 times expected) but significantly greater than those for the age-specific general male population (Steppacher and Mausner, 1974). This rate has not changed in 30 years. Surprisingly, women physicians exhibit a suicide rate slightly higher than that of male physicians, and more than three times that of women in general! (Steppacher and Mausner, 1974; Pitts, Schuller, Rich, 1979). Such an elevated rate is not unique to women physicians.

Li (1969) reported that the age-adjusted suicide rate among female members of the American Chemical Society was five times that of the general U.S. population of white females in 1959 and nearly three times that of male chemists. Mausner and Steppacher (1973) found that almost three times as many female psychologists committed suicide as expected between 1960 and 1969. The rate for male psychologists was slightly less than expected. For female physicians, Pitts et al. (1979) postulate an excess of affective disorders as responsible for their findings.

Whatever the actual causes, it seems clear that women in the professions carry a risk of suicide equal to that of their male counterparts. Pitts et al. (1979, p. 1608) report that among female psychiatrists, the suicide rate is twice that of male physicians.

Suicide rates differ rather widely by state and somewhat less by region of the country (Table 33-3). As of 1980, the Mountain states had the highest rate (16.2 per 100,000 population), with Nevada highest at 22.9. The Pacific states (except Hawaii) had the next highest rate, 14.3 per 100,000 population. The Middle Atlantic and New England states reported suicide rates below the median, 9.6 and 9.5, respectively. Except for California, the states with the highest suicide rates are not among the most populous. The distribution of these rates has varied little over the past 20 years. In 1960 (Dublin, 1963, pp. 218–219), the Pacific states led the Mountain states. At that time, the South Central states had slightly lower rates than the New England and Middle Atlantic states. Degree of urbanization bears little relationship to suicide rate (Statistical Resources Branch, Division of Vital Statistics, unpublished data, 1980).

Just as suicide rates differ between states and regions of the United States, they differ between countries. Finland has, for a great many years, had one of the highest suicide rates among developed countries, followed by Denmark and Sweden. Norway has consistently had a much lower rate than the other Scandinavian countries. At present, Denmark's (1981) suicide rate, at 30.0, is the highest reported (United Nations, 1984). Finland (24.7) and Sweden (19.4) still have high rates, and Norway's (12.8) is higher than previously but still low among the Scandinavian countries.

Differing ascertainment practices have not provided a satisfactory explanation of the differing rates. The likelihood that the differences are real and related to cultural factors was emphasized by Sainsbury and Barraclough (1968). They compared the rank ordered 1959 suicide rates of emigrants to the United States from 11 countries with the rank ordered national rates for those countries in the same year and found a product moment correlation of 0.87, significant at the .001 level. Scotland's suicide rate has trailed that of the United Kingdom for 70 years. Efforts to explain this difference (Barraclough,

TABLE 33–3   Suicide Rates by Geographic Region and State, 1980

| Region | Suicide Rate per 100,000 Population | Region | Suicide Rate per 100,000 Population |
|---|---|---|---|
| Mountain States | 16.2 | East South Central | 11.6 |
| Arizona | 16.9 | Alabama | 11.2 |
| Colorado | 16.3 | Kentucky | 12.8 |
| Idaho | 13.1 | Mississippi | 9.2 |
| Montana | 14.5 | Tennessee | 12.2 |
| Nevada | 22.9 | West North Central | 11.2 |
| New Mexico | 17.4 | Iowa | 11.0 |
| Utah | 13.2 | Kansas | 10.9 |
| Wyoming | 16.0 | Minnesota | 10.8 |
| Pacific States | 14.3 | Missouri | 11.9 |
| Alaska | 16.9 | Nebraska | 10.1 |
| California | 14.5 | North Dakota | 11.0 |
| Hawaii | 11.4 | South Dakota | 12.7 |
| Oregon | 14.6 | East North Central | 10.9 |
| Washington | 13.3 | Illinois | 9.3 |
| South Atlantic | 12.7 | Indiana | 10.4 |
| Delaware | 11.9 | Michigan | 11.5 |
| District of Columbia | 9.9 | Ohio | 11.9 |
| Florida | 15.4 | Wisconsin | 11.7 |
| Georgia | 12.6 | Middle Atlantic | 9.6 |
| Maryland | 10.8 | New Jersey | 7.4 |
| North Carolina | 11.2 | New York | 9.5 |
| South Carolina | 9.5 | Pennsylvania | 11.1 |
| Virginia | 13.4 | New England | 9.5 |
| West Virginia | 12.5 | Connecticut | 8.9 |
| West South Central | 12.3 | Maine | 12.5 |
| Arkansas | 11.6 | Massachusetts | 8.2 |
| Louisiana | 12.1 | New Hampshire | 11.0 |
| Oklahoma | 13.1 | Rhode Island | 11.2 |
| Texas | 12.3 | Vermont | 14.7 |

Source: Statistical Resources Branch, Division of Vital Statistics, National Center for Health Statistics. Published and unpublished data for 1980.

1972) have become moot, since the rate for Scotland is now inexplicably higher than that of the United Kingdom (Murphy, 1983). Despite such minor shifts, the correlation of rank ordering still holds.

In the past, the suicide rate for white males rose progressively with age (Fig. 33–2). In the past 30 years, the rate for the age-group 15 to 19 years has more than tripled. Among 20- to 24-year-olds it has more than doubled. At the same time, the rate for older white males has shown a steady decline. The age–rate structure for nonwhite males has shown a similar change at ages up to 44 (Fig. 33–3). Changes have been less striking among young women (Murphy and Wetzel, 1980). This sharp rise in suicide rates of the young was first reported from Alberta province of Canada over the same time period (Solomon and Hellon, 1980). A partial effect of the same sort has been reported from

Australia as well (Goldney and Katsikitis, 1983).

Alberta, at the beginning of the period, had a primarily agrarian economy with one of the lowest per capita incomes in Canada. Discovery of petroleum deposits brought an influx of migrant workers and the development of a large petrochemical industry. Per capita income became one of the highest in Canada. According to Durkheim's (1951) theory, these major socioeconomic changes could well account for the increase in suicides in Canada. However, no such large-scale changes are identifiable for the United States. No satisfactory explanation for the phenomenon has been forthcoming. At present, it must be regarded as a secular trend.

The term secular trend has been applied to variations in suicide rates over time. Secular in this sense derives from the Latin sae-

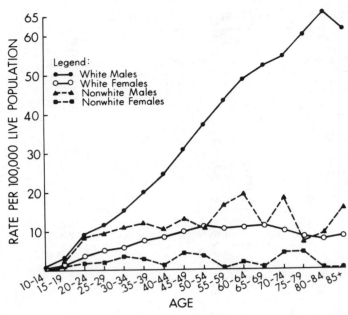

**FIGURE 33-2.** Suicide rates in U.S.A. by age, sex and color, 1950. Source: Mortality Statistics Branch, National Center for Health Statistics. Vital Statistics of the United States, (published and unpublished data).

*cularum,* generation, an age, and refers to things occurring once in a long while. No regular periodicity is implied. If an etiology is identified, the phenomenon would likely be classified more specifically. The almost universal decline of suicides during wartime in combatant countries is not regarded as a secular trend.

## Clinical Picture

At this time, suicides cannot be identified accurately in advance of the act. For this rea-son, they have had to be studied retrospectively. By conducting systematic interviews with family members, attending physicians, and others, it is possible to reconstruct in considerable detail the personality, behaviors, health history, social history, vocational and economic functioning, recent life events, and psychiatric diagnosis of suicides. Informants reasonably close to the victim are able to report the presence of psychiatric symptoms specifically inquired about. These in turn permit confident psychiatric diagnosis.

Studies of this type from three continents

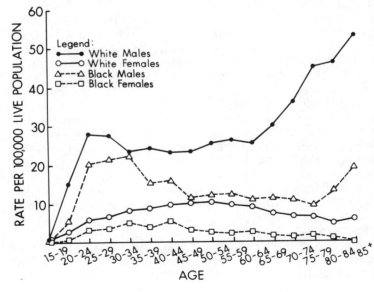

**FIGURE 33-3.** Suicide rates in U.S.A. by age, sex and color, 1980. Source: Mortality Statistics Branch, National Center for Health Statistics. Vital Statistics of the United States (published and unpublished data).

(Robins et al., 1959a, b; Dorpat and Ripley, 1960; Barraclough et al., 1974; Beskow, 1979; Chynoweth et al., 1980) show a remarkable consistency in a number of features, despite differences in emphasis (Table 33–1). A finding on which all studies agree is the predominance of clinical depression as the primary diagnosis. The proportion of victims so diagnosed has ranged from 30 per cent (Dorpat and Ripley, 1960) to 80 per cent (Barraclough, 1974). Usually the depression is well established, having lasted for several months. Occasionally it may have lasted only days to weeks. Sometimes the duration is not certain.

Few suicides have been found lacking in psychiatric symptoms. Most have been diagnosable. When a psychiatric diagnosis has not been made, it usually has been because of unavailability of informants who knew the victim well, not because there was a clear lack of symptoms. A small proportion of suicides in almost any series has been socially isolated and almost friendless, hence the paucity of information in some cases. On the other hand, social isolation of that degree is not a particularly common finding among suicides.

Beskow (1979) points out that "suicide does not just happen. It has a history," which he terms a suicidal process. The contents of the process include communication of suicidal thoughts (82 per cent), suicide attempts (27 per cent), and psychiatric hospitalization (43 per cent). Despite the clinical orientation of this monograph, the data presented do not distinguish a suicidal process from a disease process, such as affective disorder or alcoholism, that usually does not eventuate in suicide. A study of suicides alone cannot clarify the distinction.

Perhaps an example of the suicidal process is that of suicide in alcoholism (Murphy and Robins, 1967; Murphy et al., 1979). The alcoholic suicide has progressively narrowed his social field to the point where he has only one close personal relationship. It is usually a hostile dependent one. When the other person has taken all of the abuse she or he is willing to take, she or he terminates the relationship abruptly. The alcoholic tries to reestablish the relationship but is rebuffed. Contemplating life without the last remaining support, he concludes that life would not be worth living and shortly ends it. There is often an expression of shame or failure at having lost the relationship.

Further evidence of a process or progression to suicide is the fact that two thirds (Robins et al., 1959a) to four fifths (Beskow, 1979) of suicides have communicated, if not their suicidal intent, at least their thoughts of death to others. They characteristically do so to more than one person, on more than one occasion, and in more than one way. The most common means reported is the direct statement of intent. "I'm going to kill myself," or "I'm going to jump in the river." Around 40 per cent of suicides are reported to have given such clear notice (Robins et al., 1959a; Dorpat and Ripley, 1960).

Other ways of communicating intent include assertions of a desire to die, of belief that one's self or one's family would be better off for the death, reference to methods of suicide and dire predictions. Examples of the last category are such statements as, "You'll find a dead man in the street" and "You'll read my death notice in the paper on Thursday." A history of suicide attempts was found in one third of cases. The suicide attempt might have been recent or remote and belonging to an earlier episode. In almost three fourths of cases, the suicidal ideas had been expressed for less than a year and in two fifths, for less than 3 months. Where the communication was of long standing, there had been an increase in such behavior in the past year (Robins et al., 1959a).

The response of others to these communications is interesting. Even after the suicide, one fourth of the respondents expressed the view that at times they thought the communication was not genuine. The great majority were distressed and upset by it. After the initial shock and fear, respondents often came to discount the significance of the communication. "He had never talked or acted this way before. It just wasn't him. He couldn't do something like that" (Robins et al., 1959a). Apparently the anxiety generated by the communication turns to denial of its significance.

One sometimes hears the statement that there is little to fear from suicide in patients with a severely retarded depression. "They just can't get up the energy." The statement betrays a lack of knowledge. Such patients can and do commit suicide. They do not form a large part of the suicide statistics—

first, because the condition is not at all common and, second, because retarded depression is highly recognizable and likely to lead to hospitalization and vigorous treatment. Electroconvulsive therapy (ECT) is the treatment of choice.

A more frequently heard statement is that the risk of suicide is greatest when the depression starts to lift. Clinical study has not confirmed this. Persons in all stages of depression take their own lives. What is undeniably true is that the period after psychiatric hospital discharge is risky. Temoche, Pugh, and MacMahon (1964) showed that the risk of suicide in the first 6 months after discharge from Massachusetts mental institutions was 34 times that of the general population. It was nine times greater than expected in the second 6 months. The finding has been confirmed by Pokorny (1964) for a Houston Veterans' Administration hospital population and by Ettlinger (1975) in Stockholm.

Those patients who took their lives may have been insufficiently improved clinically. It is more likely, however, that they had experienced a relapse. There is often a striking decrease in supportive contact with a physician in the transition from inpatient to outpatient status. Inpatients are usually seen daily or almost daily by their psychiatrist. When discharged, they are often given a return appointment in a month to 6 weeks. This may be interpreted by the patient as abandonment. With support and surveillance sharply reduced, despair may return unnoticed. Some suicides might be prevented by closer followup.

Data from a variety of studies support the view expressed by Beskow that "suicide does not just happen." That, at a minimum, two thirds of suicides have communicated their thoughts and intentions adds to other evidence that self-destruction is usually, if not always, planned. A combination of factors sets the stage for this act, none of which is either necessary or sufficient. These include but are not limited to a family history of suicide, interpersonal conflicts, disappointments, physical illness, social or physical isolation, feelings of hopelessness, and psychiatric illness. Of these, psychiatric illness comes closest to being necessary. But the lifetime risk of suicide is hardly above 15 per cent, even in depressive disorder, alcoholism, and schizophrenia. The assessment of suicidal risk remains an art.

## Differential Diagnosis

Suicide is an infrequent event in anyone's clinical practice, so the danger is easily forgotten. Because suicide is potentially preventable, continued alertness to the danger signals is vital. Depression is the most common antecedent. It does not have to be severe for suicide to result. In addition to primary depression, that which complicates another disorder, such as alcoholism, schizophrenia, or an organic brain syndrome, can increase risk. The possibility of suicide must be kept ever in mind.

Interviews with physicians who had lost a patient to suicide showed that they readily recognized depressed mood. In these cases, however, they had often failed to identify the syndrome of depression (Murphy, 1975). As a consequence, they failed to treat it. Some recognized the syndrome but viewed it as a psychosocial phenomenon rather than as an illness. Having an explanation in terms of the patient's life situation, they did not treat. It is well to keep in mind Fawcett's (1972) pithy aphorism: "The presence of a 'reason' for depression does not constitute a reason for ignoring its presence."

When depression complicates another illness, whether psychiatric or medical, attention may be so focused on the other illness that the depression goes unnoticed. This is particularly true when depression develops insidiously. Treatment may then be directed at symptoms (such as insomnia or anxiety), rather than at the depression. It is surprisingly difficult to change the focus. But if a patient becomes irritable or noncompliant or fails to improve as expected, it is time to step back and review the case.

The alcoholic who has become progressively more isolated and dependent on a single relationship for support is at great risk when that support is withdrawn. But alcoholics are more reactive to their environment than are depressives in many ways. Those who encounter crises in health, employment, or financial security are also at increased risk. The risk is highest both in anticipation of and shortly after such events. It is in the nature of alcoholism that these crises will occur. If the alcoholic can be supported psychologically for about 2 months, an adjustment is usually made and the danger of self-destruction diminishes.

Despite the prevalence of communication

of suicidal thoughts, few attending physicians seem to have been aware of it. Both in the original study (Robins et al., 1959a) and in a subsequent study of the physician's role in suicide (Murphy, 1975), only about one in six physicians had such knowledge. Because there is some evidence that suicidal patients *will* tell a physician, if asked (DeLong and Robins, 1961), it seems likely that such patients often were not asked. In a few cases, patients denied to a physician the intention they carried out. Although it may never be known what proportion of the general population ever expresses suicidal thoughts, the findings make clear that the old wives' tale "those who talk about it won't do it" is just that. *Those who talk about it may indeed do it.* It is important to ask each depressed patient about suicidal thoughts. The fear of implanting an idea that may be acted on is unjustified. Most depressed or alcoholic patients have already thought of it. Many are relieved to be asked. It permits a discussion that the patient feared was taboo. It allows the physician a clearer view of the depth of the patient's despair. It is also important to ask family members whether there has been talk of suicide.

Vague suicidal thoughts may change rapidly to a formulated plan. It is important, then, to reassess the patient's state of mind at each contact. This is much easier to do than one might think. The inquiry might go something like this: "You told me last week that you had thoughts of suicide but not about actually doing it. Has there been any change in your thinking on that subject?" The patient who has a fully formulated plan and the means available to carry it out requires close surveillance. Admission to the closed ward of a psychiatric unit is the safest measure.

Fawcett, Leff, and Bunney (1969) have suggested that the patient who breaks off therapy on grounds that the psychiatrist isn't helping or can't help is at particularly high risk; "help negation" they called it. The time surrounding transfer of a potentially suicidal patient from one therapist to another was found to be dangerous as well. Whatever support can be mustered at these times, including hospitalization, is indicated.

About one third of suicides have made a suicide attempt. Such an act, recent or remote, in the patient with one of the high-risk diagnoses must be regarded as a warning of grave danger and treated accordingly. Hospitalization is easily accomplished immediately after the acute event. Both assessment and treatment can then be carried out.

The experienced clinician can easily recall instances in which any of the danger signals occurred but was not followed by suicide, even in the absence of intervention. This should be neither surprising nor reassuring. Most suicidal crises do not end in death. At the same time, a miscalculation is irretrievable. Overtreatment is not the mistake it might be with other conditions. Undertreatment is. Whether or not the depressed or alcoholic patient is as suicidal as he or she appears, there is considerable suffering from the illness. The likelihood of a favorable response to treatment is good.

## Treatment

At present, there is no assured way of directly changing suicidal intent. A prevented suicide is statistically a non-event. It is thus virtually impossible to prove that prevention has occurred (Murphy, 1984). Because suicide is principally a symptom of certain psychiatric illnesses, the logical approach is to treat the underlying illness. All available information indicates that depressives, at any rate, are not at risk for suicide when not depressed. For the suicidally depressed, hospitalization and ECT are recommended. For the alcoholic, residential treatment programs are increasingly effective. For the depressed schizophrenic, antidepressant medication may be added to the neuroleptic in use. Close supervision of medication is necessary, however, as the tricyclics are quite toxic in overdose. An antidepressant may help the depressed stroke victim. The delirious patient requires uninterrupted surveillance to prevent self-injury. At the same time, the source of the delirium must be found and remedied, if possible. Overmedication is a common cause. A concerned, supportive relationship with the patient, as well as with the family, is always of benefit.

It is not possible in every case to prevent suicide. A few suicides give no warning. Some individuals hide not only the depth of their despair, but also their suicidal thoughts and plans from even those closest to them. This has been called the "executive suicide" because of the decisive and self-contained way in which it is accomplished. Only in retrospect are the symptoms of depression recognized. Physicians and other professionals who kill themselves often fit this description. Much more commonly, however, suicides communicate both their distress and their suicidal thoughts to others. This is true not only of depressives, but of alcoholics as well. Some patients are chronically suicidal despite all efforts. When failure occurs, it should be in spite of the appropriate treatment rather than on account of its absence.

## ATTEMPTED SUICIDE

### Definition

Attempted suicide is any *act*, including overdose, cutting, or otherwise producing tissue injury, that is so labeled by the person doing it or by those involved in that person's care. It does not include threats, however dangerous, such as standing on a ledge of a high building. There is no utility, other than a pejorative one, in characterizing one act as a "gesture" and another as "genuine." They share the same background, purpose, and prognosis.

Journal articles and books continue to be published with titles identifying the subject matter as suicide but in which the population studied and reported on was all still living. The persistent confusion of suicide attempt with suicide in this literature is both frustrating and misleading. Incautious statements about suicide that have only, or principally, to do with suicide attempters are one result. There is more reason than semantics to distinguish between these two phenomena. Suicides are more than three times as likely to involve men as women. They are about equally frequent before and after age 40. They are most commonly associated with one of two major psychiatric illnesses. Suicides usually plan the act. They choose rapidly effective means that they use in isolation or with provisions made to forestall interruption. The purpose is to die. In contrast, suicide attempters are predominantly women (2:1). They are mostly under age 35 and are less likely to be suffering from one of the psychiatric illnesses commonly associated with suicide. They often act impulsively. They typically use ineffective or slowly effective means and include provisions for rescue: they carry out the act in the presence of others or notify others of what they are about to do or have just done. The purpose is to survive. The principal feature that the two behaviors have in common is the terminology. Attempted suicide is not failed suicide.

### Etiology and Pathogenesis

Maris (1981), in an extensive study of 266 suicides controlled by 64 suicide attempters and 71 natural deaths, explored the concept of "suicidal careers." He hoped to be able to characterize the life course of individuals dying by suicide and to produce a general theory of suicide. As it turned out, a number of historical and clinical variables he had expected to be strongly correlated with suicide were more strikingly associated with attempted suicide. These included early separation from a parent, early traumatic experiences, coming from a multiproblem family, heavy drinking, heavy drug use, "sexual deviation," negative interaction, and history of suicide attempt. These features were not altogether lacking among suicides. They were generally lowest among natural deaths. Characteristics most often associated with suicide were hardly surprises: older age, male sex, hopelessness, and view of death as escape from pain. The supposed pathogenetic features that Maris identified among suicides were more strongly characteristic of his only living group: suicide attempters. Few of this group will become suicides.

Who may attempt suicide? Diagnostically, there is an overlap with suicide. Around one fourth to one third of attempters are clinically depressed. About an equal proportion are alcoholics or abusers of other substances. Diagnoses that are uncommon among suicides, such as somatization disorder (Briquet's syndrome) and antisocial personality disorder, are seen with considerable frequency among suicide attempters. These and other personality disorders together may constitute upward of 40 per cent of a suicide attempt population (Murphy and Wetzel, 1982). In some studies, all of the attempters have been judged psychiatrically ill (Schmidt, O'Neal, Robins, 1954). In others, from 5 per cent (Ettlinger and Flordh, 1955; Murphy and Wetzel, 1982) to 20 per cent (Dahlgren, 1945) were thought not to be ill. Although the depressed patient who makes a suicide attempt may not, at the moment, be bent on self-destruction, the potential is there. To a somewhat lesser extent, the same may be said for the alcoholic.

Followup studies of attempters show that 1 per cent to 2 per cent will take their lives within 1 year of the index event and 1 per cent annually thereafter (Ettlinger, 1975, p. 100). The few followup studies that exceed 10 years suggest that the incidence may flatten off later—it does not go up endlessly. The lifetime risk of suicide among suicide attempters is perhaps a bit above 10 per cent. Such grave morbidity as there is in attempted suicide (social impairment, subsequent hospitalization, suicide) is generally attributable to the underlying psychiatric condition and not to the attempt itself.

There is a familial aspect to suicide attempt. In my series of 127 cases (Murphy and Wetzel, 1982), 34 per cent had a family history of suicide attempt and 20 per cent had a history of suicide in the family. Others have reported lower frequencies, but it is not always clear how diligently the information had been sought.

In addition to the troubled backgrounds described by Maris (1981), suicide attemp-

ters tend to have accumulated a number of problems. McCulloch (1972) described this phenomenon in a study of 511 attempters. Table 33–4 presents his findings. Proportions for the sexes have been combined for simplicity. The mean number of problems cited as major factors was 1.8 for women and 2.7 for men. It appears that more problems are required for a man to attempt suicide. Perhaps more reasons are needed to explain it to others. Patients with greater numbers of problems were more likely to have made a previous suicide attempt. They were more likely to attempt again within a year. Problems and concerns were present on several levels. Half were personal, some were interpersonal, some impersonal.

Responses to inquiry as to motivation tend to be highly idiosyncratic. They lend themselves poorly to tabulation. One strategy for constraining the free-form response is to offer a series of likely responses for endorsement. Using this method with 128 attempters, Bancroft, Skrimshire, and Simkin (1976) obtained the following frequencies: seeking help, 33 per cent; relief from a state of mind, 52 per cent; influence someone, 19 per cent; "wanting to die," 38 per cent; don't care if live or die, 34 per cent; none of these, 18 per cent. Responses overlap and often conflict. In an earlier study, Birtchnell and Alarcon (1971) reported that 46 per cent of 91 consecutive suicide attempters endorsed

**TABLE 33–4   Social Precipitants of Attempted Suicide**

| | Major Factor | | Present to Any Degree | |
|---|---|---|---|---|
| | No. | % | No. | % |
| Marital disharmony* | 131 | 60 | 159 | 73 |
| Financial problems | 172 | 34 | 253 | 50 |
| Kin disharmony | 142 | 28 | 247 | 48 |
| Drink | 144 | 28 | 197 | 39 |
| Unemployment | 112 | 22 | 144 | 28 |
| Housing difficulties | 82 | 16 | 128 | 25 |
| Crossed in love | 69 | 14 | 78 | 15 |
| Crime | 48 | 9 | 78 | 15 |
| Isolation | 48 | 9 | 71 | 14 |
| Work, fear of unemployment | 38 | 7 | 64 | 13 |
| Forced separation from spouse* | 16 | 7 | 21 | 10 |
| Bereavement | 29 | 6 | 49 | 10 |
| Sex problems | 27 | 5 | 49 | 10 |

Condensed from McCulloch JW: Social prognosis of an Edinburgh clientele, in Waldenström J, Larsson T, Ljungstedt N (eds): Suicide and Attempted Suicide. Stockholm, Nordiska Bokhandels, Förlag, 1972.
N = 511 (175 males, 336 females) except as noted.
* Married only: N = 217.

the statement that they had wanted to die at the time of the attempt. Thirty-seven per cent said that they had not, and 17 per cent were not sure. Bancroft et al. (1976) caution that the endorsement of "wanting to die" should not be taken at face value. Respondents often feel a need to save face—to make the act appear more socially acceptable. The same may be said for a number of other responses. Wanting to influence someone (19 per cent) is surely a gross underestimate.

When asked, attempters will cite more than one problem. Yet the purpose of the act is mostly the same. Behind the great majority of attempts lies a wish to make an impact on another person's awareness. Attempted suicide generally occurs in a social context. It is literally a cry for help. A specific recipient of the message is readily identifiable in most instances. Some change is sought, whether in the recipient's attitude or behavior or in the relationship. The distress is genuine, although the method of communication is unconventional. Often it follows a period of failure of more customary efforts at communication. The final straw that triggers the behavior may in itself have been trivial. To the uninformed observer, the act may appear petulant and capricious, when in fact it expresses desperation. For some, it reaches the stage of "don't care if live or die"; for a few, the genuine hope is to die.

McCulloch (1972) found the usual wish on the part of the attempters to be that another would change. Yet half of the *patients* changed their own behavior for the better in a 3-year followup. The majority of those who were better satisfied had themselves changed. Three fourths of those considered their situation improved ($p < .0001$). Only one fourth of patients whose behavior had not improved reported that their social state improved. One fourth of 266 patients who were not married reported that a key person's behavior had changed for the better. (Problems included infidelity, pathologic jealousy, drinking, gambling or getting into debt.) Three fourths of these reported their social state to have improved ($p < .01$). Interestingly, in those cases where the key person's behavior did not improve, 39 per cent of patients reported their social situation to have improved. It is not stated whether this occurred by the patient's change, termination of the relationship, or what.

Overall, at least half of the patients regarded their social situation as improved. Only 16 per cent to 17 per cent of patients repeated the suicide attempt within 1 year. (In a number of other studies, the repetition rate is nearer 25 per cent.) Men were half again as likely to repeat as women. Those most prone to do so "had been diagnosed as personality disorders, especially psychopaths, were dependent on alcohol or drugs, had poor work records and unstable living circumstances." Six per cent of men and 2 per cent of women completed suicide within the followup period. This 4 per cent toll of suicides in 3 years is consistent with the outcome for suicide attempters elsewhere.

There was a significant tendency ($p < .001$) for persons under age 35 to show more improvement in social state. In other studies, between 80 per cent and 90 per cent of attempts are by overdose. The proportion may have been even higher in McCulloch's study of a poison control center population. McCulloch found that the patient who cuts himself or who attempts to strangle or suffocate himself is likely to do badly in the months after leaving the hospital.

## Epidemiology

Attempted suicide is not a reportable act, so there are no national or local statistics. Sampling is likely to be strongly biased according to the catchment area chosen. Where most admissions are to a single facility, as in Edinburgh (Kreitman, 1977), it appears that the lower socioeconomic classes are overrepresented. Those with more means may circumvent the customary treatment program.

Attempted suicide is many times more frequent than suicide. Just how much more has been the subject of much opinion and a little research. Estimates range from 5 to 100 times as frequent. Parkin and Stengel (1965) conducted the most methodologically rigorous study in the city of Sheffield. They found attempted suicides to outnumber suicides by 9.7:1 over a 2-year period. A later careful study by Kreitman (1977, p. 160) in Edinburgh gave a ratio of about 7:1. Studies of comparable quality have not been reported from the United States.

Jacobziner (1965) compared suicides with attempts by poisoning in adolescents aged 12 to 20 years in New York City during 1960–

1961. He found a surprising ratio of about 100:1 for this restricted age-group. It may be this figure that has been cited by others without specification of the age-group examined, since there is no other documentation for it. The suicide rate among the young has more than doubled in the intervening time. Whether the incidence of suicide attempts has increased proportionately is unknown. For the population as a whole, there is no clear evidence for an attempt-suicide ratio greater than 10:1.

## Clinical Picture

A large minority of suicide attempters come from families in which suicide or attempted suicide has occurred. There is frequently a background of a broken home or social deprivation. Nearly all attempters suffer from chronic low self-esteem. Their interpersonal skills are poor. While desiring the company and support of others, they have not learned to develop and maintain such relationships. Those they do have tend to be formed with exploitative, insensitive individuals. The social class structure of the suicide attempt population is skewed toward the low end. Many of these individuals live unsatisfying, frustrated lives marred by their own ineptitude. A specific problem is often engrafted on a chronically frustrating life situation. Partly because of poor communication skills, partly because of a nonreciprocal relationship, problems seem insurmountable. The final straw may be quite small. Alcohol consumption is a frequent releaser of the act.

Attempters tend to use what is at hand. Although knives are even more ubiquitous than pills, 80 per cent to 90 per cent of suicide attempts are by overdose. Aspirin is found in nearly every medicine cabinet. It is favored by the youngest segment of the attempter population—adolescents. More often, hypnotics, sedatives, and pain-killers are swallowed. In the midst of an argument, the attempter may angrily or tearfully run to the medicine cabinet and start gulping pills. More often she (more than two thirds are women) sits brooding and then starts to swallow her medication, one or a few capsules at a time until she becomes sleepy or alarmed. She may do this in a place where others are sure to come soon. Otherwise, she will call someone and let it be known

what she has just done. The message may be direct or by means of slurred or incoherent speech. The rescue has been arranged.

About 10 per cent of suicide attempts are by cutting or piercing. Most of this is lateral laceration of the wrist. An older literature describes wrist cutters as attractive, intelligent young women who repeat the act endlessly. While such persons exist, two thirds as many wrist cutters are male as female. Proportional to the number of attempters of each sex, more males than females cut. Repetition is not particularly characteristic of them (Clendenin and Murphy, 1971; Weissman, 1975). There is a tendency for persons making more medically serious attempts to have a poorer prognosis, both psychiatrically and with respect to subsequent repetition. The patient who gives a self-oriented reason for the act (depressed, guilty, want to die) is a higher risk than the one whose behavior is in reaction to external circumstances.

## Editor's Comment

*There is also literature, somewhat controversial, suggesting that the symptom of hopelessess is correlated with an outcome of completed suicide in depressed psychiatric patients who have suicidal thoughts or a recent attempt (Dyer JAT, Kreitman N: Hopelessness, depression and suicidal intent in parasuicide. Br J Psychiatry 144:127–133, 1984; Beck AT, Steer RA, Kovacs M, et al.: Hopelessness and eventual suicide: A 10-year prospective study of patients hospitalized with suicidal ideation. Am J Psychiatry 142:5, 1985). Also, as Dr. Murphy has often stated, the closer the resemblance of the suicide attempter to completed suicide, the greater is the risk of the patient killing himself (Pallis DJ, Gibbons JS, Pierce DW: Estimating suicide risk among attempted suicides. II. Efficiency of predictive scales after the attempt. Br J Psychiatry 144:139–148, 1984).*

## Clinical Management

The majority of overdoses present little danger to life. The management of acute poisonings is best left to the clinical toxicologist. I recommend hospital admission for all attempters. Both the medical and the psychiatric seriousness of the act must be evaluated. Experts agree that the apparent triviality of the act is no guide to the overall risk.

A minor overdose may result from the unexpected interruption of a serious effort to end life. Minor lacerations of the wrist may be a trial run before a more determined effort. Without careful psychiatric assessment, the patient's potential for suicide must not be assumed. One third of suicides are preceded by a suicide attempt. Denial of suicidal intent cannot—indeed must not—be taken at face value. The patient may be seeking early release in order to complete an abortive attempt. Patients with depression, alcoholism, schizophrenia, or an organic brain syndrome are at increased risk. Treatment of the underlying psychiatric condition is central to suicide prevention.

In addition to clinical evaluation, the hospital admission provides an ideal opportunity to bring the patient and others concerned together for a frank discussion of the issues that led to the act. If each person in turn is allowed to voice his or her version of the issues, the stage is set for negotiation. The psychiatrist's role is to ensure that each person has an opportunity to express his or her views without interruption and to facilitate discussion. A resolution need not be reached. Opening the communication will usually suffice. Further psychotherapy may be offered if indicated. The great majority of attempters do not repeat the act.

The attention-seeking aspect of the attempt and the attempter should be reinforced only within clinically indicated limits. The patient should not be allowed to exploit the hospital admission for social purposes. To this end, I recommend no personal telephone or television, strict limitation of visiting privileges, and no off-unit privileges during a stay that is as short as feasible to accomplish the clinical goals. This restrictive program does not include aloofness on the part of the physician. Warmth, acceptance, and understanding are appropriate attitudes for the therapist to exhibit. Medical and nursing staff attitudes, particularly in the emergency and intensive care units, tend to be somewhat harsh and distant toward the suicide attempter. Because these people are involved in acute life-preserving activities, they tend to view the suicide attempter's voluntary endangering of his or her life as antithetical to their values. It is possible to soften this attitude by interpreting the personal distress that is the background for the behavior. Attempted suicide is a desperate act and necessitates understanding.

## REFERENCES

Bancroft JHG, Skrimshire AM, Simkin S: The reasons people give for taking overdoses. Br J Psychiatry 128:538–548, 1976.

Barraclough BM: Are the Scottish and English suicide rates really different? Br J Psychiatry 120:267–273, 1972.

Barraclough B, Bunch J, Nelson B, Sainsbury P: A hundred cases of suicide: Clinical aspects. Br J Psychiatry 125:355–373, 1974.

Beskow J: Suicide and mental disorder in Swedish men. Acta Psychiatr Scand [Suppl] 277:1–138, 1979.

Birtchnell J, Alarcon J: The motivation and emotional state of 91 cases of attempted suicide. Br J Med Psychol 44:45–52, 1971.

Blachly PH, Osterud HT, Josslin R: Suicide in professional groups. N Engl J Med 268:1278–1282, 1963.

Bleuler M: The Schizophrenic Disorders. New Haven, CT, Yale University Press, 1978.

Chynoweth R, Tonge JI, Armstrong J: Suicide in Brisbane—A retrospective psychosocial study. Aust NZ J Psychiatry 14:37–45, 1980.

Clendenin WW, Murphy GE: Wrist cutting. New epidemiological findings. Arch Gen Psychiatry 25:465–469, 1971.

Dahlgren KG: On suicide and attempted suicide: A psychiatrical and statistical investigation, Lund, A.B. PH Lindstedts Univ.-Bokhandel, 1945.

Delong WB, Robins E: The communication of suicidal intent prior to psychiatric hospitalization: A study of 87 patients. Am J Psychiatry 117:695–705, 1961.

Dorpat TL, Ripley HS: A study of suicide in the Seattle area. Compr Psychiatry 1:349–359, 1960.

Dublin LI: Suicide: A Sociological and Statistical Study. New York, Ronald Press, 1963.

Durkheim E: Suicide: A Study in Sociology. Glencoe, IL, The Free Press, 1951.

Ettlinger R: Evaluation of suicide prevention after attempted suicide. Acta Psychiatr Scand [Suppl 260], Munksgaard, 1975.

Ettlinger RW, Flordh P: Attempted suicide: Experience of five hundred cases at a general hospital. Acta Psychiatr Neurol Scand [Suppl] 103:1–45, 1955.

Farberow NL, McEvoy TL: Suicide among patients with diagnoses of anxiety reaction or depressive reaction in general medical and surgical hospitals. J Abnorm Psychol 71:287–299, 1966.

Fawcett J: Suicidal depression and physical illness. JAMA 219:1303–1306, 1972.

Fawcett J, Leff J, Bunney WE Jr: Suicide. Clues from interpersonal communication. Arch Gen Psychiatry 21:129–137, 1969.

Goldney RD, Katsikitis M: Cohort analysis of suicide rates in Australia. Arch Gen Psychiatry 40:71–74, 1983.

Guze SB, Robins E: Suicide and primary affective disorders. Br J Psychiatry 117:437–438, 1970.

Haberlandt WF: Aportación a la geneticadel suicidio. (Datos en gemelos y hallazgos familiares.) Folia Clinica Internacional 17:319–322, 1967.

Jacobziner H: Attempted suicides in adolescence. JAMA 191:7–11, 1965.

Kreitman N: Parasuicide. New York, John Wiley & Sons, 1977.

Li FP: Suicide among chemists. Arch Environ Health 19:518–520, 1969.

Litman RE, Curphey T, Shneidman ES, Farberow NL, Tabachnick N: Investigations of equivocal suicides. JAMA 184:924–929, 1963.

Maris RW: Pathways to Suicide. A Survey of Self-destructive Behaviors. Baltimore, Johns Hopkins University Press, 1981.

Mausner JS, Steppacher RC: Suicide in professionals: A study of male and female psychologists. Am J Epidemiol 98:436–445, 1973.

McCulloch JW: Social prognosis of an Edinburgh clientele, in Waldenström J, Larsson T, and Ljungstedt N (eds): Suicide and Attempted Suicide. Stockholm, Nordiska Bokhandels, Förlag, 1972.

Morrison JR: Suicide in a psychiatric practice population. J Clin Psychiatry 43:348–352, 1982.

Murphy GE: Clinical identification of suicidal risk. Arch Gen Psychiatry 27:356–359, 1972.

Murphy GE: The physician's responsibility for suicide. II. Errors of omission. Ann Intern Med 82:305–309, 1975.

Murphy GE: Problems in studying suicide. Psychiatr Dev 4:339–350, 1983.

Murphy GE: The prediction of suicide: Why is it so difficult? Am J Psychother 38:341–349, 1984.

Murphy GE, Armstrong JW Jr, Hermele SL, Fischer JR, Clendenin WW: Suicide and alcoholism: Interpersonal loss confirmed as a predictor. Arch Gen Psychiatry 36:65–69, 1979.

Murphy GE, Robins E: Social factors in suicide. JAMA 199:303–308, 1967.

Murphy GE, Wetzel RD: Family history of suicidal behavior among suicide attempters. J Nerv Ment Dis 170:86–90, 1982.

Murphy GE, Wetzel RD: Suicide risk by birth cohort in the United States, 1949 to 1974. Arch Gen Psychiatry 37:519–523, 1980.

National Institute on Drug Abuse Statistical Series. Annual Data. 1982. Data from the Drug Abuse Warning Network (DAWN). Series I, No. 2. US Department of Health and Human Services, 1983.

Ovenstone IMK: A psychiatric approach to the diagnosis of suicide and its effect upon the Edinburgh statistics. Br J Psychiatry 123:15–21, 1973.

Parkin D, Stengel E: Incidence of suicidal attempts in an urban community. Br Med J 2:133–138, 1965.

Pitts FN Jr: Affective disorder and suicide in women physicians: Other views (letter). Am J Psychiatry 136:1607–1608, 1979.

Pitts FN, Schuller AB, Rich CL: Suicide among U.S. women physicians, 1967–1972. Am J Psychiatry 136:694–696, 1979.

Pitts FN Jr, Winokur G: Affective disorder. VII. Alcoholism and affective disorder. J Psychiatr Res 4:37–50, 1966.

Pokorny AD: Suicide rates in various psychiatric disorders. J Nerv Ment Dis 139:499–506, 1964.

Pokorny AD, Smith JP, Finch JR: Vehicular suicides. Life-Threat Behav 2:105–119, 1972.

Robins E: The Final Months. A Study of the Lives of 134 Persons Who Committed Suicide. New York, Oxford University Press, 1981.

Robins E, Gassner S, Kayes J, Wilkinson RH, Murphy GE: The communication of suicidal intent: A study of 134 consecutive cases of successful (completed) suicide. Am J Psychiatry 115:724–733, 1959a.

Robins E, Murphy GE, Wilkinson RH Jr, Gassner S, Kayes J: Some clinical considerations in the prevention of suicide based on a study of 134 successful suicides. Am J Public Health 49:888–899, 1959b.

Sainsbury P, Barraclough B: Differences between suicide rates. Nature 220:1252, 1968.

Schmidt CW Jr, Perlin S, Townes W, Fisher RS, Shaffer JW: Characteristics of drivers involved in single-car accidents: A comparative study. Arch Gen Psychiatry 27:800–803, 1972.

Schmidt EH, O'Neal P, Robins E: Evaluation of suicide attempts as guide to therapy: Clinical and follow-up study of one hundred nine patients. JAMA 155:549–557, 1954.

Schulsinger F, Kety SS, Rosenthal D, Wender PH: A family study of suicide, in Schou M, Stromgren E (eds): Origin, Prevention and Treatment of Affective Disorder. New York, Academic Press, 1979, pp 278–287.

Solomon MI, Hellon CP: Suicide and age in Alberta, Canada, 1951 to 1977. A cohort analysis. Arch Gen Psychiatry 37:511–513, 1980.

Steppacher RC, Mausner JS: Suicide in male and female physicians. JAMA 228:323–328, 1974.

Temoche A, Pugh RF, MacMahon B: Suicide rates among current and former mental institution patients. J Nerv Ment Dis 138:124–130, 1964.

United Nations: Demographic Yearbook, 1982. New York, United Nations, 1984.

Weissman MM: Wrist cutting. Relationship between clinical observations and epidemiological findings. Arch Gen Psychiatry 32:1166–1171, 1975.

Wheeler EO, White PD, Reed EW, Cohen ME: Neurocirculatory asthenia (anxiety neurosis, effort syndrome, neurasthenia): A twenty-year follow-up study of 173 patients. JAMA 142:878–889, 1950.

# INDEX

Page numbers followed by i represent illustrations; those followed by t represent tables.